Peter Newby is an affable and welcoming guide, but don't let that [illegible] sents the crystallization of careful, sophisticated practical, technica[illegible] bined with a sure-footedness in and around the folk-ways of edu[illegible] with a considerable span of interests, permeated with a strong sense of why such work, and a commitment to doing it well, really matters. That Newby has done all this without compromising the complexities and challenges that make all this work important is an achievement that makes this an especially useful and enjoyable book for beginning and experienced researchers alike.

Peter Freebody, The University of Sydney

Crafting an appropriate and effective research design is a challenging task for many students, novice and experienced researchers. Users of this comprehensive text will find it very helpful in designing suitable research tools, seeking consistency in theoretical underpinnings and making critical research decisions. The text is intelligently grounded – it provides useful insight into real-life research situations and examples. It is a very accessible text, easy to read and navigate through. I would have no hesitation in recommending it to students embarking on educational research and to lecturers about to teach a course in research methodology.

Marc Schäfer, Rhodes University, South Africa

An excellent text for students studying at all levels from undergraduate to doctoral qualifications. The structure of the book leads the reader through the complete research process, highlighting the many ambiguities and challenges faced during research. Clear language makes the text accessible and helps to clarify some of the more difficult issues without minimising their complexity. This book will be a great asset to many first time as well as experienced researchers.

Sheine Peart, Nottingham Trent University

There are few things more important than good research into education, and in this book Peter Newby makes sure his readers can meet this challenge. He is a reliable, thorough and confident guide for anyone setting out on their research journey. The text is particularly helpful for researchers developing action or policy in this field.

James Wisdom, Visiting Professor of Educational Development, Middlesex University

This is an excellent, up-to-date and accessible methods text which will greatly appeal to students grappling with the research process. The style of the book is clear and user-friendly, whilst the content anticipates many of the problems which students are likely to encounter during their research in education. Comprehensive and good value for money.

Samantha Punch, University of Stirling

A refreshing approach to basic research issues, in a comprehensive research text that should stand the test with students who find some issues difficult to grasp. Its combination of theory and practical illustrations guides the reader through all aspects of the research process, the management of quantitative methodology and analysis a particular strength. The relaxed style of writing and presentation, and online features, will be appreciated by staff and students alike.

Molly Cumming, University of Strathclyde (retd)

One of the most thorough and comprehensive research text available. The author offers a thorough presentation of all aspects of the research process, draws on a wide range of real examples from practice and offers particular support to those students who struggle when presenting quantitative data in their research projects.

Liz Keeley- Browne, Oxford Brookes University

Combines comprehensive detailed coverage with accessibility and practical guidance. This will become a core text for many students of educational research.

Steve Strand, University of Warwick

A serious and important attempt to simplify the complex process of research, without restricting or overly classifying the range and power of techniques available to us.

Stephen Gorard, The University of Birmingham

I am impressed by Newby's concrete and structured way of guiding the student through the entire research process. His descriptions of complex theories and procedures is conveyed in an interesting and accessible way. Students will also enjoy the writing style and pedagogical organization of the book.

Carina Rönnqvist, Umeå School of Education, Sweden

Peter Newby provides a lucid and accessible guide to research methods for education. His approach, which sees such methods as a means to an end, is a much-need reminder that the main aim of research is to answer difficult questions and to break new theoretical and empirical ground.

Richard Andrews, Institute of Education, University of London

Research Methods for Education

Visit the *Research Methods for Education* Companion Website at **www.pearsoned.co.uk/newby** to find valuable **student** learning material including:

- Multiple choice questions to test your understanding of key terms and procedures
- Furthering your own research project encourages readers to relate the material covered in the textbook to your own research activity
- Consolidate your learning provides extra exercises and activities to be used as workshop activities or self-study aids
- Focus group video provides examples of two focus groups to help you understand how they might be run
- Refresh your knowledge of maths and statistics gives you the opportunity to test your understanding of basic mathematical and statistical concepts and refresh your knowledge where necessary
- Online glossary to explain key terms
- Interactive online flashcards to allow the reader to check definitions against the key terms during revision

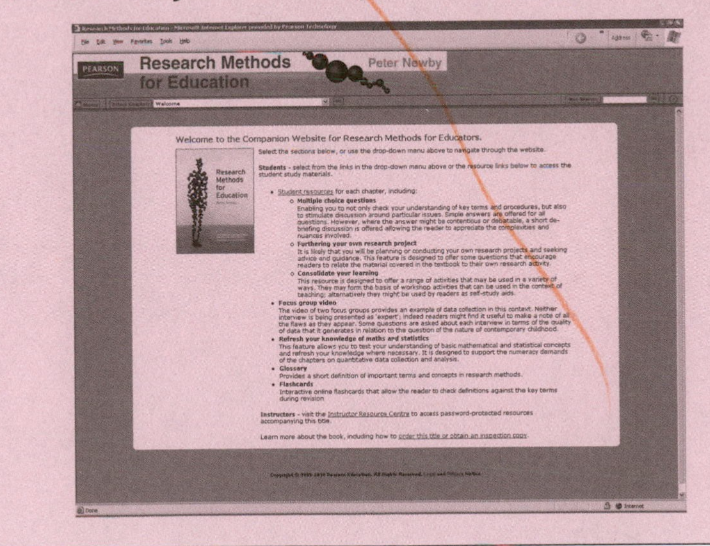

Research Methods for Education

Peter Newby

Emeritus Professor of Higher Education,
Middlesex University

Longman
is an imprint of

Harlow, England • London • New York • Boston • San Francisco • Toronto
Sydney • Tokyo • Singapore • Hong Kong • Seoul • Taipei • New Delhi
Cape Town • Madrid • Mexico City • Amsterdam • Munich • Paris • Milan

Pearson Education Limited
Edinburgh Gate
Harlow
Essex CM20 2JE
England

and Associated Companies throughout the world

Visit us on the World Wide Web at:
www.pearsoned.co.uk

First published 2010

ISBN: 978-1-4058-3574-9

British Library Cataloguing-in-Publication Data
A catalogue record for this book is available from the British Library

Library of Congress Cataloging-in-Publication Data
Newby, Peter.
Research methods for education / Peter Newby.
p. cm.
ISBN 978-1-4058-3574-9 (pbk.)
1. Education--Research--Methodology. I. Title.
LB1028.N46 2010
370.7'2--dc22

2009036147

10 9 8 7 6 5 4 3 2 1
14 13 12 11 10

Typeset in 9.5/12 Giovanni Book by 73
Printed and bound by Ashford Colour Press in the UK

The publisher's policy is to use paper manufactured from sustainable forests.

I would like to dedicate this book first to Radka. It is, I know, a small recompense for all the support you have given me. I would, as well, like to offer it to Josephine and Matilda who, I hope, will be amongst the next generation of researchers.

Contents

Supporting resources

Visit **www.pearsoned.co.uk/newby** to find valuable online resources

Companion Website for students

- Multiple choice questions to test your understanding of key terms and procedures
- Furthering your own research project encourages readers to relate the material covered in the textbook to your own research activity
- Consolidate your learning provides extra exercises and activities to be used as workshop activities or self-study aids
- Focus group video provides examples of two focus groups to help you understand how they might be run
- Refresh your knowledge of maths and statistics gives you the opportunity to test your understanding of basic mathematical and statistical concepts and refresh your knowledge where necessary
- Online glossary to explain key terms
- Interactive online flashcards to allow the reader to check definitions against the key terms during revision

For instructors

- PowerPoint slides that include a summary of each chapter, and can be used to help prepare a lecture or presentation

Also: The Companion Website provides the following features:

- Search tool to help locate specific items of content
- E-mail results and profile tools to send results of quizzes to instructors
- Online help and support to assist with website usage and troubleshooting

For more information please contact your local Pearson Education sales representative or visit **www.pearsoned.co.uk/newby**

List of Figures

List of Tables

List of Case Studies

List of Activities

About the Author

I began academic life as a geographer. An early interest in research methods gave me an insight into another world – consultancy. It was in this context that I learnt to translate theory into practice and how to construct a research strategy that was within the client's budget. My experiences here shaped my belief in what I thought higher education should be doing and my own career changed as a result. For ten years, I headed up educational development at Middlesex University. After that, I set up an education research and development centre where the focus of our work was the exploration of learning processes and frameworks that could deliver prosperity and greater social equality to communities. At the heart of much of my work was the idea of how skills should be embedded in the curriculum. Over time, my ideas moved on to explore the interaction of skill, knowledge and performance inherent in the concept of capability and through this I developed my ideas on skill complexes. This led to significant work on the development of entrepreneurship and leadership. I am now Emeritus Professor of Higher Education at Middlesex University.

Peter Newby

Preface

Writing any textbook involves selection. It is impossible to present a compendium of everything that could be said about every method of research. For one thing, the book would never get finished and, for another, with so much information it would be impossible for any reader to see the wood for the trees. All of which leads me to the first question, 'Why did I include some things and leave others out?' The answer to this is that I have a particular view on what a research training should consist of but, behind this, there is another question, 'Why bother with research at all?' Let me begin by explaining why you are expected to follow a course in research methods and, almost certainly, expected to produce some research of your own.

When students join a university, they are, invariably, presented with details of the course they will follow. This will show them what they will study at each stage of their course, where they have choices about what they can study and how they will be assessed. In many institutions, certainly in the UK, they will also be told what learning outcomes are expected. However, what is often lost in this detail is a bigger picture of the principles that underpin a university education. Perhaps surprisingly, these principles are common to many disciplines, from the sciences through the social sciences to the arts. They almost certainly inform undergraduate programmes in education. And from my perspective as author of this book, research plays a major part in giving these principles substance.

An undergraduate programme develops students so that they can, with integrity and a sense of having earned the honour, call themselves 'graduates'. Generally there are three steps in this process. Each builds an important element in the infrastructure of becoming a graduate. The first is *understanding*. Students demonstrate their ability to understand their subject by reproducing arguments, perspectives and evidence in their own words. So, if you ever wondered why you were given essays, term papers and examinations, this is the reason. The need to demonstrate understanding becomes intertwined with another principle on which graduateness is based, *critical capability*. This is concerned with how well we exercise our judgement. We develop it by assessing subject material based on our understanding and demonstrate it through the quality of the arguments we construct. The final stage of building a graduate is to develop the ability to *create knowledge*. This can only happen when we exercise critical judgement, when we see where there are gaps in our knowledge or where our understanding is flawed.

It should be clear now where a course in research methods fits in. It is the key to the final stage of becoming a graduate. As a graduate, you will be expected, wherever you work, to be able to influence development, based on a cogently argued case for change. You will not be able to do this without sound research to back up your argument. And the same argument applies if your research journey begins at the postgraduate level.

I am aware that not every student finds a course in research methods as appealing as one on educational policy or special needs or citizenship but you should remember that a university education is designed to give you the intellectual and technical skills to shape the world. I have written this book to give you the ability to do this. Recognising, however, that learning about research methods and how to use them can be challenging, whilst writing I have had the reader in mind. I have imagined a student a little daunted by the thought not only of passing a course in research methods but also of having to produce a piece of research work. I have tried to see the expression on that student's face and in the eyes, so that I can see whether my ideas are understood. I have tried, also, to write the text so that it is approachable and readable. Nothing is more off putting than reading an author who likes to show that they know more than the person studying the book. There is, of course, technical vocabulary, but it is explained. I have, wherever possible, sought to give context to what I have included, with background on some of the people associated with the techniques and approaches. I have tried also to show the utility of the methods with examples of how and where they have been used. The learning model is explanatory but I hope that the inclusion of activities, case studies and Web materials (developed and provided by Mike Radford) moves the book away from being overly didactic. Certainly my object was to engage students with both the excitement of research and the sense that they could do it themselves.

I have said that I had a student in mind when I was writing but who are you? As I imagine you, you are just beginning a research journey. You may have done research elsewhere, perhaps at school, but that was not designed to enable you to produce research that could inform and shape the world. Typically you can begin this research journey at one of three points. First, you may be an undergraduate taking a course in education. Second, you could be a trainee teacher or a newly qualified teacher who has moved into education from a specialist subject field and are taking a course of professional development over and above a postgraduate teaching qualification. Third, you might be following a postgraduate programme at masters or doctorate level, often after a period in teaching and as a means of advancing your career. While these three starting points inevitably imply that people will have different amounts of contextual knowledge, it is likely that all will have little appreciation of how to go about research in ways that other researchers will find acceptable and convincing. I have assumed little prior knowledge and, in mathematical terms, only the ability to add up, subtract, multiply and divide. The challenges in research methods (as in most other courses) are met by thinking logically. There is some mathematical formulation to enable you to make the leap to more advanced books and academic papers where statements about statistical tests are an integral part of communication.

So what has my teaching approach been? It is founded on the belief that something that is well explained is better understood. It is designed to build understanding and through this develop the confidence to undertake research. This is not a book that sets out rules and recipes for how to carry out research. I believe that my role is to build a self-belief that you are capable of research, so that when you transfer your learning to a research environment, you understand the flexibility and freedom you have and can justify your research practice.

Now a word for tutors as well as students. I have written this book as three separate sections. There is no need to start at the beginning and continue through to the end. Each section can be read independently. Part 1 gives the context for research in education.

It deals with the implications of philosophy and terminology and concepts used by research methodologists to make the research process comprehensible. It outlines three broad approaches to education research, quantitative, qualitative and mixed methods. These ways of looking at research are deeply rooted but things may change as young researchers grasp the opportunity to attack the research question without feeling the need to be bound by research convention. Part 2 examines the process of data collection and Part 3, data analysis. How you make use of the material depends, of course, on how your programme is structured. The book can be used flexibly to support the way you teach your course. In my experience, it is best to start by doing something. An easy way to begin is with Chapter 10 on reading data tables. Combined with an introduction to secondary sources (Chapter 4), it could show that much of the data needed might be available already. I would not recommend beginning at Part 1; this could kill enthusiasm for an exciting field. Instead, go back to the material as and when the issues materialise in data collection and analysis. I would continue with data collection, setting practical exercises, and intersperse this with data analysis. My object would be to give students as much 'hands on' experience as the timetable permitted but there are other ways of delivering a programme that are equally appropriate.

How I have approached writing this book is the product of many years teaching students research methods. As the character of the student population has changed, so has my approach. I hope what I have written meets the needs of present day students. While the words and the framework are mine, I have had valuable help from a number of people. In particular, I should mention Dr Liz Keeley-Browne (Oxford Brookes University), Helen Channon (University of Cumbria), Molly Cumming (University of Strathclyde), Professor Stephen Gorard (University of Birmingham), Dr Lisa Lucas (University of Bristol), Carina Rönnqvist (Umeå School of Education) and Dr Steve Strand (University of Warwick). I am grateful to Pauline Shippey and Milly Wolmark for producing by text in a form acceptable to the publisher. I would also like to record my thanks to the team at Pearson. To Catherine Yates who chanced on a throwaway remark that I knew something about research methods and to Stuart Hay, whose protestations that he 'didn't quite understand' revealed, instead, significant knowledge about research methods. A number of other reviewers contributed anonymously. All of you have helped improve the book. Any errors that remain are mine alone.

Acknowledgements

We are grateful to the following for permission to reproduce copyright material:

Figures

Figure 2.3 after *Getting better All The Time: making benchmarking work*, The Audit Commission (2000); Figure 4.10 from *OECD Online Database-two screenshots*, data from Foreign/international students enrolled under Education and Training from OECD.Stat Extracts, http://stats.oecd.org; Figure 4.12 three screenshots from the World Bank website, © World Bank 2009; Figure 9.2 from 'Lesson Observation Notes and Prompts' document from: http://education.exeter.ac.uk/pages.php?id=527; Figure 9.3 from *Problem Basing Learning: An Exploration of the Method and Evaluation of its Effectiveness in a Continuing Nursing Education Programme*, Middlesex University (Newman, M. 2004), © Mark Newman; Figures 10.3, 10.19a, 10.19b, 11.3, 11.4 screenshots from IBM's 'Many Eyes' website, Courtesy of International Business Machines Corporation, copyright © International Business Machines Corporation; Figure 11.2 from Constant Companion Method: A Kaleidoscope of Data, The Qualitative Report, 4 (l/2) by Dye, J., Schatz, I., Rosenberg, B. and Coleman, S. (2000), http://www.nova.edu/ssss/QR/QR4-1/dye.html; Figure 11.5 screenshot from SmartDraw.com's 'SmartDraw' software, Diagram created with SmartDraw. For a free trial visit: www.smartdraw.com; Figure 11.8 from The Advertising Archives; Screenshot in Activity 2.1 from www.eric.ed.gov, Education Resources Information Center (ERIC) website, 2008, http://www.eric.ed.gov. Reprinted with permission from the US Department of Education.;

Tables

Table 4.1 adapted from http://www.caci.co.uk/ACORN, CACI Limited; Table 8.6 after Mind the Gap: Are Students Prepared for Higher Education, *Journal of Further and Higher Education*, 27(1), 53–76 (Lowe, H and Cook, A 2003), Routledge, reprinted by permission of the publisher, Taylor & Francis Ltd, http://www.informaworld.com.; Table 9.6 from Toward Self-Directed Learning in Secondary Schools: What do Teachers do?, *Teaching and Teacher Education*, 17(7), 837–55 (Bolhuis, S. and Voeten, M 2001), Copyright 2001, with permission from Elsevier.; Table on page 398 adapted from http://www.pisa.oecd.org/dataoecd/30/63/39704360.xls, OECD, Table 5.4: Based on OECD (2007), PISA 2006: Science Competencies for Tomorrow's World, Volume 2: Data p. 165; Table 10.2 from http://www.hesa.ac.uk/dox/performanceIndicators/0506/sp6_0506.xls, Hesa cannot accept responsibility for any inferences or conclusions derived from the data by third parties.; Table 10.10 from Child and Youth Well-Being in the United States, 1975–98: Some Findings and a New Index, *Social Indicators Research* 56(3), 241–318 (Land, K., Lamb, V. and Mustillo, S. 2001), With kind permission from Springer Science+Business Media; Table 10.11 from *Pisa 2006 Volume 2: Data/Données*, OECD (2006) Table 6.2c: Based on OECD (2007), PISA 2006: Science Competencies for Tomorrow's World, Volume 2: Data p. 230; Table 10.13 from 'Summary of academic staff (excluding atypical) in all UK institutions 2006/07' at http://www.hesa.ac.uk/dox/dataTables/staff/download/staff0607.xls?v=1.0, HESA cannot accept responsibility for any inferences or conclusions derived from the data by third parties; Table 11.6 from http://www.transana.org/images/TransanaShortcuts.pdf, Jeffersonian Transcription Notation is described in detail in G. Jefferson, Transcription Notation, in J. Atkinson and J. Heritage (eds), Structures of Social Interaction, New York: Cambridge University Press, 1984.; Table 12.1 from The Importance of Socio Economic Status and Individual Characteristics on the Prevalence of Head Lice in School Children, *European Journal of Dermatology*, 15 (5), 387–92 (Willems, S., Lapeere, H., Haedens, N., Pastels, I., Naegert, J.-M. and De Maeseneer, J. 2005); Table 12.1a from *OECD in Figures 2007*, OECD (2007), Data from Performance under Education, OECD (2007), OECD in Figures (2007), www.oecd.org/infigures; Table 13.14 after Making it Work: Low-Income Working Mothers' Involvement in Their Children's Education, *American Educational Research Journal* 40 (4), 879–901, Table 3 (Weiss, H. et al 2003), Weiss, H. et al, American Educational Research Journal 40 (4), pp. 879–901 Table 3, copyright © 2003 by Sage Publications. Reprinted by permission of SAGE Publications.

Text

Case Study 9.1 adapted from Taken from a study undertaken by Hockey, J., Robinson, V. and Meah, A., at the Dept. of Comparative & Applied Social Sciences, University of Hull, by kind permission of the authors; Activity 13.4 adapted from Reading Achievement & Social Selection in Independent Schools in Sweden: Results from IEA PIRLS 2001 Reading Test, *Scandinavian Journal of Educational Research*, 50(2), 85–205 (Myrberg, E. and Rosen, M. 2006), 'Reading Achievement & Social Selection in Independent Schools in Sweden: Results from IEA PIRLS 2001 Reading Test', Myrberg, E. and Rosen, M., Scandinavian Journal of Educational Research, 50(2), 2006, Routledge, reprinted by permission of the publisher, Taylor & Francis Ltd, http://www.informaworld.com.

In some instances we have been unable to trace the owners of copyright material, and we would appreciate any information that would enable us to do so.

Guided tour of the website

Refresh your knowledge of maths and statistics

This feature allows students to test their understanding of basic mathematical and statistical concepts and refresh their knowledge where necessary. It is designed to support the numeracy demands of the chapters on quantitative data collection and analysis.

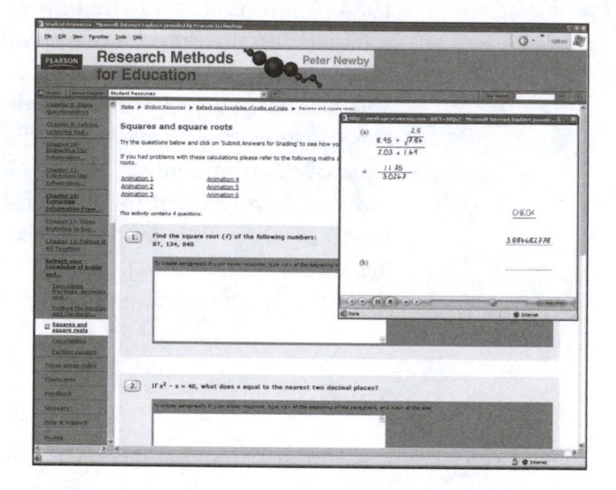

Consolidate your learning

These 'consolidate your learning' pages are designed to offer a range of activities that may be used in a variety of ways. They may form the basis of workshop activities that can be used in the context of teaching. Alternatively they might be used by readers as self study aids.

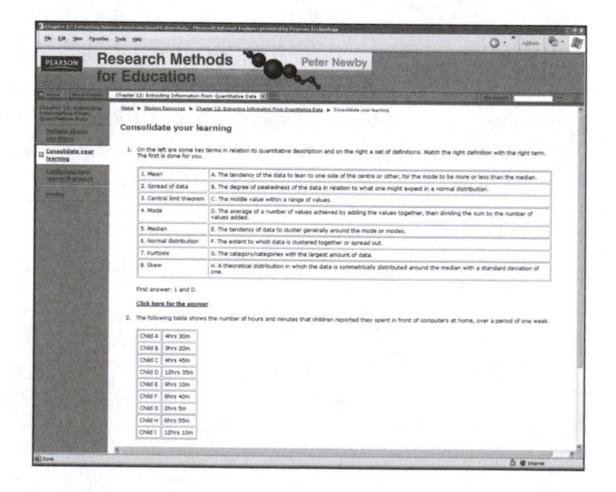

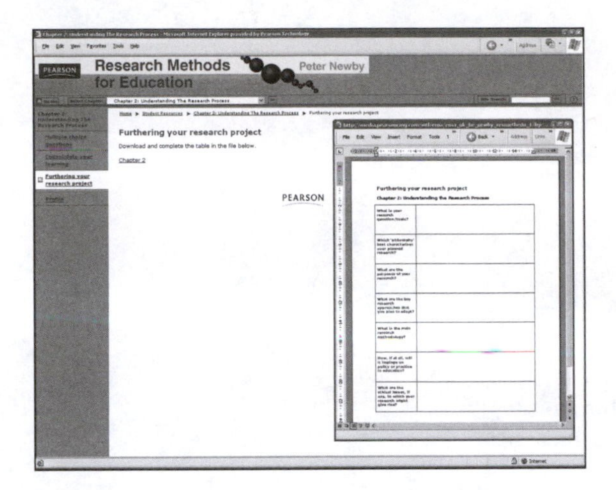

Furthering your own research project

It is likely that readers of this book will be planning or conducting their own research projects and seeking advice and guidance. The short 'Furthering your research project' feature is designed to offer some questions that encourage readers to relate the material covered in the textbook to their own research activity.

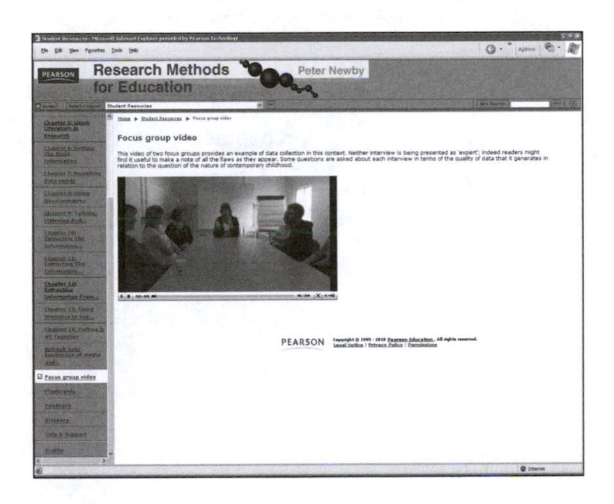

Video of a focus group

The video of two focus groups provides an example of data collection in this context. Neither interview is being presented as 'expert', indeed readers might find it useful to make a note of all the flaws as they appear. Some questions are asked about each interview in terms of the quality of data that it generates in relation to the question of the nature of contemporary childhood.

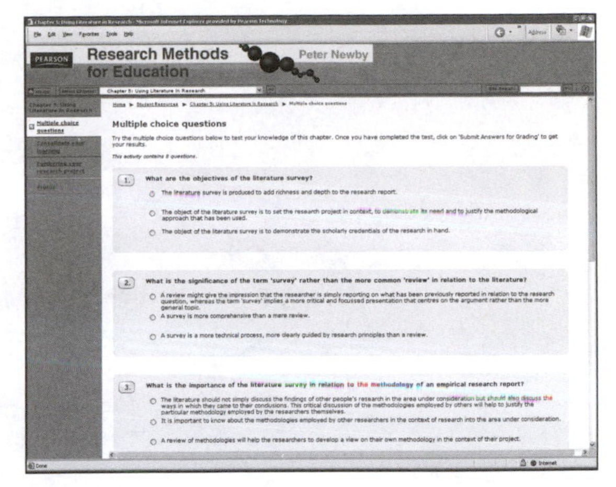

MCQs

Enable students to check their understanding of key terms and procedures, but also to stimulate discussion around particular issues. Simple answers are offered for all questions. However, where the answer might be contentious or debatable a short de-briefing discussion is offered, allowing the reader to appreciate the complexities and nuances involved.

Glossary

Provides short definition of important terms and concepts in research methods.

PowerPoint slides

For hard-pressed teachers in higher education these slides offer a first stage of support in preparing a lecture or presentation. They also provide a summary of each chapter which may be helpful to both students and teachers.

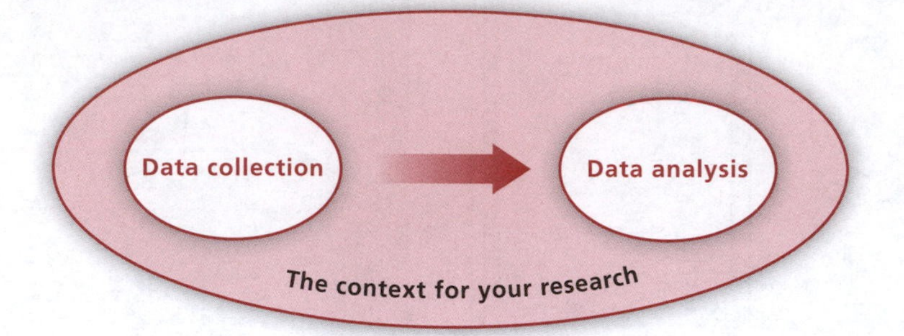
Data collection
Data analysis
The context for your research

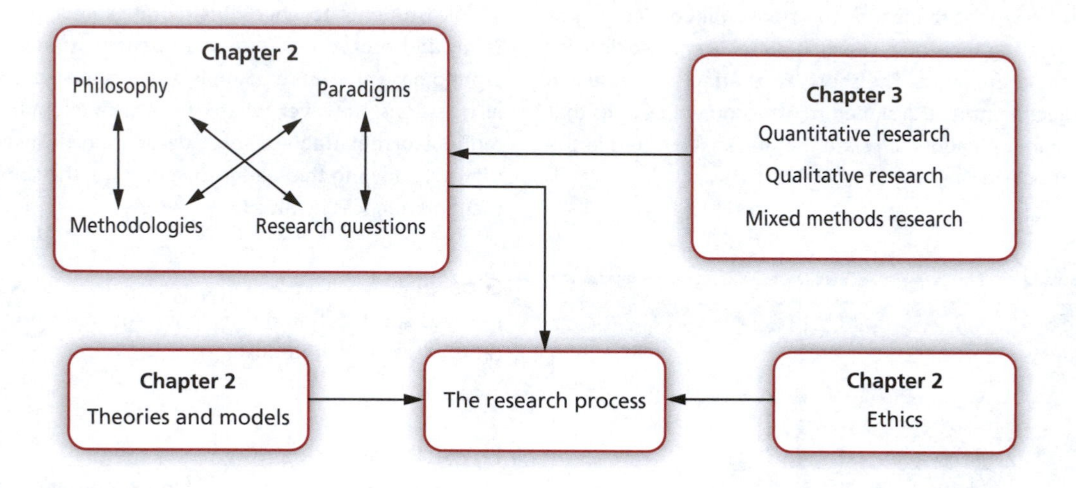
Chapter 2
Philosophy
Paradigms
Methodologies
Research questions
Chapter 3
Quantitative research
Qualitative research
Mixed methods research
Chapter 2
Theories and models
The research process
Chapter 2
Ethics

Part 1

THE CONTEXT FOR YOUR RESEARCH

This first part of the book sets the scene for research in education. Its purpose is to provide you with confidence in handling the concepts and ideas that condition research practice. These are important if you want your research to be taken seriously. While some of the material can seem challenging, it is discussed in a straightforward way. Because of the need to explain concepts and ideas to students who may not have met them before, there has had to be some simplification as well as selection.

Simplifying things in order to help people understand them can lead to concerns being ignored or glossed over. There is, however, guidance on further reading that will take you more deeply into issues. Nonetheless, there are two points of advice that I offer in respect of this section.

1. It is possible to omit much of Part 1 and go on to Parts 2 and 3, which deal with the more technical aspects of research data collection and analysis. But do note, there will be times when it will be necessary to return to Part 1 in order to understand fully why certain things should be done in a certain way and why some approaches and techniques should be used only in specific circumstances.
2. If this is your first introduction to research methods, the discussion and explanations are still within your grasp, especially if they are supported by the guidance of a tutor and class discussions.

Chapter 1 sets the scene for education research.

Chapters 2 and 3 explore influences on the research process that we undertake. These constitute the context for our research and they are shown in the figure on the previous page.

In Chapter 2 we will look at the influence of philosophy, methodology, research paradigms and research questions. The figure shows that these are highly connected issues. In fact paradigms, broad approaches to research activity, are so important in giving shape to our understanding of the research process that they are considered in depth in Chapter 3. In Chapter 2 as well we will look at how theories and models fit into the research process and how our research should rest on ethical considerations of how others are affected by our work.

Chapter contents

Chapter 1

RESEARCH: A MESSY BUSINESS

Key themes

- Learn how this book can meet your needs, whatever stage you are at in your research development.
- Why people undertake education research.
- The character of the research community in education.
- How to be successful in education research.
- Educational research is highly contested.

Introduction: Putting the book in perspective

A book on research methods – it's not exactly the sort of book you would choose for the beach, is it? Let's be clear, getting through this book will require some work from you and, at times, you might find that it's stretching you rather more than you want to be stretched. However, what is written here will help you understand what you need to know so that you can make sense of the research process. The explanations are clear and draw on your understanding of education. You will be guided through some of the more tricky research manoeuvres and there will also be practice activities to help you develop your confidence, your understanding and your technique. There is a lot to learn but when you are at the end of your journey, you will appreciate that what you have learnt is making sense at a whole series of levels. You will know about the 'proper' way of applying a technique; you will know about alternative techniques for different situations; you will know that there is always more than one route to a research destination and you will also appreciate the most important lesson that this book has to teach you, that while you can bend and sometimes break the rules, there are principles that will constrain and confine you if you want others to value your work.

And there are two other things that you will find out as well: first, that developing an approach to research issues is creative and stimulating and second, that doing your first piece of research is engrossing and one of the most enjoyable and satisfying things that you will ever do – believe me!

Think of this book as if it were a game or a puzzle, for example a jigsaw. This introductory chapter is the box that contains the puzzle. It gives some instructions and guidance on how to put it together. One thing you need to appreciate is that the research puzzle is unusual because, unlike a conventional jigsaw, it can be put together in an infinite number of ways. To this extent, it is more like a computer game in which the object is to get to the end but because of the random nature of events there are a great many routes for reaching the goal.

What does this chapter tell you about the puzzle? It will give you a perspective on research in education. As a puzzle, research can be 'solved' at various levels of expertise and this chapter will help you understand which level you, as a reader, are at. You will also appreciate that education research has not one heart but three – one whose beat provides the life-support for academics as 'searchers after truth', one for practitioners and the third for policy makers. It will help you understand that solving the research puzzle involves decisions and judgements on your part. You will see that the interest in education research does not end at the school gates. Education is seen as a way of achieving a wide range of social, economic and political goals, so it concerns a far wider community than just education professionals. Most important though, this chapter will give you guidance on the standards that you have to maintain if you want your research to be taken seriously.

Welcome to the research world.

1.1 What do you put in a first chapter?

There is no absolutely right or wrong way of putting together the first chapter of any book but there is always a way that makes sense in terms of the message that the author wants to convey. In this instance, rather than getting into the intricacies of the research process, we are going to look at who this book is for and why it will be useful at all stages in your research career. You are going to see why we do education research and just who does it, because it is important you understand this when you read education research. And you will also learn what the key objectives of any research are as well as some rules of thumb that you should know before you become a researcher.

1.2 Who is this book for?

In order to write this book, I first identified the people who might use it so that they could see how it could be valuable to them. See if you recognise yourself in Table 1.1. For everyone in the world of research this book, and this chapter particularly, has two key messages.

- First, real world research is not necessarily clear cut and well structured. It is important that you develop the skill of knowing when, where and how to compromise with what theory and accepted practice says that you should do. You can choose to work within one of the traditional research approaches and abide by their rules (we cover these in Chapter 3). You do not have to; you can mix approaches and styles of research to give you the information you need to solve your research problem but if

Table 1.1 Who can use this book?

- An undergraduate student following a course in research methods.
- A postgraduate student following a course in research methods.
- A research student planning a dissertation or thesis.
- A lecturer responsible for a taught research methods programme.
- A tutor supervising a student's project.
- A professional or academic researcher.

you do work within a set of rules, you should recognise that you are letting go of your freedom to take decisions and to construct your research programme in ways that seem best for you. The argument of this book is that you need to understand the consequences of doing or not doing something, so that you are able to make good decisions according to the circumstances.

- This leads on to the second key message. Once you have this understanding and you are confident in your judgements, then you will have the intellectual command of your subject to persuade others that the choices you have made and the way you have done things are appropriate. This word 'appropriate' is important. It does not mean 'best' necessarily, but it does mean 'justifiable' and 'acceptable in delivering results that are fit for purpose'. Once you can do this, then you will meet the prime, perhaps the only, requirement of delivering research output, namely that it is acceptable to the audience you select.

But what of the specific value to each of the groups?

(i) Students

For students following a course in research methods (and especially those who are at the start of their research journey), this book will give you a grounding in how to do research. It is more applied than philosophical (though you may be forgiven for thinking otherwise as you read the first few chapters) but never loses sight of the fact that principles underpin not only research methods but also the outlook of the researcher. It also argues that research frequently blends data and methods and can draw upon more than one approach. What you have to do as a researcher is to learn how to put together a research strategy that meets the needs of the research problem and the context for undertaking the research. At the end of your course and with the help of this book, you will be able to do this.

(ii) Research students

If you are a research student preparing a research plan, the goal for you is much the same. You need to appreciate that an academic audience can be far more fickle and precious about research than someone who is paying you a consultancy fee. However you undertake your research, it is vitally important that the infrastructure on which your research programme rests is robust. Pay particular attention to Chapters 4 and 5! A single book is unlikely to deliver everything everyone ever wants to know about research. This book is no exception but it will give you a sufficient understanding to be able to develop a research strategy and choose a research procedure.

(iii) Lecturer

If you are a lecturer teaching a research programme, the object is to give you a book and associated learning materials in which you can have confidence and which you believe your students can manage by themselves without you first having to give an explanatory lecture. This is especially important for the chapters dealing with quantitative procedures. It is also important to have a book that encourages discussion in your class because this will be important in helping your students develop the sort of flexible thinking that will produce creative solutions to research problems.

(iv) Supervisors and tutors

Those who supervise research students will have a book in which they can have confidence that their students can use to teach themselves about research methods and which can be used as a platform for launching them into more sophisticated research procedures. It will have failed though if your students do not understand what a research strategy is and how important it is that they develop one and not just produce a chapter in their thesis called 'Research Methodology' that explains how they constructed a questionnaire or why they chose to use qualitative procedures without explaining why others were not considered.

(v) Professional and academic researchers

Professional and academic researchers will dip in to this book to see what is being said about research methods today, though only you can answer whether you have learnt anything more than experience has taught you already. You have probably learnt how to manage the pressures of time and the lack of resources. It would, however, be good to think that if this book has just one message for you, it is to consider building in other approaches to the way you work. Chapters 4 and 10 might offer something new to you.

1.3 Why do we do educational research?

Let's begin by looking at the most important question, why bother to research education at all? The answers will begin the process of building a framework that will help you understand how the research process works. At one level the answer to the question is quite simple but when you start to look at the reality of research it is a little more complex than you might think. There are three broad reasons for doing research in education.

(i) To explore issues

This category includes everything from finding answers to a specific question (why do girls in the UK get better grades in mathematics than boys?) to identifying and specifying a problem or issue that should be the subject of further research. For example, if you think there could be a relationship between social conditions in a community and the educational attainment of cohorts of children, it would be interesting to know if any schools or areas bucked the trend.

(ii) To shape policy

We conduct research to collect information and use it to make a judgement that informs policy goals and indicates how we can attain them. We also carry out research to find out whether we are going in the right direction once a policy has been implemented. There is an example of this in Case Study 1.1.

Case study 1.1 Education research and policy

Education is a bit like constructing a building, you cannot get very far if the foundations are not strong. The foundations for learning are the ability to take in information, to communicate understanding and to manipulate number according to rules. More popularly we would call this 'the 3Rs', reading, writing and arithmetic. In the UK there has been concern over 'declining standards' in these basic skills for some time. In the recent period politicians and others have blamed it on social change in the 1960s and the outcomes in terms of attitudinal and behavioural changes in later decades. If we look around the world we find evidence of the same concerns. The Organisation for European Co-operation and Development (OECD) co-ordinates with Statistics Canada (the official statistics agency for Canada) the Adult Literacy and Life Skills Survey (ALL). This records tests of the proficiency of national populations in:

- Prose literacy – the ability to understand and use text.
- Document literacy – the knowledge and skills to locate and use information in text and diagrammatic form.
- Numeracy – the effective management of the demands made on us by different situations.
- Problem solving – the ability to move towards a goal in situations where routine procedures are not available.

The ALL survey builds on the earlier International Adult Literacy Survey. The headline results of the ALL survey (OECD and Statistics Canada, 2005) are that:

- Many adults worldwide have difficulty coping with literacy and numeracy in their everyday lives.
- National differences in performance are apparent; Norway performs well in all areas, Italy and the USA less well in literacy.
- Young people tend to perform better than older people.
- Men tend to perform better in numeracy tests and women in prose literacy.

The Progress in International Reading Literacy Study (PIRLS), which is co-ordinated by the International Association for the Evaluation of Educational Achievement (IEA) reported on the reading achievement of children in 40 countries in its last report (Mullis, I. et al., 2007). We cannot review all the findings here but, from the point of view of taking policy action in the UK, one stands out:

> For countries with decreases since PIRLS 2001, Lithuania and the Netherlands had decreases at the two highest benchmarks, England and Sweden had decreases at all except the low benchmark, and Romania had decreases across the distribution.

These concerns and studies constituted the context for policy development in the UK. At the time this book is being written, the Government in the UK has just received a report on teaching reading in primary schools (Rose, 2006). The report's core recommendation is:

> Despite uncertainties in research findings, the practice seen by the review shows that the systematic approach, which is generally understood as 'synthetic' phonics, offers the vast majority of young children the best and most direct route to becoming skilled readers and writers.

Synthetic phonics teaches reading by first requiring children to learn the letter sounds and then how to blend letter sound combinations to give words.

All of these reports can be consulted on-line. The Web addresses have not been given here to give you practice at finding sources.

(iii) To improve practice

Doing something better than the way it is done already is a common reason for venturing into research. You probably saw this in Case Study 1.1. The sorts of improvement that can be investigated are improving educational outcomes, achieving the same outcomes with less resource, improving behaviour and social relations, improving personal effectiveness as a teacher, and improving the performance or standing of an educational institution. The list is almost endless. If you are monitoring the introduction of the synthetic phonics approach to reading and it does not produce an improvement in children's reading standards as rapidly as expected, you would be expected to think of the reasons for this. One might be because the approach will be new to most teachers who may well have problems adjusting to it. A research programme that identifies a way of introducing synthetic phonics to help teachers adopt and adjust to the new approach could raise the performance of both teachers and their pupils.

1.4 Who are the educational researchers?

What might be occurring to you now is that these three reasons for doing research could come together in the way of a poorly fitting jigsaw. Figure 1.1 shows how that happens. We can use this model of education research to say something about who does education research. So the model is effectively a representation of the research community as well.

Let's start with the research block in the centre, *Finding Out, Answering Questions and Exploring Issues.* This is where most of the academic community sits; undergraduates taking their first steps in research, postgraduates working on their first piece of independent research and lecturers and researchers taking forward the body of knowledge with more cutting edge research. The circular arrow within the square shows that this community discusses the issues amongst itself, in journals and in books. Periodically some of the research conclusions 'escape' from this community to influence the development and character of policy. Research can be used to establish the need for policy or a change in policy; this, in the diagram, is called *Policy Judging* because the research is being used to make a judgement about the broad policy direction. If, however, the broad socio-political goals are already determined, research can be used to suggest modifications to targets and goals (and sometimes processes) in order to achieve policy ends more effectively. This is called *Policy Shaping.* It is not important to spell out the processes by which this happens other than to say that in some instances the goals are pulled out of the research community while on other occasions they are pushed into the policy arena, often with the help of the media. In the UK the *Rose Report* on reading (named after its author, Jim Rose, who was in charge of inspections for the Government's quality assurance agency for schools) was pulled out of the research community's activities because of the political concern about reading attainment (Rose, 2006). The social consequences in later life of poor reading ability led to education research on reading being examined to see what apparently worked (Case Study 1.1 deals with the *Rose Report*).

Once new policy has been introduced, policy makers and others want to know that it is working. This is *Policy Testing.* It happens in two ways. Either consultants are commissioned (these can come from the academic or commercial research communities) or the academic community judges the policy itself. Frequently both happen. What is found out

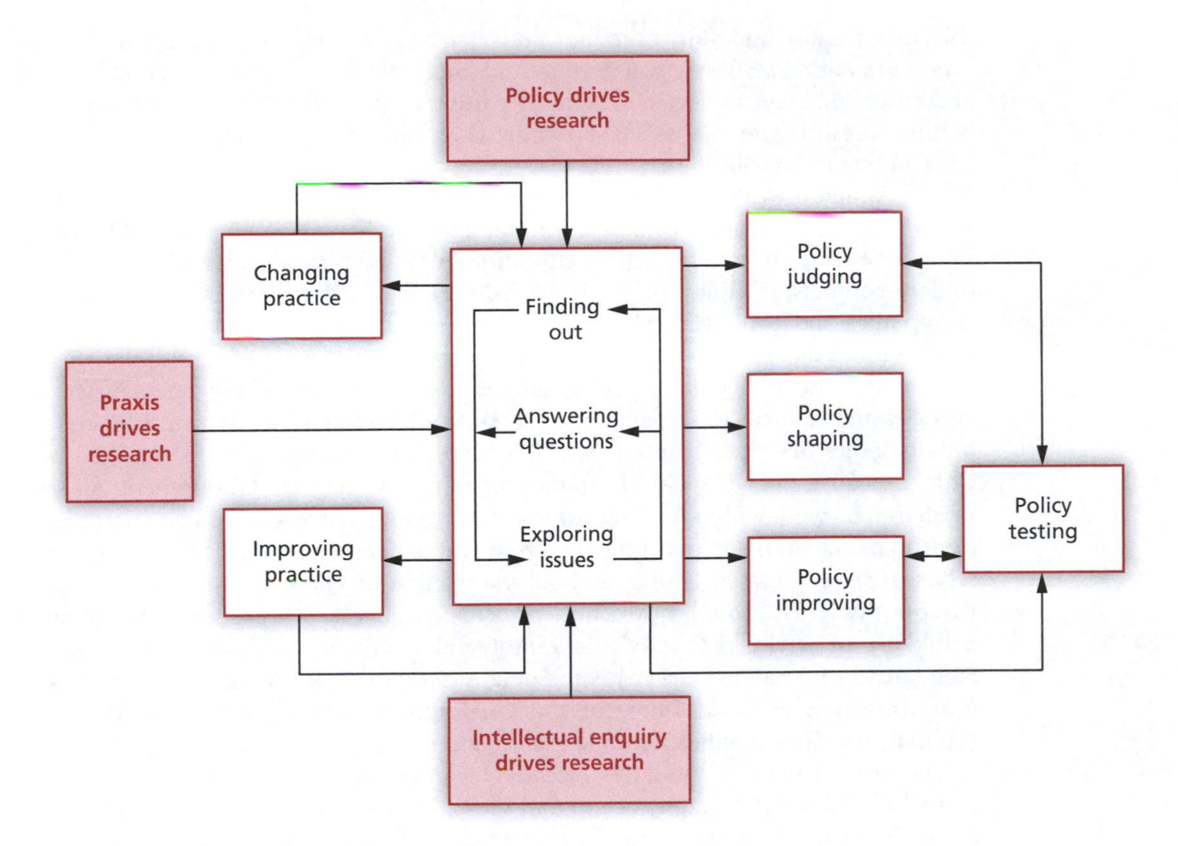

Figure 1.1 A map of educational research

can lead to improvements in policy structure and targets. Policy performance and policy evolution rely as much, if not more, on practice as they do on policy formulation.

This is where *Changing Practice* and *Improving Practice* come in. These can be applied to the following.

- Individuals, for example, teachers seeking to improve classroom performance.
- Groups, for example, a subject department in a school whose public examination results are below the national average when the school intake is representative of the socio-economic composition of an age group.
- Organisations (schools, universities, education authorities). Some of the research will be done by individual researchers and some will be undertaken by those outside the academic or professional and consultant research communities.

This simple model indicates that research can be driven by the needs of *praxis* (a concept that integrates task performance with the application of knowledge and theory and which then results in an increase in knowledge and a development of theory that can then inform practice), *policy* and *intellectual enquiry*. It presents the three areas as separate domains. The reality, however, is that the boundaries between them are highly porous. As a model, it is a crude but realistic representation of the research world and while it allows some of the groups involved in education research to be identified, it does not give a complete picture. You can, however, begin to appreciate how complex the policy development and delivery framework for education actually is. It is important to appreciate this, first, because policy drives so much research and, second, if you are involved in any aspect of policy assessment, you need to understand the range of departmental interests and ensure that you appreciate all inter-departmental linkages. The complexity of these is hinted at in Figure 1.2, which shows the Government Departments in England that have an interest in education.

The complexity of the situation in England is replicated in most of other developed states. The Department for Children, Schools and Families (DCSF) has overall responsibility for education from pre-school education, play and care, through primary and secondary compulsory education to 16–19 education. The Department for Innovation, Universities and Skills (DIUS) has overall responsibility for post-19 education. The organisations that deliver the services are nursery schools, playgroups, childminders (for early years) and individual schools, colleges and universities. These are managed by agencies and councils (in blue in Figure 1.2). Not all agencies are shown. Agencies are public bodies that operate at arm's length from Government. They are managed by a Chief Executive and work within a framework of policy set by the Government. All service deliverers work within funding streams, targets and, where appropriate, local priorities and preferences. Some schools are directly funded through the DCSF. The very act of service delivery represents policy, so how an organisation chooses to work and the relative priority it gives to tasks can effectively shape policy. Other agencies operate independently of service deliverers to monitor and maintain standards. The Office for Standards in Education (Ofsted) is the quality assurance agency for schools and early years providers and the Office of the Qualifications and Examinations Regulator (Ofqual) regulates qualifications and examinations.

The responsibility of the DCSF extends beyond teaching, teachers, pupils and students to include, for example, health and safety, buildings and finance. Other Government Departments' work impacts on young people and the education service. The Department for Business, Enterprise and Regulatory Reform (BERR) determines policy

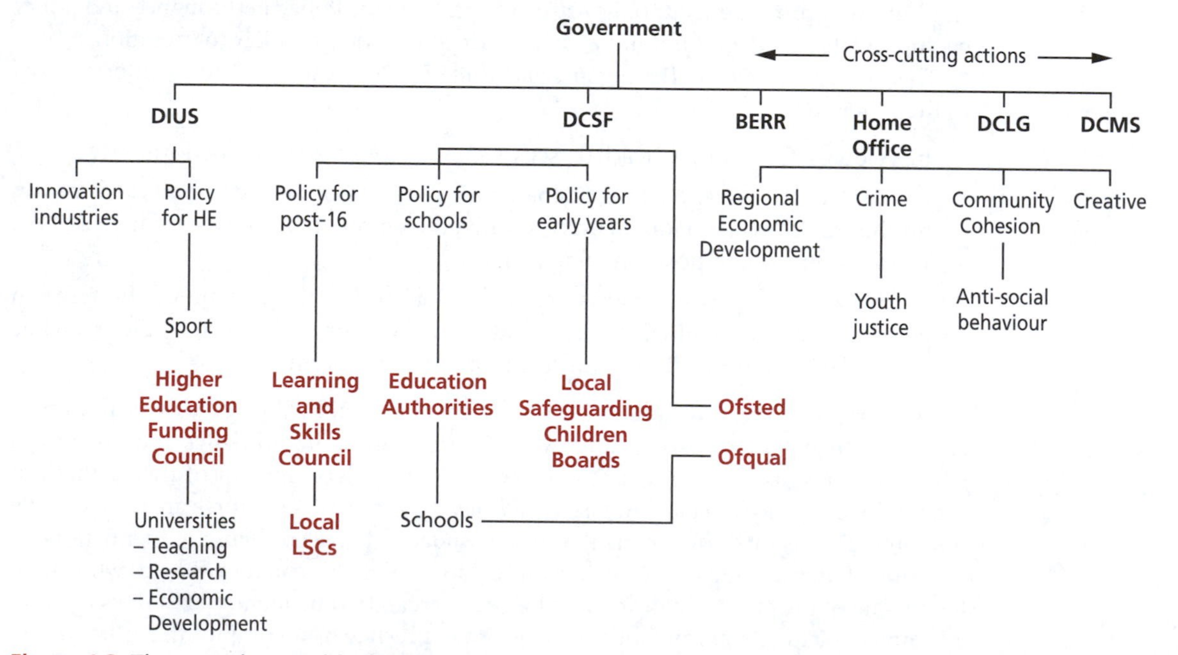

Figure 1.2 The complex world of education policy in England

for regional economic development and interacts substantially with higher education. Initiatives on enterprise emanate from BERR and the Treasury. Other departments implement cross-cutting actions. Rather than see how they intersect with education and schooling, it is easier to understand how schools are linking with those departments to address deep-rooted social problems. These revolve around issues of school exclusion, school absence, youth culture, behaviour and the Youth Justice system, community development and youth employment and arise from a key piece of legislation, The Children Act, 2004. These areas interact locally in Local Safeguarding Children Boards.

The situation in Sweden and the Netherlands is as complex as it is in the UK with a network of agencies and authorities managing the educational programme (see Figure 1.3). Note that it does not include the social and economic areas of interest to educational researchers that were set out in Figure 1.2. In Sweden the management of the system is structured according to educational level with national agencies responsible for schools, vocational training institutions and higher education. While those for vocational and higher education deal directly with the institutions that they fund, the agency for schools works with municipalities and it is these that have 'hands on' responsibility for dealing with the schools. The School Inspectorate is an independent agency responsible for monitoring standards. In the Netherlands the situation is similar. We should note though that here, several of the areas that in England are dealt with by separate ministries, are integrated into one ministry. Theoretically this should make action across these boundaries by education providers more effective. Day-to-day administration of the system occurs at an institutional level in vocational institutions and universities and by municipalities for schools. Provinces have some regulatory responsibility as well. The Netherlands, as well, has a number of agencies. The Central Funding Agency disburses money. The Education Inspectorate manages an inspection regime and the Educational Council and Science and Technology Advisory Council provide general and specific advice to government.

The implication of this breadth across departments and policy areas is that educational researchers have to be outward as well as inward looking. The complexity of education as a research area means that educational researchers not only have to be aware of policy over a wide range, they need also to have a breadth of capability, knowledge and understanding that will enable them to cope with the complex and consequently messy world of education.

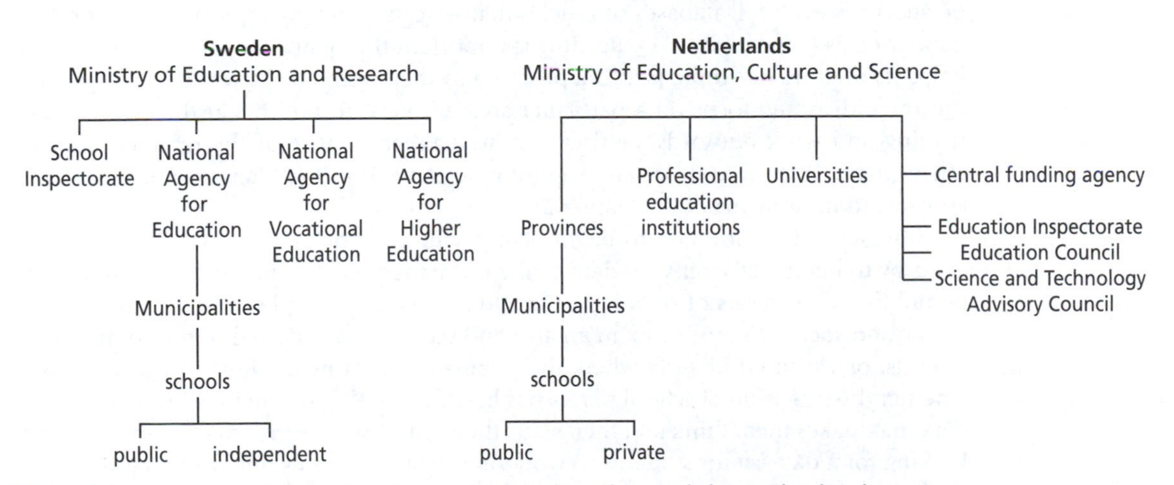

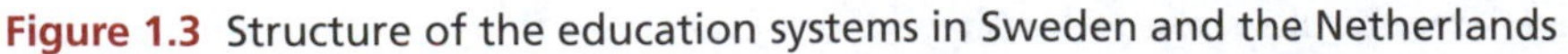
Figure 1.3 Structure of the education systems in Sweden and the Netherlands

1.5 What are the objectives of educational research?

What we have learned so far is something about the nature of educational research and the character (and breadth) of the research community. You should now be able to see where you fit into the research community (and, by implication, how you can build a career around research). For everyone in this research community, there are two fundamental objectives, each of which must be achieved with every piece of research. These objectives are the foundations of successful research, whether it is an undergraduate project, a piece of personal research to improve practice or an investigation into policy effectiveness. You need to understand these objectives because they will test you in every project and at every stage in your research career.

1.5.1 Find something out

The first objective is to ensure that we find something out. This is not always as it seems; there is plenty that can go wrong! In order to meet this objective, we have to be prepared. There are two ways of making sure that we are prepared but both amount to doing quite a lot of work before we start our data collection. We need to begin by getting a 'feel' for the field. This not only gives us background out of which we can begin to shape our own views and ideas, it also throws up whether someone has already done the work that is beginning to interest us. We can start looking from either a theoretical or practice perspective. A theoretical perspective means that we read what others have written about how the elements we are investigating should relate to each other, or about how they do relate to each other and about what should happen in order for situations to improve. If we get into a topic through our own work or practice, we will find questions such as 'How can this be improved?' and 'Why did that work well?' focusing our enquiry. Often we will read what academics have written in academic journals or what government publishes in reports and, sometimes, what journalists write in newspapers and magazines. We need to get a sense of the different perspectives people have brought to an issue. Textbooks and review papers are good for this. We have to appreciate the range of research on an issue, where the balance of research effort has been and how it has changed over time. This enables us to understand how issues emerge and perspectives evolve. Databases of articles that we can search by topic and by period are good for this (see Activity 1.1). Reading is important throughout the research process. It helps us identify our topic (see Chapter 5) and then refine it. As we start to crystallise our own ideas and focus on a particular area, we need to put this at the centre of our reading and work outwards, getting a more detailed picture of the research that has taken place. At this point, we are beginning to move into the 'literature review' that is considered in more detail in Chapter 5.

However, we do not have to begin by knowing a lot before we start. Some research starts by trying to make sense of data. Some researchers wait for major statistical series to be published, a census of population would be a good example. We could look at the ethnic and socio-economic mix in an area and see if this is reflected in the community's schools, or we could identify where the population is growing most in order to judge whether the provision of school places has kept pace. Other researchers just come across data that makes them think and then starts them on a long journey of enquiry. A lecturer looking for a data set for students to work on can stumble on something that is intriguing, where some results seem to be obeying one rule and others another. For example,

Activity 1.1 Accessing published information on the Web

We can now access many research articles via the Internet. Some are available free of charge on the Web, others are available through subscription or on a pay-per-view basis. Many educational institutions and organisations subscribe to on-line journals.

You will need to practise accessing research information via the Internet. There are two ways of going about it. Both can be time-consuming but with practice you will get better.

- If your institution subscribes to e-journals you can type in your institution's password for each journal you want to search and then access the contents of each year or volume, much as you would if you were picking volumes up off the shelf of a library. As yet, it is not as quick just to search the Internet.
- The second way is to search a database of articles taken from a range of journals. Many databases are now on-line and available through institutional subscription. In addition, here are some public databases:

There are, as well, Web search options.

- Google Scholar (http://scholar.google.com/) is available on the Web. Whichever search engine you use, there is usually a hyperlink to take you to the interface of the journal in which it is published.
- Google Books (http://books.google.com/) offers a similar facility for books.
- ERIC (http://www.eric.ed.gov/) is a major repository of education research, principally from the USA. Each entry is usually accompanied by a full précis.
- British Education Index (http://www.leeds.ac.uk/bei/) is a growing database of British research held at Leeds University.
- Australian Education Index (http://www.acer.edu.au/library/catalogues/aei.html) is operated by the Australian Council for Education Research.

Activity 1

Look up the name of one (or more) of your tutors (a) on-line via your library search facilities and (b) in each of the Web search options listed. Make a record of what each approach gives you. Now look up the tutor's home page and assess how much of the listed research output is given by each search option.

Activity 2

Use the on-line search options to see how many references each gives you for (a) phonics and (b) synthetic phonics (both are approaches to teaching reading). By looking at the references for the first two pages only, assess what proportion of the publications come from the USA, UK and Australia.

What you should learn from this is that:

1. we need to look at more than one database in order to get a rounded picture, and
2. differences in searches on different databases can be a good indication of the significance of the issue in the research and policy communities that the databases serve.

the educational attainment of children looked after by local authorities is very poor. But what if you found an authority where the young people's attainment was far higher than usual? Questions follow and answers are sought by looking at other data sets or through a field investigation.

All of this can be summarised as 'make sure that we understand our issue and where it is located in the field of education before we start'. If we want to find something out, we have to maintain this focus throughout. We have to ensure that the data and information we collect are directly linked (or as directly as we can make them) to the issue we are investigating. It is very easy when we are reading to follow up on references and then discover that we have strayed a long way from our topic. And finally, before we start, we have to have a good idea of what techniques we are going to use to extract the information and meaning from our data. So, if we want to be sure that we will find something out, we have to make sure that we have a research plan in place before we start. This should specify the focus of our research, identify our data needs, how we will obtain our data, how we will process them and place the whole programme in a time frame. Remember though, it can always be changed if conditions and circumstances alter.

To summarise, if we want to be sure that we will find something out that is new and which adds to the body of knowledge we have about education, then:

- Read to gain a good general understanding of educational theories, principles and issues.
- Read to be aware of issues that are of growing and shrinking importance.
- Read around the research topic to appreciate how understanding has grown and changed.
- Read to see how other researchers have collected and analysed data.
- Read to help develop a research plan.

1.5.2 Convince others

The second objective of research is to convince others that what we have found out is valid. Some people might say that what we find out has to be 'true' but, as we shall see in Chapter 2, 'truth' in research is a problematic concept. However, our research will be completely worthless if other people do not accept our results. We have to be clear which 'other people' we have to convince. They could be examiners, editors of academic journals, research managers who commission research or organisations that fund research. In reality, though, they fall into three groups that we can represent as overlapping sets of interest.

1. One group represents an *academic culture* with values of integrity, ethics, reliability, robustness and academic freedom.
2. The second group represents a consultant/professional researcher *contractor culture* that has an overarching need to generate revenue (which may affect the way in which results are delivered to the client).
3. The third group represents a *commissioning culture* that uses research to aid decision making. Organisations in this group (such as government departments, education agencies that manage research and training funds and institutions wanting to improve performance) identify the issues and questions that they are interested in and then contract with researchers to find information and answers. The commissioning culture shares most of the values found in the academic culture but differences are to be found in the area of academic freedom. What researchers have to understand is where the commissioning organisation is coming from. Behind the research there is usually more than a question, there is often a decision to be made. What is the benefit of introducing an initiative? Should we continue to fund this service? What are the options open to us for resolving this problem? Decisions are not neutral. They can be highly charged. They come with the interests of different groups attached to them. They can be highly political. The public presentation of the research has to acknowledge all of this.

In order to convince our audience there are two criteria we have to meet – that the results are both valid and acceptable.

(i) Validity

By now we could be forgiven for thinking that the research world is a difficult one to live in. Actually it is not that bad, just that in a few situations it can be a hard life. In general, we are likely to find it more accommodating than we might expect. If you are submitting a thesis for a research degree and, in the thesis, challenge some established positions, the likelihood of the examiner failing you is low even if they hold a different point of view. One of the benefits of academic freedom is the ability to disagree with others – but only when you can support your argument! Of course, there are situations when expressing a different point of view could be the equivalent of committing academic suicide. In the past, when academia was much smaller and some subject associations were dominated by a cabal that controlled access to journals, it could be difficult for academics to get contrary views published. This situation may well continue when not only reputations are at stake but also personal and research income. The *British Medical Journal* makes it clear that people reviewing or commenting on papers should reveal 'competing interest', which it explains as a situation where 'professional judgment concerning a primary interest (such as patients' welfare or the validity of research) may be influenced by a secondary interest (such as financial gain or personal rivalry)'. This is clearly an issue of ethics in research, an issue that we shall look at in more detail in Chapter 2. When researchers move outside established traditions they may well encounter criticism and hostility. This might apply, for example, to sociologists who look to explain behaviour in terms of the physical environment we inhabit or educationalists who approach a government department to fund research into underachievement at school and who place their proposal in the context of radical social theory. In the first case many sociologists would view the assertion that the physical environment (whether natural or man-made) controls our actions as gross misunderstanding of what it is to live in society and, in the second, radical social theory is unlikely to be something that the Secretary of State for Education feels that they can justify to an electorate.

So what makes a piece of research valid and convincing to others? These are the criteria that we have to demonstrate:

- Our data have to be *representative* of the issue we are investigating. The implication of this is that we have to pay particular attention to the processes of sampling and of choosing examples (this is covered in Chapter 6). If our sample is non-representative of the issue ('the schools were selected for the survey because I had access to them') what we will show is that we have the ability to collect data that has a high likelihood of being meaningless. Similarly, we should choose examples or case studies on the basis that they illustrate something, such as the situation in a failing school, or how a school has managed to significantly reduce truancy. Choosing a school because we happen to know the head teacher is rarely a sufficient basis for arguing the validity of our selection.
- Second, our argument and the evidence that supports it has to be *complete*, or as complete as we specify it needs to be. For example, if we are investigating how a school or college managed to improve all of its indicators of pupil attainment, we would be well advised to look beyond the operation of management processes and changes in teaching and learning process. These will have an effect but we will not know how significant they are unless we also have some information on whether staff turnover fell, changes in staff experience and qualifications and how the character of student entry shifted over time. We might find ourselves arguing that the most important factor in success is the reputation of the school and the effect this had on recruitment. Completeness comes from knowing the field we are investigating. We have to make sure that we do our reading! We can set limits to how complete our investigation is but remember, these limits have to be accepted as legitimate limits by our audience. 'The investigation focuses on pupils in the last year of compulsory education' establishes a limit that is educationally reasonable, whereas 'Restrictions of time meant that we could only survey four schools rather than the 12 planned' will rarely be

accepted as proof of anything other than the inability to build the availability of resources into the research planning process.

- The presentation of our research processes and results has to be *transparent*. Without transparency people will start to think that problems have been swept under the carpet. If they begin to do this, it is our credibility as researchers that suffers. Transparency means that we have to be as clear as we need to be in order to convince our audience. In particular we need to be clear about why we selected a particular sample size, on what basis we chose our cases, how many people responded to our surveys, and the characteristics of those who responded (as well as those who did not respond). If we use statistical procedures, we need to be clear about why we chose a particular level of probability to accept or reject a hypothesis. If we use percentages, we need to be clear about the size of the group we are studying. When our audience finds out that the 80 per cent who approved of the policy was 80 per cent of five people, most of them will think that we are trying to pull a fast one. We should also be transparent about the problems we faced. 'Data from X school could not be obtained because it failed a government inspection during the investigation' would be accepted by most people. Transparency is important because it allows people to judge our research process and our conclusions and to determine for themselves whether they are sufficiently robust. Compromises in procedure are frequently acceptable, even to professional audiences. Ultimately transparency is read as a statement about your honesty as a researcher.

(ii) Acceptability

The issue of the acceptability of our research is a complex one because it has to take account of the quality of our research work and the acceptability to our audience of our conclusions.

If our results are not valid, then they will not be accepted. Valid results are well grounded in the evidence we present and are justifiable in the circumstances in which we collect and analyse our data. If our conceptualisation and execution of our research is poor, our results will not be accepted. This is a situation faced periodically by all departments in higher education in the UK that would like to receive funding to carry out research. The Higher Education Research Council for England (it is similar in other parts of the UK) judges research and will not fund departments whose research output, as assessed by peers, is poor.

But even if our methods and methodology are appropriate, there is still the issue of the acceptability of our message. If our conclusions run counter to expectations, prevailing wisdom or the direction an organisation would like to go in, then they *may* not be accepted. In his 1999 address to the British Educational Research Association, Peter Mortimore pointed out that performance-related pay for teachers was not an initiative that could be supported by research evidence and that there was specific research that drew attention to why it would be a retrograde step (Mortimore, 1999). But it was still introduced. He drew attention to the way in which other education research has, over time, run counter to government initiatives. The implication of this is that political values are more important than good research practice when it comes to the acceptability of education research.

- If our conclusions are not accepted, the appropriateness of our procedures is likely to be questioned. As researchers we should always remember that established orthodoxies (and organisations wanting evidence to support a decision) do not like to be challenged. If we *are* challenging orthodoxy, we should make sure our procedures are robust.

1.6 Some guidelines on research

You should, by now, have picked up some messages on the position that this book takes on research. It is that:

- research throws up problems;
- problems have to be solved; and
- there is always more than one solution.

The research community is large, fragmented and has different interests, purposes and goals. Despite this fragmentation, there are objectives that are common and determine how acceptable the research world will find the research we do. Surprisingly the research world of researchers, policy makers, consultants and those who commission research is a fairly forgiving place if researchers have to compromise with what research theory says should happen. Why is this? Think about it; it is obvious why researchers take a relaxed view about research procedure; if they did not, it would be very difficult for them to undertake much research themselves. The guidelines that follow are not meant to provide you with authority to break any rule in the research rule book but they are designed to give you the confidence to argue your case and to give you an idea of what you have to do when you research in the real world.

1.6.1 Don't get into a research rut

Many textbooks on research method argue that there is a 'proper' way to undertake research. Some present only a single method, for example, quantitative procedures (see Chapter 3). Others recognise that there is a range of approaches including, for example, humanist, feminist, postmodern or, at a more procedural level, action research, evaluation or data analysis (again, see Chapter 3). These are called methodologies (a concept that we shall explore in more detail in Chapter 2). They represent a way of working and each has a set of rules, procedures and methods. These methodologies have arisen because in particular circumstances they seem to work well. The danger of working within a methodology, however, is that there are occasions, perhaps even a majority of occasions, when the requirements of the paradigm do not match the reality that the researcher has to deal with. For example, if we want to show whether changing student learning from a lecture-based programme to one built around seminars improves academic performance and all we do is observe students, ask them their views and look at their results, I would not be sure that we were actually showing what you wanted to show – even if their results improved. What if it was a 'good' year? What if the lecturer was bad and the tutor was good? Our results would show the effect of a member of staff, not the teaching method.

The best guidance anyone can be given at the start of their research career is to understand all the models of research practice but when it comes to the research itself; do not start with an ideal procedure, start with the research issue. Do not contort your research to fit in with the ideal. Let your research issue guide you in the way in which it wants to be investigated. And feel free to create a research programme that blends approaches. Research paradigms and models offer researchers a comfort zone. The real world requires researchers to deal with complexity and problems. In other words, we have to deal with reality, warts and all.

1.6.2 Audit your resources

It is too simple to think of a research programme as being just the product of a negotiation between the research issue and research paradigms. At least, it would not be too simple if we had deep pockets and all the time we wanted because we could then get close to delivering the perfection that might be required. Sadly few researchers are blessed with such abundance. Most research is probably done by people working by themselves. Some people are fortunate enough to have an assistant. Some others work as teams but, unlike the sciences, it is rare to find an education team larger than five. In the real world educational researchers are invariably faced with resource constraints and more than anything else, this means that we have to compromise with perfection. It certainly is a good idea to pre-test data collection procedures to make sure that they deliver what you want them to – but what can you do if time does not allow it? It would be good practice to test the significance of a dozen possible influences on the behaviour of a population but what if your research design, with you as the only researcher, requires a sample size in excess of 30,000 in order to do this? When we start designing our research programme we must audit the resources available to us, note when they are available and estimate the call on our resources of various procedures. We should make a list of the resources we have and those we will need. In general, we are likely to require resources for data collection (we may be able to call on friends, colleagues or students), for specialist advice (on data processing, for example). We will require access to information sources (both traditional and on-line), phones, faxes and post (and unless someone else is picking up the bill, we will have to pay for these). We will also need to know how much time we have available to pull it all together. We should now see that developing a research programme is not something we do and then implement. We have to make sure that the procedures we are using will give us the information we need *and that we can afford to use them*. If the equation does not balance, then it's back to the drawing board. That's the trouble with the real world, it keeps getting in the way of what is best!

1.6.3 Appreciate that things can go wrong

In the literature we may find awareness of problems and delays, etc. referred to as a risk assessment. Whatever we call it, we have to build in to our research the fact that disaster can strike. What we have to decide on is the chance of disaster and, if it happens, what the consequences are for our research.

We need to analyse what can go wrong with our research programme, how likely it is to occur and what the consequences are of it happening. Then what we have to do is look at our assessment in the context of Table 1.2. This shows just three states of risk: a high chance of something occurring, a moderate likelihood and a low likelihood. What might go wrong? Our computer with all our data might be stolen. The school we were going to use as a case study could get a new head teacher who might refuse permission. Our teaching duties or our commitments on other courses might be greater than we expected. How would we judge the likelihood of these? If we carry a laptop around and have never had it stolen, have we just been lucky? Is it our turn soon? Is our case study school failing in some way and is the head teacher likely to walk the plank? Or if the school is very successful are they likely to move to a better job? We can look behind the risk and begin to assess its likelihood.

The columns in Table 1.2 describe the impact of things happening. Impact is a measure of cost and consequence. If our hard drive crashes, taking what we hoped was almost the final version of our thesis with it, that is quite an impact. The consequence is that

Table 1.2 Generic risk assessment matrix

Chance of risk occurring	Level of impact/cost of occurrence to research		
	Devastating	Moderate	Low
High	Unacceptable	Unacceptable	Acceptable
Moderate	Unacceptable	Unacceptable	Acceptable
Low	Acceptable	Negligible	Negligible

we have to start writing all over again and the time it takes is either a real or an opportunity cost. Impact is expressed in terms of the recoverability of the research programme. Again there are three states: devastating, that is the programme is non-recoverable; moderate, that is the programme is recoverable with some effort; and low, when the programme is recoverable with little extra effort. We have to determine the limits to each category of recoverability. For example if our research is scheduled to last three months, up to two weeks to recover to where we were might be 'low', between two weeks and one month may be 'moderate' and anything over one month is non-recoverable. For other lengths of research programme we would choose different boundaries to our categories.

Table 1.2 also shows the acceptability of something happening without our taking any action to avoid it. Acceptability is determined by a combination of likelihood and impact. How we label each cell in the matrix is a matter of judgement. Table 1.2 is not definitive, it is just my view. For those cells labelled 'Negligible', I would not plan any mitigation measures at all. For those labelled 'Unacceptable', I would ensure that I would take action to minimise the risk, while for those labelled 'Acceptable', I would for some or if the timescale for the research was short. This is the theory. What we have to do is put this into effect. Experience (and making mistakes) are great teachers. However, we can build experience without actually researching by analysing other people's research. Start this process by looking at Activity 1.2.

1.6.4 Understand the Laws of Enquiry

These are not laws in the same way that scientific laws are laws. They have not been subjected to rigorous testing but they do seem to work. Experienced researchers can often circumvent these but they always seem to catch you out in the end. That is why both those who teach research methods and professional researchers usually have a library of materials they can refer to. And, incidentally, that is why, if you are at the start of your research career, this book should be on your shelf for a few years.

Table 1.3 sets out the Laws of Enquiry. Read them and think about them and their implications before you go on to the next paragraph.

So, you have read through the Laws (they are, of course, not really 'laws' but patterns of disruption to research that seem to occur to new researchers with some regularity). You have seen the thrust of the First and Second Laws and you have probably had to struggle a little with the Third. It is actually quite a simple message but an incredibly important one – no matter where you start with your enquiry, there is always a problem to solve or something you should know in order to continue. Research, in other words, is a problem-solving activity. Some problems you can anticipate, others do not appear until you start.

Activity 1.2 Pre-empting problems

Read any journal article that has researched an educational issue through the collection and analysis of information (that is, it should not be a conceptual or philosophical paper). It does not matter how the information was collected as long as it was, at least in part, from 'primary sources', for example, straight from the horse's mouth or by direct observation. Data collected by questionnaire would be suitable, as would interviews, written accounts, pictures and watching people and recording their actions.

- Are any problems identified by the author? If so, at what stage did they occur in the research programme and could they have been foreseen?
- Look at the research process in terms of the following stages:
  - collection of data
  - storage of data
  - processing of data
  - analysis
  - writing and reporting.
- For each stage, consider (a) what problems might have occurred; even if they did not, (b) what impact they would have had on the research (think in terms of time); (c) what contingency you would build in to accommodate them. Think in terms of the following as a start:
  - Sources of information: think about alternatives to the ones used, how many there are, their availability when the researcher needs them in an emergency, the cost and effort of setting up a second programme to generate information that might never be used.
  - The potential for obtaining information that is variable in quality: if you are employing people to collect data, what is the likelihood of their using the same procedure? What is the cost of training them? What is the cost of monitoring their work?
  - The possibility that the resources you thought would be there suddenly disappear.
  - Whether the quality of the data supports the type of analysis. Do you actually feel convinced?
  - Loss of data and loss of files: how can this happen? Are there times when it is less serious? Is there a point when it becomes catastrophic? What could you do?

Table 1.3 Laws of Enquiry

First Law
There is always something you need to know in order to understand fully what you have to do.

Second Law
You don't know what you need to know until you try to do something.

Third Law
When you know what you need to know in order to understand how to do something, you are likely to find that the first law operates again!

Implications for your work
- The only way to finish is to begin.
- Do not try to solve all the problems before you start.
- Allow enough time to solve problems.

If all that researchers had to cope with was finding things out in order to progress the research then we could manage it, but there are other aspects of research design with the same sort of issue. At a higher, strategic level, when we come to develop a research action plan, we have to go through the process of reconciling possible research methods with research issues and research resources. This is not necessarily straightforward and we may have to go around the issue several times to get them all to balance. A first pass identifies the best research methods to get to grips with the research issue but we just do not have the resources. The second pass sees us change the research methods to fit in with the resources but they sit uneasily with the research issue. In the third pass, we narrow the research issue, amend the research methods and find that they fit in with our resources.

Finally, over a period of time, we will appreciate that the research world changes. Technology creates opportunities for innovation in data collection. New methods of data analysis are developed. We have to know of their existence and understand their role on the assumption that we may need to use them some time. The danger with the Third Law of Enquiry is that we will keep on learning and understanding in order to develop the perfect research plan. One piece of sound advice is 'don't bother'. Perfection is expensive, rarely attained and if we say that we have achieved it (or even nearly achieved it), there will be someone in the research community who will want to make their reputation by pointing out what we have not done. The skill we need to develop is to know when to stop refining the research process. The key to this is our ability to marshal our rationale and present our reasons so that those who matter are convinced.

1.6.5 Appreciate the research progression

If we think that our research programme will start at the beginning and proceed in an orderly fashion until we get to the end, then we have to think again. We have had enough clues already to suggest that it will not be like this. Research is a progression but rarely a linear process. It usually progresses as a series of loops around decision points. 'If I approach the issue using this strategy, what resources will I need? Do I have enough? Can I trim my resource needs or do I need to look at an alternative strategy?' When we come to writing up our research as a thesis or as an academic paper, we will probably find that we will start with something 'straightforward', such as our review of literature, and continue either by returning to the introduction, writing the analysis and finally the conclusion or we might write the analysis and then finish with the introduction and conclusion. Once we have written our conclusion, though, we need to go back to our introduction to make sure that it highlights the issues and questions that we answer. Then we will need to go through our literature review to make sure that it places the issues we have investigated at the centre. If we do not do this, then our work will not have a good storyline and will read like a series of loosely connected passages. Well-written research should be like a good novel; it should take the reader along with it, the bits of the story falling into place in a convincing and compelling way and, not least, it should be a good and interesting read.

The guidance to take away from this is that we should not be afraid to revisit our decisions and that we should make sure we tie up all the loose ends before we embark on the next stage of implementing our research plan.

1.6.6 Understand how to allocate time

Research is like an iceberg; there is an awful lot of effort that goes into it that people do not see. Very crudely, there are four stages to the research process:

1. Planning and preparation.
2. Data collection.
3. Analysis.
4. Writing up the report or papers.

Planning and preparation is the stage that should utilise our intellectual and practical effort. Of course, there will be things in stages two and three that we may not have foreseen: a key respondent on long-term sick leave, the person who was going to offer us training and support in a software package moving to another institution, theft of digital recording equipment and no money in the budget to replace it, unwillingness of a school or college to be involved following a change of senior manager. All of these might happen but if we built in a safety net for every problem that could arise we would never get started. The most we can do, following our risk analysis, is to develop a research programme that gives us options should disaster happen. The first stage is when we do our thinking and our organisation.

At the end of the first stage, we should have a plan. All of our data collection procedures should be determined, our methods for collecting data (questionnaires, interview schedules, observation sheets) should have been designed and produced and all of those who are going to provide us with information should be in place, even if the actual dates when we will meet them have yet to be agreed. In other words, for stages two and three when we collect and analyse the data, we should be on automatic pilot, having taken all of the decisions we need to make in stage one. If we do this, we will realise that planning and preparation can take up a significant proportion of the time we have available. To give some guidance, planning and preparation for major pieces of work such as a research thesis can take up as much as a third of the time available. For smaller projects, the proportion goes down, though not always by as much as we might expect.

1.7 Finally, some things we ought to know about educational research before we start

This first chapter is all about giving us context as education researchers. In this last section we will get a perspective on the character of educational research.

The popular image of research comes from science. We could be forgiven for thinking that some scientists wear white coats just to reinforce the popular image of science. The reality, of course, is that IT analysis and modelling now takes the place of much laboratory work – and you do not need a white coat to work with a computer. The image, however, remains and it generates an interpretation that research is something that is set apart from everyday experience. When we look at educational research we have a bit of a problem with this perception because the object of study in education research is everyday experience. This places the education researcher in a very different position from the scientific researcher. While the former is still an expert, they are an expert on a topic on which a significant proportion of the population can have strong and valid opinions. It is important that we, as education researchers, understand this. So, in the public mind, while the scientist is doing good work manipulating the DNA of plants to generate medicines, the education researcher could be part of the problem with 'education today'. This is not to say that the researcher is doing poor research, just that the relative accessibility to it of education as an issue on which it has an attitude means that educational research is a highly contested area.

1.7.1 Research into education is highly political

Look back to Figure 1.2. See how many government departments have an interest in education. It is clear that educational issues cut across many departments. Each has its priorities and goals. Where these compete there is the potential for conflict. Every political party sets out its policies for these areas in the hope that they will capture sufficient popular interest to get them elected. Since only one party (or group of parties) is in government at any one time, this often means that from one election to the next the unsuccessful parties will change their policies. Education, like most social and economic issues, is a contested area. We might think that when it comes to what goes on in the classroom, the political system is too far away to have any influence but we would be wrong. In the UK the framework of what should be learnt, the allocation of time for the development of literacy and numeracy, the study of skills between 16 and 18 and even the guidance on how to teach reading have been political decisions. The outcomes of education become political footballs. Year on year improvements in student attainment in public examinations represents a collapse of standards if you are out of power and are 'a tribute to the hard work of teachers and pupils and to "our" initiatives in school management' if you are in power. Pupil selection, the access of children from socio-economically deprived areas to higher education, is a political issue in the UK. Whether 'intelligent design' should be taught as part of the science curriculum is a legal and political issue in the USA; the wearing of religious symbols is an issue in France and the lower literacy attainment, lower retention in schools and lower participation in higher education of boys are all issues in Australia, as they are in many countries. In the Netherlands truancy is a problem but who should be punished? As in the UK, parents can be fined for their child's non-attendance at school but in 2004, the Government introduced trials of a policy of putting the truants themselves into youth detention centres.

Many issues are common around the world. When you undertake Activity 1.3 you will begin to build a picture of what is happening globally and of the common threads to change. However, what we should also appreciate is that wherever there is an issue, there is a lack of consensus and when there is a lack of consensus, people struggle to ensure that their solutions carry the day. The reason, of course, that they do this is because it is through the successful use of an issue that they advance their careers, either as politicians or education managers or, even, academics. We should be aware of all of this. We might think that our research into the causes of truancy reflects a balanced academic perspective but as well as those of teachers, we will be treading on the toes of the criminal justice system, the educational welfare system and the social services system all the way up to the Government. Working in a crowded field across boundaries is interesting – but there are more people to offend. Be prepared to take criticism and stand your ground.

Activity 1.3 Global educational issues

Use the Web to identify educational issues of concern to more than one country. Use national sites in the first instance (try searches on 'educational debates' and 'educational problems') and then see what the World Bank, UNESCO and the OECD have to contribute.

1.7.2 Doing education research can make you enemies

The potential to make enemies should be apparent from the discussion above on the political character of education research. However, it is not just the politicians we have to worry about; it is educationalists and other researchers as well. We have to understand that many people's views on education are driven by deeply held values on such things as equity, excellence, social justice and wealth creation, to name but a few. Education is one of the mechanisms they can use to achieve their social and economic goals. Because of this they take a particular view of education and what it should be like. Any research that challenges the mode of education they argue for is a challenge to their values and to them. If you are working within a set of liberal educational values, you will probably engage in a balanced debate with other academics. However, if you challenge a conventional perspective, for example with the suggestion that educational provision should be segregated according to ability, then the tone of the debate may well move towards the vitriolic. Even within the academic community you will find 'camps' whose research will be mutually reinforcing. A will quote B, C and D; B will quote A, C and D and so on. This reflective referencing means that if we challenge the conclusions of one in the camp, we could well face criticism from them all.

We cannot do anything to change this situation. We should, however, realise that if we are going to research education, our best defence against those who want to rubbish our conclusions because they run counter to their own views is a robust research procedure that neutral observers will accept is sound in the context in which the research has been done. Remember this guidance; poor methodology, a conclusion that someone does not like and our work will be consigned to the recycle bin on our computer. Our reputation will have suffered as well!

1.7.3 Be careful how you read 'research'

Those involved in education are frequently driven by profound beliefs of what is right and what is wrong and they have a strong commitment to persuading others to join with them to maintain a status quo or to create change. We need to be aware that education research can be undertaken by people with a point to prove. For this reason, we should approach research publications from a sceptical point of view. Authors should have to win us round and demonstrate their credibility to us.

How do we adopt this sceptical perspective? We need to ask the right questions of every stage of the research that we are reading. Why was the research topic chosen? What is the context for the research? The possibility of there being a political dimension to research designed to improve practice may be low but if the research is designed to assess a classroom methodology developed by the researcher, then at least one person stands to benefit if it is shown to be effective. Look to see how an author explores and reviews the research issue when defining the research question. Do we think it is balanced? How far does the language introduce a sense of concern (problems unresolved or not even recognised over a long period) or define the issue within a political context, for example, testing a policy proposal of a political party? What evidence do we have of the stance taken by the author in their non-academic workings such as newspaper articles?

It is not just what is chosen to be researched that we need to look at but also at how the research was carried out. If we are reading something published in an academic journal, we should check to see if it has been judged by other academics as being of an appropriate standard, a process called 'refereeing'. Most have been. This is one of the guarantees of academic quality. Nonetheless, when we read it we need to assure ourselves that the way in which the evidence has been attained is robust and that the conclusions are warranted. You will be able to do this effectively by the time you have reached the end of this book.

Finally, we have to read very closely the words used by the author. Enthusiasm is acceptable but it can tip over to a level of commitment that begins to undermine the neutrality of the conclusions. 'The failure of particular groups of children to perform at the level expected of them' is acceptable language; a 'shocking waste of talent' says much the same thing but has an emotional content that lays bare the values of the author. When we read, look for words that are laden with values; pay attention to the author's style and see if there is a shift, especially in the conclusion, from studied neutrality towards a more committed tone.

If doing all of this sounds a tall order, it is not meant to be. All researchers should develop the skill of reading behind the words to detect other messages but we should not imagine that there is a radical manifesto behind each publication. Most work is honestly attempted and often the most serious criticism that can be made is that it is pedestrian. But then, in an army of researchers, there are bound to be more foot soldiers than anyone else.

1.7.4 Striving to be neutral

Look back at the last section on research being undertaken by people who want to prove a point and examine yourself. When you come to develop your research proposals, ask yourself, 'Why is this topic important to me?' If you are researching the role of play in education of young children, is it because you want to enhance practice or because you are concerned that an overemphasis on formal education is taking away something from childhood that you believe is important for the healthy development of a person? You need to examine where you are coming from and to decide how explicit you make that for your audience so that others can make up their own minds about your own intellectual neutrality.

Being neutral is difficult. If we believe in something, we have to manage our own values in the research process. If we are contracted to undertake research, then we have to manage not only our own values but also the expectations of the organisation that is paying for the work. Frequently the most important expectation it has is that our research will enable it to go forward with what it wants to do. If our research results suggest that there is genuinely a better alternative, then we have a duty of care to our client to make the organisation aware of it. With all of these issues we begin to realise that collecting the information is often the relatively straightforward part of research.

1.7.5 Research and changing the face of education

All young researchers in every subject can dream about making the conceptual breakthrough that changes the face of their subject. Few actually achieve it, of course, but at least in the sciences and some social sciences, it is a possibility. In education there is little 'blue skies' research. Most research is either for or about policy or for or about practice. The main things that drive education research are values, political ideals, effectiveness and efficiency. The issues with which education researchers are grappling are often large scale and there are few research teams able to work at the scale and with the size of data sets that are required. Much educational research, therefore, looks only at a segment of the issue and at this level it can be difficult to connect the work to an overarching framework that represents a completely new direction for the subject. New approaches to learning that get more students up to a threshold level of attainment are important for society, but they are not mould-breaking, like the discovery of DNA. Console yourself with the knowledge that without the new techniques, new ways of training and developing teachers and all the other educational innovations supported by education research, there would be no one to make the scientific breakthroughs or create the literary or artistic icons for our period.

If it is not with a detailed study that education researchers can have a significant impact, how can they? The answer probably lies in synthesis, in bringing together the results of many studies and demonstrating where the weight of evidence lies and the implications for education policy or practice of the distribution of the evidence. Most research projects and the books and academic papers that arise from them place the research in the context of the literature on the subject. It not far from this to a synthesis of a field of education for a research review, surprisingly a process for distilling knowledge that seems to be more common in other subjects such as medicine than it is in education. Perhaps this says something about values being more important in driving educational change in the past, rather than evidence of what works (something we would all be worried about if this were the case in medicine). The synthesis that can truly have an impact is usually issue or problem based. What can education research tell us about the benefits of streaming, or the causes of disaffection, or how schools can fulfil a community purpose? Synthesising often diverse research from different parts of the world calls for particular processes. We will look at some aspects of using literature in Chapter 5.

1.8 Is research a messy business?

The purpose of this chapter is to give new researchers an insight into the context in which educational research sits. The key message of this chapter and this book is the need for researchers to be flexible and to allow the requirements of the research issue to influence the character of the research programme. If you have already been introduced to research methods in education, either in an introductory course, or through another book or through reading research articles, you might have been led to a different conclusion. There are many books and, almost certainly, many courses that present research as a highly structured, procedurally ordered, process. The expectation is that the researcher fits a template over the research problem and then follows the rules. However, the templates are not always appropriate; you as a researcher will have to make many decisions and the research world is riven by intellectual and political positioning. Is research a messy business? Yes, it is. It is messy because:

- the real world is not as clearly defined as research templates require;
- you will rarely have the luxury of an abundance of resources to draw on, so you will have to make real choices and compromises;
- the transition from fact to opinion is not always clear cut, especially when the research is on attitudes and beliefs;
- researchers mark out their territories and defend them;
- people use research to advance themselves.

You have to stay safe. Alienating others is acceptable only when you are absolutely sure of your ground. To be a successful researcher, you have to know enough in order to make choices. For every research issue you tackle, you must draw on a broad understanding of research principles, models and methods. Without this, your choice is constrained. This book will give you the understanding you need. Because it is driven by the need to find answers rather than follow procedures, it will give you the confidence to put together research procedures that are fit for purpose. Now let's get started.

Summary

- The purpose of education research is to answer questions about educational issues. Often the research aims to inform either policy or practice. In the case of policy, it may be concerned with its development or effectiveness or impact. In the case of practice, its goal is either to improve practice or to understand whether professional practice (in the classroom or in administration and management) is effective.

- Educational research is carried out by three groups.
  (i) Academic researchers approach issues from an intellectual perspective. They try to find answers to real (and often significant questions) and while they may hope to have an impact on what education actually does, there is no guarantee of this.
  (ii) Policy research can be conducted as an academic process but, when it will directly feed into policy making or policy assessment, it is conducted by contract researchers (who may also be academics).
  (iii) Practice orientated research is commissioned by individuals and organisations that are seeking to increase their effectiveness. While we can identify these groups, the reality of the research world is that the boundaries between them can be very blurred.
- The complexity of the research world is increased by the range of topics and issues that educational research considers. We gained an appreciation of this by looking at how government in the UK managed education in its social and economic context.
- Like most research, educational research aims to find things out. As educational researchers, we have to be sure that our specific research issue or question has not been tackled before. This means that we have to stay abreast of research in education. Finding out something is of little use unless we can convince other people of its merits. To do this we have to demonstrate the validity and acceptability of our research.
- If we are to achieve this, we have to plan our research. We have to ensure that we have sufficient resources to deliver on our plan. We should look at what we intend to do and assess what can go wrong, and we should remember that the plan needs to be flexible because there will almost certainly be something that goes wrong or that we have not planned for.
- We should also remember that while all research has a political character, education research has a strong political dimension because it is concerned with the creation or outcomes of political policy.

Further reading

Brew, A. (2001) *The Nature of Research*, Routledge Falmer.
The idea that the research process is uncontroversial should be nailed firmly on the head. All research, as Angela Brew points out, is conducted in social, political and intellectual contexts which can pull the researcher in different directions. In this book she explores the idea of research traditions, the difference between research and scholarship, how we create new knowledge, ways of looking at research – as a commodity, as a learning process – and at the link between research and teaching.

References

Mortimore, P. (1999) *Does Educational Research Matter?* Presidential address to the British Educational Research Association Annual Conference, available from Education-Line, http://www.leeds.ac.uk/educol/documents/00001206.htm, accessed January 2008.

Mullis, I., Martin, M., Kennedy, A. and Foy, P. (2007) PIRLS 2006 International Report: *IEA's Progress in International Reading Literacy Study in Primary Schools in 40 Countries*, TIMSS & PIRLS International Study Center, Lynch School of Education, Boston College.

Rose, J. (2006) *Independent Review of the Teaching of Early Reading*, Final Report, Department for Education and Skills.

Scott Murray, M.T., Clermont, Y. and Werquin, P. (2005) *Learning and Living: First Results of the Adult Literacy and Life Skills Survey*, Statistics Canada and OECD.

Chapter contents

Chapter 2

UNDERSTANDING THE RESEARCH PROCESS

Key themes

Getting to grips with the research puzzle

- You do not just start research. You do not get up one day having decided to research an issue and go out to collect the information. There are influences that you have to take account of and decisions you have to make.
- We will see how research philosophy, research paradigms and ethical principles affect how we go about research.
- We will look at four important methodologies: case studies, ethnography, evaluation and action research.
- We will outline rules and principles that govern how you put your research together and how to use terminology appropriately to produce an effective research proposal.
- By the end of this chapter you will be able to start preparing a research proposal.

Introduction

If, after reading Chapter 1, you are feeling that getting into education research is like being sent into battle without adequate arms, then take heart. This chapter will begin the process of building your understanding of research so that you can acquit yourself well. You will learn about things that influence the way you go about your research and the procedures that you adopt. You will understand about the broad goals of research and how they can affect your research output. As you go through the chapter, you will find that it will:

- demystify research terms,
- show you the confusion that can arise when people use terms in different ways,
- begin the process of putting the research issue at the centre of the research enquiry and
- explore what sorts of questions research in education can answer.

Research is a very creative process. You have to bring together ideas about how to proceed, resolve questions about what you want to achieve, select the research tools you want to use, identify the issues you want to study and even the context in which you would like to study them. Figure 2.1 shows three principal components of any research process: the goals and the outcomes you can achieve, the processes you can use and the issues you can research. You have to make choices about all

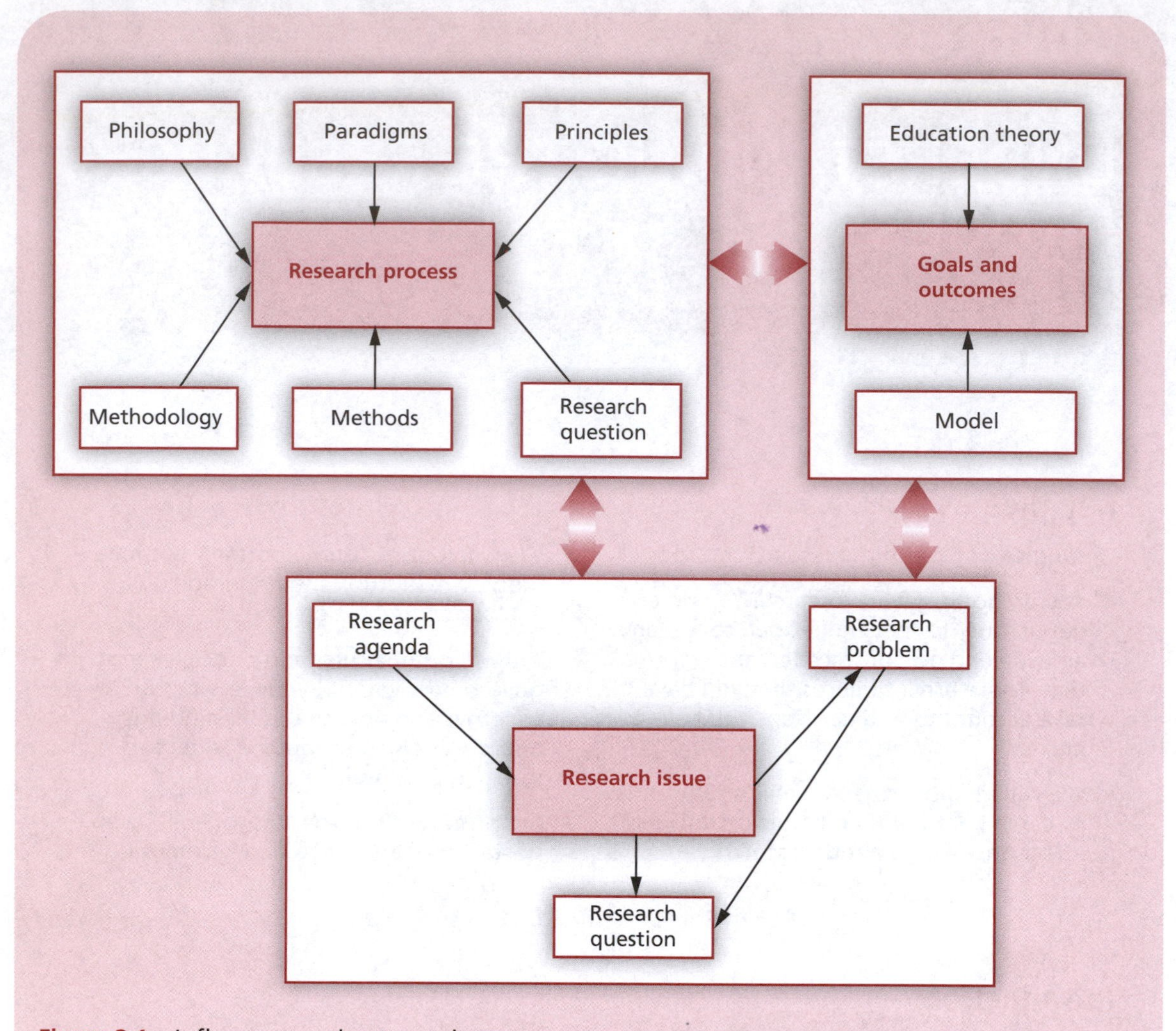

Figure 2.1 Influences on the research process

of these. Making these choices is not an arbitrary process. There is a whole series of factors that can influence your decision. These too are shown in Figure 2.1. This is what we shall examine in this chapter. We shall look first at ideas that influence the research process, then at ideas that influence the outcomes you want your research to achieve and finally ideas that influence the research issue and the research question. At the end of the chapter, you will be guided on the first stages of developing a research project.

2.1 Ideas that influence the research process

Research is not always a matter of collecting information and answering the question. Some people might think that you are not asking the right question, others that you have not used the right approach to obtain your answer. Others might question whether you have the right information to answer the question. Unless you know the decisions you have to make about the way in which you are going to do your research and unless you know on what basis to make those decisions, your work could be seriously flawed and you could be walking into controversy and an unfavourable critique of your research. In this section, you will learn about the following concepts and how they can influence the way you work:

- Philosophy.
- Paradigms.
- Research principles.
- Research methodology.
- Research methods.
- Research theory.

2.1.1 What is your standpoint? An introduction to research philosophy

Why is philosophy important to your research? Because it expresses views and values about the world; because it describes how the world is organised and perhaps, even how it should be organised. It can have an ethical dimension. It can, for instance, concern itself with equality and equity. It can have a political component, for example you should be able to trace a link between the education policies of political parties and their underpinning political philosophy and beliefs. With education philosophy we can construct a curriculum and develop a teaching approach that maximises opportunity for all, or we can do the same but have as our goal the early identification of gifted children so that, through their development, they can reach positions where they can innovate and lead in society. In other words, the philosophy is to create (and exploit) an educated elite. So philosophy shapes what you think is important. It can influence what you choose to read, what you research and how you research it.

Research as an activity has developed schools of practice, each with its own philosophical standpoint, that cross subject and disciplinary boundaries. These philosophical positions can influence not just how the research is conducted but rather more importantly what is researched and how the evidence is interpreted. If you thought that all you had to do was accurately collect some data and honestly report your findings, then think again. If you do, there are researchers who, from their own philosophical standpoint, will castigate your research naivety. If you are to defend yourself, then it is important to understand what you are defending yourself from.

This is a particularly difficult section to write because it is hard to put together a simple framework that incorporates the main philosophical positions and standpoints. Research philosophy is multidimensional; that is, it comprises approaches and beliefs that are not mutually exclusive. If we look at a philosophy one way, we can use one set of terminology and if we look at it another, then we use another. We could divide researchers into those who believe that a real world exists and those who believe it is a personal construction (that is, reality exists only in our minds), between those who believe it is their role to understand and explain and those who believe that out of understanding should come change, between those who believe that social action is the product of our exercising individual free will and those who believe that there are powerful structures in society that constrain choice. In other words, the world of research philosophy is complex and all this book can do is open a few windows to let you glimpse some of the main domains of the research landscape. The areas that we shall look at are:

- Scientism and Positivism.
- Humanism, Phenomenology and Existentialism.
- Critical theory.
- Postmodernism.

(i) Scientism and Positivism

Scientism, as the name suggests, is about science. It refers to the approach that scientists take in their research and their beliefs about what research ought to be. It argues that *proper* research follows the methods and adopts the standards that have been developed within the natural sciences. Scientism, however, is more than an approach to the collection and analysis of data. It argues that the method (its rigorous and methodical approach of observation, experimentation and testing) is the only way of generating valid statements about the real world. The implication of this is that any understanding that is developed in other ways (for example, through watching what people do) is less valid than understanding developed through scientific study.

At the heart of scientism lies the idea of predictable cause and effect, out of which can ultimately be generated immutable laws that govern the behaviour of matter. While the social sciences have not progressed this far, scientism has, nonetheless, had a significant impact.

To understand this, we can go back to the nineteenth century and appreciate the impact of the advances that science was making. Its methodical approaches to observation, experimentation and analysis created order and understanding in the natural world (and it is the organisation of these into scientific procedure that underpins the advances in bioengineering and stem cell technology today). The work of Michael Faraday, for example, demonstrates this (scientific methodology is, incidentally, also the foundation of industrial growth from the twentieth century onwards). Faraday was a self-taught scientist who became Director of the Royal Institution, the premier scientific body in the UK. Faraday's research was broad, in chemistry and in physics, but it is for his work on electromagnetism that he is best remembered. Magnetic forces and electricity were certainly known before Faraday's work but they were poorly understood. Faraday's experimentation and development created the first electric motor and the dynamo but it was his argument for a unified electromagnetic force field that paved the way for the commercial application of electricity production and consumption and, ultimately, the creation of a modern society.

It is easy to understand why others should ask why society, which was rapidly changing as a result of industrialisation in the nineteenth century, should not be subject to the same sort of analytic enquiry. In response to this historical condition, there arose, first in France, from about the middle of the nineteenth century, a research position called positivism, which believed that 'out there' was a truth that could be discovered. We will look at positivism again in Chapter 3 in terms of how it shapes the operation of the research process. In this section we are concerned with understanding how it can influence your selection of an approach to research. Positivism emphasises the power of evidence and, nowadays especially, is very much associated with the use of quantitative analysis. It works by testing assumptions and a key element in its procedure is the generation of a hypothesis (see Chapter 3). It assumes that the researcher is a searcher after truth, neutral in the whole process and uninfluenced by social and economic relationships and pressures.

These features are very much associated with a critique and development of positivist philosophy by Karl Popper in the 1930s (of whom we shall hear more in Chapter 3) and it was his influence that largely led to the application of a quasi-scientific approach to social research that is general referred to as 'quantitative methodology'.

(ii) Humanism, Phenomenology and Existentialism

The second research philosophy that we shall examine is humanism, a broad umbrella term for a range of ways of understanding the social world. If scientism believes that truth has an independent existence, for example, chemical reactions will remain the same whether or not mankind exists, humanism believes that truth is a social construction (that is, one culture's truth may not be another's). Within a humanistic perspective it is not necessary that two people should have the same view of what the 'real world' is (because the real world on which they base their decisions and actions is inside their heads). In fact, for humanist researchers, it is important to understand divergences in views. Humanism is marked by a range of traditions but common to all is a belief in the value of the human experience and particularly its significance in creating what is meaningful. If I, for example, go to Auschwitz I can be sickened by the scale of the slaughter and the images I will see but my reactions are the product only of my belief in right and wrong and my sense of humanity. If my colleagues, whose relations were killed there were to go, the experience will have a different meaning for them. It will go far beyond what I feel, perhaps even to a sense of guilt that they and their parents survived when so many did not. It is this difference that has implications not just for the way in which research is conducted but also for what is actually researched and, by further implication, what actually constitutes an appropriate research question and an answer.

Humanistic approaches to research evolved very differently from the scientific. The positivist approach would even question whether humanistic styles of enquiry constitute research at all, largely because the phenomena under investigation (emotions, viewpoints, perceptions, understandings) may not exist independently out there in the 'real world'. Not surprisingly, those who conducted investigations from a humanistic perspective in literature, the arts and the social sciences, did not like the conclusion that what scientists did was research, while their efforts were merely studies. From their perspective their approach had formal procedures that gave worthwhile results. It was, in other words, fit for purpose. Imagine we are studying what effective leadership is in terms of schools. We could look at effectiveness in terms of student outcomes but these could be the result of effective teaching and nothing to do with leadership. We could measure leadership in terms of the turnover of staff in a school (on the basis that teachers want to work with good leaders) but our results could reflect a downturn in the job market. Our best option is to go and talk to teachers and support staff and then to the head teacher to see if we can pull together themes that seem to represent the data we have collected. It was with research like this that another research tradition became established in a range of subjects (including education and even in mathematics) and this tradition has become associated with a set of research tools that go under the umbrella description of 'qualitative' (again, we will look at this in more detail in Chapter 3).

The stimulus for the humanistic tradition in research can be found in French philosophy of the 1930s but it was not until after 1945 that a new research approach began to emerge. In many ways the development of a new approach reflected many of the ideas of Thomas Kuhn (an American philosopher of science who worked in the middle of the twentieth century) on how disciplines evolve and change. In essence, he argued that ways of working are matched to the challenges of a time and that as time moves on, so ways of working fail to find answers to all of the questions we want to ask. In the case of educational research there was a sense that positivism could not provide all the answers to the questions that educational researchers were asking and a belief that behaviour was affected by how people viewed the world. Educational researchers were influenced by what was happening in sociology in the 1960s and 1970s. In sociology the research focus moved from one of looking for order (typified by Ernest Burgess, Professor of Sociology at the University of Chicago, whose work on the social structure of the modern American city influenced two generations of sociological research) to understanding variety and change in social systems. What was recognised in sociology (and other social sciences) was that there were issues worth exploring that existing positivist approaches could not manage. From the 1960s, themes of social justice and equality emerge within research programmes. While positivism could tell us how many people were poor, it could not help us to understand what it was like to be poor. This is the essence of humanistic research traditions.

The division between the scientific and humanistic research traditions has often been bitter. The situation in Sweden is typical of many other countries. Englund's review of Swedish education research (Englund, 2006) identifies the decline of the quantitative tradition from the 1970s onwards and its replacement by what we can loosely call a humanistic approach. The sorts of issue that have been important for education when investigated through a humanistic perspective include the emotional state of children, understanding the learning process, interpersonal relationships, managing change, experiencing education as a student, teacher and parent, leadership, self-representation and consumption and status. A humanist researcher would not see their main purpose as measuring these but capturing the experiences that help us understand what we might do to change, manage or reproduce those experiences. All of these are areas where people's views, feelings, emotions and concerns are treated as valid influences in understanding how they interact with the world. The research environment, from a humanistic perspective, is not black and white but a rainbow of all colours where the hues gradually merge into each other. One area where humanistic approaches are gathering momentum at the present time is in medical and nursing research (including research into education, learning and training), again areas that have long been dominated by the scientific tradition. Can you think why this might be? If you want to improve your understanding of humanistic research, look at Activity 2.1 in which you will explore what researchers do by accessing *Eric*, one of the research databases introduced in Chapter 1.

The focus of humanistic enquiry is the world we inhabit, the world we create and the world we experience. These are all worlds within our minds. There are two important schools of thought that we should be aware of: phenomenology and existentialism.

(a) Phenomenology

Phenomenology, very simply, is concerned with how we experience the world rather than ideas and concepts about how the world really is. Implied in this is a concern with the meanings we give to the things we experience. If you are a phenomenologist, then the core of what you study is individual and collective experiences of what many refer to as the 'life-world'. The world that is explored by research is a perceived and experienced world. The methods phenomenologists use are, amongst others, description, observation, reporting and reflection.

Dave Trotman, a lecturer at Newman University College, worked within a phenomenological framework for his doctoral research (Trotman, 2006). His objectives were to understand what it was like to work in primary schools (an investigation of the teachers' *lifeworlds*) and to consider how such understanding could be used in the evaluation of

Activity 2.1 Getting a feel for humanistic research

Chapter 1 introduced you to several research databases. Let's look at one of them, ERIC (http://www.eric.ed.gov). Its opening page looks like this.

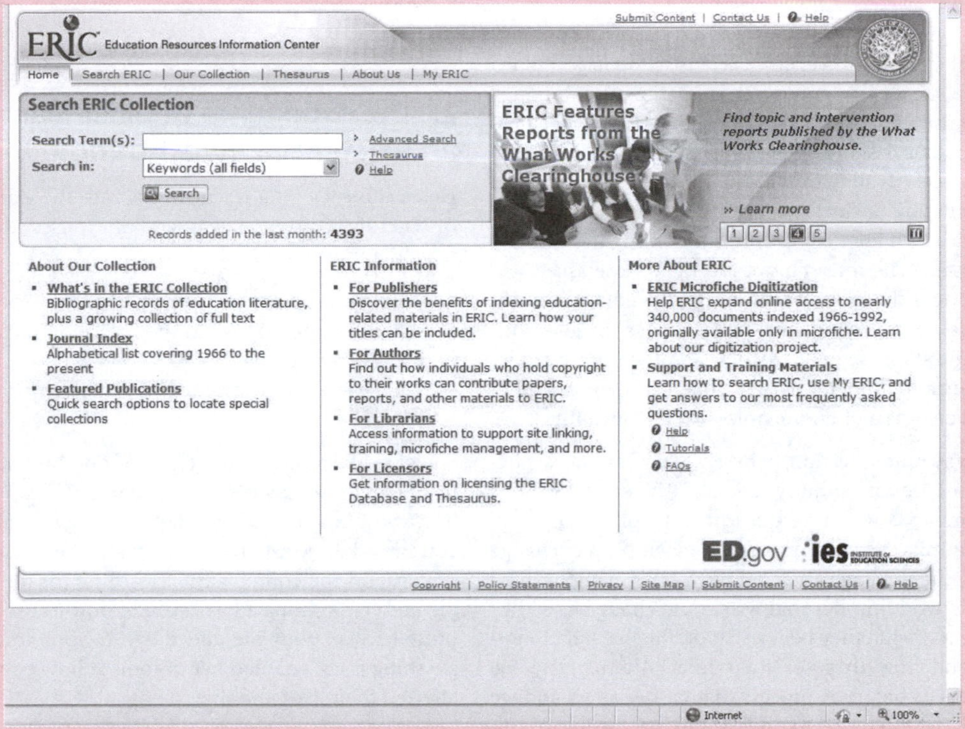

Submit Content | Contact Us | Help

ERIC Education Resources Information Center

Home | Search ERIC | Our Collection | Thesaurus | About Us | My ERIC

Search ERIC Collection

Search Term(s):

Search in: Keywords (all fields)

Search

Advanced Search
Thesaurus
Help

Records added in the last month: 4393

ERIC Features Reports from the What Works Clearinghouse

Find topic and intervention reports published by the What Works Clearinghouse.

Learn more

About Our Collection

- What's in the ERIC Collection
  Bibliographic records of education literature, plus a growing collection of full text
- Journal Index
  Alphabetical list covering 1966 to the present
- Featured Publications
  Quick search options to locate special collections

ERIC Information

- For Publishers
  Discover the benefits of indexing education-related materials in ERIC. Learn how your titles can be included.
- For Authors
  Find out how individuals who hold copyright to their works can contribute papers, reports, and other materials to ERIC.
- For Librarians
  Access information to support site linking, training, microfiche management, and more.
- For Licensors
  Get information on licensing the ERIC Database and Thesaurus.

More About ERIC

- ERIC Microfiche Digitization
  Help ERIC expand online access to nearly 340,000 documents indexed 1966-1992, originally available only in microfiche. Learn about our digitization project.
- Support and Training Materials
  Learn how to search ERIC, use My ERIC, and get answers to our most frequently asked questions.
  Help
  Tutorials
  FAQs

ED.gov ies INSTITUTE of EDUCATION SCIENCES

Copyright | Policy Statements | Privacy | Site Map | Submit Content | Contact Us | Help

Internet 100%

Put the search term 'humanistic research' into the search box. When I did it in June 2009, there were 1668 references. Scroll through the references and see if you can find any that fit these categories:

- papers that deal with identity and affective characteristics (that is, those concerned with emotion and feelings);
- papers that use the term 'humanistic' to describe a therapy or treatment;
- papers that deal with the application of humanistic ideals to the curriculum and learning process.

For the first 50 papers accessed, count how many are in each of the above categories. Then analyse what topics are dealt with in each of the categories. Write a report of no more than 200 words on the areas that humanistic research deals with.

educational practice. His approach was to work with a small group of teachers. Initial discussions explored the role of the teacher and out of this emerged a pupil focus, specifically a concern with developing the imaginative and creative capabilities of children. He went on to delve into the differences between the teachers and to seek to understand how far their approaches to developing creativity requires them to enter the children's lifeworlds. Trotman's is a well-argued case for phenomenological research but there are other examples I could have used. Phenomenology has been used as a research approach to study employability and career development, the experience of learning, group dynamics and inclusion, the value of special education settings and understanding the processes through which we assume roles. Case Study 2.1 gives an example.

Case study 2.1 Humanistic research in education

1. Assessment in higher education – a phenomenological investigation

The context for Rose Grant's PhD research is the burden placed on university teachers to manage the examination of students so that quality is maintained while the dimensions that are assessed (interpersonal and practical skills as well as intellectual capability) are increased, all within a situation where numbers of students are increasing, funding is limited and the purpose of higher education is becoming increasingly contested. The research question that Rose asked was 'How does the lecturer within a higher educational institution understand him or herself as an assessor?' This question is very particular and the key words are 'understand him or herself' because they highlight why hers was a phenomenological investigation.

But why this question, why should there be a phenomenological enquiry at all? There are various arguments that can be put forward. For instance, organizations can only change if their employees change (or if they change their employees). Changing how people work implies that we should change how they think and what they believe. To do this, we have to understand how they see their roles. Alternatively, we could see change as process that creates stress and we should be interested to understand how people reconcile the demands placed upon them in the performance and development of their roles.

How does a phenomenological stance influence the processes of data collection and analysis? Rose Grant's analytic methodology was essentially description and interpretation. Her object was to report her subjects' *experience* of being an assessor. She collected her data by interview. Her questions (such as the significance of the assessment methods they used and, how 'their choice and implementation of assessment practices impacted on their understanding of themselves as professional educators' p. 69) were directed at understanding what it was to be an assessor.

Rose Grant's findings are interesting. Despite the extent of change in higher education, her participants felt energized and challenged, not trapped. Their use of a wide range of assessment techniques was a response not only to demonstrate that they met course objectives but also to the needs and capabilities of students from diverse backgrounds. In many ways (and this is my interpretation), the research shows that creative people can resolve competing challenges and problems as long as they accept the premises that create these situations.

Source: Grant, R. (2005)

2. The experience of older learners – an existential investigation

Helen Russell's PhD research was into the experience of 'laterlife' computer learners. She posed three research questions:

- What was the nature of their learning experience?
- What interpretations did they place on their learning experience?
- What were the outcomes of the learning experience?

She gives examples of the types of question she used to uncover the existential nature of their experience. 'Have you experienced any highs (and lows) and have you shared these experiences with anyone?' helped her understand the complexity of learning for older people and 'What impact has learning how to use a computer had on your life and did you hope to achieve anything else?' enabled her to look at how computers affected their lives and their being.

If we examine these questions, they are not so very different from questions we might have asked anyway. So why do we accept this as a piece of existential research? The answer is not to be found in the questions or the method of collecting the data (interviews in her case) but in the context in which she set the issue. If we look at her paper, there is one key section ('Learning and Being') in which she presents her argument for an existential perspective. While this performs the function of a review of previous work that we find in most academic papers, it is actually far more than this. In it she assembles, by reference to theoretical, philosophical, conceptual and empirical studies, an argument that learning is fundamental to creating the 'self', that is, our natures, our characters and our lives. And the function that learning performs is that it enables us to find meaning in and for our lives.

How, then, did the 'latelearners' find meaning? Learning enabled them to sustain relationships with others and to feel part of the world. Without this engagement, they were fearful of a drift into 'nothingness'. They

▶

wanted to feel that their lives still had value and that their sense of 'being' was not predicated solely on memories and past experiences but was still developing. This we can see is a very different type of conclusion from what we might find in many other examples of qualitative research.

Source: Russell, H. (2007)

(b) Existentialism

Existentialism is more difficult to pin down because of the many people who have claimed to work within its assumptions and beliefs. Its focus is to understand the nature of human existence. It is, in many ways, a self-centred view of the world with its emphasis on freedom of choice and a belief that individuals must be responsible for creating value in their own lives. It generates a research environment in which we seek understanding by looking at the world from a personal perspective, subject to emotional pressures and driven by conviction and desire. The novelist (and academic) Alexander McCall Smith gets to the heart of the philosophy through the main character, a woman detective, in one of his books. He writes:

> Mma Ramotswe had listened to a World Service broadcast on her radio one day which had simply taken her breath away. It was about philosophers who called themselves existentialists and who, as far as Mma Ramotswe could ascertain, lived in France. These French people said that you should live in a way which made you feel real, and that the real thing to do was the right thing too. Mma Ramotswe had listened in astonishment. You did not have to go to France to meet existentialists, she reflected; there were many existentialists right here in Botswana. Note Mokoti, for example. She had been married to an existentialist herself, without even knowing it. Note, that selfish man who never once put himself out for another – not even for his wife – would have approved of existentialists, and they of him. It was very existentialist, perhaps, to go out to bars every night while your pregnant wife stayed at home, and even more existentialist to go off with girls – young existentialist girls – you met in bars. It was a good life being an existentialist, although not too good for all the other, nonexistentialist people around one.

McCall Smith, A. (2003) *Morality for Beautiful Girls*, Abacus

While existentialism could be a rationale for living life in a particular way, it has also been influential in generating representations of the world. As an artistic representation, for example in literature or film, it could (and has been) a framework for understanding society and, as such, has been investigated by researchers. The implication of this is that what we might use as data in an existential investigation suddenly expands. We can ask our subjects to represent their understanding and views of their world through creative activities such as drawing and writing. If we ask them to shoot a video or take photos, we see the world through their eyes. We can also work in metaphor, for example, if we were to ask a group of young people to use a TV programme to describe their lives, we might get better insights than by using a questionnaire. Themes that an existential approach to research could deal with might be identity and the freedom to behave in a particular way (look at Note Mokoti above. Such a theme could lead to an exploration of youth culture and deviance). Two areas of research in the USA seem to be particularly associated with an existential perspective: the nature of curriculum and adolescence. Existentialism is applied to curriculum as a design philosophy (I can find no work that uses it as an investigative tool). An existential curriculum is essentially one of self-discovery. With adolescence, it is used as a lens through which to find and look at research evidence. Case Study 2.1 provides another example of existentialism in education.

In summary, while philosophical considerations can predispose us to collect and analyse data in a particular way (many will predispose us to use some type of qualitative data analysis), their real significance is how they expect us to look at the issue we want to research. We should think of them as a mindset we adopt when we approach our research and which influences the type of issue we want to investigate and the nature of the research question we ask.

(iii) Critical theory

The next area of philosophy that we need to consider is critical theory and the various perspectives that are embedded within it. Critical theory too has its origins in the early part of the nineteenth century and, as with the other philosophical perspectives that we have looked at, it still influences the position that many people take on research. Essentially at the heart of the critical perspective is a strong political belief, usually from far left of centre.

We can begin to understand the thrust of critical theory by looking at it in relation to positivist theory. With positivism the researcher is a neutral analyst dealing with objective facts. Many critical theorists also argue that they deal with an objective reality but with all critical theorists there is one way in which they differ from positivists, they seek not just to explain but also to change. Critical theorists are not neutral; they come to research influenced by concerns (such as the social consequences of inequality) and driven by goals (for example, income equality). One of the principal philosophers of modern critical theory, Max Horkheimer, wrote that the purpose of critical theory is 'to liberate human beings from the circumstances that enslave them' (1982). It is not surprising that, with his left wing leanings, Horkheimer too was a refugee from Nazi Germany, though he returned after the Second World War. The character of research within a critical theory framework is that while any individual piece of research may not argue for change, the overarching purpose of critical theory is to expose the need for change. There is also another theme common to many of the theoretical positions they adopt, their belief that frameworks and structures in society constrain the way individuals and groups behave. These structures often derive from the exercise of wealth, influence and political power.

Critical theory analysis is sympathetic to a left wing political perspective. However, any strong political perspective can determine how people look at and research issues. It can be argued, for example, that the so-called 'neo-conservatism' (a term that originally defined those who, especially in the period before and during the presidency of Ronald Reagan, moved their political stance from left of centre to right), which has been developing in the USA as a movement of shared values over the last quarter of a century, has many generic characteristics in common with established critical theory, though its analyses and solutions are, of course, very different from those of critical theorists. It too is driven by concerns over the character of society as it perceives it; too many government interventions to resolve, for example, poverty, so that government becomes part of the problem rather than the solution. In many respects its concerns are the same as those who look at society from left of field but its prescriptions are very different. Instead of a collective or state solution to inequality, a neo-conservative solution would seek to give people the freedom to overcome the barriers themselves. We can now appreciate that, as researchers or readers of research, it is important to understand the political principles that underpin critical theory and the drive for change.

One of the most influential critical theorists of the nineteenth century was Karl Marx who died in 1883. Since the collapse of the Soviet Union and with China's adoption of an economic model that is not too distant from rampant capitalism, Marx's ideas about the nature of society and the conflicts within it do not feature greatly either in teaching or in the development of policy solutions to problems. It is, however, important to point out that his goal, the emancipation of the working class by returning to them a fairer share of the wealth that they had created, generated a model of the evolution of society that reflected the struggle for the control of wealth. There are many social scientists even today, though, who would argue that his analysis of the nature of class conflict and power relationships in society are valid today. There are many more who would accept that his ideas are still useful in understanding the world we live in, at every scale from global to local. Many of the issues that concern educational researchers can be analysed from a Marxist perspective; these might include social exclusion, racism and under-achievement in lower socio-economic groups. In a classic application of Marxist theory, Nigel Greaves, Dave Hill and Alpesh Maisuria, academics working in Kurdistan and the UK, explore the relationship between education and inequality. They argue that 'education services the capitalist economy, helps reproduce the necessary social, political, ideological and economic conditions for capitalism, and therefore, reflects and reproduces the organic inequalities of capitalism.' They come to this conclusion on the basis of empirical evidence principally from the UK. The method is very different in that the premise, that 'education services the capitalist economy', serves as the basis for assembling the evidence.

(iv) Postmodernism

The final philosophical perspective we shall consider is postmodernism. Postmodernism rejects the assumption of a single explanation of things (such as science seeks to develop) and recognises that the world is a complex place that is full of contradictions. How then does this differ from modernism? Table 2.1 sets out some of the differences between them from a researcher's perspective. Modernism is marked by the search for order as epitomised by the derivation of theory (for example, Marxism) and big themes through which to understand events (for example, the idea that we should have theories of education that would serve the needs of society and individuals is, itself a modernist 'big idea'). Postmodernists believe that all explanation involves assumptions, that the world is multi-layered, that people and organisations can play several,

Table 2.1 Modernism and postmodernism compared

Modernism	Postmodernism
Understanding comes through reason and analysis.	All analysis and explanation is based on assumptions.
Understanding is demonstrated in general laws about behaviour.	Laws cannot predict individual behaviour.
Understanding is timeless.	Understanding requires context.
Focus on the general.	Interest in the particular.
Authority with the researcher.	Knowledge creates privilege and should be shared with those who might benefit from it.
Knowledge is presented in cause-effect models.	Knowledge is assembled to reflect local conditions.

sometimes conflicting, roles and that all understanding of action is affected by the context in which the action occurs. A school where all the students meet the national standard for assessment for their age may not be newsworthy, until we find out that the majority of students do not have English as their mother tongue. Locality and identity are strong postmodernist themes while modernism is more concerned with 'grand designs' and a focus on the general. In education this might be the introduction of a national curriculum rather than giving schools the freedom to construct a curriculum that meets the needs of their community. Postmodernists are critical of the way in which the research process gives the researcher authority over those who are researched because this replicates power structures found in the world outside research. In her book *The Graffiti Subculture*, Nancy Macdonald argues that involving 'the researched' in the analysis of the research data ensures that 'interpretational authority' is shared but she also adds that when 'we collect accounts . . . we reserve the right to decree what people are *really* saying or *really* doing' (Macdonald, 2001, p. 20). Postmodernists seek ways to emancipate those on whom research is done and find ways of giving voice to those whom modernists dispossess (by virtue of their supposed neutrality in research and consequent non-involvement of those who provide data). In the modernist world, knowledge is presented in cause and effect models. Postmodernists assemble information in order to describe and, through description, understand realities, that is, what actually exists rather than what exists in an ideal situation.

'Modern' societies are viewed as being ordered in terms of class relationships and family structures; postmodern societies are seen as being fragmented, with new forms of family (single parent) and partnership (same gender). Education policy and practice is not immune from a postmodern analysis. 'Modern' education provision was characterised by uniformity. In the UK, for example, the 1944 Education Act created a framework of provision for more academically able and less academically able. After 1964 a new consensus emerged and for most children the divide was removed and replaced by a new uniformity – comprehensive schools. From the late twentieth century, however, we can see growing fragmentation in school character with more faith schools, new types of school such as academies and specialist colleges that, together with the existing grammar schools and comprehensives, give more than a hint of postmodern solutions to educational provision. Self-governance by schools removes the possibility of there being policies that all schools in an area have to meet. Nowhere is this more apparent than in the regulations governing transfer between primary and secondary schools. In the UK, the Government has set out a School Admissions Code. Three researchers at the London School of Economics were asked to review school admissions policies (West et al., 2009). They found that while most admissions practices conformed to the Code, 40 per cent did not give priority to children with medical or social needs and 47 per cent did not give priority to children with special educational needs (which the Code requires them to do when an application names a school). In fact, when they disaggregated their data, they found that the likelihood of a Voluntary Aided (faith schools) or Foundation (state funded but governed by an independent board of governors) school giving priority to a child with special educational needs was much lower than other types of schools.

Postmodernism and modernism are lenses through which to understand education practice. They are starting points for an investigation. They are not, in themselves, methods but a way of thinking about the world that influences what we choose to investigate. Modernists might emphasise efficiency and effectiveness in teaching and measure the results in terms of the proportion of schools or pupils attaining a target. Postmodernists, especially those coming with a critical perspective, would sense that a single measure would disadvantage those whose capability is not described by the measure. For example, if a school's performance is measured by the results of its pupils, then it would be a more effective use of resources for the school to concentrate on those pupils on the borderline of the standard in order to maximise the proportion of pupils who passed and to ignore those who were a long way off the standard. Postmodernists, on the other hand, might argue for a range of teaching approaches to be used, for small group teaching as opposed to whole class teaching and for learning to be more customised in order that those far from the standard would also benefit from an educational experience. While postmodern research does not specify a particular methodology or research strategy, there are two that are themselves inherently postmodern in character. They are action research, an unfolding and evolutionary process where the goal need not be specified at the start, and the case study, an affirmation of the value of the particular in a world where the general is often revered.

Postmodernism as a concept is widely used in education research. Despite the discussion above, postmodern ideas can be difficult to understand, especially when they are 'explained' by people whose own understanding is not as perfect as it might be. It can, as well, be almost impenetrable through the use of pretentious language. In 1996, Alan Sokal, a mathematical physicist, published a paper titled 'Transformative Hermeneutics of Quantum Gravity'. It is a 'dense' read, heavily peppered with postmodernist jargon – and a complete hoax. (The paper and his explanation for writing it can be found on his website, http://www.physics.nyu.edu/faculty/sokal/). Whether or not it exposed postmodernism as a shallow concept or whether it exposed the inability of postmodernists to communicate effectively is a decision you will have to make for yourselves. If you become confused, just remember the joke told by the Australian academic, Clare O'Farrell (1999, p. 11): What do you get when you cross a mafiosi with a postmodernist? The answer: Someone who will make you an offer you cannot understand.

In summary – why philosophy can be important

You have read something about different philosophical traditions that are relevant to education. Now let's summarise why you need to be aware of and appreciate research philosophies.

- You have to understand where a researcher is coming from so that you can critique research conclusions within the prescriptions of a research philosophy and to be able to comment on the appropriateness of the philosophy as a guiding framework for a particular piece of research.
- You have to decide how far your values and emotional attachment to the research issue should condition the way in which you will approach the research process. If you are committed to wider access to educational opportunity, what is your viewpoint if you have to investigate private education?
- Philosophy provides a lens through which to identify a research problem or to interpret or understand the implications of research data.
- Finally, you have to consider how far working within the confines of a research philosophy requires you to use particular research methods.

What it all comes down to is that by taking our understanding of research to a higher conceptual level, we become better at deciding how to work within and, if necessary, outside the rules and conventions of research. This research process of breaking rules in order to accommodate the research problem is, as we should now appreciate, a *very* postmodern way of working!

2.1.2 Paradigms

The next idea that may influence the way we look at or conduct our research is the paradigm. This is a way of thinking about a subject and proceeding with research that is accepted by people working in that area. This implies that both purpose and process are widely agreed within a discipline or part of a discipline and that what is delivered through research enables researchers to understand the world more effectively. The implication of this is that if you work within a paradigm, you work with a set of rules that determine your research procedures and that may even shape your research question, and that there will always be a group of people sympathetic to your approach.

The idea of a paradigm was popularised by the philosopher of science, Thomas Kuhn, to explain why science operated so successfully for long periods within a body of accepted theory and procedure, only to change radically and move in a new direction governed by a new set of challenges, goals, theories and procedures. He published his book, *The Structure of Scientific Revolutions*, in 1962 and it was this that popularised the term 'paradigm shift' to describe the move from one way of explaining and researching to another. While Kuhn's ideas about the development of science are now widely challenged because the detailed history of what was happening rarely added up to a widespread 'eureka' moment, there is still an appeal in using the concept to understand big shifts in direction.

However, the paradigm concept is also used at a much smaller scale. In business analysis, for instance, James Belohlav, a management professor at De Paul University in the USA identified different business strategies over a 30-year period which he called paradigms (Belohlav, 1996). The equivalent in education might be teaching and learning strategies that held sway over a period. For example, from the mid-1960s, comprehensive education was introduced to replace a system based on selection at the end of primary education. While this shift was the result of a political policy (in much the same way that changes from the 1980s onwards have been politically driven), how the schools organised their teaching was a matter for the senior management team. Throughout this period there have been debates between competing paradigms, such as those who believed in whole class teaching and those who believed in some sort of separation according to ability. In terms of education research, some approaches to research might also be thought of as paradigms because they constitute ways of working which researchers believe produce valid and worthwhile results. Each approach has its own rulebook and sets of procedures that have become accepted as canons of good practice. The difference between the way in which 'paradigm' is used here and the way in which Kuhn used it is that paradigms can co-exist, whereas Kuhn argued that they could only co-exist for a short period before one succeeded another to become the dominant mode of thinking.

What sort of research approaches might we consider as paradigms? This is not as easy to answer as it might seem. The reason for this is that, as social scientists, we have been rather loose in our use of terminology. In particular, we have not distinguished between a paradigm and research methodology. Look at the definitions below, taken from the Oxford English Dictionary:

- *Paradigm:* a conceptual model underlying the theories and practice of a scientific subject.
- *Methodology:* a system of methods used in a particular field.

From the definitions it should be clear that the concept of 'paradigm' functions at a higher level than methodology; it ties the way a researcher works to ideas about what it is appropriate to investigate and on what basis the research output should be considered to be a truth. In other words, it links research philosophy and the practice of research. We shall look at some research frameworks such as ethnography and case study research, when we discuss methodology. We should be aware, though, that many authors call these (and other methodologies) paradigms. In this book I refer to them as methodologies because they are more concerned with the processes of collecting and analysing data and not higher level conceptual thinking involving assumptions, concepts and values. In this section we look at *quantitative*, *qualitative* and *mixed approaches* as paradigms. We shall consider the implications of approaching research from these three perspectives in greater detail in the next chapter. Now all we have to understand is why they can be thought of as paradigms. The issues are summarised in Table 2.2.

(i) Quantitative analysis

Quantitative approaches to research can lay claim to having the strongest case for being a paradigm. These have a precise idea of how truth can be determined using a combination of statistical analysis and logical deductive reasoning to draw out inferences from the evidence presented. They know the position of the researcher in relation to the research process; they are a neutral technocrat who has no commitment to the issue under investigation other than to seek the truth (that is, the researcher is not swayed by emotional attachment to an issue or commitment to a cause). Quantitative approaches have logically consistent procedures through which to pass the evidence and reach a conclusion. The values are those of science, the assumption is that of an objective reality and the concepts are concerned with the nature of what is evidence and what constitutes proof.

(ii) Qualitative analysis

Qualitative analysis starts from quite different premises. Unlike quantitative researchers, qualitative analysts do not believe that there is a single truth. They believe that people can subscribe to different views and believe valid but different truths and their interest is in exposing these. Concerned as they are with the way in which people accommodate to the world, they accept that people make different adjustments each of which is a perfectly valid condition. They do not necessarily believe that the researcher has to strive to be neutral. Commitment to a cause such as gay rights is, for some qualitative researchers (though not all), a good starting point. In other words, qualitative research is much more catholic in its embrace of standpoints than quantitative. Evidence is not necessarily only

Table 2.2 Paradigm characteristics of principal research approaches in education

	Quantitative	Qualitative	Mixed methods
Truth	Single.	Multiple.	Either single or multiple or both.
Approach	Deductive.	Inductive.	Either inductive or deductive or both.
Researcher	Neutral.	Can be committed.	Either neutral or committed or both.
Methods	Formal procedures.	Structured procedures plus insight.	Either formal or structured or both.
Data	Number.	Any information.	Any information.

numerical. Relationships, character, emotions and all the other ways that we live our lives and express ourselves are all legitimate sources of information that can be used to make sense of the world. While, in their purest form, quantitative approaches logically deduce conclusions from evidence, qualitative approaches assemble the evidence from whatever source is relevant and identify patterns and order and use inductive reasoning to suggest what the causes are. Insights and imagination are as much tools of the qualitative researcher's trade as are more formal analyses. Given these characteristics, it is reasonable to use the term *paradigm* to describe qualitative research.

(iii) Mixed methods approaches

It is more difficult, however, to claim that a combination of qualitative and quantitative approaches in one investigation constitute a definable paradigm. The reason for this is that there are no concepts or beliefs that anchor mixed methods. As the term suggests it brings together viewpoints that should not be able to co-exist, a single reality (quantitative) with multiple realities (qualitative), neutrality (quantitative) with commitment (qualitative), deduction and induction, logic and imagination. If it has a distinguishing feature, then that feature is pragmatism. If something works, delivers what we want (in other words it is a practical way of solving problems), then it can be used.

Pragmatism, in a research context, is, essentially, problem solving. We have a problem (our research question) to which we need to find answers. If we mix methods to obtain and analyse the data which will answer the question then, as long as the answer is acceptable to our audience, mixed methods passes the pragmatic test. In fact, this type of belief emerged as a strand of philosophy in America. The first person to develop an argument for pragmatism was Charles Peirce in the late nineteenth century. His approach was essentially the application of common sense, which, perhaps, reflects the fact that for the early part of his working life he was a scientist. So, if we are pragmatic, combine approaches and use 'Does it work?' as a test of its adequacy, then we can combine methods to construct arguments that are compelling. As we said in Chapter 1, one of the skills that an effective researcher should posses is to know when to bend, ignore or break rules. When we use a mixed methods approach, we are breaking other people's rules and replacing them with our own.

The pragmatism of the mixed methods approach has potential benefits for many education researchers. This is because we are often concerned with an issue at both a significant scale (for instance, teenage pregnancy, in which the UK has very high rates in comparison with other countries) as well as the conditions that give rise to it and the experiences of those affected by it. These are different levels of enquiry and a mixed methods approach is, essentially, complimentary, with quantitative approaches dealing with the issue of scale and qualitative with the issue of experience.

(iv) Seeing the links

The links between qualitative and quantitative analysis and research philosophies should now be clearer:

Positivism predisposes researchers to a quantitative approach.

Humanistic philosophical positions and postmodernism predispose researchers to a qualitative approach.

A critical theorist could go either way or both, though commitment to a cause does challenge the idea of a disinterested researcher, one of science's key assumptions.

A mixed methods approach downplays the influence of philosophy altogether because the need for pragmatism is paramount, because of the importance placed on the issue being researched and because of the need to find an answer to a specific question.

2.1.3 Principles

Paradigms are concerned with rules. For the researcher working within a paradigm, freedom to act in a particular way may not exist. As we will see in Chapter 3, each approach has its own rulebook and sets of procedures that have become accepted as canons of good practice. However, even with rules it is possible for two researchers to work in different ways. There is, therefore, an area where researchers have freedom to take decisions and their decisions are constrained not by rules but by principles. As a researcher, we have to identify our principles and then ensure that we comply with them throughout.

Principles reflect the moral position that you have, so, in this sense, there is a link to philosophy. There are situations in which you can legitimately work outside of a principle but only if the moral good outweighs the moral loss. If we are convinced that learning by finding out is the most beneficial approach for students over the long term (because it is learning that stays and is not forgotten), then it may well be worthwhile helping one group to learn by discovery and sacrificing another by teaching the same material in a didactic way just to test whether your way is genuinely better. The disadvantage to the second group is (we believe and hope) outweighed by the advantage to all other students in the future. If, however, we ever think of breaching a principle for the sake of expediency, then we must hope that we are never found out!

How do we determine what our principles are when it comes to research? Here are some pointers:

(i) We have to consider our position with respect to honesty in relation to the data we collect and present and the results we publish. It is very easy to ignore data that does not fit in with the interpretation and explanation that we are working towards. We might also be tempted to 'construct' data that fits the ideas we are testing. From a pragmatic point of view, it is not sensible for a researcher to falsify data because if (or, more likely, when) someone else tries to replicate our results and finds that it cannot be done, it is our reputation that has been ruined. As researchers we have a moral duty to other researchers to be honest in how we work. The best way of demonstrating our honesty is to be transparent with our methods of data collection, analysis and interpretation.

(ii) We have to decide how far our responsibility extends to others that we involve in our research. Do we name and shame people if they are doing or have done something wrong? Do we maintain the confidentiality of people who give us sensitive information? Do we allow readers the ability to identify organisations that have given us access as case studies? These are difficult areas and we need to determine where we stand. One moral principle that may help us is the notion that people or organisations with whom we work should not be harmed by how we work or what we do with the outcomes of our research. However, principles can conflict with other principles and we have to determine which ones are overriding. For instance, if our research into school management suggests that there is financial corruption which, if made public, will inevitably affect the reputation of the school, should we ignore it or is the possibility of there having been criminal activity a higher moral principle?

(iii) We should think about whether it is appropriate to share the benefits of undertaking the research and publishing the results and, if so, with whom. Is it acceptable to get information from an organisation, publish the results or present a thesis and not tell the people we contacted what we found out? If we do this, then our research is rather like a smash and grab raid. It could be labelled 'intellectual imperialism' where the researcher stands aloof from the subjects and treats them as disposable suppliers of data. If our research generates benefits, who shares in these? If we are examining the educational consequences of disadvantage, have we an obligation to help our respondents understand the consequences or even to help them overcome them? We need as well to take a position on who owns the intellectual property embodied in our analysis and conclusions? If you are a student and you have been guided by a supervisor, what rights does the supervisor have to your conclusions? If your work is published, whose names are on the publication – and whose is first? Not surprisingly this is a contentious area. Of what significance are the discussions that led to the actual activity of data collection and analysis? At the heart of the issue is whether the research is the product of one person or the result of advice, guidance and even collaboration.

(iv) How far should those involved in our research be free to withdraw? This question suggests that, at least, they ought to know that they are participating. If we ask questions either directly or in a questionnaire, then at least they will know that something out of the ordinary is occurring. If we are testing computer assisted learning against classroom learning then participants may not know that they are part of an experiment. Should they? And if our participants are children, should they consent or should we just obtain the agreement of parents and, if necessary, teachers? This is, essentially, a question of when children become responsible beings and when their rights are superior to those of adults who notionally have responsibility for them. A research group from the University of Huddersfield led by Rachel Balen has explored just this issue. They use the phrase 'active beings' to describe children who are mature enough to make informed decisions and the phrase 'human becomings' to describe them at points before this (Balen et al., 2006). They point out that children's perspectives may be different from adults' but are equally valid, even if they do not wholly appreciate the nature of the research. This is an interesting argument that suggests that children can assent to participating in a research endeavour when they appreciate that the outcome can be beneficial to others but without understanding the exact nature of the benefit. The research team gave an interesting example of this – obtaining data from the children of drug addicts.

(v) If we are working in a setting such as a children's home or a prison or with a group such as the terminally ill, drug users or people with learning difficulties, we will need to find out how other professionals inform themselves about what is appropriate. If we are working in a community setting, then how far do you allow the community a say in what should be researched and how the research should be conducted? And if we allow our participants some involvement, what implications does this have for ensuring that they benefit (see point (iii))?

(vi) With the Internet so adept at providing just the sort of information that we might need, we have to consider the ethics of using someone else's work without attribution. Plagiarism is becoming a significant issue in research (and in studying in general). The American academic newspaper, *The Chronicle*, published an article with four examples of four people who, it claims, plagiarised other work in their own academic publications and asked the question, 'How many more?'

(http://chronicle.com/free/v51/i17/17a00802.htm.) The consequences of using other people's work without attribution are serious in the academic world and self-interest alone would suggest that we ought not to do it.

(vii) We have to consider what standards we want to represent us and our work. These are not just ethical standards as outlined above but also standards of presentation, writing, grammar, referencing and so on. We ought to be precise in our public statements and correct in how we express our views. Grammar and spelling checkers can help us with this but if we are not sure about our ability to express ideas, then we should do something about it. If we are writing in English, there are guides that can inform us. Quality newspapers publish style guides (for example, *Guardian Style* edited by David Marsh) and *The Times* has its style guide on-line (http://www.timesonline.co.uk/tol/tools_and_services/specials/style_guide/).

Ian Shaw, Professor of Social Work at the University of York, comes to a clear position in respect of ethics in qualitative research. His position is that codes of practice for ethics risk 'compartmentalizing ethical aspects of research, and shutting them off into a preamble to research' (p. 10). As we suggest here, consideration of ethical issues has to be embedded in the whole process of research and particularly it has to be reflected in a moral stance taken by the researcher. While his argument is stated in the context of qualitative research, the underpinning standpoint is equally applicable to any research approach. The evidence, however, produced by two Israeli researchers, Einat Peled and Ronit Leichtentritt, who looked at published research was that, in the same field of social work, 'ethical considerations are marginal in most phases of the studies that are reported in our journals' (Peled and Leichtentritt, 2002, p. 145). They question why this might be the case and conclude that it is likely that the researchers are ethical in their approach but that research training does not emphasise the need to make an ethical standpoint clear. It should be part of all research in education.

No one but you can determine the principles that will guide your work but there is guidance on which you can draw. Activity 2.2 provides an opportunity to understand more about ethical research guidelines produced by the British Educational Research Association and others.

2.1.4 Methodology

The next concept that should influence the way you do your research is methodology. But before we look at it in detail, there is something that you should be aware of. As you read more literature about conducting research, you will realise that authors fall into one of three groups:

- those who use the terms *research methods* and *research methodology* very precisely and with different meanings;
- those who see little distinction between the two terms and use predominantly one or the other to mean what the first group refers to as *research methods*; and
- those who are 'flexible' in their use of the terms and use them interchangeably.

As you will appreciate by now, one of the themes of this book is flexibility in developing a solution to a research problem. However, that flexibility should not really extend to the way in which researchers apply concepts or apply meanings to terms. If we do not use words with precision and with constancy (and I too have been at fault in not following this advice) then there is limited basis for effective communication and academic

Activity 2.2 Appreciating research guidelines

The guidelines below are from the British Educational Research Association (BERA, 1992). Look at the BERA website http://www.bera.ac.uk/blog/category/publications/guidelines/ and identify the ways in which the latest set of guidelines differ.

1. **The British Educational Research Association** believes that all educational research should be conducted within an ethic of respect for persons, respect for knowledge, respect for democratic values, and respect for the quality of educational research.

Responsibility to the research profession

2. Educational researchers should aim to avoid fabrication, falsification, or misrepresentation of evidence, data, findings, or conclusions.
3. Educational researchers should aim to report their findings to all relevant stakeholders and so refrain from keeping secret or selectively communicating their findings.
4. Educational researchers should aim to report research conceptions, procedures, results, and analyses accurately and in sufficient detail to allow other researchers to understand and interpret them.
5. Educational researchers should aim to decline requests to review the work of others when strong conflicts of interest are involved or when such requests cannot be conscientiously fulfilled on time. Materials sent for review should be read in their entirety and considered carefully, with evaluative comments justified with explicit reasons.
6. Educational researchers should aim to conduct their professional lives in such a way that they do not jeopardize future research, the public standing of the field, or the publication of results.

Responsibility to the participants

7. Participants in a research study have the right to be informed about the aims, purposes and likely publication of findings involved in the research and of potential consequences for participants, and to give their informed consent before participating in research.
8. Care should be taken when interviewing children and students up to school leaving age; permission should be obtained from the school, and if they so suggest, the parents.
9. Honesty and openness should characterize the relationship between researchers, participants and institutional representatives.
10. Participants have the right to withdraw from a study at any time.
11. Researchers have a responsibility to be mindful of cultural, religious, gendered, and other significant differences within the research population in the planning, conducting, and reporting of their research.

Responsibility to the public

12. Educational researchers should communicate their findings and the practical significance of their research in clear, straightforward, and appropriate language to relevant research populations, institutional representatives, and other stakeholders.
13. Informants and participants have a right to remain anonymous. This right should be respected when no clear understanding to the contrary has been reached. Researchers are responsible for taking appropriate precautions to protect the confidentiality of both participants and data. However, participants should also be made aware that in certain situations anonymity cannot be achieved.

Look at the guidelines for the following research bodies and identify:

(i) common elements and
(ii) how they differ.

British Sociological Association

http://www.britsoc.co.uk/equality/ Statement%20Ethical%20Practice

American Educational Research Association

http://www.aera.net/AboutAERA/Default.aspx?menu_id=90&id=717

Australian Medical Association (section 1.2)

http://www.ama.com.au/codeofethics

The Swedish Research Council has a website devoted to guidance on ethics. How many sources are relevant to educational research?

http://www.codex.uu.se/en/forskningmanniska.shtml

and

http://www.codex.uu.se/en/regler.shtml#A

debate. Research methods and research methodology are quite distinct ideas and should be used in different ways.

Research methodology is concerned with the assembly of research tools and the application of appropriate research rules. *Research methods* are the research tools themselves, for example, questionnaires, observation, statistical analysis. At its simplest, for the practical researcher, methodology is how the toolkit of research methods is brought together to crack an individual and specific research problem. In some disciplines it is still possible to talk of a dominant methodology but this is not the case in education where there are many competing methodologies, each with a distinctive combination of principles, procedure and practice. What we will appreciate is that certain methods are closely linked with specific methodologies and, by virtue of this, specific philosophies. It is impossible, in this book, to cover every methodology used in education research but it is important to say something about the principal ones.

(i) Case study

A case study is a detailed analysis of an individual circumstance or event that is chosen either because it is typical or because it is unusual or because there was a problem or because something worked well. The case study has had a mixed history as a research approach. It became established in the social sciences in the first half of the twentieth century. It was developed as an approach in sociology but was used, though not always referred to as case study, in many other subjects including geography, psychology and education. In the late 1930s it came under heavy criticism as being nothing more than description and unable to provide insights that would produce general explanations of individual and organisational behaviour. For the best part of half a century it declined in importance until a revival started in the 1970s and 1980s. This was part of the reaction against scientism in social research and a growing interest in the individual and the local. Some researchers identify it with a postmodern approach to research because it looks at particular instances rather than searches for general truths.

It is the relationship between the general and the specific that has to be resolved when we research a case study. In general, research has two goals:

- First, it aims to pick out patterns because they suggest that there are processes at work that create patterns. If we were to look at the reading capability of children aged 10 and found that a very large proportion of those who had a reading age of seven or less had not experienced any nursery education while those with a reading age of 10 or above had, we would (a) have found a pattern and (b) a possible process that had influenced the pattern. These processes constitute the general actors at work.
- Second, we are also interested in variations from the expected. Why do these pupils from this school who have not had access to nursery education have a reading age of 10 or more? What is happening locally to disrupt the expected pattern? The question is whether a study of the individual case can tell us anything about the general situation.

The answer is that it can. For example, we might ask what a study of an individual school can tell us about schools in general. We could use this information in the following ways:

- we could look at statistics that place one school in the context of others, either nationally or locally, and then see the school as being characteristic of where it is, for instance, average, above average, well below average etc.;

- we could look at one school in the context of case studies of other schools to see what common features emerge;
- we can also generalise about something like group behaviour within a case. If our case study involves surveying the attitudes or behaviour of a large group (such as all the teachers in a group), then assuming that they are not all in one category (male, young, in post a long time), we are likely to generate data that is reasonably characteristic of a typical group of teachers;
- finally, we might have an expectation of what should be the situation in our case study; we might determine this on the basis of an established theory or it might be based on our assumption about what would constitute reasonable behaviour in the circumstances. The case study becomes a test of our expectations, and, while it is a limited test, it is, nonetheless a test. If you think about it, this is the principal way of using the case study in medicine. The medical intervention is based on the theory of what should happen and on the outcomes of previous interventions.

A case study can make use of a wide range of methods, documentary sources, statistics, external reports and evaluations and so on as well as data collected by interview, questionnaire and observation. Clearly these methods can be used by other methodologies as well and, sometimes, the differences between one methodology and another can be difficult to determine. For example, a case study of pupil behaviour in a school could be little different in terms of the methods used to collect data from an ethnographic study in a school where the focus is on classroom behaviour.

The question of how case studies can be used in research requires us to look at them in two ways, first, in terms of what they can be used for and, second, how they can be used in the overall research approach. Let us look at each of these in turn.

- *What can research issues be used for?* Table 2.3 presents a matrix showing how we can represent case studies. The principal ways of using them is shown by the rows of the matrix. These are the *purposes* for which we are using them. There are three: exploration, explanation and description. We can use a case study to find out what is going on, to throw light on something that we have never met before or do not understand. This is exploration. We start by not knowing and we use the case study to establish understanding. With explanation, however, we start either with a question, 'Why?' or

Table 2.3 Characteristics of purpose and features of investigation in case study

Purpose	Unusual or typical	Issue	Critical incident	Longitudinal study
Exploration	How children manage with a new approach to teaching numeracy.	When does a child bully others?	Staff pass a motion of 'no confidence' in college management.	The effectiveness of procedures through which children are allocated places at secondary schools.
Explanation	How can counselling help in resolving behaviour problems?	The growth in reports of bullying behaviour.	The circumstances that led up to the incident.	Why some parents feel procedures to allocate school places are inappropriate.
Description	A day in the life of a typical primary head teacher.	Managing a parent's complaint about bullying.	How many hours a day staff spend on college activities.	Leisure activities of a cohort born in 1996.

with an assumption that this is what will happen. In this instance our goal is to explain some sort of outcome, such as, 'Why did the teachers take the students out when the weather forecast was bad?' Finally, we can use the case study to describe or record a situation. Given all that has been said, even in this book, about the search for generalisation, the fact that description is identified as a purpose at all may come as a surprise. If so, it will be an even bigger surprise to learn that this is one of the principal uses of the case study. How come? Well, we only have to think about the significance of practice improvement to the education system to begin to appreciate why. Case studies of good or effective practice abound on teaching, classroom management, community engagement, school organisation, institutional leadership and many, many more. (Table 2.4 has some examples.) The columns of the matrix in Table 2.3 show what can be *investigated*. Depending on the issue that we are investigating, we can look at it in the context of what is typical or what is unusual or atypical. The former will give us a picture of what usually happens and the latter what happens in more extreme circumstances. Good practice could be an example of this, as could poor performance. We can also use a case study to investigate an issue or a process, such as the admissions process to higher education and how it treats students from ethic minorities or, as another example, the interaction between schools, support agencies, the police and the youth justice system who are all involved if a young person becomes involved with antisocial or criminal behaviour. Another example of the use of the case study is to investigate critical incidents and their consequences. Such studies might include the death of teachers and pupils while on a school trip, or identifying the critical decisions that led to collective management failure, or when a teaching session went particularly well or badly. Finally, there is a particular instance of a case study, usually undertaken with government resources, that is particularly important – long-term cohort study. This follows a group over an extended period of time. It is used in medicine to track survival rates of cancer patients, especially those who have been involved in a new treatment. The National Children's Study in the USA records the relationship between environment and health for 100,000 children up to the age of 21. The Education Longitudinal Study (2002) is following a representative cohort of 2002 high school students in the USA through to employment. In the UK, the Government has commissioned an eight-year-long study (ending in 2009) on citizenship education and its effects. There have been long-term studies looking at the outcomes of full-time education in Sweden (Evaluation Through Follow Up, which began in 1961), and in the Netherlands and France (educational pathways in secondary education). A good summary of some long-term studies was prepared for the German Government as part of its policy making process, to determine whether it should instate similar studies (Kristen et al., 2005).

Table 2.4 Web location of good practice examples

Good practice issue or area	Website
Education of 14–19 year olds in UK	www.dcsf.gov.uk/14-19/index.cfm?go=site. CaseStudies Consortia&sid=53&pid=422&ctype= TEXT&ptype=Single
Exclusion and alternative education provision in UK	www.dcsf.gov.uk/exclusions/case/index.cfm
European Social Fund	http://ec.europa.eu/employment_social/esf/members/ index_en.htm (select state and look at earlier projects)
European Small Islands Network: education	http://www.europeansmallislands.net/downloads.html

- *How can case studies be used?* This is a question that relates to the overall objective of the research. What is it that we are trying to achieve? Is it to find out or to answer a question? If a question, is it generic or specific to the case? Are we trying to understand operational details within an organisation or the character of the organisation? Broadly speaking there are four ways of using a case study. A *single case study* deals with one instance only. In this instance, the case has to be representative of something, for example the typical, the extreme, the modern, the old fashioned and so on. We could, for instance, make a case study of a failing school. *Multiple case studies* can be designed to be repetitive (that is, to test the findings of earlier cases, to compare a failing school at a later point in time) or comparative (in which case the characteristics of the cases are deliberately and knowingly varied in order to assess the significance of the differences). It is also possible to differentiate between the *holistic case study* (a whole organisation study designed not only to focus on the research issue but also to appreciate the organisational culture) and an *embedded study* where details of the organisation (for example, a department) are considered in detail.

Case studies can be excellent at giving researchers a rich understanding of a situation but they are not unproblematic.

- There may be a problem of getting at the truth. If the actions we are concerned with took place a long time ago people may forget. More usually they may reconstruct their interpretation to position themselves in a better light. They may be economical with the truth and not actually tell you a lie but not reveal the whole circumstance either. These issues become significant if we interview those who were responsible for decisions. Few people are so self-confident that they will reveal their failings. Most senior people are concerned with how their legacy will be read. If people have lost their jobs, they are likely to place blame for failure elsewhere. This is a difficult issue that is resolved only by digging for more information and by giving an individual's response to others involved at the time and presenting the individual with their responses. Ultimately, however, we have to make a decision about whom to believe.
- The second problem with a case study is that we can get it horribly wrong. If we start off on a track seeking to show something, it can lead us to wrong conclusions. The research world will tell us when we are wrong but it is best to cultivate a neutral attitude.
- What are the limits of a case study? In the real world, one thing leads to another. At what point are we dealing with another issue? The answers to this problem are either to set the limits at the beginning (time period, to whom we should speak, consequential issues to be covered) or to keep going back to the main problem we want to understand each time a new dimension shows itself and to ask whether finding out more really benefits our analysis.
- Lastly, case studies that emphasise uniqueness are not really all that helpful. What is valuable about a case study is what can be transferred to other situations such as other organisations that face or might face similar problems to those in the case study or to those performing a similar role in an organisation. The case study should always seek to identify the learning that can be transferred.

(ii) Evaluation

Evaluation is concerned with whether a process or activity delivered the outputs or outcomes that were expected of it. It is extensively used, from the large scale (such as the environmental impact of construction projects for example, the Channel Tunnel), to the small scale (the adoption of a new teaching approach). It is used in many sectors including infrastructure development, finance, regeneration and development as well as education. The one common element to all is the degree of focus of the research. The concern of evaluation is to look at something specific such as project outcomes, how decisions were made, or a failure in procedure. While many evaluations are concerned with a project, this is not necessarily the case. The easiest way to understand evaluation is not to look at the areas where it has been applied but to understand the types of goal that can be set for it. There are four (see Figure 2.2), and they are not necessarily mutually exclusive.

The **first level of decision** that we have to take when setting up an evaluation is to determine what our goal is.

- At the most general level an evaluation can be conducted to *understand* what is happening. Why did things turn out differently from what we expected? Why did we not foresee these outcomes and consequences? Why does this system actually work? The issue to be resolved is 'not knowing'. Answering these questions could involve anything from a detailed description of processes and decisions (such as you would get in a case study) to an experiment conducted under scientific principles and any combination of methods in between.
- The second task is quite basic; it is to ensure *compliance*. Organisations have to comply with regulations and implement policy directives that arise from higher levels of authority. Educational institutions in most countries are inspected to ensure compliance with the requirements of state funding. Projects are evaluated to reassure those who finance them that the claimed outputs actually exist and the money has been

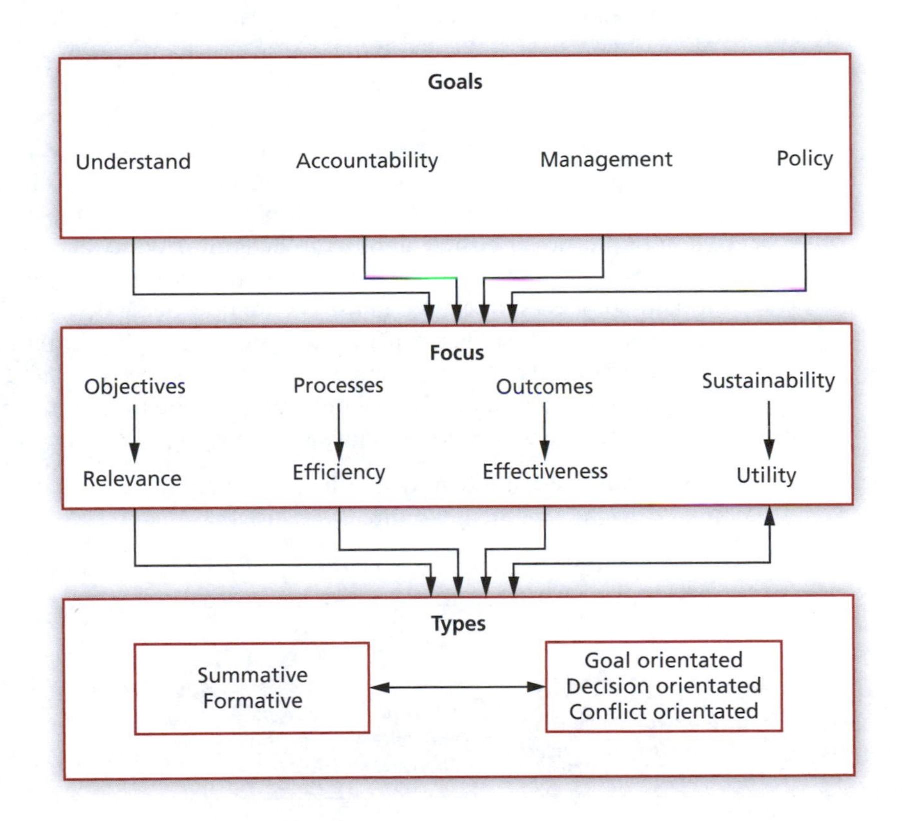

Figure 2.2 Evaluation decision making

spent appropriately. The evaluation process in these cases seeks to produce incontrovertible evidence that things are as they should be. Evaluation in this instance is an exercise in accountability.

- The third role that evaluation can perform is to *improve organisational management and practice*. In this type of evaluation, the evaluator looks at the understanding and appreciation of what is happening in context. This context might be anything the evaluator knows about from organisational and management theory to examples and instances that constitute experience in a field. In some instances the evaluation is comparative, when a process within an organisation is compared with what happens in other organisations. This approach is used by the UK Audit Commission and is referred to as *benchmarking*. Figure 2.3 sets out the procedure followed by the Commission. The key stage is that of identifying 'partners'. The Audit Commission calls them partners because of the context of its evaluations, which is to compare, as far as is possible, like with like. What it has done is create groups of organisations (such as education authorities) that are similar in terms of their socio-economic and demographic characteristics. With this model, inner urban areas are compared with inner urban areas, outer ones with outer, rural areas with rural areas and so on. Statistics are collected for every aspect of performance. At a higher operational level there are regional partnerships that benchmark practice in managing special educational needs (SEN) in the UK. In the Netherlands, the Government has set up a benchmark project to compare aspects of the Dutch education system with what happens in a select group of other countries, Germany, Flanders in Belgium, the UK, Sweden, Denmark, Finland and Norway.
- Finally, evaluation can be a tool for *policy formulation and shaping*. When used to do this it operates at two levels, first to translate experience from a test bed to a regional or national scale and second, to learn from what happens in other countries. Governments will try out new ways of doing things on a limited project basis in order to test whether they work. If they are not successful, they can be modified to improve performance but if this does not work, then failure is not expensive. Learning from other countries is almost the same as benchmarking. The difference, and it is relatively minor, lies in the fact that benchmarking is a continuous activity, while evaluation of practice elsewhere in order to determine policy actions is more of a one-off activity. This process has been extensive in education in recent years. For example, quality processes developed in the UK are now being developed by countries across the world. The Australian experiment in students paying for tuition has been adopted in New Zealand and the UK and will inevitably sweep through the developed world. Degree level education throughout Europe is being reformulated on a three-year undergraduate/two-year postgraduate framework.

The **second decision** that we take in an evaluation concerns its focus. Again there are four and, again, they are not mutually exclusive.

- First, we could be concerned with the *objectives* or goals of the project or organisation or process we are investigating. If we are concerned with objectives, then the underpinning

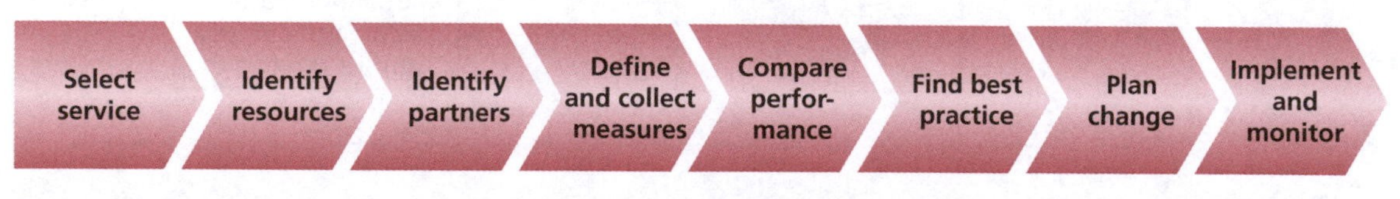

Figure 2.3 The benchmarking procedure (after Audit Commission, 2000)

issue is one of relevance and we seek to determine whether the outcomes are relevant to the current situation and, by implication, whether the objectives continue to be meaningful. After an influx of refugees a school might, for example, employ support teachers to help non-native speakers cope with lessons. Each year it could evaluate the benefits of its investment and, if it were to find that students' capability in the language of tuition had improved, it might conclude that the benefits of its programme were outweighed by the costs.

- Second, we might be concerned with *processes*, in which case the underlying issues are ones of efficiency. Are the processes producing either the quantity or quality of outcomes that are warranted in terms of the inputs? Is this organisation efficient? Is this school, set in a middle class catchment area, offering sufficient value added to its pupils in terms of their leaving qualifications? Is the investment in this new system of private finance for public services giving us value for money? Or, in the case of our example of employing support teachers, are they producing the benefits expected of them and, if not, what might be changed?
- Third, the focus might be on *outcomes*, in which case we are asking questions about effectiveness. Are the outcomes, both expected and unforeseen, delivering what we wanted to happen? Are the anti-bullying policy and associated measures actually creating a safer environment? Is the action of placing police in schools leading to a reduction in anti-social behaviour?
- Finally, our focus might be on *sustainability*. Here there is a range of questions that might be asked. Is the initiative likely to continue beyond a period of start up funding? Is there a champion who will support it? Does it continue to meet the needs of the community? Does it have a continuing utility? Will we know when it ceases to be useful?

The **final decision** that we have to take concerns the type of evaluation we wish to set up. There are two ways of looking at this and they can be combined.

- First, an evaluation can be summative or formative. *Summative evaluations* occur at the end of something, such as a project, and are concerned with whether what was supposed to happen actually did happen. *Formative evaluations* occur at one or more stages during a project or programme and have the objective either of ensuring that the project is keeping to a planned schedule or of improving performance if it does not meet expectations.
- Second, an evaluation can be goal orientated, decision orientated or conflict orientated.
  - *Goal orientated evaluation* is concerned with outcomes but, because outcomes are a consequence of the whole implementation process, from the goals that were established, through the resource inputs that were applied and the decisions that were taken to the management actions that implemented those decisions, a goal orientation must consider the whole project or programme. It has to consider not only whether goals were met (and if not, why not) but also whether the right goals were specified (and if not, why not). We could, for example, evaluate a school's attempt to stamp out disruptive classroom behaviour with a strong discipline policy. We can collect data to judge how effective it was but we ought also to consider why students were disruptive and whether curriculum change might not have been a better strategy.
  - A *decision making* focus looks at how decisions were made and the context in which they were made, from the resources available to be used to the management actions. A decision making focus might also investigate whether decisions

were reviewed and what the consequences of review were. In our example we would want to understand why the senior management in a school chose discipline as the means of managing behaviour.

- A *conflict orientation* investigates how conflicts were resolved within a project, from decisions about goals, objectives and priorities to the decision making embedded in project delivery. How far one takes the analysis through into the delivery phase is dependent upon whether conflicts at earlier stages were resolved or whether points of view were so well established in the management framework that conflicts continued. A conflict analysis is usually undertaken when a project has failed or is underperforming. The governors of our school with the discipline problems might review the implementation of the programme if behaviour did not improve and exclusions increased. An evaluation might find that the senior management team had been divided over which direction to take to solve their problem and that half were vehemently opposed to using policing and punishment strategy for improving behaviour.

What issues do we need to be aware of if we are considering using an evaluation methodology? Three stand out.

- First, evaluation is presented as being detached from delivery, systematic in its work, objective in its outlook with the evaluator independent of what is being evaluated. It clearly believes that it draws on the principles of scientific research for its inspiration. The reality, however, is that evaluation is a bit like constructing a case for the prosecution or the defence in law. You assemble the evidence and present it in a way that argues your case in the most cogent and persuasive way possible. The scientific approach lets the evidence speak for itself. An evaluator brings the evidence together and creates a perspective based on perceived insights that reconfigure the evidence to confirm those insights. The insights need not be wrong but, equally, they need not be correct. If the evaluation is internal to an activity, then there is potential if not for bias, then at least accentuation of the positive.
- Second, evaluation should take account of multiple perspectives, those who might be funding a project, stakeholders who might be involved in the delivery of a project, the beneficiaries of the project outcomes and the community in general. The balance of these can affect the character of the evaluation. To return to our example of a school's decision to institute a strict disciplinary regime, evaluation might show that pupils may not give it wholehearted approval, educational authorities may not either if it results in more pupils being excluded from schools but teachers and the community may think it an excellent idea.
- Finally, the boundaries of an evaluation must be clearly established at the outset. Because evaluations can follow what seem to be interesting lines of enquiry, it is quite easy for them to stray outside their remit.

(iii) Ethnography

Ethnography comes from two Greek words that mean 'people' or 'nation' and 'writing', so ethnography is writing about people. In an educational context we could use an ethnographic approach to 'write about' the culture of a school staff room and the relationships within it. We can observe what happens there and even ask questions, both informally and formally through interviews. The writing element describes a process that leads to analysis, synthesis and conclusions. It may seem descriptive but the writing leads to the identification of structures and processes. In our staff room we may find that that one place is recognised as being that of a particular teacher or that the chemistry department always sits together but the English department never does. The evidence is assembled to create an argued interpretation. Speculation can play an element in constructing a possible explanation and further research can seek the evidence on which to accept or reject it. The people involved in an ethnographic study can be any group from a formal structure such as an organisation to an informal group such as a gang. Ethnography is well established as a method in education research and is used to understand such things as classroom behaviour, the learning process, group values and behaviour, organisational management and change and so on.

The stages in an ethnographic study are shown in Figure 2.4. Once the issue to be researched has been identified, the first stage is to find where we can study it. In the case of our school staff room, we have to find a head teacher and a group of staff that will agree to our being with them. The selection of the study environment must be done with care. It should be representative of both the issue and the context in which the issue is normally found. As we shall see in Chapter 6, identifying our study location is a matter of sampling and the right location is important if the results of the investigation are to have any wider implications. If the context is atypical, it could still be used for an investigation but the researcher has to then make a clear judgement of those conclusions that might and those that might not be applicable to other circumstances. The process of data collection uses standard methods of observation, conversation, interviews, questionnaires and others that we will meet in Chapters 8 and 9. What makes a study ethnographic is that the researcher spends a long and intensive period in the study environment. It is this that produces the insight to make sense of the data. Analysis consists of the assembly of evidence to identify themes. At the heart of this process is the categorisation of research data and the linking up of the categories by the researcher. At this stage the

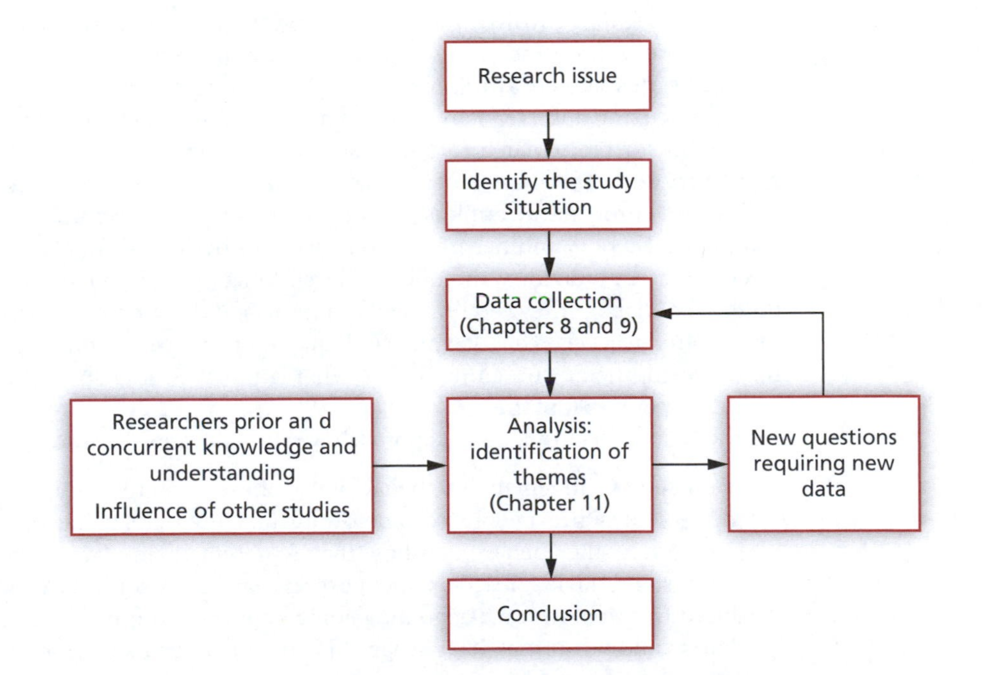

Figure 2.4 Stages in an ethnographic study

researcher often makes use of background knowledge and understanding to inform the selection of themes. But not everything may be resolved at this stage. Analysis may raise new questions that will require further data collection, so there can be a significant feedback loop at this stage. This should be built into our research schedule. The final stage is to write up a report setting out and arguing for our conclusions.

The centrality of the researcher to the process is emphasised in the sifting and sorting of the data to identify how it best fits together. There are techniques that can be used, for example classification and coding (see Chapter 11), but the structures that these represent arise from the researcher's assessment of the evidence. So the researcher is the point of synthesis and the synthesis is influenced not just by the data that is collected but also by what the researcher knows from other similar or related studies. In addition, of course, any researcher is likely to be influenced by the existence of:

- social and family structures;
- concepts such as respect, dominance and equality that frame relationships; and
- ideas and interpretations developed by other researchers, for example territoriality (the attachment to a location or the defence of a location) and identity (individual or group).

Within the ethnographic approach the objective is not to change the behaviour of individuals or groups but to act as an observer of that behaviour. This is more difficult than it may seem. If our observer status is kept hidden from the study group, then our position becomes problematic if we do not behave in ways that the group expects. Often, the option of being a 'hidden' researcher is not open to us. For example, as a 20-year-old it would be difficult not to stand out in a staff room. Being a 'hidden' researcher is likely to be a better option in studies of organisations because we can take on a formal role and do a normal job. Many other researchers use the term 'participant observer' to describe a 'hidden researcher'. It matters little which term we use, though 'participant' does have the sense of being fully involved in the interactions that are being studied.

If we are not a 'hidden' researcher, then we are visible to the group and our researcher status known to the members. (The visible researcher is also described as a 'non-participant observer'.) In this situation, the researcher has to gain the group's agreement for the research to take place and for the group to be observed. This can affect how some group members behave. This may be a particular issue at the start of the research programme but it is likely to wane as the observer becomes just part of the wallpaper. There is another problem, as well, in being visible – you can be asked to intervene at an individual or collective level. Imagine that you are observing a class of infants. At that age they certainly will not understand your role as a researcher, you are just another teacher. What do you do when a pupil asks you for help (because once you have helped, there is no going back)? What is the answer? I suspect that most people would help. Does it matter?

If we adopt an ethnographic approach we should be aware of some potential pitfalls.

- The issue of influencing the behaviour of those you are studying has already been mentioned. Once people become aware that they are being observed, they may change how they behave and how they represent themselves to the world. A bully might stop bullying, teachers might express agreement with the changes being introduced by the head teacher, young people might act with more bravado or insolence than would be normal. If we suspect this might be the case, what can be done to improve the situation? The answer is to stay longer, become part of the environment and hope that your subjects' normal behaviour reasserts itself.

- Second, there is a real issue of researcher misinterpretation. The reflective approach is so central to the analysis that one wrong inference can lead to erroneous conclusions. This is difficult to guard against. That is why research is published, so others can see how conclusions are reached and, if necessary, criticise them.
- Third, the position of the researcher as an insider can raise ethical issues. What happens if we spot something that we think is wrong? If we suspect child abuse, the chances are that we will act. If we suspect that a teacher is altering the grades that children are given in tests that reflect their attainment over the past year, what should we do then? Remember that it is our work that will be affected! With an ethnographic approach we may find that we get hold of privileged information. Can we use this in our research – and publish it? Read section 2.1.3 on principles again.
- Fourth, there is a significant potential for researchers to identify with their subjects in some way. For example, if we are studying why a school has low attainment standards and much of our research has been looking at how teachers cope with a significant annual intake of students whose first language is not the language of tuition, we might be tempted to write a report that was sympathetic to the teacher's situation rather than one that highlighted a collective failure in identifying methods used successfully elsewhere to achieve better results. The researcher is so important to ethnography that critical distance is vital if the results are to be credible.
- Finally, ethnographic research can become just a description rather than the insight into something of a more general nature. As a research approach it seeks to provide the research community with generalisations – ideas and concepts that are applicable to other situations. If we adopt an ethnographic approach, we should make sure that our study talks to a wider set of circumstances. A study of a breakdown in leadership in one college should have something to say about preventative measures for most other colleges, and probably schools as well. With an ethnographic approach, the researcher is immersed in the detail of the study but always finishes by looking at an issue with a wider perspective.

(iv) Action research

The final methodology that we shall look at is action research. The distinctive characteristic of action research is its purpose, it seeks to develop and implement change.

The origins of action research can be traced back to the early twentieth century. The earliest examples of what we might call action research never used the term itself though and they were isolated occurrences in the research world. The social scientist Kurt Lewin is usually acknowledged as having coined the term and conceptualised the essence of the research process. Lewin was another refugee from Hitler's Germany who found refuge in the USA. His work in psychology was principally concerned with the interaction of people in a group setting, what became known as group dynamics. It was this expertise that led to his being approached at the end of the Second World War to explore what could be done to ease tension and conflict amongst ethnically based gangs of young men. His paper on 'Action Research and Minority Problems' brought the term into existence, established the research approach to achieve change and laid the foundations of a research approach that was to transform the research environments of both education and business. Lewin died in 1947.

Action research is an approach that uses research findings to inform and shape personal and organisation action. It does not generate knowledge for its own sake, so to this extent it is closer to evaluation and case study than it is to ethnographic research (though even this need not necessarily be the case – this is what is meant by research being a messy business, nothing is ever really clear cut). It differs from evaluation and case study in that the knowledge they produce is usually passed out of the research environment to someone else to consider and act upon. With action research, the action is part of the research process. This gives rise to a cyclical procedure in which research generates action and action becomes the evidence base for further research. This is shown in Figure 2.5.

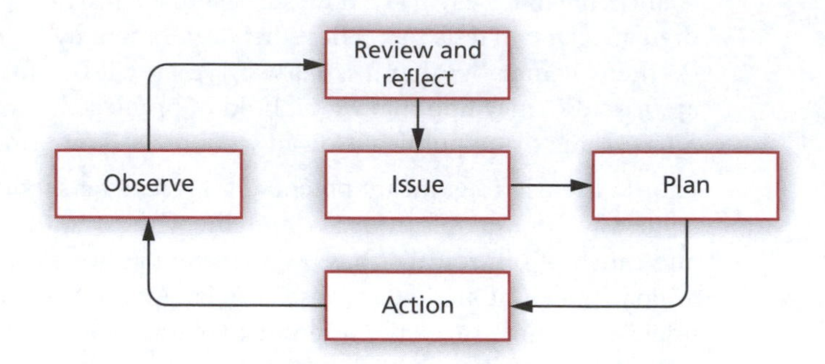

Figure 2.5 The action research cycle

Let us start with the issue that is at the centre of the investigation. This is placed at the centre of Figure 2.5. In an attempt to resolve the issue (which might be that very few students choose to study a statistics option in a research methods course), those involved in the action research programme develop an action plan. It would be appropriate in the first cycle to put a process of assessment, analysis and reflection between the issue and the action plan because it is out of this initial consideration that the first action plan arises. In our case, this could be a meeting of the course team members to discuss the problem and decide what they can do about it. The implementation of the plan gives rise to the next stage, the actions themselves. These actions are different from what went on before and the difference constitutes the driver for change and the resolution of the issue. If the course team believe that students do not take the option because they are not confident in their numeracy, they might develop numerical problem solving activities to give them confidence. The actions are monitored and observed through data collection procedures that were determined at the initial planning stage. In reality, of course, observation does not follow action, it runs in parallel with it (or just behind it – if it is too far behind, then memory can play funny tricks with recall). In our case, we will have student test data and assessments of self-confidence with numbers. Finally the data is brought together and assessed in the stage called review and reflection. The formal processes of data analysis and reporting are determined at the planning stage. These analyses, plus the experiences of those involved, become the evidence to judge what has been achieved. A crucial part of this process is to ask questions: Why did this work well and that not? Why was there a hiccup at that stage? Was everyone pulling their weight? How far have we resolved the issue? It is this question that triggers the next cycle. What can we do to resolve the issue or get closer to our goal next time? This is the second plan.

The issues that action research can address are shown in Figure 2.6. Four purposes or types of task are identified. Each of these is particularly well suited to a target environment.

- *Organisational change* may require a change in goals, practices or procedures. Achieving this, however, may require deeper change in outlooks, aspirations and attitudes. Because of action research's power in achieving organisational change, it is used extensively in business and, in some organisations, it effectively operates as

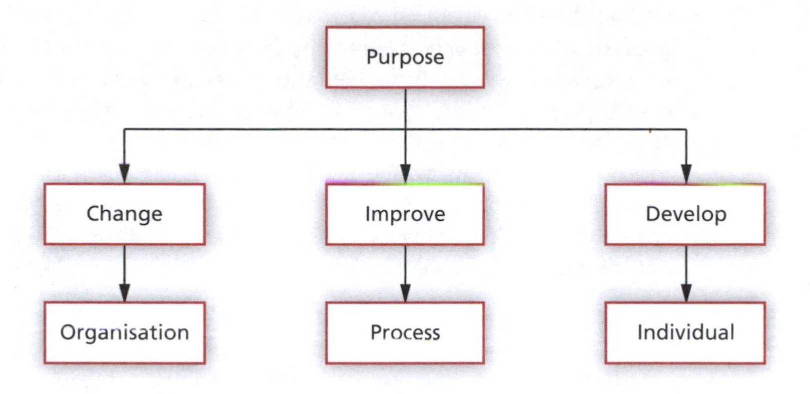

Figure 2.6 How action research can be used

management practice. Schools and colleges are organisations and it is entirely appropriate for it to be used as part of the process they use to adjust to a changing external environment. We could use an action research process to help school teachers adjust to a timetable revision in which the standard lesson is increased from 35 minutes to either 90 minutes or 150 minutes. Blocked time is both an opportunity for teachers and a problem in terms of sustaining student interest, concentration and motivations. We could explain the action research process and ask them to develop lesson plans, review the lesson outcomes using student feedback and their own reflection and amend intentions for next lessons.

- Action learning to achieve *improvement* focuses on processes. Improvement is measured by outcomes but it is the processes that generate those outcomes that are the concern of the action researcher. Typical of the processes that action research can change are those concerned with improving quality. Delivering quality is an expectation of both those who receive and those who fund education. There is one approach to management, called total quality management, that has action learning at its core and which places quality improvement at the heart of organisational activity. While there is criticism of total quality management in business (predominantly that the emphasis is so much on process that profitability is largely unaffected) it does take time to produce culture and organisational change that delivers impact. In most instances schools, colleges and universities respond to externally imposed quality indicators but there are some that have built total quality processes into the way they work. In the Netherlands, for example, the Hanzehogeschool in Groningen is using the approach and in Finland the University of Art and Design. For more information on this see the European Foundation for Quality Management's (EFQM) website: http://www.efqm.org/.
- *Development* is the last purpose for which action research is particularly suited and it is here that it has had its greatest impact in education. Development is about individual practice and action research is widely promoted as a process for individuals to improve their own practice – as a teacher, as an administrator, even as a leader. It needs not be restricted to people working by themselves. It can be a group activity but the impact is on an individual's practice. Over ten years ago, the Research Council of Norway initiated a curriculum development programme using an action research programme to build enquiry and research into the primary curriculum. You can read about the outcomes at: http://www.nysgjerrigper.no/Artikler_Engelske/AboutNysgjerrigper/.

The character of action research should be getting clearer for you now. It is a practical procedure that seeks to change things. Researchers are not outsiders. Decisions are taken on a collaborative basis, worker and researchers, teachers and students. It does not necessarily seek to produce an immediate answer. It navigates over a number of research cycles (from action to reflection) towards its goal. Its major contribution to the research toolbox is reflection, which it takes out of the personal and private domain of the researcher and exposes it to collective consensus. However, we should not imagine that it comes without its own issues. By now we should appreciate that there is no such thing as a perfect research procedure!

- Because action research is a negotiated process, it lacks the formality of many other approaches. Local circumstances, moods and feelings at a particular time can both affect the decisions that are taken. Some researchers see the potential for compromise as a lack of rigour. Others view the fact that it is practitioner led as demonstrating a lack of rigour. These, you will note, are concerns about procedure. They also reflect the arrogance of some professional researchers. What you should judge action research on are the outcomes. Does change occur? Are things better than they were?
- Because analysis and interpretation is undertaken by those involved in the actions, there can be concerns about how disinterested the analysis and explanation can be. How critical can someone or some group be of their past actions? How likely are they to seek an explanation for failure in external events and other people's actions rather than their own? Honesty in research can be difficult when it is our own credibility that is on the line.
- Finally, there can be concerns about leadership, decision making and power relationships. The idea of action research is that it is a democratic process. Inevitably though there are people who by virtue of some combination of knowledge, personality or position will begin to dominate a group. How should this be managed? Just as problematic, what if there are two or more of them? How do you manage the potential for conflict? The best solution is to agree procedures for collecting and processing data that give everyone a voice at the outset.

(v) The four methodologies compared

Table 2.5 summarises the characteristics of the four methodologies that have been considered. They each perform well in different situations. Ethnography is more academic in its character (we use it to explain and understand) while evaluation and action research are more applied and concerned with practice. Case studies can perform both roles. They differ in terms of where the researcher fits into the process, sometimes inside, sometimes outside, sometimes visible, sometimes hidden, and in the methods they use. There is, though, much more commonality in the issues they face: the need to overcome a lack of detachment in ethnography, evaluation and action research, the need to work within a boundary in case study or evaluation research and the danger of misinterpretation and lack of generalisation in ethnography and case study. It is, however, the fact that we can make these general statements that establishes them as methodologies. Distinctiveness, purpose and status of the researcher are the principles that define them and together they determine how the processes of data gathering and interpretation work. It is this combination that lies at the heart of a research methodology.

You should not, however, imagine that these methodologies are your only options. You will meet other approaches including experimentation in Chapter 3 (considered

Table 2.5 How the methodologies compare

	Ethnography	Case study	Evaluation	Action research
Distinctiveness	Researcher focus.	Learn from the particular.	Question focus.	Change focus.
Purpose	Understand, explain.	Explain, explore, describe.	Understand, test compliance, improve, inform.	Change, improve, build, develop.
Researcher status	Hidden or visible participant.	External analyst.	Outside the process but may be internal to project.	Inside the process and the project.
Methods	Observation, conversation.	Information assembly, interview.	Any.	Reflection.
Limitations and issues	• Influencing behaviour. • Misinterpretation of evidence. • Ethical issues. • Not detached. • Lack of generalisation.	• Getting at the truth can be difficult. • Wrong interpretation. • Can it be generalised?	• Not detached. • Limited perspectives. • Setting boundary to study.	• Lack of rigour. • Not detached. • Group decisions about actions can be compromises.

there because they are better understood in terms of the issues discussed in the chapter). Researching is a dynamic field that changes as researchers address new conditions and circumstances. For example, we are beginning to consider the principles that might underpin Web-based research (there is some further reading on this at the end of the chapter). It is possible for us to create new frameworks that combine methods and develop new ones and which will lead us via a new path through to an end point. We should bear in mind, as well, that there is a growing acceptance of mixed methodologies (see Chapter 3). Pragmatism in research is becoming acceptable. What we have to do, as researchers, is present a strong case for tackling the issue in the way that we have.

2.1.5 Research questions

Research questions are statements of the issue that we want to research. The research issue identifies the area of our research (such as the socialisation of young children in a classroom setting). The research question pins down the things we want to investigate ('Is the amount of time devoted to free play associated with the number of friends a child has and the number of friendship groups that they have access to?'). What is particularly important about research questions is that the way we phrase them can affect our approach to research. And this is why: research questions point us to the data we need and are also indicative of the methodology that will give us the data and process them. This is not to say that the type of research question we ask *determines* how we go about the research (in the sense that we have no options but to do it only one way), just that it predisposes us to look in certain directions at particular methodologies.

Table 2.6 summarises the types of research question that can be generated and the research approach that often follows. The intention of Table 2.6 is not only to show the association between our research question and the way we do our research but also that

Table 2.6 The link between research question and research approach

Question	Research approach
What *is* happening here?	Data analysis. Ethnographic. Descriptive.
What *did happen/has happened* here?	Case study.
What *will* happen?	Causal analysis. Research synthesis, systematic review. Descriptive inference.
What is . . . ?	Descriptive.
What should we do?	Policy analysis.
What is the effect of?	Evaluation, experimental design. Causal analysis, experimental design.
What is the cause of?	Causal analysis, statistical design.
Is this result the same or different?	Association analysis, statistical design.
Is this working? Can it be better?	Action oriented: action research, appreciative enquiry. Policy analysis.
All questions	Mixed design.

in every case there is more than one approach that we can adopt. Each of the research approaches has a theory of how it should be applied.

(i) What *is* happening here?

The assumption with this question could be that we have found data that we want to make sense of. This could be a table from a regular statistical series or a research data set that has been archived. Many countries now provide digital or documentary storage facilities for survey data and statistical series. See, for example, the UK Data Archive, the Australian Social Science Data Archive, the New Zealand Social Research Data Archive, and the South African Data Archive. Activity 2.3 will help you become familiar with data archives. With statistical data we will use data analysis techniques to identify pattern, order, discrepancies and deviations. Pattern and order represent the usual and discrepancies and deviations situations that are towards the outer limits of what is usual. Data analysis is considered in detail in Chapter 10.

We can also pose the question, 'What is happening here?' in respect of situations that are ongoing and, probably, significant. It would be an appropriate question to ask if there were a tripartite breakdown in trust between the senior management of a college, governors and staff. An ethnographic approach (see section 2.1.4(iii)) in which the researcher operated within the community and observed and absorbed the culture, tensions and issues would be entirely appropriate, as would a descriptive approach. A descriptive approach places the researcher outside the issue and its context (unlike ethnographic). The researcher is an assembler and commentator rather than an observer and analyst. The description can be based on statistical data (in which case the techniques in Chapters 10 and 12 are important) or on text such as reports, minutes and policy statements (in which case the approaches in Chapter 11 will be used).

Activity 2.3 Accessing data archives

CESSDA – access to archives worldwide

CESSDA is the Council Of European Social Science Data Archives. Via its website (http://www.cessda.org) we can connect to data archives worldwide. Not only does CESSDA act as a portal to data archives, it has also produced a 'metadata' model to provide international coherence in archiving data and which will, inevitably, inform the data collection process so that it conforms to archiving criteria. CESSDA provides access to 21 websites in Europe, 14 in North America, as well as archives in Australia, New Zealand, South Africa, Israel and Uruguay. Not all the websites have data archives. A key feature of CESSDA is the integrated catalogue, which enables researchers to search ten national archives. This is important if you are conducting international research.

National archives

If we know that we want data from only one country it is better to access that archive directly. The **UK Data Archive**'s Web address is http://www.data-archive.ac.uk. It is also a very useful access point to data archives in other European states and has an easy to navigate map at http://www.data-archive.ac.uk/findingData/map.asp.

Activities

1. Access the home page of CESSDA and navigate to the catalogue (under Accessing Data) on the left hand side. Select 'Browse by Topic' and then 'Education'. Is the archive equally strong in all subfields? Assess this by counting the number of entries in each subfield. Access the largest subfield. Identify whether the same data is available from all states. Which states have the greatest representation?
2. Access the home page of the UK Data Archive. Select 'Search Catalogue' (under 'About Data') and then 'Browse by Subject' (on the left under 'Finding Data'). Identify how many categories are of potential interest to the educational researcher. Imagine you are researching children's lifestyle and diet (your concern is obesity on the one hand and young people's concern with body shape on the other). What data sets can you identify that might help you (a) frame your own research and (b) act as a baseline to your own study?
3. Access the map of other data archives from the UK Data Archives website (click on 'Other Archives' under 'Finding Data'. Choose any archive and identify the range of data available on education.

(ii) What *did happen/has happened* here?

This question looks at events that have passed. It is the sort of question that would be asked if a school was failing to meet target outcomes, or if there was a high turnover of staff, or if an education authority or school board had managed to reduce unauthorised absence significantly. In all of these cases the outcome is known and a case study would be an appropriate approach (see section 2.1.4(i)). The case study is a mixed method approach (see Chapter 3) that can make use of a wide range of data collection techniques such as text analysis, data analysis, interview and questionnaire survey. The case study approach can be very similar to evaluation. The purpose of a case study is to bring out critical incidents (if a pupil were severely injured on a school trip) or to present exemplars of good or poor or successful or innovative practice.

(iii) What *will* happen?

This question shapes your research so that it is capable of being predictive, that is, saying what should happen in different situations. The traditional way of achieving this is to estimate the influence of different factors on an outcome. This cause-effect approach is developed using a causal analysis strategy, which is explained in more detail in Chapter 3, when we look at quantitative analysis. If a college had a model that measured the influence of different channels of communication on student choice of institution (prospectus, student visits, tutor visits to schools, web, email, text message, newspaper, posters), it could use it to determine how many extra students a fixed investment in marketing would generate when invested in each mode.

(iv) What is . . . ?

This is the simplest research question that can be put. What is the number of graduates in Russian? How many organisations are providing out of school activities in this area? How many applicants do we normally get for a teaching post? Answers to questions such as these are factual not conjectural. Either they can be found out or they cannot. All the researcher has to do is to describe what has been found. The research process is, therefore, descriptive, and can use either words or statistical methods. It is usually fairly straightforward to see how the data that will answer the question should be collected or identified. The skill of the researcher lies in getting an answer that meets the standards required in the most cost-effective way. For example, if we wanted to know how much people in an area spent on private education, we could sample the people in the area and ask them (see Chapter 6), we could go to fee paying schools in the area and ask them how many children lie in the area or, in the UK, we could use the Family Spending Survey (an annual survey on the expenditure patterns of families categorised by age, income, socio-economic status, geographical location and household composition) in conjunction with the Census of Population and derive a very accurate estimate. The last route is likely to be the most cost-effective.

(v) What should we do?

Research that helps determine a line of action is research for policy. Policy research is a multi-method approach that assesses policy outcomes or informs policy decisions. It rarely determines the decision. Policy research contains data that represents different perspectives. There might be, for example, a quantitative and qualitative description of the issue that needs to be addressed, an assessment of current policy and a description of the instruments and processes for implementing it, a statement of policy and policy implementation in other countries and an assessment of what the general public thinks about the issue. The final stage, however, is always a political assessment. This can be party political or it can be political in the sense that organisations will judge whether the payback is worth the effort.

(vi) What is the effect of . . . ?

What is the effect of this policy? How effective have we been in implementing the new ways of working? What is the impact of the new curriculum? These questions lead, in the first instance, to an evaluative approach, another mixed method way of researching. The intention of evaluation is to explore the consequences of some action. If the action is a policy, then there is little to choose between evaluation and policy research. One thing that should distinguish evaluation from other approaches is the fact that it should identify unintended outcomes as well as intended, unforeseen as well as foreseen and negative consequences as well as positive. We shall look at evaluation again in Chapter 14.

Questions about impact can, however, have a narrower focus than the ones we have just considered. What is the effect of food type at lunchtime on pupil behaviour and performance in the afternoon? What is the effect of class size on pupil performance? What is the effect of ambient temperature on pupil performance? Such questions as these may be capable of being answered by a causal analysis using an experimental or quasi-experimental design (see Chapter 3). With this the subjects are allocated to groups experiencing or not experiencing an intervention either in ways that seek to minimise the differences or in ways that randomise factors that might interfere with a direct causal relationship. This approach seeks to replicate the type of design found, for example, in medical research. It is, however, difficult to accomplish because the number of variables that can influence the research result is very large and the more that are uncontrolled the greater are the problems of interpretation.

(vii) What is the cause of . . . ?

With the previous question the concern was with identifying the effect of an intervention in the system. This question may look much the same but its focus is with the system as it is operating, not as it is affected, and its concern is to identify causal relationships in that system. The approach that will do this is, again, causal analysis but not an experimental design, instead a statistical design. The relationships are explored using a correlational method (see Chapters 12 and 13), which tests how closely related two or more variables are to each other. If many variables can be associated with each other and if the strength of their association can be quantified, then a researcher is well along the path of turning a conceptual model into one that quantitatively represents the operation of a system.

(viii) Is this result the same or different?

This question can be answered by a similar statistical design approach as above. Instead of measuring causation in the relationship, the approach measures association. We might ask the question, 'Are the degree results in education from X University the same as those from Y?' Alternatively, 'Do teachers trained at A institution have a career progression that is the same or different from the norm?' In these cases we can use a range of statistical techniques to give us an answer (again, see Chapters 12 and 13).

(ix) Is this working? Can it be better?

This question explores the relationship between process and outcome. It is often, though this is not a necessary condition, a process for improvement led by the person or organisation seeking to improve. Equally it is possible for an outsider to manage the research and guide the improvement process as a consultant. This process is called action research (see section 2.1.4(iv)). As a process it too is multi-method (see Chapter 3). At the broadest level, when concerned with strategic direction and achieving goals, action research can be little different from policy analysis, particularly if the route to achieving policy goals is not clear. It is important, however, to distinguish between analysis to inform policy (see above), analysis to improve policy and analysis to understand how policy came about. The first two stem from broadly liberal agendas; the last one, understanding policy origins, is likely to stem from a radical perspective.

(x) All questions

Many of the approaches that have been described are multi-method (see Chapter 3). If one were to look at the history and evolution of research methods, it would be clear that the process of combining methods represents the last phase of development. The idea that research must utilise particular procedures is a standpoint that only idealists would subscribe to, and the ideal circumstances that are required are not always found in real world research. The real world, as we have seen, is not like that, it is a messy place. It requires answers in unreasonable timescales and expects firm conclusions to enable decision making when these may only be supported by leaps of faith. This is not to suggest that multi-method approaches to research are inherently weak, indeed far from it. Their variety in combination may, in fact, be a strength in situations where the real world makes unrealistic demands on research. We could see the effective combination of methods as a new research paradigm. Instead of setting out to conform to orthodoxy, there is no reason why we should not start with the research that apparently needs to be done. All research questions may be susceptible to and benefit from a multi-method approach.

2.2 Ideas that influence your goals and outcomes

In section 2.2 we explored issues that we have to take a stand on and which influence how we work. In this section we shall look at different issues on which we have to take decisions and which will influence what goals we set for our research and what outcomes we seek to attain. Figure 2.7 shows the two principal issues that we have to consider, education theory and models. Both of these can influence our research goals.

2.2.1 Education theory and its influence on your goals

Before we consider the role of education theory, we need to settle a potential source of confusion, the difference between education theory and research theory. Education theory deals with the subject matter of education – child development, learning, curriculum design and so on. Research theory, which may influence the process we adopt, is a specification of procedure. Education theory derives from conjecture about what might

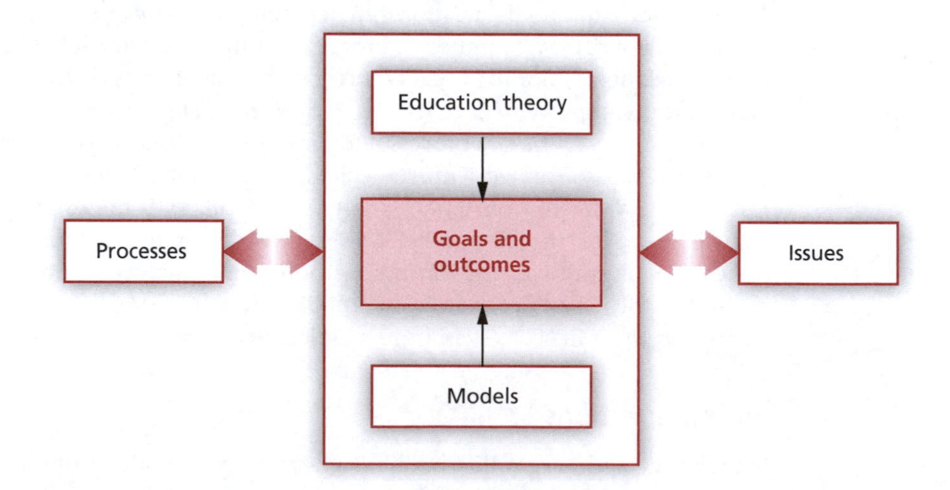

Figure 2.7 Influences on research goals and outcomes

(or should) be the case or from evidence drawn from the real world. Research theory is based on either a set of premises and consequences derived logically from them (the quantitative paradigm) or what researchers accept (the qualitative paradigm). Education theory is (or aims to be) generalisable, whereas research theory is specific to a particular type of problem or approach. Education theory can be tested, while research theory can only be benchmarked against the principles on which it is based. In summary, education theory shapes our understanding and gives us choice when making educational decisions. Research theory is a rule book whose legitimacy stems from principles accepted by the academic community and whose coherence owes as much to custom and practice as to any overarching theorisation.

Now let us look in more detail about how theory is used in the field of education. Just what is a theory? It is a generalisation that should apply in all or most cases (which is how it tends to be used in science) or in some cases or particular circumstances (which is how it is often used in the social sciences). A theory seeks to explain things in terms of cause and effect and with varying degrees of certainty. A good theory is predictive. Education theory falls into two types (there are other classifications with more than two categories but remember this is a book on research procedure and there is no time to go into detail on this issue).

(i) Normative theory

The first type of theory, called normative theory, explains how things *could or should be organised or what goals should be achieved*. Much theory in education is normative because it says how children should be educated. John Dewey, the famous liberal American educationalist who died in his 90s in 1952, argued that education was not about the rote learning of facts. His approach emphasised 'learning by doing', that is, developing an understanding through practice (for example in science). We can see in his theories the origins of the competence and capability movement in education. Maria Montessori, an Italian educationalist who, coincidentally also died in 1952, argued that education was holistic and embraced social development as well as cognitive and practical. She also derived, from her own observation and experience, a theory of education that had practical expression where children developed at their own pace in a structured educational world presenting a range of stimuli and challenges. Both Dewey's and Montessori's theories about education are normative, that is, driven by a belief about what is appropriate as an outcome. Such theories give rise to practices that deliver this outcome. Belief can be moral (the full development of a child's talents) or instrumental (the development of children's talents to meet the needs of society and the economy).

(ii) Explanatory theory

The second type of theory, descriptive or explanatory theory, explains *how things work*. The Russian psychologist and educationalist Lev Vygotsky (who died at the early age of 38 in 1934) sought to explain how learning took place by formulating a theory built around two sets of mental capabilities, one inherited and the other learnt. It is the latter, he said, that creates an understanding of the indicators, signs and symbols through which we represent the world. Language, he said, is crucial in determining the scale and quality of the word (semantic) map that each of us has and his theory argues that the semantic map is both the product of learning and the means of enabling more learning to take place.

Human capital theory is another explanatory theory. It sees investment in intellectual and practical skill development as the basis of economic growth and economic success.

It is the theory that underpins investment in numeracy and literacy at preschool and primary levels, in the development of generic skills (for instance, problem solving and group work) at secondary and higher education and investment in lifelong learning to enable people to retrain and find employment with the skills needed by modern economies. We look for evidence of the effectiveness of human capital development in international surveys of student performance.

Education theory performs a vital role; it is a framework for advancing our understanding of the subject. It shapes our thinking about the desirability of outcomes; it enables us to understand the processes at work and it helps us assess the way in which the real world works. Education theory can be constructed at a broad social scale or in the context of a specific idea. Professor Dickson Mungazi (who died in 2008) has reviewed the evolution of education theory in the USA, from the period of the Founding Fathers to the late twentieth century (Mungazi, 1999). He shows how the first influences were philosophical, including John Locke's opposition to authoritarianism, the rationalism and liberalism of the Enlightenment and the differing religious convictions of the early settlers. These shaped a new country that espoused a democratic ideal and separated church and state. Later he points out the role of the education system in meeting national goals, such as the development of a more equal society. Mungazi's thesis is that educational theory is intimately associated with the evolution of society, both as a driver and reflector of change. As he says, 'Any change in society and the values of society itself must be reflected in the educational process' (Mungazi, 1999, p. 210).

At a specific level, education theory seeks to frame our understanding of aspects of education. Educationalists draw on psychological theory to understand how education should match a child's development. Psychology too underpins our attempts to create learning theory. The theory of intelligence rests on psychology, though our understanding of multiple skills and capability draws on a broader appreciation of personality. We have theories of curriculum and behaviour management, theory that seeks to link pedagogy with specific educational outcomes, theories that define a learning process (such as experiential learning), theories of instructional design that guide authors of on-line learning materials.

So how can education theory affect our research? In two ways, it can either be the objective of our research or we can seek to develop theory through our research.

(i) Theory testing as a goal

Demonstrating the applicability of education theory or otherwise can be the focus of our research. We can take a theory, either normative or explanatory, and see if it works in our test environment. We can do this with the whole theory or, more usually, we do it with an aspect or relationship in the theory. For example, if we taught in a system that included children with physical and emotional disabilities in normal schools, we would have to adjust our teaching and learning strategies to manage diversity. We might want to conduct some research that will help us do this. We could, for example, explore whether children with limited attention spans (who often have difficulty in managing their behaviour in ways that we, as teachers, expect) learn in exactly the same ways as children with a more normal range of attention and behaviour. We could do this by taking one of the research instruments to determine learning strategies (such as Honey and Mumford's (2006) *Learning Styles Helper's Guide* and their Learning Styles Questionnaire) and give it to the children with whom we are concerned. We should be aware though that the results would require some considerable insight on our part to assess that the theory was transferable outside its usual domain of application (the boundaries of what might be considered normal). It would, however, be an interesting and perhaps significant piece of research. Look at Case Study 2.2 for an example of theory testing that has actually taken place.

(ii) Theory development as an outcome

An objective of much research is to develop predictive knowledge that is widely applicable or applies in situations that are bounded and constrained. When knowledge is generalisable to all or particular situations and predictions can be made with some degree of certainty, it assumes the status of theory. As a researcher, we can be part of the process of theory building. It is rare for anyone to develop a whole theory as a result of one piece of research; for one thing the complexity of social relationships is such that

Case study 2.2 The acquisition of causal knowledge

Our ideas on how children learn have been strongly influenced by the work of the Swiss psychologist, Jean Piaget. Piaget's theories on child development were derived from his observations of his own children's development. His theories were formulated in the second quarter of the twentieth century. Piaget argued that children's cognitive development evolved through four stages:

1. an early stage in which the child learns to differentiate self from an external world
2. a pre-operational stage characterised by the development of language and the naming of objects
3. the first operational stage in which children learn to organise objects by a single dimension (size, number, colour)
4. the fully operational stage when children develop the ability to think in an abstract way about the world.

Psychology research over the last 25 years has challenged Piaget's theory. The ability to make statements about specific cause and effect, Piaget argued, was developed in the operational stages, and abstract causal learning (that is, going beyond making the link between flame and hurt to make a connection between the abstract hot and hurt) in the fully operational stage. Now psychologists argue that causal learning develops at a much earlier age and is operational in simplistic and naïve ways before children go to school. This transformation of theory occurred because educational and developmental psychologists took Piaget's original assumptions and tested them in laboratory and field settings. The inference researchers draw from their evidence is that even the youngest children use evidence drawn from their lives to make causal statements which, if they stand the test of being validated by subsequent experience, become consolidated as knowledge. The latest research seems to suggest that children build up their cognitive and causal representation of the world using a decision making process about whether or not to accept new knowledge using a process called 'belief networks' (or 'Bayes nets', linkages between events and outcomes to which we can give estimates of their likelihood of occurring), based on the probability model developed by Thomas Bayes who lived in the first half of the eighteenth century. The study led by Elizabeth Bonawitz, an American psychologist, is typical. Her team read picture books to 4- and 5-year-old children. Each story featured an animal (a rabbit or a deer) that suffered an ailment under specific conditions. After the stories, the children were asked what caused the problems. The authors had built a statistical model of the likelihood of a child choosing a cause (this was the belief network) and their research showed that their model accurately predicted the children's choices.

For more information on this revision to classical child development theory, see the following papers: Bonawitz et al. (2006), Gopnik et al. (2001), Schulz and Gopnik (2004).

one study is unlikely to be able to deal with all the factors that might influence behaviour and, for another, such a study would require a significant amount of resource (and educational research is not especially well endowed). So most research aiming to build theory proceeds step by step, considering one influence and then another. At each stage a little bit of understanding is gained and pieced together with what others have found. In this way a theory takes shape. Theory building in education research is, more often than not, a collective process in which researchers in different institutions and different countries pool their research findings in research literature. This is one of the reasons why a literature review is such an important part of any research project. Case Study 2.3 looks at the topic of teacher burnout and shows how our understanding changes over time.

2.2.2 How models can influence your research outcomes

We have already explained above what theories are. What are models? Models are representations of reality. Models can be based on different weights of evidence. If there is an overwhelming weight of evidence, then a model can assume the characteristics of a theory. If there is little weight of evidence, say just one study, then it assumes the characteristics of a case study. Models can be developed at different stages in the investigative process. We can construct a model from our literature survey (so it is at the very

Case study 2.3 Teacher burnout

Stress is a feature of many jobs and many countries now regard high levels of stress in the workplace as a health and safety issue. Trade unions and employers both report the last 20 years have seen stress levels rise amongst teachers as the character of the education process has changed and as the pressure to achieve more has increased. Teacher burnout has become a research topic and the goal is to identify the principal causes of stress (that could be put together to constitute a theory specific to teachers) so that employers can modify the environment in which teachers work.

In 1983 Cunningham reviewed the evidence for teacher burnout, which he described as 'physical, emotional and attitudinal exhaustion' but his paper was more concerned with solutions than theorising about cause. In the same year Iwanicki looked at causal processes. By the 1990s research was beginning to focus on assessing the significance of potential causes. In 1994 Byrne looked at a number of personal and organisational factors that might be associated with burnout and identified role conflict, work overload, classroom climate, decision making, and peer support as determinants of stress, and self-esteem and external locus of control as personal factors that could mediate the causes. She also concluded that burnout was more complex than the results of her research seemed to demonstrate. In 1996, Whitaker looked at the special case of burnout in principals and in 2002 Fore looked at the case of special education teachers, while in 2000 Brouwers and Tomic explored Byrne's conclusion that stress was more complex than a simple set of causative factors when they showed that teachers' self efficacy (the extent to which a teacher believes that they are able to influence student performance) appeared to be significantly related to burnout. In 2003 Hastings and Bham looked specifically at the influence of student behaviour and showed an association between disrespect, emotional exhaustion and depersonalisation on the one hand and lack of sociability and depersonalisation and personal accomplishment on the other. In 2006, Goddard et al. showed that innovative work environments contributed more to teacher burnout.

This is by no means a complete review of the issue of teacher burnout but it does show you that after 20 years although we are getting a better picture of the issues it is by no means complete. The theory is still some way off.

beginning of our research work) and set out to test it or we can analyse our data and on the basis of our analysis construct a model (at the very end of our research). Models can be based on theoretical intuition without empirical evidence, in which case we call them normative models. They can also be constructed from empirical evidence. Summarising the concepts of theory and model:

- both can be developed from logical deduction and both can be created from empirical study;
- both relate reality to abstract thinking about reality.

In view of this summary you might well ask, 'Why do we need them both?' Theory is valuable because it can be the starting point of an investigation and it organises our understanding of a situation. This need not be an empirical situation, though in the case of education, it usually is. Models are valuable because they can abstract from and visually represent our understanding of complex situations, key players and processes in education activity and they can be a basis for testing our understanding of reality, for example, do the relationships that were found in one situation reappear in another? Mark Warford used a model as a template to research the diffusion of an educational innovation (Warford, 2005). Innovation diffusion is a well understood process but not in education. People who adopt new ideas can be categorised into innovators, early adopters, early majority, late majority and laggards. The numbers in each category are small at first, rise to a peak in early and late majority and fall off thereafter. Warford used this model to see if it applied to an educational innovation, new guidelines on foreign language teaching. His findings are interesting in that they indicate how an innovation diffusion process can stall. Two points stand out. First, although this was an educational policy initiative, it was not taken up. Second, those who had adopted the innovation reported that local education administrations were barriers to change. This is interesting research given the pressures facing teachers to change to meet new demands.

Models usually show a link between one event and another. The implication is that the link is causal in nature. You might, for example, develop a model to show what influences children's selection of meals in the school or college cafeteria. Your model can take the form of a statement or a diagram or it can be expressed in symbolic terms (see Figure 2.8). Models can be used in all research approaches, in conjunction with all methodologies and at various stages in the research process.

- We can use them to organise our understanding of previous studies and to highlight what we consider to be the key relationships. This type of model helps us shape our research programme and it may be something we seek to verify through our research.
- We can develop one to shape and represent our thoughts without reference to previous studies (much as we did for Figure 2.8). We can move directly to find the evidence for our model or we could use it as a benchmark for other studies.
- Finally we can use a model to represent our research findings.

If we are beginning to see some value models in research, our next question, perhaps, ought to be, 'How do I go about building one?' There are whole books on the procedures such as simulation, soft-systems modelling, probabilistic modelling and so on, so what we say here only touches on the topic. In broad terms we can represent reality as mathematical symbols or relationships, or as formal objects (such as people and organisations) and their relationships in a diagram or in words (look at Figure 2.8 again). Models can be representations of reality (the school meal example in Figure 2.8) or

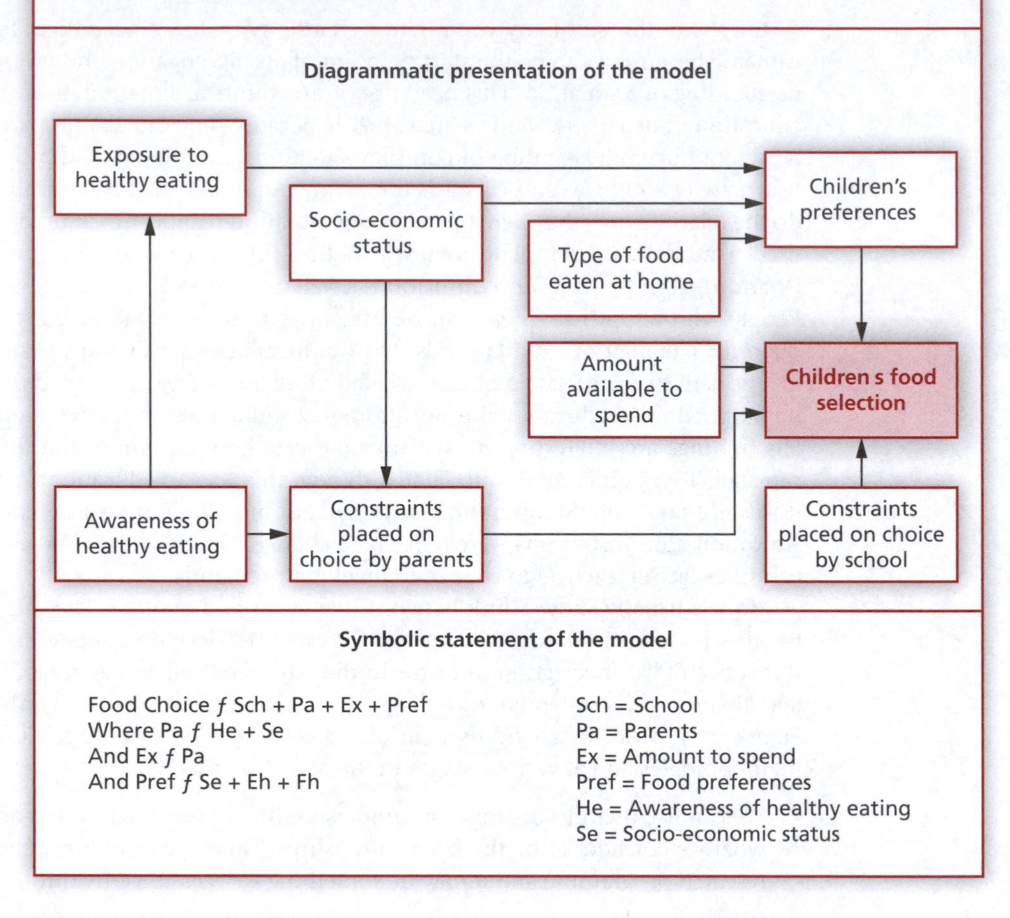

Written statement of the model
Children's selection of food is influenced by their own food preferences (which themselves are influenced by the socio-economic status of the family, the types of food eaten at home and the extent to which they are exposed to healthy eating messages at home), the amount they have to spend (which may be determined by their parents), their parents' expectations of what they will eat (which may be strong or weak dependent on the parents' socio-economic status and their awareness of the need to eat a healthy diet) and the constrains placed upon them their election by the school
Diagrammatic presentation of the model
Exposure to healthy eating
Socio-economic status
Children's preferences
Type of food eaten at home
Amount available to spend
Children s food selection
Awareness of healthy eating
Constraints placed on choice by parents
Constraints placed on choice by school
Symbolic statement of the model
Food Choice ƒ Sch + Pa + Ex + Pref
Where Pa ƒ He + Se
And Ex ƒ Pa
And Pref ƒ Se + Eh + Fh
Sch = School
Pa = Parents
Ex = Amount to spend
Pref = Food preferences
He = Awareness of healthy eating
Se = Socio-economic status

Figure 2.8 Ways of representing a model

they can be as mental constructs, representations of what people think the world is like. These are called mental models and many psychologists accept that they determine the way in which we interact with the 'real' world. We can move into mathematical modelling using some of the statistical processes we shall meet in Chapters 12 and 13. Chapter 7 deals, in part, with what we call 'variables', which can be represented as formal objects and, if capable of measurement, can be translated into a mathematical model. Once we start identifying the variables that exist in our research problem and think about how they might interact in the real or imagined world, we have started the process of modelling.

2.3 Influences on the selection of a research issue

Research agenda, research issue, research problem and research question – you could be forgiven for thinking that these terms are all alternatives for saying the same thing. Many writers use them interchangeably, indeed I suspect that I have been a little too 'flexible' on occasion in the way I have used them in this book! However, there are differences between them that relate to different stages in your thinking about research. The *research agenda* is what the research community (including those who sponsor or pay for research) think are the issues that it is worthwhile investigating. Since funding is important for so many researchers these days, it is important that they are aware of other people's priorities. Activity 2.4 is an opportunity to become aware of some research priorities worldwide. We can, of course, have our own research agenda which indicates what we will research and when. In all likelihood, however, it will fit in with topics being investigated by others and which will be part of a bigger picture of research.

A *research issue* is a theme from the research agenda. It is a topic or area where there is potential for research and, usually, benefit in undertaking the research. To all intents and purposes the term can be used interchangeably with 'research problem' and this term itself is frequently used as an alternative to 'research question'. It is, however, more accurate to see a *research problem* as having a tighter, more focused specification than a research issue. Thus disaffection might be a research issue and the research problem could be to define the nature of any link between youth culture and motivation for education.

While the idea of a research problem can 'shade' from one term to the other, there is more of a difference between research issue and *research question*. The former is more

Activity 2.4 What are the research priorities?

Go to the websites below – you can just type the organisation into your favourite search engine and then follow the link to funding or programmes. Identify the priorities in research funding that these organisations have. You can even look at reports on some of the sites to see how priorities have changed. See what differences there are, if any, in the priorities of public and non-public bodies. Are there any similarities between different states? If there are, why do you think this is?

USA

Social Science Research Council
http://www.ssrc.org/

US Department of Education
(follow the link to grants and contracts)
http://www.ed.gov/index.jhtml

The Annenberg Foundation
http://www.annenbergfoundation.org/

The Rockefeller Foundation
http://www.rockfound.org/

UK

Economic and Social Research Council
http://www.esrc.ac.uk/

The Nuffield Foundation
http://www.nuffieldfoundation.org/

The Leverhulme Trust
http://www.leverhulme.org.uk/

Department for Children, Schools and Families (DCSF)
http://www.dfes.gov.uk/research/

Netherlands

Education Council of the Netherlands
http://www.onderwijsraad.nl/english/publications

Note: Government departments can change their names, so make sure you use the current name when you search on the web.

general and descriptive of a field and the latter is specific, identifying the particular question that the research process is meant to answer. To follow through the disaffection example, a research question might be, 'Can computer gaming be used to attract boys back into learning?' Sometimes it is difficult to focus the research on a particular question and that is here we can usefully use the term 'research problem'.

No one is likely to be too critical if, on occasion, you are a little loose with your terminology in this area. However, it should be apparent that the terms ideally relate to a progressive focusing of our research from the identification of a broad area of interest or concern to a question that can be answered.

Now that these terms are a little clearer, how do they relate to each other so that that we finish up with a focus and direction for our research? Figure 2.9 has some of the answers. Research takes off when the research question is sharply defined both as text and in the researcher's mind. At this point we may not know how we are going to go about the research but we are clear on the dimensions that need to be investigated and the factors that can influence the outcome. Getting to this point is not necessarily easy and can take time. Indeed, it may even be necessary to undertake some exploratory data collection and analysis to make sure that there is an issue to be investigated. The purpose of this next section is to show how research themes arise and what can influence their selection. Our task is to specify a research question. Most people get to this point by moving from the general to the specific, from a general understanding of a topic to a specific research question.

2.3.1 Learning from a research agenda

We can begin by getting an idea what the key items on the research agenda are in your country and in other countries. There are several reasons why we should do this. If we expect to be a professional researcher then the research agenda is closely linked with opportunities to gain research funding. But the main reason why we should do it is to get a sense of the issues that are thought to be important and worth researching. We do not have to work in one of them, the most important advice we can get is to follow our own interests, but the research agenda will give a societal and policy perspective that an academic perspective will not necessarily provide. It is also important to know what the

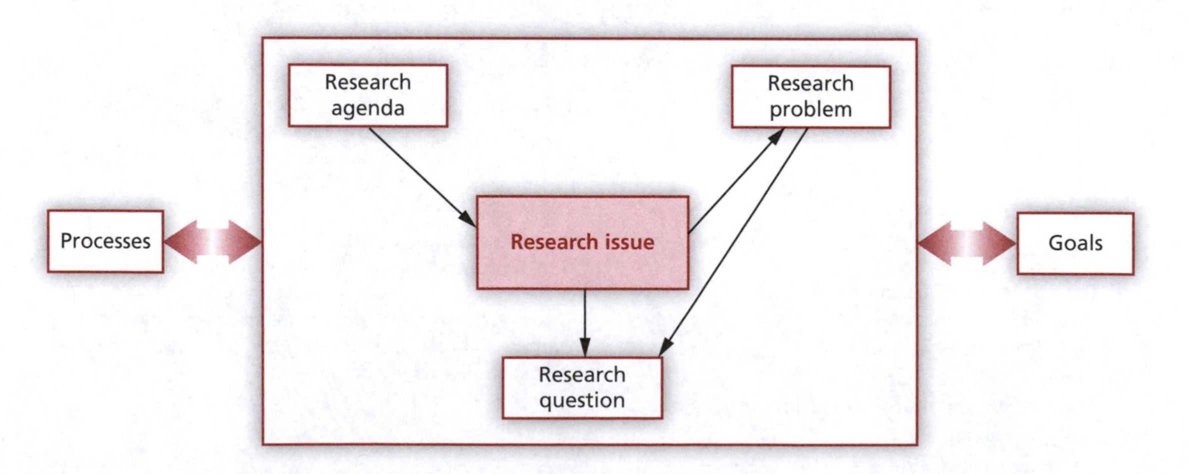

Figure 2.9 Influences on research issue and question

issues are in other countries because ideas now circulate internationally very quickly and we may get a better understanding of the up and coming agenda. Activity 2.4 will help us build up a picture of principal issues in several countries. Staying abreast of the international research agenda is something that we should do on a regular basis. Remember, the articles that are published in journals may relate to research that was completed 18 months or so ago and that was started usually at least a year before that. In other words, journals reflect an agenda that is two or three years old.

2.3.2 Determining a research issue

Our appreciation of the research agenda may lead us to the next stage, the determination of a research issue. This may be one of the themes we have identified in our or someone else's research agenda. However, our research issue need not come from this source.

Those who can generate research ideas find it difficult to appreciate that there are others who find it difficult. Students who are good at providing answers to questions they are given may struggle when they have to formulate a question themselves. Many academics recognise this is a particular capability. This is why many degree programmes conclude with an individual study that often carries great weight in the overall assessment of a student's performance.

The implication of this is that formulating a research question and generating an answer represents a different, possibly higher skill set than the one a student utilises in a course taught and examined by someone else. But where does this capability come from?

The short answer is that it seems to develop particularly well if we are working in a rich and stimulating environment. Elements of this type of environment are access to text resources, the serendipity of Internet searches, awareness of world (and local) events and, particularly, a world where discussion is rife. Discussion challenges us and requires us to justify a point of view. As a process, it shapes and develops thinking. Some people can have meaningful discussions with themselves, but most find that critical friendship is the key to taking ideas forward. Research may be an individual activity when we are collating our results or a lonely life when we are correcting or processing data but the start of the process benefits from being a highly social activity.

What being in a rich environment does is kick-start and fuel thinking. But what starts the process off? The answer is almost anything. For many researchers, though, the following are likely to be important triggers:

- not agreeing with the conclusion of another researcher;
- not liking the implications of a policy;
- being concerned at what is happening in the education system, particularly in relation to organisational and individual performance;
- consolidating the results of different research and asking questions about similarities and differences;
- being struck by the potential in another subject if applied to education;
- realising that someone else has not told the whole story or that academics have failed to give due weight to an area, especially a new area of activity.

2.3.3 Kick-starting the search for a research issue

What has just been said about the importance of a rich environment is all well and good but what if this is our first research project? What if we are in a small department where no one else is an active researcher? How, in these circumstances, do we generate research ideas? People will have their own ideas about what to do, which will be just as valid as what is suggested here. What is important is that the ball starts to roll and a momentum is created that leads inexorably to the statement of the research question. Three approaches that could start the process are: exploring our interests, reviewing our experiences and latching onto issues (see Activity 2.5). Even if you have identified a research field, do the start-up activities to see what other areas emerge. You never know, you might change, or you could generate topics for a later project.

2.3.4 Scoping the research problem

As the issue becomes more defined in our mind it becomes a research problem – that is, it is more tightly defined. The next stage is to find out just what has been published in relation to a topic, activity or issue. This is known as scoping. Sometimes scoping is the research itself. If there is an absence of knowledge and something needs to be known, then finding it out (scoping) is the answer. Mallik and McGowan (2007) did just this in relation to practice-based learning (that is, learning in the workplace), an issue of growing importance in nursing education. Their approach was to compare approaches in five health care professions in order to understand the implications of differences in practice-based learning.

We shall meet scoping again when we look at the processes of reviewing literature relevant to our research. In the meantime, there is, however, another way of using the term that will move researchers along the path to defining their research question.

Activity 2.5 Identifying a research topic

1. Identify your interests

- Create a table to show the following types of educational issue: education policy, education management and change, whole school issues, curriculum issues, classroom practice, society and education. If you want to use your own list, go ahead.
- For each category, put in three examples and rank them from most interesting to least interesting.
- Compare the 'most interesting' in the first category with the second, judge which one you would prefer to work in and then continue with all the other categories.
- Could you find something interesting to do with the last one?

2. Review your experience

- Look back over the last year of your higher education. List the topics that captured your imagination and those that bored you.
- If you have worked in education, for example, as a teacher or administrator, identify what worked and what didn't and ask if you know why.
- Think about the teachers you have had at school or college, what 'according to you' differentiated the best from the worst?
- Generate another scenario where you can exercise your judgement of your experiences.

3. Take up an issue

- Go to a daily newspaper and mark up every article or report concerned with education. Identify any contentious statements and ask yourself, 'Would I be interested in researching it?'
- Go to a weekly newspaper for teachers (for example, *The Times Educational Supplement* or *The Times Higher Education Supplement* in the UK or *Education Week, Teacher Magazine* or *The Chronicle of Higher Education* in the USA) and make a list of issues that are contested by groups with different viewpoints or problems and concerns that are reported. Do a paired comparison in order to identify the one that interests you most.

Once an issue has begun to emerge, the next stage is to assess its feasibility and after that, its value, especially its value to you. Scoping will help with this. It uses many of the same approaches as literature review but its purpose is different. It should answer questions that will help us decide whether to go forward with research and, if so, how best to do so. One thing we should remember is that answering the questions that will take us forward is no simple matter. Once we have found some information that seems to give us an answer to a particular question, we may have to go back and look again at an earlier question that we thought we had answered.

There are two dimensions to feasibility that we have to consider, first whether something is worth doing and, second, whether it can be done. The first task in scoping the research field is to find out if the research that is beginning to take shape in our mind has ever been done before. If it has, if the results are generally accepted and non-contentious (which may be a lot to ask in education) then there is probably not a lot of point in repeating the study. There are, however, exceptions to this. If a previous study was selective in some way then another may be useful. For example, if it was concerned only with selective schools, there is likely to be some value in replicating it in non-selective or if the research was limited to an area, there would be merit in a confirmatory study based on another. We can, with some advantage, turn this process round and look to see what research has been done in another country such as the USA or Australia. The USA in particular has led with many education innovations and changes and the question, 'Will it work/has it worked here?' is one that is likely to be fruitful. Even if someone appears to have tackled the issue in which we are interested before, all may not be lost. We need to look at the research and ask whether they have covered every possible factor that could influence the results. We shall look at these factors again in Chapter 7, when we will call them variables. As a start, we could ask whether published research has taken account of the influence of ethnicity, of status, of gender, of age, of family background. These are the obvious factors; there may well be others that are relevant to our field. Another fruitful avenue to follow that may help us identify a research area is a subject from which ideas can be 'borrowed' and applied to education. We should not consider this as in any way being of doubtful legitimacy. Education is an open intellectual area and cross-fertilisation with other areas such as psychology, business, sociology and, with access to educational opportunity now being so important in political terms across the world, geography too. Even subfields of education can be a source for knowledge transfer. For instance, how we think about curriculum design is probably more sophisticated in e-learning than it is in any other area of pedagogy.

At the heart of the scoping process is access to information that we then use to answer questions and identify opportunities. If we have not gone into the literature with a research idea at the back of our mind, just the process of distilling the information may help us find an answer to the question, 'What avenues are left unexplored?' More important for the busy researcher is, 'Where do we find this information?' Increasingly governments are funding 'observatories' that scope the field for us. Observatories are usually publicly funded organisations that search and become repositories for publications on particular issues or themes and are an alternative to the need to search reports, books and journal articles ourselves. They are useful because they will often present digests that will help us appreciate the field. Of course, not every field of education is covered. Table 2.7 indicates areas of education that are covered and gives examples. To access the websites, just put the terms into a search engine to get to the correct website in one or two clicks. Most of the Observatories (as opposed to databases of research) are located in EU countries and the observatory concept appears to have been stimulated

Table 2.7 Observatories for education research

Area	Examples	
e-learning	Education Observatories net.	Delphi Jura Project.
Lifelong learning	Marchmont, Exeter. Merseyside Social Inclusion.	Pascal, Learning Regions.
Pedagogy	Teaching and Learning, Nottingham.	OU Knowledge Network.
Attainment	International Observatory on Academic Achievement.	
Skills	Basic Skills Agency.	ILO, Human Resource Development.
Sport	Euroseen net, Sport Education.	
Higher education	Borderless HE – OBHE.	
Science and technology	Netherlands Observatory of Science and Technology.	UNDP ICT for Development Observatory.
Area	Northamtonshire Observatory. Enfield Observatory.	Milton Keynes Observatory.
Behaviour	Non-violence, Surrey.	EOVS, European Observatory of Violence in Schools.
Communication	EENet, Education and Technology.	Voson On-Line Networks, Australia.
Prediction	Foresight UK. UNESCO Observatory on the Information Society.	Observatory of Innovation, Cardiff.

by EU funding to cover many areas of research, development and public policy. Originally a mechanism for collecting, storing and making available digests of information, many are evolving into 'think-tanks' with a view on policy directions. Not every area of interest to educationalists is covered but diligent use of the observatories can throw up information on areas that we may be interested in. For example, search the UNESCO observatory and we will find information on early childhood, information on mathematics teaching on the Basic Skills Observatory and literacy on the Marchmont Observatory. Of particular interest to researchers looking at education in a local community setting are the locality based observatories. These are now widespread in the UK and you should check to see if you have one for any area that you are studying. As an example, the Milton Keynes Observatory gives access to detailed information on crime, social indicators and educational attainment, much of which can be mapped at the touch of a button. Even if a comprehensive local observatory does not yet exist for the area in which you are interested, there is almost certain to be relevant information on the websites of the Government office for the region, the Public Health Authority and the Community Safety Partnership.

Once we have convinced ourselves that there is at least one opportunity for us to follow, we might think that all we have to do is refine our research question and plan the research programme. Not so fast, there is another question we have to answer: 'Will the research fly? Does it have sufficient potential for our needs?' We have to answer this in terms of why we are undertaking the research. Is it for a qualification or to get research funding or to produce an academic paper for publication? To reach a conclusion on potential we have to make the following judgements.

- Does it have the potential for me to use a range of methodologies and techniques that will be expected by the people who are judging my work? A PhD will require more than a master's thesis.
- Does it enable me to construct a research strategy that is fit for purpose and demonstrates my capability in this area?
- Is the issue big enough to match up to the standards of the qualification or application? For example, it would be acceptable for an undergraduate to research one classroom but a master's student should recognise that there is a range of influences on both teacher and learner and a doctoral student should seek to grapple with at least several of these.
- Does it allow me to demonstrate my grasp of the field and my intellectual command of the subject?
- What impact will my research have? If we are replicating someone else's work, the impact is low. If we are extending someone's work then there is greater impact but if our work is new and innovative we will have the potential to make a real impact.

At the end of the scoping stage we will have taken a decision on whether or not to go ahead. The chances are that we will have decided to proceed with our research rather than go back and start again because there is still plenty left to research in education. Much of the research published in education lacks potential for synergy with other research because it is either individualistic or anachronistic. To be really effective, research has to link in with what has gone before and highlight what should come after. This is the type of research approach for a whole subject area that has built success in the natural and applied sciences and even in areas of social science. It is an approach that gives rise to synthesis as an accepted research strategy, an approach that is just beginning to appear in education. For us, however, the next stage is to frame our research question. This is the topic for the next section.

2.4 First stages in preparing a research proposal

As we have undoubtedly appreciated from these first two chapters, preparing to get involved in research is a long process. It only becomes shorter as our experience increases. We will know that we have arrived on the research scene when other people begin quoting us and our work is beginning to shape the whole research agenda. Until we reach this stage, our best course of action is to follow a structured framework out of which our research proposal and plan will arise. This is what this last section deals with. It is, at one and the same time, an activity for and an application of the key themes of Chapters 1 and 2. We will test our understanding of the following:

- our purpose in conducting research (this is not the research field or the research question but what you want to use the research for);
- research terminology;
- research planning, including risk assessment and management;
- ethical issues in research.

The significance of these issues to the research process only becomes apparent when we start to work with them. It is for this reason that this section has been introduced. It will help us explain our research ideas to ourselves and it will begin the process of building a knowledge base to support our research.

2.4.1 Why this research?

Let's start at the beginning. What is our purpose in doing this research? If we are not sure, we should look again at Chapter 1. If it is a requirement that we do research in order to gain a qualification, remember that we are likely to be judged on how rigorous we are in our research approach (which may restrict the number of research approaches we use) and how capable we are in generating data that throws light on the issue (which may expand the number of research approaches we use). Our judgement is to get the balance right and choose a topic that gives us opportunity. In making our decision we should recognise that a decision downstream in the research process is influencing a decision right at the headwaters of the whole process. This is just another example of the need to know something before we can fully understand what we have to do.

Do we have an area that we are interested in researching? If not we should plan a programme of activities that will:

(a) increase our knowledge of educational issues, especially those that are in the public arena,
(b) enhance our contacts with other students and researchers and
(c) improve our critical and evaluative capability.

If we are just stuck for some initial ideas, Activity 2.5 could help. In the end the crucial elements in developing research ideas are a wide knowledge base and a thoughtful and critical perspective. This is what you have to work at developing.

2.4.2 What is your research area?

If we have already identified the area that we think is one we would like to research, the next step is to explain why we have selected it. The reason for this is that by setting out our ideas and reasons in writing we will expose any areas of which we are not sure. While ultimately we have to convince others that our research is acceptable, we have to develop the ability to recognise flaws in our thinking and address them. The following questions may help you explain your selection:

- Why am I interested in this area?
- Why do I think that it is important?
- Is there the potential to write as much as I need to write in order to fulfil the research task satisfactorily? In other words, is there sufficient in this area to write enough for a research article or a PhD or master's thesis?
- What experience do I have of the area? Is this enough to make a judgement about its worth and potential?
- Who else thinks that there are issues in this area that are worth exploring? Are they credible enough to use in justifying my selection?

We will have to defend our decisions later on in the research process as well, when we have to justify our selection of research methods.

2.4.3 Creating the context for your proposal

The context for our research is both personal and academic. We should consider the following issues:

- Will it deliver on our personal goals? These may well be more than its sufficiency for meeting the requirements of a thesis. What is its 'impact potential'? Will it allow us to show off our capability? What is its potential for publication? Will it allow us to carve out a niche in our field or will it confine us to being foot soldiers of the research army? How many others are researching in this area – and is there room for one more? We should remember that research is a stepping-stone to authority in the academic world.
- Does the topic have a political dimension? Is the area one that is contested by educationalists or political commentators or politicians? If our answer is 'yes' to any of these, what will our position as a researcher be? Do our own values and beliefs predispose us to one position rather than another? Will this influence our approach, for example, will we work within a framework for change and, if we do, how will we create a level of neutrality in our work that ensures that it is acceptable to a wide range of researchers and that it is capable of influencing people who have not yet taken a position?
- How much do we know about the area? How do we know that our knowledge and understanding is sufficient to construct a research proposal that takes understanding further forward rather than replicate existing findings? If we are unsure how to go about this, we should read section 2.3.4 on scoping research again. Having started to build a picture of the area with references to other people's research, how should we organise it? Activity 2.6 will help us. It gives us a framework for analysing material to pick out the research perspectives and the research findings. As the volume of references increases, we may find it easier to use this approach as a first sift and to connect key themes via a 'spider diagram'. (If you are unfamiliar with these as a way of expressing association, just look the term up using a search engine. You will find that there are even computer programmes to help you.)

2.4.4 Begin to identify the research boundaries

At this stage it is important that we do not overreach ourselves. It is all too easy to set up a research programme that seeks to answer every question. However, we can only deliver what is possible within the resources available. What we have to do now is assess the resources available to us and then build in a contingency to cover us when things go wrong.

Let us begin by specifying the following:

- The total amount of time that is available to us. As a guide, allow about 15 to 20 per cent for writing up our results, about 30 to 35 per cent for preparing the research plan (this includes the pre-research reading) and the remainder for collecting and analysing our data. The one area where we should not cut back is preparing to do the research. There is a great deal of reading to do. So we should make sure that we are prepared.
- What help can we expect from others? We should be careful if we are doing the research for a qualification, there may be regulations that specify that the work should be our own. Assistance in data collection is valuable and can cut down on the time allocated for this stage but drawing on other people does mean that we have to establish a robust data collection process that ensures that if two people were collecting the same data (for example, by interview) the results would be the same.

Activity 2.6 Auditing research literature

The process of identifying the principal themes of published material is central to research. This activity will help you appreciate the insights you need to develop.

1. Make a list of at least ten publications associated with your research area that you have read. For each one, identify the following:
   - The philosophical position it adopts. It could be just one (positivist, humanist, critical theorist, postmodern) or it could be an amalgam.
   - The researcher's position, whether an outsider or an insider, neutral or committed. Do you get any sense of the researcher's values or their political position?
   - The type of research question (see Table 2.2).
   - What ethical issues are identified? Can you suggest others that you would have considered?
   - How well does it communicate with the reader? Is it accessible to the general public or do you have to know a lot about the topic in order to understand what it is saying?
2. Now look at the substantive research presented in each publication.
   - How far does it theorise about the area?
   - Does it present a model of relationships? Are these relationships specified before the research or are they an outcome of the research? This gives you a sign whether the researcher is approaching the issues from the perspective of 'finding patterns' (an inductive approach) or testing predetermined relationships (a deductive approach).
   - What is the focus of the research that is presented? For example, what aspect of the topic is put under the microscope? How central do you think this is to the area overall?
   - What are the conclusions? Can you create categories to show how the conclusions of the research can be grouped, such as for and against, the significance of social relationships or individual character.
3. Finally, write a review of the research you have analysed, identifying the research approaches and research issues. Bring out conflicts in interpretation, preferences for research approach and ensure that your judgements on these are clearly apparent.

- Do we think that we will need specialist help (for example, to assist in complex data analysis)? Will we need to pay for research publications, access to research collections, postage and printing? Do we have the resources for all of these? This is an area we should re-examine as our approach to data collection becomes clearer.
- So far we have assumed that everything goes according to plan but what if it does not? What if our case study is beset by problems halfway through our research and withdraws from the programme? What if there is a postal strike that delays sending out questionnaires? What if our computer crashes and we have not backed up our hard disk with the data? We must identify the risks and consider whether we need to build in a safety margin to cope with them. This must impact on the boundaries we set. For more on risk assessment, look at section 1.6.3.

2.4.5 Developing and justifying your research question

Our writing so far has, principally, been to enable us to understand our research area and to help us identify the issue that we would like to explore in our research programme. We are now at the stage where we have to specify our research question. At this point, we have to convince not just others but also ourselves, that the research can be done and that it is a worthwhile endeavour to do it. The following process may help.

- Outline our research theme in general terms. Show how this arises from our review of existing literature. Demonstrate how it takes forward our understanding. Does it study a new area, for example, the operation of the housing market and access to educational opportunity? Does it take a well researched area into a new domain, for example, the appearance of disaffection in primary schools? Does it deal with the delivery of a new policy, for example, the role of police in schools? We must show how our research ideas are different from what has gone on before. Are we critical of anyone or any perspective? We might think about the conclusions we can reach. How would they affect the way in which we look at the education process? We will then be able to say something about what we think the impact of our research will be.

- Specify our research question. Explain why we chose to express the issue in this way. Why did we reject other formulations of the question. The answers to this might be related to the process of data collection. After we have thought about this, we may need to go back and look again at the research question.

2.4.6 Assessing ethical issues

We should set out the principles that will guide our research work. Read again what was said in section 2.1.3. We do not have to follow this listing slavishly, other things may be as or more important to us. We could, for instance, be driven by a desire to make things better. This would certainly shape the type of research we did and the way we did it. To help us specify the principles that will guide us, we can identify all the people who have a stake in the research we are considering. These could be interviewees, people whose lives will be affected by the outcomes of our research, our self-interest and its centrality to our work. As the net expands, it could include parents, communities and even society as a whole. As the network of stakeholders widens there are possibilities that interests will conflict. It is good to be able to identify success but should we do the same with failure? A new way of working may produce benefits but it could also fail and worsen a situation. Should we 'ethically' take this risk? What principle will guide us? At the very least we should have a principle that guides us on obtaining information from people (informed consent) and integrity as a researcher.

2.4.7 Putting it all together

On the website that accompanies this book, there is a template based on this section that will help you prepare a research proposal.

Summary

- Research terms can be confusing. While authors have sometimes confused them, there is a progressive focus in the sequence of research agenda, research issue and research question.
- How we go about our research is influenced and affected by philosophy, methodology, research paradigms, theories, models principles and ethics.
- Research philosophy is something we have to understand in order to (a) appreciate where other researchers are coming from and (b) guide our own research approach. The principal philosophies that we should understand are scientism (and the positivist research approach), phenomenological and existential philosophy (which underpin much qualitative research), critical theory (with its concern for repression and inequality) and postmodernism (which refocuses our attention from big theories to local circumstances).
- We should know where our research might lead, either (a) to a general understanding and the development of a theory or model (b) to a deeper understanding

of a specific situation, the identification of key influences and even the development of a model. We should understand the part played by normative theory and explanatory theory in our research. We can test both, even if we are new to research, but any generalisations from our research are likely to be in the form of models and not theories.

- Ethical considerations should run through our work and not be just something we deal with at the beginning. We should be guided by principles and it may be a good idea to state what these are.
- You should now be able to identify a research area, demonstrate your understanding of research in that area and show how your research theme fits in. You are now in a position to begin to prepare a research proposal. As we go on to look at details of research methods, you should continue reading in your field in order to deepen your understanding of the issues.

Further reading

Research and philosophy

Bridges, D. and Smith, R. (2007) *Philosophy, Methodology and Educational Research*, Blackwell, Malden, Mass.

This edited collection of papers gives substance to many of the issue considered in this book. Chapter 2 exposes misunderstandings about positivism but, in doing so, raises doubts as to its appropriateness. David Bridges' own chapter argues that we are in a period of fluidity and change as we seek to establish education as a discipline.

Pring, R. (2004) *Philosophy of Educational Research*, Continuum, London.

Richard Pring's book is an excellent introduction to the fractured world of research philosophy. His argument that the polarisation between positivism and interpretivism and between quantitative and qualitative positions fails to recognise the actual variety and complexity of research on the ground is echoed in this book.

Ethics in research

Israel, M. and Hay, I. (2006) *Research Ethics for Social Scientists*, Sage.

Oliver, P. (2004) *The Student's Guide to Research Ethics*, Open University Press.

These two books take different approaches to appreciating the ethical position in research. Israel and Hay are analytical, drawing a distinction between regulatory compliance and ethical conduct. They explore ethical principles: informed consent, confidentiality, avoiding harm, doing good, integrity and care. Paul Oliver's book is more of a guide, with three useful chapters on ethics before research begins, during data collection and afterwards.

On-line research

Exploring On-Line Research, http://www.geog.le.ac.uk/ORM/index.htm.

This website is a sound introduction to an evolving way of researching. It gives advice on ways of collecting data, a link to resources that can inform on-line research and an excellent self-study programme on ethics in on-line research.

References

Audit Commission (2000) *Getting better All the Time: Making benchmarking work*, The Audit Commission, London.

Balen, R., Blyth E., Calabretto, H., Fraser, C., Horrocks, C., and Manby, M. (2006) 'Involving Children In Health And Social Research – "Human becomings" or "active beings"?' *Childhood*, 13(1): 29–48.

Belohlav, J.A. (1996) 'The Evolving Competitive Paradigm: Corporate strategy of the future is re-inventing business itself in search of competitive essence', *Business Horizons*, 39(2), 11–19.

Bonawitz, E.B., Griffiths, T.L. and Schulz, L. (2006) 'Modeling Cross-Domain Causal Learning in Preschoolers as Bayesian Inference', *Proceedings of the Twenty-Eighth Annual Conference of the Cognitive Science Society*, Vancouver, available at http://web.mit.edu/liz_b/www/ (accessed February 2009).

Brouwers, A. and Tomic, W. (2000) 'A Longitudinal Study of Teacher Burnout and Perceived Self-efficacy in Classroom Management', *Teaching and Teacher Education*, 16, 239–253.

Byrne, B.M. (1994) 'Burnout: Testing for the Validity, Replication, and Invariance of Causal Structure across Elementary, Intermediate, and Secondary Teachers', *American Educational Research Journal*, 31(3), 645–673.

Cunningham, W.G. (1983) 'Teacher burnout – Solutions for the 1980s: A review of the literature', *The Urban Review*, 15(1), 37–51.

Englund, T. (2006) 'New Trends in Swedish Educational Research', *Scandinavian Journal of Educational Research*, September 2006, 50(4), 383–396.

Fore, C. (2002) 'Teacher Burnout in Special Education: The Causes and the Recommended Solutions', *The High School Journal*, 86(1), 36–44.

Goddard,R., O'Brien, P. and Goddard, M. (2006) 'Work Environment Predictors of Beginning Teacher Burnout', *British Educational Research Journal*, 32(6), 857–874.

Gopnik, A., Glymour, C., Sobel, D.M. and Schulz, L.E. (2001) 'Causal Learning Mechanisms in Very Young Children: Two-, Three-, and Four-Year-Olds Infer Causal Relations From Patterns of Variation and Covariation', *Developmental Psychology*, 37(5), 620–629.

Gopnik, A., Glymour, C., Sobel, D.M., Schulz, L.E., Kushnir, T. and Danks, D. (2004) 'A Theory of Causal Learning in Children: Causal Maps and Bayes Nets', *Psychological Review*, 111(1), 3–32.

Grant, R. (2005) *A Phenomenological Investigation into Lecturers' Understanding of Themselves as Assessors at Rhodes University*, thesis submitted for the degree of PhD, available at http://eprints.ru.ac.za/300/ (accessed January 2009).

Greaves, N.M., Hill, D. and Maisuria, A. (2007) 'Embourgeoisment, Immiseration, Commodification – Marxism Revisited: a Critique of Education in Capitalist Systems', *Journal for Critical Education Policy Studies*, 5(1), available at http://www.jceps.com/?pageID=article&articleID=83 (accessed January 2009).

Hastings, R.P. and Bham, M.S. (2003) 'The Relationship between Student Behaviour Patterns and Teacher Burnout', *School Psychology International*, 24(1), 115–127.

Horkheimer, Max (1982) *Kritische Theorie: Critical theory: selected essays*, translated by Matthew J. O'Connell et al., Continuum, New York.

Iwanicki, E.F. (1983) 'Toward Understanding and Alleviating Teacher Burnout', *Theory into Practice*, 22(1), 27–32.

Kristen, C., Römmer, A., Muller, W. and Kalter, F. (2005) 'Longitudinal Studies for Education Reports: European and North American Examples', *Education Reform*, 10, Federal Ministry of Education and Research (BMBF), Bonn and Berlin.

Macdonald, N. (2001) *The Graffiti Subculture: Youth, Masculinity and Identity in London and New York*, Palgrave, Basingstoke.

Mungazi, D.A. (1999) *The Evolution of Educational Theory in the United States*, Praeger, Westport, Conn.

O'Farrell, C. (1999) 'Postmodernism for the Uninitiated', in Meamore, D., Burnett, B. and O'Brien, P. (eds), *Understanding Education: Contexts and Agendas for the New Millennium*, Sydney, 11–17.

Peled, E. and Leichtentritt, R. (2002) 'The Ethics of Qualitative Social Work Research', *Qualitative Social Work*, 1(2), 145–169.

Russell, H. (2007) 'Learning for Being: An Ontological and Existential Approach', *International Journal of Lifelong Education*, 26(4), 363–384.

Schneider, K., Bugental, J. and Pierson, J. (2002) The Handbook of Humanistic Psychology: Leading Edges in Theory, Research, and Practice, Sage, Thousand Oaks, Calif.

Schulz, L.E. and Gopnik, A. (2004) 'Causal Learning Across Domains', *Developmental Psychology*, 40(2), 162–176.

Seligman, M. and Csikszentmihalyi, M. (2000) 'Positive Psychology: An Introduction', *American Psychologist*, 55(1), 5–14.

Trotman, D. (2006) 'Interpreting Imaginative Lifeworlds: Phenomenological Approaches in Imagination and the Evaluation of Educational Practice', *Qualitative Research*, 6(2), 245–265.

Warford, M. (2005) 'Testing a Diffusion of Innovations in Education Model (DIEM)', *The Innovation Journal*, 10(3), Article 32, available from http://www.innovation.cc/ (accessed January 2009).

West, A., Barham, E. and Hind, A. (2009) *Secondary school admissions in England: policy and practice*, Research and Information on State Education Trust, London.

Whitaker, K.S. (1966) 'Exploring Causes of Principal Burnout', *Journal of Educational Administration*, 34(1), 60–71.

Chapter contents

Chapter 3

PUTTING YOUR RESEARCH DESIGN TOGETHER

Key themes

- This chapter deals with the three broad approaches that we can adopt for research in education – quantitative, qualitative and mixed methods.
- Quantitative research looks for numerical evidence on which to reach conclusions. It makes many assumptions on data collection and analysis, which may constrain some investigations.
- Quantitative research sets up questions as testable hypotheses and assesses these terms of probabilities.
- Qualitative research uses behaviour, words and images as the evidence on which to base its conclusions. Its object is to understand how people experience their lives as a means of providing rich and deep insights into why things happen as they do.
- Mixed methods research combines quantitative and qualitative approaches. It was developed as an approach to resolve research problems that were insoluble by either of the other two approaches by themselves.
- We shall also be introduced to two more methodologies, survey and analysis and experimentation.
- This chapter is a bridge to the processes of data collection in Part 2 and data analysis in Part 3.

Introduction

This chapter will help us by showing how we can put our research design together. Chapter 2 introduced us to some key influences that should shape our research. Now we shall look at approaches to research that we can draw on. The chapter presents an overview of these approaches, a sort of 'road map' to making them work for us. It sets out the principles on which they are based, the principal elements of the procedures and what sorts of thing might derail our research. The remaining chapters are then concerned with the methods and techniques that you can slot into these approaches.

As we will see in this chapter, there are a number of ways of putting a research design together. Some of them have conventions that govern procedures. Some researchers regard these as rules not to be broken. Many others come from a more flexible tradition and have, as a guiding principle, 'What works?' In getting to grips with approaches to research, we should bear in mind this division amongst researchers. We should seek to understand the approaches and their implications for our research field. We will need to decide whether our preference for one is based on its conceptual and procedural superiority, or whether it is best suited to the circumstances we face.

3.1 An overview of research approaches

Given the variety of research approaches and the wide range of research methodologies, still the best way to define and draw out the characteristics of social research is to fall back on the traditional division between quantitative and qualitative research traditions and to include the process of combining the two as an emerging 'tradition' in its own right. However, we should be aware that, in this book, this approach is a framework that is used principally to aid understanding. We make this point because the division has been represented as being unbridgeable. Exponents of each approach argued that theirs was the only true way to undertake research in education and the social sciences; the debates between them became so argumentative that the phrase 'paradigm wars' was used to describe them. Here the use of the terms 'quantitative', 'qualitative' and 'mixed methods' is nothing more than description and does not imply any superiority of one over the others.

What do we mean by quantitative and qualitative?

- *Quantitative research* implies using numerical data as the evidence base. Because we collect numerical data, we analyse them using numerical and statistical procedures and we draw our conclusions on the basis of this analysis.
- *Qualitative research* deals much more with the processes that drive behaviour and the experiences of life. We can understand this better if we think first about the numerical data used in quantitative research. This often deals with the outcomes of behaviour or activity, for example, the numbers of students who gained particular grades in a class test or the number of applications for each place in secondary schools in an area. In these cases, qualitative researchers would be more concerned to understand if some students worked harder than others and what their motivation was or, in the case of school choice, what made parents think that one school was better than another. Clearly, the nature of qualitative enquiry is different from quantitative and this difference is reflected in the character of the data (a concern with feelings and values) and also the methods used to analyse such data.
- *Mixed methods research* seeks to combine both quantitative and qualitative traditions on the basis that research issues in education are often so complex that the insights of both approaches are required if we are to gain a good understanding. An emotional response to a situation (such as anger) may be qualitative but it could be equally important to know how many people share it. As we have expressed it, this is essentially a pragmatic argument for giving mixed methods the same sort of status as quantitative and qualitative research.

Whatever framework we choose to work within, our task is to uncover some truth about the issue we are researching. Truth is central to the notion of research. As a researcher we need to convince others that our results are not false and that our conclusions are valid. We cannot do this simply by expressing our views forcefully or through the use of rhetoric. The term 'epistemology' is used in research literature. Often it is used to describe research designs, especially designs that conform to a generally accepted template. More appropriately, however, epistemology, as a philosophical idea, is the study of knowledge and, by implication, how we know what we know. It is the word 'how' that principally concerns us here because it implies that there are some ways of gaining knowledge that are more valid and some that are less and, as a result, there is some knowledge that is 'true' and some that, if not actually false, cannot be shown to be true. The issue of 'how' is important because the process by which knowledge is developed, determined and acquired is, ultimately, the basis for determining whether it is true, not true or false. However, the issue of validity is, in the end, not always absolute but often a question of what someone believes to be valid. The 'truth' that results from belief in a faith is very different from what I believe to be true from the perspective of a social scientist and both are likely to be different from what a physicist would accept as truth. The standards we apply to determining truth depend on where we are coming from, what we are using the truth for and, we should not ignore this, how many people agree with us. As an educational researcher all we can do is, first of all, convince others that the processes we used to collect our data and the analysis we used to convert them into evidence are reasonable and, then, that the argument we construct to reach a conclusion is logical. These are the steps that our research design should specify, so it is, by implication, fundamental to the truth of our research findings.

In the remainder of this chapter, we will look at the character and principles that define these three styles of research: quantitative, qualitative and mixed methods. However, we should remember that:

- no one approach is absolutely better or worse than another;
- a research approach should arise primarily out of the research question, not out of a researcher's conviction;
- circumstances can lead to a researcher modifying a style to meet particular constraints or needs;
- sharing ideas and borrowing techniques reflects a researcher's skill.

And there is one final important point that we should make. While our research question guides our research, we should not be blind to what else our research data may be telling us. Case Study 3.1 makes the same point but does so in a far more memorable way.

Case study 3.1 Good research – with a valuable lesson

The research that starts this chapter comes from psychology and concerns the processes of perception and attention. These processes are clearly important in ensuring effective learning. We can investigate how pupils or students are different in terms of their perception of the subject, their teachers, school or education and their powers of attention in class or we can look at modifications to the learning environment or to the learning process and assess what impact these have on perception and attention and ultimately on learning. For example, one of the major changes that we are now seeing in the learning environment is computer-based learning and the use of multimedia. However, this research concerns basketball.

Basketball? Read on. There is a point about good research here.

In 1999 Daniel Simons and Christopher Chabris, two American psychologists, published a paper that explored the relationship between attention and perception. Theirs was not the first paper on this subject but it was, perhaps, the most influential in bringing this topic to wider notice. Subjects were asked to watch videos of two mixed groups playing basketball and

▶

count how many times the ball moved between players of the same team. One team was wearing white shirts and the other black. Both teams had a ball and players moved around. The subjects were asked to count either the number of passes between members (what Simons and Chabris called the easy test) or the number of bounce passes or aerial passes (the hard test). The dynamics of the situation and the level of the tests meant that subjects had to concentrate and pay attention.

Simons and Chabris do not report how accurately their subjects recorded the passes, so you might ask whether it was worth reporting a procedure for testing attention and perception without analysing the results. Yes, because what the authors were testing was something far deeper than it appeared to the subjects. The subjects watched four videos. In all of them, there was an unexpected event, either a woman walked holding an umbrella or a gorilla walked through the play. In one pair of videos the woman and the gorilla were transparent and in the other pair they were opaque that is, they appeared just the same as the players. In one of the videos the gorilla was on screen for nine seconds, even pausing to stand in the middle of the players and beat its chest! Overall almost half the subjects failed to notice anything unexpected.

This chapter deals with ways of tackling research. We use the terms 'styles of' or 'approaches to' research to describe them. You may also find them referred to as 'research paradigms' (look again at Chapter 2 if you are not sure what these are). In certain instances the approaches constitute templates for how to do research, so they take some of the decision making out of the researcher's hands. But they are not all like this and even in the most constrained template, researchers have to exercise considerable judgement.

Now lets turn back to Simons and Chabris' study of what they termed 'inattentional blindness'. What has it got to do with education? Not a lot. But it does have something important to say about research and researchers, and that is that you should not be so focused on your research issue or research paradigm that, when you analyse your data, you miss what it is really trying to tell you. Make this your guiding principle: *Always look for the gorillas*.

For more information see Simons, D.J. and Chabris, C.F. (1999) 'Gorillas in our Midst: Sustained Inattentional Blindness for Dynamic Events, *Perception*, 28, 1059–1074. Available at http://www.wjh.harvard.edu/~cfc/Simons1999.pdf and watch the videos on http://viscog.beckman.uiuc.edu/djs_lab/demos.html.

3.2 Quantitative approaches to research

3.2.1 Positivism – the guiding principle

Positivism underpins what is generally described as quantitative research. While we ought to be aware that it has undergone several manifestations since being developed by the French philosopher, Auguste Compte, in the middle of the nineteenth century and while we will come across the terms 'logical positivism' and 'post-positivism', it is not necessary for us to know the detail of the changes or to appreciate the differences in the terms if our principal concern is with resolving practical research problems. Nonetheless, as background, if nothing else, we should appreciate how the ideas of positivism have shaped our understanding of what research is. Case Study 3.2 explains how Comte developed the concept to a point where it could challenge the need for the existence of God as a means of understanding the world. Positivism's legacy, however, has not been the deification of science but the more humble (yet ultimately more influential) responsibility for establishing principles to guide scientific research. The framework of principles that are set out below have their origins in the train of thought that Comte established.

Case study 3.2 Auguste Comte and the origins of positivism

The sixteenth century saw the dawn of the scientific age. By the nineteenth century the scale of scientific knowledge and its translation into technology was impacting on the way in which economy and society were structured. Clearly science was creating possibilities for humankind where none had previously existed. This awareness tripped over into philosophical discourse and it was there that Auguste Comte, a French philosopher and social analyst, made his mark. The philosophy of positivism that he developed (his *Course of Positive Philosophy* published between 1830 and 1842) placed science on a pedestal. At the heart of his thesis was the belief that truth arose from verifiable facts. Scientific method had evolved from trial and error to become more ordered in terms of (a) recording cause and effect and (b) specifying the conditions in which cause and effect might be tested. It was these ideas that he developed and expressed in relation to the sciences, society, history and politics. He saw positivism as the culmination of mankind's ability to understand the world. Ultimately it was a challenge to the existence of God. Progress in understanding, as well as material progress, came about through observation and through measurement, not through speculation and not through prayer. So Comte's praise of science raised it to a position where it could challenge beliefs that were part of the fabric of society.

While his ideas about the nature of science were held in high regard and while some still describe him as the 'father of sociology', Comte developed his ideas about positivism further to include a bizarre positivist religion. It lost him many followers. He died in 1857.

3.2.2 The character of quantitative research

The character of quantitative research can be succinctly summarised as the identification and explanation of pattern and order. While this is the goal of many other (though not all) styles of research, there are two aspects of the process that are particularly significant for quantitative research, the derivation of theory and the nature of proof.

(i) A concern with theory

Quantitative research seems to replicate the strength and success of science by reproducing some of its research principles. Its belief in an observable and measurable reality places it firmly in the positivist camp. Because the things that quantitative researchers examine are measurable and because the conditions for data collection and analysis are specified, quantitative research can be replicated. The reproducibility of research results not only in a test of the effectiveness of research procedures but it is also a platform for the generalisation of research findings. When we can repeat the same study in the same and different circumstances, we have a basis for making statements about the word that have general applicability. The ultimate purpose of quantitative research is to generate theory – truths about behaviour and relationships that are applicable in a range of situations.

However, while the generation of theory is a laudable objective for education, it is not necessary for every bit of quantitative research to lead to a theory-type statement. For one thing, the education world just could not cope with that much theory! When we say that the goal is the construction of theory, we must appreciate that the development of theory advances step by small step. An idea is tested in one location and then another. It is modified according to this circumstance and then another. And then everything has to be replicated to ensure that there are no spurious claims as to relationships and predictions. Figure 3.1 shows how this might work for the problem 'How do parents choose a school for their child?' The first researcher might explore whether they choose the school

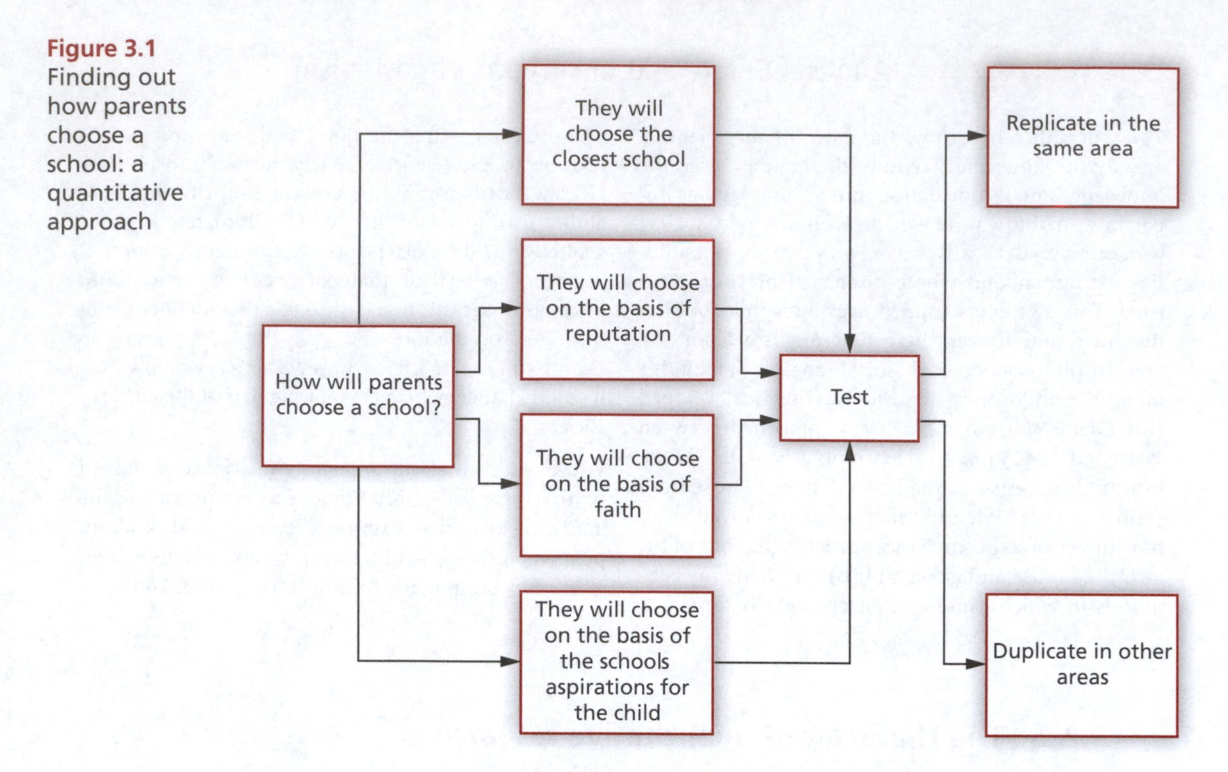

Figure 3.1 Finding out how parents choose a school: a quantitative approach

closest to where the family lives. Subsequently researchers would test this again in the same area in order to replicate the study and validate the original results. Others would explore whether the same results were found in other areas. Duplication of the research is a test of the extent to which individual conclusions are more generally valid. Another researcher might question whether parents choose a school on the basis of the school's reputation. The research would again be replicated and duplicated. Yet other researchers would look to see if parents choose a school on the basis of faith or according to what aspirations they thought the school had for their child and again the research would be both duplicated and replicated. In this way the research community would build up a picture of how significant the various potential influences actually are. If we were to think, though, that there are co-ordinated teams of researchers doing this, we are likely to be wrong. Most educational researchers work alone or in small groups and the most that they can do is identify pattern and order over a small part of the educational terrain. The researcher who brings things together to specify a theory comes along infrequently.

(ii) A concern with proof: the role of the hypothesis

The nature of proof is the second issue that makes quantitative research distinctive. Imagine that we are researching the comparative effectiveness of different ways of teaching a modern language, or the consequences for effective learning of spending different amounts of time with a teacher. How do we know whether the pattern that we think we see really exists? How do we prove to others that the pattern exists? The concept of proof lies at the heart of quantitative research.

What do we mean by proof? It all depends on the circumstances. When we fly in an aircraft we want to be sure that the theoretical relationship between thrust, wing surface and lift that the engineer is using is not a Friday afternoon theory knocked out so that the scientist can get a good start to the weekend. In science 'round about' is not good enough. Prediction here means just that, if something happens then the result that is predicted will also happen. In other words, there is a defined and stable relationship. In a criminal court, in many countries, proof is 'beyond reasonable doubt'. There are many researchers who would accept that this is a perfectly reasonable specification and, in terms of qualitative research, it probably comes closest to what is practised. The academic equivalent of a jury is that the research is published to the community of scholars who either accept it, or reject it. But for quantitative research there are ways of convincing others that our findings constitute a proof.

In science we understand that a theory is proved when there is *certainty* in a relationship. The problem for education is that it deals with people and the best that can be said of people is that there is a *likelihood* of something happening. Let us look again at the question of the factors that might influence parents' choice of school, the example that we first met in Figure 3.1. Our research on travel time might show that, as travel time increases, the proportion of children going to a particular school decreases. We might even find that some children will pass by a school in order to attend a school that is further away. Because we know the numbers of children in an area, we can say that 30 per cent of them will go to school A, 60 per cent to school B and 10 per cent to school C. We can even express this in a different way and say that for any child there is a 30 per cent chance of going to school A, a 60 per cent chance of going to school B and a 10 per cent chance of going to school C. In other words, we can use probability to say something about behaviour.

Now imagine that we wanted to go further in our research and wanted to understand in greater detail the factors influencing parental choice of a school.

- First, we have to specify the factors that might influence demand. We have already identified travel time as a possible factor as well as the reputation of the school (which is the parents' belief about how good or bad it is), whether the school is faith based and what its aspirations for its pupils are. We could add as factors the attainment of students, how many progress into higher education and the student/teacher ratio. When these factors are combined we might have a means of predicting demand for places in any one school.
- Second, we have to present these factors in a particular way. As they stand, they effectively constitute a theory of what is likely to happen. We can express this theory as a proposition, 'demand for places at a school is influenced by (a) the travel time of potential pupils plus (b) the school's reputation plus (c) whether it offers a faith-based education plus (d) the character of the school's aspirations for its pupils plus (e) student attainment plus (f) student progression plus (g) the staff/student ratio'. Such a proposition is called a hypothesis. We may have been guided by other people's research in our selection of factors but their inclusion represents an assumption on our part that this combination of factors is causative and therefore predictive of demand. We might even go so far and say that shorter travel times will be preferable to longer, a high reputation preferable to a poor one, high grades in public examinations preferable to low ones, a high proportion of students progressing to higher education preferable to a low proportion and a low ratio of students to staff preferable to a high ratio. A faith-based school may appeal particularly to parents actively practising a faith and a school's aspirations for its pupils (which might range from a traditional academic education through to a commitment to community and public service) will strike different chords with different parents and, probably, at different times too. In other words, we can be really quite specific about how the causation works to influence parental choice.

Can we prove our hypothesis? The answer to this is 'maybe' but it is not straightforward. First we have to go back to the notion of proof and what can or cannot be proved. At this point we do have to concern ourselves with philosophy and the process of logical deduction. In terms of logic, the only truth that we can establish is whether or not a conclusion is false and not whether a conclusion is true (this is because we cannot possibly test every situation for truth). The implication of this is that we have to phrase our hypothesis in a particular way, as an inverse of what we are trying to prove. If our hypothesis is that A is related to B, the inverse that we have to test is that there is *no relationship* between A and B. This is called the *null hypothesis*. If you want to understand the reasoning behind this in more detail, read Case Study 3.3. We will return to the process of establishing proof in the next section. We will meet the null hypothesis again in section 13.3.

There are two approaches to undertaking a quantitative study: either collecting our data (often through a survey) and analysing them using statistical and numerical procedures or collecting our data within an experimental setting and framework. Much, though not all, of their procedure is common. We shall deal with each in turn.

3.2.3 Putting the 'quantitative' research process together: Part I the survey and analysis approach

In this section we will look at how we generate a hypothesis, look in broad terms at how we test a hypothesis and review what we can do to prevent things going wrong with this approach to research.

(i) Deriving the hypothesis

Before we go on to look at other elements in the quantitative style of research, let us see how things are coming together so far. All research starts with a concern. In Chapter 2 we reviewed some of the influences that can act on researchers to shape their concerns, interests and approaches. Out of this there comes a research question. Sometimes this is quite broad but for a quantitative researcher, it is very specific and phrased as a hypothesis. Let us go back to our example of trying to estimate the demand for places at any school. The factors that might be at work are derived from a range of sources from other people's research, our own induction based on what a reasonable parent would do, hearsay and hunch. So far, we have come up with several possible influences. Figure 3.1 shows a selection of these and identifies a one to one relationship with school choice. At this point be clear that this does not represent all possible influences. There is no mention, for example, of attainment, progression or staff/student ratios. We could also add the nature of the curriculum, the standard of buildings and specialist facilities and, if we wanted to include class division as a factor, the socio-economic status of the parents who already send their children there. The factors that we, as researchers, choose to look at in our investigation constitute a model of what we think will explain how parents choose a school for their child (see Chapter 2 for an introduction to the concept of a model and Chapter 7 for a fuller description of the modelling process). Once we have a degree of explanation, we have the potential for prediction. We can express Figure 3.1 and our other factors as a model in another way.

School choice *f* travel time + school reputation + student attainment + student progression + staff/student ratio + moral tone set by the school + aspiration for pupils + . . .

Where *f* represents the phrase 'is a function of'.

Case study 3.3 The logic of the null hypothesis

The logic of the null hypothesis is closely associated with the work of Karl Popper. A refugee from the Nazis, Popper came to Britain in 1945 from Austria via New Zealand. He is particularly known for his ideas on the philosophy of science. It is these ideas that have shaped classical social science research.

Popper's illustration of what is and is not provable is the statement 'all swans are white'. If you assert this as a premise based on your observation of swans, it is valid and proved by experience – that is until you visit Australia, when you find that some swans are black.

In Popper's terms, premises (in our research we now call these hypotheses) logically generate conclusions. The premise that 'all swans are white' has two possible conclusions, one true and one false. If we have never visited Australia and were totally ignorant of the existence of black swans in Australia, we could accept a false conclusion. But if we did, we would have accepted the conclusion without all the facts and in doing so would have falsely accepted the premise as well. So, if we are faced with a premise that:

All swans are white

This is an Australian swan

Therefore it is white

and the swan is black, not only is the conclusion wrong, the premise also is wrong. This simple example was the key to transforming social science research. As the philosophers of social science, Len Doyal and Roger Harris (1986, p. 40), say, 'False conclusions (that is, conclusions that are false not wrong) are only compatible with . . . premises being false . . . true conclusions are compatible with any combination of truth or falsity in the premise'.

Transposing the argument to a research situation, testing a positive hypothesis (left-handed children perform better in creative subjects like art) will leave us none the wiser. Testing a null hypothesis, on the other hand (left- or right-handedness does not affect performance in creative subjects), leaves us with the possibility of demonstrating that it may be false and if the null hypothesis is false, then we have a basis for accepting that there is a likelihood of the positive hypothesis being true.

This merely states that school choice is a function of the factors that follow. While statistically this can be managed, it is a complex relationship that is being specified. It becomes much simpler if we express it as five separate relationships:

1. School choice *f* travel time.
2. School choice *f* school reputation.
3. School choice *f* student attainment.
4. School choice *f* student progression.
5. School choice *f* staff/student ratio.
6. School choice *f* moral tone.
7. School choice *f* aspiration for pupil.
8. etc.

Each of these can be expressed as an idea to be researched. For example:

- school choice is related to travel time; or
- as travel time increases, the number of parents choosing a school will fall; or
- the number of children attending a school is inversely related to the travel time to the school.

However we express the idea, the statement becomes the research hypothesis (which is conventionally referred to as H_1), that is, the issue to be tested in respect of its validity as a causal influence. Let us examine the first statement and compare it with the other two. The difference is that it does not suggest in what way travel time influences school choice, whereas the others do. In fact, the last two are equivalent except that one is expressed in more everyday language and one is expressed in more mathematical language. The first research hypothesis is called a *non-directional hypothesis* and the second and third are called *directional hypotheses* because they specify the direction of the association. This distinction is important and you will meet it again in Chapter 13. Note also the nature of the relationship that is specified in the directional hypothesis. We could test another directional hypothesis, that as travel time increases the number of parents choosing a school also increases but, in terms of reasonable behaviour, this does not make much sense. This hypothesis seems fundamentally counter-intuitive because it suggests that parents prefer their children to travel longer distances than shorter ones.

Having defined the research hypothesis, we now have to specify the null hypothesis (conventionally referred to as H_0) that there is no effect from the variable we are investigating. Remember, the null hypothesis is tested because if it proves to be false, it is the only way of knowing that the premise on which it is based is false. Table 3.1 sets out the research hypothesis and associated null hypothesis. What is apparent is that the null hypothesis does not change a great deal, whatever the research hypothesis.

Table 3.1 Research and null hypotheses

Research hypothesis	Null hypothesis
School choice is related to travel time.	School choice is not related to travel time. *or* There is no relationship between school choice and travel time.
As travel time increases, the number of parents choosing a school will fall.	There is no relationship between travel time to school and parents' choice of school.
The number of children attending a school is inversely related to the travel time to the school.	There is no relationship between the number of children attending a school and the travel time to the school.

(ii) Proof and rejecting or accepting the null hypothesis

The criteria and conditions for accepting or rejecting the null hypothesis are central to the quantitative style of research. At the heart of the decision to accept or reject a hypothesis are likelihoods and probabilities. One of the conditions that must be met before a decision can be made is that the evidence on which the decision is based must be representative of the issue being considered. This will be considered in more detail in Chapter 6 when we look at sampling. The criterion we use to identify our data is that every piece of evidence that is used to make the decision on proof must have the same chance of being used as any other piece of evidence. In our example, if there are 1,000 sets of parents selecting a school for the new academic year, every time we select a parent to provide us with information on travel time, each parent must have the same 1 in 1,000 chance of giving us the information. The reason for this is to ensure that the selection of unusual circumstances, for example a child who might travel in excess of two hours, is completely random. This randomness ensures that bias is not present. For example, if we were selecting 100 parents to ask them the expected travel time of their children and there were exactly 100 parents in the whole group who intended to make their children travel a longer distance to a more distant school, what would be the chance of selecting those parents who, in terms of our hypothesis, would be atypical? If we did

Case study 3.4 Calculating the possible number of samples of a given size

To keep the numbers a manageable size, let us assume that we wanted to know about the decision making of 20 refugee families that had moved into the study area in the last three years and that 8 of them would be selected to give their information. The general expression for calculating the number of combinations of a given size ($r = 8$) out of a total group size of n is:

$$\text{Combination } (n, r) = \frac{n!}{r!(n - r!)}$$

The mathematic symbol ! represents a calculation called a factorial. This is very simply a number multiplied by one less than the number and then two less until the final multiplication is by one. So, factorial 4 is $4 \times 3 \times 2 \times 1$. As a general expression, this is written:

$$(n \cdot (n - 1) \cdot (n - 2) \cdot (n - 3) \ldots$$

With our study the total number of refugee families (n) is 20; r, the number of families we wish to get information from, is 8; and $(n - r)$ is, therefore, 12. The answer to the question 'How many combinations of 8 families are there out of a group size of 20?' is given by:

$$\frac{20!}{8! \times 12!} = \frac{(20 \times 19 \times 18 \times 17 \ldots)}{(8 \times 7 \times 6 \ldots \times 12 \times 11 \times 10 \ldots)}$$

$$= \frac{2432903008176640000}{40320 \times 479001600} = 126{,}037$$

The answer is about 126,000, so the chance of having any sample of 8 is 1 in 126,000. If our concern is choosing people who are not typical, then this figure should reassure us. When we do this for larger samples, the numbers get very large indeed! (And that is an exclamation mark, not a factorial.)

select them, it would throw part of our model into disarray. Equally, if we selected parents who lived the furthest distance from any school, we would also have a problem. We can calculate how many combinations of potential respondents there are. See Case Study 3.4 for a worked example that shows that the odds of our choosing a sample that is unbiased is very high indeed and that we can be confident in the data that we obtain. We can, using this selection criterion of equal chances of being chosen, apply a procedure to establish with what probability the results of our selection could have been obtained by chance (this is called a statistical test and we shall look at several in Chapter 13).

We shall return to this issue of the number of combinations of a certain size when we look at sampling in Chapter 6. For now, we shall assume that the research has been conducted and the results processed using one of the test techniques outlined in Chapter 13. All of these techniques yield a result (a numerical value) that can be assessed in terms of the likelihood that it occurred by chance. In broad terms the values that result from the statistical test are influenced by the data that are collected and by the size of the sample, that is, the number of bits of data that have been collected. As our sample size increases, the number of bits of data in our analysis increases and this, in turn, is likely to have an effect on the size of the value that our statistical test produces. The reason for this is quite obvious. Subtracting one number from another is a simple measure of difference (often the basis of a statistical test). If we do this calculation 20 times and sum the resulting differences, the result is likely to be larger than if we do it five times. When you examine our value, we need, therefore, to be aware of how many bits of data went into its calculation.

Assuming that we have allowed for the size of the sample (and how we do this is considered in Chapter 13, when we look at something called degrees of freedom), we judge whether the probability that it has occurred by chance is more or less than a threshold that we will accept as being proved or not proved. This threshold is referred to as the *significance level*. Finding an answer to the question 'What is an appropriate level of significance?' could take us round in circles. What may be significant for a researcher wishing to prove a point may not be significant for someone more sceptical, such as a researcher whose conclusions are about to be challenged. Fortunately common sense and convention offer us an answer. If there is a 50 per cent probability that research results were obtained by chance, then our understanding of the issue being researched has not been advanced. If the probability is 10 per cent, then many researchers are likely to be convinced; at 5 per cent, chance is not a big player in the game and at 1 per cent, this constitutes proof that most people would accept. The next level, 0.1 per cent, has only a one in a thousand chance that chance itself had been the influencing factor.

The basic model is that proof is more convincing when chance is less likely to be an influence. Conventionally the 10 per cent significance level is a weak proof, 5 per cent a solid proof and 1 per cent convincing proof. The level of probability associated with the value resulting from the statistical test then has to be applied to the null hypothesis (not the research hypothesis because it is impossible in social research to have all the data to demonstrate that it is true). This is a straightforward process, which is outlined in more detail in Chapter 13, but there are occasions on which it can call for some mental agility. There is another way of expressing this that is sometimes found in the literature. Instead of saying that there is a 1 in 20 chance that our research result has occurred by chance, we could say that in only 1 out of 20 occasions when we get this result will we be wrong in rejecting the null hypothesis. This does not seem unreasonable, given that people do not always do what is logical (or even sensible) and that research is a messy business. The issues in educational research, especially when the numbers we are dealing with are small, can be fuzzy and indistinct and a 95 per cent probability that the results are not due to chance seems pretty good to me.

(iii) What can go wrong?

We can now appreciate that a quantitative positivist style of research requires adherence to procedure. It produces robust and compelling results as long as the researcher's decisions are appropriate. And because there are many decisions that have to be made, the potential for things to go wrong is quite high. This section highlights some of the fundamentals that have to be correct.

(a) Poor data

The process of obtaining data can be fraught with difficulty. If we intend that the conclusions we draw from the analysis of our research data will apply to other situations (that is, we want to be able to generalise our conclusions), then we have to pay particular attention to how we select our data. We should understand Chapter 6, which deals with obtaining data and pay special attention to sampling. Only a limited number of sampling procedures are appropriate if we want to extend our conclusions from the data we have analysed to a wider world.

Even if our procedure for choosing the sample is appropriate, we can still get things wrong. In general, the smaller the quantity of data that we have, the greater the possibility that we will select data that is atypical. For example, suppose that we have assessed the IQ of 100 children and were going to select a sample to represent the group. If we selected only one, then we have as much chance of choosing the highest or lowest in the group as any other. Using this one to represent the group is not particularly appropriate.

However, even with an appropriate sample size, we can still finish up with a sample that is not balanced. Let us assume that we are seeking to obtain sensitive information, for example, we might want to know from parents what the household income is, or, from students, whether their parents give them any sex education. In these circumstances we should be aware that:

- Some people may inflate their income – would you expect this to be the same rate for everybody or to be more in evidence in certain income groups?
- Some people may refuse to tell you their incomes or whether they receive sex education from their parents. Again, would you expect this to be a random effect or concentrated in certain groups?

Asking questions in the right way is considered in Chapter 8.

Failure to obtain information can produce bias and we should show that our data is not biased. We do this by examining the pattern of non-response. For example, if a school were to send a questionnaire for parents to complete, it should check on the geographical distribution of the replies by comparing the postcodes of respondents with the postcodes of the children in the school. Any marked variation would constitute bias and imply that the voice of a particular group, such as an ethnic minority, was not being heard.

To summarise, we need to:

- take care about sample size
- think about whether we are being given truthful information
- examine non-response for evidence of bias.

(b) Using the wrong statistical test

There are a large number of statistical tests, many of which seem to be doing much the same thing. However, there are quite marked differences in the tests and in the way in which they operate. We will examine some statistical tests in Chapter 13. Not all tests are the same; they perform particular tasks and make assumptions about the nature of the data that can be analysed. To make sure that we do not use the wrong test we should understand the following.

- The assumptions on which the test is based.
- What our purpose is in conducting a test, for example to test whether two things are different (boys' and girls' non-attendance at school) or to see whether things are associated (assessment score at age ten with the number of years of pre-school education).
- How the way in which we measure our data influences the type of test we use. Chapter 4 explains about data measurement.

Finally, when we put all of these things together and we are still faced with a number of possibilities that seem appropriate, we should appreciate that two different tests can (but not will) produce different levels of significance with the same research data.

(c) Preparing our data for analysis

The third thing that can create problems for us is a problem with our data. In general, two types of situation occur, one where we are dealing with a great range in our data, from very small to very large, and the other where we combine data into classes (0–19, 20–39, etc.).

Having a great range in our data set is a problem (especially if the data is bunched at one extreme) because many of the statistical procedures in Chapter 13 require our data to conform to a particular pattern, with broadly the same number of units of data either side of an average value (this is usually the mean, which we shall meet in more detail in Chapter 11). Fortunately this problem is relatively straightforward to resolve in most instances. For example, with pressure on governments to find ways of financing higher education, research that seeks to determine how far the debt students take on is related to their expectations of earning power would be of great interest. While expected earnings are likely to be within a limited range (a financial analyst might earn ten times more than an archaeologist, but most people will be somewhere in the middle), the pattern of student debt may be very different. Students from well-off backgrounds may have little or no debt. Students from the poorest backgrounds will have some debt, but often governments will not pass on some of the charges in order to encourage them to enter higher education. Many students, however, will have a high level of debt because their parents cannot afford to pay all of the fees and expenses and they are too well-off to qualify for a state subsidy. In the UK at the present time it is estimated that some students could finish their studies with debts of £25,000. In order to manage this great range (0–25,000) and the fact that there will be a concentration of students towards the top end, we could transform the data by using not the original data but a logarithm of this data (a logarithm is the power to which we must raise a base number, in our case we use 10 because this is the default base, to yield the original data value; so the logarithm of 100 is 2 because 10 must be raised by the power 2 to give 100. 10^2 is 10×10 which is 100). To see how data is transformed and large numbers made manageable, look at Table 3.2. In this table, 10 to the power 1.6989 ($10^{1.6989}$) is 50, so the logarithm of 50 is 1.6989. 10 to the power 4.3979 ($10^{4.3979}$) is 25,000. The effect of using logarithms is to transform an actual range of 0 to 25,000 to one of 0 to 4.3979, something that is much more manageable and which allows us to compress data so that it conforms more to the requirements of some of the statistical tests we might use.

Table 3.2 Logarithmic transformation of data

Actual student debt	Logarithm of student debt
0	0
50	1.6989
250	2.3979
1,000	3.0000
2,500	3.3979
5,000	3.6989
10,000	4.0000
25,000	4.3979

The second area where we might have problems is grouping data into classes. This occurs when we have a continuous data series, one where any value is potentially possible. For example, student debt is a continuous series. Someone could have a debt of £49, someone else £4861 and a third person a debt of £18,324. If we are dealing with a large number of people, it is often easier to compress the data into classes (such as £1 to £500, £501 to £1,000, etc.). But how do we choose the classes? This is an absolutely crucial question because selection of different class boundaries can produce totally different statistical results. Look at Case Study 3.5 for an illustration of this and an indication of the problems that we might face. However, Chapter 10 gives us some answers to choosing the number of classes with which to represent data and the identification of class boundaries.

(d) Drawing the wrong conclusion

Lastly, even when we have planned our whole procedure, identified a statistical test that meets our goals and is appropriate for our data, ensured that our data collection has been perfect and we are confident that our data presents an honest picture of reality, we can still reach the wrong conclusion. How?

To understand this, we have to go back to what it is we are investigating and how we conduct the investigation. Much education research uses data published by public bodies, everything from population data to data on educational standards and performance. One characteristic of this data is that it is presented at a series of spatial levels, from national down to local. Herein lies the problem because we can get different results exploring the same issue when using data from different levels. The problem arises because of the inference that individuals behave or have the same characteristics as the group as

Case study 3.5 The effect of different class boundaries

The end of year test results for all children are being presented for analysis by the head teacher for a report to parents. The results for 16 children are shown below:

46 19 40 45 36 18 41 40 19 47 46
40 39 40 38 46 9 48 28 28 32

The head teacher groups the test scores in three ways; the first has a large number of classes, the second fewer and the third a small number. The results are shown below:

0–5		0–10	1	0–15	1
6–10	1	11–20	3	16–30	4
11–15		21–30	1	31–45	10
16–20	3	31–40	8	46–60	5
21–25		41–50	7		
26–30	1	51–60			
31–35	1				
36–40	7				
41–45	2				
46–50	5				
51–55					
56–60					

Look at the results and think about them. The class interval of five shows three peaks, at 16–20, 36–40 and 46–50. The class interval of 15 shows only one peak and the class interval of 10 shows something in between. If these counts were used in a statistical process, they would almost certainly generate different results. Choosing the number of classes is a skill based as much on intuition and a 'feel' for the data as it is on procedure. Read the section on histograms in Chapter 10 closely.

a whole. In the statistical literature this is referred to as the *ecological fallacy*. Read Case Study 3.6 to see an example and to understand more.

The ecological fallacy is an issue for education researchers because of the extent to which spatially based data is used, especially with the application of geographical information systems (the use of computers for mapping, transformation and analysis). For example, we might want to look at the level of association between socio-economic status and levels of achievement at the end of compulsory schooling. If we were to look at this issue using data from local authorities, we would almost certainly have an ecological fallacy problem. The only way we can minimise the problem without complex data manipulation (which may not work anyway) is to use very small-sized areal units (such as postcodes).

The ecological fallacy has much in common with the class boundary problem that we looked at earlier. It has been shown that different combinations of spatial units will generate different statistical test outcomes. This should not surprise us. The manipulation of boundaries to gain electoral advantage, a process known as gerrymandering, has long been practised by corrupt administrations. Geographers refer to this issue of how to process spatial data so as to minimise bias and inappropriate inference as 'the modified areal unit problem'. We should not ignore this issue. It is well understood by examiners and by those who referee academic papers for journals and even new researchers should show that they understand it.

(iv) Summary

While the quantitative approach has strong procedures to guide us, we should never ignore the number of times we have to take a decision about what to do. Each decision has to be justified so that it is acceptable to our peers. We have to plan our strategy from

Case study 3.6 The ecological fallacy

The implications of the ecological fallacy have been appreciated since the 1930s. The earliest identification and exploration of the issues seems to have taken place in the USA. But even earlier than this, questions were being raised by the work of a famous French philosopher and sociologist, Emile Durkheim, who lived from 1858 to 1917. He argued, 1897, that religious belief and culture accounted for differences in suicide rates between Catholic and Protestant countries in Europe.

Durkheim's work was quantitative but not statistical in the way that we use the term in this book. The problem with Durkheim's analysis was that he had assumed that because two things occurred together (religious affiliation and variations in suicide rates), they were related. While we can understand this, the problem is actually more acute than this.

A particularly influential paper was published by the American statistician, William Robinson, in 1950 (Robinson, 1950). This demonstrated quite clearly the ecological fallacy. Robinson explored the relationship between illiteracy and being black, using 1930s data. He carried out his analysis at a broad regional level in the USA (nine regional census divisions), at the state level (48 at the time) and at an individual level. The results highlighted the problem for all researchers, not just educationalists.

Scale of analysis	Relationship between being illiterate and being black
Regional	.946
State	.773
Individual	.203

Robinson measured the relationship between being illiterate and being black using a technique called a correlation coefficient (see Chapter 13). This shows how the numbers of black residents are represented in literacy rates. The results are startling. When he used regional data on literacy rates and the proportion of black people, the results showed that the two were highly associated and that a change in one was closely related to a change in the other but when he used data for individuals the level of association was far, far lower.

This is a statistical phenomenon and while solutions to the problem are being explored, they are not yet successful and certainly not for the beginner researcher. It is better that the problem is avoided.

start to finish to ensure that the various stages and components fit together and then, almost certainly, we will have to review and revise it as we take account of the things that can cause us to be wrong in our conclusions. Table 3.3 summarises the stages. Having identified a research area, we focus on an issue and phase a research question. We unpick the question to identify what we think may be the factors at work and present them as a model to be tested. For each factor we state a research and null hypothesis and identify what data we will need to test the hypotheses and where we will get the data from. At this stage we also need to specify the statistical test we will use to ensure that the way we obtain the data is compatible with what the test requires. If not, it is back to the beginning to start all over again. We can appreciate that this procedure necessitates considerable pre-planning, so much so that it often takes up at least a quarter and often much more of the time available for the whole project. The model is fundamentally the same for the experimental approach that we shall look at in the next section.

3.2.4 Putting the quantitative process together: the experimental approach

(i) Introduction

The concept of an experiment might seem strangely alien to education, yet it need not be. However, it is true that the experimental approach in education and the social

Table 3.3 Planning a quantitative approach to your research

Activity stage	Reference section
1. Identify a research area.	2.3, 2.4.2 and 3.5
2. Isolate a research issue and question; develop a model of the factors that influence outcomes.	2.3 2.2.2
3. Understand the research done by others.	Chapter 5
4. For each factor you assess, construct a research hypothesis and a null hypothesis.	3.2.2 and 3.2.3
5. Identify your data needs.	Chapter 4
6. Identify your data sources.	Chapter 4
7. Identify how you will obtain your data/sample.	Chapter 6
8. Identify what statistical test procedures you will use.	Chapters 12 and 13
9. Review your data collection process to make sure it meets the needs of your test.	Chapters 8 and 9
10. Review problems of analysis and inference and, if unresolved, start over again.	3.2.3
11. Apply test and assess likelihood that result occurred by chance.	3.2.3 and Chapter 13

sciences is much less used than it is in the natural sciences. The reasons for this are that people are much more variable and less easy to control than quantities of a chemical or a defined measure of a physical intervention. The only social sciences where experimentation has been extensive are psychology and the hybrid area known as management science. In both cases there is a tradition of experimentation that is closely tied up with the discipline's self-perceived identity as a science. Where experimentation has been used in education, the origins of the approaches are to be found in other subjects (such as psychology). When used appropriately, though, it is a powerful technique and an asset in educational research.

(ii) How experimental approaches are similar to survey and analysis approaches

Just because an approach has a different name, it does not mean that it differs completely from others. Experimental and survey approaches share many principles. In both the concept of proof is the same. Both preface their investigation with a hypothesis. Both generate data to be used in a statistical test. Both, in other words, are clearly rooted in a positivist tradition. The differences between them are limited but significant.

(iii) How experimental approaches differ from survey and analysis approaches

The difference between the two approaches lies in how they manage the jumble of influences acting upon or through a process that can be investigated. In section 3.2.2 (i) we set out some of the influences in relation to parental choice of a school. The survey and analysis approach deals with these in a real world setting, a situation in which all the factors are operating at the same time. The experimental approach seeks to take these influences and create situations in which they can be managed, that is, reduce the joint action of the factors and the possibility that one factor is influencing another (such as the number of children going on to higher education being one of the things parents take into account when they make a judgement of a school's reputation). It is the process by which these influences are managed that constitutes the experiment.

Let us look at an example. If we wanted to assess the effect of a new reading technique for pupils who were three or more years below their expected reading age, we would want to identify what other factors other than the technique might influence our results. Figure 3.2 shows some of these. Different teachers taking the class or supporting the student could have an effect. If pupils used different classrooms, then differences in temperature, light, layout and ambience could influence their ability to work. The time of day could be a factor influencing pupil performance, especially for younger children. The attention span of the pupil may be another factor, because the technique and material may be more suited to a particular age group. The level and quality of parental support may yet be another factor. All of these are reasonable suppositions for a hypothesis, and there will be others, too.

An experimental approach seeks to deal with this situation by allowing the influence of each factor individually on reading ability to come through in the results as strongly as possible. It does this by freezing out or stabilising the influence of the other factors. This process is referred to as controlling the influence of other factors. The principle, therefore, is quite simple. If the influence of all of the factors bar one is controlled, then any change in reading ability must be due to the influence of that factor. This approach of allowing one thing to vary while others are held constant is described as *ceteris paribus*, which is usually translated as 'other things being equal'. Just how this is done we shall see in the next section.

(iv) Experimental design strategies

The principle of ensuring that other things are equal in experimental design is to apply the intervention to one group and not to another. Thus in our example, for one group of pupils their parents would be trained in a reading support programme and told for how long they should listen to and help their children. The children in the other group would have no support. The one experiencing the intervention is called the *experimental group* and the one without the intervention is called the *control group*. For something so straightforward, there are a considerable number of experimental designs. All deal with the issues of how to select and allocate the people who will provide the evidence to experimental and control groups. We shall consider the main approaches.

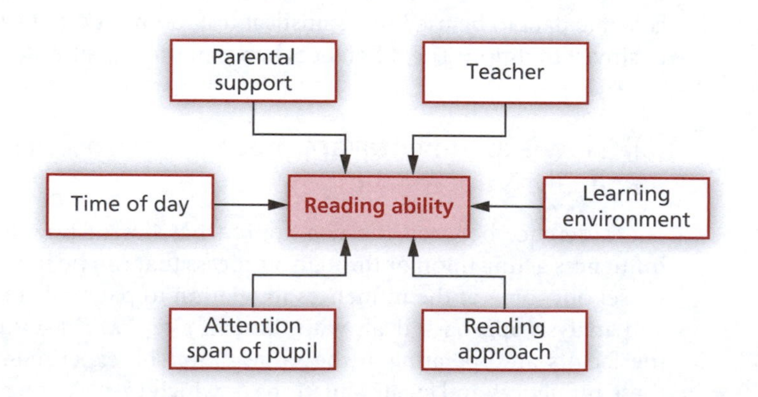

Figure 3.2 Some influences on reading ability

(a) Random allocation of subjects

The first approach is the random allocation of pupils. This is shown as allocation path (a) in Figure 3.3(a). Here experimental subjects are randomly allocated to the experimental and control groups. This is a comparative approach where the effect of the intervention in the experimental group is compared with the normal or pre-existing process in the control group. In the reading example, the experimental group would be taught with parental support and the control group would be taught without. The strength of this approach is the random allocation of subjects to experimental and control group. The implication of this is that atypical behaviours and responses by subjects are randomly distributed. This is very important for many of the statistical tests we can use.

The research procedure usually consists of three stages:

- a pre-test to establish a baseline of performance or behaviour for individuals and for all individuals combined in the experimental and control groups. The pre-test does not include any experimental intervention;
- the experimental intervention;
- a post-test procedure to identify and assess the consequences of the intervention.

This procedure is used in most experimental designs.

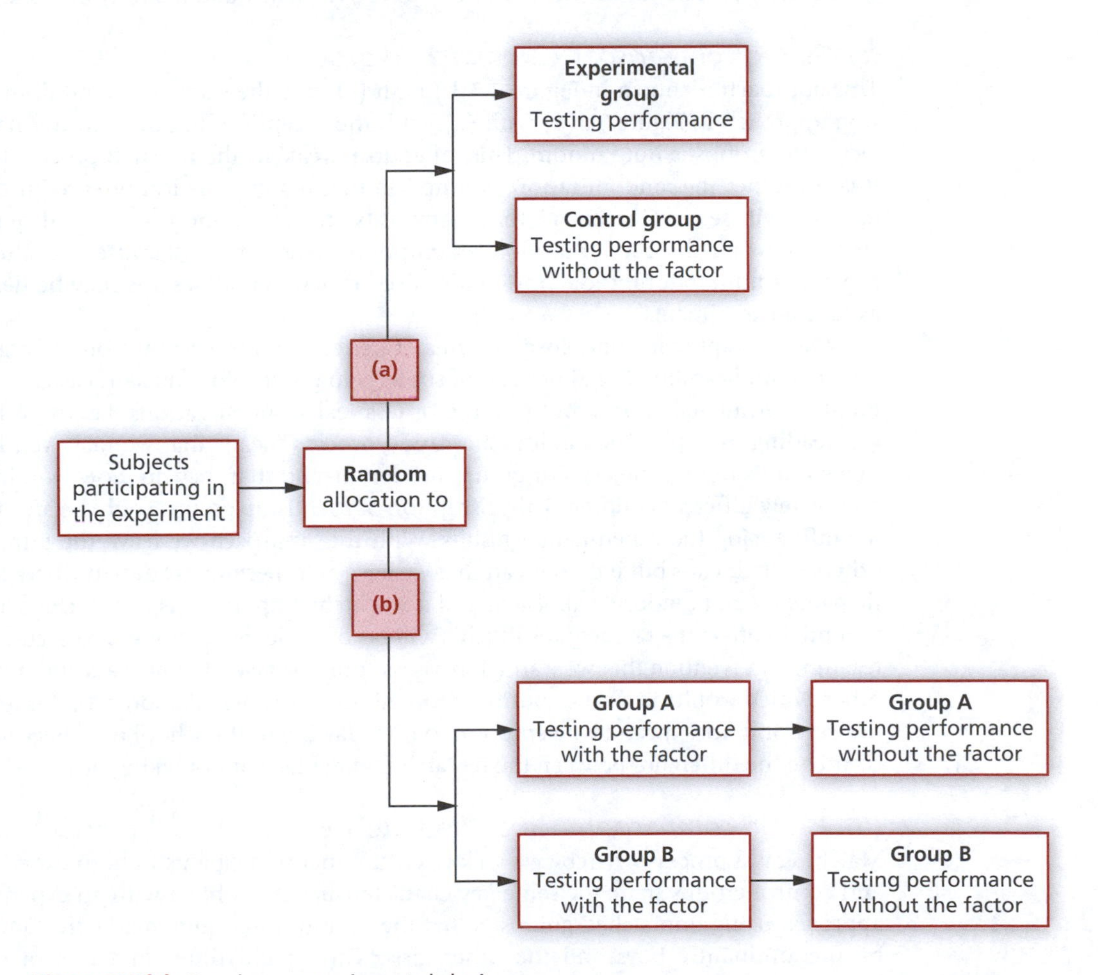

Figure 3.3(a) Random experimental designs

(b) Random allocation of subjects who experience both experimental and control conditions

The second approach to random allocation is shown in Figure 3.3(a) path (b). The concept is a strong one in that it randomly allocates subjects and then tests them in each of the two situations, experimental and control. This means that *all subjects* experience *all situations* and that the effects of both situations can be compared across both groups and for all individuals. Whereas the simple random allocation compares responses between people in the experimental and control groups, this approach allows us to understand how *each subject* responds to the experimental and control condition. This clearly is a more robust test of the intervention because it gives us data before and after the intervention on individuals (not just groups). However, we have to think about whether this approach is appropriate for our research issue. Much education research is concerned with the lasting impact of an intervention, assessing how far something can be applied on a regular basis with continuing and lasting benefit. A new reading approach example would be like this, while the application *and then withdrawal* of parental support to children might well contravene ethical principles. This particular experimental approach is more appropriate for testing a stimulus and the response it creates, where the effects are not necessarily long lasting. It would be appropriate, for example, if we wanted to assess the effect of ambient temperature or noise in the classroom on children's quality and quantity of work.

(c) Paired comparisons – unmatched groups

This approach is shown in Figure 3.3(b) path (c). It is the same as the random allocation approach in Figure 3.3(a) path (a), with the exception that the allocation of subjects into groups is not random. This, of course, weakens the research process because it contravenes the randomisation assumption that many statistical tests require (however, we will see in Chapter 13 that many tests are robust and can be used quite successfully when the randomisation assumption is not met). Because the allocation process is not random, these non-randomised experimental designs may be described as 'quasi-experiments'.

What this approach does lose in terms of perfection, however, it more than gains in terms of applicability. The allocation of subjects to groups does make it easier to implement experimental approaches in more or less real world situations. Let us go back to our reading example. The random allocation process means that we may well have to move pupils out of one class or group into another so that they are now working with completely different children. This disruption of friendship groups could be another factor influencing the experimental results. With this approach we leave the pupils with others in their class but it does mean that we have an experimental design where the participants are not randomly allocated and not matched up in terms of any characteristics that might affect the research result (this will become clearer after the next section). Any teaching intervention that we wanted to assess could be given to one class and not to another, which would act as the control group. As an experimental approach, it is less than perfect but it does mean less disruption to everyday life in the school or college and this could be the difference between the research taking place or not taking place.

(d) Paired comparisons – matched groups

Matching is a process whereby we seek to ensure that participants in both experimental and control groups share the same key characteristics. A problem with an experimental approach using unmatched groups is that they could differ quite markedly. One could be predominantly boys and the other girls. They could differ in terms of student

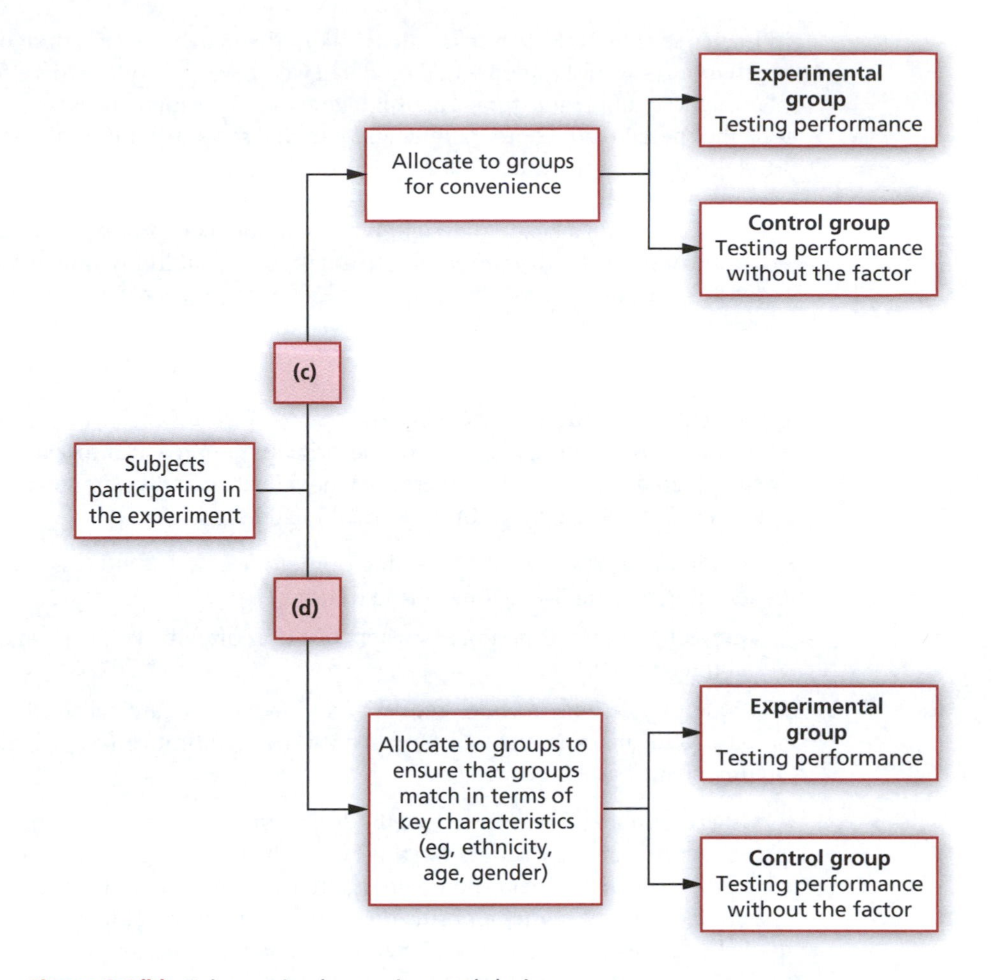

Figure 3.3(b) Other paired experimental designs

capability, or ethnicity or any other factor that could potentially influence our test results. With the possibility of variations like these, the potential for generating test results that lead to us drawing the wrong conclusion is increased. The solution (Figure 3.3(b) path (d)) is to match the subjects in the experimental and control groups in terms of key characteristics. So, for example, we would have the same number of boys and girls in each group, the same number in defined ethnic groups, the same number with given measures of intellectual capability and so on. But it is not quite as simple as this. For one thing, all the boys could be from a single ethnic group and all the girls from several groups. It is not just overall numbers that have to be matched; it is the combination of characteristics that we think will be particularly useful in terms of our research. It often means that individuals have to be matched in terms of these key characteristics. This can be difficult and is likely to mean that the selection of individuals will not be random. And this could have an impact on our selection of a statistical test.

(e) Factorial designs

The experimental approaches so far have been concerned with isolating one factor. A factorial design allows us to test two factors (or even more) together but to assess their influence separately. However, a little tweak to the matched group design takes us into a much more powerful experimental model in which we can explore this effect of a number of influences at the same time. Let us imagine that we want to assess the effect of two factors, the special reading programme and parental support for both the standard and the special reading programmes. Our design manages to ensure that the same teacher will take all classes, thus removing another source of possible influence. With this specification we have set up a factorial design. What would make it robust as an experimental approach would be to allocate pupils to our groups randomly and if we could match individuals it would be a Rolls Royce of a design. The logic of a simple factorial design is shown in Case Study 3.7. It shows how, given the right conditions, we can generate powerful conclusions.

(f) Other experimental designs

What have been outlined so far are the principal approaches to experimental design. There are many others. In fact, there are whole textbooks on experimental design. Other approaches that you may become aware of include:

- longitudinal experimentation with groups, for example a study of a new approach to teaching reading over a long period of time;
- individual subject experiments, where one or more subjects are subject to experimental intervention;
- sequential designs in which results of an intervention are collected on a continuous basis and the experiment is halted once the significance (or insignificance) of the intervention is established.

Other textbooks on research methods in education cover experimental design in greater depth than the treatment in this book. The treatment here should not be taken as an implicit statement that experimental designs are of little value in education research. The situation is rather the opposite, they are extremely valuable but they are not greatly used. There are reasons for this. First, they can be difficult to organise. The consequence of this is that cost, both in terms of money and time, can grow to considerable levels relative to other approaches. Second, the circumstances of the research may not match the quite rigorous conditions required for an experimental design. This may be true of the subjects who should be selected or the conditions in which the intervention and testing should take place. More often, however, it seems that increasingly the questions that educationalists want to ask (questions about experiences, feelings, emotions and attitudes) are not best addressed by experimental procedures.

(v) What can go wrong?

The issues that were identified as being potentially problematic in survey design are applicable to experimental design. In this section, we shall consider additional problems particularly significant for experimentation.

(a) The intervention effect

The first of these is the intervention effect. This arises when we remove the study from the real world and into an artificial environment. Any experimental situation can clearly set the issue and the event apart in the subject's mind and the question for us is what impact this has. Is the subject annoyed at the disruption to everyday life by being asked

Case study 3.7 Factorial experimental design

This experimental procedure is capable of managing complex combinations of factors all varying together at the same time. Let us continue with our study of reading capability. Our objective is to understand whether a new approach to learning to read is effective and, if it is, then just how effective.

Let us establish some definitions at the beginning of our experiment. We will use letters to represent specific experimental conditions.

- X is the process of learning that takes place at the present time. In this case the pupils have one reading period of 20 minutes at the beginning of the day and another of 10 minutes before the end of school.
- A is the use of parental support at home for 20 minutes every evening (thus A is 20 minutes of reading at the beginning of the day, 10 at the end and 20 minutes at home).
- B represents an additional 10 minutes reading in the afternoon using the existing approach (that is, X above. Thus B is 20 minutes of reading at the beginning of the day and 20 minutes at the end of the school day and nothing at home).
- AB represents 40 minutes (two twenty-minute periods) at school plus 20 minutes of parental support at home.

The table below shows the total level of reading capability as measured for the group as a whole under the four conditions (this is computed using a standard reading assessment test). By just applying a little logic to this, we can extract a lot of information.

B = 300	A = 428
AB = 624	X = 260

A − X (428 − 260 = 168) gives us the effect of parental support (because the difference between A and X is the parental support).

B − X (300 − 260 = 40) gives us the effect of increasing the reading time at school (because the difference between them is the extra 10 minutes in the afternoon).

Both show an improvement in the group's reading capability and the increase with parental support is quite marked. But what has been the effect of introducing parental support and increasing the reading time at school (that is, intervention AB)? Is it more than just adding the two effects together? We can test this assumption with the following equation:

$X + (A - X) + (B - X) = AB$ (Look at the definitions above to prove that the two sides are equivalent)

But when we use the actual numbers:

$$260 + 168 + 40 \neq 624$$

Since 624 is greater than the sum of 260, 168 and 40, we have to conclude that there is a positive interaction effect. That is, introducing parental support and increasing reading time at school has a high value-added effect on pupils' reading and is likely to be cost effective. If AB were less than the sum on the other side of the equation, there would still be an interaction effect but it would be negative.

On the basis of this analysis we might argue for a complete substitution of the new reading approach and an extension of the reading study period. But just to be sure, we ought to know what would be just the effect of 20 minutes parental support on reading capability and just the effect of an additional 10 minutes at school. With a little more algebraic manipulation we can do this.

The effect of A is given by both (A − X) and (AB − B). If we add these together and divide by 2, we get a better estimate of the effect of A. Similarly if we add (B − X) and (AB − A) and divide by 2, we get a better estimate of the effect of B.

The results show that the parental support (A) produces a learning gain of (168 + 324)/2 = 246, while extending the reading period produces a gain of (40 + 196)/2 = 118. In other words, it is the parental support that is producing more of the gain per unit of time.

The power of the factorial approach is its ability to deal with more factors than just these. As they increase, so does the complexity of the interactions. There is a particular statistical technique for analysing this type of data. It is called analysis of variance. We shall learn more about it in Chapter 13.

to participate in the experiment or upset at being selected for the control group rather than the experimental group? (We assume here that because we are working in an ethical way we have given the participants the opportunity to withdraw). How far do subjects respond to the researcher and the intervention that is being tested? The so-called 'Hawthorne effect', named after a factory in Chicago where experiments in worker productivity were conducted in the 1920s and 1930s (see Case Study 3.8), showed that subjects get better at what they are doing just because they are aware that they are part of an experiment. In contrast it is entirely possible, depending on how the experiment is set up, that if an intervention is repetitive, subjects might become bored. This could well affect results. So the question for the researcher is whether the results of the experiment are the consequence of the planned intervention or some other unanticipated intervention? Finding an answer to this is difficult. We can try to overcome these situations by having a 'blind' experiment where subjects do not know whether they are in the control or experimental groups, or in some circumstances we may not even tell them that they are part of an experiment at all. But this, of course, raises ethical issues about informed participation.

(b) Sample variation

What happens when the subjects we thought were going to take part do not? What if our experimental procedure requires a matched design and, on the day of the research, a virus takes out a quarter of our control group? What if the procedure extends over a period of time and the control and experimental groups lose members? We have to have answers to these questions. In some cases we will drop people or add others to create a matched design. In some cases we will go from a matched to an unmatched design. In some cases the best solution might be to start again with a different design. Whatever our solution, we have to recognise that we may be deviating from the ideal and this may affect the validity of our results. As ever, it is how we deal with problems and issues that will determine our credibility in the eyes of many researchers.

(c) Using the wrong test

Statistical tests not only utilise different assumptions, many are also constructed to deal with particular experimental frameworks and data types. For example the student t test that we shall meet in Chapter 13 takes different forms for matched and unmatched data. If we are sure that our groups are typical of the population at large, we can use one type of test but if we are not sure, then we have to use another. There is no getting away from the fact that making the right decision in research means that we have to know a great deal about research methods.

3.2.5 Summary of quantitative approaches

The key points to remember about quantitative approaches are that

- they deal with cause and effect and are particularly useful for resolving questions regarding outcomes rather than processes;
- many of the statistical techniques that are used to analyse data place great requirements on the way in which the data is collected;
- quantitative approaches have strict procedures;
- they are powerful, rigorous and convincing to others.

3.3 Qualitative approaches to research

3.3.1 Introduction

Qualitative research is concerned with understanding how people choose to live their lives, the meanings they give to their experiences and their feelings about their condition. It can include approaches such as:

- *Ethnography* – the processes of observing individuals or groups either as participants or non-participants and of analysing and structuring the record.
- *Action research* – a cyclical research and development procedure that moves from problem to goal, through action to reflection on the result in relation to the goal, and then moves forward by revising action or goal or both.
- *Case study* – an investigation of a single instance, usually with the goal of identifying and perhaps understanding how an issue arose, how a problem was resolved, often with the purpose of isolating critical incidents that act as decision points for change.

We should appreciate, though, that there is no reason why each of these approaches cannot include a quantitative element. They are, however, more usually associated with qualitative strategies because they do not embrace positive principles. We have already met them in Chapter 2 and they are illustrated in Chapter 14. Other authors include focus groups, interviews and document analysis as qualitative research approaches but here we look at them as ways of obtaining data rather than as a broad approach to research (see Chapters 9 and 11).

Whereas quantitative research has clear procedures that link survey and experimental approaches to common principles, the fact that data collection methods such as focus groups and interviews, appropriate to any of the three approaches set out above, can be confused with an approach to research itself indicates that qualitative research lacks a clear definition. Despite this situation, qualitative methodologies are not weak and research results are significant. The fact that it is possible to have compelling research results generated by methodologies that allow researchers to be extremely flexible in problem conceptualisation, data collection and data analysis is a paradox that we have to try to understand. If we think in terms of quality control, quantitative approaches have built a framework of rules that exist independently of the research problem. Qualitative approaches give guidance but allow researchers considerable freedom of choice. With the flexibility given to the researcher so central to qualitative approaches, this does highlight the necessity for researcher excellence.

3.3.2 How qualitative approaches are presented

It is difficult to talk of a single view of what qualitative research entails. In one way, though, there is something distinctive about qualitative approaches and that is the way in which they are often described as being 'other than' something else. Figure 3.4 presents these oppositions. The features of qualitative research are presented as the inner ring and are contrasted with the outer ring (in colour), which represents the characteristics of quantitative research. While quantitative research is described as having a hard edge and being concerned with process outcomes (assessment results, delinquency rates, literacy rates), explanation, generalisation and the derivation of laws, qualitative

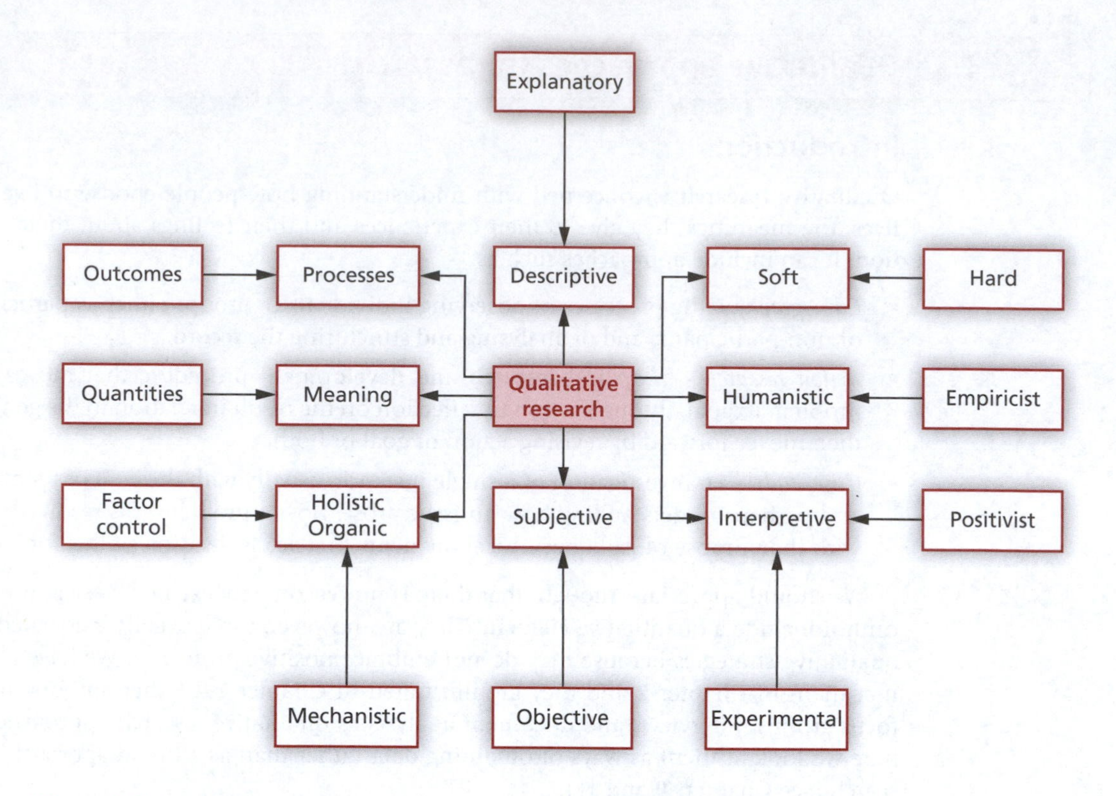

Figure 3.4 Qualitative and quantitative approaches compared

approaches are soft, descriptive and concerned with how and why things happen as they do. Quantitative approaches are objective, experimental and, within the positivist tradition, value the empirical observation of cause and effect. Qualitative approaches, in contrast, are held to stem from a humanistic tradition. They draw on insight and interpretation, and allow researchers to draw on their subjective responses to evidence. With quantitative research, numerical evidence is the basis for drawing conclusions. An issue is structured as influences (causes) and effects and the research process is presented as being strait-jacketed. But with qualitative research the emphasis is on wholeness and detailed connections between our social worlds, emotional and cognitive processes and economic circumstances, all which have to be understood in order to recreate the meaning that we give to our lives.

3.3.3 The character of qualitative research

Let us now examine the character of qualitative research and see what its distinctive contribution is to research.

(i) A holistic and integrative approach

One of the key characteristics of qualitative approaches is the willingness to use data of different types and from different sources and combine them into an analysis and interpretation of a situation. In contrast with the fragmentation of the evidence base within the quantitative method, this is a true strength of the method. Some quantitative researchers might point to the way data are combined as a point of weakness because it is not based on a single procedure against which judgements can be tested, as there is, for example, with significance testing (see section 3.2.3 (ii)). However, qualitative researchers should be confident in their response for two reasons.

- First, individual methodologies (for example, grounded theory, which we shall meet in Chapter 11) have established their own procedures that allow other researchers to see clearly what a researcher's decisions have been.
- Second, if research were a process where events and outcomes fell easily into neat relationships, the world would be a simpler place to live in. But the real world and the research world are not like this. In the discussion of quantitative research we noted that we could deal in probabilities. For example, young people from the poorest backgrounds may have only a 10 per cent chance of going to university while those from affluent backgrounds have a 70 per cent chance. However, probabilities do not tell us what we have to do to change this situation. If there is a goal of overcoming social disadvantage through access to higher education, it is necessary to understand the motives and aspirations of those who already go as well as those who do not. Understanding people does mean that you have to deal with people's feelings, values and emotions as well as their behaviours, their attachments to place and people, their fears, hopes and motivations as well as their perceptions of the world, the organisations with which they have contact and their relationships with them. What formal research procedure is there that can put all of this together? It requires sorting, evaluating, juxtaposing, contrasting and rejecting before accepting. Some of this can undoubtedly be accomplished by formal analysis but the insights that create the integration that lead to understanding are made by researchers themselves.

(ii) A naturalistic form of enquiry

The second thing that sets qualitative research apart is that it is a naturalistic enquiry. What is meant by 'naturalistic'? It means obtaining data in as natural a setting as possible. The principle behind this is to minimise the influence of an unrealistic research environment. If you want to understand more about this, look at Case Study 3.8 on quality assurance in schools, which shows how a naturalistic enquiry is an alternative to a quality assurance process that influences activity and achieves compliance without generating commitment.

It is not, however, always possible to sustain a pure naturalistic approach. Sometimes the researcher has to be known to the subjects. Certain research methods, such as focus groups, require a degree of separation of subjects from their natural world. Other methods, such as interviews, impose an artificial situation on respondents. Case studies often involve investigating behaviour in the past, so the very process of asking people to remember and to reflect creates a situation that may be far from natural.

(iii) Not one reality

Qualitative researchers often assert that they are not concerned with 'one reality'. What do they mean by this and is it a valid assertion? To understand what they mean, we have to go back again to quantitative approaches and the assumption that there is a single truth to be discovered, either a factor has an influence or it does not. The implication of this is that there is a 'real world' that has an independent, verifiable existence. All of this

Case study 3.8 Quality assurance in schools

It is not surprising that education quality assurance programmes are widespread. National governments see education as performing important tasks:

- creating the intellectual capital to support scientific, technological and business innovation;
- developing the skill base to meet employment needs;
- overcoming social disadvantage;
- creating common values and laying the foundations for a cohesive society.

Not surprisingly governments want to ensure that education is achieving the outcomes that they want. Many do this through programmes of school inspection. The World Bank has identified three approaches to quality assurance:

- state control of the curriculum and assessment of teacher effectiveness against curriculum goals;
- alignment of locally determined teaching processes against nationally determined curriculum goals and outcome standards;
- national monitoring of self-evaluation and regulation.

One of the characteristics of many quality assurance processes is that the procedures are imposed upon schools. National agencies devise regimes. Criticism by schools of these regimes usually focuses on the scale of disruption and on the way in which they configure the life of the school to the issues considered by the inspection. In England and Wales, for example, the original model was that a school inspection would normally occur every five or six years, would be of a week's duration and would involve a team of between five and twelve inspectors. The inspectors would be free to observe lessons, to meet with staff and pupils to assess the effectiveness of school policies that were statutorily required, and to assess records and documents. Schools would normally be given about two months' notice of an inspection. From the school's point of view the inspection disrupted school life for at least a quarter of the academic year. The need to show compliance with regulations and the attainment of national standards meant that the work of the school was placed in a strait-jacket for most of the time. While inspections took place in schools, they were far from being 'naturalistic enquiries' because schools and teachers prepared for the inspections and there are even cases of pupils being asked to be on good behaviour to impress the inspectors. The inspections were a clear example of the enquiry (the 'research') interfering with the process being researched.

Sweden, however, provides an interesting contrast. In the mid 1990s, Sweden began a review of the decision to decentralise responsibility for education. There was recognition of the need for quality assurance. In 2002 the role of the National Agency for Education (Skolverket) was revised to implement a new quality assurance process. At the heart of this process was self-evaluation by schools and the creation of background papers using data in the public domain and statistical and documentary records from the school. The tone of the visit is not an inquisition but a dialogue. There are relatively few lesson observations; interviews with teachers and pupils are seen as a better means of obtaining insights about the learning process. The whole process is based on the assembly of data from different sources and of different types. It is a typical qualitative research approach. As the national report on inspections for 2004 says, 'while the qualitative methods may have certain inherent weaknesses, it is the personal visits "in reality" which make the material unique and interesting' (*Educational Inspection 2004: A Summary of Inspection Results in the Swedish Report 26b*, Skolverket, p. 27). So by removing the 'threat of criticism' element in the inspection process, the Swedish approach has enabled the inspectors to visit schools without the schools feeling that they had to put on a special show. This is a more mature and, in all likelihood, more accurate and effective way of assessing the quality of education than was the case in the UK.

The UK national standards agency, Ofsted, implemented new procedures based around school self-evaluation in 2005.

seems quite reasonable. Weather systems behave according to sets of complex rules. If they did not we could not forecast the weather nor have a good stab at predicting the impact of climate change. But does all of this apply in relation to people? Is there only one explanation, only one set of relationships to be explained? Think of politics. Is every politician motivated by the public good or are some working to ensure that a rival does not gain an advantage in promotion to higher office? Does every consumer go to the nearest supermarket? How do we account for those who choose to shop at one that is further way? If the nearest supermarket is expensive and we receive social security, it is not irrational to shop for cheaper goods, even if it means travelling further. In other words, these examples demonstrate that there is no single rationality that determines the way people behave.

The task of the qualitative researcher is not to look at how people behave as an outsider but to understand how individuals see the world.

(iv) The place of theory

Now let us look at how qualitative researchers regard theory. Conventionally we say that quantitative approaches are deductive; that is, from the evidence we draw logical conclusions as to relationships. The process of quantitative research refines these, presents them first as theories (or at least a relationship that has some rational basis) and, having tested them in a variety of situations, validates them as laws (see Figure 3.5). The qualitative approach, on the other hand, is conventionally held to be inductive. In this case the evidence is brought together, reviewed, and patterns and processes identified that lead to the specification of theory. The same process of validation would generate laws. Realistically, though, no social scientist gets beyond theory, irrespective of their research approach.

It is at this point that we start to stray from conventional discussions of qualitative research. Had this book been a conventional explanation then it would have stated that qualitative research generates theory through the inductive method. Certainly the qualitative approach can be inductive and, as we shall see in Chapter 11, grounded theory is an established methodology for generating theory. However, while qualitative research is overwhelmingly inductive, it does not have to be. It is possible for qualitative research to explore theoretical statements and even to test hypotheses, though not in the same way

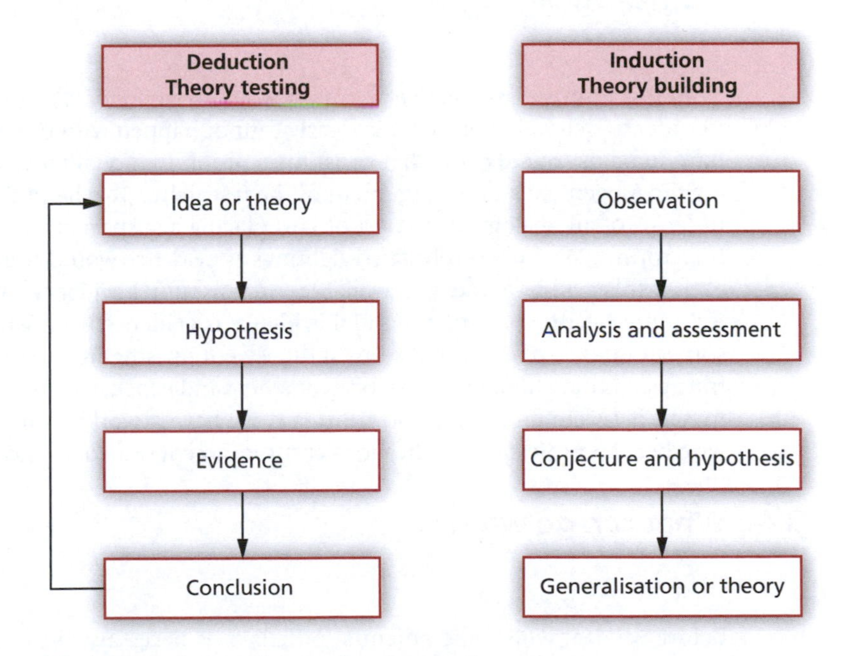

Figure 3.5 Approaches to theory development

that we would do with quantitative procedures. This represents the mindset we ought to adopt with our research, to be prepared to challenge orthodoxy and convention if our research problem requires it. A hypothesis in a qualitative approach will, though, be phrased differently from the one we would test in a quantitative study. For example, we may want to assess the relationship between motivation and academic attainment in two ethnic groups. Table 3.4 gives the research hypothesis for a quantitative approach and a qualitative approach. The difference is apparent. The quantitative test specifies the nature of the difference in the research hypothesis (motivation in group A is higher than group B) and the hypothesis that is tested is the null hypothesis. What we would hope from this is that our statistical test shows whether the levels of motivation are so different that the difference is statistically significant. The qualitative hypothesis, on the other hand, explores not only whether the levels of motivation are different but also why they are different. The educational psychologist, Alan McLean, argues that there are four drivers to motivation in respect of education: the student has to engage with the learning process (often, in the first instance, with the teacher), structure (an understanding of goals and the student tutor relationship), relevance (essentially an acceptance of curriculum values and content) and feedback (so the students can gauge their progress) (Mclean, 2003). A qualitative research project would seek to see if these issues played a part differentially between ethnic groups but, if not, the cultural dimension rather than the level of motivation could be the prime influence on attainment and this would have to be explored further.

Table 3.4 Contrasting hypotheses

Quantitative	Qualitative
The level of motivation in Group A is higher than in Group B. *Which becomes* There is no significant difference in the levels of motivation in the two groups.	The level of motivation and the motivational drivers are different in the two groups.

At this point, a quantitative approach would feed the data into a statistical procedure in order to determine proof. This clearly cannot happen with qualitative research, so we have to adjust our idea of what constitutes proof. In a qualitative approach all we have are the judgement and the argument of the researcher. It is helpful at this point to think in terms of an analogy. In a court of law, placing a suspect at the scene of a crime with fingerprints, DNA or corroborated sightings as evidence would convince most juries. But even if this evidence were not available, circumstantial evidence might still be sufficient for a jury to convict. Circumstantial evidence is evidence from which a reasonable person can infer a conclusion. If some money went missing from an office safe at the same time as I, on my limited means, bought a new and expensive car, I think I would convict myself if I were on the jury. So from law, we have a working model of proof. Proof is whether our professional colleagues or tutors accept our conclusions.

3.3.4 What can go wrong?

(i) Preface

Before we deal with some potential pitfalls, it is necessary, first, to consider briefly the debate in quantitative approaches over ensuring quality. Again the debate has to be seen in the context of not being quantitative. The criteria for judging a quantitative approach or method are validity, reliability and objectivity (see Table 3.5). Validity means that the processes of collecting data accurately reflect the aspects that they are meant to measure. Reliability means that the outcomes of measurement are stable over time, always assuming that other things remain the same. Objectivity means that the researcher is dispassionate in their judgement and, by implication, that another disinterested researcher would reach the same conclusion when faced with the same evidence.

Table 3.5 Dimensions of quality assurance

Quantitative approaches	Qualitative approaches
Validity	Credibility
Reliability	Dependability
Objectivity	Confirmability

Some qualitative researchers have decided to reject not only the methodology of quantitative research but also the terminology and have substituted their own (Table 3.5). The reason why they reject validity as a criterion for quality is that they believe that it must require the assumption that there is a single 'real world' that we research. They substitute, for example, credibility (for validity), dependability (for reliability) and confirmability (for objectivity). These may be perfectly good terms in their own rights but, in many ways, they are just as unclear as the originals. The notion of credibility requires that the subjects who provided the data believe that the interpretation is credible from their own perspective. But this can quite easily be assumed within the framework of validity because credibility is how validity is confirmed. The use of the term 'dependability' seems to add little to the idea of reliability. The only real test of dependability is whether the researcher explains the context for the research sufficiently for the audience to agree with the conclusions, which appears to be just another route to ensuring that the research and conclusions are reliable. Finally objectivity is replaced by confirmability, the assumption that others would reach the same conclusion. Given that objectivity in the quantitative sense cannot be achieved in qualitative research because there is no external standard such as statistical significance to appeal to, we have to believe ultimately in the honesty and integrity of the researcher. With sufficient information on how data were collected and analysed, we can make this judgement and understand the personal framework within which the researcher was objective.

Readers should be aware that other researchers (though not all) would contest these conclusions. Nonetheless, this book uses the old terms, 'reliability' and 'validity'.

(ii) Reliability and validity

Reliability and validity are the corner-stones of any research. We have to be sure that what we gather in represents the situation that we intended to examine and that, if another researcher were to investigate using our approach, the results would be the same. This would establish two things; first, that the approach and the techniques used are appropriate and, second, that the techniques have a rigour that any normal variation in researcher effect cannot undermine. In general the techniques of data collection that we consider in Chapters 8 and 9, which include observation, interviews and documentation, have proved their worth but there still can be problems.

One particular issue for qualitative researchers to be aware of is the influence of the relationship between the researcher and the subject. Because of the nature of the research, what may start off as a neutral relationship based on a mutual recognition of the professional role of the researcher can evolve into a more social relationship capable of influencing the behaviour of the subject, the research environment, the interpretation of the researcher and the research outcomes. Even if the social dynamics do not evolve, it is possible that the very act of being investigated may affect the subject and the outcomes. Case Study 3.9 gives two examples of this.

Case study 3.9 Two classic research effects

1. Becoming a *very* participating observer

One of the classics of ethnographic research is W.F. Whyte's *Street Corner Society* (1943). The focus of Whyte's research was the Italian immigrant community in one city in the USA. The research took place in the late 1930s. Whyte's approach was to live with and as a member of the community, to observe and to analyse. In a highly readable appendix to the text he adds a memoir describing his methodology, noting the issues he faced in his research and describing how he overcame them.

One issue that caused Whyte a problem is an issue for every ethnographic researcher, acceptance by the host community. During an election, Whyte was pressed to vote. He agreed and was given a list of names and polling stations. On that day he voted four times. It gives meaning to the phrase 'Vote early, vote often'.

2. The Hawthorne effect

The Hawthorne effect describes a situation in which outcomes contrary to those expected are caused either by a contrariness or a desire to please or achieve. The effect was first noted in studies of worker productivity at the Hawthorne factory in Chicago in the 1920s but the term 'the Hawthorne effect' was not used until the 1950s.

What the researchers in the 1920s appeared to find was that as lighting quality was reduced worker productivity increased when the opposite was expected. The researchers concluded that the workers felt they were important because they were being tested and so responded with greater efforts. Subsequent investigations have not always reproduced the same effect and questions have been raised about the limited evidence base. However, most researchers would recognise a great potential for an intervention effect, which is as much an issue for qualitative research as it is for experimental.

How can a qualitative researcher demonstrate reliability and validity? The answer is by a process called triangulation (see Figure 3.6). Triangulation seeks to validate a claim, a process or an outcome through at least two independent sources. It puts into operation a key question in the researcher's toolbox, 'Is this person lying to me?' In Figure 3.6 the first and second source of evidence confirm each other but the third does not. If we meet this in our research, we have to determine whether the confirmation provided by the first two sources is genuine or whether they have conspired to lead us to a false conclusion and that the evidence provided by the third source is closer to the truth. Of course, if this were the case, we would have gained a new piece of data, either that two people had been mistaken or had conspired. In either case, the question would be 'Why?'

How can triangulation be implemented? The following are examples:

- Repeat data collection by another researcher as a test of reliability.
- Obtaining information about the same process from two or more different people involved with the process.
- Corroborating interview evidence with documentary evidence or vice versa.

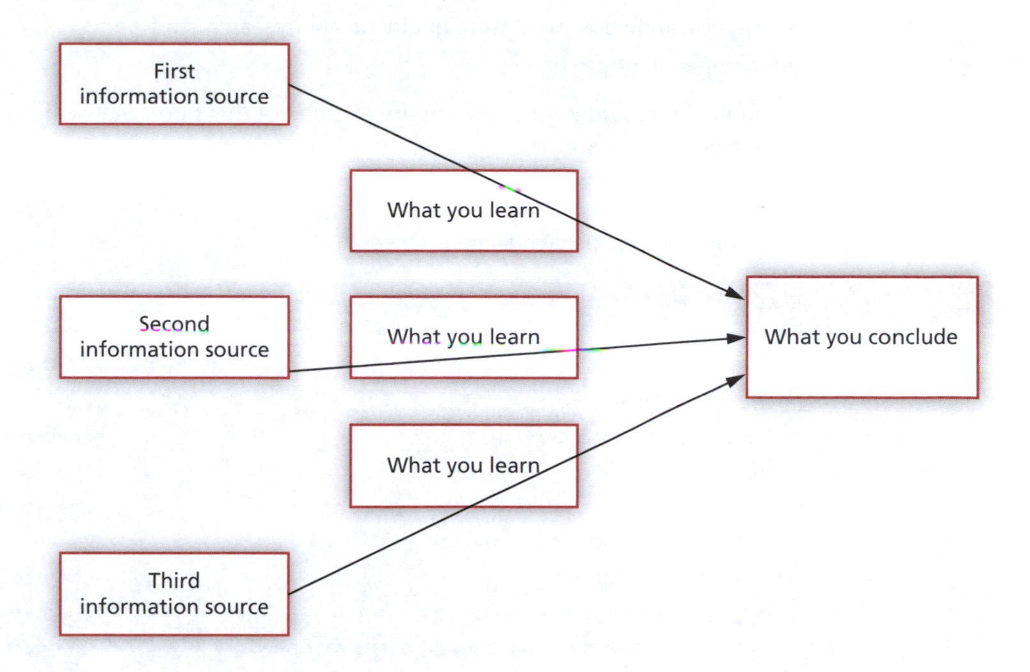

Figure 3.6 The principle of triangulation

While there may be differences in detail or nuance these are acceptable if the thrust from both sources is the same. If not, then we have to become an investigative researcher in order to expose and account for the differences.

(iii) Objectivity

Objectivity must always be a goal for every researcher, though limits can be placed on it. There could be a tension between our interpretation and our values and ethical position – for instance, if we were investigating the criminal justice system and we felt that it was being used in an unwarranted way against a particular group of young people. The researcher's ethics are always an issue and should be made explicit.

If this is done then the researcher is demonstrating integrity and integrity is the very foundation of research quality. Lack of integrity corrupts an investigation. To demonstrate integrity, we should make everything we do clear, from the values that drive us and the issues that concern us to the rationale for the decisions we take and the argument for the conclusions we reach. Only with this openness will other researchers be able to assess our motives, our methods and our judgements. In this case, they are our judge and jury.

3.3.5 Summary

Qualitative research is a powerful research approach with the potential to achieve even more than it has to date. It is enormously flexible but to realise its potential it has to be in the hands of the right type of researcher. To make full use of the qualitative approach we have to:

- believe in its value to resolve research issues;
- understand the implications of using a particular approach;

- demonstrate how we ensure quality in our research, and
- be open in all we do.

Table 3.6 provides guidance on the sections of this book that will support a qualitative research programme.

Table 3.6 Planning a qualitative approach to your research

Activity stage	Reference section
1. Identify a research area.	2.3, 2.4.2 and 3.5
2. Isolate a research issue and question.	2.3
3. Understand the research done by others.	Chapter 5
4. Identify your data needs.	Chapter 4
5. Identify your data sources.	Chapter 4
6. Consider whether to use an established methodology.	2.1.4
7. Identify how you will obtain your data.	Chapter 6
8. Identify what analytical method(s) you will use.	Chapters 10 and 11
9. Review your data collection process to make sure it meets your needs.	Chapters 8 and 9
10. Analyse data, draw conclusions.	3.3 and Chapter 14

3.4 Mixed methods

3.4.1 The idea of mixed methods research

Mixed methods research brings together quantitative and qualitative research approaches. It could include, for instance, using survey and experimental approaches together or an ethnographic approach with a case study. Mixing methods can be used for many research enquiries. Two Israeli researchers, Sara Arnon and Nirit Reichel, adopted the strategy in their study of what students understood by 'a good teacher' using quantitative analysis of data from a telephone survey and qualitative analysis where interviewees had a free response to questions (Arnon and Reichel, 2009). Scottish researchers, Edward Sosu, Angus McWilliam and Donald Gray also used mixed methods in their study of teachers' commitment to environmental education (Sosu et al., 2008). They collected data from teachers using attitude scales and analysed this using sophisticated statistical techniques to test a model of commitment that they had devised. They also collected data through interviews to explore how organisational, political and personal factors influenced individual teacher's commitment to environmental education.

It has, however, proved controversial to mix quantitative and qualitative approaches in a single research design, more so in some subjects than in others. In education and medicine the debate appears to have been particularly loud. Why should there be controversy? What is so controversial about a research design that follows a survey with a case study? Put like this, the combination seems eminently reasonable. The survey gives the general picture and the case study gives a richer understanding. However, for some researchers on either side of the quantitative/qualitative divide, the incorporation of a procedure from 'the other side' is tantamount to supping with the devil. Where does this attitude come from? A number of reasons can be identified.

- Some researchers so identify with an approach that any transgression against its principles is seen as an attack by vandals on the citadel of civilised research.
- Some subjects have a research tradition that is dominated by one approach to research. If the other approach is little known or valued, then the opportunities for combining methods are restricted and even if a researcher were to, it is likely that any resulting research papers would find difficulty in being published. Psychology, dominated for so long by a scientific methodology, possibly falls into this category.
- Some researchers misunderstand research epistemology and regard it not as a description of how research is conducted but as a rule book that specifies how *all* research should be conducted. If so, they greatly misunderstand research and look for answers to research problems in categorical rules rather than appreciating the need for the researcher to exercise judgement.
- Some researchers follow the implicit or even explicit guidance of those who fund research. The American academic Madhabi Chatterji (Chatterji, 2004) drew attention to this in the USA. Read Case Study 3.10 for more on this.
- Some traditions are given more weight when students are taught about research methods. In the UK, the Commission on the Social Sciences (an independent review of the work of the social sciences conducted under the auspices of the Academy of Learned Societies for the Social Sciences) expressed concern over the 'deficit of quantitative skills' (Commission on the Social Sciences, 2003, p. 57). For Professor Stephen Gorard and Dr Chris Taylor, both British educational researchers, the small

Case study 3.10 The *What Works* clearinghouse

A 'clearinghouse' is a repository for research and information. With the growth in knowledge and new technology, the concept is now associated with accessible on-line databases.

The *What Works* clearinghouse was set up in 2002 by the US Department of Education as a repository or what works in education. The context was the need to facilitate the adoption of educational processes that deliver good, if not always the best, results. The use of the term 'what works' indicates that there is a judgement made about what is more and what is less effective. The description of the website as a 'trusted source of scientific evidence' gives a strong clue as to the nature of the evidence that is valued. The process for assessing evidence is fully described. Two factors lie at its heart:

- the statistical significance of the result, and
- the quality of the research design.

It was this specification of a research style that Chatterji (2004) was referring to in his paper. The American Educational Research Association, the American Evaluation Association and a large number of individual researchers also protested the narrowness of the approved research design. They argued that the approach would not work in some circumstances and that there were many situations where an alternative approach would produce more credible results. More serious for the research community is the potential for the clearinghouse to distort the character of American educational research over the longer term.

Why should assessors be so specific about the research design? The answer probably has two components. First, quantitative designs fit more easily than others into cost-benefit analysis – and this is just the sort of approach to decision making that governments use. Second, for those used to taking decisions on the basis of numerical evidence, qualitative research can seem 'wishy washy', vague and unconvincing, even more so when the researchers clearly have an axe to grind!

Read more about *What Works* on www.whatworks.ed.gov.

number of quantitative studies in education is a consequence of this overemphasis on qualitative research approaches in research methods courses (Gorard and Taylor, 2004, p. 9). There is, however, another dimension to this, which is the attitude of students to numeracy and their capability in mathematics. The implication of this is that the root causes are to be found at an earlier stage in a person's education. The outcome of all of this is that students are taught more about qualitative approaches than about quantitative and are less able or inclined to use quantitative. Hopefully this book will help redress the imbalance. Quantitative approaches are illuminating and need not be difficult.

3.4.2 Mixed methods research: is it a new approach?

The main issue surrounding the mixed methods is whether it constitutes a new, distinctive approach to research that bears comparison with quantitative and qualitative approaches. There are many who say that it does. Others disagree and there are yet others who see it as a poorly disguised attempt by positivists to undermine the purity of qualitative research. We need to be aware of this debate, not least because we have to decide how important we really think it is.

(i) The arguments for

The claim that combining methods across the quantitative/qualitative divide is a new approach to research is increasingly being heard. Amongst those who have made it recently are Burke Johnson and Anthony Onwegbuzie (2004), two American researchers who referred to it as 'a paradigm whose time has come'. Stephen Gorard and Chris Taylor (2004) have called it 'a third methodological movement'.

The combination of methods is actually a lot older than this. Others have traced its use and the terms to describe it back to the 1950s, and combining methods was relatively unproblematic until the 1980s and 1990s. It is difficult to understand why it became an issue just at this time but it almost certainly has something to do with the research culture in the second half of the twentieth century. As the numbers of academics and the scale of academic work grew so camps were formed representing areas of interest and preferences for a research approach. Over time an intellectual iron curtain grew up behind which the two research traditions defined and refined their operating principles in such a way as to promote exclusion. Proper research required adherence to the rules. It was in this environment that those who brought methods together in order to understand an issue had to argue their case. The appropriate basis on which to rest their case was the construction of a third way with its own distinctive epistemology.

What does research have to look like before it can be said to possess a distinct tradition? Very simply, it should have rules of procedure. This is the case for both quantitative and qualitative approaches, though it is fair to say that those for qualitative research are less prescriptive than for quantitative and apply at the level of methodology rather than epistemology. In other words, qualitative rules tell us how to carry out a case study, for example, while quantitative analysis rests on the principle of randomness. Some order is emerging in the ways in which methods can be combined, though these are either conceptual typologies or operational guidance based on what seems to work. It is difficult at this stage to recognise a claim for a distinctive methodology, though the need to be flexible in the way we use research methods to resolve specific research issues is now much more widely accepted.

(ii) The argument that mixed methods are fundamentally positivist

There are some, however, who would counter the argument that something new is emerging when we combine research methods. Lynne Giddings, a New Zealand nurse educator and researcher, calls mixed methods research 'positivism dressed up in drag' (Giddings, 2006). She acknowledges that the youthfulness of the approach means that its theoretical and philosophical base is relatively underdeveloped but is critical of its being positioned as a new research style (a) because of its continuing reference to its parent research traditions and (b) because quantitative principles must strongly influence the research design, as she argues, 'Ideologically mixed-methods continues the privileging and dominance of the positivist scientific tradition' (p. 202). This is an unusual argument to make because inevitably good quantitative research has to conform to positivist principles and if these requirements have negative implications for necessary qualitative procedures, then it is likely that the research strategy is inappropriate. There is a sense in Giddings' assessment that hers is a defensive broadside from a qualitative researcher who feels beleaguered by the rapid growth in the dialogue on mixed methods. Her claim that quantitative methods are 'privileged' in a mixed methods approach tempts one to say, 'So what?' Equality may be a good social and economic goal in an educational setting but it does not make sense in a research context where the issue and the quality of the research findings are the key features. The real concern must be with the quality of the research design and its ability to say something meaningful about the research issue. However, while her argument may prove to be just an aside in the evolution of mixed methods research, she may well be correct in inferring that the explosion of mixed methods on the research scene is the latest example of fashion in research practice, as researchers promoting their careers join a rolling bandwagon. We will not know the answer to this until new researchers make their mark on the research world.

(iii) The argument against

The absence of an accepted conceptual infrastructure for mixed methods certainly supports the argument against the approach being a new tradition, though it is not a watertight case. Purists on both sides of the qualitative/quantitative divide will attack the combination of approaches, arguing that chalk and cheese are just not compatible. What we might care to think about, however, is that as the world evolves, frameworks that do not change will gradually lose touch with what they seek to manage. Innovation is a necessity in a changing environment, in research as in anything else. Mixed methods may not be the right innovation but the approach should not be rejected on the basis that it does not fit with what worked in the past. In research, as in life, the past is another country.

3.4.3 The character of mixed methods research

Because researchers do not agree on whether mixed methods constitute a distinctive research tradition, it is not surprising that its character is varied. Those who argue that it should be treated on an equal footing with quantitative and qualitative traditions develop typologies of combinations of methods. Pragmatists accept these typologies but do not regard them as articles of research faith to which they should adhere.

(i) Frameworks for combining methods

Dr Abbas Tashakkori and Dr Charles Teddlie, two leading American mixed methods researchers, distinguish several approaches to combining methods (Tashakkori and

Teddlie, 2003):

- *Mixed* **method** *design,* where the research approach includes both qualitative and quantitative data collection and data analysis operating in parallel or sequentially. They also include the conversion of data from one format to another (that is, from qualitative to quantitative).
- *Mixed* **model** *design,* in which qualitative and quantitative approaches are integrated throughout the study. The trigger to a mixed model design is the research question, which should take the research in directions that require both approaches.
- **Multilevel** *design,* in which one approach dominates at one level and the other at another. In terms of level, Tashakkori and Teddlie give child and family as an example. Quantitative data may be collected on the educational attainment of children in single parent families (the higher level) and qualitative data on the life experiences of children (the lower level) in order to understand how this contributes to educational outcomes. Class group and pupil group, year group and class group, and national and local are also appropriate level differentiators.

While it is useful to have a representation of options, it does not take us far in understanding the nature and value of a mixed methods approach. This is what we shall consider next.

(ii) What can mixing methods achieve?

By asking the question, 'What can mixing methods achieve?' we shift the focus of our attention from a broad approach to research towards the methods we might use. We leave behind the arguments of research purists that the combination of methods is not epistemologically possible and ask, pragmatically, 'What if . . . ?' What if we were to rephrase the question? What if we were to collect data in this way and analyse it that way? Can we construct a credible argument? What happens when we break loose from the constraints imposed by research purists? The reality is that we are likely to find that the world does not fall apart, the results seem sensible and, gradually, ideas about good ways of proceeding take shape. These ideas could become the foundations for a new epistemology even if we are not there yet.

So what can be achieved by combining methods?

(a) Triangulation

First we should note the increased potential for new ways of triangulating evidence (see Figure 3.6). Gorard and Taylor (2004, pp. 44–46) make the interesting point that the introduction of two perspectives gives us a better fix not just on the measurement of an issue but also on our appreciation of it. They point out that the use of quantitative and qualitative approaches together allow researchers to compare results in a complementary way. They cannot validate each other with any precision but they can reinforce each other. This idea of complementarity can operate in different ways in the research process. It can be used to investigate critical areas or incidents; it can also work at a higher level to provide rich detail and to improve understanding, for example, when a large scale survey is supported by a case study or a number of case studies.

In summary, triangulation takes on a different mantle when qualitative and quantitative approaches are brought to bear on an issue. It is less concerned with the accuracy of measurement than it is with the correctness of the insight and the legitimacy of the interpretation. Read the short Case Study 3.11 and you will understand this.

Case study 3.11 Getting the right interpretation

This story does not concern education but the world of design and designers. It is not written down but most designers seem to have heard of it.

Designers of a new airport terminal wished to understand how passengers and those waiting to meet friends and family used existing terminal buildings. To do this they conducted questionnaire surveys. We have to assume that the respondents constituted an accurate representation of airport users and that the subgroups of users (passengers, 'meeters and greeters', men, women, different age groups and so on) responded in sufficient numbers to make the analysis of their answers a reasonable exercise. The analysis of the responses of male passengers showed a high use of the lavatories. This did not surprise the researchers who put this down to the stress of flying. When they looked at the statistics they noticed that the use was not just a high proportion of male passengers going to the lavatories but that a large number were going several times. Either men's but not women's bladder control was particularly poor or something else was happening. And the quantitative study could tell the designers no more.

Someone thought it would be sensible to follow men and see what happened in the lavatories. This is obviously a qualitative research strategy. It also provided a new perspective and source of evidence to test the 'stress creates the need to visit lavatories' theory (thereby triangulating the interpretation). Now we have to add something here; this all took place in the early years of mass flying, when travelling by air was something that made you different from the majority of people. So, back to the story. What the researchers found was the men had assumed responsibility for managing their group through the check-in and boarding procedures. When they went into the lavatories it was not in order to use the facilities but to hear more clearly the announcements about take-off and departure gates because the airport concourse and the departure lounge were too noisy to hear them clearly. The designers found out that the solution to overcrowded lavatories was not to increase their number but to improve the public address system!

And the moral of this . . . ethnographic methods saved a costly mistake because it is more expensive to dig drains and put in pipes than it is to put in loudspeakers.

Whether this is apocryphal or an urban myth, I do not know – but it *is* a good example!

(b) Exploration of the research issue

The second thing we can do by combining methods is to unravel and to unfold an issue. There are many research situations whose boundaries, processes and internal relationships are either unknown or incompletely understood. Stacie Petter and Michael Gallivan, both at Georgia State University in the USA, identify three situations where exploration or unfolding is appropriate (Petter and Gallivan, 2004).

1. Refining our research, for example, using interviews to shape questionnaires.
2. Looking at things that are different from what was expected or at unusual or extreme results (this is one thing we are beginning to take more notice of – the unusual as well as the usual).
3. Expanding our investigation to expose and assess more issues and factors at work.

The implication of an unfolding research process is that an entire plan of action is not possible. Stage by stage, new decisions are taken to move the project forward in ways that are informed by results already obtained or questions that arise (we might recognise that this is the basis of action research, see section 2.1.4). For an individual researcher, however, this has dangers, not least of which is that the resource implications of the process are not accurately known.

3.4.4 What can go wrong?

(i) Double trouble

The answer is that anything that can go wrong with either pure qualitative or pure quantitative research can also go wrong when you mix the approaches. The issue for researchers working alone is whether they know sufficient abut each approach to be able to sidestep problems. If we are more capable with just one approach, there are three courses of action open to us. First, we can learn what we need to know (if we are more capable with qualitative research we will have to learn more about quantitative). This is all right as long as we know that there is a problem in the first place. What is more, even if we do, it may not be an effective use of our time. Alternatively we can ask the advice of an expert in the other approach. However, by far the best solution is to collaborate with someone whose expertise complements ours. This may be difficult for our first research project, which is usually an individual effort, so we should ensure that we test our ideas about a mixed methods approach with someone whose advice we value.

(ii) Linking research questions(s) with research method(s)

With a mixed methods approach, the link between our research question and the way we conduct our research may be more complex than if we were using either a qualitative or quantitative approach by itself. We combine methods in order to reflect dimensions and nuances in the research issue. Almost certainly we will pick these up from the reading that led us to identify the area as interesting in the first place. The actual specification of the research question requires great care on our part. We must explore the issue through existing research and theoretical perspectives before we can set out the research question or questions. If we have research questions, they may be sequenced, that is, in order to answer one, we have to obtain an answer to another. The nature of the research question will shape the character of our research design. Sometimes we will have the option of using quantitative or qualitative approaches, sometimes we can use only one approach. Whatever our situation, we will need a robust link between question and method. By robust, we mean that we have to be sure that the method will generate data appropriate to the question and, with a mixed method approach, it is unlikely that our research question will be just a sentence; it is more likely to be a short paragraph outlining the complexity of the issue to be explored, followed by a series of questions that deal with the dimensions of the question.

(iii) Going off-piste

Exploring virgin territory is adventurous and exciting; it is also dangerous. Yet without people doing new things, the boundaries of mixed methods research will not be pushed out. Doing things in the way that the research question wants them done is what a mixed methods approach should be all about. We should not be afraid to fail (and my view is that students should not be penalised for adventurous failure) but it is something that might happen. To use an analogy, how do you ski off-piste and still stay safe?

The answer is by looking at guidelines put forward by other researchers, judging whether you should work within them and, if you do not, then make clear why you have not and explain how you determined your way forward. What guidelines can we identify?

- In many instances one approach, either qualitative or quantitative will dominate. If there is conflict or the potential for conflict between the research methods that you choose to generate your data, then those from the dominant method should generally be preferred.

- Data sets should talk to and inform each other. If, for instance, our research is into the message that students take away from sex education classes, we could, first, survey schools to identify the character of the sex education curriculum and teaching and learning approach. We would use this data to create a typology of approaches. Next we would talk to students, perhaps in focus groups (see Chapter 11), one for each curriculum and learning type we have identified. In this way, our qualitative data informs the typology created by our survey.
- It is preferable to have flexible designs that can respond to unexpected findings or that can accommodate additional data. This does not preclude quantitative methods being dominant but we could have problems in reaching a sound conclusion if the basis on which we collected our data did not meet the quite rigorous conditions that they require. For instance, if as well as using focus groups in our study of sex education, we wanted to understand students' attitude to sexual activity between young people, we might use a questionnaire approach (see Chapter 8) and sample students in their final year to get a good representation of attitudes in our study area (see Chapter 6). When we come to analyse the data, however, we realise that the analysis of the subgroups we want to look at (for example, are attitudes of girls and boys in faith schools different from those in other schools) means that our sample size should be larger. However, a school year has passed since we last sampled and the group we sampled has now left. If we sample the next year group, we are sampling a different population and there is a chance that the passage of time or different group influences might affect attitudes.
- Mixed approaches are particularly appropriate for certain types of research:
  - going beyond showing cause and effect to understand how the cause creates the effect;
  - getting to grips with complex issues involving the interplay of behaviour, attitudes, culture and values or understanding what are called 'wicked problems', problems where attempted solutions merely produce more problems. Wicked problems in education might include social exclusion, pupil attainment and intergenerational reproduction of social values, non-attendance at school (an aspect of the first problem but a wicked problem in its own right), changing the culture in a university, school or college and drug taking and alcohol abuse amongst young people;
  - evaluation of project or activity processes and outcomes;
  - long-term longitudinal studies of behaviour or performance or attitudes and parallel studies of changes in the group's social and cultural context;
  - action research, particularly where the research takes the form of an experiment involving pre-test, intervention and post-test and where the insights of more qualitative assessments can add considerable value.

3.4.4 Summary

Mixed methods in research are growing in importance. There is now a journal dedicated to the approach (*Journal of Mixed Methods Research*, Sage). Combining methods can be powerful. They are cost-effective ways of dealing with complex issues. However, they do require us to take great care at the stage of specifying the research issue. While they require competence over a wide range of methods, this should not put us off. The methods that we are most likely to be combining are really quite robust and will take some compromise with perfection. The real danger is of not knowing when we have done things wrongly. An important member of any research project is a critical friend. Who is yours? Table 3.7 shows the issues we have to consider in mixed methods research and where they are dealt with in this book.

Table 3.7 Planning a mixed methods approach to your research

Activity stage	Qualitative analysis	Quantitative analysis
1. Identify a research area.	2.4.2 and 3.5	2.4.2 and 3.5
2. Isolate a research issue and question.	2.3	2.3
3. Understand the research done by others.	Chapter 5	Chapter 5
4. Develop a model of the factors that influence outcomes.		2.2.2
5. For each factor you assess, construct a research hypothesis and a null hypothesis.		3.2.2 and 3.2.3
6. Identify your data needs.	Chapter 4	Chapter 4
7. Identify your data sources.	Chapter 4	Chapter 4
8. Consider whether to use an established methodology.	2.1.4	
9. Identify how you will obtain your data.	Chapter 6	Chapter 6
10. Identify what analytical method(s) you will use.	Chapters 10 and 11	
Identify what statistical test procedures you will use.		Chapters 12 and 13
11. Review your data collection process to make sure it meets your needs.	Chapters 8 and 9	Chapters 8 and 9
12. Analyse data, draw conclusions.	3.3 and Chapter 14	
13. Review problems of analysis and inference and, if unresolved, start over again.		3.2.3
14. Apply test and assess likelihood that result occurred by chance.		3.2.3 and Chapter 13

3.5 Outlining your research strategy

At the end of Chapter 2, you were asked to specify your research questions. Now you are nearly at the end of this chapter, you are in a position to move on and to sketch out your research strategy.

3.5.1 Revisiting your research question

In the light of what this chapter has said about research approaches, you should look again at your research question and link it with one of the three research approaches that we have covered. Look at Activity 3.1.

3.5.2 Outlining your research approach

When you are confident about your research question(s), the next stage is to start shaping your research approach.

Activity 3.1 Furthering your research project

- Does your core research question fit into any of the types that were considered in Chapter 2 (see Table 2.2)? If the question requires data or causal analysis, you may be looking at a quantitative approach. Other types of question could be either qualitative or mixed methods, though evaluation, policy analysis and action research may predispose you to mixed methods.
- Are you concerned with outcomes or causal relationships? In which case, look towards a quantitative approach. If your research is more about understanding processes, a qualitative or mixed methods approach may be more suitable.
- Now that you have a better understanding of quantitative, qualitative and mixed methods approaches, would you like to revisit your research question? In particular, does your research question need to be unpicked and presented as a series of linked questions? If so, can these be answered at the same time or do some need to be answered before others? What sort of research approach do these questions imply?
- Take a draft of your research questions to someone whose judgement you trust. Explain why your questions take the form they do. What other formulations did you consider and reject – and why?

(i) If your research will follow a quantitative approach

In this case you need to do the following:

- Specify your research hypothesis and your null hypothesis.
- Determine whether you will use an experimental design or a survey design or some combination.
- If you are planning to use a survey design, make sure you understand about your data needs (Chapter 4), data collection (Chapter 6) and data analysis (Chapters 10, 12 and 13). Pay particular attention to the sections on statistical inference and confidence in Chapter 13.
- If you are planning to use an experimental design, set up the framework for the design, identify the permissions you need to obtain, produce the intervention (for example, a new approach to teaching or classroom management) and specify the conditions under which it must operate. Read the sections on data needs (Chapter 4), data collection (Chapter 6) and data analysis (Chapters 12 and 13). You need also to be aware of issues around inference and confidence (Chapter 13).

(ii) If your research will follow a qualitative approach

Your next steps are set out below:

- Consider what approach or combination of approaches you are going to use. Review what was said about these in Chapter 2 and look at the examples in Chapter 14. You should note that the approaches set out here are not mutually exclusive. Evaluation and case study have a lot in common. Ethnographic approaches can be used throughout all the methods.
- Identify what sort of data you will need in order to produce an answer to your question. Look at the types of data described in Chapter 4 and the ways of obtaining data in Chapters 6, 8 and 9.
- Consider how you will process your data (Chapter 12) and how you will assemble the evidence to answer your question. Remember that your question can be far broader than a hypothesis (for example, 'Why is this ethnic group under-represented in higher education?') but it can also be phrased so that it is effectively a testable hypothesis.

(iii) If your research will follow a mixed approach

The next steps are broadly the same as for the qualitative approach but at each stage you have to identify and follow through on the requirements for both qualitative and quantitative approaches.

- Link your research question(s) to appropriate quantitative and qualitative procedures.
- Determine the sequence of research approaches (will qualitative data inform quantitative analysis? Are they collected together or one after the other?), paying particular attention to the resource implications of methods that you will be using at the same time so that you are sure that you will be able to manage them.
- For each method, determine how you will collect and analyse the data.
- Consider how you will bring the data together. Will you covert it to a numerical standard, a qualitative standard (using one of the approaches in Chapter 12) or will you use an argued case?

Summary

- Quantitative, qualitative and mixed approaches to research are all appropriate for education research. Each has its own character and way of working. Quantitative research is more constraining in its requirements than either qualitative or mixed methods.
- The approach we select should be based on the research issue as the starting point, not on an abstract commitment to a particular style of research approach.
- Quantitative research can analyse data collected from surveys or from experimental situations. Both approaches require rigorous conditions in data collection.
- Qualitative research focuses on understanding people's life experience. This requires researchers to look in depth at their subjects. Qualitative research is, therefore, usually smaller in scale than quantitative.
- Mixed methods research combines both qualitative and quantitative methods of data collection and analysis. The combination of the two approaches produces understanding with deep insight over a large population. This can make it a very cost-effective research strategy.

By the end of this first part of the book you should have:

- an appreciation of factors that can influence people's approach to research;
- an understanding of the three broad approaches to conducting research (quantitative, qualitative and mixed methods) as well of specific methodologies (case studies, evaluation, ethnography and action research in Chapter 2 and survey and analysis and experimentation in Chapter 3);
- a route map of the areas that require your special attention in data collection and analysis.

As you learn more about research procedures, you should revisit your research question and your research design in order to refine and update your strategy and plan. Remember, a good researcher cycles through the process of developing a research approach several times. At each stage of reviewing the plan, and then as you analyse your data, you should ask yourself one final question:

Did I miss the gorilla?

Further reading

Mixed methods research

Teddlie, C. and Tashakkori, A. (2009) *Foundations of Mixed Methods Research*, Sage, Thousand Oaks, Calif.

At the heart of mixed methods research is the belief that it is what we find out that is important and not that there is a single 'proper' way to do research. If you want to understand the arguments for the distinctiveness of the mixed methods approach, Teddlie and Tashakkori's text is good.

Experimentation

Christensen, L.B. (2004) *Experimental Methodology*, Pearson Education, London.

The step up to reading about experimentation at a more advanced level can be a big one. Christensen's book, however, will not stress you too much. Surprisingly for a specialist book, he includes a chapter on non-experimental methods. There are three chapters on specific experimental issues (variables, validity and control techniques) and three on experimental design.

The ecological fallacy

Longley, P. and Batty, M. (1996) *Spatial Analysis: Modelling in a GIS Environment*, GeoInformation International, Cambridge.

The danger of the ecological fallacy is particularly great if we look at patterns of data in a country, region or town. The sort of analysis that is often undertaken by researchers is to look at the socio-economic in relation to school performance, or criminality or health. It is not surprising then to find that geographers have often been in the lead in seeking a solution that enables them to analyse data based on spatial units. This book gives some explanation of the approaches that are being tried.

References

Arnon, S. and Reichel, N. (2009) 'Closed and Open-Ended Question Tools in a Telephone Survey About "The Good Teacher": an Example of a Mixed Method Study', *Journal of Mixed Methods Research*, 3(2), 172–196.

Chatterji, M. (2004) 'Evidence on "What Works": An Argument for Extended-Term Mixed-Method (ETTM) Evaluation Designs', *Educational Researcher*, 33(9), 3–13.

Commission on the Social Sciences (2003) *Great Expectations: the Social Sciences in Britain*, Academy of Learned Societies for the Social Sciences, London.

Gelilke, C. and Biehl, K. (1934) 'Certain Effects of Grouping on the Size of the Correlation Coefficients in Census Tract Material', *Journal of the American Statistical Association*, 29, 169–170.

Giddings, L.S.(2006) 'Mixed-Methods Research – Positivism Dressed in Drag?' *Journal of Research in Nursing*, 11(3), 195–203.

Gorard, S. and Taylor, C. (2004) *Combining Methods in Educational and Social Research*, Open University Press, Maidenhead.

Johnson, R.B. and Onwegbuzie, A.J. (2004) 'Mixed Methods Research: a Research Paradigm whose Time has Come', *Educational Researcher*, 33(7), 14–26.

Longley, N., Holt, T., Steel, D. and Tranmer, M. (1996) 'Analysing, Modelling and Resolving the Ecological Fallacy', in Longley P. and Batty, M. (eds) (1996) *Spatial Analysis: Modelling in a GIS Environment*, GeoInformation International, Cambridge, 25–40.

Longley, P. and Batty, M. (1996) *Spatial Analysis: Modelling in a GIS Environment*, GeoInformation International, Cambridge.

McLean, A. (2003) *The Motivated School*, Paul Chapman Publishing, London.

Petter, S. and Gallivan, M.J. (2004) *Proceedings of the 37th Hawaii International Conference on Systems Sciences*, IEEE Computer Society Press, Washington.

Robinson, W. (1950) 'Ecological Correlations and the Behaviour of Individuals', *American Sociological Review*, 15(3), 351–357.

Simons, D.J. and Chabris, C. F. (1999) 'Gorillas in our Midst: Sustained Inattentional Blindness for Dynamic Events', *Perception*, 28, 1059–1074.

Sosu, E., McWilliam, A. and Gray, D. (2008) 'The Complexities of Teachers' Commitment to Environmental Education', *Journal of Mixed Methods Research*, 2(2), 169–189.

Tashakkori, A. and Teddlie, C. (2003) *Handbook of Mixed Methods in Social and Behavioral Research*, Sage, Thousand Oaks.

Whyte, W.F. (1943) *Street Corner Society: The Social Structure of an Italian Slum*, University of Chicago Press.

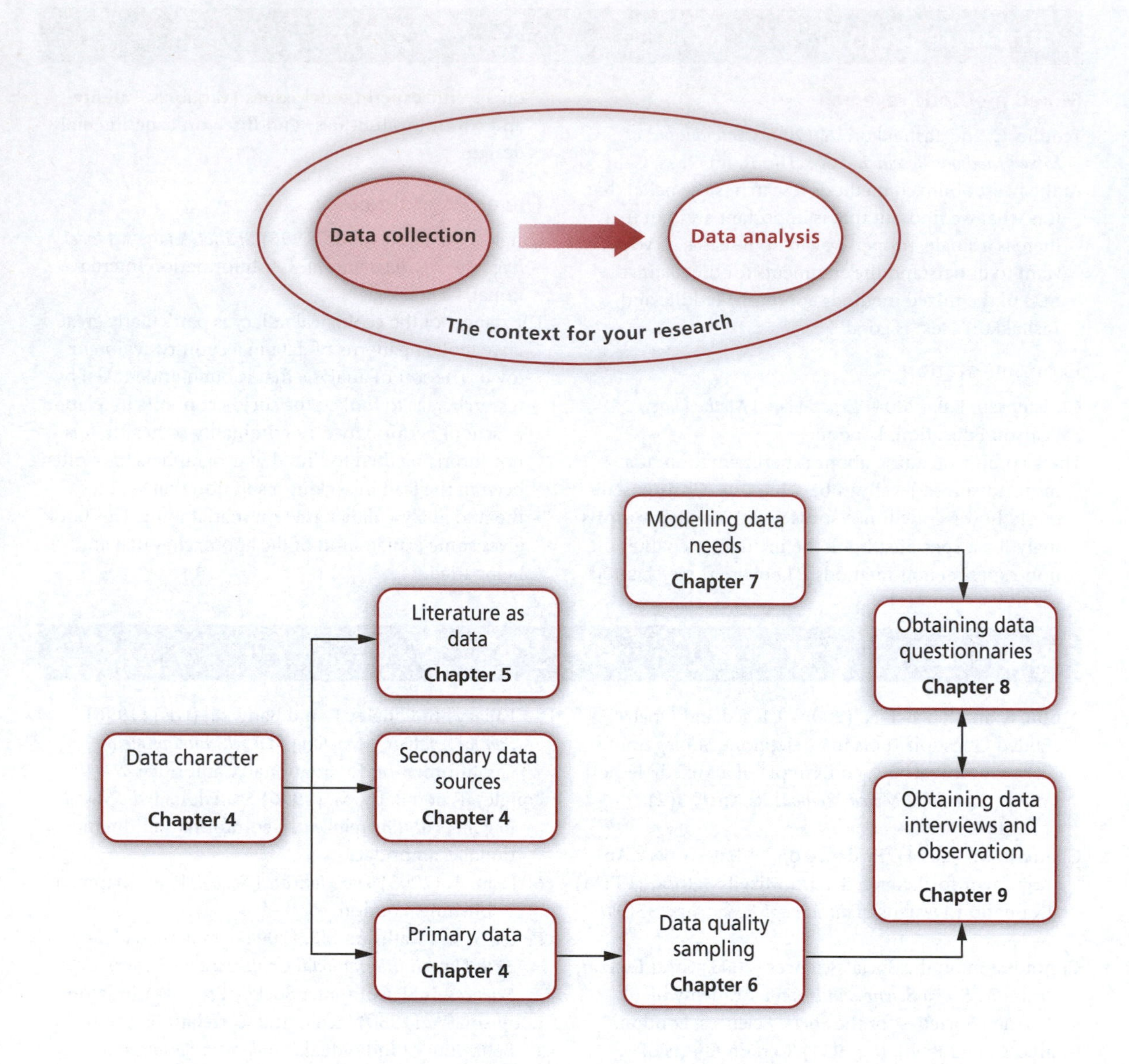

Data collection
Data analysis
The context for your research
Modelling data needs
Chapter 7
Literature as data
Chapter 5
Obtaining data questionnaries
Chapter 8
Data character
Chapter 4
Secondary data sources
Chapter 4
Obtaining data interviews and observation
Chapter 9
Primary data
Chapter 4
Data quality sampling
Chapter 6

Part 2

THE PROCESS OF DATA COLLECTION

In Part 2 we look in detail at the process of data collection. What we will learn are that there are different sources for our data and many ways of collecting them. The researcher's skill lies in combining these in order to ensure a sufficient quantity and quality of data to answer the research question. One consequence of combining methods in data collection is that research often moves towards a mixed methods approach.

We shall approach the data collection in the following way. First we shall give an overview of data in Chapter 4. This covers such things as ways in which we can categorise data and ways in which we can measure them. We shall look in detail at secondary data, because the sources of secondary data that are now available to us are so large. Chapter 5 considers literature as data and examines how we should make use of what others have written throughout our research programme. In Chapter 6, we return to primary data and how we can ensure the quality of our data when we deal with samples rather than the whole population. Chapter 7 introduces a way of looking at the research process that helps us identify the data we need to resolve our research issues by analysing the research question and representing our analysis as a model. Textbook authors do not always introduce this approach but it does sharpen our analytical skills. Finally in Chapters 8 and 9 we look at ways of collecting data through questionnaires, interview and observation.

Chapter contents

Chapter 4

DATA: ASSEMBLING THE RESEARCH TOOLKIT

Key themes

This chapter is all about understanding and practising. The objective is to help you feel comfortable exploring data sources and using new data in your research.

- The first part of this chapter is concerned with understanding the characteristics of data, specifically:
  - The difference between data and information.
  - The difference between qualitative and quantitative data.
  - How the information in data can be measured.
  - Where we can obtain our data.
  - The difference between primary and secondary data.
  - Issues we have to be aware of when accessing secondary data.
- The last part of the chapter introduces the riches of the Internet and the many sources of data for education research that exist. There are examples activities to push out the boundaries of our understanding of research.

Introduction

One of the surprising things about texts on education research methods is that they say so little about data. Other books that tell us how to do something also usually inform us about the fundamentals of the things that we will use. Take cookery books, for example. They usually give some insight into the basic elements of the process and style of cuisine. In most cases this concerns ingredients and the guidance ranges from what to look for in order to identify quality, to information about ingredients that are not part of a cultural background. But texts on research methods are, at best, limited or often silent when it comes to data. This is surprising because the volume of data that is publicly available is growing by huge leaps each year and many people are unaware of the vast riches of data that are a click or two away on the Internet. In this chapter we will examine what we can use as data and how we can measure them, look at data from several perspectives (each with their own method of classification) and finally review the wealth of data that are now available on websites worldwide.

4.1 Why do we need to look at data?

Why do we need to consider data as a separate issue? The answer is that data are the material out of which we construct our research argument. We should, therefore, understand what constitutes data and what characteristics it can have. Once we know what we can use as data, we can then consider how it might affect the way in which we phrase our research questions or how we go about structuring the research process. It is important that we know this because certain types of data lead to particular types of analysis, which themselves require certain procedures to be followed in data collection. It is not good enough to collect the data and then think about how we are going to process it to extract the information we need for our research. So, in summary, we need to consider data as part of the whole process of planning a research enquiry and, to do this, we should know what data are available and what the implications of using it are.

There is, as well, another reason why we should look at data as a research issue – and this is, possibly, the most important reason. We are, all of us, conditioned by our education and our experiences; we are limited by our knowledge, our understanding and by our imagination. As researchers, we should constantly challenge these limits by seeing how others conceive of and create data. We should venture outside our comfort zone of experience and knowledge to see what other subjects use as data. We need to be aware of what other disciplines that have an interest in our research field are doing so that their findings can become our data. For instance, if we are exploring behavioural problems in the classroom and are not aware that food type and food additives might be factors in understanding a child's ability to concentrate, then we might find ourselves in the situation of promoting solutions without understanding the cause. If we are researching child development, biochemistry and genetics may well be fields that we should get to know, given the rapid advances that have been made in our understanding about the significance of these areas for our lives (and deaths). And, if our interests as educational researchers spread this far, who is to say that we should not see blood and urine tests as part of our battery of techniques, in much the same way as we accept the use of psychometric tests? We might also ask, if it is reasonable to try to understand a child's emotional state as a factor influencing learning behaviour, what is to stop an imaginative researcher going further and drawing on reported dreams for other insights?

This is not an argument for weird research in education; most research is unlikely to stray beyond the bounds of conventional data. It is, however, a plea that researchers should feel able to break the bounds of convention and should use whatever data provide insight for their analyses. We should be encouraged to be imaginative in our approach to research and be creative in our appreciation of what data can be used. Just because it has not been used before does not mean that there should be a ban on using a new type of data in the future. Case Study 4.1 shows how an innovative approach to research and data solved a problem for some economics researchers.

4.2 The purpose of data

If we go along with the need to be imaginative about research and data, we could be forgiven for thinking that a section on the purpose of data is a little superfluous; after all, how else would we answer our research question without appropriate data? There is no

Case study 4.1 Improving understanding through proxy research

This case study is about some research undertaken by the National Bureau for Economic Research, an independent US research organisation. It is not about education but about corruption.

The issue for the researchers was how far can corruption undermine the effective economic functioning in a country and how endemic is it in society. But how do you study corruption? By its very nature it is not something that is out in the open. Asking people whether they take bribes is unlikely to get us many affirmative responses. It is like asking a waiter what the dish of the day is like. If we are told that it is excellent, we have learnt nothing. But if we are told that it is not worth having, we have learnt a lot. The trouble is, we do not know what we have learnt, is the food bad, or has the waiter had a row with the chef? Back to bribery. Asking people if they ever have to give bribes may give you some insight into the scale of the problem but it will not tell you much about the culture that allows bribery to exist.

So what did the researchers do? They looked for situations where people could behave corruptly, openly and without penalty. To do this, they chose the behaviour of diplomats and the non-payment of parking fines in New York. Their approach was to look at the number of parking violations in relation to measures of corruption scores for each nation (this was effectively a test of those surrogate measures of corruption). These measures are calculated annually by the World Bank and influence Bank lending policies. The argument was that where there was a national culture of corruption, this would carry over into the practice of diplomats not paying parking fines.

The researchers found that there was a strong link between the level of corruption as measured by the World Bank and the number of unpaid parking fines. The same analysis was conducted for London with the same results.

What conclusions did the researchers draw:

- corruption is socially and culturally determined;
- the values that create corruption are deep-seated and continue to drive behaviour in different cultural contexts;
- legal remedies are no match for these underpinning sentiments and values but financial penalties can influence behaviour.

If you wonder how this can be relevant to education, then think about the issue of how we build an ethical society and, from that, consider its implications for dealing with crime and abuse and developing a society at ease with itself and where opportunity is valued. Corruption is only one instance of an interconnected set of problems facing societies at every stage of development.

Source: Fisman, R. and Miguel, E. (2006) 'Cultures of Corruption: Evidence from Diplomatic Parking Tickets', *Working Paper 2312*, National Bureau of Economic Research, Cambridge, MA.

argument with this but what we need to unpick is the link between the data and the answer to our research question.

The simple fact is that the data do not directly produce our answers. Data is raw stuff. Think of it as being clay in the hands of the potter. Only with the potter's skill does the clay become something that is attractive or useful. Data are neutral; they just sit there waiting to be discovered and waiting for their 'message' (their informational content) to be extracted. The role of a researcher is to identify the right data and make them give up their message. In other words, researchers have to extract from data the information that is useful to their research, information that will help them answer their research question.

But that is not the end of the process; researchers also have to convert their information into evidence. In research it is not enough to assemble our data and then present them to our audiences. We have to interpret it so that people reading our work can see what conclusions we are drawing and then judge whether they would do the same. If, before we begin our research, we understand how our argument might logically progress, then we could use this insight to influence the type of the data we assemble. Supposing we were studying classroom behaviour; it might be enough to assemble data on two groups of children, those reported by teachers as being disruptive and those who were not. However, it would also be valuable to combine this with observations on parenting behaviour, family lifestyles, and classroom behaviour through the day. If similar data had been collected by researchers at some point in the past and archived, we could use it to give us a temporal perspective. If we are not aware of what data exist and what we can use, then we will always be disadvantaged.

The purpose of this chapter is to give a sense of what data are available to us as education researchers.

4.3 What types of data are there?

The information that we need in order to answer our research question is normally fairly obvious. If we are investigating on what basis young people choose an institution at which to continue their higher (university level) education there are two sources of data, either the students themselves or applications and admissions numbers to institutions, disaggregated by subject if possible. Using one or more of a range of approaches including focus groups, interviews and questionnaires, we can get the students to give us the reasons that caused them to apply where they did. If we were to use application and admission data then all we can do is *infer* students' reasoning in relation to other indicators, such as published quality assessments, composite rankings of standards as well as assumptions about the appropriateness of the culture and character of institutions. If we knew the home locations of the students we could also say something about the influence of proximity or the perceived character of institutions.

In other words, these two *sources of data* give us access to different *types of information*. Many researchers would call these two types of information qualitative and quantitative.

- *Qualitative data* are often described as referring to people's feelings and thoughts (for example, the reasons students give for their choice of institution). These are things that are valid only in terms of an individual's representation of reality.
- *Quantitative data* have a numerical value, for example the number of students who apply to an institution or the percentage of students from an area who go on to higher education. The implication of this is that quantitative data exist in a common world, are collectively understood and can be externally verified.

This division between qualitative and quantitative data is well established, extensively used and deeply rooted in all areas of social research. And yet, it is often misunderstood in terms of its implications. Describing data as qualitative and quantitative may give the impression that what we do with one, we cannot do with the other. More simply put, some people believe that qualitative characteristics are not capable of being measured. This is wrong. Qualitative data are an attribute of a person or object. It can be an opinion or the colour scheme used in a school. It is perfectly feasible (and reasonable) to count the number of people or objects who share a characteristic. We would, for example, find it valuable to know how many mathematics teachers believe that they would get better assessment results if they taught their students in ability sets. Similarly it would be interesting to know how many parents, whose children were in low ability sets, agreed with streaming. The measurement of qualitative characteristics is important for education research. It is not just the strength of a view or opinion that is significant but the number of people who hold it.

Qualitative data are inherently more complex than quantitative because they can take more forms. We shall examine these in the next section.

4.3.2 What types of qualitative data are there?

A simple quantitative/qualitative distinction is less than perfect in describing the character of data that we might use. The numerical basis of quantitative data is clear enough but it is not very helpful just to say that qualitative data are attributes. What forms can qualitative data take?

(i) Qualitative data as reported activity and beliefs

First, people can tell us about what they have actually done, who they are, what they own and what they think. This type of data is (or should be) factually accurate. Often what is reported is behaviour ('my son goes to St George's School', 'my daughter went on the trip to London') but it can also include opinions and views ('the school has improved with the new head teacher', 'my mathematics is not good enough for me to help my children'). The important thing is that the researcher obtains it directly from the respondent. While this type of data is accurate, it is not necessarily stable. Once something has happened, it has always happened but opinions and views can change and a feeling that the school has improved can be replaced by one that it is not as good as it was. These may seem unusual or even trite distinctions to draw but they have to be understood and appreciated in order to determine the type of data that is needed to answer a research question.

(ii) Qualitative data as remembered or intended activity

The second way we can think of qualitative data is as remembered or planned activity. The distinction here is between what people have actually done and what people think they usually do or might do. This sort of reporting is often associated with higher levels of uncertainty or reliability. This is an important issue for researchers. What someone *usually* does at the weekend may not be what happened *last* weekend. Knowing this may influence not just the type of information we seek but also the representative base of the people we speak to. If we are going to ask about 'usual behaviour' then we have to speak to a great many people to ensure that every type of usual behaviour is reported. One problem about asking people about usual (or frequent) behaviours (such as the usual school day or the usual sports lesson) is that individual events of particular significance may not be reported.

An American psychologist, Norbert Schwarz, provides a useful framework for understanding reports of past behaviour. He suggests that there are three dimensions to consider:

1. The duration of the period.
2. The length of time since the period or event.
3. The significance of the period or event (Schwarz, 2007).

Each of these affects the quality of what we are told. Longer periods of an experience or activity (Schwarz was interested in the experience of pain) are more memorable than short. In general, the passage of time blurs events, so that only those that have particular significance at the time or subsequently are remembered with any clarity. Evidence from elsewhere indicates that memory for detail declines rapidly the further we go back in time, with inaccuracy appearing when people are asked to reflect on what happened last week. For anything over one month, inaccuracy increases significantly. Two other psychologists, Lin Chiat Chang and Jon Krosnick (2003) looked at reported behaviour in relation to actual behaviour. This is an important issue for social researchers because questions about typical behaviours are often asked in large scale and longitudinal surveys. Chang and Krosnick asked questions about TV viewing and newspaper reading. They found that those who reported the 'typical week' overestimated their interaction with media as compared with their actual behaviour.

These findings should be a warning to us. If we ask about what people usually do or what typical activities are, we are likely to obtain poor quality data. Typical behaviour and intended activity presents many traps for researchers.

(iii) Qualitative data as inferred qualities

Finally, there is a whole set of data from which other meanings can be inferred. What image does a school that has a strict uniform code wish to project? What would you say about parents who chose a school with a uniform policy? How would you read a young person wearing the latest 'street fashion'? Would you expect an architect to wear the same clothes as a business manager?

This type of data need not be confined to people. We can audit equipment in a school and then make judgements about the range and depth of provision and which equipment is used or not used. We could infer from this something about a school's spending priorities or the approach a teacher takes in lessons. There are few real exceptions to objects and behaviours whose context gives them meaning. If we start to look at people and things in this way, a whole new world of data opens up.

We all make judgements on the basis of what we see, what we understand and what makes sense to us. Some people have turned it into a science and produce lifestyle classifications that link behaviours and values. These classifications can be useful alternatives to established classifications of social and socio-economic status. Table 4.1 shows the Acorn classification used extensively in market research. Acorn stands for '*a* *c*lassification *o*f *r*esidential *n*eighbourhoods'. The classification was first developed by CACI in the mid-1970s. It is the product of a complex statistical analysis of geodemographic data (that is, population, social and economic data with a geographical location). The classification is fundamentally different from classifications of socio-economic or social status because it shows income-related choices and values. The fundamental principle on which the Acorn classification is based is that people with similar values and similar incomes will live in much the same types of place and spend their money in much the same way. Table 4.1 shows the 2006 classification. The six primary Acorn categories have distinctive value systems that drive behaviours. *Wealthy Achievers* are most likely to support disaster relief charities and *Urban Prosperity* groups, environmental charities. *Wealthy Achievers* are twice as likely as the national average to have investments in Unit Trusts, while the *Hard Pressed* are more likely to have a funeral plan. *Wealthy Achievers* are much less likely than the average to change utility suppliers, whereas the *Hard Pressed* are much more likely to change. There is much more about Acorn on www.caci.co.uk/acorn.

Acorn is not the only option for education researchers. The Mosaic classification is available at www.business-strategies.co.uk. These alternative ways of looking at social groupings should be of interest to educational researchers because (a) they offer different insights and (b) they recognise the significance of co-location in understanding attitudes, cultures and behaviours. Look at Activity 4.1 to see how you can use them in one type of research.

Table 4.1 The Acorn lifestyle classification

Acorn category	Acorn group	Examples
Wealthy achievers	Wealthy executives	Affluent mature professionals, large houses
	Affluent greys	Old people, detached homes
	Flourishing families	Large families and houses in rural areas
Urban prosperity	Prosperous professionals	Older professionals, detached houses and flats
	Educated urbanites	Multi-ethnic young, converted flats
	Aspiring singles	Student flats
Comfortably off	Starting out	Young couples, flats, terraces
	Secure families	Working families with mortgages
	Settled suburbia	Middle income, older couples
	Prudent pensioners	Elderly singles, purpose-built flats
Moderate means	Asian communities	Crowded Asian terraces
	Post industrial families	Skilled, older family, terraces
	Blue collar roots	Home-owning, terraces
Hard pressed A	Struggling families	Older people, low income, semis
	Burdened singles	Council flats, single parents, unemployed
	Highrise hardship	Old people, highrise flats
	Inner city adversity	Multi-ethnic, crowded flats
Hard pressed B	Unclassified	

Source: http://www.caci.co.uk/ACORN/

Activity 4.1 Academic marketing: getting the right students to university

Context

The Government has a policy in England of encouraging students from disadvantaged backgrounds to enter higher education. Students apply to UK universities through an agency, the Universities and Colleges Admission Service (UCAS). This organisation monitors the socio-economic profile of applicants. Some of this data is made available to the general public but the real service is to the universities themselves.

Universities receive funding on the basis of student recruitment. They have target numbers for disadvantaged students (who are defined in terms of their postcodes) and they are rewarded for meeting their targets with additional funding. Those responsible for university admissions can monitor the postcodes of both applicants and those admitted and universities can market themselves to particular groups. If an institution appears not to be meeting its access targets, it can increase its recruitment efforts in appropriate areas.

The task

Look back to the Acorn classification (and go to the website where you can read about Mosaic) and, for both, identify the groups that a university should target if it is to meet its quota of students who come from disadvantaged backgrounds. How would you go about identifying where your target groups lived?

Go to the Acorn website, register and insert your own postcode. Describe the profile of the area in which you live. If you do not have a UK postcode, put in EN3 4SF.

Learning implications

What should you take away from this? At one level you will appreciate that universities are agents for Government policy. Just as important, however, in view of the penalties for failing to meet targets, is the appreciation that educational institutions have to operate as businesses and that this dimension needs to be taken into account in order to understand why universities, colleges and even schools behave as they do.

In terms of research practice, your use of the ACORN classification should give you a better appreciation of the value of alternative social classifications as well as an appreciation of how you can use the data in your research.

4.4 How can information be measured?

We have spent the last section looking at types of data, especially types of qualitative data. Now we shall go on to see how the information in the data can be measured. Most data are susceptible to some sort of measurement, as we shall see below. We should point out though that not every qualitative researcher collecting qualitative data (how a teacher feels about taking a particular group, for instance) wants to measure aspects of the data. If, however, someone does, the measurement process occurs after data collection, often as part of data analysis.

(i) Establishing presence or absence

At the most basic level of measurement we can establish whether or not something exists. Is there an equal opportunities policy in place? Does the school have a swimming pool? In order to work at this level of measurement, it is necessary to have mutually exclusive categories that we name, for example, equipment, outsourced services, whole-school assembly. The ones that are chosen reflect the investigation that we are conducting. Because the categories are given names, this level of measurement is referred to as *nominal measurement*. While the categories are mutually exclusive, no one is any better than another, so there is no order of precedence that arises from the logic of the classes and, because the categories are mutually exclusive, the distinguishing feature can only be present or absent. This measurement scale can be used with qualitative data (for instance, the number of undergraduate students who experience disturbed sleep patterns before an examination).

(ii) Establishing precedence

This is the second level of measurement. It is used to establish a sequenced order. We can describe the order using such words as *better, below, more than, above, smaller, longer*. We can even be more precise than this and use words like *extremely, very, quite* or *first, second, third*. The key point about this is that, while we are creating an *order of precedence*, we are not sure how big the difference or interval is between first and second or whether the difference between *extremely* and *very* is the same as between *very* and *quite*. These data are called *ordinal data*, that is, data whose numerical value derives from their order, not on the interval between them. Qualitative data can also be expressed as ordinal data (for example, parents who express a view that one school is better than another).

(iii) Establishing levels of difference

This is the third level of measurement. It is a more precise level because it establishes not just an order of precedence but also the extent of the difference between different elements of that order. For example, in a race we can identify the people who came first, second and third. This is an ordinal measure. We can also say that the person who came first ran the race in 9.6 seconds, the second in 10.0 seconds and the third in 10.8 seconds. From this we know that the third person was 0.8 seconds behind the second and the second 0.4 seconds behind the first. When we are able to specify the difference in this way using standard units of measurement, then we are using an *interval scale*. Many of the data collected as official statistics are interval data and certainly much primary data, such as IQ scores, are interval data. Many of the techniques covered in Chapters 12 and 13 are appropriate for use with interval data. Since these are strong analytical techniques that are capable of producing robust findings, the implication is that interval scale data are preferable to both nominal and ordinal data. Certainly interval scale data give us a more precise picture of some of the features in our investigation. However, qualitative data are not usually capable of being measured on an interval scale, so while interval scale data are more precise, they are irrelevant for much of the data that social scientists are interested in.

(iv) Establishing a relationship between one measurement and another

When we establish a fixed relationship between one measurement and another, we call it a ratio scale. Like the interval scale, this has units of measurement (so it is not usually applicable for qualitative data). Unlike an interval scale, however, it has a zero point that is meaningful in terms of the thing being measured. For instance, if we were examining calorific intake, or children's height and weight, or the distance teachers travel to school, or the number of seconds it would take someone to run 100 metres, all would have a zero point. This zero point would be a real zero unlike, for instance, 0 AD (or 0 BC) or 0°C. These are arbitrary zeros that exist for our convenience in structuring the world. We can have zero distance when a teacher lives at the school, but at 0°C there is still a temperature.

4.4.1 Reviewing so far

Let us take stock of what we have learnt about data. In sections 4.2 and 4.3, we have explored some of the basic characteristics of data, and how the strength of those characteristics can be measured and expressed. It should now be fairly obvious to us that while quantitative data can be expressed in any measurement scale (though conventionally interval and ratio scales are most commonly used), qualitative data are measured frequently only on an ordinal or nominal scale. It is important to understand the difference between these levels of measurement because they affect the type of statistical analysis and test that can be used. We shall learn more about these in Chapter 13. However, so far we have thought about data in a rather abstract way. Let us now become more concrete and ask, 'Where can we get our data from?'

4.5 Where can we go for data?

This question raises another perspective on data that introduces another way of classifying them. Identifying sources of data could take up a whole book – and a very boring one it would be as well! What this chapter will do is introduce us to an enormous field and, hopefully, give us the interest and confidence to go out and explore it ourselves.

Very crudely data can come from people or they can come from places. There is a general feeling amongst many researchers (and not just new ones) that data collected personally are worth more than data that already exist. In part this has to be correct because the data that we collect directly should be closely configured to the requirements of our research question. If the research question requires data on job moves by teachers plus contextual information on career aspirations, stage reached in the family life cycle and the values that individuals hold dear, then this information is so precise that there is only one way to get it and that is to go directly to teachers and ask them. Many studies, however, seem to collect data that already exist, for example, going to individual schools to find out the number of pupil exclusions when this information is already collected at an administrative level. The reality is that there is often a better way of getting the data that we require. All we need is a different mindset and the ability to combine robust data sets that already exist. If we were exploring the links between the educational performance of pupils in schools with the social conditions of the areas in which they lived, the data are ready-made for us in the UK, with school performance data available from the Department for Children, Schools and Families and national indices of multiple deprivation (that take account of social and economic circumstances, family structure, housing and so on) available from the Department of Communities and Local Government. But if we did not know this, then we will have to spend a great deal of time collecting the data and this is likely to limit the number of people from whom we can collect it.

The data we collect ourselves are called *primary data*, because we are the first people to make them available to the research community. Primary data can be both quantitative and qualitative. We shall look at how we can collect primary data in Chapters 8 and 9. Data that already exist are called *secondary data*. These too can be both quantitative and qualitative. We will say a lot more about secondary than primary data in this chapter because it is a vast domain of potentially useful information that few, especially young researchers, are aware of.

4.5.1 Primary data sources

In broad terms there are three sources of primary data:

(i) people

(ii) places and objects and

(iii) ideas.

(i) Primary data from people

Educational researchers are concerned with formal systems and structures (such as a college or an organisation responsible for administering educational provision in an area), with informal systems (such as gangs of youths or a school staff room), with interpersonal relationships and social structures (for example, in a classroom or in a family) and with individuals as pupils, as teachers, as parents, as authority figures and so on. The data they give us will take one or more of the following forms.

- *What they say:* this will include direct answers to the questions we ask, conversations that they have with us or with others, reports they write for formal presentation, emails they write to colleagues. It will include statements that represent the official position as well as things that we overhear and things that we are told in confidence. Words convey meaning, the tone of the text conveys, perhaps, a different meaning and the structure of the text can tell us something about the values and goals of the writer or speaker. People's words are some of the richest data that we can have but we should not necessarily take them at face value. People may not tell lies but they may seek to represent themselves in a better light. If someone says that they began an initiative, or if a report seeks to place some of the blame for failure on 'external forces', we should be sceptical until we have confirmed their version – this is where triangulation, which we met in section 3.3.4, comes in.

- *What they do:* behaviour is an equally important source of information. Behaviour can include the journey to school, scheduling self-directed work, the application of sanctions and the implementation of policy. Behaviour reflects processes at work (which can be compared with those that ought to be operating). It can demonstrate priorities and preferences. It can reflect relationships (power, co-operation, collaboration, friendship) and reveal emotions (fear, anger, loathing, love). It can indicate attitudes (to sexuality, the environment), motives and goals (to be first, to be rich) and values (which can be compared with those that ought to be operating).
- *What they have:* the third type of data that we can get from people is about their material possessions or about the objects that they use. People represent themselves through objects. Since the vast majority of acquisitions require choice, the very act of preferring one option to another gives a researcher an insight into the basis of the selection. We touched on this briefly in Chapter 2 when we introduced the idea of representing the world through signs and symbols. For social researchers this is an important area and has given rise to a separate area of research called semiotics, whose purpose is to understand the meanings we give to signs (we look at this in Chapter 11). However, we do not have to master this field to make use of the ideas. Possession can reflect status. What people wear can represent their self-image (or the image they would like to project), but, before we make any claims, we have to examine the context. How far does income constrain choice? How far do the expectations of the group constrain choice? For example, a teacher may feel that they have to conform when at school, rather than give vent to their personality. Having said this, look back to your school days; was the subject that teachers taught apparent in the clothes they wore? At the institution where you are currently studying, do the lecturers and heads of department and senior managers wear the same things? Do staff in business management and law dress differently from those in arts and education? If the answers are 'yes', the question becomes, 'To what extent is their choice constrained by lack of money and to what extent are they exercising choice?' If the latter, why are they choosing to represent themselves that way? Education research using semiotics is growing and its application is diverse. With research on mathematics teaching, marketing and school and college prospectuses, curriculum structure, language learning, understanding creative processes to list but a few areas, more people are beginning to explore the nature of underlying meanings and whether these meanings are more significant than what appears on the surface. Again, the advice is to be imaginative in thinking about data in relation to our own research. Look at Activity 4.2.

(ii) Primary data from places and objects

The environment that we live and work in is not neutral in research. Because it is the product of individual and collective decisions, it can be used to say things about values and priorities in much the same way that the objects we have and use say something

Activity 4.2 Being imaginative about data

The purpose of this activity is to get you to think about how different types of primary data can be used in your research. You can either try this out in relation to your own enquiry or in relation to the investigation set out below.

You have been approached by a newly-appointed Vice Chancellor of a university who has said that he wants to find out 'what makes it tick'. In your initial discussion you have found out that they are perplexed that the performance of some departments is lacklustre while others can hold their heads up in any academic gathering. She wants you to give her a sense of the mood in the place and to understand why some areas seem dynamic and others do not. You have decided to focus initially on people's enthusiasm for the job, their teaching, research and the necessary administration that they have to do, which includes everything from recruiting the students to the management of their assessment and curriculum.

- You know that group meetings can give a distorted perspective; some people may not want to put their heads above the parapet and say what they really think while others with strong opinions might hog the occasion. What would you do to ensure that people spoke with their authentic voice? How would you get people to share their perspectives with others?
- What behaviours would you observe to give your insights into collegiality, commitment, imagination?
- You want to understand how people feel about individual and institutional worth. You will ask them but what can you also do that is non-intrusive?

about ourselves. And environment is potentially an important feature in education research. Just think of the environment in these ways:

- As a place where learning takes place – the classroom, the lecture theatre, the seminar room, the library;
- As a place where educational professionals work – the classroom, the corridors, the car park, the staff room;
- As a place where pupils and students socialise – the food hall or cafeteria, the playground, the bar;
- As a home, as private space, as public space, as a preferred place for recreation or leisure.

Each of these places can be viewed in a number of ways. For example, they can be judged in terms of upkeep, or in terms of equipment or facilities. There may be an aesthetic dimension that might explain whether people find them attractive. But being attracted to a location may not be just an aesthetic response. If someone comes from a run-down neighbourhood, they may well look favourably on a place that is newly constructed and modern in design. But the environment is not just a representation of the values, interests and priorities that created it, it is also a potential influence on the way we behave. Read Case Study 4.2 to see how one researcher used place data.

(iii) Ideas as primary data

Our ideas, too, can be a primary source of data that we can use to create evidence and shape an argument. There is, however, a thin dividing line between our thoughts on a topic and our judgements on an issue and secondary data. If we begin to discuss *someone else's* comments then (a) we are using secondary data and (b) we need to quote the reference.

The essential difference between whether an idea is a primary or secondary source (and one that we have to reference) is whether we can reasonably expect an audience to know, understand and appreciate the idea and its context. From our point of view it is a judgement we have to make. We can expect more in terms of contextual knowledge of an

Case study 4.2 Emotional behaviour and environmental context

This fascinating study into children's responses to their day-care centres was carried out by a French researcher, Alain Legendre. This study was published in a journal exploring our response to the world around us and not in an education journal, so as researchers we have to stay in touch with associated fields of study. It was chosen not only to illustrate the use of place data but also the part that biological monitoring can play in educational investigations.

Legendre's purpose was to identify what environmental situations and features create an adverse emotional response in young children. The settings for the research were day-care centres in France and Hungary. Children's emotional responses were measured using changes in levels of cortisol in the saliva. Cortisol is a hormone that raises blood pressure and blood sugar and is produced in response to stress.

Saliva samples were taken from children during the day and benchmarked against samples taken at the weekend to establish a natural diurnal rhythm in cortisol levels.

Environmental and situational characteristics that were measured included the size of the group that each child joined, the sex ratios of the group, the age range in the group, the ratio of carers to children, the number of adults, the area of the playrooms, and the density of children in the playrooms. There were no measurements of aesthetic and design features such as colour, decoration, room shape, etc., though it would not have been unreasonable to have included them.

The results of the research showed that:

- stress levels, as measured by cortisol levels, increased in group situations (that is, most of the day) when they should have fallen;
- age difference affected cortisol levels; when there was an age different of six months or more in the groups, stress increased;
- the number of carers with the child affected cortisol levels, with a team of more than four carers increasing stress;
- the amount of space available to each child in the playroom affected cortisol levels, with 5 m^2 or less resulting in greater stress.

Assessments were made of the influence of other factors such as the numbers of boys and girls in the group but these were found not to have any influence on cortisol levels.

This study should start you thinking about being imaginative in your approach to research. In many ways it is a straightforward study but for education it is relatively unusual because it makes use of a physiological measure as a proxy for an emotional state. You can become more imaginative in your research by moving outside the comfort zone of what educational researchers study and how they work. You must become aware of what is going on in subjects with the same sorts of interest as education. There is, however, a word of warning to issue. There are philosophical dangers in looking at the environment as an influence on behaviour. You are venturing into a field known as determinism and many social scientists would be critical of you. At the heart of the issue is a fundamental question about how far our behaviour is constrained and how far we have free will. So if you venture into this type of analysis be very careful with your phraseology.

Source: Legendre, A. (2003) Environmental Features Influencing Toddlers' Bioemotional Reactions in Day Care Centres, *Environment & Behaviour*, 35(4), 523–49.

academic audience than a non-professional one. If we get it wrong we will be criticised for offering unsubstantiated opinions and making unwarranted assertions.

We can include ideas that can be taken for granted as primary data sources, where our comments are, as far as we know, original. If our research were into learning technology, it would be reasonable for us to talk about the ideal e-learning platform or to compare the use of a whiteboard with an overhead projector. These are things that we can reasonably expect people to know, so, equally, we can expect them to understand and appreciate our ideas. Abstract notions too can be a primary source. We can comment on national identity and multiculturalism from a value perspective or regeneration or social disadvantage from the perspective of experience, ethics or economics. We can have a view on climate change, genetic manipulation and abortion without summarising what other people have written because we can reasonably expect our educated readers to have some understanding and knowledge of the issues.

At the heart of using ideas as a primary source is our own creativity. The more thoughtful we are about issues and the more imaginative we are about asking the right questions, the more we will be able to link ideas and solve problems. We are our own resource and we should aim to develop this capability. To this end, we should be aware of issues being discussed in the academic, professional and popular press so that we can see links that others have missed. For this we need to be widely read. We should develop an analytical and questioning approach that we can use to think through issues. Activity 4.3 will show you that you are really quite good at this and that all you need is practice.

4.5.2 Secondary data sources

Secondary data is already in the public domain. Anything that is already generally available can be termed secondary data; it does not have to be published. The types of secondary data that are generally recognised are:

- official statistical sources produced on a regular basis by government or other public agencies;

Activity 4.3 Becoming a resource yourself

These are exercises you can try by yourself. It is, however, useful if you can compare your responses with other people's just to see how they approached them. For all of the exercises you can draw on your experience of being a student, your awareness of the wider world and the insights you can gain from thinking and then questioning yourself.

(i) Curriculum principles

Think about the choices of subject you made at school and at university. Identify what subjects you had to study. Why was your curriculum organised like this? If you are working in an educational setting, do the same analysis and ask the same questions. Now approach the issue from a 'what if' perspective. How would you organise a senior (11–16) curriculum and/or an undergraduate degree in a subject? How would a postgraduate masters' degree be different? Organise your thoughts and write between 200 and 300 words identifying principles of curriculum design.

(ii) Leadership

Using the same approach of drawing on your own experience and, thinking of examples you have come across, of situations that have to be confronted and the characteristics required to do the job:

- identify types of leader
- give examples
- identify leadership characteristics.

In at least 800 words, present your leadership analysis and consider whether different types of leader are appropriate in different stages of any institution or organisation's development.

(iii) Student experience

Draw on your own experience as a student at whatever level and, if appropriate, as a teacher to identify the character of a good student experience in learning. Set this within the context of any appropriate theory and your own beliefs about the purpose of education. Convert your notes into text that could be used in a research paper.

Learning lessons

What you should learn from this is (a) that your own experience can be an evidence base for you to question and examine, and (b) once you have identified the issue and isolated the right question to solve a problem, you will get an answer. It may not be the best answer but it will set you on a path of thinking that will probably lead you to a better one. One of the things you quickly learn in research is that finding the right question to ask is often more difficult than getting the answer!

- official statistical sources produced on an irregular basis by government or other public agencies;
- official statistical sources produced by public and private organisations and individuals, usually focusing on a specific issue;
- published documents, such as newspapers, journals, magazines, books, academic papers and reports, produced as hard copy or as digital material;
- unpublished documents such as reports, memoranda, minutes of meeting, letters, emails, websites, blogs, wikis;
- images (pictures and photographs), film and video.

The wealth of data that falls into this category of secondary data is truly enormous. Until 10 years ago, accessing this data could be difficult. It involved going to reference libraries to look up (and then copy down) statistical series or going to a specialist library, such as the UK's National Newspaper Library to access, for example, newspapers of the 1970s to see how educational issues were presented. Academic journal articles had to be consulted at an institutional library or obtained by post from another library and securing reports meant a trip to local or national education offices. It was not surprising that many researchers found it easier to collect primary data. The Internet, however, has changed all of this.

Across the world, organisations, particularly governments and those in the public sector, have a policy of making much information accessible. However it is not just availability that has made secondary data widely accessible, it is also the fact that there are now understandable frameworks, including some comprehensive Web portals, for accessing the data. The map of data and how to access it is becoming clearer and clearer year by year. Most academic researchers, though, including educational researchers, are not making use of this data bonanza. In part this is likely to be because they are creatures of their pasts, when they needed to create primary data because of the difficulty of accessing secondary. Those days, however, have passed and it is up to the new generation of researchers to understand the riches that can now be accessed through the Internet.

We shall look at some key sources and the data they contain but, first, it is important to appreciate some of the issues that have to be managed when we use some secondary sources.

4.5.3 Using secondary sources

There are five principal issues that we should be aware of if we use secondary data in our research. They are:

(i) the process of data collection;
(ii) the scale of data presentation;
(iii) the scale at which we use the data;
(iv) data comparison;
(v) data quality.

Each of these can affect our analysis and conclusions. It is important that we understand their impact before we use secondary data so that we can use our understanding to select the most appropriate data sets.

(i) The process of data collection

When we use secondary data we need to be reassured that it is robust and represents what it says it represents. What will reassure us is knowing that data have been collected in ways that guarantee their accuracy. For example, if someone has carried out a survey of unemployed young people aged between 16 and 18, was it done in such a way as to be representative of a wider group? (This is an issue that we shall consider again in relation to our own research in Chapter 6 when we look at sampling in relation to the collection of primary data). Table 4.2 sets out sources of secondary data and the levels of assurance that they generally command. Table 4.2 uses two terms, 'statistics' and 'data'. 'Statistics' is used specifically in relation to numerical data, whereas the term 'data' is used to refer to any data type.

A census is a survey of everyone in a community. The term is most commonly used to refer to the audits of population that many national governments conduct, usually every ten years. Because a census seeks to enumerate everyone, its principal weakness is in non-response. This is normally low in developed states. For example, the last UK Census in 2001 was estimated to have a non-response of six per cent, which was reduced to two per cent by Census Enumerators (the people whose prime task is to distribute and collect the census forms), who completed forms on behalf of some households. Actual population numbers were estimated to be accurate to between +/− 0.2 per cent.

Table 4.2 Levels of confidence in secondary data sources

Census statistics	High
Official statistics	High
Other Government statistics	High
Other public statistics and data	Variable
Data deposited in data archives	High
Corporate statistics	Generally high
Other corporate data	Variable
Self-referenced data	Low

We can also have a high level of confidence in other official statistics. These are either data collected from local government (such as data on absence from school in the UK) or sample surveys carried out (for example, on how we spend our money). Data collected by Government are assured by rigorous processes. These include the provision of definitions and templates for data collection and reviewing patterns and identifying things that are out of the ordinary. Sample surveys are assured in terms of a robust (and usually publicly accessible) sampling procedure. Other Government statistics are usually collected according to the same robust methodology.

However, the same need not be the case with other public statistics and data, particularly those coming from a lower administrative level such as a local authority. These might include surveys of parents with school age children, an assessment of need and demand for childcare, consultations on the closure of a school or the reorganisation of vocational training provision. Surveys especially are not always conducted with the same level of technical skill and professional rigour as at the national level and we should certainly investigate the procedures used. The same goes for reports. Minutes of official meetings can normally be relied upon to be accurate.

Many countries have data archives. These are databases where governments and individual researchers can deposit survey results and other forms of data (see Case Study 4.3).

Case study 4.3 Data archives: a rich resource

A data archive is a depository for research data. The controllers of an archive establish standards for data deposition. Much of the data is usually public but private researchers can place their own data in the archive. The UK Data Archive (www.data-archive.ac.uk) holds both official series of data and data collected for specific research projects. It has the following categories for education:

General	Research
Higher and Further	School Leaving
Literacy	Teaching Profession
Primary, Pre-Primary and Secondary	

These generate well over 200 data sets. Older data sets enable researchers to develop baseline data for their own research.

The Council of Europe has established a web portal (www.nsd.uib.no/Cessda/) which gives access to 21 national archives in Europe (including archives in Belgium, Denmark, Finland, the Netherlands, Norway and Sweden). Many of the national archives are searchable in English and have reports in English. For example, the Finnish archive identified almost 600 resources on education. The CESSDA website also provides access to national sites in other parts of the world and to some non-profit making sites.

Other resources include:

- Inter-University Consortium for Political and Social Research
  www.icpsr.umich.edu
- International Archive of Education Data
  www.icpsr.umich.edu/IAED
- Netherlands Historical Data Archive
  www.dans.knaw.nl
- National Digital Archive of Data Sets (UK)
  www.ndad.nationalarchives.gov.uk
- The Norwegian Historical Data Centre
  www.rhd.uit.no
- National Data Archive on Child Abuse And Neglect (USA)
  www.ndacan.cornell.edu
- Sage Publications SRM Database
  www.srm-online.nl

Data that are deposited in a data archive are usually of a high quality. Such data can come from official and public sources but even when they are deposited by research organisations and individuals they are reliable because data archives filter accessions through a quality control process. There are, as well, thematic and private data archives (for more information, see Case Study 4.3). For any data archive, it is important to check accession procedures as an assurance of standards.

Corporate statistics are also normally of a high quality because they are usually collected under a regulatory framework such as stock exchange regulations and Government regulations for the disclosure of financial accounts. We might wonder why educationalists might need to access such information. The answer is to be found in the number of commercial organisations that are entering the mainstream education sector and running schools, colleges and universities. These organisations, both for profit and not for profit, are bound by regulations concerning disclosure of information. In only rare circumstances is this inaccurate.

Other corporate data are, though, less reliable. They take the form of press releases, headline statistics and reports and profiles. Most of these are designed to give a strong corporate message that accentuates a positive interpretation. If we use such data, we should read them with care and triangulate the interpretation with other sources. If we find that the data are slanted towards a particular interpretation, then the existence of the bias itself becomes a source of information. Comparing school and college press releases with official quality assessment reports can produce interesting results, which reveal that public sector organisations are increasingly having to behave like their private sector counterparts.

We should retain the same level of scepticism in respect of data put into the public domain by groups and individuals. This is called self-referenced data in Table 4.2. For example, if we search for 'citizenship education' on the Web, we find websites that aim to support teachers of citizenship (www.citizen.org.uk), ones where teachers can share what they do (www.citized.info) and ones where people come together to argue the case for citizenship education and to offer mutual support (www.teachingcitizenship.org.uk) as well as centres of research (www.newman.ac.uk/CCE/). The data on these sites can be robust but there is no guarantee that the selection of content in any but the research sites is not influenced by attitude and values. If we are dealing with viewpoints and opinion forming in our research or with individual classroom practice, then they are a valuable source but otherwise it is probably best to find something in which our audience will have more confidence.

(ii) The scale of data presentation

The second factor we should take account of in using secondary data is that they are often collected at one scale and presented at another. Data are often aggregated upwards in geographical or organisational scale. For example, researchers might interview university lecturers about research opportunities and support but consolidate the results not at the level of individual institutions but according to whether they are vocational universities, universities that emphasise the teaching role or those that prioritise pure research. The levels at which data can be collected and presented are set out below.

- *The basic unit of data collection or survey:* this could be an individual or an organisation such as a school. This data are often privileged information for the research team only but it can be accessed if surveys are placed in data archives or depositories.
- *local area or corporate organisation such as a school:* the first unit of data aggregation (this varies according to the data set). For educational statistics in the UK, the first level of aggregation is usually the local administrative authority. However, some data may be available at smaller (and different) areas if we approach the data enquiry from a different direction. For more information on this, see section 4.6.1 on data presentation at a neighbourhood level.
- *region:* this is an intermediate level of data aggregation. England has long-established standard regions. These have recently become transformed to become centres for economic, social and environmental management called Government Office Regions (see Figure 4.1); all prepare a regional plan that seeks to create an interface between national strategic planning and local implementation planning. The East of England Plan (2006) covers economic growth, housing, transport, health, transport, social services and education. The regional level is one that educational research, both in the UK and worldwide, appears to be ignoring, yet it is increasingly an important level for policy making in the UK.
- *nation:* the highest level of data presentation is the national total. As we move up the levels towards the national aggregation, information about differences between one area and another become lost. While these differences may be random in nature, it is more likely that they reflect the operation and influence of significant economic, social and cultural forces at a local or regional level. These are lost at the highest spatial scale. However, while we lose fine grain information, we gain in terms of simplicity and the ability to identify broad temporal trends.

Figure 4.1 Government office regions in England

As researchers we should operate at the lowest spatial scale commensurate with the issue we are exploring. This ensures that we maximise the information value of the data and our ability to explain patterns. It makes little sense to use statistics on exclusion from school at a regional level unless there is some policy responsibility at this level. It is far more appropriate to seek data at the local administrative level (where there is likely to be responsibility for managing the school system) or at the school level (where responsibility for managing the pupils lies). We might think that it would be even less appropriate to look at the data at a national level but, in fact, we would be wrong. At this level an analysis represents a test of how well a government is implementing policy. It may seem a challenge to have to consider the spatial scale of data sets. However, it is usually pretty obvious at which level we should extract our data.

(iii) The scale at which we use the data (The level of analysis)

If we thought that we faced problems in terms of the scale at which we access secondary data, then we face even more when we change spatial scale to actually analyse data or present them as evidence in our argument. There are three reasons for this.

- First, every aggregation changes the informational content of data. In broad terms every data set is composed of two elements – the *message* and *noise*. The message is represented by order and pattern in the data set, which we can seek to explain. Noise is represented by random variation, people whose behaviour is so individual that it would require research into their personalities and psychological make-up to understand it. At different levels of data aggregation the balance of message and noise changes. In general, the process of aggregating data strengthens the message but only up to a certain point. After that messages can be lost or changed. An example will show this more clearly. School pupils in England are tested against national standards at various ages. The last test, at the end of compulsory schooling, is a national, externally assessed examination called GCSE. Table 4.3 shows the standards attained by pupils in one area of London. The level one standard is 5 or more grades in the public examinations at grades A* to G and the Level 2 standard is 5 or more grades at grades A* to C. Level 2 defines a narrower range of attainment. The table shows the results from 9 schools. Two schools had a 100 per cent pass rate at level 2. Three schools had a pass rate of below 50 per cent of pupils meeting the standard. This divergence in attainment should immediately start us thinking about factors at work that could produce this degree of divergence. These might include the quality of the teachers, the management and organisation of the school and the socio-economic background and family circumstances of the pupils. The table also shows the average for the local authority (47.1 per cent). This value incorporates all of the 9 schools but it cannot be used to help us understand why the variations occur within the authority. It is only of interest in comparison with the results from other local authorities. At this level, school character and processes, the most localised influences, are more random in nature. Socio-economic circumstances become influential in creating a pattern and these interact as potential influences with the type and degree of support that the local authority offers its schools. In summary, as the scale of analysis changes, so does the informational content that drives the explanation.

- The second reason why spatial scale is an issue at the stage of analysis is that inappropriate aggregation can blur messages. Figure 4.2 represents a schematic section of

Table 4.3 Attainment of national standards at 16 in an area of London 2005

		% of pupils achieving	
	Number of pupils at the end of KS4	Level 2 (5 or more grades A*–C)	Level 1 (5 or more grades A*–G)
LA average		47.1	86.5
England average		57.1	90.2
School A	159	21	87
School B	141	100	100
School C	167	19	72
School C	201	52	89
School D	205	57	87
School E	174	48	91
School F	174	31	88
School G	180	74	96
School H	238	69	94
School I	89	100	100

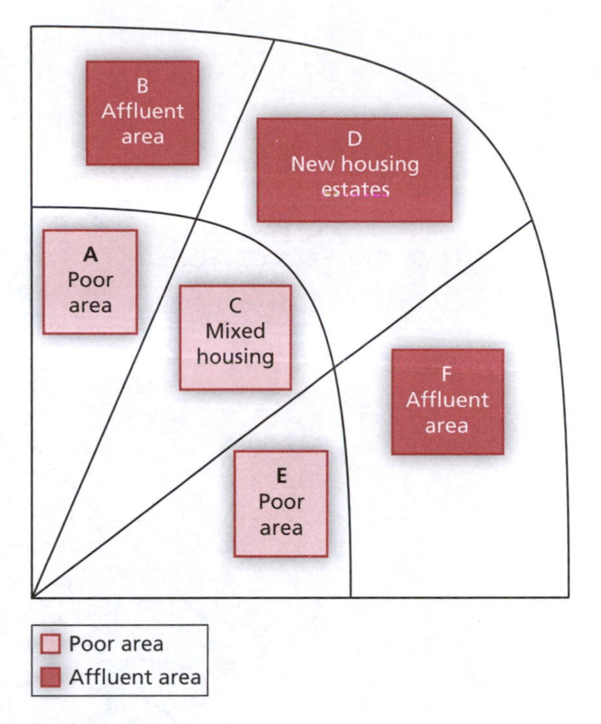

Figure 4.2 Model of urban structure

a city. Assume that the sectors AB, CD and EF are administrative units and that each part sector (A,B,C,D,E, and F) represents an areal unit for data collection. If data are presented by administrative unit (that is AB, CD and EF) then, unless we know something about the social geography of cities, we will lose information and possibly reach an incorrect conclusion. If we about think this, we will identify the reason immediately. Some of the poorer areas tend to be close to the city centre, so by combining the outer areas with the inner, we blur the messages that both areas separately can give us. So it possibly would be better to combine A with C and E, and B, with D and F so as to combine like with like. If this seems far-fetched, look at Figure 4.3. This shows the electoral districts (called wards) of the London Borough of Barnet. These wards have been grouped together as clusters (shown by the lines drawn on the map). If we were exploring the association between ethnicity and pupil attainment for our ward clusters, we would generate results that, at best, would have little meaning and, at worst, would be erroneous. Why? Because, West Hendon, with 59 per cent of its population from an ethnic minority is in the same cluster as Finchley where 41 per cent are non-white. And because Coppetts, with a 42 per cent ethnic minority population is joined together with Oakleigh and East Barnet, both of which have less than a 30 per cent ethnic minority population. The principle is that we should construct groups on the basis of similarities and not just geographical proximity or administrative convenience.

- Finally we should remember what we read about the ecological fallacy in Chapter 3 (see Case Study 3.5). Methodological studies quite clearly show that the level of data aggregation used in analysis can affect the results. Look at Case Study 4.4, which gives an insight into 'Simpson's Paradox'. This shows how aggregation can produce answers that put us on the wrong track.

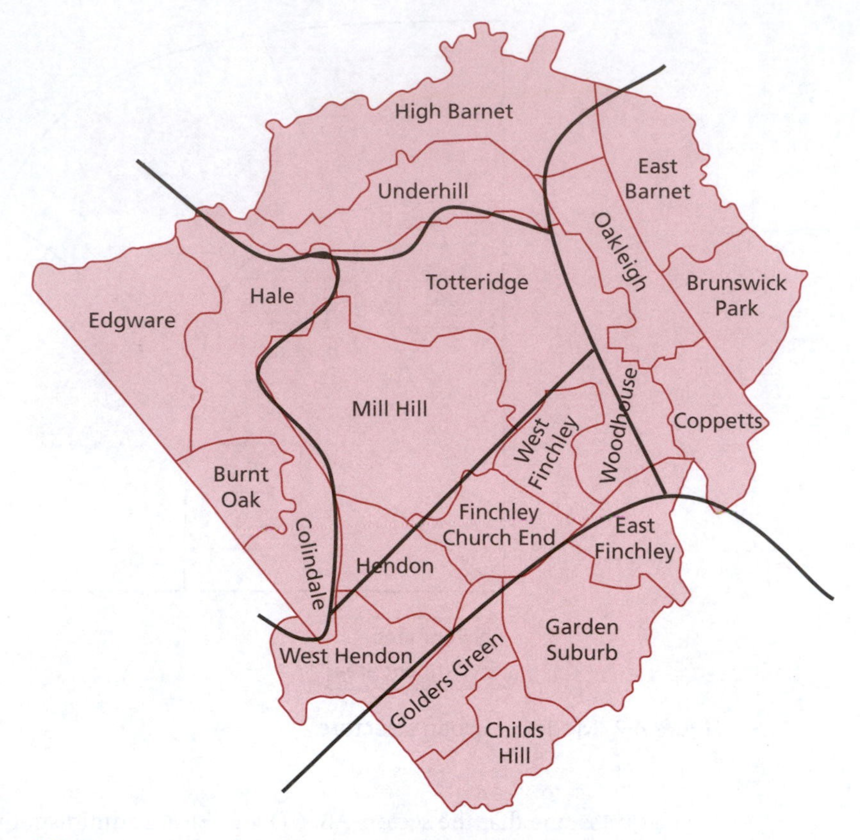

Figure 4.3 Electoral wards in the London Borough of Barnet

(iv) Data comparison

The fourth issue we should be aware of when we use secondary data is what happens when we compare data from different areas or different time periods. Comparison is a well-established method in education and social science research. If we take a fundamental educational measure such as literacy we can infer a great deal about the economic and social state of a society if we look at literacy rates country by country. If we look at literacy rates over time, then we can infer something about the social development of countries. We can use the same approach to look at regions and districts and, if the data can be reconfigured, to look at groups within society such as single parent families.

The purpose of a comparative approach is to highlight similarities and differences. In broad terms, similarities are likely to represent the same political and socio-economic processes at work and differences will represent variations in those processes. Differences can be used to shape policy and target programmes. This is the basis of attempts by governments in the UK to increase the numbers in higher education of young people from deprived communities.

Comparison, however, is of little value if the basis on which things are compared are not the same. If we use data in a comparative study, we need to reassure ourselves about the following things.

- First, we need to be sure that the definitions used to create data categories are the same. If we are using data presented by age group, are the groups the same? If not,

Case study 4.4 Aggregating data – understanding Simpson's Paradox

Simpson's Paradox describes a situation in which data aggregation reverses what is found at lower levels of data representation. This example concerns jury composition in New Zealand.

Like many societies, New Zealand is concerned to know that ethnic minorities (in this case the Maori people) are appropriately represented in the process of decision making. This is particularly important in the case of jury trials where the idea of fairness is the bedrock of the decision. Fairness requires that Maori sit on juries in proportion to their numbers in the population as a whole.

The tables below show jury composition in two towns in the North Island of New Zealand – Rotorua and Nelson. Both towns are about the same size – 32,000.

In both cases, Maori are under-represented on juries and whites over-represented. However, when you combine data for the two towns, a strange thing happens – Maori are over-represented. How could this be? The answers are to be found in the proportion that each town contributes to various totals:

- Rotorua and Nelson are about the same population, so they each contribute about 50 per cent to the total population.
- However, the contribution of each town to the combined jury pool is very different: Rotorua contributes 86 per cent of the jury pool and Nelson only 14 per cent. Since Rotorua has a higher percentage of Maori in its population, it distorts the combined measure.

	Rotorua		Nelson	
	Maori	White	Maori	White
Per cent of jury pool	23.4	76.6	1.8	98.2
Per cent of population	27.0	73.0	3.9	96.1

	Rotorua and Nelson	
	Maori	White
Per cent of jury pool	20.3	79.7
Per cent of population	15.2	84.8

The moral of this is that you should take great care when combining data to ensure that you do not generate spurious results.

Source: Westbrooke, I. (1997) *Simpson's Paradox: An Example in a New Zealand Survey of Jury Composition*, Statistics New Zealand.

what can we do? There are a number of numerical manipulations that we can use (see Case Study 4.5). If we are making an international study of qualifications at the end of full-time study, how do we equate GCSEs in England at age 16 with the more complex pre-university, senior general and pre-vocational system in the Netherlands where students complete at age 16, 17 and 18? In this case we probably do not. The only direct points of comparison between the two systems are age 18 or, turning the measure around, and looking at the number of students who do not progress in full-time education or training after 16.

- Second, we must check that the way in which data are presented do not change over time. This is particularly important in terms of spatial units. Data, for instance, are often presented according to electoral areas. These, however, change to reflect

Case study 4.5 Methods of resolving data problems

This case study deals with two typical data problems and ways of resolving them.

(i) Combining classes

The ways in which data are presented can change over time and be different for different areas. One way of resolving this is to combine statistical categories until comparison is possible. In this example, we shall look at housing rental and ownership trends (called tenure) in the London Borough of Brent between 1991 and 2005. The data is taken from the census in 1991 and from Borough estimates in 2005.

1991		2005	
Tenure type	Per cent	Tenure type	Per cent
Local authority rented	16.1	Local authority rented	9.2
Housing association	6.3	Registered social landlord	13.5
Privately rented	15.0	Other public	2.1
Owner occupied	62.5	Owner occupied and privately rented	75.2

In this comparison, there is only one common data class, local authority rented. In order to compare the situation over time, we have to make assumptions. Registered social landlords will include housing associations, so these can be treated as being in the same group. Other public housing includes accommodation provided by organisations such as the National Health Service. This should be treated as analogous to local authority rented. Since, in 2005, owner occupied and privately rented are combined, the same should be done for 1991. This is less than satisfactory but all we can do with this dataset. The revised comparison is shown below.

	1992	2005
Tenure type	Per cent	Per cent
Social housing	22.4	24.8
Of which local authority	16.1	9.2
Registered social landlord	6.3	13.5
Owner occupied and privately rented	77.5	75.2
Of which privately rented	15.0	
Owner occupied	62.5	

(ii) Apportioning classes

Imagine that we want to project demand for primary education provision for Alnwick in Northumberland and that we need to test our predictions against historical data. For this we would need to know the number of children in each year age group. This is available for the 2001 Census. Our model is that the number of children in a pre-school age group will enter the schools in Alnwick at some point in the future. For example, those aged three will enter in two years' time. This is quite a crude estimate because we are not taking account of the month in which they were born. Our argument, however, that if we test our model against historical data, we will begin to see how reliable our estimate is. However, when we go to the data for 1991, we find that it only gives a per cent of children aged 0–4. How do we resolve this problem?

▶

The first stage is to convert the percentage aged 0–4 to an actual number:

	Alnwick: Number of Children	
	1991	2001
Total population	30,081	
Per cent of population aged 0–4	5.7	
Number aged 0–4	1,715	1,274

The total population in 1991 is 30,081; 5.7 per cent of this population are aged 0–4. This is 1,715 children. We then apportion this total to the four age groups. The simplest way is to put an equal number (428/429) in each. However, this is a very crude estimate. A better estimate might be to assume the birth rate in each of 1991, 1990, 1989 and 1988. To do this, we subtract the number of children aged 0–4 in 2001 (1,274) from the number in 1991 (1,715). The difference is 440. We express this difference as a percentage of the 1991 population. The answer is 25.7 per cent. Over 10 years, this is about 2.5 per cent a year. The implication of this is that the weighting for the numbers of children will increase by 2.5 per cent each year from age 0–1 to age 3–4. We can express this weighting as 1,000 for 0–1, 1,025 for 1–2, 1,050 for 2–3 and 1,075 for 3–4. We use four figures just to get rid of the decimal points. This will produce the numbers for each age group shown in the table below. However, this is an approximation because 2.5 per cent a year over 10 years compounds itself, so we have underestimated the population in our base year of 1991. We could also improve our prediction by applying infant mortality rates and migration effects to our totals and adjust them accordingly but this is much more complex.

	1991		2001
	Equal allocation	Weighted allocation	Actual numbers
0–1	428	413	270
1–2	429	423	318
2–3	428	434	360
3–4	429	444	326

Summary

Manipulating data is a skill all researchers should develop. It usually requires nothing more than a little logical thought and some simple *arithmetic* manipulation.

changes in population distribution and even though the name may remain the same, boundaries may have shifted quite markedly. What can we do in this case? If the boundary change over the period we are investigating represents only a small proportion of the population and the groups included and excluded do not change markedly the overall balance of the population, we are probably safe in turning a blind eye to the problem and using the data as found. If not, then we have two choices, either to construct our own estimate of what would be the case if the boundaries had not changed, or to see if the data are presented in another spatial format that is stable over time. This is an issue to which solutions are now being developed. In England and Wales, for example, some data are now being presented in a format called *Super Output Areas* that are fixed over time, thus removing the problem of boundaries that change. They have another advantage, as well. Electoral divisions vary in size. The smallest, for example, can have as few as 100 residents or as many as 30,000. This range can make comparison difficult. However, there is another problem that researchers face with districts with the smallest populations – the most recent data are not available because individuals could be identified. This is unacceptable.

It is the advent of modern data management techniques that has enabled Government geo-statisticians to create Super Output Areas. Three layers of Super Output Area are being developed:

- a lower layer with a lower population of 1,000 and an average population of 1,500;
- a middle layer with a lower population of 5,000 and an average population of 7,200;
- an upper layer (that is not yet developed) with a lower population expected to be about 25,000.

Scotland and Northern Ireland have equivalent structures called Data Zones and Super Output Areas respectively, though in each case the population limits are different from those in England and Wales. As an educational researcher, particularly if you are at the beginning of your career, you should remain aware of developments in the spatial organisation of data and ways of accessing such data.

(v) Data quality

The final issue we should consider when using secondary data is its quality. Most of the consideration of secondary sources so far has been in terms of numerical data but data in other formats (such as written reports) brings its own problems too. These are usually issues of bias or appropriate representation. This is not to say that numerical data sets are not biased. Of course they can be. The bias can arise from poor procedure (usually sampling, see Chapter 6) but also by choosing to ask one question and not another (see Chapter 8). 'Would you like to see more selective schools?' is likely to get a more positive response than 'Would you like to see the top ten per cent of children go to a selective school?' because many parents would like their children to attend such a school. The second question, however, adds a note of realism.

What other formats might we use as education researchers? Documents such as policy statements, reports and press releases, videos of child behaviour, pictures, witness statements are just a few of the non-statistical sources that we might draw on. Some of this data may be less neutral than numeric data because they can go through a process, either individual, group or organisational, that seeks to emphasise a perspective or bring out an interpretation. A quality inspection report may say that a school is only delivering a moderate standard of education to the pupils but the head teacher's press release might report the praise given for improvements in attendance and the school's sporting achievements. And this is the issue with processed data. It may not be untruthful but neither is it always as truthful as it could be (though if we are able to identify the 'spin' on information, this too can be data for us). What follows are some pointers that we should take account of.

- Is this type of data factually correct? If it is in the public domain and comes from a source that values its reputation (such as a commercial company), it is unlikely to be deliberately incorrect. However, it may not give the full picture, so it is very important that we look to see what others who might take a different stance have to say. If there is something that underpins the data that we have access to (for example, a report that has given rise to a press release), we would be advised to get hold of the report.

- Do we have to accept the arguments, explicit or implied, in secondary output? We would be foolish to accept anything uncritically. Even academic papers that have been peer reviewed before publication should not be accepted as being a definitive statement. Remember what we learnt in Chapter 2 about influences on research outlook. We would not expect a structuralist to interpret data in the same way as a liberal educationalist. Sentiment, values, beliefs about what should be and self-interest, all colour how people present their views.
- If processed data are potentially so corrupted, is there any value in looking at them in the first place? Oh yes! We can use this sort of data to understand how decisions are reached, how people are influenced and how opinions are formed. We can extract information that helps us produce a timeline of how a situation evolved. The very fact that what is made public is a partial view gives us potential evidence for demonstrating attitudes, objectives, interests, values.

Secondary processed data are a rich resource; we just have to use them appropriately.

4.6 National data sources

Now we are going to look at the actual data that are available. The numbers of data sources that we can access via the Internet are truly breathtaking for the educational researcher. We shall review, first of all, on-line resources relating to data within specific countries. It is impossible, however, to deal with every country and we would be overwhelmed if we were to try to deal with every data source of potential value to education researchers. There are just too many to list, let alone describe. The implication of this is that this and the following sections should be read in a particular way. Do not expect to find definitive specifications. Do not expect to find answers to this sort of question: 'What is the Web address for data on school enrolments in Denmark?' There are several reasons for this.

- First, national sites do not always have the same data. Just because the UK has data on exclusions from school does not mean the same is true of every country.
- Second, websites change as governments restructure their executive frameworks. One thing that seems to be happening is that government, at whatever level, is consolidating its data resources so that they can be accessed through one or just a few Web portals. Different countries are at different points along this road and what exists today is likely to be different in a few years' time.
- And the last reason why we should not expect to find specific answers to 'where is' type questions is that I do not know the answers myself. If I need to know, I start searching, and that is what every researcher has to do. The data we want is likely to be stored somewhere.

So what can we expect from this and subsequent sections? The intention is to help us appreciate the possibilities with Internet access to secondary data for educational researchers and the potential that they can realise. In this section we shall look at data availability in the UK, Denmark, Finland, Norway, the Netherlands, Sweden and the USA.

4.6.1 The UK

Devolution of power to Scotland, Wales and Northern Ireland has meant that while some data are available for the country as a whole, other data are only available through sub-national sites for England, Scotland, Wales and Northern Ireland. This is important to know because education is a devolved responsibility to sub-national administrations. In general, however, there is a common pattern to the data.

(i) National Statistics (www.statistics.gov.uk)

This website is the principal portal for secondary data. Some data, especially at a regional level and above, are available for all parts of the UK, while local data are mainly available for England and Wales. Similar data exists for Scotland and Northern Ireland. Data are available as (a) raw statistics (for example, Standard Table S104, which looks at population in terms of ethnic group and religion with data presented at a range of spatial scales from wards (the lowest electoral unit), through local authorities to counties, regions and national units) and (b) as digests (for example, *Regional Trends* (published on behalf of the Office for National Statistics by Palgrave Macmillan) which gives regional profiles for population, housing, the labour market and thematic analyses drawing out regional comparisons for demography, education and training, labour market, housing, health, lifestyle, crime, transport, environment and industry). Not all of the data can be accessed via the Web.

The website is, as might be expected, complex. Others might disagree and say that if we want to understand what complexity is, we should look at the EU website. Certainly the National Statistics site is nothing in comparison with the EU's but it can be difficult to find the data we want. Three are four routes we can follow (see Figure 4.4).

- First, we can browse the site by theme. Amongst things of interest to educationalists we can look at crime and justice, the economy, health care, the labour market, population and migration and social and welfare issues as well as education and training. Each theme takes us to the following output: headline summaries from research (called 'story results'), articles and reports, data results, data from official publications, such as *Regional Trends* or *Social Trends* (called 'product results'), which may include raw data. Sometimes the data are recalibrated to suit particular circumstances. For example, we could be referred to the *Focus On . . .* publications, a series of commentaries and statistical digests and analyses on, for example, London, health, ethnicity, families, gender, older people, migration, social inequalities and Wales.
- Second, we can access data through their location by following the 'Neighbourhood' route. This is an outstanding route and resource for educational researchers looking at issues in a local context. It gives us a choice to look at a range of data for a locality or specific data for a locality. The first option gives information for 'Lower Layer Super Output Areas' (LLSO, the smallest spatial units – for a description of super output areas, see section 4.4). For the LLSO I live in there are 455 separate tables. The population of this LLSO was 1,586 in 2001. This gives some indication of the detailed level of analysis that we can undertake. The second option allows us to choose the type of area – local authority, ward, super output areas by level, education authority, primary care organisation, 'New Deal for the Communities Area' (these are areas that suffer from multiple deprivation and are a focus of public action to alleviate social and economic disadvantage), parliamentary constituency and parish. Not all information is yet available for all areas. For one education authority, there were 339 data sets. The range of data available to us is truly staggering.
- Third, we can search for data. This takes us to data and product resources. A search for 'pupil numbers' brought up references to *Social Trends* and product references

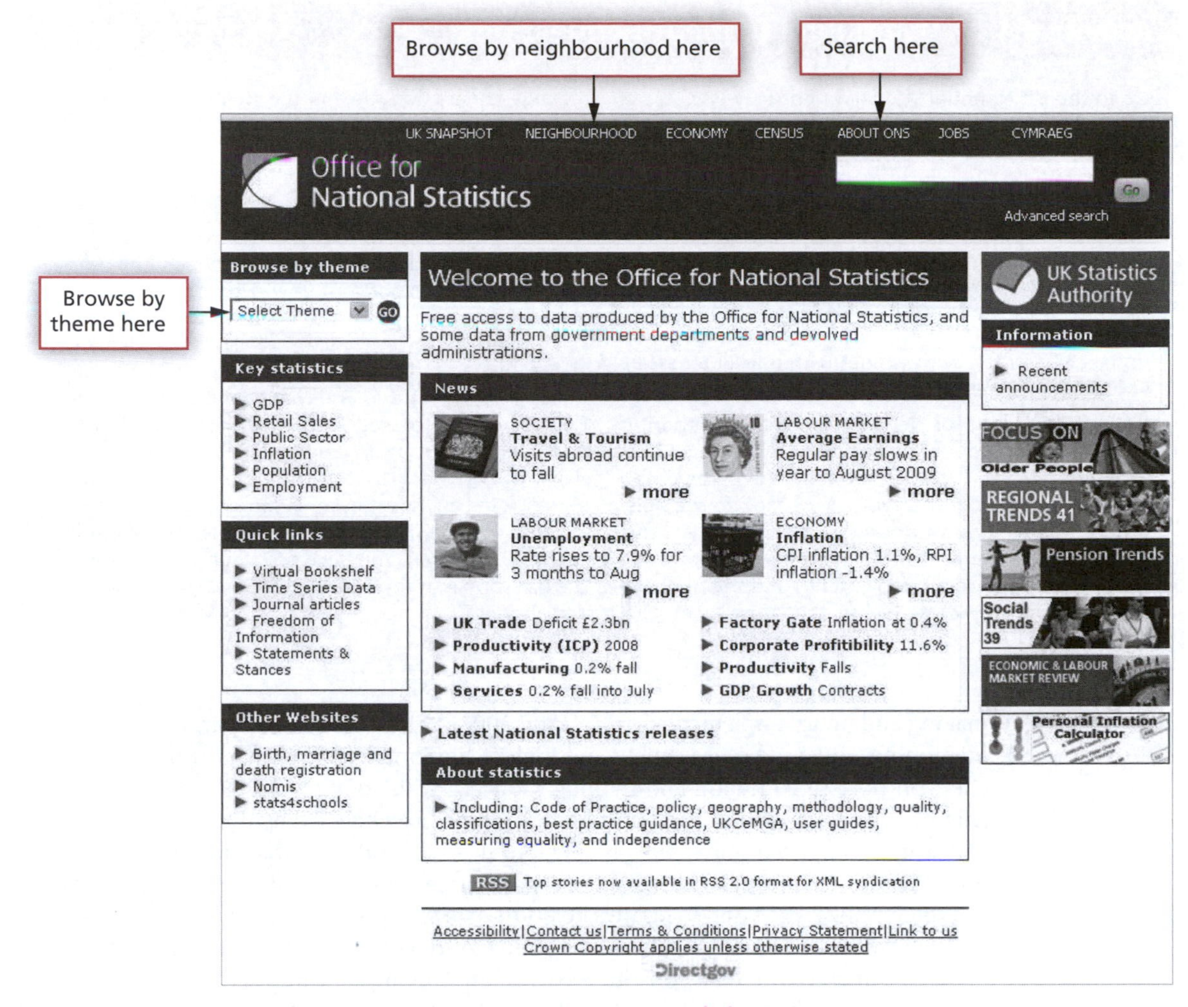

Figure 4.4 Options for identifying data on the National Statistics website

including pupil projections for Scotland. 'Exclusions' provided references to *Social Trends* and also identified detailed data in spreadsheet format held on the website of the Department for Children, Schools and Families. However, not every bit of information on Government websites is yet accessible through the National Statistics portal.

- Fourth, and reflecting the fact that public data are not yet completely linked, we can search via an external Web engine. A search for 'pupil numbers gov uk' via Google brought up a range of key resources by the fifth hit.

The only way through, to appreciate what data are available, is to begin to use it. Activity 4.4 begins this process.

(ii) The Department for Children, Schools and Families (DCSF)

The DCSF is the Government Department responsible for education and training. Via its website (www.dcsf.gov.uk) we can access the *Research and Statistics Gateway*. The Department for Children, Schools and Families website is a very useful entry point into research reports commissioned by the Government and detailed statistics that inform policy

Activity 4.4 Using data to identify questions

Go to the UK National Statistics website (www.statistics.gov.uk) and navigate to the Neighbourhood search page. Enter the search term 'Tower Hamlets' to get data on the education authority. The location of Tower Hamlets is just to the east of the City of London. Go to the section for data on *Education, Skills and Training* and open the page for *Key Figures*. Start by looking at the percentages of 15-year-olds with 5 or more GCSEs (the national qualifications at age 16) at A* to C, the percentages with no passes and the percentages with a level 5 pass in English, Mathematics and Science.

Now do the same for Newham Education Authority. The London Borough of Newham is right next to Tower Hamlets. What are the differences in the data? What do they suggest to you? Now look to see how different the two authorities are. Look at the *Benefits Data* (per cent receiving the Job Seeker's Allowance and per cent Lone Parent's and the per cent of age group 16–24 receiving the Allowance), the teenage conception rates in the Healthcare data set and the Local Authority summaries for the Indices of Deprivation. You do not have to understand (yet!) how these indices are constructed. To guide you, look at the first one in the table, the average score for all areas in the Borough.

There are, naturally, differences between the Boroughs. In 2005, 14 per cent of Newham's 16–24-year-olds were receiving the Job Seeker's Allowance and 32 per cent of Tower Hamlets, while Tower Hamlets had a teenage conception rate of 43.2 births per 1,000 in the age group and Newham one of 53.4 per 1,000. However, overall Tower Hamlets is the fourth most deprived area in England and Newham the eleventh. Go back to the data on education and training. If you investigate in more detail, you will see that Newham is performing rather better than might be expected. You have now identified an issue. The question is, 'Why is this?' Your task as a researcher is to answer it.

making and policy implementation. In early 2007, for example, the Department was commissioning work on disengagement and underachievement amongst young people and its effect on post-16 education and training. Concern with young people classified as NEET (not in education, employment or training) is high, as witnessed by the five major pieces of research completed since 1999 and the four related to the issue that are currently underway. The research programme website is one that researchers should look at to understand emerging policy issues and to appreciate up-to-date synopses of research issues.

The statistics part of the website is a source of detailed statistical data for use in our research. Much of the data constitute part of an ongoing research series. Data are published in two stages, first as provisional figures (even governments make mistakes in data collection and presentation) and as revised figures. We can search for data in four ways.

1. *By keyword*; for example, absence from school brought up 36 publications dating back to 1994 concerned mainly with pupil absence but with some on teacher sickness.
2. *By subject*; there are five starting points: education and skills; employment, jobs and careers; health, well-being and care; science, technology and innovation; and Government, politics and administration (see Figures 4.5(a) to (c)). Each of these is as a branching hierarchy. The screen dump of the section of the website shown in Figure 4.5 shows how, by clicking on an item, we can drill down to more detailed levels. In addition, this approach to searching reveals some of the connectivity that education has beyond the framework of education institutions. The link between education and work is shown with the statistics on careers (qualifications and adult participation in learning) and data on the New Deal programme (operated by the Department of Work and Pensions and aimed at getting young people and the long-term unemployed back to work). However, it is the Education and Skills track that will interest most researchers. Pre-school data include detailed information by local authority on provision for under 5s. For schools, there is data on management and finance, performance, attendance, staff and reclassification of much of the data by types of school. Altogether, there are almost 700 data sources in this category.

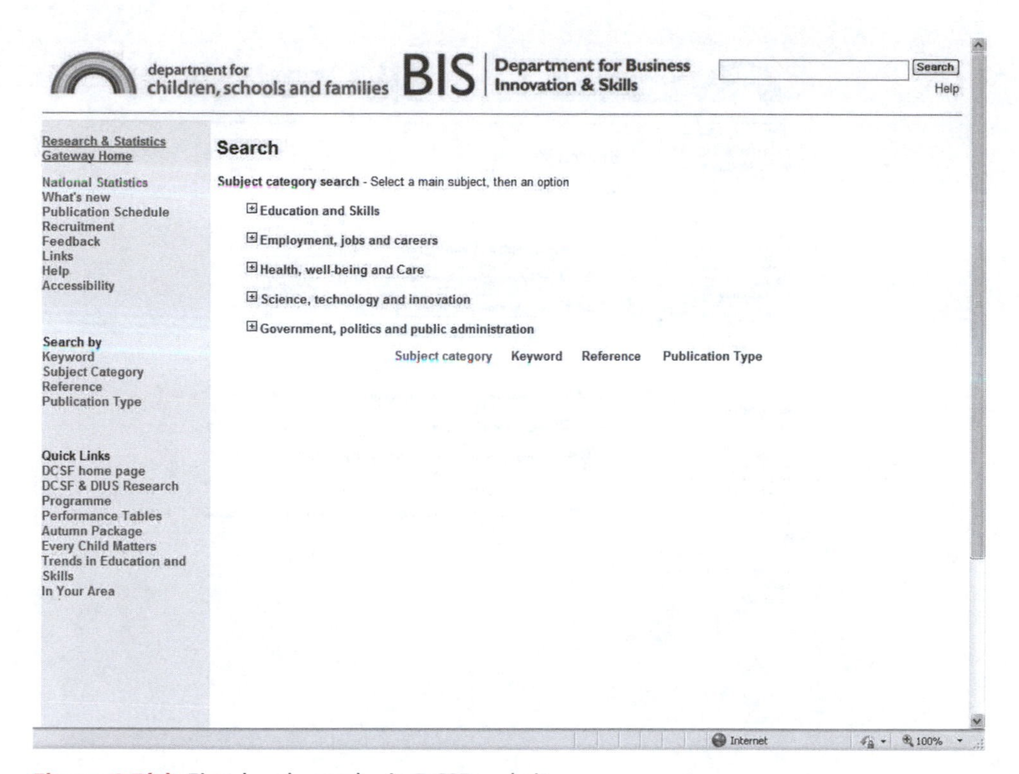

Figure 4.5(a) First level search via DCSF website

department for
children, schools and families
BIS
Department for Business
Innovation & Skills
Search
Help
Research & Statistics
Gateway Home
National Statistics
What's new
Publication Schedule
Recruitment
Feedback
Links
Help
Accessibility
Search by
Keyword
Subject Category
Reference
Publication Type
Quick Links
DCSF home page
DCSF & DIUS Research
Programme
Performance Tables
Autumn Package
Every Child Matters
Trends in Education and
Skills
In Your Area
Search
Subject category search - Select a main subject, then an option
Education and Skills
Pre-school learning
Schools
Further and Higher Education
Special Educational Needs and additional support
Skills and Competences
Employment, jobs and careers
Health, well-being and Care
Science, technology and innovation
Government, politics and public administration
Subject category
Keyword
Reference
Publication Type
Internet
100%

Figure 4.5(b) Second level search via DCSF website

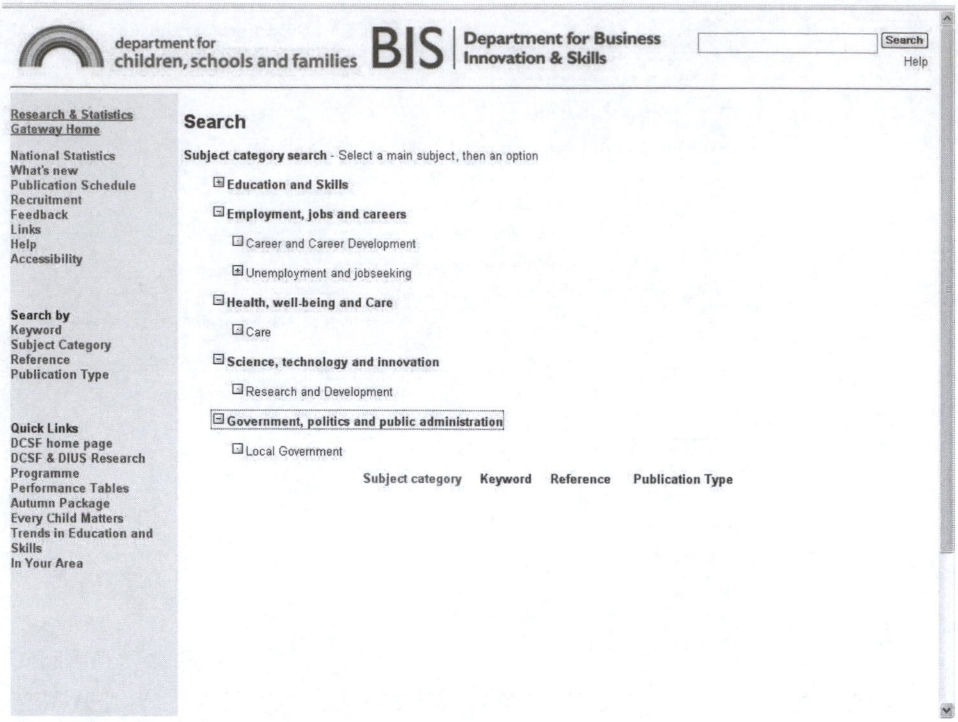

department for children, schools and families BIS Department for Business Innovation & Skills

Search
Help

Research & Statistics Gateway Home

National Statistics
What's new
Publication Schedule
Recruitment
Feedback
Links
Help
Accessibility

Search by
Keyword
Subject Category
Reference
Publication Type

Quick Links
DCSF home page
DCSF & DIUS Research Programme
Performance Tables
Autumn Package
Every Child Matters
Trends in Education and Skills
In Your Area

Search

Subject category search - Select a main subject, then an option

- **Education and Skills**
- **Employment, jobs and careers**
  - Career and Career Development
  - Unemployment and jobseeking
- **Health, well-being and Care**
  - Care
- **Science, technology and innovation**
  - Research and Development
- **Government, politics and public administration**
  - Local Government

Subject category Keyword Reference Publication Type

Figure 4.5(c) Second level search via DCSF website: further data options

3. *By publication type:* this will give us all of the publications of a particular type. The categories are statistical first releases, statistical bulletins, statistical volumes, research reports and briefs, time series, economics and other statistics. Statistical first releases are the initial releases of periodic surveys (which are often reissued in revised form subsequently). These first releases include such things as special education needs, student loan applications, admission appeals for schools and children accommodated in secure homes. Statistical bulletins are data that government statisticians and researchers have processed to explore an issue of concern or interest. Often these derive from a need to assess the outcomes of policy or to explore where new policy may be needed. Examples include the characteristics of low attaining pupils, permanent exclusions from schools and class sizes and pupil teacher ratios. Statistical volumes are collected data on a particular theme that are published on a regular basis. Amongst the most useful are likely to be *Statistics of Education* (with sections on expenditure, schools, post compulsory education and training, qualifications, population and international comparisons) and *Higher Education Statistics for the UK*. These data appear first as separate series of statistical first releases. Research reports and briefs are the product of government-funded research initiatives. They are focused pieces of academic policy-related research. For example, in 2007, the UK Department for Children, Schools and Families published reports on the social, emotional and behavioural skills of secondary pupils, on family and parenting support and on engaging parents in raising achievement. Time series are data sets (usually released annually) where a year on year comparison is valuable in order to establish trends or patterns in time. They include series on pupil attainment, average teacher salaries, total numbers of teachers, class sizes and expenditure per pupil.

Other statistics are frequently derived from other government departments and include data on children's services and the use of actions such as fast track procedures and parenting orders to deal with truancy. These illustrations can only give a feel for the enormous wealth of data and information that awaits education researchers.

4. *By text reference*; we would use this search route if we had already obtained the reference from a Government or other publication. References are listed for current year publications.

(iii) Other Government and public sources

There are many other Government departments that produce data relevant to education research (see Table 4.4). The *Department for Communities and Local Government* has information on the socio-economic context of education provision with statistical data on cities and regions, community development, equality, housing and local government. The *Youth Justice Board* has data detailing the work of Youth Offending Teams, essential if we are studying the link between school, home and potentially criminal behaviour. The *Home Office* has statistics and reports on crime, policing and anti-social behaviour while The *Cabinet Office* currently houses the *Social Exclusion Task Force* which has been responsible for much of the policy thrust on social exclusion. The *Higher Education Statistics Agency* (HESA) provides data on institutional performance, students, staff, finance and post-qualification destinations of students and UCAS (the organisation that manages university enrolment allows us to access data on applications by subject, institution, age, home of application, ethnicity and social status). *Government Social Research* is a portal to data from a range of departments and sources. Many of the sources given are non-British (for example, the Bibliography of Nordic Criminology). Many of the sources are non-governmental but amongst those that are supported by Government are the *Economic and Social Data Service* (ESDS), which is a collaboration between the UK Data Archive (www.data-archive.ac.uk) and three other centres. (For more on data archives, see Case Study 4.3). ESDS has responsibility for managing longitudinal surveys such as the National Child Development Survey. The *Question Bank* is another database that stores surveys, not survey results. The *Policy Hub* is a civil service website concerned with policy; it contains excellent material on policy development and a superb review of evaluation methodology in the *Magenta Book*. (The title was given to distinguish it from the *Green Book*, which is the Treasury's set of guidelines for the economic appraisal of policy and

Table 4.4 Other public sources of data

Organisation	Website
Department for Communities and Local Government	www.communities.gov.uk
Youth Justice Board	www.yjb.gov.uk
Home Office	www.scienceandresearch.homeoffice.gov.uk
Cabinet Office	www.cabinetoffice.gov.uk/social_exclusion_task_force
Higher Education Statistics Agency	www.hesa.ac.uk
UCAS	www.ucas.com
Government Social Research	www.gsr.gov.uk
Economic and Social Data Service	www.esds.ac.uk
Question Bank	www.qb.survey.ac.uk
Policy Hub	www.policyhub.gov.uk
Observatories	Many regional and local examples

projects.) Of particular note, as well, are the routes through to other resources at different levels of Government. For local government there is the Local Authorities Research and Intelligence Association and Info4local Government, another information portal into Government information sources. Finally, we should note the existence of numerous regional and local observatories, which assemble national data at a regional and local level. As examples, we can look at the observatory for the East of England (www.eastofenglandobservatory.org.uk) and for the London Boroughs of Enfield (www.enfield-observatory.org.uk/enfieldobservatory) and Barnet (www.barnet.gov.uk/index/council-democracy/informationobservatory.htm).

4.6.2 Denmark

The statistics Denmark website (www.dst.dk) is published, in part, in English. Data on a range of subjects are available on-line and more detailed tables are available after registration (www.statbank.dk). Figure 4.6 shows some of the tables available. The means of extracting the data is clear and straightforward. The extraction system allows us to pivot tables (a technique for manipulating rows and columns to get different data analyses) as well as outputting the data graphically. The range of data available without registration is laid out in Table 4.5. Data on social conditions includes child maintenance, housing and others that can be used to describe the social context for education.

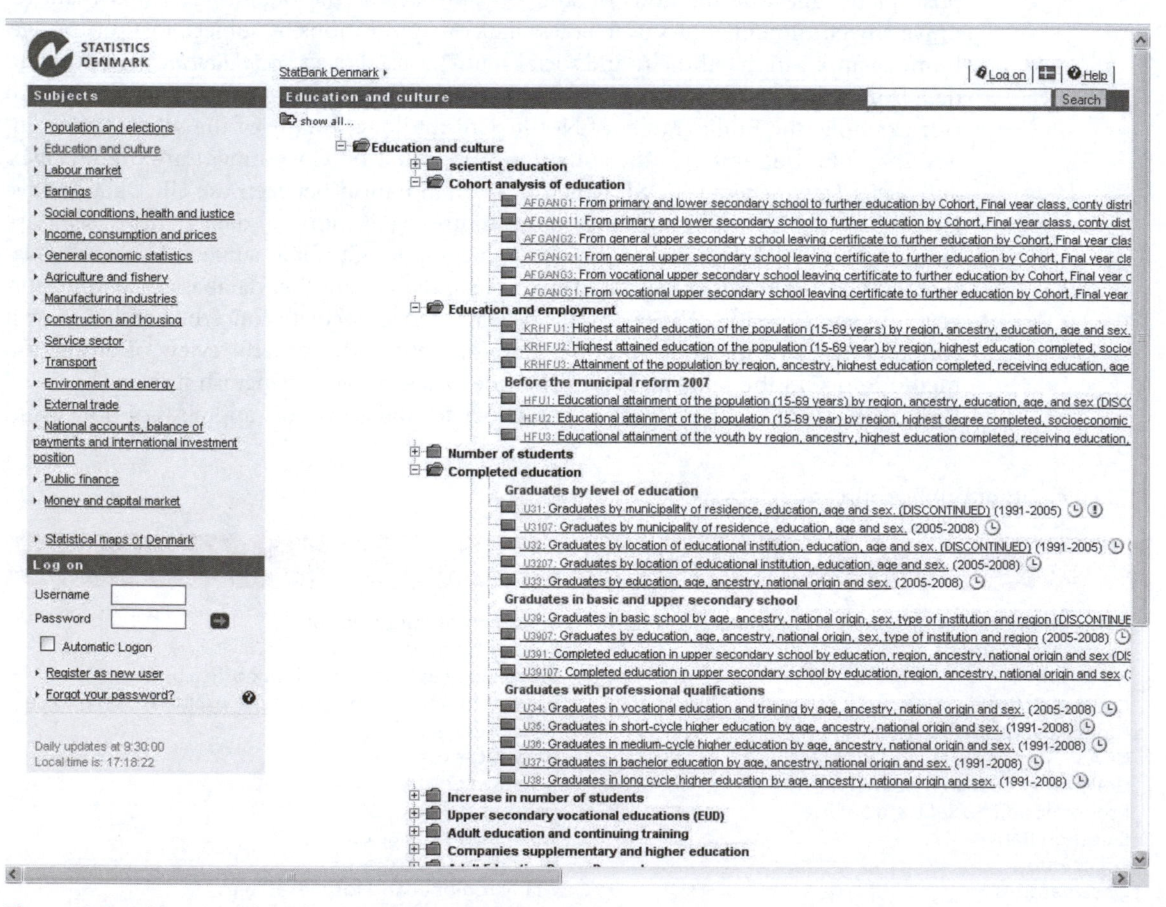

Figure 4.6 Education data from Statistics Denmark

Table 4.5 Education data available at Statistics Denmark

Theme	Tables
Cohort analysis	Three data sets covering primary and lower secondary, general upper secondary to further education and vocational secondary to further education for 2004–5.
Education and employment	Six data sets, highest education level attained, regional data, structured by age/sex/status for periods 1991–2006.
Number of students	10 data sets describing students by level of education, students by school and by professional qualifications for 1991–2005.
Completed education	10 data sets showing completions by level of education, by school and by professional qualifications for 1991–2005.
Increase in number of students	10 data sets showing entrance by level of education, by school and by professional qualification for 1991–2005.
Upper secondary vocational education	4 data sets showing numbers of students, entrants to vocational education, dropouts and completions for 1997–2005.
Adult education and continuing training	12 data sets showing competencies studied for, course participants, full-time equivalents and private education for 1996–2005.

4.6.3 Finland

The following websites provide information about statistical data, and other information about education in Finland:

(i) *Statistics Finland* (www.tilastokeskus.fi/index_en.html or www.stat.fi/index_en.html). This site describes the types of data held. For education follow the public sector link under *data collections*. The site describes data held on schools, the autumn audit of schools and pupils, educational finance, student employment, teachers and staff) but it does not give access to the data files. There is an email contact.

(ii) *Ministry of Education* (www.minedu.fi): This site describes educational policy and summarises the character of the educational system.

4.6.4 The Netherlands

Statistics Netherlands' website (www.cbs.nl) gives access to data in both Dutch and English. The English version is more restricted in scale but is growing. It is possible to search for data in the following ways.

- By *theme* (Figure 4.7(a)). The most relevant themes for education research are education, health and welfare, labour and social security, leisure and culture, population and security and justice. Each of these themes takes us to a new screen with four, at present, tabs – new data, figures (for education these are the education levels of the working population and institutions and students), publications and methods. This is a good route to get the feel of the data (Figures 4.7(b) to 4.7(d)).
- By the *figures (statistical data) by theme*: In this case we can look at key figures and then figures by theme (as before).
- By searching the *Statline database* (access via the *figures* link). This route enables us to search (a) by area of interest using keywords (a search on young people's leisure identified two tables) and (b) by area.

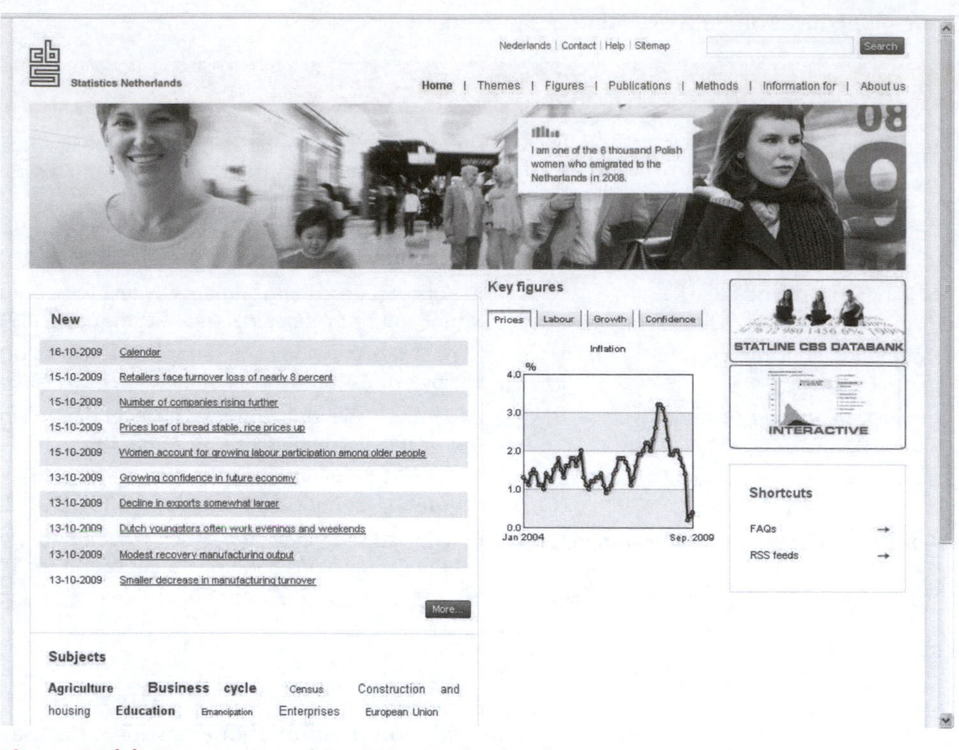

Figure 4.7(a) Home page of Statistics Netherlands

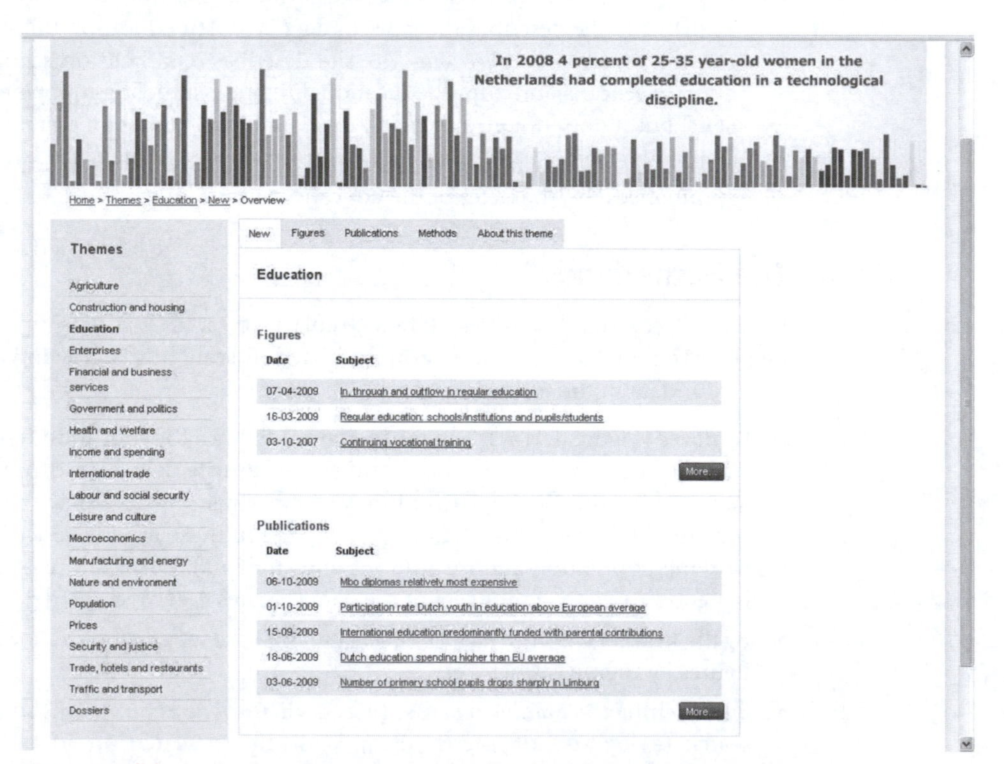

Figure 4.7(b) Home education page of Statistics Netherlands

Nederlands | Contact | Help | Sitemap Search

Statistics Netherlands

Home | Themes | Figures | Publications | Methods | Information for | About us

For the first time in ten years, the number of pupils in Dutch secondary education decreased in school year 2007/'08.

Home > Themes > Education > Figures > Overview

New | Figures | Publications | Methods | About this theme

Themes

- Agriculture
- Construction and housing
- Education
- Enterprises
- Financial and business services
- Government and politics
- Health and welfare
- Income and spending
- International trade
- Labour and social security
- Leisure and culture
- Macroeconomics
- Manufacturing and energy
- Nature and environment
- Population
- Prices

Education

Key figures

- In, through and outflow in regular education →
- Education level working population →
- Institutions and students →

All tables in the databank StatLine

http://www.cbs.nl/en-GB/menu/themas/onderwijs/cijfers/kerncijfers/institutions-and-students-kc.htm Internet 100%

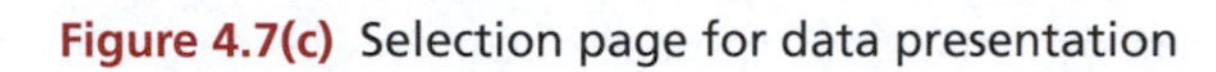

Figure 4.7(c) Selection page for data presentation

Statistics Netherlands

Home | Themes | Figures | Publications | Methods | Information for | About us |

StatLine database > Tables by theme > Select data > Show data Search: Search term | Theme

In, through and outflow in regular education

Table explanation Changed on April 07 2009. Frequency: yearly. change selection Link Download Print Help

Table Graph Map

Subjects: Pupils and students
Periods: 2006/'07*
Gender: Males and females
Origin: number

Transferred to:	Enrolment in the base year	Enrolment in the next year	Primary education	Special needs primary education	Special schools	First class years of secondary education	Special secondary education	Practical training	Vmbo full-time gr. 3+	Vmbo theoretical basis, part-time	Havo full-time gr. 3+	Havo part-time	Vwo full-time gr. 3+	Vwo part-time	Bol full-time	Bol part-time
Enrolment in the next year		3 705 091	1 552 472	44 933	64 663	390 259		27 021	217 405	2 786	145 275	7 824	161 240	2 906	335 803	11 280
Enrolment in the base year	3 677 298	3 345 996	1 346 764	44 138	60 668	386 940		26 942	216 495	2 026	144 087	6 497	160 441	2 328	316 409	5 987
Primary education	1 548 774	1 538 086	1 345 714	8 876	4 542	177 661		1 293								
Special needs primary education	46 304	45 950	271	34 615	1 465	5 714		3 885								
Special schools	61 228	57 130	779	647	52 967	870		355	384		69		13		401	23
First class years of secondary schools	394 293	389 016			802	202 483		458	102 424	47	38 804	12	43 002		881	4
Special secondary education																
Practical training	27 330	23 800			109	84		20 915	183						1 672	2
Vmbo full-time, gr. 3+, unqualified	121 939	118 015			625	55		36	110 852	680					4 315	23
Vmbo full-time, qualified	101 879	95 407							59	34	9 462	216			74 030	28
Vmbo theoretical, part-time, unqualified	1 879	961								765					136	
Vmbo theoretical,part-time, qualified	906	484										165			277	6
Havo full-time, gr. 3+, unqualified	102 091	99 624			111	62			2 557	67	90 115	2 554	222		3 647	12
Havo full-time, qualified	39 778	35 866											2 270	183	1 412	6
Havo part-time, unqualified	4 517	2 619								14		2 177			352	6
Havo part-time, qualified	2 539	1 505												78	34	

Figure 4.7(d) Search results

4.6.5 Sweden

The Statistics Sweden website (www.scb.se) is again available in English as well as Swedish. The routes into the data are again by theme (in this case called subject areas) and by searching the statistical database. The website currently gives access to more data sets in English than the Dutch site. There are 45 data sets for education and research covering education of the population, financial aid, research, higher education and the school system and day care. The search route takes us either to a listing of detailed data sets or to a free word search. Access without registration limits data output to 1,000 data cells. To get access to more data we have to register. Registration is free.

4.6.6 The USA

The USA is rich in data resources and only a few can be reviewed here in order to give a sense of what is available. This description is confined to education but data on society, culture, population and so on is widely available.

(i) US Census Bureau

www.census.gov/population/www/socdemo/education.html

Via this website we can access summary data on the following:

- Educational attainment (e.g. attainment for people aged over 15 by ethnicity).
- Fields of training (e.g. average monthly income by education).
- School costs ('school' here refers to post-secondary education and includes, for example, an analysis of enrolment by sex, ethnicity, age, marital status, work status, income).
- School enrolment (here 'school' refers to enrolment of children aged 3 and over and includes, for example, numbers and per cent enrolled or not enrolled in types of school by age and gender).
- School district demographics: searchable by map (see Figure 4.8) or by name. The map search allows us to identify the area and the label based analysis allows us to extract detailed demographic data on an individual or comparative basis. Other data sets are available including estimates of the numbers of families in poverty in each school district of the country.

(ii) National Centre for Education Statistics (www.nces.ed.gov)

This is an excellent searchable resource that allows us to identify data in the following ways.

(a) By institution using the data tools: we can search for public school districts, public schools and private schools and, for each, obtain detailed data.

(b) By tables and figures: a search for non-attendance identified 29 tables, some dating back to 1975. There is an option to search by keyword. In order to make full use of this rich data source we need to know either the name of a school or school district or a zip (post) code.

(iii) California (www.ed-data.k12.ca.us)

California is presented as an illustration of data availability at state level. On this site we can:

(c) Find information on any school, school district or administrative county. The search can be by name or by zipcode. The data output includes a profile of the school,

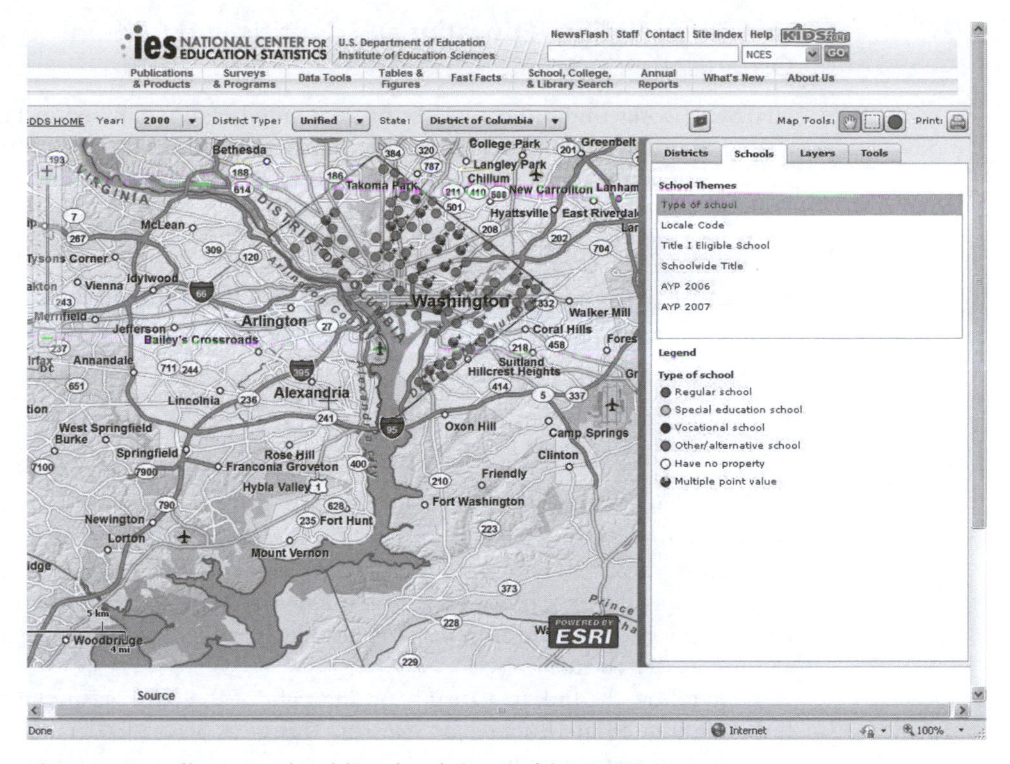

Figure 4.8 Colleges and public schools in Washington DC

performance monitoring, pupil performance and pupil withdrawal. There is a facility to compare schools.

(d) Find profiles for the state, county, district and school.

4.6.7 International data sources

International data sources are often used in comparative studies of countries. The data are compiled by international agencies and organisations from national statistics. For this reason, they tend to be less detailed than data from national agencies. The main requirement of international data sources (other than they have what we want) is that the data they present should be broadly comparable. This has two components. First, the framework used to collect and present the data should be comparable. If it is not, comparison becomes very difficult and we have to resort to procedures such as those described in Case Study 4.5. Second, the rigour with which the data are collected has to be such that the data are credible. This, of course, is the responsibility of the national government or agency. In general, issues about data quality are related to the level of a country's economic development. Infrastructure problems (such as accessibility), lack of personnel and lower levels of literacy in rural populations inevitably limit data collection and thus affect overall data quality. The international agencies that collect the data do assist by developing common frameworks and advising on collection systems.

Some aid and research agencies from economically advanced nations collect their own data or refine data collected by state agencies. These data are often better quality but restricted in their national coverage.

(i) United Nations Educational, Scientific and Cultural Organisation (UNESCO)

UNESCO works under the auspices of the United Nations. Based in Paris, it works to share information and to help member countries develop what we would now refer to as their cultural and social capital. In the field of education, a fundamental platform for economic and social development, it seeks to:

- increase early childhood provision;
- increase the numbers of children receiving free primary schooling;
- increase learning opportunities for young people and adults;
- raise literacy rates to 50 per cent;
- remove gender disparities in schooling;
- improve the quality of education.

The opening page of the UNESCO website (http://portal.unesco.org/) gives details about the organisation and its services on the right hand side and, on the left, lists the themes, areas and communities it is involved with. The first of the themes is education. The opening page of the education theme (see Figure 4.9(a)) identifies the levels of education it is concerned with, key themes (such as literacy, HIV/Aids and teacher education), as well as area links.

If we follow the link to statistics, on the right of the page we are taken to is another link, this time to the *Institute for Statistics.* This gives access to detailed data. Note, this website changes frequently.

Figure 4.9(a) UNESCO opening page

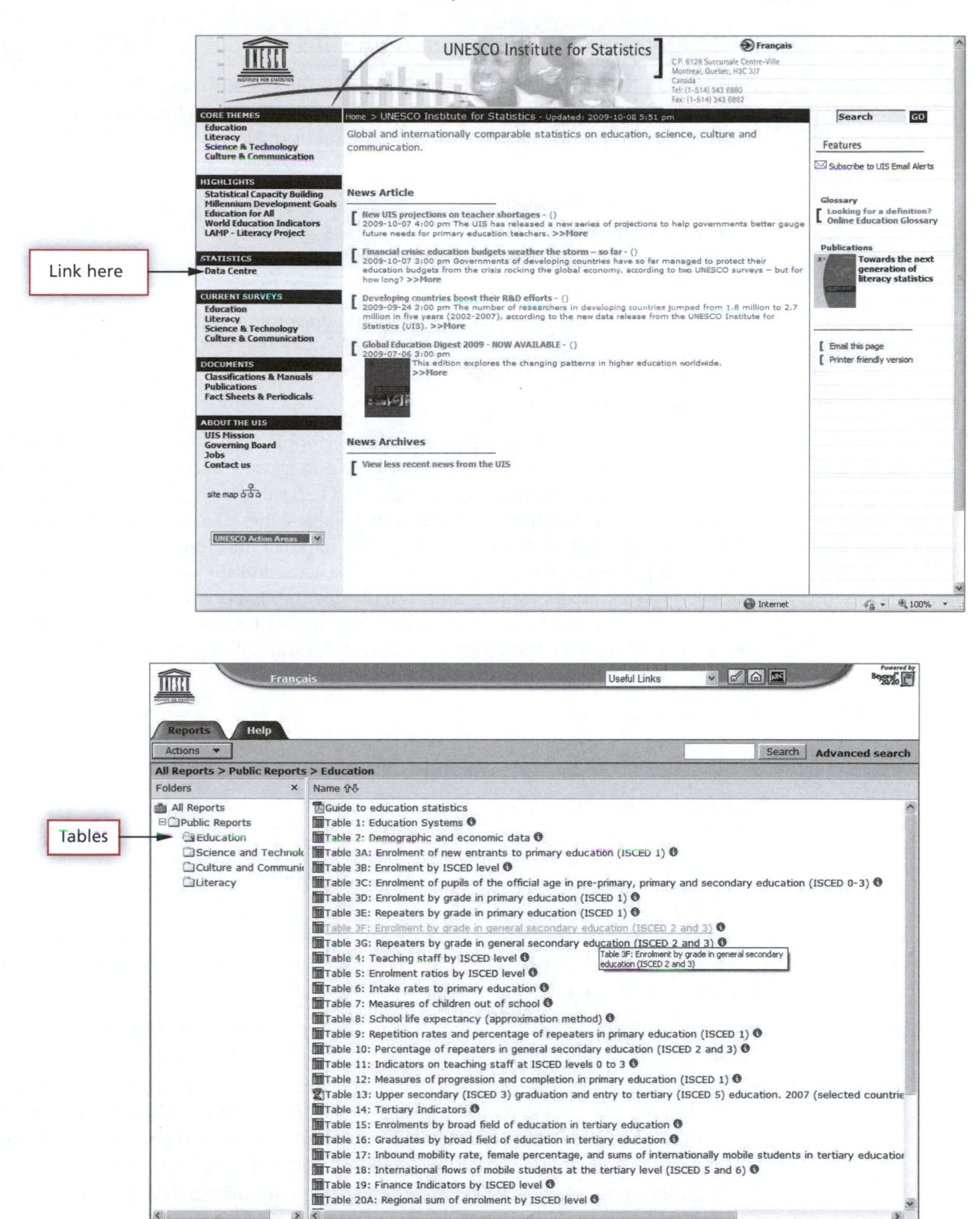

Figure 4.9(b) UNESCO statistics

(ii) International Bureau of Education (IBE)

The IBE is a specialised UNESCO centre (www.ibe.unesco.org/). Its principal concern is with curriculum development. It functions as a research and networking organisation but, for us at this point, it is primarily a source of information, data and expertise. It is a useful portal for:

- country specific information;
- searchable database of reports;
- searchable curriculum banks on HIV/Aids education and living together;
- world data on education (see section 4.8.1);
- archives of the International Conference on Education.

(iii) Organisation for Economic Co-Operation and Development (OECD)

The OECD's purpose is to support economic development and through that to raise living standards. It produces data and reports on a range of topics, including education, and works to change governmental attitudes and behaviour. While it has a separate section on education, much of its work contextualises the education sector. Education relates to the OECD's work on economy, both national and international, on innovation (developments in biotechnology, ICT and science and the concept of a knowledge economy), on social and welfare issues, employment, migration and health.

The OECD's interest in education (www.oecd.org/education) focuses on the contribution of education to the creation of knowledge capital and its role in supporting economic growth. Its principal themes are:

- the learning society;
- outcomes of learning;
- quality;
- tertiary education;
- futures for education;
- family policies;
- social cohesion;
- skills.

Most important for us, at this point, are the statistics that we can access. The principal reports and statistics are:

- *the family database*: this is currently being developed and will present over 50 indicators of family condition;
- *education on-line database (http://www.oecd.org/document/54/0,3343,en_2649_39263238_38082166_1_1_1_37455,00.html)*: this gives data on student enrolment, overseas students, graduates and expenditure. It is a searchable database and provides information on the major developed and trading nations of the world (see Figure 4.10);
- *Education at a Glance*: a periodical summarising educational data for OECD members. Tables are accessible on-line.

(iv) Eurydice

Eurydice is an information network supported by the EU that makes available comparable data and information on education systems and policies in member states plus

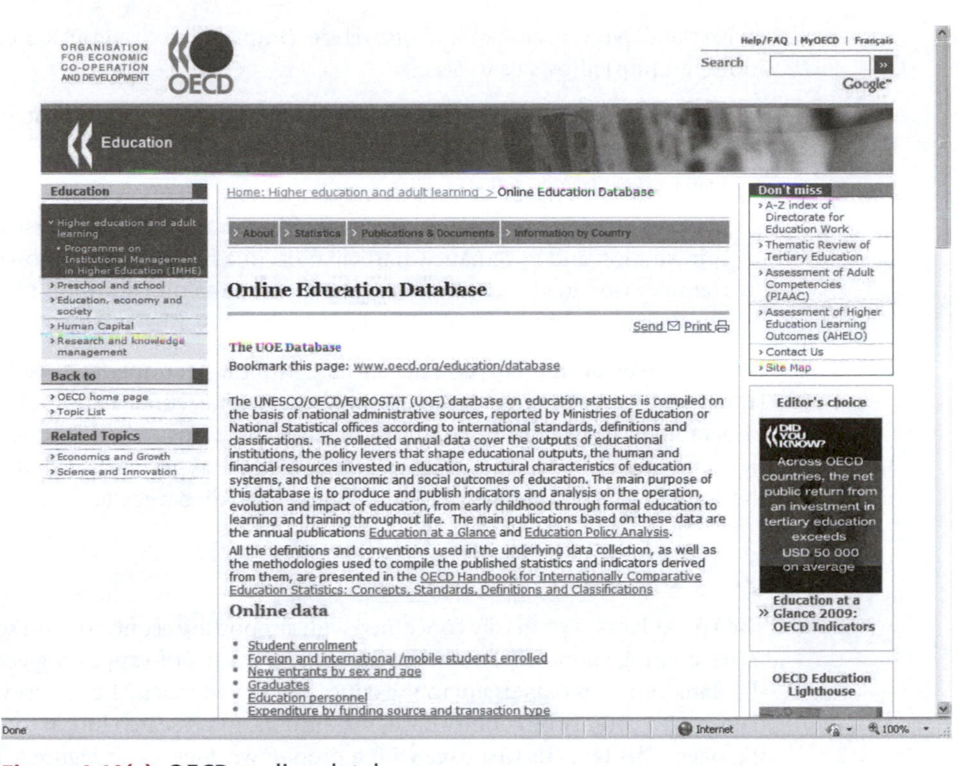

Figure 4.10(a) OECD on-line database

OECD.StatExtracts

Complete databases available via SourceOECD, OECD's iLibrary.

Search

Foreign / international students enrolled [1]

Current data selection: Country [30 / 54] Year [4] Level of education [1 / 11] Programme destination [1 / 3] Foreign or international category [3 / 7] Programme orientation [1 / 3] Gender [1 / 3] Country of origin [1 / 224]

Data extracted on 19 Oct 2009 08:18 UTC (GMT) from OECD.Stat

Level of education: 905060: Total tertiary education
Programme destination: 900000: Total
Programme orientation: 900000: All educational programmes
Gender: 90: Total males+females
Country of origin: 9000: Total: All countries

Year	2004			2005			2006			2007		
Foreign or international category	20: Non-citizen students of reporting country	10: Non-resident students of reporting country	30: Students with prior education outside the reporting country	20: Non-citizen students of reporting country	10: Non-resident students of reporting country	30: Students with prior education outside the reporting country	20: Non-citizen students of reporting country	10: Non-resident students of reporting country	30: Students with prior education outside the reporting country	20: Non-citizen students of reporting country	10: Non-resident students of reporting country	30: Students with prior education outside the reporting country
Country												
Australia	199 284	166 954	(m) 0	211 255	177 034	(m) 0	217 055	184 710	(m) 0	244 309	211 526	(m)
Austria	33 707	26 928	30 114	34 484	27 001	31 058	39 329	30 366	35 059	43 572	32 430	(m)
Belgium	37 091	19 329	29 648	38 242	21 054	(m) 0	40 607	24 854	33 927	41 351	25 202	32 88
Canada	112 816	110 990	(m) 0	(m) 0	(m) 0	(m) 0	148 164	75 546	(m) 0	132 246	68 520	(m)
Czech Republic	14 923	(m) 0	(m) 0	18 522	(m) 0	(m) 0	21 395	17 057	(m) 0	24 483	20 175	(m)
Denmark	17 160	9 882	(m) 0	17 430	10 251	(m) 0	19 123	10 952	(m) 0	20 851	12 695	(m)
Finland	7 915	(m) 0	10 344	8 442	(m) 0	10 992	8 955	(m) 0	11 514	10 066	(m) 0	12 68
France	..	(m) 0	(m) 0	(m) 0	236 518	(m) 0	247 510	(m) 0	(m) 0	246 612	(m) 0	(m)
Germany	260 314	(m) 0	198 665	259 797	(m) 0	204 603	261 363	(m) 0	207 994	258 513	(m) 0	206 87
Greece	(m) 0	(m) 0	(m) 0	15 690	2 872	(m) 0	16 558	(m) 0	(m) 0	21 160	(m) 0	(m)
Hungary	12 913	11 705	(m) 0	13 601	11 909	(m) 0	14 491	12 381	(m) 0	15 110	12 946	(m)
Iceland	489	(m) 0	(m) 0	484	(m) 0	(m) 0	715	(m) 0	(m) 0	783	(m) 0	82
Ireland	(m) 0	(m) 0	12 698	(m) 0	(m) 0	12 889	(m) 0	(m) 0	12 740	(m) 0	(m) 0	16 75

Figure 4.10(b) OECD on-line database detail of statistics

Switzerland, Norway and Iceland. Its website (http://eacea.ec.europa.eu/education/eurydice/index_en.php) allows us to access:

- *Thematic studies*: in September 2009 it published one on integrating immigrant children into schools, for example;
- *Descriptions of national education systems;*
- *Data series*: with comparative analyses of, for example, quality assessment, school administration and governance, participation in education, educational funding, teacher training, workload *and teacher numbers in* Key Data on Education in Europe (published annually), plus publications on language teaching, higher education and ICT.

Data that was on the Eurydice server has, in part, been migrated to the Eurostat server (http://epp.eurostat.ec.europa.eu/portal/page/portal/eurostat/home). There is a wealth of data here. To find data on education, click the 'statistics' tab and look under 'Population and Social Conditions'. Figure 4.11 shows the types of data that are held. They are the sources for the analyses presented on the Eurydice website.

(v) World Bank

The World Bank is primarily concerned with supporting economic and social development in developing countries. Education is seen as a means of supporting economic lift-off, so the Bank provides data useful to the educational researcher. The easiest way to access these data is on a country by country basis, via the data and research link at the head of the opening page. This takes us to a page with a drop down menu (see Figure 4.12). Selecting *data by country* takes us to an overview page. On the right is a link to education resources. The search in Figure 4.12 shows the results for Bangladesh. We can also search by:

- *themes:* education expenditure, vulnerable populations, education outcomes, school age populations;
- *groups of countries:* Caribbean, Islamic, OECD;
- *World Bank:* lending;
- *Countries at a glance:* statistical summaries on a national basis. Not all of the country profiles contain the same information. This is largely due to lack of governmental infrastructure.

4.6.8 Review

The enormous scale of secondary data available to us over the Internet should, by now, be apparent. We can use these data in the following ways:

- to set the context for an issue we are going to investigate at a detailed level using primary data we correct ourselves;
- as a large data set to be analysed using statistical analysis to identify patterns and issues;
- to compare one area with another in order to identify and explain similarities and differences.

To use them, however, we have to feel confident – confident in our ability to find out what is available; confident in being able to access the data; and confident in being able to pick up the 'messages' of the data. Confidence comes with familiarity. Activity 4.5 will help with this.

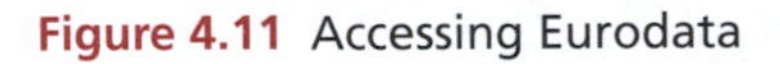

Figure 4.11 Accessing Eurodata

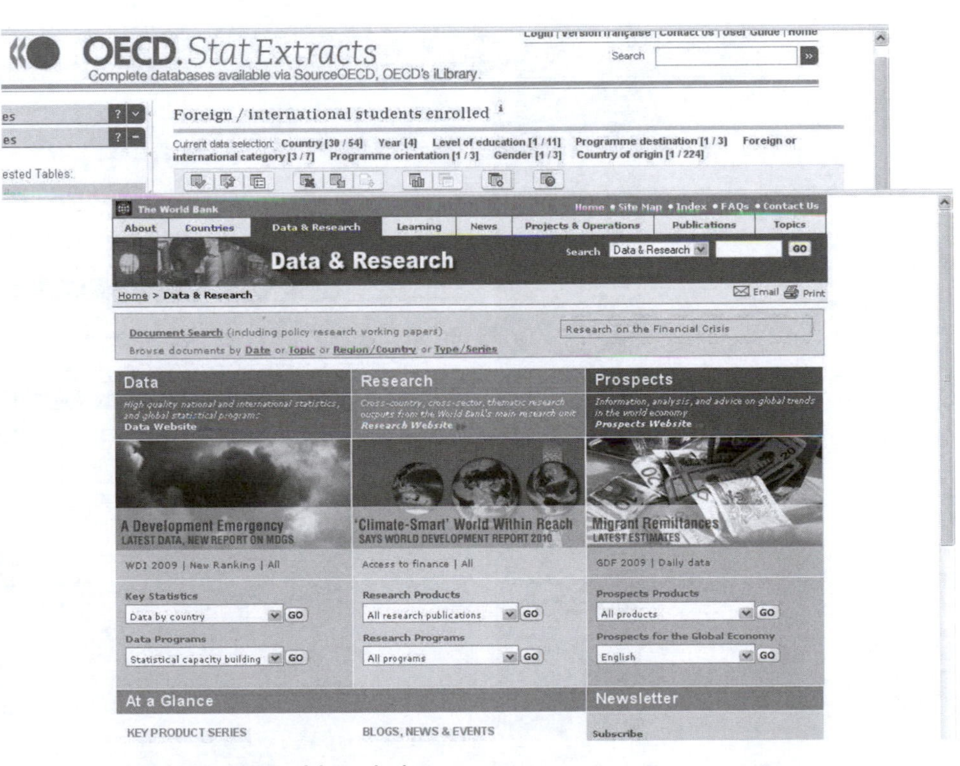

Figure 4.12 Accessing World Bank data

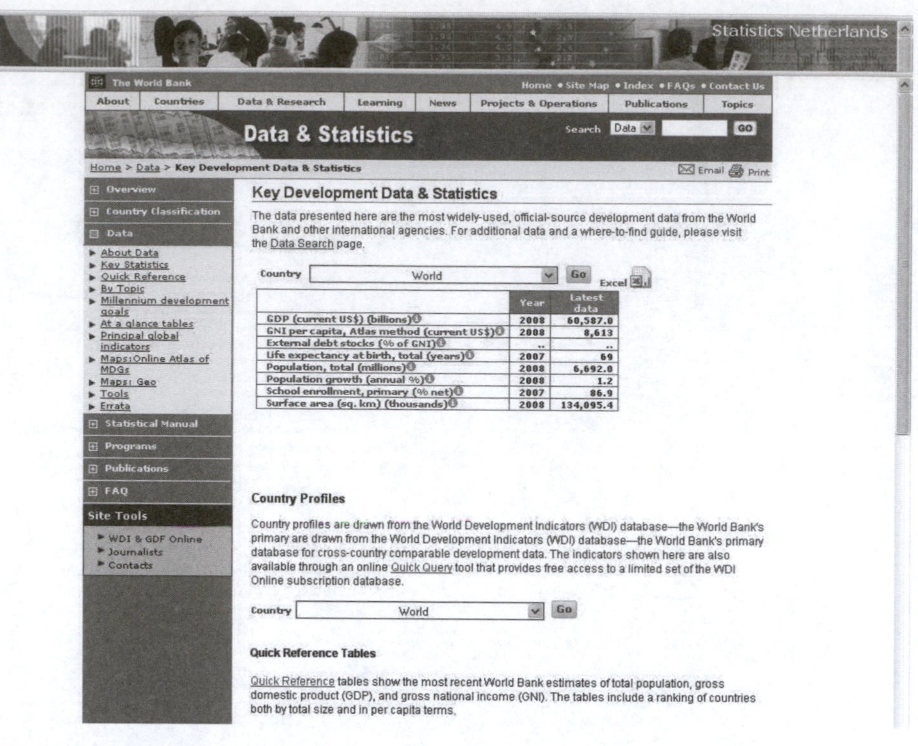

	Year	Latest data
GDP (current US$) (billions)	2008	60,587.0
GNI per capita, Atlas method (current US$)	2008	8,613
External debt stocks (% of GNI)	..	..
Life expectancy at birth, total (years)	2007	69
Population, total (millions)	2008	6,692.0
Population growth (annual %)	2008	1.2
School enrollment, primary (% net)	2007	86.9
Surface area (sq. km) (thousands)	2008	134,095.4

Figure 4.12 (continued)

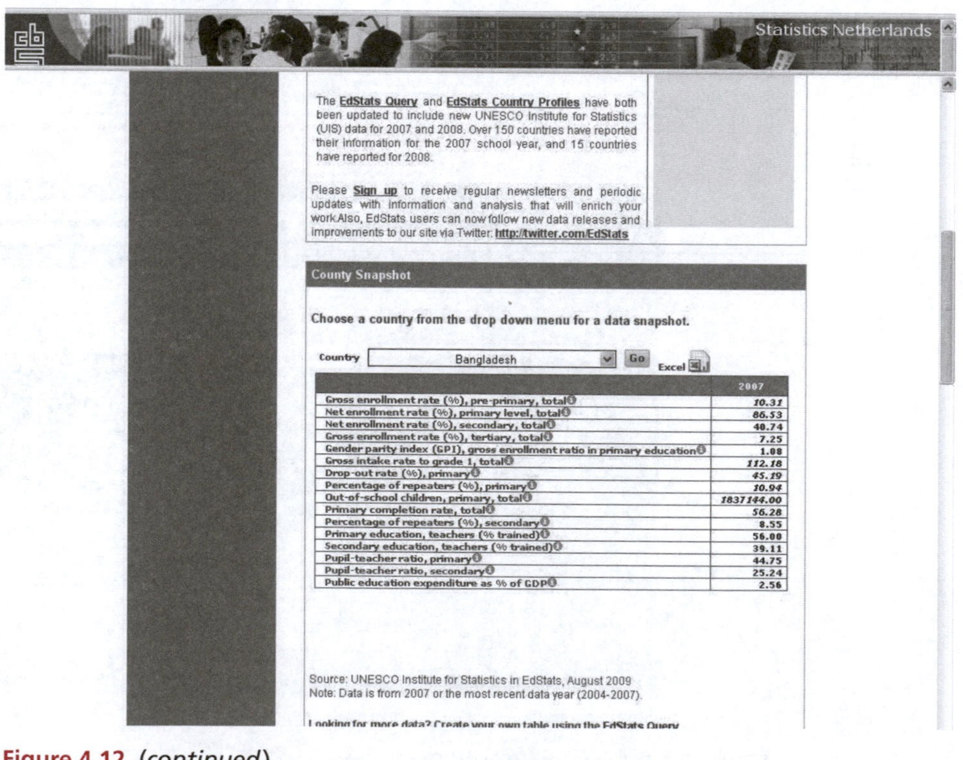

	2007
Gross enrollment rate (%), pre-primary, total	10.31
Net enrollment rate (%), primary level, total	86.53
Net enrollment rate (%), secondary, total	40.74
Gross enrollment rate (%), tertiary, total	7.25
Gender parity index (GPI), gross enrollment ratio in primary education	1.08
Gross intake rate to grade 1, total	112.18
Drop-out rate (%), primary	45.19
Percentage of repeaters (%), primary	10.94
Out-of-school children, primary, total	1837144.00
Primary completion rate, total	56.28
Percentage of repeaters (%), secondary	8.55
Primary education, teachers (% trained)	56.00
Secondary education, teachers (% trained)	39.11
Pupil-teacher ratio, primary	44.75
Pupil-teacher ratio, secondary	25.24
Public education expenditure as % of GDP	2.56

Figure 4.12 *(continued)*

Activity 4.5 Increasing your awareness of data sources

1. Select any national data set. Follow through the links from the home page. In your own words describe the structure of the website. Pay particular attention to the way in which data can be accessed and the levels (school, education district/authority, region/state, nation) at which data are presented. Is the same data presented at each level?
2. Search for data on the following topics in any national data set:
   - Performance of pupils at key points in their education. Is there any differentiation by gender, school type, ethnicity?
   - Absence/truanting from school.
   - People with qualifications. Can you differentiate between those with academic and those with vocational qualifications?
   - Data on pupils with special educational needs.
   - Data on pre-school learning/early-years education and childcare; does this data give you any appreciation of trends in provision over time?
   - One other topic in which you have a particular interest.
3. See if you can answer the following questions:
   - In which country, Australia, Denmark, the Netherlands, Sweden and the UK, have graduate numbers increased most in absolute and percentage terms since 2000?
   - Has the growth been more amongst men or women? (Hint: if you are using the right database, you can manipulate the data from the side panel.)
   - The phrase *school life expectancy* describes how many years children and young people can expect to spend in education based on current trends. Use the UNESCO website to identify the school life expectancy for boys and girls from primary to secondary in the following countries: Jordan, Yemen, China, Hong Kong, Sweden, the UK, India and Pakistan. Can you suggest explanations for any differences? How has school life expectancy changed over time? How would you go about determining whether your explanations are valid?

Summary

The purpose of this chapter was to make you more adventurous in your use of data. However, one of its main messages is that you should treat your data with scepticism until you are convinced that it is giving you legitimate answers.

Key points to take away from this chapter:

- The goal of research is to extract the information from the data.
- Information can be qualitative or quantitative in character.
- Qualitative and quantitative information can be used in the same research programme.
- Data can be collected at different levels of measurement, which may affect the type of analysis that can be used.
- There is a distinction between the data we collect ourselves (primary) and the data we use that has been collected by someone else (secondary).
- Secondary data can include books, academic papers, newspapers, film, pictures, videos, blogs, etc. as well as statistical data.
- The Internet has made secondary data widely available, so much so that much research can be undertaken using solely secondary data.

Further reading

O'Dochartaigh, N. and Sleeman, P. (2007) *Internet Research Skills*, Sage, London.

Stacey, A. and Stacey, A. (2004) *Effective Information Retrieval from the Internet*, Chandos, Oxford.

The Web contains a wealth of data for the educational researcher. Alison and Adrian Stacey's book will take you through the processes of how to find information and how to assess its quality and the quality of the website that hosts it. They also offer useful tips on how to drill down to the information you need. Niall O'Dochartaigh and Patricia Sleeman's book is also worth dipping into. Any book that begins with, 'Why not just search Google?' knows how to grab our attention. It is written by people who not only know the Web but also understand the research process from personal experience. There is a very useful section on accessing discussion groups, news and blogs.

References

Chang, L.C. and Krosnick, J.A. (2003) 'Measuring the Frequency of Regular Behaviours: Comparing the "Typical Week" to the "Past Week"', *Sociological Methodology*, 33, 55–80.

Schwarz, N. (2007) 'Retrospective and Concurrent Self-Reports: The Rationale for Real-Time Data Capture', in Stone, A.A., Schiffman, S.S., Atienza, A. and Nemling, L. (eds), *The Science of Real-Time Data Capture: Self-Reports in Health Research*, Oxford University Press.

Chapter contents

Chapter 5

USING LITERATURE IN RESEARCH

Key themes

- How to use other people's research in your work.
- How other people's research can be misused.
- How to set up a strategy for a literature search.
- Writing a literature review.

Introduction

There is often an assumption that the data we assemble and collect ourselves is what research is all about. Well, it is certainly important, no one would deny that, but the work that other people have done on and around our topic is important too. We shall look at how we use other people's research in this chapter and what we shall find is that staying in touch with the wider research field will occupy us throughout the research process.

Many books on research methods restrict their guidance to what is called 'the literature review'. This chapter is much broader. A literature review is, without question, a key part of anyone's research. But to do justice to our research we need to embed it in the wider research environment and to achieve this we need to use other people's work throughout as a foil to our own ideas and to highlight the significance of our approach and findings.

5.1 How can we use other people's research?

To say that we have to set our work in the context of other people's research is all well and good but what does this actually mean? In this section we shall see how we use other research in four very different ways:

1. To stimulate research thinking.
2. To scope a research topic.
3. To identify a research method.
4. To synthesize our research findings.

Each of these impacts at different points in a research programme and appears at different points in a research report.

5.1.1 Stimulate research thinking

The first way of using other people's research is to stimulate our own thinking. Getting started on a research project can be difficult and stressful, especially if we are new to research. It is very rare for a research idea just to materialise in our brains. We usually have to work at a topic for it to take shape. In this section we extend what was said in section 2.4 and consider how we can use it to get us thinking.

The number of questions that we can generate is influenced by the amount, variety and quality of ideas and information that we are exposed to. The more we know about research in education (and in areas that link with education), the more research opportunities and unresolved issues we will be able to identify. Most educationalists accept the importance of stimulus. Imagine what this book would be like if there were no visual variety in layout and colour or if there were no activities to get you thinking about issues. If the text were just 'how to do this' and 'how to do that', the book would be profoundly boring. If lecturers just summarised bits of a subject without giving insights into problems, personalities and progress, students' brains would clog with boredom. We accept that the link between stimulus and personal development should inform everything from the character of the curriculum and the goals of the syllabus to the detail of learning activities. However, I have not found any observations on its importance for us as individual researchers. Stimulus in a learning environment is important. It keeps us interested. It stretches our imaginations. However, while we can see it in the context of an environment in which children (or we) find ourselves, we do not think of it in relation to one we create for ourselves. This is the core of the point, the world is one that we can configure to meet our needs. As researchers we should be part of a wider community that exchanges views and ideas. We should be active in reading around our subject, appreciating the policies that impact not only on our current field of interest but also on education in general. We should be aware of the wider debates in education research, the issues that governments prioritise for research as well as the views on our research field of professionals and academics in other areas. In other words, we should place ourselves at the centre of flows of information and ideas so that out of this rich environment come new ideas, new insights and new research directions. Being aware of what is being discussed in education research should be part of every researcher's ongoing activity because it is an important input in identifying the research field.

Case study 5.1 From research to practice improvement – the role of research literature

The purpose of this case study is to show how the goal of using education research to improve educational practice can actually occur. It is this sort of linkage, between ideas and evidence in the research literature on the one hand and policy initiatives and practice development on the other, that a literature survey should seek to identify.

The idea of stimulus in the environment is central to early years education. Certainly there is much empirical evidence linking the amount and variety of stimuli to cognitive and behavioural development. It is not the intention of this case study to look at this evidence directly but to see how it has been used to assess the quality of early years care and learning environments. This takes us into an area of testing and assessment in education that has developed as a result of the close association of aspects of education research with psychology.

The idea of environmental assessment has come about as a result of the synthesis of much theoretical work on child development and the exploration of the implications of theory in applied research and in the 'real' world. For a clear example of this approach, you could read the paper by three researchers from Queen Maud's College of Early Childhood Education in Norway, Ole Lillemyr, Oddvar Fagerli and Frode Søbstad, published by UNESCO in 2001: *A Global Perspective on Early Childhood Care and Education: A Proposed Model.* Many of the ideas contained within this model are reflected in the rating scales developed by the *FPG Child Development Institute at the University of North Carolina* at Chapel Hill in the USA. The team here has devised four scales, each for an environment at a different child development stage:

- Infant/Toddler Environment Rating Scale (from 0 to 2½);
- Early Childhood Environment Rating Scale (from 2½ to 5);
- Family Child Care Environment Rating Scale (from 0 to school age);
- The School-Age Care Environment Rating Scale (from 5 to 12).

Each of these scales incorporates measures relating to the health and safety of the environment, the opportunity for children to build relationships, but central to the measures is access to stimulus. Each scale identifies academic research that validates the inclusion of a measurable item. In terms of stimulus, the early childhood scale measures the level of stimulus in the following ways:

- through the arrangement and design of the physical environment;
- through language and the availability of literature;
- through the types and range of activities that children are given;
- through the structure of the daily schedule.

These scales, and others besides, are used to assess children's environments and, in some cases, to make design changes to improve the scores (this assumes that better scores represent better environments for children's development). In a presentation to the *World Forum on Early Care and Education* in 2001, three Swedish pre-school teachers, Yvonne Södelund, Ulrica Ericsson and Yvonne Holmgren, described how they had used the Early Childhood Environment Rating Scale to evaluate practice in a pilot project of early years care and education settings and to help staff identify what changes they could make to improve the quality of the experience for children.

If you wish to explore development and use of these scales further, there is a wealth of material available. A good starting point, because it takes a more critical stance, are the 2004 conference proceedings of the Centre for Early Childhood Development and Education (CECDE), Dublin, available on the Internet at http://www.cecde.ie. The paper by Lillemyr et al. is available at http://unesdoc.unesco.org/ulis/. For more information on the environmental rating scales, see http://www.fpg.unc.edu/~ecers/.

Case Study 5.1 looks at stimulus from a different perspective. The study shows how research findings can be used to improve educational practice, one of the goals of carrying out the research in the first instance. When you have read it, look at Activity 5.1.

Activity 5.1 Working in a rich environment

Work on this activity after you have read Case Study 5.1. This shows how the results of educational research were used to construct tools to measure how far children's environments deliver the features that the educational research says are important. We are going to do something like this for your research environment.

Stage 1: The audit

- Go to your library and make a list of (a) all the education journals that are currently taken, (b) how many education journals the institution subscribes to on-line and (c) other journals that can provide insights to education researchers (look especially at journals in sociology, psychology, social work, criminology, urban studies).
- Find out how many research seminars the education department organised last year (or is organising for the current year).
- Search the Internet to find education discussion lists (these are services that enable people with similar interests to communicate with each other). As a start, in the UK, look at *JISCmail (www.jiscmail.ac.uk)*. Stop when you reach 50, it will not take long! At least ten per cent of your results should be lists based in other countries.

Stage 2: Reflection and personal assessment

- Before you conducted the library audit, how many journals had you browsed through in the previous month?
- How many times had you accessed journals electronically?
- How many of the research seminars were you aware of?
- Did you know that there are Internet discussion lists?

If a good performance is to look through five journals, go on-line five times, be aware of 25 per cent of the meetings organised by the education department and to know that academic discussion lists exist, then judge your performance as excellent, good, fair or poor.

Stage 3: The action plan

If your personal assessment is that you did not do particularly well, then you are relying on other people to create a stimulating environment for you to work in. If this is the case, you need to take more responsibility.

- Identify five journals (library and Internet) that you will browse every three or four months.
- Identify one seminar or meeting to attend each term or semester. It does not have to be in education.
- Join at least five discussion lists.

5.1.2 Scope the research topic

Once a research idea has begun to take hold, we should then start to use research literature in a different way. The second way we should use other people's research is to scope our own research question. Our purpose is more focused. It is no longer to be stimulated by the richness of educational research but to appreciate what is already known about the field that we intend to investigate. In particular, we need to appreciate the themes that have already emerged, the directions that people think are currently important and the controversies that have not yet been resolved. This appreciation is central to a core element of each and every research report, the literature review. We shall say much more about this in the section 5.4.

5.1.3 Identify the research method

The third way in which we should read other people's research is to understand the methods they used to collect and analyse their data. At this point we are digging down even more deeply into the research literature. Our focus is the overall approach and methodology as well as the detail of the methods. The question we need to ask is whether the data are a reliable description of the situation. We need to look critically at what other researchers have written. Just because something has been published does not mean that it is beyond criticism. We should examine closely what approaches to data collection and analysis other researchers have used for two reasons. First, to convince ourselves that their conclusions are valid. If the methodology is inappropriate, the conclusions are unwarranted. If the methods of data collection (for more on this, see Chapters 6, 8 and 9) are not robust, then the conclusions should be hedged with caveats. If the analysis does not probe the complexity of an issue, then the level of understanding revealed is likely to be simplistic. We should not skip over the section that deals with methodology, otherwise we may be badly misled by the research.

The second reason why we should look closely at what researchers say about their research approach is to see if particular methodologies are preferred (and why). We should look to see what works where. We do not need to break new ground if other people have done some of the work for us already.

5.1.4 Synthesize research findings

The final way in which we use other research is to create a bond between our research results and what is already known. It is very unlikely that our research will have taken place without any reference to an existing context. One of our duties as researchers is to show the relationship between our conclusions and what others have said. Most research papers and reports deal with this in their conclusions and readers will expect the author's view to move from the detail of the research analysis to placing the research conclusions in the research landscape. Unless we start off our work by knowing something of the geography of this landscape, we are unlikely to identify, with any confidence, how our work takes understanding forward or conflicts with established views.

Research is read at both a general level (for an awareness of the movement and debates) and a specific level (to inform the research topic being investigated). Reading research is a skill that we have to develop. At one level, the skill is mundane, to extract the maximum amount of information in the minimum time. However, we also have to ensure that we read the most relevant material. We shall learn more about how to do this in section 5.4. Before we get to this, however, it is important to appreciate how authors create the bond between their own work and other people's. Look at Activity 5.2.

5.2 How might other people's research be misused?

Now let us look at the other side of drawing on other people's research, the potential for it to be misused. If it is important to appreciate how we can use other people's research, it is just as important to understand how it might be misused. We need this perspective for two reasons, first to make sure that we do not misuse other people's results and arguments and, second, to be able to identify when others do.

Misuse of other people's research can, of course, be an issue of ethics in research. The purpose of research is to go some way (the journey is almost never completed) to finding a correct answer to a research question. The condition that delivers this is the researcher's

Activity 5.2 Reading research

The purpose of this activity is to understand how authors use other people's work in published research.

1. Take any academic research paper published in a refereed journal.
   - Analyse how the paper is structured – look at the headings. You will probably find terms like 'introduction', 'research approach', 'methodology', 'research findings', 'results', 'discussion', 'conclusion'. Whatever words are used, there is likely to be a beginning, a middle bit dealing with methods and research outcomes, and an end.
   - In each section, identify the references to other people's work and classify each reference according to its function in the text. It could indicate the importance of the issue, setting the context for the research, demonstrating appropriate techniques, showing the gaps in our knowledge or understanding, showing an association between existing knowledge and the study's research outcomes. Now assess each reference in terms of whether the author has a neutral view of the other person's work, approves of it or is critical. You may find it helps to construct a grid of your analysis like the one below.

Section	Reference	Purpose	Viewpoint

   - Look at the table to see if you can identify a pattern in the relationship between the section the reference is in and its purpose. If you can, you will be able to see how the author is constructing an argument and using other people's work to support it. If you cannot, either it is a very bad paper or your classification of the purposes does not match the author's intentions. Go back and try again.
   - Now look at references at the beginning and end of the paper. How does the author tie in their conclusions with other people's? How many references are used in both sections? Why do you think these references were more important to their own study?
2. You should repeat this activity several times until you are confident that you can read academic research at various levels, for its results, for its structure, for its argument.

integrity, truth and honesty. There is, however, a 'real' world outside the 'ivory tower' that houses our research intentions. Commissioned research has to satisfy the client. Students want to get a good grade at assessment. New academic researchers want to make a name for themselves in their area. Established researchers have a body of knowledge and a position to defend. No one should be under any illusion that the research world is without temptation. This section identifies some ways in which other people's research may be misused.

5.2.1 Ignorance

The first way in which people can mislead other researchers is to ignore (or be genuinely unaware of) relevant work. Leaving information out can distort analysis as much as putting false information in. Being unaware of research findings is an issue for every researcher. The more interests someone has, the more of a problem it becomes. How can we stay abreast of a rapidly expanding field, especially now with the growth in the number of research journals and the fact that the Internet has made published work so much more readily available? There are strategies that we can adopt.

- Each time we start a research project we should ensure that we scope the field in a methodical way. A process for doing this is outlined in section 5.4.
- We can identify the key journals in a field and make sure that we read contents pages of each edition. It is even easier now that we can sign up for email alerts from publishers on nominated topics.

- Another option is to read a review journal, that is, one whose purpose is to synthesize research in a field rather than to publish the outcomes of a research project. The *Review of Educational Research* and the *Review of Research in Education* both do this. The *Education Review* (USA) is devoted to book reviews.
- Finally, when the number of publications we have to read becomes overwhelming, we have to specialise.

Despite these actions, we may still miss important contributions to our field. All we can do is have them drawn to our attention. If we are part of a research group, this is more likely to happen.

5.2.2 Misunderstanding

The second way we can mislead others is to misrepresent research because we misunderstand it. Let us look at an instance of this that has been brought to light. There is real concern in both North America and Europe about the number of teachers teaching subjects for which they are not qualified. There are many worries: that the teachers might misunderstand a concept or explanation and teach their students something that is factually wrong; that the teachers might rely too much on teaching aids like textbooks so that lessons become predictable and dull; that the teachers lack the background to communicate the excitement of a subject. This concern is particularly important, for example, in mathematics, sciences and modern languages where there are often shortages of subject specialists. Some researchers have argued that being taught by a non-specialist in the sciences leads to lower levels of attainment, a fall in the numbers of students choosing these subjects at university and a decline in the skill base that underpins innovation. An American researcher, Ingersoll (1999) looked at the issue in the USA. His research showed that being taught by a non-specialist was widespread. At the time of his study a third of all secondary mathematics teachers had no background in mathematics, a quarter of secondary English teachers had no background in the subject and about 20 per cent of secondary science teachers lacked an appropriate background in the subject they were teaching. What is significant for us though is that he showed that the assumptions people made about causes were largely incorrect. In other words, other researchers had *misunderstood* the real nature of the problem. He was able to show that the assumptions that the situation was due to (a) teacher unions who sought to ensure that established long-serving teachers retained their jobs even if their professional profiles did not meet local needs and (b) teacher shortages (where there are not enough teachers in particular subjects) were incorrect. His analysis suggested that it would be more fruitful to explore the organisation and management of schools and the staffing decisions taken by principals as being more significant in explaining the prevalence of the problem.

Misunderstanding can occur when some of the participants in an exchange of views are not experts. We might, for example, be likely to have misunderstandings in relation to discussions of ethnicity, religion and multiculturalism where some people argue on the basis of research evidence and others on the basis of personal experience. We might also expect to find misunderstanding in comparative education research, especially when the comparisons are across national boundaries, when people fail to appreciate the nuances of culture or the realities of the local political and organisational structure. Sometimes people claim that others misunderstand a situation when the reality is that each has a different understanding that is the result of a different philosophical standpoint. Another American educationalist, Stephen Friedman (2000), took a contrary view to Ingersoll and argued that knowing how to teach was more important than having a good knowledge of the subject. Wherever we stand on this, both viewpoints owe as much to belief and commitment to a point of view as they do to evidence. This highlights the need for researchers to be aware of and to understand the philosophical and personal perspectives that can create these 'misunderstandings'; they can be important.

5.2.3 Selective referencing

The misuse that we have discussed so far has not crossed the boundary of having a malicious intent, a goal other than integrity and the search for truth. The next example of misuse, selective referencing (or citation bias), crosses that boundary.

Selective referencing is the quotation of research that has a particular viewpoint. Being partial, it can distort the balance of an argument. The assumption with research is that the researcher is a dispassionate observer of the evidence. The researcher brings together the evidence, makes a balanced judgement and draws conclusions. But in the real world people come with viewpoints, positions, hunches, beliefs, each of which can move a researcher from a position of studied neutrality.

How does selective referencing work?

- At one level it works by omitting some of the references supporting a position that the author disagrees with while including those that support the author's position. The ability to spot this depends largely on the reader's knowledge of the field. Yet another reason why being widely read is important!
- More pernicious is the situation in which researchers with the same broad outlook reference each other's work. At the level of building a framework of understanding about a topic, this is legitimate but when it is used to build reputations and to strengthen citation indices (these are calculations of the number of times an article or book is referenced by someone else and they are used to establish authority and leadership in a field by an author or journal), the whole process undermines the integrity of academic research.

Selective referencing has been identified as a problem in some disciplines. Studies in medical research have identified a cultural bias with European research being cited worldwide less than American. A recent study of ecology research showed that citation was influenced by the outcome of the study (proof rather than failure to prove), by the length of the article, by the number of authors, and their country and university affiliation. A 20-year analysis of citation in scientific journals showed that authors have a tendency to cite papers that are cited by papers they have read. While I am unaware of any studies that have explored citation bias in education research, this is no guarantee that it does not exist. For this reason, it is important to be able to identify it. Activity 5.3 may give you some insights.

5.2.4 Misrepresentation

The final way in which work can be misused is to misrepresent the findings or the process. This is a far more serious issue in the world of professional and academic research than misunderstanding the implications of someone else's research or being ignorant of it.

Misrepresentation of someone else's work is far beyond being what the academic community would accept as being a legitimate critique and when someone is accused of misrepresentation, it is a serious matter. Because, for some people, a philosophical

Activity 5.3 Analysing referencing

The purpose of this activity is to show you how to follow up reference (citation) linkages and to assess how far the references represent a balanced picture of research.

1. Identify an author who has written more than three journal articles and select any one article appropriate to your research or to your studies. List all the references.
2. Identify other articles written by the same author. List the references and note mutual citations of other authors.
3. Identify papers written by authors who have been referenced more than once. Look at the references in these papers and identify if any cite (a) the first author or (b) other authors cited by the first author.
4. It may help if you set up a matrix to show the number of co-citations.
5. Follow the linkages between authors as far as you can and judge the extent to which authors co-cite each other.
6. Search the literature to see who else has published in the area. Have any significant papers (especially those by authors in other countries) not been referenced?

Note: there are suggestions on ways of searching the literature in a field in section 5.4.

After you have done this, ask if there is any evidence of mutual citation (where authors cite each other) and, if there is, is it warranted? Look to see if any work has been ignored. If so, ask why. Did it reach a different conclusion? How far would you say that there is a group of researchers who are working together? If there is evidence, does it represent a malign influence pushing a particular perspective, or merely that the pool of researchers is small and know (and value) each other's work?

Author #1	Author #2	Author #3	Author #4	Author #5
Author #2				
Author #3				
Author #4				
Author #5				

position is important in determining what is 'right' and what is 'wrong' in education, the purpose of an argument is to stack up the evidence to support the 'right' conclusion. In these circumstances, truth can become a casualty.

A case of misrepresentation was alleged in the USA recently. The background is the genuine concern, in most economically advanced countries, about the competence of children from lower socio-economic backgrounds in the basic skills that enable people to function adequately in society. In particular, there has been concern over reading skills. Not surprisingly educational research that seeks to assess the effectiveness of strategies for teaching reading is of more than academic interest. Because of this, proponents of different approaches to teaching can engage in furious and at times acrimonious exchanges. Nowhere was this more true than in the USA where, as in other parts of the world, the lines of conflict were drawn between those who argued for phonics as an approach to teaching, versus others. In one exchange between authors, things came to a head in 2000 with the publication of a paper titled 'Misrepresentation of Research by Other Researchers'.

While the issue erupted in 2000, it had clearly been simmering for some time before. On the one hand was Barbara Taylor, Director of the Minnesota Center for Reading

Research, and others who take the view that teaching reading requires an integrated strategy that pays regard to the context of the student as well as the teaching strategy. On the other hand was Barbara Foorman, Director of the Center for Academic and Reading Skills at the University of Texas Health Science Center, Houston and others who published an academic paper in 1998 that showed the importance of phonics in an integrated approach to teaching reading. The accusation of misrepresentation was made by Foorman et al. (2000) in response to a paper in the journal *Educational Researcher* by Taylor et al. (2000). Foorman et al.'s paper is hard-hitting. The language is certainly strong with claims, for example, of the distortion of facts. Table 5.1 sets out some of the claims

Table 5.1 When is criticism misrepresentation?

Claim of misrepresentation	Rebuttal
Taylor et al. criticize us for a 'simple solution to the complex problem of raising the literacy of young children in high-poverty neighbourhoods'.	We have never maintained that a single solution exists to this problem, let alone a 'simple solution'.
Researchers investigating beginning reading should exercise extra caution to delimit findings from their own studies.	We agree with this, which is why our discussion section cited nine specific limitations of the study.
Taylor et al. criticize us for presenting results prior to publication.	Their critique was posted on a public website 10 months before publication. We also note that some members of B. Taylor et al. discussed their critique with a reporter long before we were aware of its existence. The reporter believed a scandal had been unearthed, but eventually decided there was nothing to write about. In fact, the results of the Foorman, Francis, et al. (1998) study were presented at two invited symposia prior to publication. In retrospect, the order of events may appear unfortunate. But the reality is that in virtually all areas of research, including education, presentation prior to publication is the norm.
In contrast to the implications of B. Taylor et al., (this can be inferred to mean that Foorman et al. did not respond to criticisms of their work).	We have responded in writing and by personal communication to numerous misrepresentations of our research by the media, by policy-oriented organizations, and by reading professionals. For example, . . . we sent Gerry Coles a disk containing our data. Coles proceeded to selectively drop classrooms in our dataset so that he could write his essay (Coles, 1999). *(See also Coles, 2000.)*
When the authors of this widely publicized study use their results as the basis for promoting specific commercial programs . . . , they contribute to the impression that students' reading problems will be solved if a school simply buys the right program.	This article is a critique of commercial reading programs and the focus of policymakers on these types of programs.
B. Taylor et al. imply that the Foorman, Francis, et al. (1998) study is to blame for 67 phonics bills: 'Since 1996, when information about the Foorman, Francis, et al. study was first publicized, 67 bills to make phonics the law have been proposed in states around the country.'	There is considerable evidence that explicit teaching of the alphabetic principle is a necessary (but not sufficient) component of reading instruction for children. If Foorman, Francis, et al. (1998) never existed, the pendulum in the reading wars would still be swinging towards the phonics side.

of misrepresentation that Foorman et al. make. The evidence presented in Table 5.1 does not do full justice to the claims of misrepresentation by Foorman, nor does it adequately represent the views of Taylor or any of the others who are criticised by Foorman. What it does do, however, is highlight some of the issues that Foorman and her co-authors claim constitute misrepresentation. In the left column is the claim of misrepresentation paraphrased or quoted from Taylor et al.'s paper and in the right column Foorman et al.'s rebuttal of that claim. Some of the issues are methodological, some a matter of principle, some a matter of interpretation and some a matter of research practice. However, the most serious assertion by Foorman et al. is that their opponents 'have taken part of the puzzle and blown it out of proportion *to fit their story*' (p. 33). This gets to the heart of the issue, and is a claim that Taylor et al. have written a paper that is more concerned with defending their position than anything else.

This is, as might be expected, a complex issue but there is no getting away from the fact that, tied up with the dispute, are philosophies of education, reputations and, in all likelihood, access to opportunities. People come to evaluation and criticism of other people's research with their own 'stories'. In this particular case, we must all make our own minds up on whether the claims of misrepresentation are justified (and the references are there to be read) but whenever there are debates in the pages of an academic journal, we should look to see how far criticism is balanced and fair minded and how far it is designed to support a position.

5.3 Strategies for literature search

The first sections of this chapter have looked at the big picture in getting to grips with research literature; first how we can use this literature in our own work and, second, how to read research literature to make sure that we can make the most important critical judgement – whether it is accurate, honest and truthful in its representation of the field. In this next section, we move on to the process of gathering the literature together. Broadly there are two approaches to this. On the one hand, there is following our noses and benefiting (or not) from serendipity. On the other hand, we can take a more structured approach, which downplays the element of luck. We will follow this approach! The elements in this structured approach are to:

- map the issue;
- use questions to frame and direct the search process;
- know the sources;
- select search options;
- follow leads;
- review the outcomes.

5.3.1 Mapping the issue

What do we mean when we talk about 'mapping the issue'? The answer is that we need to construct an overview of the topic, showing how cause and effect, influence and consequence, occurrence and intensity are all related. We need to set out our current understanding of the research topic, as well as our hunches and ideas, in order to guide our search for research literature. We can structure our map by identifying:

- factors that directly affect the issue;
- factors that influence a process or outcome that itself affects the issue;
- factors that seem to be associated with our issue, that is, they occur alongside it but do not necessarily influence it;
- actors involved in the process of making things happen;
- actors who are affected by things that happen;
- actors who have a stake in what is going on;
- organisations, individuals, groups and areas who win and those who lose.

It is not essential for *every* piece of research to identify *every* one of these elements. There is no guarantee that every one is applicable. What they are is a framework for starting the thinking process. This is what every researcher should do, think about the issue before starting the research itself. We should examine our own experience if it is relevant; we should put ourselves in the place of those who are involved with the issue and empathise with their positions so we can think how they might feel and react. We should question the issue: who, what, when, how, why? What we are aiming to produce is *our own understanding* of the influences and factors at work so that we have a framework against which we can test what other researchers have said. We are not producing a template to guide our research but a framework to test the existence of research literature that deals with the dimensions we have identified. Case Study 5.2 gives an example of this initial brainstorming process.

Mapping the issue, however, can move beyond producing a list of factors and influences. We can set out how we think these factors relate to each other, which one is a direct influence and which one a secondary influence, what happens first in a process and what happens later. It is at this point that we move beyond guiding our search for appropriate literature to shaping a model that can explain a situation. We then use this to help direct our literature search.

Figure 5.1 illustrates this and takes our example of researching the experience of overseas students (Case Study 5.2) a little further. This diagram looks specifically at some issues that a foreign student in higher education might have. In the centre of the diagram are some concerns or situations that might be experienced (for instance, racism or accommodation problems). On the right are areas of university action and responsibility and on the left the tutor's responsibility for teaching and learning. What we are trying to do here is understand how student issues are recognised and managed. Thus the university accommodation bureau is there to allocate accommodation and resolve problems. The bureau implements university policy – is it better to house all foreign students together or to mix them with home students? The former allows better provision of support services but can create a ghetto. In either case, there may be incidents of racism. Is there a procedure for dealing with this? The university might recognise the role of an induction programme for foreign students in helping them establish friendships but what if a tutor sees that a student is isolated in a class? We need to see if the link between the academic and support side of the university is strong. The same link needs to exist if a student is not coping well academically. If it is a matter of just understanding the way teaching and learning works, this could be dealt with in induction but if it is language, language support should be provided. We could produce another map, this time with the tutor in the centre of the

Case study 5.2 A framework for a literature search

Context

University students in many places are encouraged to spend part of their study period at a university in another country. At one level it is believed that the experience broadens outlooks, while the process of coping with a different culture and educational system increases students' capacity to manage when they return home. In addition, many will improve their language capability and enhance their social skills as well as gaining new knowledge and insights into their subjects from different viewpoints. Some students take the whole of their qualification in a foreign country, committing themselves to overseas residence for up to three or four years. In the UK, for example, there were 330,000 overseas students studying at UK universities in 2005–6. About 150,000 of these were supported by the EU's Erasmus programme, which financially supports study abroad programmes.

For many universities worldwide, the fees generated by foreign students are an important funding stream. Foreign students often pay higher fees than national students and the resources they generate support smaller group teaching, better resourcing for IT and libraries and more opportunities for staff to do research. In these circumstances, universities want to ensure that they understand the experience of foreign students so that they can intervene to ensure that they do not withdraw.

Issue

The Vice-Chancellor (or Provost) of your university has asked you, in your capacity as an educational researcher, to carry out a study to understand how foreign students are managing in their programmes and how satisfied they are with their experience.

First steps

We recognise that there is probably some literature on this (there is) but we need something to guide our search. Our first step is to think about our experience of going to university and then to imagine what it would be like if we were to arrive in a foreign country knowing no one. What would be our concerns?

- We might be worried about our ability to manage the language in an academic context. Grammatical errors, using the wrong words, expressing ideas in simple language can all reduce the impact of a written or spoken argument.
- They might do things differently here. Will there be a tutor we can see if we are concerned about our progress? Will there be seminars? Will we be expected to answer questions in lectures? How do exams work? What if we are asked to work in groups with others when we have never done this before?
- How will we get on with other students? How will we make friends? What if other people do not like us because we are British, Swedish, Dutch, Black, Asian . . . ?

Then we ought to put ourselves in the shoes of the tutors, some of whom might say:

- These foreign students, they take up so much more time that I would rather spend on my research. Why should I have to explain how they should work in our education system? If they do not know how to write an essay, it should not be my job to tell them.
- Foreign students make the class more interesting to teach.
- These foreign students expect to be spoon-fed and told everything. It's just parrot learning!
- Foreign students are more hard working than other students.
- I'm not going to adapt my lectures to make them more multicultural and international.
- I'm worried that all these foreign students will lead to a lowering of quality.

Back to the research

These ideas start to give us a structure for a literature search. They give us things to look for in the literature – teaching methods, friendships, language ability and so on. We do not have to identify the details as expressed here, we can generalise and see if other people have assessed things like cultural shock, conflict, learning approaches, learning support and so on. We can extend our exploration by thinking about what institutions might do to help foreign students settle in. Try doing this yourselves.

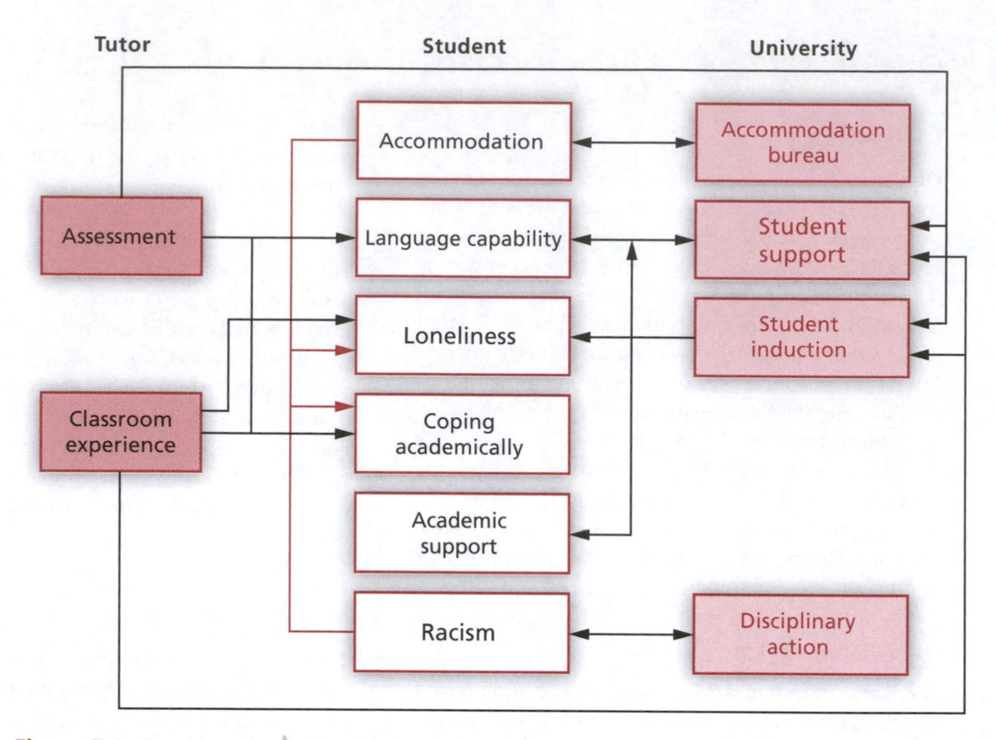

Figure 5.1 Creating a relationship map

diagram. Its focus might be a tutor who is unwilling to change to meet the needs of foreign students. What linkage map can you construct for this situation?

5.3.2 Posing questions

Implicit in the process of mapping the research issue is the need to ask questions. Essentially relationship mapping as described above is an approach for outlining and describing linkages within a system. A system can be broadly defined, for our purposes, as a set of components that interact with one another, either directly or indirectly. The components could be actors such as university tutors, foreign students and university departments. They could be the bureaucratic processes that define an organisation's operational structure or the social relationships that ensure an organisation functions effectively. Educational research at whatever level deals extensively with systems. Questions such as, 'Why are some classes noisy and disruptive?', 'How do students choose which subjects to study?', 'Why do some teachers burn out early?', 'How many nursery schools should we provide?' and 'Why is the takeup of on-line learning so poor amongst older workers?' are all questions that require us to define who is involved, what influences them, how they interact, whether everyone and everything behaves in the same way – and, if not, what are the factors and influences that create differences.

Asking questions should be something we do throughout the research planning and literature searching process. The information we need to progress our work is easy to identify once we ask the right questions. Finding the answer is usually straightforward; it is asking the right question that is the difficult part.

The nature of the questions we pose varies according to where we are in the research programme.

- At the start, when we are mapping out the issue, our questions are designed to identify possible causation and association.
- In the next stage, our questions should help us identify the literature. They take the form, 'What is the evidence for foreign students experiencing more problems with accommodation than home students? Do foreign students prefer to live with people from the same national or cultural background?' These questions are designed, first, to help us find answers in the literature and, then, if there are no answers, they may well become questions for our own research to answer. The questions are translated into search terms for our literature search (see section 5.4.4 below).
- Questioning is also important when we collect and analyse our data. It will shape the process ('What ways are there of processing this data?') and test our solutions ('Are these outcomes what we would have expected? If not, have we done something wrong?').

The questions we construct are the outcome of our ability to think in a variety of ways – creatively, logically, analytically, holistically. Ultimately our ability to be effective researchers on a long-term basis depends on our ability to continue asking questions.

5.3.3 Identifying sources

Mapping an issue and asking questions are the infrastructure on which we build our literature search. Information that is relevant to the issue we want to investigate will exist. The problem we face is how can we find it. There are a number of ways into the literature.

(i) Going in through gateways

Gateways (sometimes referred to as portals) do not identify the research literature directly but they may point us to sources that may have the information we want. However, because they are the most general level of search, they can be blunt instruments and there is no guarantee that they will take us to the level of detail we require. Table 5.2 lists some gateways.

(ii) Databases

The second way of accessing literature is via databases (see Table 5.3). These bring us closer to the documentary and other sources we want. Some databases are public (for example, the British Library's *Inside* and the US Government's *ERIC*), while others are private (for example, Ingenta and Jstor). Some are free, some are subscription and a few have a free trial. In general, the public and publicly supported databases (that is, those deriving the bulk of their funding from state finance) provide access to a wide range of literature while the private databases (that is, those that are privately financed) only contain material from journals produced by specific publishers. Those that are subscription services may be available through an institutional subscription (check with your own library or information service).

For some researchers it may be worthwhile to purchase a copy of an on-line bibliographic search engine. These can speed up the research process quite significantly. They are designed to search many of the databases listed in Table 5.3 (and more besides) as

Table 5.2 Educational gateways

Name	Website	Gives access to
The Educational Portal (USA)	www.theeducationportal.com	Practically orientated websites for themes such as early childhood, special educational needs, home schooling, educational theory.
Pinakes	http://www.hw.ac.uk/libwww/irn/pinakes/pinakes.html	Gateway to subject related websites. Sits above sites such as Intute (see below).
BUBL Information Service	http://www.bubl.ac.uk/	Provides links to Web resources. Over 100 education websites catalogued.
Intute	http://www.intute.ac.uk/	Searchable database providing access to other information sources as well as publications.
Department for Children Schools and Families (UK)	www.dcsf.gov.uk	Information for employers, local authorities, parents, school governors, teachers and young people about education and training.
Technology Studies in Education (USA)	lrs.ed.uiuc.edu/tse-portal/index.html	Links to sites offering guidance on developing a research proposal, including guidance on how to assess websites as sources.
Archives of Scottish Higher Education (UK)	www.gashe.ac.uk	Searchable database of archival material, largely without access to primary sources.
Library of Congress (USA)	www.loc.gov/rr/international/portals.html	Links to portals for countries worldwide.
Braintrack (USA)	www.braintrack.com	Links to universities worldwide.
General education database (UK)	www.world-education-database.org	Private Web portal with links to national ministries of education and other education portals.
Asian Focused Portal (Thailand)	www.shambles.net	Private Web portal with a standard framework of educational and commercial weblinks.

well as major library sites (such as the Library of Congress in the USA). They have the functionality to import references, receive alerts from data sources and create a library of resources downloaded on-line or from scans. They also enable users to write notes on the record. Their value is not limited to accessing and storing references. When it comes to writing the literature review (or any other text), they can set the reference into format required. Accurate citation is particularly important and this software will save many hours searching for missing commas, full stops and extra spaces. Table 5.4 lists some of the principal software.

(iii) Reviews

The third way of getting to the literature we want is through pre-existing reviews. If these exist, we are fortunate but it does not mean that we should not continue to look for other published material; there is no guarantee, after all, that the review is comprehensive and,

Table 5.3 Educational databases

Name	Website	Access	Comment
INSIDE	www.bl.uk/inside	Free trial	Searches journals and reports in the British Library.
ERIC	www.eric.ed.gov	Free	Searches records of journals and reports. Summarises record.
British Education Index	www.leeds.ac.uk/bei/	Free	Record of journal articles and papers. Record provides summary and may give access to full text.
Education Network Australia	www.edna.edu.au	Free	Searchable database of documentary and non-documentary sources worldwide.
EBSCO	www.ebsco-com	Subscription	Record of journal articles. May be available through institutional subscription.
INGENTA	www.ingenta.com	Subscription	Record of journal articles. May be available through institutional subscription.
JSTOR	www.jstor.org	Subscription	Record of journal articles. May be available through institutional subscription.
ERA	www.informaworld.com/smpp/subjecthome~db=ai	Free trial	Educational research abstracts. May be available through institutional subscription.
International Centre for Distance learning	www-icdl.open.ac.uk/	Free	Searchable specialist database.
Google Scholar	http://scholar.google.com/	Searches free. Subscription for literature access.	Searchable database primarily of articles and books. Sometimes gives access to text.
Web of Knowledge	http://isiwebofknowledge.com/	Searches free. Subscription for literature access.	Links together large number of databases. Scientific focus.

Table 5.4 Bibliographic search software

Name	Web address
Biblioscope	www.biblioscope.nl
Bookends Plus	www.sonnysoftware.com
End note	www.endnote.com
Procite	www.procite.com
Refworks	www.refworks.com

certainly, there may well be other work published afterwards. What existing reviews do provide, however, is a picture of the main research avenues. These might give structure to our own search, analysis and review. The following are useful sources for educational researchers.

- **Review journals**: these are journals devoted to reviewing, summarising and commenting on areas of research. They do not publish original research studies. While they can identify new directions for research, their principal function is to present an overview so that academics and research professionals can take stock and make judgements about future progress. In looking at review articles, we need to ask ourselves these sorts of question: Does what we know add up to a convincing explanation? Where are the gaps in our understanding? Does this method work? Can we define good practice? Is this approach producing the results we expected? The main review journals in education are both American and produced by the American Education Research Association. Both tend to reference research published in North America more than research from other areas. This is something that we should be aware of and rectify in our own investigations. The *Review of Educational Research* is published quarterly. Its articles are often quite narrowly focused. In June 2007, for example, Peter Stevens published an article reviewing the literature on race, ethnicity and inequality in English secondary schools (Stevens, 2007). The articles frequently have a pronounced critical dimension that reflects the values of the author. Schutz's article 'Home Is a Prison in the Global City: The Tragic Failure of School-Based Community Engagement Strategies' (Schutz, 2006) clearly falls into this category. Because of this critical dimension, there can be subsequent commentaries on articles from people with a different perspective. One instance of this concerns schema theory. The concept of schema can be traced back to Piaget but has subsequently been developed and revised by psychologists and educationalists. A schema is a framework that allows us to organise our knowledge and understanding of the world. They have been used to develop literacy programmes. In 2005, McVee et al. published a paper (McVee et al., 2005) that resulted in critical commentaries by Krasny et al. (2007) and Gredler (2007) and a subsequent rebuttal by the original authors (McVee et al., 2007). In contrast to the *Review of Educational Research*, the *Review of Research in Education* is an annual publication and its papers, in recent years, have been themed. In 2007, the theme was diversity and there were papers on race, social justice and sexuality. In 2006, the theme of 'rethinking learning' saw papers on disciplinary learning, socio-cultural research and learning, inclusive learning and informal learning amongst others.
- **Databases**: The second source of review literature are review databases. The *What Works* website in the USA accesses a database of reviews of what research appears to show are effective teaching and learning strategies. Whereas review journals synthesise substantive or conceptual contributions, *What Works* evaluates instructional programmes and strategies from the point of view of their impacts. The reviews are based on field tests in the public domain, often in research literature (which is cited), and are judgemental in that they assess the quality of the evidence and the strength of impact of an intervention. The Early Childhood section, for example, reviews ten programmes: Curiosity Corner, DaisyQuest, Dialogic Reading, Direct Instruction, Interactive Shared Book Reading, Phonological Awareness Training, Phonological Awareness Training plus Letter Awareness Training, Ready Set Leap, Shared Book Reading and Sound Foundations. For each, there is an assessment of the learning benefits that are summarised in the 'current topics' section. Studies of *Interactive Book Reading* (where adults read to a child or children and engage them with the material)

Table 5.5 Sources of reviews in education

Name	Website	Comment
Review of Educational Research (American Educational Research Association)	http://rer.sagepub.com	Thematic reviews. Recent reviews 2006–7 include: teacher recruitment and retention, race, ethnicity and educational inequality.
Review of Research in Education (American Educational Research Association)	http://rre.sagepub.com/	Thematic reviews. Recent reviews 2006–7 include: youth, technology and media culture, learning in informal contexts and a whole issue exploring dimensions of social justice in 2007.
Futurelab	www.futurelab.org	Reviews of the application of IT and ICT in reading and learning.
Evidence for Policy and Practice Information and Coordinating Centre	http://eppi.ioe.ac.uk/cms/	Reviews of evidence-based practice. Previous reviews include: emotional behaviour and disorders, cost-benefit analysis of early childhood care and education.
Office for Standards in Education (Ofsted)	www.ofsted.gov.uk	Occasional reports on teaching, learning and classroom strategies.
Department for Children, Schools and Families	http://www.dfes.gov.uk/	Reports and studies to inform policy development and policy implementation.
What Works	http://ies.ed.gov/ncee/wwc/	Practice orientated website. Reports structured around seven themes: beginning reading; character education; drop-out prevention; early childhood education, elementary school math; English-language learners; middle school math.
British Educational Research Association (BERA)	http://www.bera.ac.uk/index.php	Periodic reviews closely linked with policy issues.
NSPCC (National Society for the Prevention of Cruelty to Children)	http://www.nspcc.org.uk/InformWD/informhub_wda36433.html	Research reports, and general and specific reading lists.

found clear improvements in reading and writing but a range of results in language skills, from improvements to a decline. *Dialogic Reading*, where the child and adult swap roles as reader, listener and being engaged, was found to have positive effects on oral language.

- **Other Reviews**: There are a number of other organisations (shown in Table 5.5) that produce reviews. The *Evidence for Policy and Practice Information and Coordinating Centre* has the same objectives as the *What Works* website in the USA but differs in that it draws on qualitative as well as quantitative research. There are over 70 reviews on its website, dating from 1996. Recent reviews have covered the life contexts of young people (Accidental injury, risk-taking behaviour and the social circumstances in which young people (aged 12–24) live; a systematic review of the evidence for incentive schemes to encourage positive health and other social behaviours in young people) and teaching and learning strategies (The effect of ICT teaching activities in science lessons on students' understanding of science ideas and a systematic review of strategies to raise pupils' motivational effort in Key Stage 4 Mathematics). *Futurelab* is a not-for-profit organisation whose focus is educational ICT. There are 15 reviews on its website exploring the role and potential of ICT in thinking and creative skill development, subject knowledge and skills (languages, science), learning for different groups (primary, teachers, 14–19, students with learning difficulties) and assessment. Other organisations produce occasional reviews. *Ofsted*, the quality assurance agency for teaching in England and Wales, has produced reviews on literacy and on children whose behaviour is challenging. The *Department for Children, Schools and Families* in England and Wales funds research to inform policy actions. As part of this work it has recently produced reviews on independent learning, speech and language in early years, increasing participation of 17-year-olds in education and training, and learning skills. The *DfES* website is an excellent source of research reports and is easy to search. *BERA* has produced a limited number of reviews. The *NSPCC* site provides general reading lists on a range of topics relating to child protection, including the law, to introductions to the topic, domestic violence, sex offenders and domestic violence as well as historical perspectives.

(iv) Key journals and texts

The final sources to be searched are key journals and texts. Many of these will be subsumed within the databases identified above. There are clearly too many journals to identify individually but there are some that ought to be noted because they represent journals that are significant either for the topic or for the area. The 'national' journals below are all refereed and have a general spread of articles.

- **UK**: BERA publishes the *British Educational Research Journal (BERJ)* plus *Research Intelligence*, which has some short methodological articles, and has an *Occasional Paper* series.
- **Netherlands**: The Netherlands and Flemish Educational Research Associations publish *Pedagogische Studiën*.
- **Sweden, Denmark, Norway, Finland**: The countries of Scandinavia publish the *Scandinavian Journal of Educational Research*.
- **USA**: The American Educational Research Association (AERA) publishes four journals. The *American Educational Research Journal* publishes papers of social, institutional and pedagogic interest. *Educational Evaluation and Policy Analysis* publishes papers on research for policy and research about policy. *Educational Researcher* contains some general papers but because it reports news about the association it has a 'newsletter' feel. The *Journal of Educational and Behavioural Statistics* is strongly quantitative in its methodology.
- **Europe**: The *European Educational Research Journal* has a focus of the developing 'Europeanisation' of educational policies and practice as a result of EU policy initiatives agreed by member governments.

As well as these journals, there are many others devoted to a particular topic, such as early years, mathematics education, work-based learning and so on. They are too numerous to mention here. It is also worth noting that there are a growing number of free-to-view open access on-line journals. The American Educational Research Association publishes a list at http://aera-cr.asu.edu/ejournals/.

5.3.4 Select search options

Having identified where we might find our literature, the next step is to identify it. For this we have to determine our search options. One thing that every researcher finds when searching through literature is that it is very easy to get lost by following leads and then not knowing where you have been. What we have to do is bring order into our searches. We do this by translating our map of the research issue and our questions into concepts and terms that we can use in the actual search process. This is not a difficult task and the terms to use are, usually, quite obvious. With our study of foreign students we could use terms like 'problems', 'adjustment', 'discrimination', 'expectations', 'preparation', 'language ability', 'homesickness', 'stress', all in conjunction with the phrase 'foreign students'. We need to make a list of our search terms and our search environments or sources, just to be sure that we methodically work through the various combinations. If there is a keyword list in the search domain, then we have to benchmark the terms we develop against the keywords. This may result in another term or terms for subsequent searches.

The actual specification of search terms can take several forms.

- **Simple search:** using whole words, such as 'foreign students homesickness'. This is the simplest form of search. It will usually throw up appropriate references but there will be many irrelevant hit as well. The proportion of irrelevant hits is usually higher for Internet searches (for example with Google Scholar) rather than for database searches. We should be aware when using this approach that some words have more than one spelling (centre and center) and that not every search engine will include plurals as well as singular forms. If more than one word is enclosed in quotation marks ('foreign students'), many search engines will search for the phrase. If the quotation marks are not included, each word is identified. If we wanted to look for problems suffered by foreign students, putting the whole phrase in quotation marks would be restrictive. 'foreign students' near 'problems' will produce better results.
- **Spreading the options**: we can increase the chance of a hit if we apply rules to the search process.
  - Putting ~ in front of the search term will identify similar words: *~foreign students* finds international students and overseas students.
  - Putting * after the search term means that words or phrases with different endings are included in the search. *Educ** identifies education, educate, educational, educative.
  - We can select a number range in our search by separating the limiting numbers with two dots. Thus *'foreign students' near problems 2000 . . . 2007* will only select documents including articles published within the year range 2000 to 2007. Using 'near' means that the phrase 'foreign students' and the word 'problems' only have to be near each other, not next to each other.
  - We can suppress a word by putting – between two words (the latter is not included), *'foreign students' – fees* will omit references where fees are linked with foreign students. We can also include words by putting a + sign in between words, so *'foreign students' +fees* will include references to papers including the two.
  - Putting *and*, *or*, and *not* between two words will find paragraphs of text on websites containing the requested combinations.
  - The phrase *allintitle:* will find titles of articles, books and anything else held in the database (such as reports) containing the requested word or phrase; *allintitle: foreign students ~problems* will find titles containing the phrase 'foreign students' plus problems, issues, concerns, worries, etc.
- **Alternative searches**: the types of search considered so far are called Boolean searches (named after George Boole, a self-taught nineteenth century mathematician

who developed a mathematical system for expressing logical expressions, a system that is now referred to as Boolean Algebra). Some websites (such as the US National Criminal Justice Service, http://www.ncjrs.gov/index.html) permit other forms of searching such as pattern and concept searching. These simplify the process of including some of the operators identified above. A pattern search will look for words with similar spelling and a concept search for associated concepts.

Searching the Web is a skill that all researchers should develop if they want to make use of the rich resources that are available. More guidance is usually available on the 'help' pages of a search engine's website (for example, for Google go to http://www.google.com/help/basics.html).

5.3.5 Second level searching by author and citation

The search guidance so far has advised on developing a search framework and then identifying resources. When we bring these together, references and information that are relevant to our interests and research should begin to emerge. At this point we need to develop a further search strategy. Up to this point, though we have tried to make our search a reasoned and ordered process, there has always been a great deal of uncertainty in the results that are obtained. In general, we must expect only a small proportion of our searches to be centrally relevant to our own work. However, when we find material that is relevant, we can then dig deeper along the vein of relevance that we have exposed.

When we have found a particularly relevant article, we can use this to prise open the literature. First, we can follow up on references by the first author to them as well as to other authors. Second, we can follow up other references contained in the work and by drilling down a parallel author chain. This approach is shown in Figure 5.2. The searches are in the vertical dimension and the citations in the horizontal. The first author is shaded blue and the sequence A to A1–A3 in the first column shows the search identifying other papers by author A that are not referenced in the original paper. The columns to the right of this represent papers identified as a result of following up citations. Thus A to B to C (the top line) is a citation of the author's own work and A to (shaded) B, C and D is the citation of three papers by a second author. The figure also shows that the second author self-cites a paper that is cited in paper A2 by the first author. You should now be able to work out how the third author fits in. This sort of diagram is important in picking up the relationships between authors.

Following links in these ways can be very productive. We have, however, to be strict with ourselves and recognise when we are straying outside the field of greatest relevance to us. This type of search can easily spiral out of control. A further point to note is that different search engines are more appropriate for different academic disciplines and themes. Any search engine is only as good as its database and Google Scholar, for instance, like many, has a strong core of scientific work.

5.3.6 Reviewing outcomes

The final stage of the literature search process is to review the outcomes. We need to do this to make sure that the strategy we have adopted is actually paying dividends. The questions we need to ask are:

- Is the literature we have found central or peripheral to our research issue?
- Are the number of references we have identified sufficient payback for the time we have invested?

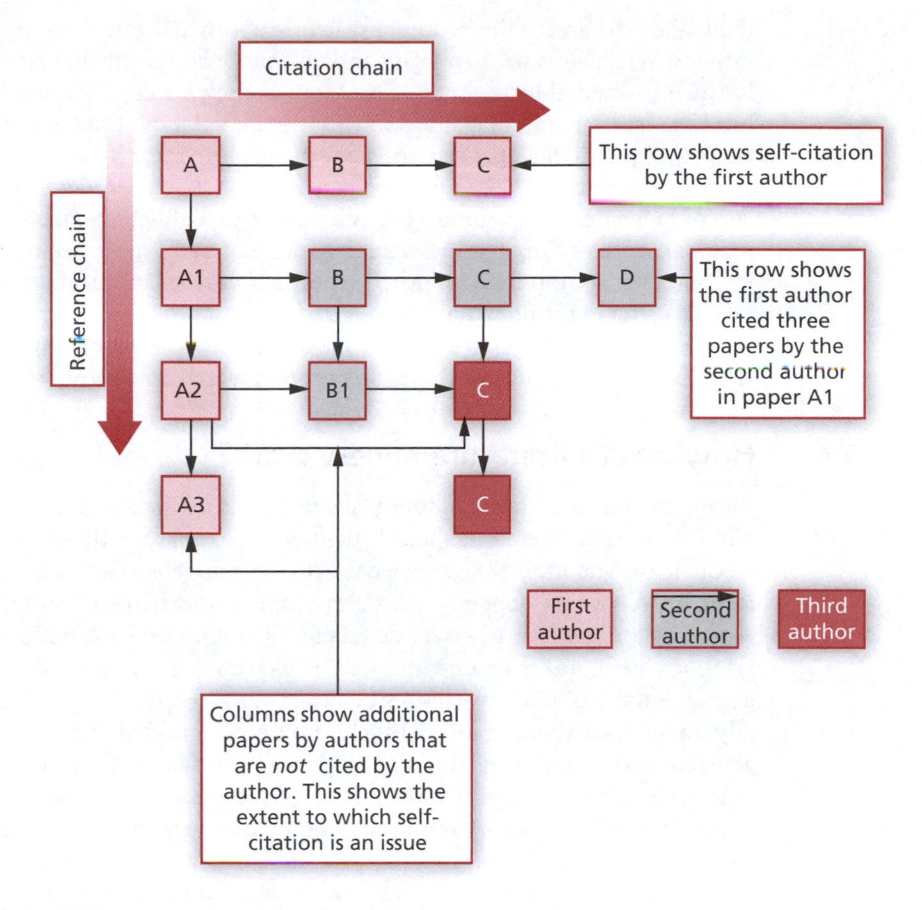

Figure 5.2 Approaches to author searching

- Are the references in well-regarded publications and have they been anonymously refereed?
- Is the topic thought to be important by other researchers?

Negative answers to these questions do not necessarily mean that we should change our research topic but they should cause us to reflect on whether other people are seeing a blind alley where we see a research project. However, negative evaluations might also mean that we have a search strategy that is flawed and that we need to revise it or to start again. In either case, it is better to find out sooner rather than later.

5.4 Preparing a literature review

Having begun to identify relevant literature, the next step is to start to shape it into a literature review appropriate to the needs of the research. A literature review is the means by which we tie our research intentions and outcomes to what other people working in the field have done. It is central to most research projects, from an undergraduate dissertation to a paper submitted to an academic journal. Often, by those just starting out on their research careers, the literature search is poorly done and poorly written up. At one extreme, researchers set their sights too low and just record what is written in textbooks. While it is acceptable to use these as a source, they are usually several years (at best) behind the research and may not deal with the material in a way that is appropriate to the research topic. At the other extreme some people think that it has to be a record of virtually everything written on the topic. Unless everything that is written is relevant, this shows a lack of judgement in selecting work and themes to highlight. Some people think that only material produced in their own country is relevant and many seem to believe that it is a free-standing section in the research report rather than an integral part of the argument. One function of the literature search is to demonstrate the need for the research.

Now that we know what it should not be, we need to find out how to do it properly and to use it to not only improve the quality of our research but also our standing as researchers.

5.4.1 How does a literature review work?

Ideally the literature review should take place before the research issue is identified. Ideally the research literature should identify a gap that we decide to fill with our own research programme. However, what actually happens may be far removed from the ideal. As we saw in Chapter 2, interest in a topic to research arises from many sources and, especially for new researchers, undertaking a literature review is not usually one of them.

So if a literature review does not start off a research enquiry, what is it? As the name suggests, it is the process of assembling literature pertinent to a topic or to an enquiry. It is usually undertaken after the research field has been identified and, in many cases, after the actual research question has become fairly clear. It fulfils a number of purposes that we shall examine in detail shortly but its overriding purpose is to connect the research we intend to do with the wider research community. There are good reasons for this. It reflects the culture of a community in which knowledge is shared. It provides a context through which others can evaluate our reasoning and our conclusions. But perhaps most importantly it demonstrates to us, as well as to others, that what we are intending to do has not been done before.

5.4.2 What should we use the literature review to achieve?

In this section we will turn from why the academic and research communities expect a literature survey to how we, as individual researchers, can use it to justify our research and establish our expertise in the area and to demonstrate our credibility as researchers.

(i) Justify our research

The first thing we have to do is convince our peers that the research we are proposing does not exist, is needed and will take forward an understanding of the issue. How we do this is very much tied up with the way in which we want to develop our argument and this will clearly be heavily influenced by the topic itself and how complete our understanding is. In order to create a good argument we will have to devote a substantial amount of time to reading widely, acquiring a good set of references and testing our understanding against other people. These can be research supervisors or colleagues whose views we [illegible] Read Case Study 5.3 to see how some Belgian researchers presented their literature review.

The issue, however, is not just how we present a literature survey but how well we present it. What needs to come across to the reader is the argument rather than the literature. The reader should be able to look through the literature review to see us at work and then make a judgement about our research capability. Below are listed some poorer ways of presenting a literature review and how they might be read by others.

Case study 5.3 A literature review that works

This literature review is a compelling argument for the research that was carried out. The study on the effect of different approaches to education on outcomes in mathematics and language attainment in primary schools was undertaken by researchers at the Catholic University Leuven in Belgium and published in the *British Educational Research Journal*.

The article contains 57 references, of which seven are to the work of the authors. The earliest reference is to a 1983 paper and 18 of the references are post-2000. The references are spread throughout the text, with 23 in a review of the field, 16 in a section arguing for the research questions, 13 in the sections dealing with methodology, two in the analysis of results and 19 in the concluding discussion. Some papers were referenced more than once. We can see from this analysis that the literature review was not confined to one section but performed three purposes:

- to set the context for the work and to argue the need for research questions to be answered;
- to justify a particular methodological approach;
- to contribute to an advance in understanding of the topic.

The introduction to the article sets the scene for the research enquiry. It establishes that we know that there are variations in attainment in the short term but that long-term effects are unclear. The authors clearly identify and justify their research questions.

Author's text	Comment
. . . research has found substantial evidence of significant variations in students' achievement scores across primary schools and classes . . . as well as across secondary schools and classes . . . (pp. 419–420)	Establishes what we know and justifies claims with 11 references.
On the other hand, only a few follow-up studies have been undertaken concerning the continuing effects of schools and classes (p. 420)	Establishes a weakness in the research position.
Such research is important because it could . . . shed new light on educational practice and educational impact (p. 420)	Makes a claim for research. Following text establishes that conclusions on the long-term effect are mixed and, by implication, establishes a need for more work.
This article addresses the effect of Flemish primary schools and classes/teachers upon language and mathematics achievement at the end of primary schooling (short-term effects) and during the first two years of secondary education (long-term effect). (p. 421)	Outlines the research agenda.

The authors concluded that while differences between primary schools and classes have a short-term effect, this is eroded when pupils transfer to secondary school.

Source: Pustjens et al. (2007)

- **An accumulation of references:** In this situation researchers include everything that they can find on a topic. The literature survey is overwhelmed by citations of other people's work. It is a bibliographic list rather than a survey with a purpose. It suggests that the researcher has missed the point about a literature review and thinks that the priority is to show what has been read rather than make the review work in the interests of the research project. It produces a text that is hard to read and hard to follow because of the number of references that are given and suggests that the author lacks the ability to discriminate.

- **A free-standing literature review:** In this, the literature review can show the qualities of insight and understanding that other researchers look for but it lacks connectivity with the research argument. Where it occurs in dissertations, theses and project reports it can suggest to readers that its inclusion is more a consequence of a pro forma approach to producing the work, closely following a generic template that has been given for guidance rather than seeing the literature review as an important part of the case for justifying the work. As guidance we would not recommend calling a section 'Literature Review' in order to make sure that, by giving it another title, it forces us to recognise the role that it should be performing.
- **Mixing literature of different types without regard to the argument:** Work in most fields falls into two quite distinct types. On the one hand, there is theoretical and conceptual literature, which deals with the most general level of understanding and explanatory relationships, while, on the other, there are empirical investigations, which are rooted in the real world. Empirical investigations can link with theoretical work as both a starting point and finishing point of an investigation. Conceptual and philosophical analyses explore issues from a perspective of applying or exploring principles. This type of literature may represent an explicit or implicit argument for policy while empirical work constitutes the evidence base. It is important to recognise these types of literature and to use them in ways that support an argument. If they are mixed without a strong linkage between them, this reveals an inability to discriminate and a lack of understanding how the literature fits together in terms of making a claim and providing the evidence. A policy related argument can be made by empirical demonstrations of a problem. For example, if we wanted to explain the need to improve attainment in full-time education, we could point out the financial implications of not having a job or being in education or training in the period immediately after leaving school (estimated in the UK in 2000/2001 at £97,000 per head). The solutions to a problem may arise from theoretical statements or philosophical analyses. An empirical research programme should relate to a higher level of understanding, for example, an untested theory or the application of theory or a generalisation from another study to a new situation, or they can show how effective the outcomes of interventions are. It is the ability to link these levels of analysis and types of literature that shows not only command of the field but also the ability to develop and sustain an argument.
- **Believing that all academic prose is good:** Academics write in order to bring their ideas to a wider audience but some also want to demonstrate to that audience that they are leaders in the field. One way of doing this is to write in such a way that readers, finding the ideas complex and difficult to understand, believe that the author must be better than they are. If we do this in our research then we run the risk of producing text that is unintelligible and/or pretentious and of substituting jargon for prose. What is more, if we copy the style without understanding the meaning, we can make complete fools of ourselves. Academic writing should always be accessible. Of course, the intended audience shapes the accessibility but if an academic finds it difficult to understand another academic's writing, then there are only two reasons for it, either the reader is stupid or the author is pretentious. For anyone, even those carrying out their first research enquiry, the academic literature should be accessible. Look at Case Study 5.4 for examples of what to avoid.

(ii) Demonstrate our capability

The second way in which we should use the literature review is to communicate to those who matter, supervisors, examiners and the academic community, something about ourselves as academic researchers. In particular, we want them to appreciate our quality

Case study 5.4 Academic writing – not like this!

There is a balance to be achieved between a writing style that is informal and everyday and folksy (*I'll, should've*) and overbearing and unintelligible. Academic writing should, like all good writing, be clear; it should communicate complex findings and ideas simply. Notwithstanding this, while much academic writing is neutral, there are times when it pays to be passionate.

Bad academic writing has been criticised for a long time but recently criticism has given rise to debate as those criticised justify their approach to writing. Criticism of academic communication really took off in 1995 when a New Zealand academic, Dennis Dutton, editor of the journal *Philosophy and Literature*, initiated a 'Bad Writing' contest. The contest ran for three years and each year about 70 nominations were received. Having read many of the nominations, any one of them could have been chosen as the winner. Here is an example.

> It thus relatavises discourse not just to form – that familiar perversion of the modernist; nor to authorial invention – that conceit of the romantics; nor to a foundational world beyond discourse – that desperate grasping for a separate reality of the mystic and scientist alike; nor even to history and ideology – those refuges of the hermeneuticist; nor even less to language – that hypostecised abstraction of the linguist; nor, ultimately, even to discourse – that Nietzchean playground of world-lost signifiers of the structuralist and grammatologist, but to all or none of these, for it is anarchic, though not for the sake of anarchy but because it refuses to become a fetishised object among objects – to be dismantled, compared, classified and neutered in that parody of scientific scrutiny known as criticism.

From my perspective this suffers from the following:

- it is a rhetorical style that only comes alive when it is read slowly with emphasis to bring out the rhythm;
- it uses concepts (*hermeneuticist, Nietzchean*) that readers have to be familiar with, thus excluding a great many;
- it uses words not in common usage (*relativises*), when simpler ones will do;
- it uses words spelled incorrectly (*hypostecised* [hypostasized]);
- it is too long (the sentence is 126 words);
- it is not clear and has to be read many times before a semblance of the sense begins to emerge;
- overall, it is pompous.

Much of the writing that has been criticised comes from the word processors of academics exploring their subjects through the concepts and frameworks of critical theory. In 2003 the critical theorists hit back with the publication of *Just Being Difficult?* (Cullen and Lamb) and claimed the need for a specialist language through which to communicate their analyses, arguing that other subjects, such as computer science and medicine, were not stigmatised by the use of such language. However, there is a difference between a technical vocabulary and an obfuscatory language that excludes those who do not know or understand the codes. Our research findings should be accessible and inclusive!

and level. We cannot tell them that we are good but we can present ourselves through our work in such a way that they reach that conclusion. The list below presents some of the messages that we can send out.

- **Good communication:** The text that we produce should be grammatically correct and the words correctly spelled. We have to know our audience and pitch the tone of our writing to meet its expectations. Broadly this means that we should write as other academics write (unless they write like the people in Case Study 5.4!) and we learn how to do this by reading journals and by writing papers and essays. We also have to make sure that our work is well presented in terms of page layout, headings and citations. The best thing is to develop a template and stick to it. If we make one or two mistakes in anything, our audience is likely to overlook our transgressions, but repeated errors will cause them to doubt our capability and when this happens, they will find substantive as well as presentational errors.
- **Awareness of the field:** The review gives us an excellent opportunity to demonstrate our skills in bibliographic search and our ability to identify relevant material. What

has to come across is not our ability to collect a great volume of references but our skill in choosing to use some but not others to make our argument. This does not mean that we should only search for a few references. This is a dangerous strategy because there is no guarantee that we shall identify the most appropriate ones. Bibliographic search is a sifting process.

- **Organisation of ideas:** The review should not be a description and summary of the texts. What we have to do is assemble the issues that our references addressed and the conclusions they came to around themes that are relevant to our argument. Look at Case Study 5.3 again and see how two clear themes emerge, one identifying research that demonstrated short-term impacts and the other showing (a) that there was less research on long-term impacts, (b) that the research itself was inconclusive. If we are writing an academic paper two or three themes may be sufficient but if we are undertaking research for a major project such as a dissertation or thesis, then it is likely that we will need to explore more themes. The important thing is that the way in which we organise our material should create an argument that shows the need for the research, establishes the importance of the research and creates the conditions for us to specify the research questions. If we do this successfully, then it demonstrates one more thing, that we have an intellectual command of our field.
- **Critical ability:** Those who read our work are looking to see if we can tell the good from the mediocre and the innovative from the ordinary. They want to see if we can identify the people and the papers that change an interpretation, identify a new field and establish new thinking as opposed to those that follow and fill in the gaps. The ability to distinguish one from the other shows critical ability. It is a straightforward task to cast doubt on the quality of work and research outcomes. For example, the quality of the sampling (see Chapter 6) can let papers down and can limit our confidence in their claims. Authors may make assertions without supporting evidence. We should also be watchful for authors who support their own methodology by quoting others who have used the same methodology rather than justifying the research approach in terms of research principles. Unless there are clear principles guiding the approach, all this does is create a self-referencing structure without any foundations or substance. If several studies come to different conclusions we should seek to explain why. Criticism, however, is not only negative. We should acknowledge those who break new ground and create new agendas. We should highlight those whose methodology is beyond reproach (and show how it has influenced our own approach). In order to show our judgements we should raise our game in terms of how we express our ideas. 'Good' and 'bad' are hackneyed and carry no weight in a sentence. We should use words like 'influential'; 'outstanding'; 'limited'; 'frankly disappointing'; 'interesting but . . . flawed, limited, etc.'. It is our range of vocabulary and flexibility and strength of expression that convey colour, provide richness and allow subtlety of view to come through. The words we use represent not just our insights but also our interest and excitement within the topic.

5.4.3 Conducting the literature review

In this section we set out the framework of a typical literature survey and review. This is not a template to be followed at all costs. The approach reflects an academic's thinking. For some people it will generate a review that lacks theatre, surprise, and emotion, all qualities that make text enjoyable to read. We make no claim that these should be part of a review; whether they are or not is dependent both on the topic and the ability of the researcher to write in a particular style. It is because most people cannot do this, or do not want to take the risk of doing it, that the framework is academic in character.

(i) Define the review in terms of the research issue

This section summarises advice given earlier in the chapter. The purpose of the review is to establish that the research will be worthwhile. We have to present an argument for this. In most cases the argument is that there is a gap in our knowledge or understanding or that there is unfinished business. Ideally before we start a literature search we should have an idea of the themes we want to explore. This is not always possible, however, and it may be necessary to do some reading before creating the themes to follow up. The following questions may help in framing the argument and the search.

- *Why is this an issue/problem?* With an educational topic there is a strong likelihood that behind the substantive research issue lies a further issue of, for example, opportunity, social disadvantage, cost, standards. We should look for the wider agenda, which often identifies a societal interest in our work.
- *Is there a political dimension?* If there is a political dimension it could mean that there are policy alternatives. We should explore what research supports the policy position and try to identify what it is in the research that leads to different policy solutions.
- *When did this issue first arise?* The interest here is to establish a chronology, to see how the issue has changed over time and to explain why it has grown or declined in importance.
- *Who has an interest in the topic?* Identify the stakeholders in an issue – parents, teachers, people who want to create change in order to advance their careers, taxpayers and so on. Who is actively pursuing their interest? How is this affecting the presentation or resolution of the issue? Following through these questions in the literature allows us to represent stakeholder perspectives.

(ii) Conduct the review

The next stage is to examine the literature and codify it. Where does it contribute to our understanding of the issue? In terms of the theory or methodology or conclusions? Has it identified an interesting or a novel data source? How does it relate to the questions we want answered? Examine the quality of the conclusions. This means we have to convince ourselves that the methodology used to collect the data is robust and that the inferences drawn from the analysis of the data are valid in their own right and not spun to reflect the interests and concerns of the author.

(iii) Organise, summarise and synthesise

Once we have identified the themes to structure our argument, we should identify how each of our references contributes to them. The references may be relevant for more than one theme. We should create a record of the reference, summarise what it says and in that summary identify how it contributes to the themes. At this point, we should note other points that occur to us. As our database of references grows, we should begin to summarise the points that emerge. We should look for developments over time, conflicts of outcome, disputes between authors, arguments and controversy.

(iv) Write the review

The final stage is to move on from our thematic summaries and notes and produce an integrated review. At this point we have to remember that we have to convince our readers of the need for our research. The review should convince them through the logic of our argument. Sometimes this is substantive, sometimes it is methodological. For example, if we want to explore (a) how much and what type of training teachers have had in sex education, (b) their judgements on its effectiveness and (c) how their training is reflected in their approach to the task, our argument is likely to be that this is an under-researched area. In bringing together the themes, we could possibly explore to what extent there is a consensus emerging in some areas but not the one we want to study. For instance, that we know what happens in primary schools but not secondary, or that approaches to classroom discipline are well documented in one country but not another. We should support the case for our research by exercising our judgement about other people's work. We could comment on the credibility and the results in the context of the methodology. Our adverse criticism could be a reason for questioning the results and demonstrating the need for additional work. Whatever our approach to research we should be clear that it is insufficient to describe the research that has taken place. Our database of sources is the evidence we use to justify our own work.

The language of a literature review should be formal. Abbreviations (*didn't, haven't*) should normally not be present, unless they are being reported. Grammar checkers should be used to identify problems with expression (*should of* instead of the correct *should have*) but beware, they are not always as accurate as they think they are! Description is not enough, discussion is vital. We should identify contradictions in results, disagreements between authors, how work builds together to create an understanding and explanation.

Finally, the review that we write should be anything but dull. It should reflect the excitement that we have in the topic; it should have a wide sphere of vision and be able to relate to all parts of the research report. If we write a separate research review at the beginning of our project, we will almost certainly have to revise it for the finished report in order to bring out the connections. The review section should build on the identification of the issue in the introduction to the research report and tease out themes that lead to the specification of research questions. Sometimes these themes identify no need for further research but some will have to support the research questions we pose. The review, in particular, should hold the interest of readers and propel them to the same conclusions that we reach. A good piece of advice is not to fill their hearts with foreboding by calling the section 'Literature Review'. This sounds dull to start with. A report of research should be interesting, so give it a title.

Summary

- The literature review should inform all parts of a thesis, dissertation or research report.
- Literature survey is an ongoing process throughout the research.
- We should be sceptical about published work, even work published in refereed journals, and we should assure ourselves that it represents an honest statement of the topic.
- The literature survey is more effective if guided by a pre-established strategy.
- On-line resources ease the process of identifying references.
- The literature review is the means by which we establish the need for the research.
- Literature review is more than a description of the literature.
- The books, articles and reports we review constitute the evidence we use to make a case for our research.
- The review should be focused, not a compendium.
- We should write the review so that it reads like literature and not a piece of dull academic prose.

Further reading

Fink, A. (2005) *Conducting Research Literature Reviews: From the Internet to Paper*, Sage, Thousand Oaks, Calif.

Hart, C. (2004) *Doing a Literature Search: A Comprehensive Guide for the Social Sciences*, Sage, London.

Chris Hart gives sound advice on managing searches and how to find materials. Though the passage of time makes some of his sources look outdated, he still gives a clear introduction to a wide range.

Arlene Fink's book may fool you into thinking that it is just a slimmed-down version of Chris Hart's or just another book on research methods (it has sections on sampling, variables and measurement scales) but it is quite different. Its focus is on reviewing literature and everything in the book is introduced to help us reach judgements about the quality of what we read.

References

Coles, G. (1999) 'No End to the Literacy Debate' [commentary], *Education Week*, 27 January, 55.

Coles, G. (2000) *Misreading Reading: The Bad Science That Hurts Children*, Heinemann, Portsmouth, NH.

Cullen, J. and Lamb, K. (eds) (2003) *Just Being Difficult? Academic Writing in the Public Arena*, Stanford University Press.

Foorman, B.R., Francis, D.J., Fletcher, J.M., Schatschneider, C. and Mehta, P. (1998) 'The Role of Instruction in Learning to Read: Preventing Reading Failure in At-risk Children', *Journal of Educational Psychology*, 90, 37–55.

Foorman, B.R., Fletcher, J.M., Francis, D.J. and Schatschneider, C. (2000) '*Response*: Misrepresentation of Research by Other Researchers', *Educational Researcher*, 29(6), 27–37.

Friedman, S.J. (2000) 'Research News and Comment: How Much of a Problem? A Reply to Ingersoll's "The Problem of Underqualified Teachers in American Secondary Schools"', *Educational Researcher*, 29(5), 18–20.

Gredler, M.E. (2007) 'Of Cabbages and Kings: Concepts and Inferences Curiously Attributed to Lev Vygotsky' [commentary on McVee, Dunsmore and Gavelek, 2005], *Review of Educational Research*, 77(2), 233–238.

Ingersoll, R.M. (1999) 'The Problem of Underqualified Teachers in American Secondary Schools', *Educational Researcher*, 28(2), 26–37.

Ingersoll, R.M. (2001) 'Rejoinder: Misunderstanding the Problem of Out-of-field Teaching', *Education Researcher*, 30(1), 21–22.

Krasny, K.A., Sadoski, M. and Paivio, A. (2007) 'Unwarranted Return: A Response to McVee, Dunsmore and Gavelek's (2005) "Schema Theory Revisited"', *Review of Educational Research*, 77(2), 239–244.

McVee, M.B., Dunsmore, K. and Gavelek, J.R. (2005) 'Schema Theory Revisited', *Review of Educational Research*, 75(4), 531–566.

McVee, M.B., Dunsmore, K. and Gavelek, J.R. (2007) 'Considerations of the Social, Individual, and Embodied: A Response to Comments on"Schema Theory Revisited"', *Review of Educational Research*, 77(2), 245–248.

Pustjens, H., Van de Gaier, E., Van Damme, J., Onghena, P. and Van Landeghem, G. (2007) 'The Short-term and the Long-term Effect of Primary Schools and Classes on Mathematics and Language Achievement Scores', *British Educational Research Journal*, 33(3), 419–440.

Schutz, A. (2006) 'Home is a Prison in the Global City: The Tragic Failure of School-based Community Engagement Strategies', *Review of Educational Research*, 76(4), 691–743.

Stevens, P.A.J. (2007) 'Researching Race/Ethnicity and Educational Inequality in English Secondary Schools: A Critical Review of the Research Literature Between 1980 and 2005', *Review of Educational Research*, 77(2), 47–185.

Taylor, B.M., Anderson, R.C., Au, K.H. and Raphael, T.E. (2000) 'Discretion in the Translation of Research to Policy: A Case from Beginning Reading', *Educational Researcher*, 29(6), 16–26.

Chapter contents

Chapter 6

GETTING THE RIGHT INFORMATION

Key themes

- The right data sources and the right sample lay the foundations for good research.
- Important primary data sources.
- Why we sample.
- The differences between different sampling approaches and how to apply them.
- How to determine sample size.
- What can go wrong with a sample.
- Modification of sampling procedures to meet project needs.

Introduction

Chapter 4 has given us a better understanding of what education researchers mean by data. In this chapter we shall understand a little more about what we call information. To draw a distinction between the two may seem a little like nitpicking but it is an appropriate one to make. While it probably matters little in terms of actually doing research, it is more significant in terms of understanding the process of doing research.

As we saw in Chapter 4, we either collect data ourselves (this is called primary data) or someone has already collected it for us (and this is called secondary data). Our job as researchers is to make data answer our research question. To do this we have to extract and exploit the information that is contained in it. There are four steps to this:

- First, we have to be sure that we get data from the right source. This is what we shall consider in this chapter.
- Second, we have to be sure that we get good quality information from our sources. We shall look at this in Chapters 8 and 9 when we consider survey techniques.
- Third, we have to process the data to extract the information from it that we want. This is the content of Chapters 10 to 13.
- Fourth, we have to use the information to create the evidence that we use to argue our case. We will look at this in Chapter 13.

6.1 From data to information

The foundations of any research are getting data from the right sources and making sure that their quality is good. A simple example will illustrate the point. We can have the best questionnaire in the world on the effect of bullying on a child's life at home and out of school but if the parents who receive it do not have any children who are being bullied, we will not get the data we need. The converse is equally true. If we give a poor questionnaire to the right people, our data will be poor. In each of these two cases, the informational content in the data is poor and no matter what processes we use to extract and amplify the information, it will always be poor. This chapter deals with the foundations of good research. We have to understand (a) the principles that will get us the data that will give us good information and (b) to make sure that these principles are effectively implemented within the resources available. If we cut corners on these foundations, the quality of our research will be undermined.

In this chapter we shall identify criteria against which we can judge the appropriateness of our data. We have to recognise though that delivering quality comes with costs attached. The implication of this is that we have to make a judgement about the trade-off between data quality and cost. We will look at this issue as well. However, central to the whole process of getting good quality data is sampling. This is what will concern us most of all. To see how important sampling is, read Case Study 6.1.

Case study 6.1 How you benefit from sampling

If you knew that there was a website that contained 11,000 images of people clad in nothing more than their underwear, you could be forgiven for thinking that it was trading, at the very best, on the fringes of decency and that in all likelihood its business was pornography. On both counts you would be wrong; you would probably be surprised to learn, as well, that these 11,000 people took their clothes off so that you (and I) would benefit.

They took part in updating the UK National Sizing Survey. This is a collaboration between the Government and the UK fashion industry. It is a database that retailers and designers use to ensure that clothes are designed and manufactured to specifications that people will fit into. If you wondered why it is important to update sizes periodically, then all you need to know is that since the early 1950s, our waists have increased by 6 inches (15.2 cm) and our height by 1.5 inches (3.8 cm). If designers get the measurements right, retailers maximise the number of people who might buy the clothes.

The 11,000 who took their clothes off in the public interest were selected to represent both sexes between 16 and 90. Because other factors influence size besides age and gender, the sample was also structured on the basis of ethnicity, socio-economic status and geographical location. Variations in these factors could influence retailers targeting niche markets.

The findings are not only useful for retailers, though. With 38 per cent of women and 44 per cent of men being overweight, the data confirms that the messages of health education are not getting through to the public. But if you think the problem is bad here, then it is worse elsewhere; on average, UK women are taller, lighter and have smaller waists than women in the USA. A healthy diet and moderate drinking will not only improve our figures, they will also mean that our careers as researchers will be longer.

6.2 What is the 'right source' for information?

The theme of this chapter is that to get 'good information' that will answer a research question, we have to get it from the right source. But what is the right source? In general, the right source:

- is authoritative; and
- is stable over time.

Let us look at each of these in greater detail.

(i) An authoritative source

There are two elements to being an authoritative source; first is knowledge of the issue being researched and second is credibility as a source of information. Let us think, for a moment, of how we acquire knowledge and we will probably come up with this sort of list:

- from direct experience;
- from others (either by being told or by reading); or
- through the media.

We can place what we learn on a continuum that ranges from absolute certainty, through not being sure to utter disbelief. The ideal source is one about whom or which we have absolute certainty. We can be pretty sure about the grade results of a school or college or when an education authority tells us that the schools in its area are short of five mathematics teachers. We can equally be sure that we do not want to use as a source something that we know to be wrong. Look at Case Study 6.2 and make up your own mind.

Most of the sources we use are likely to be ones on which we can rely. There may be some about whom we are not sure but this is where triangulation comes into its own (see section 3.3.4). However, there may be circumstances when a knowledgeable source offers us information that is questionable. Imagine a situation in which we are interviewing head teachers in a school district about the policies they have introduced and the practices they implement to raise pupil achievement. One head teacher tells us that the results at another school are the consequence of the school implementing a selection policy, something that is not permitted, and not by improving teaching and learning methods. How do we react to this as information? It falls into a broad category of rumour and opinion that generally should not be used as evidence unless it can be substantiated. A comment to the same effect from another head teacher makes it more plausible but only a dissection of the school enrolment process and an analysis of its outcomes over several years will give us information that we can totally trust.

The second element in being authoritative is credibility. Establishing the credibility of a source of data means that we have to take account of the experience, role and position of the source in relation to our research issue. If we wanted to quantify the need for early years provision in an area, then the Director of Social Services, the Director of Housing and the Director of Education in the area are likely to be able to provide us with information. However, if we wanted to know what works in terms of improving young children's

Case study 6.2 Data interpretation and the creation of information

In late May 2007 a new museum opened in Kentucky in the USA. Its aim is to explain how the world evolved. Its website promises:

> A fully engaging, sensory experience for guests. Murals and realistic scenery, computer-generated visual effects, over fifty exotic animals, life-sized people and dinosaur animatronics, and a special-effects theater complete with misty sea breezes and rumbling seats.

This is just the sort of modern presentation that we would expect from a state of the art exhibition. For most people, however, brought up to believe in rational explanation arising from scientific endeavour, the museum is a challenge. The basis of its presentations is that the first book of the Christian Bible, *Genesis*, offers an explanation for evolution that is as valid as Darwin's theory. (Actually, the originators of the museum believe that it is more valid.) We are promised a 'Walk through the Garden of Eden' and, having 'come face-to-face with a sauropod, a dinosaur of incredible dimensions', we are invited to rest at 'Noah's Café . . . a perfect stopping place for tired and hungry tourists'.

The museum was developed by an organisation called Answers in Genesis (AIG), whose second line of its mission statement says: 'We relate the relevance of a literal Genesis to the church and the world today with creativity.'

AIG makes an important point when it says:

> '. . . There aren't separate sets of "evidences" for evolution and creation – we all deal with the same evidence (we all live on the same earth, have the same fossils, observe the same animals, etc.). The difference lies in how we interpret what we study.'

For most people it is on a less sound footing, though, when it argues that:

> 'The Bible – the "history book of the universe"– provides a reliable, eye-witness account of the beginning of all things, and can be trusted to tell the truth in all areas it touches on.'

Reports of the museum in the media have been glowing in their praise for the quality of the presentation but many have been disturbed by the creationist message, often using humour to make their point. The BBC correspondent, Martin Redfern, reporting on the museum in a broadcast in April 2007 asked the museum about the Grand Canyon, which conventional wisdom says took over a million years to be formed. 'Not so,' he was told by 'Young Earth' creationists, 'All those rocks were deposited by flood waters at the time of Noah'. Those of you who remember your Bible will recall that the flood was God's punishment for a sinful world. Redfern commented that, 'Here at least, sin and anger have turned into something surprisingly beautiful!'

The Economist (2 June 2007, p. 54) observed, tongue in cheek, that:

> '. . . The debate about the origins of everything is presented even-handedly. Some people trust God, accept that the universe is 6000 years old and will go to heaven. Others trust human reason, think the Big Bang happened 14 billion years ago and, having abandoned God, are quite likely to start browsing the Internet for pornography or committing genocide.'

Ultimately, as AIG says, it is how you use the data that is important; '"facts" don't speak for themselves, but must be interpreted'. This is the role we all take on when we undertake educational research – and that is why we should always know the background of the person making the interpretation.

sociability and communication, we should talk to early years teachers. In other words, it is position in relation to the issue that is important, not position in a hierarchy.

However, let us return for a moment to opinion. Above we said that opinion should not normally be used as data but there are circumstances when it is valid. When someone in authority says 'We have to' or 'I think we should . . . ' then it is reasonable to use this as information because it comes from a source who can make things happen. Power is important, even when those who exercise it are wrong. Equally, if sufficient numbers of people say, 'I think that . . . ', then even their unsubstantiated views become legitimate information, irrespective of whether they are right or wrong. So a source can be credible if they have the possibility of changing situations, and this possibility comes from individual authority or a collective voice that can influence political and decision making processes.

In summary, the features of an authoritative source are:

- knowledge of the issue;
- trustworthiness in relation to the information being given;
- power or authority in relation to the issue;
- organisational or political authority in relation to opinion.

(ii) Stability over time

An authoritative source should give the same information even after a period of time. For example, a school whose data on unauthorised pupil absences for a given week were changed half a dozen times, should raise some questions about data quality. A teacher who said one day that 20 per cent of students would not pass the assessment and on another that 50 per cent would not, is not the authoritative source we would want. Factual information about an event or a period, values and attitudes should normally be stable over time. This does not, of course, mean that with the passage of time, the numbers of unauthorised absences cannot change or the proportion of pupils expected to pass an examination cannot fall, because in this case we are dealing with events at two points in time and not one.

This establishes an important principle. If the conditions around an event change, then the reported event can change. If they do not, then the event should not change. We met this principle in section 3.2.4 when we examined the experimental approach to research. It is called *ceteris paribus* and is important in relation to opinions and attitudes. If we ask students whether or not they like mathematics at the beginning and end of a course, we might reasonably expect individual judgements to move. We could explore this further by investigating grades received by students and whether they liked the teacher. However, were we to ask students their views of mathematics on two occasions close to each other in time before the course, then we would not expect their views to change. If they did, we are either asking the wrong question or the right question badly . . . or some of the students are having fun with us.

Stability in the data we acquire is important in respect of the claims we make for our research. Imagine that we are researching the impact of before-school clubs on pupil behaviour and performance. (Before-school clubs are initiatives to provide a safe environment and appropriate activities before school opens for children of working parents.) Our research results appear to show that children who are provided with breakfast perform better than children who breakfast at home. This would be an important finding that could affect child and education policy. But policy is rarely decided on the basis of a single piece of research. What would be necessary is for the results to be replicated for the same children and for the research to be duplicated with other children. As we saw in Chapter 3, replication and duplication are the processes that convince us that our findings are correct. In this way, we would show that the original conclusions were stable over time with the same group and that the group was not atypical because the results were stable when the issue was examined elsewhere.

In summary, data stability:

- is a precondition for a reliable analysis;
- ensures that our work can be replicated and verified by others; and
- can only exist when external conditions and circumstances do not change.

6.3 Perfection is not always an option: putting the research plan together

If getting the right data from an authoritative source is the bedrock on which good research is based, the question then arises, how perfect does everything have to be?

To answer this, we return to the points briefly made in section 1.6.6. Of course, what would be ideal is always best but what is ideal often runs foul of the real world in which we all live and work. There has to be a balance between what is ideal and what is possible.

It is important that we do the following for each research project we are involved with.

- Plan the whole research programme. Specify the data required, identify the data sources, determine the quantity of data required for the analysis and the number of sources needed to generate this quantity. Note here that we have to work backwards because, in order to convince others with our explanation, we may need a specific amount of data to generate the information we require. We have to plan forwards and, following this, backwards. We also should specify the way in which the data will be processed and analysed in order to release the information content. Finally, for each of our activities, data collection, data analysis and data reporting, we have to enumerate the resources required to carry out the task and the time each one will take. It is a good idea to plot these quantities against a timeline. Figure 6.1 shows a research timeline presented as a *Gantt Chart* (named after an American engineer, Henry Gantt, who developed them in the early twentieth century as a means of managing large-scale projects).
- Look at the resources available to the researcher or to the research project. Read again section 2.4.4, which deals with resources we might require. Pay particular attention to the availability of these resources over time.
- Judge whether the total amount of resources are sufficient for the research task as described. If they are, judge whether they match the peaks and troughs of research need. If they do not, can the research procedure be reshaped or the resources reallocated?
- If there is a serious mismatch, revisit the research procedure to see if another approach can deliver worthwhile results within the resources available. The following approaches constitute a cost-effective strategy for data assembly that can reduce costs considerably.
  - See if others have published on the issue. Several studies all reaching the same conclusion might remove the need for research altogether or it might be sufficient to warrant only a small piece of your research. For example, research exploring the association between disaffection and juvenile criminality probably does not need to determine the characteristics of disaffection because they are already widely known. In other words, it is a waste of resources to reproduce existing findings.
  - See if secondary data, especially statistics from central or local government, exist that can answer some part of the research question. Read section 4.6 for an introduction to the variety of secondary data available.
  - Only go to primary sources to fill the gaps. Obtaining data firsthand is expensive, so it is only worth doing if other sources do not exist or are inadequate.

This short section is vital in terms of the way in which we should shape and then plan our overall research design and strategy. It should be apparent that the process of research planning may require several iterations of looking at how the research can be conducted satisfactorily within the resources available. Activity 6.1 will help you see how

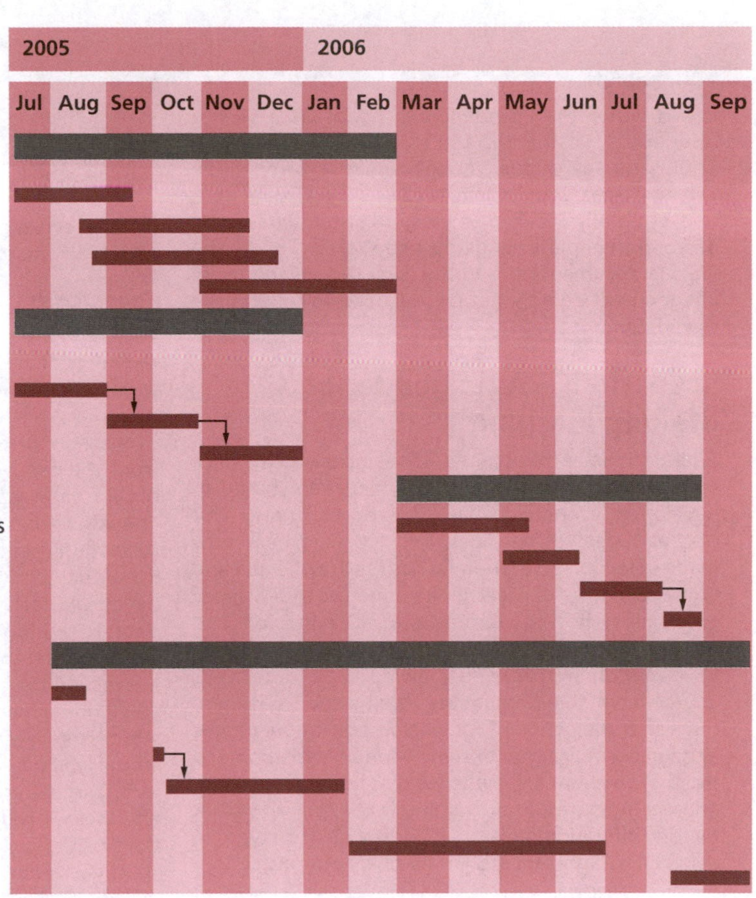

Observation of user activity

1.1: Identify groups
1.2: Focus groups
1.3: Web surveys
1.4: Analysis and report

User trends analysis

2.1: 3rd party data collection
2.2: Data analysis
2.3: Report writing

Design evaluation

3.1: Identify demonstrators
3.2: Build mockups
3.3: Evaluation trials
3.4: Analysis and report

Dissemination

4.1: Website build
4.2: Conference/workshop feedback
4.3: Delphi exercise
4.4: Journal/conference paper presentation
4.5: Final report

Figure 6.1 Example of a Gantt chart

Source: Research Student Handbook, University of Wales Institute, Cardiff, section 9, p. 6.

Activity 6.1 Before you do the work yourself

The purposes of this activity are:

- to increase your familiarity with secondary data sources, and
- to help you determine how far such sources remove the need for you to collect your own data.

Below, there are three scenarios. For each one try the search suggested and then build up a table showing, on one side, how the data meets the requirements of the scenario and, on the other, how it does not. Where the data set does not meet the requirements, explain how you would go about getting the data or justify why the effort of getting the additional data outweighs the benefits of having it available to the analysis.

Scenario A – Young people's family responsibilities

There is an awareness that the idea of childhood being a time when parents create an environment of care, taking decisions on behalf of children and when the main activities of children are to go to school, play and socialise is not one that necessarily applies to every child. Your interest as a researcher is to find out whether children take on responsibilities usually assumed by a parent or guardian and, if so, in what circumstances. You are, in particular, concerned to understand whether this happens in particular family structures or particular ethnic groups.

Your search

Go to either the Economic and Social Data Service (esds.ac.uk) or the UK Data Archive (data-archive.ac.uk) and search for 'young people as carers'. You will find that your search returns several data sets; one, especially, looks to be useful: 'Longitudinal Study of Young People in England and Wales'. Follow the link via documentation to the 'User Guide' and make a judgement about whether you need to collect your own data.

Scenario B – Age, gender and lifelong learning

Globalisation in the recent past has increased the pace of economic change. Industries that were based in developed economies have moved off-shore. Our clothes, washing machines, TVs and so on are now made in low wage economies such as Brazil, India and China. One of the great policy concerns in advanced economies is how to promote innovation in goods and services that will sustain wealth creation. In order to have an economy based on knowledge, a society needs a knowledgeable population. What evidence is there that, after the period of compulsory education, people engage periodically with some form of education and training? Is there any evidence that the willingness to engage in education or training is age related? What factors influence individual decisions? This type of research is important in shaping policy options.

Your search

See how many of these questions you can answer in respect of either Sweden (www.scb.se/default_2154.asp), or the USA (//nces.ed.gov) or the Netherlands (www.cbs.nl/en-GB/default.htm). Follow the links on these websites to see what detail of data you can come up with – not all sites will give you the same quality. Don't forget the question about factors shaping individual decisions. Has anyone carried out research on this in the country you are investigating or will you have to do it yourself?

Scenario C – Social circumstances and improvements in educational performance and attainment

All countries seek to improve the effectiveness of schools and student attainment. This is one of the foundations of developing a knowledgeable society. The evidence is clear, however, that schools are not all the same. We can propose three possible causes:

- The organisation of the school, school leadership and teaching may not be up to scratch.
- The pupils may be chosen from a lower ability range.
- Social conditions and circumstances may limit pupils aspirations and adversely affect their motivation to learn and commitment to learning.

Is there evidence that social conditions are a factor and is this changing?

Your search

You could answer this question by looking at the attainment of individual pupils in the context of their social and family backgrounds. This would, however, require a lot of resources. If you raised the unit of analysis from the individual to the school and from the family to the neighbourhood, you could obtain data that gave you insights into the issue. The skill here is to combine two data sources. For information on attainment in the UK, you could go to individual schools but there is an easier way. Schools have to report their performance annually and the data is published on the Web (www.dfes.gov.uk/performancetables). Go to this source, choose a year, a level and then an area. It is easiest to select an area you know, then you will be able to identify the schools more easily. If you follow the link to the school, you will see that it gives detailed information, including the address. Note down the data you need and the postcode. To find out about the social conditions of the pupils, you have to make an assumption that most pupils will be drawn from the immediate locality. This need not necessarily be the case but it is one of the penalties of assembling secondary data to answer questions. Go to the UK National Statistics portal (www.statistics.gov.uk) and follow the neighbourhood link. You will be taken to a search page. Fill in the postcode of the schools you have selected. You will be presented with a wealth of data on the locality. Which ones could you use as indicators of social and economic conditions?

This approach made an assumption about where the pupils lived in relation to the school. Which of the following would be your preferred way of improving your data, and why?

- Increasing the number of schools to ensure that a wide range of performance standards are looked at in context.
- Targeting areas with widely different socio-economic profiles and looking at the performance of schools in each.
- Selecting a sample of pupils from the school, inputting their home postcodes and combining data from the areas identified.

you can take costs out of a research programme. However, if the resources available cannot support a worthwhile research programme, then the research should be ditched. Poor research is worthless and only spoils the field for others.

6.4 Sampling: being able to say something sensible

As well as being authoritative, the people and organisations that give us data have to be representative of something meaningful. A city administration that manages to turn around education provision in schools would be representative of good systems organisation and management. A survey of the views of a selection of early years senior practitioners in the UK on the quality and value of their professional qualifications could be representative of judgements nationwide of the ability of universities and colleges to organise professional education in a sector that they have long ignored. A survey of what happened (in terms of student grades and performance) in Sweden following the removal of selection procedures for entry to secondary education could indicate what might happen in England if the same policy were to be adopted. (The School Admissions Code in England and Wales seeks to ensure equity in access to schools. It is overseen by a newly created agency, the Office of the Schools Adjudicator.)

In order for our data to be representative, we have to ensure that we can explore a more general agenda or issue through the data that we collect. If we deal with everyone or every organisation in a group, for example, *every* school operating and recognised as a city academy in the UK, or *every* teacher dismissed for having an inappropriate relationship with a pupil in a given period, the issue of being representative is not a problem because we are considering what statisticians call the *population*. However, if the population is all PhD students currently registered with Swedish universities or teachers in their first year of employment in the Netherlands, then the task of contacting them may not be so easy. In situations like this we select people or organisations from the whole population in a process that we call *sampling*.

This section deals with probably the most important stage in the research process. In it we shall look at the following:

- why we sample;
- the basic principle of sampling, linking the sample to the population;
- different approaches to sampling and the circumstances in which they are used;
- how many people or organisations to include in a sample;
- what can go wrong with samples.

6.4.1 Why do we sample?

As we shall see later in this chapter, it is possible to gain strong and important insights into the issue we are studying by using secondary data, either official data published by a government or public agency or data collected by another researcher, perhaps even collected for a different purpose. Investigation of existing sources should always be a starting point in data collection because collecting data ourselves involves effort and can be complicated. However, there will be situations when we have to do this and very often sampling is the only alternative open to us. These are the circumstances in which we usually have to collect our own data.

(i) Where there is a mismatch between the research question and existing data

We do not have an alternative but to collect our own data when we can find nothing to help us in our search of secondary data sources. However, even if there is secondary data, it may be too old. Education systems and the social and economic context in which they sit can change rapidly, so the pictures of situations that data represent can become out of date. The older the data set is, the more the picture is historical rather than current, and is useful only as a baseline against which to benchmark new data. As a rule of thumb, it is inadvisable to use data more than five years old for a current problem and even this has to be reviewed in the light of the research issue.

A further problem may concern a mismatch between the scale of the secondary data and the scale of the research problem. Data may exist, for example at a national scale, but if the issue is being investigated for a particular locality the national picture may not be too relevant. Local circumstances can have a significant impact. For example, in terms of an investigation into compulsory education up to the age of 16, variations in socio-economic status, in lifestyle, in ethnicity and in the mix of types of school can all create a local pattern of educational outcomes that is very different from the national one.

(ii) When we risk becoming overwhelmed with data

We also have to look to sampling as a solution when the population is so large that to contact everyone is not possible. We may be able to identify every probationary teacher or every child being cared for by public authorities or every nursery school but contacting each person or organisation with a request for information is not really an option for an individual researcher or even a small research team. The management system to trace who has been contacted and who has or has not responded would be complex and probably cumbersome, and, in a fast-changing world, there is no guarantee that the people responding at the beginning of the process are facing the same conditions as those responding at the end. And when all the data is collected, the task of collating and then processing it is enormous and will take time. Much research, in any field, has a window of opportunity framed by public concern and policy considerations. If we miss this window, we miss the opportunity to make a contribution.

(iii) When we have to live within our means

We also sample when the cost of reaching the entire population is too great for our resources. It is obviously cheaper in time and money to contact 400 primary schools rather than the 18,000 there are in England. Sampling then is a way of living within our resources and it enables individuals or small teams of researchers to research large-scale issues that would otherwise overwhelm them.

(iv) When speed is of the essence

Contacting an entire population takes time, so when information is required quickly, sampling is the obvious solution. In England, childminders are required to be registered.

Checks are made with the Criminal Records Bureau and, broadly, if the check identifies a record that is sufficiently serious, that person is disqualified from registration. Since childminding is often carried out within someone's house, checks are made on others living in the house. However, they are not carried out on household members living away from the house (for example, children living in their own accommodation or estranged spouses). (For more information on this, see The Childcare (Disqualification) Regulations 2007.) Imagine a situation where it is discovered that an ex-husband visits his ex-wife, a childminder, when children are there and that, unbeknown to her, he is registered under the provisions of the Sexual Offences Act. A government would want to know quickly how widespread this situation is. There are almost 70,000 registered childminders in England. It is impossible to survey them all but a sample of 2,000 will give a very reliable estimate (to within plus or minus two per cent of the actual number) within a time period that the public would accept.

(v) When we are dealing with an unknown population

Finally, there will be situations when the size of the population is not known and again we can sample in order to manage this. Examples might be the numbers of children riding bicycles to school, teachers who would like to retire early and the number of car parking spaces provided on all university campuses. The only option in this case is to sample and to make contact with those who can be identified. This poses problems for analysis and relating the findings of the sample to the population but it is all that the researcher can do. There are also many situations in which we can estimate the size of the population (for example, children under 16 who have one or more parents with AIDS) but the only realistic solution to finding out how this impacts on their lives is to carry out a sample.

6.4.2 The framework of sampling

Sampling is effective because it seeks to link the findings from a selection of respondents or instances to the entirety of respondents or instances. What the different ways of sampling actually do is justify both (a) the link between the sample and the population and (b) the inferences that the researcher draws on the back of that link. In broad terms, the researcher ascribes to the population the characteristics of the sample. For example, a survey of the value a sample of university lecturers placed on external quality assurance processes could be used to represent the value ascribed by all university lecturers.

Table 6.1 sets out the basic elements that researchers have to consider in the sampling process.

(i) First, there is the *target population* (often just referred to as the population)

The target population is all instances that meet the requirements of the research issue. The target population is therefore determined by the research issue. For example, if we were examining the attainment of ethnic minority students in Holland who experienced the same learning environment as their Dutch counterparts in middle level vocational education, our target populations would be (a) colleges with a mixed entry of ethnic minority and (b) native Dutch students aged 16–20. (If we think about why we would do this, it is because of the possibility that students attending colleges with no ethnic minority students might have a higher social status than students who attended a college

Table 6.1 Elements in the sampling process

Element	Definition	Issue
Target population	All of the potential sources of data determined by the research issue.	Size may be known or unknown.
Sampling frame	Every instance that can be used to generate research data.	Not every instance may be identified.
Sample	The instances that are selected to provide information.	Extent to which it is representative of the population.

with ethnic minority students and social status can be a factor that affects attainment.) If, on the other hand, our research question was whether ethnic minority students were disproportionately represented in post-16 vocational education, then our target population is all post-16 students. It should be clear from this that it is how we specify the research question that has a direct and controlling influence on the target population.

(ii) The second element in the framework is the *sampling frame*

This is each element or person in the population that we can identify and reach in order to collect research data. There are many situations in which the sampling frame and the population are the same. When this happens, we can draw the most accurate samples possible because we can list every element in the population. In our examples above the sampling frames would be (a) all colleges with ethnic minority students in the first case and (b) all students in middle level vocational education in the second. In the first case, if we sample institutions themselves, the sampling frame and the target population are the same (it is unlikely that we will overlook a college). However, in the second case, it may well be beyond our resources to list every student in order to draw our sample. As we shall see, though, there are ways round this sort of problem. There is another situation as well where the sample frame may be an inadequate representation of the population. There is an example of this in Activity 6.2.

Activity 6.2 Researching childcare

If we were researching all forms of childcare in an area, we could define our population in terms of organisations listed in a directory such as *Yellow Pages* or a classified telephone directory. However, while these sources will give us an immediate population to sample, the likelihood is that they will not identify all the organisations and carers. As a sampling frame they are, therefore, limited.

Test this out in an area known to you. We could use both of the following websites as our sample frame.

- Go to Yell.com: identify childcare providers.
- Go to childcare.gov.uk: identify childcare providers.

The crucial thing about the sampling frame is that it should identify every element of the population in order to make the sampling robust and in order for us to be specific about the nature of the relationship between the sample and the population.

When we are unable to identify and enumerate every element in the population, the sample frame changes in character and is only *indicative* of the link between sample and population. We may have an estimate of the number of men and women with HIV/AIDS but we cannot identify and enumerate each one. If we carry out a sample of HIV/AIDS sufferers, we have to *assume* that it is representative, we cannot prove that it is.

(iii) The third element in the framework is the *sample* itself

There are several types of sample and approaches to sampling. The differences between them are largely a consequence of (a) the research issue and the specification of the research question, and (b) the ability to identify and enumerate each member of the target population. Figure 6.2 sets out the different approaches to sampling. There is a broad division between two approaches.

- The first is probability sampling (also called EPSEM – Equal Probability of Selection Method) in which all elements in the sampling frame have an equal chance of being chosen for the sample. These generally are the most robust approaches because we can use them to make statements about the likelihood of things in the parent population and about the significance of differences between one sample and another. It is the ability to do this that makes for strong conclusions. They are a fundamental requirement of the scientific/positivist approach to social science research (see section 3.2) and underpin methods of data analysis that we shall meet in Chapters 12 and 13. In each case the target population is known or can be accurately estimated and can be sufficiently enumerated to allow a reliable sampling frame to be devised.
- The second set of approaches shown in Figure 6.2 has the common characteristic that the samples are not drawn on the basis of equal probability of selection, so with these we cannot draw conclusions about the likelihood of things in the population. All we can do is describe the sample. If we use one of these methods we cannot use the techniques of data analysis described in Chapter 13. The alternative name for these approaches is 'purposive' because they are usually used to achieve a particular object or purpose. We use these methods to resolve different research questions as compared with probability samples. In some cases the purpose is to obtain data

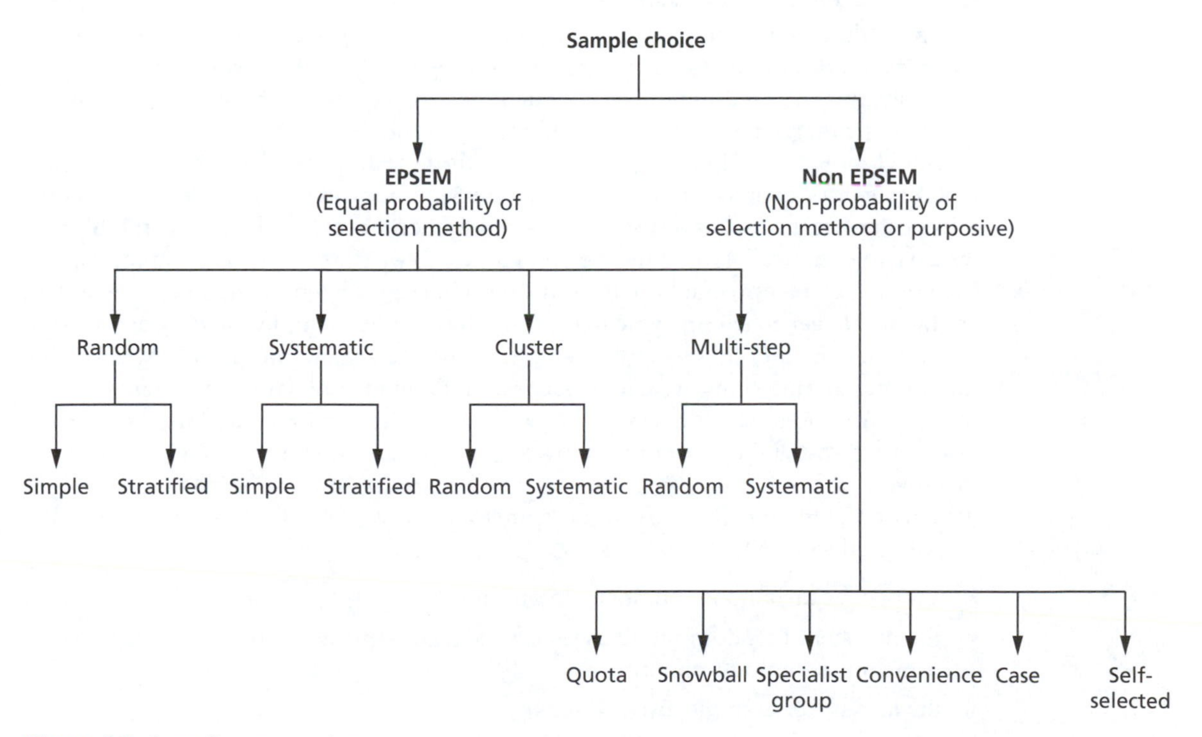

Figure 6.2 Sampling procedures

under difficult circumstances when probabilistic methods are just not feasible. These non-probabilistic approaches to sampling are more commonly a feature of qualitative strategies to research (see section 3.3) but they can be used together with quantitative approaches in some research designs.

In the following sections we shall examine each sampling approach in turn.

6.5 Probability based sampling

First we shall look at probability based approaches to sampling. These are the most robust sampling methods and are so designed that there is a clear link between the sample and the population from which it is drawn. Because of this, we can express how confident we are in our analyses in probabilistic terms and how close our survey results are to those of the population. Social Science has traditionally regarded the ability to do this as its basis for proof because it is the only research approach that generates a quantitative estimate of the likelihood of things being the same or different.

6.5.1 Simple random sampling

Simple random sampling is straightforward to apply and the data it generates is robust. Every instance of data has the same probability of being selected. In a population of 100 people, each person has a 1 in 100 chance of being selected. If our research was into staff/student ratios in private primary and lower secondary schools in Denmark, then each of the 429 schools would have the same chance of being selected for the sample. The procedure would be straightforward (see Figure 6.3). We would give each of the schools an indicator or reference number, 1 through to 429. The next step is to generate a list of numbers randomly that will enable us to select the schools for our sample. There are two ways in which we can produce these random numbers. Either we can go to a printed table of random numbers, such as those found in most books of statistical tables (see, for example, Lindley and Scott, 1995), or we can generate the numbers ourselves using the Internet. If we use a table of random numbers (see the extract in Table 6.2) we have to determine, randomly, the point at which we start. If we started at the top left each time the process would not be truly random, even though the numbers themselves are randomly generated. Imagine that we are drawing five samples, starting at the same point each time and following the same sequence each time, we would use the same numbers each time. If this were to happen we could not really claim that the process was random. An unbiased approach would be to cast a die four times, add up the face values on each cast and count either along or down to reach that number. However, all of this is very 'old technology' given that there are a large number of random number generators on the Internet that we can configure to the specific needs of the sample. Usually we will need to specify:

- a range for the random numbers (in our case 1 to 429);
- the number of random numbers to be generated (equivalent to the sample size plus some more for non-response);
- the layout (for example, five columns);
- the sequence (random, ordered low to high or high to low).

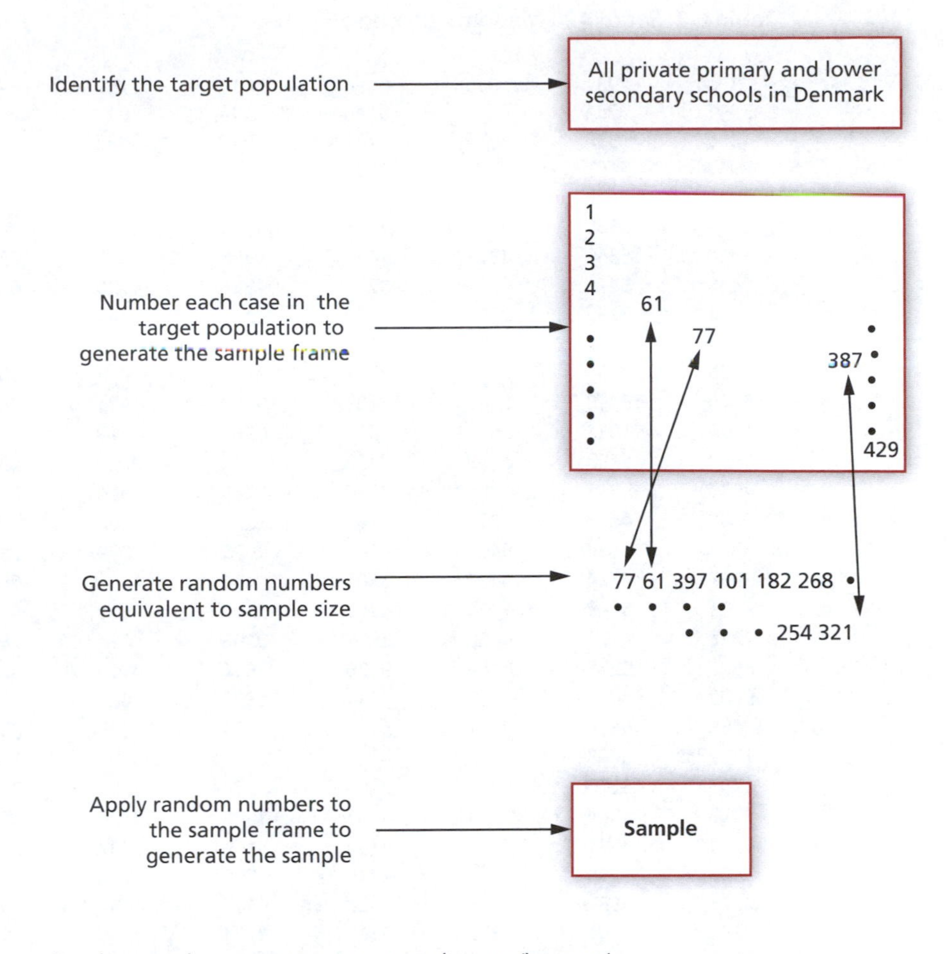

Figure 6.3 Generating a random sample

The random numbers are used to identify the schools. Once these have been selected, we then contact them to request the data that will answer our research question.

In drawing a simple random sample we have to take account of one decision we might have to make, what if the same data source were chosen twice? Fortunately this is less of a problem if we use a random number generator rather than a random number table because we can usually suppress duplicate numbers. But what do we do when we meet this situation? The answer is that we will almost certainly reject the second selection. Think of it in terms of the respondent to be contacted. There would be some head scratching on receipt of a second request for information that was accompanied by a note saying, 'We know that you have already sent us this information but please send it to us again'. This decision means that we have chosen to sample *without replacement*. There may be situations when it is appropriate to sample with replacement, that is, count the same set of data more than once, but they are rare. In general, reusing data reduces the efficiency of the sample, that is, the sample is a poorer description of the population. Think of it like this. If, in our sample of 429 Danish schools, we allow replacement and if we have 10 duplicate samples and if each of these is one of the

Table 6.2 Set of 400 random numbers

6898	2062	9065	1396	5011	2752	4751	5381
3441	6637	7416	5440	934	3814	2063	3256
5290	656	2950	3721	9650	9425	8708	9396
5753	5657	5558	9835	9214	9356	2965	1586
7073	2526	3492	3494	1592	4031	6715	5314
6299	9355	8071	7125	6551	3227	2013	2774
3854	5949	4921	7442	2805	945	2279	2473
3465	5479	2397	8279	1835	6790	6343	5258
8472	7795	3914	8332	2429	2304	2853	6209
1124	6784	4413	2426	1263	4529	5797	7140
6666	2296	7294	8765	3751	7437	9679	5425
5940	2418	8165	8609	9190	491	7827	1960
407	1082	5546	2356	6300	273	4801	2906
8090	5893	8188	7158	1474	9040	4340	1305
4933	467	1294	3829	6979	3906	7349	5685
9100	4507	9873	584	5227	3400	1285	2369
5097	170	9406	6943	2075	999	7911	2465
9956	4724	8424	8306	451	4842	5862	4490
5914	5848	7730	4305	5306	4010	4916	2701
2218	5477	6406	2897	9165	3094	7865	2122
8522	9272	8146	9526	6516	4350	9289	3367
9752	9072	9065	5314	2323	5687	6091	6148
2888	5889	8591	5070	7154	223	6380	2366
1237	6468	2458	6679	600	1003	7284	3629
4200	3300	5915	3100	4558	6303	7900	3788
3285	8684	2503	5767	1868	9128	9492	7061
6205	3877	7060	4142	8166	3247	3697	8824
9558	795	422	2713	568	9078	3006	4975
7076	9387	363	9628	5489	5430	685	84
5253	41	2320	9769	9471	9855	3926	1039
7108	787	5463	7679	4479	5904	7682	1485
8546	2915	4479	7564	2535	3883	8820	6450
7567	3602	4083	7541	8943	4458	6955	1666
94	834	8058	2899	5015	3325	7028	8452
2018	6683	8643	9694	9092	4831	621	6171
6585	8665	2298	7701	4233	1256	7290	3542
6709	6638	3779	9173	383	5266	7034	4795
9639	3846	9138	9533	2008	1392	678	8500
3686	4047	1934	2911	1846	3959	6252	1085
4264	2861	7578	2912	5706	2222	28	5784
9935	2617	2640	7130	7295	1426	4288	2109
7792	2183	8830	364	8657	5041	3690	695
3904	2806	9415	4414	4459	612	1502	3450
7641	8958	3576	5182	8652	3479	1254	5230
4928	3357	226	6351	7891	8928	4547	812
5235	3512	8858	8422	7304	281	174	4852
3023	5336	1790	6651	8885	1450	3099	3981
7083	8251	3747	5771	2737	5573	949	6301
2019	6205	2182	8571	1138	7813	2120	4856
3662	440	2416	3463	8696	9455	5867	6534

10 lowest staff/student ratios, the picture we get of all of the schools will be distorted. It is this potential for distortion that means that sampling with replacement is less efficient than sampling without replacement.

Summarising simple random sampling

- The size of the population must be known and the elements that make up the population (schools, students, teachers, etc.) must be identifiable.
- Random selection means that every element of the population must have the same chance of being selected.
- The process generates data that is appropriate for advanced statistical analysis.
- It can be costly to collect data if the elements in the sample are widely spaced and we have to travel to the person or place selected in order to collect our data.

6.5.2 Systematic sampling

Systematic sampling is the use of a predetermined sequential procedure to identify the cases that will be part of the sample. This is not a random procedure as described above but the outcomes that it produces are so similar to those generated by random sampling that they are usually considered alongside it.

Systematic sampling overcomes one of the potential problems of random sampling, the cost of accessing the sources of data and of actually collecting the data. The cost of data collection is something that researchers have to consider because we all have to live within our resources. Let us think about this in a little detail. Imagine that we are sampling households in an area. If we identify each household, we can use a random approach to generate our sample. However, there is no guarantee that they will be close to each other and every likelihood that the households will be geographically spread. This is, of course, not a problem if they are accessed by mail, phone or email but if we have to travel to them, it becomes an issue. If we are seeking to understand why some adults in the UK are lifelong learners and some are not, it would, for instance, be an issue for us to consider. We could generate a random sample using names and addresses from the electoral register (which is maintained by local authorities and updated annually) but we would be likely to spend more time travelling than collecting the data. It would be more effective, especially in terms of our use of time, to carry out a systematic sample.

The first steps are exactly the same as they would be for a random sample.

- First, we identify the target population that meets the requirements of our research problem. If we want to know whether engaging in lifelong learning is related to age, we must ensure that we survey an area with a broad range of ages. If our concern is whether ethnicity plays a part, then this should be reflected in the way in which we specify our population.
- The next step is to give each street or block of apartments and house or flat a unique identifier. These should be allocated to reflect a walking route (because this will minimise the effort of going out to collect the data) and they provide the basis for carrying out the sample of houses and flats.
- The difference with random sampling comes in the next step, the way in which the data sources are selected. When we know the target population and the size of the

sample, it follows that, logically, we also know the proportion of housing units that must be contacted to give us the data we require. A numerical example will show this.

Target population	*10,000 households*
Size of sample	*400 households*
Proportion of housing units to contact	*400/10,000 = 4%*

Once we have determined the size of the sample (and we shall see how to do this later in this chapter), we know the proportion of the total population to be sampled. In this case, the sample size is 400 households out of a total population of 10,000 houses. This means that we have to make contact with just 4% of the houses (400/10,000). With random sampling we would have drawn 400 random numbers to identify the sample cases, with systematic sampling we do it differently.

- This proportion (4 per cent) is used to determine the selection of the houses that are contacted: 4 per cent means that 1 house in 25 is contacted. Once we know this, the rest is straightforward. The first step is to establish some means of identifying houses. It is easiest to give each one a unique number. The process for doing this is shown in Figure 6.4, which shows a portion of the Swedish town of Jönköping taken from Google Earth. Moving up and down each street, we give each house a number. We continue this until every housing unit in the sample area is numbered. Starting with the first identifying number, we draw a random number between 1 and 25 to determine the first household to contact. Figure 6.4 shows that we selected the 25th house in the sequence. After contacting the inhabitants and obtaining our data, we count 24 households along our route and select the 25th (number 50 in the sequence).

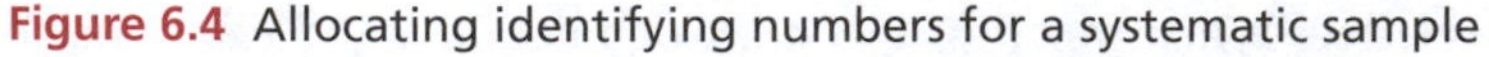
Figure 6.4 Allocating identifying numbers for a systematic sample

Source: adapted from A portion of the town of Jönköping, Sweden, using Google Earth, © 2009 Google Imagery © 2009 DigitalGlobe, GeoEye, Lantmäteriet/Metria, Map data © 2009 Tele Atlas.

This process is repeated. If a household refuses to take part or is absent, we then move to the next available household.

Systematic sampling can be adapted to many situations. It can be used to sample pupils in a classroom, a telephone survey of parents with children at a school, students entering a university library, primary schools in an area, education districts and many more.

Summarising systematic sampling

- The size and sometimes the spatial distribution of the target population must be known in order to devise the sample frame.
- After the first data source has been identified randomly, the systematic procedure of sampling *1 in n* generates results that are the equivalent of a random sample.
- Statistical tests (see Chapter 11) can be used on data generated by a systematic sample.
- Use of a systematic sample can generate significant savings in time and cost in comparison with the equivalent random sample.

6.5.3 Stratification

Stratification is a *procedure* that is applied to random and systematic sampling rather than a separate approach to sampling. We shall first look at how to stratify a sample and then at the benefits of stratification.

Stratification works by separating the population (and thus the sample frame) into categories. These categories are usually meaningful in terms of the analysis that we subsequently intend to carry out. For example, it would be reasonable to think of populations structured by gender, or age group, or family size. It would be equally reasonable to structure a sample by type of school, university department or year of first enrolment at college if these are the factors we intend to investigate in our research. The crucial thing is that we should know what proportion of our total population is male or female, or is a single child or has siblings, or is a primary school or secondary school. The classification can have more than two classes; for example three age groups each split by gender. All that is necessary is that we should know, *before we start*, what the proportion each group is of the total. The purpose of stratifying like this is to minimise the use of resources in data collection without affecting sampling quality. What we are doing is breaking up the sample into units that are more homogeneous than the population overall. Because there is less variety in each unit or stratum, we need make contact with fewer cases than if we were to sample the population as a whole or, as in the example below, we would obtain sample results that are a far more accurate representation of the population.

The proportions in each stratum or unit are then used to allocate the sample. Let us imagine that a population of schools is classified into four types of curriculum specialisation: business studies, sports, science and other. The information we have for our school population is that 18% specialise in business studies, 27% in sports, 36% in science and the remainder (19%) in other subjects. If our sample size is 280, then we have enough information to stratify our sample. The simple rule is that each stratum accounts for the same proportion of the sample as it does for the population. Table 6.3 shows the results for our example. The total sample of 280 schools is built up from 50 specialising in business studies (280 × 18%), 76 in sports (280 × 27%), 101 in science (280 × 36%) and 53, the remainder. The schools are sampled either randomly or systematically.

Table 6.3 Stratifying a sample

Curriculum	% of population	Total sample	Category sample
Specialisation		*Size*	*Size*
Business Studies	18	280	50
Sport	27	280	76
Science	36	280	101
Other	19	280	53
			280

Why is it worth considering stratification as a sampling option? The answer is that it is highly cost-effective and produces results that are more accurate than a non-stratified sample. In terms of managing the sampling process, it may be easier and less costly to make contact at a single time with those to be sampled from a single group or stratum. If, for example, we were looking at housing conditions and their relationship with children's academic progress, it might make sense to stratify our sample by house type and the number of bedrooms. This would, at least, save time in walking around and making contact because houses of the same type are often geographically close to each other. It is also possible that stratification will yield sampling results that are closer to the actual characteristics of the population. An example will show the principle at work here. Our study population consists of 16 values:

2 8 6 4 4 8 6 2 6 2 8 4 8 2 4 6

A random sample of four (6, 6, 2, 4) generates an average of 4.8. This compares well with the average of the whole population (16 values) of 5.0 (80 divided by 16). However, were we to stratify the sample into four classes, A, B, C and D, we would find:

A:	2	2	2	2
B:	4	4	4	4
C:	6	6	6	6
D:	8	8	8	8

A random sample of 1 in each stratum would produce a mean of 5.0 (20 divided by 4).

This example has obviously been structured to work and to demonstrate the principle but statistical theory demonstrates that the appropriate selection of strata or groups/categories minimises the impact of random variation. The implication of this is that if we have the same sample size as a random sample, we will have a better estimate of the population *or* if we want the same sort of estimate of the population that a random sample would give us, we can have a smaller sample size. Either of these is a gain that is worth considering.

Summarising stratification

- The groups (strata) that are used must be meaningful in terms of the research issue or analysis.
- The relative size of each group in relation to the total population must be known.

- The sample size of a stratum is determined by the stratum's proportion of the total population.
- Samples are chosen by a random or systematic procedure.
- Overall sample size may be reduced by treating each stratum as a population and determining the sample size for each stratum separately.

6.5.4 Cluster sample

Cluster sampling is the random selection of groups to represent the variety in the population. As with stratification it has been developed as an alternative attempt to optimise the use of resources in data collection. However, while with stratification the groups are chosen by the researcher (usually to reflect the analysis that will be carried out), with cluster sampling the groups are not chosen but selected on a random basis.

Figure 6.5 shows how stratification and cluster sampling differ. In this example the population is all state secondary schools in England.

- With a stratified sample we are interested in the types of school. These are shown on the left side of Figure 6.5. The numbers of each type (comprehensive, grammar, city

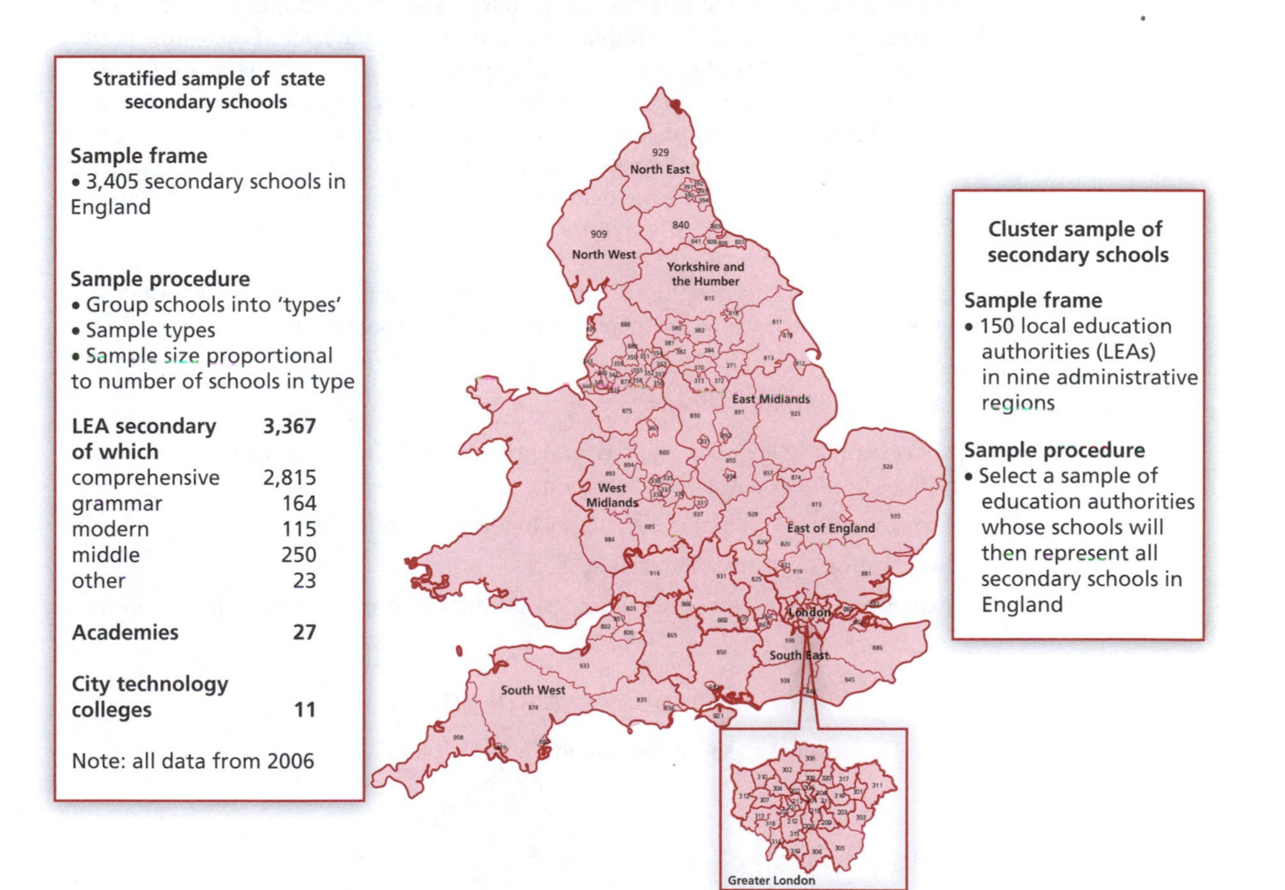

Figure 6.5 Stratified and cluster sampling compared

technology colleges, academies, etc.) determine the weight that each has in the total sample. Thus, if the total sample is 400 schools, grammar schools (equivalent to gymnasia in many other European countries) would be 164/3,367 per cent (that is, 4.87% = 19 schools) of the total.

- Cluster analysis works differently. In this case the sample frame is the 150 local education authorities in England. A number of these are sampled and their schools are taken to be representative of all the schools in England.

We can now see from this example that *stratification* seeks to segment the population horizontally (the types of school are found throughout England), while *clustering* segments the population vertically (it assumes that all school types are found in each area). In terms of sampling theory, stratification seeks to maximise homogeneity in the sample (that is, schools in any one type are more similar to each other than to schools in other types), while cluster sampling seeks to replicate the variety found in the population as a whole.

Cluster sampling is likely to produce benefits in terms of reduced cost. With the example in Figure 6.5, it is far easier to identify local education authorities than it is to identify the 164 grammar schools in England – and then to repeat this for all the other types of school. However, the theoretical evidence suggests that cluster sampling is not as effective in reproducing the features and characteristics of the population as stratification. Indeed, because clusters are unlikely to replicate the character of the whole population, there is a strong likelihood that cluster sampling may produce weaker estimates of population characteristics than simple random sampling. Because of this uncertainty, cluster sampling should only be preferred over other methods when cost, time or ease of access to data sources are a major consideration or when it is not feasible to identify and enumerate individually all possible data sources. However, on the plus side, because the selection process is random, this enables us to make use of the statistical procedures in Chapter 11.

Case Study 6.3 illustrates the use of cluster sampling in research. It describes three studies, each of which shows a different aspect of cluster sample design.

Summarising cluster sampling

- Cluster sampling is not as effective at representing the true characteristics of a population as random or systematic sampling.
- Cluster sampling has major advantages in terms of time and cost.
- Clusters should be diverse in character.
- Clusters and respondents are selected by random or systematic sampling procedures.

6.5.5 Multi-stage and multi-phase sampling

These two approaches to sampling extend the principle of cluster sampling that we have just met.

(i) Multi-stage sampling

Multi-stage sampling is very similar to cluster sampling in that it drills down through the population to the data sources. It begins in exactly the same way as the example we saw in Figure 6.5. However, it differs from cluster sampling in that individual schools are

Case study 6.3 Cluster sampling in health education

Many studies in the field of health education make use of cluster sampling to gather data. Usually this is because the researchers are interested in a *national picture* of a health related issue. Cluster sampling provides an efficient procedure for identifying respondents and gathering data in this situation.

More than one cluster

Samdal et al. (1998) looked at how children's perception of school was associated with their satisfaction with school. The context for their study is the ability of schools to influence children's health and behaviour that affects health (such as smoking and drinking). The authors drew on a World Health Organisation (WHO) survey and extracted data for four countries: Finland, Latvia, Norway and Slovakia. All countries in the WHO survey used the same cluster sampling procedure. Schools were treated as the primary clusters and randomly sampled and, in some cases, classes constituted a second level cluster to be sampled. The response rates were 81 per cent for Finland and Norway and almost 90 per cent for Latvia and Slovakia. The authors concluded that student satisfaction is strongly affected by how fairly they feel they are treated, by how safe they feel and by how supportive their teachers are.

Combining methods: clusters with stratification

Kloep et al. (2001) used cluster sampling in a study of young people's drinking behaviour. The samples were drawn using schools as primary clusters in three countries, Norway, Scotland and Sweden. In each case the samples within the schools were stratified by age (12-, 14- and 16-years-old) and whole year groups completed a questionnaire. This is an important example to note because it shows that we can mix sampling approaches. The cluster approach allowed the survey team to generate a total response of 4,066 school students. The survey results show that students living in rural areas (the target group) do not drink much alcohol but those that do see it as part of their induction into a drinking society.

Age as a cluster: another approach

Lintonen et al. (2001) also researched alcohol use amongst children in an attempt to find predictors of heavy alcohol use later in life. Their sample frame was the 1999 Finnish Adolescent Health and Lifestyle Survey. They too used a cluster analysis but structured their clusters differently from the surveys above. Because they wanted to choose young people of the same age born at the same time, they identified 14-year-olds born in 1984 on 3–8 July, 26–31 July and 6–11 August. This span of five weeks limited the age variation in the sample and provided enough subjects to enable them to undertake a statistical analysis. They identified all young people born on these dates as the primary cluster and surveyed them all in a single stage cluster sample. The response rate for boys was 74 per cent and for girls was 85 per cent. They concluded that smoking, little parental control and ample money to spend are predictive of heavy drinking in later life.

These three studies show how cluster analysis enables small groups of researchers to cope with large populations. Unlike random or systematic sampling, not every member of the population has to be identified in advance, though the size and the overall characteristics should be known. Cluster sampling is also useful for international comparative surveys because research teams in different countries can adopt the same methodology.

sampled (cluster sampling identifies an area and then uses all schools in that area as the sample). The key principle with multi-stage sampling is that the random selection of data sources extends all the way through to the identification of individual data sources, whereas with cluster sampling it ceases when the final data cluster is identified. Thus, if the final stage of cluster sampling is a year group in a school, the whole year group is used as the data source. With multi-stage sampling, the final stage would be to randomly sample pupils from the year group.

Like cluster sampling, multi-stage sampling is effective in managing large populations and, especially, populations distributed over a large area. By concentrating the actual process of data collection, the procedure allows resources to be concentrated, with the likelihood that effort and costs are reduced. Case Study 6.4 describes the use of multi-stage sampling in the Family Spending Survey.

Multi-stage sampling can also be used effectively by individual researchers, as the Greek researcher, Theodora Papatheodorou, has shown in her study of the methods used by Greek nursery teachers to manage behavioural problems. Figure 6.6 is a diagrammatic representation of the process she used. First she randomly sampled regions, selecting three out of 10. The regions selected are shown in blue in Figure 6.6. From the three regions, she then selected nine sub-regions. She sampled 25 teachers out of all those

Case study 6.4 Multi-stage sampling

The Office of National Statistics in the UK produces an annual publication, *Family Spending*, which shows household expenditure for a wide range of items. *Family Spending* is extensively used by social and economic researchers to estimate such things as disposable income, retail turnover in an area and shifts in expenditure patterns. An education researcher might use it to see how much different households were spending on education and how this had changed over time or to get a picture of the lifestyles of different social groups in order to understand better such things as social exclusion. Detailed data can be used to add substance and understanding to young people's and their parents' lifestyles (for example, by examining expenditure on various forms of gambling, going to clubs and the cinema, subscriptions to cable TV and so on). However, it is the sampling procedure that is of interest to us at this point.

The *sample frame* consists of a postcode address file called the 'small user' database. A 'small user' is defined as any address that receives fewer than 50 postal items a day. This definition excludes large businesses and organisations such as hospitals and colleges. The database is updated twice each year.

The *sample design* is multi-stage.

- First, the UK is divided into a number of *Primary Sampling Units* (PSUs). The PSUs contain the basic data sampling units, the small user address file. The source of these data units is the Post Office's list of addresses nationwide. The PSUs are clusters of addresses from the small user address file.
- Second, the PSUs are *clustered* by administrative area, initially grouped by Government Office Regions and, within each region, by metropolitan and non-metropolitan districts.
- Third, the PSUs are *stratified*, initially into four bands on the basis of the socio-economic status of the head of the household* and each band is then further stratified into two groups on the proportion of households without access to a car.
- Within each Government Office Region, each PSU is therefore classified into one of 48 classes on the basis of the clustering and stratification process.

The *sample* identifies 672 PSUs. PSUs are selected randomly in proportion to the number of PSUs in each category. The survey is continuous over a 12 month period. When the 672 PSUs are identified, each one is allocated to one month of the year. Thus in any one month, 56 PSUs are used. At the time the PSU is used, a random sample of 18 respondents from the PSU is drawn. The total sample size for the year is, therefore, 12,096 addresses.

As with all surveys, there are rules to deal with problems (such as more than one household at an address or defining what makes a household ineligible for selection). In your samples, you should try to identify what might cause problems so that you can set up rules beforehand rather than make them up as you go along.

*Each country has its own definition of 'head of household' (or an equivalent term). In the UK the definition is one that continues to evolve to reflect changing social relationships. Prior to the 1980s, the head of household was assumed to be a man in a household where there was a man and a woman. In the case of cohabitees (for instance, young people sharing accommodation), the head was the person who was responsible for paying for the accommodation. A decade later, as the once assumed relationship between household and family was breaking up, the head of household was defined as the 'household reference person', the person named as owner or on a rental agreement. Where two or more people were named, the household reference person was the one with the highest income. The 'highest income householder' is now used as the principal indicator.

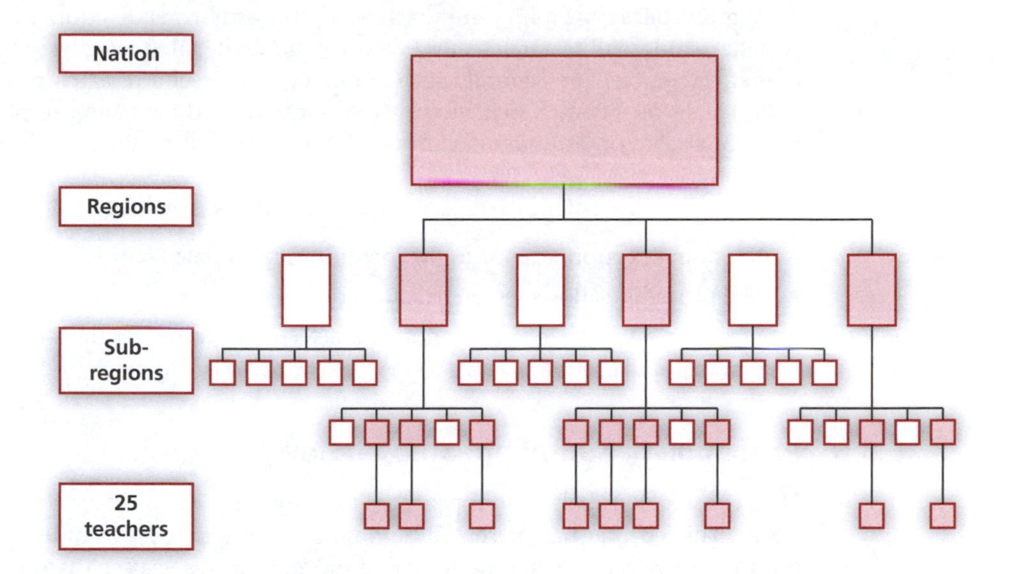

Figure 6.6 Diagrammatic representation of multi-phase sampling by Papatheodorou

employed in each of the sub-regions, giving a total sample population of 225 teachers to represent all nursery teachers in Greece. A total of 154 teachers responded to her survey. Her goal was to understand which management approaches were used in what circumstances. Teachers described their approaches and Papatheodorou classified them as behavioural, cognitive or punitive. All three approaches were found to be used by teachers and Papatheodorou's assessment was that there was more of an emphasis on resolving short-term problems than resolving the long-term issues that might underlie them.

(ii) Multi-phase sampling

A variant on multi-stage sampling is *multi-phase sampling*. With this approach the population is sampled at two levels, a general level and at a more detailed level for a smaller (but still randomly drawn and representative) set of the data population. The procedure allows the findings at the more detailed level to be applied to the more general level. An example will help illustrate this. Let us imagine that we are investigating teacher recruitment and teacher retention. We could use a cluster approach to identify our sample, first selecting areas and then the sample schools within them. Having identified our sample schools, let us say 88, we then ask each head teacher to complete a survey. This would ask about staff turnover in general and in particular subjects, about the numbers of applicants for posts both currently and historically, about how well qualified the applicants were and so on. The second phase would be to treat the 88 schools in our first sample as a population and conduct a survey of teachers in a sample of these. If we manage this process well, we can apply the results of the second survey to the wider population. We would ask questions about job satisfaction and what affected it, the quality of management and support, problems of pupil behaviour, whether teachers had been approached with job offers, how long teachers intended to stay and why they would move. In other words, we would look at the issue from the perspective of teacher experience and seek to relate that to the broader picture of staffing given us by the head teachers.

A multi-phase sampling approach is well worth consideration by individual researchers and small research teams because it allows detailed insights to be collected in a cost-effective way. For example, at the more general level a research programme might collect data on people's behaviour, while a carefully drawn sub-sample could collect additional data on attitudes, feelings and emotions that might drive those behaviours.

Summarising multi-stage and multi-phase sampling

- Random selection extends to the identification of data sources.
- The procedure allows researchers to gather detailed insights with limited costs.
- Errors in estimates of population characteristics are higher than for samples of the whole population.

6.5.6 Probabilistic sampling: an overview

Having looked probabilistic approaches to sampling we should reflect on what we have learnt. This chapter has presented random sampling as a set of individual approaches but the reality is that when we look at these approaches, we see that probabilistic sampling is a flexible and adaptable process. Probabilistic sampling procedures are not set in stone; they can be shaped to suit the conditions of the research enquiry. While this may have implications for data analysis (Chapter 13 explains the sampling requirements of various statistical tests), all researchers should remember that their first task is to collect sufficient data of good quality and if this requires the development of a new approach to sampling, then so be it. The only requirement of random sampling is that the principle of random selection should be embedded somewhere in the approach.

Table 6.4 summarises when to use probability sampling approaches and what to be aware of. As population size increases, simple random sampling becomes unrealistic and we should look at other approaches. Systematic sampling is usually the first alternative but as the spatial extent of the study grows, then even this becomes too expensive to manage. With very large populations cluster and multi-stage sampling methods are often the only realistic alternatives. Stratification can be used with any method but it can take time to identify accurately the information that is used to stratify samples. Each method has specific issues that we should be aware of. In general, however, we should note the approaches we use for smaller samples (simple random and systematic) produce more accurate estimates of the population than the approaches we use for larger samples (cluster and multi-stage).

6.6 Non-probability based sampling

One of the problems of using non-probability based approaches to sampling is that, in comparison with probability based approaches, they are often seen as less rigorous and a poor second. It is difficult not to argue that they are less rigorous. Obviously because they do not have that probabilistic link between sample and population, we cannot express our conclusions in terms of the likelihood (or probability) of their being proved. We have to rely instead on the quality and strength of our argument. However, we should be critical of the idea that they are second best because they are not meant to be used in the same situations and for the same research problems as probability based

Table 6.4 Summary of probability sampling approaches

Sampling approach	When to use it	What to watch out for
Simple random	For smaller studies where the population can be defined and itemised.	• Costs increase with sample size. • If using a table of random numbers, ensure that selection of first is random.
Systematic	For larger populations where we can create a sequence in the data, e.g. people passing a point, houses in a street.	• Need to know size of population to determine sample fraction. • Selection of first survey point should be random.
Stratification	To achieve a more accurate sample (or to save cost if you are happy with less accurate results).	• Link stratification to factors that might influence or be associated with outcomes (e.g., age and attitude, social status and behaviour). • Setting up a stratified sample frame can be costly.
Cluster	For large populations where we can 'drill down' to identify groups to represent the whole population.	• Higher sampling error than random sampling. • Clusters should not be uniform in character.
Multi-stage	As for cluster sampling.	• As for cluster sampling. • Individual members should be known and identifiable in final clusters.

procedures. They have been developed to solve different problems in accessing data sources and to be used in specific and quite different circumstances.

In the next section, we look at a range of approaches to sampling that are not based on the probability assumptions that we have met so far.

6.6.1 Quota sampling

The first approach we shall look at is quota sampling. We consider it first because, in many ways, it is more like random or systematic stratified sampling than it is to other non-probability approaches that we shall look at. The main difference is that the data sources, usually people, are not chosen at random.

Quota sampling is used in the following situations:

- when the size and the characteristics of the population are known but it is not possible to enumerate every person or element in the population (Table 6.5 shows an example);
- when we need to identify people or elements in the population with specific characteristics that are related to our research issue.

We shall now examine how quota sampling works. Quota sampling is used extensively in market research consumer surveys and opinion polls. Of all the sampling techniques it is probably the most used. With quota sampling, the researcher identifies groups that are relevant to the research issue. If our research, for instance, was into parents' satisfaction with holiday play schemes for their children, then we might want our sample to reflect the number of children in a household. The reason for this is

Table 6.5 Constructing a quota sample

Household type	% of households with children	Quota
1 parent, working, 1 child	1.8	5
1 parent, not working, 1 child	4.8	14
1 parent, working, 1+ children	0.7	2
1 parent, not working, 1+ children	2.6	8
2 parents, both working, 1 child	23.2	70
2 parents, 1 working, 1 child	14.0	42
2 parents, not working, 1 child	2.7	8
2 parents, both working, 1+ children	36.8	110
2 parents, 1 working, 1+ children	12.6	38
2 parents, not working, 1+ children	0.8	1

that parents with more children may have different needs from parents with fewer children. The groups that we use to structure the population and define the sample are also likely to be frameworks through which we analyse the resulting data. In all likelihood, we would group our parents into those with one child, those with two, those with three and those with four or more and use this classification to process the data we collect. Let us assume that the proportions are as given in Table 6.5. From the family types we are using to classify our parents, it is possible to see our research questions:

- Does the number of children in the household affect parental satisfaction with holiday play schemes?
- Does whether a parent is working affect parental satisfaction?
- Does the number of parents in a household affect parental satisfaction?
- Are levels of satisfaction of working parents different from those of non-working parents (this is called the interaction effect) and does this differ for the number of children in the household?

The percentages in the second column of Table 6.5 represent the proportion of all households with children in a population of 2,000 households. If the sample size is 300 (we shall see, when we look at how to calculate sample size, that this implies we are happy to establish levels of parental satisfaction plus or minus 5 per cent), we multiply the household type percentages by 300 to give the sample size for each household type. Thus, for a single working parent with 1 child:

$$1.8\% \text{ of } 300 \text{ is } 1.8/100 \times 300 = 1.8 \times 3 = 5$$

Having established the size of each quota, we then identify locations where we can expect to meet the sort of people we are interested in. It could be a combination of locations at different times, outside school gates or in a shopping centre at the weekend. The surveyor identifies likely respondents (excluding, for example, those who appear to be too young or too old) and the first question is always to establish whether or not they meet one of the quota categories ('Do you have children? Does your child/do your children attend holiday play schemes?').

Before we leave this example, look again at the quotas. There could be problems here. In the quota sample that we have constructed it is difficult to use a sample of one to establish the views of a whole category. In this situation, we can either:

- scale up the whole sample (we would need at least 15–20 in the smallest category (this would make the whole sample between 4,500 and 6,000); or
- we can choose to be *non-proportional* and have a minimum size or equal quota per group. This places more emphasis on the data analysis and the comparison of behaviours, judgements and attitudes rather than on the characteristics of the population; or
- we can merge categories (and quotas). This is what we would be likely to do in this instance. But even then we may have to increase our sample size.

Quota sampling can be very effective and it is relatively straightforward but before we go down this route, there are some other things to take into account.

- First, while it is usually fairly easy to begin filling up the quotas, it can take a frustratingly long time to find the final subject (likely to be the working single parent with more than one child).
- Second, it is important to think how the data, once collected, will be analysed.
- Third, if we want to say something sensible in our conclusions, we have to base it on a reasonable number of people (as a rule of thumb, not less than 30 per group). Even then, the sample size we start with might not be the sample size we finish up with – after we have started to process our results, we might find that we need more respondents to make the issue clear.
- Finally, while quota samples can generate good results, this is not guaranteed. It all depends on how good the selection of cases in the sample is. Bias is possible. Read Case Study 6.5 for an example.

Summarising quota sampling

- Quota samples differ from stratified sampling in that respondents are selected, not randomly drawn.
- Statistical analysis of data is usually limited to description.
- Quotas can be difficult to complete so they are not always as cost effective as they might appear.

6.6.1 Snowball sampling

Our second purposive sampling method is snowball sampling. This is used to identify respondents in otherwise hard to reach groups. Examples in education might be gay teachers, science teachers who believe that creationism should be taught as part of science, identifying migrant teachers (through friendship networks) and identifying head teachers who are respected by their peers. The snowball sampling technique works by an interviewee or respondent identifying other possible respondents for the researcher. The assumption is that people with the attitudes, beliefs of behaviours that we are interested in are more likely to know others with similar attitudes, beliefs or behaviours than the general population or even us as researchers. With this approach it is important to identify several initial contacts in case one of the referral chains goes cold. Researchers have

Case study 6.5 Quota samples can go wrong

Polling attitudes and opinions is a regular feature of modern life. Rarely a week seems to go by without an opinion poll on something appearing in newspapers or being reported on radio or TV. Opinion polls are now a key element in the political process. While some countries, including France, Spain and Portugal, ban polls immediately before an election, the UK does not. This means that when people vote there is an immediate test of the accuracy of the polls and this is when pollsters are most likely to be seen to get the result wrong.

Having made this point, polls are generally remarkably accurate. Normally the sample size for polls is between 1,000 and 2,000 because samples of this size generally deliver the accuracy that the polling companies want. Quotas are set for age, sex, socio-economic status and region of the country. However, despite using broadly the same methodology, pollsters in 1992 got the national election result very wrong and underestimated the gap between the victorious Conservative Party and the Labour Party by 9 per cent. Two days before the election the polls were still forecasting a Labour victory by 19 per cent.

How did the polls get the result so wrong? Post-election analysis suggested the following reasons:

- There was a very late swing from Labour to the Conservatives.
- The quotas did not accurately represent the socio-economic structure of the population with the result that lower socio-economic groups (and Labour supporters) were over sampled. This was identified as a problem when the results of the 1991 Census of Population were published.
- Quotas were established on the basis of age, sex and socio-economic status while housing tenure was ignored (the Conservative Government had allowed tenants of local authorities to buy their residences and owner occupiers were more likely at that time to vote Conservative).
- Interviewers were biased in the selection of respondents. They identified easy-to-reach people in the quotas they were given (for example, by standing outside transport interchanges where the retired were not sampled or in shopping centres where those at work were not sampled) and these, it seems, were less typical of the category overall.
- Conservative voters were more likely to report their intentions as 'don't know'. The context for this is that the Conservative Government under Margaret Thatcher had been deeply unpopular.

to have a very good understanding of the issue and a sense of where initial contacts might be found. They have to appear credible to the contacts, otherwise there may well be a reluctance to expose a sensitive friendship or contact network. For this reason the approach is probably best used by established researchers. Anyone conducting their first research enquiry should think seriously whether there is an alternative approach.

While snowball sampling is presented here is purposive in nature, we should be aware that sampling concepts and theory are always moving forward. This is the case with snowball sampling and the development of what is being called *respondent driven sampling*. This seeks to establish estimates of a snowball sample's reliability using a mathematical procedure to model the population. By bringing snowball sampling much closer to probabilistic principles, it is probably one of the most important developments in sampling theory in recent years. It is too advanced to deal with in an introductory text such as this but it can be followed up by reading the work of the American sociologist, Douglas Heckathorn (see, for example, Heckathorn, 1997).

Summarising snowball sampling

- It is used to access hard to reach populations.
- It is based on a referral process in which one contact identifies other contacts.

- Access to a contact network may be difficult for a researcher who lacks credibility in the eyes of those being researched.
- Recent developments in statistical theory have led to a probability-based version being developed.

6.6.3 Specialist group sampling

There are occasions when a research project needs input as comment, observation or a description of behaviours or activities from a closely defined group. For instance, in policy research, experts could comment on proposed policy initiatives, for example on the likely effectiveness of educational interventions to improve parenting and overcome social exclusion. If we research children with behavioural problems, it would be sensible to sample parents of such children. Likewise, if we wanted to understand the emotional burden of trying unsuccessfully to turn around a failing school, the people who can provide the answers would be head teachers who have experienced the situation. The purpose in going to a specialist group is to obtain the insights that only the members can provide. The intention is not to obtain a balanced or representative sample but a rich understanding. This approach is important when bringing together a focus group, a group that is brought together in a led discussion and which comprises people with understanding, insight or experience of what is being researched. Focus groups will be considered in Chapter 9.

The selection of people to join a specialist group should be criterion based. For an expert it would be reputation and status within a field. This can be tested by asking one expert which others they would recommend, a type of snowball process. Where the research is more concerned with experience and intimate knowledge of a situation, the selection criteria are likely to include the degree of exposure to the situation. Each research project will generate its own criteria.

There are particular circumstances in which specialist group sampling is important. One has already been noted, constructing a focus group. Another is prediction and what is called 'foresight planning'. This is a process whereby people work collaboratively to develop scenarios of what the future might be like. Case Study 6.6 has an example of this particular approach to explore what would be appropriate vocational education in the Netherlands.

Summarising specialist group sampling

- The object is to obtain insights and understanding that arise through experience.
- Selection is based on predetermined criteria or acknowledged expertise.

6.6.4 Convenience sampling

Convenience sampling is the use of data sources that just happen to be around. They are selected because they are easy to access. They are widely found in undergraduate research and are not unknown in professional research. However, the fact that 'I used this school because I knew the head teacher' is unlikely to generate research results in which the researcher, let alone the research community, can have much confidence. Nor if we stop people and ask them to take part in our survey is this likely to produce results that are representative of anything than the willingness of some people to help.

Case study 6.6 The Delphi technique

The Delphi technique was developed as a method for establishing the degree of consensus about future trends. Its initial application, in the 1950s, was in the context of the Cold War and it was used to assess things like the likelihood of a nuclear strike, weapons development and strategic alternatives in the arms race. Since then it has found many other applications.

The approach is very simple. A group of experts are asked a series of questions about an issue. The questions largely require respondents to exercise judgement and state opinions. The responses are collated and fed back to the sample group who have an opportunity to revise their views. This process continues until respondents do not change their positions. In summary, the approach does three things. First, it gathers information; second, it provides feedback and third, it allows revision. As a technique it may seem unremarkable but when people who are actually close to opinion forming and decision making take part, it becomes a powerful tool for best-guessing the future.

Simone Zolingen and Cees Klaasen used the Delphi approach in a study of key qualifications for school leavers in the Netherlands. Key qualifications are general in character (what in the UK would be called skill-based qualifications). The assumption is that they are transferable and need to be long lasting, as compared with specific knowledge for economic sectors, which may be subject to rapid change. As the authors point out, however, there is little clarity on what the character and content of these key qualifications should be. They set out to explore the following issues:

- The nature and relevance of key qualifications for the employment of school leavers.
- Whether school is the best place to acquire such qualifications.
- What form the curricula should take.

Zolingen and Klaasen began their study with a literature search that helped define the issues. They interviewed a small group of school leavers who had recently started work in order to understand the issue from their perspective. This is an example of a specialist group sample.

They then identified 53 experts from different fields (education, industry and curricula bodies). They assessed the expertise of work-based experts against the following criteria:

- at least two year's experience;
- extensive knowledge of the issue;
- views on what qualifications are desirable;
- knowledge of how these companies were connected with vocational education;
- knowledge of the careers of school leavers;
- knowledge of personnel issues in their company.

In the first round, the experts completed a questionnaire. For the second round they met in a discussion forum.

The Delphi technique, as described here, is useful in getting different groups to understand each other's perspective. The value of the conclusions, however, is only as good as the quality and appropriateness of the participants. The value of the technique is getting the right people to take part. These usually fall into one of the following groups: specialists and experts, people with a high standing in their field and people with viewpoints and perspectives that shape opinion. These people are unlikely to respond to requests to take part in a Delphi survey unless it comes from a source that they value or respect. For this reason, a Delphi approach run by a new researcher is not likely to generate much interest among these groups. However, expertise is not limited to the famous. It would be possible to involve pupils who do not attend school regularly in a Delphi survey to understand what could be done to make school more appealing. Can you think of other examples?

If these are the problems with convenience sampling, why do we use it?

- Convenience sampling is useful in a preliminary study of an issue, to identify what may be the key features to investigate in more detail or to test out the effectiveness of the survey procedure and survey instruments.
- It is acceptable as a sampling method when the size of the population is not known or when the population is very small.
- It is a last resort when the time frame for the research is short, for example, when a school or college is going to be closed.

Summarising convenience sampling

- The selection criterion is the convenience of the researcher.
- The circumstances in which convenience sampling should be used are restricted.
- Results from convenience samples should not be generalised.

6.6.5 Case studies

A case study is a study of an individual organisation, situation, event or process. The idea of a case study as a sample can be problematic inasmuch as the study may be of a unique event. In 2003, for example, the head teacher of a South London school was jailed for embezzling £500,000 (about €740,000) of her school's funds. A case study could explore the circumstances that allowed this to occur. But theft, especially on this scale, is a rare event. So is it appropriate to call such a study a sample? This sort of case study is less concerned with representativeness than with relevance. It may not be representative of other schools but it is relevant. In particular, it is relevant to a possible future situation that the governors of a school would wish to avoid.

However, lest we should imagine that all case studies are of unique situations, it is worth noting that case studies can also be type exemplars, for example, a successful school, a typical career path, a modern curriculum. To this extent a case study is representative and, being representative, constitutes a sample. In this circumstance a case study must be drawn so as to maximise its relevance to the group overall. Relevance however can lie anywhere on a range from being typical, at one end, through providing guidance to being an exemplar at the other end. American professor of education, Burton Clark, studied university change (1998) and included case studies of universities that had transformed themselves to develop an entrepreneurial culture. This is an example of a case study being an exemplar. Professor John Fitz of Cardiff University and two colleagues (Fitz et al., 2002) undertook a large-scale study of changes to school systems in England and Wales. To give substance to their general analysis and to enable readers to understand the implications of the types of change, they presented four case studies of different education authorities. These are examples of case studies typifying a more general situation.

The selection of a case study, therefore, depends upon its purpose. We have identified three:

1. To understand a critical issue or situation, often something that is rare.
2. To illustrate what is common, usual or typical.
3. To illustrate what is possible, an exemplar.

Each of these types of case study speaks to a wider community from which it is chosen but in different ways. The critical issue is usually about avoiding undesirable futures. The *typical* is something that a person or organisation can be benchmarked against. The *exemplar* is about raising aspiration, what is possible and how futures can be achieved and the *rare* is to understand how something occurred, so that similar situations can be avoided in the future.

Summarising case studies

- Case studies perform different functions.
- These differences mean that the bases of selecting a case study are themselves different, so the role of the case study has to be understood before the case study can be selected and studied.

- Though individual, case studies should always have a wider relevance than to the body from which they are drawn.

6.6.6 Self-selecting samples

While most sampling approaches adopt a 'push' strategy, where the task of the researcher is to identify data sources, self-selecting samples have a 'pull' strategy. With these samples the researcher makes available a participation opportunity and respondents choose to take part. There are many self-selecting surveys. Newspapers, radio and TV stations have them. Websites offer opportunities to 'take part in our survey' when they want feedback on usability; many times they are a marketing opportunity. A typical survey was one commissioned by the BBC in February 2007. The BBC wanted teachers to tell them how they used broadcast and on-line material in their teaching. The commissioning organisation contacted teachers' organisations who put details on their websites inviting teachers to visit the survey website and complete the survey. As a sampling procedure they have many disadvantages.

- The population from which they are drawn is not known with any accuracy.
- Respondents are usually the most interested and represent, therefore, only a subset of those who have views.
- They are often large scale, so follow-up can be difficult.
- The results have no statistical validity whatsoever.

In the context of this damning assessment, we should ask why such a flawed system ever saw the light of day and what value there is in using it. There are obvious benefits to media organisations. Programme makers use it to involve their audience and create audience participation. This encourages the audience to return and helps keep viewing or listening figures high. Newspapers choose topics (and sometimes phrase questions) in ways that appeal to their core readership. This appeals to readers' values and reinforces the paper as an outlet for their opinions. Again, the benefit is to the bottom-line of the papers.

But when should academic and professional researchers use it? A Web survey is certainly convenient for the researcher because completed surveys can be fed directly into a database for analysis. It could be used within an organisation to allow members to express their opinions about how it is run or its development strategy. It is often used to allow students to express their views of a course. It can also be used for a preliminary exploration of a field, where the object is to identify issues that can be explored further within a representative sample. In this case the fact that enthusiasts or those with strong opinions are more likely to respond is a positive advantage. If the issue is sensitive, then a self-selecting sample may be the most effective way to generate a database for more detailed surveys. For this reason the method appears to be used more in health education research than other areas of education research. The sort of example we might meet is young people self-reporting smoking, drug use and sexual activity.

Summarising self-selecting sampling

- They are not likely to reflect population characteristics.
- They are more prone to giving atypical results.
- They should be used in preliminary investigations or where access to respondents may be a problem.
- The results should always be treated with caution.

6.6.7 Non-probabilistic sampling: an overview

Non-probabilistic sampling in most cases meets the needs of particular circumstances. Table 6.6 shows what these are. Only quota sampling can be said to be a realistic alternative to probability sampling techniques. It has its advantages (it is usually quicker to collect the data than with probability approaches) but it does mean that many statistical techniques should not be used because they are based on the assumption than the data is collected on the basis of equal probability. As we shall see, however, some of these techniques are pretty robust and this assumption can be dropped without affecting the quality of the results significantly. Other non-probabilistic techniques are truly purposive and should not be used as an alternative to random-based approaches. With each technique we need to be aware of the population in order to judge whether those being surveyed are appropriate. For this reason, we should really be experienced before applying some of the techniques (such as the use of specialist groups or snowball sampling). Convenience samples are not always convincing. The fact that people 'just happen to be there' is not a convincing reason for choosing them (though this has not stopped a great many psychologists using their students for research purposes!). With both specialist groups and case studies it is important to have clear criteria for selection. Self-selected

Table 6.6 Summary of non-probability sampling approaches

Sampling approach	When to use it	What to watch out for
Quota	Small to medium sized samples where it is important to isolate the views/actions of well-defined groups. Usually quicker to collect sample data than with probability samples.	• Many analytical statistical procedures are based on the assumption that the data is collected on a random basis. Quota sampling does not meet this condition. Note, however, that with some techniques this assumption can be relaxed without affecting the analysis greatly.
Snowball	Where the population is hard to reach or where the population is defined by personal knowledge or reputation.	• Researcher must be credible to gain entry to a network. • Need to have sufficient awareness of the issue being investigated to judge whether contacts and leads are appropriate.
Specialist group	When the research calls for a specialist perspective or input. Frequently used for futures analysis.	• Develop criteria for selection of group members. • Put in place a policy of what to do if members drop out in the survey process.
Convenience	Use for preliminary studies or when the population is small or when time is of the essence.	• Do not attempt any statistical predictions unless the group is demonstrably representative of a larger population.
Case study	To represent a particular situation (good, bad, typical) or to understand the process that has led to an outcome.	• More a case of selection according to the features under investigation rather than sampling. • Justify selection.
Self-selecting	Targeted studies. Especially appropriate for Web-based surveys.	• Demonstrate how representative group is of larger population. • Ensure against multiple completion of survey and take care to check that a group does not 'fix the vote'.

samples are fraught with problems: how do you stop people completing the survey several times? How do you prevent a group with a particular interest from rounding up its members and getting them to complete the survey? Both of these will generate bias. With any sample, however, it is important to show that the group is representative of something other than itself. We have to be able to talk about a population. If we cannot do this on the basis of a sample, it hardly seems worthwhile collecting the sample in the first place.

6.7 How should we choose which sampling method to use?

How do we choose which sampling method to use? The principal condition that we have to satisfy is that we should use the method that gives us the best results for the circumstances of our research. In selecting a method we should take account of the following points.

- *The purpose of our research:* If we specify a hypothesis that we want to disprove on the basis of probability (the likelihood of the hypothesis being wrong – see Chapter 3 again), then our choice is highly constrained; we must use a probabilistic sample. We should only use snowball, specialist group, convenience and self-selecting samples and case studies for the purposes for which they are intended. For general surveys the choice is usually a random approach or quota sampling.
- *The nature of our analysis:* If we intend to use a statistical procedure to infer a relationship or to determine the characteristics of the parent population, we again constrain our choice and must use a probabilistic sample.
- *When speed is of the essence:* We can choose between a probabilistic or non-probabilistic sample. In general it takes more time (and cost) to collect data using random approaches than with quota sampling.
- *When resources are limited:* Our choices are limited in the same way as when we have to sample quickly.

6.8 How large should a sample be?

The next question is how large should our sample be. This is difficult to answer at this stage because the answer depends on understanding something about the character of a statistical population that we call the normal distribution. We shall look at this in more detail in Chapter 12. There are several ways of determining sample size, but the most precise relies on being able to calculate some statistical measures of our sample that we shall only meet in Chapter 12. Because of this a detailed answer to the question, 'How large should a sample be?' is given in Appendix 1.

However, there is another solution to determining sample size, which is to use sample size calculators that we can find on the Internet. There are several on-line calculators for determining sample size but using them is not necessarily as straightforward as it may seem. For one thing, we have to know the size of our population and as we saw there are some probability-based approaches to sampling that allow us to drill down through our population to draw a sample without necessarily having a precise knowledge of the population size. In addition, the calculators are not always clear which sampling method they are predicting for. If they do not say, then we should assume either a simple random or systematic procedure. We also have to be aware that the sample size calculators usually assume that what we are interested in investigating is divided into only two classes, *a* and *not a*. This last assumption is the basis, for example, of polling the popularity of a political party (such as the Green Party in the UK, Sweden and the Netherlands), where we either support or do not support the party. While we can configure education data into this *a* and *not a* classification (for example, young people with a criminal record and those with no criminal record, or classroom assistants who have an educational qualification and those who do not), we are far more likely to be dealing with data that is divided into more than one class (such as age groups, attainment levels, number of days' unauthorised absence) or is actually a continuous value (such as measures of IQ or age). In these cases, if we use an on-line calculator we implicitly have to restructure our data into two classes. In the long run, this may be less than satisfactory in terms of its effectiveness in estimating sample size when compared with some of the approaches we shall meet in Chapter 12. Having said this, however, on-line calculators are far quicker than any other method.

Sample size calculators are often available as free resources from commercial companies. Amongst the most straightforward to use are those provided by:

- *Creative Research Systems* – www.surveysystem.com/sscalc.htm.
- *Raosoft* – www.raosoft.com/samplesize.html.
- *National Statistics Service (Australia)* – www.nss.gov.au/nss/home.NSF (access via statistical references).

Table 6.7 gives sample sizes with particular margins of error for populations of known size based on various assumptions. The sample sizes are derived from on-line sample size calculators. The population from which the sample is drawn is shown in the left-hand

Table 6.7 Sample sizes under various assumptions

Population	Within 5% of actual value 90% of occasions	Within 2% of actual value 90% of occasions	Within 5% of actual value 95% of occasions	Within 2% of actual value 95% of occasions	Within 5% of actual value 99% of occasions	Within 2% of actual value 99% of occasions
50	43	49	44	49	47	49
100	74	95	80	96	87	98
150	97	138	108	141	123	145
200	116	179	132	185	154	191
250	131	218	151	227	182	236
300	143	255	169	267	207	280
400	162	324	196	343	250	365
500	176	387	217	414	286	446
1000	214	629	278	706	400	806
2000	239	917	322	1091	500	1351
3000	249	1082	341	1334	545	1743
4000	254	1189	351	1501	571	2040
5000	257	1264	357	1622	588	2271
10000	264	1447	370	1936	624	2938
20000	267	1560	377	2144	644	3444
50000	270	1636	381	2291	657	3841

column (it ranges from 50 to 50,000). The other columns show the conditions that affect the sample size. Each column has two conditions: the amount of error we are prepared to accept (which we call the confidence *interval*) and the level of assurance that we will be within this margin of error (which we call the confidence *level*).

- The *confidence intervals* shown in the table are 5% and 2%. The best way to understand these is in terms of the opinion polls that we read in newspapers. If these report that '42% of people will vote for . . . ' and that 'the margin of error is 2%', it means that between 44% (42 + 2) and 40% (42 – 2) will vote for . . .
- The *confidence levels* shown in Table 6.7 are 90%, 95% and 99%. These mean that for 90% of the time we want our samples to be within the error we specify or, for 95%, our samples should be within the error 95% of occasions and the same for 99%.

Putting these two conditions, confidence interval and confidence level, together we see that for any sample size we are demanding greater levels of accuracy in our sample as we move from left to right. So, if our population is 200, we need 116 respondents to meet our condition (the proportion of the population who will vote for a political party or the proportion of schoolchildren who will have school dinners) of being within 5% of actual value for 90% of occasions. Now let us look at the figures in the table. Some of them make sobering reading. We should note the following:

- The sample sizes increase from left to right in the table because the sampling conditions become more rigorous from left to right.
- The increase in confidence interval from 5% to 2% produces a marked increase in sample size that is particularly apparent in larger samples.
- The increase in confidence level, from 90% to 95% and 99% has a more limited but still significant effect on sample size.
- It is barely worth the effort of setting up a sample design if the population is 100 or below and the benefits of sampling are questionable if the population is 200 or below.
- Most individual researchers can cope with a sample size of 200 to 500. These are shown in red in Table 6.7. These demonstrate the trade-off between accuracy and the ability to manage a survey single-handedly. As the size of population grows, we have to limit the levels of accuracy we aspire to.

It is important to understand the significance of sample size in relation to the value we can place on research conclusions. A review of research on thinking skills published in academic journals carried out by researchers at Newcastle University (led by Professor Steve Higgins) as part of an initiative to identify effective practice (Higgins et al., 2005), specifically draws attention to sampling as an issue that was considered when deciding whether to include research in the assessment or not.

> Researchers and journal editors should note that studies were often excluded because basic information . . . (such as number of pupils involved) was not included in the published papers. Moreover, the details of sampling strategies and full sets of results were frequently omitted. Abstracts sometimes referred to data which was not then reported in detail. (p. 4)

The point is well made, especially in the context of Table 6.7, that without information on sample size, population size, sample method and confidence limits and levels, we cannot assess whether the researchers have reached a correct, incorrect or even valid conclusion. Activity 6.3 will help you appreciate the value you can place on other people's research.

Activity 6.3 What level of reliability can you place on research results?

This activity applies your knowledge of sampling techniques and practice to published research. Prepare a:

1. checklist of sampling techniques
2. template to show the sampling technique used in a research paper and, for probability samples, the confidence interval and level selected, the sample size and the population.

- Find five journal articles that have used sampling techniques. For each one, complete the template as far as possible. Where you have the information on sample and population size and confidence level, use a sample size calculator (such as http://www.surveysystem.com/sscalc.htm) to check the confidence interval. If you find a study with a small sample size, you might be surprised.
- For each article, judge whether the sampling method is appropriate. Pay particular attention to the non-probability approaches that are used.
- How many articles provide information on population and sample size that allow you to assess the reliability of the conclusions?

6.9 What can go wrong with a sample?

Let us look now at what can go wrong with a sample. Making the theory of sampling work in practice may not always be straightforward. Things can go wrong which can affect the quality of the data collected. However, unless we are faced with a complete disaster the situation can normally be salvaged. In this section we shall see what we can do to resolve problems when things go wrong.

6.9.1 Not enough people take part

We have calculated the sample size, identified the data sources and then, after all our hard work, a lot of them do not bother to reply. Faced with this, what can we do?

- First, we should realise that this is common and not a comment on our work. We should also have realised, because it is common, that it is likely to happen to us. We should have looked at other people's response rates for similar samples and surveys and built in a non-response rate. For this reason, it is always good practice to report in detail on sampling procedure when writing up research. Typically face to face contact will generate a higher response rate than 'phone or postal contact. When response rates get to 20% or below, as they can with postal contact, we have to consider whether the sample is representative (see the section on bias below). When we draw a sample we assume that the people who do not respond are much the same as those that do. If we have a response rate of 80% this is probably a fair assumption but when the response rate gets very low, we cannot be sure about this at all. What we have to do is build non-response into our sample. If our sample size is 100 and research shows that, with effort, we are likely to get a 40% response rate, then our sampling frame should have at least 250 contacts. You can do the calculations yourself:

  Sample size × 100/percent response

  If we still have a low response, we should demonstrate that our sample is still a good representation of the population.

- If we have not built in a margin to our initial sample, then we can extend our sampling frame subsequently and undertake an additional sample. If there is little time between the two samples, there is unlikely to be a problem but as the time gap increases, so do the risks because, with time, people can change their beliefs and behaviours. It would be an unwise politician who called an election on the basis of an opinion poll that was six months old. However, unless we are dealing with a volatile issue, the risk is not likely to be great unless the gap is measured in years.

6.9.2 People drop out

This is a problem we might face if we are undertaking a longitudinal study, that is, one where we need to go back, sometimes on several occasions, to our data sources. We can understand the problems: people die, people retire, schools are subject to quality inspections and so have other priorities, there is an outbreak of an infectious disease and potential respondents are quarantined. If we think this is not likely, imagine the impact on your research into new students settling in at university when there is an outbreak of meningococcal meningitis where we are sampling students (as there has been). University health authorities usually limit student interaction. Faced with this, these are the options:

- Build the likelihood of drop out into the sample from the start. The implication of this is that we over-sample from the beginning. As long as we can afford it, this is not a problem.
- If we have not done this, then we can replace like with like (another university in the case of our study of students settling in). This is not the best solution since we are assuming that the same sample characteristics will generate the same response pattern.
- If this is not an option, then we can weight the data from any category that is under-represented. We will know which categories these are by comparing the sample to the population. In our survey of students, we might find that male and female representation is acceptable in the sample but that overseas students are under-represented. If this is just one case, there is not likely to be a problem but as the under-representation increases, we have to hope that the (few) cases we are left with are still typical of the category. This would be a problem, for example, if the university with the outbreak was small and the next smallest was twice the size.

6.9.3 The sample is biased

In this situation the sample is large enough but is not representative of the population. It is good practice for every sample that seeks to reflect the characteristics of a population to compare the sample and the population in terms of the proportions in the various classes. The solutions are as follows:

- First, look at the accuracy of the sampling frame (the characterisation of the population from which we have drawn the sample). Some frames date because they do not keep up with the changes in the population. If we are using a census, the results can be up to ten years old. We could find ourselves with a situation in which the sample, if it is accurately drawn, is a better representation of the population than the sampling frame we used! Here we have to update the sampling frame. In many cases, however, statisticians revise census data annually on the basis of known trends.

- Another source of bias, especially with quota sample or on-street surveys, occurs with the surveyor selecting the sample. People often find it easier to talk to people around their own age, so the solution may be to have a variety of surveyors. We may be able to prevent this problem by monitoring surveyor samples and acting to change surveyor behaviour if we identify selection bias.
- It is possible that the sampling procedure itself may produce bias. It is always possible within a random sample that we can draw an eccentric sample that reflects the extremes of a distribution (for example, in our study of students settling in, it is possible, though unlikely, that we could draw a sample of the oldest students in the institutions rather than the more typical students who had just left school). While this is an acceptable sample (because there has to be a probability, albeit a very remote probability, that the names of the oldest students will be drawn), when we find that we have an eccentric sample, the best thing is to start again. With a systematic sample, there may be a periodicity in the data. An example will show what we mean by this. If we are drawing a 1 in 4 sample of students and the sampling frame is structured female, male in sequence, then we will finish up with all one gender. The solution here is to randomise the sampling frame or change the systematic draw.

Summary

Sampling is the bedrock on which research is based. If the sample is bad, the analysis and research results are worthless. The following points are the principal messages from this chapter:

- Quality research is founded on quality data.
- Data should be obtained from authoritative sources. If we are not sure whether our source is authoritative, we should triangulate the information we are receiving.
- We should choose a sampling procedure to meet the needs of our research question.
- Probabilistic sampling methods enable us to claim that we have proved something. Non-probabilistic approaches rely on our ability to argue a case to convince others.
- We may have to modify our preferred sampling approach when we examine its resource implications.
- Sampling can be a flexible procedure. The approaches described here can be modified.
- We need to calculate or estimate a sample size. The calculation needs to take account of the likely response rate.
- Finally, if the sample goes wrong, all is not lost. We can recover if we do not panic!

Further reading

From purposive to probabalistic sampling

Heckathorn, D.D. (1997) 'Respondent Driven Sampling: A New Approach to the Study of Hidden Populations', *Social Problems*, 44(2), 174–199.

Douglas Heckathorn shows how the use of a statistical modelling approach called Markov Chain Analysis can be used to give probability estimates for a snowball sampling procedure. His work was on drug users and he used one user to identify others. He classified those who were identified according to their ethnicity and was able to calculate the probability that a contact would identify someone of the same or different ethnicity. This data can be manipulated mathematically to estimate the size of the drug user population.

For more information on respondent driven sampling, visit www.respondentdrivensampling.org. This website has the opportunity to download a programme that undertakes the statistical analysis and the accompanying manual.

Probabilistic sampling

Barnett, V. (2002) *Sample Survey Principles and Methods, 3rd Edition*, Arnold, London.

Sheaffer, R.L., Mendenhall III, W. and Ott, R.L. (1996) *Elementary Survey Sampling*, Duxbury Press, London.

For a fuller introduction to statistical theory in sampling, see Vic Barnett. Sheaffer et al. take us into the higher reaches of probability sampling approaches and provide significant detail on stratification, systematic and single and two-stage cluster sampling. There is a useful chapter on *estimating* population size and a good section on how to conduct a sample when the questions are sensitive or have a high likelihood of not being answered truthfully.

References

Clark, B.R. (1998) *Creating Entrepreneurial Universities*, UNESCO, Pergamon, Oxford.

Fitz, J., Taylor, C. and Gorard, S. (2002) 'Local Education Authorities and the Regulation of Educational Markets: Four Case Studies', *Research Papers in Education*, 17(2), 125–146.

Heckathorn, D.D. (1997) 'Respondent Driven Sampling: A New Approach to the Study of Hidden Populations', *Social Problems*, 44(2), 174–199.

Higgins, S., Hall, E., Baumfield, V. and Moseley, D. (2005) 'A Meta-analysis of the Impact of the Implementation of Thinking Skills Approaches on Pupils', in *Research Evidence in Education Library*, EPPI-Centre, Social Science Research Unit, Institute of Education, University of London.

Kloep, M., Henday, L.B., Ingelsrigsten, J.E., Glendinning, A. and Espnes, G.A. (2001) 'Young People in "Drinking Societies" Norweigan, Scottish and Swedish Adolescents' Perceptions of Alcohol Use', *Health Education Research*, 16(3), 279–291.

Lindley, D.V. and Scott, W.F. (1995) *New Cambridge Statistical Tables, 2nd Edition*, Cambridge University Press.

Lintonen, T.P., Konu, A.L. and Rimpelä, M. (2001) 'Identifying Potential Heavy Drinkers in Early Adolescence', *Health Education*, 101(4), 159–168.

Motika, R.T. and Chason, W.M. (1995) *Performance of Angoff Model IV Linear Test Equating using Total Test and Content Dimensional Sub-Test Designs in Small Groups of Examiner*, ERIC reference ED382687, full text available at //eric.ed-gov (accessed May 2007).

Papatheodorou, T. (2000) 'Management Approaches Employed by Teachers to Deal with Children's Behaviour Problems in Nursery Classes', *School Psychology International*, 21(4), 415–440.

Samdal, O., Nuttlam, D., Wold, B. and Kannas, L. (1998) 'Achieving Health and Educational Goals Through Schools – a Study of the Importance of the School Climate and the Students' Satisfaction with School', *Health Education Research*, 13(3), 383–397.

Shah, C. and Burke, G. (1999) 'An Undergraduate Student Flow Model: Australian Higher Education', *Higher Education*, 37(4), 359–375.

Van Zolingen, S.J. and Klaasen, C.A. (2003) 'Selection Processes in a Delphi Study About Key Qualifications in Senior Secondary Vocational Education', *Technological Forecasting and Change*, 70, 317–340.

Chapter contents

Chapter 7

MODELLING DATA NEEDS

Key themes

- How to open up a research question and dig down into the research issue.
- How to model a research enquiry.
- How to define the variables for a research enquiry.
- How to define the data (indicators) that will describe the variables.
- What standards our data must reach.

Introduction

In this chapter we shall look at how we can 'break open' our research question and through this devise a model of the factors that we think may be influencing our research issue. We will also see how this process enables us to be more precise about our data needs. The chapter is an important link between our previous discussions of data character and types in Chapter 4 and the approaches we can use to collect our data that are considered in Chapters 8 and 9. This chapter continues the theme of ensuring that the data we collect are of good quality. In Chapter 4, we saw that there was a wealth of secondary data that we can use. Secondary data are, undoubtedly, an enormous resource for educational researchers for local investigations, for national investigations and for international comparative investigations. However, using secondary data is not without risk. There is no doubt that the vast bulk of secondary data are of excellent quality and collected according to well-established and high-standard audit, census and sampling procedures. So, if this is the case, where is the risk? It comes from the possibility that there is a gap between the data needs generated by the research question and the information that is available. It may be that the data are presented at the wrong spatial scale or that the categories used for the data are not quite right for our investigation. In other words, there may be an element of compromise between what we want for our research and what is available. If the compromise that we, as researchers, have to make becomes so great as to call into question the meaningfulness of our analysis and conclusions, then, in these situations, we have to collect our own data.

7.1 The route to data

The step that we now have to take is to move from the research question to collecting the data that we need to answer our question. We know that one of the steps we should take (because we considered it in Chapter 6) is from whom (or what) we should get our data and how we should identify them (or it). If we were ever to imagine that this was a relatively straightforward process, just a matter of asking some questions, read Case Study 7.1. However, before we can identify our data sources we have to be much more specific about the implications of our research question.

Let us suppose that we have been retained as an educational consultant to look at the teacher supply over the medium term. There are two areas for us to research, the first is teacher retention and the second is teacher recruitment. Let us further imagine that there is satisfactory information about teacher retention and that a decision has been taken to concentrate the research on the likely supply of young graduate teachers. This, broadly, is the topic identified by Anthony Stones for his PhD research in New South Wales, Australia (Stokes, 2007). The context for his research was that the range of employment opportunities for graduates has increased over time and, as a result, the proportion of graduates studying education and intending to become a teacher fell from 21.3 per cent of the total in 1983 to 9.7 per cent in 2004. This context informed the way in which the research question was *deconstructed*. The particular perspective that he emphasised was why students chose *not* to study education. From the topics that were investigated, we can see that his research focus was on the criteria that influenced career decision making.

Case study 7.1 What I say is not what I mean

There are two types of social science researcher, those who believe what the person opposite is saying and those who are sceptical, who record what they are told but always ask themselves the question, 'Why is this person telling me this?' This case study shows what happens when the people who believe what they are told are in a position to influence decisions.

In recent years the message about the need for healthy eating has been growing stronger and stronger. Most supermarkets in the UK now have a ready meal selection, which is calorie concerned and pays attention to the balance of ingredients. Organic foods are now more widespread. Even the fast-food chains reacted and, in 2005, put more salads and fruit on an equal footing with burgers and fried chicken on their menus. While the salads remain, the fruit has disappeared from many of them. The reason, of course, is that the restaurants could not sell it and a high wastage rate meant higher costs and lower profits. It was a commercial decision. Yet before we just accept this, we ought to ask ourselves, 'Wasn't it a commercial decision to introduce it in the first place?' The answer, of course, is that it was, so we ought to ask another question, 'How was the decision made?' Concern over a healthy diet represented a market opportunity but no company jumps in without researching the nature and extent of the opportunity – and this is where things began to go wrong. The market researchers asked the wrong questions. A spokesman for the American chain, Wendy's, said, 'We listened to consumers who said they wanted to eat fresh fruit but apparently they lied' (*The Guardian*, 23 August 2006).

From a research perspective, the problem was that the researchers were not sufficiently sceptical. If the whole world is concerned about obesity, 'junk food' and the need to eat healthily, it is not surprising that someone will say that they want fresh fruit but that deep down they would really rather have something that is starchy, sugary and filling.

There is a message in this for all researchers – dig deep to make sure that the answers stack up.

These were identified through a literature search and by just thinking about the issues prior to data collection. The decision criteria selected are presented in Table 7.1 (factors are ranked from high to low). The interesting aspect of this study was that students were asked what sort of salary increase would persuade them to become teachers. For those who were unsure whether they wanted to teach, it would take a salary increase of 20 per cent to make over 50 per cent of them change their minds and for those who did not want to teach, the salary increase would have to be over 40 per cent to make over half of them change.

Table 7.1 Career decision factors in a sample of Australian students

Factor	Average rating on 1–5 scale
Interest in work	4.67
Job satisfaction	4.59
Job security	4.21
Attitude and support of employer	4.20
Desire to help others	4.04
Level of salary	3.96
Support of family	3.95
Possibility of promotion	3.90
Attitude of peers and friends	3.74
Low level of stress	3.58
Hours of work	3.52
Number of holidays	3.34
Attitude of general public	3.13

What can we learn from this that can inform our own research?

It is this – the overarching question or issue has to be broken down into specific questions that determine the process of generating data. In this example of career decision making, we can infer the progression set out in Figure 7.1. At the top level, the overarching issue was, 'Why did the number of students entering education programmes decline?' The more focused question was, 'What was the basis on which students chose their careers?' This led to the identification of types of influence and, finally, the specification of factors to test (structured around rewards, social attitudes and personal costs). The process of breaking down the research question is an analytic one. It is informed by the literature but, finally, it is a process of critical and analytical thinking. It is this stage that very often determines how strong or weak a piece of research is.

The remainder of this section gives advice on how this process can be tackled. Figure 7.2 sets out how we can approach our research. The first step is to determine whether our research approach is deductive or inductive. We first met these terms in Chapter 2. They are important concepts because they determine not just how we shape our data collection and research argument but also how we think research should be conducted. Each approach leads to a different route. The difference between them is the point at which we conceptualise an explanation of the issue we are investigating. With a deductive approach it is at the beginning and with an inductive approach it is either at the end or periodically during the process.

- The *deductive approach* requires us to dissect and reconstruct our research question in order to identify the elements (or variables as we shall call them from now on) that

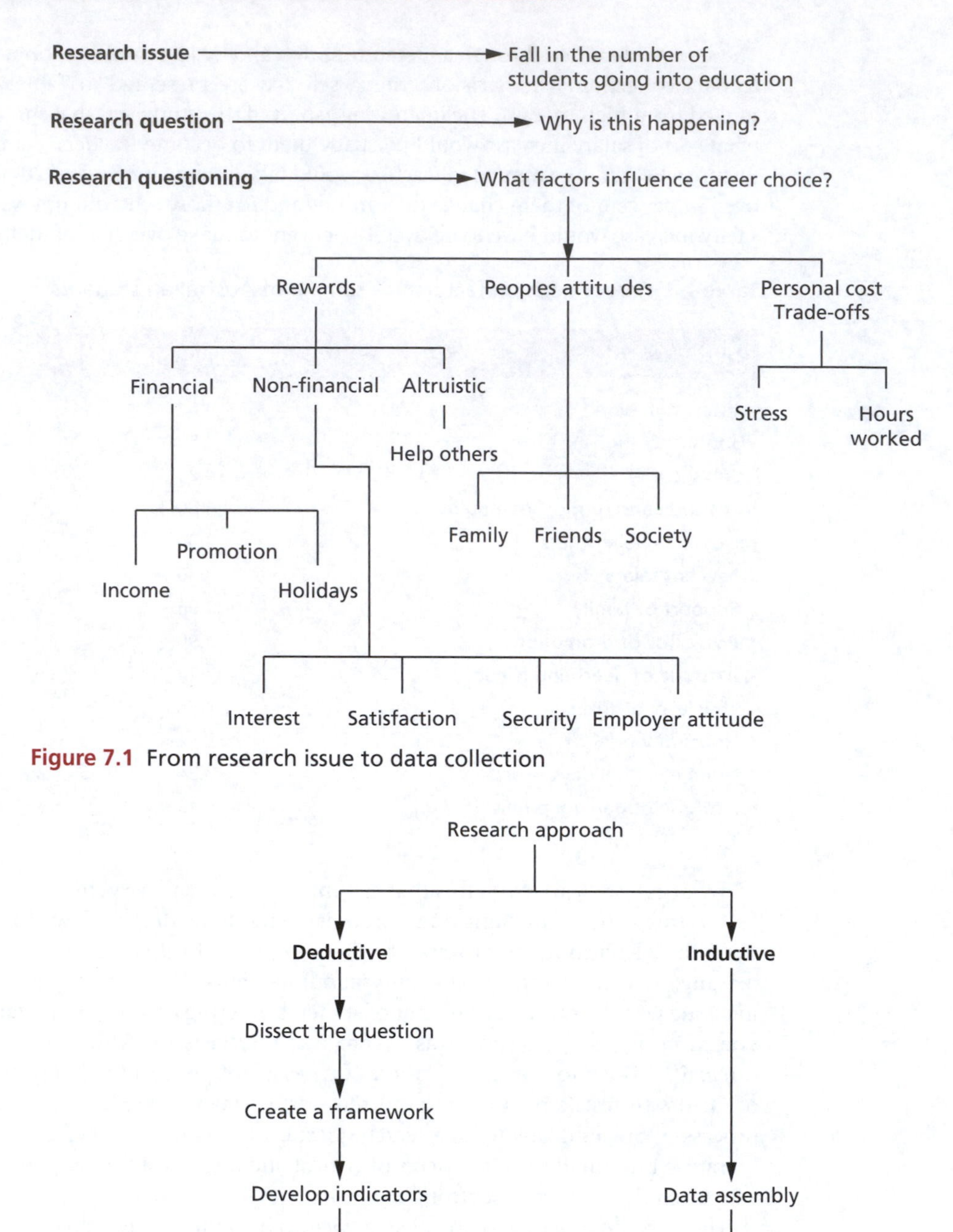

Figure 7.1 From research issue to data collection

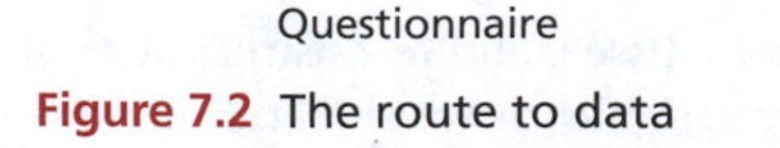

Figure 7.2 The route to data

we think work together to explain what it is we are investigating. This is the approach used in the career decision making study. We have to measure these variables and to this end we identify what are called indicators, things that can be measured and which represent the variable. It is these that generate our data.

- An *inductive approach* puts the explanation together at the end stage of the research. Once we have assembled our data, we sift, combine and organise it in order to produce a convincing explanation. We can reach the same endpoint as a deductive approach but it may not always be possible (or necessary or even desirable).

As researchers, however, we should be guided more by the needs of our research question than any adherence to a deductive or inductive approach. In particular, we should feel confident in combining the deductive and inductive approaches in any way that leads to a convincing solution to our research problem. There is no need to slavishly follow an 'ideal' research design but when we deviate from model approaches, we should explain why – and the reasons we give should be sound in research terms.

7.2 Dissecting the research question

In section 2.2.5 we looked at a number of research questions and considered how the nature of the research question steered us towards a particular way of going about the research (see Table 2.6). While our research question encapsulates the issue and indicates the nature of our interests and concerns, it is a long, long way from directing us to the data we need. Figure 7.1 shows how one researcher closed the gap. In this section, we shall learn how to do this through a process of breaking down the research question into further questions that sharpen our appreciation and lead us to the data we need.

The way we do this is to ask four types of question that help us understand the character of our research issue. The questions are:

1. **'Who'** questions seek to identify a source for our data.
2. **'What'** questions seek to establish the reasons for or the consequences of an event or process. They are often interested in establishing the trigger or inputs to an event or the outcomes or outputs from a process.
3. **'Why'** questions are used to explore processes at work.
4. **'When'** questions are used to establish sequence in a process.

Not every question need be asked in every enquiry. The sorts of question we might ask are shown in Table 7.2. The questions are still phrased in general terms. What we have to do is to apply them (and others that are appropriate) to a specific research issue. In this way we will begin to appreciate the dimensions and complexity of our research issue. Activity 7.1 gives an opportunity to practise this.

The questions we generate result from our own analysis of and thoughts on the issue informed by our background knowledge. We follow this by further reading around the issue in order to sharpen, clarify or even develop new questions. This process of analysis and reading informing each other continues until we are clear in our own minds that (a) the questions we are asking are the ones that address the issues we are interested in, (b) the questions are capable of being answered and (c) the questions are sufficiently focused, so that they clearly identify the information that is needed to answer them.

Table 7.2 Questions for exploring the research question

What is happening/ What is this?	What happened?	What will happen/ What is the effect?	What should we do?	Is this working?
Who is involved?	Why did it happen?	What is creating change?	What is the goal?	What was the object?
Who is in authority?	Who was involved?	What are the outcomes?	What must happen to achieve this?	What has happened?
What are the consequences?	Who was affected?	What can intervene to affect to affect the process?	Who is responsible for . . .?	What has happened that was not intended?
What influences the decisions?	Who gained?	Who will be involved?	What has to change?	Are the consequences beneficial/bad?
Who is the constituency?	Who lost?	When does/will it happen?	Who wins/loses?	Who has gained/ lost?
Who stands to gain/ lose?	When did it happen?			How could it be better?
	Should it have happened like that?			Why did it happen like this?
	What went wrong/ right?			

Activity 7.1 New approaches to learning in higher education

Traditionally learning in higher education is accomplished through a combination of face to face contact between students and tutors and student private study, within frameworks often established by tutors. While this model still exists, it is beginning to be eroded. The reasons for this are threefold.

- First, the significant growth in student numbers in many parts of the world has meant that tutors can no longer give the same level of attention to individual students.
- Second, university identities and status are determined by their visibility in research terms. For academics, their research contribution is often the key to career progression. In these circumstances individuals and institutions seem to rebalance the effort that goes into teaching and research.
- Third, the cost of employing academics is high (relative to institutional revenues). This, in combination with other processes, has led to an increase in the ratio of students to tutors.

It is not surprising that both institutions and academics have sought new ways of managing the staff–student interaction. The most significant developments in the last decade have occurred with the introduction of virtual learning environments (VLEs). In broad terms, these establish new ways for tutors and students to interact. Some of this is synchronous but most is asynchronous, that is, student and tutor do not have to be present at the same time. In this situation the tutor establishes a programme of work for students to follow and provides support with reading, testing and perhaps on-line communication.

The question we should ask of this innovation is, 'How suitable is it for higher education?' Treat this as your research question. Your task is to dissect the issue and construct a series of further questions that you think should be answered in order to reach a satisfactory conclusion. The word you have to crack open is 'suitable'. To give you a start you can range over everything from the outcomes achieved by traditional forms of teaching and learning, through the nature of the higher education experience, to the purpose of higher education.

When you have created our own list of questions, read the paper by Koskela et al. (2005) on this very topic. Look to see how many of your questions they asked. If there are differences between your and their questions, can you say why?

At this point, we should be in a position to see how all our questions link together to create a complete explanation. The corollary of this is that we should also have an overview of the facets and dimensions of the issue and how they all link together. How we represent this is what we shall consider next.

7.3 Putting the jigsaw together

The detailed research questions we develop point us to the data we should collect and they represent our best guess at the information we will need. The relationship of the questions to each other will say something about the influences and forces that we think are at work in our research issue or the dimensions that need to be tackled. In many instances we will have sufficient to construct a prototype explanation, a model, of what might be happening. How we represent this model will be dealt with in this next section.

The modelling approach is found in all approaches to research, quantitative, qualitative and mixed methods (though we should remember that the approach of much qualitative research is, first, to assemble the data, then sort and distil them prior to devising a model). It brings together the hypotheses or ideas or questions that are being tested. One of the most common ways of representing a model is as a process, a set of influences on actions or activities or events and the outcomes that result. We call this type of model a 'systems model'.

7.3.1 What is a system?

We are all likely to be familiar with the idea of a system from working with computers, where the system is either a set of commands that interact with each other (software) or a combination of hardware that allows us to input, output and transfer information. The systems that we shall deal with are essentially the same and are based on the idea that what happens in one place, or to one person or to one group affects what happens elsewhere. This process of one thing affecting another is called 'system interaction'. There is considerable literature on the idea of systems and their application in different subject areas, for example understanding the complex causation that might lead to climate change and the idea that a creature, plant, economy or city functions as a system. In education, we are familiar with the term 'education system', the framework of education provision that takes children in at the age of around 4 or 5 and enables their intellectual and emotional development so that they can emerge at between 16 and 25 equipped to function in society. The education system continues to provide further learning and development opportunities for adults. However, the systems that we are usually concerned with in our research are usually at a far smaller scale than this. For instance, understanding bullying as a set of influences and factors that create the bully and the bullied, or the conditions and reasons that interact to give rise to a high proportion of nursery teachers and assistants leaving their posts in their early thirties.

There are two types of system, *closed* or *open*.

- A closed system has a boundary, across which there are no interactions whatsoever. The computer programmes we use are closed systems. They may interact with other programmes but only within a boundary set by the programmer. Realistically, in education, we have no closed systems.
- Everything we deal with is an open system and has the potential to interact with everything else. The selection of a school may be affected by the location of the

school relative to where the parents live (or parent lives) as well as its educational programme. A child's performance at school may be affected by the level of parental support as well as the quality of teaching. Parental support may be related to socio-economic status. Socio-economic status may affect where we live. We can represent this as a diagram (Figure 7.3). This diagram is a first stab at representing a system. The situation we face in education, as in all the social sciences, is of clusters of strong interactions with fewer links joining the clusters together either directly or indirectly. Figure 7.3 shows the elements of a system:

- processes at work, shown by the arrows (for example, socio-economic status affecting where parents live by virtue of how much they can afford to pay for housing);
- entities or connections or states (school, parental support) that initiate, create or influence a process or are affected by a process;
- processes that can be classified as inputs (creating, interacting, influencing – socio-economic status mentioned in the first bullet point) or outputs (a changed state that may be an input elsewhere, a child's performance at school, for example, being affected by the quality of the school and the type and level of support offered by parents).

A system is a dynamic process. We need to reflect this in the way we think about research. A question we need to ask ourselves, therefore, is 'What happens when the system we identify keeps on working?' Even with a model as crude as that in Figure 7.3, we can see that the process is likely to produce 'sink' schools, that is, schools to which many parents do not want to send their children. In social terms, this is an *unstable state* that will create a strong likelihood of undesirable consequences. In educational terms we would like to achieve a more stable state where a child's performance is not adversely affected by the school they attend or the parents they have. What inputs would we have to add to Figure 7.3 to achieve this? By asking this question, we can begin to look for evidence of schools that defy our model and then identify the factors and processes at work that create the difference.

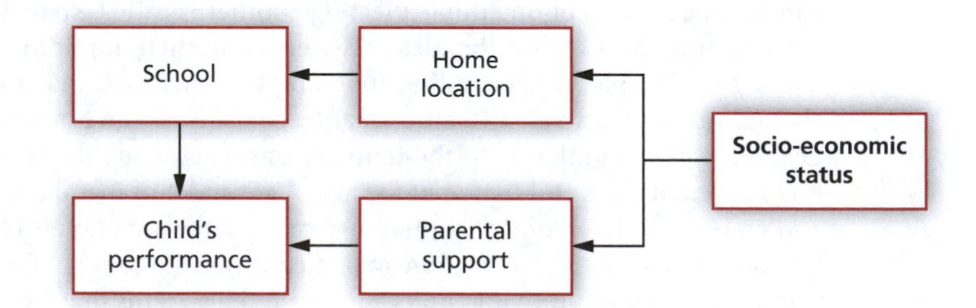

Figure 7.3 School choice and child performance represented in system terms

7.3.2 Presenting a research issue in a systems setting

We can use the systems model, therefore, to pull together the factors that we think are at work in regard to our research issue. We get to these factors by deconstructing our research issue into a research question and then fragmenting that research question into smaller units by questioning our research question, as shown in Figure 7.1. But how do we go about breaking up our research question and representing the factors we identify as a system?

The process of developing a systems representation of the issue to be investigated is not complex. It consists of four stages: reading, thinking, organising and representing.

(i) Reading: the preliminary reading that we do for any research identifies how others have approached the issue. When we read we should (a) identify as many perspectives and insights as we can and (b) establish how far these perspectives and insights are supported by other researchers. The particular focus of our reading should be to isolate what other people regard as the processes at work. Once we have the process we can begin to isolate the causation or influence and consequence.

(ii) Thinking: during this stage we should be doing two things. First, we should be considering and assessing the work of other researchers. Does it stack up? Are there any conflicts (and if there are, can they be resolved or are some researchers just wrong)? Is there a weight of evidence? We should also consider whether some factors that seem to be influential are, in fact, spurious. For instance, if research shows that pupil attainment in private schools is higher than in state schools, should we assume that state schools are worse? It all depends whether the research also shows that pupils from families in higher socio-economic groups achieve more than those from lower status groups. If they do, and if those going to private schools are predominantly from higher socio-economic groups, then what proportion of the difference in performance between private and public schools is due to the socio-economic character of the pupils? Interrelationships like this are important and, as we shall see in Chapter 13, there are statistical techniques that can help us find the answer. Second, we should be looking for what is missing. Are there links that other people have not explored? Are there other influences at work? If our interest is in factors affecting pupil performance, we will find research assessing family circumstances, school character, teaching quality and so on, but studies of where the child is in birth order are few in number. Is it a potentially significant factor?

(iii) Organising: The next stage is to structure the results of our reading and thinking about the issue. This can be a complex process but approached systematically, it can also be quite straightforward.

- First, set out the processes or outcomes identified by other researchers. In terms of pupil performance, it could be just pupil attainment, or high pupil attainment or low pupil attainment or value added (by the school).
- Next, identify the inputs to these processes and classify their role. Are they causative (creating or initiating a process) or do they influence or interfere with a process? This sort of classification is often highly judgmental, usually because our ideas are speculative and what we want to evaluate in our research.
- Then, identify the nature of the impact. Is it positive or negative? Does it predispose decision A, B or C? At the same time assess the strength of the impact.
- Finally, we add in our own conjectures and ideas. At this point, we have the material for the final stage.

(iv) Representing: There is no right and wrong way of representing system interactions. The most simple is shown in Figure 7.3, where the entities, the things that are affected and the things that cause them to change are shown in boxes and the processes (inputs and outputs) are shown by arrows. One way to show all of the information we have gathered is to use different colours for different studies and superimpose them on one diagram. Some solutions work well and others less well. If the diagram becomes too crowded, we have to do something different. What should emerge is something that represents our view of the research to date and which highlights (and is implicitly a rationale for) the research we wish to do. Case Study 7.2 gives an example of this.

The process of representing our thinking about a research issue is improved by practice. Activity 7.2 will help you think in a 'systems' way and construct a model of a research issue.

Case study 7.2 Developing a theory of leadership

Organisational change is a crucial concern of management. The last 20 years have seen educational systems across the world being subjected to enormous pressures. Performance assessment (of pupils, students and institutions) is commonplace and institutional rankings are watched closely by institutional managers. Quality assurance procedures operated through external agencies are found at all levels from preschool to higher education. Policy initiatives to encourage interagency working are becoming more common. The Children's Act (2004) in the UK and the 'Every Child Matters' initiative is not so different from 'No Child Left Behind' in the USA. The 'Training for the Indigenous Education Network' programme in Australia has some similar features and evidence of interagency working at a practice level is now common in many EU states. Couple all of this with the need to meet the requirements of Government initiated and controlled curricula and it is clear that the face of change has been (and still is) rapid.

Change can be costly, stressful and difficult to accommodate. For this reason, there has been much concern with the ability of institutional managers and leaders to guide schools and colleges through difficult times. This is the context for the research by Holtkamp and others to assess a theory of leadership. The process was broadly similar to that outlined in section 7.3.2. Their paper begins with a review of leadership theories and concepts in education (equivalent to the 'reading' stage in 7.3.). This sets the scene for an argument for a new leadership theory, whose difference is that it explicitly includes a female dimension. The outline model as represented by Holtkamp et al. is reproduced below.

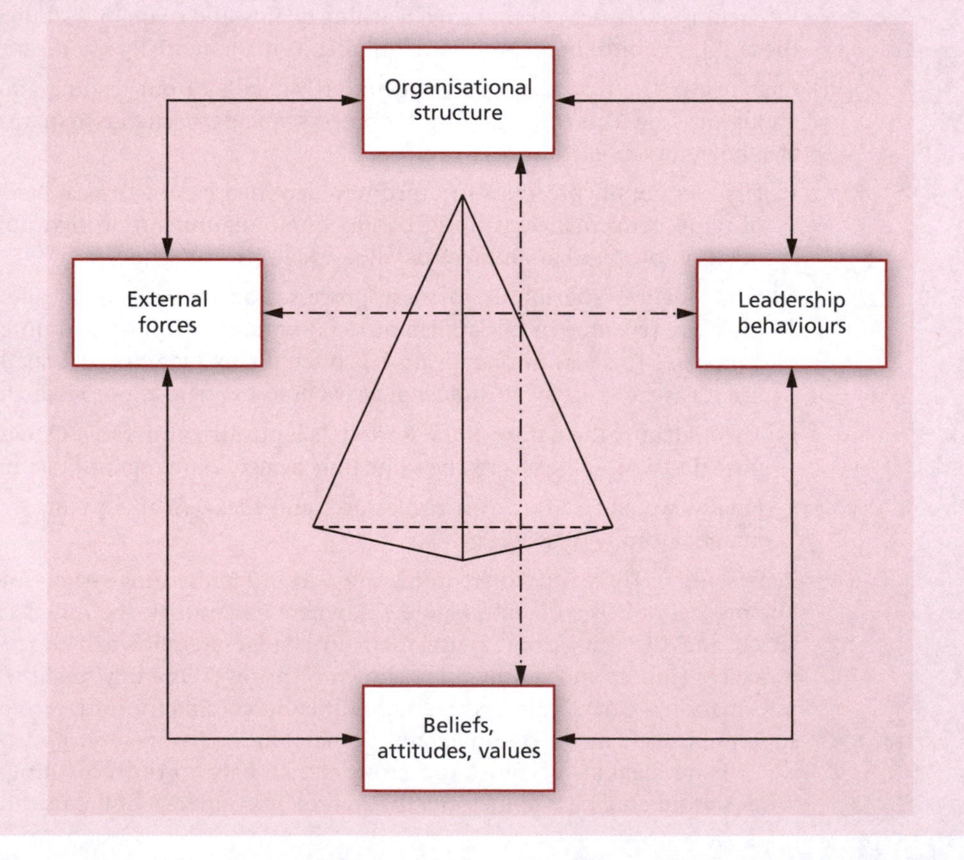

The entities of the model are:

(a) beliefs, attitudes and values
(b) external forces
(c) organisational structure and
(d) leadership behaviours.

The model shows that these entities interact and that while leadership behaviour is the outcome, there are feedback processes (the consequence of experience) that can affect the influencing factors where the leader has control (that is, beliefs, attitudes and values and organisational structure). The strongest interactions are shown by the solid lines (organisational structure and leadership, organisational structure and external forces, external forces and beliefs, and leadership beliefs). The relationships between external forces and leadership and organisational structure and beliefs exist but are weaker. The tetrahedron, as the centre of the diagram, shows the four dimensions of the model as being equally important.

The researchers used this model as the starting point for an empirical study. They sought evidence (in the form of an established rating scale, *the organisational and leadership effectiveness inventory,* which consists of 96 statements about leadership) from school principals and assistants in the USA. Their sample of 374, according to sampling theory (see section 6.8 and Appendix 1), ensured that their estimate of population characteristics was accurate 95 times out of 100. An inventory such as the one they used has, as with psychometric tests, been subject to validation, that is, it has been shown to measure what it purposes to measure.

The high level statistical analysis they conducted enabled them to confirm that their theory was a good representation of how school leaders felt about and practised leadership. We should note also that the way they depict their theory shows many of the attributes of a systems model.

Activity 7.2 Constructing a systems representation

You might look at papers in academic journals and ask, 'Where is the systems diagram?' It is true that more papers do not include it than do. First, we have to exclude all those following a broadly inductive approach. For the rest, a systems diagram may be a valid way of representing the research issue. Just because it was not published should not lead us to assume that it was not used by the researcher(s) to identify the variables they wanted to study and to show how the variables interacted. This activity practises systems thinking by reconstructing the research issue in a systems format. You can do this with any appropriate academic paper but if you want to be fairly certain of coming up with the right sort of analysis, start by reading Gary Marks' paper (2006) on low achievement. He sets out the entities for you to represent quite clearly. In the first paragraph there are things to put on your diagram. The section on 'Previous studies' should enable you to devise quite a full diagram. As you construct it, think about whether there is anything else that you would insert.

After you have thought about the issue by yourself, look at the research on attainment funded through the Department for Children, Schools and Families in the UK and its predecessors. Go to the website www.dcsf.gov.uk and navigate to the research and statistics homepage. Follow the Quick Link to the research page and select, as your keyword, 'attainment'. Can you enrich your diagram through this source?

7.4 From influences to variables

In the explanation so far, we have used terms such as 'influences' and 'factors at work'. These are all well and good but they are somewhat nebulous. Now is the time to call them by their proper name, *variables*. In this section we shall look at what roles they can take on in a systems model.

A systems diagram, as we know, shows the sequence of influences for the issue we are investigating. These influences can often vary in their intensity or strength. For instance, if we were examining the effect of classroom temperature on pupils' work rate, then we would monitor different temperature levels. If our research were into influences on the quality of educational outcomes, then we would almost certainly want to examine how different amounts of funding made an impact. Because these influences can vary in quantity or intensity, we refer to them as research variables. A variable is anything that can have a different value. It is important to appreciate the functions that they perform in our explanation. This is what we shall consider next.

7.4.1 Types of variable

Variables can be classified into three types based on their function in a systems model.

- First, there are those that are changed by other influences. The move from a primary school to a secondary school can, for some children, be a traumatic experience. If we were researching this, we would want to measure in some way children's emotional state before, during and after the move. Because it is the emotional state that is changed, we call it the *dependent variable* (because it depends on the influence of other variables). If you look back to Figure 7.3, you will immediately appreciate that the variables to which the arrowheads are pointing are dependent variables.
- The second type of variable is called an *independent variable*. In our example of moving from primary to secondary school, the move itself is the independent variable. We might, however, want to think in greater depth about influences on a child's emotional state. It could be that the parents use the transition to move house. If they separate or if a grandparent dies this could have an effect. Each of these would be independent variables. Independent variables influence the dependent variables. Some discussions of types of variable refer to independent variables as *causal variables*, on the basis that they cause the change in the dependent variable. Use of the word 'causal' is so much a part of custom and practice in discussions of research practice that it is difficult to say that it is incorrect. The term, however, does imply a relationship that operates in every case, whereas the reality is that it will happen in the majority of cases or in some cases when other conditions are met. In other words, the relationship between independent and dependent variables is rarely deterministic but probabilistic. For this reason, if we want to call them anything other than independent, we should refer to them as *explanatory variables* because this is what we are hoping they will do.
- The third type of variable is an *intervening variable*. Thinking about school transfer, we could suggest that if children transfer with friends the emotional impact will be less than if they go to a completely new school where they know no one. Knowing others would be an intervening variable because it intervenes to affect whether the emotional impact of school transfer is high or low. An intervening variable can take one of two forms. Figure 7.4, which describes an aspect of youth policy, intervening to improve the employability and increase the employment of unemployed young people, shows a set of intervening variables. The outcome of the policy intervention is shown by the box 'reduction in youth unemployment'. Youth unemployment is such an issue that most developed nations have several programmes aimed at tackling it. In our example, we will assume that we are focusing on one publicly funded programme. This is the input to the process and is the independent variable. However, it is not just the funding that is important, but also how the programme is delivered. To this extent the 'how' is an intervening variable (shown in Figure 7.4 by the box

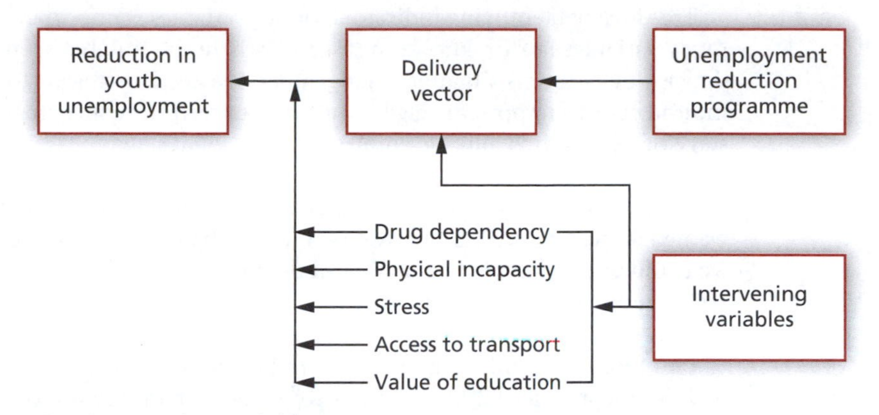

Figure 7.4 Intervening variables

'delivery vector'). There may be many ways of looking at this, but an obvious one is to differentiate between government agencies (such as Job Centre Plus in the UK), partnerships between local and central government (such as Connexions in England and Wales) or NGOs (Non-Governmental Organisations). Each of these constitutes a delivery vector. The assumption here is that there may be differences in the method of delivery that could affect standards and outcomes. Figure 7.4 also shows intervening variables interfering with a process. The following could be filters that affect individual outcomes: drug dependency, physical incapacity, stress, access to transport, value placed on education, aspiration and motivation.

Now that we have understood the types of variables and once we identified the variables that are significant for our research, the next stage is to collect our data. However, before we can do this, we have to be specific about how we wish to represent our variables.

7.4.2 Developing indicators

An indicator is something that represents or stands for a variable in our research. It is something that we can capture and measure in our research. Sometimes the link between variables and data needs is quite obvious. If we are investigating whether the attainment of girls is greater than that of boys or whether students give higher ratings for teaching satisfaction to younger lecturers than to older, the independent variables in each case are obvious – gender and age. We use gender and age to indicate girls and boys and older and younger. In other words, they are *indicators* of the variables. But not all variables are this easy to represent. Let us go back to our school transfer research example. We know that our independent variable is 'emotional state'. However, there is no ruler that we can place up against a child that will measure emotional state. We have to identify something that we can use as an indicator. We could give each child a standard emotional test that generates a numerical indication of their emotional state before and after transfer. Alternatively, we could observe children in a classroom setting and note down whether they seemed happy, contented, unhappy by observing every 15 minutes whether they were laughing, crying, smiling, angry, etc. and counting the frequency for each category. An indicator, therefore is something that we can measure, whereas a variable is not necessarily capable of being measured.

This idea of identifying indicators for our variables is important, because there will be many variables in our education research where the link between the variable and our data is not clear or is a matter of judgement. We need, therefore, to explain our choice of indicators. This important stage is the link between the conceptual/theoretical/planning stage of our research and the empirical/operational stage.

Indicators generate data that are proxies for our variables. That is, they represent the variables though they may not be exactly the same as the variables. For example, if we wanted to measure student motivation but only had access to data collected by the school, we could use the number of times a student was recorded as being late or absent (on the assumption that poor motivation was more likely to be associated with lateness and absence). This is what we mean by the indicator being a proxy.

Our research is only as good as the indicators we choose. In most cases the selection will be uncontroversial but where there is more than one option, the choice has to be justified. One of the challenges facing teachers is the spread of abilities in their class. One of the policy decisions that schools take is whether pupils should be grouped by ability in some or all of the subjects that are taught. Not surprisingly, whether whole class teaching or grouping students by ability produces better results is a topic for educational research. In 2005 Judith Ireson and colleagues published a study on the effects of grouping by ability on pupil attainment (Ireson et al., 2005). While their finding, that when 'students follow essentially the same curricula, ability grouping has little impact on attainment' (p. 454) contributes to the debate about selection and grouping, we are more interested at this time in their approach to the research and the indicators they used for the concept of 'ability grouping'. They needed to measure 'grouping' and they chose to reflect two attributes.

- First, they determined the *extent* of grouping and developed a two-fold classification of mixed ability teaching: partial grouping and complete ability grouping. Using this classification they could assess the proportion of classes that were taught in a group mode.
- Second, they reflected the extent of a pupil's *experience* of grouping, in terms of number of years in a five-year period.

Using these indicators, they thus developed an estimate of grouping at the level of the school and at the level of the individual pupil. Their indicators enabled them to measure the variable they were interested in, ability grouping.

We can appreciate, with this last example, that our variable (the concept of ability grouping) has become more complex (than, for instance, age or gender) but what we also have to understand is that there are far more complex concepts that we have to grapple with in social research. What is *quality* in education? Is *pupil attainment* only concerned with examination grades, or should it include social and personal dimensions as well? How *good* is a school, college or university? How *effective* is a teacher? What is *social exclusion*? The level of difficulty in cracking the problem of ability grouping is minor in comparison with these issues, each of which can be explained in several different ways. They are much more complex and they have many dimensions. Which ones do we choose to represent as an indicator and which do we omit? The task is almost certainly likely to be too great for a lone researcher. Fortunately, many of these concepts have been researched and standard indicator sets produced.

The indicators that are generated for complex concepts such as those above are called *compound indicators* because several indicators come together to represent the different attributes of the variable. Read Case Study 7.3 for an example of this. The composition

Case study 7.3 Measuring deprivation

The concept of deprivation is an important one for education researchers to understand. On the one hand education is seen as a vehicle for relieving deprivation. Progression through the education system and through vocational training is seen as a means of providing people with a broader range of economic opportunities and futures. For those coming from a deprived background, it is a parental 'escape route'. On the other hand, the effectiveness of the teaching and learning process is affected by deprivation. Head teachers are concerned by low pupil attainment and class teachers by problems of discipline and commitment.

But what is deprivation? It is far more than teachers' moans about 'kids from the problem estate'. It is a complex variable that we have come to understand better as we have appreciated its range of dimensions.

The most recent (2007) estimation of deprivation area by area in the UK is the Scottish Index of Multiple Deprivation (SIMP), (2006). The methodology of this index combines weighted measures of attributes of deprivation. These attributes are called domains in the SIMP. For each domain there is a set of indicators.

Each domain is given a weight in the calculation of a single index. The process of creating indicators ranges from the calculation of simple percentages to advanced statistical analysis. Domain indices are combined via a ranking and mathematical transformation procedure. It is the combined ranked values that are weighted and added together. Housing makes the lowest contribution to the index (2.3% of the total) and income and employment the highest (27.9% each).

Domain	Attribute
Current income	Number of adults (16–60) claiming income support Number of adults (over 60) claiming guaranteed pension credit Number of children (0–15) dependent on a claimant of income support Number of adults claiming Job Seekers Allowance Number of children (0–15) dependent on a claimant of Job Seekers Allowance
Employment	Unemployment count averaged over 12 months (men under 65, women under 60) Income incapacity claimants Severe Disablement Allowance claimants Compulsory New Deal Claimants not included in the unemployment count
Health	Standardised mortality ratio Hospital episodes related to alcohol use Hospital episodes related to drug use Comparative illness factor Emergency admissions to hospital Proportion of population being prescribed drugs for anxiety, depression or psychosis Proportion of live single births of low birth weight
Education, Skills and Training	School pupil absences Pupil performance at Stage 4 (Scottish Qualifications Authority) Working people with no qualifications 17–21 year olds enrolling into higher education 16–18 year olds not in full-time education
Geographic Access to Services	Drive time to a doctor Drive time to a petrol station Drive time to a post office Drive time to shopping facilities

▶

Domain	Attribute
	Drive time to a secondary school Public transport time to a doctor Public transport time to a post office Public transport time to shopping facilities
Housing	Persons in households that are overcrowded Persons in households without central heating
Crime	Recorded crimes of violence Recorded domestic housebreaking Recorded vandalism Recorded drug offences Recorded minor assault

of an indicator is a matter of choice and judgement. The fundamental requirement of any indicator is that it should validly represent what it purports to represent and that it should be reliable (in space and time) in representing it. Many composite indicators are collected by public agencies or bodies and are usually compiled to assess some aspect of public policy. In this situation it is possible to select attributes or change definitions in ways that give a positive assessment of the variable. Take what appears to be a simple concept like unemployment. In the UK, after the Second World War, the calculation of unemployment was conceptually simple – those registered as unemployed as a percentage of the total of employees and unemployed. After the boom years of the 1960s, with unemployment rising, the definition was changed to the number of registered unemployed over 18 as a proportion of the work force (that is, employees, self-employed, those in the armed forces, those on government training programmes and the unemployed). Why were these changes made? Because they reduced the apparent level of unemployment. The changes reduced the rate because (a) the numerator, the number of registered unemployed, fell (the school leaving age was raised to 16 in 1972, so unemployed 14- to 16-year-olds did not count) and (b) the denominator was increased with the inclusion of the self-employed, armed forces and those in training). In 1983 the definition was changed again so only those claiming unemployment benefit were counted. Again this led to an apparent reduction in unemployment. Clearly what researchers must do when using indicators, especially composite indicators, is to examine what is included.

Compound indicators are used in public policy in three ways:

1. To define the extent and/or location of a problem, for example, this is why the Governments of England and Wales, Scotland and Northern Ireland have devised an index of deprivation that identifies localities where deprivation (evaluated on a range of dimensions) is high (see Case Study 7.3).
2. For comparative analysis: for example, the *Physical Quality of Life Index* combines a measure of adult literacy with infant mortality and life expectancy.
3. For longitudinal analysis, that is, looking at how situations in different countries or regions change over time, the *Index of Social Progress* (developed by Professor Richard

Estes of the University of Pennsylvania) combines 40 indicators covering education, health, economy, environment, social conditions, welfare, demography, arms expenditure, status of women and cultural diversity. The 2000 report on Europe shows that Sweden and Denmark had the highest index score (107), Belgium, Netherlands and the UK had an index of between 95 and 97 and that the average score for all of the states of Eastern and Western Europe was 87.4, which was marginally above the score for the USA (Estes, 2003).

GESIS, the German Social Science Infrastructure Service, is an excellent source of information on social indicators (http://www.gesis.org/en/index.htm then access services, data and social indicators).

Compound indicators are important for educational researchers because we can use them to provide a single measure of complex variables. Deprivation, poverty, the digital divide and social exclusion are all issues that impact on education, in terms of education provision, access to education, experience of education and educational attainment. Each of these is multi-faceted and multi-dimensional. There is no simple measure for any of them. The Social and Cultural Planning Office in the Netherlands has used an index to the measure quality of life of Dutch citizens (Life Situation Index, published biennially as *The Social State of the Netherlands)*. This index brings together measures of housing, health, leisure activity, consumer durables, sport activity, vacation, social participation and mobility. The United Nations' *Human Development Index* integrates measures of life expectancy, education and standard of living. In the UK, the Department of Communities and Local Government produces the *Index of Child Well-Being*, a compound of measures to reflect material well-being, health, education, crime, housing and environment. The Index is calculated for localities and seeks to reflect the quality of life of children. By using these indicators and many other measures, they can be associated with such things as educational progression, educational attainment, access to higher education and even school quality reports. They become, in terms of our categorisation, an independent variable which is assessed in terms of its impact on the dependent variables (such as educational attainment and access to higher education).

7.4.3 Identifying variables through data analysis

In many of our studies we will collect data on the characteristics of our respondents. Amongst the most common characteristics are gender, age, employment or job type, housing and type of accommodation. We use this information in the following way. We pick out all the data relating to males and analyse them and then do the same for females. We then compare the processed data to see if there are any differences between them, in other words we are assessing whether the variable gender has any influence. If there is some pattern in the different behaviour or responses of males and females, we would then seek to identify an explanation. If, for example, boys performed better in mathematics tests, we would want to know whether the cause was internal to the boys or external, the consequence of their learning environment. When we use respondent characteristics in this way, we call them *control variables,* because we use them to control the analysis of our data. Read Case Study 7.4 for an example of this.

However, we should always be cautious about our findings. Even if our analysis does reveal a pattern, it could be a spurious one. Imagine that we are researching the career aspirations of teachers and one of the choices is 'leave the profession'. We collect our data and analyse it by gender and find, to our surprise, that while only 5 per cent of men wish to leave, 60 per cent of women do. On digging deeper, we find that the decision to leave

Case study 7.4 Using control variables to analyse data

In 2007 **Educational Research and Review**, an on-line journal, published a paper from four Nigerian academics on academic staff research productivity. This is an issue that most university vice-chancellors are interested in because it is the means by which universities establish their reputations.

The methodology adopted is robust. The researchers constructed a stratified random sample of 480 staff out of a population of 3,120. This proportion suggests that the results they obtain from their sample will be within +/− 4% of the actual results 95% of the time. The stratification was based on faculty structures.

The researchers identified the following variables:

- *dependent variable:* research productivity, which was estimated as a composite variable (whose indicators are not given);
- *control variables:* gender, marriage status (married, single), area of (subject) specialisation (arts, science and technology, social science, management studies, agricultural science, education, medicine and law).

They used the control variables to analyse the results of the different sub-groups and found that:

- men and women are significantly different in their research outputs, with men's being greater;
- married staff and single staff are significantly different in their research outputs, with married staff producing more;
- there is no significant different between the outputs of the different academic groups.

The interpretation the researchers gave to these results at times challenges a western perception. In terms of the gender difference, they suggest that men are by nature stronger and more resilient to undertake 'strenuous activities' such as research. Their result is not unusual but there may be a better explanation. For the married/single difference, they express surprise that it is not the single staff who are more productive since they have fewer responsibilities. However, they suggest that because married staff are more 'settled', their circumstance allows them to be more productive. From an outsider's viewpoint it would have been useful to have known the gender breakdown of those who are married and single. The question is, is being married or single a variable in its own right, or is it a spurious association because most of the single staff are women? This is the sort of complication that researchers should look out for and it is a reason for using sophisticated statistical tools to analyse data and not just rely on simple tests of difference. Read the article yourselves and make up your own minds.

Source: Usang, B. et al. (2007)

increases with age. Looking back on our sample, we see that our male teachers are predominantly young and our female teachers are old. Gender may have an effect but it is masked by the effect of age.

This example shows the danger in much education and social science research. The issues we investigate are so complex and the influences upon them so multi-faceted that it can be difficult to isolate the influence of one variable. As a research community we have coped with this in two ways:

- First, we have developed (and used) a greater range of qualitative approaches to gain insights into the issues (see Chapter 11). If we are concerned to understand more about low achievement, we could gain a deeper understanding through case studies of family lifestyles than we could by profiling the socio-economic characteristics of low achievers and their families. It is partially because of the complexity of education that we have seen such an increase in qualitative studies in the last 20 to 30 years.
- The second way we try to manage complexity is by developing more powerful analytical (usually statistical) tools (see Chapter 13). For example, we know that processes operate at different levels. A pupil's overall academic performance is affected by what the school does as well as by what is within their control and family circumstances.

Recognition of this situation throughout the social sciences led to the development of multi-level analysis. These powerful techniques allow us to gain insights into complex issues in ways that help us to shape policy actions. Read Case Study 7.5 for more about this.

7.5 Getting good quality data: an introduction

So far in this part of the book we have found that getting good information is dependent upon:

- finding the right people to give it to you, that is, people who are knowledgeable about the issue and who, by being representative of a group, allow us to make valid statements about that group;

Case study 7.5 Measuring a school's effectiveness

The idea that we should evaluate the benefits we receive from public services is becoming more accepted globally as governments seek to evaluate whether the money invested is well spent and delivers outputs and outcomes that represent value for money. In education, we can view quality assessment and assurance as a first stage in assessing effectiveness. Now there is often a second stage, assessing value added.

We are familiar with the concept of value added as a tax. An organisation, a manufacturer or a retailer for example, takes in inputs, does something to them and sells them for a higher price. If we make a purchase, we pay a tax at the point of consumption on the difference between the cost of the inputs and the value of the outputs. This represents the value added.

But how do we apply this to education? We can see it at work in the following situation. If two children, with the same abilities and backgrounds go to two different schools and have different levels of attainment, the schools must be a key influence in this change. One school is clearly adding more value than the other.

Professor David Mayston of the University of York is an expert on exploring the concept of value added in public services. Since 2002 he has produced three major reports on the topic for the UK Government, two for the Department for Education & Skills (the predecessor of the Department for Children, Schools and Families) and one for the Treasury. In an important report (Mayston, 2006) for the DfES, which is clearly designed to inform policy thinking on approaches to the measurement of value added, he reviews the strengths and weaknesses from a statistical point of view of various approaches to measuring value added. The review is wide-ranging and includes not only the Department for Children, Schools and Families' current approach but others that have included a wider range of explanatory variables including gender, socio-economic disadvantage, where English is a second language, peer group and social pressures, and school resourcing. While he does not recommend any particular method, approaches based on *multi-variable analysis* (where a number of variables are interacting with each other to influence the value added) and *multi-level analysis* (where different variables, such as the effects of the pupil, the class the pupil is in and the school, operate at different levels) appear to give more robust and insightful findings. He notes that most estimates of value added resulting from multi-level analysis suggest that the school effect is about 10%.

Are these more powerful approaches likely to supplant the existing national approach for measuring value added that results in the publication of school performance statistics? The answer is 'probably not'. These are now established and allow us to see trends over a period. They give a measure of value added but it seems not to be as effective as some others. Where might we see the more advanced statistical assessments being applied? The answer is that they are more likely to be used for detailed assessments of special programmes and new initiatives such as the Academy Programme that creates all-ability, publicly funded independent schools.

- ensuring that we have broken down our research question into smaller and smaller questions so that we can identify the variables that will answer our questions and the indicators that will reveal those variables to us.

Now we are going to begin the process of finding out how we can actually collect this data. The options available to us are really quite wide ranging, from obtaining our data in a highly structured way to obtaining them using more flexible and opportunistic means. Some of the decisions we make about which method to use are influenced by the nature of the environment we are working in and the nature, particularly the sensitivity, of the issue we are investigating. For example, if we are investigating an aspect of institutional organisational failure, it might be unwise to announce both the purpose of our research and our presence because the tendency of people who are involved in failure is to gloss over or even suppress the evidence. If, on the other hand, our investigation involves dealing with school children then we have to make clear the issue we are studying, who we are and the methods we will use not just to the school but to the parent/s as well. In both cases, we have to understand that there are critical issues about the subjects knowing the purpose of our research. As we have suggested, though, we might come to different decisions in different circumstances.

However, our choice is influenced not only by the relationship between the research topic and the research environment, but also by the nature of the data we expect to collect. The data collection methods we can use are not equally appropriate for all types of data. We cannot even say that if we are collecting data on behaviour, use this approach, and if we are collecting data on opinions, use this other method, because some opinions, for example, are best revealed by behaviour rather than being expressed in writing or through speech. And, in addition to all of this, we have to judge whether we have the time or the resources to use a particular method. It all seems very complex but in reality the selection of an approach is usually straightforward and in most cases we do have alternatives. On top of this, the people we are dealing with are usually only too willing to help – though this, as we shall see, can be a problem on some occasions.

7.6 The options for data collection

We have four ways of collecting our data (see Table 7.3):

- **Questionnaires:** structured formats that generate a response by asking individuals specific questions and with the researcher not involved.
- **Interviews:** a question-based format where the researcher asks individuals the questions.
- **Group interviews and discussions:** a session led by one or more researchers which involves probing groups of respondents using a question, discussion or stimulus/response format.
- **Observation:** where the researcher, who may or may not be known to the subjects, collects data using approaches that range from structured to opportunistic. Observation takes place in or captures real time in the research environment.

  Interviews also take place in real time though the location of the interview need have nothing to do with the issue being researched. Group sessions are likely to

Table 7.3 What data collection methods are good at

Questionnaire	Interview	Group sessions	Observation
• Getting data from a large number of people.	• Opening up an issue.	• Preliminary research.	• Obtaining data from those with limited verbal skills.
• Obtaining data in a structured way.	• Hearing the respondent's voice.	• Group perspectives.	• Audit of behaviour and actions.
	• Assessing response validity.	• Assessing stability of opinions.	• Identify patterns of which subjects unaware.
	• Smaller numbers of people.	• Exploring motives, values and drivers.	

occur in an environment removed from the research issue. Questionnaires are flexible in terms of when and where they are completed. There are other data sources we can use, for example, documents, but obtaining this data is more of question of assembly than collection.

As we shall see there are variations within each of these four categories and we shall meet these in the next two chapters. At this point we need only to know the circumstance in which each method is best used. Table 7.3 sets these out. However, before we discuss what these situations are, we should remember that if the circumstances require us to use a less appropriate alternative we have to reach a decision whether the compromise in data quality is so great as to undermine the validity of the measurement (and of our analysis and interpretation).

7.6.1 Questionnaires

The principal situation in which we use questionnaires is when we want to access a large number of people. Scale is particularly important for hypothesis-based quantitative research where we need minimum numbers in categories in order to draw statistically valid conclusions. In this situation, where we have to process large amounts of data, we need that data to be structured. Questionnaires do this admirably. Chapter 8 considers questionnaires in detail.

7.6.2 Interviews

Interviews can range from asking different respondents a series of common questions to a conversation around a topic. Their most important characteristic is flexibility. If a question is misunderstood, it can be rephrased. If a point is made that throws new light on an aspect of interest, then we can explore it further. It is this ability to re-ask questions that helps researchers establish whether they are being told the truth or a version of the truth that places the interviewee in a good light. This ability to probe and open up an issue is not the only reason for using an interview approach. The particular strength of the interview is that the respondent's voice is heard and the words chosen, the phrasing used, the pauses and exclamations, and the tone of the reply could all nuance the interpretation of the response. Interviews are dealt with in detail in Chapter 9.

7.6.3 Group interviews (focus groups) and discussions

Focus groups can be used at an early stage in an investigation to obtain insights prior to constructing a questionnaire. As a method of collecting data they can be used to gain a collective perspective speedily. Because a focus group is discussion based, it provides a way of establishing how stable people's views and opinions are. Its real strength, however, is that it can be used to explore the deeper significance of the responses given by members. It can be used to determine motives and values but this usually requires an approach that goes beyond discussion. We look at focus groups and how to manage them in Chapter 9.

7.6.4 Observation

Direct observation of people's actions, behaviour and attitude is an alternative to asking them about it. Observation is preferred when we are not sure that verbal responses (often from memory) will be accurate. This is especially true if the variable we are interested in alters in intensity or duration and not just presence or absence. For example, observation will show us how long a pupil's attention span was before signs of boredom set in. We can use observational approaches as well with groups whose ability to verbalise is limited. This would include young children and infants and people with profound or severe learning difficulties. Observation is dealt with in Chapter 9.

While it is appropriate to see these approaches as alternatives best suited to particular circumstance, we should also look at how they can be brought together in our research strategy to deliver better quality information. If our research is into awareness of drugs and drug use amongst 13- to 15-year-old children, a questionnaire given to an appropriate sample would give us the broad picture but a focus group would give us deeper insights and a richer picture. In this way we can combine scale and depth in our analysis and demonstrate that our detailed insights are applicable to a wider population.

7.7 What constitutes good data?

What we have learnt so far in this chapter is that we can model the issues in our research using a systems approach and, using this, we can identify the type of variable that we are dealing with. We know also that we use indicators of our variables to give us the data we need. All of this will point us to the right sort of data but we still have to determine how good the data are.

There are two ways of looking at 'goodness' in data terms. When both are satisfied, then we can say that we have good data.

- First, we require goodness in measurement. We need to be measuring what we expect to be measuring (that is, we have hit the right target).
- Second, we require that our data be susceptible to explanation. This is more about explanation than data but the two are connected. What are we looking for in terms of goodness in explanation? Very simply, our explanation should fit the facts. If we start our investigation with a model of what the situation might be (see section 7.3), data that supports the model meets the standard of goodness. With an inductive approach

to research, where examination of the data gives rise to interpretation and explanation, the criteria is met when the situation is found to be reproducible, that is, when other researchers reach the same conclusions using data from other studies. Meeting this standard of goodness in explanation is affected by the complexity of the issue, the more complex the issue, the harder it is to agree an explanation. And this is the reason we are introducing the idea of goodness in explanations at this stage – it has to be part of every researcher's consideration before data collection begins. This is why, in this chapter, we explained how to break down the research question. Case Study 7.6 gives an example of goodness in explanation at work. Goodness in explanation is actually quite a complex area of scientific philosophy which this short paragraph hardly does justice to. For more detail, read Peter Lipton's book on the topic (Lipton, 2004).

We have to be sure that we have measured accurately and with the right level of detail.

How do these two conditions actually work? If we are monitoring interactions amongst preschool children with a view to creating a typology of social development and if one of our measurements is 'spoke with other child/children', then this is likely to be a fairly blunt (and ineffective) measuring tool because it will not differentiate the child who spoke once from the ones who spoke many times, or the one who spoke to one other child from the one who spoke to different children. The consequence of this is that our second way of looking at goodness, goodness in explanation, is unlikely to be met because our data will not allow us to show how types and amounts of interaction are associated with types and levels of social development.

Before we move on to look at data collection in detail (in Chapters 8 and 9), we should be aware of how our data collection can go wrong. Goodness in measurement has two components – accuracy and precision. Together they ensure that our measurement of data is valid.

- *Accuracy* refers to the way in which we describe the attribute in which we are interested. For our measurement to be accurate, there must be a constant mathematical relationship between our measurement and the true value.
- *Precision* means that we or other researchers, using the same approach to gather data, should be able to replicate our measurements. This, of course, assumes that the context in time and place is unchanged. If it is not, then the change itself could be a variable.

Table 7.4 shows how accuracy and precision can interact in any investigation. Accuracy and precision have two states, either they are accurate or not accurate or precise or not precise. There are four possible combinations of these states. These combinations are shown as ticks (when data are accurate or precise) and crosses (when the data are not accurate or not precise). Out of the four possible combinations, only one is acceptable for analysis and for creating an explanation – when our data are both accurate and precise. In all other situations we have a problem. Imagine

Table 7.4 Combinations of accuracy and precision

	Accurate	Not accurate
Precise	✓✓	×✓
Not precise	×✓	××

Case study 7.6 Edging towards a good explanation

In the UK the academic attainment of boys is noticeably poorer than that of girls. The situation is broadly similar in many countries with an established and effectively functioning educational system. The question for us as researchers is how far is gender the cause of this and how far is it the consequence. For it to be the cause we would have to show that girls' intelligence (IQ) was greater than boys. This is a tall order. The best available evidence suggests that the differences are too small to account for the differences in performance. Because IQ tests are a compound indicator, there is a raised potential for measurement error but since different tests come up with broadly the same answers, we are unlikely to make much headway if we continue down a route dominated by genetic gender differences.

So, if not gender itself, what? These are the avenues that have been explored:

- **The subjects studied:** If males and females were to study different subjects, this could affect the results and produce the imbalance. Indeed, when we look at the data there is strong evidence for this. At 'A' level (the assessment level prior to entry to higher education), for example, the numbers of boys taking physics and chemistry has been significantly higher than girls for well over a decade (perhaps longer if we were to check the data). In 2006, the most popular 'A' level subject for boys was mathematics and, for girls, English. The issue for researchers is whether it is the way these are assessed that creates the gender gap (see below) or whether gender differences influence choice and/or performance. Again, there is evidence that girls' reading performance was better than boys', while boys performed better in problem solving tests. The issue for educational researchers is how far this represents a gender predilection for different ways of working that arises from a genetic blueprint, or is it just learnt behaviour?
- **Subject Assessments:** do different assessment cultures and practices have a part to play? Is an A grade in mathematics exactly the same as an A grade in history? This may be more of a factor in higher education (where institutions have more autonomy in assessment schemes) than in schools (where there is a stronger specification of national standards, though even here the approach to assessment between different subjects can vary).
- **Disaffection** could affect performance if we can show that more boys are identified as disaffected than girls. Indeed this is the case. If exclusion is used to indicate disaffection, then four times the number of boys are permanently excluded compared with girls. Disaffection works by reducing the time spent in class and the commitment to schooling. Disaffection must reduce the overall level of performance of boys relative to girls but (i) the proportion of children permanently excluded from secondary schools is only 0.24% of the school population (2005–6) while the number of children with fixed period exclusions (which will include many of those permanently excluded) is 10.40% and the question is whether this is sufficient to create the gender gap (ii) exclusion rates for 16–18 year olds drop significantly, yet the gender gap in performance at 'A' level remains (iii) is disaffection merely a symptom of something else?
- **Socio-economic status:** could be a further influence (and if it is, it is likely to interact with disaffection). Using the number of children who have free school meals as an indicator of status, those receiving free school meals have about 50% chance of reaching the national standard of attainment at age 16 compared with those not eligible from free school meals. However, for both groups, the gender gap still exists, so status is another route for us to explore, additional to gender.

Where are we beginning to look for deeper explanations of the gender gap? We are looking at family background and early years parenting practices; at family background and youth culture and the formation of the concepts of masculinity and femininity and at differences in approaches to learning (though how do these arise?). This list is not exhaustive and there is still much work to be done to explain the gender gap. There is an issue, though, whether it may be better, in the long run, to devote our resources to enhancing and supporting teaching and learning practice as a means of reducing the gap rather than try to fully understand why it arises in the first place.

a dartboard or circular target such as that shown in Figure 7.5. Our object is to hit the centre. If our aim were precise but not accurate, our darts would be clustered away from the centre, for example in the outer segment of number 1. If they were accurate but not precise, they would be distributed within the inner ring. If they were neither precise nor accurate, they would be spread randomly over the board. Only when they are clustered in the red bulls'-eye can we reasonably say that they are both random and accurate.

It is important, therefore, that we should be aware what the problems of measurement can be before we start.

(i) *What can go wrong in terms of accuracy?*

- Measurement problems can occur if more than one person is collecting the data. They may not be working to the same rubric, so it is important that the framework for data collection is specified in advance. This usually requires some preliminary work and pre-testing of the methodology. The same sort of problem can arise with a single investigator, who allows the basis for data collection to evolve.
- A second thing that can generate measurement inaccuracy is an interaction effect between researcher and those being researched. A desire to please may lead to a respondent giving more positive answers to questions. Hostility can have an opposite effect. Knowledge of being watched can lead to people behaving differently from normal. We will see how to manage this interaction effect at other points in chapters 8 and 9.
- Inaccuracy also occurs when the measuring instrument is erratic. A thermometer that does not register the correct temperature is of little use. Researchers can find that they have constructed a broken thermometer at any time but its likelihood is greater in two circumstances, the first, the measurement of attitudes on a numerical scale and the second, the construction of composite indicators. The

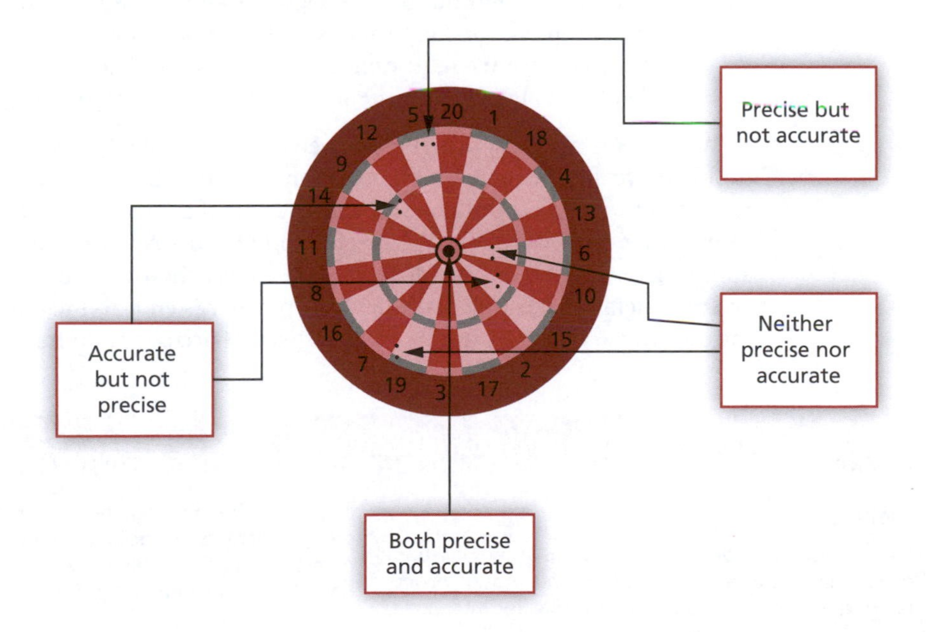

Figure 7.5 What is good data?

problem with attitude scaling is that we can never be sure that one person's 'very' is not another's 'quite'. Imagine two students doing a mathematics test. They get the same answers for each question and therefore the same test score. They were also asked to judge each question (the research was into whether the range of questions sufficiently discriminated between those with a high level of capability and those who were less capable). Where one answered very difficult or easy, the other answered quite difficult or easy. The inference is that they are making the same judgements but that they are using different terms to describe them. The problem for us is that these terms constitute our measurement scale. There are ways of establishing valid scales but they are not always applied. With composite scales there are two possible sources of error – what is included and how the elements are combined. For example, just how do we estimate value added in academic development and how do we combine this with something that is just as difficult to measure, the social responsibility of pupils? For some researchers, these are crucial issues and the best test of the validity of their estimates is the critical assessment and approval of peers.

(ii) *We can make errors in precision in the following ways:*

- First, they can arise because of poor sampling practices. If our sample is biased, with too many respondents in one group, then making the same mistake again will only produce the same result. The appropriateness of the sample design and the sampling procedure is crucial in guaranteeing the precision with which our data are obtained.
- Our data can also suffer if the methods we use to collect them are not robust enough for the purpose. We might, for example, ask children whether they have even been bullied and accept the answer 'yes' or 'no', when our research might require a categorisation of type and a measure of intensity. This is a consequence of using the wrong measurement scale. If we are investigating barriers to taking up training opportunities amongst unskilled mature workers, a questionnaire would capture *our* suppositions and perceptions while a focus group (or interview) is more likely to capture the feelings and concerns of the workers. The likelihood of error is greater with the first than with the second.

While there are ways of trying to overcome the difficulties set out above, the worst problem we face as a research community is not being sufficiently critical of the research output. We should be sure that the data that are produced are a valid portrayal of the issue. For this we need to be able to judge the selection of respondents and the appropriateness of the procedure used to collect the data. To do this, we must have access to detail that is often lacking. Transparency is crucial if research is to be convincing. Activity 7.3 takes us further into the issue of accuracy and transparency.

Activity 7.3 Accuracy and transparency

Part 1

As a research co-ordinator, you have to assign questionnaire administrators, interviewers and group leaders for data collection. You appreciate that for interviews, questionnaires administered by interview and focus groups there is a social interaction between those collecting the data and those giving it. You are also bound by legislation (and good practice) relating to

▶

equality of opportunity for the people who apply to work for you. In assigning people to the following data collection tasks, what would inform your decisions?

1. A survey of voter intentions in a multi-ethnic community.
2. The lives of women in a first generation, non-host language speaking immigrant community.
3. Rural lifestyles.

Part 2

Having thought about the factors that you should take into account in pairing data collectors with data providers, put the following term into any Web search engine: *interviewer response effect.* Make a list of all the interactions that researchers have tested and their significance.

Part 3

The final task in this activity is to identify at least ten papers dealing with an aspect or aspects of education that interest you and which use interviewers or group facilitators. For each one, consider whether there could have been an interviewer response effect. If so, is the possibility examined by the author(s)?

7.8 Taking stock and preparing for the next step

By this point in our research journey we should know the following:

- Whether we are going to deal with a whole population or just a sample.
- If a sample, how we are going to identify the people, organisations or groups to take part.
- Our research question and the detailed questions that point us to our data needs.
- How our variables might be (or are not) linked to each other.
- The attributes of the variables that we believe are relevant to our study.

Figure 7.6 represents this point in our journey. It shows that there are two areas of uncertainty that we have to resolve. We have to find the right sources to give us the data we need. If we do not have the right sources, we can never get the right data. We looked at this in Chapter 6. As well, we have to find the right data. How we go about this was the theme of this chapter. The process of finding the right data begins with our specification of the research issue or question. We have seen that there are many potential sources for this but most will take us through a literature search, the theme of Chapter 5. The next stage sees two decisions made in tandem. We determine our research approach and we dissect the research question. Unless our approach is pure induction, we should think of representing our thinking in diagrammatic terms. This allows us to define the nature of our variables. Finally, we have to deconstruct our complex variables to isolate the attributes necessary to resolve our research question. This allows us to determine the indicators.

While this may appear to be a straightforward sequence, we should bear in mind that solving our two areas of uncertainty, the right sources and the right data, are inextricably connected. We have to move between them, making sure that the decisions we make for one are compatible with the other. If they are not, then we must revisit our decisions and remove the incompatibilities. Only when we are confident that our procedures are robust can we move to the next stage, actually collecting our data.

It is important to understand that the foundations of our research should be deep and solid, so at this point we shall review what we have to do to ensure that this is the case.

- Is our research driven by moral principle or ethical purpose? We reviewed some positions that researchers have taken in section 2.1.1. The desire to achieve change in a situation is no bad thing but it presents dangers for researchers – of preferring some

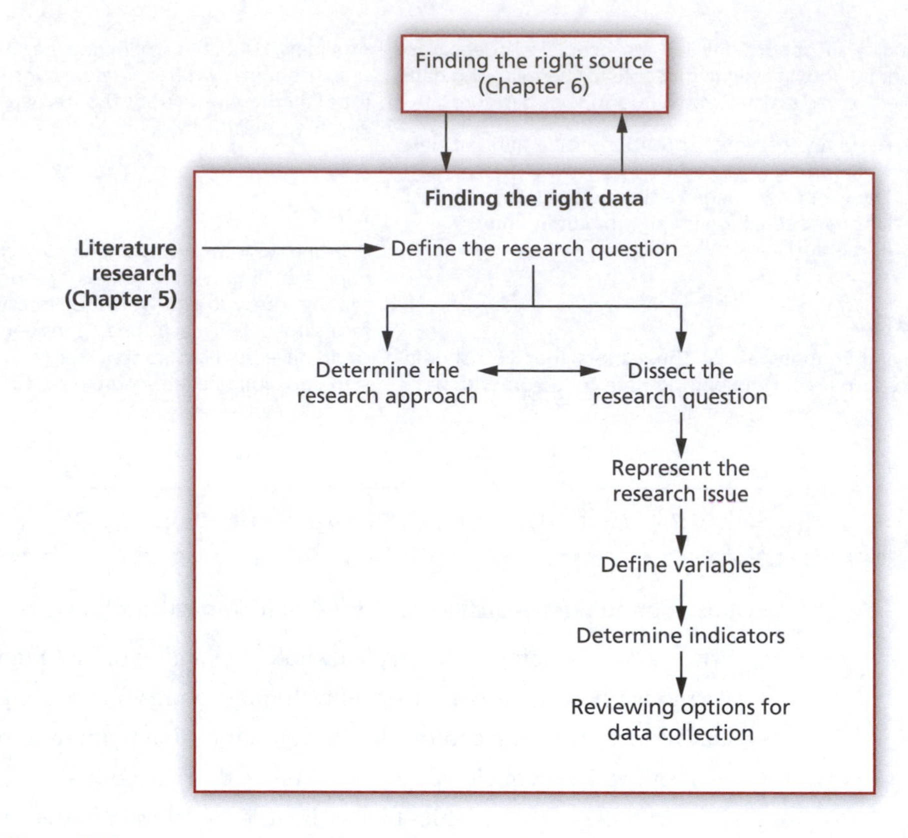

Figure 7.6 Operationalising the research question

data to others, of interpreting results in line with our views when other interpretations are also possible. The defence against this is to make our position clear and to ensure that our methodology is robust.

- The way we approach our research is influenced by a number of factors:
  - Do we believe that all research (or all research on this topic) should adopt a specific paradigm?
  - Do we think that we should adopt paradigms used by others?
  - Do we think that our approach should be determined by the circumstances of the issue, including the availability of data?

We looked in detail at quantitative and qualitative paradigms in Chapter 3. The issue for us as researchers is not about which one should we choose but whether there is no choice (because the one we use is determined by how we think research should be conducted). If our choice is not constrained, what we do is a response to the situation we face. The flexibility this implies, however, and the compromises we may be forced into, create dangers.

- Are we clear about our research question? We introduced this in section 2.2.5, where we related types of research question to particular research approaches. In this chapter we saw how important it was to break down the research question so that we could identify the variables at work and the indicators that would yield data.

- In Chapter 6 we saw how important it was to understand just how the data sources we would approach were representative of something. This is important if our research conclusions are to have any value or worth in another situation.
- In this chapter we learnt that the procedures we use to collect data can influence the quality of the data that we collect. Another pitfall for us to negotiate!

The consequence of all of this for our research is that we should move backwards and forwards, testing out our possible courses of action. If the research process has deep foundations, our own research methodology should have foundations that are equally deep. The consequence of this is that data collection should not proceed until all the ramifications have been explored and a way forward emerges that will produce good data.

Summary

- The quality of our research is determined by the quality of the data we collect. Quality data comes from the right people and is the right data to answer our research question.
- The link between the research question and the data we need has been the theme of this chapter. Modelling the research issues was introduced as a way of ensuring that we get to the right data.
- We saw how the process of 'questioning the question' enabled us to identify factors and influences that might be at work in our issue. We learnt that the proper term for 'factors' and 'influences' is *variable*.
- Variables can have different dimensions. For every dimension that is relevant to our investigation we need an *indicator*. Indicators describe variable attributes. We can draw on established compound indicators for complex variables.
- We judge how good our data are in terms of accuracy and precision.

Further reading

Systems modelling

Checkland, P. (1999) *Soft Systems Methodology: A 30-Year Retrospective and Soft Systems Thinking, Systems Practice*, Wiley, Chichester.

The name 'Peter Checkland' is synonymous with systems modelling. His work focuses on 'soft systems', essentially a process developed to cope with questions or problems where there is no clear answer. This, for instance, could be, 'How do we reduce teenage pregnancy?' In this book, Checkland describes the origins and development of soft systems thinking as a preface to the text published 20 years ago. The process he describes is easy to understand and highly applicable to educational research.

Goodness in explanation

Lipton, P. (2004) *Inference to the Best Explanation*, Routledge, London.

Peter Lipton's text on scientific philosophy is readable and the arguments he sets out are attractive and reflect the way that, intuitively, many researchers appear to work. The argument rests on the link between explanation and evidence. Assuming that the evidence is correct, then out of all explanations there will be a 'best explanation'. Much of social science research is likely to work within this framework. If circumstantial evidence of a crime points a finger at a particular person and no others, the best explanation we have is that they did it. What this comes down to is that in seeking to explain something, we collect data that we use to accept that our explanation is correct.

References

Estes, R. (2003) 'European Social Development Trends: Development Challenges of the "New Europe"' in Vogel, J. (ed.), 'Good Times and Hard Times in Sweden During the 1990s', *Report 100: Living Conditions Series,* Statistics Sweden, 435–468 (available at http://www.sp2.upenn.edu/~restes/praxis/Estes_Papers.html).

Holtkamp, L., Irby, B.J., Brown, G. and Yang, L. (2007) 'Validation of the Synergistic Leadership Theory', *Journal of Research for Educational Leaders*, 4(1), 102–138 (available at www.education.uiowa.edu/jrel).

Ireson, J., Hallam, S. and Hurley, C. (2005) 'What are the Effects of Ability Grouping on GCSE Attainment?', *British Educational Research Journal*, 31(4), 443–458.

Kelle, U. (1997) 'Theory Building in Quantitative Research and Computer Programs for the Management of Textural Data', *Sociological Research Online*, 2(2) (available at http://www.socresonline.org.uk/socresonline/2/2/1.html).

Koskela, M., Killti, P., Vilpola, I. and Ternoven, J. (2005) 'Suitability of a Virtual Learning Environment for Higher Education', *Electronic Journal of e-Learning,* 3(i), 21–30 (available at www.ejel.org).

Lipton, P. (2004) *Inference to the Best Explanation,* Routledge.

Marks, G.N. (2006) 'Influences on, and the Consequences of, Low Achievement', *Australian Educational Researcher*, 33(1), 95–115 (available at www.aare.edu.au/aer/contents.htm).

Mayston, D. (2006) *Educational Value and Programme Evaluation*, Research Report RW87, DfES.

Stokes, A. (2007) 'Factors influencing the decisions of university students to become high school teachers', *Issues in Educational Research*, 17(1), 127–145.

Usang, B., Akuegwu, B., Udida, L. and Koley, F. (2007) 'Academic Staff Research Productivity: A Study of Universities in South-South Zone of Nigeria', *Educational Research and Review,* 2(5), 103–108 (available at www.academicjournals.org/ERR).

Chapter contents

Chapter 8

USING QUESTIONNAIRES

Key themes

- The types of question we can construct.
- How to administer questionnaires and get them to respondents.
- How to generate a good response.
- How to collect good data.
- Thinking about data analysis as part of questionnaire design.

Introduction

Questionnaires are amongst the most popular of data gathering instruments. We encounter them on a regular basis in our daily lives. They come unsolicited through the post and appear as pop-ups on our computer screens. With so many questionnaires in existence, we might think that they are easy to put together and effective as a way of obtaining data. However, one of their most common characteristics is that they are poorly constructed. We can find problems with the way questions are asked and there are many examples of poor layout, such as routes through the questionnaire that take respondents to a dead end before the questions are finished and questions that do not allow for all possible responses. Like a scalpel in a surgeon's hands, a questionnaire needs a sensitive touch. In this section we shall learn what to do in order to produce a questionnaire that will get us good data to work with.

8.1 Constructing the question

There are two broad categories of question that we can use, closed questions and open questions. Each is used in particular circumstances for specific tasks and most questionnaires are a blend of the two.

8.1.1 Closed or structured questions

These are questions that are constructed in such a way that the respondent has no leeway in terms of a personalised input. All the responses fall into categories that are determined beforehand by the researcher. In terms of the character of the data collection, the respondent finds the questions easy and relatively quick to answer. They are, therefore, effective in obtaining a large data harvest. From the viewpoint of the researcher, collation of the responses is straightforward and the data can be entered readily into a spreadsheet for subsequent processing and analysis. Typically we would use closed questions to obtain data about gender or age, to ask people to rate something on a scale ('How far do you agree with the following statements . . . ?') or to rank a series of options ('Please place the following criteria parents might use in selecting a secondary school for their child in rank order, 1 for the most important . . .).

8.1.2 Open or unstructured questions

Open questions, in contrast, have no response framework imposed on them by the researcher. Respondents are given space where they can answer the question in their own words. Open questions are valuable in giving a sense of the respondent's open voice, though we cannot be absolutely sure of this because they may have been affected by the experience of completing the questionnaire. For instance, if we are answering questions on an emotive issue such as the transportation of food and flowers around the world, we might initially think that the environmental impact means that we should buy things that are locally sourced. However, if the questions also cover what we know about the system of production and the significance of the trade for the lives of those who work in the sectors, we might begin to think that the economic development and the impact on people's life chances for poor parts of the world outweigh the environmental considerations. Completing such a questionnaire may affect the position we adopt.

As researchers we use open questions to do certain things.

- First, we can use them to obtain a richer picture of some aspect under investigation. If we were researching the demand for early years childcare, it would be important to understand what factors influenced parental choice. A question such as, 'Please describe how you went about selecting your childcare?' would give us the data in the respondents' own words (and the space we leave in the questionnaire is an indication of the detail we want).
- Second, we want to be sure that the structured questions we have asked have not omitted a significant response. We can often do this by adding a category 'other' to our list and asking those who mark it to give some detail. On other occasions we can ask a supplementary question. If part of our questionnaire is concerned with the workload of teachers and we have asked questions on the number of hours worked in

the past week and what they did, we could finish the section by asking them how typical this was and their views on their work/life balance.

- Third, we usually want to use direct quotes from respondents that they give in open questions to reveal insights and to give personality to a written report. Not only does this provide an authentic voice, it adds emotion and passion and enables us to convey in a powerful way issues and perspectives that are important to the interpretation and explanation.

Table 8.1 gives examples of open and closed questions. All the closed questions give no freedom to respondents to reply in their own ways. Closed questions can be used for straightforward categorisation (Are you male/female?), to collect information about which people might feel sensitive if you asked them to give specific quantities (for example, income, age) and to extend people's thinking about an issue (factors influencing university choice). We should be aware that responses to some questions (such as income) frequently contain an aspirational element. We should check whether there has been overstatement by benchmarking our results against national surveys of income. Open

Table 8.1 Types of question

Closed questions	Open questions
• Are you: male ☐ female ☐	• What do you think are the three most important things that make for a good lecture? 1. 2. 3.
• Please indicate how much income from all sources (e.g. from parents, regular part-time work) you receive each week under £5 ☐ between £5 and £10 ☐ between £10.01 and £20 ☐ between £20.01 and £30 ☐ between £30.01 and £40 ☐ between £40.01 and £50 ☐ between £50.01 and £70 ☐ over £70 ☐	• What are your favourite school meals?
• Please identify the five most important factors in terms of their importance in choosing a university at which to study. Place 1 next to the factor you think most important, 2 next to the second most important and so on. • The university's reputation ——— • The department's reputation ——— • The research done in the department ——— • The department's quality assurance rating ——— • The number of applications for each place ——— • What the department says about teaching and learning ——— • The success of students in getting jobs ——— • The quality of the social life ——— • The town it is in ——— • How close it is to my home ———	• Tell us how the building work at school affected you. • What do you think are the principal issues that the college has to address?

questions can be structured (limiting people to three factors) but, whatever format, all allow people to use their own words. This, however, is an issue if people's ability to express their thoughts is limited. Certainly age is a factor to consider here; responses from young children should normally be obtained in ways other than questionnaires. And if we are researching learning disability, we should consider whether questionnaires are the most appropriate means of collecting data. Language capability may also be a limiting factor in using questionnaires if we are dealing with lower socio-economic groups or people with low educational attainment. It certainly will be a factor if a response is expected in a language other than someone's first language (for example, if a South Asian or East European parent whose English is limited is asked to respond in English).

Our choice of whether to use open or closed questions should be determined by the issue, by the respondents we expect to have and by the balance between the two types that we want in our questionnaire as a whole. There is no compelling evidence that one or the other is better at collecting quality data. Indeed, the evidence is rather more robust in suggesting that they are equally good. An American research group led by Howard Schuman explored this issue in the context of how people perceived the threat of nuclear war (Schuman, 1986). They concluded that while open questions produced a larger range of responses, the categories they formed were small in size. In other words, the responses were highly individual. If there is interest in obtaining a greater breadth of response within a closed question structure, the method is to add 'other' as a category and to ask respondents to add detail.

While Table 8.1 gives a hint about the types of information that we can collect, it is worth going into this in more detail. We will do this in the next section.

8.2 Accessing information

In this section we will look at types of information and what sorts of questions are suitable for accessing them. It is worth refreshing our memory about the framework within which we are working in order to clarify the difference between data and information. We first met it in Chapter 6. The framework is shown in Figure 8.1. Our purpose in asking questions is to get at the information that we know (or hope) exists and which will help us resolve our research issue. The information we hope exists is defined by the research issue. We identify the information that we think will be useful to us and phrase

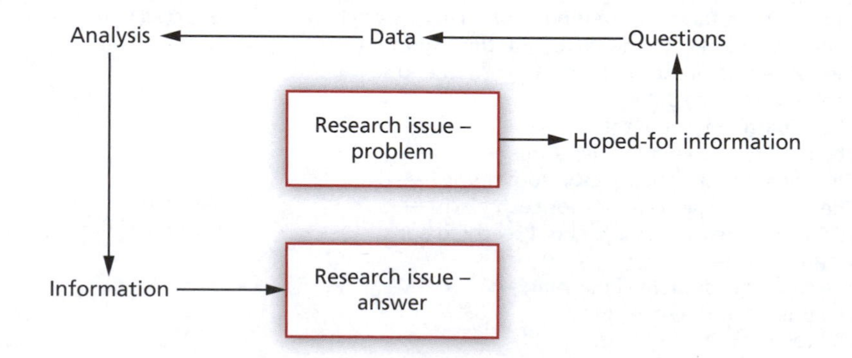

Figure 8.1 Data and information in the research framework

our questions to obtain it. Once we have asked our questions, we collect data. The purpose of our analysis is to release the information content of the data and use it to provide some sort of answer to our research problem.

With this background, let us now look at what types of information we might be interested in. Table 8.2 shows types of information and the question type that can be used to gather it.

Table 8.2 Information types and question types

Information type	Question type
Factual knowledge	Both closed and open.
Understanding	Principally open but scenario choices can be constructed for closed questions.
Schemas and mental models	Both closed and open.
Analysis	Both closed and open.
Implementation of ideas	More likely to be open but scenario choices can be constructed for closed questions.
Values	Both closed (select options) and open.

(i) Information about people's factual knowledge

This includes basic questions such as age, questions about behaviour (When did you last skip school?) and events of experiences (What happened at the staff meeting? What do you think happened when the pupils left?) Knowledge information requires recall by and sometimes conjecture (for what people *think* they know). It can be collected using closed or open questions. Which ones are used depends on other factors such as the scale of the research and the resources available for preparing the data for processing – the fewer the resources, the less attractive are open questions, because it takes a great deal of time to organise and analyse the responses. Much of the information sought by researchers will be knowledge based.

(ii) Information about what people understand

Understanding requires conjecture. The sort of question we might ask is, 'Why do you think that happened? Why do you think the School Governors voted against the proposal?' With these questions respondents have to assess a range of circumstances and to make a judgement that places an event in context. It is, by implication, a higher level of analysis and decision making that is taking place. It is possible to construct scenarios from which respondents can make a selection but most researchers are likely to opt for open questions.

(iii) Information about people's schemas and mental constructs

This information requires subjects to apply one set of information to another. If our researcher is interested in school organisation and management, we could ask teachers to give three examples of strong leadership or to judge whether senior management decisions constituted strong leadership. In these cases we are asking them to assess situations against a model that they have. If we were to ask pupils about the importance they placed on the subjects they studied, we would be asking them to apply a model and we might be interested in this to see how it was related to performance and behaviour. It is possible, with this type of information, to construct response frameworks that cover the judgements that people might make and so make use of closed questions. However, free response with open questions (and subsequent classification) is also possible.

(iv) Information arising from people's analysis of situations

We are likely to generate analytic information when we ask people to explain choices, preferences or to explore alternatives. Research for policy is, for example, likely to require analytic information. If a school were thinking of changing its academic structure from a departmental system to a faculty system or its pastoral structure from a year-based system to a house-based system, we would want to know what our staff thought were the strengths and weaknesses, costs and benefits of each. Again, we can use both open, free response questions and closed questions (where we list the strengths, weaknesses, costs and benefits and ask staff to make their selections).

(v) Information exploring implementation of ideas: capability and values in action

This information is particularly important in problem-based research (for example, a college that has received a poor quality report or a school that is thinking how to work co-operatively and effectively with social services) and policy research (how can we deliver an effective anti-bullying policy). The sort of question we would ask here is, 'How would you . . .?', 'What would happen if . . .?', 'What is the best way . . . ?' The questions go beyond knowledge to ideas. They are more likely to be open than closed but it would be possible to construct alternative outcomes or scenarios and ask people to choose, which would be better. In looking at the answers to this sort of question, we have to assess how far respondents are making a disinterested judgement and how far they are expressing a preference (which reflects self-interest).

(vi) Information about values and judgements

Here we are interested in (a) exposing people's judgements and (b) exploring those judgements as a means of identifying their values. Getting people to express agreement or disagreement with a point of view, or a decision or an action or a policy, falls into this category as does expressing preference for a set of alternatives. For example, faced with a major financial deficit, a university might ask lecturers to prioritise possible actions such as asking full-time staff to teach more hours, asking full-time staff to have more students in their classes, deciding not to run low enrolment classes – all in the expectation that the salary bill for part-time staff would fall. We could ask pupils whether they approve of school policies on bullying, exclusion, unauthorised absence and we could present them with complex scenarios that test their judgements in ambivalent situations (a girl excluded for persistent lateness and non-attendance resulting from her taking on the role of primary carer for her siblings – and keeping the situation to herself).

Understanding the types of information we can access gives us a different perspective on questionnaire design. It helps us think about our research and places at the forefront of the process the need to answer the question, 'What do we need to know?' By understanding that there are types of information, we can ask ourselves which ones we might need in our research and once we have identified the need for a particular type of information, it (a) is often far easier to identify who might be in a position to give it to us and (b) makes it more straightforward to draft the questions. Activity 8.1 provides an opportunity to think about these issues.

We are now in a position when we can think about the phrasing of the question. We know the broad types of question we can use and we should know the nature of the information we need. We may think that asking a question is straightforward but as you might have guessed, it can be tricky.

8.3 Using the right words in your question: the problem

If you have not constructed a questionnaire before, this may seem a strange title for a section whose relevance is not immediately apparent. After all, if we want to know something, we just ask it. Actually, it is not as simple as this. There is a wealth of evidence that

Activity 8.1 Designing a questionnaire to explore lifestyles

The context for many of the decisions that school teachers have to make and the actions they take about the children for whose education they are responsible are the lifestyles and social and family circumstances of those children. While this context is important at all ages, it is particularly potent for young people on the edge of adulthood. Sometimes researchers want to know aspects of this context in order to better understand the issue (for example, if the issue were underperformance, it would be valuable to know about paid work, socialising and exposure to drink and drugs). It is also valuable for teachers, especially if they have a pastoral role, to have insights into the lives teenagers lead.

Imagine that you have been asked by a teachers' union to design a questionnaire that can be used by teachers to appreciate the lifestyles of their pupils. The intention is that head teachers should be a able to authorise its use in their schools. You are not required at this stage to produce the questions. What the Steering Committee of the project wishes to see are the types of information you think will give teachers the insights they require. Using the framework outlined in section 9.3, outline the information you would collect to indicate the young people's social life outside school. For this age group (16–18), the Steering Committee has also asked for some sense of how prepared young people are to enter an adult world. Your initial thoughts are that you might explore their knowledge of the political system, their commitment to family and willingness to share in family life, their feelings about prejudice and their moral values. What sort of information would help you here? As you start to untangle the issues in your own mind, go back to the information framework and ask:

- What facts do I need to know about their lives and lifestyles?
- For which issues do I need to show whether their understanding is accurate?
- Are there any schemas or mental constructs that I need to expose?
- Do I need to ask them to analyse situations or events? If so, where will this help meet my brief?
- Are there any areas where appreciating the young people's values are important?

In your exploration of the issue, you may decide that some types of information are not required. If so, explain to yourself how and why you reached this decision.

Because understanding the lives of young people is so important, you will not be surprised to learn that a survey similar to the one you have been thinking about was conducted in 1998 and 2003 in the UK (except Northern Ireland). You should look at the 2003 Young Person's Social Attitudes Survey questionnaire to see what sorts of information the researchers felt was required and compare it with your own. The two will almost certainly be different but that does not mean that yours is not as good. The Young Person's Social Attitudes Survey is available at: //qb.soc.survey.ac.uk/surveys/ypsa/ypsa03.htm.

For background on youth policy and studies in the Netherlands, visit the website of the Netherlands Youth institute at http://www.youthpolicy.nl/.

the words we use in constructing a question affect the responses that we get. If we have a belief that we want other people to sign up to, this is very useful knowledge because we can manipulate respondents to answer in a particular way. It is also important knowledge for honest researchers who have an ethical commitment to reveal the facts as they find them because we have to make sure that we do not unintentionally bias our results.

Let us look at some evidence of this issue because this will give us an insight into good practice in question phrasing. In a discussion paper on survey questionnaire construction issued by the US Census Bureau, the author, Elizabeth Martin, gives an example (Martin, 2006, p. 3). A national sample of people in the USA were randomly assigned one of two questions on free speech:

- *Question 1:* Do you think the United States should *allow* public speeches against democracy?
- *Question 2:* Do you think the United States should *forbid* public speeches against democracy?

One word was changed – from the positive 'allow' to the negative 'forbid' but the result was that 20 per cent more people who answered Question 2 were in favour of free speech than for Question 1.

Another example, this time on attitudes to euthanasia, was reported by a group of Swedish Researchers led by Joakim Hagelin (Hagelin et al., 2004). Again the method was to give two groups of respondents different questions. One group was given three options to reflect attitudes to euthanasia: 'positive', 'negative' and 'don't know'; the other was given five options: that there should be 'no legal sanctions' for euthanasia (that is, it should be permitted) and four types of legal penalty, with some explanation of the circumstances in which they would be applied. 'Don't know' was not offered as an option. The responses are shown in Table 8.3. What can we tell from this?

- First, people were more prepared to respond to a general question about euthanasia than to a specific question about its legality. Only 2 per cent did not respond to questionnaire 1, while 10 per cent did not respond to questionnaire 2. (Note, the percentages in the response categories are percentages of those who chose to respond, not of the whole sample.)
- Second, the proportion supporting a legal penalty for euthanasia (and, by implication opposing euthanasia) in questionnaire 2 was far higher than those who expressed a negative attitude in questionnaire 1.

Table 8.3 How attitudes to euthanasia are affected by question type

Per cent of respondents choosing different options			
Questionnaire 1		Questionnaire 2	
Positive	43	No legal sanction	38
Negative	14	All penalty options	62
Don't know	43	—	
Per cent of sample who did not respond			
	2		10

- Third, suppressing the 'don't know' category forced those with this attitude either not to respond or to oppose euthanasia. Whoever said that attitudes were stable?

The implications of these two studies are significant for questionnaire design. They show quite unequivocally that:

- The tone of the question (general versus specific) can influence the number of respondents who are prepared to voice an opinion.
- The way we phrase the question can affect the responses we get. This is particularly true if the issue polarises opinion.
- 'Don't know' as a response category is a lazy option for some respondents. If we use it in our questionnaires, we need to be certain that it is a genuine option and we should develop a device that seeks to prevent a 'lazy response' by our subjects. For example, we could ask them to explain why they marked the 'don't know' category.

For a third example of the impact of question phrasing, read Case Study 8.1. Perhaps more than the others, this brings home the significance of the way in which we use words.

From these examples, what are the issues that we have to be aware of?

1. Where there is confusion about an issue (praying and smoking) or where the issue is emotive, the way we word questions is important. This does not mean that it is not important for other questions, only that it is less likely to have an impact.
2. Different ways of phrasing questions (positive/negative, reflecting general attitudes/exploring penalties) may tap different dimensions of a complex issue and may not be true alternatives to each other.
3. The whole question of the words we use is surrounded by a high level of uncertainty. While we can understand that people are more prepared to allow things than to forbid them, circumstances may change this. High levels of concern about terrorism, for example, might see more people prepared to forbid free speech. Where there is potential for uncertainty, this must be tackled before the questionnaire is given to people. This is an important issue that is only rarely reflected in published research that uses questionnaires. Where there is a possibility that it exists, good practice suggests that questions ought to be asked in different formulations at a pre-test stage and only used if the responses are more or less the same. If they are not, then more investigation is required before an appropriate version of the question materialises.

Case study 8.1 Questions: it's how we ask them

One of the classic texts on questionnaire design is by Seymour Sudman and Norman Bradburn. Sadly it is little referenced now, mainly, I suspect, because it was first published in 1982. (There is a revised edition published in 2004.) However, their work provides truly valuable insights into the complex area of how to ask good questions. They bring the importance of this home with the story that follows.

> Two priests, a Dominican and a Jesuit, are discussing whether it is a sin to smoke and pray at the same time. After failing to reach a conclusion, each goes off to consult his respective superior. The next week they meet again. The Dominican says, 'Well, what did your superior say?' The Jesuit responds, 'He said it was all right.' 'That's funny,' the Dominican replies, 'my Superior said it was a sin.' Jesuit: 'What did you ask him?' Reply: 'I asked him if it was all right to smoke while praying.' 'Oh,' says the Jesuit, 'I asked my superior if it was all right to pray while smoking.'

Source: Asking Questions: A Practical Guide to Questionnaire Design, Sudman, S. and Bradburn, N.M. (1982) Jossey Bass, p. 1.

8.4 Using the right words: guidance on using existing questions

Constructing questionnaires is not all doom and gloom. We do face uncertainty and we may be confronted with problems that appear insuperable but there is guidance that is likely to give us a smoother ride.

The first thing we should do is to find out whether someone has written a question similar to the one we want to ask. We should not create new questions just for the sake of it. Questions with a pedigree are valuable because it means that other researchers have found that they deliver the data required. Where do we get these questions from? There are two principal sources.

8.4.1 Question banks

These are similar to data archives except that the emphasis is on access to the questions and not necessarily the results of asking these questions. Table 8.4 gives some useful online sources. The purpose in looking at these sources is not to find a complete questionnaire that we can use but to find individual questions that target an indicator we are interested in. Why bother to construct a new question on ethnic identity when many national surveys already have perfectly good ones? The Economic and Social Research Council (ESRC) database is searchable by topic, by survey and by year. It accesses questions from a large set of public surveys, many of which are relevant to educational researchers. The iPoll database holds US public opinion polls stretching back 65 years. This is an enormous wealth of questions. While it is clearly a significant resource, it is a subscription service. DANs is the Dutch Data Archiving and Networked Services website. It contains not only questions but also the data that is collected. It is similar to the UK Data Archive in that individual researchers can deposit their survey instruments and data (see Case Study 4.3 for more on data archives). The searchable archive uses a 'fuzzy' logic, which means that it searches terms and concepts similar to the one put into the search box. While there is an English version of the site, which can be searched in English, the results are mainly in Dutch. As an alternative to searching, the data sets can be browsed by subject area: life sciences and medicine, humanities, social sciences, behavioural sciences and socio-cultural sciences. Data are presented in SPSS (Statistical Programme for the Social Sciences) formats. STILE is a specialist database, Statistics and Indicators on the Labour Market in the e-Economy. Its archive is structured by language, by country and by topic. While many of the substantive questions are of little relevance to educationalists, diligent searching will identify questions on, for example, training,

Table 8.4 A selection of question banks

Name	Web address
ESRC Question Bank (UK)	qb.soc.surrey.ac.uk
IPOLL Databank	www.ropercenter.uconn.edu
DANS – Data Archiving and Networked Services (Netherlands)	www.dans.knaw.nl/en/
Finnish Social Science Data Archive	www.fsd.uta.fi/english/index.html
STILE	www.stile.be/surveydb/

equal opportunities, health and safety and such contextual areas for education as social exclusion and flexible working. The Finnish Social Science Data Archive allows searching and browsing by title, by topic and by key word. Topic themes relevant to educationalists include child research, education, educational psychology, educational research, family studies and youth studies. Data are not available on-line but have to be ordered.

8.4.2 Individual researchers

The second source of questions is to approach the researchers who used them. To do this, first we usually identify relevant journal articles. On occasion questions themselves are printed in the journal article and often the gist of questions can be inferred from the text. While the latter may be acceptable, it will not give us the actual wording of questions. For this we have to approach authors directly. Many have contact details in the journal. If this is our first research project, it is possibly unwise to do this without the support and guidance of our research supervisor. This will improve our chances of a successful outcome. If we decide to approach people we have to be sure that their research is relevant to ours, that their questions might be useful and that we appear credible in their eyes. If someone emailed me asking, 'Please send me all you have on . . .' (or words to that effect), my response would be (if I had one), 'Get real. Do the work yourself'.

We should not feel that it is more important to develop questions ourselves rather than use ones developed by someone else. This is now established policy for UK Government statistics, where the platform of sharing the same question amongst different surveys is called 'harmonisation' (see www.statistics.gov.uk/about/data/harmonisation).

There are three reasons for sharing questions. First, the value of the questions has been proven. They deliver good data because respondents understand them. The second reason is no less important. They act as a bridge between different enquiries. They allow those enquiries to be knitted together to make something that is potentially bigger than the separate parts. Finally, two (or more) different surveys asking the same question act as a check on each other's accuracy. If the results of one differ by more than an acceptable margin of error, then the survey process can be reviewed to see if anything has gone wrong or to establish if there is a change in the conditions that the questions probe. If we, as individual researchers, use established questions, then these benefits are open to us.

With the existence of transnational surveys and data sets (see, for example Case Study 8.2 on Eurostat) and as the Internet allows researchers in one country to research a topic in the context of results from other countries, there is an issue of whether questions work properly if translated from one language to another. There is some research on this and while it is the field of health and not education the findings are likely to be generally valid. Arnold Huisman (a Dutch medical researcher) and his co-workers (Huisman, 2007) translated a questionnaire from English to Dutch and assessed its effectiveness. The English questionnaire looked at the impact on patients' quality of life of a chronic cough (that is, one lasting more than eight weeks). The English questionnaire was structured for self-completion by patients. It was translated into Dutch twice by two different researchers. The results were combined. To test the effectiveness of their translation, it was translated back into English by a native English speaker. The original and the translation from the Dutch were virtually identical. Having established the accuracy of the translation, the questionnaire was given to Dutch patients together with other health outcomes questionnaires. The research team then analysed the patient responses from all surveys and were able to show that:

- the outcomes as measured by the questionnaire reflected the measurements of other health outcome questionnaires;

Case study 8.2 Developing a European perspective

International comparative studies could be the subject of a textbook in its own right. They can be fraught with difficulties, the main one being to ensure data are sufficiently comparable to allow them to be compared. This means, for example, having to adjust data to compensate for differences in definition, or to make allowances for the geographical scale of the data units or for the fact that time periods are not the same. Many of these problems disappear or become less significant when countries agree to work to common standards. Delivering these common standards has been one of the great achievements of Eurostat, the European Statistics Agency.

To appreciate the scale of the achievement, it is necessary to explore the Eurostat website[1]. As an example, however, we might look at the data on education and training (a subset of population and social conditions). There are data sets on levels of education, school enrolment, students, foreign languages, expenditure and lifelong learning. Each area is further broken down. Expenditure, for instance, has information on spending on human resources, annual expenditure per student, private expenditure on education as a percentage of GDP and total expenditure on education. Each set of tables is backed up by a comprehensive set of definitions and frequently, reference to the UOE Data Collection Manual[2] (see below). This is where the link to questionnaire design becomes important. The definitions of terms are usually based on the International Standard Classification of Education, ISCED 1997, developed initially by UNESCO. UOE questionnaires are statistical returns developed for common use by the OECD, UNESCO and the EU and conforming to ISCED definitions. These definitions should be central to the frameworks for data collection that we, as educational researchers, use.

It is important to point out, though, that for educational researchers, the real benefit of Eurostat is access to comparable data over a large geographical area and with the ability to explore education data at a regional (sub-national level), where the regions are defined so that they can be compared, then the possibilities for combining and comparing regions and for looking at education in different social and economic contexts becomes immense.

[1]http://epp.eurostat.ec.europa.eu

[2]http://www.uis.unesco.org/template/pdf/wei/Manuals/UOE2007manual_volume%201.pdf

- the level of variation in patient responses to individual sets of questions was low;
- when patients were given the questionnaire on a second occasion, shortly after the first, their answers were largely the same; and
- when patients whose coughs had improved were given the questionnaire again, the improvement was reflected in their responses.

The conclusion we draw from this is that when a questionnaire is an effective instrument for collecting data in one language, it is likely to be as effective in another language if it is well translated, that is, when linguistic equivalence is established. This issue is one that should particularly concern educational researchers dealing with cross-cultural international comparisons.

8.5 Using the right words: guidance on keeping it simple

Realistically, however, for much research in education, we cannot use existing questions and we have to construct specific questions to meet our specific data collection needs. When we have to do this, there is one principle that should guide us – keep things simple. This way most people will understand most things. But what do we have to do to achieve this?

8.5.1 Match the vocabulary and ideas to the respondent

When we construct questions we need to have in mind the sorts of people we shall be talking to because people's command of language can be very different. For example, a non-native speaker may well have a narrower range of vocabulary and a weaker grasp of grammar (for example, tenses) than a native speaker. And the reality is that not all native speakers will be the same either. Age, the level of education received, the type of job, social background, where someone lives are all clues that researchers should use in order to phrase a question appropriately. If we were exploring how pupils felt about school, the questionnaire we would use for a 9-year-old should be very different from the one we would use with a 14-year-old. If our research were into lifelong learning amongst unskilled and semi-skilled workers, the questionnaire could be quite different from one given to school teachers. The key points to bear in mind when developing a question for a particular group or set of respondents are:

- be aware of the likely reading habits of our targets – as a guide UK tabloid newspapers have a reading age of about 12. (Reading age tests used in education compare the achievement of any single child with that of a representative sample of children in a specified age range. The underlying assumption is that reading improves with age, though whether our reading capability at age 40 is much different from that at age 20 is a debatable point. Reading ages are not normally calculated for beyond age 15 or 16. Some tests (for example, Wide Range Achievement Test) evaluate capability in basic skills and can be used with older people);
- be aware of our respondents' appreciation of the issues – parents, for example, may be able to explain how they chose a school for their child but may find it difficult to comment on what principles a school should use to select its pupils;
- be aware of our own reading capability and understanding – do not use jargon, technical words, abbreviations that are part of your world but are not likely to be known by your target respondents.

8.5.2 Keep it short and simple

The reasons for making questions short and straightforward can best be appreciated by thinking what they would be like if they were long and complicated. They would, in technical terms, give rise to cognitive overload, that is, they would be hard to understand. Respondents would have to think about what the question was driving at before they could begin to answer it and in this situation there is always a chance that some might misunderstand. What specific guidance can we give?

(i) *Do not introduce more than one issue or idea into the question.* If the question were, 'Do you think before-school supervision and activity and after-school supervision and activity should be provided on school premises to help working parents and should they pay?', we can imagine the confusion: where one or both of the parents do not work, they could either say 'we do not need it' and answer 'no' or be altruistic and answer 'yes'. Where a parent can deliver a child to school but not collect them, they might say 'yes' (because over provision is better than no provision) or they might say 'no' (because only after school care is required). Parents requiring provision at both ends of the school day are likely to answer 'yes'. But all of these answers are complicated by the addition of 'and should they pay?' Some parents might think that being at school should be a free good, others might think that payment should be related to income. Others might worry that 'I'll have to pay more if others pay less'. The outcome is that whatever the responses, all the researcher will get to analyse is a mess.

(ii) *Do not be long-winded or over-explain.* If a question is too long, it may be difficult for a respondent to deconstruct it, identify its essence and then assess how other elements relate to it. Elizabeth Martin (Martin, 2006) gives the following example:

> During the past 12 months, since January 1, 1987, how many times have you seen or talked with a doctor or assistant about your health? Do not count any times you might have seen a doctor while you were a patient in hospital, but count all other times you actually saw or talked to a medical doctor of any kind about your health.

It is possible to convert this into something like a decent question. If we start with the completely redundant elements, we can get rid of the last part of the last sentence, after 'but'. This has the advantage of removing the confusion between a doctor and medical doctor (we still have the uncertainty as to what an 'assistant' is). The phrase 'might have seen' is confusing. Either we saw a doctor or we did not. If we want a 'rough idea' (never a good strategy), we will keep 'During the past 12 months' and delete 'since January 1, 1987' but if we want precision we will do the reverse. What is left is likely to generate data we can work with. The question then becomes:

> Since January 1, 1987, how many times have you seen or talked with a doctor about your health? Do not count any times you saw a doctor while you were a patient in hospital.

8.5.3 Never resort to double negatives

If we use double negatives respondents will have to think deeply about what is being asked and some will invariably get the interpretation wrong. Imagine a questionnaire where respondents are asked: 'Do you agree or disagree with the following statements. Please tick the appropriate box.'

- The first statement, 'Teachers should provide weekly reports on their pupils' is relatively straightforward. If we disagree, then we can say, 'Teachers should not provide weekly reports.'
- The second statement is more problematic, 'Teachers should not be expected to provide individual tuition to pupils outside timetabled sessions'. How can we express our disagreement with this? 'Teachers should not be expected not to provide . . .' or 'Teachers should not be expected . . .' We know what we want to say, 'Teachers should be expected to provide . . .' but the process of constructing a double negative to construct a positive creates a barrier.

8.5.4 Keep it short

The problem with long questions, other than the fact that respondents might get lost in the convolutions of grammar and long sentences, is that they might not read to the end. If they miss an instruction, this creates a problem of data interpretation for the researcher. It is also serious when respondents are asked to select from or rank a list. The issues here are: (i) whether people can discriminate between many options and (ii) on what basis they discriminate.

There is evidence that items placed at the beginning of a list receive more 'hits' than items placed lower on a list. There are two solutions to this problem. Either the number of items should be restricted (the guidance is that the effect kicks in when the list starts to exceed six to eight items). The other solution is to overcome the effect of selecting the first items by reversing the selection for half of the subjects or by randomising the list for each subject. The cost implications of this can be significant since, in either case, the sample would have to be increased to allow for the random distribution of first-order bias.

The second issue, the basis on which people make this selection, has also been researched. We have considered the order effect (also called the primary effect) above. Two others have been identified: 'recency' and social acceptability. *Recency* is the tendency for recent experience to influence a person's response. As long as the experience is individual, the effect is unlikely to be significant as it is so random. However, if it affects a population or just a part of a population, then it will be significant. If we were surveying teachers about their enjoyment of their work, we should be more concerned about results obtained in winter than in summer, because dark days, bad weather, colds and flu are all potential influences on responses. *Social acceptability* is the tendency for people to give responses that they feel are socially acceptable rather than ones they truly feel. If, for example, we were researching multiculturalism in the curriculum, some teachers might feel that they have to agree that it should be a feature while deep down believing that school is not a place to form social attitudes.

8.6 Guidance on using the right words: dealing with sensitive issues

Dealing with sensitive issues is both a problem and an opportunity for questionnaires. It is a problem because, no matter how good the questionnaire is, it cannot replicate the warmth and emotional contact of actually being with people and helping them through what may well be a draining experience. Against this, it is an opportunity, because of its neutrality, impersonality and distance, for people to express their feelings. Questioning people about sensitive issues (such as how teachers and classmates cope with the death of a pupil, exploring a person's sexuality, assessing the extent of violence in the family) raises quite significant questions of ethics. Will any of the participants be damaged by the experience? How secure is the information from prurient eyes? What should the researcher do if there is evidence of unresolved harm or criminality? These questions would daunt even seasoned researchers and so are unlikely to be within the capability of those just starting out. There are, however, issues of principle that, as abstract concepts, we can ask people to consider, despite their sensitive nature. Euthanasia is a case in point. The care of people in the final stages of a terminal illness is a matter faced by medical staff on a daily basis. It is not surprising, therefore, to find that there have been many surveys of medical staff on euthanasia in the context of pain relief and end of life care. A survey of Italian doctors in 1999 showed that only a minority of doctors endorsed it. A survey of Norwegian doctors revealed similar findings. An international survey of Scandinavian physicians showed that Danish and Swedish doctors were more liberal. While education research is unlikely to deal with anything as difficult as euthanasia, how people respond to sensitive issues is something that we, as researchers, must be aware of.

Methodological studies suggest that the following are the key dimensions that we should consider when asking questions about issues that people might find difficult or sensitive.

- The importance of the issue to the respondent. Things that are important to us generate strong reactions. If we were researching why a school was underperforming in terms of student attainment, it would be significant if we were to find that staff teaching mathematics, sciences and modern languages were implacably opposed to the school's policy (initiated by the head teacher) of whole group teaching.
- Direct experience of or exposure to the issue generates knowledge, and helps us position that knowledge (for example, good/bad). It can also generate an emotional response (for instance, if we have direct experience of child abuse, either through having suffered it or having identified it).
- Regularity/frequency of the issue in a personal context will affect how we view it or how we respond to it. If the principal or vice chancellor of a university comes round to speak to us two or three times a year and if we have the opportunity to run into them at coffee or lunch, we are more likely to have a favourable impression than if the opposite were the case.
- The social perspective in a person's reference group may well affect us. If our immediate subject colleagues think that we should revamp the curriculum, the chances are that we will go along with it.
- The social perspective in the broader community may influence our views on bigger issues. For instance, support for capital punishment has fallen steadily over the past 50 years in many developed countries.

While we must consider the implications of these issues in our research, we still have to produce the question. Our key ally in producing the questions is the privacy of the questionnaire and the anonymity we should afford the respondent. A study by Anthony Ong based on his doctoral research (Ong and Weiss, 2000) explored the relative significance of these in relation to student cheating. The research procedure began with a class test in which books and support materials were left scattered around. The students were told to ignore them but they were marked so that researchers would know if students had accessed them. The second stage of the research presented the students with a questionnaire on student behaviour, one question related to cheating. Table 8.5 shows some of the questions they asked and the proportions acknowledging the behaviours. Half of the respondents were told that their responses would be anonymous (that is, the researchers would not be able to identify individuals with a response) and the other half was assured that their responses would be given in confidence (that is, the researchers would know what they had said but would not release the information). These conditions established (for the respondents who cheated) whether they could be identified as cheats. In each group the researchers were able to identify the students who cheated ('the peekers' in Table 8.5). The design of the research was sophisticated. In methodological terms, Ong could identify the impact of a strong guarantee (anonymity) as compared with a weaker guarantee (confidentiality) and assess each in relation to the nature of the question.

Overall, guarantees of anonymity produced a higher response for questions about behaviour frowned on by society than conditions of confidentiality (look at the

Table 8.5 Proportions of subjects answering 'YES' to questions under conditions of anonymity and confidentiality

Question	Anonymity	Confidentiality
Are you between 18 and 25 years old?	.83	.76
Have you ever, even once, been charged by the police for driving under the influence of alcohol?	.25	.15
Do you or does anyone in your house own a gun?	.21	.28
Have you ever tried marijuana?	.22	.31
Do you speak more than one language reasonably well?	.83	.76
Were you born in California?	.31	.52
In the past year, have you ever, even once, used unapproved material in an exam, quiz or other form of test?	.47	.13
'Peekers' only	.74	.25
Have you observed anyone engaging in physical abuse of campus property within the last year?	.11	.17
Are you an only child?	.09	.09
Have you ever, even once, taken something from a store without paying for it?	.69	.60

proportions admitting to driving under the influence of alcohol and shoplifting). This is confirmed when the responses of those who cheated were extracted: 74 per cent of cheats (the 'peekers') admitted cheating under conditions of anonymity, while only 25 per cent admitted it under conditions of confidentiality. Where behaviour could be reputation enhancing (gun ownership, use of marijuana), confidentiality allowed some respondents to overstate the situation.

What conclusions can we draw from this research:

- under-reporting is likely for sensitive issues;
- anonymity and confidentiality will both aid the process of obtaining responses but anonymity has the greater impact;
- people will respond to direct questions of a personal nature;
- responses to questions on sensitive issues are indicative and are not an accurate estimate for the population.

8.7 Guidance on using the right words: avoiding bias

We will only get good data to work with if we ask good questions. As we have seen, we can ask questions in such a way that we influence the response. If this happens, then the response is not solely that of the respondent. We have, in other words, biased our data. In most cases this happens because of oversight but there may be some situations where it is actually a strategy within the questionnaire design. It is clearly not good research practice but where it happens (and when people do not notice it), it is evidence of a skilled (but corrupt) researcher at work. When might this happen? In situations when producing a particular answer benefits the person or people who commissioned the research. Read Case Study 8.3 and make up your own minds.

Bias can occur in questions when they are presented or contextualised in such a way that it is made difficult for the respondent to agree or disagree with it. For example, if the question were, 'Now that English is the first foreign language that people in many other countries learn, there is no reason to require pupils to study a modern language. Do you agree or disagree?', it would almost certainly influence responses. From a research perspective, the fact that other people learn English is only one of several factors that should influence why children in the UK should learn a foreign language.

Case study 8.3 Do the ends benefit the means?

Internet gambling is a big business and also a political issue. The manipulation of public opinion for and against it is obviously important in either rejecting or accepting legislation to control or forbid it. Surveying public opinion is the bread and butter of market and opinion researchers.

One opinion poll in the USA reported a survey of 20,054 people of voting age – a survey size that generated a margin of error of +/− 0.6%, that is, the percentages giving particular answers were accurate to within 0.6%. The headline results of the survey were:

78%	were not in favour of Internet restriction on gambling
71%	did not want to stop on-line gambling in casinos based overseas
77%	did not want the Government to spend resources to prevent on-line gambling
54%	found gambling personally acceptable for everyone
87%	agreed that the Government should not tell people what to do with their time and money
83%	agreed that adults should be allowed to take reasonable risks

Convincing figures – until you start to examine the questions. Let us look at some of them.

> The United States Congress is currently (2007) considering legislation that would attempt to abolish on-line gambling. With the assumption of something that is morally offensive to almost everyone, such as child pornography, do you think it is appropriate for the federal government to restrict what adults do on the Internet in the privacy of their own homes?

Comment: It is a long question. It suggests that on-line gambling is not morally offensive (whether it is or not). It asks respondents to consider gambling in the context of child pornography and thereby weights views in favour of gambling. It introduces the notion of privacy and the right to do what one likes in private.

> More than 80% of Americans believe that gambling is a question of personal choice that should not be interfered with by the Government. Do you agree or disagree that the federal government should stop adult Americans from gambling with licenced and regulated on-line sportsbooks and casinos based in other countries?

Comment: It is a long question. It is a leading question because it could be difficult for someone of undecided opinion to vote against 80% of Americans.

> Many gambling experts believe that Internet gambling will continue no matter what the government does to try to stop it. Do you agree or disagree that the federal government should allocate government resources and spend taxpayer money trying to stop adult Americans from gambling on-line?

Comment: Another long question. The opening statement could influence responses. The phrase 'spend taxpayer money' is emotive. One of the principles of professional practice of the American Association for Public Opinion Research is that 'we should not knowingly select research tools and methods of analysis that yield misleading conclusions'. In your judgement, do the questions meet that principle?

Source: www.onlinegamingmythsandfacts.com/polls.htm (accessed 9 January 2008).

Bias can also occur when an issue is associated with a person, an event or an object that is clearly established with their/its own image in the eyes of respondents. If we ask, 'Organised sporting activities, such as those provided by David Beckham's Football Academy, can help overcome disaffection. Do you agree or disagree?' our respondents are likely to be influenced by the David Beckham association. This is called a 'prestige' effect. The reality is that the question is perfectly valid without it (and the evidence is that such programmes can counter disaffection).

Another way of affecting responses is to impute the question rather than state it directly. For example, the direct question is, 'Should pupils be taken out of school by their parents for a family holiday?' The imputed question (called an elliptical question because respondents can fill in the missing words to create a question) is, 'Parents should not take their children out of school for a family holiday'. The research evidence is that the latter construction generates more extreme views than the former. The guidance for avoiding bias is to pare the question down to its essentials. There should be nothing in the phrasing that competes as an additional trigger to the stimuli of the questions.

8.8 The question of scaling: the principles

There are many occasions in education research where the intensity with which a view is held or the level of commitment to something or someone or the degree of interest in an idea is of interest to us. The measurement of emotional responses such as these has led to the development of a whole area of survey methodology that is widely referred to as attitude measurement or attitude scaling. This is such an extensive field that all we can do here is to give an indication of the issues that researchers should consider and introduce two of the more important techniques. Any researcher wishing to make attitude measurement a significant part of their research agenda should explore this field in greater detail. This section really does cover only the nursery slopes.

8.8.1 Words or numbers?

Scales are used to differentiate the strength or intensity of a person's response. We could, for example, ask children how they respond to meals provided at school, teachers to the perceived importance of the range of tasks and duties they are asked to take on, and parents to their judgements about the schools attended by their children. It would be of interest to know that some dishes were more liked and others less liked or that these children expressed these preferences and those children had other preferences. In order to reflect these differences we need the equivalent of a questionnaire ruler to measure what each child thinks. Normal rulers are calibrated in metric or imperial units but the units we use with scales have to be based on a more abstract unit of difference that everyone intuitively recognises and applies and which each person has internalised. The concept of a scale works because it draws on a set of common experiences, expectations and beliefs. There is a possibility that because there is a strong cultural determinant to these; a scale that works in one context may not work in another, or may function differently in another. An exploration of adolescent values in Britain might produce very different results from one conducted in Nigeria just because what is socially acceptable as values and behaviour may well be very different.

But how can we express the range of views that people can hold? There are conventionally three ways of doing it.

(i) First, we can translate the scale into a simple *linear measurement*. Figure 8.2 gives two examples of this. Both lines are the same length but the top scale is *longer* than the bottom (because 'not at all' is more extreme than 'not a lot' and 'to the exclusion of other subjects' is more extreme than 'a lot'). The limits of the scale are set in *verbal* terms and rely on the words we use sitting in a semantic space that is more or less common to all of us. Subjects are asked to make a mark on the line to indicate their own position (on liking to study mathematics). This may give a spurious sense of accuracy. How precise should the measurement be – to one or two decimal places? There is also the question of how long it would take to extract the data from the measurement scales. We would have to use a ruler to measure each response and for many researchers this is one task too many.

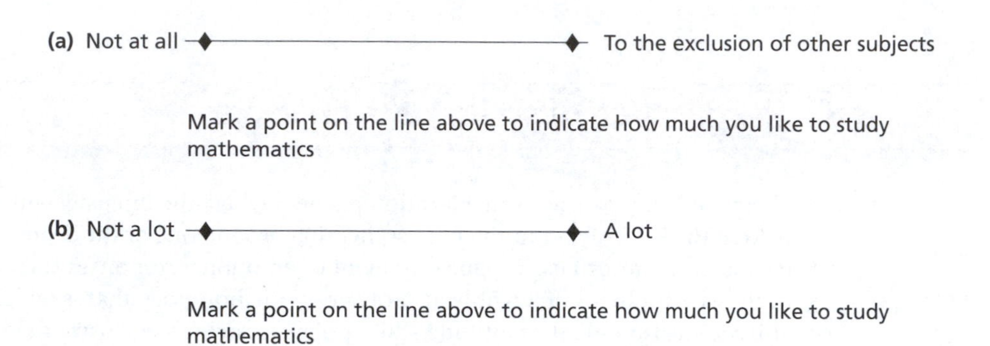

Figure 8.2 Scales as a linear construct

(ii) Second, we can define the scale in terms of a *numerical progression*. This is shown in Figure 8.3 (a)–(e). Words still define the end points of the scale but steps are constructed so that the scale is broken up into unit lengths. We intuitively know that the steps in (a) and (b) are different in size because the length of the scales is the same (both begin and end at the same point) while the number of steps is different. Example (c) shows another way of representing the scale, as spreading out from a mid-point. A numerical scale has the advantage for researchers that the data is easy to extract. While the data are coarse (there are only five or seven steps between the extremes as opposed to the infinite number of steps in Figure 8.2), there is a very real question of our ability to differentiate attitudinal and value based conditions at fine levels. The unit scales may be a better reflection of the way we think and judge. There is a problem that we have to face, however, and that is whether the distance between the scale items (that is between 1 and 2, 2 and 3, and 3 and 4, etc.) is always the same. If this is confusing you, then think back to what we said about measurement scales in section 4.4. Are we measuring on an ordinal or an interval scale? Unfortunately for us it is actually the former and this will affect the type of numerical manipulation and analysis we can perform. For instance, it is advisable not to calculate average values until the data has been transformed. This, however, becomes less of a problem as sample numbers increase.

	1	2	3	4	5	
Not at all						To the exclusion of other subjects

(a) On the scale above, mark how much you like to study mathematics

	1	2	3	4	5	6	7	
Not at all								To the exclusion of other subjects

(b) On the scale above, mark how much you like to study mathematics

	−1	−2	−3	0	1	2	3	
Not at all								To the exclusion of other subjects

(c) On the scale above, mark how much you like to study mathematics

	A little	About the same as other subjects	A lot	
Not at all				To the exclusion of other subjects

(d) On the scale above, mark how much you like to study mathematics

	Not much	A bit below other subjects	About the same as other subjects	A bit above other subjects	A lot	
Not at all						To the exclusion of other subjects

(e) On the scale above, mark how much you like to study mathematics

Figure 8.3 Scales as numerical and verbal constructs

(iii) Third, we can construct the scale using *words* (see Figure 8.3 (d) and (e)). Like the use of ordinal numbers, this creates a series of units in the scale. However, the problem that was apparent with the numbers is even more pronounced with words as the scale units because there is no pretence at equal intervals. In fact, we have to start from the positions that the intervals are not equal. This does limit our ability to analyse the data unless it is manipulated to allow us to do so. This can be done through a procedure referred to as item analysis that looks at the pattern of responses for each scale. This, however, is a topic for another text.

How do we choose which type of scale to use? This is a 'fuzzy' area and there are no clear guidelines of the sort that we should use this scale in these circumstances. All we can do is highlight some of the issues to consider so that they can be considered in the context of a specific research problem.

- Do we need specifically to identify a mid-point? If so, we should use a numerical scale with a zero mid-point or a verbal scale with an apparent mid-point. But we should remember that a mid-point can be a 'lazy option'. We look at this issue in greater detail in the next section.
- It is possible to have the best of all worlds by using a scale with an uneven number of scale positions (5 or 7 are common). The third or fourth scale positions (see 8.3 (a) and (b)) can be variously interpreted as a mid-point or a point where the respondent is ambivalent between the options.
- Should we use words or numbers? Numbers have the advantage that we understand them and we can make the assumption that people with the same view will mark the same position. When we process the numbers, however, what do they represent other than being closer to or further away from an end point? We find it easier to describe in words than numbers. If we use a verbal scale we must take steps to demonstrate that people use descriptors such as 'a little', 'not much' and 'very' in much the same way.
- Do we want to minimise the number of keystrokes when we transfer our data from the survey form to a digital file? If so, we should use a simple numerical scale (1–5 or 1–7) – half the key strokes of a scale with a neutral mid-point!
- How many scale positions should we use? The more scale positions we have, the more potential there is for people to use them differently. Individually we tend to lose the ability to discriminate between scale positions and the number increases. Conventionally, few scales are longer than seven scale units. Seven and five scale units are common. For children, even these scales may be too long. We look at this issue in greater detail below.

8.8.2 Odds or evens?

There has been discussion about the value of having a mid-point in the scale. The reason for having one is that there may be some people who genuinely cannot choose between the options. However, when a mid-point is inserted, there is evidence that responses can gravitate towards it because there is comfort in the average and it is easier to check it rather than think deeply about the issue and decide on which side you sit. This is particularly true if people do not have a lot of commitment to the survey. Where there is no mid-point in a scale, tests suggest that rather than abandon completing the scale, subjects will decide where they fit, one side or the other. Which way we decide to go, an odd or even number of scale units, may, in the end come down to the number of people we want to complete the scale. The smaller the number of subjects, the more we want people to express an opinion, so we are more likely to use a scale with an even number of units in order to force them to do so. With a larger sample size, we might expect (hope) that a more positive or negative view will emerge through the fog of regressing to the centre.

8.8.3 How long should the scale be?

A scale can vary from just two positions (Yes, No; Agree, Disagree; Good, Bad) to an infinite number of positions (the linear scale above). In most cases, however, there will be a series of intervals between the end points. How many should there be? The circumstances of the survey will affect the answer. The topic may restrict the number of units, particular subjects certainly will. Young children or people with learning difficulties may well find it difficult to cope with more than three scale positions, such as Bad, Don't know and Good. With other groups of subjects, however, such a scale would not give us much worthwhile data to work with. On the other hand, when scales move into double figures, we have to ask whether people will discriminate so finely. With five or seven scale points there will be a lot of overlap between people whose views are in the same general area. As the number of scale points increases, the possibility of people with the same views marking different scale positions increases. The tried and tested numbers of scale positions are five and seven.

8.9 Methods of scaling

What we have dealt with so far are the issues we have to consider in determining our approach to scaling. Now we shall consider some actual approaches to opinion and attitude scaling. There are a great many methods we could consider. However, we shall only look at two that use rating scales of the sort that we have discussed so far. At this point we should emphasise the distinction between a rating scale used as a measurement device and an attitude scale that combines rating scales to give a single statistic to represent a person's viewpoint. The former can be used to provide specific information about a person's viewpoint in a questionnaire. An attitude scale is a collection of rating scales that represent the full range of viewpoints on a topic. The individual rating scales that comprise the attitude scale have been tested to ensure that, when combined, the numerical value that results is representative of a person's attitude on the whole spectrum of attitudes. We shall see this distinction in the first example below.

8.9.1 Likert scales

Rensis Likert was an American psychologist who gave his name to the technique he developed in the early 1930s (it was actually part of his PhD thesis). The fact that his scaling procedure is still being used 70 years on shows that it is a robust, tried and tested method.

Likert scales consist of a set of statements each of which is judged on a rating scale. Likert's original rating scale was five units long:

- strongly disagree;
- disagree;
- neither disagree nor agree;
- agree;
- strongly agree.

It is possible to use scales of different length and with an odd or even number of scale positions (Likert also used scales six units long). The integrity and effectiveness of the scale as a measurement device does not appear to be affected.

The statements that are used in Likert scales relate to the topic under investigation. There are many Likert scales available from publishers or from academics. The benefit of using a pre-existing scale is that we know it works and that we can easily construct a statistic to indicate a person's position on the spectrum of attitudes. For example, if we wished to assess how many children in a year group fell into the gifted and talented spectrum, why bother to review the research on the topic in order to isolate our variables and select our indicators when the *Gifted and Talented Evaluation Scale* and the *Scale for Identifying Gifted Students* are available to purchase? So the first instruction to anyone researching attitudes and opinions is, look to see if anyone has been there before you. There will be occasions, however, when we have no option but to construct our own scales. The procedure is set out below.

Stage 1: Develop the statements

Two Irish researchers, Houston Lowe and Anthony Cook (Lowe and Cook, 2003), found that they had to develop their own statements for their research on how well prepared students were for university. Table 8.6 presents their results for the reasons students gave for going to university. What is immediately apparent from the responses to each statement is that the statements themselves reflect a broad spectrum of attitudes. 'Like the idea of going to university' and 'Better than the dole' (unemployment benefit) reflect a more positive attitude than 'To find a partner' and 'Postpone the need to work'. What we are ideally looking for in terms of the pattern of responses is a single peak for each question. When this happens it suggests that (a) respondents are only responding to a single stimulus and (b) we have drawn a sufficiently large sample. To understand why this should be the case, we have to understand something that we have not yet covered, the normal distribution (we look at this in Chapter 13). This is yet another example of the 'laws' we referred to in section 1.6.4 coming into play. At the present time, we just have to accept that what we are looking for is a single peak. Where there is more than one peak (for example, 'To enjoy myself before starting work'), we have a difficulty. Do the two peaks suggest that we have not sampled enough people and that were we to increase the sample size the respondents would be concentrated between the two existing peaks? This is not likely where the two peaks are either side of the scale mid-point. More

Table 8.6 Students' responses to reasons for going to university

	Numbers of students				
	Strongly agree	Agree	Undecided	Disagree	Strongly disagree
Like the idea of going to university	20	58	15	6	1
Better than the dole	25	33	11	16	16
To enjoy myself before starting work	4	27	20	34	15
Seems like the normal thing to do	4	21	13	47	15
Parental expectations	3	19	11	45	21
To get away from home	3	16	16	45	21
Friends are going to university	2	15	11	51	22
Postpone career decision	1	9	15	52	23
To find a partner	1	3	15	38	44
Postpone the need to work	1	5	6	39	49

Source: After Lowe and Cook (2003).

likely, there are two distinct groups of students each with a different outlook on life which affects their reaction to this statement. Only further investigation will reveal the answer but, if there are two groups, we have to reject the statement in our attitude scale because it is multi-dimensional, not uni-dimensional.

Stage 2: Tap the attitude range

We have to ensure that the statements we use reflect the whole range of possible attitudes. To get to this situation we need to think about the issue, read what others have researched on the topic and from this construct a set of statements to reflect a wide range of positions. It is often better if the process of constructing the statements is done with the help of others. The statements can reflect different reasons for going to university as long as the reasons fall on a continuum of very positive to not very positive. 'Because all my friends are going' shows less commitment to the idea of going to university than 'Because I really enjoy studying'. We would expect this to be reflected in the way people answer. Someone who gave a high score on the first scale would be unlikely to give the same score to the second.

Stage 3: Test the spread

After the statements have been constructed, they should be assessed for (a) the range of views they tap and (b) the extent of any clustering, that is, too many statements tapping the same viewpoint. For this, we will need a group of people who will assess each statement in terms of how it reflects the range. The members of the group should be people with an appreciation of the range of possible viewpoints and some background in constructing attitude statements. Approaches we can use are to ask our helpers to place the statements in rank order from reflecting a positive to a negative view (problematic when the number of statements gets into double figures) or to ask them to rate each statement (on a five or seven point scale) in terms of how much it is for or against the attitude we intend to explore.

Stage 4: Choose the statements

The last step is to discard some statements. What we require are statements that discriminate between subjects. There are statistical procedures that can be used to do this but for a small set of statements (say up to 15), eyeballing may give a fair indication of which ones to include and which to discard. There are two actions that we should take:

- First, if our helpers have ranked the statements, we will not want to keep ones whose rank position is very unstable because this shows that there is some uncertainty about the strength of attitude that the statement is indicating.
- Second, we need to be certain that the statements reflect the attitude range and are not bunched. Rating the statement in terms of how positive or negative it is will help here. In broad terms we should aim to have an even progression of statements through the attitude range. We should reject statements where our judges are polarised and discard those that are too similar to others. As the end of this stage we should have a Likert scale that will perform effectively. However, we will not have the statistical analysis to demonstrate this to others. For this, we have to master an area called reliability analysis, which, again, you will have to read in a specialised text.

8.9.2 Semantic differential

The semantic differential sounds worse than it actually is. It has certain advantages over other approaches. It is very easy to use. There is a lot of evidence on which scales actually work. There are simple analytic approaches that can give insights as to what is happening. Finally, there are more advanced and sophisticated analytic approaches that provide strong evidence of the forces at work in the data.

The semantic differential takes a concept and subjects rate that concept on a series of Likert-type scales whose end points are adjectival opposites such as Good/Bad, Exciting/Dull, Stimulating/Boring. As an example of how it might be used, let us imagine Lowe and Cook's research on why students choose to go to university being conducted with students in their senior years at school. Table 8.7 shows some of the scales that the students would be asked to complete for the concept of university. We could also ask the students to complete the scales for the concept of a traditional university and a modern university. And if we wanted to understand how different universities were seen, we could ask them to complete the scales for named universities. Table 8.7 shows scales with seven units. It is important that the unit positions are given names in order to act as a guide to respondents. Note that the scales do not necessarily have to deal with what might be the most obvious characteristics of universities (for example, as places of learning we could use 'Learned/Ignorant'). We can use scales such as this but we are trying to delve into people's understanding of the concept at a deeper level – that is why we use some of the scales that seem, at first sight, incongruous. They do actually generate a response and it is usually clear, from the way people mark the scale, that many are using it in the same way.

How do we choose the adjectival opposites that form the semantic differential scales? We can offer the following guidance.

(i) The three dimensions: the key concept in semantic analysis

There are two factors to bear in mind when selecting the scales – the purpose of the investigation and what other researchers have found works. Before we consider these, however, we should understand a key feature of descriptive semantic space that was

Table 8.7 Semantic differential scales

Think of the idea of a university. Now put an x on each of the following scales where you think it fits on that scale.

	Very	Quite	A little	Neither/Nor	A Little	Quite	Very	
Happy								Sad
Difficult								Easy
Smooth								Rough
Cold								Warm
Lively								Placid
Dishonest								Honest
Entertaining								Boring
Common								Sophisticated
Positive								Negative
Strong								Weak

identified early on in semantic differential studies and has been confirmed by many studies subsequently. While the adjectives exist in a space of many dimensions, a three dimensional space (see Figure 8.4) is effective in locating the vast majority of descriptive words. The three dimensions are: evaluation (for example, Good/Bad, Attractive/Unattractive), potency (Strong/Weak) and activity (Active/Passive, Fast/Slow). What this means is that the adjectives we use embody different combinations of these three dimensions. We actually make use of this characteristic on a daily basis to provide nuanced commentaries, observations and interpretations. For example, 'worthless', 'useless' and 'ineffective' can be used as synonyms but they are subtly different in meaning and we can make use of these differences to test how people perceive something. This is what Stephen Kroeger and Linda Phillips explored in their research into individual plans to research pupil behaviour (Kroeger and Phillips, 2007). In selecting a spread of descriptive scales, we should seek to ensure that these three dimensions are represented in a balanced way.

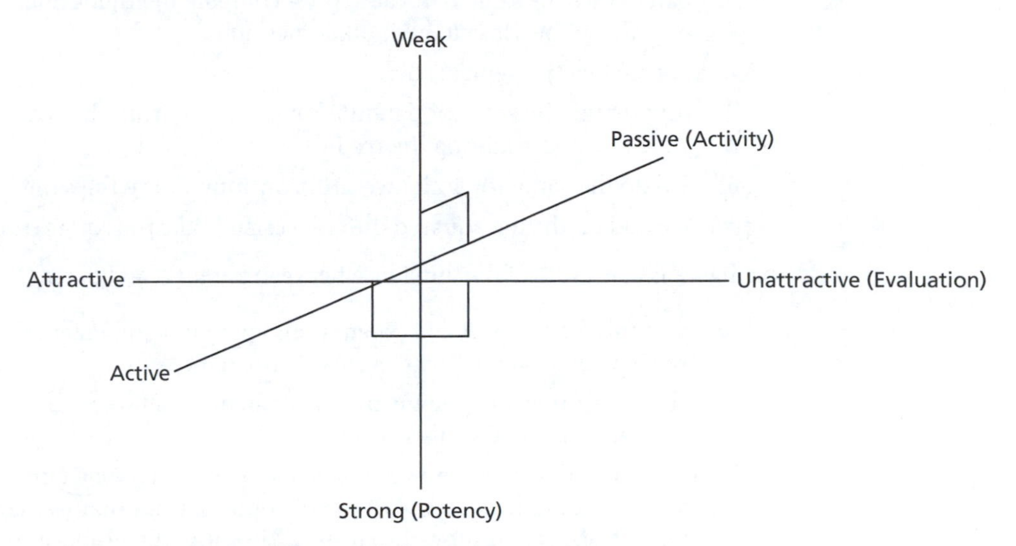

Figure 8.4 Semantic differential dimensions

(ii) Choosing the scales

How can we do this? We can start by looking at a seminal work by one of the founding fathers of the semantic differential, the American sociologist, David R. Heise. One of his earliest works was to profile popular English words (Heise, 1965). In 1958, three other American researchers had produced an atlas of semantic differential profiles (Jenkins et al., 1958). Both publications give the weightings of adjectives in terms of the three principal dimensions, evaluation, potency and activity. Our goal should be to include a range of scales so that all of these dimensions are covered, usually several times. The next step after this is to conduct a thorough literature search (a) to identify how other researchers have deconstructed the concept we intend to research (this can suggest adjectival descriptors) and (b) to identify any that have used this technique. If their scales work, we should consider using them. A wider literature survey of the technique itself (rather than the subject we intend to research) will also throw up successful scales. Finally, we should think about our topic and identify other concepts that may be useful to our research. We use all of these sources to build a set of scales and, from the list we have, we should reduce it to between 15 and 30. Below this number we may not be tapping all the nuances we require, above it and fatigue will set in amongst the subjects.

The semantic differential is easy to operationalise. Respondents understand quite readily what they have to do. Completion of the scale can be done on an individual basis but, equally, it can be done by groups. This makes data collection very effective. Analysis is straightforward, either using some of the methods considered in Chapters 12 and 13, or using a specific measure of 'difference' to show how respondents (or even stimuli) cluster together. Let us see how this works.

Imagine that our research is into parents' ideas of education and learning. In particular, we want to see what sort of image they have of the value of education and learning. We could give a selection of parents in a town a range of ten semantic scales against which to judge 'the value of education'. What we want to do is see how far the parents differ in their judgements and whether they cluster together in their attitudes. How can we show that one person is similar or different to another? The method is quite simple.

- Each parent uses the same ten scales. If we compare their judgements on each scale, we can measure how close to each other they are.
- We compare their judgements by:
  - (i) subtracting the score of parent A on scale one from the score of parent B on scale one and squaring the result.
  - (ii) We do the same for scale two and continue doing the same up to scale ten.
  - (iii) We add up the ten squared differences and take the square root of the result.

This figure is a measure of the difference between parent A and parent B.

- We repeat this for parent A and parent C and parent A and Parent D and so on until we have compared parent A with every other parent.
- We then do the same for parent B and then parent C and so on until every parent has been compared with every other parent.
- This yields data that shows how close everyone is to everyone else. With even up to 20 people, we could make sense of the data but beyond that we have to use a programme such as SPSS to show the clusters. This not only produces the cluster analysis, it will also calculate interpersonal differences.

The semantic differential continues to be used in social and educational research. See Case Study 8.4 for an example.

8.9.3 Which rating scale to use?

In possibly the majority of research situations that new researchers will face, Likert and semantic differential scales are alternatives to each other, so the selection of one rather than the other can be due to nothing more than personal preference. Whichever one is chosen, it is important to ensure that there is some 'quality control' in the selection of the scale terms – and it is this that may swing the choice one way or the other. The scale terms (statements in the case of a Likert scale and adjectival pairs in the case of the semantic differential) should not be plucked out of the air and used. Not only do they have to relate to the issue, they should also constitute a reasonable representation of attitudes. In the case of Likert scales, this does mean that we should go through quite a long testing procedure unless we use a scale already developed and tested by someone else. (It is fair to say, though, that many published studies appear not to have gone through this testing procedure without undermining the integrity of the results). With the semantic differential, as long as we choose adjectival pairs that reflect a balance of

Case study 8.4 Using rating scales in research

Different approaches to obtaining data have their strengths and weaknesses. One of the skills of a researcher is to be able to combine approaches in order to gain insights that using a single approach would not produce. This is what a small research team (Elias Avramidis, Phil Bayliss and Robert Burden) from the University of Exeter did in a study that looked at the inclusion of children with special educational needs in a mainstream school.

The success of any new policy depends on many factors but amongst the most important is the extent to which those responsible for implementing it actually believe in it. This is what the research team did by exploring the attitudes of teachers in a mainstream school. The study measured attitudes in two ways:

- A series of statements judged by Likert scales exploring beliefs, including:
  - Inclusion offers mixed group interaction which will foster understanding and acceptance of differences.
  - Isolation in a special class has a negative effect on the social and emotional development of a student with special needs.
  - The challenge of being in an ordinary classroom will promote the academic growth of the child with special needs.
- A set of semantic differential scales exploring teachers' emotional reactions, including:
  - anxious – relaxed
  - worried – self-assured
  - negative – positive.
- A series of statements judged by Likert scales to measure teacher intentions, including:
  - I will accept responsibility for teaching children with severe learning difficulties within a whole-school policy.
  - I will change my teaching processes to accommodate children with severe learning difficulties.
  - I will engage in developing skills for managing the behaviour of children with severe learning difficulties.
- A series of statements judged by Likert scales to measure the skills teachers thought they had, including:
  - I feel confident in diagnosing/assessing specific needs.
  - I feel confident in collaborating with colleagues to provide coherent teaching programmes for students with SEN.
  - I feel confident in implementing Individual Educational Plans.

The teachers who completed the survey were drawn from 23 schools in one area. Over half of them had been teaching for more than 14 years. The main conclusions of the research were:

- Overall teachers were generally positive towards the concept of inclusion.
- The experience of teaching children with significant disabilities generated a more positive attitude.
- Teachers trained in special needs had a more positive attitude.
- Teachers who believe themselves to be skilled had a more positive attitude.

Reflecting on this research, we can say that creating self-belief, giving teachers experience and special training are key factors in effective policy implementation.

Source: Avramidis et al. (2000).

the three underpinning dimensions of meaning, evaluation, potency and activity, we are likely to ensure that we reflect a wide range of views. Doing this can be less time-consuming than establishing the appropriateness of a set of statements. However, as research becomes more advanced, there is some methodological evidence that semantic differential scales may provide a better representation of viewpoints. In a study of how teachers react to academically gifted students, a British and an Australian academic, Professor John Geake and Professor Miraca Gross, stated that they preferred the semantic differential because:

- they believe that the agree/disagree character of Likert scales generates neural activity in different sides of the brain and has a tendency to produce 'middling' judgements, and

- more down to earth, they think the object of the Likert scale is so obvious that it affects responses (Geake and Gross, 2008).

In a comparative test of the two methods a Norwegian team, led by Oddgeir Friborg, found that when 334 students completed the two scaling procedures, the semantic differential data indicated that the students were more consistent in their judgements, that they clustered more and that the patterns determined by the semantic differential data produced a better fit with the data (Friborg et al., 2006).

8.10 The structure and layout of questionnaires

If the first step in getting a good response to questionnaires is to find people who are prepared to answer our questions, the second is to ensure that they answer them. How the questionnaire appears to them is a key aspect of this. In this section, we shall identify some goals that we should set ourselves and suggest what we can do to achieve them.

8.10.1 Capture their interest

People who are interested in our work are more likely to agree to take part in our survey. The interest can be a general interest in the topic or a professional interest (for example, science teachers wondering what pupils' (and their parents') perceptions of science are). In the majority of cases, they should believe that the research is worthwhile and that it will deliver some benefit.

The way to achieve this is to explain succinctly, emphasising the purpose and possible outcomes of the research and the significance of their contribution. This should be done in a pre-survey communication (if one is sent out) and reinforced in the introduction to the survey. If there are different sections we might also explain briefly the point of the questions we are asking.

8.10.2 Build up their commitment to the survey

A common problem with questionnaires is non-completion. This raises issues. Do we include the information given? Do we count respondents as non-respondents if under half is completed? How do we manage different numbers of subjects responding to different questions when we analyse our results? It is far better to minimise non-response than to deal with these sorts of issue.

We can go a long way to achieving commitment to the survey with our sequencing of questions. We should try to make our respondents feel that it is a waste if they do not complete the questionnaire. This is what we can do:

- Put straightforward questions, ones to which they know the answer, at the beginning. This is why questions on gender, age, etc. that create the respondents' profile are often at the beginning.
- Put sensitive questions towards the end. If we need to ask about income, then this is better placed after people have responded to substantive questions on the research topic and have begun building commitment.

- Put difficult questions, ones that require thought rather than a quick response, towards the end.
- Do not put open-ended questions at or too close to the beginning because people have to think about how they want to respond. It is also good practice not to put in lines on which people can put their responses. This is likely to limit answers; just leave a blank space.

8.10.3 Make it look easy

If a task does not look easy, then inevitably people will not jump at the opportunity of taking it on. This applies as much to completing questionnaires as anything else. It is particularly an issue if the potential respondents are volunteers. So how can we make the questionnaire look easy?

- Create the right mindset amongst the respondents by telling them that they are the experts, they know the answers to the questions and that all their answers are given in confidence. In other words, create the impression that everything is straightforward.
- Then make everything straightforward. Provide clear instructions as to how they should answer the questions (tick, mark, write in). For closed questions, use boxes for respondents to mark.
- Do not make respondents answer more questions than they need to. Route them through the questionnaire to take them past sections that are not relevant. For example, 'If you answered YES, go to Q14'.
- Do not make the questionnaire look long. Maximise the number of questions per page but do not overcrowd the pages. Consider using both sides of the paper.
- Give the questionnaire a professional feel by creating an attractive layout. There are many questionnaire construction programmes with design tools and layouts that will help.
- Do not go overboard on design, for example, by using different templates or too many different typefaces (use one to convey instructions and another for the questions).
- Consider the respondents. Older children can complete a longer questionnaire than younger. People who are being paid will complete a longer questionnaire than volunteers. Case Study 8.5 looks at a questionnaire completed by people with a learning disability.

8.10.4 Make it easy for yourself

It is surprising how many investigators do not consider their own interests at the design stage. A few simple actions at this stage can make things much easier later on.

- How will the data be analysed? We must make sure that the questionnaire delivers data in the form and format that the analytical techniques require.
- How will the data be put into a form for analysis? If the questions are closed and we have access to an optical character reader (OCR – a device that scans a questionnaire page, reads the boxes that have been marked by the respondent and loads it into a data file for subsequent analysis), we can put the data straight into a spreadsheet. If we do not have an OCR, then the data has to be inputted manually. Figure 8.5 shows how this is done. Conventionally the rows of a spreadsheet are our subjects and the

Case study 8.5 'Does he take sugar?' Tapping the views of the learning disabled

Who better to give a view on the quality of service provision than users of the service? But what if the services are for those with a learning disability? If someone is less capable in thinking and has a simpler view of the world in which we live, how reasonable is it to ask them to complete a questionnaire? While this is a challenge, it is one we should meet because if we do not, we are discriminating and conspiring to prevent them from making a contribution to society. The problem is not theirs, it is ours – to create a questionnaire that they can respond to.

This was the problem faced by the Social Services Inspectorate for Wales and the Welsh Audit Office. They did not duck the issue by asking service providers or carers, they wanted the views of users. How did they go about it?

1. *They offered reassurance.*
   - There won't be anything in our report that would lead to you being recognised.
   - Tell us what you think. It is not a test and there are no right or wrong answers.
2. *They used simple, conversational language – short sentences and words that respondents would know.*
   - Please say how old you are.
   - Are you asked how things are going by your social worker/care manager?
   - Do you have a big say about what you want for the future?
3. *They made it easy to respond with both closed and open questions.*
   - Do you go to any of these? *Day centre* ☐ *College* ☐ *Leisure centre, e.g. for swimming, gym, sport* ☐
   - What other help have you been given by social services (for example, a support worker, help with money, etc.)?
4. *They used pictures to lessen the formality of the questionnaire.*

   - Where do you live?
5. *They offered advice on how to complete the questionnaire.*
   - Tell us what you think. It is not a test and there are no right or wrong answers.
   - If you like, you can ask someone you trust to help you fill it in.
6. *They made it easy to return the survey.*
   - Please send it to us in envelope provided. There is no need for a stamp.

What are the key lessons for questionnaire design that we can take away from this? There are two.

- Be clear about the information we want.
- Put ourselves in our respondents' shoes.

If you would like to see the questionnaire, it is available at http://www.joint-reviews.gov.uk/assets/DocumentsEnglish/1.07.2_learning_disability_survey.pdf (accessed April 2008).

columns are our questions. We will find it far easier to input the data if we put the column number next to the question or the response boxes. Check also whether there are any specific requirements of the tools that you will use or formats that are required (for instance, column separation between questions). Open questions that will be analysed by computer-based methods may also require particular formats.

- Make sure that response pages do not get separated. Questionnaires should, at least, be stapled. Preferably they should be produced in a booklet format. This conveys our commitment to the research to the respondents.
- If questionnaires are being completed by different groups (such as teachers in different schools), colour code them. This makes it considerably easier when sorting them into groups (especially if the analysis will be done manually). It also has the added advantage that it will stand out on the crowded desk of a respondent!

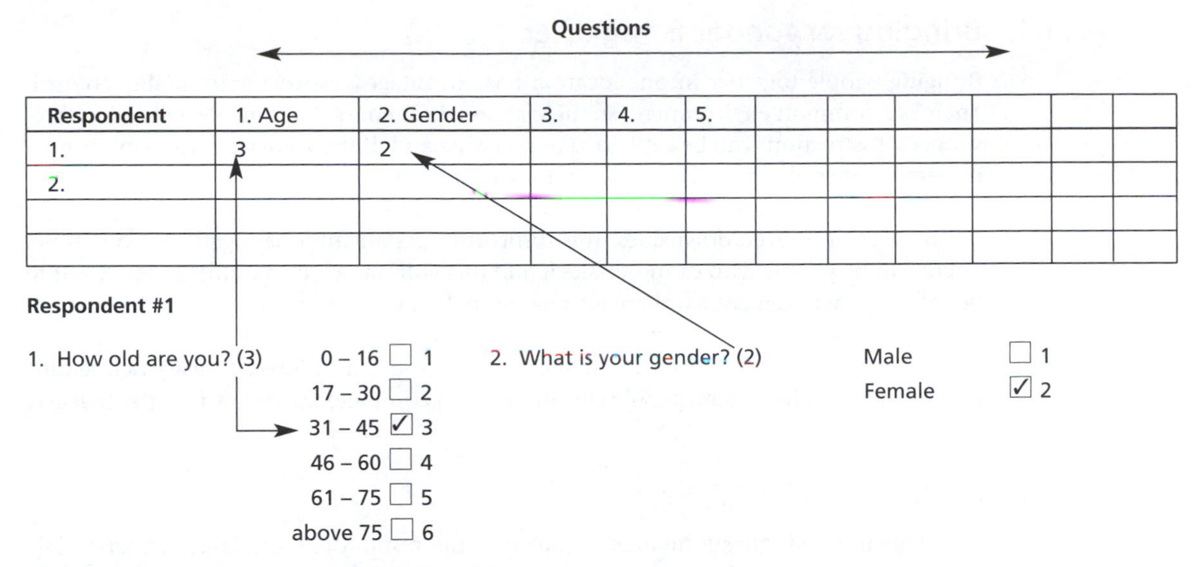

Figure 8.5 From questionnaire to spreadsheet

8.11 Administering the questionnaire

Constructing a questionnaire requires one set of decisions, how to get it in front of respondents requires another. And the two sets of decisions affect each other. We have four ways of putting questionnaires in front of our subjects: by bringing the subjects together, by taking the questionnaires to them (where they work or in their homes), by mailing them and by sending them by email or providing access to them by the Internet. Each has its pros and cons that are summarised in Table 8.8.

Table 8.8 Questionnaire administration summarised

Modes of administration	Advantages	Disadvantages
Single location	• Common experience. • Better quality control. • Good completion.	• Difficult to get everyone together. • Managing finishing times.
Drop and collect	• Reasonable completion rates. • Help on return visit. • Target respondents.	• High surveyor costs.
Post	• Cheap. • Contact large numbers.	• Low response rates. • Costly to improve response. • Sampling issues.
Computer assisted	• Push or pull approaches. • Directly read into computer analysis.	• Sampling issues.

8.11.1 Bringing respondents together

Bringing people together in one location has advantages, especially in quality control. There is a common environment, so there are no differences that can affect individual responses. Instructions can be explained to everyone and, if there are any problems or misunderstandings, these can be quickly addressed and the same advice or solution given to everyone. The outcome of this is high rates of completion.

There are, however, downsides. It is difficult to get all subjects together at one time. There will be people who cannot make it and this will impact on sample design. Getting people together is an issue if there is to be more than one questionnaire. Group sizes are usually smaller than with other approaches. At a very practical level, there may be a problem with people finishing at different times. If some are allowed to leave before others, this may result in some people choosing not to complete the survey in order to leave.

8.11.2 Drop and collect

With this method, questionnaires are taken to the respondent and collected later. This can produce quite high completion rates because of the face to face contact and the knowledge that someone will be knocking on the door asking for a questionnaire. The return visit also provides an opportunity to provide advice and guidance on questionnaire completion. It is this approach that is often used in a national census. There is another advantage. Respondents can be targeted, so hard-to-reach groups can be accessed.

The downside of this system is that numbers of respondents are directly proportional to the numbers of people dropping and collecting questionnaires. The method is, therefore, costly, especially when people are not in and we have to make return visits.

8.11.3 Postal questionnaires

Sending a questionnaire through the post is straightforward once a database of contacts has been constructed. It is cheap and a large number of people can be contacted. Because there is no face to face contact, the questionnaire has to be straightforward and length will affect the response rate.

While the cost of administration is low, the cost of getting responses can be quite high. Postal questionnaires can have initial response rates of below ten per cent. Achieving higher rates is expensive in terms of the cost of second and subsequent mailings. Low response rates raise the issue of the sample being biased, so there is an additional cost in assessing this.

8.11.4 Computer assisted delivery

Finally, we can use modern technology to help us. We can either push the questionnaires through email or pull the respondents in to complete an on-line form. The email questionnaire is most like the postal questionnaire, with broadly the same advantages and disadvantages. We could use emails to draw people into an on-line form but this is likely to reduce response rates. Electronic surveys tend to be predominantly closed questions because the effort of typing responses to open questions may reduce response rates. However, technology can be used to read freestyle responses into computer programmes for text analysis. One of the benefits of computer-based responses is that they can produce higher response rates to sensitive questions. If sampling can be properly managed, computer-based responses can be cost effective.

8.11.5 How and when to use the methods

The circumstances of the research will dictate how we administer our questionnaires. The factors we should take account of are:

- How are we going to process the data? If we intend to use statistical techniques to relate and compare data with each other, we must have a correctly drawn probability-based sample (see section 6.5) that must be large enough so that the groups we compare are never less than 20 (30 is much better). If we want to know the characteristics of a population (for instance, what teachers think of the curriculum they teach), we should have a sample that accurately reflects the population. Both of these imply a large sample, which points us towards a mail, email or, if we have the resources, a drop and collect questionnaire. If we use mainly open questions, it is likely that we are after a rich picture (for instance, if we were investigating what gave teachers job satisfaction and what made them dissatisfied), we would be more likely to use a drop and collect method or bring them together.
- What sort of sample do we need? If the sample is drawn from a national population (for example, heads of educational services in local authorities), it is unlikely that we will get them together at once and drop and collect will be expensive. What we are left with is a postal or email questionnaire. We can improve the likelihood of getting a response with these approaches with a good letter of introduction which explains the purpose of our enquiry. If we are sampling schoolchildren on a national basis, some form of cluster sample will be appropriate (see section 6.5.4). With this approach, we would sample classes or pupils within classes, so we could bring the students together or use drop and collect.
- What resources do we have available? The more resources we have the more options we have. If resources are limited (maybe just us), we either limit ourselves to a small number of respondents (using, say, a drop and collect approach) or we send out a large mailing. As a rule of thumb we should mail out five times the number of questionnaires that we hope to analyse. So, if we base our analysis on a response of 500, we should mail out 2,500.
- Take advantage of circumstances. For instance, if there is a gathering of the group we wish to administer a questionnaire to, we should take advantage of the opportunity. If we wanted to know what teachers who are members of unions felt should be union priorities, we could administer the questionnaire at a conference of union members. We should be aware though that these may be union activists whose priorities may be different from other rank and file members. Others we are likely to bring together to administer questionnaires are schoolchildren. This is particularly so if we are administering the questionnaire through the school. We have to consider the staff in the school and make the task straightforward for them. Rather than have a random sample of children, it is likely that we will sample years or classes and administer the sample in class groups.
- Is it likely that our respondents will need advice and support to answer our questions? The groups this might refer to are children, those with limited learning disabilities and the elderly. If our questionnaire deals with technical or professional

issues that our respondents may not be familiar with, we should include these people as well. In these conditions we would bring the people together or administer the questionnaire using the drop and collect method. If our research was into using the Internet to create a stronger partnership between parents and schools, we would need to know (a) the level of technical provision at the children's homes, (b) the level of parents' technical understanding and (c) their interest in working in partnership with the school. Given that many of the questions would be technical in nature, we could administer the questionnaires in two ways, either at parents' open days (when they come to talk about their child's progress) or using a drop and collect approach. The latter might be preferable because it would include those parents who do not attend open days. It is possible to provide support via email or the Web but this is not likely to be effective for the groups or topics described.

8.12 Piloting the questionnaire

Even by applying everything we have learnt – and more – we can still produce a questionnaire that is less than effective. That is why, when we have produced a draft questionnaire, we should test it to identify any flaws and failings. A process for testing a questionnaire is set out in Table 8.9.

We should begin the pilot by having some people with expertise in questionnaire design look over the first draft. This may well remove many of the potential problems. They will be able to point out any leading or respondent-influencing questions, problems of routing through the questionnaire, questions that lack clarity or where there are opportunities for respondents to add detail. They will advise whether the question will produce the data we need to answer our research question and whether we have been too optimistic with the amount of data we want (if it is too long, respondents will not complete it). New eyes will see issues that are not apparent to us. Two or three people is all that it takes.

Table 8.9 Procedure for pre-testing a questionnaire

Group	Activity	Action
Experts	Assess first draft of questionnaire.	Revise first draft.
Users	Complete questionnaire.	Review for correct: • interpretation of questions • routing.
Users	Return questionnaire in manner required by protocol.	Revise protocol if returns not 100%.
Users	Detailed feedback on questionnaire.	Revise as required.

After this we revise the questionnaire and take it to some users to complete. We will not be using their responses, so (unless it is a national sample) we should ensure that they are not in our sample frame. We do not have to sample in order to identify them, just find some people with similar characteristics to the population we will sample. For instance, if we are producing a survey for teachers in schools a, b and c, we could get some teachers in school d to complete the questionnaire. When we have received the completed questionnaires, we should go through them to determine that the questions have been appropriately answered and to ensure that respondents have answered the questions we required of them. We should, with the pre-test, be able to identify which respondent completed which questionnaire. While this may not be necessary in the final survey, it is important at this stage so that we can go back to the respondents to probe more deeply into how they completed the questionnaires.

The sorts of issues we should follow up are:

- whether the questionnaire was straightforward to complete or whether it caused them any confusion;
- about questions that caused them any difficulty in responding;
- whether they felt the questionnaire touched on all the topics that they think important (if not, ask them what other questions/issues should be introduced);
- about the layout, sequence of questions, the visual impression, their feelings on seeing it for the first time.

One approach (and we shall learn more about it in Chapter 9), is to sit with respondents as they complete the questionnaire and ask them to comment on the questions as they answer them.

We should, as well, ask at least some of the respondents to follow the instructions for returning the questionnaires. This is most important for postal questionnaires. It is one way of ensuring that we have put a return address on the form (and not just the covering letter – things can get separated) and that the address is correct. Having done all of this, we should be able to put a questionnaire out into the field that most people will be able to use. But every questionnaire is a learning experience and there will be something that, with hindsight, we will wish we had changed.

8.13 And finally

Questionnaires are amongst the most used of data collection instruments in social science and education research. There are good reasons for this. They can generate lots of data and they are apparently easy to use. However, there are considerable differences between good and bad questionnaires, that is, those that are effective in their task and those that should never have seen the light of day. The difference, though, between good and bad questionnaires can be slight, so with forethought all researchers should be able to produce questionnaires that are effective and efficient. Now you should try – look at Activity 8.2.

We should always remember, however, that there are alternatives to questionnaires. And it is these that we shall look at in the following chapter.

Activity 8.2 Putting it all together – creating your first questionnaire

You are working at your desk when you get an indication that you have just received an email. You open it and see that it is from a colleague in another country. On reading the message, you find that they are inviting you to work with them and other specialists on a survey of the use young people make of new technology. The survey is to be conducted in EU states. You read that there is to be a meeting in two weeks' time and the participants are asked to bring a draft questionnaire. They have attached the brief for the survey. You reply that you will be there.

Now you have to prepare the questionnaire. The brief for the survey is to see:

- how far access to and use of computers and new technology varies for young people (aged 15–16) throughout the EU;
- how young people use computers and how confident they feel with the technology;
- the attitudes of young people to computers and new technology.

In preparing your questionnaire you should:

- think about the issues and jot down your ideas;
- search to see if others have researched the topic and, if so, look at their work;
- think about the age of the respondents and how this might affect the way you ask the questions;
- consider how a very large survey would be processed and how this may affect the questions.

When you have drafted your questionnaire, you can see how the professionals approached the task. Look at http://pisaweb.acer.edu.au/oecd/PISA2000_Computer_Questionnaire.doc.

The research was undertaken as part of the OECD Programme for International Student Assessment (PISA). This programme conducts periodic studies of the performance of students in OECD countries on a standard test. Look at the website: http://www.pisa.oecd.org. It is one that you may find useful if you are interested in comparative education analysis.

Summary

- Developing a questionnaire requires that we think 'in the round'. How we deliver our questionnaire can affect our question types and layout. How we process data for analysis should be reflected in the questionnaire layout.
- We should have a balance between closed and open questions that takes account of (a) our respondents and their ability to manage different question types and (b) our analysis and the resources we have available. For us, there is a trade-off between new data and high cost.
- We should know what type of information we require from a detailed analysis of our research question.
- We should not think that all questions have to be new ones. If there is a tried and tested question, we should use it.
- Questionnaires should look appealing and should not be off-putting to respondents because they are too long. Respondent interest and commitment is inversely related to the length and complexity of the questionnaire.
- Biased questions give useless data.
- Scaled questions are useful but they have to be well constructed.
- Remove problems before they can affect results by piloting the questionnaire.

Further reading

Bradburn, N., Sudman, S. and Wansink, B. (2004) *Asking Questions: The Definitive Guide to Questionnaire Design*, John Wiley, Chichester.

Oppenheim, A.N. (2000) *Questionnaire Design, Interviewing and Attitude Measurement*, Continuum, London.

Shaeffer, N.C. (1999) 'Asking Questions About Threatening Topics: A Selective Overview', Chapter 7 in *The Science of Self-report: Implications for Research and Practice*, Stone, A.A., Turkkan, J.S., Bachrach, C.A., Jobe, J.B., Kurtzman, H.S. and Cain, V.S. (eds), Lawrence Erlbaum, Mahwah, NJ.

There are many texts on questionnaire design that could be suggested. However, I always recommend Oppenheim. First published in 1966, it has stood the test of time and is a particularly good introduction to a wide range of attitude measurements. Bradburn's book contains much practical advice and Shaeffer's article gives good guidance on a tricky issue.

References

Avramidis, A., Bayliss, P. and Burden, R. (2000) 'A Survey into Mainstream Teachers' Attitudes Towards the Inclusion of Children with Special Educational Needs in the Ordinary School in one Local Education Authority', *Educational Psychology*, 20(2), 191–211.

Friborg, O., Martinussen, M. and Rosenvinge, J. (2006) 'Likert-based vs. Semantic Differential-based Scorings of Positive Psychological Constructs: A Psychometric Comparison of Two Versions of a Scale Measuring Resilience', *Personality and Individual Differences*, 40(5), 873–884.

Geake, J. and Gross, M. (2008) 'Teachers' Negative Affect Toward Academically Gifted Students: An Evolutionary Psychological Study', *Gifted Child Quarterly*, 52(3), 217–231.

Hagelin, J., Nilston, T., Han, J. and Carlsson, H.E. (2004) 'Surveys on Attitudes Toward Legalisation of Euthanasia: Importance of Question Phrasing', *Journal of Medical Ethics*, 521–523.

Heise, D.R. (1965) 'Semantic Differential Profiles for 1,000 Most Frequent English Words', *Psychological Monographs*, 79(8), whole edition.

Huisman, A.N., Wu, M.Z., Uil, S.M. and van den Berg, J.W.K (2007) 'Reliability and Validity of a Dutch Version of the Leicester Cough Questionnaire', *Cough*, 3(3).

Jenkins, J., Russell, W.A. and Suci, G.J. (1958), 'An Atlas of Semantic Differential Profiles for 360 Words', *American Journal of Psychology*, 71, 688–699.

Kroeger, S. and Phillips, L. (2007) 'Positive Behavior Support Assessment Guide: Creating Student-Centered Behavior Plans', *Assessment for Effective Intervention*, 32(2), 100–112.

Lowe, H. and Cook, I. (2003) 'Mind the Gap: Are Students Prepared for Higher Education?', *Journal of Further and Higher Education*, 27(1), 53–76.

Martin, E. (2006) *Survey Questionnaire Construction*, Research Report Series #2006-13, Director's Office US Census Bureau, Washington DC.

Ong, A.D. and Weiss, D.J. (2000) 'The Impact of Anonymity on Responses to Sensitive Questions', *Journal of Applied Social Psychology*, 30(8), 1691–1708.

Schuman, H., Ludwig, J. and Krosnick, J.A. (1986) 'The Perceived Threat of Nuclear War, Salience, and Open Questions', *Public Opinion Quarterly*, 50, 519–536.

Chapter contents

Chapter 9

TALKING, LISTENING AND WATCHING: OTHER APPROACHES TO DATA COLLECTION

Key themes

- The strengths and weaknesses of interview, collective interviews and observation.
- The procedure for setting up and conducting interviews, collective interviews and observation.
- The difference between types of interview and interviews and focus groups.
- The role of the researcher in the data collection process and the pressures that researchers face.
- Ethical issues associated with these methods of data collection.

Introduction

As we saw in Chapter 8, questionnaires are, even with open-ended questions, a highly structured data gathering process. Their benefit is that the data they collect directly address the research question; their downside is that if the researcher fails to cover aspects of the research issue in the formulation of the questionnaire, important data are not collected. The methods that we shall look at in this section, interviews, focus groups and observation, are more flexible than questionnaires and allow the investigator to open up and explore avenues of enquiry. In other words, the route for data collection is not fixed; it can change as the process of collecting the data changes our understanding about the issue being researched. This is a powerful opportunity – the problem is that many 'opportunities' can lead only to dead ends. So when we are considering data collection methods and thinking about which ones to use, we should always remember their potential to distract us and blur the focus of our research enquiry. Having said this, they can also expose new and perhaps more significant questions.

While we shall deal with interviews, focus groups and observations separately, we should note that there is nothing written in research methodology to say that they should be used in a mutually exclusive way. (If anything they work well together with each other and with questionnaires.) A common strategy is for one approach (for example, questionnaires) to be used to establish a broad picture. Another approach, for example, focus groups, is then used to understand the mindsets and behaviours of particular groups. Alternatively, focus groups can highlight issues that become the basis of a questionnaire. Such combinations are now standard practice in research design. Talking, listening and watching are the backbone of data collection.

9.1 Talking and listening: introduction to individual and group interviews

There is often a thin line between a questionnaire and an interview. If a questionnaire is administered by asking subjects the question, then has it actually crossed the line to become an interview? Such questions are often the very essence of methodological debate. However, our purpose with this text is the practice of research, so while there *is* a distinction between questionnaires (the bulk of which will be self-administered) and interviews (which usually require two people, the interviewer and the respondent), there may be occasions when the methods of one are combined with the methods of the other. Sensible researchers, though, will know how to manage the combination. We have already seen, in Chapter 8, the principles and procedures for conducting a questionnaire survey. In this section we shall deal with individual and group interviews.

Let us begin by drawing out the distinctions between questionnaires and interviews:

- Questionnaires are structured tools that can manage data collection for large groups.
- The means and process of data collection are different. Questionnaires are prestructured, interviews can be flexible: questionnaires are usually self-administered, interviews generally require a minimum of two people.
- Questionnaire data are often capable of being processed in a quantitative way while interview data are more usually explored using qualitative methods.
- Interviews take longer to administer than questionnaires. If we were surveying 100 students with a questionnaire and another 100 through an interview, how much longer would it take to do the interviews than administer the questionnaires?
- The flexibility of interviews and their ability to expose issues creates an understanding of processes, events and emotions, all of which makes them particularly suitable in qualitative research.

With this understanding as a context for the way in which we can use interview approaches, in this section we shall:

- profile different types of interview;
- consider some ethical consequences of the invasive character of interviewing;
- appreciate the critical role of the interviewer as the instrument of data collection;
- look at alternatives to verbal stimuli and verbal responses;
- consider what can go wrong with interviews and how to avoid problems.

9.2 All interviews are not the same

Yes they are, inasmuch as an interview means that a researcher asks someone else questions. However, there are different types of interviews with different protocols and which are used in different circumstances. Figure 9.1 shows the range of interview types.

Interviews can be conducted either with individuals or with groups on a collective basis. Individual interviews are ranged along a spectrum of how structured they are, that

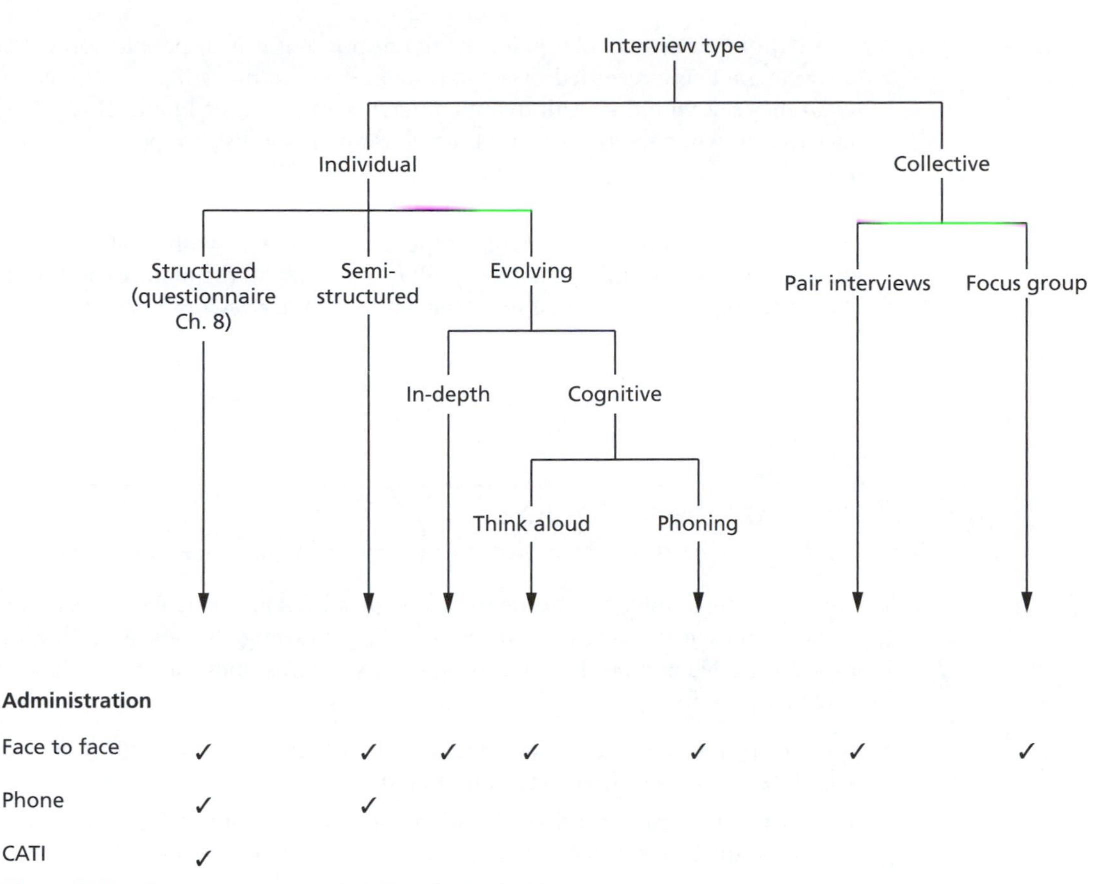

Figure 9.1 Interview types and their administration

is, how much freedom the interviewer has to deviate from the script and ask supplementary questions. The most structured interviews are based on an interview schedule that provides interviewers with a script and precise question wording. They are, effectively, spoken questionnaires. There is little to add to the guidance given in Chapter 8, other than (i) the interviewer cannot deviate from the script and (ii) the refusal and non-completion rates are lower than with sending surveys by post or drop and collect but the labour cost is greater. Structured questionnaire interviews are extensively used by market researchers.

The types of interview we shall consider in more detail in this chapter are semi-structured, the two forms of 'evolving' interview (evolving because the direction of the interview is determined by the answers given by answers to preceding questions) and the two forms of collective interview.

Figure 9.1 also shows ways in which the interview can be administered.

- Because a person-to-person relationship constitutes the heart of the interview, *face to face* is the most common approach.
- *Telephone* interviewing is only appropriate for structured or semi-structured interviewing because, unlike the other approaches, it does not require a face to face experience. We also have to consider the process of recording responses. It is much easier to tick boxes than summarise conversation. There is always the possibility of recording the interview but this raises (a) questions of its legality if permission is not asked

and (b) questions over the quality of the response if it is. If people know that their answers are being recorded over the phone, they are more likely to be guarded in what they say, with the result that the interview can become bland. This is less likely face to face, when interviewer and interviewee can establish a rapport.

- *Computer assisted telephone interviewing* (CATI) should only be used with structured interviews because of the need to key in responses in real time. There are experiments with computer-based interviewing (especially associated with health and trauma) but the work is not sufficiently advanced to cope with all the nuances and contingencies that social research requires. Asynchronous interviewing (asking questions in one time period and receiving responses in another) is possible but little used.

9.3 Semi-structured interviews

The semi-structured interview fits between the questionnaire (where there is no freedom to deviate) and the evolving interview (which has known goals but not necessarily any known or expected end points). It is more invasive than a questionnaire. It is structured inasmuch as:

- there is an interview guide with topics to be covered (as opposed to an interview schedule which has a fixed set of questions);
- most semi-structured interviews will have starter questions and guidance and what themes to introduce if the interviewee does not introduce them;
- there will be guidance on interviewer behaviour, including guidance on the clarification that can be offered and the extent to which the interviewer can stray beyond the brief with follow-up questions. For an example of an interview guide, see Case Study 9.1.

From the point of view of data collection, the interview guide is structured to reflect the research questions and collect data on an indicator that can be used to answer the research questions. In addition, interviewers have the freedom to clarify people's understanding and to ask follow-up questions to explore a viewpoint, to determine knowledge or to open up other explanations and answers to questions that were not foreseen when the research questions were determined. Look at Activity 9.1 for practice on follow-up questions. This ability to ask additional questions produces data that will enable the investigator to appreciate the issue better.

Against this, as with all interview approaches, there is a trade-off between the quantity of data collected and its richness. The data are indeed rich and deep but, unless resources are abundant or the data are obtained from few people, we will find it difficult to use all of the data in our analysis. This contrasts with questionnaires, where the data for each person are 'thinner' but the scale of the data collection allows it to be segmented into meaningful chunks (for example, the behaviour or attitudes of teachers as compared with technical and administrative staff, or the career intentions and aspirations of pupils in private schools as compared with those in state schools). The higher cost of interviews as compared with questionnaires is not just a consequence of employing more people for longer. There is, as well, a cost of training interviewers, debriefing them and monitoring the data they collect. If a research programme cannot afford a burst of interviewers at the right time and has to make do with fewer

Case study 9.1 An interview guide

This guide is taken from a study carried out in 2002/03 by three British sociologists, Jenny Hockey, Vicki Robinson and Angela Meak, on how heterosexual relationships are made. The full data from the survey are available through the Economic and Social Data Service (www.esds.ac.uk). The researchers interviewed 71 people from three generations of 22 families.

INVITE EXAMPLES IN EACH CASE. ASK HOW GRAND/PARENTS/CHILDREN VIEWED THEIR DECISIONS/ACTIONS IN PARTICULAR INSTANCES.

1. How did you find out about 'sex'/periods, etc.? Do you think that boys/girls were treated differently?

PROBE AROUND SOURCES OF SEXUAL KNOWLEDGE.

2. When did you first notice/become 'interested' in boys/girls?
3. What was/is courtship like for people of your generation? What do/did you get up to?

(ACTIVITIES: CINEMA, MEALS, OUTINGS, CLUBS, DANCING, HOLIDAYS, SEX?)

4. How did you know when you'd found what [sic] you thought was the 'right one'? What was 'right' about them?
5. The first time you slept together/were intimate together, was it (a) what you expected? (b) what your partner expected? (Was this on your wedding night or some other time or place?)

PROBE AROUND LOCATIONS (IF EXPERIENCED WITH MORE THAN ONE PARTNER).

6. Do/did you find yourself comparing other partners to your 'true love'? How have earlier or subsequent partners compared with this person sexually, emotionally, etc.?
7. Tell me about your wedding day. How did he/you propose? What was planning for it like – was it a big event or low key? How did you feel? What are your enduring memories of your wedding day(s)?
8. How did your courtship compare with day-to-day life after you decided to set up home together? Think about having to share each other's physical, psychological and emotional space and also sharing them with other people (in-laws, children, etc.)?
9. What impact did the arrival of children have on your relationship? Do you feel that you became less of a partner/husband/wife and more of a parent? Was there an 'identity' shift? What was the impact on your sexual relationship?
10. How did you make your choices about how to socialise your children? Did you replicate or reject existing family models? Do you feel that you treat your sons and daughters the same, or do/did you have different rules for the girls/boys? (E.g. re sex and social lives – going out, etc.)
11. How do/did you feel about the possibility of your children being sexually active in your home? OR Do/did your parents let your partners stay over?
12. How do you feel about the possibility that your parents are still sexually active, or that they are while you're in the house?
13. As you've got older, do you think that your relationship has become less physical and more emotional/companionship, etc.? If so, do you think that the latter has been a compensation for a waning sex life? How has your sex life changed from when you were younger, if at all? OR Do you think imagine that sex will hold the same place for you as you get older? When do you think that it might change?
14. Are there other moments that had a significant impact on your relationships – either by testing it/them or bringing you closer together? For example, starting or leaving work, changing body image/confidence, taking up an 'interest', children leaving home, moving house, becoming a grandparent, separation, divorce, loss, retirement?

INVITE EXAMPLES IN EACH CASE. ASK HOW GRAND/PARENTS/CHILDREN VIEWED THEIR DECISIONS/ACTIONS IN PARTICULAR INSTANCES.

15. What were the best and worst moments in your relationships? How did you and your partner(s) respond when difficulties arise?
16. How important is talking through things with your partner?
17. Who do you talk to when you're having problems or share the good times with? Partner, parent, sibling, friend, grandparents, etc.?

▶

18. What is okay to take outside the relationship? 'Bedroom moments', emotional or sexual difficulties, etc.?
19. How did/do your experiences of relationships compare with the expectations you had when you first started discovering men/women?
20. How have your relationships with your partners differed to those with your friends? What do you get from one and not the other?
21. What do you see as the key ingredients for a successful relationship?

Activity 9.1 Putting the questions and following up the answers

The keys to successful interviewing are to use a tone and words that the interviewee will be comfortable with. This requires a high level of empathy: the best interviewers put themselves in the person's shoes and try to imagine how they would speak, how they would react, how they would feel and they use this awareness to phrase the questions and to determine what follow-up questions to ask.

Look at the interview guide in Case Study 9.1. Imagine how you would ask the questions of a woman in her 80s. Imagine what sort of world she inhabited in her late teens, probably just after the Second World War. What sort of attitudes prevailed to sex and marriage? How would she feel about answering questions on these topics?

Now put yourself in the woman's shoes and write out your answers to questions 7 and 8. Then compare them with what the interviewer actually said by reading the interview (extract one) at www.eds.ac.uk/qualidata/support/interview/semi.asp. Your questions will be different, so look to see how the interviewer kept the pace of the interview going in a conversational way.

interviewers over a longer period, then there is a danger that the answers given by those later in the interview cycle might have been affected by conditions in the wider world. For example, if our research is into the choices young people make with respect to their futures and the media report on the high salaries in the financial sector and low starting salaries in teaching while interviewing is ongoing, later interviewees may be affected by what they read, hear or see. The possibility is that this will sway some people's replies and influence the results that we obtain. Finally, there is always the possibility that respondents will construct replies that place them in a better light. The principal defence against this is for the interviewer to be aware of the possibility, to have good background information, to follow up with questions that reflect knowledge of a different interpretation and, if all else fails, to triangulate the response through other interviews or documentary sources.

The advantages and disadvantages of semi-structured interviews are set out in Table 9.1.

Table 9.1 Semi-structured interviews summarised

Advantages	Disadvantages
• Reflects research questions.	• Time-consuming.
• Can clarify misunderstanding.	• Train interviewers.
• Allows questioning to explore issue.	• Need for scepticism.
• Rich data.	• High cost.

9.4 In-depth interviews

In-depth interviews are more loosely structured than semi-structured. They can evolve according to the interviewer's take on the interviewee's response. We should immediately appreciate, from this, that the interviewer needs not only to be skilled but, just as important, they must be knowledgeable about the issue. Without this knowledge and understanding, follow-up questioning may not be sufficiently penetrating. It is not necessary that the interviewer should know the answer to a question (unless the purpose is to test the veracity of the respondent). More important is to have an understanding of what happened in similar circumstances elsewhere or, if this is not possible, to have sufficient insight and understanding of the human condition to judge the answer that is given. Interviewing skills grow with experience. For this reason, in-depth interviews are unlikely to be a realistic option for researchers at the beginning of their careers.

When should we use this type of interview? It is particularly good at exploring feelings and beliefs or at obtaining a rich understanding of how an issue unfolded and what it meant to the respondent or how a decision came to be taken. As a technique it is much used in policy research where decision making and futures estimation are important. It is also used with opinion shapers to find out how an issue or area will evolve or to give their views on an event. This is where the approach comes closest to the sort of interview we might see on a news programme on TV. Behind all of this is the purpose of the research, which may be to reconstruct (and explain) events, to construct futures, to move opinion and to discern meaning and significance in relation to the issue or concern at the centre of the investigation. Vaughan Robinson and Jeremy Segrott, two geographers at the University of Wales, Swansea, used in-depth interviews to understand the decision making processes of asylum seekers to the UK. This research (Robinson and Segrott, 2002), conducted on behalf of the UK Home Office, took place at a time when much of Europe was concerned about the volume of in-migration and while it would be difficult to identify specific cause and effect between the research and policy outcomes, it certainly will have informed operational practices within the UK consular and immigration services. They conducted in-depth interviews with 65 people (some of whom had been granted refugee status or leave to remain, some of whom were awaiting deportation and others who were awaiting a decision on their application to remain). What they found was that the refugees were responding to a range of 'push' factors, including persecution and violence and that their priority was to reach a place of safety rather than a *specific* place of safety. Their interviews also revealed the processes by which they reached the UK. The asylum seekers were in the hands of agents. In some cases the agents offered them a 'menu' of destinations and prices, in other cases the agents only dealt with access to the UK. Where asylum seekers chose the UK, their decision was influenced by its image as a safe and tolerant refuge, links (including colonial links) with the UK and the ability to speak English. The researchers found that the asylum seekers did not have a clear appreciation of asylum procedures or benefits, so their decisions to come to the UK were unaffected by such considerations.

With the in-depth approach, the role of the interviewer is not to slavishly follow a structure but to stimulate a response. Interviewees should be helped to find their own way through the issue, express things in the sequence they want to follow and use words that they want to use. The interviewer can kick-start the process and move it along but control and manipulation of the response is not really an option, as it is with semi-structured interviews. Robinson and Segrott (2002) used a 'topic guide' that highlighted the issues they wanted to cover. In relation to understanding the migrants' choice of destination, these included:

- Did research participants choose a particular destination country?
- Did the choice of destination alter during the journey itself?
- Was help sought from facilitators in the country of origin?
- Who was this, i.e. an individual or an organisation?
- Did such facilitators offer a choice of destination? What kind of guidance/advice did they give on possible destinations?
- Did they help with travel documents, i.e. passports?
- Was help sought from facilitators in the UK?
- Did the research participant consider seeking refuge in a neighbouring country, rather than a more distant country like the UK? Which country was this? If this option was not pursued, why was this the case?
- What other countries were considered besides the UK? Why were these countries considered?
- Were they unable to gain entry to them?
- Were some of these other countries rejected as options by asylum seekers themselves?
- What were the reasons for these decisions?
- How does the UK differ from other considered destinations?
- Did research participants intend to settle in the UK, or did they intend a temporary stay?

These are clearly issues to be addressed in the discussion rather than questions to be put directly to their respondents.

The advantages and disadvantages of in-depth, unstructured interviews are summarised in Table 9.2. In-depth interviews provide an opportunity for a detailed exploration of an issue. They are particularly useful for case studies, policy research, action research and research where a timeline is important and where opinion and meaningfulness are significant. They are extensively used in feminist research where the interview has been used to encourage or stimulate actions that can change the circumstances and life trajectory of some of the women who participate (see Case Study 9.2). While it can be used to collect factual information, it is particularly valuable where the research is concerned with the values and mindsets that lie behind the facts. In researching the decision of a school in England to seek academy status (one where private funders assume a degree of influence over schools), we would want to know what values, beliefs and

Table 9.2 In-depth interviews summarised

Advantages	Disadvantages
• Issue-based.	• Time-consuming.
• Good for explorations of what people find meaningful in their lives.	• Requires common interviewing protocol.
• Emphasis on free-response of interviewees reduces influence of interviewer.	• Interviewer has to be credible.
	• Respondent may not take part.
	• Interviewee may change reality.

Case study 9.2 Interviewing as a means of empowerment

It has long been appreciated that the process of being asked a question can cause us to think about something in a different way. We can also take our research a stage further by getting people to behave in a different way.

Colleen Reid, Allison Tom and Wendy Frisby, all academics at the University of British Columbia, brought together low income women to explore poverty and health. Within the framework of a series of group meetings and activities (recreational, social, educational and political), there was a research component that explored the consequence of participating in the research for the women involved. The interviews revealed:

- a reduction in isolation – 'knowing you're not alone';
- a growth in empowerment as they shared problems and analysed causes;
- a sense of powerlessness as they sought solutions and discussed the barriers to action.

However, the process (meeting, discussing, being interviewed) did have successes at an individual level as some women grew and felt able to implement personal solutions – joining community organisations, returning to education, taking up employment training. There were also collective successes, in education and in learning about entitlements. While the processes of meeting and discussing were clearly central in raising awareness, the process of being interviewed explored the journey the women had made and this contributed to their self-belief, self-esteem and their capacity for action.

Source: Reid et al., (2006).

expectations drove the decision and whether there are any conflicts between the decision makers and the decision influencers (the school governors, the senior management team) and those whose roles and interests may be affected (the teachers, the local authority, the community and the unions).

Inevitably, interviews take time to arrange and administer, so there is a clear relationship between the scale of the research and its cost. Interviews may be conducted over a period of time but this again raises the issue of the stability of responses. Small groups of researchers often carry out interview research but this requires that interviewers have to be knowledgeable to be credible and well-prepared and briefed to ensure the operation of common standards. This also requires that the results of the interviews are audited to ensure that there has been no deviation from guidelines. Finally, we should note two problems in respect of the informants. First, a question of access; what if one or more informants does not wish to be interviewed? Documentary sources may provide some evidence, but the question for the researcher is whether someone's absence undermines the research. Second, in post-event questioning (whatever the outcome of an issue), many people will reconstruct reality and present a version of events that places them in the best light. Interviewers should always remain sceptical.

9.5 Cognitive interviews

Cognitive interviewing was developed as a procedure to aid recall in the mid-1980s. Its initial applications were in police work where the object was to improve the accuracy of eyewitness testimony. This approach is called a 'probing cognitive interview'. More recently a variant has been developed called 'thinking aloud'. This is frequently used to solve problems and to understand the problem solving process.

9.5.1 Probing cognitive interviews

While much of the early work on cognitive interviewing was in forensic psychology and criminology, applications in relation to education and to children have begun to emerge. Much of this work has been in the area of child abuse but it has also been used to explore social relations amongst primary school children. For instance, the research of a team led by Dr David Estell (Estell et al., 2002) looked at the social relationships between young children and their relationship with academic achievement. Their approach was to ask the children (between 6- and 8-years-old) whether any 'hang around together a lot' (p. 520) and to follow up by getting them to identify who the children were and whether the respondent was part of a group). It is, however, fair to say that relative to other approaches, it is underused in substantive educational research.

The objective of the probing cognitive interview to get the interviewee to visualise the location of an event as an aid to recalling circumstances, actions and outcomes, remember feelings and emotions and explain the reasons behind the actions and the feelings (in Estell et al.'s case, this was to visualise the class and the groups within it). As with other unstructured interviews, probing cognitive interviewing is flexible and gives considerable freedom to the interviewer. There is, therefore, no single protocol or set of standard practices. We can, however, identify processes that interviewers weave together to deliver results.

- *Establish the context:* place the interviewee in the location where we want them to be, at the time of an incident, just before, some time after. Obtain descriptions of the physical setting, who else was there, the interviewee's feelings.
- *Do not interrupt:* encourage the interviewee to focus. Allow silences to continue. Remove external distractions.
- *Break up the pattern:* memory retrieval is usually segmental. Ask people to go backwards in time, ask them what another person might see, all in an attempt to 'find' missing memory. Go over events several times, cross-checking each version against the others. Probe discrepancies.
- *Ask interviewees to visualise:* and then describe what they see.

Probing can and almost certainly will be *ad hoc,* driven by responses that the interviewer thinks will benefit from further development. It is, however, an advantage for researchers to have considered what responses might be obtained, what sort of insights are required and to produce an *aide-mémoire* so that these points are not overlooked in the interview.

The analysis of the interviewee's responses usually requires a complete transcript of what was said. For this reason, interviews are usually recorded or videoed. It is best to have back-up equipment so that if one piece fails the interview is not wasted. Chapter 11 deals with how transcript data can by analysed, including computer-based analyses.

Probing cognitive interviews could be used to help our understanding of many issues relevant to education. For example, we could investigate violence amongst young people (why do some people stand and watch a fight rather than step in to stop it?), how teachers cope with stress or student and employer views about work experience or placement, in fact any topic where recall of a specific situation is required or could be used as data. Because they go behind the events to understand the motivations and emotions they add considerably to the researcher's depth of insight. However, they usually take place in an unfamiliar setting for the interviewee and there is a possibility that this may influence the response in some way. It is important, therefore, for interviewees to be completely at ease with the research intentions and the interviewer. The interviewer's social skills are extremely important.

9.5.2 Think aloud interviewing

Think aloud interviewing differs from other forms of cognitive interviewing in that its purpose is not to establish factual accuracy but to gain insight into thought and analytical processes. For example, there is concern in many countries about underachievement in mathematics. Is it the nature of the subject, the way it is taught or the way people reason? Think aloud interviewing has been used to explore the issue by asking pupils to explain what they are doing when they try to solve mathematical problems. Irenka Suto and Jackie Greatorix used the same approach to understand what was going on in examiners' minds when they were assessing scripts (Suto and Greatorix, 2008).

It is, conceptually, a simple procedure. As people undertake a task they are asked to describe what they are thinking. The role of the interviewer is to keep the narrative going with prompts (e.g. 'And now what?') and follow-up questions when something of potential interest is mentioned but skipped over by the interviewee. The method has much in common with the teaching technique of the same name. Using this method, Irenka Suto and Jackie Greatorix identified five marking strategies:

1. *Matching*, where the examiner identifies a correct answer or response.
2. *Scanning*, often a precursor to matching where the examiner reviews sections of script to see if it contains gradeable material.
3. *Evaluating*, looking at the work as a whole to see what merit it contains and whether it can be given any marks.
4. *Scrutinising*, looking in detail at work to see at which point an error was made or whether a candidate was following a correct procedure as a means of seeing what credit can be given.
5. *No response*, where a candidate has written nothing.

While the think aloud procedure seems straightforward, it is not without its problems.

- Some respondents might find the verbalisation of their thought processes difficult. We can imagine that this might be the case with younger children, people with learning difficulties and even some older people. If the think aloud approach is selected for use, the task must be within subjects' capabilities and the instructions they are given must draw them into the right analytic and descriptive mindset. For instance, most children would find it straightforward to describe what they are doing and then lead to the thought process with the question, 'And why are you doing it like that?'
- However, even the involvement of the interviewer can also be a problem. Too many questions can affect concentration and can alter the problem solving process. Where the line falls between getting the respondent across the starting line and interventions that affect the pace and direction of the race has to be a matter of judgement.

How have think aloud methods been used in education research and with children? The focus in all cases is on solving a problem or resolving an issue and the goal is either

Case study 9.3 The 'Think Aloud' approach

Understanding the nature of 'giftedness' and developing ways of teaching gifted children to realise their potential have become significant in educational research in the last two decades. Berkowitz and Cichelli (2004) chose to study the reading strategies of two groups of gifted children, high achievers and low achievers. The study, in New York, drilled down to ten subjects using a set of well-founded sampling and search procedures. The children were all given the same texts to read and asked to say what they were thinking as they read aloud. If they became engrossed in the reading task, they were prompted to think aloud. The interviewers asked questions like, 'Could you elaborate on what you meant by . . .?' At the end, they were given the opportunity to add anything further. This research procedure provided rich data. It enabled the researchers to link the children's ways of thinking and their emotional states with the tasks that they were performing. For the researchers it established a 'cause-effect' relationship.

The researchers concluded that gifted high achievers (i) are more homogeneous in their use of reading strategies than gifted underachievers, (ii) are more skilled in using strategies and (iii) make more use of a range of strategies. The differences observed by the authors have implications for helping gifted children realise their potential.

to improve something or to build models of problem solving or decision making. The areas where research has been most abundant are:

- learning for disabled children;
- gifted children;
- acquiring literacy and reading skills;
- approaches to subject teaching;
- development of on-line learning platforms and packages;
- methodology, especially questionnaire testing.

Case Study 9.3 provides an example of think aloud approaches in use.

The approach has been used most extensively, however, in a methodological context, to provide feedback on what was in people's minds when they responded to a questionnaire. The argument for using the think aloud technique was well presented by Laura Desimone and Kerstin Le Floch in 2004. They showed how it could be used at the piloting stage to improve questionnaire design. Alice Bell (Bell, 2007) provides an excellent example of why it is a valuable technique. Her guidance for nurse researchers gives sound advice for anyone conducting questionnaire research with children and affirms that questionnaires can be used with children as young as seven. She outlines the strengths of using think aloud procedures in testing questionnaires and provides two examples of how their use led to questionnaire improvements:

- where children misinterpreted personal computer as meaning personal, for their use alone;
- where children did not understand the abbreviation 'pc' for personal computer.

These are useful examples because they show that even the smaller things can trip us up! Amy Homes and Lorraine Murray used the approach in their review of ethnicity classifications in the Scottish Census (Homes and Murray, 2008). Ethnicity is an important area for survey designers because, as their report shows, the potential for causing offence and confusion is great. They asked interviewees a question, allowed them to answer it and then asked them what was in their minds when they responded. Their report is well worth reading not just to see the cognitive interview method at work but also to become aware of how important it is for social researchers to deal sensitively with issues of ethnicity.

9.6 Collective interviews

Collective interviews, as the name suggests, are where more than one person is interviewed at the same time. They include focus groups. The move from one to more than one completely changes the dynamics of the interview and brings its own problems, not least the need to avoid one or a few people dominating. But the benefits include the opportunity to interview more people with the resources available and the likelihood that interaction between interviewees will release more useful data.

9.6.1 Pair interviews

Pair interviews (sometimes called dual interviews) bring two people together to answer questions. The pairs can be selected on any basis relevant to and appropriate for the investigation. Sometimes the pairs are randomly selected, sometimes the selection is on the basis of who is available at particular times. It is equally possible for the pairs to be self-selecting or the pairs can be chosen as the basis of the investigative unit (for example, parent and child, student and tutor, mentor and mentored). In whatever way, the pairs are selected, it is crucial that the research framework explains and justifies the basis of the selection. Gill Highet used self-selecting pairs of young people aged 13 to 15 as the basis for her data collection on research into young people's use of cannabis (Highet, 2003). She notes that the pair approach provided emotional support for the participants in talking about a sensitive issue. In particular, she reports that the approach especially helped young men verbalise their views and emotions. From a practical point of view pair interviews were easy to set up and to sustain. They generated good quality data because the pair achieved a better balance in the power relationship between interviewer and interviewees. Getting this right is vital not just for pair interviews but for all interviews. The social skills of the interviewer are clearly important and while questions have to be put, the interviewer has to create a situation where the responses become more of a chat between interviewees than a direct response to the question. In this way the issue is explored and new ones, perhaps, exposed. For example, Gill Highet asked two girls, both non-smokers, whether they had heard of people trying cannabis first and then moving on to smoking cigarettes regularly. The responses were:

Naomi Em, I've never heard of it.

Natasha I think it's more likely to be the other way about – you need something stronger.

Naomi I don't see how they could get cannabis and they couldn't get cigarettes.

Natasha Maybe they just thought, 'Oh aye, I've had enough' to start with the strong stuff and then like, maybe take a step back and then start smoking instead 'cause they're still getting attention fae [for] it and they feel cool.

Naomi Maybe they think that smokin's nothing – it's no' going to harm you – but it really does, you can get cancer an' a' that. [Continues.]

While paired interviews can deliver excellent data, the method is not without its problems. These are principally practical in nature. Amongst the problems reported by researchers are:

- distractions if the interview is not isolated from other activities;
- lack of commitment from one of the interviewees;
- an interviewee leaving the session before the interview was completed;
- one interviewee dominating the other;
- unwillingness to reveal feelings on a sensitive issue (which, in one instance, were revealed in a one-to-one situation).

Notwithstanding these issues, some of which can be minimised by preparing the ground beforehand, pair interviews have a distinctive place in the suite of methods we can use.

9.6.2 Focus groups

The use of focus groups by all the major political parties in the UK as a means of aligning political standpoints and policy with public attitudes has brought the technique a degree of disrepute but their success in doing this makes them a worthwhile and powerful method in the educational researcher's armoury. Focus groups take three broad forms:

1. *Group interviews:* where questions are given to group members and their responses noted. While there is little interaction between respondents, there is a danger that those who answer the question last may be influenced by earlier responses.
2. *Group discussions:* where a starting question about an issue leads to a discussion (therefore going beyond just answering the question). The process is built around a series of topics introduced by the focus group co-ordinator. This approach is often associated with voting by the group on an issue, for example when the topic is first introduced and after it has been discussed.
3. *Exploration of individual views* in a group context. This is particularly useful to understand the stability of people's viewpoints and to identify arguments that sway positions.

While these three types of group are identifiable, it is not unusual to find elements of more than one in any group session. Because they are managed experiences all, to some extent, are structured. However, the strength of the focus group is that the structure should not be limiting. Discussion should flow to allow issues and perspectives to emerge and to be discussed. Custom and practice has led to the emergence of guidelines for managing a group. These are, however, only guidelines and they should be used to help us think about the way we run a group and what outcomes we want.

- *Setting up a group:* the selection of group members is central to the success of the research project. A group constitutes a sample and has to be looked at in this way. We can select members on the basis that they are representative of a broader community, or they can be knowledgeable about an issue, or they can have been affected by an event or circumstance, or they can be concerned about a problem. Each of these conditions constitutes a valid framework for choosing people, but the selection process does not stop there. Should the groups mix social status or gender (there is some evidence that higher status members and men dominate in group sessions) or should they have a uniform status? One consequence of the latter is that more group sessions may be needed.

- *Giving thought to the setting:* where the group takes place should not advantage any single member. The location and the setting should be one where everyone feels comfortable. What is appropriate for teenagers may not be as suitable for head teachers. The layout of the space should support interaction and not establish hierarchies. It is more difficult to speak from the back of a room than the front, so a layout in which everyone faces inwards is often the best option. It is also useful to offer refreshments before the session starts as a means of breaking the ice.
- *Conditions for success:* it is important that the person (or persons) running a group (usually called the moderator) appreciates that people want to talk. They have chosen to be there because they have views and opinions. If the moderator does not engage everyone, those who wanted to speak but did not will be disappointed. For group members, coming together is a social event, an opportunity to meet people and join in discussion and the social dimension has to be realised. If members are to move beyond stating their positions into explaining, justifying and judging others, then the group has to develop a collective sense of trust. Setting ground rules is a useful foundation for this – how do people show that they want to speak? When should they yield the floor? How should aggression be dealt with? Finally, once people have spoken, they find it easier to speak again. Everyone should speak at the beginning, during the introduction to the session. A useful starter is for everyone to explain why they were interested in attending.
- *Managing the process:* the group moderator is central to achieving a worthwhile outcome. The moderator sets both the tone and the atmosphere. They have to be neutral, not passive – dull is not an option! The moderator has to show personality to give life to the group and to maintain interest and commitment. At the same time, they have to be a manager, encouraging the more reticent to speak, testing ideas, exploring the implications of viewpoints and summarising positions.
- *Stimulating thinking:* it is important to move beyond statements into explanations and justifications. How to ensure that this happens should be planned before the group takes place. Questions are an obvious stimulus but pictures, videos and task activities (for example, drawing tasks) have also been used. A successful focus group moves beyond answering questions.
- *Producing a record:* the discussion is the data so we have to make sure that it is recorded. Audio recording is the minimum (and it is probably best to have two recorders in case one malfunctions). Video recording is useful to capture the non-verbal communication. The group should have an observer who makes notes during the session and the moderator and observer should produce reflective reviews at the end of the session. All are potential sources of data.

Despite their obvious value as a research tool, focus groups have had a limited use in education research and many of the studies seemed not to exploit their full potential. A criticism of much current use of focus groups (not just in education research) is that data collection remains at a surface level, is limited to answering questions in a group setting and that the potential for interaction within the group to expose the backgrounds to and values underpinning views and opinions is not realised. Achieving this requires thought at the planning stage. It is not difficult to get people to give opinions, it *is* difficult to help them articulate why they hold those opinions. How we can do this is shown in the next section.

There are, however, examples of excellent practice. In particular we should note research into critical pedagogy and action research. Both have a goal of working with people to achieve change. Action research seeks to improve a process or a situation and hence outcomes. Teachers frequently use action research to enhance the learning experience of students. The teacher identifies a baseline of student performance, motivation and attitudes to learning, varies the teaching and then measures the same indicators again. Critical pedagogy has the objectives of delivering greater social justice and emancipation. In both cases there is normally a strong element of empowerment when used in an educational context. Much of the research in critical pedagogy is informed by the work of radical thinkers, like the Brazilian Marxist Paolo Freire. Freire developed the concept of 'conscientisation', in which learners are helped to identify the root causes of their social condition (rather than merely address the symptoms). Freire's ideas fall solidly within a field that has been called emancipatory learning, the idea that education, knowledge and understanding are fundamental to overcoming disadvantage and achieving social and economic change. Not all educational research and development can be mould-breaking in this way but finding things out without there being a purpose behind the research can seem a bit pointless. Case Study 9.4 explores the use of focus groups and other methods to inform policy action.

9.7 Beyond the standard question

While the question/response format is ubiquitous in interview situations, both individual and group, it is not the only stimulus open to researchers. In this section we review some other approaches that have been used to obtain responses.

9.7.1 Pictures

Artistic representations, shapes and photographs have all been used to elicit responses in interviews. The content of the image is directly related to the nature of the investigation. The benefits of using pictures from a research strategy perspective is that they provide a common stimulus for each interviewee, that is, a potential source of variation is removed from the range of influences. The use of pictures also stimulates recall. Pictures can be particularly important when dealing with groups whose verbal skills may be limited. This would include children and people with learning difficulties.

Pictures can be used to assess the importance that people ascribe to objects. This is what Harvey Ells did in his study of food choice by children and young people (Ells, 2001). He interviewed 7- and 8-year-olds and 14- and 15-year-olds in their classrooms and usually in pairs. The children were shown pictures and photographs and asked to comment on what they saw. The advantage of using pictures was that it was significantly cheaper than taking respondents to food stores and food service outlets. Ells' paper deals with a range of methodological issues and how they were (or were not) resolved. For instance, he reports that pictures were used particularly successfully with young children, though in small group interviews some children did exaggerate their responses. Pictures have also been used as a stimulus for storytelling ('Tell me what is going on here'). The basis for using pictures in this way comes from psychology where the *thematic apperception test* is used to explore personality and motivation. In this type of test (called, generically, projective techniques) subjects interpret a set of ambiguous images; their

Case study 9.4 Sexual attitudes and sexual health amongst three ethnic groups in the UK

The context

The UK has the highest rate of teenage pregnancy in Europe. Teenage pregnancy and sexually transmitted diseases (STDs) impact on all of us, whatever our lifestyles. We pay, through taxation, the costs of health care and treatment. We meet, through taxation, the support for single person families. Taxation revenues fall through periods and days lost from work. The examples could continue. It is, therefore, in all of our interests that we understand behaviours that can lead to teenage pregnancy and STDs. As part of this research effort the UK Government's Teenage Pregnancy Research Unit commissioned research on Bangladeshi, Indian and Jamaican young people. These three groups were chosen because teenage conceptions amongst Jamaican and Bangladeshi young women are higher than the national average and those for Indian young women are lower.

The methodology

The first stage of the research programme was 75 in-depth interviews that established individual stories and experiences. The data from the interviews informed focus groups whose purpose was to explore implications for service provision and delivery. The groups were organised so that young people, parents, service providers and community support organisations for each ethnic group discussed the issues separately. Ground rules for the group were set out and the purpose of the research and the outcomes of the interviews were presented. The themes explored in the groups were:

- How people obtained information about sex and relationships.
- When was the right time to become sexually active?
- What are the consequences of teenage pregnancy?
- What are the barriers to communicating about sexual health?
- How should services be designed to ensure accessibility?

These issues were discussed in a variety of ways – in pairs with feedback to the group, whole group brainstorming, and discussion and small group discussion. The discussions were recorded.

The findings

The research study was detailed and thorough and the summary here cannot do justice to the richness of the report.

- Cultural factors and family are strong influences on young people and their attitudes to teenage pregnancy.
- Gender differences are apparent in behaviour and attitudes. Males and females often receive different messages about sex from within the family.
- Young people's attitudes are often more relaxed than their parents'. Parents feel powerless to maintain cultural norms but they used religion, education and social advancement as a means of minimising shifts in attitude amongst their children.
- Knowledge and use of reproductive health services was patchy but if they were to be used ethnic role models and culture-specific resources were felt to be important.

Source: French, R.S. et al., (2005).

interpretations are used to gain insight into their views of the world and their relationships with other people on the basis that they 'project' their unconscious into their narrative. Outside psychology, projective approaches have been used to help people express opinions and to determine and understand attitudes. Miriam Catterall and Patrick Ibbotson have reviewed how a range of projective techniques might be used in education research (Catterall and Ibbotson, 2000). While much of the stimulus material is visual, they point out that verbal stimuli and role-play can also be used to explore people's viewpoints. Their assessment of the advantages and drawbacks of using such techniques is summarised in Table 9.3. On the advantage side, projective techniques are easy to use in combination with other approaches, such as questionnaires or focus groups. When

Table 9.3 Advantages and disadvantages of projective techniques for data assembly

Advantages	Disadvantages
Versatility	Ethical – may be used to obscure real purpose of research.
Active respondent involvement	May tell us more about popular culture than personality.
Respondent enjoyment	Stability of interpretation.
Overcomes barriers to responding	No common templates of materials.
Creates insight	

used with focus groups they can be a means of getting to a deeper level of understanding than is possible by simply asking questions such as 'Why do you say that?' or 'Why do you think that?' This versatility means that they can be used effectively with both a qualitative and quantitative design. The difference from the respondent's perspective is that projective techniques are different from what most people would expect of data collection. The different approach to data collection is intriguing, requires more active involvement than, say, a questionnaire and, in consequence, is likely to be more interesting. As Catterall and Ibbotson say, 'Projective techniques can also be fun to complete once respondents get over the initial surprise, self-consciousness and embarrassment at what they are expected to do' (p. 249). This can, however, be a double-edged sword because it might be the case that they are most suited to younger rather than older subjects or those with a more outgoing personality. For sensitive topics (such as abuse, sex, death), projective approaches may be a means of overcoming some people's reticence in talking about the issue or of discussing how it affects them. They can also be used to help subjects empathise with someone else's perspective. What is it like to be bullied, to be old or to go to a new school? Catterall and Ibbotson used completion of speech bubbles in a cartoon showing students being told by a lecturer about an assessment, not only to reveal their own views about the type of assessment but also to get students to think of assessment from the point of view of the lecturer. Finally (and this is, for many researchers, the real benefit), projective techniques throw up ideas and insights that may not have occurred to us when we designed our questionnaire or set up our interview schedule. On the other side of the equation is the fact that some researchers might use projective approaches to probe into areas that might be distressing for the participants. If our intention is to expose deep feelings that might otherwise not surface, this could be an invasion that might be detrimental to the well-being of the subject. Properly we should take advice from an expert (usually a psychologist) before we implement a projective approach. From a data perspective, there is concern that projective approaches tell us more about the subject's take on modern culture (which is why they are used extensively in consumer research) than give us insights into attitudes and emotions. Many of the stories that people tell about the images are similar. This supports the concern about cultural-based interpretations but there is a further methodological issue to concern us, the fact that different data analyses can give different results and the possibility that different researchers using the same analytic method can deliver different interpretations. For many quantitative researchers this would lead to the method being dismissed but we should be aware that when it comes to insights into the way people think, we have to accept that people are different and those differences can lead to more than one interpretation.

Another approach used by researchers has been to give subjects cameras and ask them to take photographs that highlight issues relevant to the research investigation. Tuula Heinonen and Maria Cheung used cameras in their study of the lives of rural women in China (Heinonen and Cheung, 2007). Their contacts were trained to use cameras and were then brought together after they had taken their photographs. They selected photographs that were the most significant for them and, in groups, they described the pictures and then explored why they were taken and what made what was in the picture important to them. What is revealed was an insider's view of life in a Chinese village. Putting it in context, the alternative as a research strategy was a long period of observation, but always as an outsider (see section 9.10).

9.7.2 Video and film

The use of moving images is an extension of still images. Jill Cheeseman and Barbara Clarke used video stimuli to understand children's mathematical thinking (Cheeseman and Clarke, 2007). They videoed mathematics lessons and then asked their interviewees to reconstruct what they were doing as they watched the video (essentially a 'think aloud' approach). Broadly the same approach was used by Howard Tanner and Sonia Jones, two Welsh researchers, who wanted to establish whether ICT improved mathematics learning. Their research tested the use of technology such as whiteboards and data projectors. At the heart of their research was video-stimulated reflective dialogue (VSRD), in which lesson videos were shown to pupils in groups to stimulate dialogue and discussion. The findings were clear: interactive oral work was stimulating; 'fun' and explanatory feedback were important; the technology was perceived to be modern (as compared, for example, with OHPs) and produced clear text and diagrams; the opportunity to try things out, make mistakes, erase the screen and start again was valued. Using mini write-boards (dry wipe boards) and, for older pupils, video feedback, was a strong stimulus for reflection. This last point raises the question whether this research technique ought to be used more to support student learning.

The advantage of using still or moving images is that they remove differences in experience as a variable in the research design. When should they be used? This is a more difficult question to answer. Clearly they act as a stimulus in situations where it might be difficult to generate a response to questions. They could be used with children or with people whose experience of what is being investigated is limited. The latter is important because it allows the researcher to present a stimulus image that is closely related to the type of data that is required to answer the research question (for example, in the study above where the researchers could focus on different forms of ICT in use in the classroom). This is clearly a benefit in terms of research design because it seeks to make the issues being investigated the principal variable. Projective techniques could be used to add detail and depth to many questionnaire designs but from a methodological point of view it is important to be able to show a link between the results of analysing the questionnaire data and the insights from the projective technique. This may not be easy if the sample size of the group completing the projective test is too small.

9.7.3 Activities

Activities that interviewees or focus group members are asked to perform are the final category of alternative stimulus. Asking people to represent what their understanding is, what they feel and what their emotions are pictorially is one approach that is common.

Using dolls, drawing images and organising images (for example, selecting photographs or postcards to represent how lecturers feel about their college) have also been used. In education research such approaches are especially common with young children whose verbal skills may be insufficiently developed to provide researchers with the data they need. Activity-based stimulus requires subjects to be actively involved and to think about what they are asked to do (questions are usually responded to immediately). This may promote recall and organisation of ideas. It is especially useful when dealing with issues that are hard to verbalise or which the respondent is uncomfortable with. These approaches are, for instance, widely used in explorations of abuse or trauma (such as bullying or the death of a family member). Drawing was used by Fiona Leach and Shashikala Sitaram in their research into sexual harassment of schoolgirls in India (Leach and Sitaram, 2007). Working in groups the girls drew maps to show where they had seen or experienced abuse taking place. The researchers wanted to understand what the girls felt about the different types of abuse. Their approach was to construct an 'abuse spider', where each leg of the spider represented a type of abuse. The girls placed coloured stickers on the legs (each colour represented a level of seriousness) to represent how serious they felt the abuse was.

The representation of the world using alternative approaches may require the researcher to view the data as a metaphor. This, of course, requires a different type of analysis and an understanding that underpins the ability to understand the language of metaphor. Much of the work on metaphor analysis has been based on language, where there can be an issue about when words are being used in an everyday conversational sense and when they have a deeper meaning. For a discussion of this complex area (yet one that is increasingly important for qualitative analysis), Rudolph Schmitt's paper (Schmitt, 2005) offers a good introduction to the way in which the concepts can be operationalised. He suggests that we can see metaphor in the following ways:

- As a means of representing our results: he gave an example of medical provision, which could be represented as a 'franchise', as a 'mission' and as a 'nurturing process'.
- To describe the research process, for instance, thinking of qualitative data as a 'kaleidoscope' of colour whose pattern emerges only when viewed through an analytical process.
- Identifying metaphors used by interviewees.

Schmitt points to other ways of using metaphor in research but they are not likely to be as useful for the beginning researcher.

Professor Kara Chan's research on children's perceptions of material possessions begins to use metaphor (Chan, 2006). The research issue she explores is of interest to both educationalists from the perspective of value development and to marketers from the perspective of selling to children. Her method was to give each child a sheet of paper, blank but for a stimulus statement: 'This child has a lot of new and expensive toys' and 'This child does not have a lot of toys'. The children were asked to draw something that illustrated the text. The drawing activity was then followed up by a short interview. The drawings were then analysed and 28 categories of objects and facial expressions (these were the metaphors) were devised to represent the meanings that the children were expressing. Branded goods were a metaphor for being well-off, for instance, while patches on clothes and toys were a metaphor for being poor. Chan was able to show that even very young children could express emotional attachment, social meaning, personality and self-image. As this work shows, the interpretation of the data to create (and extract) meaning is a crucial step. We shall look at this again in Chapter 11.

9.8 Ethical issues

While all research generates ethical concerns, obtaining data through interviews and focus groups can pose particular questions. We shall explore this here.

9.8.1 Consents

People should consent to take part in research programmes. Their consent should be informed but what does this actually mean? Certainly they should be aware of and understand the purpose of the research. They should know why they particularly have been chosen. They should know how their information will be used and how identifiable and locatable it will be. They should know the limits of their involvement – will they see research results, will they be able to comment upon the analysis and conclusions and, if necessary, be able to refute them or withdraw their contribution? All of this is fairly standard, until the last point. Expert or key informant, or what are called elite interviews (talking to a head of education, or someone with a high profile and considerable authority and responsibility), pose particular issues. Depending on the issue, it might be quite easy to identify respondents, despite any guarantee of anonymity that might have been given. If the research output is critical of someone's role or contribution or is blamed for an action or an outcome, should there be a power of veto? How important is the research relative to someone's position, prospects or even job security?

From another perspective, we have to be sure that someone is able to give informed consent. With children the situation is quite clear. Up to a legally stated age (usually 18 in EU states as established by family law), parents or guardians have to give consent. However, there are complications that create 'grey' areas. In the UK, children can take the decision to leave school at 16 (though this is due to be raised in 2013). In Italy, Finland, Denmark, France, and Sweden children can marry at age 16, though in Sweden the parental responsibilities continue. In the Netherlands only women over 16 with a child may take responsibility for themselves. Usually the 'grey area' is between the ages of 16 and 18, but when girls under 16 in the UK can have an abortion without their parents' consent in some circumstances, there may be situations below age 16 when a child's and parents' interests conflict. If we are researching underage pregnancy and the actions girls take, whose consent should we seek for an interview, the girl or her parents? The answer is that whatever the research, the researcher should always adopt a precautionary principle and negotiate access with the parents. There are, however, research fields where we should be sure that the parents understand or are able to make a decision. If the problem is one of parents speaking a foreign language, then the solution is to interpret the request. But what if the parent is a registered drug addict and the child is identified as a carer and tells the parent to sign the form? What if the parents themselves have learning difficulties?

In summary, consent is more than a signature on a form. We must be sure that people understand in what (and on what basis) they are participating. However, events can change and challenge even this position, so consent given at one time may not be consent throughout the entire research programme.

9.8.2 Disclosure

Confidentiality is a normal condition under which people give us data. Normally maintaining confidentiality is not a problem but what happens in a focus group? While we can recruit participants on the basis that what is said in the group is confidential to the group, not everyone might subscribe to the same ethical standards. Imagine a focus group to consider sexual identity with young adolescents in a school. Of course the researcher has to reinforce the confidentiality message, even to the extent of getting participants to sign a non-disclosure agreement, but what if one of the participants talks about the experience outside the group and identifies one of the group members as admitting to being gay. Should the researcher take it up with the pupil who has disclosed the information (over whom they have no authority) or with the head teacher, thereby breaching confidentiality? Should the pupil be reprimanded or punished? Acting after the event is always difficult. It may be that a better approach would be to role-play the issue (and others) with the group before the focus group discussion. That would represent a commitment to the duty of care to the participants and could well shape attitudes to the importance of sticking to an agreement.

There is another situation in which confidentiality is a challenging issue and it too involves a conflict with a duty of care. Researchers can learn a great deal of sensitive information (which may not even be relevant to the investigation) especially in one-to-one interviews. What should a researcher do, having agreed to treat what is said in confidence, if they learn that the respondent is self-harming or that another pupil is carrying a knife? Do these constitute circumstances where the confidence can be broken? The first course of action would be to try to get the interviewee to seek help but if this is not successful then, on balance, acting to secure the safety of the interviewee or the wider community delivers a benefit that exceeds the cost of a broken commitment.

9.8.3 Risk

Interviewing can be risky. Going to people's houses and meeting people on estates is a necessary part of the data collection process if, for instance, we are researching aspects of social exclusion. The leader of a research team has a responsibility to look after its members. As a minimum, we should know where members are going when they are off-site. There should be procedures that require them to phone in before and after a meeting. They should normally visit in pairs. Again, the ethics require planning to foresee problems and to produce solutions to situations we hope will never occur.

9.9 Reviewing interviews and focus groups

Despite all the caveats and discussion of things that can go wrong, most interviews and focus groups work well and produce useful data. This is because people try hard to give us what we want. The question can be poorly phrased but respondents will answer it trying to see what we want. Our role as researchers is to capitalise on this goodwill, appreciate that with the passage of time our interviewees have an investment in the process and ensure that we remove the problems, niggles and barriers to effective communication.

What we have to do to make sure that things go well is:

- match the type of interview to the research problem by exploring the problem and reviewing how others have tackled it;
- determine what sort of data we require and what sort of stimulus will produce it;

- consider our interviewees and their ability to vocalise their feelings and manage alternative stimuli (see Case Study 9.5 for how one researcher configured data collection when she worked with children);
- construct a framework for managing our interview;

Case study 9.5 Obtaining data from children

The way we work with adults may not be appropriate for other groups, including children and people with a learning disability. The solution in such cases is to ensure that the process of collecting data is meaningful to the survey participants. This case study describes how a British research group that included Dr Samantha Punch worked with 13- and 14-year-old children in a study of the problems they faced and how they coped with them.

The topic itself is one that even adults would have difficulty engaging with. It is never easy to address one's own demons and it is particularly difficult for young people whose self-understanding is limited and whose self-belief may be challenged when they confront problems. The research therefore raises ethical issues, which Dr Punch acknowledges. In particular, she notes issues of confidentiality and the fact that those engaged in the research had to be prepared to take on the role of advisor as to what course of action might be appropriate.

The methods she used to obtain data were as follows.

- *Group and individual interviews:* group interviews were used with single sex groups because of research evidence that boys and girls dealt with their problems in different ways. The group size varied between three and six. Interviews took place in school and residential home settings. Follow-up discussion showed that the school samples preferred group interviews and the residential home samples preferred the individual interviews. This highlights an issue of vulnerability when exploring sensitive issues with children.
- *The secret box:* Dr Punch needed to know what problems the young people faced but appreciated that she would be unlikely to be made aware of them in a group or even individual session. Her solution was to ask the young people to write them down and post them in a 'secret box'. When she discovered that even then some children reported that they had problems that they had not revealed or which they thought they might experience in the future, she introduced an even more 'secret box' that was to be opened only after the interviews. Many of the responses were concerned with puberty and the social context (for instance, drink and drugs).
- *Stimulating discussion:* getting young people to talk about how they managed their problems required more than a series of questions from the facilitator or interviewer. Dr Punch's solution was to use video clips from soap operas, problem page letters, and a set of 'common phrases' that adults use in reaction to young people's problems. This last stimulus was used as an ice-breaker to create group bonding since phrases such as 'you'll understand when you grow up' and 'it's not the end of the world' invariably produced laughter!
- *Tasks and activities:* these were used to stimulate discussion. They included grouping problems into categories ('big, middle and small worries'), spider diagrams on which young people noted how they coped with problems and listing whom they would turn to in respect of different types of problem.

The outcome of this approach was twofold.

- First Dr Punch and her group obtained the data she wanted. They were able to identify the types of problem experienced by young people and how they dealt with them. Those in residential homes were more knowledgeable about agencies and more confident about talking to them but some young people felt that there was a stigma to making contact with them. Many young people also felt that adults trivialised their problems but friends were a good source of advice.
- Second, the children appreciated the sensitivity with which the issues had been broached and discussed. The whole methodology rebalanced the power between researcher and subject and between young people and adults. But, perhaps most importantly, they enjoyed the experience. Amy thought it was 'brill' and Lisa said that 'it was good, I felt I could say anything'.

Source: Punch (2002).

- assess whether this framework will deliver the depth of insight we require of our data and, if not, consider how we can reach that depth;
- review issues with an ethical dimension at all stages of the data gathering process.

When we have done this, we should again consider whether we shall have sufficient data to answer our research question. If not, we should consider what other data we can obtain. One approach might be to go out and observe. This is what we shall consider in the next section.

9.10 Watching and listening: an introduction to observation as a data collection method

For all education's commitment to qualitative research, observation comes a weak second to talk-based investigations when we see what is published. This is surprising, first, because verbal communication is a limiting factor for some groups which are of interest to us (young children, for example) and, second, because we have plenty of evidence that what we see influences our judgements more than what we hear. A good (and very influential) example of this appeared in 1968 when an American psychologist, Robert Rosenthal, and a high school principal, Leonore Jacobson, published a short (only 11 paragraphs long) but ground-breaking paper on how teachers' expectations of their pupils become self-fulfilling. The summary for their paper states:

> Within each of 18 classrooms, an average of 20% of the children were reported to classroom teachers as showing unusual potential for intellectual gains. Eight months later these 'unusual' children (who had actually been selected at random) showed significantly greater gains in IQ than did the remaining children in the control group.

What Rosenthal and Jacobson identified was an effect but not the process that caused it. Their findings began a programme of observational research into how children pick up the clues as to what is expected of them and how they are regarded. Of course, obvious praise or criticism has an impact but the wealth of research evidence suggests that non-verbal communication is rather more important. Elisha Babad quotes one example:

> When a student fails to answer a teacher's question, the teacher would continue to be in eye contact with that student for a brief period (measured in seconds or milliseconds) before turning their eyes away. It turns out . . . that the duration of this eye contact following failure varies as a function of teacher expectancy: the duration would be longer if the teacher expects the student to be capable of answering the question and shorter in the case of a low expectancy.
>
> (Babad, 2005, p. 290)

Small clues, such as brief eye contact over a long period, can contribute to lower academic attainment and progression in children from lower socio-economic groups, social and ethnic stereotyping and that ill-defined but possibly pervasive concept, institutional racism. There does not have to be a notice saying 'You are not very good'; pupils will pick up the signs from a run-down and poorly equipped school. Such signs say eloquently 'You are not worth spending money on'. And since pupils respond to this behaviour and to these clues, we should pay more attention to observation as an approach to data collection because behaviour is an important source of information.

Observation can deliver worthwhile data but only if it is done well. There is a sense amongst some new researchers that observation is easy, all you have to do is walk around until something strikes you. The very great danger of this is that it is the most unusual things that are the most striking and the most unusual things are not usually the most useful for understanding and explaining ordered situations and relationships. Observation is an organised process with structures and protocols that are the guarantee that data are valid and reliable.

9.11 What can we use observation to do?

Observation has a long history as a research method. Anthropologist Bronislaw Malinowski opened up a new type of field research (later called ethnography) in 1914 with studies of native groups in Papua New Guinea. His total immersion approach was adopted and reconfigured for use in developed societies by the Chicago School of Sociology, which flourished at the University of Chicago between the First and Second World Wars. William Foote Whyte, author of *Street Corner Society* (Whyte, 1943), one of the seminal works that used observational methodology in an urban setting, was a graduate student at Chicago. Perhaps the most famous attempt to record the nature and condition of society in a country is the UK's Mass Observation Project (see Case Study 9.6). Elsewhere, in psychology, observation was being developed as a means of enquiry quite independently. Perhaps the most famous research (and the most important for educationalists) was Jean Piaget's observation of his own children, which was to lay the foundations of our understanding of child development. Piaget observed his children in the natural setting of their home lives, though he did test out his evolving ideas on child development in play-type activities. As Gerard Duveen (2000) observes in his analysis of Piaget's observational approaches, '. . . some of the observations . . . are straightforward records of his children's activity, many . . . are also records of interventions . . . A rearrangement of things around the child would produce a new situation in which the child's reaction could be observed . . .' (Duveen, 2000, p. 88). Duveen notes that his methodology combined sound ethnographic with clinical practice.

While much educational scholarship in these early years of the twentieth century was based on the exploration and implementation of philosophical ideals ('what should be' and not 'what is') there were examples of educationalists using observation to source their data. For example, Marion Kirkpatrick's discussion of rural schools (in the USA) published in 1917 is clearly a reflection based on his own experience. Partly descriptive autobiography (the first day as a schoolteacher in rural Kansas), rather nostalgic, anecdotal, strongly reflective and contemplative, it was written as a guide for those who were beginning their careers. It gives a picture of education, rural life and farming communities at the beginning of the twentieth century. While the analysis does not result from structured observation, it is, nevertheless, the distillation of experience and contains insights, so we should regard it as an authentic research document. By the middle of the century, it was clear that developments in observation methodology in anthropology, psychology and sociology were making their way into education and that educational research was becoming conceptually and methodologically better founded. It was in this

Case study 9.6 The Mass Observation Project

Mass observation, as the name suggests, is an attempt to capture the mood, views and behaviours of people in everyday life. In 1936 Britain experienced a deep constitutional crisis. It may seem of little importance in our more relaxed times but the possibility of the marriage of the King to an American divorcee sent Church, Crown and Parliament into turmoil and created a crisis resolved only by the King's abdication.

It was not the crisis itself that led to the Mass Observation Project but the sense that the media were presenting a 'sanitised' view of the events from a perspective of upper class and middle class duty. The personal and emotional dimension was missing and the views of ordinary working people were not known (because they were irrelevant). Yet among many working people there was affection for the King who, as Prince of Wales, had highlighted the plight of the unemployed during the Great Depression of the 1930s. This was the situation in which three young men, Tom Harrison, Humphrey Jenning and Charles Madge, set up Mass Observation in 1937.

Their approach was to recruit an army of volunteers who listened and watched and then recorded in notebooks, on camera and on film what people said and did. The aim was to produce an 'anthropology of ourselves'. Observation continued during the Second World War and into the 1950s. The post-war period was, however, becoming very different from the 1930s. The end of rationing (introduced in the war) gradually led to the evolution of a consumer culture and Mass Observation followed the trend, eventually to become a market research organisation.

The archive of Mass Observation was taken by the University of Sussex, a newly-founded university in 1970. In 1981, the University initiated a new project with the same goal of producing 'the science of ourselves'.

The archive is available on-line (on a subscription basis) at http://www.amdigital.co.uk.

There is a considerable amount for researchers interested in educational history and for those concerned with the present day. There are observations on children and childhood, education, family relationships and teachers.

The last word in this case study is a report from the archives. Children in 1937 were asked to write about 'the greatest person that ever lived'. One 17-year-old wrote:

> I believe A. Hitler to be the finest person who has ever lived. My reasons are manifold; firstly, only a great man of fine character could work himself up from the ranks of the army to the position of Fuhrer . . .
>
> Secondly he is . . . a Methodist; and I am a Methodist: he is a teetotaller and I am a teetotaller . . . having so much in common between us, I cannot help but admire him.
>
> Thirdly, one has only to go to Germany to see the great work he is doing for his people . . .
>
> Hitler stands for all that is fine about modern Germany.

The report continues with a strong anti-Semitic theme. Attitudes such as this need to be understood if they are to be confronted. Bigotry exists today and so mass observation could still be an important means of confronting it.

period that we start to see an expansion of education journals (for example, *Education Review* in the late 1940s and the *Scandinavian Journal of Education Research* and *Educational Research* in the 1950s) that provided a platform for the publication of observational studies.

How have education researchers responded to the opportunities afforded by an observational methodology? A number of areas can be identified.

- *Child development:* amongst the topics that have been studied in recent years are social competence of children, interaction between children and their teenage mothers, between children and carers (foster mothers, childcarers), development outcomes and home environment, friendship patterns (in the context of desirability) and the behaviour of gifted children.

- *Socialising behaviours:* themes investigated include play and social interaction, role play for citizenship, learning to be friends, sibling synergy and teacher and school governor socialisation.
- *Anti-social behaviours:* studied using observational techniques include drug use, hazardous drinking (amongst university students!), teaching for active citizenship, aggression and peer rejection, homelessness, attention-deficit hyperactivity disorder and many studies on disaffection.
- *Group cultures:* have been explored in terms of cultural diversity and learning, subject cultures and disciplinary learning, new technology and learning, enhancing ethnic diversity in higher education and youth cultures.
- *Territoriality:* studies around this theme often intersect with youth culture, socialisation and anti-social behaviour. Other themes researched are: gender construction amongst immigrants, organisation of work teams and groups, teenagers' appropriation of space and gangs.
- *Practice observation:* for practice improvement and the maintenance of quality standards is well established in medical and teacher training, teaching and lecturing, co-teaching (teaching a class jointly) and the assessment of vocational and practical skills.

While these themes are ones that can be picked up from the research literature, observational research is not limited to them. It can form part of any investigation, quantitative or qualitative in nature. The data that are collected can be processed into usable information from which we can draw our research conclusions using either quantitative or qualitative methods. When we develop our data collection strategy, we should see if there is a role for observation. In order to do this, we have to appreciate its characteristics.

9.12 Characteristics of an observational approach

Observation has certain characteristics that distinguish it from other approaches and we need to see whether they can be met in relation to our own research. There is, however, a caveat to this; there is possibly more flexibility in how we collect data through observation than many other approaches, which, as we have seen, can be constrained by principle or by custom and practice. We should not, therefore, be afraid to test the limits of an observational approach.

(i) A naturalistic setting

The first thing we should note about observation is that it takes place in a natural setting for those being observed. Thus, for example, we would observe pupils in a classroom, young children playing in a playground, members of a school or college at the institution, senior management team in a meeting, young people at leisure, family life at home and so on. In all of these situations, the setting is one that people normally inhabit as part of their day-to-day activities. There is another type of 'natural setting' that we ought to understand, one that is recognised and accepted for what it is but which is not part of the normal experience. For example, if, as part of an investigation into socialisation, we were to put a group of infants into a room with play facilities and then video what happened, their environment would be unknown but the equipment and the setting would be, so it could be classified as a 'natural setting'. The key conditions of the idea of a natural setting are that there are no conditions or variables that are not usually present which could influence or disrupt what is being observed.

(ii) An unfolding investigation

A second characteristic of observational approaches is that the pathway to an end point is not predetermined. Observation is an emergent procedure. It is discovery based. As we learn more our ideas develop and our thinking changes. There are few limits on what we can do and where we can go. An observational approach is flexible; it can merge very easily into other methods of data collection or alternative data sources (such as statistical series or documents). With this opportunity, however, comes a great danger. It is easy to mistake a line of thinking that opens up a route that we believe will lead us to answer the question, only to find that it is a cul-de-sac.

(iii) A holistic viewpoint

Observation takes a view of the whole circumstance. While there is a focus to an investigation, the context is an equally important source of data that aids understanding and interpretation. It might, for example, be difficult to understand bullying at school without reference to home life or to appreciate a tutor's approach to teaching without understanding the academic culture of the subject. The implication for the researcher is that it is important to know the background in order to give depth and perspective to the subject.

(iv) A changing world

Most (but not all) observation takes place over a period of time. This is often a precondition for effective data collection in a naturalistic setting. While changing conditions are part of the natural setting, they are a potential agent of influence; in fact they may be the factor being investigated. For instance, if we were looking at the amalgamation of two schools, we should be interested in observing the reactions of teachers and administrative staff. Not only does amalgamation create extra work, it also reduces the number of posts. Both are stressful situations. The issue for the researchers is to be able to partition the dynamics of the world into background noise and significant influences.

(v) The significance of unique events

Every observational setting is, by definition, unique. What we have to do as researchers is demonstrate that out of our unique observations there is something that is meaningful for and relevant to other contexts. For this to be true, two things have to happen. First, the observations must produce patterns from particular events, it must infer linkage between outcome and probable cause. In other words, it should, inductively, produce generalisations. Second, it must be able to show that the setting for the observations is, itself, not unusual or atypical. A classroom or a youth centre are unique but what goes on within them is replicated to some degree elsewhere. How we select our observational settings is important (see case study selection in section 6.6.5).

9.13 Ways of being an observer

An observational approach gives us quite clear choices of method, each of which has implications for how we generate our data and whether we influence the setting. The first distinction we should make is whether we are a remote observer or a close observer. Close observation takes place in the setting. Remote observation is separated from the setting. Most remote observation is by video link, either in real time or recorded. Claire Cameron (Cameron, 2007) provides an interesting example of remote observation. Most video studies directly analyse video evidence. What Cameron and her co-workers did, on a project called 'Care Work in Europe', was to observe care workers in Denmark, England and Hungary and edit the observations into videos which were shown to specific groups – children, care workers, 'experts' and parents. The videos were used to stimulate discussion of practice and the discussions were themselves audio recorded and videoed as the data to be analysed. While remote observation allows us to examine and re-examine our data, it does not engage with the full authenticity of the setting, even when conducted in real time. For example, it gives us a focused view and does not enable us to see the full extent of the setting; it does not allow us to see things out of the corner of our eye and direct our attention to it; it isolates us from environmental conditions and restricts our view of background activity and noise. The process of editing a video introduces a judgement into the research process. While these things may be problematic, they have to be judged in the context of whether they remove noise or interfere with the message. The chances are, it will be the former.

Close observation falls into four types: we can either be involved or not in the setting we are investigating or known or not known as an investigator to the people in the setting (see Table 9.4). Other terms are also used for these categories. Other texts say that we are 'obtrusive or overt' if we are known to those we are observing or 'unobtrusive or covert' if we are not known, and describe us as 'participant' if we are actively involved in what we are researching or 'non-participant' if we are not involved.

(i) Active and known

In this situation the researcher is immersed in the activities of the group and is known as a researcher to those who are being studied. W.F. Whyte's classic study, *Street Corner Society*, is an example of this. Whyte spent long periods with the group he was researching but was clearly different from though accepted by the group. He took part in group activities but stood outside the group to study it. This approach, where a researcher is actively involved in a community but known not to be a member of that community is much the same as that conducted by anthropologists who were responsible for developing the ethnographic approach. The issues around implementation are very similar to

Table 9.4 Types of observation

	Obtrusive	Unobtrusive
Participatory	Active and known	Active and not known
Non-participatory	Inactive and known	Inactive and not known

those confronted by early ethnographers. Fundamental to getting good quality data is the need for a bond of trust to exist between the group and the researcher. This takes time to develop, so this type of investigation is rarely for a short duration. Trust can be built, first, with someone or some people with authority and then transmitted to others in the group. The bond of trust is frequently initiated through discussion about the project and the process of data gathering. Without the project being valued by the group, the researcher will not be accepted. Despite this acceptance, problems may still arise if there are status differences between researcher and researched and those problems may be exacerbated if there are ethical differences as well. Robert Power describes the ethical and value conflicts he experienced while working on illicit drug abuse (Power, 1989). At the level of personal values, he comments on the use of smoking as an ice-breaker when one is not a smoker. He raises the question of paying drug users to take part in research, knowing how the money is likely to be used, or giving them rewards such as queue jumping to gain access to treatment. He records his personal experience of being asked to 'collect drugs . . . and to deliver packages' while 'on one occasion, a drug user, who had a warrant out for his arrest, signed a letter and asked me to post it from my holiday in Italy to the court concerned' (p. 49).

(ii) Active and not known

Being an active participant in a group yet being covert places us in an excellent position to obtain strong, robust and compelling data. It circumvents the need to build trust and it can generate unusual insights. In 1986 an American anthropologist, Jack Weatherford, published a book, *Porn Row,* that dealt with his experience of working in a porn shop in Washington. In it, he recounts how the shop was used by other researchers, including one whose topic was child abuse. This researcher paid her interviewees. She used a snowball sampling method (where respondents helped identify and recruit other respondents, see section 6.6.2). What the researcher was unaware of was the fact that the women helped each other make up stories. Many of the interviewees, in other words, had no personal experience of being abused but the payment was a useful source of income. Ethically it may be sound to reward people for their time but we should always remember the Latin phrase, *caveat emptor,* let the buyer beware!

Covert participation such as Weatherford's is not without its problems and issues. Amongst these is the question of safety and security. Dennis Rodgers spent a year in Nicaragua researching life amongst the poor. He has written a compelling account (Rodgers, 2007) of how his research led him into gang membership. Facing danger, a knife fight, stealing, street fighting with other gangs, drug taking, gun fights, using grenades and gaining a reputation for 'fighting dirty' – no ethical consideration of a PhD proposal can prepare a researcher for these experiences (and one can only hope that he did not mention them in his letters home!). Fortunately educational researchers are rarely faced with such dangers. However, as the American researcher Robert Labaree (2002) shows, being an insider researcher raises its own issues. His work, on university governance, was undertaken while he was a member of the senate of the university where he worked. This situation raises an issue, both for the researcher and, as importantly, for the reader. Being an insider certainly gives access to information, some of which may be privileged, and produces insights, for example into power relationships and decision making outside the public arena, that otherwise would not be available. But being part of the power structure can lead us to form relationships with others to shape events and direct the very processes that we are studying. When we are actively involved, our involvement and how we view an issue can influence our interpretation of the evidence.

This last point is a serious methodological issue for the investigator. How active do we have to be to be taken seriously yet not change the character of the world we are investigating? And for the reader, what reliance can we place on research undertaken by an interested party? If we find ourselves in this situation, we have to make clear how we have resolved the conflict and this requires, at the very least, that we recognise it and make explicit our own values.

(iii) Inactive and known

In this observational approach the observer is visibly an outsider to the group. The group is aware of the observer but has no interaction at a process level with them. This is typically the approach used in studies of children, as exemplified by Gun Persson's work on interactions between children (Persson, 2005). His work on whether children showed both aggressive and beneficial behaviour to other children was undertaken over three years in three day-care centres in Sweden. Data were collected in two-month periods and in each period each child in the study was observed six times for a 20-minute period. Each observation was in a natural setting, inside or outside, and on each occasion the child's behaviour was not constrained by the investigation. He noted that 'children who show a readiness to unselfishly intervene on behalf of a peer are generally not inclined to make use of aggression in their interactions with peers' (p. 89) while, for others, social 'nonaltruistic behaviour was sometimes positively related to aggression (p. 90). All forms of social behaviour increased with age, a fact that he suggests is due to increasing competence in developing strategies that yield material and social benefit. Boys and girls could only be differentiated in terms of altruistic behaviour, where girls outperformed boys and only then in the third year of observation. He suggests that the reason for this difference is to be found in the development of empathy.

Persson's approach, relative to many others that have been published, is well conceived, well structured and well organised. It is a rigorous application of an observation strategy. Not all observation, however, has to be as structured as this. Indeed, if we are not sure what we are going to meet, it probably cannot be.

Gillian Ballinger was faced with this situation when she examined how well prepared students were to study a degree in English at university (Ballinger, 2003). As a tutor on a first-year undergraduate programme, she was aware that students found the adjustment to university learning difficult. They were concerned about feeling disorientated and disorganised, how to manage literary context and theory and how to analyse texts, as well as their ability to manage the volume of work in the time available. While a research methodologist might question the detail of her method, there is no doubt that her approach of finding out what went on in English teaching at school was a sound one. She chose two schools in which to observe classroom teaching and found the same approaches in each. She found contrasts between school and university (see Table 9.5).

Despite these differences, Gillian Ballinger felt that there were similarities that would prepare students for the transfer: a discursive approach to enable individuals to establish and justify their own viewpoints, an appreciation of the importance of context to literature and the importance of the audience and staging in understanding plays. Her paper concludes with some general guidance for university tutors. While the investigation is not as rigorously set up as Persson's, it is certainly valid as a means of appreciating the learning environment that provides the basis for university transfer, and her analysis of differences and similarities is clearly informed by a sound understanding of the purpose as well as the methods of higher education teaching.

Table 9.5 Contrasts between learning at school and university

School	University
Close examination of text.	Increase in text coverage, need for time management.
Importance of the teacher's opinion.	Importance of literary theory and cultural/historical context.
Commentary at the beginning of school courses.	Development of autonomous thinking and argument.
Seating in rows, not conducive to interaction.	Discussion – active involvement in lectures and seminars.
High level of preparation for the examination.	Little preparation for exam.

This idea of observation as a learning process is taken further by Seonaidh McDonald who reviewed shadowing as a mean of gathering data (McDonald, 2005). Shadowing is more usually thought of as a work experience activity but, because it involves someone following someone else over an extended period of time, it is admirably suited as a means of data collection. McDonald identifies three ways of using shadowing:

1. *As experiential learning:* the traditional way of looking at shadowing; in research terms we might use it in an initial stage of an investigation to build up our background knowledge;
2. *To record behaviour:* we follow people in order to collect data on their behaviour that will be useful for our research. Three American researchers, led by Professor Vernon Polite, followed 58 school principals to assess the transference of learning from a professional development programme into work practice. An interesting perspective on their research is that they fed back their analysis to their subjects to shape their further development (Polite et al., 1997).
3. *To see the world from another perspective:* this approach is less instrumental than recording behaviour, where there is often a strong analytic framework (reflecting data needs and variables to be tested). The emphasis is on the lived experiences of the subjects and the purpose is to understand the world through their eyes. This moves the research strategy firmly into the realm of phenomenology (see section 2.1.1). As McDonald says, 'shadowing has made a leap from being used as a neutral measuring and recording (quantitative) tool to the means of generating a narrative to first develop and then share insight into a role (qualitative)' (p. 466).

Shadowing as a method for education researchers can be used to understand how people perform roles, spend time and interact with others. It could be used in a study of school management, teacher burnout or student workloads. It is an approach that can be used with others; the researcher need not be a mute observer but can, for instance, ask questions to gain understanding.

(iv) Inactive and not known

In this situation the researcher does not participate in group activities and their other role as a researcher is unknown to the group being researched. Given these conditions it is obvious that the group size must be sufficiently large for the research not to stand out. Typical studies using this approach are observing people shopping or in crowd situations (such as at sporting events). It has also been used in studies of children in hospital, where a white coat can create an appropriate disguise. Because so many educational settings are small in scale (it is difficult to remain unknown in even a large school), it is not extensively used in educational research. However, it could be. For example, there is concern in some cities in the UK that the conversion of areas to rental accommodation for university students would lead to a significant change in the character of an area and create conflict with local people. This issue could be explored by unobtrusive non-participant observation. The approach could also be used in a study of how students or pupils used physical space, for example a library or Internet cafés. Ronald King's approach of hiding in a Wendy house to observe children in a classroom is unlikely to be repeated (King, 1978) but his reflection on his research procedures (King, 1984) is well worth reading in order to appreciate what research decisions have to be made. A modern, technological approach to unobtrusive non-participant observation is the surveillance of public communal areas. Not only are systems in widespread use in towns and cities in the UK, they are extensively used in educational institutions as well. It has, for example, been used to study bullying and other aggressive behaviour and the nature of social interactions amongst children. While there are ethical issues associated with the use of remote observation, from an operational point of view the strength is that it is a highly cost-effective naturalistic investigation (as long as those being observed are unaware of or have forgotten about the surveillance system). The downside is that the visual range is restricted and, without an audio system, verbal interaction is not recorded.

9.14 How to proceed with observations

In structuring a recording procedure, we have to make two decisions. First, what is it that we are going to record? Second, at what point do we structure and code our observation?

(i) What will we record?

The prime influence on this is obviously the thing we are investigating. The question we pose requires specific data if we are to answer it. Those data must be relevant to the issue. Our opportunities in respect of data can be divided into four categories: context, behaviour, verbal interaction and image. The actual recording of data is dependent on the research issue and the chosen indicators. Notwithstanding this, context data should normally always be recorded.

- *Context data* records the conditions of the setting before, during and perhaps even after the observation. It should be a full description of the physical environment, including items that might not apparently be relevant to answering the question (for example, temperature, paint colour) and activity in the setting before the observation started. The purpose in collecting this data is to assess, over repeated observations, whether anything in the environment appears to be affecting the observed characteristics.
- *Behaviour* includes actions by a person alone or as a group of two or more. We might be interested in where people go, who they are with, what they do (and in what sequence), what they look at and how they look. We should be interested not only in movement in space but also by non-verbal communication – gestures, stance, eye

movements and so on. When the research objective is focused, this is reflected in the observational approach. Sannelee Bolhuis and Marius Voeten (Bolhuis and Voeten, 2001) observed how Dutch secondary teachers taught their subjects in order to understand the potential for and barriers to self-directed learning for the students. They placed an observer (who had a laptop with a program to record observations) in the classroom, fitted the teacher with a microphone so that all that was said could be heard by the researcher on headphones and tape recorded the teaching sessions as well. They found that 30 per cent of teaching time was 'traditional', where the emphasis was on knowledge transmission, 5 per cent on developing independent learning (what they called process oriented teaching) and 43 per cent on engaging actively with the students (which they called activating teaching).

- *Verbal interaction* is important both in terms of the content and the character of the communication and between whom the communication occurs. Communication data can convey information about attitude, mood and status, it can reflect interests and concerns and it can be used to interpret actions and behaviour. Talk can be conversational, discursive, explanatory, persuasive, confrontational and positional in character. A group of Dutch medical educators conducted an interesting study on verbal interaction (Visschers-Pleijers et al., 2006). Their interest was in a model of learning that is extensively used in medical education, problem-based learning. The concept behind this is that being confronted with a problem creates a need to identify specific knowledge and need-driven knowledge is more effectively anchored in the memory than knowledge acquired through transmission, for example in lectures. In problem-based learning, new knowledge is assembled and combined with existing knowledge to solve problems. As a method of learning, it is argued that it is a better means of ensuring transference than classroom learning. What the Dutch team did was observe the verbal interactions of four seminar groups with the object of assessing how far the students' time was spent on learning activities, especially those that advanced their ability to collaborate in resolving problems – a skill we should all value in our doctors. They found that 80 per cent of the time was spent on learning interactions, with cumulative reasoning accounting for 63 per cent of the time alone. This simple approach throws light on the effectiveness of the learning process. Observation can be extensively used in classroom and playground studies, decision-making meetings and social interactions.
- *Image* (presentational data) is an object, experience and context through which people present themselves to the outside world. Such data include what we own, what we choose to use, what we consume, how we dress, how we travel, where we travel, how we spend our time. How we choose to use our time and money says something about our values, our status and even our aspirations. If we were to think that this is not relevant for children, then the research by a team led by a British sociologist, Christopher Pole, into 'pester power' should make us think again. Their findings (summarised on the *Cultures of Consumption* website at http://www.consume.bbk.ac.uk/researchfindings/newconsumers.pdf) show that (i) even for young people fashion is a marker of identity, (ii) children as young as six understood 'pop' culture and (iii) that access to 'labels' influenced being excluded or included. Pole describes and comments upon the methods used in the research elsewhere (Pole, 2007). The research team drew together data from discussions with and questions to young children, children's drawings and observation, such as wardrobe audits. The context of his commentary on the research approach is the move away from neutral observation to understanding the lifeworld and lived experiences of children. This makes the child much more of an

active participant in the research process and brings children into much closer contact with the researcher. As Pole says, 'Social research with children is now conducted within a highly charged context' (p. 70) and, when the research theme is how children wish to present themselves, clothe themselves and represent their bodies, discussions about parts of the body and how they are displayed raise concerns about how far legitimate research can go before it crosses a boundary of more general social concern for child welfare. Yet the issues with which Pole is concerned, children's consumption and their use of their own bodies, exist in other areas of interest to education, not the least sexual identity, sexual awareness and the whole area of sex education. Understanding the lived-in world of children and young people poses significant ethical and methodological problems for educational researchers.

(ii) When do we code our observations?

We look at the process of coding (organising) our data in Chapter 11 but the question 'When do we code?' is important to consider now because it has implications for the way in which we record our observations and the way we are thinking about the whole of our investigation. We can either code while we are observing or we can code afterwards. Whichever we choose, however, there are some things that should be common to both. The following procedures should be the norm:

- Context description (see section 9.15).
- Contemporaneous notes.
- Post-observation reflection.

Even when we are coding while observing, we should have a means of recording descriptions and comments that are not covered by the recording schedule. While much of this recording might be descriptive, conveying a richer picture narrative, it is also possible that we shall notice things that we should look out for on other occasions. It is more than likely that we shall begin to consider ideas that start to make sense of our observations. Post-observation reflection takes this further. Because we are looking back over our observations, hindsight allows critical distance to begin to shape perspective. We can think of our last observation in the context of earlier ones, identify similarities and differences, allow for context and so on. This reflective approach begins as a conversation that we have with ourselves and becomes an integrative tool that guides our analysis.

The data produced by these procedures are raw data. They have to be manipulated and organised before they begin to release their information. Data coding is a stage in this process. Coding requires that the data are put into some sort of framework, for example, a classificatory or categorical framework. Table 9.6 shows part of the coding sheet used by Bolhuis and Voeten in their study of teaching and learning approaches in Dutch schools (see section 9.15). If coding takes place at the same time as observations are made, it is obvious that a framework needs to be in place. The framework can be generated in one of two ways:

- *either*, it can be specifically derived for the research, which implies that there should be a preliminary study to develop and test the framework;
- *or*, a pre-existing framework can be used.

If we have to develop a framework for our research, we should (a) think about the types of activity we might observe and begin to construct a framework from this and

Table 9.6 Part of the coding framework used in a study of teaching and learning practice

Observational categories	Description of observational categories in six main groups of behaviour
1. Explaining	The teacher is talking and students are expected to listen.
e1 Subject matter	The teacher explains, clarifies, demonstrates, illuminates the subject matter.
e2 Drawing attention	The teacher draws students' attention to the subject matter.
e3 Reviewing subject	The teacher reminds students of explanations given on the subject matter in previous lessons.
e4 Previewing subject	The teacher tells students what subject will be dealt with in this and/or coming lessons.
e5 Relevance	The teacher explains and illuminates the outside-school significance of subject matter.
e6 Evaluation	The teacher explains how learning results of students will be judged, assessed, awarded.
e7 Learning	The teacher explains and demonstrates how to learn, and how to diagnose and monitor learning.
e8 Learning goals	The teacher explains and demonstrates the learning goals.
2. Questions	The teacher asks students questions.
q1 Subject matter	The teacher poses a question on subject matter.
q2 Reviewing	The teacher asks students a question reminding of subject matter that was dealt with before.
q3 Checking	The teacher asks a question to ensure the lesson can go on, like 'You got it?' or 'Ok?'
q4 Learning activities	The teacher asks what learning activities students have undertaken or planned.
q5 Diagnosing/monitoring	The teacher asks students to think about, analyse and supervise their learning.
q6 Relevance	The teacher asks students about the importance of the subject matter.
q7 Repeating	The teacher repeats the question they posed before when no (adequate) answer followed.
q8 Continuing	The teacher deepens the question, going into the students' response.
q9 General question	The teacher asks something not directly related to the subject matter or learning process.

Source: from Toward Self-Directed Learning in Secondary Schools: What do Teachers do? *Teaching and Teacher Education*, 17(7), 837-55 (Bolhuis, S. and Voeten, M 2001), copyright 2001, with permission from Elsevier.

(b) read extensively around the field and use other people's conclusions and assertions as the basis of our own search for indicators.

There are, however, some well-established pre-existing frameworks that can be used. One of the most extensively observed behaviours is teaching and most institutions that train teachers, as well as many schools, will have a framework for teacher observation. Many of these have an implicit (sometimes an explicit) link to a theory concerned with the purpose of education and effective teaching and learning. Look at Activity 9.2, which shows a series of criteria against which to observe lessons and the judgement criteria used by Ofsted (the quality assurance agency for schools and colleges in England). Whether we develop our own framework or use someone else's we should always be able to (a) identify and (b) justify criteria that underpin the observation process. England has a system of publicly-funded subject centres to bring together subject specialists in teaching and learning at university level. *Escalate*, the subject centre for education (which covers both teacher training and researching and studying education) has a checklist of

Activity 9.2 Whose quality?

One of the concerns of educationalists is that the basis on which schools are publicly judged can distort the education that is offered to children and work to their disadvantage. Once standards are established against which schools are assessed, head teachers are thought to shape the way teaching is provided and pupils are managed in order to demonstrate that the school meets (or exceeds) those standards. But is this actually the case? In this activity you have two pieces of evidence. One, on the left in the table below, are the criteria used within a school for lesson observation. This is the practice in which, usually, a senior or experienced member of staff observes the teaching of colleagues. Often this is a subject expert such as a head of department. Sometimes lessons are observed by a member of senior management, especially if there is an external inspection due or if there are concerns about the competency of the teacher. On the right are the criteria used by Ofsted for assessing and grading the lesson. Your task is to:

1. Consider how far the school's observation criteria are designed to meet the Ofsted criteria. Look first to see whether the same words are used and then look at the sense of each text to see whether there is any conflict between them.
2. Think about good and bad lessons that you have experienced. What made them good or bad? Are those factors reflected in either set of criteria?

Think of the following situations:

(a) a lesson in a school that selects only the brightest pupils
(b) a class which has a wide range of abilities
(c) a class where 30 per cent of the pupils have only been in the country for less than two years and whose command of the language is limited.

How far will the Ofsted criteria cope with these situations?

	Ofsted judgement criteria	
Lesson observation criteria	**Description**	**Characteristics of the lesson**
• Lesson plan has clear goals which are achieved. • Teacher shows good subject knowledge and understanding. • Pupils are engaged with subject. • Activities reflect individual pupil needs. • Variety of teaching methods to enable all pupils to learn effectively. • All pupils are stretched. • Assessment records are complete and inform pupil development. • Individualised Education Plans are referred to during the lesson. • Support staff and resources are effectively used to support learning. • Challenging behaviour is managed effectively. • Pupils are encouraged to reflect and helped to become independent learners.	**Outstanding (1)**	The lesson is at least good in all major respects and is exemplary in significant elements, as shown by the significant progress made by all of the learners.
	Good (2)	Most learners make good progress because of the good teaching they receive. Behaviour overall is good and learners are well motivated. They work in a safe, secure and friendly environment. Teaching is based on secure subject knowledge with a well-structured range of stimulating tasks that engage the learners. The work is well matched to the full range of learners' needs, so that most are suitably challenged. Teaching methods are effectively related to the lesson objectives and the needs of learners. Teaching assistants and resources are well deployed and good use is made of time. Assessment of learners' work is regular, consistent and promotes progress.
	Satisfactory (3)	The lesson is inadequate in no major respect, and may be good in some respects, as shown by the satisfactory enjoyment and progress of the learners.

▶

Lesson observation criteria	Ofsted judgement criteria Description	 Characteristics of the lesson

• Pupils make progress over time.
• Pupils enjoy their work and show a good attitude.
	Inadequate (4)	**A lesson cannot be adequate if:**
		• most learners, or a significant specific minority of learners, make less than satisfactory progress;
		• learners' overall behaviour or attitudes are unsatisfactory, spiritual, moral, social and cultural development are neglected, and learners' overall personal development is poor;
		• the health or safety of the learners is endangered;
		• the teaching is unsatisfactory. Unsatisfactory teaching is likely to have one or more of the following:
		  • weak knowledge of the curriculum leading to inaccurate teaching and low demands on pupils;
		  • work badly matched to the pupils' starting points;
		  • ineffective classroom management of behaviour;
		  • methods which are poorly geared to the learning objectives or which fail to gain the interest and commitment of the learners;
		  • inadequate use of resources, including assistants and the time available;
		  • poor assessment.

criteria that underpin 'good practice observation' and which is applicable to many models of teaching observation at all levels (see Table 9.7). The key elements of this are:

- there should be an introduction that sets out what is to be achieved and a conclusion that summarises what has been achieved;
- the lesson should be planned and not be an *ad hoc* reaction to circumstance;
- the teaching approach should enable students to achieve what is to be achieved and should actively involve students;
- the teacher knows the material;
- the material should challenge the students;
- the teacher should have good communication skills and should have a rapport with the students.

How are criteria such as these translated to the observation form? They are a complex set of ideas and having a separate space for each criteria is likely to result either in some being omitted or a failure to enter a further record on sections already completed while wanting to see if there is anything that can be said about an incomplete section. The Education Department at the University of Exeter has an interesting solution,

Table 9.7 *ESCALATE* good practice criteria

Openings and closings

- All sessions should have a clear introduction which indicates the aims and learning outcomes of the session and time plan.
- The session should be closed within the timetable time with some kind of conclusion or summing-up, summary of learning outcomes achieved and setting of work/reading for students to complete in their study time.

Planning and organisation

- The class begins and ends on time.
- Planned activities occur within the time allowed.
- There is evidence of planning of student learning.
- The tutor addresses the particular learning outcomes that students are expected to achieve, these relate to the overall aims and objectives of the unit/course, and these outcomes are communicated to the students.

Methods/approach

- The approach to organising and stimulating student learning is suitable to achieve the learning objectives set.
- The method adopted is justifiable in comparison with alternative approaches which may be taken.
- The approach ensures adequate student participation which is planned and not incidental.
- The approach is explained to students and understood by them.

Delivery and pace

- In a tutor-led session: the pace and delivery is appropriate for the students present; sufficient time is given to explain key concepts; neither too rushed nor too slow.
- In student led activities: explanations to students of activities is well-paced; sufficient time is allowed for student activities.

Content

- The tutor demonstrates a good command of the subject being taught.
- The content is appropriate to the level being taught and the needs of the students, is up-to-date and accurate.
- The tutor is able to respond to students' questions, provides authoritative and accurate guidance on reading and further study.

Intellectual stimulation

The class is conducted in a constructive learning environment in which the material of the lesson challenges the students and encourages them to develop their skills and move beyond their existing levels of understanding.

Student participation

Students have opportunities to participate in the learning process in an active way that promotes their understanding, which gives them an opportunity to ask questions and relate the material to their own learning development.

Use of appropriate learning resources

Which learning resources are appropriate depends very much on the topic being taught. Examples include:

- texts
- video and film
- visual material such as posters, pictures, diagrams, samples
- computer based learning packages
- multi-media packages.

Good teaching does not necessarily involve high-tech equipment, more important is having the right stimulation for learning. The students' own knowledge and experience are often the most valuable resources.

Use of accommodation and equipment

- Best use is made of the accommodation and equipment available.
- Suitability of the room/lab/studio for the type of learning activity being undertaken.
- Seating arrangements are effective.
- Any health and safety issues have been identified and dealt with.

▶

Table 9.7 *(continued)*

Overall style and ambience

- Good communication with students.
- The tutor can be heard and understood clearly.
- The tutor communicates an enthusiasm for the subject; is lively and encouraging to students.
- Explanations are given at the appropriate level in clear language.
- Respect for students' own culture, language and religion: the diversity of the student body requires staff to be sensitive to the different cultural backgrounds of the students.
- Rapport with students: students are encouraged by the tutor, a good relationship exists with the group and students receive positive feedback.

Acknowledgement of students' special needs

Where students have special needs or disabilities the tutor takes these into account and accommodates those needs in the presentation of material and in their response to the students.

half-way between a pre-code and a post-code (see Figure 9.2), with observations timed for at least every three to five minutes and a set of prompts to inform observation by reminding the observer of what to look for.

The alternative to devising a customised pre-coded observation form is to use one that already exists. Because so much observation research with children is about capability in social situations, many coding systems have been devised. It is impossible to list them all but Kenneth Merrell, a leading American educational psychologist, identifies six that have a general application (Merrell, 2008, p. 62):

- *Child Behaviour Checklist* – a rating scale for use in school.
- *Behaviour Coding System* – to analyse coercive and aggressive behaviour in school.
- *Social Interaction Scoring System* – for general social behavioural problems.
- *Family Interaction Code* – for home observation.
- *Child's Game/Parents' Game* – observation in 30 second units in a research setting of child/parent interaction.
- *Teacher Behaviour Code* – to observe changes in parent teaching behaviour after training.

Another framework with a general application is the *Social Interactive Coding System* developed, in 1990, by a team led by Dr Mabel Rice of the University of Kansas' Language Acquisition Studies Lab and used to measure the relationship between language and social interaction for children with impaired language capability (see Rice et al., 1990).

All of these can be used by education researchers but they are only a few of the many that are available. The *Fast Track* website provides a listing of many of these (http://www.fasttrackproject.org/allmeasures.htm). (*Fast Track* is an action-based project in the USA whose purpose is to research and then intervene to prevent serious antisocial behaviour amongst adolescents.)

There are fewer coding systems in the public domain with an *explicit* educational application but we should be aware of the Flanders Interaction Category framework (see Table 9.8) because it is used to codify interactions between pupil and teacher in a teaching and learning setting. The framework is based on a teaching and learning model that engages the pupil. At the heart of the observation schedule are processes of initiating action and responding. It was developed by an American educationalist, Ned Flanders, in 1970 and used between 2001 and 2003 by Dr Mark Newman (then at Middlesex University and now at the University of London Institute of Education) for a

LESSON OBSERVATION NOTES

Trainee:	Date:	Class:
School:	Time:	Topic:

Lesson Plan

☐ Learning objectives and outcomes
☐ Teaching strategies
☐ Pupil activities relevant to LO
☐ Opportunities for assessment
☐ Planned differentiation
☐ Pupil progression

Timing	

Behaviour management	***Range of questioning***	***Appropriate***	***Opportunities for***	***Develops***
Positive reinforcement Use of voice Waiting for quiet Remind off task pupil Scanning the class	Open Closed Differentiated Supplementary Probing/challenging Responses extend thinking	Language Clear explanations Modelling Timing/pace	discussion reflection active involvement addressing misconceptions	thinking skills enquiring/predicting, problem solving pupil independence

Observer:

Figure 9.2 Teaching observation schedule from the University of Exeter

Table 9.8 Flanders interaction categories

	(Who is talking?) Teacher	Pupil
Response activity	Accepts and clarifies an attitude or the feeling or tone of a pupil in a non-threatening manner. Praises or encourages. Accepts or uses pupils' ideas. Asks questions.	Pupil-talk – response.
Initiating activity	Lecturing. Giving directions. Criticising.	Pupil-talk – initiation.
Silence or confusion		

study into problem-based learning in nursing education. It has ten data coding categories, seven relate to the teacher, two to students and one to silence. Data is recorded in these categories on a systematic basis (for example, every minute). This allows a quantitative assessment of the nature of the interaction to be built. Newman used the Flanders coding to understand how teacher and pupils worked in problem-based learning (where a problem determines the learning need). The results of observing two lessons, one a lecturing approach and the other a problem-based learning approach, are shown in Figure 9.3 (Newman, 2004). The contrast is obvious. Pupil talk and response accounts for about 20 per cent of the lecture-based lesson and about 66 per cent of the problem-based lesson.

This ability to structure observation is important because, as we saw with Newman's work, it can generate quantifiable data. To this extent, pre-structured observations are analogous to closed questions since both generate counts of data. In the same way, open questions and post-observation coding have much in common too. Both are essentially inductive, allowing the pattern to emerge after the response or the observation, and both are particularly useful at an early stage of investigation when instruments and approaches are being tested. When observations are post-coded, the procedures common to all observational approaches assume a great significance. All detail, not just apparently significant events, should be recorded. The consequence of post-coding observations is that we shall collect a great deal of data that subsequently we will not use. Because of this, the process of sifting the data to pick out the nuggets that help resolve our research issue is very important. We shall look at how we can do this in Chapter 11.

9.15 Observation issues to be aware of

Observation is not just about going out with a recording sheet and pen and getting on with the job. It has to be a carefully conceived and structured activity. As we have seen, there are decisions to be made but even when we have determined how we want to proceed, there are issues we have to consider and traps we can fall into. In this section we shall consider three types of issue, ethics, bias and method, as they apply to observational research.

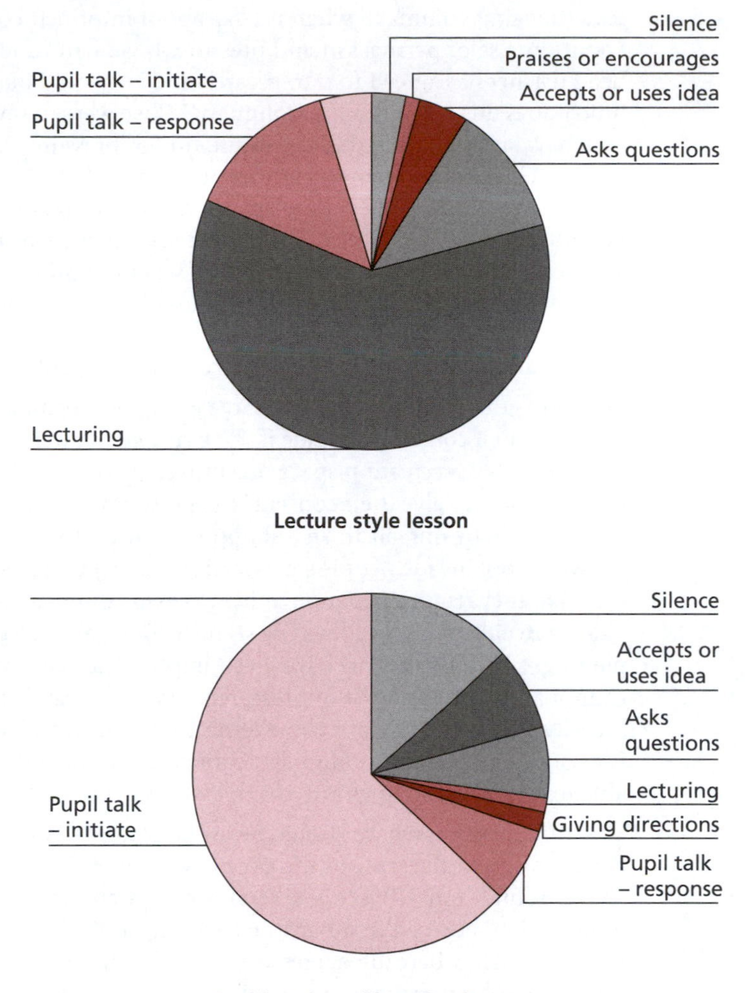

Source: Newman (2004).

Figure 9.3 Classroom interaction using Flanders interaction analysis

(i) Ethical issues

All research should be undertaken with the consent of those involved in giving us data but observational research raises some specific issues about consent. We will consider three situations: observation in organisations, observation in crowds and observation over time.

- Much of our observational research could be within an organisational setting – a school, a college, a university, an education administration unit, a publicly-funded external quality assurance organisation to list but a few. Of course we would need to gain consent at an organisational level (for example, the head teacher of a school) and also of those being observed (and if there were pupils, that would be their parents). The issue that should concern us is the relationship between the organisation and those observed. The Scottish Education Research Organisation (SERA), specifically uses the term 'voluntary' when it talks about informed consent. This raises concerns about the use of persuasion and pressure. If we write a letter to parents saying, 'The head teacher has agreed to our research and we would like you to agree as well', how much does this influence the 'voluntary'? If we were to say to a parent, 'All other parents have agreed', does this constitute undue pressure? But within this issue of authority relationships there is another problem lurking. Imagine that we are observing organisational roles in a college against a background of organisational change: how far will those we observe (for example, senior managers and administrators) behave and act according to their perception of what the principal expects rather than their own preferences? Our solution in this situation should be our regard for anonymity, not just in reporting our findings but also in ensuring that the names of those we observe are not known to others. This can be a difficult task.

- A second ethical issue arises with large group observation. This is rare in educational research but it could be an issue if, for example, we were observing in a school or college cafeteria or recreation space or a university campus. In these situations would we expect people to give their consent? In reality, it would be unrealistic in the same way that it would be unrealistic in a shopping centre. However, we do have to ensure that (a) we do not invade people's personal space, (b) we respect their privacy and (c) ensure that they retain their anonymity. The issue of privacy also arises in the context of video surveillance. Should we use security footage for research purposes? While people might be construed to have given implied consent for its use for their safety, we cannot argue the same for our research. Market researchers justify the use of a shop's security videos in much the same terms as they justify observation in public places, it is anonymous and has no impact at the time on the individual. This may be extendable to education settings but it is not without a potential challenge.
- The third ethical issue we should be aware of arises from the methodology we adopt. Participation in the lives of the people we are observing can create challenges. W.F. Whyte found himself voting several times in an election; Denis Rodgers stole and fought when he lived in a barrio in Nicaragua. While education research is unlikely to require us to become aggressive, it may well confront us with moral dilemmas. What if we observe something that is illegal or is wrong? Is there ever a point at which the benefits to the research of not being a whistle-blower outweigh the moral compromise that is involved? Activity 9.3 puts us in the position of having to resolve moral dilemmas.

Finally, we should ask ourselves whether consent once given should automatically last until the end of the project? Of course people have the right to withdraw but somehow this is not the same as renewing consent over a long period of observation. In most cases this will not be an issue but suppose our study group is learning impaired and the programme they are on sets them up to become independent decision makers. At what point should we ask for their informed consent?

(ii) Bias in observation

The second issue we should be aware of is bias. This can occur in a number of ways. We have already touched on a major source of bias, observer influence in section 3.23 when we looked at experimental approaches and discussed the 'Hawthorn Effect'. We cannot get away from the fact that by just being there, even if we are not actively involved, we can affect what happens. How do we avoid this sort of bias? By having a mix of observers of different gender and ethnicity; by observing at random intervals; by constructing a

Activity 9.3 Researching the desire for lifelong learning

The nature of work, the pace of business evolution and the pace of life itself are all changing rapidly. The skills we acquired when we were young may not be those we require now and are likely to be irrelevant at some point in the future. Upskilling is in the interests of both employee and employer. Enlightened employers recognised that any learning activity promotes an interest in learning that could lay the foundations for significant skill and capability development. The vehicle maker Ford established EDAP (Employee, Development and Assistance Programme) in the late 1980s. Ford's liberal interpretation of learning included (and still includes) golf lessons and flower arranging as well as programmes with a more direct benefit to the company, such as language training and technical updating. It became a model followed by many other employers.

But what of an organisation whose view is more short term? You are researching the character of learning and training in an organisation and are particularly interested in how the system set up by the organisation manages personal and organisational goals. Some of the workforce is employed on a full-time contract and others are employed on a regular basis on a sessional contract. Your approach is to observe on-the-job training and to ask questions. Permission for the research has been granted by the chief executive and you are carrying out your research at a branch plant. So with the necessary permissions in place, you approach employees. One after another they tell you that they are unavailable or ask you to come back later. You decide to talk with the site manager (with whom you have already spoken), only to find that he too is 'unavailable'. You go back to the head office and shortly after receive a call to meet with the site manager. At that meeting, you are given a proposition – speak to the people identified by the manager and report back on what you find out. Are you being asked to spy?

How would you respond, knowing that your research career depended on getting good data? It is easy to be sanctimonious when it is not your future at stake!

If you would like to find out what really happened (plus examples of other moral dilemmas faced by researchers) read the paper, 'A Different Kind of Ethics' by Jason Ferdinand and others (Ferdinand et al., 2007).

checklist of things to observe (though even this is not a guarantee); by increasing the number of observation sites – and even then we cannot be sure that we have solved the problem.

While we may just have to live with the possibility of observers affecting the observed, there are other forms of bias of which we should be aware and, if present, assess their significance for our research conclusions.

- First, there is the possibility that some behaviour may be situationally specific. If we are researching the educational value of play with a view to developing collaborative toys and games, the nature of the play environment (classroom, playground, home, after school club) may well affect the character of play activity. We may also find in our research into disruptive classroom behaviour that a pupil with a record of poor behaviour will behave far more normally with one particular teacher.
- A second form of bias is a tendency to see what we want to see. This can, of course, happen when we are analysing our data; patterns that support our research hunches may well be accentuated even though they do not deserve it. Just as serious is bias at the observation stage. Four American researchers reported on this in a study of shoplifting (Dabney et al., 2006). They observed people, via video surveillance, as they came into a shop. Because of the number of people involved, they followed every third shopper. This approach, however, was costly and was revised to be every third shopper who was dressed in clothes in which goods could be concealed. There was one discretionary element for observers. If the third person was not dressed in concealing clothes but exhibited typical shoplifting behaviour within 15 seconds (such as actively looking for employees and surveillance systems, fidgeting with

packaging), they could be followed. What the researchers noted was that after the revised shopper selection process was introduced, the proportion of African-Americans and Hispanics in the sample increased. The conclusion reached by the research team was that social stereotyping was creating observational bias. This is an issue for educational researchers to be concerned about and we should reflect on our data to see if it is present.

- The third area of bias we should be aware of is partisanship and over-identification. If we are observing in conflict or choice situations, then it is difficult to remain neutral if we wish to understand the processes and experiences involved (see Case Study 9.7 for an example of this). The implication is that if we want to reach this level of understanding we have to take sides. While this immediately introduces bias (after all, the perspective is one-sided), there must also be a concern that identification with the group might lead to a potential (and not an impartial) representation of the group to the academic community and society. Now the situations where this might arise in an educational setting are probably few and far between but they will exist. It might occur if we are studying gang formation, cultures and conflicts. Alternatively, we might be looking at an attempt by a university to renegotiate the staff employment contract and wish to understand the tactics of either university management or unions, or by school governors in England to take a decision to change from local education authority control.

(iii) Other issues

There are two other issues that we should be aware of: sampling and disengagement.

Many new researchers think of observation as a data collection technique where sampling is not an issue. It is. What is more, as with all methods of data collection, decisions about sampling have to be taken in conjunction with the way in which data are collected. The first decision is *where* are the data to be collected? Are they contrasting locations (for example, an all boys' school and all girls' school), in which case we are effectively setting up a quasi-experiment? Or are they type examples, in which case we are setting up case studies? The location has to be chosen so that the results of our research produce something more than just a unique description. Second, within the data collection process we have to decide how we observe. Is it *ad hoc*, just what comes along, or do we set out to collect data on specific events or specific people? Third, are we intending to develop a quantitative assessment of observed characteristics or behaviours? If so, then we need to be able to relate the number of observations to the total of all potential observations. Chapter 6 on sampling gives ways of doing this.

The second issue, disengagement, is something that researchers who spend a long period with a group have to face. In many ways it is an ethical issue because our leaving should not cause problems for the group. Yet the loss of the researcher who has become a community member can do just that, especially if the researcher has been an active participant. And this, of course, raises a further issue, should observational research leave the observed unchanged? Disengagement from a community means that we have finished taking from that community. It can represent some observation as a greedy, self-serving and self-centred practice. This, of course, is another ethical issue. What can we do to resolve it? We can give something back (for example, our results) but if our research is empowering, we create change. This need not be wrong, as radical ethnographers would argue, but it is something on which researchers should form a view.

Case study 9.7 Trading bias off against data

While we should seek to avoid bias within our research procedures, there are some occasions when, in order to obtain data, we have to accept that it may occur. John Drury and Clifford Stott, two British sociologists, found themselves facing just this dilemma in their research into crowd disturbances. The purpose of the research was 'to understand the development of behavior and perceptions within a crowd – for example, how participants turn from peaceful protest to violence.' To do this, they argued, 'researchers need to examine the *interaction* between crowd and police. This means studying not just crowd participants' behavior but also how they understand their social context, including the behavior of other groups involved in the crowd event' (Drury and Stott, 2001, p. 49). The research approach was to participate in such events. The paper presents their reflection on their participation in two demonstrations. In 1987 Margaret Thatcher's Government campaigned in a general election for a change in the way that local government revenues should be raised, from a tax on the basis of property values to a per capita charge. The consequence was four years of often violent demonstrations against the measure. Clifford Stott participated in the most serious of these in London in March 1990. Two years later, John Drury took part in a demonstration against the construction of a motorway in east London.

Drury and Stott reflect on how their research could have been biased and what they sought to do about it. They identify three forms of potential bias.

- Partiality of access, where taking part in an activity seems the best way to gather a rich supply of authentic data. The implication of this is that the perspective through which the data is collected is one-sided.
- Partiality in observations, where over-identification with the community can lead to selective data observation.
- Partiality in analysis, possibly the consequence of the first two sources of bias but it can also result from the desire to interpret data in line with a particular political or value perspective.

For both events in which they participated the authors sought to overcome bias by collecting evidence from other sources (news reports, the police, reports from other demonstrators). In each case, they triangulated their own observations with the other sources. They sought to avoid partiality in analysis by distancing the participant from the data synthesis and analysis. While they were promised access to police officers in order to interview them this was not, in the event, forthcoming. For the roads protest they did, however, obtain data on the police perspective from, amongst other things, a student project and a tape recording of a meeting between police and protest leaders.

What do we make of all this? First, the authors make clear not only where bias could occur but also how they managed it. This constitutes excellent practice because it allows all those who read the research to make up their own minds about its validity. Second, they are probably correct in arguing that their involvement in the protest movements gave them access to insights and understanding that would not have been open to them if they had been neutral observers. Whether this allows them to claim that 'what was lost in data from the out-group (the police) was more than made up for with data from the in-group (the protesters)' (p. 61) is more controversial. Third, while they sought to repair the imbalance in data from the two sides, the approach of using a student project (for which Drury supplied an interview schedule) does raise questions of ethics, in particular the issue of consent.

Source: Drury and Stott (2001).

Summary

- Data collection is part of a whole system of research. Decisions about data collection cannot be taken in isolation, they have to be taken in conjunction with decisions about research objectives, selection of sources and data analysis. Each impacts on the other. In this chapter we have learnt about some techniques of data collection – how to do it. At this point we need to stand back and see a bigger picture.
- Data collection is a rigorous process. While flexibility is important, unless data collection is a structured activity, the data collected are likely to be worthless.

- Data are not confined to words. Images, behaviour, possessions are all potentially useful.
- Data collection methods are not mutually exclusive. Interviews, focus groups and observation perform different tasks and work well together.
- The methods we have looked at are invasive. Because of this ethical issues arise. While principles, such as those outlined in Chapter 3, can guide us on many questions, there are some situations that will require others to help us reach a judgement. It is the moral responsibility of researchers to know when further guidance should be sought.
- Now you are at the end of Part 2 of this book, you know about:
  - primary and secondary data sources;
  - how you should use literature throughout your research programme;
  - how data selection and sampling are fundamental to the quality of your research;
  - the need to conceptualise your research problem; and
  - how you can collect data using questionnaires, interviews and observation.

You are, in other words, well-prepared to go out and collect your data. How you process the results is what we shall look at in Part 3.

Further reading

Interviewing

Wengraf, T. (2001) *Qualitative Research Interviewing*, Sage, London.

Asking questions is, in comparison with in-depth interviewing, a straightforward process. In-depth interviewing requires not only great social skill (putting people at their ease so that you get the information you want) but technical and procedural skill. There is not just one type of interview and each one has its own standards of practice. Tom Wengraf provides an excellent introduction to all of this and gives some of the best exemplification of how interview data can be processed that I have seen in a text.

Focus groups

Bloor, M., Frankland, J., Thomas, M. and Stewart, K. (2001) *Focus Groups in Social Research*, Sage, London.

Fern, E.F. (2001) *Advanced Focus Group Research*, Sage, London.

Greenbaum, T.L. (1998) *The Handbook for Focus Group Research*, Sage, London.

The keys to ensuring focus group research is successful are:

- managing the group so that members want to spend time with you, and
- enabling the group to give you the insights you need and want.

There are many texts on conducting a focus group and they tend to make the same points about the group's composition (a sampling issue), the preparation that needs to be done and actually working with the group. The texts identified are all sound on this. They also highlight aspects of good or up-to-date practice.

Bloor et al. – getting group members to engage with the issue by giving them focusing exercises.

Fern – how to use groups to achieve particular research objectives (such as an initial exploration of an issue or gaining an understanding of what something was like or how people felt about it – see Chapters 7 and 8).

Greenbaum – reaching beyond the stage of asking questions by getting the group to think in different ways about the issue. Greenbaum looks at projective techniques (for example, associating the issue with an animal or a car) and provoking techniques (where we push beyond the first response – see Chapter 8).

On-line research

Fielding, N., Lee, R.M. and Blank, G. (eds) (2008) *The Sage Handbook of Online Research Methods*, Sage, London.

Hine, C. (ed.) (2005) *Virtual Methods: Issues in Social research on the Internet*, Berg, Oxford.

The Internet will soon become an established means of collecting data. We have protocols for sampling and interviewing in circumstances that we have considered here but what we need is something similar, that other researchers regard as good practice, for when we obtain our data via the Internet.

The collection of papers edited by Fielding et al. is much more of a heavyweight text than Hine's. For the researcher wanting to work through the Internet, there are sections on designing Internet research, data capture, Internet survey, virtual ethnography and the Internet as an archival source.

Image-based research

Pink, S. (2007) *Doing Visual Ethnography*, Sage, London.

We touched on the use of image-based data but before making use of this sort of material, it is important to look at a specialist text. Sarah Pink's book is the pick of the bunch. She deals with photographic and video output from the perspectives of their production and interpretation and non-visual ways of representing findings. Throughout there is a strong theme of philosophical, ethical and moral issues that are embedded in the use of visual data in a text-based intellectual world.

Metaphor analysis

Schmitt, R. (2005) 'Systematic Metaphor Analysis as a Method of Qualitative Research', *The Qualitative Report*, 10(2), 358–394.

The interpretation of deeper meanings is known as 'metaphor analysis'. The idea that what we say and produce can reveal deeper insights about us has a long tradition in the arts and philosophy but, for social researchers, the foundations for a research approach were laid by two Americans, a linguist, George Lackoff, and a philosopher, Mark Johnson, in their book *Metaphors We Live By* (1980, University of Chicago Press). Translating their ideas into operational research practice with rules and procedures remains an issue for qualitative researchers. Rudolph Schmitt has begun to do this.

References

Babad, E. (2005) 'Non-verbal Behaviour in Education', Chapter 7 in Harrigan, J., Rosenthal, R. and Scherer, K. (eds) *A Handbook of Non-verbal Behaviour Research Methods in the Affective Sciences*, Oxford University Press, New York.

Ballinger, G. (2003) 'Bridging the Gap Between A Level and Degree: Some Observations on Managing the Transitional Stage in the Study of English Literature', *Arts and Humanities Higher Education*, 2(1), 99–109.

Bell, A. (2007), Designing and Testing Questionnaires for Children, *Journal of Research in Nursing*, 12(5), 461–469.

Berkowitz, E. and Cichelli, T. (2004) 'Metacognitive Strategy Use in Reading of Gifted High Achieving and Gifted Underachieving School Students in New York City', *Education and Urban Society*, 37(1), 37–57.

Bolhuis, S. and Voeten, M. (2001) 'Toward Self-Directed Learning in Secondary Schools: What do Teachers Do?' *Teaching and Teacher Education*, 17(7), 837–855.

Booker, B. (2002) *Stakeholders' Meanings of Effective School Leadership: A Case Study in a New Zealand Primary School*, EdD thesis, Griffith University (Australia), available at http://www4.gu.edu.au:8080/adt-root/uploads/approved/adt-QGU20061023.151530/public/ 02Whole.pdf (accessed March 2009).

Cameron, C. (2007) 'Understanding of Care Work With Young Children: Reflections on Children's Independence in a Video Observation Study', *Childhood*, 14(4), 467–486.

Catterall, M. and Ibbotson, P. (2000) 'Using Projective Techniques in Education Research', *British Educational Research Journal*, 26(2), 245–256.

Chan, K. (2006) 'Exploring Children's Perceptions of Material Possessions: a Drawing Study', *Qualitative Market Research*, 9(4), 352–366.

Cheeseman, J. and Clarke, B. (2007) 'Young Children's Accounts of Their Mathematical Thinking', *Mathematics: Essential Research, Essential Practice, Volume 1*, Proceedings the 30th Annual Conference of the Mathematics Education Research Group of Australia, 192–200, available at www.merga.net.au (accessed January 2008).

Dabney, D., Dugan, L., Topalli, V. and Hollinger, R. (2006) 'The Impact of Implicit Stereotyping on Offender Profiling: Unexpected Results from an Observational Study of Shoplifting', *Criminal Justice Behaviour*, 33(5), 646–674.

Dengin, N.K. (2001) 'The Reflexive Interview and a Performative Social Science', *Qualitative Research* 1(1), 23–46.

Desimone, M. and Le Floch, K.C. (2004) 'Are We Asking the Right Questions? Using Cognitive Interviews to Improve Surveys in Education Research', *Educational Evaluation and Policy Analysis*, 26(1), 1–22.

Drury, J. and Stott, C. (2001) 'Bias as a Research Strategy in Participant Observation: the Case of Intergroup Conflict', *Field Methods*, 13(1), 47–67.

Duveen, G. (2000) 'Piaget Ethnographer', *Social Science Information*, 39(1), 79–97.

Ells, H. (2001) 'Talking Pictures in Working School Lunches: Investigating Food Choice With Children and Adolescents', *British Food Journal*, 103(6), 374–382.

Estell, D.B., Farmer, T.W., Cairns, R.B. and Cairns, B.P. (2002) 'Social Relations and Academic Achievement in Inner-City Early Elementary Classrooms', *International Journal of Behavioural Development*, 26(6), 518–528.

Ferdinand, J., Pearson, G., Rowe, M. and Worthington, F. (2007) 'A Different Kind of Ethics', *Ethnography*, 8(4), 519–543.

French, R.S. et al. (2005) *Exploring the Attitudes and Behaviours of Bangladeshi, Indian and Jamaican Young People in Relation to Reproductive and Sexual Health*, a report for the Teenage Pregnancy Unit NO. RW53, available at www.dfes.gov.uk/research/data/uploadfiles/RW53.pdf (accessed January 2008).

Heinonen, T. and Cheung, M. (2007) 'View from the Village: Photonovella With Women in Rural China', *International Journal of Qualitative Methods*, 6(4), 35–52.

Highet, G. (2003) 'Cannabis and Smoking Research: Interviewing Young People in Self-Selected Friendship Pairs', *Health Education Research*, 18(1), 108–118.

Homes, A. and Murray, L. (2008) 'Cognitive Question Testing Scotland's Census Ethnicity Classification', *Scottish Government Social Research*, available at www.scotland.gov.uk/socialresearch.

Irenka Suto, W.M. and Greatorix, J. (2008) 'What Goes Through an Examiner's Mind? Using Verbal Protocols to Gain Insights into the GCSE Marking Process', *British Educational Research Journal*, 34(2), 213–234.

Jones, K. (2007) 'The One About Princess Margaret', appendix to 'How Did I Get to Princess Margaret? (And How Did I Get to the Worldwide Web?)', *Forum Qualitative Sozial forschung/Forum Qualitative Social Research*, 8(3), AN.3, available at http://www.qualitative-research.net/fqs-texte/3-07/07-3-3-e_app.pdf.

King, R. (1978) *All Things Bright and Beautiful: A Sociological Study of Infants' Classrooms*, Wiley, Chichester.

King, R. (1984) 'The Man in the Wendy House: Researching Infants' Schools', chapter 5 in *The Research Process in Educational Settings: Ten Case Studies*, Burgess, R.G. (ed.), Falmer Press, London.

Kirkpatrick, M.G. (1917) *The Rural School From Within*, J.P. Lippincott, Philadelphia and now available from ERIC (ED392563).

Labaree, R. (2002) 'The Risk of "Going Observationalist" : Negotiating the Hidden Dilemmas of Being an Inside Participant Observer', *Qualitative Research*, 2(1), 97–122.

Leach, F. and Sitaram, S. (2007) 'Sexual Harassment and Abuse of Adolescent Schoolgirls in South India', *Education, Citizenship and Social Justice*, 2(3), 257–277.

McDonald, S. (2005) 'Studying Actions in Context: A Qualitative Shadowing Method for Organisational Research', *Qualitative Research*, 5(4), 455–473.

Merrell, K.W (2008) *Behaviour, Social and Emotional Assessment of Children and Adolescents*, Lawrence Erlbaum, New York.

Newman, M. (2004) *Problem Basing Learning: An Exploration of the Method and Evaluation of its Effectiveness in a Continuing Nursing Education Programme*, Middlesex University.

Persson, G. (2005) 'Developmental Perspectives on Personal and Aggressive Motives in Pre-Schoolers' Peer Interactions', *International Journal of Behavioural Development*, 29(1), 80–91.

Pole, C. (2007) 'Researching Children and Fashion: An Embodied Ethnography', *Childhood*, 14(1), 67–84.

Polite, V., McClure, R. and Rollie, D. (1997) 'The Emerging Reflective Urban Principal', *Urban Education*, 31(5), 466–489.

Power, R. (1989) 'Participant Observation and its Place in the Study of Illicit Drug Abuse', *British Journal of Addiction*, 84, 45–52.

Pramling, N., Norlander, T. and Archer, T. (2003) 'Conceptualization of the Unknown by 6, 9 and 14-year-old children in a Story-Telling Context: In Search of a "Heffalump"', *Childhood*, 10(3), 379–392.

Punch, S. (2002) 'Interviewing Strategies With Young Adults: The "Secret Box", Stimulus Material and Task-based Activities', *Children and Society*, 16(1), 45–56.

Reid, C., Tom, A. and Frisby, W. (2006) 'Finding the "Action" in Feminist Participatory Action Research', *Action Research*, 43(3), 315–332.

Rice, M.L., Sell, M.A. and Hadley, P.A. (1990) 'The Social Interactive Coding System (SICS): An On-line, Clinically Relevant Descriptive Tool', *Language, Speech and Hearing Services in Schools*, (21), 2–14.

Robinson, V. and Segrott, J. (2002) *Understanding the Decision-Making of Asylum Seekers*, Home Office Research Study 243, available at http://www.homeoffice.gov.uk/rds/pdfs2/hors243.pdf (accessed January 2009).

Rodgers, D. (2007) 'Joining the Gang and Becoming a *Broder*: The Violence of Ethnography in Contemporary Nicaragua', *Bulletin of Latin American Research*, 26(4), 44–61.

Rosenthal, R. and Jacobsen, L. (1996) 'Teachers' Expectancies: Determinants of Pupils' IQ Gains', *Psychological Reports*, 19, 115–118.

Schmitt, R. (2005) 'Systematic Metaphor Analysis as a Method of Qualitative Research', *The Qualitative Report*, 10(2), 358–394.

Suto, I. and Greatorix, J. (2008) 'What goes through an examiner's mind? Using verbal protocols to gain insights into the GCSE marking process', *British Educational Research Journal*, 34(2), 213–233.

Visschers-Pleijers, A., Dolmans, D., Leng, B., Wolfhagen, I. and Vleuten, C. (2006) *Medical Education*, 40(2), 129–137.

Weatherford, J.M. (1986) *Porn Row*, New York.

Whyte, W. (1943) *Street Corner Society; the social structure of an Italian slum*, The University of Chicago Press, Chicago.

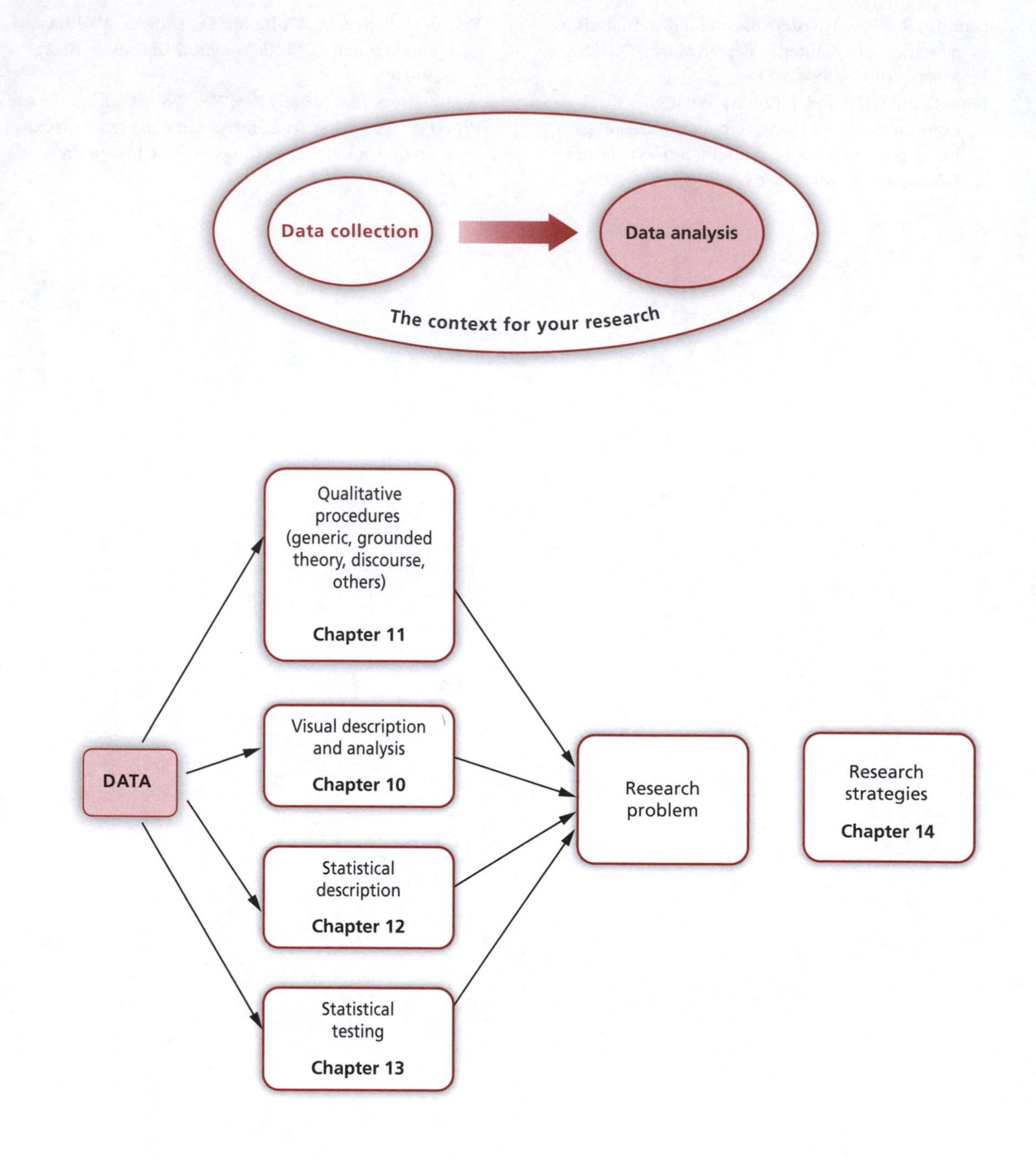
Data collection
Data analysis
The context for your research
DATA
Qualitative procedures (generic, grounded theory, discourse, others)
Chapter 11
Visual description and analysis
Chapter 10
Statistical description
Chapter 12
Statistical testing
Chapter 13
Research problem
Research strategies
Chapter 14

Part 3

THE PROCESS OF DATA ANALYSIS

In this final part of the book we turn to how we can process our data. The object of this exercise is to get our data to release the information we need to answer our research question. As we shall see, there are many approaches open to us (and even the ones we consider here are far fewer than the whole range). It is important that we are familiar with many methods and confident about using them because one of the research skills we should develop is the ability to construct an analytical package that does what we want, dovetails with our methods of data collection and is informed by any philosophies and paradigms we are working within.

How should we look at data analysis? When we get into the details of the methods, we will see that there are procedures we should follow. As a generalisation, quantitative methods are more tightly constrained than qualitative but qualitative approaches, too, have ways of working that are established and, in many ways, expected. Nonetheless, there is flexibility in applying research methods that we should make use of when the circumstances of our research require it.

There is also another way in which we should think about data analysis. Essentially what we are doing is filtering our data though a procedure in order to focus our information on our research problem. This idea of data analysis as a filter is one we should pursue a little further. A filter acts like a sieve and we know that the size of our mesh determines the size of the particles that can get through. While we are not yet at the stage of breaking down our data on the basis of particle size, we should remember that we are often dealing with both the big picture and smaller scale effects. As an example, if our research were into classroom behaviour, one of our findings might be that many teachers would not confront what they considered to be unacceptable behaviour. If we follow up on this by asking 'why', we might find that the head teacher was ineffective in dealing with children sent to him for admonishment or punishment. We might subsequently find that there was a failure in leadership but that this could be partially accounted for by the fact that the number of pupil exclusions was reflected in school performance measures and that school governors wanted to improve the school's image. It is important that we remain aware of the possibility of this scale effect within our research enquiry.

The filters through which we can pass our data are

- Visualisation techniques
- Statistical description
- Statistical testing
- Generic and specific approaches to the analysis of qualitative data.

The book finishes by returning to the templates we can use to frame our research and that we first met in Chapter 2. Our purpose here is to show, with some examples, how studies were set up as a prelude to a final section on developing a research programme.

Chapter contents

Chapter 10

EXTRACTING THE INFORMATION FROM STATISTICAL DATA

Key themes

- How to 'read' a data set.
- How to reorganise data in order to make the message more apparent.
- Visual displays of simple data sets.
- Describing complex data sets.

Introduction

If collecting good data is a necessary start to producing good research, then making them release their information is equally important. Sometimes this is straightforward and it is obvious what the data mean. However, there are occasions when the message that the data contains is blurred, unclear or even hidden. It is our task as researchers to release the information and apply it to our research question. This is what we shall do in this chapter in relation to statistical data, both published and obtained through primary research.

At this point, it is worth reviewing what we said in Chapter 4, especially sections 4.9 and 4.10. Here we saw that there was an enormous wealth of statistical material portraying educational systems and outcomes that is published by national governments and international agencies. In addition, national governments produce social and economic data that can be used to contextualise educational research, for example, data on family life, demography and the demand for education places and economic growth and the need for skills. International agencies assemble data that place education in the context of development, gender inequality and migration. These data often have to be reorganised or portrayed in a different way for their message to be revealed and for it to have impact. In certain ways this process is like enhancing a digital photograph, sharpening the image, removing a figure, getting rid of red-eye; we do not change the fundamentals but we do produce a better picture. But it is not only data produced by governments and international agencies that we can manipulate. We can use the same approaches with our own data. So, what are these methods?

10.1 Reading a data set

The first step in getting the information out of data is to look at them. Often, however, the data we are faced with can be difficult to penetrate. In this section we shall look at some of the problems we might encounter and how we can overcome them.

Reading a data set is often referred to as scanning and sometimes as 'eyeballing'. This can have the connotation of being a less than perfect, 'quick and dirty' method that has the potential to lead to incorrect conclusions. We should say at the outset, therefore, first, that while the approaches to scanning described here may be quick, they certainly are not dirty; second, there is a framework we can use to scan data; and third, scanning is primarily a procedure to throw up things that are worthy of further interpretation.

The methods we shall look at are:

- Visual inspection.
- Shaping.
- Stripping out.
- Compressing.
- Re-ordering.
- Reconstructing.

10.1.1 Visual inspection

The purpose of looking at a data table is to get it to reveal its information, but looking at a data table is not as easy as just looking; it's *how* you look that is important.

Some tables reveal all immediately. Table 10.1 does just this. It shows the number of students (by total and by gender) and the number of teaching and clerical staff in Iranian secondary schools over an eight-year period from Iranian year 1365–66 to 1384–85 (1998 to 2005). We can see that, year on year, the numbers of students and staff increased. The message is straightforward – but even this message poses questions.

Table 10.1 Upper secondary school students and staff in Iran

	Student			Teaching and clerical staff	
Academic year	Total	Male	Female	Teaching	Clerical
1365/66 . . .	1,277,921	768,322	509,599	64,649	21,032
1370/71 . . .	2,030,986	1,192,340	838,646	87,964	34,690
1375/76 . . .	3,480,635	1,817,665	1,662,970	117,690	64,839
1380/81 . . .	3,985,150	2,020,296	1,964,854	161,291	105,467
1381/82 . . .	3,828,524	1,940,924	1,887,600	167,570	105,962
1382/83 . . .	3,817,744	1,944,229	1,873,515	171,759	106,507
1383/84 . . .	3,772,585	1,917,888	1,854,697	176,810	102,514
1384/85 . . .	3,763,037	1,917,183	1,845,854	188,777	108,302

Source: Iran Statistical Yearbook 1384/85 (2005/06), Table 15.12.

In 20 years, the numbers of students has trebled; why? Iran has a young population and a high birth rate. But this is not the whole story. Look at the numbers of male and female students at the beginning and end of the period. Far more girls are going to school now than in the past. Not surprisingly, the number of teachers has increased as well but not by the same amount as the number of clerical staff. The ratio of teachers to students is not so different at the beginning and end of the period but for clerical staff it has almost halved. Why is this? Is it because teachers refuse to do administrative work or because the system was underresourced at the beginning of the period? We can only guess at the answer.

There are many tables that we, as researchers, will come across that will be just like Table 10.1. They will reveal a message and also intrigue us by posing further questions. For this reason inspection of data tables can often be used as the start of a research enquiry. However, there will also be data tables that require us to work harder before we can understand what it is they are trying to tell us. Table 10.2, produced by the Higher Education Statistics Agency (HESA) in the UK, is a case in point. At first sight it looks straightforward, a simple table with two variables, the subjects that were studied and entry qualifications. But the complexity starts to kick in when we read the title and when we look at the entry qualifications.

First, let us consider the title. The table deals with *young entrants* to full-time first degree courses from *low participation neighbourhoods.* The context for this table is the assumption that education is a means of creating a more equal society and that participation in higher education provides a route to higher value employment and social and economic advancement. The reason for collecting the data is to evaluate the extent to which UK universities are committing themselves to Government policy to encourage young people from poor backgrounds to enter higher education. 'Low participation neighbourhood' is an indicator of poor background and HESA has defined these areas using small area statistics from the 2001 national census. Low participation neighbourhoods can be as small as a few postcode areas or may be the larger part of a local authority. This is the information we have to hold in our head when reading the table. We are also told that the figures are percentages, but of what? We will come back to this shortly. Let us now look at the entry qualifications. The categories are a bit of a mishmash because some constitute a scale (that is, they can be arranged in a sequence from high to low or vice versa) and others can be put in any order we like. Standard entry qualifications are subjects studies at the Advanced Level General Certificate of Education (A levels) and the Higher Grade of the Scottish Certificate of Education (Highers). Students' performances in these examinations are converted into points; higher numbers of points are achieved by a combination of studying more subjects and gaining higher grades. Categories 02 to 13 constitute a scale (the number of points increases). The other categories do not constitute a scale (like the subjects of study along the top), because no one sequence is intrinsically better than another. Now let us return to the actual percentages. Our first task is to work out what these are percentages of. Do they sum to 100 per cent along the rows or the columns? If they do, our task is a little easier because we can begin to look for patterns in terms of the interaction of rows and columns – but they do not! So all they can be is a percentage of another data set. What can this be? It is the total on which the cell value is based. For example, the cell value in blue falls in the row for foundation and access courses and the column for computer sciences. The actual value, 26.6, shows that, of those who applied for a course in computer sciences and were accepted on the basis of an access qualification, 26.6 per cent were from low participation neighbourhoods. Because every cell is constructed like this, the consequence is that no cell can be compared directly with another cell because there is no guarantee that the

Table 10.2 Qualifications and subjects of study of young entrants to first degree courses from low participation neighbourhoods 2005/06 (after HESA Table SP6)

Entry qualifications	Percentage Subject of study																		
	1	2	3	5	6	7	8	9	A	B	C	D	E	F	G	H	I	J	All subjects
01 A levels/Highers with unknown tariff pts	5.1	17.2	20.0	15.8	19.3	19.8	21.3	18.3	9.2	20.9	21.5	18.1	19.6	19.1	17.6	14.1	19.3	21.3	**17.7**
02 Tariff pts up to 100		18.0	18.1	9.5	20.3	17.7	19.4	15.8	14.1	19.3	19.8	16.4	15.0	19.7	17.9	19.4	17.5	19.4	**18.0**
03 Tariff pts 101–160		19.9	18.9	4.5	16.5	21.2	20.8	14.5	16.6	20.9	22.8	15.4	20.3	20.7	19.5	16.0	21.1	27.9	**18.5**
04 Tariff pts 161–200		16.3	19.7	5.5	18.6	19.5	15.8	13.4	12.7	18.1	21.1	12.9	16.2	18.2	19.6	15.8	19.3	15.6	**16.7**
05 Tariff pts 201–230		17.1	17.3	11.0	17.6	14.8	18.4	13.8	10.8	17.5	23.2	15.3	15.7	18.0	15.5	14.7	17.4	16.2	**16.5**
06 Tariff pts 231–260	4.7	15.5	16.6	9.4	14.3	13.1	16.1	10.6	10.3	15.6	18.3	13.3	15.7	16.2	16.0	13.5	17.2	24.1	**15.0**
07 Tariff pts 261–290	8.5	13.1	14.6	6.0	18.2	12.8	16.1	12.4	9.1	14.0	21.2	12.5	11.8	13.1	10.9	12.5	15.5	19.0	**13.8**
08 Tariff pts 291–320	13.8	13.2	15.0	5.4	14.0	17.1	14.5	11.0	9.3	13.4	18.6	11.8	10.6	12.5	12.8	12.3	15.8	14.4	**13.3**
09 Tariff pts 321–350	11.2	12.1	11.9	6.9	10.7	14.0	13.9	11.1	11.0	11.6	15.0	10.3	12.0	11.5	11.5	10.0	16.8	16.0	**11.8**
10 Tariff pts 351–380	7.6	10.8	11.2	11.5	9.5	12.8	15.6	10.5	6.2	10.0	13.2	10.5	13.0	9.1	8.6	10.6	17.6	16.1	**10.7**
11 Tariff pts 381–420	6.8	9.7	10.0	12.5	10.4	11.7	14.3	9.0	8.2	7.7	11.9	11.0	8.0	7.8	7.8	9.2	17.6	12.1	**9.4**
12 Tariff pts 421–480	6.2	10.3	10.4	9.7	9.3	10.1	13.2	7.0	6.8	7.3	11.6	10.5	8.1	8.8	7.5	9.3	14.2	8.9	**9.0**
13 Tariff pts 481+	7.9	14.3	8.3	14.8	6.9	9.4	7.9	8.6	6.9	7.6	10.6	8.5	8.9	8.0	6.6	9.3	13.9	12.4	**8.5**
14 VCE or GNVQ only		26.6	21.4		32.4		24.3	19.3	9.7	30.4	24.6	18.1	17.5			25.5	27.6	28.7	**22.2**
15 VCE or GNVQ and A levels or Highers	17.6	16.6	17.9	8.5	18.3	19.9	19.7	14.7	10.8	19.1	19.2	15.8	18.6	16.7	18.7	17.7	20.0	26.5	**17.5**
16 Baccalaureate	6.5	12.6	9.8		9.4		10.9	8.2	9.7	6.9	7.9	11.9	17.4	5.4	6.0	8.3			**8.4**
17 Foundation or access course		27.7	20.3		17.4		26.6	17.1	18.4	20.7	21.0	17.7	9.9	18.9	14.2	12.2	17.2		**14.3**
18 BTEC, ONC, SCOTVEC or equivalent		18.7	23.5	14.7	32.6		23.6	21.8	18.7	19.9	24.4	21.2	23.2	31.4	29.6	20.5	23.9	25.7	**21.6**

19 Higher education qualification	14.3	23.7	24.7	16.6	25.1	17.6	23.7	21.7	20.6	27.2	26.1	22.9	22.4	16.0	27.7	20.2	22.9	27.7	**22.7**
20 No previous qualification					31.8							18.9				18 6			**21.8**
21 Other qualifications not given elsewhere		27.7	17.3	7.3	11.2		20.6	13.2	15.4	25.3	18.4	17.8	14.2	18.6	13.4	24.8	21.0	18.7	**19.2**
22 Unknown qualification	0.0	27.8	20.3		20.9	18.6	27.9	21.2	21.5	19.5	20.0	22.5	13.2	19.1	22.4	12.9	21.2	32.8	**20.9**
All qualifications	**7.3**	**14.8**	**14.9**	**9.5**	**13.1**	**12.6**	**19.0**	**12.6**	**10.5**	**13.8**	**16.3**	**14.3**	**14.8**	**11.5**	**11.0**	**14.6**	**18.4**	**19.9**	**14.0**

Subject of study

1 Medicine and Dentistry, and Veterinary Science
2 Subjects allied to Medicine
3 Biological Sciences
5 Agriculture and Related Subjects
6 Physical Sciences
7 Mathematical Sciences
8 Computer Sciences
9 Engineering and Technology

A Architecture, Building and Planning
B Social Studies
C Law
D Business and Administrative Studies
E Mass Communications and Documentation
F Languages
G Historical and Philosophical Studies
H Creative Arts and Design
I Education
J Combined Subjects

Percentages based on populations of less than 20 have been suppressed and are shown as a blank cell.

Source: from http://www.hesa.ac.uk/dox/performanceIndicators/0506/sp6_0506.xls, Hesa cannot accept responsibility for any inferences or conclusions derived from the data by third parties.

denominator used to calculate the percentages is the same. For the purposes of comparison, however, we can look at the column and row totals.

The column totals represent the proportion of young entrants from low participation neighbourhoods entering each subject area in 2005/06. Table 10.3 ranks these column totals from low to high. The question for us as researchers is whether there is any pattern here and, if there is, whether there is any meaning to it. If we divide the table into two, the nine subjects with the highest percentage from low participation neighbourhoods and the nine with the highest, then:

- lowest percentages: four of the nine subject areas are sciences and mathematics (medicine, mathematics, physical sciences and engineering), two are humanities (history and philosophy and languages) and two are vocational (agriculture and architecture);
- highest percentages: two are broadly vocational (subjects allied to medicine and law), two are sciences (biology and computer science) and the remainder are general areas of study (though with some preparation for working life).

There is possibly an explanation behind this pattern. Can you think what it might be? Begin by thinking about the target group, young people from low participation neighbourhoods and then imagine yourself in that situation. What is the likelihood that you will have good grades in mathematics and physics? Would you gravitate more to an academic subject or to one that offered you some sort of career future?

Where does this leave our interpretation of the cell values? In a bit of a limbo. We can try to see if there are problems in relation to column or row totals but if there are, they

Table 10.3 Percentage of young entrants to full-time first degree courses from low participation neighbourhoods by subject

Subject code	Subject	Percentage
1	Medicine and Dentistry, and Veterinary Science	7.3
5	Agriculture and Related Subjects	9.5
A	Architecture, Building and Planning	10.5
G	Historical and Philosophical Studies	13.1
F	Languages	11.5
7	Mathematical Sciences	12.6
9	Engineering and Technology	12.6
6	Physical Sciences	13.1
B	Social Studies	13.8
D	Business and Administrative Studies	14.3
H	Creative Arts and Design	14.6
2	Subjects Allied to Medicine	14.8
E	Mass Communication and Documentation	14.8
3	Biological Sciences	14.9
C	Law	16.3
I	Education	18.4
8	Computer Sciences	19.0
J	Combined Subjects	19.9

are none too clear and inspection will not reveal them. But let us reflect on how we have got this far. We can summarise what we did as a series of rules.

1. Read the title of the table closely. Identify the variables and relate them to column and row headings.
2. Understand all the terms in the title and the context that has led to them being analysed in the table. Think about educational, social and economic situations.
3. Understand how variables are structured in rows and columns. In Table 10.3 there is only one variable each side. With some tables we can find up to four variables on each side, so we have to be able to read the hierarchy in which they are presented.
4. Do the variables constitute a series or are they independent categories that could be presented in any order?
5. Look to see if there are column or row totals. Do the cell values sum to one of them?
6. Is there any apparent pattern to the cell values? If not, is there a pattern if you rearrange the table by row or column totals?

Activity 10.1 gives you the opportunity to practise this type of analysis yourself.

10.1.2 Shaping data tables

There are occasions when we have the opportunity to make our own selection of data from primary sources. It is important to appreciate that there may be different ways of displaying it in table form. The implication of this is that different formats may vary in their 'readability', that is, some may be more difficult to interpret than others. Tables 10.4(a), (b) and (c) illustrate this. They show three ways of tabulating the same data. The data are taken from the education and culture statistics set of Statistics Denmark. They show percentages of children in different age groups engaging in sport and cultural activities. Table 10.4(a) contains exactly the same data as the other tables but because it is arranged as a list, it is much more difficult to take in its characteristics. This is what we mean by readability. Tables 10.4(b) and 10.4(c) have the rows and columns reversed. Which do

Activity 10.1 Reading tables

Benchmarking one's own performance against others is an accepted way of improving standards in business performance. It is now found in education with the construction of league tables of schools and universities. League tables, however, are only as good as the data used to compute them and many tables are heavily value based. There is, however, a benchmarking process that is well-conceived and whose data is robust. PISA, the Programme for International Student Assessment, is operated through the Organisation for European Co-operation and Development (OECD). The approach is to administer a standard test to young people aged 15 (that is, to students at the end of the period of compulsory schooling in most states) to evaluate their knowledge of and capability in specific subjects. The focus of the test is usually reading, mathematics and science. PISA tests were conducted in 2000, 2003 and 2006 and are scheduled to be repeated in 2009, 2012 and 2015. You can read more about PISA (and even attempt some of the tests) on the website: www.pisa.oecd.org.

Your task is to make sense of the table below, which is taken from Table 5.4 of the 2006 survey. The letters in the table give reasons for missing data. What patterns do you detect (a) in the performance of students (look at the differences between public and private schools) and (b) in the non-availability of data? You can read what the OECD statisticians said on page 230 of the 2006 report (available from the website).

▶

Percentage of students and student performance on the science, reading and mathematics scales, by type of school

Results based on reports from school principals and reported proportionate to the number of 15-year-olds enrolled in the school

	Government or public schools (Schools which are directly controlled or managed by: i) a public education authority or agency, or ii) a government agency directly or a governing body, most of whose members are either appointed by a public authority or elected by public franchise)				**Government-dependent private schools** (Schools which receive 50% or more of their core funding – funding that supports the basic educational services of the institution – from government agencies)				**Government-independent private school** (Schools which receive less than 50% of their core funding – funding that supports the basic educational services of the institution – from government agencies)	
		Performance on the				Performance on the				Performance on the
		Science scale	Reading scale	Mathematics scale		Science scale	Reading scale	Mathematics scale		Science scale
	Percentage of students	Mean score	Mean score	Mean score	Percentage of students	Mean score	Mean score	Mean score	Percentage of students	Mean score
OECD										
Australia	w	w	w	w	w	w	w	w	w	w
Austria	90.7	511	491	506	8.4	503	479	488	0.9	c
Belgium	w	w	w	w	w	w	w	w	w	w
Canada	93.0	532	524	524	4.3	578	578	582	2.7	c
Czech Republic	96.2	514	482	510	3.5	492	481	487	0.2	c
Denmark	76.1	492	493	511	22.8	507	499	521	1.1	c
Finland	97.6	564	547	549	2.4	c	c	c	0.0	a
France	w	w	w	w	w	w	w	w	w	w
Germany	94.3	514	494	502	5.5	555	535	544	0.2	c
Greece	94.9	469	455	455	0.0	a	a	a	5.1	545
Hungary	84.2	500	478	485	13.1	533	516	529	2.7	c
Iceland	98.9	490	484	505	1.0	c	c	c	0.1	c
Ireland	41.8	488	494	483	54.8	519	530	511	3.4	558
Italy	96.4	476	469	462	1.2	c	c	c	2.4	c
Japan	70.1	537	501	528	1.0	c	c	c	28.9	526
Korea	53.7	524	554	549	31.5	505	543	527	14.8	552
Luxembourg	85.6	490	481	495	14.4	465	470	460	0.0	a
Mexico	89.7	402	402	398	0.0	c	c	c	10.3	455
Netherlands	33.0	524	505	526	67.0	527	509	534	0.0	a
New Zealand	95.5	527	518	519	0.0	a	a	a	4.5	603
Norway	98.1	484	482	488	1.9	c	c	c	0.0	a
Poland	98.4	497	507	495	1.0	c	c	c	0.6	c

Portugal	91.1	471	469	463	6.9	484	470	479	2.1	c
Slovak Republic	92.3	487	465	491	7.2	506	484	507	0.5	c
Spain	65.3	475	446	466	24.6	503	482	495	10.1	537
Sweden	91.7	501	504	501	8.3	531	539	522	0.0	a
Switzerland	95.5	511	499	530	0.9	c	c	c	3.6	513
Turkey	99.5	424	447	423	0.0	a	a	a	0.5	c
United Kingdom	93.8	510	492	492	0.2	c	c	c	6.0	597
United States	92.6	485	m	470	0.8	c	m	c	6.6	554
Partners										
Argentina	67.5	364	342	354	24.8	441	430	430	7.7	447
Azerbaijan	99.1	382	351	475	0.0	a	a	a	0.9	c
Brazil	92.4	375	378	353	0.0	a	a	a	7.6	482
Bulgaria	m	m	m	m	m	m	m	m	m	m
Chile	46.9	409	412	385	44.9	447	453	418	8.2	514
Colombia	82.7	379	378	361	5.1	431	440	415	12.3	412
Croatia	98.6	494	478	467	0.6	c	c	c	0.7	c
Estonia	98.1	531	500	514	1.4	c	c	c	0.6	c
Hong Kong-China	7.5	570	562	575	90.7	541	535	546	1.9	c
Indonesia	60.7	403	403	404	13.5	352	344	341	25.8	389
Israel	73.4	449	435	438	20.3	471	457	461	6.3	475
Jordan	80.6	410	390	373	1.3	c	c	c	18.1	468
Kyrgyzstan	99.4	320	283	308	0.0	a	a	a	0.6	c
Latvia	100.0	490	479	486	0.0	a	a	a	0.0	a
Liechtenstein	c	c	c	c	c	c	c	c	c	c
Lithuania	99.3	487	469	485	0.7	c	c	c	0.0	a
Macao-China	3.8	463	453	473	68.5	504	487	517	27.6	535
Montenegro	99.8	412	393	400	0.0	a	a	a	0.2	c
Qatar	91.1	338	301	304	0.1	c	c	c	8.8	434
Romania	100.0	418	396	415	0.0	a	a	a	0.0	a
Russian Federation	100.0	479	440	476	0.0	a	a	a	0.0	a
Serbia	99.4	436	401	436	0.6	c	c	c	0.0	a
Slovenia	97.7	517	493	503	2.3	c	c	c	0.1	c
Chinese Taipei	65.0	549	509	567	0.0	a	a	a	35.0	501
Thailand	83.5	422	417	418	6.1	389	385	379	10.5	433
Tunisia	98.2	388	384	368	1.8	c	c	c	0.0	a
Uruguay	84.9	416	397	414	0.0	a	a	a	15.1	496

Note: Values that are statistically significant are indicated in bold (see Annex A3).
a The category does not apply in the country concerned. Data are therefore missing.
c There are too few observations to provide reliable estimates (i.e. there are fewer than 30 students or less than 3% of students for this cell or too few schools for valid inferences).
m Data are not available. These data were collected but subsequently removed from the publication for technical reasons.
w Data have been withdrawn at the request of the country concerned.
x Data are included in another category or column of the table.

Table 10.4 Danish children's sports and exercise activities by age

(a) By activity

		2004
Football	7–9 years	34.9
	10–12 years	39.8
	13–15 years	27
	7–9 years boy	49.6
	10–12 years boy	53.2
	13–15 years boy	36.6
	7–9 years girl	16.8
	10–12 years girl	27.3
	13–15 years girl	17.9
	Unknown	60
Handball	7–9 years	17.9
	10–12 years	15.9
	13–15 years	13.5
	7–9 years boy	10.3
	10–12 years boy	16.5
	13–15 years boy	8.5
	7–9 years girl	27.4
	10–12 years girl	15.3
	13–15 years girl	17.9
	Unknown	20
Other types of ballgames by groups	7–9 years	1.9
	10–12 years	5.5
	13–15 years	5.1
	7–9 years boy	2.6
	10–12 years boy	5.8
	13–15 years boy	6.1
	7–9 years girl	1.1
	10–12 years girl	5.3
	13–15 years girl	4.2
	Unknown	0
Badminton	7–9 years	9.4
	10–12 years	19
	13–15 years	21.9
	7–9 years boy	11.1
	10–12 years boy	25.2
	13–15 years boy	26.8
	7–9 years girl	7.4
	10–12 years girl	13.3
	13–15 years girl	17.9
	Unknown	0
Tennis	7–9 years	1.9
	10–12 years	8
	13–15 years	9.6
	7–9 years boy	1.7
	10–12 years boy	9.4
	13–15 years boy	12.2
	7–9 years girl	2.1
	10–12 years girl	6.7
	13–15 years girl	7.4
	Unknown	0

▶

		2004
Other types of ballgames individual	7–9 years	0.5
	10–12 years	4.2
	13–15 years	2.8
	7–9 years boy	0.9
	10–12 years boy	6.5
	13–15 years boy	3.7
	7–9 years girl	0
	10–12 years girl	2
	13–15 years girl	2.1
	Unknown	0
Swimming	7–9 years	41.5
	10–12 years	34.9
	13–15 years	16.3
	7–9 years boy	41.9
	10–12 years boy	37.4
	13–15 years boy	15.9
	7–9 years girl	41.1
	10–12 years girl	32.7
	13–15 years girl	16.8
	Unknown	40
Gymnastic, aerobic	7–9 years	26.9
	10–12 years	16.6
	13–15 years	11.2
	7–9 years boy	22.2
	10–12 years boy	10.8
	13–15 years boy	4.9
	7–9 years girl	32.6
	10–12 years girl	22
	13–15 years girl	16.8
	Unknown	20
Athletics	7–9 years	0.9
	10–12 years	2.8
	13–15 years	3.9
	7–9 years boy	0
	10–12 years boy	2.2
	13–15 years boy	3.7
	7–9 years girl	2.1
	10–12 years girl	3.3
	13–15 years girl	4.2
	Unknown	20
Dance	7–9 years	11.3
	10–12 years	9.3
	13–15 years	10.7
	7–9 years boy	4.3
	10–12 years boy	2.9
	13–15 years boy	3.7
	7–9 years girl	20
	10–12 years girl	15.3
	13–15 years girl	16.8
	Unknown	40

▶

Table 10.4(a) *(continued)*

		2004
Spinning	7–9 years	0.5
	10–12 years	0.3
	13–15 years	0.6
	7–9 years boy	0
	10–12 years boy	0
	13–15 years boy	0
	7–9 years girl	1.1
	10–12 years girl	0.7
	13–15 years girl	1.1
	Unknown	0
Weight training	7–9 years	0.9
	10–12 years	1.4
	13–15 years	6.7
	7–9 years boy	0.9
	10–12 years boy	1.4
	13–15 years boy	6.1
	7–9 years girl	1.1
	10–12 years girl	1.3
	13–15 years girl	7.4
	Unknown	20
Martial arts	7–9 years	4.2
	10–12 years	4.8
	13–15 years	3.9
	7–9 years boy	6
	10–12 years boy	7.2
	13–15 years boy	4.9
	7–9 years girl	2.1
	10–12 years girl	2.7
	13–15 years girl	3.2
	Unknown	0
Bicycle race	7–9 years	1.4
	10–12 years	4.8
	13–15 years	6.2
	7–9 years boy	0.9
	10–12 years boy	5
	13–15 years boy	8.5
	7–9 years girl	2.1
	10–12 years girl	4.7
	13–15 years girl	4.2
	Unknown	0
Roller-skate, skateboard	7–9 years	11.3
	10–12 years	8.7
	13–15 years	9
	7–9 years boy	11.1
	10–12 years boy	10.8
	13–15 years boy	11
	7–9 years girl	11.6
	10–12 years girl	6.7
	13–15 years girl	7.4
	Unknown	0

▶

		2004
Riding	7–9 years	9.4
	10–12 years	11.4
	13–15 years	5.1
	7–9 years boy	2.6
	10–12 years boy	0.7
	13–15 years boy	0
	7–9 years girl	17.9
	10–12 years girl	21.3
	13–15 years girl	9.5
	Unknown	0
Canoe, kayak, rowing	7–9 years	0.5
	10–12 years	1
	13–15 years	1.7
	7–9 years boy	0
	10–12 years boy	1.4
	13–15 years boy	3.7
	7–9 years girl	1.1
	10–12 years girl	0.7
	13–15 years girl	0
	Unknown	0
Yachting	7–9 years	0.5
	10–12 years	1.7
	13–15 years	3.9
	7–9 years boy	0
	10–12 years boy	2.9
	13–15 years boy	7.3
	7–9 years girl	1.1
	10–12 years girl	0.7
	13–15 years girl	1.1
	Unknown	0
Scout	7–9 years	14.6
	10–12 years	13.5
	13–15 years	7.3
	7–9 years boy	13.7
	10–12 years boy	11.5
	13–15 years boy	8.5
	7–9 years girl	15.8
	10–12 years girl	15.3
	13–15 years girl	6.3
	Unknown	0
Other	7–9 years	6.6
	10–12 years	10
	13–15 years	14.6
	7–9 years boy	7.7
	10–12 years boy	9.4
	13–15 years boy	17.1
	7–9 years girl	5.3
	10–12 years girl	10.7
	13–15 years girl	12.6
	Unknown	20

Table 10.4(b) By age, by year and by activity

		Football	Handball	Other types of ballgames by groups	Badminton	Tennis	Other types of ballgames individual	Swimming	Gymnastic, aerobic	Athletics	Dance	Spinning	Weight training
7–9 years	2004	34.9	17.9	1.9	9.4	1.9	0.5	41.5	26.9	0.9	11.3	0.5	0.9
10–12 years	2004	39.8	15.9	5.5	19	8	4.2	34.9	16.6	2.8	9.3	0.3	1.4
13–15 years	2004	27	13.5	5.1	21.9	9.6	2.8	16.3	11.2	3.9	10.7	0.6	6.7
7–9 years boy	2004	49.6	10.3	2.6	11.1	1.7	0.9	41.9	22.2	0	4.3	0	0.9
10–12 years boy	2004	53.2	16.5	5.8	25.2	9.4	6.5	37.4	10.8	2.2	2.9	0	1.4
13–15 years boy	2004	36.6	8.5	6.1	26.8	12.2	3.7	15.9	4.9	3.7	3.7	0	6.1
7–9 years girl	2004	16.8	27.4	1.1	7.4	2.1	0	41.1	32.6	2.1	20	1.1	1.1
10–12 years girl	2004	27.3	15.3	5.3	13.3	6.7	2	32.7	22	3.3	15.3	0.7	1.3
13–15 years girl	2004	17.9	17.9	4.2	17.9	7.4	2.1	16.8	16.8	4.2	16.8	1.1	7.4
Unknown	2004	60	20	0	0	0	0	40	20	20	40	0	20

		Martial arts	Bicycle race	Roller-skate, skateboard	Riding	Canoe, kayak, rowing	Yachting	Scout	Other
7–9 years	2004	4.2	1.4	11.3	9.4	0.5	0.5	14.6	6.6
10–12 years	2004	4.8	4.8	8.7	11.4	1	1.7	13.5	10
13–15 years	2004	3.9	6.2	9	5.1	1.7	3.9	7.3	14.6
7–9 years boy	2004	6	0.9	11.1	2.6	0	0	13.7	7.7
10–12 years boy	2004	7.2	5	10.8	0.7	1.4	2.9	11.5	9.4
13–15 years boy	2004	4.9	8.5	11	0	3.7	7.3	8.5	17.1
7–9 years girl	2004	2.1	2.1	11.6	17.9	1.1	1.1	15.8	5.3
10–12 years girl	2004	2.7	4.7	6.7	21.3	0.7	0.7	15.3	10.7
13–15 years girl	2004	3.2	4.2	7.4	9.5	0	1.1	6.3	12.6
Unknown	2004	0	0	0	0	0	0	0	20

Table 10.4(c) By year, activity and by age

		7–9 years	10–12 years	13–15 years	7–9 years boy	10–12 years boy	13–15 years boy	7–9 years girl	10–12 years girl	13–15 years girl	Unknown
2004	Football	34.9	39.8	27	49.6	53.2	36.6	16.8	27.3	17.9	60
	Handball	17.9	15.9	13.5	10.3	16.5	8.5	27.4	15.3	17.9	20
	Other types of ballgames by groups	1.9	5.5	5.1	2.6	5.8	6.1	1.1	5.3	4.2	0
	Badminton	9.4	19	21.9	11.1	25.2	26.8	7.4	13.3	17.9	0
	Tennis	1.9	8	9.6	1.7	9.4	12.2	2.1	6.7	7.4	0
	Other types of ballgames individual	0.5	4.2	2.8	0.9	6.5	3.7	0	2	2.1	0
	Swimming	41.5	34.9	16.3	41.9	37.4	15.9	41.1	32.7	16.8	40
	Gymnastic, aerobic	26.9	16.6	11.2	22.2	10.8	4.9	32.6	22	16.8	20
	Athletics	0.9	2.8	3.9	0	2.2	3.7	2.1	3.3	4.2	20
	Dance	11.3	9.3	10.7	4.3	2.9	3.7	20	15.3	16.8	40
	Spinning	0.5	0.3	0.6	0	0	0	1.1	0.7	1.1	0
	Weight training	0.9	1.4	6.7	0.9	1.4	6.1	1.1	1.3	7.4	20
	Martial arts	4.2	4.8	3.9	6	7.2	4.9	2.1	2.7	3.2	0
	Bicycle race	1.4	4.8	6.2	0.9	5	8.5	2.1	4.7	4.2	0
	Roller-skate, skateboard	11.3	8.7	9	11.1	10.8	11	11.6	6.7	7.4	0
	Riding	9.4	11.4	5.1	2.6	0.7	0	17.9	21.3	9.5	0
	Canoe, kayak, rowing	0.5	1	1.7	0	1.4	3.7	1.1	0.7	0	0
	Yachting	0.5	1.7	3.9	0	2.9	7.3	1.1	0.7	1.1	0
	Scout	14.6	13.5	7.3	13.7	11.5	8.5	15.8	15.3	6.3	0
	Other	6.6	10	14.6	7.7	9.4	17.1	5.3	10.7	12.6	20
	None of above	9.4	10.4	19.7	11.1	7.2	22	7.4	13.3	17.9	0

you find is better at communicating the sense of the data? Visually 10.4(b) is harder to read because of its width; 10.4(c) shows the characteristics of the table in one glance. With this table it is easier to compare data down columns (how children of different ages participated in an activity) and across rows (how children of the same age spent their time in different activities). When faced with options for displaying data, tables whose shape and extent can be appreciated 'at a glance' should be prioritised.

10.1.3 Stripping out

The third approach to scanning the table is to relate our research question, and specifically our information needs, to the data table. Often we will find that only part of the table addresses our specified needs. Our task is to isolate this data (this is the process of 'stripping out') and focus our attention on it. Let us see this process at work.

Imagine our research is into interagency working in supporting children. The context of our work, in the UK, is the 'Every Child Matters' policy. This seeks to ensure that the agencies that have an interest in or responsibility for children's welfare act in a co-ordinated and integrated way and that there are no cracks between them that children could fall through. The policy expects agencies to work together to resolve such problems as truanting, the welfare of children in the family, bullying and youth criminality. Different agencies have different responsibilities in these and other issues but to resolve the issues they need to collaborate. Imagine the position from the viewpoint of a head teacher. There is a need to maintain contacts with children's social services, the youth justice system, the police, health service agencies, youth employment and advice agencies – and these are just the main ones. Now imagine that the head teacher needs to do this for every area in which the pupils live. From this perspective, interagency working becomes much more complex. But how big is the problem? Table 10.5(a), which shows pupil movements across education authority boundaries in London, may give us some answers but, as it stands, it is far too complex. With 33 administrative units (local education authorities) the matrix gives over 1,000 potential pieces of data. We need to focus on the core information – just how many pupils are educated in the borough in which they live? By answering this question, we will get an idea how many agencies in different authorities head teachers will have to become involved with. Fortunately these data are easy to access; they lie on the diagonal but even here it is difficult to read, so we have to extract it (Table 10.5(b)). Alphabetical listing helps us find the position for any authority but is not useful when 'reading' the data. For this, we should arrange the data as an ascending or descending series (Table 10.5(c)). Now we have some sort of answer to our question about the scale of the issue. For some authorities it is much more of a problem than others. The head teachers in Kensington and Chelsea (an education authority in London) have over half of their pupils living in another authority but those in Tower Hamlets (another authority) have about 5 per cent. Are more head teachers like the ones in Kensington and Chelsea or like Tower Hamlets? We cannot answer this directly but, on balance, because about 60 per cent of the authorities have between 30 per cent and 55 per cent of their pupils living outside the authority, we can say the issue of cross-boundary liaison is quite significant. And why is this important? Look at it from the perspective of a head teacher first. With pupils from five authorities, the head teacher will have to deal with *five* sets of children's services, *five* sets of youth justice boards, *five* sets of police services (and many more local policing teams) and so on. And each of the other agencies will have to deal with schools

Table 10.5(a) Cross border movement of secondary[1] school pupils[2, 3] resident in London, 2007[4]

		percentage of pupils												
	Resident LA \ School LA	Camden	Greenwich	Hackney	Hammersmith and Fulham	Islington	Kensington and Chelsea	Lambeth	Lewisham	Southwark	Tower Hamlets	Wandsworth	Westminster	Barking and Dagenham
	City of London	3.9		1.3		5.2	2.6	3.9	1.3	37.7	35.1		6.5	
202	Camden	71.2	–	0.1	0.8	9.4	0.7	0.3		–	0.1		10.7	
203	Greenwich	–	71.4	–	–	–		0.1	2.3	0.6	0.1	–	0.1	
204	Hackney	2.0	–	55.9	0.1	14.6	0.1	0.3	–	0.2	13.5	–	1.2	–
205	Hammersmith and Fulham	0.5		–	51.2		7.2	0.1		–	–	8.9	1.4	
206	Islington	17.1	–	2.5	0.7	63.9	1.0	1.3		0.4	0.4	–	1.9	–
207	Kensington and Chelsea	1.2			23.6	–	45.4	0.4		0.1	–	5.4	10.7	0.1
208	Lambeth	0.1	0.2	0.1	0.6	–	1.0	49.2	0.7	13.5	–	14.6	5.6	
209	Lewisham		11.3	–	0.1		–	0.7	69.0	5.5	0.1	0.1	0.3	–
210	Southwark	0.1	1.6	–	0.2	0.1	0.2	6.5	8.4	74.7	0.3	0.7	4.1	–
211	Tower Hamlets	0.1	0.8	1.3	0.1	0.2	0.1	0.2	–	1.2	94.2	–	0.4	0.1
212	Wandsworth	–	–	–	5.5	–	0.8	2.9	0.1	0.4		72.0	0.7	
213	Westminster	2.2			4.3	0.6	10.2	1.5		0.3		1.5	71.5	–
301	Barking and Dagenham	–	–	0.2	–	0.1		–		0.1	0.7	–	0.1	84.2
302	Barnet	2.3		–	0.1	0.1	0.1	–		–	–		0.4	
303	Bexley		4.8	–	–	–		–	0.2	0.3	–	–	–	
304	Brent	3.1		–	1.7	–	1.2	–	–	–	–	0.1	3.3	
305	Bromley	–	0.7		0.3			0.3	1.8	0.3		–	–	
306	Croydon	–	–	–	0.1	–	–	2.2	0.2	0.4	–	0.9	0.2	
307	Ealing	–		–	2.2	–	0.9			–		0.1	0.2	
308	Enfield	0.4	–	0.6	–	0.5		–		–	0.1	–	0.1	–
309	Haringey	2.0	–	2.8	0.1	2.3	0.1	–		–	0.1		0.3	–
310	Harrow	–			0.7		0.2					–	0.1	
311	Havering	–	–	–		–				–	0.1		–	3.1
312	Hillingdon	–			0.4		0.3			–	–	–	–	
313	Hounslow	–			0.8	–	0.2			–		–	–	
314	Kingston upon Thames				0.4			–		–		0.5	–	
315	Merton	–	–		1.1		0.1	1.5	–	0.2		8.1	0.2	–
316	Newham	0.1	–	0.2	–	0.1	–	–	–	0.1	1.9	–	0.1	0.6
317	Redbridge	–	–	0.1	–	–		–			0.6		–	2.4
318	Richmond upon Thames				2.6		0.4	–				0.3	–	
319	Sutton				0.1	–		0.1		–		0.5	–	
320	Waltham Forest	0.3		0.7	–	0.2	–	–	–	–	0.3		0.1	0.1

1 Includes: maintained mainstream secondary schools (including middle deemed), City Technology Colleges and Academies.
2 Includes: solely registered and main registration of dually registered pupils. Excludes pupils reported to be boarders.
3 Aged 11–15 as at 31 August 2006.
4 Excludes: unmatched records (i.e. with missing or invalid postcodes).
(x suppressed data) (. not applicable)

Source: DFES.

Table 10.5(a) *(Continued)*

percentage of pupils																			
Barnet	Bexley	Brent	Bromley	Croydon	Ealing	Enfield	Haringey	Harrow	Havering	Hillingdon	Hounslow	Kingston upon Thames	Merton	Newham	Redbridge	Richmond upon Thames	Sutton	Waltham Forest	Outside London
									1.3										1.3
4.1		1.6		0.1	–	0.1	0.3	0.2			–			–	–	–		–	0.1
–	18.8	–	5.5	–	–				–					0.1	–			–	0.8
0.4	–	0.2		–	–	1.7	5.7		0.1		–		–	0.6	0.3			2.2	0.6
0.1		1.9		–	5.7	–	–	0.1		0.1	14.6	0.3	0.7			6.9	–	0.1	0.1
3.1		0.1		0.1	0.1	1.2	4.4			–	–			–				–	1.7
0.2		4.8		0.1	1.7	0.1		–		0.2	4.3	0.1	0.3			1.4		–	0.1
–	–	–	0.5	9.2	–	–	0.1				–	0.1	3.1	–		0.1	1.0	–	0.1
–	1.2	–	8.7	2.0	–	–	–					–	–	–	–	–	0.2	–	0.6
–	0.1	–	0.7	1.8	–		–				–	–	–	0.1	–	–	0.1	–	0.1
–	–	–	–	–		–	0.1		0.2					0.6	0.1			0.1	0.1
–		–		0.9	–		0.1	–			0.4	3.1	6.9			4.7	1.2		0.1
0.8		5.5		–	0.4	–	–	0.2			0.8	–	–	0.1	–	–			0.1
–				–		–	0.1		8.3					2.4	3.4			0.1	0.4
80.1		5.9			–	3.6	2.8	1.2		–					0.4			–	3.1
	86.0		4.3	–			–				–			–	–	–	–		4.1
7.6		74.0		–	2.8	–	–	4.7		0.5	0.3	–		–	–	–		–	0.5
	3.1		84.3	4.9									–	–			0.3		4.0
–	–		4.6	76.5	–	–	–				–	–	1.2			–	8.6	–	4.8
0.3		1.7			77.9	–	–	1.1		5.0	8.9	0.3		–		0.1		–	1.3
5.5		0.3		–		86.8	2.9	–						–	0.1	–		0.2	2.5
3.1		0.4		–	–	13.1	74.7		–					–	0.1			0.4	0.4
5.4		8.3		–	1.1	–	–	72.3		6.2	–	–			–	–		–	5.5
–						–	–		87.9					0.3	0.9			0.1	7.4
0.2		0.2	–		3.9			0.7		85.0	2.8	–	–	–		0.1	–	–	6.3
–		–		–	2.0		–	–		0.6	76.8	1.1	–			9.8	–		8.4
		–		0.1	–						0.5	77.0	3.1			6.9	3.4		7.9
–		–	–	3.4		–				–	–	4.7	67.1	–		0.1	12.1		1.1
–	–	–	–	–		–	0.1		0.9		–			92.3	2.1	–		1.1	0.3
0.1	–			–		0.1	0.1		1.5				–	2.3	86.0	–		0.8	5.9
		–		–	0.1			–		0.1	12.0	3.7	1.3			75.9	–		3.5
			–	3.9								3.1	3.5			–	80.7		7.9
0.1		–	–			1.1	0.5		0.3					1.4	5.7			88.1	1.0

Table 10.5(b) Diagonals extracted

City of London	
Camden	71.2
Greenwich	71.4
Hackney	55.9
Hammersmith and Fulham	51.2
Islington	63.9
Kensington and Chelsea	45.4
Lambeth	49.2
Lewisham	69.0
Southwark	74.7
Tower Hamlets	94.2
Wandsworth	72.0
Westminster	71.5
Barking and Dagenham	84.2
Barnet	80.1
Bexley	86.0
Brent	74.0
Bromley	84.3
Croydon	76.5
Ealing	77.9
Enfield	86.8
Haringey	74.7
Harrow	72.3
Havering	87.9
Hillingdon	85.0
Hounslow	76.8
Kingston upon Thames	77.0
Merton	67.1
Newham	92.3
Redbridge	86.0
Richmond upon Thames	75.9
Sutton	80.7
Waltham Forest	88.1

Table 10.5(c) Diagonals re-ordered

Kensington and Chelsea	45.4
Lambeth	49.2
Hammersmith and Fulham	51.2
Hackney	55.9
Islington	63.9
Merton	67.1
Lewisham	69.0
Camden	71.2
Greenwich	71.4
Westminster	71.5
Wandsworth	72.0
Harrow	72.3
Brent	74.0
Southwark	74.7
Haringey	74.7
Richmond upon Thames	75.9
Croydon	76.5
Hounslow	76.8
Kingston upon Thames	77.0
Ealing	77.9
Barnet	80.1
Sutton	80.7
Barking and Dagenham	84.2
Bromley	84.3
Hillingdon	85.0
Bexley	86.0
Redbridge	86.0
Enfield	86.8
Havering	87.9
Waltham Forest	88.1
Newham	92.3
Tower Hamlets	94.2
City of London	

and childcare teams in more than their own borough. It is a system that, unless managed well, has the potential to fail many children.

Stripping out data, like other methods of reorganising data, can also leave us with new questions. In this case, is there any pattern in the authorities at the bottom and at the top? If we were to explore this further, we would want to know whether authorities with higher proportions of incoming pupils:

- were surrounded by authorities with few schools on their borders;
- had higher levels of pupil attainment than surrounding authorities;
- had a similar socio-economic profile to surrounding authorities;
- had a large proportion of children attending private schools.

In summary, stripping out data may answer an immediate question, but it is likely to highlight other questions that need to be answered.

10.1.4 Compressing data

The information contained in data is revealed as a pattern for which we seek an explanation. The pattern does not have to be of the type 'boys do this and girls do that'. While gender, demography and status are relevant variables, patterns can be more subtle. For example, the personality types of some head teachers could be the factor that underpins the delivery of good teaching and learning in some (but not all) schools and, in others, it could be the reason behind teacher turnover. The search for pattern is the starting point of data exploration. The problem, as we have seen already, is that the balance between 'message' and 'noise' in the data often favours noise. This occurs because there is a relationship between the visibility of the message and the scale at which the data are presented. What do we mean by scale? Imagine that we have pupil attainment data for all the pupils in an area. If we look at a data file of individual cases there is so much detail that we will not be able to see any pattern. What we do is compress it and, depending on how we compress it, different patterns will emerge.

- If we put them into classes (0–20, 21–40, 41–60, etc. where the values are attainment scores) and count the number of pupils in each class, then we might see a pattern (we would expect to see a curve revealing that there are more average pupils than high or low attaining ones. If this were not the case then we should be extremely suspicious of the tests we gave the children in the first place).
- If we compressed the data by putting them into postcode classes, we might find that different postcodes had very different patterns of pupil attainment. However, if the classes or postcodes are too small, the pattern may still not be visible, so we have to combine classes or postcodes still further until we can read the message clearly. Putting it another way, the categories or classes we choose and their size are the lenses through which we look at the data.

Table 10.6 shows this process at work. Table 10.6(a) shows the number of schools and the number of pupils in the Netherlands by the type of school in 1994/95 and 2004/05. As it stands, the table is difficult to read. We can understand what it should be telling us but its message is not clear. However, when we consolidate the non-public schools and primary and secondary schools, as in Table 10.6(b), we can begin to understand something of what the data wants to tell us. First, the number of schools in both categories has fallen in the ten years since 1994/05. Second, in both the number of students has risen. We can draw one conclusion from this and raise a number of questions. We must conclude that school sizes in both categories have increased. But what are the questions in the data?

- We might expect pupil numbers to increase because of the natural increase in population but has the increase been the same in both categories? There are two percentages we can calculate that will give us the answer.
    - First, we can calculate the percentage by which each category has increased:

      State-funded religious and private schools

$$\frac{2004/05 - 1994/95}{1994/95} \times 100 = \frac{88{,}780 \times 100}{646{,}620} = 13.7\%$$

Table 10.6(a) Schools and pupils funded by the state in the Netherlands

Regular education: schools/institutions and pupils/students		No. of schools	No of pupils
Total primary education – public	1994–95	2,686	459,700
	2004–05	2,410	493,560
Total primary education – Protestant	1994–95	2,365	410,550
	2004–05	2,177	438,300
Total primary education – Roman Catholic	1994–95	2,311	482,050
	2004–05	2,167	538,750
Total primary education – other private education	1994–95	498	98,760
	2004–05	560	129,610
Secondary education – public	1994–95	182	186,920
	2004–05	191	241,840
Secondary education – Protestant	1994–95	228	221,530
	2004–05	144	214,340
Secondary education – Roman Catholic	1994–95	391	294,710
	2004–05	168	239,810
Secondary education – other private education	1994–95	225	173,210
	2004–05	165	241,860

Note: In the Netherlands there are wholly state funded public schools and state-subsidised private and religious foundation schools.

Source: Statistics Netherlands.

Table 10.6(b) Schools and pupils funded by the state in the Netherlands with the categories consolidated

		No. of schools	No of pupils
State – funded religious and private schools	1994–95	2,868	646,620
	2004–05	2,601	735,400
State – funded public schools	1994–95	6,018	1,680,810
	2004–05	5,381	1,802,670

State-funded public schools

$$\frac{2004/05 - 1994/95}{1994/95} \times 100 = \frac{121{,}860 \times 100}{1{,}680{,}810} = 7.25\%$$

Clearly the rate of increase in student numbers is greater in the religious and private schools.

- Second, we can calculate each category's share of the pupil total in each year.

State-funded religious and private schools

$$\frac{\text{1994/95 religious}}{\text{1994/95 religious \& public}} \times 100 = \frac{646{,}620 \times 100}{(646{,}620 + 1{,}680{,}810)} = 27.8\%$$

Repeat the calculations to see how the share has changed.

- The next question is whether all sub-categories have changed at the same rate – and it is here that we find some interesting patterns between the different types of school and the different levels of education. Our approach is to inspect the detailed data against the broad pattern we have established. As a guide, look at religious versus non-religious schools.
- Finally, we ought to ask whether these data include all pupils in the Netherlands. Could there be some schools that are not state assisted? How could we test for this? One way is to identify, through population statistics, the numbers of children of school age in our target years and see how these totals compare with our own.

What does this data analysis tell us? That the educational system in the Netherlands, as in many other countries, is constantly evolving as parents make choices for their children. For a review of these changes, see the OECD paper by Frans de Vyder (de Vyder, ND).

10.1.5 Re-ordering data

Another approach for making a data set more readable is to reorganise it. Table 10.7 shows a very simple way of doing this. The data are produced by the OECD and are extracted from a table showing expenditure per head for different levels of education. The choice of early childhood education reflects the concern in many countries to tackle the social and economic consequences of deprivation. On the one hand having a child in school or care gives parents the opportunity to work and to provide more effectively for the family and, on the other, children are placed in a stimulating environment where the foundations for subsequent academic progress and attainment are laid. In Table 10.7(a), however, it is impossible to pick out patterns. The simple expedient of turning an alphabetical listing into a table where countries are ranked on the basis of their expenditure makes things much clearer (Table 10.7(b)). What can we pick out as the main messages?

- The difference between the lowest rank (Mexico) and the highest is over $6,000. That is, the UK spends four times as much on early childcare education as Mexico.
- 10 of the 25 countries for which we have data spend plus or minus $500 of the OECD average on early years education. In other words, this is a fairly balanced distribution. There is another indicator of this; can you see it? Look at the number of countries outside a spend of plus or minus $500 of the OECD average. This idea of a balanced distribution could be important if we wished to conduct a more advanced statistical analysis (see Chapter 13 for more on this).

While there is a relationship between how rich a country is and its position in the ranking (Mexico and Korea have lower per capita incomes than the USA or UK), it is not the only one. How do we explain Switzerland and Japan spending less than $4,000 when other countries spend more? Why do Belgium, France and Ireland spend about $3,000 less than the UK and why are the UK and USA so much higher than other countries? Before we reach any conclusions, we have to be sure that the basis on which the data are collected are the same. If they are then we have to look for the answers in the political priorities behind the spending.

Ranking is not the only way to re-order data. Any way that creates a pattern that can be interpreted is useful. In most cases the criteria we can use will be known beforehand. All that is necessary is that we 'attach' the criteria to the observation of data group. Table 10.8 shows an example of this. The table provides data on the proportion of pupils in each London borough that is eligible for free school meals. This measure is a

Table 10.7 Expenditure per child in US dollars on early childhood education in OECD countries in 2004

a. Alphabetical listing		b. Ranked listing	
Australia	—	Australia	—
Austria	6,106	Mexico	1,794
Belgium	4,915	Korea	2,520
Canada	—	Slovak Republic	2,575
Czech Republic	3,178	Czech Republic	3,178
Denmark	5,323	Switzerland	3,581
Finland	4,282	Japan	3,945
France	4,938	Poland	4,045
Germany	5,489	Hungary	4,231
Greece	—	Finland	4,282
Hungary	4,231	Norway	4,327
Iceland	6,114	Sweden	4,417
Ireland	4,948	Portugal	4,461
Italy	5,971	Spain	4,617
Japan	3,945	**OECD average**	**4,741**
Korea	2,520	Belgium	4,915
Luxembourg	—	France	4,938
Mexico	1,794	Ireland	4,948
Netherlands	5,807	New Zealand	5,112
New Zealand	5,112	Denmark	5,323
Norway	4,327	Germany	5,489
Poland	4,045	Netherlands	5,807
Portugal[7]	4,461	Italy	5,971
Slovak Republic	2,575	Austria	6,106
Spain	4,617	Iceland	6,114
Sweden	4,417	United States	7,896
Switzerland	3,581	United Kingdom	7,924
Turkey	—	Canada	—
United Kingdom	7,924	Greece	—
United States	7,896	Luxembourg	—
		Turkey	—

Source: OECD sourced via www.freestatistics.org.

well-used measure to indicate deprivation and disadvantage. The first two columns show the percentage of pupils in each borough eligible for free school meals. If the table were just these two columns, it would be difficult to read; there is too much information for us to see any pattern. So how can we reorganise our data? The obvious way is in geographical terms. All we need do is create a two-fold classification, inner and outer London. In this table we have used the official categorisation of boroughs but even if there were not one, we could create our own. Our first task is to tag each borough as inner or outer London (columns 3

Table 10.8 Nursery and primary schools pupils in London Boroughs eligible for free school meals, January 2006

London borough	% of pupils eligible	Outer London borough	Inner London borough	Outer London boroughs ranked		Inner London boroughs ranked	
Barking and Dagenham	24.0	o		Kingston	7.2		
Barnet	19.7	o		Richmond	9.1		
Bexley	10.1	o		Bexley	10.1		
Brent	27.1	o		Havering	11.4		
Bromley	12.0	o		Bromley	12		
Camden	42.6		i	Merton	12.1		
City of London	23.8		i	Sutton	12.8		
Croydon	21.2	o		Harrow	16.6		
Ealing	23.7	o		Hillingdon	17.5		
Enfield	24.7	o		Redbridge	17.7		
Greenwich	33.1	o		Barnet	19.7		
Hackney	38.8		i	Croydon	21.2		
Hammersmith and Fulham	42.8		i	Hounslow	21.8		
Haringey	32.5		i	Ealing	23.7		
Harrow	16.6	o		Barking	24	City	23.8
Havering	11.4	o		Waltham Forest	24.3	Wandsworth	27.1
Hillingdon	17.5	o		Enfield	24.7	Lewisham	27.9
Hounslow	21.8	o		Brent	27.1	Haringey	32.5
Islington	41.9		i	Greenwich	33.1	Newham	32.5
Kensington and Chelsea	38.5		i			Southwark	34.2
Kingston upon Thames	7.2	o				Westminster	36.1
Lambeth	36.8		i			Lambeth	36.8
Lewisham	27.9		i			Kensington	38.5
Merton	12.1	o				Hackney	38.8
Newham	32.5		i			Islington	41.9
Redbridge	17.7	o				Camden	42.6
Richmond upon Thames	9.1	o				Hammersmith	42.8
Southwark	34.2		i			Tower Hamlets	52
Sutton	12.8	o					
Tower Hamlets	52.0		i				
Waltham Forest	24.3	o					
Wandsworth	27.1		i				
Westminster	36.1		i				

and 4). We then pick out each group separately and rank them in terms of the proportion eligible for free school meals (columns 5 and 6, 7 and 8). Immediately the association between geographical location and eligibility for free school meals is apparent, from under 10 per cent in Kingston and Richmond (next to each other in south west London) to over 50 per cent in Tower Hamlets (the old dock area just east of the City of London and the traditional first stop for immigrants).

Many of the data investigations we can carry out will show a spatial pattern. However, just because we have shown a spatial element to the pattern does not mean that we have found a cause. Our arguments have to be more sophisticated than that. Space itself is neutral, it is how we value and use location that is important. The factors that we are looking for are often associated with access – but accessibility is much more than just transport. We have to think about access to job opportunities, to well-qualified teachers, to welfare and social services. So we have to dig deeper and understand the processes at work that create the pattern. In our case free school meals are used as a proxy for relative poverty but poverty does not have a single cause. Some people may not wish to enter the labour market, others may want to but may be discriminated against and yet others may be unable to because they are unable to speak the language or because they are prevented by legislation. The advice is always to go beyond the first pattern, particularly if it is geographical in character, and see if other factors are at work.

10.1.6 Reconstructing data

The last method we shall look at that can help us understand the message in our data is to reconstruct it in another form. We had an introduction to this when we looked at the interpretation of Table 10.5. In this case we used percentages to standardise our comparisons. This is a particularly useful method when we are dealing with data over a period of time. In this case the percentages we calculate are called *index numbers*.

Let us look at an example. Table 10.9 presents some data from Norway on pupil numbers in total (column 2), numbers receiving additional training in their mother tongue and a bilingual education in their mother tongue and Norwegian (column 3) and those receiving additional training in Norwegian. The context for these data are, in educational terms, how we manage non-native speakers in our educational systems. This, however, sits within (a) a broader social context consisting of the acceptance of migrants and refugees in a community, the social costs of managing society if there is no support of an early age, the opportunities that we forgo if we do not make best use of migrants' talents and (b) the need to monitor trends and assess the implications of policy and practice interventions. To return to Table 10.9, we can immediately see what the data in columns 1 to 4 are telling us, how these numbers changed over the 16 years from 1992 to 2007. We can see, in each case, that the numbers generally increased. What we cannot tell easily is the rate at which they increased. Index numbers help us do this.

The method of calculation is straightforward.

$$\text{Index No.} = \frac{\text{Year total}}{\text{Base year total}} \times 100$$

The Index number for the total number of pupils in 1993/04 is:

$$\text{IN} = \frac{466{,}605}{463{,}309} \times 100 = 100.7$$

Index numbers are a means of comparing different series on a standardised basis. In each case the base year is assumed to be 100. If we look at columns 5 and 6 in Table 10.9 we can immediately see differences in the rate of increase for the total number of pupils and those receiving additional training and a bilingual education. The increase for the latter is much greater – over the entire period about four times as great.

If we look at the rate of increase in the numbers receiving additional training in Norwegian, we have to start with 1997/98 as our base year should always be the same.

Table 10.9 Pupils in Norwegian schools with training in their native language and in Norwegian

1	2	3	4	5	6	7	8	9
School year	Pupils, total	Pupils with mother language training and/or bilingual education	Pupils with additional training in Norwegian	Pupils total	Pupils with mother language training and/or bilingual education	Pupils, total	Pupils with mother language training and/or bilingual education	Pupils with additional training in Norwegian
1992/93	463,309	10,045	—	100	100			
1993/94	466,605	9,933	—	100.7	98.9			
1994/95	470,779	10,204	—	101.6	101.6			
1995/96	477,236	11,276	—	103	112.3			
1996/97	487,398	12,770	—	105.2	127.1			
1997/98	558,247	15,810	24,599	120.5	157.4	100	100	100
1998/99	569,044	17,008	25,311	122.8	169.3	101.9	107.6	102.9
1999/00	580,261	17,306	28,242	125.2	172.3	104	109.5	114.8
2000/01	590,471	18,176	31,113	127.4	180.9	105.8	115	126.5
2001/02	599,468	18,611	32,855	129.4	185.3	107.4	117.7	133.6
2002/03	610,297	18,734	33,833	131.7	186.5	109.3	118.5	137.5
2003/04	617,577	19,695	35,374	133.3	196.1	110.6	124.6	143.8
2004/05	618,250	19,713	35,632	133.4	196.2	110.7	124.7	144.9
2005/06	619,640	20,717	37,342	133.7	206.2	111	131	151.8
2006/07	619,038	22,166	39,963	133.6	220.7	110.9	140.2	162.5
2007/08	616,388	22,084	39,856	133	219.9	110.4	133.7	162

What we can see here is that the growth in pupils with additional training in Norwegian grew at the fastest rate (column 9) compared with those receiving a bilingual education and the total number of pupils.

The index numbers we calculated are straightforward. We can also use the concept to combine information from different data sets. For example, if we wanted to bring together measures of children's welfare into an index of well-being, we could draw on (depending on the country) a range of health, social, economic and educational data. What we might actually use and how we might combine them depends on how we define 'well-being'. A Professor of Sociology, Kenneth Land, led a team that attempted this for the USA (Land et al., 2001). They defined seven dimensions of well-being: social relationships, material well-being, health, safety, educational attainment, participation in community and emotional and spiritual well-being (see Table 10.10). For each they identified a number of indicators, 28 in all. The judgements they had to make were (i) which data sets to use, (ii) what weighting to give to the different dimensions and (iii) how to combine different measurement scales. The task is not difficult but does require a rationale for the decisions. Using this index Land and his colleagues were able to show that, overall, the well-being of children and young people in the USA was no better in 1998 than it was in 1975. It would also be feasible to construct one for administrative areas in the UK. Activity 10.2 is an opportunity to attempt this.

Table 10.10 28 national indicators of child well-being in the USA

Domain	Indicators
Material well-being	• Poverty rate – all families with children. • Secure parental employment rate. • Median annual income – all families with children.
Material well-being and health	• Rate of children with health insurance coverage.
Material well-being and social relationships	• Rate of children in families headed by a single parent. • Rate of children who have moved within the last year.
Health	• Infant mortality rate. • Low birth weight rate. • Mortality rate, ages 1–19. • Rate of children with very good or excellent health (as reported by their parents). • Rate of children with activity limitations (as reported by their parents). • Rate of overweight children and adolescents, ages 6–17.
Health and safety/behavioural concerns	Teenage birth rate, ages 10–17.
Safety/behavioural concerns	• Rate of violent crime victimisation, ages 12–17. • Rate of violent crime offenders, ages 12–17. • Rate of cigarette smoking, Grade 12. • Rate of alcoholic drinking, Grade 12. • Rate of illicit drug use, Grade 12.
Productivity (educational attainments)	• Reading test scores, average of ages 9, 13, 17. • Mathematics test scores, average of ages 9, 13, 17.
Place in community and educational attainments	• Rate of preschool enrolment, ages 3–4. • Rate of persons who have received a high school diploma, ages 18–24. • Rate of youths not working and not in school, ages 16–19. • Rate of persons who have received a bachelor's degree, ages 25–29. • Rate of voting in presidential elections, ages 18–20.
Emotional/spiritual well-being	• Suicide rate, ages 10–19. • Rate of weekly religious attendance, Grade 12. • Percent who report religion.

Source: Land et al., 2001, pp. 249–50.

Activity 10.2 Constructing a well-being index for England

Complex concepts such as standard of living, lifestyle, quality of educational provision and satisfaction are rarely evaluated using simple data sets. The reason for this is that there are many aspects to their character. When faced with this situation, statisticians try to reflect the many sides to this character by using indicators for different character aspects. These indicators are then combined into a composite indicator.

Using the following sources, see which data sets you might use to construct a composite index of community well-being. This activity will test your ability to source data.

Source	www
Neighbourhood Statistics	neighbourhood.statistics.gov.uk
Department for Children, Schools and Families	dcsf.gov.uk/gateway
National Statistics	statistics.gov.uk (select browse by theme)

Having made your selection, how would you combine the data sets? Hint, you will have to convert everything to a common measurement scale.

10.2 Portraying data

Another approach to reading data and seeing the messages contained within them is to transform the data from numbers into a visual representation. Why should we do this? Well, there is considerable evidence that we can assimilate and make sense of visual images more easily than number blocks. It is a process we use in our everyday lives. The patterns we identify (or recognise) are bigger than the elements that comprise them. Numbers only have a relationship to other numbers up or down a numerical scale; when reorganised to present a visual stimulus we can judge them in terms of their proximity (clustering), shape, colour and categorisation, amongst other things.

This is why data visualisation is so important in data analysis. The surprising thing is that so many texts present it as the 'nursery slopes' of data analysis, aimed particularly at readers unable to manage quantitative analysis. There are two main reasons why we should dismiss this position. First, graphical methods are very useful in an initial exploration of the data. If a pattern is identified, it can help us determine our next steps, for example, an assessment of the significance of relationships between the variables. The second reason is equally important. Graphical methods have high levels of communicability, even to non-experts. Graphical presentations get our message over far more effectively than mathematical statements. We should, therefore, treat data visualisation with the seriousness it deserves.

10.2.1 Stem and leaf diagrams

The stem and leaf diagram (also known as 'stem plot') has its origins a century ago but it only gained prominence when it was presented as one of a range of approaches for exploratory data analyses by the American statistician John Tukey in 1977. The method is used to get an impression of a set of data. It is easy to implement and can be modified to suit individual circumstances. There are, now, computer programs for reformulating data into a stem and leaf plot but it is often just as easy to use a traditional pencil and paper approach, even for large data sets.

The concept is straightforward. It assumes that most data can be broken up into two component parts:

- a '*stem*', the part of the number which is common to other data units and which gives the general location in the data set; and
- a '*leaf*', the part which is most individual and which gives the specific value in the data set.

An example will show this. If some of our data are 28, 34, then the tens (20 and 30) are the stems and the units (8 and 4) are the leaves. We would write these numbers like this:

Data		*Data components*	*Stem*	*Leaf*
34	⟶	30 + 4	30	4
28	⟶	20 + 8	20	8

We would portray more data like this:

Stem	*Leaf*
30	1, 4, 4, 5, 9

Table 10.11 Mean scores in student performance on the mathematics scale, PISA 2006

	Mean score		Mean score
OECD		**Partners**	
Australia	520	Argentina	381
Austria	505	Azerbaijan	476
Belgium	520	Brazil	370
Canada	527	Bulgaria	413
Czech Republic	510	Chile	411
Denmark	513	Colombia	370
Finland	548	Croatia	467
France	496	Estonia	515
Germany	504	Hong Kong-China	547
Greece	459	Indonesia	391
Hungary	491	Israel	442
Iceland	506	Jordan	384
Ireland	501	Kyrgyzstan	311
Italy	462	Latvia	486
Japan	523	Liechtenstein	525
Korea	547	Lithuania	486
Luxembourg	490	Macao-China	525
Mexico	406	Montenegro	399
Netherlands	531	Qatar	318
New Zealand	522	Romania	415
Norway	490	Russian Federation	476
Poland	495	Serbia	435
Portugal	466	Slovenia	504
Slovak Republic	492	Chinese Taipei	549
Spain	480	Thailand	417
Sweden	502	Tunisia	365
Switzerland	530	Uruguay	427
Turkey	424		
United Kingdom	495		
United States	474		
OECD total	**484**		
OECD average	**498**		

Source: PISA 2006, volume 2, Table 6.2c.

This shows that we have five data units with a stem of 30. Stems and leaves do not have to be tens and units. Stems can be hundreds and leaves tens and units, or stems can be hundreds and tens and leaves units. It all depends on the character and spread of the data.

Tables 10.11 and 10.12 show the method in operation. Our data show average scores in a mathematics test in 57 countries. The data are drawn from the 2006 PISA

Table 10.12 Stem and leaf diagram of data in Table 10.10

a. Consolidated data	b. Differentiated data
54 9 7 7 8	54 9 7 7 8
53 0 1	53 0 1
52 7 0 0 3 2 5 5	527 0 0 3 2 5 5
51 0 3 5	510 3 5
50 4 5 6 1 2 4	504 5 6 1 2 4
49 1 6 0 0 5 2 5	491 6 0 0 5 2 5
48 6 6 0	486 6 0
47 6 6 4	47 6 6 4
46 6 2 7	46 6 2 7
45 9	459
44 2	442
43 5	435
42 7 4	427 4
41 7 5 1 3	417 5 1 3
40 6	406
39 9 1	399 1
38 4 1	384 1
37 0 0	37 0 0
36 5	365
35	35
34	34
33	33
32	32
31 8 1	318 1

programme. Table 10.11 shows the scores for each country. Because the score values are in hundreds, we use the hundreds and tens as the stem. Thus 420 has 42 as its stem and 0 as its leaf. Table 10.12 shows the data arranged as a stem and leaf plot.

What strikes us about the pattern?

- Look first at column (a), the consolidated data. The first thing we notice is that scores are bunched towards the top end. The pattern is, therefore, asymmetrical; in statistical terms we call this 'skewed'.
- Second, there are two peaks, at 520 and 490 (statistically we say that this pattern is 'bi-modal'). This pattern is of interest to us because it may be significant in research terms. There are two things that might create this pattern. The countries with stems of 52 may have something in common and those with stems of 49 may have something in common but the things they may have in common are different for the two groups. Here the difference would be in the underlying processes that produced the data – mathematics teaching in these countries. However, the pattern could also be produced by the samples of pupils who took the test not being broadly similar in each country. Here the difference would be the result of the way in which the data were collected.

- Third, the distribution is elongated. Statistically, this is called a 'long tail'. This could indicate either that the countries with low scores tested less able pupils or, more likely, that the school system is less capable of developing the mathematical skills of the students.

We have used the stem and leaf approach to establish the shape of the data set and to identify its key features. This has enabled us to pose further questions and to suggest reasons for the patterns. It has been easy to do this and it has been quick. There are, however, questions that we can still put to this data. In Table 10.12b, the countries are divided into two groups, OECD members and partners. Is there any pattern amongst these? It is easy to test this by differentiating the two groups in terms of colour. What is our conclusion? Well, more of the tail consists of OECD partners but partners are also represented at the top end as well. What we might conclude from this is that partnership itself is not a factor in explaining the pattern, though level of economic development may be. The important thing to note here is that we have used the stem-leaf visualisation to help us ask questions that take our analysis forward.

10.2.2 Bar graphs and histograms

Bar graphs (also known as bar charts) and histograms are similar to each other. Both show the relative importance of categories of data (for example age groups, or numbers gaining a pass grade in different subjects). They do this by representing the number of observations (units of data) in a category. Because of this, some texts refer to them as frequency diagrams. Both represent numerical values as columns whose height is proportional to the numerical value. Determining the scale of the column is critical and its length is determined by three things:

- First, the range in the value of the data. If the smallest value is 8 and the greatest 72, we would use a more detailed scale than if the smallest value were 80 and the longest were 2,020. If we tried to use the same scale for both, we would (obviously) need a very large piece of graph paper! Our solution is to compress the larger range of data into a smaller linear scale.
- Second, the size of the diagram we want to produce. This also affects the length of our linear scale. With large diagrams we can show more detail but this may be at the expense of the overall picture.
- Third, the number of graphs we want to fit on one sheet of paper.

These practical issues can only be sorted out on an individual basis. In terms of visual communication, we can be advised that if the scale is too small differences are not apparent but if it is too large, differences that may not be great are magnified. We can often find examples of the latter in the portrayal of economic and financial data, especially when a portion of the scale is deleted in order to magnify a minor upturn or downturn in a data series (this is usually done in order to make a rise or fall in the graph look more impressive than it actually is).

Despite the same methodology being used in calculating the height of the column for bar graphs and histograms, they are, in fact, different.

- A bar chart is used when categories are discrete and separate, for example males and females, primary schools and secondary schools. To represent the fact that the categories are discrete, we usually leave a space between the columns.

- A histogram is used when a measurement scale that is continuous (such as age) has been broken up into classes into which we put counts or frequencies of occurrence. It is, therefore, similar to a stem and leaf diagram.

Bar charts and histograms can be constructed by graphical analysis programs as well as by hand. Figure 10.1 shows a bar chart of the data below it. The data are taken from survey results on children's activities undertaken by the Australian Census Bureau. Figure 10.1 was produced using MS Excel. Three categories of activity are shown: organised sports, selected other activities (which include riding bikes, watching TV and playing electronic games) and computer activities. The bars show the numbers of children engaging in the activities in three survey years, 2000, 2003 and 2006. The pattern is clear and interpretation is helped by the use of colour. We can see the relative importance of the three groups of activity both by year and over the three years. The Australian survey also broke the total down by the gender of the children. Depending on the way the data are arranged in the spreadsheet, we get some very different results as bar charts. Figures 10.2(a)

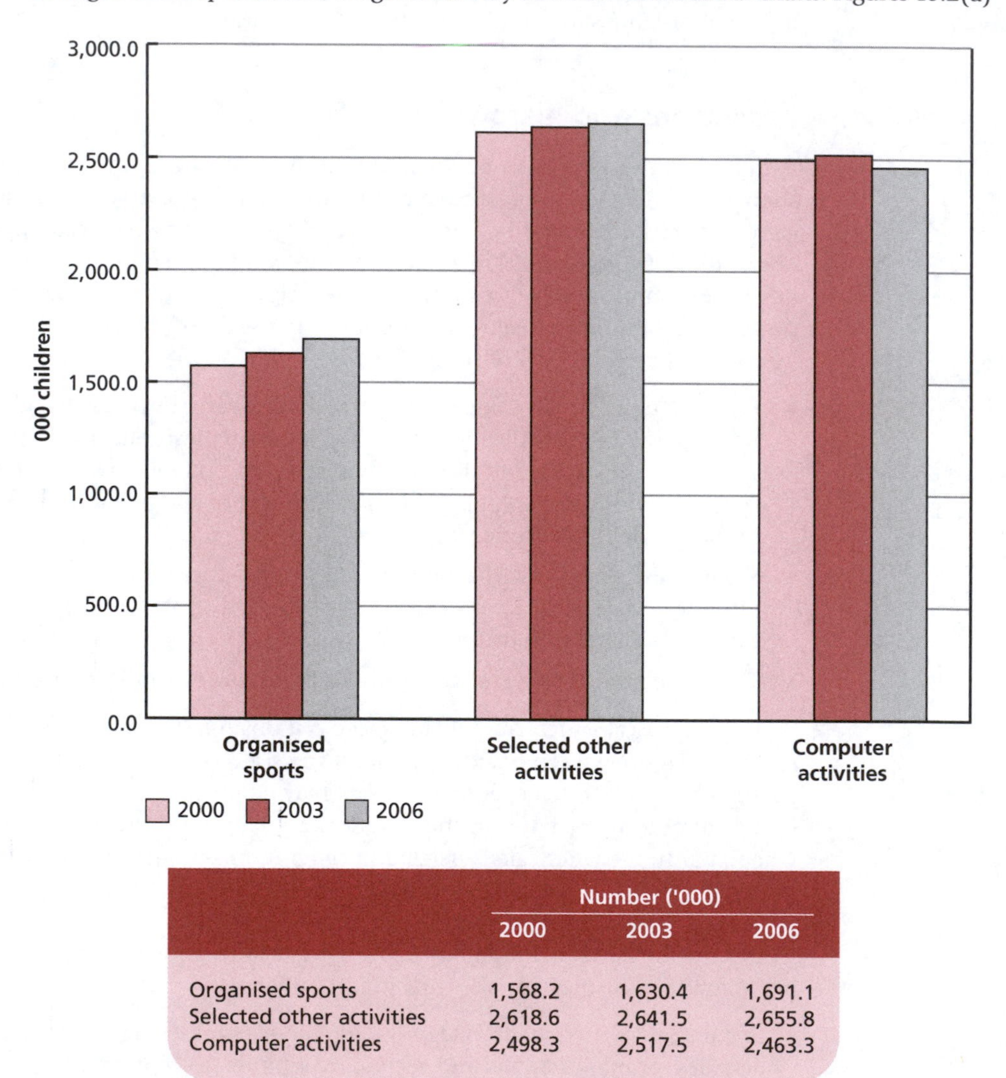

	Number ('000)		
	2000	2003	2006
Organised sports	1,568.2	1,630.4	1,691.1
Selected other activities	2,618.6	2,641.5	2,655.8
Computer activities	2,498.3	2,517.5	2,463.3

Figure 10.1 Australian children's participation in cultural and leisure activities

Source: Australian Bureau of Statistics.

and 10.2(b) shows two different bar charts which are the result of presenting the data in different ways. These figures were produced by the Calc program in the Open Office Suite. The problem with this presentation is the over-use of colours which makes it difficult to see the patterns. It would almost be better to present each one, as two separate graphs. The lessons from this are that (a) visual communication is important and (b) we should manipulate our data to produce the best visual effects.

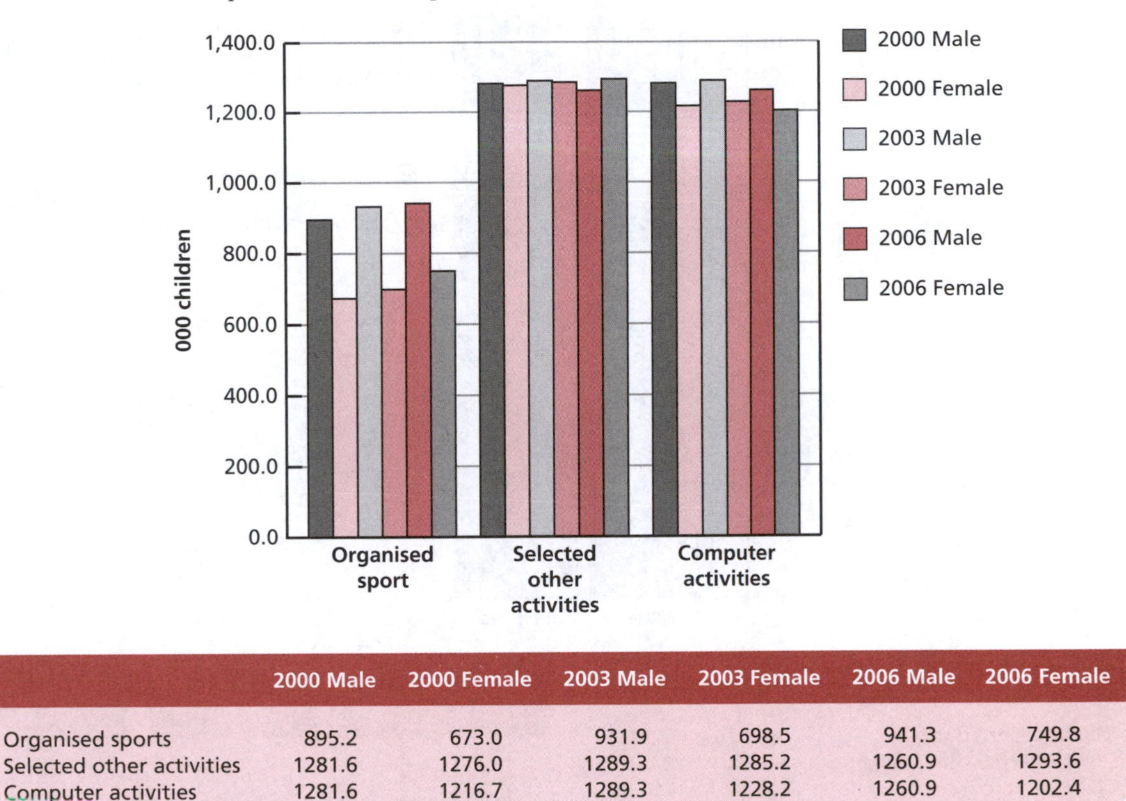

	2000 Male	2000 Female	2003 Male	2003 Female	2006 Male	2006 Female
Organised sports	895.2	673.0	931.9	698.5	941.3	749.8
Selected other activities	1281.6	1276.0	1289.3	1285.2	1260.9	1293.6
Computer activities	1281.6	1216.7	1289.3	1228.2	1260.9	1202.4

Figure 10.2(a) Participation in activities, Australian children 2000–2006

For those without access to these programs, it is possible to produce histograms on-line. Figure 10.3 shows a histogram of the average of scores in mathematics for students in different countries. This is the same data used in the stem and leaf diagram above. This is an attractive analysis because not only does it show the shape of the distribution (the dominance of high scores), it also allows us to see which countries scored what, thereby giving us an insight into another dimension of analysis (the level of economic development and the score). Figure 10.3 was produced on IBM's Many Eyes system (www.many-eyes.com). Registration is required.

A very special type of histogram is the age-sex pyramid. This is used to portray the gender composition of a country or area for each age group. Figure 10.4 shows a population pyramid for the Netherlands. It follows the convention that (i) the age group is shown on the vertical axis, (ii) gender is on the horizontal axis and (iii) females are on the right and males on the left. This diagram is taken from the website of Statistics Netherlands. Like some other countries, Statistics Netherlands has an interactive viewer that allows users to move backwards and forwards in time. Figure 10.4 shows the projected demographic structure of the Netherlands in 2030. What it reveals is a typical mature population structure with a low birth rate and a low death rate (population only

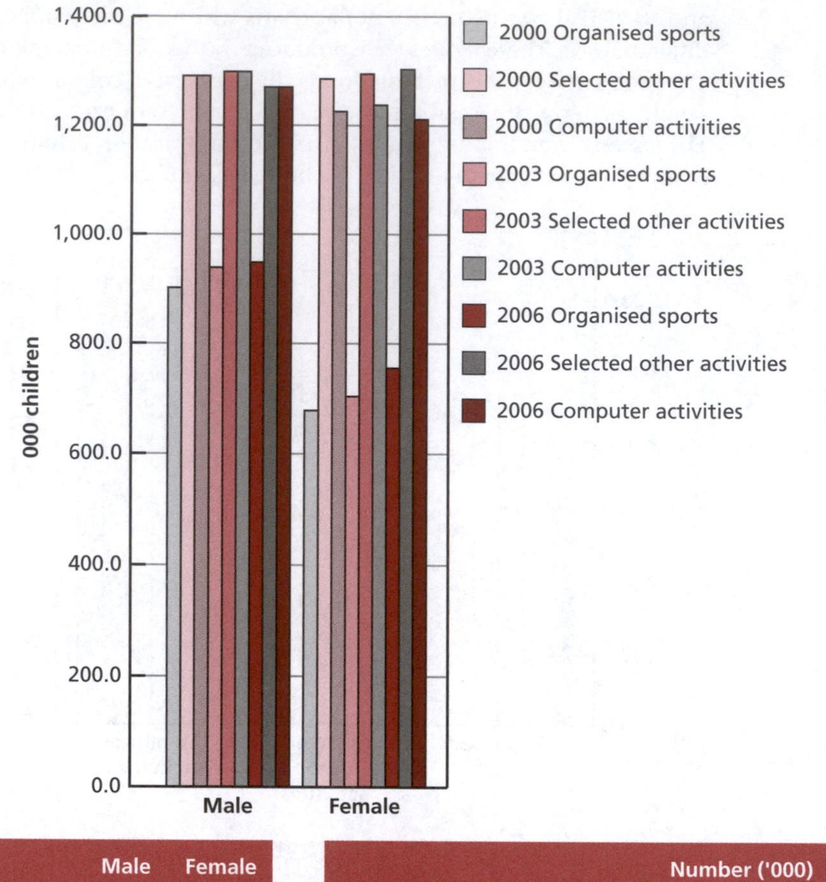

	Male	Female
2000 Organised sports	895.2	673.0
2000 Selected other activities	1281.6	1276.0
2000 Computer activities	1281.6	1216.7
2003 Organised sports	931.9	698.5
2003 Selected other activities	1289.3	1285.2
2003 Computer activities	1289.3	1228.2
2006 Organised sports	941.3	749.8
2006 Selected other activities	1260.9	1293.6
2006 Computer activities	1260.9	1202.4

	Number ('000)		
	2000	2003	2006
Organised sports	1,568.2	1,630.4	1,691.1
Selected other activities	2,618.6	2,641.5	2,655.8
Computer activities	2,498.3	2,517.5	2,463.3

Figure 10.2(b) Participation in activities, Australian Children 2000–2006

starts to decline rapidly from the age of 70). To understand the bulges between 28 and 40 and between 56 and 65, we have to go back to the conditions at the times those people were born. The end of the Second World War was 65 years ago and in many countries birth rates grew rapidly with the removal of that threat. The bulge between 28 and 40 was the period when those born after the war had their children.

Another useful source of national demographic structures is the US Census Bureau. On its site, we can access demographic data for most countries of the world. Figure 10.5(a) and (b) show population pyramids for Germany in 1991 and 2006 and (c) shows India in 2006. These have been chosen to show particular features of population pyramids.

- The pyramids for Germany and India for 2006 are characteristic shapes for two types of society, developed and developing. The 'beehive' shape for Germany shows a mature

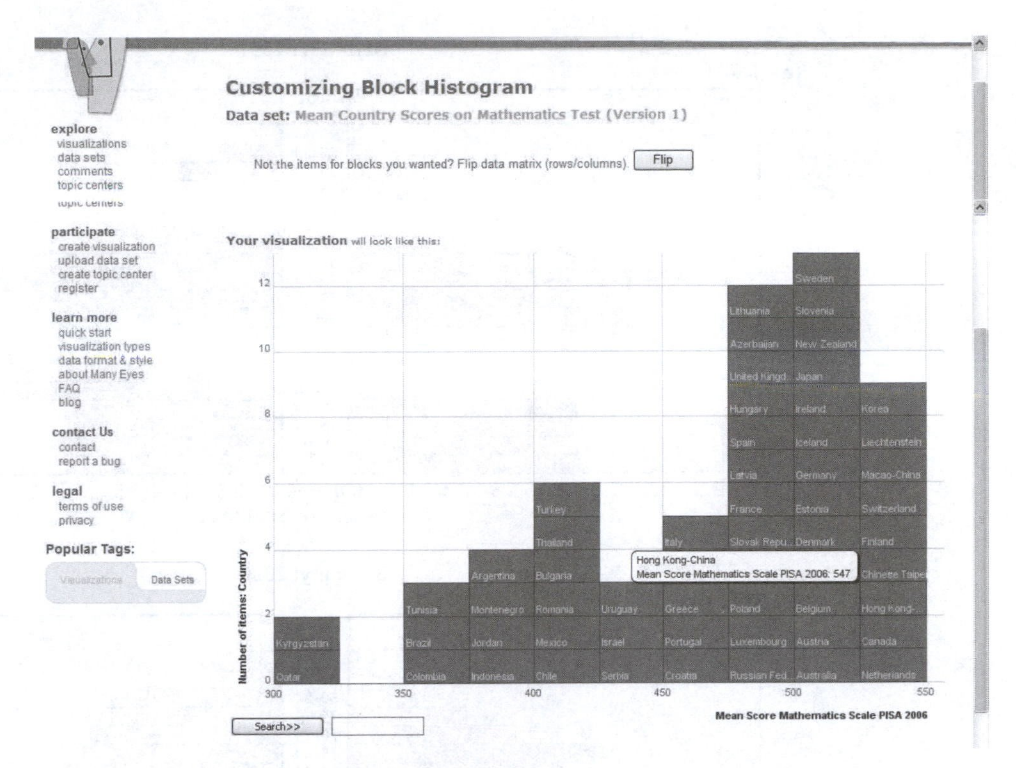

Figure 10.3 Histogram of stem-leaf data (Table 10.11)
Source: from Screenshot from IBM's 'Many Eyes' website, Courtesy of International Business Machines Corporation, copyright © International Business Machines Corporation

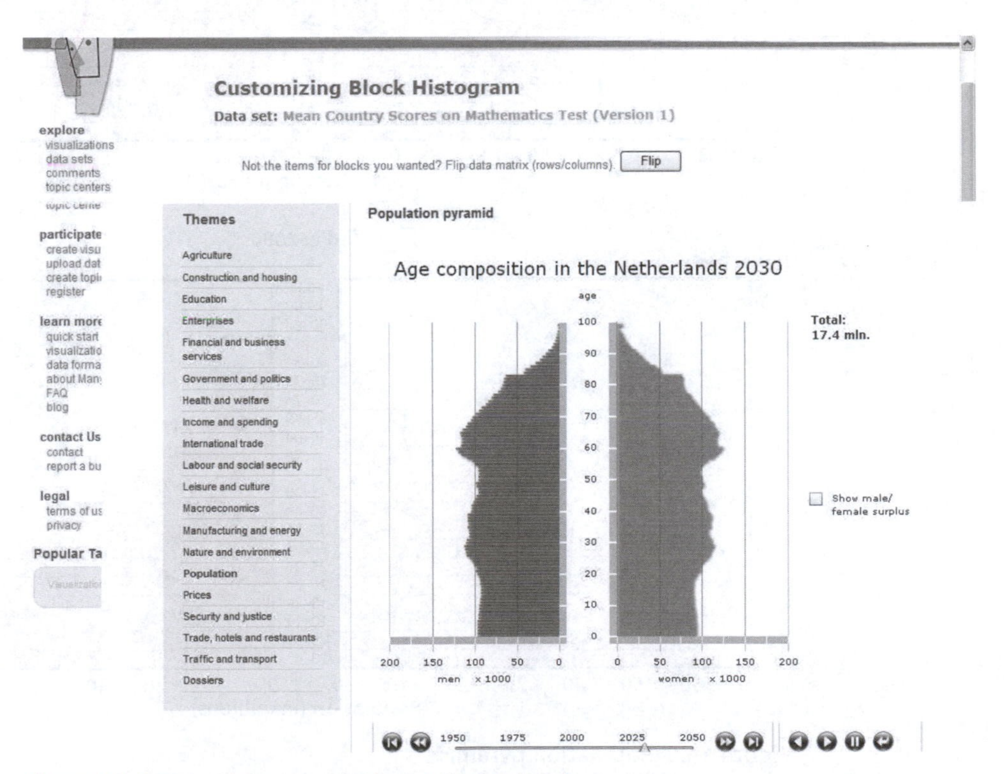

Figure 10.4 Population pyramid, the Netherlands

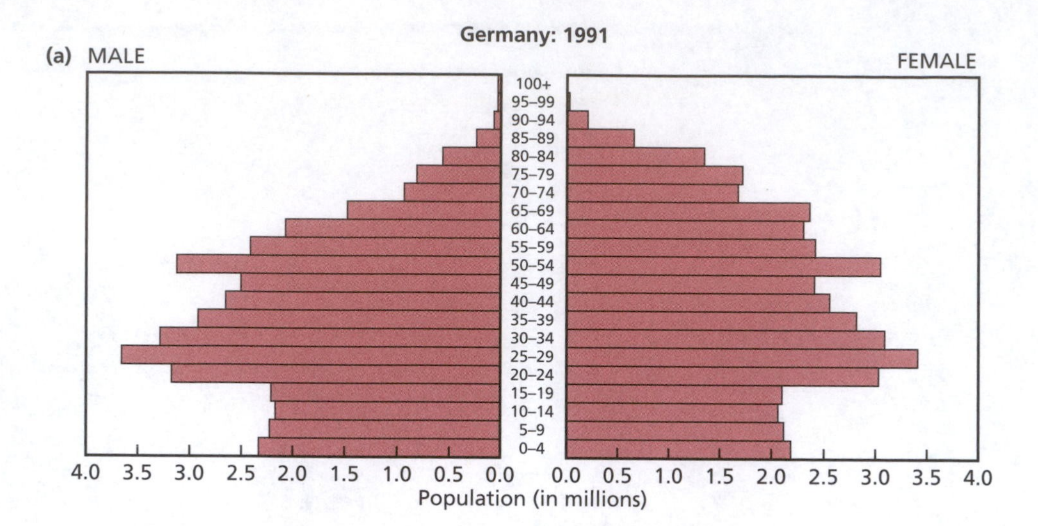

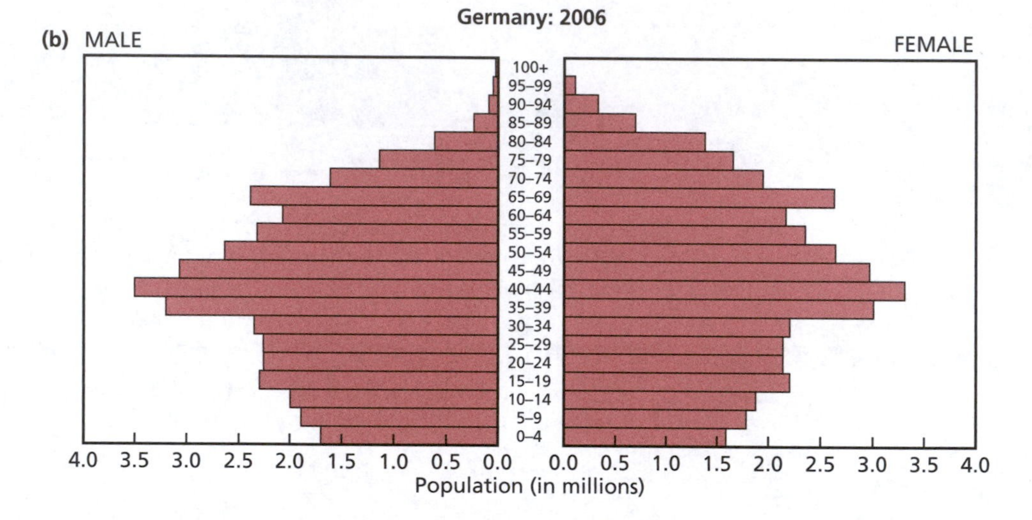

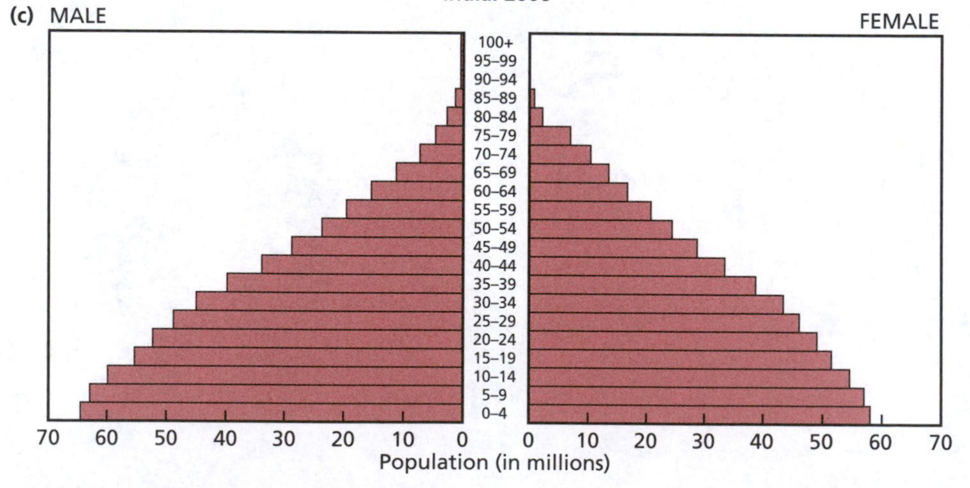

Figure 10.5 Population pyramids
Source: US Census Bureau, International Data Base.

population with a low birth rate and death rate. The triangular shape of India's pyramid shows a youthful population with a high birth rate and high death rate.

- Comparison of population structures over time will tell us something about the dynamics of the population. Those in the 0–4 category in Germany in 1991 were in the 15–19 group in 2006. If we compare the sizes of the bars for the two years, we see that the sizes of both male and female groups have increased. There can be only one cause, in-migration.
- Pyramids allow us to look back in time. The fall in birth rate between the 35–39 and 30–34 age groups in Germany (2006 pyramid) should make us ask the question, 'What happened in the early 1970s?' Was it economic decline in the old German Democratic Republic or changing attitudes as a result of the introduction of the pill?
- In Germany in both 1991 and 2006, there are more males born than females. This is as nature intended. If we look at the raw data, for every 100 females in the 0–4 age group, there are 105 males. In India, there is an imbalance between males and females, but it is more pronounced. The data show that for every 100 females there are 110 males. The question we should ask is 'Where did the females go?' And the answer is not very palatable. They were born and then they were killed.

The examples of population pyramids we have looked at so far have been downloaded from the Internet. We can even do this for local authorities in England and Wales via the Census website (www.statistics.gov.uk/census2001/population_data.asp) and for Scotland via SCROL (Scotland's Census Results OnLine at www.scrol.gov.uk/scrol/common/home.jsp). Often, as researchers, we have to look at smaller areas such as civil wards or areas we define using small area statistics. In these cases, we have to create our own pyramids. Activity 10.3 is an opportunity to do this and it gives us an idea how we can use this method of portraying data in educational research.

10.2.3 Cumulative frequency graphs

Cumulative frequency graphs are based on the same tables we use to construct histograms. Histograms show the *frequency* of occurrence in each class, for instance, the numbers of students scoring different marks in an examination. If we can sequence our classes in some meaningful way, we can construct cumulative frequency graphs, which show the proportion of our population with all of the data characteristics up to a particular point. If we sequence our mark categories from low to high, we can use the data to create a cumulative frequency graph. We could see how many students gained a mark of 0 to 10, how many 0 to 20, how many 0 to 30 and so on. In other words, we can only construct cumulative frequency graphs for continuous data series. Before we look at the technique itself, however, we should understand why should we want to construct cumulative frequency graphs at all.

The answer is that we use them to show where concentrations in our data occur. The cumulative frequency approach is particularly useful when considering issues that have an equity (or inequity) dimension. Let us see what we mean by this. If we have a data set that shows us the wealth of people in a country, we can produce a graph showing what proportion of people own what proportion of the wealth. An even distribution of resources will produce a graph that is a straight line – 10 per cent of the people have 10 per cent of the resources, 20 per cent have 20 per cent, 30 per cent have 30 per cent and so on. *Unequal* distributions are shown as a cumulative frequency curve that deviates from this straight line and the greater the deviation the greater the inequality. For example, in Slovakia, the richest 20 per cent of the population earn about 32 per cent of the income. In the UK, the proportion is about 43 per cent. Measuring inequality is a specialist area with its own techniques which are beyond the remit of this book, but the pattern of a

Activity 10.3 Thinking about population

The table below gives demographic data on the age/sex structure of the two areas in England, East Dorset and Luton. Your task is to construct population pyramids in one of the following ways:

- by hand
- using a spreadsheet by combining separate tables for males and females
- using an online service (such as Statisticum, www.statisticum.org).

Then answer the following questions:

- Will the need to provide secondary education places in both locations in 5, 10 and 15 years be the same, grow or contract?
- Is the population over 55 going to be the same, increase or decrease? If the planning rate of home care provision is 6.5 per 1,000, what is your estimate of the number of home carers for the over 65s in both locations in 10, 15 and 20 years' time? How many vocational training places would you provide and when?
- Can you explain the differences in the two pyramids? Would your explanation make any difference to your estimates of school and vocational training places?

	East Dorset			Luton		
Age range	Total	Males	Females	Total	Males	Females
0–4	3,759	1,899	1,860	13,284	6,776	6,508
5–9	4,605	2,353	2,252	13,528	6,902	6,626
10–14	5,002	2,594	2,408	13,872	7,152	6,720
15–19	4,315	2,273	2,042	12,934	6,346	6,588
20–24	2,857	1,531	1,326	14,758	7,284	7,474
25–29	3,078	1,483	1,595	13,563	6,795	6,768
30–34	4,390	2,038	2,352	15,212	7,760	7,452
35–39	5,458	2,530	2,928	14,512	7,292	7,220
40–44	5,635	2,712	2,923	12,602	6,370	6,232
45–49	5,476	2,655	2,821	10,521	5,354	5,167
50–54	6,739	3,155	3,584	10,886	5,427	5,459
55–59	6,012	2,907	3,105	8,706	4,405	4,301
60–64	5,215	2,451	2,764	7,883	4,119	3,764
65–69	5,370	2,618	2,752	7,128	3,742	3,386
70–74	5,238	2,447	2,791	5,620	2,743	2,877
75–79	4,689	2,086	2,603	4,260	2,012	2,248
80–84	3,270	1,339	1,931	2,748	1,001	1,747
85–89	1,846	671	1,175	1,615	491	1,124
90 and over	834	237	597	758	180	578
Totals	**83,788**	**39,979**	**4,380**	**184,390**	**92,151**	**92,239**

small proportion having a lot (or being responsible for a majority of the problems) is found extensively in social data. We can find references to it as the 80:20 rule, though this is more a metaphor rather than the actual ratio. Recognising imbalance in distributions is important for social researchers.

How do we actually construct cumulative frequency graphs? The method is straightforward.

- First, arrange the classes in sequence from low to high (or vice versa) and lay out the data as a table which shows the number of units of data in each class.
- Second, add the data in the second class to those in the first. Note the result. Then add the data in the first and second classes to those in the third and continue to the end.

The procedure is shown in the tables in Figure 10.6. The data in the table is from the grades awarded students in a whole school year. The grades are broken into 10 classes and the numbers of students in each class are shown in the second column. The third column shows the number of students up to the grade. Thus one student gained a mark 0 to 10 and two student 0 to 20, and so on. Figure 10.6(a) shows the histogram for the data and Figure 10.6(b) the cumulative frequency curve for the data. This type of graph is also called an *ogive* (possibly from an arabic word meaning 'arch' which describes the shape of a particular cumulative distribution). The ogive shown in Figure 10.6(b) gives the amount of data in any class that is *less than* the total (for instance 135 students have marks between 0 and 60). It is also perfectly reasonable to construct an ogive *from* the total and create a curve that, at any point, shows the amount of data that is more than the lowest quantity (we just sum from high to low – in our example, 77 students scored a mark higher than 60). A particularly useful feature of ogives is that we can convert the data in the distribution to percentages and show the proportion of the data set up to a class. This is useful when we compare data sets.

Ogives are shown as continuous lines because the data (though broken into classes) is continuous. We assume, for example, that there is a gradual progression in the number of students 0 and 100. Most spreadsheet percentages will allow the construction of ogives. Figures 10.6(a) and (b) were constructed using the spreadsheet in MS Excel. Activity 10.4 uses ogives in a very typical way with examination grade distributions. The data are taken from a UK examination board and refer to examinations (A levels) taken by students at

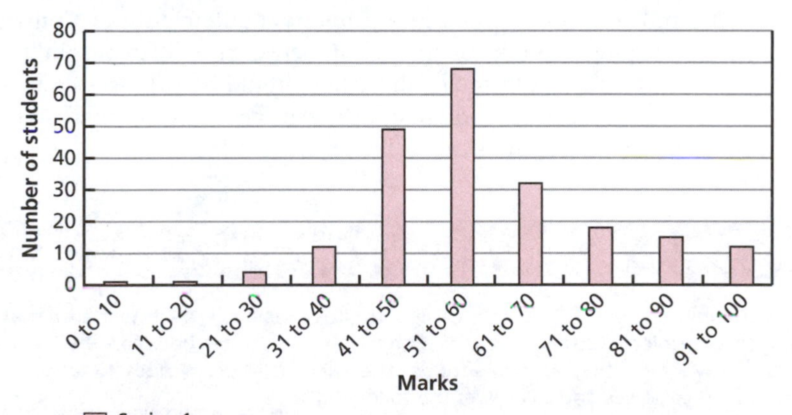

Marks awarded	Number with marks	Number with marks up to class
0–10	1	1
11–20	1	2
21–30	4	6
31–40	12	18
41–50	49	67
51–60	68	135
61–70	32	167
71–80	18	185
81–90	15	200
91–100	12	212

Figure 10.6(a) Histogram of marks awarded

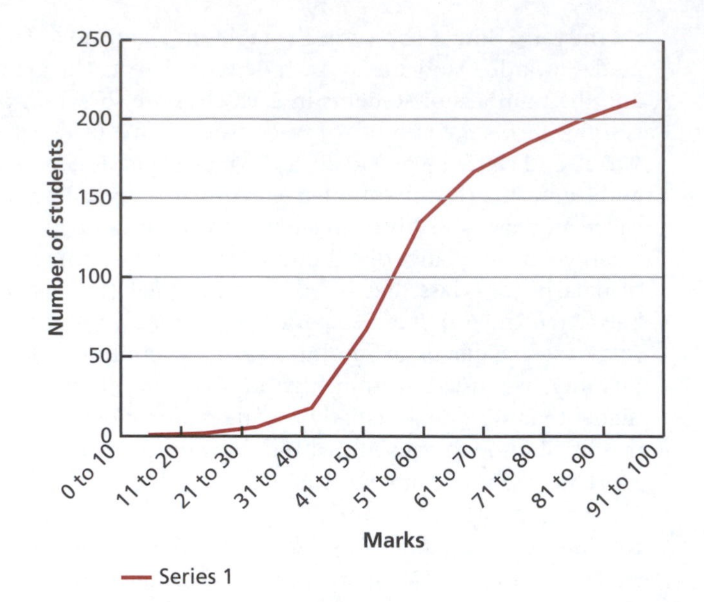

Figure 10.6(b) Ogive of marks awarded

the age of 17 or 18. The table in Activity 10.4 shows the grades obtained (A is the best and U the poorest) for three subjects at different times. Constructing ogives may only be a staging point in our analysis. If there are no differences in the curves there is nothing to explore but if there are, then they should be (a) assessed to see whether they are large enough to be important and (b) explored to see if they can be explained. This is something we shall look at in Chapter 13.

Activity 10.4 Do the same standards apply?

The data below show the grades awarded to students in three subjects (Business Studies, English Literature and Mathematics) at two sittings. Use the data to construct ogives and to answer the following questions.

- Is there any evidence that different subjects have different assessment distributions? Could this imply different standards of assessment or different cultures?
- Is there any evidence that assessment distributions differ between the 2006 and 2007 assessments? If there is, does it matter?

How would you assess whether different examination boards appeared to have the same standards in assessing the same subjects?

		Grade A	Grades AB	Grades ABC	Grades ABCD	Grades ABCDE	Grades ABCDEU	No. of Entries
2007 January	**Business Studies**	9.6	41.7	69.1	90.4	97	100	230
2006 May/June	**Business Studies**	17.8	43.3	70.2	89	97.5	100	22,577
2007 January	**English Literature**	30.8	50	88.5	96.2	100	100	52
2006 May/June	**English Literature**	24.2	48	72.6	91.5	98.8	100	8,482
2007 January	**Mathematics**	22.2	53.3	75.4	88.6	96.4	100	167
2006 May/June	**Mathematics**	35.3	56.6	75.1	87.9	96.6	100	9,137

10.2.4 Pie charts

Pie charts are amongst the most recognisable and most used graphical ways of displaying data. Pie charts are used to show the relative importance of different elements in a distribution. For example, we can use them to show the age or gender structure of graduates in different countries, or the proportion of students gaining different grades, or the proportion of pupils in different class sizes. The production of a pie chart by hand is straightforward. All we have to do is convert our raw data into percentages of the total and then use these percentages to define the sizes of segments of a circle. Table 10.13 sets out the calculation. The data shows the composition by grades of academic staff in English universities in 2006/07. There are five categories of staff: professors, senior lecturers and researchers, lecturers, researchers and other staff. For each category we know the number of staff and the sum of these, 169,005, is the total number of academic staff employed by English universities. Our next step is to convert the number in each category as a percentage of the total. Thus 16,485 are 9.70 per cent of 169,995. We then use these percentages to define a segment of a circle: 9.7 per cent of 360° is 35°. Using a protractor, we then mark off the number of degrees around a circle we have already drawn and draw lines from the centre of the circle to the circumference.

Table 10.13 Procedure for creating pie charts

Category	Number	% total	% 360°
Professors	16,485	9.70	35
Senior lecturers/researchers	33,650	19.80	71
Lecturers	51,930	30.55	110
Researchers	36,740	21.60	78
Other	31,190	18.35	66
Total	169,995	100.00	360

Source: from 'Summary of academic staff (excluding atypical) in all UK institutions 2006/07' at http://www.hesa.ac.uk/dox/dataTables/staff/download/staff0607.xls?v=1.0, HESA cannot accept responsibility for any inferences or conclusions derived from the data by third parties

There is, however, an easier way to construct pie charts by using the graphics option in a spreadsheet. Figures 10.7(a), 10.7(b) and 10.7(c) were drawn in just this way. These data were selected to show the strength as well as the weaknesses of pie charts as a method of extracting the information from data. Their strength is that they immediately show dominant categories, in this case white and other ethnic groups. The weaknesses are that:

- we lose precision – we can only hazard a guess at the dominance of white students (about 80 per cent of the total) and our estimates for other groups are likely to be wide of the mark;
- we lose the ability to determine the relative importance of categories as the number of categories increases – and the ethnic composition shown here is a very crude one;
- it is difficult to compare one pie chart with another – are there more Asian/British Asian men or women undertaking full-time research?
- pie charts cannot deal with complex data sets (that is gender and ethnicity at the same time). With three sets of data, we produced three pie charts. If we wanted also to look at students enrolled on taught postgraduate and undergraduate courses we would construct another six pie charts. With nine pie charts to compare, there is just too much information to take in.

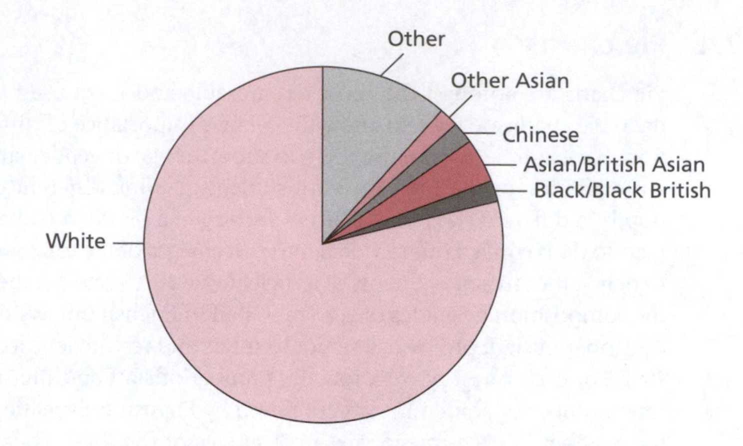

Figure 10.7(a) Ethnicity of full-time research students, total UK 2006–07

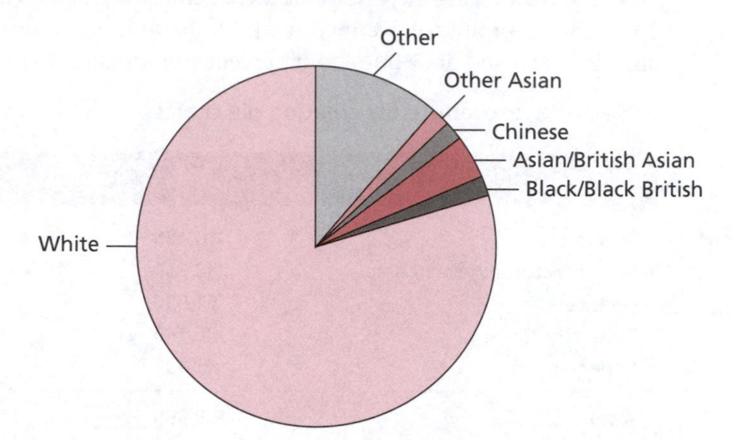

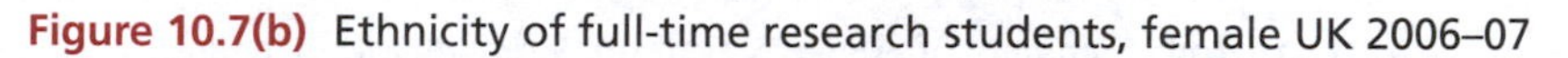
Figure 10.7(b) Ethnicity of full-time research students, female UK 2006–07

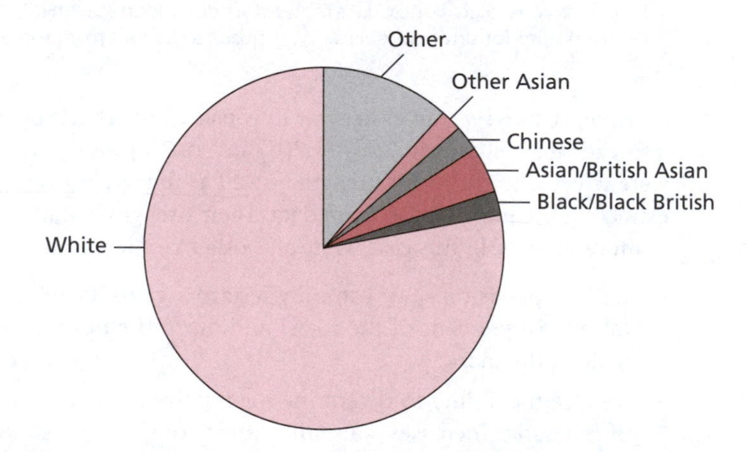

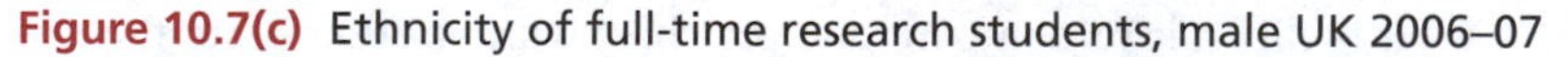
Figure 10.7(c) Ethnicity of full-time research students, male UK 2006–07

So when should we use pie charts? The answer is, as little as possible, because they are less effective than other methods (such as bar charts) and certainly they should be avoided when the number of categories is greater than five or when we are presenting more than four sets of data.

10.2.5 Line graphs

Line graphs take us into a more sophisticated area of graphical data analysis. So far, the data we have looked at has consisted of only one variable. Look back over the methods we have used and notice that stem and leaf, bar charts and histograms, ogives and pie charts all deal with a single variable. With line graphs we can see how two variables change at the same time. In technical terms this represents a move from considering univariate data (one variable) to bivariate data sets (two variables). The purpose of the graph is to show how the two variables are related. However, for this to be a valid investigation, there has to be some underpinning relationship or set of processes that links one variable to the other.

Time is such a variable. Normally what we are dealing with is an observation at a particular point in time. From this we can draw a graph of the variable in time. Figure 10.8 shows Dutch unemployment rates over a 22-year period. The base data are shown in the table below. Figure 10.8 was produced by a spreadsheet package. This graph only connects the data points. Most packages will smooth the lines. This is acceptable as a presentation technique.

From the line graph, we can immediately pick up the main messages. Over most of the period there has been a substantial fall in unemployment. Over most of the period, female unemployment has been higher than male. While the lines tend to follow each other, there was a period in the middle to late 1980s when the trend in male and female rates was divergent.

Line graphs are good at communicating information. They point us towards things that can or should be explained. Their weakness is the extent to which our interpretation can be manipulated. Figure 10.9 shows us the problem. Here there is an implicit test of the assumption that more highly educated people are responsible for the growth in Internet use. However, the graph shows the number of Internet users mushrooming while the number of graduates is a flat line. The reality is that the number of graduates increased by 50 per cent in just seven years. The problem arises (a) because the vertical scale is configured to the number of Internet users and (b) because of the scale difference in the two data sets. The number of Internet users is, for instance, between 80 and 120 times the size of the number of graduates in a year. Often we meet the reverse of this – steep slopes on our line graphs that result from the exaggeration of the vertical scale, something that often results from a section of the scale above 0 being cut out. The only solution in our case is to produce two graphs.

In summary, line graphs are effective communicators of patterns and trends. Several graphs can be plotted on the same axes for effective comparative assessment. While we should concentrate on 'reading the line', we should not ignore the axes. Manipulation of these can lead us into mistaken interpretation.

10.2.6 Scatterplots

Scatterplots (also known as 'scattergraphs') also deal with bivariate data, data sets with two variables. Unlike line graphs, however, where there is only one quantity of variable (b) at any point of variable (a) (or vice versa), scatterplots can have *more than* one quantity of any variable for the other. If this sounds confusing, then it becomes clear when we construct the scatterplots. Figures 10.10(a), 10.10(b) and 10.10(c) show plots for data on children looked after by a selection of London boroughs in 2007. 'Looked after children' are those placed in local authority care. There is concern about this group because of the fear that the absence of a stable home environment can be a platform for underachievement and deviant behaviour. Column 1 (page 437) in the data table for the scatterplots shows the proportion that misused substances, Column 2 the proportion cautioned or

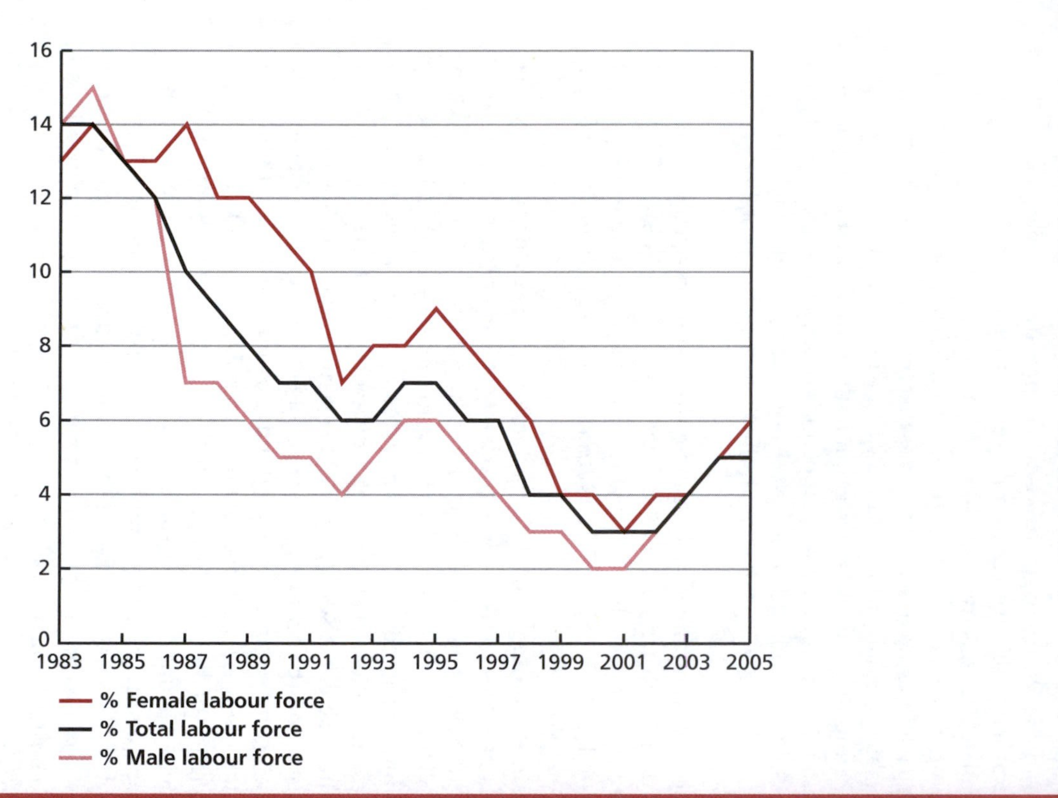

	1983	1984	1985	1986	1987	1988	1989	1990	1991	1992	1993	1994	1995	1996	1997	1998	1999	2000	2001	2002	2003	2004	2005
Unemployment, female (% of female labour force)	13	14	13	13	14	12	12	11	10	7	8	8	9	8	7	6	4	4	3	4	4	5	6
Unemployment, male (% of male labour force)	14	15	13	12	7	7	6	5	5	4	5	6	6	5	4	3	3	2	2	3	4	5	5
Unemployment, total (% of total labour force)	14	14	13	12	10	9	8	7	7	6	6	7	7	6	6	4	4	3	3	3	4	5	5

Figure 10.8 Dutch unemployment 1983–2005

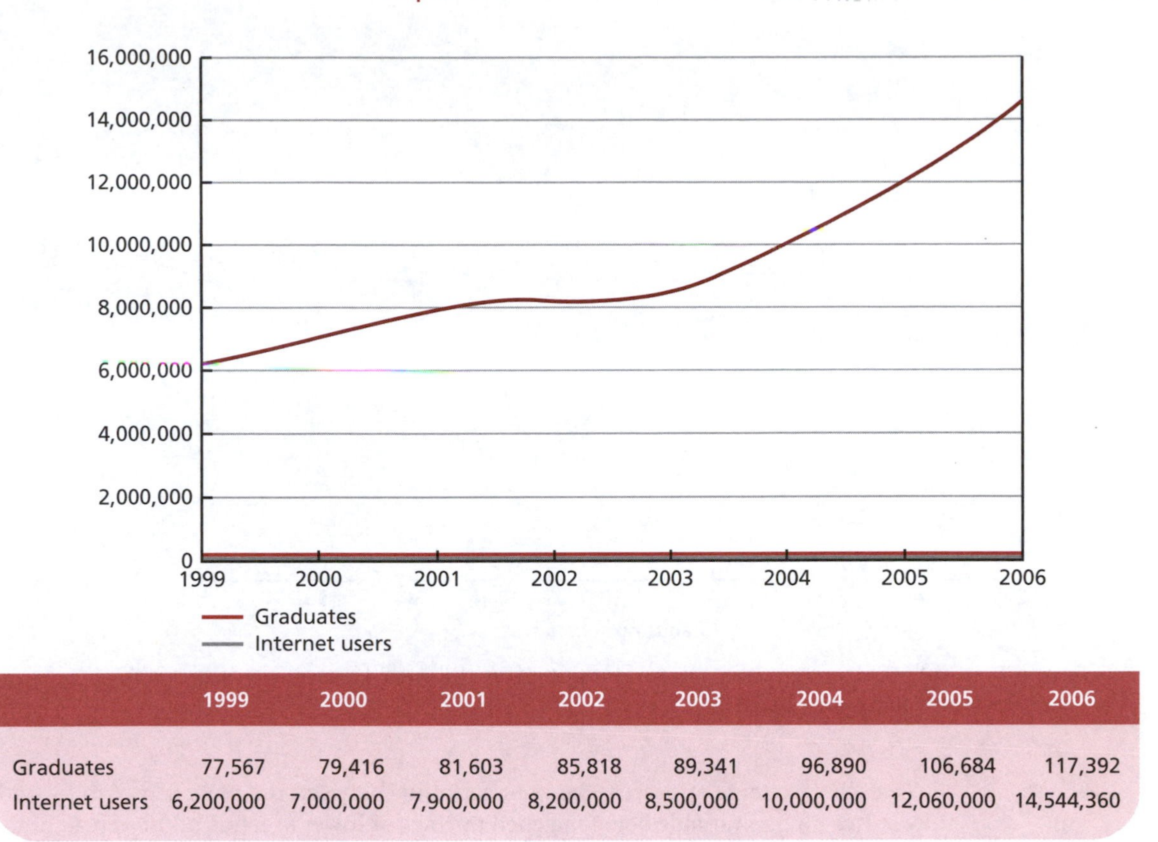

	1999	2000	2001	2002	2003	2004	2005	2006
Graduates	77,567	79,416	81,603	85,818	89,341	96,890	106,684	117,392
Internet users	6,200,000	7,000,000	7,900,000	8,200,000	8,500,000	10,000,000	12,060,000	14,544,360

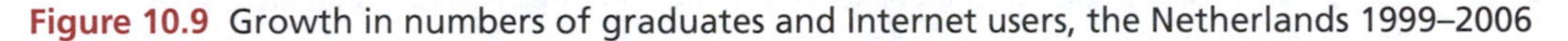

Figure 10.9 Growth in numbers of graduates and Internet users, the Netherlands 1999–2006

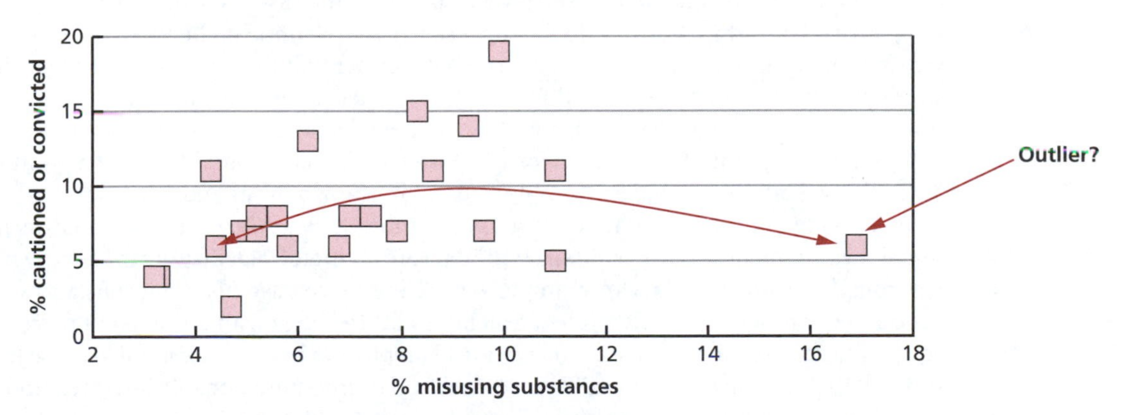

Figure 10.10(a) Scatterplot: outcomes of looked after children, London boroughs 2007 (criminal activity and substance abuse)

convicted and Column 3 the proportion with five or more GCSEs at grades A* to G (the final assessment stage of the UK National Curriculum). Figures 10.10(a), (b) and (c) show pairs of data plotted against each other. Again a spreadsheet was used to process the data.

(a) shows the per cent cautioned or convicted against percentage misusing substances.

(b) the per cent with five GCSEs against the per cent abusing substances.

(c) the per cent with five GCSEs against the per cent cautioned or convicted.

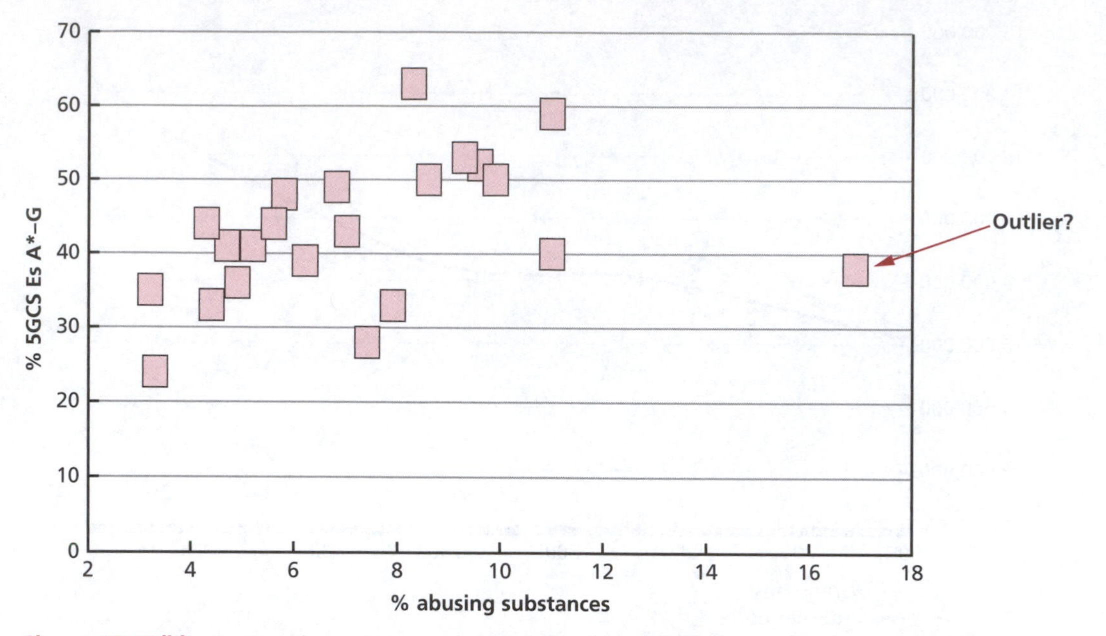

Figure 10.10(b) Scatterplot: outcomes of looked after children, London boroughs 2007 (education and substance abuse)

In each case there appears to be an association between the pairs of variables, with low scores on one variable being matched by low (or lower in terms of the spread of the distribution) on the other. There is clearly a relationship here between all combinations of data pairs. Because an increase in one is associated with an increase in the other, we call this a positive relationship. If the reverse had been the case, we would have called it a negative relationship. We may not be surprised at the relationship between police convictions and cautions and substance misuse but the fact that there is a positive relationship between each of these and educational outcomes is more intriguing. We can see now why it is called a scatterplot. For each, there is a general trend but no single line that will join up the points. Some points form a cluster, others are more isolated. If a point is 'by itself', we call this an *outlier*. Possible outliers are shown in (a) and (b).

Identifying outliers is an important stage in exploring data. They could show errors in initial measurement or data recording. If the data are accurate, then they are even more interesting. In Figure 10.10(a), for example, why is the percentage misusing substances in the outlier borough four to five times greater than the borough with the smallest percentage (connected by the blue line). But, as with all graphs, we have to be careful because the scales of the axes can exaggerate differences and lead us into unreasonable interpretations. For this reason, if we are using IT-based visualisation, it is always safest to test the data on another system, just to make sure that there is no error in data processing by a program. Figure 10.11 shows the same data as for Figure 10.10(c) using the Many Eyes visualisation tool. This may not be any better than one produced by a spreadsheet but one advantage of the 'Many Eyes' system is that the raw data can be retrieved by clicking on the data point. Do the plots look the same? This is the type of decision we have to make many times as researchers. Do the data points form a group or are there some that are very extreme in their location? If there are, we would call these outliers and they could be the product of unusual circumstances or errors in measuring. Does the representation of the data distort the message? Sometimes the answers are clear; where they are not we may require a more rigorous analysis. We shall meet some of the methods we can use in Chapter 13.

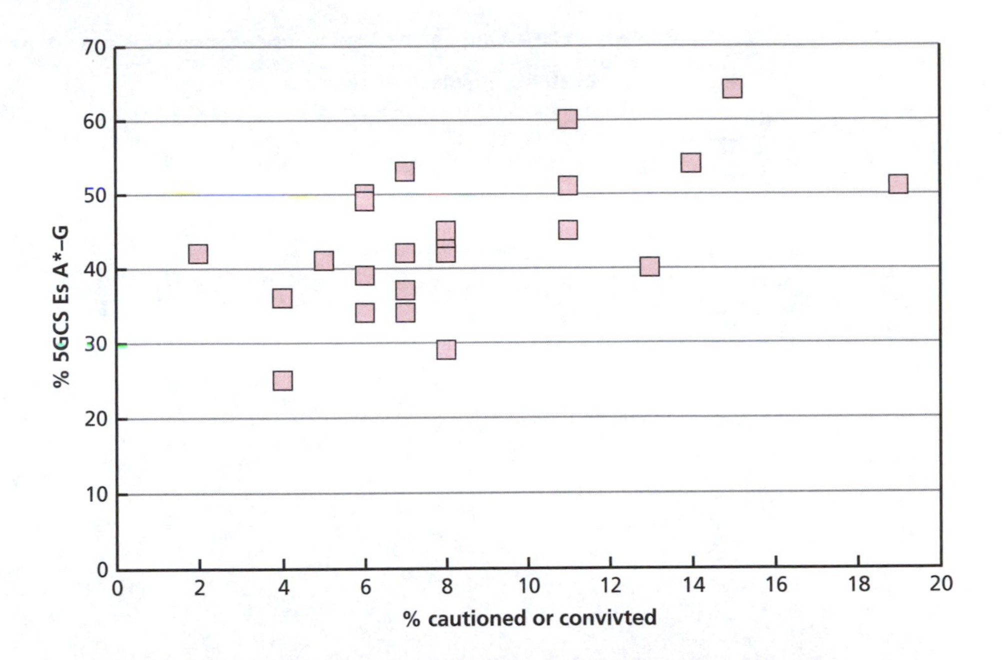

% identified as having misused substances in year	% cautioned or convicted during the year	% with 5 GCSEs A* to G
9.6	7	52
0.0	0	–
6.8	6	49
4.4	6	33
9.9	19	50
16.9	6	38
8.3	15	63
4.7	2	41
11.0	5	40
5.8	6	48
4.9	7	36
5.2	7	41
4.3	11	44
7.9	7	33
11.0	11	59
8.6	11	50
3.3	4	24
5.2	8	41
3.2	4	35
7.0	8	43
5.6	8	44
7.4	8	28
9.3	14	53
6.2	13	39

Figure 10.10(c) Scatterplot: outcomes of looked after children, London boroughs 2007 (education and criminal activity)

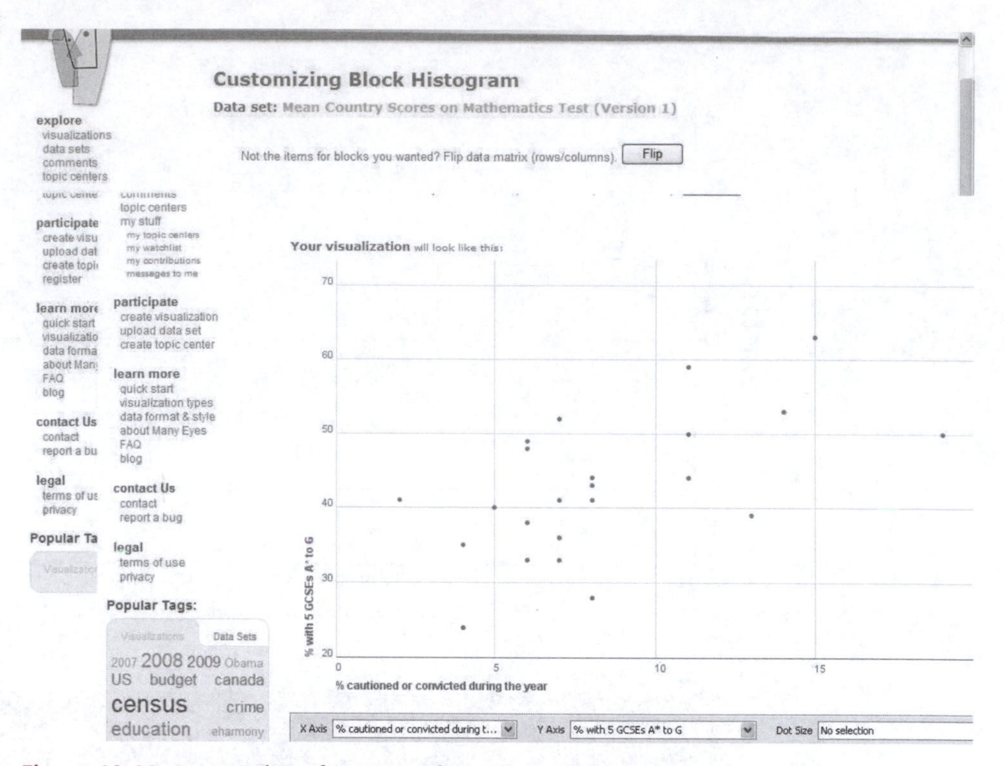

Figure 10.11 Scatterplot of GCSE performance against cautions/convictions

When would we use a scatterplot?

- As an initial exploration of data to see if there were any patterns that might suggest relationships that should be explored further. For instance, we would be interested in a plot of data that took the form of a curve or fell along a straight line. In this case, we might then go on to a correlation or regression analysis (see Chapters 12 and 13).
- To differentiate between the usual (a cluster) and the unusual (an outlier) and to investigate both because both can have an important message. The usual shows us what is happening in the majority of cases and the unusual shows us what is happening in extreme cases – and, as we have seen in Figure 10.10, outliers are an indication of things being done well or disastrously!

10.2.7 Moving up a gear: three-dimensional scatterplots

Often our data comprises more than two variables. We saw one way of dealing with this above, where we plotted all combinations of data on separate scatterplots. We can also plot data on three-dimensional scatterplots.

Three-dimensional scatterplots use three axes, conventionally labelled x, y and z. They are becoming more used with the increased sophistication of data visualisation programs. What these programs do is plot the data as a projection, so that perspective is used to create the impression of depth. Many commercially available data analysis programs will offer this visualisation option. Standard spreadsheets do not. However, there are packages that can be used on-line.

Figures 10.12(a), (b) and (c) show the scatterplots for the looked after children data in Figure 10.11. These were produced through Wessa.net (Web-enabled scientific services and applications). The initiative is the work of Professor Patrick Wessa and can be accessed via http://www.wessa.net. The software plots three views of the data set. Figures 10.12(a) and

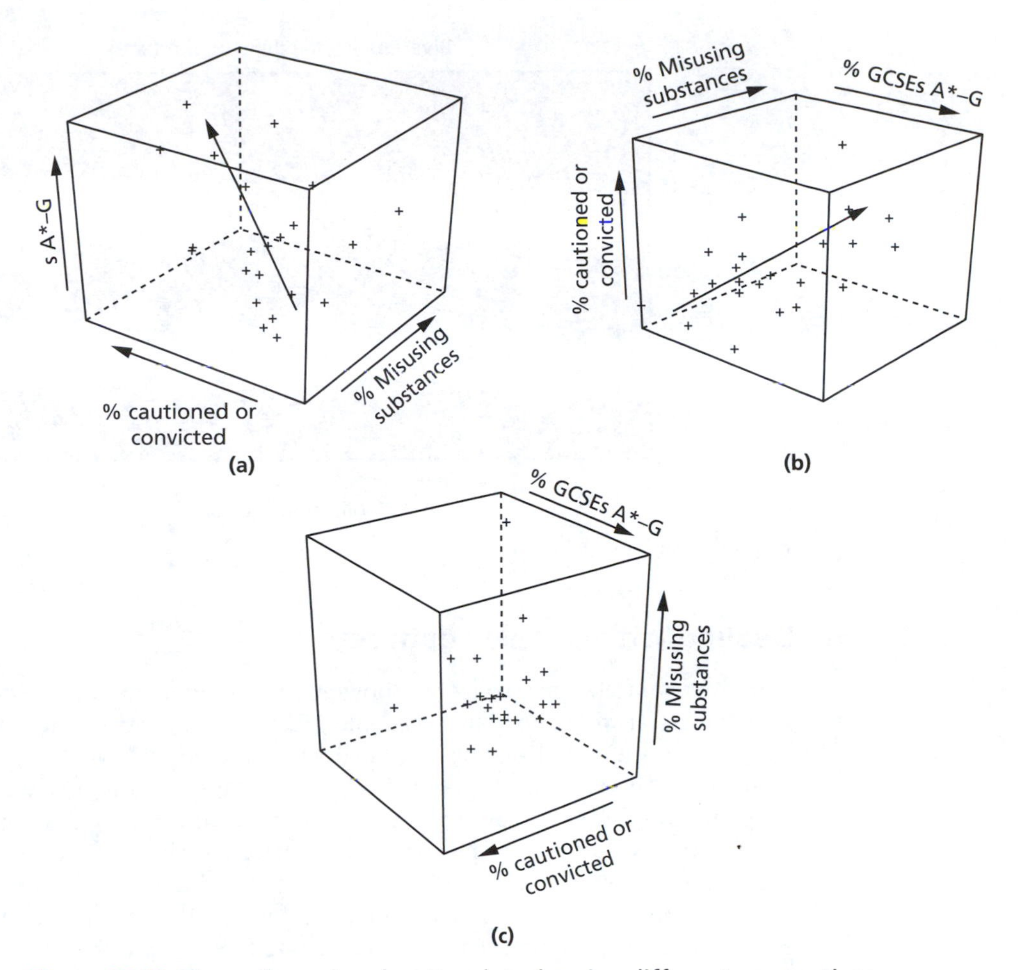

Figure 10.12 Three-dimensional scatterplots showing different perspectives

10.12(b) show rising trends (marked by the arrows). All views are necessary because some may not show the pattern clearly. Figure 10.12(c) shows clustering influenced by the variables less clearly than (a) or (b). The program also produces 'maps' of the two variable distributions called *density plots*. These show the concentration and intensity of data points. The data points are interpolated by *isopleths* (contours). Figure 10.13 is a density plot of Figure 10.10(a). It plots the percent misusing substances on the horizontal axis and the percent cautioned or convicted on the vertical axis. It shows an 'island' with a ridge running in a south east–north west direction. The elongated shape of the island indicates that as misuse increases so do cautions and convictions. But what about the ridge? Imagine a section along the length of the line in Figure 10.13. It would show a steep rise up to the top of the ridge and then a more gentle slope down. The core of the relationship between the two variables is the peak of the distribution, where the shading gives way to lighter tones. This is where the strongest relationship between drug misuse and convictions is. The pattern of spread around the core is shown by the outer isopleths and as we move away from peak of the ridge, the influence of the core relationship weakens and other influences, which may be individual or random, become stronger.

What three-dimensional plots offer us is new insight into and perspectives on the patterns that may exist in our data. They reinforce the fact that much research is about looking for order. What we have seen so far is how we can look for order in simple data sets but our research can be more complex than this. When this happens, our visualisation must become more sophisticated.

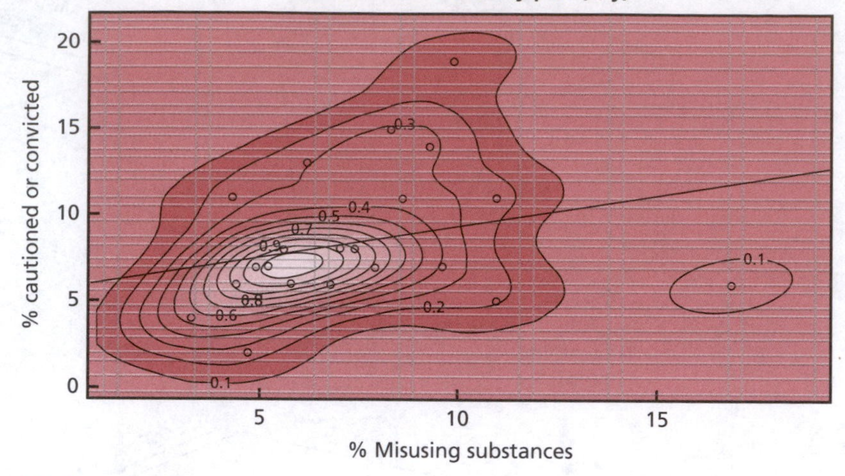

Figure 10.13 Density plot

10.2.8 Dealing with complex data sets

Our review of techniques so far has shown us how to look for patterns in relatively simple data sets, anything up to three variables. Traditionally, beyond this point, researchers have used a numerical or statistical analysis to understand what the data are telling them. We shall see some of these techniques in Chapter 13 but it is important to point out that advances in computing power are producing data visualisation methods that can give us insights into the message of complex data. This section is not at the cutting edge of visualisation but it is in advance of where education and much social science research currently sits. This much is apparent from the fact that the number of papers in education journals that make use of these methods is miniscule.

The types of data set we are likely to encounter will either be hierarchically organised or assemblies of simple data sets. Hierarchically organised data have multiple categorisations. For example, teachers can have worked for one year, two to five years, six to ten years or over ten years and can be classified by ethnicity and by gender. This type of structure is shown in Figure 10.14. This is quite a simple hierarchical structure of three levels but even with only the highest level of ethnic categorisation used in the census in England and Wales, it still creates a table with 40 cells, which is a lot of data to manage. Let us now see how we can visualise complex data sets.

(i) Star plots

Star plots (also known as 'polar', 'radar' or 'rose diagrams') can be constructed with spreadsheet software. The concept is simple. It assumes that any place, organisation, person or idea can be profiled on a number of dimensions. People, for instance, need not be just male/female, young/old or in a certain socio-economic group, they can also drive to work, catch a bus or walk, or have lived at the same address for five, ten or 20 years. What we have to do first is create the profile dimensions. How many should there be? If the number is too few, we lose richness in our description; if it is too many we are swamped by detail and lose the ability to discriminate. Generally researchers seem to use between 8 and 12 profile dimensions. These dimensions are then plotted as radii at equal intervals around a point. If there are 12 profiles, they are plotted at 30° intervals and if there are 8,

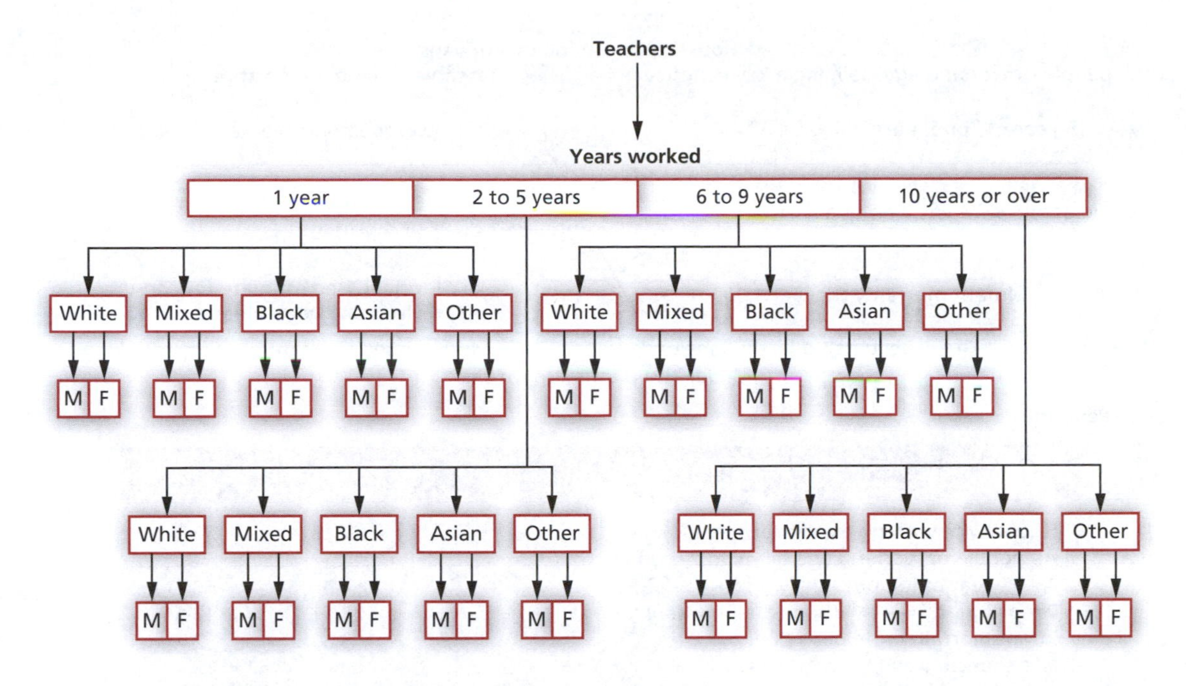

Figure 10.14 Hierarchical data structure

they are plotted at 45° intervals. The score on a profile dimension is represented by the length of a line from the central point. When all lines have been drawn, the end points are joined together to show a shape.

These are the principles underpinning the star plot. Fortunately, we do not have to draw them by hand because most spreadsheet programs will do it for us. The effectiveness of the method can be seen in Figures 10.15(a) and 10.15(b), which profiles two areas in England, Penwith in Cornwall and Richmond in London. The difference between the two areas can clearly be seen in the different shapes that are produced. The value of this method is apparent when we produce plots for many areas. In this case we can use shape to classify areas into the same group. Classification is very important in the research process.

(ii) Metaphor mapping

Metaphor mapping is based on the same principle as the star plot, that a dimension is represented by a line and the set of dimensions by an overall shape but here the difference ends. Whereas star plots create a geometrical shape, metaphor mapping creates shape that is recognisably something else. The best known application of metaphor mapping is the Chernoff face, in which the descriptive dimensions are represented by facial features. The technique was developed over 30 years ago by an American statistician, Herman Chernoff (Chernoff, 1973). The reason for its development was that social scientists wanted more and more to get to grips with the patterns in multi-variate data sets (that is, those with a great many variables). Inspecting raw data or even part-processed data can overload us. However, when data is displayed graphically, we appear much more able to manage the complexity and identify the patterns.

One of the classic examples of the application in use was by the Los Angeles Community Analysis Bureau who, in 1973, mapped life in Los Angeles (Figure 10.16(a)). The map

Households with no cars or vans
All people of working age claiming a key benefit
100
Rateable value per m²: offices
All 15-year-old pupils achieving 5+ A* – C
50
Average hours worked: female
People aged 16–74 with: no qualifications
0
Owner occupied: owns outright or mortgage
Infant mortality rate per 1,000
Model-based estimate for consumption of fruit and vegetables
Life expectancy at birth: females
Model-based estimate for binge drinking
Model-based estimate for smoking

— **Penwith**

	Penwith	Richmond
Households with no cars or vans	27.13	23.7
All people of working age claiming a key benefit	17	7
All 15-year-old pupils achieving 5+ A* – C	57.4	66.1
People aged 16–74 with: no qualifications	29.81	13.64
Infant mortality rate per 1,000	3.8	2.7
Life expectancy at birth: females	82	83.1
Model-based estimate for smoking	23.5	19.3
Model-based estimate for binge drinking	15.2	12.3
Model-based estimate for consumption of fruit and vegetables	27	37.1
Owner occupied: owns outright or mortgage	68.33	68.7
Average hours worked: female	30.08	34.97
Rateable value per m^2: offices	54	167

Figure 10.15(a) Star diagram, Profile of Penwith

Note: Each ray corresponds to a social, educational or economic dimension. These correspond to the ones in the data table. The first one is placed at 12 o'clock and the others at equal intervals in a clockwise direction. Each ray is marked as a scale, in this case 0 to 100. The scale points on each ray are joined to give the shape profile for the area. This method seeks to differentiate areas from each other in terms of their shape profile.

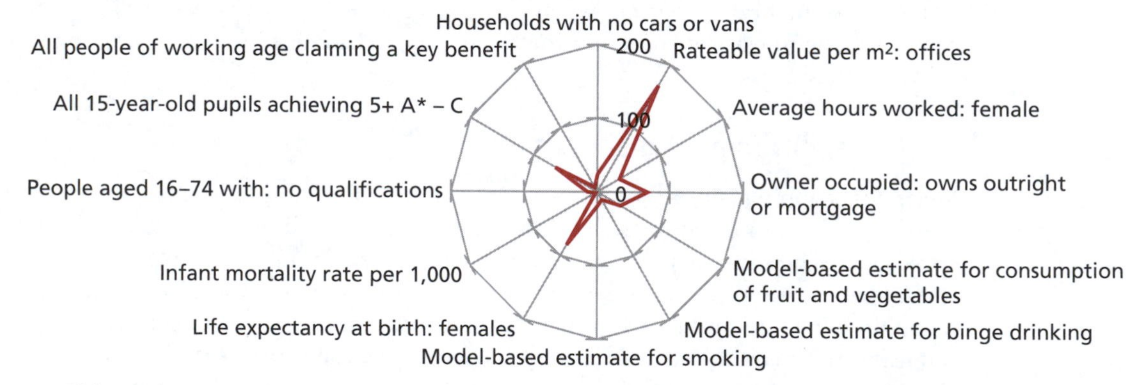

Figure 10.15(b) Star diagram, Profile of Richmond

plots four variables; affluence (face shape), unemployment (mouth shape), urban stress (eyebrow and eye) and predominant ethnicity (colour). The map is effective in showing the patterns and associations of poverty. While the Los Angeles map is well known, it is a poor example of the potential of the approach because many more variables can be included. A standard Chernoff face has 18 features onto which variables can be mapped.

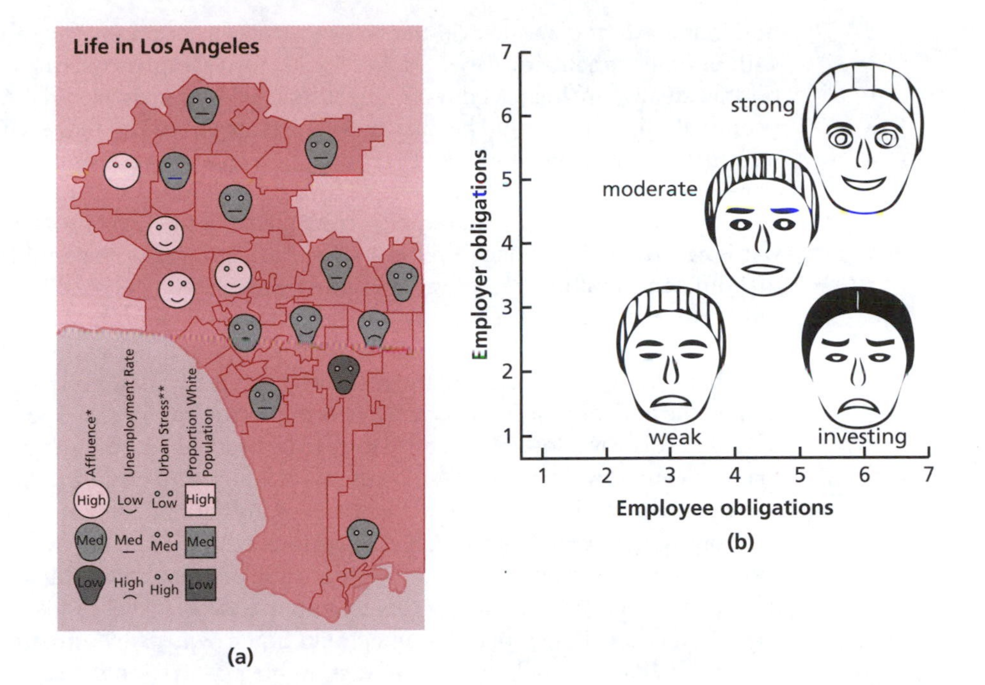

Figure 10.16 Chernoff faces

Often fewer variables are used. The reason for this is that even four facial variables each with five levels or conditions generate 625 facial forms. Figure 10.16(b) shows characteristic faces that describe four types of psychological contract between employers and employees (Rigotti and Mohr, 2005). The idea of a 'psychological contract' was developed by management researchers to describe how employees and employers understood their obligations to each other. However, it has a far broader application than this. For example, there is a psychological contract between pupils and teachers. Some of the obligations are explicit – a duty of care, attendance at school, teaching the specified curriculum, others are unwritten but expected – good behaviour, appropriate work rates, after school activities. The faces in Figure 10.16(b) reflect aspects that are better in the relationship between employer and employee with a happier appearance and things that are worse with a sadder appearance. The sad appearances show an intention to move employment quickly, low levels of job satisfaction, poor health, irritability. The reverse is the case with the happier faces. This example shows that the technique can handle not just social, economic and demographic data, but also emotions, attitudes, hopes and expectations, all of which are key dimensions to understanding such things as achievement and underachievement, teacher burnout and parent satisfaction with the education their child or children receive.

The construction of Chernoff faces has been held back by inadequate computing and mapping capability but with the expansion of the visualisation of large data sets we can expect data analysis programs to build in the Chernoff facility. We will then be able to use them to handle and categorise complex data sets that are beyond the limits of star plots.

(iii) Matrix chart

A matrix chart is a means of displaying and manipulating multivariate data sets whose numerical base can take any form. It can be used to compare variables that are measured only in two states (larger and smaller, present or absent), as categories (men/women, ethnic groups) as well as interval data. It is, therefore, very adaptable. As its name suggests, the basic structure of the chart is a matrix of cells, with one variable on the horizontal axis and another on the vertical. The cells of the matrix can then be plotted with another variable or variables. We could, for example, construct a matrix chart to portray quality in higher education institutions. One axis would be the institutions (nominal), the other would be quality criteria (categorical) and for each criterion at each university we could put a symbol to represent the quality score (interval if we put the raw score or ordinal if we use the rank score for the institution).

Simple forms of matrix chart can be constructed in MS Excel but it is not a straightforward procedure. IBM's Many Eyes is a more sophisticated system and has the advantage that different combinations of variables can be displayed (that is, different combinations can be tested). Figure 10.17 shows a matrix chart of data from Mexico using data from David Gallardo of the Consejo Nacional de Evaluacion de la Desarrollo Social in Mexico. The chart shows three variables; the level of social disadvantage on the vertical axis, location on the horizontal axis and home ownership as the bubble size. The controls at the bottom of the display allow different variables to be brought into the analysis. It is this feature that shows us how the method can be used – as a means of exploring data and looking for associations as well as a method for communicating our interpretations. In Gallardo's example, we can see that the administrative units are separated out by level of social disadvantage and that the bubbles show the proportion of home ownership. The bubbles are all the same colour. We can change this to colour code the level of disadvantage or, more usefully, an overall index of disadvantage. But home ownership is not the only variable we can analyse. We can also look at the average number of occupants in each house and we can change the bubbles from the actual value to the percentage each is of the row total.

The matrix chart is primarily a means of exploring data to see what messages it has for us. It should be used in the early stages of an investigative process. It does reveal pattern but in many cases we can bring out the significance of the pattern better with numerical techniques.

(iv) Other approaches to portraying multivariable data

We saw that many of the techniques for portraying data that we can use (such as bar charts) show only one variable. We call this type of data *univariate*. When we portray two variables, we refer to our data as *bivariate*. With more than two variables we call our data set *multivariate*.

The portrayal of multivariate data using symbols (referred to in the technical literature as 'glyphs') is a major area of research and development in computing. The reason

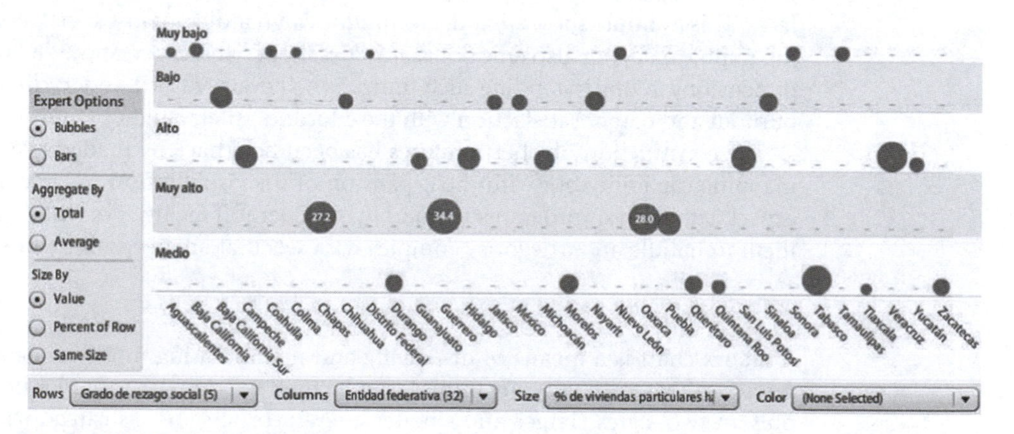

Figure 10.17 Matrix chart

for this is that businesses are seeking to make much more effective use of the data they hold or can access for business processes such as marketing and product development and this is driving the technical advances. The databases held by organisations can be enormous. Police forces throughout the UK, for example, have had access to a national database since 1974. In addition, they have access to a DNA database, a fingerprint database, a firearms database, a database of individuals posing a serious risk to the public and the possibility soon of access to a facial images database. The process of finding relationships, associations and patterns in this wealth of data is called 'data mining'. This is where graphical display can be used, to quickly identify things that should be explored further. Access to these resources requires programs that can sort and sift all categories of data, statistical, written, spatial and temporal. Typical of these is the software used by some Dutch police services, DataDetective. In Amsterdam, in areas where data were analysed, there was a 15 per cent fall in criminal activity and when it was used to forecast robbery in the street, there was a significant drop in levels. What the technologies do is find associations within and between databases and present their analyses in graphical and cartographic formats. They are used not just to find past patterns but also to predict patterns and it is this that is the key to much crime reduction.

What other glyphs have been developed that we have not met so far?

- *Divided bar chart:* if we wanted to test whether the UK government's objective of widening access to higher education was being met we could construct a bar chart to show the numbers of students in any year and then divide the chart on the basis of the proportion of postcodes designated as those to be targeted for wider participation. Figure 10.18(a) shows just this.
- *Metroglyphs:* these are rays that come out of a point or circle. The location of the line represents a variable and its length the quantity of the variable. They were developed by an American botanist, Edgar Anderson (Anderson, 1957). Figure 10.18(b) shows one of his original glyphs. They are clearly very easy to construct and are based on the same principles underpinning the star plot and Chernoff faces. Each line represents a

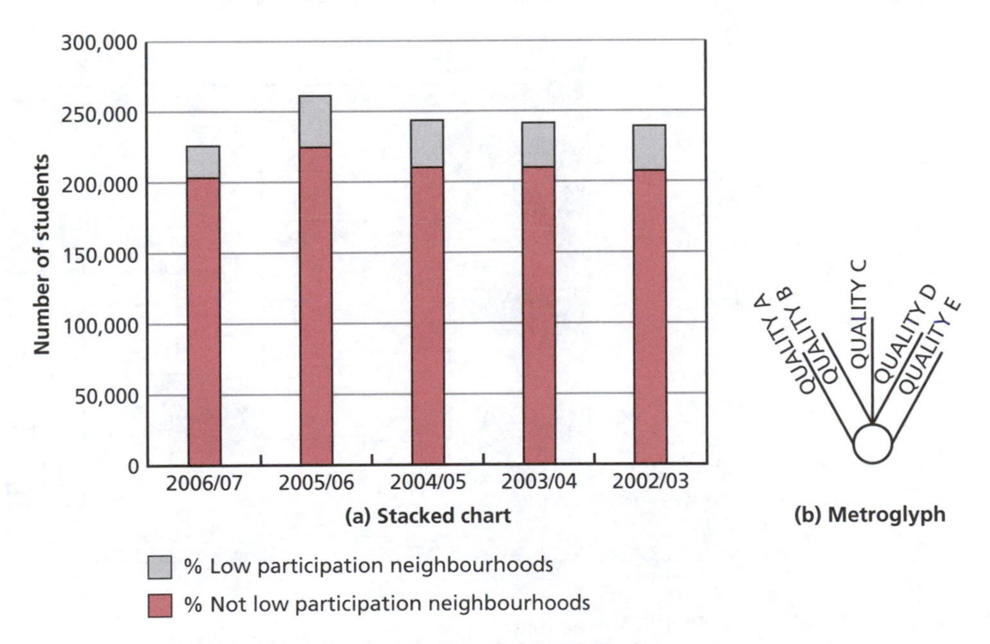

Figure 10.18 Other ways of representing multivariate data

different variable and the length of each line the quantity of the variable. However, unless there are special reasons for using this way of representing data, it is probably more effective to use a star plot because (a) shape is a stronger feature for the star plot and (b) standard office programs will draw star plots for us.

- *Tree maps:* these represent hierarchical relationships in data as sets of nested boxes, where each box represents a variable whose scale/size is reflected in the size of the box. Figure 10.19(a) shows a tree map of US data on disability and academic progression produced through IBM's Many Eyes system. The diagram shows students who had a disability broken down by (a) the relative numbers of students by type of disability, (b) the number with a disability between 1994 and 2005 where data is available and (c) those who dropped out and those who completed a diploma course. The power of the technology is shown when we look at Figure 10.19(b). The data is now reorganised to show the pattern by year. Note at the top of the display, 'year' has been dragged across to make it the prime variable. We can also change those who gained a certificate to those who gained a diploma by altering the right hand bottom tab. If we wanted to see the pattern of disabled students who gained a qualification, we could set the bottom left tab to 'certificate'. As well, the program allows us to pass over our data cells and reveal the data on which they are based and also to zoom in on areas. Tree maps are clearly an acceptable and powerful tool for visualisation.

10.2.9 Using visualisation methods

This session has introduced many graphical methods for data visualisation. Some are likely to be unfamiliar to new researchers, others, like pie charts, may be well known.

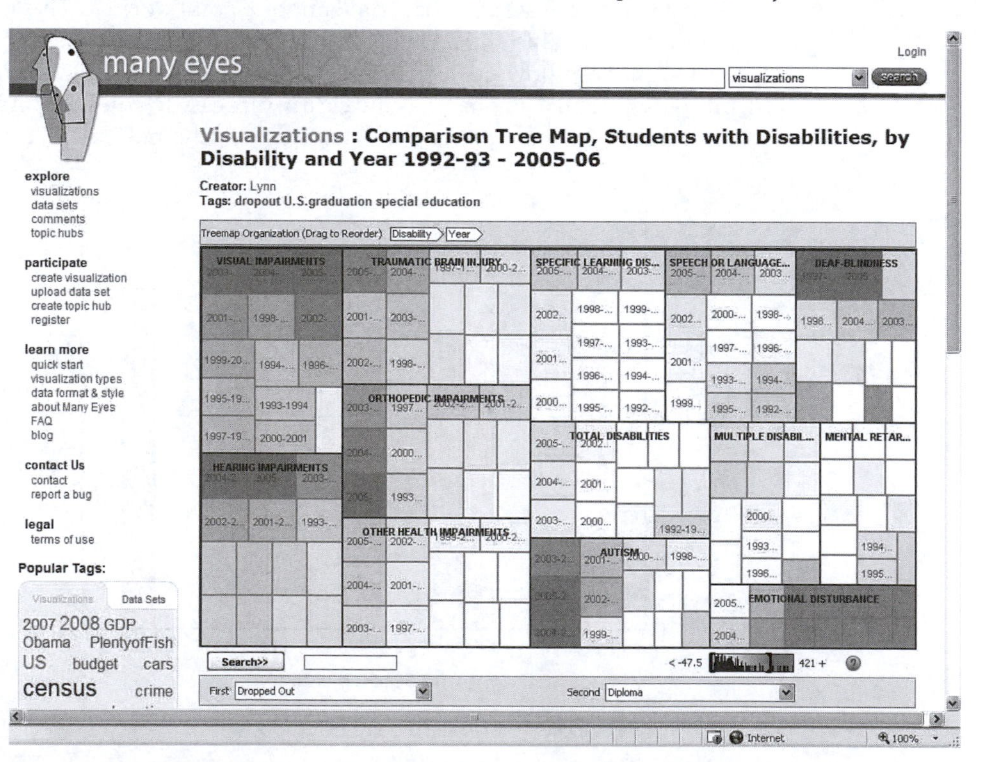

Figure 10.19(a) Tree map

Source: from Screenshot from IBM's 'Many Eyes' website, Courtesy of International Business Machines Corporation, copyright © International Business Machines Corporation

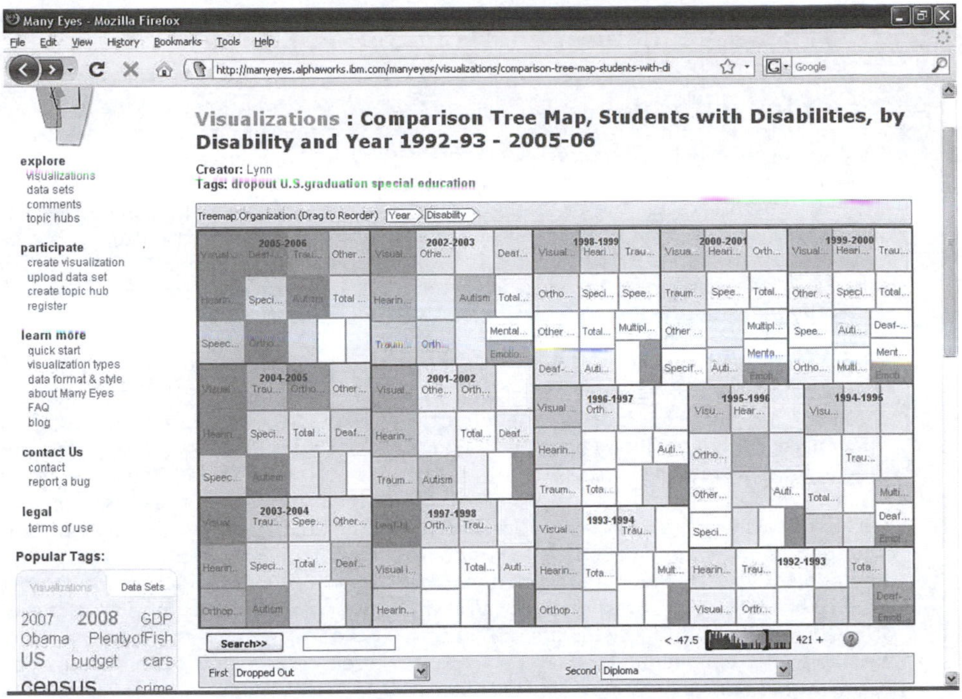

Figure 10.19(b) Revised tree map
Source: from Screenshot from IBM's 'Many Eyes' website, Courtesy of International Business Machines Corporation, copyright © International Business Machines Corporation

The danger is that familiarity may inhibit us from using other methods, ones that might be more appropriate to either the data we have or our research needs. In this section we shall offer some guidance on how to make use of these visualisation methods. There are two things we must consider, how many variables we have and whether our intention is to explore data or to portray the results of our exploration.

We have looked at visualisation methods that will handle one, two or three or more variables.

- For single variables (age or ethnicity or assessment grades, for example) we can use stem and leaf diagrams, bar charts, histograms, and cumulative frequency plots (ogives).
- For pairs of variables (ethnicity paired with assessment grades or obesity paired with family income or teacher recruitment over time), we can use a scatterplot or a line graph.
- For three or more variables (ethnicity, gender and assessment), we can use three-dimensional graphs, star plots, Chernoff faces, matrix charts, concept maps and tree maps.

In terms of how we are going to use the methods, all can be used to portray data and all can be used to explore data but some are better at one thing than the other.

- For data exploration, stem and leaf diagrams, scatterplots and all the multidimensional methods are particularly appropriate.
- For portraying suppositions or conclusions, bar graphs, histograms, line graphs and scatterplots are all effective. Pie charts are better at portraying data than exploring data but are not particularly effective for either.

Activity 10.5 is an opportunity to develop your skills in data analysis and visualisation.

Activity 10.5 Reading the message from data

A. Complex data tables

1. You have been asked to prepare a short report for your vice chancellor on aspects of your university's performance on the UK higher education indicators. The indicators are available at www.hesa.ac.uk then follow the link (on the right side of the page) to performance indicators.
   - Identify the data structure of Tables 1a and 1b. What is the difference between these two tables in terms of the students each describes?
   - Answer the question 'Over the period 2002/03 – 2006/07 has the proportion of students from low participation neighbourhoods in London's universities increased/decreased or stayed the same?'
2. You are researching the role of education in modernisation of the state and social and economic development. One of the indicators that you are using of educational progress is literacy. Visit the UNESCO website and follow the literacy links to the table on regional literacy rates. UNESCO: http://stats.uis.unesco.org/unesco/ReportFolders/ReportFolders.aspx.
   - Describe the data structure of the table. In particular, explain the classification of regions.
   - In which areas is the literacy rate highest and in which three areas is it lowest?
   - Are there areas where the male and female literacy rates vary markedly? Match these areas with states that share the same characteristic.
   - Use the chart button at the head of the table to portray the data. What do you think of the result? Can you suggest an alternative method of visualisation?

B. Data portrayal

The table below gives a range of data for pupils in selected schools in a London borough. Your task is to visualise the data (either in its entirety or by selection) to see what patterns emerge. Key Stage 2 is the final stage of primary education (age 10/11), Key Stage 3 is assessed at age 14 and Key Stage 4 at age 16. Value added is calculated on the basis of pupil data. It seeks to assess the contribution of the school experience to a pupil's development as measured by academic tests. As a guide, you may want to start by looking at each column separately, then at pairs of columns and then at combinations of three or more columns. This is an exercise in data exploration.

School	Column 1	Column 2	Column 3	Column 4	Column 5	Column 6	Column 7	Column 8	Column 9
A	0.295	8.6	30.5	279.7	98.5	999.5	86	91	92
B	0.256	12.3	29.9	417.8	99.1	998.1	86	91	90
C	0.331	8.4	33.9	394.9	98.9	1009	101	101	99
D	0.220	7.4	34.9	309.6	99.5	1008	95	96	95
E	0.314	8.2	32.3	340.3	99.1	1007.4	95	96.5	99
F	0.189	7.3	35	364.9	98.8	992.5	96	97	98
G	0.170	6.5	36.1	364.4	100.3	993.8	101	100	103
H	0.178	5	36.2	250.8	101	975.1	102	103	99
I	0.118	7.7	35.8	353.4	98.7	992.6			
J	0.311	8	33	308.4	99.7	1032	90	89	90
K	0.022	5.1	45.4	517.1	103.1	1010.5	88	92	89
L	0.346	10.8	28.8	292.4	98.7	996.2	85	90	89
M	0.026	3.5		466.1					
N	0.165	8.9	29.1	244	98.9	979.3	102	102	104
O			35	374.1	100.6	1003.6	99	98	97
P	0.201	6.1	34.1	382.4	100	1024.3	103	105	101
Q	0.165	4.9	36.5	394.4	100.7	1000.7	124	123	129
R	0.002	3.3		414.1					
S	0.237	8	32.5	334.6	98.9	1000.9	93	97	99

Column 1 Per cent of pupils with special educational needs (SEN), both with and without statement of need.
Column 2 Per cent half days lost through absence.
Column 3 Average point score for pupils at key stage 3, 2004.
Column 4 Average point score for pupils at key stage 4, 2006.
Column 5 Value added between key stage 2 and key stage 3, 2006.
Column 6 Value added between key stage 2 and key stage 4, 2006.
Column 7 Mean verbal test score.
Column 8 Mean quantitative test score.
Column 9 Mean non-verbal test score.

Summary

Data interpretation and presentation has, for a long time, been relatively ignored as an area of analysis. It is, however, the foundation on which sound analysis is built. The methods, techniques and strategies that we have looked at in this chapter are the starting points for a long journey of practice and adaptation; practice because using them has to become second nature and adaptation because the approaches have to be selected to suit the occasion and modified to match the data. What should be apparent from this chapter is that the field of visualisation is moving forward rapidly. The innovations seem to occur in the sciences. They have been adopted in the fields of business and management. So far, the social sciences, including education, have lagged behind.

- Data are the researcher's raw material. As researchers we have to extract the information from the data, understand its meaning and apply it to our research problem.
- We cannot achieve this unless we read data correctly. Simple tables are straightforward enough, but many data, especially those from official sources, are complex. They can have a wide range of categories and multiple levels of categories, usually with one nesting inside others. Both of these situations create data tables whose scale is so great that we cannot take them in in one glance.
- When data tables are large and complex we need to adopt strategies for making them give up their information. These strategies include:
  - inspection to identify the data structure;
  - shaping and rearranging tables to make them more readable;
  - stripping out data that is not needed;
  - compressing data by combining categories;
  - re-ordering data to make comparison easier;
  - reconstructing data in another form.
- Our object is to identify pattern and order in our data. We do this because we are interested in what is usual, what is exceptional and what is related. Visual inspection of data does not always reveal everything to us. In the past we used the techniques we shall meet in Chapters 12 and 13. However, improvements in computing power mean that we now have another way of looking at data, by visualising them.
- There are many ways of portraying data. We have to choose a method that reflects the nature of our data.
  - If we are dealing with one variable, we call this *univariate* data.
  - If we are dealing with two variables, we call this *bivariate* data.
  - If we are dealing with more than two variables, we call this *multivariate* data.
- Methods suitable for univariate data include stem and leaf plots, bar graphs and histograms, and cumulative frequency graphs or ogives.
- Bivariate data can be represented on line graphs and scatterplots. It is possible to add a third (or more) variable by altering the form of the plot of the two principal variables. The scatter plot then becomes a means of portraying multivariate data.
- Other visualisations for multivariate data include:
  - divided bar charts;
  - star plots;
  - metroglyphs and Chernoff faces (metaphor mapping);
  - matrix charts;
  - tree diagrams;
  - tree maps.
- The range of visualisation types is increasing and we should remain abreast of the opportunities. Most of the visualisations can be performed by readily available software.

- Visualisation is not only important for revealing the structures within the data, it is essential as a tool for communication, our interpretation and understanding.
- As researchers, it is important that we stay abreast of development and innovation in data visualisation because it is likely to become as important as established methods of data analysis such as the statistical tests we shall look at in Chapter 13.

Further reading

The field of data visualisation is fast moving and many books will become out of date very quickly. William Jacoby's slim text, *Statistical Graphics for Visualising Data*, Sage, Thousand Oaks, Calif., 1998) is a useful first introduction because it explains and develops some of the basic principles. For a history of visualisation, the website of the Department of Mathematics and Statistics at York University (Canada) has an excellent review from the earliest maps to 2004 (http://www.math.yorku.ca/SCS/Gallery).

To keep up to date, just type in the search term 'data visualisation/vizualisation' into your search engine.

References

Anderson, E. (1957) 'A Semi-Graphical Method for the Analysis of Complex Problems', *Proceedings of the National Academy of Sciences*, 13(3), 923–927.

Chernoff, H. (1973) 'Using Faces to Represent Points in a K-Dimensional Space Graphically', *Journal of the American Statistical Association*, 68, 361–368.

De Vyder, F. (ND) *Dutch Education: A Closed or an Open System*, OECD, available at www.oecd.org/dataoecd/1/33/191730.pdf (accessed May 2008).

Land, K., Lamb, V. and Mustello, S. (2001) 'Child and Youth Well-Being in the United States, 1975–98: Some Findings and a New Index', *Social Indicators Research*, 56(3), 241–318.

Lengler, M. and Eppler, R. (2007) 'Towards a Periodic Table of Visualisation: Methods for Management', *IASTED Proceedings of the Conference on Graphics and Visualisation in Engineering*, (GVE 2007), Clearwater, Florida, USA, available at www.visual-literacy.org (accessed June 2008).

Macduff, C., McKie, A., Martindale, S., Rennie, A-M., West, B. and Wilcock, S. (2007) 'A Novel Framework for Reflecting on the Functioning of Research Ethics Review Panels', *Nursing Ethics*, 14(1), 99–116.

Rigotti, T. and Mohr, G. (2005) 'German Flexibility: Loosening the Reins Without Losing Control', chapter 5 in *Employment Contracts on Well-Being Among European Workers*, de Cuyper, N., Isaakson, K. and de Witte, H. (eds), Ashgate, Aldershot.

Chapter contents

Chapter 11

EXTRACTING THE INFORMATION FROM QUALITATIVE DATA SETS

Key themes

- Criteria for assessing quality in qualitative research.
- A generic qualitative method for processing data.
- The classification and coding of data – the core of the qualitative process.
- How to build data into coherent blocks of knowledge.
- How different qualitative methodologies approach data analysis.

Introduction

One of the assumptions that new researchers can often make is that because qualitative data takes the form of words, objects, pictures, actions and behaviours and does not require numerical processing, they are inherently easier and more straightforward to analyse than quantitative data. This is a myth that we should nail immediately, not the least because it is often associated with the assumption that qualitative analysis is 'easier' than quantitative (and the implication that it is, as a consequence, less robust). Looking at this from the opposite perspective it is exactly because qualitative data are non-numeric that qualitative analysis is *more* complex than quantitative. The implication of this is that qualitative research cannot consist of a sequence such as, 'We asked them and now we are telling you what they told us'. This approach is naïve. Good qualitative research is far more sophisticated than this. It has to be much more than mere reportage. Commentary that is the product of understanding the field and insights into the structure of the data is an essential element.

11.1 Qualitative research: a complex field

The complexity of qualitative research arises from two things, the range and variety of the data and the epistemological position (see Chapter 3 *passim*) adopted by researchers. The data that we can collect can take the following forms.

(i) **Words** that can exist as printed text, or that we collect through formal interviews or that arise in discussions or that are overheard. They can take a printed form or exist in a virtual world. The communicative element that we are interested in consists of the words themselves and the emphasis they are given. The words can convey factual information and through selection and pronunciation, social and cultural insights. Pauses, emphasis and speed of speaking can provide further data.

(ii) **Behaviour** that we can observe *in situ* (this is called naturalistic observation) or that we can stimulate as a result of the way we structure our research (think of a focus group or a task-based activity). We can choose what behaviour we want to observe and identify how, where and when to observe it or we can chance upon it, so that it is unanticipated and incidental to our research design.

(iii) **Objects** that are given and received, or that are possessed, used, desired or rejected can all tell us about cultural affiliations, values, likes and dislikes, preferences and relationships. Football shirts worn on a game day tell us about allegiance. Wearing hip-hop fashion tells us about identity (see Marcia Morgado's analysis of hip-hop, Morgado, 2007). Banning 'hoodies' from a shopping centre (it happened in the UK in 2005) tells us about outsider views and reactions. Objects can have symbolic meanings (the analysis of this is called iconography) and these can be explored in relation to individual ownership and use as well as in relation to the social and cultural processes involved in their production.

(iv) **Visual images**, still and moving, can be used in different ways. If they are produced by our subjects (photographing their community or children's drawings of home and family), we use them to say something about our subjects' values, concerns fears or condition. If we, as researchers, produce them (videoing a focus group), we use them to capture other data variables. If they already exist (images of teaching and learning over the past century), we use them to say something about the producers, their production or about the socio-economic conditions at the time of production or that are responsible for their continuing existence).

While not every educational researcher will assemble data from this complete range, most researchers will not limit themselves to one source. For qualitative researchers, it is the sheer diversity that constitutes the challenge and makes qualitative research a complex and difficult field.

If this were not enough, our options when it comes to assembling and analysing data complicate the issue even more. To appreciate this point, we have to refresh our understanding of some of the issues we considered in Chapter 2 where we first met the distinction between quantitative and qualitative paradigms. It was here that we first noted that it was legitimate, in qualitative research, for the researcher's own value position to influence not just the research questions but also the answers to those questions. The consequence of this is that while there are characteristics that bring qualitative researchers together, there are epistemological, political and social perspectives that produce debate (and division) that is every bit as fierce as that which once existed between quantitative and qualitative protagonists.

There is, therefore, a sense that qualitative research is more a federation of practices than an integrated framework for conducting research. Notwithstanding this, there are process characteristics (that is, how the research is conducted and the data analysed) that are common to many of the approaches (even if they are sometimes given a different name). It is these in relation to data processing that constitute the heart of this chapter.

11.2 Delivering quality in qualitative research

One of the problems with much published research (quantitative as well as qualitative and in all branches of the social sciences) is that the process by which the results are generated is not transparent. This is not to say that the process of data collection and analysis is bad, just that the reader cannot judge whether the findings and conclusions rest on a sound methodological foundation. Anthony Onwegbuzie and Larry Daniel, two American educational researchers, categorise the failings as:

1. A failure to legitimise research findings in terms of either validity or reliability (see section 3.3.4 and Chapter 3 *passim*).
2. A failure to assess whether data are trustworthy.
3. Generalising conclusions to situations nor warranted by the sample.
4. Failure to comment on the scale and size and strength of the relationship between variables (in quantitative analysis this is known as 'the effect size', see section 13.3.6).

Onwegbuzie and Daniel's position is uncompromising and many qualitative researchers would regard their argument as one that sought to organise and judge qualitative research programmes by using positivist principles. Their response is to argue that concepts should be redefined for qualitative research. Thus validity might be explored in terms of concepts such as credibility, transferability, dependability and conformability. Certainly from the point of view of those reading research, it can be difficult to assess the implications of research findings without knowing what the sample size is and how the sample was drawn. We cannot judge how transferable a case study is unless we know whether it was carefully selected or just happened to be around. Similarly we cannot judge the value of results unless we get insights into how the data was used to construct an explanation or argument. Onwegbuzie and Daniel are explicitly critical of an 'anything goes' attitude that they judge exists in the qualitative research community. If such an attitude does exist, the consequences for qualitative research is serious, especially if it is geared to informing policy or transforming practice because it will not be taken seriously by those with the power to make decisions. It is for this reason that there has been some discussion in the qualitative community about the criteria and standards against which to judge qualitative research.

Liz Spencer and colleagues from the National Centre for Social Research in the UK (a charity associated, since 2007, with the London School of Economics and Political Science) undertook a review of the issue of quality in qualitative research on behalf of the UK Cabinet Office (Spencer et al., 2003). The authors note the divisions in qualitative research: '. . . while some consider Lincoln and Gubba (two American researchers who have been leaders in the movement to specify quality criteria for qualitative research) to have completely reformulated quality criteria . . . [o]thers maintain that they have retained the same basic criteria as used in quantitative research and remained within a positivist paradigm' (Spencer et al., 2003, p. 39). In other words, there are some researchers who will be bound by procedure and criteria and others who will not because they believe that the criteria and procedures mimic quantitative research. The approach of Spencer and her colleagues is to accept the divisions on the issue (divisions which, by implication, will marginalise some qualitative research traditions from a policy and practice influencing role) and classify qualitative research on the basis of its acceptance or rejection of the applicability of quality criteria. They identify the following three approaches to qualitative research.

1. The rejection of quality criteria on the basis that, because there is no single 'correct' way of representing reality, there can be no 'correct' way of collecting and analysing data. It is this category that Onwegbuzie and Daniel criticised on the basis of 'anything goes'.
2. An acceptance of the concept of quality, which is to be judged in terms of the particular character of qualitative research. We met this argument in section 3.3.4 and noted there the issue of the use of different words to describe quality issues for qualitative research and the discussion whether they represented a meaningful distinctiveness or just a semantic difference. This is closest to Onwegbuzie and Daniel's position.
3. Rejection of the position that quality can be thought of in terms of the credibility of a study and its replacement by a mix of an ethical standpoint, a political viewpoint, a desire to improve and emancipate or a commitment to the issue and to those being researched. In other words, the idea that quality in qualitative research is being honest and sincere. We shall see examples of this approach when we look at 'critical' qualitative research. However, because the researcher is committed to a viewpoint, there are other qualitative researchers who would not accept the findings.

Despite these different positions, as readers of research we need some assurance that the research has been done well. The solution by the researchers from the National Centre for Social Research is to present a framework against which research can be assessed without constructing a strait-jacket that forces qualitative research to conform to a specific model. The framework they developed is guided by four principles that for most researchers will be unproblematic.

1. Research should contribute to advancing knowledge or understanding.
2. The research design should address the research question.
3. Data collection, analysis and interpretation should be rigorous, systematic and transparent.
4. Research claims should be credible with plausible arguments about the significance of the evidence.

These themes have been embedded in this book.

The research team translated these principles into 18 questions to ask of research. Table 11.1 summarises the questions that relate to data collection and analysis. The questions are all phrased in such a way that we can reach a judgement on how convinced we are by a piece of research and, if we have misgivings, where their source is. For each question, the research team identifies indicators. Not all of these have to be present, but sufficient have to exist to enable us to have confidence. Most of the indicators (for example, for sample design) can be assessed through the text, but some (for example, literature review) require pre-existing specialist knowledge.

For researchers new to qualitative research, the framework has two advantages. First, it helps us read the research output and appreciate whether the research process is adequately developed and explained to allow us to have confidence in the findings. Second,

Table 11.1 Quality indicators for qualitative research

Appraisal questions	Quality indicators
1. How credible are the findings?	• Can the reader see how the researcher arrived at their conclusions; the 'building blocks' of analysis and interpretation are evident? • Do the findings/conclusions 'make sense' and do they match other knowledge and experience?
2. How has knowledge/understanding been extended by the research?	• Is there a literature review that summarises knowledge and key issues raised by previous research? • Are the aims and design of the study set in the context of existing knowledge? • Are findings presented in a way that offers new insights? • Is there a discussion of the limitations of evidence, what remains unknown or what further information/research is needed?
3. Scope for drawing wider inference – how well is this explained?	• Is there a discussion of what can be generalised to wider population and how the sample was drawn/case selection made? • Is there a description of the context of the study so that its applicability to other settings can be assessed? • Is there a discussion of how hypotheses/propositions/findings may relate to wider theory and/or a consideration of rival explanations? • Is evidence to support claims for wider inference supplied?
4. How defensible is the research design?	• Is there a rationale for the study design and an explanation of how it meets the aims of the study? • Are reasons given for different stages of research, the use of particular methods, data sources, etc? • Is there a discussion of the limitations of research design and the implications for the evidence?
5. How well defended is the sample design/target selection of cases/documents?	• Is there a description of study locations and how and why they were chosen? • Is there a description of the population and how the sample relates to it? • Is there a rationale for the selection of sample/settings/documents?
6. Sample composition/case inclusion – how well is the eventual coverage described?	• Is the profile of sample/case described? • Is there a discussion of any missing coverage? • Are reasons for non-participation and non-inclusion of cases/documents given? • Are access and methods of approach described and how these might have affected participation/coverage discussed?
7. How well was the data collection carried out?	• Is there a discussion of who collected data, what procedures/documents used for collection/recording and evidence of checks on origin/status/authorship of documents? • If interviews/discussions/conversations were not recorded, were justifiable reasons given? • Are the conventions for making field notes given? • Is there a discussion of how fieldwork methods or settings may have influenced data collection?
8. How well has the approach to, and formulation of, the analysis been conveyed?	• Do we know the form of the original data? • Are the reasons for the data management method/tool/package given? Are they reasonable? • Can we see how descriptive analytic categories or labels have been generated and used? • Can we see how analytic concepts/typologies have been devised and applied?

▶

Table 11.1 *(continued)*

Appraisal questions	Quality indicators
9. Contexts of data sources – how well are they retained and portrayed?	• Are background details of study sites or settings given? • Are participants' perspectives placed in a personal context? • Are the origins/history of written documents given?
10. How well has diversity of perspective and content been explored?	• Are diversity/multiple perspectives in the evidence shown? • Are negative cases, outliers or exceptions discussed?
11. How clear are the links between data, interpretation and conclusions?	• Are there clear conceptual links between analytic commentary and the original data? • Is there evidence of how/why particular interpretation/significance are assigned to specific aspects of data? • Can we see how explanations/theories/conclusions were derived and how they relate to original data? • Are cases which do not fit with the explanation considered?
12. How clear are the assumptions/theoretical perspectives/values that have shaped the form and output of the research?	• Are assumptions made explicit? • Are ideological perspectives/values/philosophies made explicit and is their impact on the research design and choice of methods explained? • Is the possibility of error or bias explored?

Source: After Spencer, L. et al. (2003b).

we can turn this whole process around and see just what we have to do in order to produce research findings that our professional community will find convincing. In the context of this chapter, questions 8 to 12 in the table are important. If this information is to be presented in a thesis, report or journal article, we have to be sure that our processes are sound and our decisions with respect to data analysis accurately recorded. Just what these processes and decisions are we shall see in sections 11.3 and 11.4. Activity 11.1 will show you how far other researchers have met the quality test.

Activity 11.1 Learning to differentiate research output

The questions in the quality framework in Table 11.1 are generic and could, perhaps with some tweaking, be used for almost any style of research. For this activity, however, you should only use it in relation to qualitative or predominantly qualitative research.

Go to any educational research journal and select five articles that use a qualitative methodology. Their approaches to research need not be different and the articles can be selected from a single volume. Assess the articles against questions 3, 5, 6, 7, 8 and 13. If authors fail to address the quality indicators, is there any pattern to this failure?

As a comparison, go to the website for the Qualitative Report, an on-line journal, at http://www.nova.edu/ssss/QR/. Read the following two papers from volume 13, number 1:

Gonzalez, L., Stallone Brown, M. and Slate, J.R. (2008) 'Teachers Who Left the Teaching Profession: A Qualitative Understanding', pp. 1–11.

Tercanlioglu, L. (2008) 'A Qualitative Investigation of Pre-Service English as a Foreign Language (EFL) – Teacher Opinions', pp. 137–150.

On the basis of all the academic papers that you have read, write a short paragraph to advise editors of journals how they should strengthen their peer review and selection processes.

11.3 The qualitative method process: an overview

Despite the divisions in qualitative methodology (and they are deep, with opposing viewpoints sometimes expressed, as we shall see, in quite vitriolic language), the methods for creating order out of the rich and complex data sets used by several different approaches are remarkably similar. In many respects this is not surprising because one of the things they usually have in common is a welter of data of often quite varied form. We can appreciate the problem faced by all areas of qualitative research if we think of it in terms of a metaphor. If we were to mine a valuable mineral, tin, copper, gold, we have to accept that the majority of our resource is thinly dispersed in surrounding rock. To get at it, we have to mine the rock, crush it and use either physical processes (sorting, sifting and grading) or chemical processes (the addition of chemicals that precipitate the valuable mineral) to extract the mineral at a high enough concentration to make its exploitation economic. We do something similar with qualitative data. First, we break it up into small units. Some we throw away and others we put together in different ways to see which structure best conveys the meaningfulness of the data. In this process of atomising our data and then selectively reconstructing, we move between two types of analysis. In the first we take the data at face value. We call this *manifest analysis* because the explanation is manifested or apparent in the source data. The second type of analysis is *interpretive*. With this approach we do not accept the data at face value and seek to go behind and inside it to identify hidden meanings. These are latent within the data, so we find this level of analysis referred to as *latent analysis*. For example, Marcia Morgado's study of hip-hop (Morgado, 2007) goes beyond a description of clothes and how they are worn to explorations of identity, defiance and being outside a group and within a group.

Let us now look at the generic process of qualitative data analysis in a little more detail. Figure 11.1 sets out the broad stages. Preceding analysis, there is the stage of data collection. This was covered in Chapters 7, 8 and 9. The process of qualitative analysis is one of shaping data into a form where it can be interpreted in such a way that it at least contributes to an understanding of the research issue (even if it does not wholly answer the research question) and this interpretation is accepted by at least a proportion of the professional audience. This process has four stages:

1. *Preparing the data:* putting it into a form that can be manipulated:
2. *Identifying basic units of data:* essentially a classification procedure as classes of significance to the research issue are constructed and named;
3. *Organising data:* a sequential procedure in which links between data units are built, evaluated and, perhaps, rejected for the whole procedure to start again. This 'clumping' of data can take place at different levels. Basic data units are aggregated into first level clumps and first level to second level and so on as long as the data and interpretations warrant it.
4. *Interpretation of data:* this is a test of the meaningfulness of the basic data structure and data aggregation. An interpretation need not be acceptable and can lead to data analysis being repeated.

In Figure 11.1 are two boxes on either side of the analysis core. These represent influences upon the analysis and the dotted lines show that they need not be present. On the left side is existing information about the issue, both research findings and professional debates. On the right side are the researcher's personal perspective. These two boxes constitute context and they are present throughout the research process.

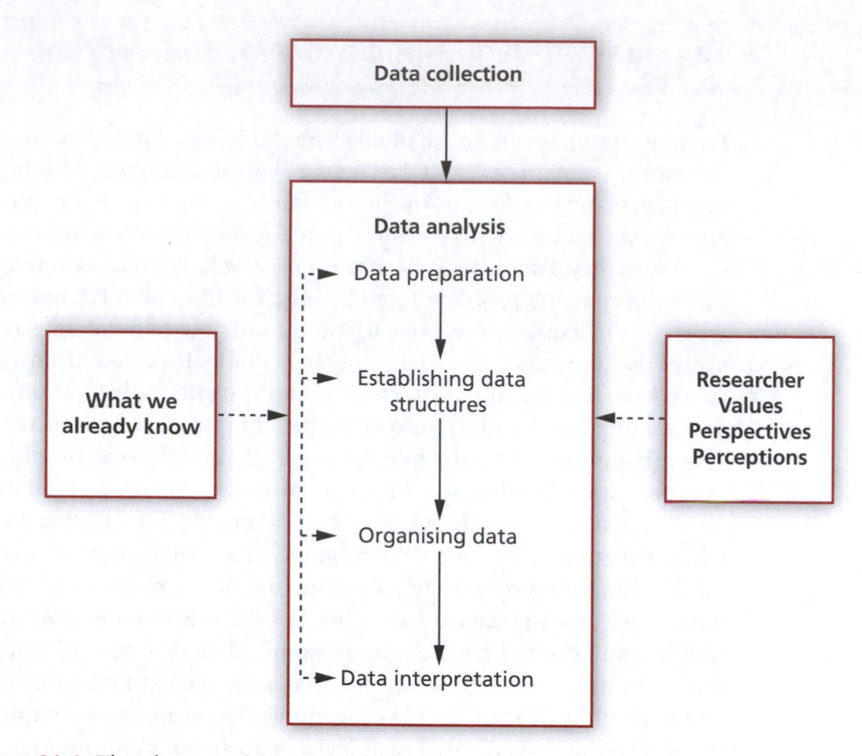

Figure 11.1 The data analysis process

In the following sections we shall explore the stages in the core of qualitative data analysis in more detail in order to gain insight into how the process is operationalised.

11.3.1 Preparing the data

The first stage in quantitative data analysis is to assess whether the data are in a form that can be analysed. In some cases they will be. For example, visual data such as videos (of a class activity, behaviour and so on) or photographs (taken by the subjects being researched) constitute our raw material and, with this, we would normally move directly to the second stage, coding (section 11.5). Text-based data (reports and other documents) are also usually in a form we can work with immediately. There are, however, data types that have to be transformed before we can work with them.

1. *Observations:* field observations and associated notes may not be in a form in which they can be used directly. We need ordered data and when we are in the field our observation sheets can get crumpled or covered in coffee. We can use an observation sheet to make a note of an idea that has just occurred to us. They can become separated from our descriptions of the setting. If we are using original manuscripts, typescripts or products, they may be too valuable to be worked upon directly. What we have to do in these cases is some combination of the following:
   - copy the original data;
   - link observations with information on who was observing and details of the setting;
   - transcribe shorthand notes and comments into text readable by others.

2. *Speech:* interviews, conversations, speeches and presentations that have been captured on an audio recording medium can be analysed directly but it is more usual for them to be transcribed into a text format. This, however, requires decisions to be made.
   - Are only the words transcribed or do we include speech fillers, such as 'umm', 'er' and 'ah'?
   - Do we transcribe speech in dialect directly or do we transform it into something more like standard language?
   - Are we only interested in the words or is the way they are spoken also of interest?
   - Are questions important? If so, they have to be recorded at the time or video recording used.

Dr John Bailey, a British medical researcher who uses qualitative methods, argues that the issues that underpin these questions are fundamentally methodological and are concerned with how far the researcher wishes to report an authentic voice and how completely communication (words, tone, emphasis, gestures, mannerisms and so on) should be recorded (Bailey, 2008). If we are researching young people how important is it that we record how they actually speak in 'street talk' rather than in grammatical English? If we use the latter, what information will we miss? In reaching decisions about the character of our transcription we have to think about what type of data we need in order to get to grips with our research issue. There is, therefore, no single 'correct' transcription. The fact that we have to take these decisions shows that transcription is not just a technical matter. This highlights a further issue, that transcription is often reduced to audio typing by a clerical assistant. While it is acceptable to use research resources to do this, we should not imagine that the typescript itself is the transcription; it is just the base layer onto which we, as the researchers, have to graft other aspects of communication, such as sighs, laughter, smiling, scowling and so on. And then we have to represent the meaning of all of this. Look at Activity 11.2.

A final point that should be made in relation to preparing all types of data for analysis is that it may not be necessary to use all the data that we have. There can be no hard and fast rules on this but as a guideline we go into our data knowing what our research question is. It is legitimate not to use data that is not relevant to our question. Data selection is an important part of data preparation and, as a guide, we should look at and review all the data we have as a first step. Selecting out data is important in resource terms (allow three to six hours to transcribe an hour's worth of recording) but there is a

Activity 11.2 Eats, shoots & leaves

Lynne Truss's book, *Eats, Shoots & Leaves: the Zero Tolerance Approach to Punctuation*, explains the role of punctuation in conveying meaning. Look at the sentences below and see how many meanings you can convey with a change of emphasis and use of pauses.

The tourist saw the astronomer with the telescope.

The landlord painted all the walls with cracks.

Visit the cemetery where famous people are buried daily except Thursday.

Woman without her man is a savage.

Dog for sale eats anything especially fond of children.

They were alright.

With thanks to the people who put these sentences on their websites.

downside. The benefit of a researcher personally transcribing everything is that it is an important engagement with the data. Insights into data structure and meaning are rarely instantaneous, they usually require time to develop.

11.3.2 The mystery of coding

Our goal with qualitative data is to reorganise and reconstruct it in such a way that we extract information from it. The implication of this is that information lies deep within the data. Of course, this is not always the case and what we see or what we are told provides all the understanding we require. If we work with our data at this level though, we should, as a matter of course, triangulate the information from another source.

Our desire to reveal messages buried in data should not blind us to the fact that our data can mislead us. Case Study 11.1 provides an example and is a warning to us that a good researcher will always view results with scepticism.

11.3.3 How coding works

Forewarned about the dangers we face, let us now explore how coding works. The object of coding is to 'name' units of data. The name or code we give to data should, in some

Case study 11.1 Predictive texts

This is not about fast-moving fingers on a cell phone keypad, but about the claim that some religious texts are encoded to foretell the future. As rational people, we probably treat the claim that the Bible can be used for prediction with a judgement that is well beyond scepticism. However, in 1994 the American peer reviewed journal, *Statistical Science*, published a paper that made the startling claim that the book of Genesis contains letter sequences that spell words with related meanings, which they demonstrated by identifying named people and their dates of birth or death. Their intriguing finding was popularised in two books, *The Bible Code* by Michael Drosnin and *Cracking the Bible Code* by Jeffrey Satinover. Now software exists to allow each one of us to make our own predictions (for an example of the Bible foretelling the sinking of the Titanic, go to: www.research-systems.com/codes/howto/videos/Titanic.htm).

The search for hidden messages has also extended to other areas. Led Zeppelin's 1971 hit *Stairway to Heaven*, when played backwards, apparently says, 'Oh, here's to my sweet Satan. The one whose little pack would make me sad, he'll give those with him 666'(note, 666 is a *highly* symbolic number), while Britney Spears' song, *Baby One More Time* is apparently an invitation to, 'Sleep with me, I'm not too young' when played backwards.

All of this is clearly a challenge to people who may accept religion as an act of faith but believe that foretelling the future is little more than superstition. But rescue from this predicament came in 1999 when statistical science published another paper on the subject from a team led by Professor Brendan McKay of the Australian National University. This paper set out a set of technical reasons why the earlier results were spurious. In an earlier test, Professor McKay was able to show that *War and Peace* gave just as good results. He followed this up by demonstrating that, in *Moby Dick*, the assassinations of the Indian Prime Minister, Indira Gandhi, the American Presidents, John F. Kennedy and Abraham Lincoln, the Israeli Prime Minister, Yitzhak Rabin and even the death of Princess Diana, are predicted. *Moby Dick* may be a classic novel but the author was no soothsayer. Case proven!

If you want to know more about false messages, look at Professor McKay's webpage: http://cs.anu.edu.au/~bdm/dilugim/. If you want to hear the songs sung backwards: http://www.thepeek.com and search for 'hidden messages'. Remember the lesson, we can often find what we are looking for in our data. Stay sceptical.

way, be connected with the issue under investigation, so that when the codes are put together (this is a process that ranges from rejecting data to combining codes) we obtain insight that was, with the raw data, not available to us. Where do these codes come from? There are three sources:

1. We can use a coding structure already devised by someone else. Examples include the Family Therapist Coding System (Pinsof, 1981), the Interpersonal Process Code (Rusby et al., 1991), the Social Interactive Coding System (Rice et al., 1990), the Facial Action Coding System (Ekman and Friesen, 1976). Case Study 11.2 gives examples from the Interpersonal Process Code. Other sources can be found in published research papers.

Case study 11.2 The interpersonal process code

This coding structure can be used to analyse interactions in the home, in the play environment or in a laboratory setting. It is an 'omnibus' framework, that is, it seeks to cover all ages and all interpersonal behaviours. It is appropriate to use it with children.

The code looks at and records three broad aspects of behaviour (these are referred to as *dimensions*):

1. Activity.
2. Content – classified as positive, neutral or negative.
3. Affect or emotional tone.

It also records who is interacting with whom, who initiates the interaction and who is at the receiving end.

1. *Activity codes* are classified according to the setting. Two coding frameworks are shown below.

Family interaction	Playground interaction
1 = Work	1 = Free play
2 = Play	2 = Participation
3 = Read	3 = Parallel play
4 = Eat	4 = Alone
5 = Attend	
6 = Unspecified	

2. The template for *Content codes* is set out below.

Activity type	Positive	Neutral	Negative
Verbal	Positive talk	Talk advise	Negative talk
Non-verbal	Co-operative	Social involvement	Non–co-operative
Physical	Positive physical	Physical interaction	Negative physical

The manual* gives definitions and illustrations of all of these situations.

3. The coding of *Affect* is derived from observation of facial expressions, voice tone, and body language. The six categories are:
   1. happy
   2. caring
   3. neutral
   4. distress
   5. aversive
   6. sad.

The interpersonal process coding framework is typical of predetermined codes in that it has to strike a balance between recording detail and representing broad behaviours. The benefits of using such a coding system are that someone has done the hard work for us and the method has usually been tried and tested. The choice for us as researchers is often between building something bespoke ourselves or walking into a coding salesroom and getting something off the shelf.

*Rusby. J., Estes, A. and Dishion, J. (1991) *The Interpersonal Process Code (IPC)*, Oregon Social Learning Centre, Eugene, Oregon (available at http://www.oslc.org/resources/codemanuals/interpersonalprocesscode.pdf).

Case study 11.3 Coding with pre-determined themes

Sylvain Bourdon is a Professor of Education at the University of Sherbrooke in Quebec and an expert in mixed methods research. His research interests encompass the transitions of young people to another life or education stage, alternative schooling, lifelong learning and learning through work. It was in the context of these interests that he explored a feature found throughout the developed world – the replacement of state service provision (such as care of the elderly) by social enterprise (that is, companies or organisations that operate on a 'not for profit' basis) and the employment of graduate students by such organisations. He and his research team identified over 1,000 social enterprises and captured data to create a profile of the sector. They used this framework to sample 43 organisations from which they would gain deeper insights (this is a typical mixed methods strategy). The research objectives were to understand how working in a social enterprise related to the students' career goals and what the expansion in their roles meant to the social enterprises. The data they collected was in the form of interviews, questionnaires and field notes, all of which were transcribed for analysis. The coding was done by members of the team. They all worked to a common framework which reflected their investigative interest: education histories, work histories, personal relationships (for the students), organisational structure, goals, culture, resourcing (for the social enterprises). The basic framework is set out below:

The individual	The organisation
• Schooling/training history. • Work history. • Working conditions. • Work organisation. • Schooling – working relations. • Friends – relationships. • Family life. • Work – rest of life relations. • Future perspectives. • Perception of community sector.	• History and development. • Mission and goals. • Structure. • Clientele, members. • Financing. • Others.

The purpose of this coding was not to build theory but to sort and organise data so that the search for patterns would be easier. In other words, it was to create profiles of types of student and types of social enterprise. This is a typical early-stage analysis.

Source: Bourdon, S. (2002).

2. We can devise a coding system before our analysis based on theory and existing knowledge. This is sometimes referred to as *concept mapping*. Effectively, what we are doing is constructing a schematic model that shows relationships between variables and then using our data to test it. Read Case Study 11.3.
3. Third, we can allow the coding structure to emerge from our data. This is where the 'mystery' is and we shall consider it in more detail below.

Before we do this, however, it is worth noting, from a methodological perspective, contrasts between the approaches. The first approach is either diagnostic of situations (that is, looking at situations through the lens of established practice and solutions) or confirmatory of relationships that are generally accepted. The Facial Action Coding system, for example, can be used to infer the emotional state of infants. The second approach, where the codes arise out of a theoretical perspective, is deductive and the third approach is inductive. We draw these distinctions not to complicate the situation but to show how complex the research field is and, particularly, how the neat assumption of qualitative equals inductive breaks down on detailed examination.

11.3.4 The downside of coding

Let us now turn back to the process of coding. We referred to it as a 'mystery', why? The reason is that it is not extensively explored as a process in the literature, nor do many authors explain it when they report their work. This makes understanding how to operate the process difficult for researchers who have never done it before. It also creates an environment in which poor practice can become established. On top of this, even when performed with reasonable competence, coding can and usually does 'wreck your head', as Helen Marshall, an Australian sociologist, puts it (Marshall, 2002). Through discussions with other researchers, she identified the following problems:

- It is a messy business with no clear boundaries and an overwhelming amount of data that produces a miserable experience involving frustration, confusion and self-doubt (Marshall, 2002, p. 60).
- There is no end to the amount of coding that can be done and, as a result, considerable uncertainty about when to stop. And as we search, the only guideline for the point where the cost of extracting more information from the data exceeds the benefit that the information brings comes down to experience. This is not a great deal of help when you have never done it before.
- The final problem for researchers is a consequence of everything that has been said before. With no clear boundaries of when to stop, a coding process that eats up time and the need to meet deadlines, it is not surprising that Helen Marshall's respondents reported that the whole process created pressure and led to work that was less than thorough.

In the next section we shall see what we can do to overcome these problems.

11.3.5 Making coding work

The issues, especially for the researcher new to qualitative analysis, are how to stay in control of the coding process and how to stay calm and collected. Coding (and what happens subsequently) can be a confusing process but by (a) exposing the questions we have to ask and (b) the judgements we must make, it becomes a more manageable process even if it does not absolutely remove the confusion.

We can break down just the coding process into six types of activity. The important thing to remember is that the process we shall learn about is not necessarily one where we start at the beginning and progress through the stages until the end when we produce a result. More likely, we will start, progress part of the way through the process, think about what we are doing and start again, incorporating some new ideas. And the likelihood is that we shall have to do this several times.

(i) Stage one: know who does what

It is important that every data source, every data collection activity and every coding activity is identified and recorded. If two people are working on the data, we need to know which data each worked on and what they did. We should also record when it was done and the start and finish times (all of them). We may never need the information but if we suspect something is not quite right (for example, drift in the application of the coding criteria), we need to be able to go back and understand the circumstances. This stage is rarely reported in the literature but it is good housekeeping.

(ii) Stage two: don't start yet

While we may have acquired a richer appreciation of the issue we are researching during data collection, we should not imagine that this is a sufficient basis for getting stuck in to the coding. We probably have not seen all of the data, certainly not together at one time. Our ideas may be warped by the interview we have just conducted. The first activity we should undertake in relation to our data is to use it to refocus our thinking. To do this we should review a range of the data – look at the video evidence from different places or on different days, read reports, read through transcripts, making sure that they come from the beginning, middle and end of the data collection process and, if they are transcripts of interviews, that they are from different types of respondent. As we do this, points will occur to us. We should note these down, because, at the end, they may be the basis of our first attempt at coding. Making our acquaintance with a reasonable range of data in this way helps us appreciate its scope. It gives us an idea of the dimensions and scale of our task and the extent to which some of our data may be irrelevant to our research purpose.

Celia Godfrey, a research officer at the Royal Children's Hospital in Melbourne Australia, adopted this approach in her PhD research into early educational intervention with disadvantaged families (Godfrey, 2006). Her study utilised a mixed methods approach. She combined interviews with parents, interviews with staff at a Child and Family Services centre, field observation notes and psychological tests on the children. Godfrey makes clear the repetition that characterises the early stages of coding: 'This . . . analysis began with each transcript being read many times in hard copy and annotated in terms of the ideas conveyed . . . The thematic codes used by the researcher emerged from the data and were not pre-determined according to theoretical or other expectations' (Godfrey, 2006, p. 44).

(iii) Stage three: think about what we want the coding to do

We can code in several ways; each reflects a different character of the data.

- Coding can highlight facts or describe situations or events. Not surprisingly this is referred to as *factual or descriptive coding.*
- We can also look into our data and *interpret* what it means. Sometimes the interpretation is a summary of the data and just re-expresses what the data appears to be telling us. In this case we are operating at or close to the surface of the data and taking it, more or less, at face value. At other times our interpretation may be more conceptual or abstract or broader in scope than the data itself, in which case we are operating at a deeper level. The interview data from the parents in Celia Godfrey's research (see above) was analysed at face value. One parent said, 'Oh, I'm not sure, um, a bit of confidence and a bit of time just with me. Because we, with having five children it gets a bit, quite, you know hard to find time. Just to spend time with my child . . . was probably the main goal'. This was one of five responses coded to the theme of 'Provide some special one-on-one time with Mum' (Godfrey, 2006, p. 73). We should bear in mind, though, that we can move from descriptive to interpretive coding. For example, a study of children's play on housing estates began with

observations of play (using a pre-existing coding framework that recorded age, gender, play activity and play environment) and concluded by inferring some of the drivers for selection of play locations such as safety and preferring to congregate with other children and be part of a social group (Wheway and Millward, 1997).

(iv) Stage four: coding and tagging the data

The process of putting a generic name (the code) to a unit of data is called *tagging*. We should make clear at the outset that coding and tagging is an iterative process, that is, we have to go round and round several times before our final coding solution begins to emerge. In a nutshell, the process starts by our creating codes. There is no rule that tells us how to do this. The codes are, at this stage, our best guess. The codes either emerge from the data or are based on existing templates or the findings of previous research or any combination of these. We apply these first stage codes to our data and where we match a code to data, we tag the data with the code name. As we go through the data we learn more and gain more insights. This, almost certainly, will lead us to extend our coding structure and refine the codes. Once this happens, we have to return to our data, apply the new codes and tag the data. And the process continues. As an example of the outcome of this process we can look at the coding framework developed for a study of adolescent parenthood. The authors, Patricia Ann Wright and Anita Ann Davis, two academic psychologists, looked at how teachers think about students who become parents. The broader relevance of their study lies in the fact that teachers are often an important means of support to the students. They gathered their data though interviews and went through the process described above until they generated a set of stable codes that could be applied to all the interviews. One of the themes to the interview was, what did the students worry about? Their analysis enabled them to identify 12 concepts: responsibility, vulnerability to violence, gangs, absent father, finances, graduation and college, peer acceptance, baby's father, dating troubles, lack of love, unavailable mother and drugs. In one interview a teacher said, 'At 17, you just ought not to worry if your mama is in an alley somewhere with a pipe in her mouth. But, they do.' This was coded as 'drugs'. Another said, 'You hear all these kids talk about, well, "I can't play out in my yard, or my mom won't let me go out after night, or I'm not allowed to go here". I think for some of these kids, its just basic survival.' This was coded as 'vulnerability to violence' (Wright and Davis, 2008, pp. 680–681).

The coding process lies at the heart of transforming data into information. For anyone who has never done it before, it is riddled with uncertainty. Practice and experience give us confidence and the advice that follows is designed to fast-track new researchers through the learning process.

- *What is a unit of data?* A unit of data is the portion of data that is coded and to which we attach a tag. It is anything we want it to be. It can be as long as a paragraph, it can be just a word. It can be what someone has chosen to photograph or it can be the facial expression of someone in a photograph. A useful way to start with text is to take paragraphs and summarise in one or two words the key points. In this way we can start to see the units. In the study by Wright and Davis whole sentences were tagged.
- *Do we have to tag all of the text?* No, some data may well be redundant in terms of the research topic. In all forms of text, from reports and minutes of meetings to transcriptions of interviews, there are likely to be filler words, phrases, sentences and even longer sections.

- *How many codes should there be?* There is no answer to this. At first we should not restrict ourselves to a particular number on the grounds that, at a later stage we can always get rid of some. At that later stage, if we are coding manually, it can be difficult to cope with many more than about 50 codes. And the danger of using computer technology is that, at the time, it can appear to be easier to create another code rather than think more deeply about what is being said and whether an existing code is applicable. Methodological literature has tried to help us by creating the concept of 'saturation' (a point at which coding has extracted maximum 'goodness' out of the data) but it is rarely explained or illustrated. Glen Bowen, an American qualitative researcher, developed a rule of thumb that 'a data category was considered saturated if it was reflected in more than 70 percent of the interviews, confirmed by member checks (interviewee feedback on the analyzed data), resonated with key informants, and made sense given prior research' (Bowen, 2008, p. 148). This is a useful indicator because transparency about the number of codes we have is necessary if we are to ensure that the audience for our research is not to believe that finality in the analysis was determined by frustration or the need to meet deadlines rather than an obvious and natural completion to the analysis.
- *How should we make the tags?* If we are doing this by hand, the best way is to make several copies of the data and then annotate and copy. If we are dealing with text, we could use a selection of highlighter pens. It is likely that as we progress through the text some of our ideas may change, which will affect the coding. In this case we note the change from old to new thinking, identify the data we have been working on as Mark 1 coding and start over again with a clean copy. There are also computer programs we can use to help us handle the data. When we use these, the tagging process is usually one where we highlight text or a portion of an image or a section of speech and then click on a code.
- *Should data only be tagged once?* If we can devise a coding framework that is mutually exclusive all well and good, but it is difficult. It is possible that we will start like this but then things will get messy and codes will overlap. In fact, it is almost inevitable that this will happen because as our coding framework grows, we cannot hold it all in our minds. However, it is a good goal to set ourselves to work towards removing this overlap at the end of each pass through our data. It will help us to be clearer about our concepts and though it may require us to create more codes, there is a benefit in the long run.
- *How do we work through the data?* Do we work through it case by case, looking at each video of children playing in turn or reading each person's interview transcript in turn or do we look for aggression in all the videos of co-operative play (or in the responses to question 4 and then all the responses to question 5)? The answer is that we have to strike a balance between following our noses and being systematic. If something occurs to us when we are marking up one piece of text, we should make a note of where we are and what we are going to do, then we should examine the other texts to see if there are similar meanings. For example, if we are coding transcripts of teachers' interviews about managing pupil behaviour and one teacher mentions that some pupil behaviour deteriorates through the day, we should go back and see if anyone else has made any allusion to the time factor. This could be important and could be related to energy levels and dietary habits. We should always have by our sides a record book or even a template of what analysis we have done on what data. As a guide, most people seem to begin by looking at sets of data in the round. Some then follow their noses, others continue to look at one set of data after another but look at

them several times over to make sure that each is reviewed in the context of our developing ideas. Lesley Reid, at the University of Edinburgh, provides a good example of how this occurred in her study of how teachers assess pupils' writing (Reid, 2007). She noted that 'interviewees were prompted to talk freely on three (sic) related issues:

- their own teaching career backgrounds;
- their knowledge and experience of writing pedagogy;
- knowledge and experience of writing assessment;
- their views of the role of pupils in the assessment process' (pp. 136–137).

These themes provided the framework for first level descriptive coding. The research team then met to discuss the project, their ideas were shared with the participants and out of this there emerged additional coding to cover, for example, 'length and type of experience. The 'writing pedagogy' codes were branched to include comments about resources used and teaching approaches adopted (for example genre-based, process focused). Teachers' comments about writing assessment were coded under technical skills, planning, vocabulary use, creativity, writing structure. Their comments about the role of pupils in the assessment process were coded under 'written and verbal feedback, motivation, prioritizing criteria' (p. 137). Teachers were interviewed a second time after they had met again to discuss assessment practice and additional codes were developed from this to cover 'primary/secondary sector differences, the effect of formative assessment practices and the importance of the context of text production' (p. 137).

- *How do we know that our coding is accurate?* Well, coding is all a matter of interpretation so it is possible that our interpretation may be different from someone else's yet still be valid. This might be the case if I adopted a neutral stance to the data and someone else came with a critical perspective. However, it is a good idea to get someone else (or some other people) to code some examples of the data and to compare the outcomes. The differences can be discussed and used to inform our own coding framework.

The process of coding and tagging data is not a clean one. It will go slowly at first as we feel our way around the data. There are likely to be false starts – but this is no bad thing because each time we learn something new. However, it does (usually) all come good at the end!

(v) Creating links and themes

In essence the coding and tagging process refines, re-orders and reduces in scale the data we began with. Our marking up of the data and our marginal comments may look complex, even a mess, but even on a first pass through, we have reduced the quantity of information. The example we gave above from Wright and Davis gave an example of coding for 12 student concerns, identified by teachers, that the researches categorised as 'worries'. With this process, we may well begin to see the start of a pattern emerging. The next stage in the process is to create links between the categories. We do this by looking for similarities and establishing differences between the codes we have created. The effect of this is that we begin to build themes of associated concepts. When we do this, it is a major step in creating order and identifying patterns and meaning in our data. How do we go about this?

- First, we should create a list of all of our codes then review our data to confirm that they are appropriate. We do this because it is almost inevitable that, as we move through the data, we create codes – and some of these may be better than the ones we have already developed.

- At this point, we have a coding structure in which we have reasonable confidence. It is at this point that we often compare our coding structure and tagging results with what others produce. Our next step is to assess the quantity of data in each code. We want to ensure that our coding structure is not too coarse so that we have lots of data in a few codes nor too fine so that we have a lot of codes with little data. In neither case will we get a good sense of the information in the data set. If we are assessing the amount of data in each code by hand, the best way is to transfer the tagged data onto a record card and mark its location or origin on the card plus the name of the tag. When we have done this for all of the tags, we assemble the cards into separate piles. This allows us to do the following:
  (a) compare the data in each pile to confirm the consistency of the tagging process
  (b) look at the largest piles and ask whether they contain subsidiary concepts or facts
  (c) look at the smallest piles (and it is likely that we will finish up with a 'pile' of one or two cards) and ask whether the code has a meaningful role to play.

We may, at this stage, restructure our concepts. Again, there is technology that can help us with this.

- Our next step is to look at the codes and see if we can detect any common or overarching themes. In all likelihood we will approach this from different directions. We could begin by comparing each of our coding categories in relation to the others and asking, 'Why is this one different from that one?' Our answer, 'Because it is . . .', will establish characteristics which may themselves be capable of being grouped. In other words, by establishing how codes are different, we might be in a position to identify some that have features in common. We could also try to construct our own framework. Which codes deal with events, emotional states, environments, processes, values? We could take our piles of cards and ask, 'How similar or different are these two categories?' and then use our answer to place them relative to each other. This grouping of codes is a process that takes time and it needs time if it is to be effective. What we are trying to capture and represent are the threads that hold the data together. This is a creative process. It requires knowledge, understanding and insight. We half see solutions but then they become shrouded in mist but, with time, links, patterns and meaningful explanations do emerge. A group of doctoral students (Dye et al., 2000) has described this process as moving from 'raw data bits' to 'final category array'. Their model is reproduced in Figure 11.2. The 'raw data bits' represent the initial tagging. The 'initial category set' represents the first stage of bundling codes together. These were progressively reviewed and refined until an overarching framework (final category array) was produced (the red square). Other themes are shown relative to each other within the overarching theme. What this representation emphasises is that categories overlap. Clean and neat solutions are rarely an option.

In coding, experience is the great teacher. Activity 11.3 provides an opportunity to make a start with some authentic data.

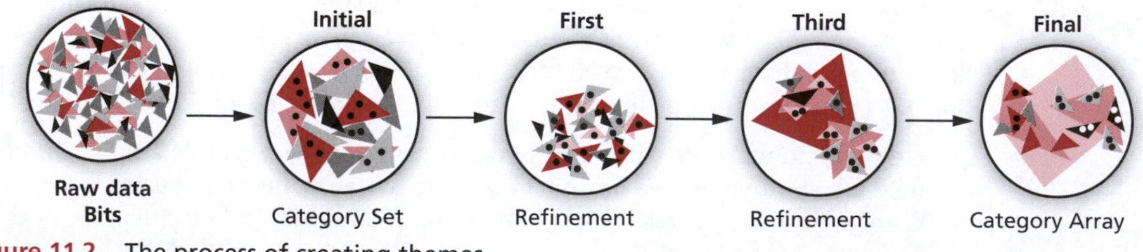

Figure 11.2 The process of creating themes
Source: From Dye et al. (2000).

Activity 11.3 Bullying in school

Most of what we read about bullying amongst young people is about our own country. It does not take much research, however, to realise that what goes on in our country is replicated in many others. Visionary is an EU-funded project that brings together experts to address the problem and explore strategies to solve it (www.bullying-in-school.info). It collects reports that demonstrate that bullying is a worldwide issue. One report, from *The Independent* on-line edition (South Africa) noted that 'Schools in Garteng are beset by racialised groups, gambling, bullying and pupils who aren't scared to use weapons on one another' and reported research that 'children who bring ipods, PsPs and expensive cell phones are targeted by children who want those items, while in poorer areas, violence happens over money and food' (www.int.iol.co.za, search for 'bullying' report, 11 May 2008).

In October 2004 Maraumo Maria Malematsa submitted a thesis on bullying in a South African school as part of the assessment for her Master's degree in Education (M.Ed.). A transcript of one of the interviews is reproduced below: Your task is to code it to bring out the salient issues.

1. **R: Good morning, relax madam, as I have already explained to your son do you**
2. **agree that I use a tape recorder to interview you?**
3. P: Err . . . but ag, yes you may proceed.
4. **R: Tell me about your son's behaviour at home.**
5. P: I have serious problems with him even my neighbors are complaining.
6. **R: What type of problems?**
7. P: It has started after marrying his step father and losing my job.
8. **R: And**
9. P: He will just sit there and sulk not talking to anyone even his sisters. My
10. husband after being paid will come home drunk. He will start by accusing him
11. with things he had not done. At first he used to keep quite then now because
12. he swears at him calling him names like I am not your father, you're hopeless
13. you will not make it in life and stupid my son answers back.
14. **R: What do you do?**
15. P. I sometimes intervene but I am always caught in the middle. My husband
16. will swear and then attempt to beat us. One day he tried to beat me, my son
17. run outside and throws him with stones. He was so furious since that day
18. when he is drunk they fight. I am worried because my son is no longer happy.
19. He hangs out with a group of boys. They are so troublesome, I receive
20. complaints from neighbours that they take their children's money, tease them,
21. beat or even ask them to do nasty things. They will sit at the corner when a
22. girl passes they tease at her, call her names and if she does not respond they
23. laugh at her.
24. **R: And what else?**
25. P: I think here at school they have called me complaining that he had taken
26. money from one boy. Daily during break he will go to the toilets ask money or
27. take money from other boys but he targets same boys. If they don't oblige he
28. will beat them after school. He will force others to write homework's for him
29. especially clever girls.
30. **R: Hmm . . .**
31. P: Their group will beat other children at the street. I am so worried he is now (Transcript page -1-)
32. out of hand I have tried to call his uncle to talk with him but all in vain. But I
33. think the cause of this bully behaviour is how my husband treats him. I think
34. he feels not loved because he will not even sit with us or view the television. I
35. really don't know what to do. I am just afraid that he will end up in jail or
36. commit suicide.
37. **R: You have said the cause of this bully behaviour is my husband.**
38. **According to you is your son a bully?**
39. P: He does not act like other kids. Now and then, the school or neighbours
40. complain about him. I don't know really but bully is not maybe a person/child
41. who takes money by force from others or maybe beat small boys?
40. **R: Ja, you are right.**
43. P: So he is a bully. And I still say my husband is a cause, there is no peace in
44. our house. It frustrates him.
45. **R: Where do you think they bully mostly?**
46. P: At school because he spends most of his time at school.
47. What should the school do
48. P: Maybe try to talk with children who beat others or take their money. But I

49. think if you have more children like my son call a parents meeting maybe we
50. can came up with a better solution.
51. **R: What else can we do?**
52. P: Involve other children who see what bullies do daily ask about their
53. opinions. Maybe you can draw up a plan and tell all the children that bullying
54. is not a fine thing. But mam to my problems I think I am going to discuss them
55. with child protection unit people. My sister has told me about them they say
56. they help. Maybe my husband will stop drinking and swearing. Please keep
57. on talking with my son maybe he will gain some confidence.
58. **R: I will do so. According to you what should the school do to stop**
59. **bullying?**
60. P: The school principal should talk to teachers. A planning on how to stop
61. bullying should be written. Parents and school leaders should be called and
62. asked for their opinion. I think even in the classrooms bullying should be
63. taught so that other learners should know that it is not right to bully. If a
64. learner had bullied his or her parents should be called or the school should
65. have a special punishment. To stop bullying I think punishment must be used.
66. But I think teachers too must stop bullying or maybe some are not aware that
67. they hurt learners. I think they should learn more about bullying.
68. **R: Thank you very much, bye.**

11.3.6 Coding as a team

So far we have thought about the data coding process more or less as an individual activity. Much qualitative research, however, is undertaken by groups of researchers. This changes not the goal of coding but its organisation.

The principal issue to be resolved is that there has to be a common understanding of the coding criteria and the coding process across all members of the research team. The reason for this is quite obvious. Without it there will be chaos. Because of the need for a shared understanding of the coding criteria and their common application, the development of the criteria is a much more organisationally complex process than it at first appears. The common understanding has to be 'grown' within the team. A group of American qualitative researchers in disease control and prevention has described the procedure that it follows (MacQueen et al., 1998). The procedure is built around two processes:

- allowing the codes to arise from the data by first creating codes based on the specific research issues or questions and then analysing the broad swathes of text that this identifies in order to identify data specific concepts; and
- progressively involving more of the team in the decision making.

The whole process is likely to be interactive; it is rare to hit the jackpot of an effective coding structure first time round. MacQueen et al. describe the process of stages of testing (and learning about) the efficacy of the coding structure.

- A small number of team members develop a first-draft coding framework which is then reviewed by the research team.
- A small number of team members apply the structure to the data. If there is a high level of agreement between the codes, the coding structure is released for wider usage. These are periodic checks to ensure consistency.
- If there is a poor level of intercoder agreement, the reasons are reviewed by the code designers and the coders. If the reason is that coders misunderstand the code criteria, then retraining and redrafting produces a solution. If the reason is that

codes are ambiguous, then the criteria are reviewed by the team and more sharply conceptualised.

- As the coding structure is stabilised and released for use, consistency checks are conducted on a regular basis.

11.4 Using software to help

We have assumed, so far, that all the data processing is done by hand. It is certainly a good idea to have some experience of doing it this way because it gives us a good feel for the data but with a lot of data it can not only be a long process, it can also be a tedious one as well. However, since the middle of the 1990s there have been major developments in software that certainly increase productivity and, it is claimed, accuracy as well. In this section we shall review what help technology can offer us in three areas: transcription, early stage thinking and data coding and analysis.

11.4.1 Technology and transcription

The principal issue in the context of applying technology in the transcription stage is the direct transfer of speech to text.

Voice recognition software generally has to be 'trained' to the voice of a speaker. If there is more than one speaker (as in an interview) then the results of using such software are usually less effective than typing the words out. One solution to this, used by an American researcher, Jennifer Matheson, was to dictate what both questioner and respondent said (Matheson, 2007). Her procedure was to:

- record the whole interview on a digital platform;
- transfer the recordings to a computer;
- train the voice recognition to software;
- listen to the digital recording in chunks and dictate what is said into the voice recognition software.

Matheson's paper contains much sound advice.

The problem that Matheson was seeking to overcome, 'a useless jumble of words', is likely to be resolved in the not too distant future. We can see where the developments are going in mobile telephony. We can receive text messages as voice mails. Now we can also dictate text messages by downloading the software, though this too requires training. The field, like much technology, is fast-moving and we can expect to see the burden of manually transcribing speech lifted from the shoulders of qualitative researchers in the not-too-distant future.

11.4.2 Technology and early stage thinking

There will be occasions when we have textual data but no clear idea, despite having read it through, of themes or emphases. Alternatively, we might want to examine text to see how particular ideas are explored. There are text analysis programs that can help us with this type of preliminary assessment.

Textanz (www.cro-code.com) performs word and phrase counts. If we were researching the teacher experience, for example, we could search for the word 'stress' and synonyms for 'stress' to see how many times they occurred. This could give us an indication whether this was a concept worth pursuing.

Concordance (www.concordancesoftware.co.uk) performs similar functions and allows us to compare words in their context. Perhaps more useful at an early stage are approaches that present data visually. There are two that we can use on IBM's Many Eyes website (http://manyeyes.alphaworks.ibm.com/manyeyes).

Word Clouds shows word frequencies. The IBM version does a simple count of the most frequently occurring words and presents them alphabetically with the word size proportionate to the word frequency. It will also look for the frequency of word pairs. Figure 11.3 shows a word cloud for a UK school inspection report. If we place the cursor over any word when we are using the program, the frequency count and its context is highlighted. The search option in the program allows us to look for letter sequences (for example, all words beginning with 'p').

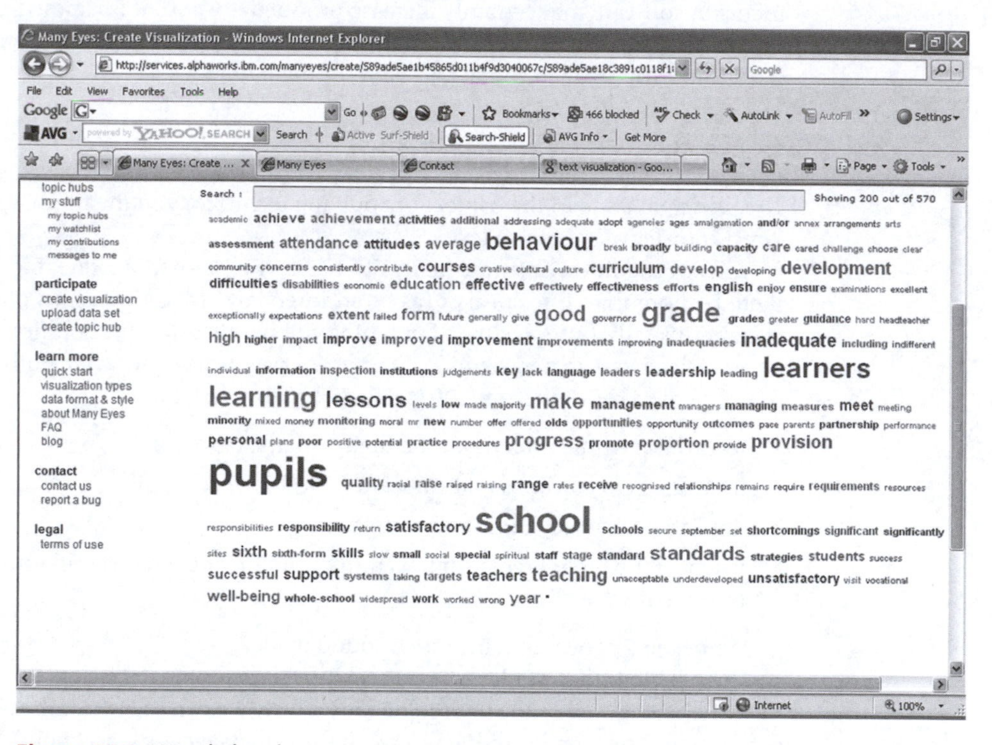

Figure 11.3 Word clouds

Source: from Screenshot from IBM's 'Many Eyes' website, Courtesy of International Business Machines Corporation, copyright © International Business Machines Corporation.

Word Trees shows the contexts in which words are used. Figure 11.4 shows a word tree from the same school inspection report for the word 'behaviour'. From this we can see with what themes and ideas 'behaviour' is associated in the report. This presentation seems to suggest (a) that behaviour is an important indicator and (b) that behavioural problems seem to be endemic.

These visualisations do not provide answers but they can help us get to grips with our data.

11.4.3 Technology and data coding and analysis

The greatest impact of technology has been in the area of data coding and analysis. Bolinger et al. (2004) note that one of the strengths of computer assisted qualitative data

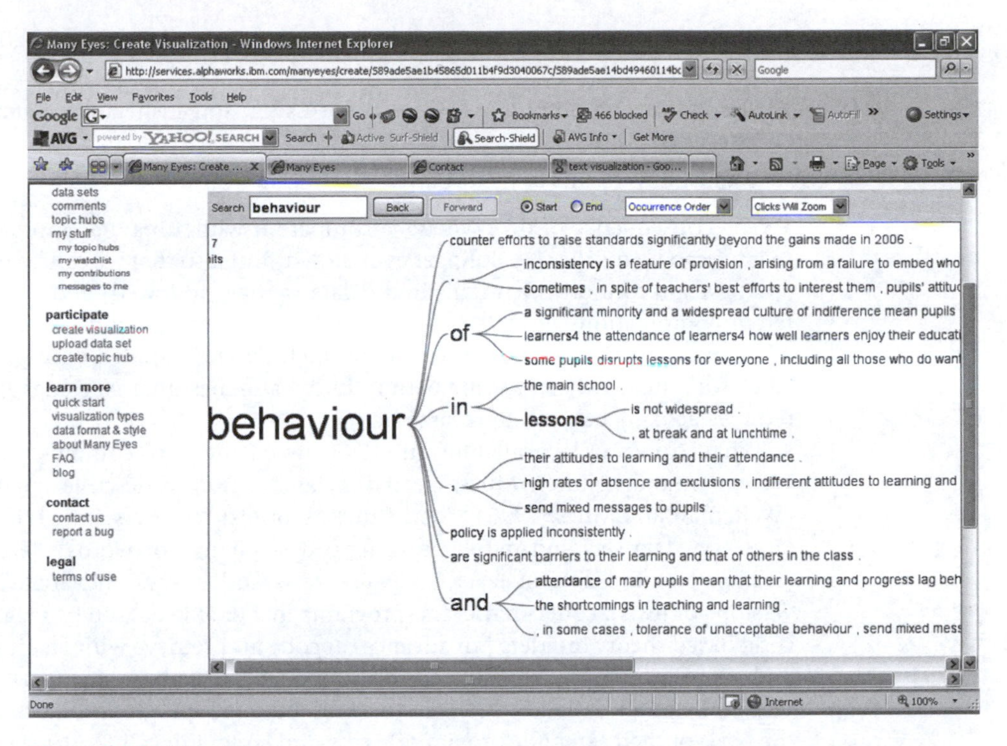

Figure 11.4 Word tree
Source: from Screenshot from IBM's 'Many Eyes' website, Courtesy of International Business Machines Corporation, copyright © International Business Machines Corporation.

software analysis (CAQDAS): is 'the ability to organise data and its analysis efficiently' (p. 250). They note, amongst other things, the automation of clerical tasks, speedier access to data and the ability to handle complex searches. All of this amounts to a faster data analysis and a clear record of the process of and stages in the analysis. To this extent, most software (and there is a lot) would meet Spencer et al.'s (2003) criteria for quality in qualitative research, particularly the points in section 12 in Table 11.1.

What do the software packages actually do? Ann Lewins and Christina Silver are funded (in 2008) by the UK's Economic and Social Research Council to support the effective use of CAQDAS. Their Working Paper (Lewins and Silver, 2006) identifies the elements found in most CADQAS packages.

- They act as 'containers' for the project. Some store the data internally, some access data that is stored elsewhere. It used to be that local operating systems could not manage large databases but local computer memory is now so large that this is ceasing to be the case.
- They provide rapid access to data.
- They enable us to search data, either in its original or tagged form. Searches can be complex and usually display data in context.
- They enable us to code data, though we have to define the codes. They are in this regard a 'mechanisation' of qualitative research. Insight and creativity remain in the domain of the researcher. Coding frameworks are to hand and enable us to be more consistent in our coding.
- They allow us to search the data set to apply existing codes (this is called 'autocoding') and to move between descriptive and interpretive coding.

- They allow us to annotate the coding process by recording our thoughts and hunches on memos.
- Results can be outputted to word processing, spreadsheets and statistical analysis packages.
- Many allow results to be displayed diagrammatically.

The consequence of this, when we compare it with a manual approach, is not only that we can be quicker (as Bolinger et al. noted) but also that we can be better organised (we have a record of which trails in the data we have followed) and we can explore different combinations of codes in our search for an explanation (many of the systems allow us to search in ways that we can on the Internet (so-called Boolean searches) with 'and', 'or', 'not', etc., and some permit 'fuzzy' searches, that is, things that are like the term we actually put into the search box).

What software is available? In 1995 two American computer scientists, Eben Weitzman and Matthew Miles, created a classification to describe qualitative software (Weitzman and Miles, 1995). Their structure of text retrievers (programs that can scan large text data sets and retrieve specific text sequences or words), textbase managers (storage and indexing of texts, images of texts and images and archiving of changed versions of texts), coders retrievers (programs that enable data to be tagged with codes), code-based theory builders (an advance on code and retrieve with facilities for grouping and naming groups of codes, creating hierarchical coding structures, making notes within the program) and conceptual network builders (programs that associate codes on the basis of their semantic proximity) is, by and large, still valid today. Figure 11.5 shows the software that they classified. Even then there was much overlap between the sets. Since then four things have happened.

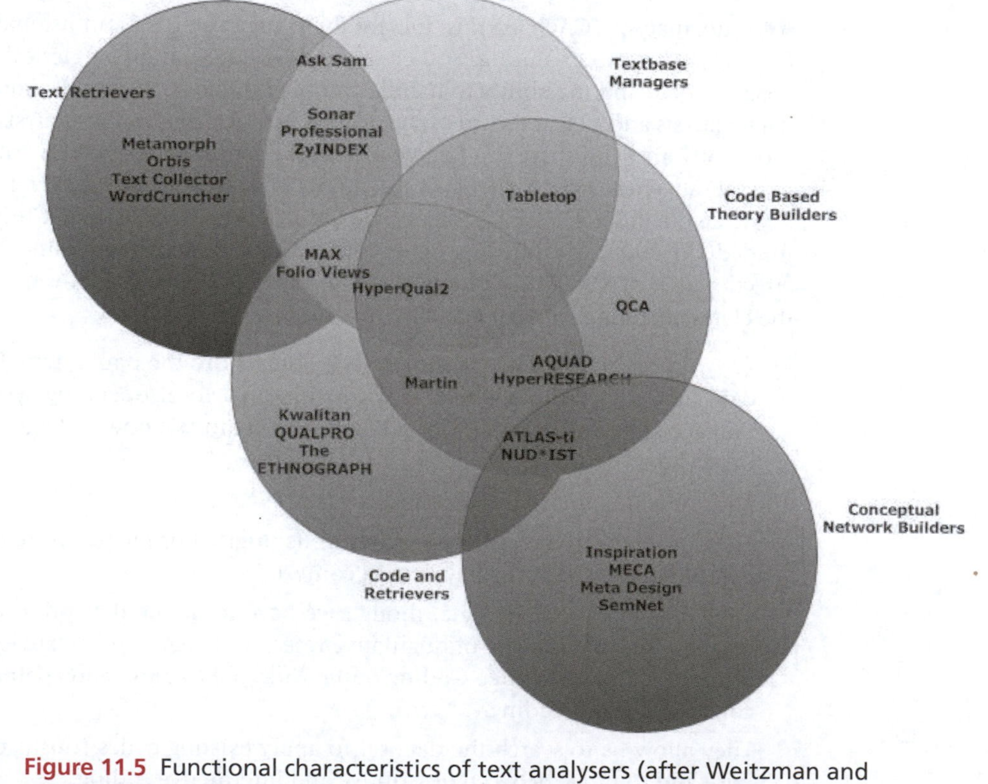

Figure 11.5 Functional characteristics of text analysers (after Weitzman and Miles, 1995)

First, the number of software solutions has increased (though some in Weitzman and Miles' sets have been taken over or disappeared). Second, the range of functions they perform has increased. Third, the differences between them have shrunk. Fourth, specialised software has appeared.

Table 11.2 shows some of the current qualitative analysis software. It can be divided into two types, general purpose software (such as the first seven in the table) and specialist software (the remainder). The general purpose software usually manages a range of inputs, coding, searching and autocoding, theming, and data visualisation. The specialist programmes deal with data types (video, digital, text) or archiving or pro forma mark ups. Other programs are listed at the following websites:

http://www.eval.org.resources/QDA.htm

http://www.intute.ac.uk/socialsciences (and input search 'qualitative analysis').

Table 11.2 Features of text analysis software

Software	Features	www
The Ethnograph	Code and retrieve text.	http://www.qualisresearch.com/
MAXQDA	Code and retrieve text and digital data, data visualisations, geo referencing.	http://www.maxqda.com/
AQUAD	Code and retrieve text and multimedia.	http://www.aquad.de/eng/index.html
Kwalitan	Code and retrieve text and multimedia.	http://www.kwalitan.net/engels/
ATLAS-ti	Code and retrieve text and multimedia, data visualisations.	http://www.atlasti.com/
Nvivo	Code and retrieve text and multimedia, visualisation and theory building.	http://www.qsrinternational.com
HyperResearch	Code and retrieve text and multimedia, visualisation and theory building.	http://www.researchware.com/
Framework	Code and retrieve text. Aids theory building with framework template layout. Audit trail explicit.	http://www.natcen.ac.uk
Qualrus	Code and retrieve text and multimedia, visualisation and theory building.	http://www.ideaworks.com/qualrus/index.html
QDA Miner	Code and retrieve text with option to quantify results.	http://www.provalisresearch.com/
C-I-SAID	Code and retrieve text with option to quantify results.	http://www.code-a-text.co.uk/cisaid.htm
Transana	Digital audio and visual data.	http://www.transana.org/
Folio Views	Information retrieval.	http://www.thefiengroup.com/
ELAN	Multimedia annotation.	http://www.mpi.nl/tools/
QCA	Numeric and text data, code and analyse, numerical outputs. For comparative analysis.	http://www.compasss.org/
ZyIMAGE	Searchable archiving system.	http://www.zylab.com/
Ask Sam	Searchable free-form database.	http://www.asksam.com/

▶

Table 11.2 *(continued)*

Software	Features	www
Concordance	Text analysis.	http://www.concordancesoftware.co.uk/
Super HyperQual	Text data coding and analysis.	http://home.satx.rr.com/hyperqual/
Orbis	Text retrieval.	http://www.notabene.com/
Sonar Professional	Text retrieval and document management.	http://www.virginiasystems.com/index.html
Texis and Metamorph	Text search engine.	http://www.thunderstone.com/texis/site/pages/metamorph.html
EXMARaLDA	Transcription and annotation of spoken language.	http://exmaralda.org/en_index.html
Anvil	Video annotation.	http://www.anvil-software.de/

How do we choose which programme to use? Ann Lewins and Christina Silver have expanded their Working Paper (Lewins and Silver, 2006) into a book that should be read by anyone beyond the beginners' stage in qualitative research. It deals in considerable detail with the processes outlined here and illustrates them in relation to three leading programs; *ATLAS-ti, MAXqda* and *Nvivo*. The general advice with respect to selecting software is to examine what programs offer in relation to what the research enquiry requires. For example, if we are going to use one of the specific approaches to data analysis that we look at later in this chapter rather than the generic approach we reviewed in Section 11.3, it is important that the technology works in the way the technique requires. If, however, you are at the start of your research journey (as many readers of this book will be), this advice is not particularly helpful. Most people in this position will make their choice in one of the following ways: if they are part of a university, then they will choose the one the university subscribes to or, if not, then price is the criterion. Realistically, when we are learning and gaining experience, this is a perfectly acceptable strategy. However, as we embark on a major piece of work (such as doctoral research or a funded piece of academic or professional research), we should review the software options in more detail because some of the programs are based upon quite distinct method (and methodological) differences. As the German sociologist, Udo Kelle, has pointed out, *The Ethnograph* is rooted in phenomenological and ethnographical approaches, *MAXqda* has its conceptual origins in Max Weber's concept of 'ideal types' and *AQUAD* was influenced by a 'Popperian methodological approach' (Kelle, 1997). We cannot escape the fact that, in much qualitative research, methodology, software and interpretation are inextricably linked.

The increasing sophistication of most generic software packages has seen concerns grow about their potential to distance a researcher from their data. Indeed the range of options within programs has probably led to more 'experimentation' with the data, that is, sorting and sifting data and generally trying things out just to see what emerges. This image of 'experimentation' is picked up by a Czech social scientist, Zdenek Konapasek. His argument is that modern software is more than a tool, it is a 'virtual environment for . . . practice-based knowledge making' (Konapasek, 2008). He points out that the technology is 'the interface in which and through which we do thinking'. He could also reasonably argue that it is also an aid to our creative thinking.

Notwithstanding Konapasek's representation of the consequences of technology for qualitative research, it is clear that computer assisted qualitative research and analysis is sufficiently well established for continued innovation in product development. Hyperlinking within data is becoming established. This is likely to drive the need for inbuilt multi-dimensional analysis and visualisation of relationships. It is, however, the automated transcription of the spoken word that will make a qualitative strategy more attractive for many researchers.

11.5 Coding, theming and explanation in context: an introduction to qualitative approaches

Qualitative analysis, so far, has been presented as a generic approach. However, this is something of a simplistic assumption, as we shall see in the following pages. Qualitative researchers can approach their data from a large number of competing positions, each legitimate but each possibly producing different explanations. On the one hand are researchers who believe there is a single reality in the world they study (and, by implication, a single, correct explanation of events). On the other hand there are many more researchers who believe that the researcher constructs one out of countless explanations. Then there are some, like Gerald Cupchik, a Canadian psychology professor, who see a halfway house where there are common patterns of daily life (Cupchik, 2001). Realism, constructivism and constructivist realism – the field of qualitative research can resemble a jungle that poses many dangers for the innocent researcher. But as if this were not enough, there are differences in the way we can go about our research. Some qualitative researchers adopt a deductive approach and others (many more) have an approach that is inductive. Then there are those who approach qualitative research from the perspective of critical theory who believe that 'facts' should be looked at from the perspective of power and authority relationships and that the realist/constructivist debate is an irrelevance. Add to this the fact that researchers come with their own personal baggage, their subject culture, their research preferences, their personal goals (the box on the right side of Figure 11.1) and we see that qualitative research is not just an exceedingly complex field, it is one that is in a constant state of flux, shifting and developing all the time. It is *impossible* to construct a simple representation of qualitative research because the field itself is not coherent. All a book like this can reasonably do is pick out some islands of (relative) stability and describe how data analysis happens there. This is what the next sections do.

Before we look at approaches to qualitative analysis in detail, it will be helpful if we set out *some* of the situations in which we can use them and see what alternatives we have if we want to use them in these ways. Table 11.3 sets out the nature of our research enquiry and what approaches might be considered. At this point we should emphasise that if your type of enquiry does not match what is in this table, it does not mean (a) that you should panic because the table cannot show every type of enquiry and (b) that you cannot use any of the methods that are shown in the table. It is also possible that some of

Table 11.3 What do we want to find out?

Study type	Research approaches
I want to understand my subjects' experiences of life.	• Grounded theory. • Narrative analysis. • Phenomenography. • Content analysis.
I want to understand how people construct and represent themselves and their worlds.	• Conversation analysis. • Semiotics. • Discourse analysis.
I want to understand my data in the context of power and equality relationships.	• Critical discourse analysis.
I want to test what others have found.	• Template analysis. • Discourse analysis. • Narrative analysis. • Content analysis.
I want to test out the applicability of a concept or theory.	• Template analysis. • Discourse analysis. • Narrative analysis. • Content analysis.

these types of enquiry can be combined but at this stage our intention is to keep things as simple as possible.

- If we want to get insights into our subjects' worlds (sometimes we see this described as 'life worlds'), then the four approaches in Table 11.3 are possibilities. Phenomenography is the only approach that puts this goal in the foreground, so if we want to use the other approaches we must ensure that our data collection is appropriately structured.
- The second approach, how people construct themselves and their worlds, takes as its assumption that people see themselves (and may want to be seen) in particular ways. One head teacher might want to be seen as caring and supportive, another as a chief executive of a mid-size organisation. One young person who has left school with poor or no qualifications and has no job, may see themselves as a failure, another who has excellent grades but who was not admitted to a top university may also see themselves as a failure. The three approaches, conversation, discourse and semiotic analysis, have different starting points. Conversation analysis looks at how we use verbal interaction to achieve our objective, discourse analysis at how written or spoken text and semiotic analysis can use speech, text, images and objects.
- The third approach, how broad social structures that reflect who wields and exercises power over whom and which influence our interpretation of our data, pushes us towards critical discourse analysis. This idea of 'critical' as an approach can be applied to other types of qualitative analysis (such as critical narrative analysis) but they are not considered here.
- The fourth and fifth approaches, testing other people's findings and testing theory, are effectively the same issue and the approaches we might use are the same. Template

Table 11.4 National assessment systems: ages of assessment

	National standardised assessment system	At school entry	During compulsory primary education	During compulsory secondary education
England	Yes	5	7,8,9,10,11	14
Ireland	Yes	No	7,10	
Northern Ireland	Yes	4/5	8,11	14
Scotland	Yes	Varies	Varies and 8,10,12	Varies and 14
Wales	Yes	4/5	7,11	14
France	Yes	No	8	11,15
Germany	No	6	No	
Hungary	Yes	6	10	12,14,16
Italy	Yes	No	No	
Netherlands	Yes	No	12 (most)	14,15
Spain	Yes	No	12	16
Sweden	Yes	No	9	12,14,16
Switzerland	No	No	No	No
Australia	No	(No)	Varies	Varies
Canada	(Yes)	No	Varies	Varies
Japan	Yes	No	12	15
Korea	Yes	No	12	15/16
New Zealand	Yes	5/6	8/9	12/13
Singapore	Yes	No	10,12	
USA	Yes	Varies	Varies	Varies

Source: Reproduced form Table 9.1, *National Standardised Assessment,* INCA at http://www.inca.org.uk/pdf/table9.pdf (accessed 26 October 2009).

analysis ensures that the specifics of how other people have worked are reflected in our approach. For the other approaches, we use other people's findings or theory constructs to direct what we look for in our analysis.

Let us now look at these approaches in detail.

11.6 Template analysis

Template analysis epitomises the fluidity of qualitative research with different approaches, all with common elements, bearing the same name. It differs from many other qualitative analysis approaches because, unlike these where the strategy is to let the codes emerge from the data (bottom up), the strategy with template analysis is based on working top down, at least in the initial stages.

In general, a template is a predetermined framework of concepts that are represented as codes and the template we will use will be specific to our research issue. Where does a template come from? The answer is from one of the following three sources:

1. It is one that has been used before. If this is the case we are using it either to test the applicability and reliability of the method or to see whether results obtained in an earlier study are applicable elsewhere.
2. Alternatively, it could arise from the nature of the research question. If we were evaluating a policy or a process (such as a policy on the transfer of children from primary to secondary school or the process of transfer in a particular area), the template is likely to be dependent on the objectives or goals of the policy.
3. Finally, it can come from any combination of existing knowledge about an issue and the philosophical perspective that the researchers choose to work within. Most template analysis research seems to have its origins here. We shall look at two examples of this in more detail.

11.6.1 Using a template to analyse literature

The first example of template analysis shows the use of templates in a developing area of educational (and social) research, the synthesis of research evidence. This has long been standard practice in medical research (where, for example, different tests of medical interventions are brought together to see whether the results conflict or are confirmatory). This type of research is called 'metanalysis'. It was used by an American educationalist, Wayne An, in a study of what he calls 'high stakes testing' (An, 2007). This he describes as 'when . . . results are used to make important decisions that affect students, teachers, administrators, schools and districts'. A typical example would be the existence of national tests for specific age groups that are then used as an index of quality, a measure of organisational and management effectiveness and as a tool to guide parental selection of a school. How ubiquitous such tests are is shown in Table 11.4, which reproduces an analysis presented on the INCA website (International Reviews of Curriculum and Assessment Frameworks). Germany has the least high stakes testing and the UK, Hungary and Sweden the most. Without doubt such testing is important and leads to such questions as whether school standards are improving, the impact on the curriculum, the impact on pupils and the consequences for teachers. An explored whether the research showed if high states testing had any effect on the curriculum, the expectation being that the curriculum would become configured to deliver good test results. He looked at 49 separate studies and assessed them against a coding template that he devised. His basic coding structure was built around three categories, subject matter content, pedagogy and structure of knowledge, and he looked for evidence that change had occurred in these three areas. He assessed the reliability of his own coding by having 2,090 samples from the 49 texts coded by other people. The intercoder reliability was almost 90 per cent.

An's is an effective approach in a growing area of educational research and while his substantive results are less important than his method in a methodological text, they are nonetheless, of interest. He found the following significant consequences of high stakes testing:

- contraction of content and move to teacher-centred pedagogy in 70.3 per cent of studies;
- increase in teacher-centred pedagogy and knowledge fragmentation in 65.7 per cent of studies;

- contraction in content and increase in knowledge fragmentation in 64.7 per cent of studies;
- content expansion and increased knowledge integration in 26.5 per cent of studies;
- increase in student-centred pedagogy and knowledge integration in 17.1 per cent of studies;
- content expansion *and* contraction in 16.3 per cent of studies;
- content expansion and increased teacher-centred pedagogy in 16.2 per cent of studies;
- content expansion and increased pupil-centred pedagogy in 16.2 per cent of studies.

As An points out, the bulk of the evidence outlined above shows that high stakes testing harms the curriculum. However, we should not ignore the fact that a minority of studies showed improvements in curriculum (if a pupil-centred pedagogy, greater content and integration of knowledge are felt to be better in educational terms). The question we should now be asking is this, 'If testing works in some situations and not others, why not?' An has pointed out the anomaly, the next research agenda is to find out why it exists.

11.6.2 Using a template to study interview data

Most of the data that qualitative educational researchers use comes from what people tell them and the interview is a particularly important source of this data. The next example of template analysis uses interview data but there are some interesting twists to the study.

The authors, Jennifer Fereday and Eimear Muir-Cochrane, are a research nurse and nurse educator respectively in South Australia. Their research area was the feedback nurses were given about their work. Nurses used this as evidence for their continued professional registration (in the medical world it is paramount that practitioners demonstrate continuing competence). From focus groups with nurses and clinical managers the two researchers collected a wealth of data on how performance feedback was given, received and used. They subjected this to an initial template analysis. The template was derived from two sources:

- the research questions – how nurses received, judged and used the feedback and its value and utility; and
- the concept of social phenomenology developed by Alfred Schutz (Schutz 1967). While this is too large a topic to explain here, it is, in essence, an assumption that our life circumstances and our social interactions create shared meanings and understanding, which (a) establish an apparently objective world and (b) establish our experience (knowledge) that we use to communicate with, assess and judge others and operate in the shared world.

Drawing on these two sources, the coding framework they constructed consisted of six categories of code: motives, social relationships, the meanings of social actions, systems of relevance, ideal types and 'common sense'. In social relationships, for example, they differentiated three interactions: 'we-relations', where there was interaction, 'thou-relations' where the relationship was not reciprocal and 'they-relations' where the relationship lacked individuality and personal identity and rested on a shared understanding of what is common, typical or expected. This template is straight out of Schutz's conceptualisation of social phenomenology. Two other features are of methodological interest in this study.

First, the process of creating the template structure and data collection were concurrent. Thus the template may well have informed the data collection process. Second, the template evolved as the data was assessed. In effect, an inductive approach was then used to create additional codes. The research programme continued to identify themes. The key conclusions reached by the researchers are interesting because of their general applicability to anyone receiving feedback, from lecturers whose classes are observed to students whose work is graded. Fereday and Muir-Cochrane identified the following:

- The seniority of the person providing feedback was important in determining the credibility of the feedback for those new to the process.
- When people worked together, the credibility of the feedback was greater.
- Familiarity bred trust and respect.
- When feedback showed that the giver understood the total work context, its credibility was greater.
- Shared experiences made feedback more credible.
- Delays in giving feedback or absence of follow-up reduced the credibility of feedback.

11.6.3 Using templates to interface data collection and analysis

Some of the data used by qualitative researchers is not collected by free-form interview but via structured and semi-structured interviews. However, the software tools that have been developed for analysis have not reflected the possibilities of linking the coding process (in data analysis) with a structured process of data collection. In other words, the interview process can reflect a coding structure. So, for instance, Fereday and Muir-Cochrane could have linked the six categories of code to specific questions (that is, tagged the questions) and then applied the second level coding to the individual responses.

This issue has been picked up by an agency, the Centers for Disease Control and Prevention of the US Department of Health and Human Services. It has created a software package (EZ-Text), which links a question in a survey to a template in the analysis engine. Thus each question and each individual's response to that question is treated as a separate database entry. The programme also permits the definition of codes against which to assess the data and their application to the data. While the programme has been designed for semi-structured interviews, it is capable of handling large segments of free-form text. The tool (developed by Carey et al., 1998) is available on a free download from the Centers for Disease Control and Prevention at http:www.cdc.gov/hiv/topics/surveillance/resources/software/ez-text/index.htm.

11.7 Qualitative content analysis

The second qualitative research approach we shall examine is content analysis. This is a set of procedures that can be applied to any message medium (text, spoken word, actions video recordings) to identify what is being communicated, by whom and to whom. It is concerned with the significance and meaningfulness of the communication. Thus it is concerned not just with words but also on the concepts and ideas that are being communicated.

It began its existence as a quantitative tool to explore communication, the implication being that the greater the frequency of occurrence of content (a word or phrase) the more important was that element of the message to the communicator. If a school or university prospectus uses words like 'friendly', 'pastoral care', 'caring', 'sociable' and 'welcoming' more than any others, we have a quantitative representation of what it wants to communicate. Quantitative content analysis is possible even with standard word processing packages but more sophisticated programs (such as some of those found on IBM's Many Eyes website) can show associations. There are also programs that will find pairs of words or word sets within a defined range of text. Qualitative content analysis, in contrast, creates a coding structure based on the researcher's interpretation and identification of meaning in a message, and in this case it might conclude that the emphasis on the social at the expense of the academic might imply that its standards and aspirations are not high.

It is not surprising to find that the caring professions (particularly health and social care) use qualitative analysis extensively because so much of their concerns are with interactions and emotional states. Two nurse educators, Hsiu-Fang Hsieh from Taiwan and Sarah E. Shannon working in Seattle, USA, reviewed how researchers were applying it (Hsieh and Shannon, 2005). They distinguished three approaches:

1. *Conventional content analysis*, which works by coding the data collected by the researcher – essentially the coding approach that we saw in section 11.3.
2. *Directed content analysis*, which begins with a theoretical or hypothetical proposition and uses this to construct a coding structure – essentially the process that we met when we considered template analysis in section 11.6.
3. *Summative content analysis*, which selects keywords based on previous research or the interest of the researcher in the text. This approach is more individual than the others (that is, it is more distinctive from other approaches to qualitative analysis than other types of content analysis). Its object is to understand how words are used in context. As the authors say, it 'is an attempt not to infer meaning but, rather, to explore usage' (p. 1283). It has been used in studies of death and dying, where emotional impact often means that people can only talk about it through euphemism. This is not unusual in teaching and will certainly be familiar to teachers who are asked to take classes on sex education but who have not been trained in personal and social education.

It can be difficult to see much daylight between qualitative content analysis and other approaches to qualitative analysis, even some of the other approaches we shall meet later, such as grounded theory. But there are features that set it apart, though whether they are sufficiently compelling for it to be categorised as a method in its own right is debatable.

The first feature to note is that the analysis can be and often is quantified. This is an important statement that, perhaps, ought to be more generally found in qualitative research. Counts of words that define or describe an element or feature of a message are indicators. Whether such counts are valid indicators is another matter. But what could they indicate? Either the message at face value, that the school is caring, in our example, or a deeper message, that the school is primarily for non-academic pupils, which might be incorrect. However, some qualitative researchers would exclude content analysis from their qualitative research toolbox when quantitative summaries are included. Activity 11.4 provides an opportunity for you to judge the value of quantitative indicators in qualitative research.

The second feature that creates distinctiveness is the focus of the enquiry. Klaus Krippendorf, a German communications scientist working in the USA, who has been

Activity 11.4 Should we quantify qualitative codes?

Children are an important segment of the economy. They are significant consumers both in terms of what their parents spend on them and in their own right. The UK bank, Halifax, conducts an annual survey of the money children receive each week from their parents ('pocket money'). In 2006, the average for children aged 7 to 16 was £8.20 with more for girls (£8.66) than boys (£7.72) and more for children in London (£11.71) than for children elsewhere. Advertising is an important means of communicating with consumers. Our broader interest as education researchers should mean that we are interested in the message contained in advertisements targeted at children.

This is the issue that an American professor of nutrition, Carol Byrd-Bredbenner, investigated. She looked at the content of advertisements broadcast on Saturday mornings in 1993 and 1999. Her template was one that had been used in other studies. It was used to record information about the advert, length, type (commercial product, TV programme) and product advertised. In addition it coded the following for food: the type of food, the individuals in the advertisement and compliance with advertising industry guidelines. The results were as follows:

- A fall in advertisements for products from 69% of the total in 1993 to 55% in 1999.
- An increase in food advertising from 69% of the total product advertising in 1993 to 78% in 1999.
- An increase in the total of fats and sweets from 36% of the food advertisements in 1993 to 53% in 1999 and fast-food restaurants from 23% in 1993 to 28% in 1999. There were no advertisements for vegetables, fruit and protein-rich foods.

Your tasks are:

- To judge whether the quantification of qualitative data counts as a valid indicator in qualitative research. You should review other literature on this topic. A useful starting point is the website of the Advertising Education Forum (http://www.aeforum.org). What else would a qualitative researcher want to know?
- To identify where else this type of approach could be used (e.g. analyses of classroom behaviour).

Source: Byrd-Bredbenner, C. (2002) *Family and Consumer Sciences Research Journal*, 30(3), 382–403.

highly influential in the development of content analysis, has identified the following areas where the method can be used effectively (Krippendorf, 2004). He refers to these areas as 'types of logic'.

- *Extrapolations* of:
  - (a) *trends* (see Carol Byrd-Bredbenner's study described in Activity 11.3)
  - (b) *patterns*, to see whether two or more data sets show characteristics (in education, for example we might look at press coverage of academic standards when assessment grades improve year on year)
  - (c) *differences*, the obverse of our search for patterns. Do two data sets (such as a school prospectus now and one ten years earlier) exhibit different characteristics?
- *Establishing Standards:*
  - (a) *identifying* a feature to prove that it exists in a communication (in education this could be a satisfactory specification of a pupil's misdemeanour when parents are informed that their child is to be suspended from school
  - (b) *evaluation* of communications to show the level of factual accuracy or the existence of bias (for example, in newspaper reporting of educational outcomes)
  - (c) to reach *judgements*, an issue of great concern to education at the present time is plagiarism. Content analysis can be used to demonstrate stylistic and language use differences.

Whether the potential to use quantitative assessments (content analysis was originally a quantitative approach) or its value in certain types of study make content analysis sufficiently distinctive as a method to warrant a place in a separate category is debatable. Certainly, as it explores relationships amongst concepts, it comes closer to other types of qualitative analysis. What is apparent, however, is that its use is widespread in the social sciences, from law to psychology and it is especially strong in media studies. In education and research into young people it has been used to explore topics as varied as the character of young people's personal information on MySpace (Hinduja and Patchin, 2008), group learning processes (Malatalo-Siegl, 2008), school evaluation in the Netherlands (Blok et al., 2008) and the quality of life of 'street children' in South Africa (Vuyisile, 2006).

11.8 Grounded theory

Grounded theory is an approach to social science research that makes use of coding as a means of extracting the information from data. It goes further than the approach to coding we looked at in section 11.3, however, in that its object is to generate theory from the data (theory that can be tested through later research), rather than just make sense of the data. Its approach is distinctive, too, in that the bottom up process of sifting primary data (that is, the data we collect ourselves) can be informed after our preliminary analysis by secondary data and even new primary data and other research conclusions.

The approach takes its name from the fact that the theory that is generated is *grounded* in real world data. In other words, it is not a generalisation or idealisation of reality. It is not what should be, might be or could be under certain circumstances. It is what is. Whether what the process produces is really theory can be a moot point. There is, however, no doubt that what it seeks to produce is a statement or conclusion that should be applicable or can be tested in similar circumstances.

Grounded theory is arguably the most popular (and, if not the most popular, then one of the most referenced) qualitative research methods. In fact, with its holistic view of the process of theory building, it can reasonably be referred to as a methodology. It was developed in the 1960s by two American sociologists, Barney Glaser and Anselm Strauss, for their work on dying while in hospital. Their interest in the topic was a reflection that both had experienced family bereavement in the recent past and the approach they developed was influenced by their research backgrounds. Glaser had a quantitative background and Strauss' background was rooted in social psychology and symbolic interactionism. This assumes that meaning is created through interaction between people and that our understanding of meaning and meaningfulness affects the way we act. The implication of this idea is that beyond 'reality' is a world of symbols that are socially and culturally created. We shall meet this idea again when we look at another method of qualitative analysis, semiotics, later in the chapter.

The method that Glaser and Strauss developed is a combination of (a) coding and assembling data into themes, followed by the comparisons of outcomes with previous results (the constant comparative method) and (b) the need to understand a sensitive topic such as dying through experiential and phenomenographic data. Their method was a mix of quantitative rigour, which was represented in the procedure to be followed, and 'soft' data. This clearly was a product of their respective origins. Grounded theory embraces the richness of the qualitative world with a rigour and within a framework that owes much to quantitative research.

But grounded theory is more complex than this because we should refer not to grounded theory but to grounded theories – and for many researchers it is important to distinguish between them. Equally, however, there are others who believe that arguing over the differences between them is akin to counting the number of angels that can stand on a pin-head, that is, it is ultimately pointless.

11.8.1 Classic grounded theory

Classic grounded theory is the version developed by Glaser and Strauss and described by them in *The Discovery of Grounded Theory* (Glaser and Strauss, 1967). Because it makes use of the coding process, we can best understand its distinctiveness by seeing how Glaser and Strauss' approach is different from template analysis.

- It is inductive in its approach, that is, it starts with the data and seeks to find pattern in the data, not impose frameworks upon it. Template analysis begins deductively as the analytic frameworks are predetermined. Grounded theory has to be rooted in what the data is telling us whereas template analysis has the potential to distort what messages might lie in the data.
- It challenges and tests decisions that we have already made about coding. It seeks to question or verify the applicability of codes both in relation to new primary data and also in relation to previous research findings. It evaluates its own procedure and also existing conclusions. Template analysis requires no such procedure. Compared with grounded theory, it is a static and unchanging procedure.
- It anticipates that researchers will constantly be thinking about their data, their codes and the interrelationships between them. It recognises that reading, thinking and rereading is often a stimulus to creative insight about relationships, themes and structures. For this reason it expects researchers to note down their thoughts. This is called 'memoing'. Template analysis does not make this assumption. It is more a process for extending a framework of understanding to new situations or testing the general applicability of such a framework.
- It moves forward in a distinctive way through the coding and theming process with specific stages, often with feedback from one stage to another. Template analysis is much simpler and requires us only to assess the data in terms of the specification of a pre-existing template.
- Theorisation to explain patterns in the data is an integral part of the process. Template analysis can remain at a descriptive level.

Understanding how the analytical and data generalisation process works is central to appreciating the contribution of Glaser and Strauss to qualitative analysis. The actual techniques used are much as described in section 11.5, so it is the *process* that establishes its distinctive contribution. The process has three stages and two generic processes that transcend the stages (Figure 11.6). The three stages are:

1. *Substantive coding:* this is also called 'open coding' and is the initial coding stage. The goal is to develop a set of codes that summarises the *researcher's* assessment of the data. The expectation is that the researcher approaches the data without preconceptions and reacts to the data on its own terms. The process is an interactive one. Normally the researcher reads through or observes the data, noting down any ideas or observations (this is the memoing process which continues throughout). After the initial read through and having digested the implications of the memos, the next stage is to identify data units and

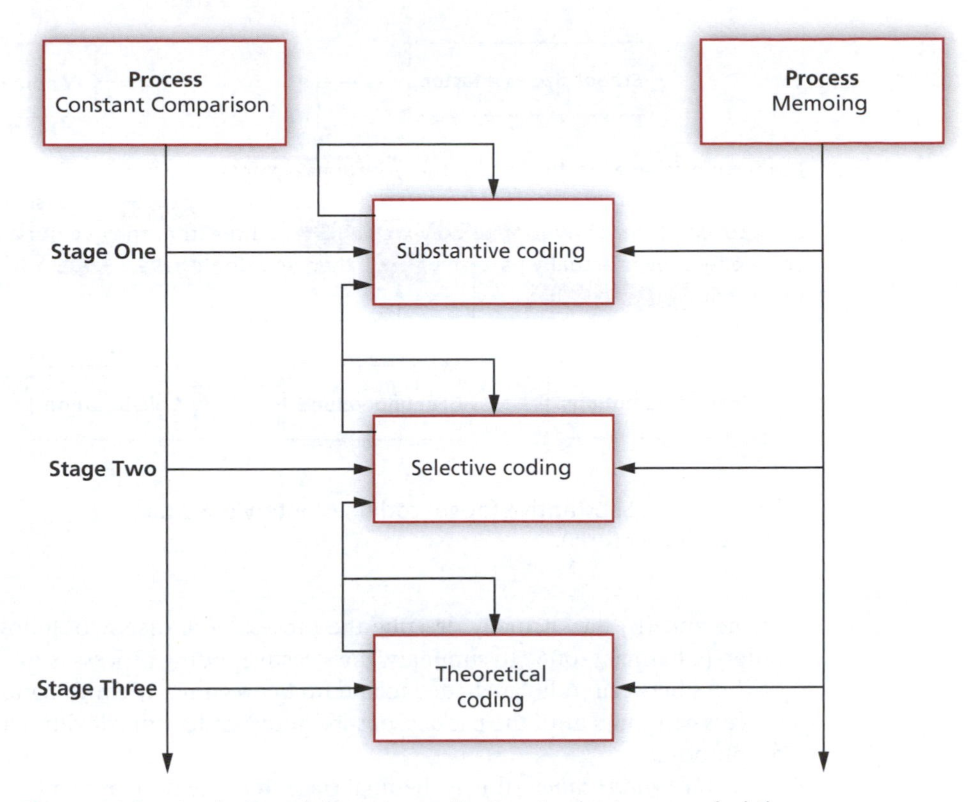

Figure 11.6 Analysis and data generalisation in classic grounded theory

describe them with a code. This is essentially the process we saw in section 11.3. What are the data units and where do the codes come from? The data units are those segments of the data that contain something of meaning in the context of the research. They can be anything from an expression or word, through a sentence to a paragraph or a longer section of data. For example, if we are investigating why parents do not act before legal proceeding are taken against them for not ensuring that their children go to school and we are told that, 'I couldn't make sense of the letters that I got', we might code this as 'complex communication/difficult language.' The codes come out of the text and may be words used in the text or terms chosen by the researcher. The codes will undoubtedly be influenced by where the researcher is coming from. Dr Barry Brooker's study of what stakeholders in a school understood by leadership uses open coding from the classic grounded theory approach to analyse interview and documentary data. Figure 11.7 shows an example of this first stage coding process (Brooker, 2005, p. 58).

2. *Selective coding:* this moves us forward into a process of grouping codes together on the basis of some overarching idea. If a parent told us that 'I didn't get any letters brought home', with the implication that the child failed to deliver them, we might code this as 'failure to ensure effective communication'. With the other code, 'complex communication/difficult language' we might put it into a higher level code called 'poor communication'. The process seeks to find a link between codes that will bind them to a core idea, the theoretical code. Because grounded theory assumes that a core idea exists, it can be a trying process. It is, perhaps, for this reason that Kathy Charmaz uses the terms 'initial' and 'focused' coding to describe the processes of substantive (initial) and selective (focused) coding because (a) they make no assumption that there is a single unifying

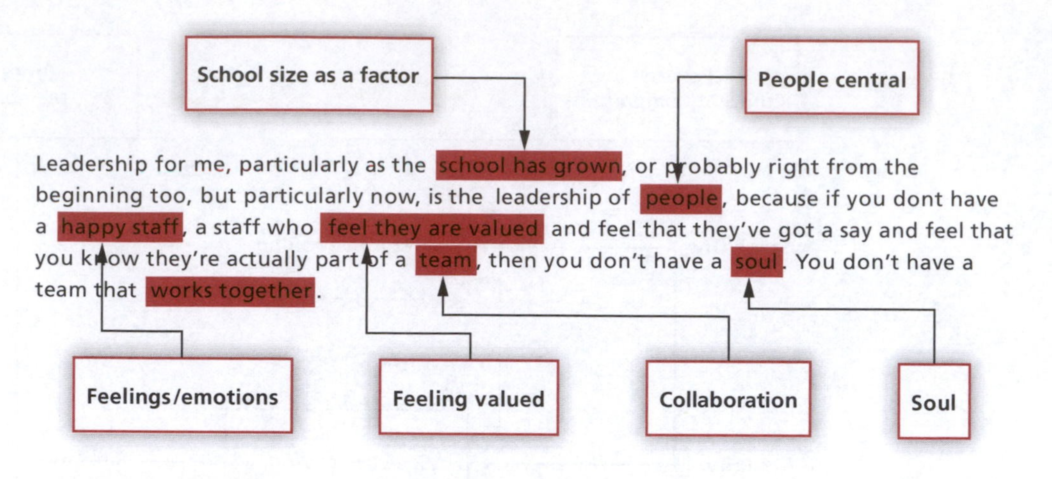

Figure 11.7 Substantive (open) coding of interview data
Source: Brooker (2005).

theme and (b) they actually describe the process of a 'first stab' followed by 'creating order' (Charmaz, 2006) In summary, the selective coding process is one in which possible links between codes are batted to and fro between many combinations of codes. The process continues until the package of substantive codes linked with selective codes is fit for purpose.

3. *Theoretical coding:* this is the final stage. It is the development of a core idea that links all the codes together. Our aim is to develop an explanation that fits the selective codes. However, we should not assume that a theoretical code is a single word or even a phrase. It probably will be a statement that explains the relationship between the codes as variables. Such a statement is in other words, the theory that grounded theory seeks to develop. The statement we seek to construct is an explanation of the structures that we have isolated and relationships between them. In our example so far, we might conclude that 'parents whose child does not attend school are concerned about their child. Their inaction is because they do not understand the sequence of events leading to prosecution and a key reason for this is poor communication practice by the school and authorities'. This is the theoretical statement. In edging towards a theoretical statement, we seek to explain 'why?' In other words, the theory is causal or implies causality. In trying to explain 'why' we may find that certain things are not as clear or as well specified as we would like. For this reason it is permissible (and expected) that we go back and reclassify and recode. Case Study 11.4 gives an example of the derivation of a theoretical code.

Let us now take a closer look at the two *processes* identified in Figure 11.6.

- *Constant Comparison:* our grounded theorisation is built upon the coding process. One of the problems with coding is that we can overwhelm ourselves with codes. Our process has to be (a) effective in capturing the meanings in the data set and (b) it has to be efficient in the way it does this. What do we mean here by 'efficiency'? Putting it simply, we have to get as much meaning out of the data as we can with the minimum number of codes. We can never know when we have achieved this but the constant comparative method is our means of getting close to an optimal solution. The approach works in the following way. Let us assume that we are coding responses to a series of questions that subjects could answer in their own way. We

Case study 11.4 Grounding beer drinking in theory

You may think that we can get all we need to know about alcohol consumption from statistics and quantitative analysis. We can certainly find out a lot but no quantitative analysis will tell us how having a headache in the morning is an indication that we had a good time last night and why, if we cannot remember last night, we should think that it is such a good idea to do it again at some time in the not too distant future. The answers to these and other equally difficult questions are to be found in the realm of qualitative analysis.

An Australian marketing lecturer, Simon Pettigrew, took on this challenge. He wanted to understand beer drinking as a social phenomenon and interviewed nearly 450 people in three Australian states in order to do so. In terms of data collection, he makes some interesting points about the imbalance of men and women in his sample. He noted 'the tendency for females to be more cautious and resistant when talking to unknown researchers' even when the researcher was a woman which he attributed to the fact that 'a female approaching another unknown female departs from the social norms associated with public drinking'. Nonetheless, over 400 interviews, varying in length from 20 to 90 minutes, generates a lot of qualitative data.

The interviews were transcribed and imported into a proprietary analytic program, NU*DIST (a forerunner to NVivo). With this scale of data it would be almost impossible to manage it without technological assistance. The approach Pettigrew used as the basis of his analysis was grounded theory. What were his steps in procedure?

1. First he decided on his unit of analysis, that is, the amount of text he would look at and code. He chose to code on a line-by-line basis. He had over 300,000 lines to code!
2. The first stage, substantive coding, was conducted line after line. He generated 201 codes, which described the social and demographic characteristics of the respondent and others concerned all aspects of the consumption process from the image of the beer, through self-image, to the social nature of drinking. Some of these codes were influenced by the researcher's existing understanding of marketing and branding.
3. In the next stage, selective coding, he began the process of grouping the codes. Here the technology was able to help a great deal because it could select types of response and he could assess how significant they were. He gives the example of picking out what men thought of women who drank beer.
4. He does not describe in detail the processes of memoing and constant comparison but they are clearly there in his approach.

So what was the outcome of his research? It was all about individuals managing their image and using beer to communicate group membership, to strengthen their self-image and to enhance their esteem in the eyes of others. And it is not just the beer that influences this image, it is also where we drink it. And what should not surprise us is that all this is what *other* people do, but *we* drink a beer because we like it. It is this explanation that is the theoretical code.

This study is not just a 'bit of fun'. It is potentially very important for education. It shows that we need to look below the surface to really understand issues. How far does the reading material we give to 2-, 3- and 4-year-olds create a sense of being different for a child being brought up by a lone parent? It shows that we need to look beyond what educational researchers are doing in order to discover substantive and methodological insights. With this study we go from marketing to semiotics (see section 11.11.4). perhaps we should ask what aspects of studying the learning process would benefit from a marketing perspective. Is this the key to attract the attention of those who are disaffected?

might begin by looking at the first subject's response and coding it. We then move to the second subject and repeat the process. At this point we would see if (a) the codes we gave to the second subject are applicable to the first (we will already have done the reverse of this because we would know what codes we had developed for the first subject) and (b) whether the two sets of codes overlap. If the codes overlap, we would define new codes to ensure that no idea or element can be coded into two codes. If one seems to be a sub-case of another, we would start to pencil in a hierarchy. With the third subject we apply the codes from the first two subjects and see if there are any more we would like to create. If we do, we would go back and apply these to the first two subjects. This process continues with all subjects and is essentially the same whatever data sets we have and however we choose to work with them. In reality (though Glaser might argue otherwise), in undertaking this process a researcher is not cocooned with just the data set and isolated from the world of scholarship. That is, the process is not conducted in isolation. Experience, knowledge and understanding are all brought to bear on the comparative process. While the process is as we have described it here, examples in the literature of the process at work are virtually non-existent and most researchers appear to gain experience on a trial and error basis. Nonetheless, the constant comparison of subject with subject and data with emerging concepts (selective and finally theoretical codes) is one of the engines that push grounded theorisation from one stage to the next. It is, however, an engine that can grind exceedingly slowly and can become tedious and mind-numbing. Two Norwegian medical researchers, Tove Giske and Barbara Artinian, report that it took them 18 months to code their data using the constant comparative approach – and their sample consisted of interviews with just 18 patients (Giske and Artinian, 2007)! While constant comparison is the method we use to edge towards being effective and efficient, it does not tell us when we are there. Grounded theorists use the concept of 'saturation' to help identify this point. Saturation is achieved when new data does not create new insights (that is, it fits into existing categories). In his work on community based anti-poverty projects in Jamaica, Glenn Bowen reports that the use of the constant comparative method led to his sample size of interviewees growing from 24 to 36, so it can also have an effect on the scale of research activity (Bowen, 2008).

- *Memoing:* the second process that drives grounded theory forward is memoing. This is such an obvious process that it hardly seems worthwhile giving it a name but it is very important. As we work with our data, ideas occur to us and we have to make sure that we do not lose them. Memoing is the process of recording these ideas. It is such a useful and important method of recording thoughts and hunches and the evolution of our analytic ideas and frameworks that it is found extensively in other qualitative methods. Barry Brooker wrote in a memo:

> During the interview the principal was keen to soften any references to areas that were not going as well as she would really like . . . it did leave me wondering whether some actions she undertakes, which seemed to be purely for caring, human reasons, are also done for management and political reasons.
>
> (Brooker, 2005, p. 57)

Melanie Berks and her colleagues at Monash University in Australia identify what we can do with memos:

- Record the how and why of our decisions.
- Comment on the data, which helps us extract meaning (this is Brooker's example above).
- Record thoughts and ideas that may be useful subsequently in framing an analysis.
- Open up the study to other researchers – and other interpretations (Berks et al., 2008).

If grounded theory had stopped here, it would have been a fine achievement and testament to a successful collaboration between two researchers from two different research traditions. Since Glaser and Strauss' work became known, however, qualitative research has expanded greatly and with this expansion has come innovation and change in method.

11.8.2 Grounded theory – mind the gap

If a methodology is never to change, either it has to be regarded as good practice (in other words, researchers are pragmatic and decide that it delivers worthwhile results) or researchers have to believe that there is a correct way of doing things based on philosophical or logical principles (this, for instance, would apply to positivism which underpins much quantitative research). However, neither of these conditions applies to grounded theory. In the 1960s qualitative research was overwhelmingly descriptive. Grounded theory was different and offered a framework that organised procedure, allowed comparison and enabled us to develop explanatory ideas that could be evaluated in other contexts. It not only appealed to qualitative researchers, it won converts. The 1970s and 1980s was a period of growth and consolidation. The amount (and quality) of qualitative research increased but as this happened, variants on the procedure began to appear.

When Anselm Strauss, the same Strauss who had worked with Glaser in the 1960s, published *Qualitative Analysis for Social Scientists* in 1987 he had been working within this developing paradigm for almost 40 years. His book gave the field a methodological coherence that it had previously lacked. He was at pains to point out that the differences in his approach to grounded theory compared with those of Glaser were minor – but the differences were appearing. He also observed that grounded theory 'is not really a specific method or technique. Rather it is a style of doing qualitative analysis' (Strauss, 1987, p. 5). Perhaps this statement shows that he was growing beyond the original conceptualisation of grounded theory. It was, however, the book he published with Juliet Corbin in 1990 (with whom he had been collaborating on medical sociology for almost 20 years), *Basics of Qualitative Research: Grounded Theory Procedures and Techniques*, that exposed the gap. This book was much more focused on the method of grounded theory and, prophetically, it begins with a quote from the philosopher and educationalist John Dewey: 'If the artist does not perfect a new vision in his process of doing, he acts mechanically and repeats some old model fixed like a blueprint in his mind' (Strauss and Corbin, 1990, p. vii). In other words Strauss and Corbin saw grounded theory as an approach that was still evolving to meet different situations and respond to new ideas about how social research should be conceptualised. It was an explicit rejection of the idea that grounded theory had to be conducted exactly as Glaser and Strauss had represented it all those years earlier.

What were the differences that were appearing?

(i) There was an acknowledgement of the fact that a researcher cannot analyse data as an isolated process. To this extent a researcher can never be a neutral observer and must come laden with baggage, which, for some, is conceptually and philosophically heavier than for others.

(ii) While both methods use the same terminology to describe the analytic process (code, comparison, core categories developed as a precursor to theorisation), the words paper over differences. As Walker and Myrich point out, 'They [Strauss and Corbin] have taken what would appear to be a laissez-faire perspective when compared to Glaser' (Walker and Myrich, 2006, p. 551). In other words, they were recognising the need for flexibility to suit circumstances. A change to method, however, means that it is possible to produce a different theoretical interpretation from that which Glaser and Strauss' original method would have generated. Which raises the question, 'Who's right?'

But how significant are these differences? Strauss and Corbin still have three stages to their approach and, while they give the three stages different names from those used in classic grounded theory, they perform really quite similar functions.

- The first stage, *open coding*, tags units of data. With Strauss and Corbin, however, this usually requires line-by-line coding rather than 'chunks of text' coding.
- The second stage, *axial coding*, groups open codes, much the same goal as Glaser and Strauss' *selective coding*. There are, however, some procedural differences. It may be helpful to give an example of axial coding. Two American researchers in special education, Jeannie Lake and Bonnie Billingsley, explored the nature of conflict that can arise between parents and schools. They conducted open-ended interviews, with parents, school officials and conflict mediators exploring the cause, circumstances and resolution of disagreements and used grounded theory to process their data. The open coding generated labels such as 'lack of factual information', 'lack of legal information', 'misunderstanding of parental rights', 'not understanding the operation of educational systems' and 'inability to judge program quality' (Lake and Billingsley, 2000, p. 243). These were bundled together to create an axial code called 'knowledge'. The process *is* this straightforward but it requires an excellent command of language to define the umbrella concepts that describe the axial code. At this stage two brains are often better than one!
- The third stage, *selective coding*, is the selection of a theme to be the core theme on which the explanation rests. Again, the object is not so different from the purpose in classic grounded theory.

And, for the record, Strauss and Corbin's model also incorporates the constant comparison and memoing processes.

To the outside observer, therefore, it may not seem that the differences between the classic approach to grounded theory and what Strauss and Corbin were saying were all that great. In fact, many pragmatic researchers accept the differences with a shrug and an assumption that 'needs must'. But to some, the differences were important and not only could not but also should not be papered over.

You do not write, as Glaser did, 'Strauss' book is without conscience, bordering on immorality' without feeling that you have been betrayed (Glaser, 1992, p. 5). Glaser's response to Strauss and Corbin was a defence of the classic approach but its effect was to fuel debate. Methodologists have sought to define, understand and bridge the differences. Udo Kelle (2005) says that while Glaser may have a point, it is overstated.

What was not happening, however, was any slowing up in the use of grounded theory. Researchers recognised the debate, largely ignored it and went ahead with their research, using the method as they saw fit. This has given rise to what Bill Warburton has called 'the extended grounded theory family' (Warburton, 2005), that is, a whole series of variants on classic grounded theory that have been developed to meet the needs of particular situations or philosophical perspectives. In many regards this continued use and adaptation of grounded theory shows the attachment of the academic community to the approaches. However, there is a sense amongst some researchers (see, for example, Jones and Noble, 2007) that there is a lack of rigour in its implementation and that 'anything goes'. This is a potentially serious criticism and we should ensure that it is not levelled at us. The best way to ensure this is to (a) be transparent and (b) report our method in some detail. Activity 11.5 is an opportunity to practise this.

Activity 11.5 First steps with grounded theory

In 2001, the decennial census in the UK estimated that there were 175,000 young people whose task it was to care for relations, principally grandparents, parents and siblings: 13,000 of them did this for over 50 hours a week. In 2004, the organisation *Carers UK* published a profile of young carers based on a sample of over 6,000. The survey showed that:

- Over half lived in one parent families.
- Most of those cared for are mothers.
- Physical health was the reason for half of the care needs and mental health problems for 29%.
- 60% of young carers provide domestic help, 48% general and nursing care (with 18% providing intimate personal care), 81% provide childcare and 82% provide emotional support.
- 10% of young carers care for more than one person.
- 65% of young carers have provided care for three years or more.

Just these statistics are painful enough and while we might guess at the impact on the carers, there is no substitute for direct engagement with them. Your task is to apply any variant or combination of grounded theory to the young carers' own voices and to prepare a short report explaining and demonstrating your method and summarising your findings on the consequences of being a young carer. The data, available on the Web, are of two types: a film made by young carers and a blog and discussion group used by young carers.

Film: There2Care: http://uk.youtube.com/watch?v=a73iPj_EHE.

Discussion: The Princess Royal Trust for Carers: http://www.youngcarers.net/community/forums.

Source: Dearden, C. and Becker, S. (2004) *Young Carers in the UK*, The 2004 Report, Carers UK, London.

11.9 Discourse analysis

Like grounded theory, discourse analysis is a complex field. The problem for new researchers is that it is used by a range of subjects (from linguistics to psychology and including education) and in each case there are differences in the way in which it is conceptualised and operationalised. This effectively creates a whole series of different discourse analyses. Many approaches focus on the way in which we use language, while others treat communications as a means of representing deeper meanings. The consequence of this is that there is not one single discourse analysis. Rather, it is a federation of approaches that share a common focus, communication, but need not share methods or even beliefs about the nature of evidence. How then can we understand this potpourri of approaches? The answer is to identify what makes them individual. The result of this, however, is that there is not a simple framework that we can use to represent the field of discourse analysis. Instead, we have to accept that we are dealing with a cluster of approaches held together by a belief in the significance of communication as a source of insight.

This section begins with an overview of discourse analysis and then considers some different approaches within the discourse analysis family.

11.9.1 Discourse analysis: an overview

Discourse analysis is concerned with the way in which we use language. At one level, language is a tool for basic communication and, at another, it is a means of representing an understanding of ideas and also developing those ideas. In 1822 Charles Babbage, a British mathematician and engineer, set out ideas for something he called a 'difference engine'. What he proposed we now call a 'computer'. However, a computer, early in the twentieth century, was a person who managed and manipulated statistics. While we use the 'computer' today to describe what sits on our desks, the term is not a particularly accurate description of what many of us actually use it for, word processing, graphic design, surfing the Web and playing music and video. It does not take too much imagination to think that one day soon we will be calling it something different. Language evolves to reflect and enable intellectual and material innovation. At the same time it is the means through which we construct messages that others will interpret with the meanings we intend, that is, we use language to create shared beliefs and expectations. This last idea probably requires a little unpicking for its sense to be clear. The words we use have a meaning. Over time, meanings become stable (though they can change in the future). Take 'community'; what images and values does this conjure up? We might imagine a rural scene of village life, where a small-scale location focuses interaction amongst the people. Or we might imagine an urban scene where an ethnic group has chosen to live together. In both cases, geographical scale is important and we might use terms such as 'togetherness', 'supportive' and 'sharing' to express processes and values that are tied up with the idea of community. The word, then, expresses a way of living which, when we deconstruct it, is one we value. A scale or so up from the community is the nation. Again it is a concept we value. Within a nation, we are 'the same as' and 'different from'. However, while both community and nation can be argued over, the idea of nationhood is far more contested. In Belgium, the Flemish and the French may feel more similar to their neighbours than they do to each other. In Britain, political devolution has strengthened Welshness and Scottishness and may have weakened Britishness. In England, the idea of a nation whose identity rests on shared culture and language has its roots in the tenth century. In Italy and Germany, the idea of a nation was still an aspiration in the nineteenth century. So when we use the words 'community' or 'nation/national', context is clearly important. And now, with the EU, nations are progressively sharing actions to create, of all things, a community but a community that is very different from the one we looked at initially. Our interest, from the perspective of discourse analysis, is that the use of the term 'community' within a European context represents an attempt to imbue the supra-national idea with the warmth and affection that we associate with its use at the local level. The debate over what is to be shared and how it is to be managed and the relative importance of national and supra-national institutions will, inevitably, either redefine what community means or lead to a new concept and a new word.

While this example may not have immediate implications for the processes of education, there are others that do. For example, take the concept of partnership. This has a general-use meaning of working together for a common good and a legal meaning of a business enterprise structured in a particular way. In the UK, its use in public service provision has been growing. From the 1980s onwards, funding for regeneration and development was offered to public and private institutions signing up to a *partnership* agreement. Since then, the term has been extended to cover normal working relationships of both a collaborative or contractual nature that have, to some degree, always been around. *Partnership for Schools* is the body that delivers the UK Government's 'Building Schools for the Future' and 'Academy Development' programmes. The former is a programme for financial investment in schools and the latter a programme for developing state-funded schools managed through an independent governing body. The Partnership for Schools Board of five people has representatives from the private and public sectors and the civil service (but not actually education and, at one stroke, stretching the concept of partnership to breaking point). The *Independent/State Schools Partnership* programme is a funding initiative to strengthen collaboration and raise standards between the two sectors. The *Safer Schools Partnership* is a mechanism for creating effective links between schools, the youth justice system and the police service. *School Sports Partnerships* seek to establish collaboration in sports development amongst local schools as a means of accessing public and National Lottery funding. In these and other partnerships, the heart of the partnership association is access to funding, which somehow does not fit easily with what many would understand by partnership, that is, collaboration for a common good.

What all these examples show is that we use language to achieve outcomes and re-frame realities and that the way we use language is not always the way that we have used language in the past. This is what discourse analysis is concerned with and, more than many, we as educationalists should appreciate that words are an extremely strong weapon in enabling us to attain the futures we want.

Margie Wetherell, a Professor of Social Psychology, and her co-authors identify four ways in which we can look at and analyse discourse (Wetherell et al., 2001, pp. 6–10).

1. *A focus on words and the way we express ourselves.* In this situation we are interested in how context (such as social situation, cultural background, group affiliation) influences how we use language. While this could include the study of dialect and the historical evolution of language, more relevant for the educationalist might be how young people create language that enables their discourse to be hidden from others. In 2005, the BBC published a *Lexicon of Teenspeak* on its website (http://news.bbc.co. uk/1/hi/magazine/4074004.stm). Parent Line Plus, a UK charity, has published a 'jargon buster' on its website (http://www.gotateenager.org.uk/default.aspx?page=jargonbuster). So, if you are in the dark when someone you interview says, 'He's my blud and dis my yard', you now know where you can go for help. This new way of speaking even has a name – multicultural London English. But it is not just 'teen speak' that we should be interested in. We could, for example, set the meaning in context. If a school is criticised in a report for unruly pupil behaviour and lack of pupil achievement but damned with faint praise for its well-written policies, there is more than a strong inference that aspirations are not translated into action and it is the context that tells us this. And there is an interesting point on which to end this first way of looking at discourse. The words 'young people' and 'youth' should be interchangeable. Yet when we search the Web using the term 'young people speak' we get very different results than if we use 'youth speak'. Try it and see what the implications of using 'youth' are.

2. *A focus on language in use* is the second type of analysis. Here the focus is on interaction between subjects and how language, the words, expression, emphasis, is used. This may involve the detailed analysis referred to above but because language is batted back and forth, we are interested in how one contribution shapes a response and how the interaction between people creates meaning or understanding. Three Dutch researchers show this method in use in their study of the way in which special needs pupils solve mathematical problems (Aalsvoort et al., 2006). They video-recorded the interactions of pupils and teachers as the pupils solved the problems ('sums') and analysed them in terms of 'materials used; questions raised during the sum; supportive activities, e.g. offering help when the student seemed to fail in solving sums independently; and task structure, e.g. learning to apply strategic knowledge by using spatial and numeral representation of 1s and 10s correctly' (p. 306). Their results are interesting because they indicate that 'students can be more effective partners in processes that elicit mathematisation if they are allowed to take part in the meaning-making of the strategies involved in doing the sums (Aalsvoort et al., 2006, pp. 315–316). The implication of this is that learning is effective when they are allowed and encouraged to find their own way of expressing ideas and testing their interpretations with the teacher.

3. *Focus on language pattern:* Here, in the third type of analysis, the focus shifts from the way language is used to the context in which it is used. We saw in the first approach to discourse analysis that context helps create the meaning. Surfing, for example, means different things when we are on the beach or on the Internet. When we talk about language pattern, however, we usually mean more than just individual words, rather the character of the whole set of text or script. Two researchers at the University of Central Arkansas in the USA, Shoudong Feng and Tammy Benson, looked at the language patterns of pre-school children. The setting for their study was a computer suite in a pre-school centre that they attended in order to give them a good start when they moved to formal school. They videoed almost four hours of activity at times when the children had a free choice of what they could do. From the recordings they extracted sections where the children interacted with each other and coded the type of interaction. The coding system they used was intended to show how the language met the children's immediate needs and desires. This was based on Michael Halliday's thesis that language meets seven objectives for children (Halliday, 1973):

- they can express wants;
- they can give instructions and so manage other people's behaviour;
- through language they can get on with others;
- they can use it to describe themselves and how they are feeling;
- through language they can find out about their world and things in it;
- they can be creative and construct imaginary worlds, and
- they can give information and instructions.

What the researchers found was that almost all the children's speech fell into these categories, though managing other children's behaviour, using language to find out about their environment and giving information and instruction were dominant. Their analysis raises an issue about whether the results reflect the development stage that the children have reached or whether the nature of the environment constrained behaviour and thus language use (and development). If the latter, we have to pay more attention to the character of the environment and the nature of the activity in early years learning.

4. *A focus on the link between language and the nature and structure of society:* this type of analysis seeks to understand how language is used to bolster our positions in a social setting. At a macro level, it is used to show how language is a vehicle that can be used to maintain privilege and assert status. As Wetherell says, 'Controversy is basic to this form of discourse analysis because it involves the study of power and resistance' (p. 9). Sarah Ohi, an Australian academic, worked within this perspective in her exploration of the early years literacy programme in the Australian state of Victoria. She identified that the literacy model that was proposed was founded upon assertion and not an actual analysis of evidence. Her discourse analysis of the policy documentation and teaching manuals showed that:

- there were few direct connections to primary sources of research evidence;
- implementation was heavily influenced by US example and there was no attempt to assess whether the Australian situation created specific difficulties;
- there was no invitation or opportunity for teachers to assess primary evidence (because references were not cited and when they were they were not always referenced in the text);

- there was no invitation for teachers to assess the model and this contributed to a sense of being deprofessionalised (Ohi, 2008). We shall meet this type of approach to discourse analysis again when we look at critical discourse analysis in Section 11.10.3

11.9.2 From text to image

We should remind ourselves that discourse analysis does not have to be limited to text-based material. Visual data (videos, drawings, photographic images) can also constitute a discourse. Putting this into the context of the four approaches to discourse analysis described by Wetherell (Section 11.9.1), the majority of the image-based discourse analysis (and it should be noted that the quantity is much less than text-based) is related to a focus on pattern and the association with the nature and structure of society (points 3 and 4 in the section above).

Fiona Ormerod and Roz Ivanic, both then members of the Literacy Research Group at Lancaster University, explored how children 'make meaning'. They looked at this through project work, where interest, choice and control were managed by each child and were reflected in the output. Their analysis looked at the materials children included in their projects, the models they constructed, the images they drew, those they cut out and used and the graphical quality of their writing and image framing. They noted that 'the choice of materials and the ways in which they are used to construct images can appear to communicate, in a very subtle way, something of the child's attitude towards the subject represented' (Ormerod and Ivanic, 2002, p. 76). They note, for example, that 'in Denise's project on pigeons and doves, her use of a *soft pencil* and *gently rounded repeated strokes* seems to communicate a *sensual appreciation and protective fondness* for the beautiful fragile creature that she is depicting'. In another instance they observe, 'In the football project produced by Robbie and four of his friends, there is a cutting of a photo from a magazine, showing a player committing a foul, and next to it the word "Fowl" is *written boldly, in large letters, using thick black fibre-tip pen* . . . The *distinctive* way in which the word is written appears to communicate both *confidence* in the writer's *knowledge of the rules* of the game and a strong sense of *shock and disapproval*' (pp. 76–77). In both cases the emphasis is mine and not the authors'. We can see with these examples that through the way pictures and words were constructed and the way they created emphasis the authors were able to gain insight into how children were learning to express their knowledge and understanding.

11.10 Other approaches to qualitative analyses

It is at this point that qualitative data analysis becomes even more fragmented. So far we have looked at:

- a *process* used by many approaches, coding;
- an *approach*, grounded theory, which uses coding and which builds up an interpretation from the data itself;
- *discourse analysis*, where the focus is on understanding communicative intent, communicative actuality and the consequences of both.

We have skirted around some methodological issues (such as whether discourse analysis is a method or a paradigm) in order to focus on where and how the approaches are used. But while we have sought to represent qualitative analysis in a coherent way, it will be apparent that the more deeply we move into it, the more fragmented it becomes. We just have to accept this.

11.10.1 Narrative analysis

Narrative analysis looks at statements produced by individuals. These can be people or organisations. The narrative can be spoken or written. Thus, for example, children's accounts of their day at school and school prospectuses designed to give parents an understanding of the education their child will receive can both be subject to narrative analysis.

While there is variation between disciplines in the way in which narrative analysis is conceived, the feature common to all is that the research data is a narrative that presents an individual perspective. As an aside, this raises the issue that interviewing to produce a narrative must allow the personal voice to come through, that is, research interests and the researcher should not inhibit the way an individual wishes to respond.

The thinking behind narrative analysis is that the personal voice reflects the priorities, concerns, values and attitudes of the narrator and gets us closer, as researchers, to an individual's personal experience or an institutional perspective (in the case of a school, for example). Narrative is, of course, a form of discourse. Its distinguishing feature is that the teller determines the sequence through which the data are revealed. There are different types of narrative. Some report a sequence of events with a beginning and an end, some are hypothetical reactions to stimulus ideas and some report things that happen on a regular basis. In each case, we need our data in a particular form, namely that it should be the writer's or speaker's own voice. The consequence of this is that narrative analysis conditions the type of data we collect and the way we collect it. This is a good example of why it is far better to plan our research procedure in detail and not to blunder through, making decisions about method as we go.

But exactly how is narrative analysis carried out? To get to grips with this we have to understand that, in broad terms, narrative analysis can deal with three types of data.

1. *Research interview data:* the interview is normally conducted in such a way as to minimise interviewer interaction or interruption. Questions are phrased to encourage the interviewee to speak for longer periods and to be responsible for the sequence of the narrative. The type of instruction that might be used is, 'Tell me about . . .'
2. *Existing narrative* that exists in report or story form. We could, for example, use as our data quality inspection reports, written statements of policy, responses to policy options, emails and blogs written by members of our target research community.
3. *Written accounts* constructed for the research. Gwendolyn Lloyd did this in a study on how mathematics teachers in training got to grips with their professional role (Lloyd, 2008). She asked her subjects to compose fictional narratives that dealt with classroom situations that supported and conflicted with curriculum statements on recommended teaching themes and approaches.

Once we have the data, the framework within which we analyse it is rather different from the tagging approach we considered earlier. Analysis can range along a continuum from being more tightly focused to being more loosely focused. We shall look at examples of each in turn.

More focused approaches usually adopt a way of looking at the narrative developed by an American Professor of Linguistics, William Labov. Heather Richmond, a Canadian teacher educator, used Labov's approach in her study of the experiences of adult learners. She collected her data through focus groups and individual interview. This yielded accounts that were expressed in the learners' own words and in the sequence and with the emphases that they wanted. She organised each narrative into a 'storymap'. This is a pictorial or tabular representation that seeks to place the narrative into various categories: time (past present and future), personal state (ranging from disorganised and confused to organised and clear) and experience (self, family, community and schooling). Each storymap was then looked at through Labov's frame (see Richmond, 2002). This consists of four categories:

1. Orientation – a description of context, when and where something occurred, the nature of the location, who was there.
2. Abstract – a summary of an event, story, narrative.
3. Complicating action – evaluation of the event/action in terms of significance or meaning for the subject.
4. Resolution – what happened as an outcome at the end of the narrative.

These categories are perspectives through which to process the data. What we have to be aware of is that the 'facts' are presented in order to achieve a specific perception, which may colour the attitude of the listener to the narrator. Where this is identified, it is additional research evidence. It does, however, move the analysis away from a consideration of structure towards interpretation of meaning and intent. Richmond's paper is methodological in character and does not go into substantive research findings. However, Ilze Grobler also used the approach for her PhD study of teaching and learning in higher education (Grobler, 2006) and showed the change that happened to learners as they moved to a collaborative learning approach and the importance of reflection in creating (or as Grobler expresses it 'co-constructing') knowledge. Qualitative research gives us quite different insights into the learning process compared with those from quantitative research. The latter may tell us what works (or what produces good outcome measures) but qualitative research tells us what the process is and why it does or does not work.

More loosely focused approaches to narrative analysis are not any less rigorous but they are less wedded to a procedure. They often make use of the coding procedure we met in section 11.3 and it can, in fact, often be difficult to distinguish what makes a piece of research a generic piece of qualitative analysis and what makes it a narrative analysis, other than that the data are personal narratives. Heather Fraser, a Canadian social work researcher, adopts a less formalised approach in her review of how to undertake narrative research (Fraser, 2004) and she makes some very specific points about the culture and standpoint of narrative research. She argues that narrative researchers have to find a way between the idea that action is conditioned either by circumstance or by individual decision making, and the approach of narrative research is that of the chef who sees cooking as an art form and does not try to stick to recipes. She clearly makes the point that narrative researchers have to process their data in ways that extract the most or best information and should not be constrained to follow any particular procedure. Her guidance for analysing narratives is that we consider it in four stages, interpretation, comparative experiences, the political dimension and the identification of common patterns.

- *Interpretation:* this is the stage in which we seek to pick out the salient features of what we are being told. We have to read the narrative at an overall level to see if we can characterise the story as a 'type' and also at a more detailed level (perhaps even read it on a sentence by sentence or line by line basis) in order to identify important themes. She gives an example of how these two levels of interpretation can intersect. In the middle of a narrative a respondent said, 'And I realised years ago that I always had this feeling because I'd received so much charity in my life that I had to give back to society'. Fraser called her story 'paying the debt'. Table 11.5 shows questions that she thinks a researcher might usefully ask of the data at this stage. These direct us to a close reading of the narratives and enable us to gain insight. Is there, for example, a persuasive intent? Is there obvious difficulty in talking about something?

- *Comparative experiences:* at this point we want to see if the narrator places their story in any cultural or social context. Does the narrator talk about themselves (what Fraser calls the intra-personal experience), or about relations with others (the interpersonal)? Are there references to popular culture (for instance 'a lot of people think . . . ') or social relationships? In this process we are not putting these interpretations on the narrative but looking to see if the narrative itself makes reference to them.

Table 11.5 Narrative analysis questions

Stage	Questions
Interpretation	• What are the main points? • What contradictions emerge? • What are the vocal inflections? What might they signify? • Are some words used instead of others? What might this signify? • Are some words emphasised? What non-verbal gestures are there? • Are there gaps, pauses, silences? What do they suggest – thinking, distress, boredom?
Comparative experiences	• Identify themes, e.g. interpersonal relations. • How do the themes relate to other aspects of the narrative? • Are there examples of adherence to transgressions of social and cultural norms and conventions? • Is there evidence of cultural preference?
The political dimension	• Is there evidence of a value stance or political leaning in the narrative? • How might other theorists analyse the narratives? • What do the narratives say about the lived experiences of particular social groups? • How can you ensure that you are not selecting evidence to match your academic perspective?
Common patterns	• What common themes emerge? • On what basis have these themes been identified? • What differences are there between individuals? What relevance is this? • Is there evidence of sensationalism in the narratives? Is this relevant? • Are narratives that challenge established findings given due weight?

- *The political dimension:* the next stage takes this further by looking for evidence of a value base in either or both moral or political terms. Fraser suggests (Table 11.5) that it is appropriate to look for evidence on the experiences of groups. She suggests by class or gender or age or race amongst others. This could equally be family structure or class size.
- *Common pattern and differences:* in the final stage we try to identify common themes to and differences between narratives. Her questions here are far more general than at earlier stages and are designed to challenge us and our conclusions. She seeks to remove the possibility of bias by asking, 'What would other theorists say?' 'Are relevant portions of the narrative interpreted fairly?' 'Are narratives that challenge established findings or the researcher's preconceived ideas given full weight?'

It will be clear that Fraser's less formalised approach has elements that we can see in other approaches to the analysis of text. Progressively moving away from the detail of the narrative, compare and contrast assessment and placing the accounts in a social, political and cultural context are all found elsewhere.

Because narratives are individual constructs (that is, produced without influence or interference by real people), this focuses the researcher's attention on why the particular elements of the narrative were selected (and not others) and why they were presented in the way they were (and not others). In particular, a researcher will have to determine the importance of elements and how this is reflected in their location in the narrative. Here we have to acknowledge that there may be differences between speech and written text, between reportage and argument and between factual and rhetorical styles. Narrative analysis clearly requires a different set of understandings and insights compared with other discourse analysis and novice researchers should understand the implications of these genres before tackling the method.

11.10.2 Conversation analysis

The essential difference between narrative and conversational analysis is that narrative analysis is one person speaking and conversation analysis is more than one person speaking. At the heart of conversation analysis is the interaction between the parties and it is this that constitutes the data for analysis and assessment. Why this focus on the interaction between speakers? The interaction in conversation can tell us about the warmth or distance between the participants (something that is important in negotiations or useful to know about if we are trying to defuse conflict between groups of young people). If we want medical staff to have a sensitivity to people in distress, then conversation analysis can reveal the difference between good and bad practice – and this sort of learning can be applied to the teacher who is trying to resolve an issue of bullying. In summary, we can say that it is through conversation that we establish social relationships and make things happen. That is why conversation analysis is a perspective that qualitative researchers should understand.

What sets conversation analysis apart is not only the fact that it focuses on the verbal interaction between people but also the method that it uses to do this. It notates the interaction to describe and record its character. To do this, most conversation analysts use a system devised by an American sociologist, Gail Jefferson (see Table 11.6). This shows the way the conversation moves between speakers and is managed. It differentiates between simultaneous and overlapping speech, where one speaker follows another (contiguous utterances), the length of the interval between utterances and the character of the delivery. Table 11.6 shows the mark-up options supplied with Transana software which is

Table 11.6 Jeffersonian transcription notation

Symbol	Name	Use
[text]	Brackets	Indicates the start and end points of overlapping speech.
=	Equal Sign	Indicates the break and subsequent continuation of a single utterance.
(# of seconds)	Timed Pause	A number in parentheses indicates the time, in seconds, of a pause in speech.
(.)	Micropause	A brief pause, usually less that 0.2 seconds.
. or ↓	Period or Down Arrow	Indicates falling pitch or intonation.
? or ↑	Question Mark or Up Arrow	Indicates rising pitch or intonation.
,	Comma	Indicates a temporary rise or fall in intonation.
-	Hyphen	Indicates an abrupt halt or interruption in utterance.
>text<	Greater than/Less than symbols	Indicates that the enclosed speech was delivered more rapidly than usual for the speaker.
<text>	Less than/Greater than symbols	Indicates that the enclosed speech was delivered more slowly than usual for the speaker.
°	Degree symbol	Indicates whisper, reduced volume, or quiet speech.
ALL CAPS	Capitalized text	Indicates shouted or increased volume speech.
underline	Underlined text	Indicates the speaker is emphasizing or stressing the speech.
:::	Colon(s)	Indicates prolongation of a sound.
(hhh)		Audible exhalation.
• or (.hhh)	High Dot	Audible inhalation.
(text)	Parentheses	Speech which is unclear or in doubt in the transcript.
((italic text))	Double Parentheses	Annotation of non-verbal activity.

Source: Transana Keyboard Shortcuts and Transcript Notation, Henne, R. (and subsequently modified by Woods, D.), http://www.transana.org/support/documentation.htm (November 2008).

used to analyse video or audio data files. The character of speech is shown by symbols for rising or falling speech, speed of speech, loudness of speech, stress on words and syllables and non-verbal actions.

In what sort of situations can conversation analysis be used by educational researchers? Bethan Benwell, an English language academic, and Elizabeth Stokoe, a social psychologist, used it to study university seminars (Benwell and Stokoe, 2002). Many university educators believe that seminar discussions are important not only in establishing student knowledge and understanding but also in the intellectual development that marks out 'graduateness'. What Benwell and Stokoe found was not just a reluctance by students to engage in discussion, but resistance in adopting what they called 'an intellectual identity', that is, being 'into studying' and not trying to establish a persona that it is 'cool' not to enjoy learning. Most tutors will imagine that if students are at university, they are there to learn, they enjoy learning and that they will pursue learning of their own volition. The assumption is that students have 'an intellectual identity'. What is not clear is whether resistance to students adopting this identity that the research highlighted has its roots in wider society or in the tension which the researchers observed between tutor and students over the management of the sessions.

In another study, Rebekah Willett, a British educationalist, used conversation analysis to show how 8- and 9-year-old children were beginning to understand and define their genders (Willett, 2006). In terms of issues where it might be used in education research, we can look at Jonathan Clifton's exploration of communication in a business setting. He quite clearly shows 'the machinery of talk with which leadership is enacted' (Clifton, 2006, p. 202). With organisational management and leadership so important now throughout the educational sector, particularly in countries where schools are gaining more freedom from public administration, the processes of exerting authority should be better understood, so that institutional managements can be better trained. Case Study 11.5, though not educational, is an excellent example of the use of conversational analysis to understand organisational failure.

11.10.3 Critical discourse analysis

Critical analysis is marked out by a concern with power and the exercise of authority and the extent to which this results in inequality. Critical discourse analysts see language as a means of demonstrating and exercising power. Many researchers adopting critical discourse analysis as an approach do so from a radical perspective and see their research as a challenge to a status quo that reinforces discrimination and embeds inequality. This simple description smoothes over many divergent perspectives and anyone wishing to engage with critical discourse analysis should read further to understand the differences and the disagreements. This section indicates these approaches in broad terms and shows how they have been used in educational research.

As Rebecca Rogers and others comment in their review of critical discourse analysis in educational research, it 'sets out to describe, interpret, and explain the relationships between language, social practices, and the social world' (Rogers et al., 2005, p. 376). They concluded their review by noting that most studies limited themselves to analysing how power was reproduced and how it could be challenged. They also commented that the methods used were not clearly described. This is a criticism in relation to transparency that we have met before. If readers cannot see the process, they cannot judge the output.

What sorts of area have educational researchers looked at? Helen Oughton looked at the UK Government's strategy for up-skilling adults, 'Skills for Life' (Oughton, 2007). The context for this policy is twofold, meeting the needs of economies that require an updated knowledge and skills base, and secondly, the economic and social cost of those who, by virtue of their educational attainment, find themselves towards the margins of society. Oughton's data were documents concerned with explaining the goals of 'Skills for Life' and the curriculum that was specified. Her focus was numeracy. Her conclusion is that the documentation presents numeracy as 'a set of competences to be achieved in

Case study 11.5 One of our aircraft is missing

In clear but moonless conditions the aircraft hit the top of a mountain range near Alice Springs Air Station. The pilot had over 10,000 hours of flying experience and the co-pilot nearly 4,000 hours. The air accident investigation noted a high cockpit workload and problems in communication between the crew. Ten years after the accident, data from the cockpit voice recorder were reviewed to see what light conversation analysis could throw on the communication problems.

Below is a section of the text from the transcript and the same text marked up using Jeffersonian notation.

What is immediately apparent is the fragmented and disjointed character of the speech, with breaks at which the co-pilot could respond. The conclusion of the conversation analysis was that the ways the pilots communicated created a context for error:

- Their talk overlapped.
- There were situations when the co-pilot did not respond.
- The pilot corrected what the co-pilot said when there was no problem.

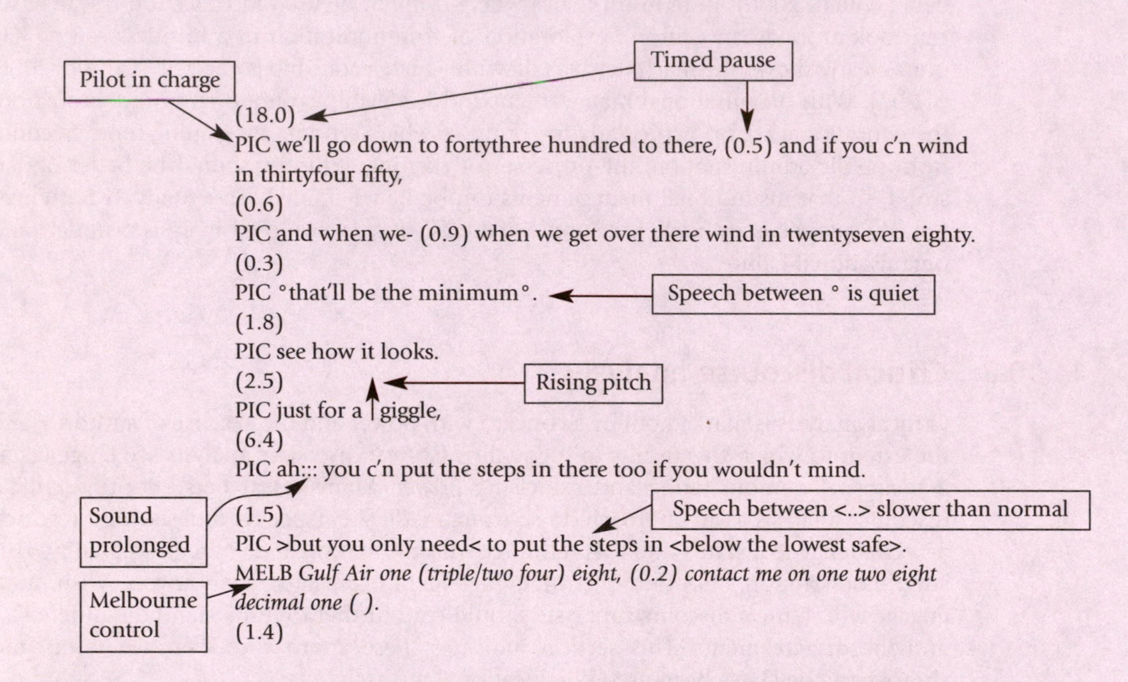

The overall judgement was that the two were not working as a team. This was the context in which the pilot instructed the co-pilot to set the altitude alert. The co-pilot set 2,300 feet, which the pilot acknowledged. The correct setting should have been 3,100 feet. The aircraft hit the mountains at 2,250 feet.

Source: Nevile, M. and Walker, M. (2005) 'A Context for Error: Using Conversation Analysis to Represent and Analyse Recorded Voice Data', *Aviation Research Report 132005/0108*, Australian Transport Safety Bureau.

response to employer demand' (p. 273) when it could have been justified on the basis of 'empowerment, personal achievement and critical literacy' (p. 273). This conclusion reflects a great gulf between those who see education as a means of being employed and those who see it as a process of personal development that comes from being self-motivated. It is the contrast between a programme whose outcomes are measured by the number that can pass a test and one where success is measured by the number that go on to further study.

Inge Askehave, a member of the Department of Language and Culture at Aallborg University, looked at the market orientated focus that many universities are now embracing (Askehave, 2007). Her data were international prospectuses from four countries, Finland, Scotland, Australia and Japan. She showed that international prospectuses adopted a common structure with common elements, each of which conveyed a message and which, together, conveyed an impression (marketers might call this the 'brand'). Her detailed analysis of one university's brochure exposes the image being created: 'natural beauty, historic feel and friendly atmosphere' (p. 731). She digs deeper into the text and shows that the 'university' is projected as supportive and enabling. Her method is clearly outlined and her analysis, from an educationalist's viewpoint, is interesting. Again, as with Oughton's work, we find a representation of education that is economically functionalist (in this case the functionalism is a focus upon the student as a 'customer' rather than as a learner) and very different from the liberal tradition that many academics espouse.

Donald Gillies shows that this shift in educational purpose is deeply rooted in British educational policy. Gillies explores the concept of 'excellence' and notes its association in modern times with a 'crisis narrative', a sense that problems exist (because of an absence of excellence) which must be addressed by policy action (Gillies, 2007). He identifies linkages between quality inspection in Scottish schools and the European Foundation for Quality Management's idea of excellence. What Gillies does most effectively is to show the sleight of hand with which the term is used in different circumstances and that while, as an idea, it is difficult to object to it, its implementation may have consequences that may be objectionable (in particular, the application of a business quality model that measures quality in terms of assessment outcomes and which serves to distort the education process and adversely affects children's experiences and achievements).

What do these studies show us? Very simply, that words are used to frame an issue, that language is used to identify a solution and that the continuous reiteration of words and phrases sets the agenda and, over time, shifts a status quo. And this is the power of critical discourse analysis, it can help us understand what is happening and deflate the bubble. It is not, however, a method of research for the novice.

11.10.4 Semiotics

The idea of semiotics and the interpretations we put on objects, features and events has been touched on before (in section 2.1.1 *passim*). In this section, we shall look at how semioticians work and on research that has relevance for education. Our intention is to give an appreciation of what it is aiming to achieve, not an account of its procedures.

Semiotics takes as its starting point that we understand the world as a series of signs and symbols and that when we see, for example, a palace, we understand not just as a grand building but a symbol of wealth and status. Semiotics is, for this reason, traditionally described as being 'the science of signs', in other words it is concerned with how we create and transmit meaning. Semiotics developed as a field of research practice in the early part of the twentieth century. There were two separate traditions, one in the USA and the other in Europe. There was little intellectual exchange between them and the one only really understood the existence of the other in the second half of the century. It was the European tradition that began to have the greater impact in the social sciences because it came out of the same sources as post-modernism and post-structuralism (again, see section 2.1.1). The ideas became part of popular culture with the publication of Umberto Eco's *The Name of the Rose*. Eco is an academic semiotician and his book incorporates semiotic themes. Dan Brown's *The Da Vinci Code* does the same.

The purpose of semiotics is to identify signs in text, images, film, in fact any medium through which we can communicate. There are three types of sign.

1. *Icons* are representations of something real. A photograph, for example, is an icon. Icons can take the form of images (our photograph), drawings (a sketch map, for example) or metaphors.
2. *Index* – an index is an indicator of something else. If our joints ache and we have a fluctuating temperature, it could indicate that we have 'flu.
3. *Symbols* are constructed and agreed within a socio-cultural context. Symbols require interpretation. Our palace example above shows what we mean by this. Symbols are all around us. Look at the washing instructions on your clothes, for example. And when you are browsing the Internet, which symbol do you press to go to your home page? A cowrie shell and the €20 or £20 note in your pocket are all symbols of value. The advertisements we see on our TVs and in our newspapers and magazines often embrace symbolism. It does not take much imagination, for example, to understand the symbolism in the advertisement in Figure 11.8.

These are the basic structures that semioticians work with and they use them to deconstruct communication, in other words break it up into its component parts. The thing to be communicated (a fact, an idea, a value) is called the *signified* and the sign that communicates is called the *signifier*. A crown, for example might be the signifier for monarchy and the monarchy (or the king or queen) is what is signified. At this point we have to introduce the idea of shades of meaning and to do this, we draw a distinction

Figure 11.8 Symbolisation in marketing
Source: The Advertising Archives

between *denotation* and *connotation*. We understand what we mean by a 'lesson', a coming together of students and teachers with, hopefully, a learning outcome. This is what the idea of a lesson denotes. But when the music teacher, art teacher, biology teacher or mathematics teacher all close their eyes, the image they see in their mind's eye may well be very different. The differences they attach to the core concept constitute the *connotative meaning*. So for the biology teacher, a lesson takes place in a laboratory, for the art teacher in an open space where students work at their own pace and so on. All are lessons but the lessons are not all the same because the connotations for each are different. Connotation can also be judgemental. If two teachers are talking about a pupil and one says, 'Oh, her', it represents recognition, but if she says, 'Oh, *her*', with the emphasis on 'her', it says something beyond recognition that implies something bad.

Semiotic analysis is more complex and detailed than this but this overview is sufficient for us to understand the method's approach. Now let us look at how semiotic research may be useful to educationalists.

The Norwegian education researcher, Marit Holm Hopperstad, used a semiotic approach to understand aspects of child development (Hopperstad, 2008). She wanted to develop insights into how children made meaning and explored this by analysing their drawing and play activity. Her study shows how we can use semiotics with groups who are unable to verbalise what is happening or their reactions or emotions. Her theoretical position was that drawing implies the selection of forms in order to make or represent a meaning, so the artwork that is produced is a semiotic object. What Hopperstad wanted to do was to understand how play informed the construction of the artwork. Her method was to observe children drawing and she videoed their activity. Her observation notes, the video record and the children's drawings constituted her data. She analysed their talk by linking talk and conversation sequences to particular art outcomes. Hopperstad's work is fascinating but too detailed to consider here. From a substantive point of view, what emerges from her study is that children work and rework meaning in their drawing and methodologically we see that drawing can be used to understand children's ability to make meaning.

Another area where educational researchers can usefully use a semiotic approach is in understanding young people's search for and creation of identity because this may well be the context for understanding behaviour. Research on topics as diverse as adolescent magazines (Corrie, 1999), suicide behaviour (Anderson et al., 2005), body shape (*Social Semiotics*, 2005) as well as the more obvious area of clothes (Morgado, 2007, on hip-hop style) all help us appreciate in what ways young people can construct an image and create an identity that should be recognised by those they want to recognise it. This type of research, though outside education, is relevant to educationalists.

11.10.5 Phenomenography

Phenomenography sets out to understand how individuals perceive the world in which they operate. It makes no assumption that there is a single real world and accepts that there can be many worlds, all real to individuals. In many ways the actual methods used for data analysis in phenomenography need not be very different from those outlined in sections 11.3 to 11.6. What is different about phenomenography is its starting position. In order to appreciate how others see the world phenomenography has to be successful in data collection. There are no specific phenomenographic methods of data collection so, using whatever method is appropriate (interviews, diaries, personal accounts), the researcher has to be sure that they understand what the subject is saying and also has to be sure that the subject is saying what they are actually experiencing. In other words, there is an additional stage in data production, interaction between researcher and subject, that produces mutual understanding and agreement.

Phenomenography was developed by a Swedish professor of education, Ference Marton, as a means of understanding learning from the student's point of view. It was Marton who developed the framework of deep and surface learning, something that every student of education is (or should be) aware of. Deep learning has the outcome that the knowledge is retained (which implies it is understood) and can be applied in new or different situations. Surface learning is typified by rote learning, retained for a short time then forgotten and therefore incapable of being used elsewhere. Given the assumptions behind university level education, that students should be capable of independent and self-directed learning, able to transfer their knowledge and understanding to other situations and skilled in analysis, synthesis and argumentation, it is not surprising that it should come under investigation and equally not surprising that the student's perspective should be placed at the forefront. As a concept deep and surface learning was rapidly accepted by educationalists worldwide and it was this conceptualisation of learning that probably explains the spread of phenomenography as a method. Marton's analytic method has much in common with other approaches. Essentially the data are investigated and 'categories of description' identified. These categories have the character of being (a) elements common to subjects and (b) generalisations that result from groupings of ideas into themes.

Many of the studies using a phenomenographic approach are studies of the learning or teaching process. A New Zealand educationalist, Lois Ruth Harris, used the approach to study teachers' understandings of students' commitments to learning (Harris, 2008). Her starting point was that we know something about student disengagement from education, especially its social and demographic associations, but we know little about the circumstances in which students engage with what education can offer. Harris collected her data through interview. Phenomenographers try to come at their data without any preconceptions and to achieve this they state their viewpoint before commencing their analysis. Harris even went so far as to limit her reading on the subject to methodological and not substantive texts. She analysed the interview texts to identify ideas and themes relevant to engagement. She picked out the most frequently occurring themes and identified passages that typified the theme. From these she extracted a generic theme, called a category of description. The outcome of her research was that she was able to distinguish six dimensions to engagement in learning.

1. Participating in classroom activities and following school rules.
2. Being interested in and enjoying participation in what happens at school.
3. Being motivated and confident in participation in what happens at school.
4. Being involved by thinking.
5. Purposefully learning to reach life goals.
6. Owning and valuing learning (Harris, 2008, p. 65).

Phenomenography has gained wide acceptance in education research because of its application in understanding the learning process. It is not necessarily limited, however, to learning. There is no reason why it cannot be applied to other situations where it is valuable to reconstruct an individual's view of the world. What is it like to be classified as a 'failing teacher' and to be in danger of losing one's job? What is it like to be a male teacher in a girls' school (or vice versa)? What is it to enjoy learning in a culture where this is not accepted? Understanding each of these situations better might lead to our managing them better when things begin to go wrong.

Summary

1. Qualitative analysis is not an easy option. There are many approaches that can be adopted. Each has its own views about the nature of reality and the nature of the evidence provided by the data. These have to be understood because if they are not we can finish up making assertions and drawing conclusions that are not warranted by the philosophical foundations of the method. Compared with the comfort of established research procedures and standards of judgement that exists in positivist research, qualitative research is a minefield for the unwary and dangerous for the naïve.
2. Most qualitative research is presented as taking place in natural settings (though data collected through focus groups may, at times, fall outside this categorisation) and as being within an interpretivist tradition. The implication of this is that the researcher has to deal with many realities and find a way through them that seems to make sense.
3. We must not assume that qualitative research lacks rigour. There is as much need to demonstrate the quality of qualitative research as there is to ensure the quality of positivist research. Without demonstrating quality, what purports to be research is just speculation. The best test of quality is transparency in procedure. Much published research lacks this. There is considerable flexibility in the way in which data can be collected and analysed. We should take advantage of this flexibility if either or both our research question or research issue require it. Flexibility, however, reinforces the need for transparency since it does mean that academic peers rather than established research procedure are our test for quality.
4. The number of qualitative approaches that we might use is large, larger even than the set we have considered in this chapter. The approaches vary along a number of dimensions:
    - How predefined the methodological structure is – from highly structured approaches such as grounded theory, to more loosely structured approaches such as phenomenography.
    - What influences methodology – from philosophical positions (as with critical discourse analysis) to conventions about research procedure, conversation analysis, for example.
    - The nature of the evidence provided by the data, from evidence of reality to evidence about what people say about reality.

    The way these approaches have been represented in this chapter is not definitive. Other authors have, quite legitimately, presented their explanations in different ways.
5. While there are methods that have distinctive approaches (conversation analysis, for example), many could draw on what we have set out as core processes. Semiotics, grounded theory, discourse analysis and critical discourse analysis, for instance, all:
    - use a range of data;
    - transform data into a form suitable for analysis;
    - code data;
    - generalise from the data to produce themes.
6. The processes of data analysis, from coding to theming, can all be undertaken on computer. This becomes a realistic option for more than small amounts of data. Commercially available and free Web resources can also be used for early stage explorations of data.

7. The choice of approach for data exploration and analysis should be made on the basis of the research issue and the assumptions of the method.
   - Do you think you are dealing with people's experiences (in which case you might consider, amongst others, phenomenography, content analysis or grounded theory) or what people say about their experiences (look towards a type of discourse analysis)?
   - Do you think that the message is explicit in your data (perhaps conversation analysis) or will you have to dig deeper (perhaps semiotics)?
   - Do you want to test other people's findings (consider template analysis) or develop your own (any other method)?
   - Do you think that the conclusions should stem from the data or can you interpret the data in the context of other findings (that is, Glaser's model of grounded theory or Strauss' model)?

These are the types of question that have to be asked of any qualitative research project. If they are not, then it is easy to make the wrong choice. Qualitative analysis may have fewer 'must have' conventions in respect of procedure but its assumptions dictate the shape of the research.

Further reading

Grounded theory

Charmaz, K. (2006) *Constructing Grounded Theory: A Practical Guide through Qualitative Analysis*, Sage, Thousand Oaks, Calif.

Corbin, J. and Strauss, A. (2008) *Basics of Qualitative Research: Techniques and Procedures for Developing Grounded Theory*, Sage, Thousand Oaks, Calif.

The latest edition of the text originally written by Strauss and Corbin is still an excellent introduction to implementing grounded theory. Kathy Charmaz's book covers the same ground, though in less detail.

Discourse and conversation analysis

Andersen, N.A. (2003) *Discursive Analytical Strategies*, The Policy Press, Bristol.

Fairclough, N. (2003) *Analysing Discourse*, Routledge, London.

McClure, M. (2003) *Discourse in Education and Social Research*, Open University Press, Buckingham.

Rapley, T. (2007) *Doing Conversation, Discourse and Document Analysis*, Sage, London.

Discourse analysis is a complex field. These four books will take you to different parts. Each takes a different approach.

McClure provides a broad overview with case studies showing discourse analysis in different contexts. After reading in the introduction to Chapter 5 that 'like any other texts, research texts . . . are fabrications', you begin to look at research literature in a different way.

Rapley provides a sound introduction to some important approaches to qualitative analysis. Chapter 3 is insightful in terms of ethical guidelines and advice on recording conversation and Chapter 4 on the practicalities of recording outlines a procedure that will ensure you will obtain data. Chapters 6 to 9 look at ways of extracting meaning from the data. Examples are well drawn to make points clear.

Fairclough's book has a much more 'hands on' approach. More than with McClure, you will have to get used to the technical terminology used in discourse analysis but the ideas are well explained.

At the heart of Andersen's book are the theoretical positions that determine the various approaches to discourse analysis. This is a book to read if you are unclear of your own philosophical position. It is, however, not for the faint-hearted.

Narrative analysis

Webster, L. and Mertova, P. (2007) *Using Narrative Enquiry as a Research Method: An Introduction to Using Critical Event Narrative Analysis in Research on Learning and Teaching*, Routledge, Abingdon.

Often we are interested in turning points in people's lives or the impact and effect of critical incidents. This book shows how to conduct such an investigation. Usefully, there is a whole chapter of examples of narratives so that researchers can see what they should aim to produce.

Semiotics

Harnson, C. (2003) 'Visual Social Semiotics: Understanding How Still Images Make Meaning', *Technical Communication*, 50(1), 46–60.

Van Leewen, T. (2005) *Introducing Social Semiotics*, Routledge, London.

Van Leewen's book is a highly readable overview of what can be a complex subject. It takes a broader view than just analysing material as signs, signifiers and signified and shows how people assemble resources to communicate an impression, an idea, a belief. It defines and explains the principles of social semiotics and outlines the frameworks used in analysis.

Visual imagery is a growing area of data analysis, yet examples of how to go about it are few. Claire Harnson, an American analyst, has written a short review of images from a semiotic perspective in the journal *Technical Communication* (available as a download from Amazon USA). With examples to explain principles and questions that will point researchers in the right direction, her paper is an excellent introduction to a difficult area.

References

Aalsvoort, G., Harinck, F. and Gossé, G. (2006) 'Script Identification: A Way to Understand How Students Choose Strategy During Mathematization?' *European Journal of Special Needs Education*, 21(3), 301–319.

An, W. (2007) 'High Stakes Testing and Curriculum Control: A Qualitative Metasynthesis', *Educational Research*, 36(5), 258–267.

Anderson, M., Standen, P. and Noon, J. (2005) 'A Social Semiotics Interpretation of Suicidal Behaviour in Young People', *Journal of Health Psychology*, 10(3), 317–331.

Askehave, I. (2007) 'The Impact of Marketisation on Higher Education Genres – The International Student Prospectus as a Case in Point', *Discourse Studies*, 9(6), 723–742.

Bailey, J. (2008) 'First Steps in Qualitative Data Analysis: Transcribing', *Family Practice*, 25(2), 127–131.

Benwell, B. and Stokoe, E. (2002) 'Constructing Discussion Tasks in University Tutorials: Shifting Dynamics and Identities', *Discourse Studies*, 4(4), 429–453.

Berks, M., Chapman, Y. and Francis, K. (2008) 'Memoing in Qualitative Research: Probing Data and Process', *Journal of Research in Nursing*, 13(1), 68–75.

Blok, H., Sleegers, P. and Karsten, S. (2008) 'Looking for a Balance Between Internal and External Evaluation of School Quality: Evaluation of the SVI Model', *Journal of Educational Policy*, 23(4), 379–395.

Bolinger, J., Johnston, L. and Brackenridge, C. (2004) 'Maximising Transparency in a Doctoral Thesis. The Complexities of Writing About the Use of QSR NVIVO Within a Grounded Theory Study', *Qualitative Research*, 4(2), 247–265.

Bourdon, S. (2002) 'The Integration of Qualitative Data Analysis Software in Research Strategies: Resistances and Possibilities', *Forum Qualitative Social Research* (on-line journal) 3(2), http://www.qualitative-research.net/fqs-texte,2-02/2-02bourdon-e.htm (accessed July 2008).

Bowen, G. (2008) 'Naturalistic Inquiry and the Saturation Concept: A Research Note', *Qualitative Research*, 8(1), 137–152.

Brooker, B. (2005) 'Stakeholders' meanings of effective school leadership: A case study in a New Zealand primary school', unpublished doctoral thesis, Griffith University, Australia. Online at http://www4.gu.edu.au:8080/adt-root/public/adt-QGU20061023.15153.

Carey, J., Wengel, P., Reilly, C., Sheridan, J., Steinberg, J. and Harbison, K. (1998) *'CDC EZ-Text': Software for Collection, Management and Analysis of Semi-Structured Qualitative Databases (Version 3.06)*. Developed by Conwal Incorporated for the Centers for Disease Control and Prevention.

Charmaz, K. (2006) *Constructing Grounded Theory: A Practical Guide Through Qualitative Analysis*, Sage, London.

Clifton, J. (2006) 'A Conversational Analytical Approach to Business Communication: The Case of Leadership', *Journal of Business Communication*, 43(3), 202–219.

Corrie, D. (1999) *Girl Talk: Adolescent Magazines and Their Readers*, University of Toronto Press.

Cupchik, G. (2001) 'Constructivist Realism: An Anthology that Encompasses Positivist and Constructivist Approaches to the Social Sciences', *Forum Qualitative Social Research*, 2(1), Art. 7, http://nbn-resolving.de/uru:nbn:de0114-fqs0177, accessed July 2008.

Dye, J., Schatz, I., Rosenberg, B. and Coleman, S. (2000) 'Constant Companion Method: A Kaleidoscope of Data', *The Qualitative Report*, 4(l/2), available at www.nova.edu/SSS/QR/QR4-1/dye.html (accessed July 2008).

Ekman, P. and Friesen, W. (1976) *Facial Action Coding System: A Technique for the Measurement of Facial Movement*, Consulting Psychologists Press, Palo Alto.

Fereday, J. and Muir-Cochrane, E. (2006) 'Demonstrating Rigour Using Thematic Analysis: Hybrid Approach of Inductive and Reductive Coding and Theme Development', *International Journal of Qualitative Methods*, 5(1), Art. 7, available at http://www.valberta.ca/~iiqm/backissues/5_1/5_ltoc.html (accessed July 2008).

Fraser, H. (2004) 'Doing Narrative Research: Analysing Personal Stories Line by Line', *Qualitative Social Work*, 3(2), 179–201.

Gillies, D. (2007) 'Excellence and Education: Rhetoric and Reality', *Education, Knowledge and Economy*, 1(1), 19–35.

Giske, T. and Artinian, B. (2007) 'A Personal Experience of Working With Classical Grounded Theory: From Beginner to Experienced Grounded Theorist', *International Journal of Qualitative Methods*, 6(4), 67–80, available at http://ejournals.library.valberta.ca/index.php/IJQM/article/view/992.678 (accessed July 2008).

Glaser, B. and Strauss, A. (1967) The Discovery of Grounded Theory: Strategies for Qualitative Research, Aldine, Chicago.

Glaser, B. (1992) *Basics of Grounded Theory Analysis: Emergence vs Forcing*, Sociology Press, Mill Valley, Calif.

Godfrey, C. (2006) *Responses to an Early Childhood Educational Intervention with Disadvantaged Families: An Exploratory Study*, thesis submitted to Victoria University in partial fulfilment of the requirements of the degree of Doctor of Psychology (Clinical Psychology), available at http://wallaby.vu.edu.au/adt-VVUT/public/adt-VVUT20070509.155333 (accessed February 2009).

Halliday, M. (1973) *Explorations in the Functions of Language*, Edward Arnold, London.

Harris, L.R. (2008) 'A Phenomenographic Investigation of Teacher Conceptions of Student Engagement in Learning', *Australian Educational Researcher*, 35(1), 57–79.

Hinduja, S. and Patchin, J. (2008) 'Personal Information of Adolescents on the Internet: A Quantitative Content Analysis of MySpace', *Journal of Adolescence*, 31(1), 125–146.

Hopperstad, M. (2008) 'How Children Make Learning Through Drawing and Play', *Visual Communication*, 7(1), 77–96.

Hsieh, H-S. and Shannon, S. (2005) 'Three Approaches to Qualitative Content Analysis', *Qualitative Health Research*, 15(9), 1277–1288.

Jones, R. and Noble, G. (2007) 'Grounded theory and management research: a lack of integrity?', *Qualitative Research in Organizations and Management*, 42(2), 84–103.

Kelle, U. (1997) 'Theory Building in Qualitative Research and Computer Programs for the Management of Textual Data', *Sociological Research Online*, 2(2) at http://www.socresonline.org.uk/socresonline/2/2/1.html (accessed July 2008).

Kelle, U. (2005) '"Emergence" vs "Forcing" by Empirical Data? A Crucial Problem of Grounded Theory Reconsidered', *Forum Qualitative Social Research*, 6(2), Art. 27, available at http://nbn-resolving.de/urn.nbn.de:0114-fqs0502275 (accessed July 2008).

Konapasek, Z. (2008) 'Making Thinking Visible With Atlas.Ei: Computer Assisted Qualitative Analysis as Textual Practices', *Forum Qualitative Social Research*, 9(2), Art. 12, available at http://nbn-resolving.de/urn:nbn:de:0114-fqs0802124 (accessed July 2008).

Krippendorf, K. (2004) *Content Analysis: An Introduction to its Methodology*, Sage, Thousand Oaks, Calif.

Lake, J. and Billingsley, B. (2000) 'An Analysis of Factors that Contribute to Parent School Conflict in Special Education', *Remedial and Special Education*, 21(4), 240–251.

Lewins, A. and Silver, C. (2006) 'Choosing a CAQDAS Package: A Working Paper', available at http://caqdas.soc.survey.ac.uk/index.htm (accessed July 2008).

Lewins, A. and Silver, C. (2007) *Using Software in Qualitative Research: A-Step-by-Step Guide*, Sage, London.

Lloyd, G. (2006) 'Preservice Teachers' Stories of Mathematics Classrooms: Explorations of Practice Through Fictional Accounts', *Educational Studies in Mathematics*, 63(1), 57–87.

MacQueen, K., McLelland, E., Kay, K. and Milstein, B. (1998) 'Codebook Development for Team-based Qualitative Analysis', *Cultural Anthropology Methods* (renamed *Field Methods*), 10(2), 31–36.

Malatalo-Siegl, K. (2008) 'From Multiple Perspectives to Shared Understanding: A Small Group in an Online Learning Environment', *Scandinavian Journal of Education*, 52(1), 77–95.

Marshall, H. (2002) 'What Do We Do When We Code Data?', *Qualitative Research Journal* 2(1), 56–70, http://www.latrobe.edu.au/aqr/journal/1AQR2002.pdf.

Marton, J. (2006) 'The Integration of Images into Architecture Presentations: A Semiotic Analysis', *Art, Design and Communication in Higher Education*, 5(1), 21–37.

Matheson, J. (2007) 'The Voice Transcription Technique: Use of Voice Recognition Software to Transcribe Digital Interview Data in Qualitative Research', *Qualitative Report*, 12(4), 547–560.

Morgado, M. (2007) 'The Semiotics of Extraordinary Dress: A Structural Analysis of Interpretation of Hip-Hop Style', *Clothing and Textiles Research Journal*, 25(2), 131–155.

Morgan, C. (2006) 'What Does Social Semiotics Have to Offer Mathematics Education Research?' *Education Studies in Mathematics*, 61(1–2), 219–245.

Ohi, S. (2008) 'The Teacher's Role in the Research-Policy-Prexis Nexus', *Australian Journal of Education*, 52(1), 95–109.

Onwegbuzie, A. and Daniel, L. (2003) 'Typology of Analytical and Interpretational Errors in Quantitative and Qualitative Educational Research', *Current Issues in Education*, (on-line) 6(2), available at http:/ cie.ed.asu.edu/volume6/number2/ (accessed July 2008).

Ormerod, F. and Ivanic, R. (2002) 'Materiality in Children's Meaning Making Practices', *Visual Communication*, 1(1), 65–91.

Oughton, H. (2007) 'Constructing the "Ideal Learner": A Critical Discourse Analysis of the Adult Numeracy Core Curriculum', *Research in Post-Compulsory Education*, 12(2), 259–275.

Pettigrew, S. (2002) 'A Grounded Theory of Beer Consumption in Australia', *Qualitative Market Research*, 5(2), 112–122.

Pinsof, W. (1986) 'The Process of Family Therapy: The Development of the Family Therapist Coding System', pp. 201–284 in *The Psychotherapeutic Process: A Research Handbook*, Greenberg, L. and Pinsoff, W. (eds).

Radford, L. (2000) 'Signs and Meanings in Students' Emergent Algebraic Thinking: A Semiotic Analysis', *Educational Studies in Mathematics*, 42(3), 237–268.

Reid, L. (2007) 'Teachers Talking About Writing Assessment: Valuable Professional Learning?' *Improving Schools*, 10(2), 132–149.

Rice, M., Sell, M. and Hadley, P. (1990) 'The Social Interactive Coding System (SICS)', *Language, Speech and Hearing Sources in Schools*, 21(2), 2–14.

Richmond, H. (2002) 'Learners' Lives: A Narrative Analysis', *Qualitative Report*, 7(3), available at http:// www.nova.edu/ssss/QR/QR7-3/richmond.html (accessed August 2008).

Robertson, S. (2005) 'Re-imagining and Re-sampling the Future of Education: Global Knowledge Economy Discourses and the Challenge to Education Systems', *Comparative Education*, 41(2), 151–170.

Rogers, R., Malanchavavil-Berks, E., Mostey, M., Hui, D. and O'Garro Joseph, G. (2005) 'Critical Discourse Analysis in Education: A Review of the Literature', *Review of Educational Research*, 75(3), 365–416.

Rusby, J., Estes, A. and Dishion, T. (1991) *The Interpersonal Process Code*, Oregon Social Learning Center, Oregon.

Schutz, A. (1967) *The Phenomenology of the Social World*, Northwestern University Press.

Social Semiotics (2005) 'Thinking Fat: Special Issue of Social Semiotics', *Social Semiotics*, 15(2).

Spencer, L., Ritchie, J., Lewis, J. and Dillon, L. (2003) *Quality in Qualitative Evaluation: A Framework for Assessing Research Evidence*, Cabinet office, London.

Strauss, A. (1987) *Qualitative Analysis for Social Scientists*, Cambridge University Press.

Strauss, A. and Corbin, J. (1990) *Basics of Qualitative Research: Grounded Theory Procedures and Techniques*, Sage, Newbury Park, Calif.

Vuyisile, M. (2006) 'The Quality of Life of "Street Children" Accommodated at Three Shelters in Pretoria: An Exploratory Study', *Early Child Development and Care*, 176(3–4), 253–269.

Walker, D. and Myrick, F. (2006) Grounded Theory: An Exploration of Process and Procedure, *Qualitative Health Research*, 16(4), 547–559.

Warburton, W. (2005) 'What Are Grounded Theories Made Of?', available at http://eprints.soton.ac.uk/16340/ (accessed July 2008).

Weitzman, E. and Miles, M. (1995) *Computer Programs for Qualitative Data Analysis: A Software Sourcebook*, Sage, Thousand Oaks, Calif.

Wetherell, M., Taylor, S. and Yates, S. (2001) *Discourse as Data*, Sage, London.

Wheway, R. and Millward, A. (1997) *Children's Play: Facilitating Play on Housing Estates*, Chartered Institute of Housing.

Willet, R. (2006) 'Poofy Dresses and Big Guns: A Post-Structuralist Analysis of Gendered Positioning Through Talk Amongst Friends', *Discourse*, 27(4), 441–455.

Wright, P. and Davis, A. (2008) 'Adolescent Parenthood Through Educators' Eyes: Perceptions of Worries and Provision of Support', *Urban Education*, 43(6), 671–695.

Chapter contents

Chapter 12

EXTRACTING INFORMATION FROM QUANTITATIVE DATA

Key themes

- The questions that statistical description can answer.
- The three key characteristics of data sets, how *typical* any value is, how *spread out* the data are and the *shape* of the data set.
- Describing data expressed through different types of measurement scale.
- Expressing the degree of association between one data set and another.
- Assessing trends over time can show a pattern.
- Working with real data sets.

Introduction

It is almost inevitable that, at some point in our research, we will have to deal with numbers. Even if our research is firmly rooted in the qualitative tradition, it is likely that we will need to demonstrate the significance of our study in a broader context. If, for example, our research was into understanding why some children have difficulties with numeracy (with a view to developing a teaching approach that helps them conceptualise mathematical concepts), we could show the significance of our research in terms of the cost of remedial support at later stages in the educational system, the proportion of pupils who failed to reach a standard or the percentage of adults whose numerical capability was insufficient to enable them to function effectively in society. We could estimate the cost to the economy of inadequate numeracy. All of these numbers are simple descriptors of situations but without them our study cannot be benchmarked in terms of its broader importance. But while our research would be of significance, its real value arises when we use the insights we have gained and develop a new approach to teaching that will help students learn. This is what a joint British/Dutch research team that looked at strategies for solving mathematical problems used by English and Dutch 9- and 10-year-old pupils did (Anghileri et al., 2002). They were able to show that the approach of the Dutch pupils (and the teaching approach that underpins this) was more effective than that of the English. And the only statistics they used to explore the performance data were averages and percentages.

It is not just the demonstration of the fact that quantitative analysis can help us draw conclusions that is important here, it is also that the methods used were so simple. There are, of course, more complex procedures for answering questions like, 'Is the difference between these two sets of data significant?' And we shall meet some of them in Chapter 13. What Anghileri and her collaborators did was show a marked difference in performance just by describing the data mathematically. And this is what this chapter is all about, using statistical summaries to draw out the characteristics of data sets so that, by inspection, similarities and differences can be identified and assessed.

12.1 What can we achieve by describing data?

Description as a research procedure achieves three things.

- First, it is a summary of what it is that we are looking at and summaries allow us to pick out the key points to identify characteristics that locate something (such as the degree to which a policy has been attained, practice improved or a social problem alleviated), so that we can look at them in relation to other instances. Summaries focus on the message and suppress the noise.
- Second, description is the means by which we show our understanding. Descriptive analysis is the process through which we move towards an understanding and our description is a statement of where we have reached in our understanding. We cannot show our understanding without describing it and the description of data is a powerful tool at our disposal.
- Third, we can describe a position in time. This creates a platform for establishing difference between now and a point in the past or the future and is the basis for further exploration of our understanding about the dynamics of a situation. Without description we cannot take our thinking further and move from an understanding of 'What is?' to formulate such questions as 'What might be?', 'What should be?' or 'What could be?'

Now that we have established why description is important, let us look more closely at the sorts of enquiry we can undertake with descriptive analysis.

12.1.1 Overcoming information overload

If we are confronted with a mass of data, it overloads us; we cannot assimilate it. UK universities, for example, are assessed on more than ten performance measures each year. Some have an equity dimension (per cent of students from schools and colleges in the state sector, per cent from lower socio-economic groups, per cent from low participation neighbourhoods). Others profile mode of attendance, type of degree, continuation rates (that is, failure), employment outcome and other university activities such as research. The quantities of data are enormous. Our immediate response is to simplify the data. One way of doing this is to compress the indicators into a single indicator for each institution. This would enable any institution to be compared with any other. This is what many newspapers in the UK do each year. The Higher Education Statistics Agency says that '[no] meaningful league table could fairly demonstrate the performance of all higher education institutions relative to each other' (see www.hesa.ac.uk/index.php/content/view/1168/141/, accessed August 2008). Notwithstanding this counsel of perfection, the rest of the world cannot handle a data matrix of 169 rows (the number of universities) and a number of columns that probably stretches into the hundreds. Even broken up into separate indicators, it is impossible to grasp the message of the data. Summary statistics profile the data set. What helps us understand the data is, 'What universities are typical on any one measure?' 'What are the best performing universities and what are the worst?' This type of question, as we shall see, is fundamental to descriptive analysis. And such questions are important because, when we have answered them, we can then ask the next question, 'Why are these so good and those so bad?' And so our research begins.

12.1.2 Profiling a situation

The second way we can use summary information is to create a profile. For example, if we wished to create a profile of British higher education we could, for each measure, say what the best and worst score was on each performance indicator. A group of British educational psychologists, led by Peter Smith, created a profile of those who were bullied at school (Smith et al., 2004). They categorised them as 'non-victims', 'escaped victims', 'continuing victims' and 'new victims' and used a variety of self-report and teacher reports to create the profile. The indicators they used included how much they enjoyed school, their likes and dislikes about school, patterns of friendship, whether they had ever bullied, their scores on a behavioural profile (that measured emotion, conduct, inattention, peer relationships, social behaviour), school attendance and the outcomes of being bullied. Their results, presented as percentages and average scores, revealed that the groups differed in their adjustment to school and the way they functioned in school. The results also showed that continuing victims of bullying were judged by teachers as having high rates of conduct disorder, hyperactivity and emotional problems. The benefit of this research is that it gives us insights not only into bullying but also into the link between being bullied, classroom disorder and, perhaps, exclusion.

Another approach to profiling is to assemble statistics from national sources. This is what Pamela Meadows and Daniel Roegger, two researchers under contract to the UK's Department for Work and Pensions, did in order to profile low income homeowners (Meadows and Roegger, 2005). This is the sort of research that in education we should be aware of because we need to understand the dimensions and consequences of low income for educational attainment and processes. Using data from the *Parents and Children Study*, the *Family Resources Survey*, the *Survey of Housing, Family Spending*, the *British Household Panel Survey*, the *House Condition Survey* and the *Poverty and Social Exclusion Survey*, they were able to create a profile of low income homeowners in terms of income levels, house value, mortgages, repossessions, age, size and condition of home, their neighbourhood, patterns of consumption, savings, wealth and debt. While 60 per cent of low income homeowners are over 60-years-old, this still leaves about 5.5 million households who are under 60, a significant proportion of which will have children or young dependants.

12.1.3 Looking for links

The third type of investigation we can undertake is to look for links between variables in order to push forward our ability to explain. If two or more variables are associated, we could be taking the first steps in creating a model with some explanatory power. When children start to mix with other children, usually when they attend nursery or primary schools, the incidence of cross-infection increases. In some instances the potential harm from infections is so great that we immunise against them. Where cross-infection does occur, for example with colds, there is some benefit to the discomfort as the antibodies that develop create resistance against reinfection. In some cases, however, there is discomfort without benefit. Head lice infections ('nits') are a case in point.

An Australian study of primary school children found that 13% of children were infected with head lice, 3.3% had evidence of having been infected and that the incidence of infection in individual schools varied from 0 to 28% (Counahan et al., 2004). A review of studies of head lice published in a letter to the journal *Emerging Infectious Diseases* confirmed (i) the worldwide prevalence of head lice (ii) the incidence varied between 0.48 and 22.4% in Europe, from 0 to 58.9% in Africa and 3.6 to 61.4% in North and South America (Falagas et al., 2008). There was, as well, one theme common to many of the studies, that girls were more likely to be infected than boys. This is the sort of link we need to explore in more detail.

A Belgian study has done just this (Willems et al., 2005). A sample of just over 6,000 school children in Ghent (30% of the population) revealed an infection rate of 8.9%. The following additional data were also collected:

- Personal data – age and sex.
- School data – school, class.
- Hair length, colour and type.
- Family data – number of children in the family, socio-economic status.

The results are shown in Table 12.1. This profile suggests association between variables. More girls than boys had hair lice. Infestations decreased from kindergarten to 6th year primary classes and increased with hair length and members of children in the family. They were higher for lower socio-economic groups. We have, here, the basis for a conceptual model but before we put it together we need think whether the associations are direct or indirect. Why should gender *per se* be an influence? Only because girls might have longer hair. To what extent are large families associated with lower socio-economic

Table 12.1 Incidence of hair lice

	%		%
Boys	6.8	Straight hair	8.6
Girls	10.7	Curly hair	10.6
		Frizzy hair	8.1
Under 5	9.1		
6–7	9.2	Fair hair	7.7
8–9	9.5	Red hair	9.1
10–11	7.0	Brown hair	10.0
Over 12	8.6	Black hair	8.2
Kindergarten	10.2	1 child in family	7.8
1/2 year Primary	9.7	2 children in family	7.6
3/4 year Primary	8.0	3 children in family	8.6
5/6 year Primary	6.1	4 or more children in family	13.9
Very short hair	5.1	Unemployed parent(s)	17.6
Short hair	8.5	Manual worker	12.4
Medium length hair	11.5	Non-manual worker	5.8
Long hair	10.6	Professional worker	5.2

Source: Willems et al. (2005).

status? Further investigation is clearly required but the use of simple descriptive statistics has taken our understanding forward. And why should we as educationalists be interested in this research on head lice? Because we want to understand the reasons for absence and the causes of bullying, amongst other things.

12.2 Describing with numbers

In Chapter 10, we learnt how to represent data graphically. In section 10.2.2 we saw how we could use histograms to represent the pattern in the data. We shall do exactly the same in this chapter and learn how to make numerical statements that represent data characteristics and form.

If we look back to Figure 10.6(a) we can see that there is a definite shape to the pattern in this data. As we shall see, this shape and its characteristics are important in quantitative analysis because it is the link between data description which we cover in this chapter, and more advanced statistical analysis that we look at in the next.

Let us look in a little more detail at some of the characteristics of a distribution. We need to understand what these are because they can be used to describe how one distribution differs from another. There are four aspects of the shape of the distribution that we should focus on: where the centre is, the spread of data around the centre, the height of the distribution and whether or not it is symmetrical.

- The first thing that we should notice about a distribution is that there is a centre, the point around which the observations are equally distributed. Imagine the distribution as a balance, with the same weight of observations on each scale. We can describe where this point is using measures such as the mean, mode and median. All express the 'averageness' of a distribution. We often use this measure to say something about our data. For example, we might say that the average score of pupils in school A on a language test was 48 and in school B it was 61. When we express the performance of the pupils in this way, we think we are identifying a difference that may be important.
- The second characteristic of a distribution that can interest us is that there is a spread of data around the centre. In some cases most of the data will be close to the centre and in other cases the data will spread widely from the centre. In describing data it is useful to be able to capture the extent of the spread of the data. We can measure this spread. As Figure 12.1(a) shows, it is perfectly possible to have two collections of data centred on the same point but with different spreads and it is important, when we describe our data, to be able to tell people about this difference.
- The third feature of a distribution is how high it is. In Figure 12.1(b) the distributions are of different heights, though in both they have the same centre and the same spread. This relationship between height and spread is called *peakedness*. We can produce numerical descriptors of peakedness as well.
- Finally, the fourth characteristic a data distribution may have is that it can be symmetrical or that it can lean to the left or right side. This is shown in Figure 12.1(c). This imbalance between left and right is called *skew*. The coloured curve is skewed to the right and the black shade to the left. We can describe skew in numerical terms as well.

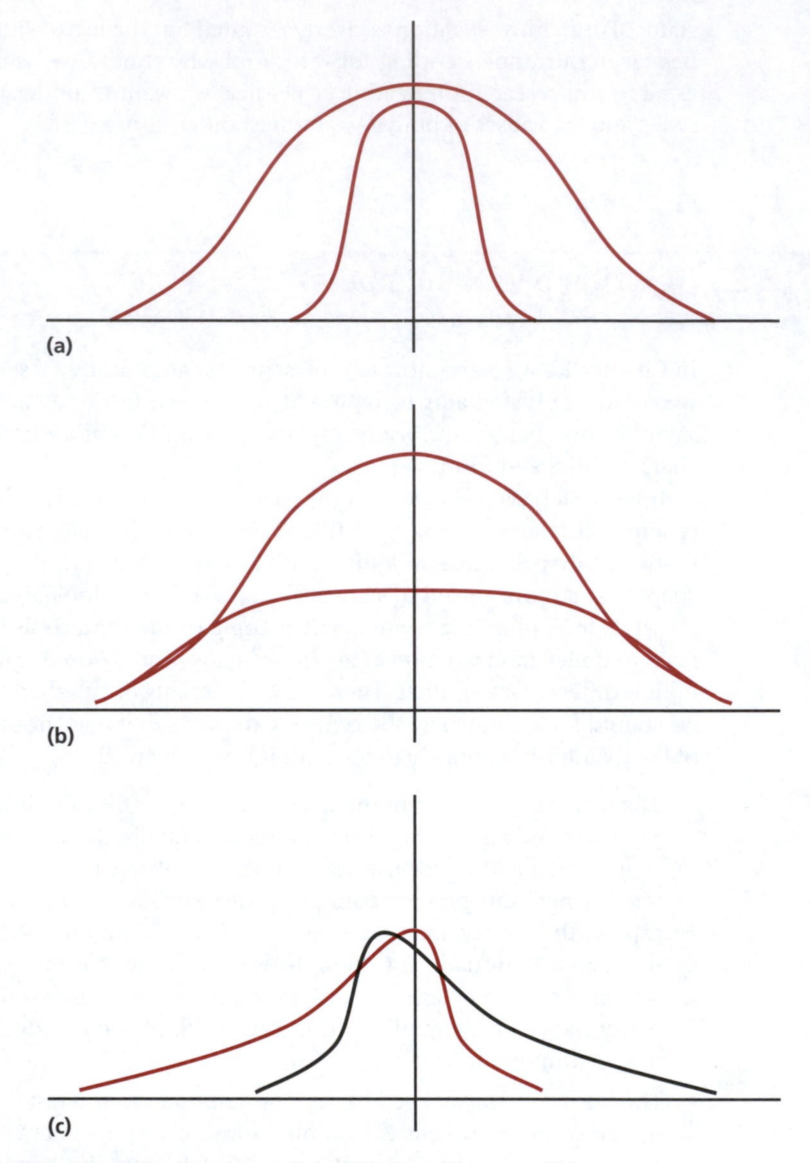

Figure 12.1 Data distributions with different characteristics

It is important that we describe our data sets accurately because our description can highlight that it may be worth investigating further. Why do pupils in two schools score such different grades? If test sores are all concentrated around the average does this mean that *all* the students are much the same or is the examiner only using part of the mark scale? While we shall look at each of our characteristics in turn, we should be aware, at the outset, that central tendency and spread are the most important. The final points we should make about the numerical descriptors we shall meet is that (a) in calculating them, we shall use different measurement systems and that (b) in describing some of these features of distributions, we shall combine indicators from these different measurement systems. This is not at all difficult but it may be useful to refresh memories by reading section 4.4 again.

12.3 Finding where the centre is

We use the idea of a centre to demonstrate typicality. We say that something in or near the *middle* is more representative than something at the edge of a group, that when *more people* believe something, it is characteristic of the group as a whole. We talk about average when we mean *usual*. 'Middle', 'more' and 'usual' are all different words we use to express typicality and each one is different. Statistics is the same and each of these ideas has a statistical equivalent. In this section we shall learn how to calculate them, what they mean and how to use them.

12.3.1 The mean – the most used

When we talk about the average, we usually mean the mean. For most people, it is the measure of centrality that is most frequently used. Its method of calculation normally requires little or no explanation; it is 'wired in' to the way in which we think about the world. We know what an average temperature is. When the newsreader talks about the average rate of inflation or unemployment over the last three or six months, we understand what is meant. In both cases, it is the mean. Calculating the mean is simple and most of us know how to do it – add up all of the values and divide the total by the number of values. We can express this using statistical notation.

$$\bar{x} = \sum_{1}^{n} \frac{x}{n}$$

where $\bar{x}$ is the mean of x
x is a single value
$\sum_{1}^{n}$ represents the process of summing all the values of x from the first (1) to the nth
– indicates the division process
n is the total number of xs

As you read articles and books you will come across this sort of notation. It is not (usually) put in to confound us. It is a shorthand way of saying 'this is how I did the calculation' and it can be important for us to know this because some calculations can be done in different ways (especially with statistical tests) and each way should be used only in particular circumstances. As researchers, we should be able to read what the notation is telling us. As we can see, with this example, it need not be too difficult.

Table 12.2 shows the number of free school meals taken in primary schools in a Scottish education authority on a census day in 2008. Data from 53 schools are shown. With this amount of data it is difficult to get a sense of the typical, so calculating the mean value is important. But calculations from official data sets like this can be tricky. The left-hand column has several asterisks. These indicate either where the number was four or less or where it could not be worked out. We have to decide on what basis to calculate the mean.

- If we choose to ignore the schools for which we have no information, then we divide the total number of pupils taking free school meals (2,077) by 46 to give a mean of 48.2.
- If we count the schools, we can assume either that no one had free school meals (we divide our total by 53 to give a mean of 39.2) or that four in each school had free school meals (which would increase our grand total by 28 pupils and give us a mean of 39.72).

Table 12.2 Free school meals taken in primary schools in a Scottish education authority (2008)

49	49	72	72	40	40	93	93
1	1	31	31	42	42	8	8
10	10	65	65	15	15	25	25
17	17	24	24	28	28	8	8
102	102	2	2	47	47	16	16
22	22	35	35	*	0	63	63
21	21	*	0	14	14	103	103
21	21	*	0	*	0	62	62
51	51	59	59	118	118	86	86
10	10	7	7	31	31	60	60
84	84	42	42	74	74	95	95
25	25	62	62	15	15		
*	0	91	91	52	52		
*	0	*	0	79	79		

Which mean value should we take? First, we should investigate to see if we can identify the reasons for the missing data. If, after this, we still have no solution, we have to decide whether to ignore the schools for which there are no data and just use the data we have (which may overestimate the true mean) or set the missing values to zero (which may underestimate the true mean). In some cases it may be better to overestimate (for example, if allocating funding) but generally we should go with the data we have, while noting that our best estimate of the mean may be within a range.

While there may be issues with missing data, the method of calculating a mean is actually straightforward. Much of the data we have to work with, however, may be grouped into classes (which statisticians refer to as 'bins') because this is the way the data is presented to us by official sources. This poses a problem. How do we calculate a mean in these circumstances? It is quite simple. We assume that the data in each class is evenly distributed and then represent each class by its mid-point. Table 12.3 shows the number of nursery and primary school teachers by age. What is the mean age?

- Our first step is to look at the age groups. Most of the classes have a range of five years, 25–29 for example. Two have no limiting boundary, under 25 and over 60.
- The easiest classes to deal with are those with an age range of five years. What we do is determine the mid-point of the class. The easiest way to do this is to add the upper class boundary to the lower class boundary and then divide by two. So 30 plus 34 equals 64 and half of 64 is 32.
- Where the class does not have a value for class boundary we have to create one. At the lower end, we assume that teachers start at age 21 and, at the upper end, that they retire at 65.
- Our final step is to assume that every teacher has the age of the mid-point of the class. We have to do this because we do not know from our table their actual ages. It will give us the most reliable estimate. If we used the lower limit of the class we would underestimate the total ages of teachers in the class and if we used the upper limit we

Table 12.3 Age of teachers in schools in England 2006

	Numbers of nursery/primary teachers in each age group	Class mid-point	Product of class frequency and mid-point
under 25	9,500	22.5	213,750
25–29	30,100	27	812,700
30–34	24,400	32	780,800
35–39	17,000	37	629,000
40–44	17,000	42	714,000
45–49	19,400	47	911,800
50–54	28,200	52	1,466,400
55–59	19,300	57	1,100,100
60 +	1,800	62.5	112,500
Total	166,700		6,741,050

would overestimate the total ages. We then multiply the number of teachers in each class by the mid-point of the class to give the total ages of teachers in the class.

- To calculate the mean age of teachers, we sum their ages (6,741,050) and divide this by the total number of teachers (166,700). This gives a mean age of 40.44.

This method is quite simple and well within the capability of anyone aiming to do research in education but sometimes the technique can get in the way of the implications of the result. This might be the case here. Let's look at the data again. What stands out? The number of nursery and primary teachers rises from first entrants (213,750 in the under 25 group) to 780,800 in the 30–34 group then falls (629,000 in the 35–39 group) and then rises again, peaking in the 50–54 age group. The mean age actually falls in the trough. So, in this case, the mean age (40.44) of teachers does not identify the *most usual* teacher. This is something we need to watch out for. The mean is susceptible to the influence of extreme values and to the character of the data distribution. Our calculations are perfectly correct but the mean gives a better indication of typicality when the pattern of the distribution falls off on the lower side of the mean much the same as it does on the upper side, in other words when the distribution is symmetrical.

12.3.2 The median

One of the ways we think about something being typical is for it to be in the middle. This is what the median identifies, where the middle is.

To find the median, we must, first of all, rank the data. This is the most time-consuming part of the process. Take the data in Table 12.2. We have to rearrange these in rank order from the lowest to the highest. This is what we have done in Table 12.4 with the data on free school meals from the first column in Table 12.2. There are 46 data units ranked from 1 (pupil in a school with free school meals) to 118. The median item is the middle one, the one that splits the distribution into two. If there were an uneven number of data units (say 47), it would be easy to find the median because it would be the item ranked 24, which has 23 values on either side. With an even number of data units it

Table 12.4 Identifying the median item

1	15	25	42	62	91
2	15	25	47	63	93
7	16	28	49	65	95
8	17	31	51	72	102
8	21	31	52	74	103
10	21	35	59	79	118
10	22	40	60	84	
14	24	42	62	86	

is marginally more difficult. The median value with 46 data values lies between the 23rd (which has 22 values above it) and the 24th (which has 22 values below it). The 23rd and 24th items are shown in colour. We estimate the median value as half the distance between them. The difference between 40 and 42 is 2, half is 1, 1 plus 40 is 41. This compares with a mean of 48.2 for the same data set.

We can also estimate the median from grouped data. To show the method, we shall use the data on the ages of nursery and primary school teachers (Table 12.3) in Table 12.5.

- Our first step is to find the class that contains the median teacher, that is, the 83,350th teacher if they were all arranged in rank order of their ages. To do this it is easiest if we calculate the *cumulative frequency* of our data set. That is, we add the numbers in a class to the numbers in all preceding classes. This is shown in Table 12.5. The cumulative frequency for the 25–29 group is the frequency for the group (30,100) plus the frequencies of all preceding groups (9,500), a total of 36,900. The process continues with all groups.
- The second step is to identify the category that contains the median teacher. There are a total of 166,700 teachers, so the median teacher is number 83,350. The median teacher, therefore, is found in the 40–44 age group (shown in red). We know that the median teacher is in this group because there are 98,000 teachers up to the age of 44 and only 81,000 up to the age of 39. Since 81,000 is less than 83,350 the median teacher cannot be below 39-years-old and because 98,000 is greater than 83,350, the median teacher cannot be older than 44.

Table 12.5 Identifying the median item from grouped data

Age group	Frequency	Cumulative frequency
under 25	9,500	9,500
25–29	30,100	39,600
30–34	24,400	64,000
35–39	17,000	81,000
40–44	17,000	98,000
45–49	19,400	117,400
50–54	28,200	145,600
55–59	19,300	164,900
60 +	1,800	166,700

- The third step is to identify where in the category the median item is. Here we again assume that the data in the category are evenly distributed. What we have to determine is the difference between the cumulative frequency up to the median category (81,000) and the median value (83,350). In our case this is 2,350. We then express this as a percentage of the frequency in the median category (17,000) and multiply this percentage by the range of the median category (5). In other words, we are saying that if our median teacher is 2,350/17,000 per cent of the total in the group (actually 13.8%), the age of the median teacher is 13.8% of the range of the age group (13.8% of 5), that is, 0.69. All we do is then add this lower age limit of the group (40) to give a median age of 40.69. We can express this procedure in a fearsome-looking but quite straightforward formula:

$$\text{Median} = \frac{LV + \frac{n}{2} - CF}{f} \cdot r$$

LV = value of the lower limit of the median class
n = total number
CF = cumulative frequency of class below median class
f = frequency in median class
r = range of median class

In our example:

$$\frac{40 + \frac{166{,}700}{2} - 81{,}000}{17{,}000} \cdot r = \frac{2{,}350}{17{,}000} \cdot 5 = 40.69$$

- An alternative to the calculator method is to draw an ogive (see section 10.3 for the method of how to do this) and read off the 50% value. The benefit of this approach is that all the calculation can be done via a spreadsheet. Figure 12.2 shows an ogive

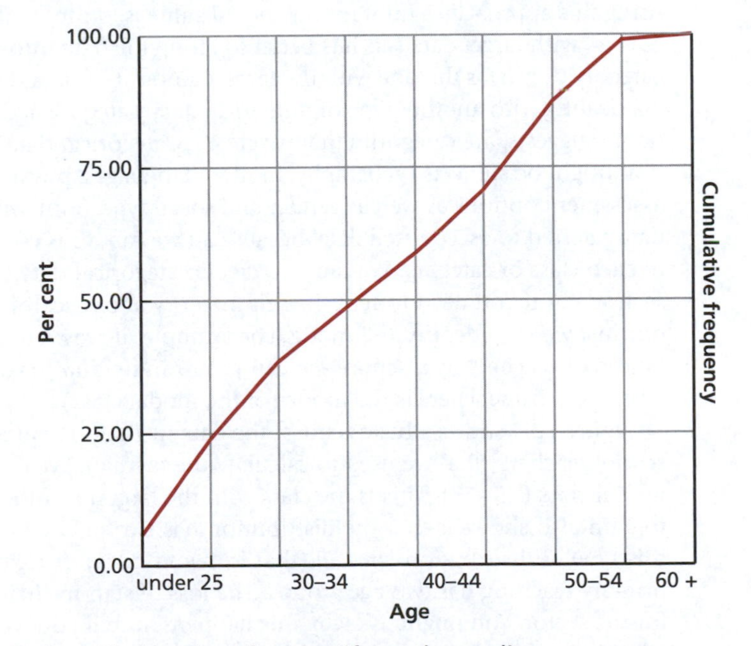

Figure 12.2 Graphical method for identifying the median

created via Calc, the spreadsheet program in the Open Office Suite. We can find the median value, 50%, and read off the median age, about 40.7. This graphical method is less precise than the calculation method but it is fast.

Unlike the mean, the median is not affected by extreme values. Each value has the same weight as every other value. What does this mean? If there were 40 items, the 1st and the 40th have the same influence when we identify the median. If we were calculating the mean and the largest value (the 40th item) was an outlier that was three times as large as the 39th value, it would exert an undue influence on the value of the mean. The reason for this is that we are using two different measurement scales. With the mean, we use an interval scale. With the median we are often using an ordinal scale (that is, one based on rank order and not a standard unit of distance). Because this is a weaker measurement scale (that is, it is less precise), the median is a less precise estimator of central tendency. But against this, it is easy to calculate, is not distorted to the same extent as a mean can be by extreme data values and allows us to rapidly assess our data.

12.3.3 The mode

What is most common is another way of describing what is typical. The mode does this. It is the most straightforward of the measures of central tendency; it is the easiest to describe and identifying the mode does not stretch the intellect. But there are issues to be aware of.

The mode is the data value that occurs most frequently. If we had the following sequence of data units: 12, 14, 15, 15, 16, 16, 16, 18, 18, 20, 24, the mode would be 16. Identifying the mode can be as simple as this but with some data sets, this method does not generate a useful measure of central tendency. Look at the data in Table 12.4, for example. This is arranged so that we can identify the most frequently occurring data values. They are 2 × 10, 2 × 15, 2 × 21, 2 × 25, 2 × 31 and 2 × 62. A data set with six modes is not very useful to us. And when we get several hundred more units of data in our data set, using this approach to hunt for the modal value is, quite frankly, a waste of time. For this reason, with larger data sets it is better to group the data into classes. The modal class (or category or bin) is the one with the largest amount of data. This clearly indicates that we are dealing with another type of numerical data, categorical data. Categorical data, as the name suggests, are categories that we create. Categorical data that we can meet in education might be subjects (geography, modern languages, physics, etc.), types of school and assessment options as well as gender and social type. Sometimes we can find this type of data referred to as 'counted data' because all we can do is count the number of instances in each class or category. We can also create categorical data from interval scale data (see section 4.4 if you need to refresh your memory about scales of measurement) and if we do this, we can identify the mode. For example, if we were investigating the travel distances of teachers to a school we can group individual travel distances and the group with the most teachers is the mode (or the modal class).

Figure 12.3 shows a histogram of the data in Table 12.3 (ages of nursery and primary school teachers) that we used to calculate the median. We can immediately pick out the modal class (25–29). This is the class with the largest number of teachers. What the histogram also shows is that the distribution has two peaks, at 25–29 and 50–54. We call this type of distribution *bimodal* (that is, two modes). It clearly shows that nursery and primary teaching has two age groups. The loss of staff in their early 30s is a serious issue for the sector. You might ask why this happens and, if you were in this situation, what it would take for you to stay in teaching.

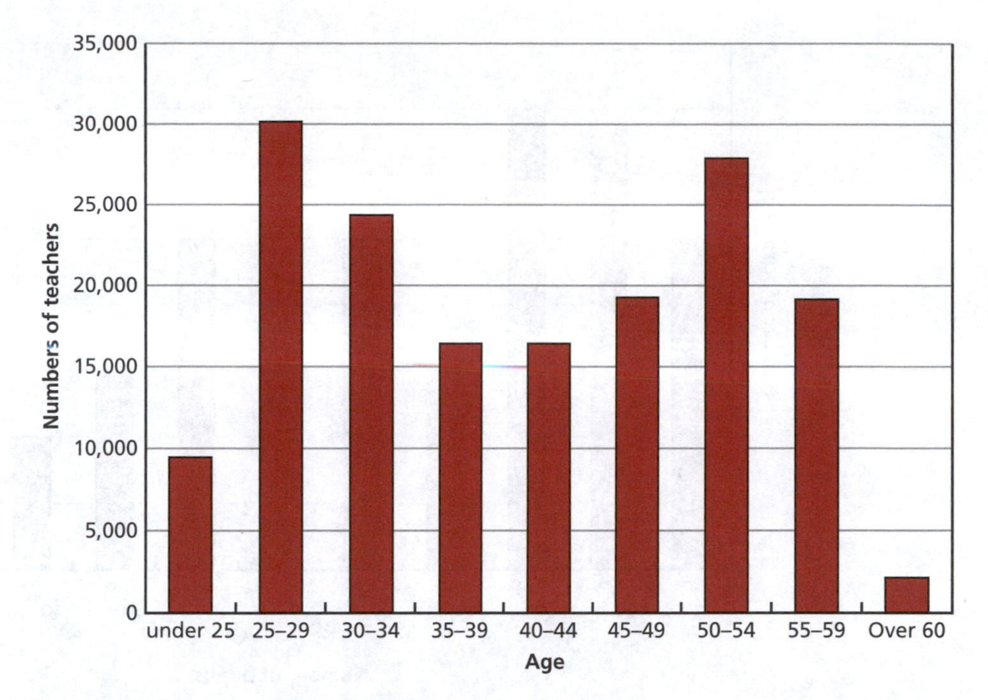

Figure 12.3 Ages of nursery and primary school teachers

We can also use the data on pupils taking free school meals (Table 12.4) to identify the mode. This, however, involves us in an additional step, creating the class boundaries that we use to represent the data. This is where we have to exercise our judgement, as we shall see with the following examples.

Figure 12.4(a) shows the data with 11 classes. This gives two modal classes, 10–19 and 20–29 pupils per school, with two subsidiary peaks. If we reduce the number of classes to 5 (Figure 12.4(b)), the modal class moves to 19 and under. Now if simply changing the number of classes can do this to a statistical indicator, what can we do in order to identify what the 'right' number of classes should be? This is actually a complex mathematical area and clearly there has to be a relationship between the number of data units and the number of classes (and, by implication the class interval) in order to show sufficient detail (that is, neither suppress information nor swamp interpretation with detail). There are some rules of thumb, however.

- Sturges' rule states that the number of classes is given by the equation:

  $1 + 3.3 \times \log n$ where n is the number of observation

  Herbert Sturges, an American statistician, developed this rule of thumb in 1926.

- An alternative is to use the equation:

  $5 \times \log n$

  This equation appears as custom and practice in some social sciences and appears to have no formal or identifiable source.

Both of these formulations have been criticised because they have no basis in statistical theory. Because of this it is better if we do not use them. The Rice rule (so called because it was developed by staff in the Statistics Department at Rice University in the USA)

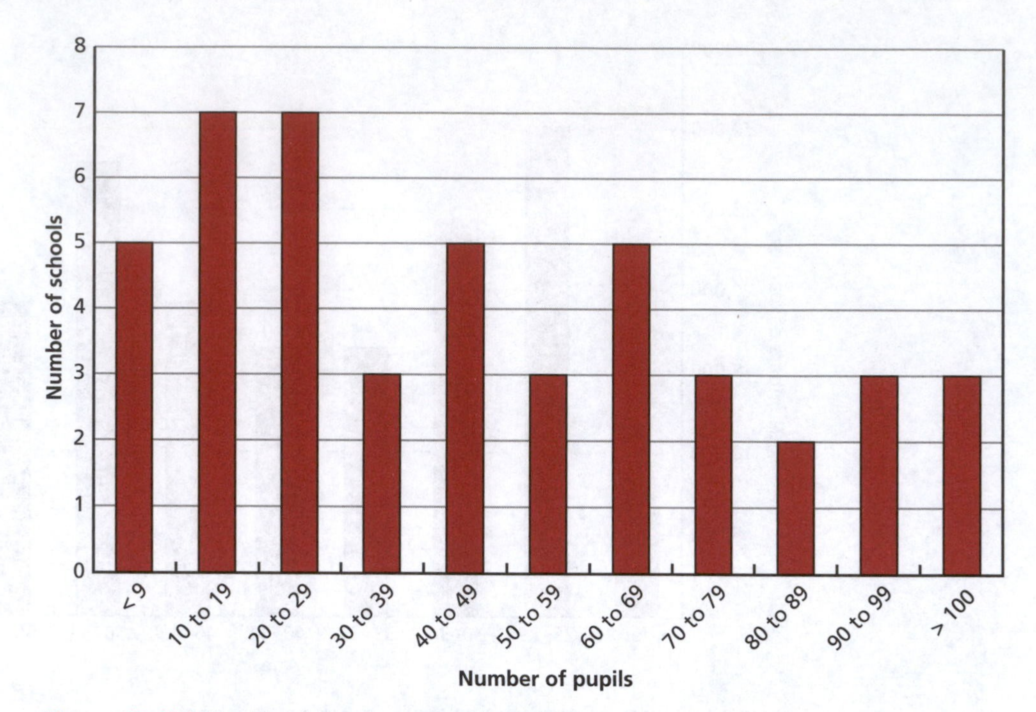

Figure 12.4(a) Pupils taking free school meals

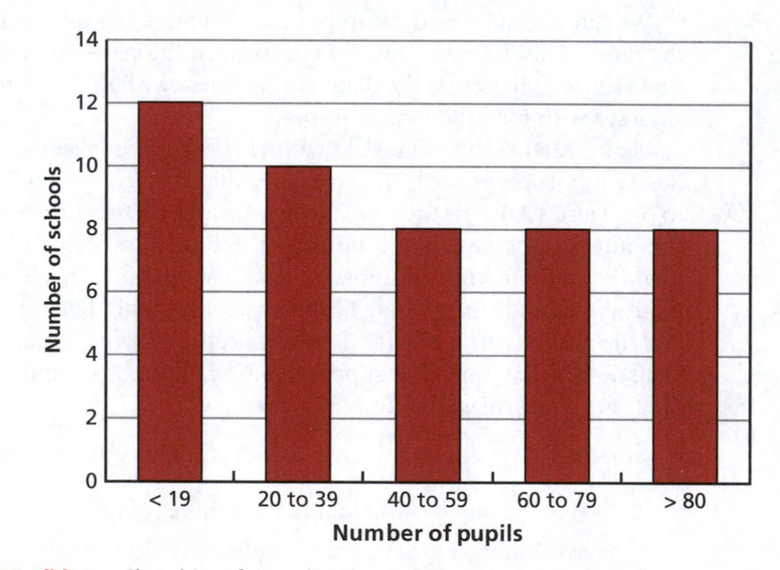

Figure 12.4(b) Pupils taking free school meals (revised categories)

seems to give results that approximate to more advanced rules that are beyond this text to explain. The Rice formula is:

$2\sqrt[3]{n}$ where n is the number of data units

Table 12.6 shows the number of classes each method would generate for data sets of different size. As the data sets increase in size, the Sturges model compacts the distribution,

Table 12.6 Number of classes generated by different rules of thumb

	Size of data set			
	25	50	100	200
Rice	6	7	9	12
Sturges	6	7	8	9
5 × log	7	8	10	12

which will lead to a loss of detail. The *5 × log n* model may overestimate the ideal number of classes with small amounts of data. Both of these conclusions assume that the Rice model gives more appropriate results. Figure 12.4(c) shows our school meal data with 8 classes. This shows detail and gives a sense that the distribution is more skewed than multimodal.

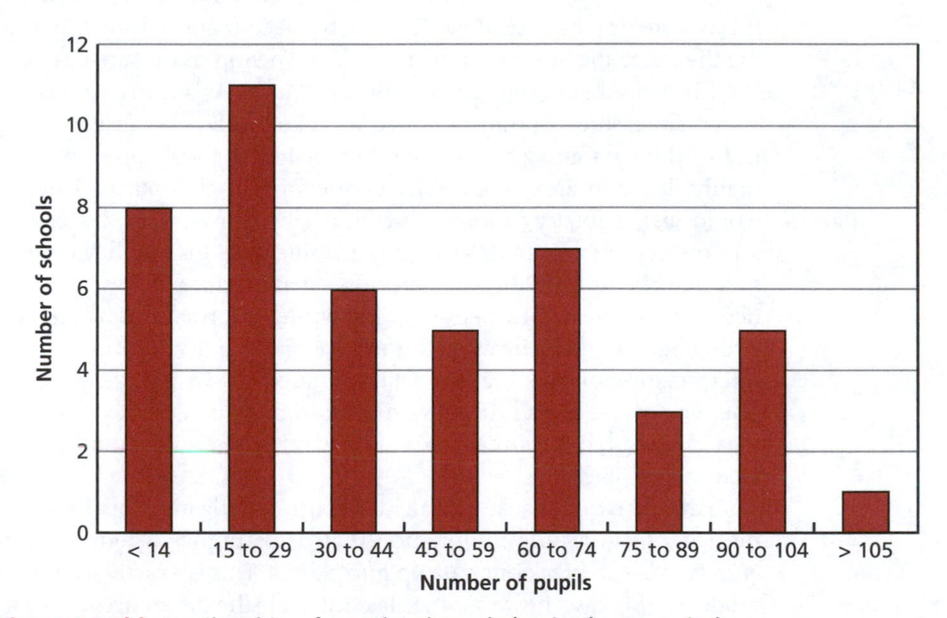

Figure 12.4(c) Pupils taking free school meals (revised categories)

12.4 Measuring spread

Having an estimate of where the centre of a data set is located is not a great deal of use unless we know where the rest of the data are. Are they close to the centre, spread out a long way from the centre, or what? Knowing how 'spread out' the data are is important. It can tell us how useful a measure of centrality is (it is not much use if the data is very spread out). If one of our samples is bunched around the centre and another is spread out, we would want to know why. Are the people we spoke to really like that or did we mess up with our sampling?

There are two ways we can measure how spread out the data are, one uses the median as its reference point and the other the mean. We shall look at each in turn.

12.4.1 The range as a measure of spread

The range of a data set is associated with the median as a measure of centrality. The range measures the spread of the data. It is easy to compute. Imagine a race; there is a competitor who is first and another who is last. There, in a nutshell, is the concept of range, from the first to the last, the smallest unit of data to the largest.

(i) Using interval data

Let us look at Table 12.2 again. This shows the data on the number of children in a selection of Scottish schools receiving free school meals. The smallest number in the left-hand column is 1 and the smallest in the right-hand is 0. Remember that we had to make assumptions about how to deal with missing data and it seems a reasonable assumption that there is at least one school where no children receive free meals (and even if this were not the case, the difference between 0 and 1 is no big deal). So in determining the range the bottom of the range is 0. The top of the range is 118.

This measure of range gives us the *total range*. As a measure it is susceptible to erratic extreme measures. In statistics these are called *outliers* because they exist way beyond the rest of the data. Imagine that our data included a two form entry primary school in a highly deprived area where three-quarters of all children had free school meals. This would give a total of some 270 children, which is vastly larger than the majority of schools in our table. In this case it is genuine data, that is, they represent an actual situation that results from the same processes that produce the rest of the data. However, outliers are also created by people giving wrong information, by researchers keying in the wrong figures and by investigators misunderstanding a response. Outliers can distort our interpretation of data. If a data set has a range of 147 and the bottom value is 7, we have one idea of the spread. If the next to bottom value is 82 we get a completely different idea of spread. It is for this reason that we also determine another measure of range, the *interquartile range*.

Again, it requires just a straightforward investigation of the data to determine this measure. First, a little information that helps unpick a term that may be unfamiliar, *quartile*. We can break our data up into classes. This is exactly what we did when with the mode. In this case, however, the class interval (the difference between the lower limit of the class and the upper limit) was always the same. Now, imagine this whole process reversed, so that each class contains an equal number of data units. In this case, the class widths would vary in size. The divisions that are normally used are:

- Ten classes, where each class holds 10% of the data. We call these classes *deciles*.
- Five classes, where each holds 20% of the data. We call these *quintiles*.
- Four classes, where each holds 25% of the data. We call these *quartiles*.

So if our data set consisted of 200 data units, we could have 10 classes with 20 units of data in each, or five classes with 40 or four classes with 50. In our case, we are dealing with quartiles. If our data do not divide so easily as this, we have to work around the problem. Table 12.7 shows the school dinner data in Table 12.2 divided into deciles, quintiles and quartiles. Where the number of observations does not divide equally by the number of classes, we have to adjust the number, usually by going up or down one. The

Table 12.7 Deciles, quintiles and quartiles

(a) Deciles		(b) Quintiles		(c) Quartiles	
Class number		Class number		Class number	
1–8	5				
9–15	5	1–15	10		
16–21	4	16–29	9	1–16	11
22–25	4	30–51	9	17–40	12
26–40	5	52–76	9	41–68	12
41–51	5	77–118	9	69–118	11
52–62	5				
63–76	4				
77–91	4				
92–118	5				

class intervals have to be adjusted so that the whole data range is covered. If there is a gap between one value in one class and the next value in the next class, the difference has to be split between the class intervals. All of this is a fairly common sense procedure.

While this procedure has shown how we can divide our data up, when we look at the quartiles, we can be far more precise in our identification of the interquartile range. *The interquartile range* is the range from the bottom of the second quartile to the top of the third quartile, that is, the quartiles immediately below and immediately above the median. The interquartile range represents the 50% of the data set in the middle of the distribution. We can, however, still be faced with problems.

From Table 12.7 column(c), we can *estimate* the interquartile range as 17 to 68 (a range of 52). But if we look at the *actual values* in our distribution they are 17 and 65, a range of 48. However, because we had to adjust the numbers in our class to take account of the fact that 46 is not exactly divisible by four, even this interquartile range is an overestimate since it contains 24 out of 46 observations, 52% and not 50%. We can have a range of 50% of the data values if we use 23 of them. How do we do this? The answer is to calculate where a theoretical bottom and upper value would be by taking 11.5 (half of 23) data units from a theoretical median (41) and adding 11.5, giving 19 to 64 (a range of 45).

The method we choose depends on the degree of accuracy we require. The 'theoretical' method is the best. However, we will often use the concept of interquartile range to get a rough and ready impression of the data. Speed may be more important than precision. However, it does not take a great deal of effort to create a more precise measure.

(ii) Using grouped data

We can also estimate spread using grouped data. The easiest way is to construct an ogive and read off the data. Look at Figure 12.2 and identify the range and interquartile range for the data on the ages of teachers.

If we want a precise measure, we may have to use the original data (Table 12.5). For the range, we can make reasonable assumptions, the youngest teacher will be aged 21 and the oldest 65. For the interquartile range we have to make some calculations. With 166,700 teachers in the population, we know each quartile should hold 41,675. We can find the quartile with the 41,675th teacher (30–31), identify the precise age within this quartile and then find the quartile with the 125,025th teacher (50–54) and identify the precise age within this quartile.

To do this, we use the method we used earlier to find the median:

- Identify the quartile with the 41,675th teacher.
- Subtract the cumulative frequency of the groups below the quartile with the 41,675th teacher from 41,675 (41,675 − 39,600 = 2,075).
- Express the difference as a proportion of the number in the category containing the 41,675th teacher (2,075/24,400 = 8.5%).
- Determine 8.5% of the width of the category containing the 41,675th teacher (8.5% × 60 months = 5.1).
- The lower quartile of interquartile range is 30 years 5 months.

We repeat this procedure for the upper band of the interquartile range. The result is 51 years. The interquartile range is 30 years 5 months to 51 years (a range of 20 years 8 months). As we shall see later, this information is useful.

How can we use this information? To tell us that 50% of the teaching population is between 30 years and 5 months and 51-years-old and that the difference between the lower limit of the range and the median and the upper limit and the median is virtually the same. In other words, the core of our distribution is symmetrical around the centre. This is an important finding because it suggests that we could be dealing with a particular type of probability distribution that we shall read more about in the next chapter.

12.4.2 Standard deviation as a measure of spread

We use the standard deviation to measure the spread of our data in association with the mean. It is useful in exactly the same way that the interquartile range is, but there is one other way it is useful as well, and it is important. The standard deviation has important characteristics that allow us to express ourselves in terms of probability. In other words, it enables us to go beyond describing what has happened to talking about the likelihood of something. Let us leave it in these rather vague terms at present and note, in conclusion, that just as we could use the median with ungrouped and grouped data, we can do the same with the standard deviation. We shall look at how to calculate each in turn and what its implications are.

(i) Using raw data

The principle of the standard deviation is really very simple, it measures how different each unit of data is from the mean. Let us imagine a data set of five numbers:

2, 3, 4, 5, 6

The mean of these numbers is 4. Now let us measure the difference between each unit of data and the mean. For 2, the difference is 2, for 3, the difference is 1 and for 4 it is 0. For 5 the difference is −1 (4 − 5 = −1) and for 6, −2. Now, what happens when we add all these numbers up to measure the total amount of difference (or deviation) in the data set? The answer is obvious – it is zero, because the negative numbers cancel out the positive ones. This is not a good measure of deviation but it is not a problem because, in mathematics, we can get rid of negative numbers by squaring them. However, because we do it to negative numbers we have to do it to positive ones as well. So our differences from the mean now become:

$$2^2 + 1^2 + 0^2 + -1^2 + -2^2 = 4 + 1 + 0 + 1 + 4 = 10$$

At this point in our calculation of spread we have to take account of the fact that some data sets are only 5 digits, some are 50 and others 50,000. Clearly the size of the data set is going to affect the value of the overall deviation so we have to 'remove' the effect of size as best we can. The best way to do this is to calculate the mean deviation for each data set. In our case we divide the total deviation (10) by the number of data units (5). The answer is 2. If we had 50 units of data in our set we would divide the total deviation by 50. We call this figure (the sum total of all the mean squared differences from the mean) the *variance*.

We have not finished, however, because there is a loose end in our mathematical argument. We used the device of squaring numbers to get rid of negative values. This has the effect of overstating the value of the difference in the data set and we have to reverse the effect. We do this by taking the square root of our mean difference: $\sqrt{2} = 1.414$. This is the standard deviation. The variance is the square of the standard deviation. You will come across this again in Chapter 13.

We know sufficient about statistical calculation to be able to express this whole process in a formula:

$$\delta = \frac{\sqrt{\Sigma(x - \bar{x})^2}}{n}$$

Where

δ = standard deviation (sigma, lower case)
$\sqrt{}$ = square root
x = a data unit
$\bar{x}$ = mean
Σ = sum of all (sigma, upper case)
n = the number of data units

An easier formulation of this formula if we calculate a standard deviation manually is:

$$- = \frac{\sqrt{\Sigma x^2}}{n} - \bar{x}^2$$

In this formula we:

- Square all the values of x, sum them and divide by n.
- Square the mean and subtract it from the sum of the squares of x divided by n.
- Take the square root.

Using our example of just five values of x:

x	x^2
2	4
3	9
4	16
5	25
6	36
Σ	$90/5 = 18 - 4^2 = \sqrt{2} = 1.414$

(ii) Using grouped data

Now let us look at how we can calculate the standard deviation for grouped data. Table 12.8 shows a frequency distribution of the heights of 10-year-old girls. To understand the procedure for calculating the standard deviation, we shall set out our data in a computation table (Table 12.9).

The original data are in columns A and C. Column B shows a value of the mid-point of each height category. Column D is the product of multiplying the mid-point of each category by the frequency in the category. Column E is the square of the mid-point value and Column F our estimate of the sum of square, the product of multiplying the frequency (Column C) with the square of the mid-point (Column E).

Step 1: Calculate the mean $-$ ΣColumn D/ΣColumn C

$= 141.23$ cms

Step 2: Calculate the mean sum of squares $-$ ΣColumn F/ΣColumn C $= 20027.34$

We then substitute this data into our formula:

$$C = \frac{\sqrt{\Sigma x^2 - \bar{x}}}{n} = \sqrt{20027.34 - 141.23^2}$$

$$= \sqrt{20027.34 - 19945.91}$$

$$= \sqrt{81.43}$$

$$= 9.02$$

Our best estimate of the standard deviation is 9.02.

Table 12.8 Heights of sample of girls age 10

Height in cm	Frequency
90 to 100	4
>100 to 110	11
>110 to 120	34
>120 to 130	237
>130 to 140	1,328
>140 to 150	1,652
>150 to 160	454
>160 to 170	35
>170 to 180	3
>180 to 190	2
>190 to 200	2
over 200	–
	3,762

Table 12.9 Layout for calculating standard deviation from grouped data

A Height mid-point in cm of group	B Mid-point	C Frequency	D B × C	E B^2	F (C × E)
91–100	95	4	380	9,025	36,100
101–110	105	11	1,155	11,025	121,275
111–120	115	34	3,910	13,225	449,650
121–130	125	237	29,625	15,625	3,703,125
131–140	135	1,328	179,280	18,225	24,202,800
141–150	145	1,652	239,540	21,025	34,733,300
151–160	155	454	70,370	24,025	10,907,350
161–170	165	35	5,775	27,225	952,875
171–180	175	3	525	30,625	91,875
181–190	185	2	370	34,225	68,450
191–200	195	2	390	38,025	76,050
Σ		3,762	531,320	75,342,850	

(iii) With small samples

The formula we have used so far to calculate the standard deviation can be used when we are studying the whole population and when our sample size is large (as in the case of our age data). When our sample size is small, however, there is an increased chance that it will not be an adequate representation of the population. We get round this by applying a correction factor, Bessel's correction (named after an early nineteenth century German statistician, Friedrich Bessel). As a general rule we should apply this correction when our data set or sample size is less than 30. The correction is to use (n − 1) and not n as the divisor in the equation:

$$C = \frac{2\ \overline{\Sigma x^2}}{n} - \bar{x}$$

(iv) How can we interpret the standard deviation?

To interpret the standard deviation (normally written as δ) we have to understand it in the context of an ideal situation. This ideal is called the *normal distribution* (see Figure 12.5). This is one of a family of distributions with broadly the same appearance, a symmetrical, peaked curve. The normal distribution is often called the *bell curve*. The following characteristics of the distribution were identified in the eighteenth century through empirical investigations into gambling and associated probabilities. What was established theoretically was that the normal distribution had a mean of 0 (so the deviation in the values below the mean and above the mean are exactly the same) and a standard deviation of 1. What was particularly important for statistics (and so for us) was that, in the normal distribution, it was further established that within this one standard deviation there were 68% of the data units of the distribution. Just think about this and

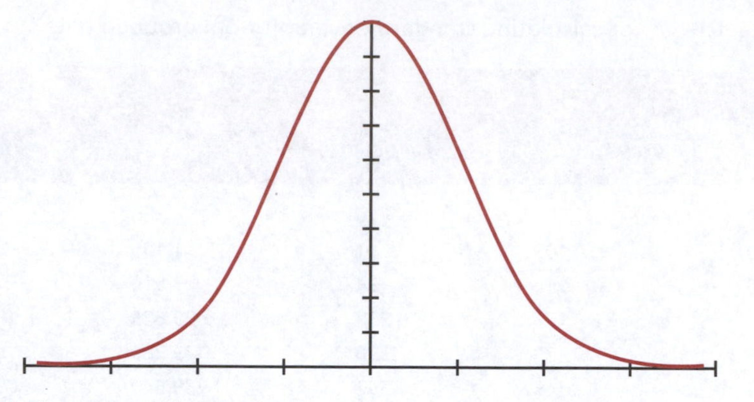

Figure 12.5 The normal distribution

remember that, in these early days, this was all to do with gambling and people were interested in the chances of different outcomes occurring. This finding puts us in a very interesting position, just at the point where we move from describing characteristics of shape to describing and judging likelihood, in other words, we are at the doorway that leads into the world of probability. If we know that 68% of outcomes lie within one standard deviation, then we also know that there is a 68% chance of one of those outcomes occurring.

Later in the century another important discovery was made which allowed this important feature of the normal distribution to be extended to the real world. Let us imagine we have a group of 30 children that we wish to sample to test their IQ. If we want our sample size to be 5, there are 142,506 ways of combining 5 students out of the 30. Now the interesting thing is that if we were to draw each of these samples and calculate the mean IQ of the group, we would find that there were more combinations that would produce a mean value at or close to the true mean and fewer combinations that would produce a mean that was very different from the true mean. Visualise this for yourself, a peak of samples in the centre close to the true mean and the number of samples falling away as we move away from the true mean. In other words, it is a normal distribution. Let us summarise this. If we draw all of the samples of a given size from a population, the distribution of the means of these samples will be a normal distribution, *irrespective* of whether the parent population followed a normal distribution. So the parent population need not be normal but the distribution of sample means (the so-called *sampling* distribution) is always normal. This has important implications for sampling, which are further developed in Appendix 1.

So how, then, do we interpret the standard deviations we have calculated for our data. Let us look again at the data on the height of 10-year-old girls. We saw that the mean height of girls was 141.23 cm with a standard deviation of 9.02 cm. This means that 68% (remember this was established theoretically) of our population will lie within 9.02 cm of our mean, that is within the range 132.21 cm to 150.25. Actually it is not exactly 68% but we do not need to be absolutely precise at this point.

But this is not all we can do to use our new knowledge about the standard deviation. We can also estimate how confident we are in our estimation of the mean. Of course, we can only do this if we have sampled our data, because if we were dealing with the population we would be completely sure. And if we are not confident in the value of our mean when we are working with the whole population, we are not very good at pressing the keyboard of our calculator or computer. If we are dealing with a sample, we can calculate a value called the standard error of the mean which will enable us to say within what limits the true mean will lie. The formula for this is:

$$\text{Standard error of } \bar{x} = \frac{\delta}{\sqrt{n}}$$

It is not important to understand how this formula is derived but the underlying principle is that it is the sampling distribution (the distribution of all possible samples of a given size) from which the sample is drawn that is important. So for any sample statistic, there is a 68% chance that the true value lies within one standard error. For statisticians, however, 68% is pretty hit and miss. Something more accurate is usually required. Again, the characteristics of the normal distribution provide the solution. If we double the standard deviation (2δ), then we account for about 95% of the population and if we treble it (3δ), we account for about 99%. Again, these figures (developed through statistical theory) are not precise but are sufficient for our purpose at present.

Let us examine this with our age data:

$$\text{One standard error of } \bar{x} = \frac{9.02}{\sqrt{3762}} = 0.15$$

$$\text{Two standard errors of } \bar{x} = \frac{2 \times 9.02}{\sqrt{3762}} = 0.29$$

$$\text{Three standard errors of } \bar{x} = \frac{3 \times 9.02}{\sqrt{3762}} = 0.44$$

The sample mean height of 10-year-old-girls is 141.23 cm. Our best estimate of the population mean is that it is:

- 141.23 ± 0.15 (141.08 cm to 141.38 cm) with a 68% probability (one standard error).
- 141.23 ± 0.29 (140.94 cm to 141.52 cm) with a 95% probability (two standard errors).
- 141.23 ± 0.44 (140.79 cm to 141.67 cm) with a 99% probability (three standard errors).

Note that as the probability goes up the range within which the true mean sits increases as well. If we think about it, this is what we would expect.

There is one other statistic that we should be aware of, the *coefficient of variation*. This simple measure expresses the relationship between the standard deviation and the mean. It is particularly useful when comparing different data sets because it allows us to express the spread as a proportion of the mean. The coefficient of variation is given by the formula:

$$\text{Coefficient of variation} = \frac{\delta}{\bar{x}}$$

Because the coefficient of variation is standardised according to the size of the population or sample, it measures the relative degree of spread. In our age data the coefficient is:

$$\frac{\delta}{\bar{x}} = \frac{9.02}{141.23} = 0.06$$

Sometimes the coefficient is expressed as a percentage (in this case it would be 6%, that is the standard deviation is 6% of the mean). How might we use this statistic? Imagine we were analysing assessment grades in academic courses. For each subject we can calculate the mean score and the standard deviation and, for each, the coefficient of variation. What would a comparison of these show? With a large number of students taking each examination, we would hope to see the coefficients of variation being much the same for each subject. If they were not, this might be an indication that some subjects had an assessment template that encouraged full use of the marking scale and others did not. We could calculate the coefficient of variation for each examiner in a subject and, as quality control, identify who was out of line.

12.5 Leaning distributions

Distributions are not always symmetrical about the central point. They can lean one way or the other. This 'lean' is called *skew*. If they lean to the left (that is, there are more data units than expected in the right tail of the distribution) they are positively skewed and if they lean to the right (that is there are more data units than expected in the left tail of the distribution) they are negatively skewed. The existence of skew may tell us something about our sampling processes and outcomes if we expect our sample to be normally distributed on some measure. If we had data on the social composition of entrants to higher education, we could look at how many each institution drew from lower socio-economic groups and socially disadvantaged backgrounds. We could express this in terms of under recruitment or over recruitment or expected recruitment (that is, a skew one way or the other or no skew) and classify institutions on this basis. Skew can be described using quantitative measures.

12.5.1 Using the range and median

We can visually determine whether skew exists by inspecting a histogram of the data and see if it leans to one side or the other. We can also use our measures of range in association with the median to get a more quantitative estimate of skew. Figure 12.6(a) shows a symmetrical distribution. Here the first quartile (Q_1) is equal to the fourth (Q_4) and Q_2 is the same as Q_3. In each of these quartiles there are 25% of the data values. In Figure 12.6(b)

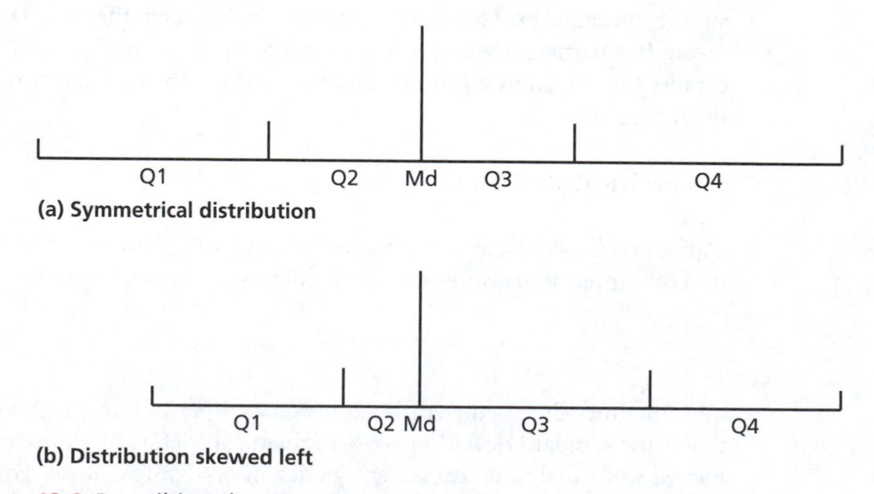

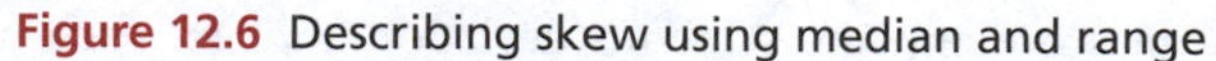
Figure 12.6 Describing skew using median and range

the distribution is skewed left. Each quartile still has 25% of the data values but the range of Q_2 is less than Q_3. From this we can devise some rules:

- If the range of $Q_1 + Q_2$ is less than $Q_3 + Q_4$, there is a positive skew.
- If the range of $Q_1 + Q_2$ is greater than $Q_3 + Q_4$, the skew is negative.
- If the range of Q_2 is less than Q_3 the skew is positive.
- If the range of Q_2 is greater than Q_3, the skew is negative.

While these relationships describe the skew, they do not actually measure it. For this, we have to use the mean and standard deviation.

12.5.2 Using the standard deviation and mean

The precise measure of skew is given by the formula:

$$\sum \frac{(x - \bar{x})^3}{\delta}$$

This is usually corrected to take account of sample size:

$$\frac{n}{(n - 1)(n - 2)} \cdot \sum \frac{(x - \bar{x})^3}{\delta}$$

Where n is number of data units
x is an individual unit of data
$\bar{x}$ is the mean of the data set

This formula is quite straightforward but, fortunately for us, it is also the one used by common spreadsheet programs such as MS Excel and Open Office Calc. A symmetrical distribution has a value at or near 0. The direction of skew is indicated by positive and negative results.

For many advanced data analyses it is important that we demonstrate that our data are normally distributed, that is, we demonstrate that skew is not present to any significant degree. So if our statistical analysis requires normality, we should be able to demonstrate it.

12.6 Flat and peaked distributions

Skewed distributions lose their symmetry by leaning one way or the other. What happens, however, when distributions retain their symmetry but deviate from the normal decline away from the mean? In this situation our distribution can vary from being excessively peaked or excessively flat. Figure 12.7 shows this situation. The peakedness is called *kurtosis*. If a data set is excessively peaked, this is referred to as positive kurtosis or the distribution is *leptokurtic*. If it is excessively flat, we call it negative kurtosis or say that the distribution is *platykurtic*. In Figure 12.7 we can see that a leptokurtic distribution has the limits of the interquartile (or even the full) range close to the median or mean and that a platykurtic distribution has a wide range.

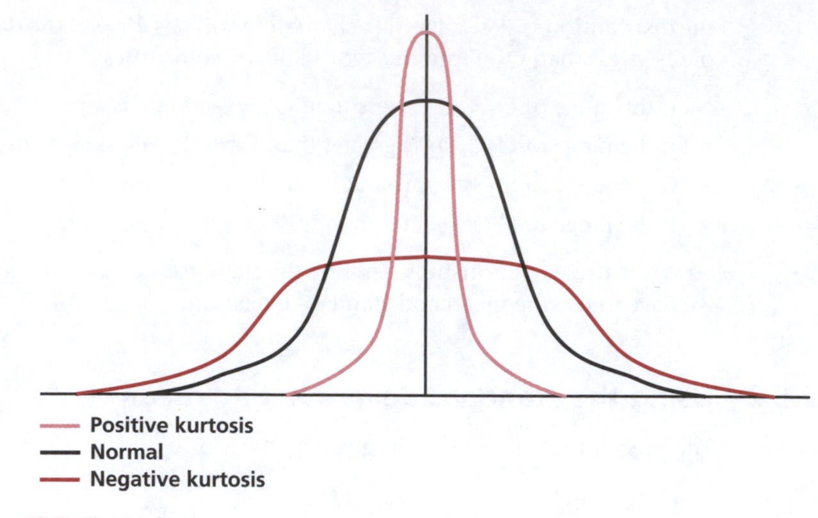

Figure 12.7 Kurtosis

Again, we need to understand this characteristic of our data set if we use advanced statistical methods that require our data to be normal. As we move towards a leptokurtic or platykurtic distribution we lose the characteristics of the normal distribution. The formula used to calculate kurtosis is extensive and it serves little purpose to reproduce it here since the calculation is easily done by a spreadsheet program. The value for a normal distribution is 0. Positive values reflect positive kurtosis and negative, negative kurtosis.

12.7 Using skew or kurtosis in our research

Skew and kurtosis are often ignored in descriptive statistics, yet they are important in directing our research effort. In general terms, we use measures of descriptive statistics in two ways, either comparatively or to ask ourselves what the implications are. Let us consider each in turn.

Our measures of central tendency, spread, skew and kurtosis can be used in a comparative way which we can use to take our investigation further. If, for example, we were working on school exclusions and we analysed our data on the basis of school size (grouping schools into bands of similar size), we would be interested if any of our measures varied markedly from one group to another. We might for example, ask why the spread was so much greater in this size group or why the measure of kurtosis for another size group was so different. If we could reconstitute our data to explore exclusions by age of pupil, the identification of marked differences in these measures would drive our investigation forward by asking the questions 'Why?' and 'How?'

While the importance of comparative assessment applies to all our descriptive measures, skew and kurtosis are, as we have seen above, important for another reason also. They represent deviation from the normal distribution. Why is this important? Because the characteristics of the normal distribution are the link between description and our entry into more powerful statistical approaches to the exploration of association between variables and the estimation of causal relationships. And this is where quantitative analysis can really get interesting.

But what if our measures of skewers and kurtosis show a marked deviation from the normal distribution? Do we just shrug our shoulders and say, 'It can't be helped. We'll just have to stop our investigation'. The answer is 'No'. Deviation can make the interpretation of subsequent statistics more unreliable and we can make some allowance for this. There are techniques of data analysis that make no assumptions about the shape of our data and we can use these. However, if we have to use techniques that require our data to be normal, there is something we can do – we can mathematically transform our data. We have met this procedure before.

One of the more common transformations that we use is not to base our calculations on the absolute values of the data, but to use the logarithms of those values. The effect of this is to reduce the importance of differences between the values of extreme data units. It will, therefore, reduce skew but not kurtosis. This is better than nothing.

Table 12.10 shows the effect of this transformation on a data set consisting of the body mass index of a group of children. The effect of using the logarithm of the data rather than the base data is effectively to normalise the distribution in terms of skew. It marginally increases the kurtosis measure. We would, in this case, be advised to use the transformed data in any subsequent analysis exploring causes or consequences.

Now that we have looked at these descriptive approaches, test out how they might be used in Activity 12.1.

Table 12.10 The effect of transforming data

	Body mass index	Log BMI
	10.6	1.025
	15.2	1.182
	16.0	1.204
	16.1	1.207
	16.2	1.21
	16.7	1.223
	16.9	1.228
	17.1	1.233
	18.1	1.258
	18.2	1.26
	18.7	1.272
	19.4	1.288
	19.6	1.292
	19.7	1.294
	20.4	1.31
	21.6	1.334
	25.9	1.413
	28.6	1.456
Skew	**1.622**	**−0.207**
Kurtosis	**2.046**	**2.294**

Activity 12.1 Making data give up its secrets

This activity is an opportunity to practise some of the methods of describing the characteristics of a data set. The data we shall use (see table below) are taken from *Statistics Norway* (http://www.ssb.no/english/subjects/04/02/utlaerer_en/) and show the total number of teachers of given ages each year over a 12-year period.

1. Identify the modal class for the total number of teachers from 1992 to 2003. Is it always the same? If not, can you suggest why it shifts?
2. Calculate the mean and median ages for teachers in 1992, 1995, 1999 and 2003. Do the values support your interpretation of the data based on modal classes? Comparing the means and medians, is there any suggestion that the distributions are skewed?
3. Calculate the standard deviation of the data for 1992, 1995, 1999 and 2003 by hand. Are the results much the same for each year? Then enter the data into a spreadsheet and repeat the calculation using the spreadsheet. Are the results the same?
4. What is the standard error of the mean for the four years? Write down what the standard error implies for any one of your years. Are the results much the same for the four years?

		Age				
Year	Total	–29 years	30–39 years	40–49 years	50–59 years	60– years
1992	94,057	7,585	21,114	36,139	18,788	6,188
1993	94,746	7,933	19,746	36,189	20,702	6,049
1994	95,370	8,513	18,950	35,217	22,896	5,870
1995	96,520	9,106	18,683	34,321	24,971	6,111
1996	99,335	9,706	18,649	33,307	27,314	6,454
1997	106,078	11,805	20,298	33,466	29,544	6,820
1998	109,100	12,520	21,006	32,871	31,123	7,029
1999	110,540	12,378	21,511	31,987	32,273	7,585
2000	112,060	12,127	22,274	31,000	33,369	8,303
2001	108,277	11,962	23,198	29,608	34,563	8,946
2002	107,989	10,621	24,071	27,858	35,435	10,004
2003	107,860	9,487	24,957	26,425	35,860	11,131

Source: Statistics Norway.

12.8 When time matters

The data we have looked at so far have all related to a single variable, the numbers of children having free school meals, height, the ages of teachers, for instance. These data represent a snapshot at one time. But as researchers we often deal with more than one variable. In this section, we shall look at an important second variable, time itself.

Time series analysis, seeing how something such as absence from school changes over time, often plays an important part in educational investigations. We might, for example, look at the outcomes over time of policy initiatives or trends in behaviour such as smoking and teenage pregnancy, or pupil attainment. We are interested in how things change over time and whether the change has a pattern to it. In this section, we will consider how we can describe and determine patterns in a time series. Table 12.11

Table 12.11 Live births in England and Wales

Year	31 March	30 June	30 September	31 December
1996	157.3	158.1	169.9	164.2
1997	158.1	163.3	164.9	156.8
1998	155.8	158.6	166.1	155.4
1999	152.1	157.3	160.1	152.4
2000	148.7	150.7	155.0	150.1
2001	145.5	148.8	153.0	147.4
2002	143.3	147.2	155.0	150.6
2003	147.4	155.2	162.9	156.0
2004	155.2	157.4	165.4	161.7
2005	154.3	159.8	170.2	161.7
2006	159.5	166.2	174.9	169.0

Source: Birth Statistics: Review of the Registrar General on Births and Patterns of Family Building in England and Wales, 2006, Office for National Statistics, Table 2.1.

presents data showing the number of births in England and Wales over the four quarters of the year from 1996 to 2006. As we know this data can be represented as a graph. Figure 12.8 is a graph of this data, drawn using Calc in the Open Office Suite. There is a pattern to this data that seems to reproduce itself over a short period. This is referred to as its *periodicity* and we can see it in Figure 12.8 as the line peaks every fourth quarter. In addition, successive peaks are lower than the ones preceding them for about half the period, then the opposite happens (the change occurs around 2001). The same is true with the bottoms of the troughs. This suggests another periodicity over a longer period. What can we do to see whether our eyes are deceiving us and to emphasise the periodicity of the data?

A simple yet often effective analysis is to calculate a moving average (also known as a *running mean*). This is a straightforward process. If we look at the data for 1996 in Table 12.11 we can demonstrate the method with a basic three period moving average. We would normally start with three period set because this has the effect of smoothing the pattern without distorting the shape. The calculation is to look at three time periods,

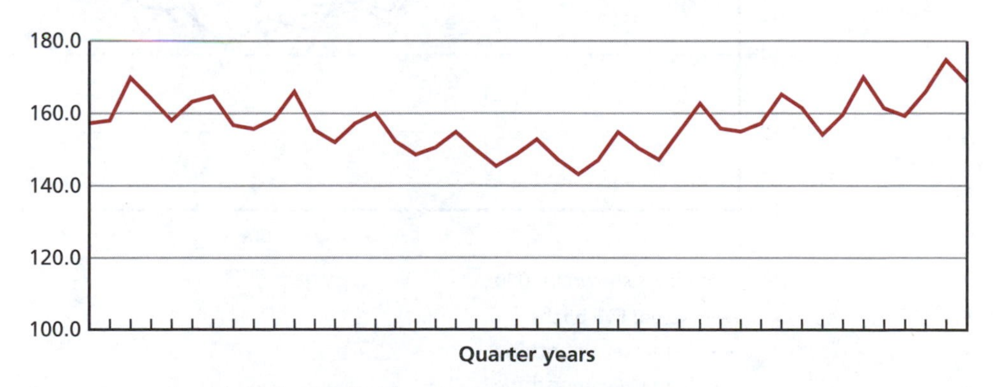

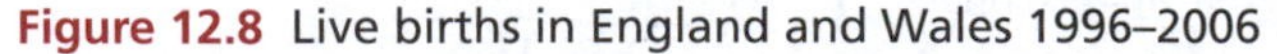
Figure 12.8 Live births in England and Wales 1996–2006

total up the number of live births over these periods, find the average for the three periods and use this as the value for the middle period. Thus:

Period ending

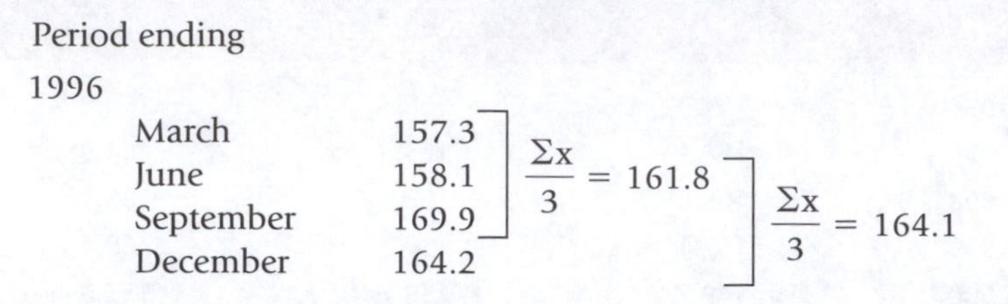

1996

March	157.3		
June	158.1	$\frac{\Sigma x}{3} = 161.8$	
September	169.9		$\frac{\Sigma x}{3} = 164.1$
December	164.2		

We add together March, June and September totals and divide by three to give a revised June figure (161.8). Then we add June, September and December and divide by three to give a revised September figure. We continue this for all of our periods and then plot our revised figures.

We can do this calculation for any length of period. Figure 12.9 shows the results for a moving average over three quarters (black) and over five quarters (dotted line) plotted against the raw data (blue). Note the difference between Figures 12.8 and 12.9 – the *y scale* in Figure 12.9 has been shortened deliberately to exaggerate the vertical difference. This has been done to demonstrate the following points:

- The five period moving average reduces the peaks and troughs and brings out the long period trend.
- The three period moving average suppresses the marked peaks and troughs but retains the shape of the distribution (for example, peaks usually coincide with peaks on the original data and troughs with the troughs).
- This is not the case with the five period moving average where it sometimes peaks at points where the original data set has a trough. This phenomenon is referred to as *phase shift*.

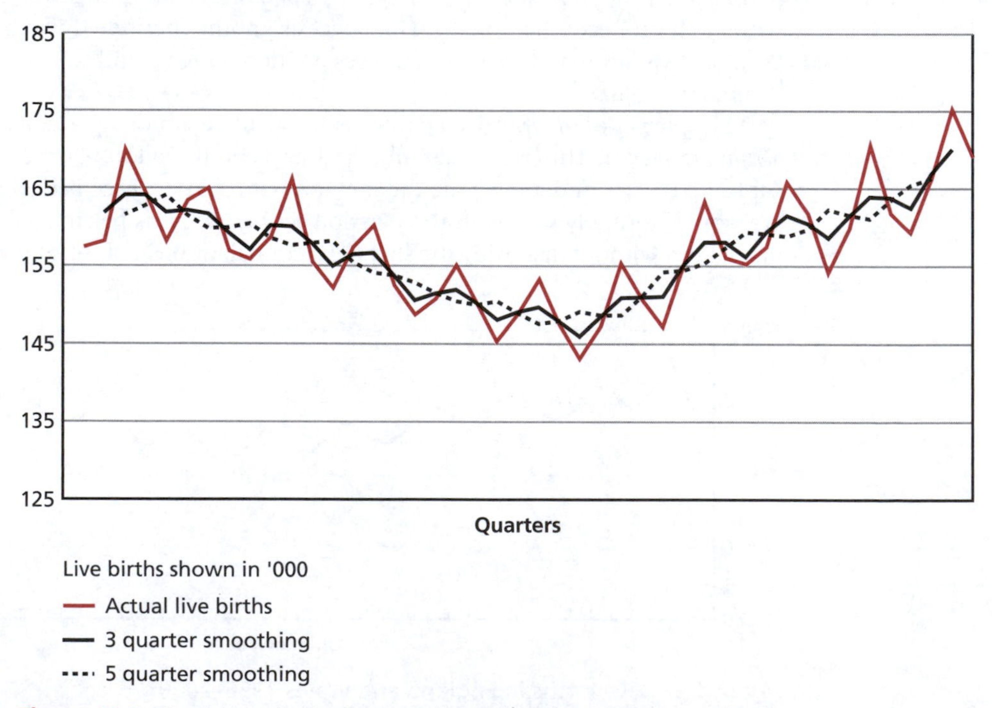

Figure 12.9 Live births in England and Wales 1996–2006 (smoothed)

This analysis confirms what we suspected when we first looked at the data. It becomes particularly useful when we are dealing with a great many data plots where the seasonal periodicity (or short term periodicity) can be masked by influences that are more pronounced than the trend but which occur on a random basis.

If we want to explore the periodicity of the data in more detail, we can look at the difference between the moving average and the original data. The difference is called the *residual*. If the original data is greater than the moving average, the residual is positive and if it is smaller then the residual is negative. Why would we do this? We have to understand that what we are doing with our moving average is to emphasise the trend. Sometimes, however, it is what happens around a point in time that is equally interesting. If a head teacher has a long run of data on annual school enrolments, this can be used to establish a long run trend, even to the extent of predicting enrolment for the forthcoming year. If the school then introduces a marketing campaign, there is a baseline against which to judge its effect. Figure 12.10 is a plot of the residuals between the base data and the five period moving average. Two things stand out. The peaks of the residuals are broadly the same and the bottoms of the troughs are broadly the same. From this, we can deduce that the seasonal effect of birth rates that are higher than the trend in late summer is 5,000 to 6,000 and of lower birth rates than the trend is 6,000 to 8,000 in late winter. If we wanted to, we could make a 'seasonal adjustment' by adding or removing these figures.

The moving average is an easy introduction to time series analysis and it shows us how we can go about identifying if there are different periodicities. We can see that there are periodicities in the data of Table 12.11, one short about six months and the other long over 20 years. We have seen that we can identify tipping points and cycles from peak to peak. This distance between peaks is called the *wave length* and it is the conceptual link between our analysis and more advanced approaches.

How can we improve on our descriptive analysis? There are three ways of making our exploration of time series more sophisticated. We shall outline them here but operationalisation is best done with a computer package.

1. **Weighted moving averages:** Our moving average treated each data unit as having the same weight. For example in a three period moving average, each period has a notional weight of one. We multiply this weight by the period total (which does not

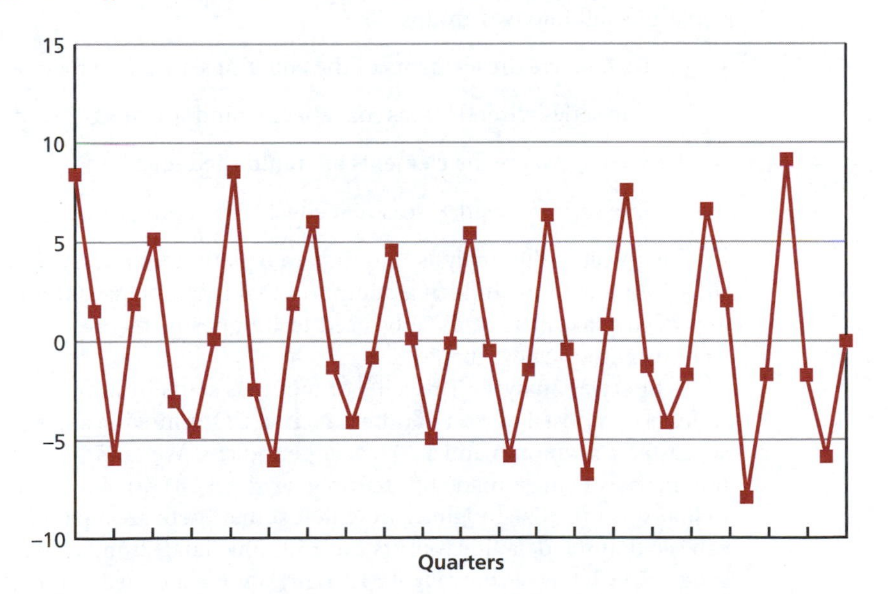

Figure 12.10 Plot of residuals

change the total) before adding the three years together and dividing by three. We can, however, apply a weighting function that gives each unit of data a different weight. We do this particularly if we are smoothing over long time periods (say five periods or more) to prevent 'phase shift' (we met this idea above) when a downturn in the actual data is converted to an upturn in the smoothed data or vice versa. Our object with applying a weighting function is to make the underpinning pattern in our data clearer. The usual approach is to weight values according to their distance from the central value, with the weighting decreasing as we move away from the central point. In our five period moving average, for example, instead of weighting each data unit as 1, we could allocate weights of 1/10 to the first and fifth values, 1/5 to the second and fourth and 2/5 to the third, a ratio of 4:2:1 from the centre to the extremes. Table 12.12 shows how this is done. The data is taken from Table 12.11. The base data are the actual totals for each quarter. The weights emphasise the value that is to be plotted. We take .4 of this total and enter the indicated proportions of the other periods. Note that the weights add up to 1. Column 3 is the base data weighted and column 4 is the sum of all the weighted data shown as plotted for the third period. There are many sophisticated exponential smoothing functions we can use as well.

Table 12.12 Method of calculating weighted moving average

Base value	Weight	Base × weight	Plot value
157.3	.1	15.7	
158.1	.2	31.6	
169.9	.4	68.0	163.9
164.2	.2	32.8	
158.1	.1	15.8	

2. Data decomposition: These methods start with the idea that there are mathematical equations that can describe the data sets. The object of this approach is to extract the underlying pattern, often with the object of predicting future states. In broad terms the equations fall into two groups:

- the first, where the elements of the equations are *added* together:

  Time series = trend + seasonal effect + random effect

- the second, where the elements are multiplied together:

  Time series = trend × seasonal effect × random effect

The object of this analysis is to find an equation that best describes a pattern through time (often with the hidden assumption that it can be used for forward planning). This approach makes use of the advanced techniques in regression and correlation that we shall meet in the next chapter.

3. Spectral analysis: This suite of methods starts from the assumption that any time series is composed of a set of different curves. Our moving average analysis, for example, suggested a six month and a 20+ year periodicity. We can illustrate the principle of spectral analysis using a made up example. Figure 12.11(a) shows a time series. It does not matter what the data might represent, just that there are a pattern of data over time. We can see that the data line follows the 150 value apart from a slump in the middle of the series. Now let us see how Figure 12.11(a) was constructed. Look now at Figure 12.11(b).

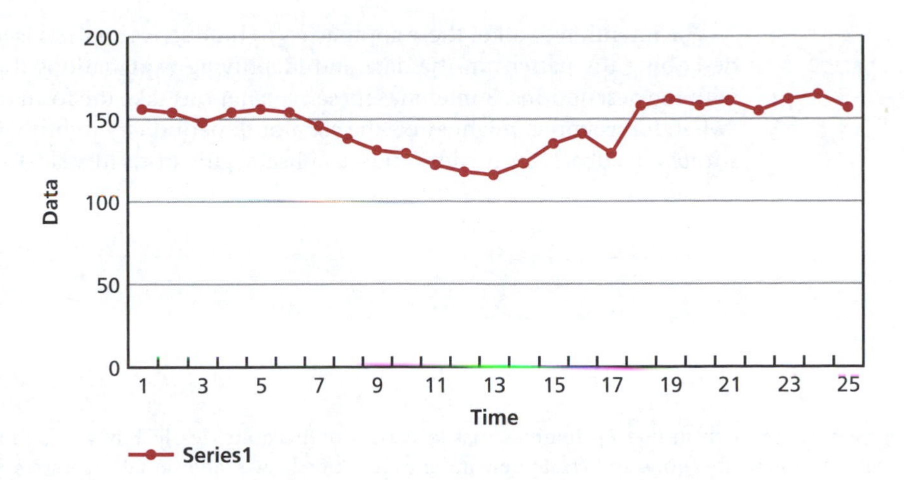

Figure 12.11(a) Time series data plot

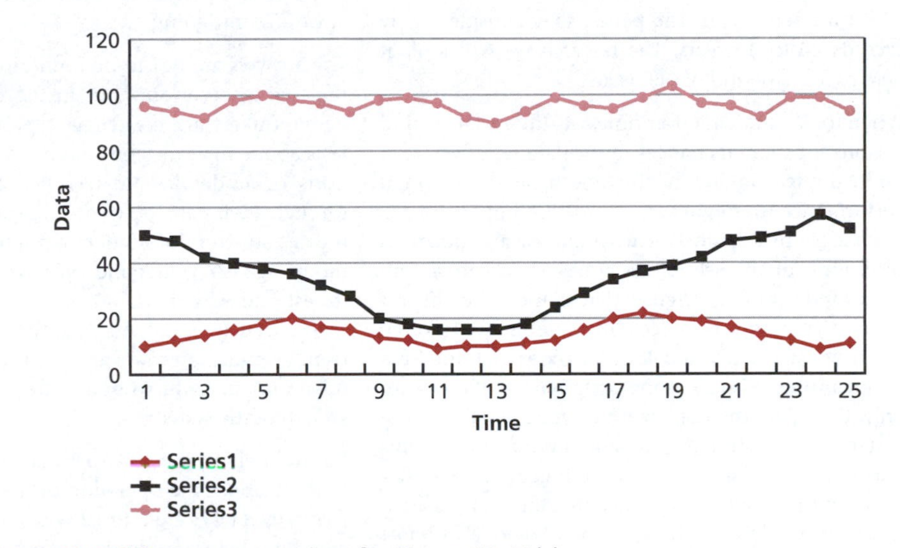

Figure 12.11(b) Component data for Figure 12.11(a)

This shows the data that were used to construct Figure 12.11(b). The bottom data set shows a periodicity of about 12 units of time. The middle curve shows a periodicity of 24 units of time and the top line shows a periodicity of 6 units of time. These periodicities represent the wavelength. In addition, we should note that the heights of the curves (that is, from the trough to the peak) are different. This is called the *amplitude of the curve*. With this example we have started with some made up data and combined them to create the data set in Figure 12.11(a). Spectral analysis starts with the data set and then tries to find the set of curves that will best describe the data. It decomposes the time series into a set of curves that differ in (a) wavelength (the distance between the peaks) and (b) amplitude (the vertical distance from the peak to the trough). The object is to identify the waves that, when added together, account for most of the variability in the data set. With this approach we can see that we not only get a very good description of the data but also a powerful technique for prediction.

The intention of all of these approaches to time series analysis is to find a good way of describing the pattern in the data and identifying explanations that can be associated with the descriptions. Sometimes these explanations take the form of external influences (what, for example, might affect the six month periodicity in births?), while others constitute a feedback loop within the data itself (girls born in year 0 are likely to produce children in 20 to 30 years' time). Case Study 12.1 shows a time series analysis that threw up some interesting questions.

Case study 12.1 Trends in the number of students at German universities

Sometimes research throws up findings that take an analysis in new directions and create new insights. A German researcher, Volker Mueller-Benedict, reported a research programme that did just this (Mueller-Benedict, 2000). When educational researchers deal with time series data, the period they consider rarely exceeds 20 to 30 years. The research we will look at here covers a period of 160 years.

When looking at data over time, we often want to find reasons for sudden changes in the data set. If we were, for example, looking at outcome measures of pupil performance we might want to ascribe improvements to changes in a national curriculum or a major reorganisation of the school system. Such events are almost random in occurrence, that is, it can be difficult to establish that they reflect any periodicity. However, when we step back and look at big social and economic processes, such as the performance of the economy, then patterns may begin to emerge. We can see patterns of growth and recession, booms and slumps but, surprisingly we can also find longer term periodicities in the economy. The idea that they exist is associated primarily with the work of a Soviet economist working between the First and Second World Wars, Nikolai Kondratiev and, for this reason, they are sometimes called 'Kondratiev waves'. What Mueller-Benedict did was to look for long waves over 160 years of student entry to German universities using spectral analysis. He looked at four subject areas: Protestant theology, law, medicine and education. He chose these because they were subjects that had been continuously taught over the whole period. In each case we can chart the influence of specific events, the collapse of the Weimar Republic and hyperinflation in the 1920s, the rise of National Socialism and German reconstruction in the 1930s, the boom that followed the unification of Germany in the late nineteenth century. The figures, taken from Kondratiev's paper, show all of this quite clearly. But within this data he also identified two additional processes that created long waves, one of 35–40 years' duration and the other 13 to 18 years long and only present in the twentieth century. His interpretation of the underpinning processes at work is intriguing.

The answers are not to be found in the conditions of the German economy but in the way in which academic careers are created. A typical academic career lasts about 40 years (the length of the long cycle). Cohorts of academics are recruited and move *en bloc* through their careers, creating peaks and troughs in the age structure of academic populations. When the modal age is 45, demand for new academics is at its lowest and when it is 60 or more, demand is at its highest. So in a stable situation (much of the nineteenth century) they are apparent. They still existed in the twentieth century but the effect was masked by the growth of the system.

But what about the 13 to 18 year cycle? Here we have to think about the operation of the labour market. In Germany it takes eight to 12 years to go through higher education before someone can enter the academic job market. Allow for the need to satisfy demand over a period of time (four to ten years is not unreasonable) and the 13 to 18 year cycle is found to be the period necessary for supply processes to meet demand. And this process became more apparent in the twentieth century because it was fuelled by the increasing social mobility that led to a growth in student numbers.

The implication of this work for educational researchers is that our methods of analysis of quantitative data may confine us to short and medium term interpretations and that within at least some of our data sets there may be lurking deeper processes that we need to understand if our attempts at modelling and predicting situations are to be effective.

12.9 Describing relationships between data

In Chapter 10 (section 10.26), we looked at scatterplots, graphical representations of how one variable changed at the same time as another. We could, for example, plot the number of times teachers used audio visual and IT systems in lessons in a week and plot this against their ages. But how can we summarise and describe these relationships? We could treat the variables separately and calculate their means and standard deviations. In our example, we would calculate the mean of the number of times AV and IT were used and the mean age of the teachers. However, this rather misses the point when the characteristic that we are interested in is that a change in one variable is related to a predictable level of change in the other. When a scatterplot shows a trend, it is useful to be able to describe this trend. To do this we construct what is called a *regression line*. This is a line fits the data and represents the trend.

We can construct a regression line in a number of ways:

- We can fit it by eye. This is the easiest, quickest and least accurate method.
- We can interpolate a median line. Figure 12.12 shows the method.
  - First, divide our data into three equally sized groups, using the horizontal axis as our baseline.
  - Next, identify median points for the first and last groups by (a) finding a median value on the x axis and constructing a vertical line – shown as a dotted line and (b) finding a median value on the y axis and constructing a horizontal line. Because there are seven values in each section, the median item is the fourth when counted along the axes.
  - Where the lines cross is the median point for the cluster.
  - Last, join the two points together for the regression line.

  This approach is marginally more accurate than fitting a line by eye.
- We can identify a line using an approach called the 'least squares' method. What this does is identify a regression line that minimises the sum of the distances between the regression line and every variable. If we think about it, this is very much the same approach we used to calculate the standard deviation. We shall look at this in more detail. It sounds difficult but we can actually do it quite easily by spreadsheet.

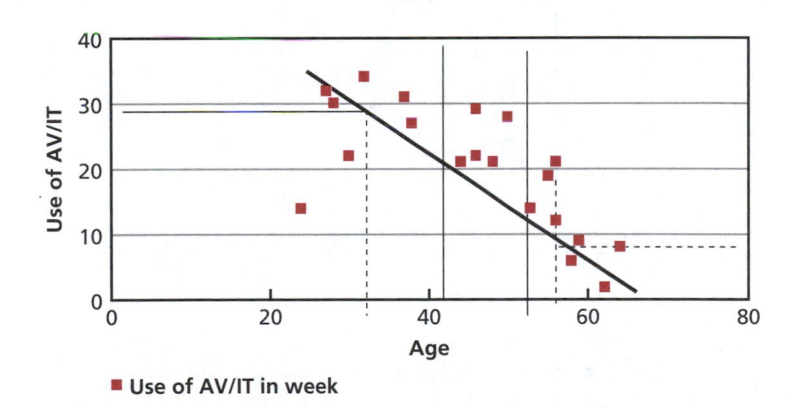

Figure 12.12 Estimation of medial regression line

Let us understand the principle first. Because we have two variables, we have to decide whether we are going to minimize the *vertical* distances between each data point and our regression line or the *horizontal* distances. This is depicted in Figure 12.13. It is important that we understand the implications of this, because each will produce a different line.

- If we minimise the sum of the *vertical* distances (shown as dotted red lines in Figure 12.13), then we are using the x values to interpolate values of y (that is, x values are used to predict the y values). This is referred to as a regression of y on x.
- If we minimise the sum of the *horizontal* distances (the red lines) then we are using the y values to interpolate values of x. This is referred to as a regression of x on y.

Both approaches are possible, though conventionally we regress y on x (usually because x is regarded as the independent variable and y the dependent).

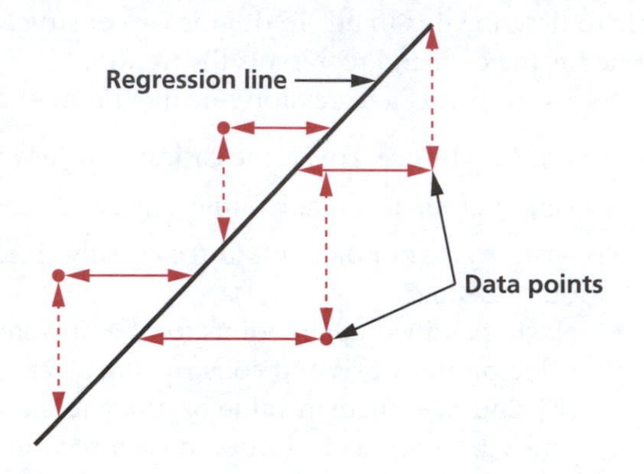

Figure 12.13 Regression options

How do we actually construct our regression line? Well, it turns out that the most accurate method is also the easiest. Figure 12.14 shows a scatterplot of data showing the relationship between deprivation and academic performance for administrative units (counties) in the east of England. The blue line is the regression of y on x calculated and drawn using Calc (within the Open Office spreadsheet). All we have to do is put our data into the spreadsheet, create the plot using the graphing facility and then add the regression line to our data plot. We can do the calculation by hand but it takes far longer.

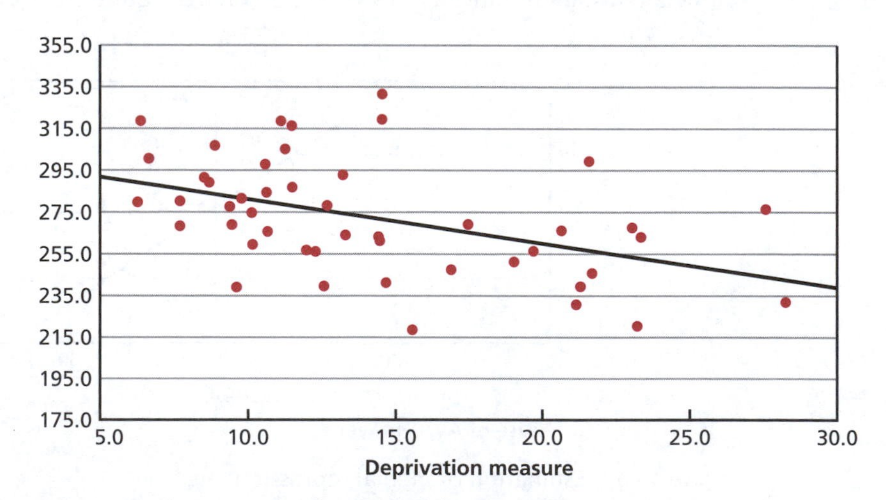

Figure 12.14 Academic performance and deprivation

However, while our line represents the pattern and shape of the data, it does not measure the strength of the association. To do this, we need to calculate another statistic that reflects how predictable the y variables are in relation to any value of x. This statistic is called a *correlation coefficient*. Let us see how a correlation coefficient works.

Figures 12.15(a)–(c) show the limits of a correlation coefficient. If our values of x and y fall on a straight line, our coefficient is 1. This means that for every unit increase in s, there is a constant proportionate increase in y. There are, however, two extremes +1, shown in Figure 12.15(a), where the increases in both are positive and −1, shown in Figure 12.15(c) where an increase in one is related to a decrease in the other. If the range of the coefficient is +1 to −1, what happens at 0? This is shown in Figure 12.15(b), which shows a random scatter of data with no relationship between the variables. With this framework to help us, the correlation coefficient (known as r) for the data in Figure 12.14 is −0.45. Again, the correlation coefficient was calculated using a standard spreadsheet program. What does the figure tell us? First that it is an *inverse* relationship and second, that there is a spread of data around the predicted values of y, that is, y values are not always the same proportion of x. This clearly is a far more typical situation for the sort of data that we shall meet in our educational research and there are good reasons for it. We cannot predict exactly how a change in the level of deprivation will affect the academic performance of every child in an area because:

- The measure of deprivation is a blunt measure and not specific to any one child.
- Some families cope better on low incomes than others and some on higher incomes are less concerned with their child's education than others in the same situation.

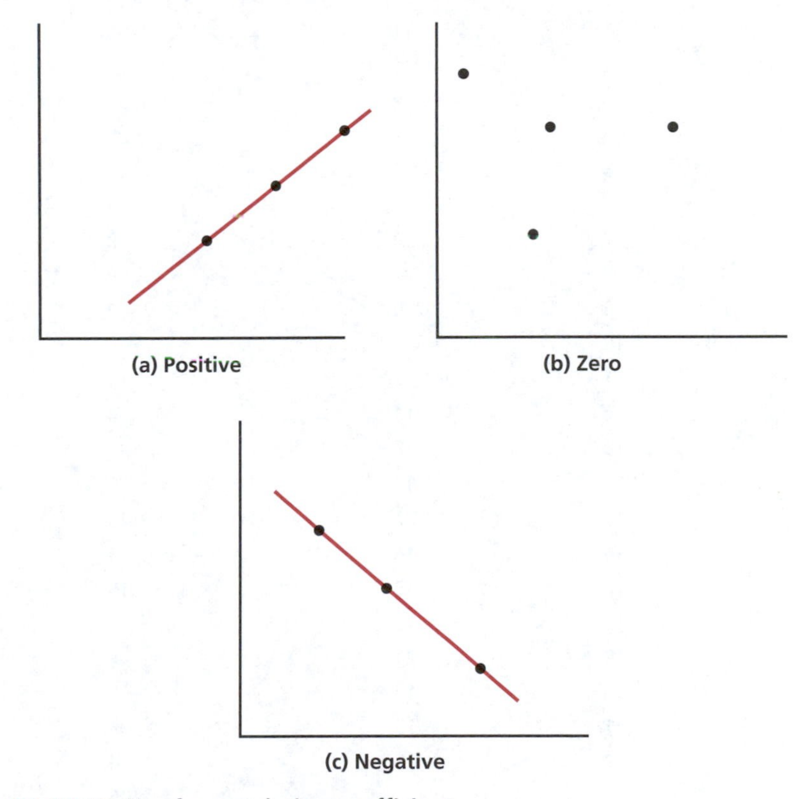

Figure 12.15 Limits of a correlation coefficient

- Children themselves are not all the same. They have different skills and capabilities, not all of which are reflected in academic testing. And on top of this some may be just going down with an illness on the day of a test and others may be just plain grumpy and not in the right mood.

These sorts of circumstance apply to most of the data that we meet in education so it will be a rare situation that one of our correlation coefficients gets close to + or −1. Far more typical is the −0.45 that we obtained in Figure 12.14 but even here we can see that there is a clear association between the two variables. We will see how to understand what a correlation coefficient is telling us in Chapter 13 when we meet something called the *coefficient of determination*.

When we use a spreadsheet to calculate a correlation coefficient we use interval data. But as we know, there are circumstances in which the data we have are ranked. Fortunately, we can also calculate a correlation coefficient with ranked data. The method of calculation is quite different from the one in spreadsheets (usually this is the Pearson coefficient, named after the statistician who developed it). When we have ranked data we calculate a Spearman coefficient (developed by an English psychologist, Charles Spearman). The interpretation of the correlation coefficient is, however, exactly the same. Table 12.13 shows the rankings of countries on the basis of their

Table 12.13 Rankings for 2003 PISA mathematics tests in state and private schools in 22 countries

State schools	Private schools	Difference in rankings squared
1	11	100
2	1	1
3	9	36
4	9	25
5	2	9
6	3	9
7	4	9
8	5	9
9	6	9
10	7	9
11	7	16
12	14	4
13	18	35
14	12	16
15	22	49
16	16	0
17	13	16
18	19	1
19	21	4
20	17	9
21	15	36
22	20	4
		406

PISA mathematics test results for state and independent private schools. The calculation is straightforward:

- Set out the table with the area (or person or organisation) ranked on the two variables.
- Square the difference in rank values (for example $(1 - 11)^2 = 100$.
- Sum the squared differences: 406.
- Substitute this in the formula:

$$1 - \frac{6 \Sigma d^2}{n^3 - n}$$

where d^2 is the rank difference squared
n is the number of pairs of data

$$= 1 - \frac{6.406}{10,648 - 22}$$

$$= 1 - \frac{2,436}{10,626}$$

$$= 1 - .229 = .771$$

The correlation coefficient (in this case identified as r_s (after Spearman) is +.771. This is a strong correlation and suggests that when mathematics teaching is good in private schools in a country, it is also likely to be good in state schools in that country. The implication of this may be that mathematics is more embedded in the culture (or parental expectations) of some countries than others and so more highly regarded. While the calculation of the Spearman coefficient is easy, with large data sets it can become a chore. Fortunately there are a number of online calculators available on the Internet.

12.10 Thinking about data description

This chapter acts as an important link between the data we have to work with and the final conclusions we draw in relation to our research questions. The approaches to data analysis that we have looked at are usually known as descriptive techniques and we use them to produce a *descriptive analysis*. This is not so different from what we do in qualitative analysis. We can use these descriptive analyses in two ways which reflect our approach to conducting our research enquiry.

- We can come to a data set with no (or at least few) preconceptions of what we will find or what we should be looking for. Our descriptive analysis will show us what is usual and what is unusual. This could be the start of identifying our research question. Why does this area have student outcomes that are so different from other similar areas? Why is student satisfaction so much better in that department?
- We can come expecting to find particular differences, for example, why boys' attainment is lower than girls', why the academic attainment of some ethnic groups is greater than others. These positions are established by previous research or theoretical analysis. We want to test them as propositions and so construct hypotheses.

Whichever approach we adopt, inductive or deductive, descriptive analysis can help us.

Summary

- We can use numerical statements to (a) summarise the appearance of our data and (b) summarise relationships in our data.
- We can describe central tendency (using mean, mode and median), spread (using range and deviation), skew and peakedness.
- In terms of relationships, we have looked at time series, regression and correlation (and regression and correlation also say something about the appearance of the data).
- Different types of data (interval data and data counts) require different approaches to calculating descriptive measures and give us much more flexibility in selecting data for analysis.
- Every method that we have considered is straightforward and easy to understand. This is significant given many people's predisposition to give up on numeracy. All the techniques are within the capability of every educational researcher.
- In many instances the laborious computational work is taken out of our hands when we put our data into spreadsheets. All we have to do is understand the methods conceptually.
- Overall, in this chapter we have added significantly to the toolbox of techniques at our disposal. We may not use them in every investigation but they are there for us when we need them. Just as important as this is that these techniques are a stepping-stone to even more powerful ways of looking at data. We shall look at these in the next chapter.

Further reading

Salkind, N.J. (2008) *Statistics for People (Who Think) They Hate Statistics*, Sage, London.

This easy-to-understand book covers the material we have looked at in this chapter. Its attraction is that it makes use of spreadsheets to do the calculations.

References

Anghileri, J., Beishvizen, M. and van Putten, K. (2002) 'From Informal Strategies to Structured Procedures: Mind the Gap', *Educational Studies in Mathematics*, 49(2), 149–170.

Counahan, M., Andrews, R., Buttner, P., Byrnes, G. and Speare, R. (2004) 'Head Lice Prevalence in Primary Schools in Victoria, Australia', *Paediatrics and Child Health*, 40(11), 616–619.

Falagas, M., Matthaion, D., Rafailidis, P., Panos, G. and Pappas, G. (2008) 'Worldwide Prevalence of Head Lice', *Emerging Infectious Diseases*, 14(9), available at http://www.cdc.gov/EID/content/14/9/1493.htm (accessed September 2008).

Meadows, P. and Roegger, D. (2005) 'Low Income Homeowners in Britain: Descriptive Analysis', *Research Report No. 251*, Department for Work and Pensions, HMSO.

Mueller-Benedict, V. (2000) 'Confirming Long Waves in Time Series of German Student Populations 1830–1990 Using Filter Techniques and Spectral Filter Techniques and Spectral Analysis', *Historical Social Research*, 25(3/4), 36–56.

Smith, P., Talamelli, L., Cowie, H., Naylor, P. and Charham, P. (2004) 'Profiles of Non-Victims, Escaped Victims, Continuing Victims and New Victims of School Bullying', *British Journal of Educational Psychology*, 74(4), 565–581.

Willems, S., Lapeere, H., Haedens, N., Pastels, I., Naegert, J.-M. and De Maeseneer, J. (2005) 'The Importance of Socio-economic Status and Individual Characteristics on the Prevalence of Head Lice in School Children', *European Journal of Dermatology*, 15(5), 387–392.

Chapter contents

Chapter 13

USING STATISTICS TO SAY SOMETHING SIGNIFICANT

Key themes

- The principles underpinning a statistical test of significance.
- The types of question we can use statistical tests to answer.
- The factors we have to take into account in choosing a test.
- How to interpret test results.

Introduction

This chapter will help us reach a judgement about our research evidence. If we stop to think about the process of making judgements, for example, how we judge some things better, some things worse, some people good and some bad or some accused guilty and some innocent, we probably imagine a process of looking at the evidence, balancing the pros and cons and then reaching a decision. Our decision, however, is likely to be influenced by our feelings about the subject, our likes and dislikes, our beliefs of what is right and what is wrong, our sense of the boundaries between what is acceptable and what is unacceptable. In other words, our rational assessment is fed through an emotional interface to produce our judgement and our judgement is a very personal thing. Our goal in this chapter is to remove the subjective element from the decision making.

13.1 Statistical testing: thinking about it in the right way

How can statistical procedures be used to inform such a subjective process? The answer is that they can but it all depends on the types of question we ask and the types of evidence we use. Let's assume we have two objects, 'this' and 'that' and two questions to answer, 'Which is taller?' and 'Which is better?' At the outset we can say that everyone should agree which of 'this' or 'that' is taller but we can have no certainty about judgements of which one is better. This, of course, is because my idea of what makes something better may be different from yours. I might prefer an apple to an orange but you might prefer an orange to an apple and who is to say that I am right and you wrong or vice versa? However, what if we were to deal not with individuals but with groups? Our question could then become, 'How *many* think this is better than that?' Having put the question in this way, we have created a situation in which everyone should agree, on the basis of the evidence, that more people prefer this or more that. We may not agree with the majority view but we have to accept that there *is* a majority view.

It is often easier to draw conclusions from our research if we can represent our data in a quantitative way. Sometimes this can be done with a direct measurement (height, weight, age), often it is the numbers (of people, schools, pupils, teachers, etc.) possessing a quality (gender, aptitude, performance, professional qualifications, preference) that we use. In other words, we can measure things we are interested in using different types of measuring instrument or scale. And some of these scales can help us convert essentially subjective judgements (such as 'better') into quantifiable data.

Having produced our quantified data, we have not reached the end of our research enquiry. We can all agree that one number is bigger than another but is the difference somehow significant? Does the difference in the numbers tell us anything other than that the numbers are not the same? This is a really interesting (and also a very powerful) question. Faced with two schools, one with an unauthorised absence rate of 5 per cent and the other with a rate of 10 per cent, and the question, 'Is the difference significant?', we might answer, 'It could be but I need to know more'. Just what might it be helpful to know? It would be helpful to know about their sizes because some absence will be random in occurrence and the more pupils in a school, the more random occurrences there will be, but this should not affect the proportion of random occurrences. It would also be useful to ask what types of schools they are. If one is a regular state-maintained secondary school and the other is a reception unit for pupils suspended from school, we are not comparing like with like. It is not important, however, to ask about the family and social backgrounds of the pupils. This may be a factor in *explaining* the difference but it is not a factor in explaining the significance of the difference between the two measurements.

Let us explore this idea a little more. If 49 per cent of people prefer this to that and 51 per cent that to this, does this suggest that there are two separate groups of people with their own clear preferences or would you think that the preference for one or the other was randomly distributed throughout the population? At this point, most people would not be convinced that the difference was significant and that there was only one group. But what if 20 per cent preferred one and 80 per cent the other? It is more likely that people would agree that the difference was important and that there were two groups. The questions for us as researchers are at what point do we begin to suspect that there might be two groups and at what point are we sure that there are two groups? Putting it another way, at what point does the difference between the numbers become significant? This question is at the heart of this chapter and, as we shall see, we can use statistical tests to help us reach a conclusion.

But what is a statistical test? The answer to this question is that it is a procedure we follow to help us reach a decision about our data. We use a test to establish whether things are the same or different (for example, whether any difference in the student outcomes from mixed or single sex schools is important enough for us to change the character of the way we educate children) or whether things are related to each other (for example, does improving the ratio of teachers to students improve outcomes for students?). At the core of the procedure is an estimation of probability; the probability, for example, that the improved academic performance of girls in a group of single sex schools is to be found in every all girls' school. With probabilities we can be more certain about our judgements. If the performance of girls in 90 per cent of single sex schools were better than girls' performance in mixed sex schools, most people would find that figure pretty convincing, some might even say that it is a significant difference. And this is what a statistical test does; it helps us establish the significance of our findings.

13.2 From spread to significance

The journey we are going to make now is an important one in our research lives because it will move us into a completely new approach to quantitative methods. It will take us from the position we reached in Chapter 12, where we used quantitative approaches to *describe* our data, to one where we can answer the question, 'What is the significance of our findings?' But it is not just being able to answer the question that is important to us, it is also the fact that we can know the chances of our getting the answer wrong. That puts us in a very strong position when it comes to drawing conclusions.

If we imagine that this all sounds very difficult, then we should think again because we have already covered the basics when we learnt how to calculate the standard deviation in Chapter 12. What we now have to do is work through some logical developments of the principles underpinning the standard deviation and, as we do, the basic principle of assessing the significance of our findings (this is called *significance testing*) will begin to take shape.

Let us begin by refreshing our understanding of standard deviation. This, as we saw, is a measure of spread about the mean of a distribution. Now whether we are talking about the marks obtained by students in an assessment, or expenditure on teachers' salaries, or the travel time of pupils to school or scores on a scale that measures dysfunctionality in family life, there will be common characteristics. In particular, there will *always* be more people who are more typical than atypical. (If this is not the case – for example, we have a distribution that is bimodal, with two peaks, then we are clearly dealing with not one but two populations. We met exactly this situation in Chapter 12, Table 12.3 where we found that the mean of the distribution fell between two peaks.) Because of this tendency for the concentration of values to decrease as we move away from the mean, we feel entitled to make a big assumption – that the characteristics of our observed data satisfy the requirements of it being a normal distribution (to refresh you understanding of this, read section 12.4.2).

This is an important step because what we can do is use the normal distribution as a model for our research data. We can understand now why we want to demonstrate that our research data conforms to the normal distribution and why we calculate measures for skew and kurtosis. And because we know that the normal distribution has given proportions of data units within 1, 2 and 3 standard deviations of the mean, we can use it as the basis for statistical testing.

There is, however, a caveat to this. There are other statistical distributions that can and are used for statistical testing but the underpinning principles of a statistical test are pretty much the same. All we have to know is which distribution to use, which is effectively the same as saying which test we should use. So, as we progress the argument, bear in mind this discussion. The world is often more complex than when it is first presented, but if it is not presented simply at first, it is often difficult to grasp an idea and then move forward with it to understand more complex issues.

13.2.1 Setting out in a new direction

Some people may have the impression that mathematics is all about equations and procedures that are set in stone and that the totality of these produces a discipline in which imagination is not required at all. If so, they would be quite wrong. Mathematics values creativity because, while there are rules and procedures, mathematicians create the logical environments and develop the rules to fit these environments.

So why this first paragraph? It is to get us to understand that what we sometimes have to do is get out of the groove we are in and begin moving in a new direction. Let's do just this.

Many of the variables we might want to investigate will, when the whole population is involved, conform to the normal distribution. We could, for example, expect this to be true for measures of intellectual intelligence (the whole population is involved), or the performance of students of a given age in a city on a standard assessment (because a large number are involved) or the expenditure per student by higher education institutions (when there are enough of them). Obviously, however, the population sizes of each are different, the largest measured in millions, the smallest in tens or hundreds, yet they are all normal distributions. If we wanted to, how could we ever compare them? Well, we could manage it with computer graphics. Imagine a normal distribution, a symmetrical bell-shaped curve, in our mind's eye. We can shrink the horizontal axis of the largest population and shrink the vertical axis in proportion and the shape and size should be the same as for a smaller population. If the distributions are normal, one should fit exactly over the other. In other words, *every* normal distribution will have the same shape. Figure 13.1 shows a normal distribution. Note the bell-shaped curve and the symmetry around the central point (the mean, where the horizontal and vertical axes meet).

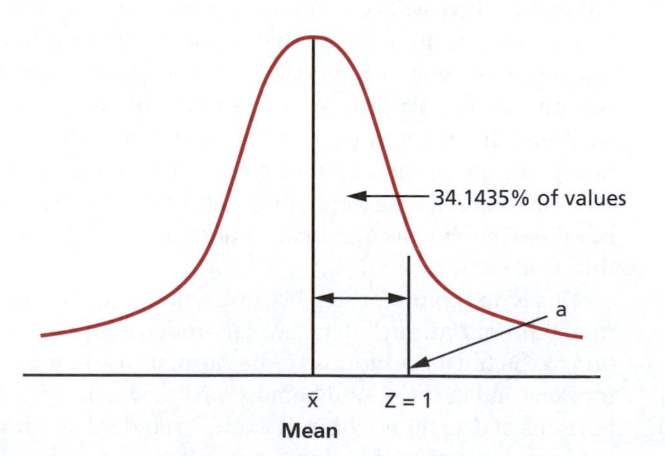

Figure 13.1 Understanding the idea of Z

The next step may not seem to have much point now but it connects with something we learnt in Chapter 12. What we have to do is understand a characteristic of the normal distribution and we need to do this because it is the link to understanding the idea of statistical testing. We can measure along the horizontal axis and, for each unit we measure, we can calculate the proportion of the distribution between the origin (the centre of the distribution where the x and y axes intersect) and any point. In other words, for every miniscule distance we travel along the x axis, we can measure the proportion of the distribution between that point and the origin (the mean). From this we could produce a table of measurements for each unit of distance along the x axis. Welcome to the Z table! The *Z table*, also called the *normal distribution function*, shows the proportion of the normal distribution for a series of standard units from the mean. Figure 13.1 shows this. Moving from the mean to point (a) shows the proportion of the population or sample in the area under the curve between the mean and point (a). Figure 13.1 shows this proportion as 34.1435% of all the data in the distribution. Table 13.1 is an extract from a Z table. The Z values are given in the first column (these are notional units of distance along the x axis). In the second column are the proportions of the distribution between the mid-point and values of Z and in the third column are the proportions between values of Z and the extreme of the distribution.

Stay with the argument for a moment longer and all will become clearer. Let us look at three values of Z. When Z is 1.0, 34.1435% of values are accounted for. When Z is 2.0, the proportion is 47.725% and when it is 3.0, the proportion is 49.865%. These proportions are only half the distribution, the right-hand side. For each value of Z, there is an

Table 13.1 Values of Z

Z value	Percent of distibution between 0 and Z value	Percent of distribution between Z and the limit of the distribution
.1	3.9828	46.0172
.2	7.9260	42.0740
.3	11.7911	38.2089
.4	15.5422	34.4578
.5	19.1462	30.8538
.6	22.5747	27.4253
.7	25.8036	24.1964
.8	28.8145	21.1855
.9	31.5940	18.4060
1.0	34.1435	15.8565
1.2	38.4930	11.5070
1.4	41.9243	8.0757
1.6	44.5201	5.4799
1.8	46.4070	3.5930
2.0	47.7250	2.2750
2.2	48.6097	1.3903
2.4	49.1802	0.8198
2.6	49.5339	0.4661
2.8	49.7445	0.2555
3.0	49.8650	0.1350

equivalent proportion on the left-hand side. If we add the proportions from the right and left sides together, then either side of the mid-point there are:

68.29% of values when Z is 1.0
95.55% of values when Z is 2.0
99.93% of values when Z is 3.0

At this point, something might strike you. These percentages are virtually the same as the proportions we saw in Chapter 12 that were 1, 2 and 3 standard deviations from the mean. Actually, in Chapter 12 we only used approximate values and the values above are the actual ones. Remember this while we go on to look at another way of looking at the Z distribution.

As well, for each of our values of Z, we can show the per cent of the values lying beyond any point a. Thus, for example, when Z is 1.0, 15.865% of the values are greater than Z. These values are given in column 3 of Table 13.1. When we look closely at columns two and three, we will see something that should strike us as so obvious that we will wonder why we have not spotted it before. Each pair of values sums to 50%. This is not surprising because the two together are exactly half of the distribution.

The question now for us is, 'What can we do with our research data so that we can make use of the Z table and the fact that in a normal distribution a given proportion of all the data values will lie within a specified distance of the mid-point?' Let us go to the next section.

13.2.2 Standardising sample data

If an education authority in an urban area recognised that it could play an important part in reducing traffic congestion and improving environmental quality by ensuring that children attended their nearest school, it is entirely feasible for it to carry out the following research to test what impact this policy would have. First it would allocate each child to its nearest school using an appropriate geostatistical program. (*Geostatistics* or *spatial analysis* explores the way in which patterns occur and relationships exist over an area. Geostatistics has grown rapidly with the growth in computing power and is extensively used not only in geography, geology and biosciences as we might expect, but also in marketing and business analysis.) Next, the education authority would calculate the shortest road distance between every child's home and the school (easily done using the same program). Then it would calculate the mean travel distance and the standard deviation. With this data it could ask questions like, 'What is the probability of a child living more than 2 km from the school?' (it would want to know this because the likelihood is that beyond this distance all children will travel to and from school by car) and 'Acknowledging that parents may want to select a school on the basis of something other than proximity, what is the furthest distance a child will travel if we allocate 50%, 60%, 70% and 80% of children to the closest school?' To answer these questions, what we do is standardise our data by converting specific values into Z values. The formula we use to standardise our data is straightforward:

$$Z = \frac{x - \bar{x}}{s}$$

Where Z is our data expressed as standard units.
x is our data unit
$\bar{x}$ is the mean of our data
s is the standard deviation of our data

Let us just consider what this formula is doing. We are subtracting the mean from any unit of data and expressing the result as a proportion of the distribution's standard deviation. Z is, effectively, units of a standard deviation. Since a standard deviation is always 68.29% of a normal distribution (we know this from the theoretical work done in relation to gambling almost 300 years ago), we have put our data into a form where it can be directly compared with a normal distribution. Let us return to our two questions on the consequences of allocating children to the closest school. If our mean travel distance for all children is 3.5 km, the standard deviation 2.7 km and the question is, 'What is the probability of a child living more than 2 km from the school?', the Z value of our data unit is:

$$\frac{2.7 - 2}{3.5} = 0.2$$

If we look at column three of Table 13.1 (column three because our question was the probability of a child living more than 2 km from school) we see that the proportion living beyond 2 km is 42.0740. However, we have to remember that this table only gives us half of the distribution (look at Figure 13.1 again to see what we mean), so we have to double our figure to give 84.148. Therefore the probability is 0.842 (the proportion has been rounded to three decimal places).

For the second question, we have to work the table in reverse and find the Z value equivalent to our proportions. Table 13.1 is a little crude for this but we can make a good stab at it. Let us take 70% as an example. In Table 13.1 we can look for 70% in column two (column two because that gives the proportion of the distribution between the mean and Z and it is this that will enable us to determine the distance). However, look as we might, we won't find it. Until we realise that, again, we have to deal with both sides of the distribution. In fact, what we have to look for is 35% (half of the 70% in half of the distribution). We see in the table that Z = 1 gives us 34.1435% and Z = 1.2 gives us 38.4930. Our best guess from this table is that Z is 1.05 or thereabouts. Let us now put these figures into our formula and see what we get:

$$\frac{2.7 - x}{3.5} = 1.05$$

$$2.7 - x = 1.05 \times 3.5$$

$$-x = 3.675 + 2.7$$

$$= 6.375$$

So our answer is that if we allocate 70% of children to their nearest school, the furthest any one of them will travel is 6.375 km (we can ignore the '−' sign above because the side of the distribution we look at does not matter in this instance).

If you have sharp eyes you may have noticed something different about the equations we have used here. It is a technical matter but if we do not explain it, you could be confused when you read quantitative research paper and books. Some terms in this formula are different. For example, we have used S to stand for standard deviation, rather than δ that we have used before. Why? The answer lies in convention. Statisticians use different symbols to signify values derived from a population and values derived from a sample. The formula for Z set out above is the formula that denotes the data is a sample of the population. If we were dealing with data for the population as a whole, we would write the formula:

$$Z = \frac{x - \mu}{\delta} \qquad \text{where } \mu = \text{mean}$$

$$\delta = \text{standard deviation}$$

We have actually started to do something interesting in this section and that is to use the characteristics of the normal distribution in our analysis and to inform our conclusions. Let us see what else we can do with it.

13.2.3 From percentages to probability

It is a short step now to be able to make statements about the likelihood of an event. Let us assume that teachers are preparing a year group for a national mathematics assessment. Because the assessment will be of all children at the same school stage, we can reasonably assume that the results will be normally distributed (a whole year group is likely to be in excess of 120 students). The teachers have the statistics for the previous year's national test, a mean of 49 and a standard deviation of 19.4. They have conducted a number of class tests to reflect what students will be asked to do in the national assessment and have accumulated the scores for each pupil. The question they want to answer is how their pupils are performing in relation to the national distribution. (There are a number of reasons why this is an important question, ranging from wanting to know whether they have been teaching them the right sorts of thing for the test to knowing that they will be judged by the proportion that achieve a particular grade or higher). To answer their question, they select two pupils, the third best in the group to represent the best students (they choose the third because this is more conservative than choosing the best) and the pupil with the lowest grade. The marks for each pupil are 87 and 28.

What they do is look at how their students perform in the context of the previous year's results. These are their findings:

Pupil	Z calculation	Z value
Best	$\frac{87 - 49}{19.4}$	1.959
Worst	$\frac{28 - 49}{19.4}$	−1.082

Now let us think about these Z values. Table 13.1 shows that when Z is 1.959, only about 2.3% of the population exceeds this score (the right-hand column). A value of −1.082 (the worst student) is exceeded by about 85% of the population. The teacher was pleased with these results because their worst student is better than the worst nationally and their third best student is in the top 3% of students nationally. The evidence is that their pupils, on the whole, perform somewhat better than the rest of the population. The issue is whether their students perform significantly better than the national student set. We cannot quite answer this yet but we are getting closer to an answer.

The teacher also calculated the mean mark for all their students. This was 60.35. They calculated the Z value as:

$$\frac{60.35 - 49}{19.4} = 0.5851$$

With this Z value, about 72% of all the values in a normal distribution fall below it. (In Table 13.1 this is given by taking the value in the right-hand column from 100% or adding 50% to the value in the left-hand column). Most people would find this result pretty convincing: 50% of the teacher's students got below a mark of 60.35 and nationally about 72% got below this mark.

Now there is a different way of looking at this value of 72% and that is to say that in 72% of all national tests, the national mean value will be lower than the teacher's class mean. Or, putting it another way, only in 28 years in 100 will a national test average exceed theirs. This is starting to sound interesting because it is expressing the result in a way that brings out the significance of the difference.

We have not yet quite reached the point of implementing a significance test (we look at these from section 13.6 onwards) nor yet pinned down what we actually mean by 'significance' in a research context (we look at this in section 13.4.1) but we have seen the principles underpinning the idea of significance testing. This, quite simply, is to:

- establish a statistical distribution as a model;
- examine the research data in the context of the model;
- use the distributional characteristics of the model to make probabilistic statements about the data.

And while we have used the Z distribution to give us insights into the idea of testing, we should not ignore the fact that creating Z values for our survey data can be used to answer important research questions.

Finally, in this section, we should point out that there are several websites with calculations for Z that will remove the need for calculating values by hand and looking up the results in tables. How easy can it get!

13.2.4 What types of question can we ask?

Well, it just gets easier and easier. While the number of *research* questions may be very large indeed, when we put them into a form for statistical testing, there are only two broad types: 'Are these the same?' and 'Are these related?' Let us look at each in turn.

(i) Are these the same?

Let us imagine that we have constructed a study in which pupils from two classes sit the same science test. (This is essentially the PISA research process that we met in Chapter 10.) The purpose of our test is to evaluate the teacher effect so, as far as possible, we match the pupils in terms of socio-economic and family background and an indicator of mathematics ability based on the preceding year. From the results we can calculate some of the descriptive statistics (such as median, mean, range and standard deviation) we met in Chapter 12. These will indicate differences between the two student groups but they won't give us a clear answer as to whether the differences we see are significant. In fact, until we start expressing our findings in terms of probabilities, we cannot produce an answer that both we and other researchers will be convinced by. For this we need a statistical test. It does not matter how we phrase the question, 'Are these the same?' or 'Are these *significantly* different?', the two are effectively the same question. Each is testing the same hypothesis – are these two samples drawn from the same parent population or are they from two different populations, one taught by a good science teacher and one taught by a poor science teacher? This, in a nutshell, is what lies at the heart of much significance testing. There are some complications to this that we have hinted at before but they apply equally to our second type of question, so we will look at them afterwards.

(ii) Are these related?

This is quite a different question from our first one. Things can be related without being the same and, as many researchers have found out, things can be associated without being related in any way whatsoever. Let us think about this issue of association and relatedness a little further. If we were to take the profile of live births in England and Wales that we looked at in Chapter 12 and compared that with admissions to primary education four years later, we would be surprised if we did not see the same sort of pattern. Clearly the two sequences of data are related. Now let us examine another *apparent* relationship. A 1979 study of childhood respiratory disease showed that children whose parents (or parent) smoked had a stronger lung function than those whose parent(s) did not smoke. If these were related, we would act on the results and put children into smoke-laden atmospheres. The fact that we have not suggests that we do not believe it, that the relationship is spurious and that all we have is an association but not a relationship. The reality is that spurious relationships are not all that difficult to find. The 1930s saw the first research showing a 'relationship' between the number of babies born and the number of storks nesting. In 2004, three German researchers (Hofer et al., 2004) were able to show a statistically significant relationship (in general terms, this is one where the probability associated with an event is sufficiently large as to be convincing to a reasonable researcher) between storks nesting and out of hospital births (but not between the number of storks and the number of hospital births). There was nothing wrong with their computation and the individual data on the number of storks nesting and the number of babies born was accurate but what was wrong was the fundamental assumption that storks have anything at all to do with babies. All a bit of fun no doubt, but it is a good example to demonstrate that a relationship implies causation between the variables, association does not.

What about the complications we mentioned earlier? Let us look at them.

- First, we have to go back and examine this idea of association and add a caveat to the conclusion above. If we seek to establish through a statistical test whether two samples (such as our two groups of students who took the science test) are different from each other, we assume that if we show that they are not different, that they are (close to being) the same. Very often we call the tests that do this 'tests of association'. But in this case what is being tested is whether data are drawn from the same population or whether they represent two different populations, not whether there is causation. Association has different implications according to the circumstance in which we use it, so we have to be careful how we use it.
- Second, we have to be specific about the actual hypothesis that we are testing when we use statistical techniques. The reason for this is that we are working within a positivist framework. To refresh our minds of what the implications of this are, we should read again section 2.2.1. One thing we have to note is that our hypothesis, the one we actually test, has to be constructed as a 'null hypothesis'. Look at section 3.2.3 for details on this. The hypothesis we seek to test is one of no significant difference between the variables.
- Third, if we reject the null hypothesis, we should have ready an alternative hypothesis. This is often called the *research hypothesis* – and it is the one we are really interested in. The way we phrase the research hypothesis has important implications for the procedures we follow with statistical tests. If our null hypothesis is that 'there is no difference between A and B', our research hypothesis could be one of the following:
  - 'there is a difference between A and B';

- 'A is greater than B';
- 'B is greater than A'.

We cannot have more than one research hypothesis, so effectively we have to choose between a difference between A and B and one of the other two. In making the choice, these are the things we have to bear in mind:

- saying that there is a difference is a weaker prediction than saying what sort of difference it is;
- saying that A is greater than B or B greater than A requires us to have an idea of why this should be so. In other words, we should have an idea of the processes involved. These processes constitute a model of how we believe A acts upon B or B upon A. Our specification of the research hypothesis is an important stepping-stone in assembling proof for a model or a theory.

We shall have more to say about our research hypothesis in the next section.

13.3 Determining a test result

In this section we shall deal with issues that affect our choice and interpretation of a statistical test.

13.3.1 What do we mean by statistical significance?

Well, the first thing to appreciate is that statisticians use the word 'significant' differently from the way we use it in normal speech. When we hear about 'significant casualties' in a news broadcast, we know that they are large. If a government is defeated in a vote in parliament, we would accept that this important event is 'significant'. If statisticians, however, calls a difference 'significant' they do not mean that it is important nor do they mean that it is large. So what do they mean?

Statistical significance is concerned with the correctness of our judgement about our null hypothesis. If a researcher says that the evidence that a method of teaching reading improves the reading ability of children and that the improvement is statistically significant, what they are saying is that the evidence is such that the conclusion they have reached is probably true. Now the question is, on what basis do they reach that conclusion? The answer is that they are sure that the teaching method is the reason for the improvement and that it is highly unlikely that their result occurred just by chance. This idea of chance takes us immediately into the realm of probability and we have to understand the nuances we put on this word 'chance'. One sense of chance is that something can be likely (or unlikely). For example, we might be told that there is an 80 per cent chance that it will snow today or there is a 2 per cent chance that a child attending a private school will receive a criminal record (I don't know whether that is the case, I just made it up to make the point!). But there is also another way of using 'chance', when we hear, 'It's just chance if you get a place to read medicine there'. The implication in this case is that it could not have been predicted, in other words it was the product of a random set of processes (it must seem like that when a university is heavily oversubscribed and all the students have high grades for the assessments they took at the end of their school careers). These two ways of looking at chance are built into the idea of statistical significance.

If we express the likelihood of something (that these children are better at mathematics than those because of the way they were taught) in probability terms (the mean score of children taught this way is 15 per cent higher than those taught using another approach), then we can reasonably ask the question, 'Is this difference significant?' To understand how statisticians have reasoned this question (we say 'reasoned' because the issue is one of logic and not numeracy), we have to go back to our hypothesis, which is, as we know, a null hypothesis. In this case our null hypothesis would be something like, 'There is no difference between the two groups that have been taught in different ways'. The question we ask ourselves is, 'Is the null hypothesis true?' The evidence we have is that children do better with the new method. But we cannot take a decision yet because there is another thing to consider. If our comparison were based on 5 students in each group, we would be hesitant about being definitive in our claims. It is entirely possible, for example, that the 5 students who were taught using the new approach just happened to be bright students (that is, our sample was not balanced). If there were 20 students in each group, we would be more confident in our claims that the new method constituted a breakthrough and if this was a large test with 5,000 students we would almost certainly be justified in saying 'case proved'. It is clear then that the difference has to be interpreted in the context of sample size. What we will find with our statistical tests is that when our sample is small, the difference between groups has to be large and when our sample is small, even small differences can be significant.

So let us go back to our question, how does a statistician determine whether the result of a statistical test is significant? All statistical tests will generate two important values. One is the *test statistic*. This is the number that results from putting our test data into the formula for the test. The other is a *probability value* associated with this statistic and it is the one we are interested in. Remember that we are testing a null hypothesis that there is no difference between the two groups. This is the same as saying that both groups are drawn from the same population. Just think about this for a second. If the two groups are from the same population then, assuming that our sampling is sound, the means should be much the same. If the means are very different and if the null hypothesis is correct, then we must be sampling from different ends of the population, one side is those who are better at mathematics and the other those who are poorer. We ask ourselves what the likelihood of this is and answer, 'Not very likely'. What the probability value shows us is the chance of getting a set of results like those we have if the two groups are actually drawn from the same population.

As you might expect, however, it is not quite as straightforward as this because of what we can and cannot do with the null hypothesis. (For a discussion on why we cannot prove that the null hypothesis is true but we can prove that it is false, read section 3.2.2, especially Case Study 3.3). The question we ask of the null hypothesis is, more accurately, 'What is the likelihood that it is *not* true?' Our probability statistic tells us the answer.

Some examples will help us to understand this. If we have a probability of 0.1 from our test, this means that the null hypothesis has a 0.1% chance of being 'true', or, in other words, a 99.9% chance of not being true. If our probability is 0.999, this means that the null hypothesis has a 99.9% chance of being 'true', or, in other words, a 0.1 chance of not being true.

We can find in the research literature different ways of expressing the interpretation of the probability level. They are all much the same but they can throw you if you have not met them before. Here are three more ways of saying what we have just explained, all taken from published material. In each case significance is explained in terms of:

- the probability of rejecting the null hypothesis when it is true (or when we should not have rejected it);
- the probability that the differences are due to chance;
- the probability that if we were to draw the samples again we would get the same result.

We still, however, have not pinpointed the idea of *significant difference.* How do we know whether our probability value of .0365 is significant or not? Let us return to an argument that we have touched on before. If we were researching whether teachers who undertook no educational duties or activities in their lunch break exercised better class control after lunch than teachers who patrolled playgrounds or marked work and our test generated a probability value of 0.5000, would we accept that undertaking no lunchtime work led to more effective behaviour management if it occurred 50% of the time? We would clearly be unwise to because the implication is that for the other 50% of time the two groups of teachers would either be the same or those who worked during the lunch break would be better. So, how many times would those who did not work at lunchtime have to be better at managing their classes than those who worked before we think that the difference is significant? If it happened 999 times out of 1,000 most people would be convinced. If it happened 75% of the time many people would accept that the teachers who did not work were better at controlling their classes – but not statisticians. Statisticians are conservative and while they would accept 99.9% as convincing, there is a lower limit below which convention says they do not go. That limit is usually 95% (statistical programs present this probability value as 5%, a 1 in 20 chance, because the hypothesis they use is a null hypothesis).

Why do statisticians work with this limit? Now this is an interesting question because it shows how custom and practice can become so embedded in a subject that it becomes an established truth that is not to be challenged. The level of 5% was established in 1925 by Ronald Fisher in his book *Statistical Methods for Research Workers.* This has been described as the most influential statistics book in the twentieth century. Whether this is true or not I am not qualified to say, but what is evident is that much of what Fisher wrote in that book has been republished in texts in the intervening years, including this book. He later wrote 'it is a common practice to judge a result significant, if it is of such a magnitude that it would have been produced by chance not more frequently than once in twenty trials. This is an arbitrary, but convenient, level of significance for the practical investigator' (Fisher, 1925, p. 191). The 5% level came about because he wanted to use Karl Pearson's tables of probability values for statistical tests in his 1925 book. However, Pearson and Fisher had been at war over Fisher's use of a statistical test since 1922 (though it is fair to say that the two had been feuding for some time before this) and permission to use the tables was refused. Fisher got round the copyright issues by printing only the probabilities associated with the tails of the distributions between 0.1 (10%) and 0.01 (1%) and saying: 'We shall not often be astray if we draw a conventional line at .05.' And we have been following this advice since.

To summarise, the range within which statisticians normally work for statistical testing is between 95% (95 out of 100 or 5% with a null hypothesis), and 99.9% (999 out of 1,000 or .001% with a null hypothesis). Conventionally 95% is used more. However, before we accept these conventions, we should understand something of the history of statistical testing. Much of the work on developing statistical method was carried out in industrial quality control processes and in medical testing. Drug manufacturers, for example, work necessarily at very low margins of error. We would not be very happy taking a drug if we knew that there was a 1 in 10 chance that the manufacturing process got the dosage wrong. Similarly, car component manufacturers have to work to high standards because failures cost money. With social sciences, however, extremely robust standards are not necessarily called for because the things we investigate are more 'fuzzy' and much less clear cut. We know from many studies that the educational outcomes of children from single parent families are poorer than those from two parent families. Writing in the *Lancet*, Swedish researchers led by Gunilla Weitoft have shown that health outcomes are poorer also (Weitoft et al., 2003). Their data shows that the death rate of girls from single families was 22.1 per 1,000,000 and for boys it was 49.1 compared with 17.0 for girls in two parent families and 29.6 for boys. Their studies showed 'increased risk of psychiatric disease, suicide or suicide attempt, injury or addiction in children in single parent households' (p. 294). The increased risk that was established is statistically significant (at the level of 95%) but (and this is an important but) there were also circumstances where differences existed but they were not as marked but might have entered the conclusions had a less rigorous (90% or even 85%) level been selected.

The implication of this is truly important for researchers. We have to think about significance in two ways, first as statistical significance and second as significant in the context of the research topic. Where we find interesting results whose probability would indicate we should not reject the null hypothesis, we should think again and consider whether our result is 'significant' because the assumptions of statistical significance are too rigorous for the data we can collect on the issue. We should always remember that when we are dealing with people, differences may not reach conventional statistical levels but they are, nonetheless, personally and societally important. However, whatever level of significance we choose as our benchmark, we have to justify it, either in conventional statistical terms or in terms of our research topic.

13.3.2 The link between our hypothesis and our test

Now let us look at our hypothesis in a little more detail and understand how important this is in understanding the idea of significance. We know that for reasons of logic we have to test a null hypothesis and that every null hypothesis has a *research hypothesis*. The nature of our research hypothesis affects the type of probabilistic statement that we make. Let's put some terminology in place first before we explain it. There are two ways of expressing the research hypothesis.

- Saying that there is a difference between two samples (but not what the difference is) is referred to as a *two-tailed test*.
- Saying that A is bigger than B or vice versa is called a *one-tailed test*.

What do one- and two-tailed refer to? Figure 13.2 explains this. The tails referred to in one- and two-tailed tests are the tails of the probability distribution that we are using for our test (usually the normal distribution or some variant of it). A significant difference between two sets of data is established when the likelihood (or probability) of the difference being the result of chance is low. These probabilities are found at the extremes or tails of the probability distribution.

- In a one-tailed test, only one side of the distribution concerns us, the left deals with one research hypothesis (A is greater than B) and the right with the other (B is greater than A).
- With a two-tailed test (when our hypothesis is only that A and B are different), we deal with both sides of the distribution.

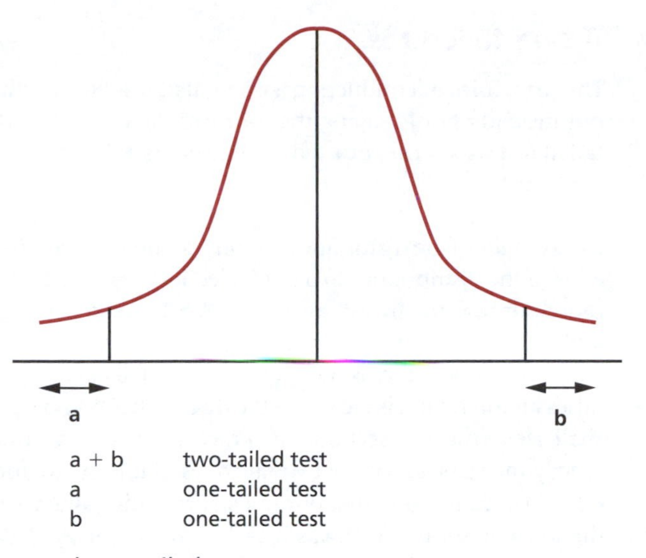

Figure 13.2 One- and two-tailed tests

This distinction, as we shall see, is important, because it ties in with something we learnt in relation to Z tables, that sometimes, depending on what we are trying to determine, we have to double the probabilities associated with an event or outcome. This may sound difficult but it is not as long as we are clear about the exact research hypothesis that we are using. Let us now look at the implications of this. All will become clearer in the following sections.

13.3.3 A two-tailed test

Acknowledging this caveat, that there may be circumstances in education research where being less rigorous than is conventionally the case may well be justified, let us now see what happens in a two-tailed test. Figure 13.2 shows this situation in general terms. If our level of acceptance or rejection of the null hypothesis is set at 5% (we will use the formulation found in statistical programs, rather than the 95% we have used so far), in a two-tailed test we allocate 2.5% of our probability to each side of the distribution because we are sampling both sides of the distribution, that is, we are not specifying in what way our two data sets might be different. If it were 10%, we would allocate 5% to each side.

Let us look at this in terms of our Z table (Table 13.1). We cannot be exactly accurate with this table but we can get pretty close (if we use an on-line checker or a more detailed set of tables, we can and should be more accurate). Look at column three and find the Z value closes to 2.5%. It is between 2.2750% ($Z = 2$) and 3.5930% ($Z = 1.8$). So 2.5% of the values in the distribution give a Z value of just below 2 (actually 1.96). If our test statistic is greater than this we should reject our null hypothesis because in more than 5% of cases where we obtain this test value from our samples, the difference does not occur by chance. If our test statistic fails to reach the critical level (that is, our research hypothesis cannot be accepted), we cannot accept our null hypothesis. All we can say is that there is not enough evidence to reject the null hypothesis.

13.3.4 A one-tailed test

The principles of conducting a one-tailed test are exactly the same as for a two-tailed test but instead of only saying that our two data sets, A and B, will be different, with a one-tailed test we say that one will be bigger than the other and specify which one will be bigger. This has an important consequence for rejecting or not rejecting the null hypothesis.

In the two-tailed test we saw that we split the critical acceptance/rejection level between the two tails of the distribution. In our example we put the 5% we are interested in into both ends of the distribution. In a one-tailed test, we only look at one half of the distribution because our research hypothesis is that A is bigger than B (or vice versa). Look again at our Z table (Table 13.1) and we see the implications of this. Again we look at column three to find where 5% probability is. We can see that it falls between 1.6 and 1.8 (actually 1.645). This raises an interesting issue about the discriminatory power of one- and two-tailed tests, as we shall see in the next section. The process of rejecting or nor rejecting the null hypothesis is exactly the same as for the two-tailed test but what are the implications of using one or the other? Let us imagine that our test statistic (the value we obtain from putting our data into the formula for the test) was $Z = 1.8$. With a one-tailed test we would reject the null hypothesis because the critical value of Z is 1.645 (our value is 1.8) but with a two-tailed test we would not reject the null hypothesis because the critical value of Z is 1.96 (and our value is 1.8). So the way we phrase our research hypothesis is very important indeed.

13.3.5 Choosing between a one- and two-tailed test

What are the implications of using a directional or non-directional research hypothesis? To come to some conclusions about this we should first look at the implications of reaching the wrong decisions with our test statistic (that is, getting a sample where the difference actually is produced by chance).

Table 13.2 shows a two by two matrix of the 'truth' of the null hypothesis and the conclusions we can reach.

- If the null hypothesis is true, we make a correct decision if we do not reject it and an incorrect decision if we reject it. This is called a *Type I error*. If in a study of lunchtime support provided by teachers, we would make a Type I error if we concluded that not working at lunchtime led to better class management when the real situation was that there was no difference between them.
- If the null hypothesis is false, we make a correct decision if we reject it and an incorrect decision if we do not reject it. This is called a *Type II* error. Again, in our example, we would make a Type II error if we said that class management in the afternoon was not affected by whether the teacher did or did not work at lunchtime when the reality is that not working would lead to better class management.

Table 13.2 Type I and Type II Error

	Null hypothesis	
Decision	True	False
Reject	Type I Error	Decision correct
Do not reject	Decision correct	Type II Error

Which, if either, is the more serious mistake to make? Imagine a man is being tried for a capital offence. If he is innocent but he is found guilty, this is Type I error. If he is guilty but found not guilty at trial, this is a Type II error. Is it better to hang him if he is innocent, or release him if he is guilty? Most people would say that the finality of the former (a Type I error) is the more serious. The implication of this is that we should do as much as we can to avoid a Type I error.

Let us now think about this in relation to the value at which we will reject or fail to reject our null hypothesis. Table 13.3 helps us here. It shows us the risk associated with making a Type I or Type II error at various critical levels of rejecting the null hypothesis. It shows that the risk of making a Type I error increases as the critical level becomes less rigorous (that is, there is less risk at 0.01% than there is with 0.1%). It also reveals that the risk of making a Type II error decreases as the critical level becomes less rigorous (that is, there is more risk at 0.01% than there is at 0.1%). This situation has three implications:

- First, there is a trade-off between a Type I and Type II error when we change the critical value at which we test our hypothesis. Perhaps it is for this reason that many researchers stick to 5%.
- Second, if we wish to minimise a Type I error (to execute an innocent man or incorrectly reject a true null hypothesis) then we should choose a lower critical value as our benchmark.
- Third (and this is particularly important in terms of our determining whether our research hypothesis is directional or no-directional), at any given critical value, a two-tailed test includes a Type I error in both tails of the distribution. For example, at the 5% critical value, a two-tailed test is effectively testing both halves of the distribution at the 2.5% level.

Most statistical packages for computers have, as their default, a two-tailed test (that is, the direction of any difference is not specified). It is usually straightforward to reinterpret the test statistic as a one-tailed test. However, there are some arguments against doing this.

Table 13.3 Where the risk is with Type I and Type II Errors

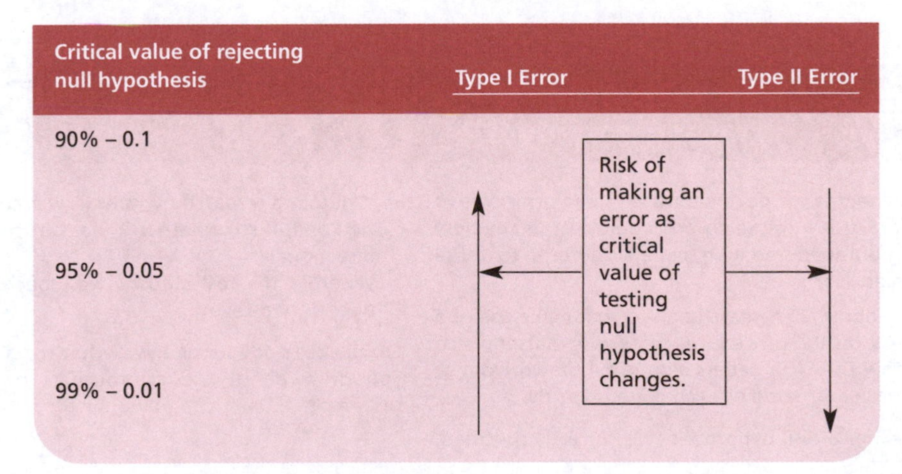

Critical value of rejecting null hypothesis	Type I Error		Type II Error
90% – 0.1	↑	Risk of making an error as critical value of testing null hypothesis changes.	↓
95% – 0.05	↑		↓
99% – 0.01	↑		↓

- First, the research hypothesis may specify the wrong direction (bigger than rather than smaller than) leading to the wrong side of the distribution being tested. You may say that this is no big deal since all we have to do is change the direction of our research hypothesis. However, while this might take us from a state of not rejecting the null hypothesis to one where we reject it, it does raise questions about how we derived our research hypothesis in the first place.
- Second, the use of a one-tailed test without specifying that it is one-tailed can lead to great confusion in the literature.
- Third, we may be tempted to use a one-tailed test when a two-tailed test just fails the critical value at which we would reject our null hypothesis. The idea of a statistical test is to place as much decision making as possible in the hands of procedure and out of the hands of the researcher, so to use a one-tailed test like this is unethical. No doubt it happens because researchers like to show that their results are significant!

In summary, there are no hard and fast rules about when to use a one-tailed or two-tailed test but there are conventions. These are (i) to use a two-tailed test in preference to a one-tailed and (ii) to use the 5% critical value for significance, other things being equal (though we can argue for something less robust).

Activity 13.1 provides an opportunity to asses how far academic authors specify the sorts of thing that we have identified as good practice.

13.3.6 But is it always about significance?

When we ask about the significance of our test result, we are assessing the likelihood that the result occurred by chance. But is this always what we should be interested in? Let us imagine we have a situation of two new ways of teaching reading that we wish to compare against the existing method we use. Two schools that are matched in terms of their intakes take part. In each, one third of the group is the control, one third taught using new method A and one using new method B. Each group size is 30. With method A, all children show a moderate improvement. With method B, half the children show a great improvement, the rest show some or a little improvement. Our test reveals that the significance of the difference between A and the control is much the same as B.

Activity 13.1 How clear are researchers about the basis of their testing procedure?

In this chapter we have identified some principles of good practice in research procedure. Let us see how many published research papers conform to these principles.

Identify about 20 research papers that make use of a statistical testing procedure. It does not matter which tests they use. The papers should be drawn from at least three journals. For each paper identify:

- Whether a null hypothesis was correctly specified.
- Whether a research hypothesis was correctly specified and, if so, whether it was directional or non-directional.
- Whether the test statistic was specified as being one- or two-tailed.

On the basis of your analysis, what conclusions would you draw about the rigorousness of educational research?

This is undoubtedly an important finding but which test has a greater impact overall on reading improvement? By looking at the data a different way we can interpret the result differently. In this case, we look at the size of the impact and not the significance of the difference as a way of differentiating the two methods. Let us understand this in a little more detail. With both methods the difference is significant at about the 2% level, in other words we would get our results only 2% of the time if our samples were actually from the same population. But we still do not know which of the two new methods produces the better results. All we know is that both are better than the control method.

We can actually determine this though if we look at something called the *effect size.* This is an estimate of the *scale of the impact* that interventions make and not on the significance of the difference. The concept of effect size is used extensively in assessments of interventions in the learning process because it is especially important that interventions that produce the greatest leaning benefits are adopted. To measure effect size we have to know the standard deviation and the mean. The statistic that is generated, *Cohen's d,* is calculated as:

$$d = \frac{\bar{x}\text{ intervention group} - \bar{x}\text{ control group}}{\delta}$$

where $\bar{x}$ is the mean

δ is the standard deviation

Calculation can either be straightforward (if the standard deviations are the same) or rather more complex if we have to use both standard deviations. The latter situation is more usual but fortunately there are several on-line calculators that can be used which do the job for us. If we assume our research data generated the following mean reading scores and standard deviations:

Control	$\bar{x}$	84.2	δ	22.7
Method A	$\bar{x}$	94.9	δ	21.0
Method B	$\bar{x}$	104.8	δ	39.5

then d is .49 between A and control and 0.64 between B and control. As a benchmark, 0.2 suggests a small effect, 0.6 a moderate effect and 0.8 or above a large effect. The implication of this result (remember both new approaches have the same statistical significance) is that method B has the greater effect and that if we were investing in training for teachers we should train them in method B rather than method A.

13.4 Choosing a statistical test

Table 13.4 (see p. 581) shows the tests we shall consider in this chapter. While they are only a small selection of test that are available, it is important, even with this restricted selection, to understand the criteria we have to take account of when we choose one.

Selecting which statistical test to use can be daunting. Choose the wrong one and our results are not worth the paper they are printed on. The number of tests potentially available to us is large and knowing which one to use (or not to use) is a skill that researchers develop. Fortunately there are some simple rules that we can apply that will help us to reach a satisfactory solution.

13.4.1 The issues to consider

There are four factors we have to consider in determining whether a test is appropriate for the data we have. We shall consider each in turn.

(i) The question we want to answer

As we saw earlier, there are two broad types of question we can ask: one asks whether two sets of data are the same and the other seeks to establish whether two sets of data are related. The tests we use for both are different and specific to their type. We shall use this distinction between tests that compare and tests that relate to frame our selection of a test. The issues that we shall go to consider apply equally to each type of test.

(ii) The number of variables that we have

Every test must have at least one dependent variable (for example, pupil attainment scores or IQ scores, or the salaries of teachers or the structure of teaching or the numbers of para-teaching professionals). The only test we can carry out in this case is to compare our data with the population from which it is drawn. In other words it is a test of the *accuracy of our sample*. Little published research reports this, which means that we have to take a great deal on trust.

Most studies will have both independent and dependent variables (see section 7.5.1 if you would like to refresh your understanding of these terms). In general terms, we can have any combination of variables, one independent with two dependent, two independent and three or more dependent. As the number of variables increases, so does the complexity of the investigation. More variables mean more factors to be investigated, more things that are influencing others and more things to be influenced. There are two ways we can approach this type of situation. First, we could choose to break complex systems down and look at pairs of relationships. Let us imagine that we are investigating student achievement. What sets of factors can we identify that might be at work? We could look at factors relating to the teaching process, those concerned with learning, those concerned with school organisation and others that reflect the culture and atmosphere of the school. We could identify quite easily 20 or 30 variables that we could measure and relate to pupil achievement outcomes and what this would show us is that some factors had a greater influence than others. What it would not do, however, is reflect the connectivity that exists between variables. We would, for example, fail to pick up any association between family circumstance, peer relations and their influence on an individual's propensity to learn and on violence within and outside the school. We would not understand how learner support builds confidence and brings success and how success can change culture. In other words, what testing pairs of variables does not do is get to grips with how systems work. So our second approach is to use more sophisticated statistical tools that can handle more than two variables at the same time (in some case considerably more than two variables). These tests are able to assess how variables vary with each other and function as a system. With advances in computing power over the last 20 years, this is now a straightforward task.

(iii) The number of data sets we have

The third thing we have to consider in selecting a test is the number of data sets we have. As we saw above, the number of variables we consider increases the complexity of our research question; the number of data sets we use in our investigation adds another sort of complexity. Fortunately the tools (statistical tests) that we have handle this complexity together with the complexity arising from the number of variables. For example, we could survey students on their career intentions. One approach would be to sample the population of boys and then the population of girls. This would give us two samples. Alternatively, we could sample the population and split our sample into two, boys and girls. This would give us two variables. At this simple level there may not be much difference between the two but the point we have to bear in mind is that as the number of groups in our research programme increases, so we have to move to more sophisticated tests that will allow us to look at differences between the groups as well as differences between variables that are found in all the groups. If we think of this visually, we might imagine a matrix in which the columns are the groups (for example students in ten schools) and the rows are all other variables (such as attainment). If this starts to look like a spreadsheet then we can begin to understand how the various statistical packages want their data provided. Some of the spreadsheets we work with can become quite complex as we build in hierarchies of variables.

(iv) The measurement scales for our variables

The last factor that influences the choice of test is the scale of measurement that is used to quantify the variables. Section 4.4 reviews measurement scales. In summary, the strongest measurement scale (because it contains most information about the variable) is the *interval scale* (such as age or IQ). Less powerful (we used this with the idea of the median and quartiles) is the *ordinal scale* in which we rank variables according to the presence of a characteristic. Finally, there is the *nominal scale*, in which we count the number of instances in named classes (for instance, the number of children under 5 and between 5 and 10). The nature of the measurement scale is important because it gives rise to two quite distinct groups of statistical tests, *parametric* and *non-parametric*.

- Parametric tests require that the data are measured on an interval scale. This means that we can calculate and compare parameters such as the mean or standard deviation.
- Non-parametric tests do not do this and so work with less precise ordinal or nominal measurements.
- Parametric tests also require that the population and sample are normally distributed. This can be a big ask! We can be confident that IQ measurements will meet the specification as long as our sample is large enough but what about the distribution of wealth or incomes? Non-parametric tests make no such assumptions and so are often called distribution-free tests.

The consequence of these differences is that we have to build in to our research planning the way we are going to collect and analyse our data. If we fail to do this, we run the risk of coming unstuck. (Just ask your tutors how many times students have asked them, 'I've got this data; how can I analyse it?') And there is another thing that we have to take into account. The implication of the fact that non-parametric tests work with weaker measurement scales is, inevitably, that they are less robust than parametric tests in determining the significance of an association between variables. In general, if we use a non-parametric test and we want to get a test result as robust as for a parametric test, we would have to increase our sample size. This difference between parametric and non-parametric tests reduces as sample size increases. With 100 in the sample, they are effectively as powerful as each other. For smaller samples how much larger should the sample be for a non-parametric test? The statistician Erich Lehmann suggests that sample size should be at least 15% greater than for a parametric test (Lehmann, 2006). For the method of computation for sample size, see Appendix 1.

To summarise the effect of the measurement scale:

- The way the data are measured will influence the selection of a test.
- Tests fall into two groups, parametric and non-parametric.
- Parametric tests require data to be normally distributed. Non-parametric make no assumptions.
- Interval data can always be re-expressed as ordinal or nominal (categorical) data. Thus, for every parametric technique we can substitute a non-parametric technique.
- Non-parametric techniques are unstable as a discriminating tool with small samples. The sample used in a test should not normally be less than 30.

13.5 An introduction to tests

In this section we shall look at the tests we can use for our two basic questions, 'Are these the same?' and 'Are these related?' In each case, these questions require us to have at least two data sets to compare. Table 13.4 shows the tests we shall consider and summarises the conditions in which they should be used. Note how the table is arranged.

- The first column gives the questions that the tests answer. There are only two broad types of question (see section 13.3).
- The second column gives the context for the test. A 'goodness of fit' test compares our observed data with another data set. This could be the population from which it is drawn (in which case we test how good our sample is) or the data as we would expect them to be if they were arranged according to some principle we establish (this could be setting up the data as a normal distribution). Context also describes the samples themselves. If we have two or more samples and they are independently drawn (that is, one does not influence the other), then we can see what tests we can use. The number of variables we are dealing with is also considered under context.
- The third column gives the measurement scale.

This table can be used, therefore, to help researchers select a scale. First we have to decide which type of question we are asking. Next we have to look at the way we have sampled, the number of variables we have and so on. And finally we have to consider on what scale our data will be measured. This broad sequence should help us to focus on which tests are appropriate and can be used to identify tests that are not considered here.

Because most calculations will be completed using a statistical package, our approach is to explain what the test does and to illustrate this in broad terms with examples. There are few detailed computations. With this background, showing which tests are appropriate in what circumstances, it should be straightforward to follow the requirements set

Table 13.4 Choosing a test

Question	Context	Measurement scale	Test
Testing for differences	Goodness of fit.	Interval.	t test
	Two independent samples.	Interval.	t test
	Method samples.	Interval.	t test
	Goodness of fit.	Nominal/categorical.	χ^2
	Two independent samples.	Nominal/categorical.	χ^2
	Goodness of fit.	Interval/nominal as cumulative distribution.	Kolmogorov-Smirnov
	Two independent samples.	Interval/nominal as cumulative distribution.	Kolmogorov-Smirnov
	Small sample size.	Nominal/categorical.	Fisher's test
	Three or more independent samples.	Interval.	One way ANOVA
	Two variables each with two or more conditions.	Interval.	Two way ANOVA
Testing for relationships	Two variables (samples or populations).	Interval/ordinal.	Correlation coefficient
	Three or more independent variables:		
	– one varies, others held constant	Interval/ordinal.	Partial correlation
	– all variables together	Interval/ordinal.	Multiple correlation
	– progressively adding variables.	Interval/ordinal.	Stepwise multiple regression
	Two variables.	One dichotomous.	Biserial correlation
	Grouping correlation measures.	All scales/all variance.	Principal components analysis
	Grouping correlation measures.	All scales/common variance only.	Factor analysis
	Multi-level relationships.	Nominal/categorical.	Log-linear analysis

out in the manual of whatever statistical package is being used to input the data and then follow the guidance for interpreting the test statistic.

13.5.1 Calculating the test statistics

Most researchers will use one of the following commercially available products for data processing and analysis:

- **SPSS** statistics (www.spss.com): now in Version 17, the *Statistical Package for the Social Sciences* is a long-established software package that will handle data for studies up to advanced research. There are a number of on-line support resources. Amongst the best are:
  - University of Sheffield: www.shef.ac.uk/scharr/spss/index2.htm
  - University of Birmingham: www.statsguides.bham.ac.uk/

  - University of California Los Angeles: www.ats.ucla.edu/stat/spss/notes_old/default.htm, with video instruction.
- **Minitab** (www.minitab.co.uk). Minitab will handle most analyses that education researchers require. On-line support websites can be found at:
  - University of Birmingham: www.statsguides.bham.ac.uk
  - Queen Mary University of London: www.stu.qmul.ac.uk/primer/minitab/minitab_t.htm.
- **Stata** (www.stata.com). Stata includes powerful multi-level modelling and multi-variable analyses. Support can be accessed via:
  - University of California Los Angeles: www.ats.ucla.edu/stat/stata
  - Princeton University: //dss.Princeton.edu/online_help/stats_packages/stata/stata.htm.
- **SAS/STAT** (www.sas.com). SAS/STAT has a similar range of tests to other packages. On-line support is available at www.ats.ucla.edu/stat/sas/.

If access to a commercial package is a problem, there are free packages available. Those that compare well with commercial packages are:

- **OpenStat:** www.statpages.org/miller/openstat. *OpenStat* comes with a downloadable text and sample files.
- **SISA:** www.quantitativeskills.com/sisa. *Simple Interactive Statistical Analysis* is an on-line resource that calculates statistics for some of the tests we consider here.
- **Statpages:** statpages.org. *Statpages* has links to calculation for almost all of the tests we consider here.

13.6 Testing for difference

Before we look at the tests that we can use for establishing difference (or sameness, they are two sides of the same coin), we should make one point very clearly. Most researchers will not restrict themselves to one test. They do this for the following reasons:

- Their data will be based on different measurement scales, counts of people, interval data such as income or age, quasi-interval data from rating scales and so on. Because of this, they will need either to reduce everything to a common scale or use different tests. Most choose to do the latter.
- If the data is subdivided and then tested (for example, if different age groups or categories of teacher and teaching assistant are used as populations in their own right), data may not fulfil the requirements of some tests. In particular, sample size may be small. This might restrict the use of non-parametric techniques. If this might be an issue, it should be foreseen at the planning stage and the overall sample size increased accordingly.
- Finally, different tests may be used at different stages of the enquiry. Some of the more straightforward tests might be used to establish the accuracy of the sample while more sophisticated tests are used to explore and identify significant associations within complex data sets.

For these reasons, it is important that education researchers know more about statistical testing than they need to for any research enquiry. And, with time and experience, knowledge of tests will increase to way beyond what is considered in this text.

13.6.1 Student's t test

The first test we shall look at is Student's t test. This is a well-established and robust test. 'Student' was the pen name of William Gossett. Employed as a young graduate by the Guinness brewery in Dublin in 1899, he spent his early years researching brewing from a business perspective – essentially, what mix of ingredients produced the best beer. He worked with small samples of data and it was because of this that he made an impact in the world of statistics. We have to understand that the advances in statistical method at this time were being made by Karl Pearson. Pearson was a statistician who dealt with large samples, so anyone concerned with small sample sizes was breaking new ground.

Gossett developed the t test in the first decade of the twentieth century with the help of Pearson and improved it with the help of Ronald Fisher. Given the animosity between Pearson and Fisher (see section 13.4.1 for background on this) this was no mean feat. The t test looks at the difference between two means (for example, the mean amount of money spent at lunchtime by pupils who stay in school and those who leave the school premises). Immediately, from the fact that we are using the mean, we know that the t test works with interval data. However, we need to know more than the difference between mean values before we can establish the significance of that difference. If one mean is £1.57 and second £4.80 the difference could be significant, yet, in another case, if one mean is £1.89 and another £6.37 the difference may not be significant. What else do we need to know to answer the question whether two means are significantly different? Figure 13.3 will help us understand what we need to do. The diagram shows four distributions A, B, C and D. Let us imagine that A is one sample (those who stay in school for lunch) and B, C and D our second sample. Let us make it clear, B, C and D are not three samples, they are three examples of our second sample. Obviously if B were the sample, the chances of the mean of B being significantly different from the mean of A is less than if either C or D were the sample. Clearly the difference is not just the difference between the means but the extent to which the distributions overlap. This is what Gossett started to look at in his research because it seemed to be the way in to making a statement about probability. His approach, however, was not to look at the standard deviations themselves but at the likelihood that the sample means were an accurate estimation of the population mean. If we look at just one sample, this measure is called the *standard error of the mean* (read section 12.5.2 (iv) for an explanation of this). With two samples we do not look at the standard error of the mean of each one but the *standard error of the difference.* We know that the standard error of the mean gives the range within which the mean will lie with a given

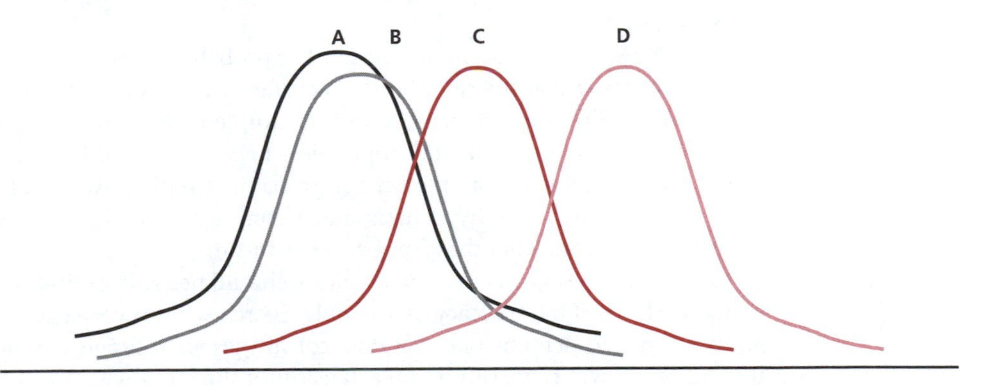

Figure 13.3 Understanding the t test

probability. The same is true of the standard error of the difference in the means. To calculate this, we need to know the standard deviations of our samples. What these terms mean will become clearer when we see them in action.

Let us now look at the circumstances in which we can use the t test. It is important to know these because the circumstance changes the formula we use.

(i) To see whether our data is an accurate sample of the population

Here we assume that we know the population mean. The formula we use is:

$$t = \frac{\bar{x} - \mu}{s/\sqrt{n}}$$

where $\bar{x}$ is the sample mean
μ is the population mean
s is the sample standard deviation

Let us see what this formula tells us. The top line says that it is subtracting the sample mean from the population mean. This is a measure of the difference between them. The bottom line is the standard deviation of our sample divided by the square root of our sample size. This is an estimate of the standard error of our sample mean and it shows the limits within which the mean will fall with a 68.29% probability.

The test generates a statistic, t, that we interpret for its significance. We can interpret it through three sources:

1. a book of statistical tables (see, for example, Lindley and Scott, 1995);
2. an on-line look-up;
3. a statistics package.

The test statistic has to be interpreted according to the size of the sample. This is because this test, in common with most of the tests we shall look at, generates a test statistic that is a function of sample size, thus large data sets are likely to produce large test statistics. We do not use sample size itself, however, but something called 'degrees of freedom'. The degrees of freedom in a test are always the sample size less one. So in a sample of 58, there are 57 degrees of freedom. The explanation of degrees of freedom as a concept is difficult (the mathematics are complex) but it is to do with the fact that once a certain number of parameters of a data set have been established, only a given number can vary without altering the character of the data set. In many ways, it is easiest to accept it as an act of statistical faith and remember that it is $(n - 1)$. However, as we shall see with some other statistical tests, what n is in the context of degrees of freedom is not always the same.

Now let us think about our test result. The probability value generated by the test tells us the likelihood that the sample is an accurate sample of the population. If we generated a probability statistic of 0.38 with a sample of 30, we would *not* reject our null hypothesis that the sample and population mean are *not different* (in fact the statistic suggests it is a very good sample). If our probability statistic were .021, we would almost certainly reject our null hypothesis and examine our sample to see what had gone wrong. Think about what these probabilities mean.

Good practice suggests that the literature should be replete with examples of the t test being used to test the accuracy of a sample. Searches, however, suggest the opposite. It is good practice to demonstrate that data constitutes an accurate sample because without this being shown, there can be no extension of the arguments from the analysis of the sample to the population. The failure to observe good practice was noted by American researchers, led by Linda Zientek, who reviewed quantitative research in teacher education (Zientek et al., 2008). They comment: 'For readers to make well-informed decisions on the basis of a study, the essential elements of study's design sample and analysis should be reported' (p. 209). Only 9% of articles included what was required to replicate the study and only 17% compared sample characteristics with population. When this does not happen, there is no evidence for generalising the results. It is poor practice.

(ii) To see whether one sample differs from another, when the samples are independently selected

Now let us look at another way in which we can use the t test. This is the situation in which the t test is most used, to compare samples that have been drawn independently of each other. This situation arises if we have conducted two samples (for example, if we sampled the ages of staff teaching chemistry in higher education with the ages of staff teaching classics) or if we compare two samples from two different studies (what we found in our study of the ages of chemistry teachers with what someone else found). The test, effectively, is asking whether both samples are drawn from the same distribution (or population). The t test formula in this case is:

$$\frac{\text{difference between the means}}{\text{standard error of the difference}}$$

The first line of the formula is known to us, a simple subtraction of one mean from the other. The second line takes a little more explaining. Because we are dealing with two samples and not a sample and a population, we will have two standard errors of means. If we look at the difference between these two standard errors, then it is obvious that there will be another standard error, the standard error of the difference between the means. This is easily calculated by pooling the mean variances. (The variance of a distribution is the square of the standard deviation, that is, it is the sum total of all the squared deviations between the mean and every unit of data). We can write our formula as:

$$t = t = \frac{\bar{x} - \bar{y}}{\sqrt{\frac{s_{\bar{x}}^2}{n_1} + \frac{s_y^2}{n_2}}}$$

where $\bar{x}_1$ and $\bar{x}_2$ are the means of the two samples

s_1 and s_2 are the standard deviations of the two samples

n_1 and n_2 are the populations of the two samples

This form of the t test is used extensively. Most researchers (and statistical packages) make the assumption that sample sizes and variances (the squares of the standard deviations) are unequal. If they are not a different formula (not given here) should be used.

Examples of the use of the t test to assess differences between samples abound in the literature. Welsh researchers used the t test (in Minitab) to compare boys' and girls' daily nutritional intake. They found a significant difference at the 95% level between boys' and girls' energy intake (Thomas et al., 2007). Adedeji Tella used it to compare the difference between boys' and girls' motivation to study mathematics and found the difference to be significant at 95% (Tella, 2007). Two Swedish researchers, Asa Ahlin and Eva Mörk, used the t test in an interesting way to assess whether the characteristics of municipalities in Sweden that officially reported school expenditure were significantly different from those that did not. This was an important test because it determined whether the conclusions from those that reported could be extended to other municipalities. The test did not detect a significant difference (Ahlin and Mörk, 2007).

(iii) To see whether one sample differs from another when the two samples are matched

Matching (or pairing) is a process to reveal data characteristics across two or more samples. One way of doing this is when we use the same data units twice. If, for example, we were assessing students' knowledge of current affairs, we could test them, have several lessons and then test them again. If we wanted to test the effect of teaching approaches (one might be a conventional lesson the other could be a computer-based learning package), we might use another approach to matching our samples. In this case we would match the pupils on variables that we felt were important. These, for example, could be measures of intelligence, age, gender, socio-economic status. In their work on language development in young children two Dutch researchers, Leesbeth Schlichting and Henk Spelberg, used a matched sample, one drawn from the population of young children and the other from a population of children with a language impairment. The context was the development of a set of indicators for language development. The two researchers wanted to assess whether indicators that had been developed were an effective discriminator of language development and for this they matched their samples in terms of age, sex and socio-economic background. Differences between the two groups as evaluated by the t test were significant at either 94% (language comprehension) or 99% (sentence development and expressive vocabulary) (Schlichting and Spelberg, 2003).

When we use the t test in this way, with matched samples, we are not concerned with the difference between the means of the two distributions but the mean of the difference between the two situations for the individuals taking part. So if we were looking at a class of 15 students and their knowledge of current affairs before and after a lesson, we are less interested in the means for the group before and after the lesson and more interested in the change in individual scores between the two tests. The test statistic then becomes:

$$t = \frac{\text{means of the effect}}{\text{standard error of the effect}}$$

$$t = \frac{\bar{x}}{s/\sqrt{n}}$$

where $\bar{x}$ is the mean of the effect

s is the standard deviation of the effect

n is the number of participants

13.6.2 χ^2 (chi-square)

The chi-square (also written as 'Chi-Squared') test is extensively used by social science researchers. This is not surprising because it is easy to understand and interpret. Unlike the t test which uses interval data, chi-square requires data to be in a *counted form* (numbers of people in different socio-economic groups, number in categories 1–5, 6–9, etc.). This means that chi-square is a non-parametric test. The most commonly used form of chi-square (and the one found in most statistical packages and which we shall consider here) was developed by the British statistician Karl Pearson (originally Carl Pearson, but when he was at the University of Heidelberg his name became changed).

What the chi-squared test does is compare the actual distribution of data with a theoretical distribution of the same size. We shall see how we put this into operation with some examples later. While it works with a different type of data from the t test, it makes the standard assumption that samples are randomly drawn and, like most non-parametric tests, its discriminatory ability weakens as the sample size becomes smaller.

The issue of sample size with chi-square is an important one so we should understand it in a little more detail. As sample size decreases, so the number of counts in each of our groups or categories for instance people with an IQ of 70 to 80 is likely to fall. When the values in categories (in chi-square we call these *cells*) become low (generally below 5) the test becomes a poor discriminator of significance. As a rule of thumb, a limit of 10 per cent of the total data counts should be in cells with fewer than five counts. If this does occur, we have two solutions, either to increase the sample (and we should have thought of this at the start of our planning!) or we combine cells. However, it is not just at low sample sizes that we experience difficulties. When the sample size is large (over a thousand), chi-square has a tendency to show differences as significant. It may be that there is a better test that we could use but with large samples it may be safer to use a higher level of significance, say 99 per cent. There is an implication in this that we should be aware of. Many of the data we use may be expressed in percentages. Can we calculate chi-square using percentages rather than actual totals? As a general rule the answer is 'no'. If the actual number of counts is small, say 35, and if we use percentages, chi-square thinks that our sample is three times as large, with the consequence that it overstates the probability statistic. If the actual data count is between 90 and 110, then there is probably no impact. With large sample sizes, using percentages will give us a more conservative test statistic but the overall result is that we will not know where we are with our test.

Let us now see how chi-square can be used.

(i) To test goodness of fit

We can use chi-square to see whether our data conforms to a particular distribution. In education research, the most usual distributions we might use are equal probability (with the same number of observations in each category, for example, in each year group of a school are the numbers of children who bring packed lunches much the same), with the normal distribution and with a population distribution (for example, do the parents of the children at this school conform to a national distribution of socio-economic status). In each case our null hypothesis is that there is no significant difference between the observed distribution and the expected distribution. Our research hypotheses are that (i) our data are not evenly distributed, (ii) that they are normally distributed or (iii) that they match the population characteristic. Note that the chi-square test is a two directional and not a one directional test.

How should we set out our data? First we have to determine our expected distribution. If we were researching educational attainment of different status groups in Sheffield, an old industrial city in Yorkshire, we would determine an indicator for status.

This could be housing type. The proportions of households living in different tenure types are:

Owner occupied	60.15%
Social housing	30.28%
Privately rented	8.52%
Rent free	1.04%

If our sample consisted of parents in the tenure groups we could reconfigure our sample into the Sheffield pattern. Assume our sample is:

Owner occupied	96
Social housing	37
Privately rented	14
Rent free	3
	150

If these were distributed according to the whole population in Sheffield, our *expected distribution* would be:

Owner occupied $150 \times 60.15\% = 90.22$
Social housing $150 \times 30.28\% = 45.42$
Privately rented $150 \times 8.52\% = 12.78$
Rent free $150 \times 1.04\% = 1.56$

Our observed and expected distributions are then:

Tenure group	Observed	Expected
Owner occupied	96	90.22
Social housing	37	45.42
Privately rented	14	12.78
Rent free	3	1.56

From this table it is now clear why we call the values in each group 'cell values'. The test statistic is quite straightforward to calculate:

$$x^2 = \frac{\Sigma(O - E)^2}{E}$$

where O is the observed value
E is the expected value
Σ is the sum of the calculation for all the cells

So, for example, the calculation with our data is:

$$\frac{(96 - 90.22)}{90.22}, \text{ etc.}$$

It is worth continuing with this example to show the effect of a low cell count. If we use the data as shown above we will obtain the following values from our statistical calculator:

χ^2	3.35
Probability	0.3407

If we combine the last two cells (privately rented and rent free), our values are:

χ^2	2.42
Probability	0.2982

With only three categories, the difference in observed and expected categories ranges from +18% to −18%. With four categories, the difference increases to +91%. As we see above, small cell values can magnify differences (usually to the detriment of the test) and are reflected in the probability statistic.

How do we interpret these test statistics?

- As with the t test, we use the concept of degrees of freedom. With the t test we saw that degrees of freedom were n − 1, where n was the number of data values. We use the same idea with chi-square but we must think carefully what are our data units. If we were doing a t test, there would be 150 of them but with chi-square we have bundled them into bins labelled 'owner occupied', 'social housing', etc. These are our data units and there are either four of them with our raw data or three of them with our consolidated data. With our raw data we have (4 − 1) degrees of freedom, with our combined cells we have (3 − 1) degrees of freedom.
- The probability values are outputted from online calculators (statistical packages available on university networks will do the same). How do we interpret them? We have to bear in mind that we are testing a null hypothesis, that there is no significant difference between our two distributions. The probability value (often just labelled *p* or *pr* in output from statistical packages) is the chance that the sample is drawn from the population if the null hypothesis (that there is no difference between the two distributions) is correct. We have to set the probability level we obtain in our test against the threshold level that we established at the outset of our test. Let us assume that we established a threshold level of .05. This means that there is only a 5% chance of drawing the sample that we are testing when the null hypothesis (that there is no difference between the sample and the population) is true. Now in our case, this probability is either 30% (rounded from .298) or 34% (.340). Neither of our probability values is close to a point at which we would reject the null hypothesis, which, given that we want our sample to be a good one, is a good result.

For a small number of values, these calculations are easy to do with a calculator. These were done using an on-line calculator. Often the advantage of an on-line calculator or commercial statistical package is that they will provide degrees of freedom and the test probability level. Without these, we have to lookup the test statistic in a table of values or use a table on-line.

(ii) To see whether one sample differs from another or others in terms of a second variable when both are independently selected

This is a very common test situation. Imagine that we wished to compare the diet of pupils with free school meals and those who pay for their meals. We might base our assessment on their selection of food at lunchtime. We could brief our researchers on the data collection process, to sit with pupils and assess their meals as predominantly healthy, predominantly unhealthy (high fat/low vegetable content) and mixed. The school will advise us on which of our respondents have free school meals. With this research programme we will generate a data set in the form of a 2×3 matrix (see Table 13.5).

This form of chi-square is referred to as a *two way classification* because there are two variables – (i) healthy eating and (ii) who pays for school meals. The method of calculating the chi-square statistic is exactly the same as with our earlier example:

$$\frac{\sum(O - E)^2}{E}$$

However, in this case we derive the *expected distribution* in a different way.

The expected value for any cell is the product of that cell's row and column probabilities. This sounds complex but it is, in fact, extremely straightforward. The row probability is given by row total as a proportion of the grand total (that is, the total number of cases) and the column probability by the column total as a proportion of the total number of cases. The product of this is given by:

$$\frac{\text{row total} \times \text{column total}}{\text{grand total}}$$

An example will show what an easy calculation this is. If the row total is 22, the column total 37 and the grand total 226, then substituting these in our formula, we find that our cell expected value is 3.6:

$$\frac{22 \times 37}{226} = 3.6$$

This chi-square statistic can be calculated manually or by an on-line calculator or by a statistical package. If the calculation is not done by hand, care must be taken to use a calculator or package that deals with two way data and not one way. The benefit of using an on-line or package calculator is that most will generate the chi-square test statistic, the number of degrees of freedom and the probability value for the statistic with the given degrees of freedom. If we calculate the statistic manually (and it is straightforward as long as we can multiply, divide, add up and subtract in the right order), we should know how to determine the degrees of freedom. Even this is easy:

$$\text{rows} - 1 \times \text{columns} - 1$$

Table 13.5 Data format for a two way chi-square analysis

	Predominantly healthy	Mixed	Predominantly unhealthy	Totals
Pupils with free meals				Σ free
Pupils without free meals				Σ no free
Totals	Σ healthy	Σ healthy	Σ unhealthy	Grand total

In our example:

$$(2 - 1) \times (3 - 1) = 1 \times 2 = 2$$

Chi-square is easy to understand, simple to operationalise and is a robust method that has stood the test of time so it is not surprising that it has proved to be popular amongst education, social and business researchers. A Finnish researcher, Professor Päivi Tynjälä, used the test to look at the learning experiences and learning outcomes of students taught in a traditional way and those taught on a constructivist way. She was able to show that those who learnt in a constructivist environment acquired more diversified knowledge (Tynjälä, 1999). Because she only had one degree of freedom, she chose to test her data for significance at the 99% level.

In another study, Andre Brouwers and Welko Tomic of the Dutch Open University, used chi-square in a study of teacher burnout and its relationship with self-efficacy, the extent to which a teacher believes they can affect student performance (Brouwers and Tomic, 2000). They measured three dimensions of burnout: emotional exhaustion, depersonalisation and personal accomplishment and evaluated self-efficacy on a Likert scale (see section 8.10.1). They were particularly interested in how burnout and self-efficacy changed over time and developed a series of models to represent this. The relationship between these models and the data set was tested using chi-square. This is a sophisticated analytic study with important implications for the process of managing the education system and teachers. We should remember, however, that their conclusions rest upon a simple but valid application of a robust statistical technique, chi-square, that is equally available to new researchers.

Activity 13.2 is a chance to test your ability to interpret χ^2 output.

13.6.3 The Kolmogorov-Smirnov test

The Kolmogorov-Smirnov test (KS test) is actually an amalgam of ideas from two Russian statisticians who were active in the middle part of the twentieth century. It is more extensively used in the sciences and engineering than in the social sciences and it does much the same as chi-square, so we might ask ourselves, 'Why are we considering it?' The reason is that it can handle large numbers and so gives us greater confidence in the results than chi-square.

How does the KS test work? It requires the data set to be represented as a cumulative distribution. We met this concept in Chapter 10 when we looked at ogives (see section 10.3.3). The test does not assume that data are normally distributed, so it is non-parametric. Figure 13.4 will help us appreciate what the test does. Unlike chi-square, which looks at

Activity 13.2 Getting to grips with χ^2

Working out chi-square a Nigerian researcher, Michael Ejieh, looked at an issue faced by many educators in developing countries (and by many parents in small countries). Should children be educated in their mother tongue or in a global language? He investigated the attitude of primary level student teachers and found that they had a generally negative attitude to educating in the mother tongue. He used chi-square to test whether their attitude (two categories) was related to their subject of study (four categories).

- How many degrees of freedom is this?

His χ^2 statistic was 3.019. Is this significant at the 95% level?

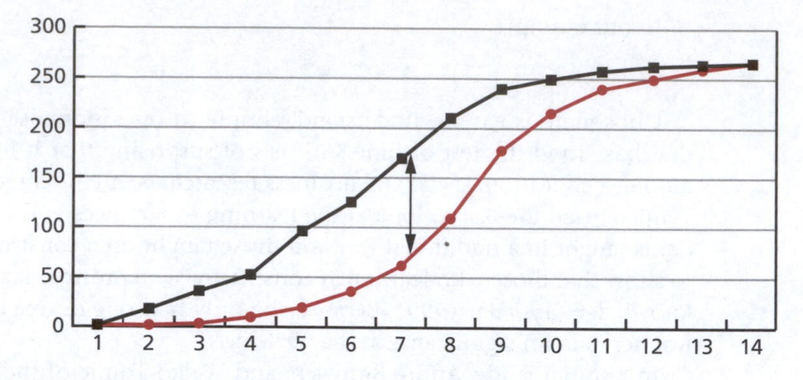

Figure 13.4 How the Kolmogorov-Smirnov test works

the difference between two distributions over their whole length, the KS test focuses on the *maximum difference* between two distributions when they are plotted cumulatively. In other words, it is another approach to assessing the scale of the difference between two distributions.

Figure 13.4 shows two such distributions. The KS test identifies the maximum difference between the two cumulative distributions and tests its significance. There is a caveat that we should note about the test. It is *less sensitive* if the maximum difference is at the tail of the distribution. In this case, comparison with another test such as chi-square may be warranted.

Let us now see how we can use the test.

(i) As a test of goodness of fit

As with chi-square we can use the KS test to assess whether a data set conforms to a theoretical population. This might be a normal distribution but there are situations where another distribution might be used. While you may read of this in an academic paper, it is unlikely that a new researcher would address this issue.

The *procedure* for this test is as follows:

- Recalibrate the data according to the theoretical distribution. If this is the normal distribution, calculate Z values for the sample data (see section 13.2).
- Set out the data as two cumulative distributions and identify the maximum difference (D).
- Test D against a critical value for the sample size and level of significance.

It is, of course, easier if a statistical package does all of this for us (such as SPSS, Minitab and the free program, OpenStat) and there are on-line calculators as well. However, if neither of these is feasible, it is possible to use statistical tables (Neave, 2000) or even to calculate the critical value ourselves (see Appendix 2).

The KS test was used as a test of goodness of fit between a sample and a theoretical distribution in a study of teaching and learning styles in China. The two Chinese researchers, Zhou Li and Fan Zhi-Zhong, looked at the teaching styles of native English speakers and the learning styles of native Chinese learning in English. They wanted to establish whether, on each of eight learning styles, their student sample was normally distributed. The reason for doing this was that they wanted to conduct further tests on the data and the procedures they wanted to use required an assumption of normality. They took their survey data and compared it with the same data recalibrated as a normal distribution and tested the difference between them using a KS test. The p values of their test statistics ranged from .097 to .659. From this they concluded that the students were normally distributed on the different learning styles. They repeated the KS analysis for the teachers' teaching styles and were able also to show that the distributions too were normal. This gave them confidence to continue their analysis of assessing how far teaching and learning styles matched. Their results showed a clear mismatch between teaching and learning styles and this clearly has implications for effective teaching and learning when teachers and learners are from different backgrounds or cultures. From a methodological point of view, it is worth noting that the researchers also used chi-square and t test. This reinforces the point that no analysis should normally be limited to one test.

(ii) To see whether one sample differs from another when they are independently drawn

This is a very common situation in which researchers find themselves and, above, we have seen that we can use a t test and chi-square to do exactly the same thing. The KS test can be used in the same way and is an alternative to chi-square. The procedure for this test is broadly similar to the test for goodness of fit with the differences that (a) data have to be put into a comparable format if sample sizes are different and (b) the calculation of significant values for D are different. The procedure is:

- Express each cell or group as a proportion of the whole sample for both data sets (or use raw data if the samples are the same size).
- Set the data out as a cumulative distribution between 0 and 100% (or use raw data if the samples are the same size) and identify the maximum difference (D).
- Compare this with a critical value for D that takes account of significance level and sample size. Note that the calculation takes account of the sample size of each distribution.

Again, this procedure can be accomplished using statistical packages and on-line calculators.

The KS test was used in this way by three Croatian researchers, led by Ivan Prskalo, in a study of the impact of the Bologna process (the co-operation by EU member states to create transparency and commonality in European higher education) (Prskalo et al., 2007). Their study group was pre-school and primary trainees and the focus of the study was their preparation in physical education. In particular they were interested to discover whether the Bologna process has affected either absolutely or relatively instruction hours of teacher trainees. In a detailed analysis of how curriculum hours were used before and after the Bologna changes, they were able to show that the changes that had occurred were significant at the 90% level. They go on to discuss the implications of the changes in terms of the preparation of trainees for the workplace.

13.6.4 Fisher's test

We know that chi-square is less robust with small samples, so what can we do in those cases? Well, if there are only two variables with two states (2 × 2 tables), we can use Fisher's exact probability test. It is called 'exact probability' because it determines the exact probability of expected values. Surprisingly, it is little referenced in educational research but, especially for students dealing with small samples, it should be the test of choice for 2 × 2 tables.

The test itself is named after the English statistician, Sir Ronald Fisher, who introduced it in the 1930s. The mathematics of the test are actually quite complex but there are a number of on-line calculators as well as statistical packages that make it a simple test to administer. What is required is that we set our data as a 2 × 2 contingency table. With 2 × 2 tables, there is one degree of freedom (rows −1 × columns −1).

Imagine that I am concerned about gender imbalance in grading students' work and that my colleagues and I are giving the work of women students lower grades than we give to men. I might look at the end of term grades given by several of my colleagues and for each I would produce a 2 × 2 table (such as Table 13.6). This shows that there were:

- 31 men and 24 women;
- that 12 men (38% of the total) were given the highest two grades and that 4 women (17% of the total) were also given the highest two grades.

On the face of it, there is a strong case for agreeing that there is a gender imbalance in our marking but to be sure we need to test our assumption. As usual our test hypothesis is a null hypothesis, that there is no significant difference between the marks given to men and women and our research hypothesis is that we are systematically undermarking women. This is a one-tailed test (because our research hypothesis is directional). Using an on-line calculator, we obtain a test statistic for a one-tailed probability of 0.07, so we do not reject my null hypothesis if I use the conventional level of significance of 0.05%. If I had obtained these figures, however, I would be concerned that we were so close to the critical value and I would want to conduct more research. One thing I could do is go back in time and look at the grades given by this colleague in the past. I would add these data (for this year) to the grades awarded last year and conduct another test and I would repeat this by adding in data for the year before that as well.

Table 13.6 2 × 2 contingency table for Fisher's exact test

	Male	Female
Highest two grades	12	4
Other grades	19	20

13.6.5 Analysis of variance (ANOVA)

So far we have looked at tests of goodness of fit and ones that enable us to compare two samples. What happens if we have three or more samples? If we are investigating whether student performance in standard tests is different in different types of school, it is likely that, in most countries, there will be three or more types of school to sample. We could test all combinations of school, A with B and C and B with C. With three this might just be possible but with more it becomes more time-consuming. However, if we were to look not at a general measure of achievement in the schools but at achievement in specific subjects, then what might have looked manageable at the beginning starts to look like a mountain. Enter the analysis of variance, an approach to data analysis first introduced by Sir Ronald Fisher in the decades between the two world wars.

The analysis of variance test (ANOVA) is important because not only is it a powerful test, it is also a stepping-stone to even more powerful procedures. How does it work? It does exactly what it says in its name. Variance, as we know from Chapter 12, is the square of the standard deviation. Because the test deals with data that involve the mean, we can immediately identify the test as parametric (because to calculate the mean we need interval data). What the test does is examine the difference between the means by comparing variances. We might ask if it examines differences between means, how does it differ from a t test? The answer is that the t test does this by looking at the means themselves, ANOVA looks at the variances. So ANOVA does much the same as a t test but (a) it does it in a different way and (b) it can deal with more than two data sets at a time.

How does ANOVA work then? If we were investigating measures of student performance on different modules (we wanted to know whether tutors were all marking to the same standard), and we had data for three modules, we can imagine a spreadsheet in which the columns represented the modules and the rows, student grades. The test assumption is that there is no difference in student judgements between the modules (note, this is also our null hypothesis). We can, with this data calculate three *types* of variance:

1. One, called the *within-groups variance*, for the modules individually (this would give us three measurements of variance, one for each module).
2. Another, called the *total variance*, for all the modules combined (that is, based on every student judgement for every module).
3. The third, called the *between-groups variance*, is a residual calculated by subtracting the total of within groups variance from the total variance.

The analysis of variance test compares the variance from different sources. One source is the module (for any one student we can compare any mark with the mean mark for that module) and the other is the set of marks for every module (for any student we can compare any mark with the mean mark for all three modules). In our example there is one variable (modules) and we would compare the sum of the variances for the individual modules with the sum of the variances for all the observations treated as one data set.

(i) One way ANOVA

One way ANOVA is used to test for difference when there is only one variable. Table 13.7 shows data from three schools. Each cell entry is a score in a geography test. The question is whether the data all come from the same population (our null hypothesis that there is

Table 13.7 Data for one way ANOVA

School A	School B	School C
58	87	64
73	54	57
27	77	51
56	45	40
32	40	58

no difference between the schools) or whether the school effect produces differences (our research hypothesis, in this case a two directional hypothesis). To assess these we have to calculate and compare three variances:

1. The between groups variance (A:B:C).
2. The total variance.
3. The within groups variance.

This calculation is easily performed using a statistic package, an on-line calculator or even a spreadsheet. Table 13.8 shows the output for the data obtained from an on-line calculator. The format is typical. We should focus on three things.

- *Degrees of freedom*: This is more complex than we have seen before. The rule here is that we lose one degree of freedom for every time the procedure calculates a mean. We calculate four means but, in each case, we have to be clear what *n* is. First, we calculate a mean for the whole data set. The total degrees of freedom are given by $n - 1$, where n is the total of observations. In this case n is 15, thus giving $15 - 1 = 14$ degrees of freedom. Second, we calculate means for each of the three schools. This is the within groups' degrees of freedom. There are 5 observations in each school so the degrees of freedom for each school is $5 - 1 = 4$ and for all 3 groups $= 12$. This leaves 2 degrees of freedom $(14 - 12)$ for the between groups analysis.
- The *F ratio* is the test statistic. It is the ratio of two variances, the between groups variance divided by the within groups variance. The F value in our example is the ratio of 163.8/290.5. These two values are derived from the sum of squares divided by the degrees of freedom. F is the test statistic that we look up if we are using tables of significance to see what its associated level of probability is.
- Most calculators, however, will perform this for us. In this case the probability is .583. Putting this another way, 42 per cent of the times we reject the null hypothesis, the null hypothesis would be correct. This is such a high error rate that we cannot reject the null hypothesis.

Test your own ability to interpret F ratios with Activity 13.3.

Table 13.8 Output from one way ANOVA

	Degrees of freedom	Sum of squares	Mean square	F	P-value
Between groups	2	327.600	163.800	0.5639	0.5834
Within groups	12	3,486.000	290.500		
Total	14	3,813.600			

(ii) Two way ANOVA

Two way ANOVA is used where there are two variables, each with different conditions. We met this situation before when we looked at the chi-square test but an example will refresh our understanding. Three American criminologists used the test to look at the part played by sex, ethnicity and community in self reports by young people of involvement in youth violence in different American cities (Peterson et al., 2007). The relationships they tested are set out in Table 13.9. They differentiated violence into two types:

Activity 13.3 Interpreting data for ANOVA

While our example used made up data, three South African researchers used ANOVA to look at the effects of streaming boys and girls in mathematics classes. They sampled nearly 1,500 students in four schools, one mixed but with segregated classes, one mixed with mixed classes and two single sex, one for boys and one for girls. Individual pupil data were mathematics test scores. Tables 1, 2 and 3 show the results. Your task is to:

- specify the null hypothesis for each table
- specify at what probability level you reject or do not reject the null hypothesis
- express our acceptance/rejection of the null hypothesis
- look at all the results and suggest what an effective policy response might be.

You can read what the authors say in the original paper at: www.sajournalofeducation.co.z??a/index.php/saje/article/view/2004/126.

Source: Bosire et al., 2008.

Table 1 Comparison of all students by school type

	Sum of squares	df	Mean square	Fisher F value	Significance (*p*)
Between groups	1,248.495	3	416.165	41.524	0.0001
Within groups	12,297.296	1,227	10.022		
Total	13,545.791	1,230			

Table 2 Comparison of girls' attainment by school type

	Sum of squares	df	Mean square	Fisher F value	Significance (*p*)
Between groups	204.762	2	102.381	11.636	0.0001
Within groups	3,132.295	356	8.799		
Total	3,337.056	358			

Table 3 Comparison of boys' attainment by school type

	Sum of squares	df	Mean square	Fisher F value	Significance (*p*)
Between groups	917.288	2	458.644	44.180	0.0001
Within groups	9,021.254	869	10.381		
Total	9,938.541	871			

general and serious, and looked at the effects of sex (male/female), ethnicity (5 groups) and community (11 locations). The two way ANOVA tests they conducted were:

- Sex plus community by violence (22 by 2 data set).
- Ethnicity plus community by violence (55 by 2 data set).

Their research shows aspects of ANOVA that are valuable to the researcher:

- The test can deal with complex data sets.
- The analyses can throw up interesting perspectives.

Table 13.9 Layout of data for two way ANOVA

	General violence	Serious violence
Sex	Data on involvement in general violence by gender.	Data on involvement in serious violence by gender.
Ethnicity	Data on involvement in general violence by ethnicity.	Data on involvement in serious violence by ethnicity.
City/community	Data on involvement in general violence by community.	Data on involvement in serious violence by community.

Both tests were significant. For sex there was an interaction with where people lived in respect of general violence but this was not the case for serious violence. While there was a relationship between ethnicity and violence (higher than White for African-American, Hispanic and Native American and lower than White for Asian), when they combined ethnicity with where people lived, the locality effect was stronger than ethnicity and they concluded that 'it is not the case that minority youths are always more violent than are white youths' (p. 403).

This example shows the strength and flexibility of the test but how does it work? The principles underlying two way ANOVA are exactly the same as one way ANOVA, in that we are concerned to apportion the variances between different sources and compare them. Let us look at how this would work in a study we might set up. We have a research methods module that we teach to students at the start of their research careers. We teach the same module to undergraduates and to postgraduates. Undergraduates use it as the basis for project work. Postgraduates receive further training prior to undertaking their own research. We have three ways of delivering the module, as a conventional taught class, as a computer-assisted learning package and as a problem-based learning programme. (This type of programme sets up issues and students have to find out what they need to know in order to resolve them. It claims deeper understanding amongst its benefits but some teachers are concerned that students following this approach lack an integrated perspective). We select undergraduates and postgraduates to follow a tuition programme. Table 13.10 shows the framework for collecting our data on student performance.

Table 13.10 Data framework for two way ANOVA

	Undergraduate	Postgraduate
Conventional class	Test results for undergraduates taught conventionally.	Test results for postgraduates taught conventionally.
Problem-based class	Test results for undergraduates taught using problem-based method.	Test results for postgraduates taught using problem-based method.
Computer-based learning	Test results for undergraduates taught using computer-based method.	Test results for postgraduates taught using computer-based method.

These are the questions we can ask:

- Does the level of the student (undergraduate/postgraduate) affect student performance?
- Does the teaching and learning approach (conventional/problem based/computer based) affect student performance?
- Is there an interaction between student level and teaching and learning approach that affects performance?

With a one way ANOVA, there were only two outcomes, either we accepted or rejected our null hypothesis. With two way ANOVA, there are many more outcomes because we have at least three null hypotheses (we say at least three because, as you will find out if you go on to more advanced statistical methods, there are more ways of looking at variance than just these three ways). In our example, these are:

1. There is no significant difference in performance between undergraduates and postgraduates.
2. There is no difference in performance between the three teaching and learning models.
3. There is no interaction between level of student and teaching and learning models.

Now let us see what the outcomes could be:

- We reject the null hypothesis for student level but do not reject the others.
- We reject the null hypothesis for teaching and learning models but do not reject the others.
- We reject the interaction null hypothesis but do not reject the others.

Table 13.11 shows a typical output table from a statistical package (such as SPSS) for two way ANOVA. The crucial cells to look at are those highlighted in colour. *Student Level* refers to the undergraduate/postgraduate test, *Learning Model* to the three teaching and learning models and *Student Level*Learning Model* to the interaction effect. Many ANOVA programmes will also produce graphs of the relationship between variables (very often variables are called 'factors' in ANOVA). These bear an uncanny resemblance to the regression lines we met in Chapter 12 (see Table 12.12). This is because ANOVA is part of a whole set of models that explore linear relationships amongst variables. It is these that we are going to turn to when we look at statistical tests that can help us answer our second question, 'Are these related?'

Table 13.11 Typical output table for two way ANOVA

Source	Sum of squares	Degrees of freedom	Mean square	F	Significance
Corrected model					
Intercept					
Student level				F	S
Learning model				F	S
Student level * learning model				F	S
Error					
Total					
Corrected total					

Before we move on to this, let us look at our example using some data. Table 13.12 shows the output from an on-line ANOVA calculator. The upper part of the table shows the raw data – the scores for six undergraduate and postgraduate students (A1 and A2) on each of the three learning models (B1 to B3). The lower part of the table shows the output statistics. We had three null hypotheses:

1. Student level (rows): there is no significant difference between undergraduates and postgraduates. The probability statistic for this is 0.098. If our critical level is 0.05 (95%), we would not reject our null hypothesis (but with only six subjects, we should not be too dogmatic in our judgements).
2. Learning model (column): there is no significant difference in student performance in the three learning situations. The probability statistic here is 0.042, which is within the 5% level, so we can reject our null hypothesis. When we look at the data there is evidence that students perform better on the conventional learning model.
3. Interaction between student level and learning model (r × c): The probability statistic here is 0.34. We cannot reject the null hypothesis.

Table 13.12 ANOVA output

	Values entered		
	B_1	B_2	B_3
A_1	22	37	26
	47	54	39
	36	66	53
	49	59	49
	37	48	33
	54	40	37
A_2	54	61	54
	35	68	37
	41	52	49
	42	46	58
	27	40	61
	52	59	56

	ANOVA Summary				
Source	SS	df	MS	F	P
bg	1305.2222	5			
rows	312.1111	1	312.111	2.91	0.098366
columns	754.8889	2	377.444	3.52	0.042340
r × c	238.2222	2	119.111	1.11	0.342717
wg	3219.3333	30	107.311		
Total	4524.5556	35			

bg = between groups; wg = within groups (error)

The outcome of our analysis is that the learning model is the prime factor in determining outcome grades and while there are differences between undergraduate and postgraduate students in grades these are not significant at the 95% level. There is no evidence that undergraduates do better than postgraduates with any learning model or vice versa.

ANOVA is an adaptable and powerful technique. It is based on identifying and measuring associations between data sets on the same basis we test relationships between data sets. This underlying statistical model is called the linear model. We will now look at its use in the identification of significant relationships.

13.7 Testing relationships

In sections 12.9 and 12.10 we saw that we could describe a relationship between two variables diagrammatically in a regression line and numerically in a correlation coefficient. In this section we want to see how we can test the significance of relationships and then what statistical models we can use to describe the complexities of some of these relationships.

13.7.1 The significance of a correlation coefficient

A correlation coefficient (see section 12.10) shows how strong a relationship is between two variables. But is this all we need to know to understand what it is telling us? If we have two correlation coefficients, one of .80 and the other of .43, we know which one is the stronger. However, if we were also to know that .80 was based on 6 data pairs and .43 on 400, then would we think again? The correlation coefficient .80 is still stronger but is only based on 8 pairs of values. There is a chance that we have sampled some non typical values, so that correlation coefficient may be spuriously high. With 400 values, we may still have sampled some from the extremes of our distribution but the likelihood is that this influence is swamped by more typical values. Because of this, the correlation coefficient is likely to give a more accurate representation.

Sample size is clearly important when we interpret correlation coefficients and we can take account of sample size and produce a statement about the significance of the coefficient. If a correlation coefficient is significant at whatever value we choose, then we are saying that the relationship between the two variables is a significant relationship. How can we test a correlation coefficient for significance? The most usual test is the t test.

We start with our null hypothesis, in this case that there is no relationship between the variables. The test statistic is straightforward:

$$t = r. \sqrt{\frac{n - 2}{1 - r^2}}$$

where n is number of pairs of variables used to calculate the correlation coefficient

r is the correlation coefficient that we calculated

However, it is even easier to do the calculation on-line or through a statistics package. Table 13.13 shows the results for our two examples. We should note the following:

- Sample size (n) and the correlation coefficient (r) are given in the first two columns. The top row is our sample of 6 and the bottom row our sample of 400.

Table 13.13 Assessing the significance of correlation coefficients

n	r	Degrees of freedom	t	pr (two-tailed)
6	.8	4	2.67	0.056
400	.43	398	9.5	< 0.001

- The degrees of freedom are always the number of pairs minus 2, one for each variable.
- The results of the t test are given in the last column, which shows the probability that the statistical relationship occurs by chance. In the case of the sample of 6, it is about 5%; in the case of the sample of 400, it is about 0.1%. What this is telling us is that our lower correlation coefficient is, in fact, far more significant.

The test that we have used here can also be used with Spearman's rank correlation coefficient (see section 12.10).

There is another way in which we can assess how accurate our sample correlation coefficient is as an estimate of the population correlation coefficient. This is to establish the limits within which the population correlation coefficient lies with a certain level of confidence. *Confidence* is expressed as a probability. It can be any level of probability but 95% is the convention. With a 90% probability the confidence interval (the range between the confidence limits) will be larger than 95% and with a 99% probability the interval will be smaller. Most researchers stick to the middle!

How do we obtain (and interpret) a confidence interval? The calculation is based on the z table that we met early in this chapter. The good news is that there are many on-line calculators as well as statistics packages that will produce the answers for us so we do not have to resort to doing it ourselves. Let us use the coefficients we tested for significance in Table 13.12.

- Look first at the correlation coefficient of 0.43 based on a sample of 400. Our on-line calculator determines that at a 95% level the coefficient ranges from 0.347 to 0.506 (remember, the coefficient was significant at about the .01% level). How do we interpret this? Many people would say that this means that 95% of the time the true mean falls within the range .347 to .506. It may be a little fussy to make this point but this is not quite right. The confidence limit is established on the basis of sampling and we should more accurately say that in 100 samples, 95 will contain the population mean. The difference between the two interpretations is subtle yet meaningful.
- Now let us look at our other set of data. Here the coefficient of 0.8 was based on 6 pairs of data. Our on-line calculator determines that at a 95% level the coefficient ranges from −0.032 to 0.997. This implies that despite the fact that the coefficient was significant at about the 5% level, it is virtually worthless because the confidence interval is so great.

There are two other points we should make about confidence intervals and limits. First, they can be calculated for other measures (such as mean, regression lines). Most calculation can be done for us using statistical packages. Their interpretation is the same as above. The second thing to note about confidence intervals is what they tell us about sample size and sampling. We know from our example above that the confidence interval is large with a low sample size and becomes smaller as sample size increases. Let us imagine that we have a correlation of 0.7. With a sample size of 20, the confidence limits are from .374 to .872. With 100, they are from .584 to .788 and with 500 from .653 to .742. As researchers with limited resources, we have to get the best estimate of correlation at the lowest cost and there is clearly a trade-off between accuracy and cost. It is for this reason that we should take particular care to determine a sample size that will give us the accuracy we need. If you have not done it yet, now is the time to re-read section 6.8 and follow this up by reading Appendix 1 now that we have covered more technical material.

13.7.2 Analysing more than two variables using regression and correlation

We saw both in Chapter 10 and Chapter 12 that we can portray the relationship between more than a pair of variables. Now we can see what we can do to analyse complex data sets. We shall look at three approaches: partial correlation, multiple correlation and stepwise correlation.

(i) Partial correlation

If we were researching factors affecting unauthorised absence from school we might hypothesise that factors that influenced absenteeism might be a student's performance and attainment, being officially reprimanded, suffering bullying, lacking friends and experiencing economic disadvantage. Each of these is an independent variable that can influence the dependent variable, unauthorised absence from school. Partial correlation works by holding all independent variables constant and allowing one to vary so that only its variation influences the dependent variable. We can see how useful the technique can be in identifying the relative importance of independent variables.

For each of our independent variables we would need an indicator or indicators. Table 13.14 shows some that we might consider. Our data set consists of data on each student for each of these variables in two school years.

Table 13.14 Independent variables for partial correlation

Factor	Indicator
Performance and attainment	End of term score in mathematics. End of term score in English.
Reprimand	Number of times removed from class. Number of times kept behind after class. Number of times reported to senior staff member.
Bullying	Self-report of verbal abuse. Self-report of physical abuse.
Friendship	Number of close friends reported by class teacher.
Economic disadvantage	Eligible for free school meals.

Partial correlation varies the first indicator (mathematics score) against unauthorised absence for all of our subjects while the other variables are held constant. (This is done by mathematical manipulation of data; the process is too complex to describe here. What is important is that we understand what is happening and not how it is happening.) This process is repeated for the other eight variables. The effect of this is to show the relative importance of each independent variable.

The computation is easily done on a statistical package and it produces interesting results. A group of American educationalists used the approach to study how aspects of the lives of low income working mothers were related to their children's education (Weiss et al., 2003). This is an important issue given the policy thrust (in the UK especially) to see employment as a way of relieving child poverty and overcoming the likelihood of adults reproducing the inequalities of their own childhoods. The researchers collected data on 390 children drawn from three different cities in the USA. Table 13.15 sets out how the variables they used related to mothers' involvement. Note how low correlations were significant at 95 and 99% levels. This shows the importance of sample size. The results have policy and practice implications. They show that ethnicity was not an influencing factor, that part- and full-time work influenced involvement in different directions – part-time work was positively associated and full-time work negatively associated – and that mother's education and age were positive influences, that is, better educated and older mothers were more involved with their children's education. From a research design perspective, what is equally interesting is the way in which the researchers used qualitative methods (interviews and observation) to gain an understanding of the processes at work in the mothers' lives. These data were analysed using a coding methodology on QSR NUD*IST (now Nvivo, see section 11.6.3). The benefit of this two-pronged approach was, as the authors say, that 'emergent findings from one method helped to shape subsequent analyses performed by another method'.

While partial correlation offers insights, it misses something as well. It is rather like undertaking a two way ANOVA but not looking at the interaction effect between the variables. Multiple correlation helps us do this.

Table 13.15 Partial correlation coefficients of mother's involvement with child's education (after Weiss et al., 2003, Table 3)

Independent variable	Partial correlation coefficient	Significance level
Mother's years of education	.17	0.01
Mother's age	.11	0.05
Location 2	−.14	0.05
Part-time work or education	.13	0.05
Full-time work or education	−.13	0.05
Status of mother's partner	0.06	NS
Location 1	0.02	NS
European American	−0.01	NS
African American	−0.02	NS
Latino American	−0.01	NS

(ii) Multiple correlation

Partial correlation allowed only one variable to vary at a time. Multiple correlation does the opposite, all independent variables are allowed to influence the dependent variable at the same time. So, in our example of unauthorised absence, *every* measure in Table 13.15 would be built into a (very complex) correlation equation. Interpreting the results is just the same as for every other correlation coefficient since they will vary between +1 and −1. As with all other correlation coefficients, they can be tested for significance and confidence limits can be established.

Having established the concept, let us see how the technique has been used. Heinrich Stumpf and Julian Stanley used the multiple correlation technique in a study that explored predicting graduation rates (Stumpf and Stanley, 2002). They identified seven variables that, individually, were highly correlated with graduation rates. These were various grades gained by students on the American College Test, the Scholastic Assessment Test (both are tests used by institutions to assess capability to benefit from higher education) and grade averages from high school. They used these seven independent variables together and performed a multiple regression against the numbers of students graduating. The multiple correlation they obtained was .72 from a sample size of 350. We can guess from what we learnt in section 13.8.1 that this is significant, but what are the 95% confidence limits? Use an on-line calculator to determine them (an Internet search for 'correlation confidence limits on-line calculator' should bring up several). If we square the correlation coefficient, this gives the proportion of the variance in the data set explained by the model. (The reason for this is that the correlation coefficient is calculated on the basis of the sum of squared differences between every data point and the regression line that represents the correlation coefficient. This is more or less equivalent to the way variance is calculated. It is not important to understand this, so it may be easier just to accept it rather than try to understand why.) When we square the correlation coefficient, we call the resulting statistic the *coefficient of determination*. In this case, the coefficient of determination for the multiple correlation accounts for $.72 \times .72 = 52\%$ of the variance. It is a good indicator of the explanatory power of the set of independent variables. It can be calculated for all correlation coefficients. When we have the answer to the proportion of variance explained, we should always ask the questions, 'And what about the variance that isn't explained? How can we go about finding out what factors are at work there?' In general, we will find that statistical analysis gives us some of the answers but not all. It will answer some questions and will often lead us on to ask others.

The example above is a good use of the technique but we should still treat the results with some caution. This is largely because we do not know how stable the variables we put into the correlation model are over time. What do we mean by this? The model relates a measure of output from higher education (graduates) with measures of input (the attainment of those coming into the system). Since both the independent variables (the input measures) and the dependent variable (the output measure) are surrogates of the same thing (which we might variously describe as IQ or the ability to do well in tests), it is not surprising that we get a high correlation coefficient. If there is no change in the character of those applying to higher education, then we might accept that this correlation model is an accurate predictor of output. There is, however, a strong move in some countries (the UK included) to expand the number of young people from disadvantaged backgrounds entering higher education. If we keep the same correlation model, we would find with this policy that the correlation coefficient goes down as the policy becomes more successfully applied because of the likelihood that students from disadvantaged neighbourhoods will have poorer academic qualifications. Quantitative analysis will give us clear answers but we always have to think about its implications.

(iii) Stepwise correlation

Let us review where we are with advanced correlation techniques. Partial correlation allows us to see the influence of one variable amongst a set of variables. Multiple correlation allows us to see the effect of all variables working together. But what if one or more of our independent variables were not strongly correlated with the dependent? Or, more seriously, what if one or more of our independent variables interacted with another important independent variable to reduce the correlation coefficient? How would we know which variables were contributing most to the explanation of the variance? This is an intriguing question. Neither of our approaches deals with this and tells us the sequence in which we should combine our independent variables. What we need is something in between partial and multiple correlation.

There is a way of actually doing this with a method called stepwise correlation. This works by computing a series of correlation coefficients. It works like this:

- First, it chooses the variable with the largest individual correlation with the dependent variable. It then looks through all the other independent variables and adds in the one that, together with the first, explains more of the variance in the data set than any other combination of independent variables. In other words, the first two variables explain more of the variance in the data set than any other combination of two variables.
- Next, it repeats the procedure and identifies a third variable that, together with the first two, account for more of the variance in the data set than any other combination of three variables.
- The method continues by progressively adding in other independent variables on the basis of the contribution they make to accounting for the variance of the data set.

If this sounds like a lot of computation it is because all possible combinations of remaining variables have to be tested at each step. In the first step it identifies the largest correlation, in the second step it retains the first variable and then identifies one other so that together they account for most variance. At the third step it takes the first two variables and then identifies a third variable so that with the other the three account for most variance, and so the process continues. It is fair to say that this is a little-used technique amongst educational researchers. While it solves a problem, much quantitative analysis has moved on to using other techniques that are briefly described in section 13.8.

13.7.3 Correlation when measurement scales are not the same

Before we look at these more powerful techniques that extend the correlation model, we should consider one further correlation coefficient. The correlation coefficients that we have looked at so far have all been based on the measurement scales of the variables being the same, either interval or ordinal. What do we do when they are different? The answer is to use a different correlation coefficient. The most usual circumstance we meet is with interval and *dichotomous data*. Dichotomous data is a special form of counted or nominal data when there are only two categories. For example, if a questionnaire gives only 'yes' or 'no' as an answer this would be a dichotomous variable. If we wished to indicate gender, we could use '1' and '2' for male and female. Similarly, if we wished to show that the head teacher of a school had or did not have a management qualification, we could represent it in the same way.

How would we use this structure to calculate a correlation coefficient? Our research into management effectiveness in a school might produce several indicators – number of staff days lost through illness, grading of external quality reports, value added by the school to pupil achievement. One of our independent variables might be a management qualification for the head teacher. The correlation coefficient we could use in this case is the frighteningly termed 'point-biserial coefficient'. Ignore the fact that the words are difficult. All the calculation is done by technology and we interpret the results in exactly the same way as with all other correlation coefficients. So it is no more difficult to use than any of the others.

Let us see how it might work with an example. Table 13.16 shows data on the number of days of staff absence in 30 schools. The data set has been divided into whether the head teacher has or does not have a school management qualification. The hypothesis we are testing is that there is no difference between staff absence in schools where head teachers have a qualification and schools where the head teachers do not. The research hypothesis is that schools where the head teachers have a qualification have lower rates of staff absence. These data were inputted into an on-line calculator. The correlation coefficient was −.51. (It is negative to show that those teachers without qualification had more days of staff absence at their schools). The probability associated with this coefficient is 0.001981, which means that we should reject our null hypothesis.

Table 13.16 Data and output for point biserial correlation coefficient

	Schools where head teacher has no qualification	Schools where head teacher has a qualification
Number of days of staff absence in Survey Period	9	6
	17	12
	5	9
	18	0
	22	0
	37	14
	41	8
	22	22
	39	21
	28	2
	26	9
	22	16
	13	3
	18	1
	9	30

Point biserial coefficient −0.51
Probability (one-tailed) 0.001981

The point biserial correlation coefficient is extremely useful for education and social researchers because we often have data with a two-fold classification. An American research group led by Marcus Boccacini used point biserial coefficients in a study that explored the ability to predict who young offenders might be (Boccacini et al., 2007). They took 447 young people involved with the youth justice system and tested them on two scales:

1. One that measured antisocial processes (self-centredness, callousness and the tendency to behave impulsively).
2. Another that measured childhood psychopathy (personality disorders).

They then correlated each individual's scores on these two scales with whether or not they had been charged with specific offences. It was this 'yes/no' element that made the point biserial coefficient the one to use. There were 68 correlations each for the antisocial processes and psychopathy scales, 136 in total. With this number of correlations at, for example, the 95% level, we can expect some six or seven of them to be significant by chance. Though just which ones they might be we have no way of knowing. Because of this likelihood, on the basis of the coefficients they obtained they were unable to reach any firm conclusions about the broad relationship between criminality and what these tests measured. Indeed, some of the correlations suggested that higher test scores might be associated with a lower propensity to engage in criminal activity! We might ask why their results failed to confirm a hypothesis that many would find intrinsically appealing? It could be that the simple categorisation of whether the people had or had not committed the named offences was too crude and that a composite measure would have yielded a better result as it would differentiate single from multiple offenders. It could also be that by testing only those who had a criminal record they were not dealing with a large enough population and that had they included people who had no record, the greater range in test scores might have generated higher correlation coefficients. This assessment makes an important point. Just because we have not rejected our null hypothesis does not mean that our research hypothesis is wrong. What may be at fault is the way we have gone about the research (though this is not to say this was the case with Boccacini's group).

13.8 Beyond the foothills of quantitative analysis

We have now reached the end of our journey in quantitative analysis. We have looked at some robust techniques that have proved their value over many years. You can now demonstrate how much you have learnt from this chapter by tackling Activity 13.4.

There is, however, much more to learn. There are more powerful techniques (such as factor and principal components analyses and log-linear analysis, which you may have read about in academic papers) that can address seemingly intractable questions. Increasingly these techniques are being used by education researchers and, should there be another edition of this book in several years' time, it may be appropriate to discuss their use. But this is to look forward. Looking back, quantitative data analysis has changed significantly in the last 30 years. In 1980, much of the analysis that we have looked at here would have been done by hand. This meant that researchers were limited in what they

Activity 13.4 Choosing techniques and methods

In 2006, two educational researchers at Goteborg University in Sweden, Eva Myrberg and Monica Rosen, reported on a study that looked at reading achievement amongst third grade pupils (age 10) in public and private schools. The underlying issues that the research tackled was the extent to which affluence and social status led to a privileged allocation of educational resources with the consequence of differential educational outcomes and implications for the quality of education in public schools in the context of a national goal of equality in educational provision.

Their method was to conduct the same test with students in public and private schools. Because private schools only accounted for 3 per cent of the total, pupils in this sector were over-sampled in order to produce robust research data. Out of a total of 10,632 pupils tested, 1,034 attended private schools.

A selection of Myrberg's and Rosen's test results are set out below. Your task is to complete the tables, either by calculating the test statistic and assessing its significance or by assessing the significance of the test statistics that are given.

Question 1

What statistical test would you use to compare whether the difference between the means was significant? Use the test and assess whether the difference was significant.

Measure of reading ability

	Mean	Standard deviation
Public school pupils	522	79
Private school pupils	539	81

Question 2

The researchers wanted to see how far the social backgrounds of the pupils were different. The two tables below show the percentages in each category for the two groups. Use the χ^2 test to assess the significance of any differences.

Per cent of pupils' families with income

Annual income in krona	Public schools	Private schools
Under 180,000	9.7	6.5
180–269,999	12.8	10.7
270–359,999	17.4	16.1
360–449,999	28.0	19.6
450–539,999	15.6	14.6
over 540,000	16.5	32.4

Per cent of pupils with number of books

Number of books at home		
0–10	3.3	1.0
11–25	6.7	2.2
26–100	26.4	17.6
101–200	22.4	21.2
Over 200	41.4	58.0

How many degrees of freedom are there in each table? The researchers used χ^2. Can you think of another test to use? (Hint – look at the categories. Both are ascending series.) Process the data using the test. Interpret the probability statistic and give the confidence limits at 95%.

Question 3

The researchers also looked at family practices in reading to children. The tables below show some specific results. How many degrees of freedom are there? What is the significance level of each χ^2 statistic? If you were planning a reading support programme for a public school in a low income neighbourhood, how would you recommend parents could best be involved? Remember the parents may be the barrier to progress.

▶

Per cent of pupils in category

Parental involvement	Public schools	Private schools	χ^2	df	pr
Telling stories					
Never/almost never	12.1	9.7			
Sometimes	50.4	45.0			
Often	37.6	45.3	7.803		
Reading to child					
Never/almost never	1.6	1.0			
Sometimes	28.4	19.8			
Often	70.0	79.2	12.165		

Source: Myrberg, E. and Rosen, M. (2006) 'Reading Achievement and Social Selection in Independent Schools in Sweden: Results from IEA PIRLS 2001', *Scandinavian Journal of Educational Research*, 50(2), 185–205.

could do. Students' t tests, chi-square, correlation and regression and even two way ANOVA and multiple and partial regression were done with a calculator. Factor analysis, one of the more advanced techniques mentioned above, may have been developed 80 years earlier but no one did it by hand. For that you needed someone who could help input data into and interpret output from a mainframe computer. Use of powerful multivariate techniques was restricted.

The situation today has changed out of all recognition. Researchers have access to a mass of software that removes the effect of computation (and the chance of a keying error). Laptops will run the programs. The process of doing quantitative research has been transformed. In many ways, undertaking quantitative research is now considerably more straightforward and almost certainly involves less effort than qualitative research. But this encouragement for researchers to look to quantitative approaches comes with a caution. Not only do we have to be aware of what the techniques do, we also have to be aware of what conditions they require for their data and the assumptions that a test requires. For this, we have to look outside the black box that is the statistical program and be clear that the assumptions it makes are the same as we require. Before we use a package test, we should read what it says on the label.

This chapter has brought us almost to the end of our research journey. All that remains to be done is to see how the research package comes together. This is what we shall look at in Chapter 14.

Summary

- We have learnt how the standard deviation is the bridge between describing our data and being able to assess the significance of our results. A key aspect of this is the Z table, which gives the probabilities within the normal deviation for all values of Z. We have learnt how to convert our data into Z values and seen how we can then make probabilistic statements about our data.

- We have seen that statistical testing only answers two types of question, 'How different are these'? and 'Are these two related?' We refreshed our memory about the way in which we phrase the question in a statistical test, noting that all a test would allow us to do is reject a null hypothesis.
- This chapter introduced the idea of a level of significance, expressed in probabilistic terms, for rejecting or not rejecting the null hypothesis – what is the probability that this result has been produced by random processes? We found out that statisticians conventionally use the 95% (5%) or 99% (1%) thresholds but added a warning note that social scientists could be a little more flexible.
- We also learnt that significance was not necessarily the only indicator of a statistical test that we should examine. We pointed out that significance testing ignores the effect size of a relationship, which may be more important in some situations. As well, we looked at confidence level, something that is particularly important with small sample sizes.
- We learnt that the alternative to the null hypothesis is the research hypothesis and that we should understand the implications of specifying it as a two-directional or one-directional hypothesis, in particular how critical it is for interpreting the level of significance.
- We have been introduced to a range of statistical tests and now understand that we choose a test primarily on the basis of the question we want answered and the character of our data. This chapter has made it clear that there are many more tests available than it described but the tests introduced here are a good foundation for reading research literature and for researchers beginning their research careers. We have learnt that even if we have complex data sets there are tests that are within our capabilities to use as new researchers, so we should not necessarily confine ourselves to 'easy' questions.
- Perhaps, however, the most important thing to have learnt from this chapter is that technology has taken the difficulties of computation and assessing significance out of our hands and that undertaking quantitative research is not only more straightforward, it is also, arguably, easier than qualitative research.

Further reading

Cohen, L. and Holliday, M. (1996) *Practical Statistics for Students*, Paul Chapman Publishing, London.

Neave, H.R. and Worthington, P.L. (1988) *Distribution Free Tests*, Unwin-Hyman, London.

Advising on further reading for statistical analysis could be a lengthy undertaking, so great is the range of methods and texts available. Instead, I have chosen only to direct you to the next level.

Cohen and Holliday's book is included because, although it covers some of the material we have considered, it deals with more tests that a new researcher might use. It is written in a straightforward way that, if you have followed this chapter, you will manage. Neave and Worthington's book also provides more tests for the beginning researcher but in their case, all are non-parametric.

After this level, the analytic path leads onto multivariate analysis, statistical procedures based on different theories of probability (especially Bayes' theorem) and non-linear modelling.

References

Ahlin, A. and Mörk, E. (2007) 'Effects of Decentralisation on School Resources: Sweden 1989–2002', *Working Paper 9*, Uppsala University, Department of Economics, Uppsala.

Boccacini, M., Epstein, M., Poythress, N., Douglas, K., Campbell, J., Gardner, G. and Falkenbach, D. (2007) 'Self-Report Measures of Child and Adolescent Psychopathy as Predictors of Offending in Four Samples of Justice-Involved Youth', *Assessment*, 14(4), 361–374.

Bosire, J., Mondoh, H. and Barmao, A. (2008) 'Effect of Streaming by Gender and Student Achievement in Mathematics in Secondary Schools in Kenya', *South African Journal of Education*, 28(4), 595–607.

Brouwers, A. and Tomic, W. (2000) 'A Longitudinal Study of Teacher Burnout and Perceived Self-efficacy in Classroom Management', *Teaching and Teacher Education*, 16(2), 239–253.

D'Abrera, H. and Lehmann, E.L. (2006) *Non-parametrics: Statistical Methods Based on Ranks*, Springer, New York.

Fisher, R.A. (1925) *Statistical Methods for Research Workers*, Oliver and Boyd, Edinburgh.

Hofer, T., Przyrembel, H., Verleger, S. (2004) New Evidence for the Theory of the Stork, *Paediatric and Perinatal Epidemiology*, 18(1), 88–92.

Lehmann, E.L. (2006) *Nonparametrics: Statistical Methods Based on Ranks*, Springer, New York.

Lindley, D. and Scott, W. (1995) *New Cambridge Statistical Tables*, Cambridge University Press.

Myrberg, E. and Rosen, M. (2006) 'Reading Achievement and Social Selection in Independent Schools in Sweden: Results from IEA PIRLS 2001', *Scandinavian Journal of Educational Research*, 50(2), 185–205.

Neave, H. (1980) *Elementary Statistics Tables*, George Allen & Unwin, London.

Peterson, D., Finn-Aage, E., Taylor, T. and Freng, A. (2007) 'Youth Violence in Context: The Roles of Sex, Race and Community in Offending', *Youth Violence and Social Justice*, 5(4), 385–410.

Prskalo, I., Fiudak, V. and Neljcik, B. (2007) 'Educating Future Pre-School and Primary School Teachers to Teach Physical Education: Bologna Process in Croatia', *Kinesiology*, 39(2), 171–183.

Schlichting, J. and Spelberg, H. (2003) 'A Test for Measuring Syntactic Development in Young Children', *Language Testing*, 20(3), 241–266.

Stumpf, H. and Stanley, J. (2002) 'Group Data on High School Grade Point Averages and Scores on Academic Aptitude Tests as Predictions of Institutional Graduation Rates', *Educational and Psychological Measurements*, 62(b), 1042–1052.

Tella, A. (2007) 'The Impact of Motivation on Students' Academic Achievement and Learning Outcomes in Mathematics Among Secondary School Students in Nigeria', Education Journal of Mathematics, Science and Technology Education, 3(2), 149–156.

Thomas, N-E., Cooper, S-M., Graham, M., Boobler, W., Baker, J. and Davies, B. (2007) 'Dietary Habits of Welsh 12–13 year olds', *European Physical Education Review*, 13(2), 247–256.

Tynjälä, P. (1999) 'Towards Expert Knowledge? A Comparison Between a Constructivist and a Traditional Learning Environment in the University', *International Journal of Educational Research*, 31(5), 357–442.

Weiss, H. et al. (2003) 'Making it Work: Low-Income Working Mothers' Involvement in Their Children's Education', *American Educational Research Journal*, 40(4), 879–901.

Weitoft, G.R., Hjern, A., Haglund, B. and Rosen, M. (2003) 'Mortality, Severe Morbidity and Injury in Children Living With Single Parents in Sweden: A Population-Based Study', *The Lancet*, 361, 289–295.

Zhon, L. and Fan, Z-Z. (2007) 'Discrepancy Between Native English Speaker Teachers' Teaching Styles and Chinese English Learners' Learning Styles', *US – China Education Review*, 4(9), 15–20.

Zientek, L., Caprano, M. and Caprano, R. (2008) 'Reporting Practices in Teacher Education Research: One Look at the Evidence Cited in the AERA Panel Report', *Educational Researcher*, 37(4), 208–216.

Chapter contents

Chapter 14

PUTTING IT ALL TOGETHER

Key themes

This chapter looks at examples of actual research strategies. By the end of the chapter, and the book, you will have:

- Appreciated how many research strategies require research questions to be formulated in a specific way.
- Looked at research through the perspective of six research frameworks: hypothesis testing, experiment, ethnography, case study, action research and evaluation.
- Seen how researchers have put together research methods within these frameworks.
- Begun the process of developing your own research programme.

Introduction

Grasping the ideas, understanding the methods and appreciating the issues covered in this book is an enormous undertaking. There is, however, one more key point that remains to be emphasised. This is that the research has to be conceptualised as a whole before we start. This has been touched on before (for example, when we talked about the need to think about how data were to be analysed at the same time as identifying how we would obtain our research evidence) but what is different now is that it is the core theme of this chapter.

The guidance for reading this book makes it clear that the sections and chapters do not have to be mastered in sequence. However, there is clearly a sequence in the way in which it is organised. By and large this reflects the way in which many social science researchers will put together a research programme. The process, however, is far more than a sequence of free-standing stages. Conceptualising the research process is far more than deciding on the research question, deciding what data are needed and where they will come from and then analysing them. Certainly starting the process without knowing the route to be taken is more than likely to be a recipe for research disaster. Organising a research programme means that we should:

- have a plan for what should happen at each stage;
- understand the possible implications that a procedure at one point might have for a decision we have to take subsequently or even previously;
- appreciate that we can get blown off course by unforeseen circumstances and

that we should build flexibility into the way we arrange things to ensure that when things do go wrong we still have an exit route.

The capability to do all of this rests firmly upon having a sound appreciation of a wide range of research methods but it is fair to point out that our capability is enhanced by practice and experience. By this point in the book we can assume that the foundations of an understanding of research methods are well on the way to being laid. The purpose of this chapter is to start building the experience that turns students into effective researchers.

14.1 The research question: a pointer to strategy

The process of developing a research strategy has two stages.

- First, we have to develop our *research question*. This is not always as easy as it might seem. What we think is important is often a function of what we know about a topic and its context, so as we read more about a topic the research question evolves along with our growing knowledge, understanding and insight. Framing our research question is not an activity to be crossed off a research planning list, it is a process. Unless we give the process time to work, we can finish up with a shallow research question that lacks the potential to produce research findings that will have an impact. In section 2.1.5 we saw how research questions pointed us in different directions. In the examples that follow, we are going to look at how this works in reality. As we know, our research question is a way of focusing our attention on a broader issue. Given that there are often different ways of looking at, approaching or being intrigued by an issue, an important task for a researcher is to convince the audience that the thrust of the enquiry is legitimate and relevant to a mix of educational, political, social, economic or moral contexts. We have, then, to see the research question in the context of a scene setting argument. The examples that follow show this in action.
- Second, our research question guides us towards a broad research strategy. Operationalising this strategy means that we combine approaches to data collection and methods of data analysis. While particular research strategies predispose us to working with particular data collection and analysis methods, there are no hard and fast rules to this. There is considerable flexibility in how we go about the process of answering the research question and usually there are alternatives to the way that might first suggest itself. While these alternatives are rarely discussed in research literature, we should explore them, if only to convince ourselves that the obvious approach is the best one. One will, however, begin to take shape. It will be influenced not only by our research question but also our understanding of data availability, the resources we have, our knowledge of what methods might work and what methods have been used.

In the following sections we shall look at seven established research strategies. Using examples, we shall show how the way the researchers looked at an issue and phrased the research question set them on a path that culminated in a way of working that conformed to an accepted research strategy. One thing that we should make clear, however, is that not all research fits into an approach to conducting research that is graced with a particular name. Much research takes bits from here and there and mixes them with methods that are closely associated with established strategies. This is perfectly acceptable. We should not be hung up on the assumption that only named ways of working are acceptable. The world and education research is infinitely more complex than can be addressed using just a few named strategies. If it helps to understand the thrust of this argument, then the following metaphor may help. Think of the seven research strategies that we shall look at as peaks on a plain of research practice. At the top of the peak is the purest form of the strategy but, as we descend and move towards a different peak, pure research practice becomes modified and while it retains some of the elements of what is pure practice, it is a mixture of different research approaches and ideals. It is not debased, it is just different and appropriate to the context of a specific, perhaps unique, research issue.

Let us now return to the peaks. They are all frameworks within which people can work at the start of their research careers. Our intention is to understand why they were appropriate to our examples and to see how the researchers worked within the research approach. The research strategies that we shall examine are:

- Case study.
- Evaluation.
- Ethnography.
- Action research.
- Experimentation.
- Hypothesis testing.
- Research question.

14.2 Case study

(i) Phrasing the research question

The education sector is complex because it strives to meet a range of goals which, if they do not actually conflict, can come perilously close to doing so. This is particularly the case with universities. They are independent institutions but many are dependent on state funding; they are responsible for developing high level skills required by employers but they are staffed by academics whose career progression rests on research output and, like many organisations, they have significant demands on their resources and, for many, those resources are inadequate for a truly effective response. This is a picture repeated in many countries. It is not surprising, therefore, to find that the ways universities position and manage themselves has become of interest to researchers.

Wim Westera and two colleagues investigated a particular type of response to this challenging situation, collaboration between institutions in an attempt to create capacity to deliver research and teaching and to save costs (Westera et al., 2004). Collaboration is an obvious response. It enables institutions to benefit from specialisation and economies of scale. One university, for instance, develops one set of teaching materials and allows others to use them and, in turn, is allowed to use materials developed elsewhere. They noted a trend for institutions to seek to work together 'to reinforce their position in the educational market' (p. 317). However, they claim that 'all too often strategic alliances appear to be nothing but hot air' (p. 318). We should note that we are given no evidence for this, so there is a gap in the argument they make. The implicit conclusion, nonetheless, from their argument is that either we should seek to understand why some succeed or that we should understand why many fail. They chose the former and focused on a case study of 'one of the very few university alliances in the Netherlands that actually succeeded in building up a mutual win-win situation' (p. 318), the *Knowledge Engineering Web,* in which five universities worked together.

At this point we should recognise that the study of one thing that worked was the logical outcome of the way they shaped their argument for the research. They could have adopted other approaches but their interest was in looking at an island of success in a sea of, if not failure, then performance below expectations.

(ii) Implementing the case study strategy

The purpose of a case study is to understand why what happened actually happened. The reason for a case study is the importance of what happened. In the UK, in 2008, the national test results for school students were many months late. We need to know the operational details of why this happened to ensure that procedures are put in place to prevent it happening again. At another time, we may want to research school effectiveness and leadership. Rather than review the literature we may want to develop our own insights. It would be appropriate for us to undertake a case study of a school that on all criteria appears to be successful, and if we choose one serving a poor community, so much the better. In both of these cases what happened and why is important and 'what happened and why' is at the heart of the case study approach. For this reason the case study is used extensively in teaching where it acts as a substitute for learning by experience.

Westera and colleagues' study of the Knowledge Engineering Web in the Netherlands is an attempt to learn about the conditions that created success (Westera et al., 2004). This was, potentially, an important learning exercise as the experience could inform collaborative activity between organisations that normally compete and it could apply to organisations far broader than just universities. The study examines the evolution of the network through time. They document the growth in the number of institutions and lecturers involved. They demonstrate the growth in the quantity and range of learning materials produced for students of knowledge engineering and artificial intelligence. They show how this success took some six years to materialise and that there were important stages of alliance building and consolidation before the production of learning materials. They explored the barriers to development and assessed programme management. The evidence base for this deconstruction of success was documentation, discussions with key personnel and, one suspects, close involvement with the project. This perhaps is one weakness of the research, the fact that the relationship between the authors and the collaborative project is not made explicit. The reader has to judge, therefore, whether there is sufficient critical distance between the analysis and the process of participation. The issues are essentially the same as those facing participant observation and there is always a danger that success may be overstated. Nonetheless, if insights are the product of a reflective analysis, it is an established technique.

Key features of a case study

- Demonstrate the benefit of looking at just one example and show its advantages over a sample of many instances.
- Present the context for the research in such a way that a case study is the obvious if not the only research strategy to adopt.
- Examine the case over time and describe what happened – what worked and what went wrong.
- Obtain data from documentation, people (interviews), developers, users, managers.
- Put an interpretation on what has been found out. Identify critical events, times, stages and key people in achieving success or capturing failure.

14.3 Evaluation

(i) Phrasing the research question

One feature of school life that is beginning to change in many developed countries is that schools are becoming less isolated from other agencies concerned with social and behavioural issues. Society is thus taking a more holistic view of how to deal with problems that may have a cause in one part of a child's world but have consequences in others. Typical of society's concern is antisocial behaviour and how to tackle it.

Rachel Sandford, Rebecca Duncombe and Kathy Armour, all at Loughborough University in England, looked at this very topic. They observed that 'sport/physical activity programmes are popular tools [to confront antisocial behaviour], based on a prevailing belief in their potential to instil positive attitudes, traits and values, and to secure a wide range of benefits for young people who are disaffected with, or disengaged from, one or more aspects of society' (Sandford et al., 2008, p. 419). However, they also noted that 'there is a lack of robust, empirical evidence to support those beliefs' (p. 420).

Having established need, these researchers could have gone in different directions. They could have made a quantitative assessment of outcomes on a national scale; did people experiencing a sport/physical activity intervention in their lives offend less? Instead, they chose to look in detail at two specific programmes. In both cases it was an evaluation of what has happened. The path they chose was to look at projects that sought to involve young people with physical activity.

There is an important point emerging here. Above we looked at case study as the *strategy* for resolving a question. Here, evaluation is the strategy and the projects are case studies, that is, a case study is the *lens* through which we look at the data. There is a subtle difference though with the case study we looked at above. There, the interest was in what we could learn from the case study, what went right and what went wrong. Here, our interest is in whether an approach is effective in delivering policy goals.

(ii) Implementing the evaluation strategy

Evaluation can answer two types of question, often both at the same time.

- It seeks to find out about and understand outcomes. This approach is called *impact evaluation*. It may try to do this in the context of goals or objectives, in which case there is a strong policy dimension to the evaluations.

- There is, however, often a need to go beyond a demonstration that something has been achieved and explore the processes involved. This leads to evaluation answering such questions as, 'Could we have done better?' or 'What was the reason for failure (or success)?' This approach is called *process evaluation*.

Evaluation can take many shapes. On the one hand it can be experimental, with a quantitative assessment of a null hypothesis. On the other hand, it can probe an issue and employ whatever methods seem appropriate to assembling the data that will place the issue in perspective and produce the insight to demonstrate that we understand what happened and are able to act on our judgements.

The approach adopted by Rachel Sandford and her colleagues who looked at the role of sports to counteract disaffection (Sandford et al., 2008) was to focus on two programmes, the HSBC/Outward Bound project and Youth SportTrust/BSkyB 'Living For Sport' programme. The first is a programme that offers a residential outdoor activity programme to 30 Year 9 children from five schools in a deprived area in the East of London. The second is a national programme that offers schools themselves the opportunity to offer programmes that 'have included climbing, abseiling, horse-riding, skiing, tennis, football, martial arts, aerobics and circus skills' (p. 424). The programme ends with some sort of competition and a celebration party. With over 7,000 young people having been on the programmes in the projects they looked at, the researchers had access to sufficient data for the quantitative assessment they wanted. Their approach was to examine student profiles and behaviour before and after involvement with the sports programmes. These profiles (which covered attendance, behaviour, confidence and self-esteem) were produced by teachers periodically during the programme period. All the evidence they collected, from the objective number of referrals to the impressionistic teachers' views of behaviour and attitude, points to an improvement in student behaviour. But as they suggest, the need now is to understand what was happening, in particular the processes responsible for the improvement.

Evaluation is, however, a flexible strategy, and need not be confined to questions about policy. Another example will show us how an evaluation strategy can be a way of shaping understanding in order to develop principles of good practice. Rob Bowker, an English academic, is interested in teaching and learning strategies, in particular how well understood the strategies for learning outside the school environment were (Bowker, 2002). There is a belief that school trips are beneficial, as much in improving social relationships, group dynamics and individual motivation as in knowledge acquisition. Realising these benefits, however, is dependent on the teacher having a clear idea of what should be achieved and structuring the visit to ensure that the goals are achieved.

The focus for his research was the Eden Project, a reconstruction of global biomes in climate-controlled environments in the south west of England. Bowker identified five questions:

1. What are the Eden Project's educational aims?
2. What are the learning objectives of schools visiting the Project?
3. What strategies are used by schools visiting the Project?
4. What strategies are used by the Project to communicate their messages?
5. What strategies are effective in achieving the school's objectives and the Project's aims?

His approach was to base the research on schools that organised their own visits. This clearly is a better test of the ability of teacher and the Eden Project to understand each other than if the schools had made use of the Eden Project's own visit programme. Data was obtained from pupils, teachers from eight primary schools and through an analysis of the presentation methods used by the Eden Project.

Three schools identified specific curriculum links as the purpose for their visit, others identified social benefits. Obtaining data from pupils was achieved by observation on the day of the visit and follow-up interviews in schools. These had to be tailored to the age of the children and use was made of visual prompts. The focus of the questioning was to see how far the children appreciated the purpose of the Eden Project, how effectively the displays communicated that purpose and what differences existed in pupil response according to the way the visit was managed.

What Rob Bowker did, on the basis of his study, was to conceptualise a complex relationship between the visit location (in this case the Eden Project), teacher and pupil and deduce conditions for effective learning based on what he learnt from the pupils. He concluded that effective strategies included:

- a high adult/child ratio of 1:4 or even 1:2 to provide effective guidance and focus;
- structuring activities within the child's ability to concentrate (about 40 minutes, he suggests);
- making the purpose of the visit clear to children beforehand;
- introducing some prior knowledge before the visit;
- using an adult to mediate the child's experience, for example, by asking questions;
- providing opportunities for interactive learning at the site; and
- allowing free time.

Key features of evaluation

- Evaluation can be used to assess policy, shape policy, improve practice and develop concepts and models.
- Be clear about the purpose of the evaluation. Spell this out as, 'What I need to find out'.
- Many evaluations require a mixed methods (quantitative and qualitative) methodology.
- Identify (i) outputs, (ii) outcomes that were anticipated and (iii) outcomes that were not anticipated.
- Examine what happened against what was supposed to happen.
- Obtain data from management reports, minutes, official publications, observation of beneficiaries, interviews with managers and beneficiaries.
- Make judgements about the findings, for example, 'Is this an effective use of time and money?'

14.4 Ethnography

(i) Phrasing the research question

Ethnography is a research framework that can operate as a means of configuring the whole approach to research (the research strategy) or as a means (perhaps together with other methods) of collecting data. We shall explore its use as an overarching strategy.

The resolution of conflict and injustice is central to the way societies operate. Legal frameworks protect and punish but in some circumstances they are inadequate. Physical bullying at school might be such a case. It is assault and so a criminal act but many schools (and police services) prefer to use other means (such as restorative justice where offenders are made to hear the real impact of their actions) rather than criminalise young people. At a larger scale of social conflict, other approaches have been tried. In South Africa the Truth and Reconciliation Commission operated on a national scale with a form of the restorative justice model and the process has been central to healing the wounds between ethnic communities. But reconciliation as a state of mind evolves and what was acceptable may change over time.

This was the premise adopted by Krisztina Tihanyi and Stephanos du Toit, two South African researchers, and the driver for change that they examined was the education experience. As they point out, 'The lives of young South Africans present an interesting paradox: they have no first hand experience of Apartheid, yet they are surrounded by its economic and social legacies' (Tihanyi and du Toit, 2005, p. 25). Their research was 'whether the racial integration of South Africa's education system has presented a space or opportunity for reconciliation' (p. 25). In other words, is the education process moving reconciliation on and helping the different communities live more at ease with each other?

They could have sought answers from a mass survey of young people but it is doubtful whether this would have generated any insightful results because it takes more than a questionnaire to penetrate feelings and emotions to the level needed to gain answers to the question. Instead, they spent time in schools and saw what was happening. Their strategy was ethnographic and the schools they studied were sample cases, that is, they were selected to represent different aspects of the school system.

(ii) Implementing the ethnography strategy

Ethnography really deserves far more space than we are able to devote to it here. It is a far more complex set of research practices than just living with and observing a group. It raises questions about the relationship with the group. Is the research negotiated or imposed? Is the researcher a neutral observer (which places the researcher more in the descriptive or interpretive camp) or is there a perspective through which data are collected and processed that puts the observer in the critical ethnography camp?

The reason for an ethnographic approach is to:

- Avoid respondents telling us what they think they should say or what we want to hear. (This does not, of course, preclude ethnographers from asking questions.)
- Use behaviour and verbal interaction as an indicator of priorities, values and goals.
- Mix methods appropriate to the needs of the study.

Krisztina Tihanyi and Stephanos du Toit used this approach in their study of reconciliation in South African schools (Tihanyi and du Toit, 2005). They first identified schools that represented a range of ethnic and socio-economic mixes and sought permission to work with their students. Of the eight schools they identified, they had to give up two because of interference with the research approach by school principals. They were able to substitute one. This shows the need to have a strategy in place and time in hand for when events do not go according to plan. In addition to observation, they collected data through questionnaires (whose results were used to stimulate discussions, a sort of focus group approach) and through individual interviews. The discussions were videoed and the interviews recorded. On the basis of this data the researchers were able to profile the schools on how they were approaching the issue of reconciliation and creating a multicultural society. They identified the following types:

- Schools with internal segregation, where 'racial tensions simmer' (the sample case was a school where coloured students were the majority and black students the minority).
- Schools with colour-blind multiculturalism, where the language of multiculturalism and inclusion ('diversity is valued') dominates the discourse but where behaviour (white pupils with white, black with black, coloured with coloured) suggests that divisions still exist.

- Schools with mainly white students in denial of the social changes, where 'race is not a problem' and race and politics rarely come up in discussion or conversation.
- Schools with predominantly black students involuntarily excluded from integration and where, by virtue of poor access to resources, the possibility of attracting students from other communities is a non-starter. The students had to establish their positions on racism, apartheid and reconciliation by themselves, in the context of both the past (which made them angry) and the future, with a sense of resignation ('At the end of the day we won't survive without whites').

Key features of ethnography

- Offers deep insight into issues.
- Data collection can be opportunistic as well as planned.
- Evidence from behaviour, interaction and representation (of self, of others, of organisations) is as important as evidence from discussions.
- Data are analysed separately before they are synthesised into an explanation.

14.5 Action research

The essence of professionalism, in whatever sphere, is a commitment to both effective practice and to delivering a service that meets a client's needs. For lecturers these two dimensions come together in their teaching. The commitment to meeting students' needs often means asking students to do things that they might not want to do. Effective practice suggests something other than repeating tired old lectures.

Christina Bergendahl, a Swedish chemistry lecturer, grappled with these issues when she discussed the relationship between teaching methods adopted by staff and knowledge and skills outcomes for students (Bergendahl, 2003). What she wanted to understand was how teaching and assessment methods could help students' learning outcomes match the tutor's learning objectives.

As she explains, the complexity of this topic meant that it was better to start her research journey without knowing what the end might look like rather than design a research programme that makes assumptions about what is best and which would lack the flexibility to change when the assumptions prove wrong. Her research strategy is one that has been used in business contexts, where the goal is known (for example to improve profit) but the route is uncertain. The model is one where change is initiated (seeking cheaper suppliers) and, if the outcomes are in the right direction, the strategy is continued. In the academic world, we call it action research. Bergendahl's first step was to initiate an innovative approach to laboratory teaching. This was the 'action', reviewing the outcomes was the 'research'.

(ii) Implementing the action research strategy

Action research is a process of learning by doing. The purpose of this is typically either to improve effectiveness or quality in the delivery of a service or product or to learn why something is working the way it is. It is a popular research strategy amongst teachers and educationalists because:

- it can be used for small scale enquiry by one person;
- it is a mechanism for engaging people with their work and frequently has the benefit of increasing commitment and motivation;
- It makes use of reflective practice in which we consider outcomes in relation to goals or expectations. Action research embeds reflective practice in its processes. Reflective practice raises the question for action research to answer and may even determine the nature of the action.

We find this cycle of action and reflection in Christina Bergendahl's work on teaching chemistry. Her question was whether different approaches to laboratory learning would have different outcomes for students. Her approach was to set up a quasi-experiment in which three groups of students were given different approaches to experimentation: a set of procedures to be followed, an open-enquiry/problem solving approach and a revised open-enquiry approach with more direction. She tested student attitudes to laboratory experimentation before and after and found that the open-enquiry approaches were received more positively.

The outcome of this research then led her to consider how approaches to teaching, learning and assessment could enhance the development of higher order thinking skills. With a further group of students she introduced a variety of teaching and assessment methods and collected data from student notes, assessment responses, observation and interviews on their impact on thinking skills. From this data she was not able to identify any single approach that worked best for all students but she was able to show that combinations of different approaches that required students to interact with the learning process in different ways had the most impact on the development of higher order skills.

What we should appreciate from this is that her action research strategy utilised a quasi-experimental framework followed by an action research reflective model. This is yet another instance of the fact that we can mix methods and methodologies with strategies to meet the needs of the circumstances.

Key features of action research

- Action research is designed to improve outcomes and/or processes while, at the same time, enabling personal and professional development.
- Its core procedures are (i) learning by doing and (ii) reflection as the key to unlocking all learning.
- It makes use of both quantitative and qualitative methods of data collection and analysis.
- The experience of those involved in the action process is important in understanding the outcomes.
- Action research is cyclical. After one cycle of action research another begins. The 'actions' in action research are often incremental and not wholesale changes.

14.6 Experimentation

(i) Phrasing the research question

Assessing the effects of an intervention or controlled change in circumstance is an approach that is widely found in the natural and behavioural sciences. The strict laboratory conditions that make it so successful there are not often available to education researchers and so when we are faced with the sort of question experimentation deals with ('Do these fail less often?'), we have to follow the principles but accept that our ability to control external variables is limited. We should refer to this as quasi-experimentation, though we do not always do so.

An important process outcome for higher education is to enable students to function as autonomous learners (this is one of the higher order skills that Christina Bergendahl was concerned to develop in her chemistry students). For some groups of students, such as trainee teachers, it is important not only that they achieve this goal but also that they are effective autonomous learners because, without this capability, their effectiveness as teachers will decline with time. Two Belgian researchers, Wil Meeus and Peter Van Petergem and a Dutch colleague, Joost Meijher, explored how they could improve the capacity of their teacher education students to function autonomously. Their approach was to introduce a portfolio method of assessment. The authors give an example of what they mean by this: 'During her practice, she gathers evidence of her competency – e.g. lesson plans, a video tape of an interesting intervention, a summary of the pupils' learning progress, etc. Furthermore, she uses these materials to reflect explicitly on her competency' (Meeus et al., 2008, p. 363). However, to judge its impact, they needed a benchmark against which to assess it. This meant that some students had to continue with the old model of working and assessment (the traditional dissertation). In this way they set up a quasi-experiment where the main influence on learning outcomes was the mode of production of the materials to be assessed and the learning processes that underpinned each.

There is always an ethical issue with this approach to experimentation that we should note. How do we minimise the disadvantage to any who might be disadvantaged? Is there a level of disadvantage that should not be tolerated? If so, should this be zero? Of course, the implication of zero disadvantage is that partial changes should never happen and that it is better to have total change with the possibility that everyone is worse off than they would have been. The alternative is that no change will ever occur. When faced with this sort of circumstance our solution, perhaps, should be to ensure that no one is worse off than they would have been had the intervention not occurred.

(ii) Implementing the experimentation strategy

The purpose of experimentation is to show an effect as a result of manipulating inputs to a process. Underpinning this in the social sciences is a wish to move beyond the association of inputs and outputs to infer causation. This was exactly the situation that Wil Meeus and his colleagues were faced with in their study of dissertation models. The way they approached the issue of testing two approaches to dissertation production (traditional and portfolio) shows great concern with extraneous influences. Their approach was to set up the two dissertation models for two groups of students, one group had free choice and the other was given the portfolio approach. Table 14.1 shows how the

Table 14.1 Allocation of students to dissertation model

	Traditional dissertation	Portfolio dissertation	
Course A	93	28	121
Course B	—	53	53
	93	81	

students split up for the test. Of the 121 students in Course A, 93 followed the traditional model and 28 the portfolio model. All students in Course B followed the portfolio model. The numbers following each dissertation model, though not equal, are not greatly dissimilar. This is important because some statistical tests can become unstable in a comparison of greatly different sample sizes.

The problem for the researchers was to be sure that not all the good students had opted for one model and the weaker students for the other. This is important because student capability would (or should) have a significant impact on performance. The researchers resolved this issue by looking at grades given to students in an earlier module (teaching practice). They did this by conducting two *t tests*:

- comparison of students from Course A and Course B in the portfolio group;
- comparison of students from Course A in the traditional and portfolio groups.

In neither case was there a significant difference in the student performance levels. They could, therefore, be confident that student capability was evenly distributed between the dissertation and portfolio models.

The second issue that the researchers faced was that supervision quality could affect outcomes. If better supervisors looked after one group and less effective supervisors were with another then this could skew the results. It is difficult to judge supervision standards before the event, so the researchers identified dimensions of supervision practice that might affect student performance. These dimensions were:

- work experience of supervisors;
- learning as knowledge acquisition;
- learning as the ability to use knowledge;
- teaching as a process of encouraging and stimulating students;
- learning as a co-operative and collaborative activity;
- learning as a process of self-direction;
- confidence in students' capacity for self-direction.

For each of these dimensions, the researchers constructed a set of scales (between 4 and 10 for each dimension). These scales constitute the indicators. They compared how the supervisors in the two groups compared in each dimension and found that there was no significant difference in any apart from confidence in the students' capacity for self-direction. They looked at this in more detail by investigating the differences between:

- Course A teachers vs Course B teachers.
- Course A teachers in the traditional and portfolio groups.
- Course A and Course B teachers in the portfolio group.
- Course A and Course B teachers in the traditional group.

None of these differences was significant, though this could be due to low sample size. It was clear that variation in supervision was unlikely to influence student outcomes.

How, though, to measure the outcomes? The researchers were not interested in academic performance as measured by student grades but by the relative ability of the methods to build the capacity for autonomous learning. They measured this using two existing scales:

- The Reporting Autonomous Studying Questionnaire.
- The Inventory of Learning Styles for Higher Education.

The students rated themselves on these scales before and after the dissertation experience.

The Reporting Autonomous Studying Questionnaire was used to deliver an overall estimate of metacognition (how aware we are ourselves of our own learning). The Inventory of Learning Styles generated measures of the students' abilities in cognitive processing (inference, decision making and other aspects of information processing), learning orientations and mental learning models. The researchers processed the data from the two surveys separately using a type of analysis of variance (actually an analysis of co-variance which allows the inclusion of additional variables). The result of these statistical tests, the researchers conclude, is that the portfolio approach has a greater impact on metacognition than the traditional dissertation. They conclude that 'the learning portfolio is more successful in increasing students' capacity for autonomous learning' and that it 'is more likely to bridge the gap between higher education and the job market'.

Key features of experimentation

- Experimentation seeks to identify the effect an intervention has on outcomes to a process.
- Set up the research design so that there is a control against which the experimental results can be judged.
- The control can be the same experimental subjects before and after the intervention or different subjects under two different conditions.
- Intervening variables should be identified and, where possible, controlled for in the research design.
- Experimentation is heavily dependent on quantitative analysis.

14.7 Hypothesis testing

Immigration is an emotive issue. In 2006 the best estimates were that EU states received about 1.8 million people from outside the EU. In addition, a further 1.2 million EU citizens moved to another EU state. Immigration brings many economic advantages. Because it is the young, most go-ahead and best educated who are more likely to move country, immigration is a significant contributor to economic growth. However, alongside economic advantages there are social consequences. Immigrants group together and form social enclaves. Some elements of the host society express concerns about the cost of social security support and the provision of public housing. In the longer term however, immigrants often diffuse into the host population and adopt its cultural values. In modern society one of the principal vehicles for achieving this is education. But how good are schools at coping with immigrants and how good are immigrant children at coping with new schools and new languages?

This was the issue three Finnish researchers, Karmela Liebkind, Inga Jasinskaja-Lahti and Erling Solheim, addressed in their study of how Vietnamese children aged 13 to 18 adjusted to school in Finland. Their approach was to review the literature in this area and from their analysis of this they developed a model of adjustment processes (Figure 14.1). This model shows how adjustment to school is an interaction of positive and negative

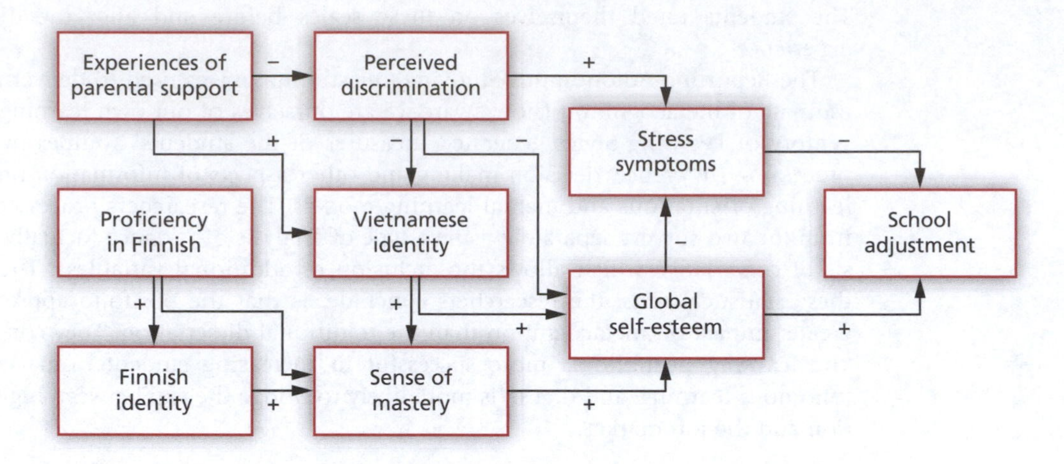

Figure 14.1 Model of interactions in school adjustment

processes (marked + and − in Figure 14.1). For example, proficiency in Finnish directly produces a sense of being in control in the system. As well, it can lead to an assumption of Finnish identity, which reinforces the sense of being in control. This sense of mastery heightens self-esteem, which results in a positive adjustment to school. Stress does the opposite. Stress is increased by a feeling of being discriminated against. Discrimination also reduces self-esteem with a consequential increase in stress. They translated their model into five hypotheses that they could test.

- Vietnamese youth were not expected to be significantly less adjusted to school than their host-population peers.
- Perceived discrimination decreases self-esteem and increases psychological distress.
- Parental support enhances ethnic identity and increases school adjustment.
- Ethnic identity alleviates psychological distress and enhances self-esteem and sense of mastery and improves school adjustment.
- Proficiency in the majority language improves school adjustment.

Examine these hypotheses. The first is a null hypothesis. The other four are research hypotheses that focus on the influence of particular variables.

(ii) Implementing the hypothesis testing strategy

Of all the approaches to education and social science research, this is the one to which new researchers are usually first introduced. There are probably three reasons for this. First, because of the heritage of positivism and the influence of Karl Popper (see sections 2.1.1 and 3.2). There was a period when social science research, across all subjects, was moving rapidly to a situation of quantitative dominance and this influence is still felt. The second reason why students are guided towards a hypothesis testing mode is that it does always require that the whole project is considered before data collection begins, and forward planning whatever strategy we employ. Thirdly, it requires that researchers root their research in an existing framework of knowledge and for those taking this first step in research it is easier (and safer) to do this than to launch into some new conjecture.

The Finnish researchers set out to test their hypotheses by collecting data from 175 Vietnamese school students, the test group, and 337 Finnish students, the comparison group. The students were given the same survey instruments, series of attitude scales to measure:

- school adjustment;
- stress symptoms;
- self-esteem scale;
- sense of mastery;
- parental support;
- cultural identity;
- perceived discrimination;
- proficiency in Finnish.

School adjustment is clearly the dependent variable in the model and the others are independent variables. Each student was measured on these scales and additional demographic data (age, sex, length of residence in Finland) were also collected. The data was analysed in the following way.

- First a form of ANOVA was used to look at differences within and between the two groups. None of the demographic factors was related to school adjustment though, not surprisingly, the length of time a Vietnamese child had been in Finland was related to lower stress, higher self-esteem, proficiency in Finnish and sense of being in control. However, the analysis did show that the Finnish students were less well adjusted to school than the Vietnamese.
- The second stage of the analysis was to correlate all of the independent variables with each other. The correlation coefficients then represented the strength of the + or − linkages in the model. The results are shown in Figure 14.2. The researchers concluded that their model fitted the data, though three relationships were not significant: national identity did not increase the sense of mastery, proficiency in Finnish did not affect Finnish identity and Vietnamese identity did not affect self-esteem.
- The third stage was to revise their model. This is shown in Figure 14.3.

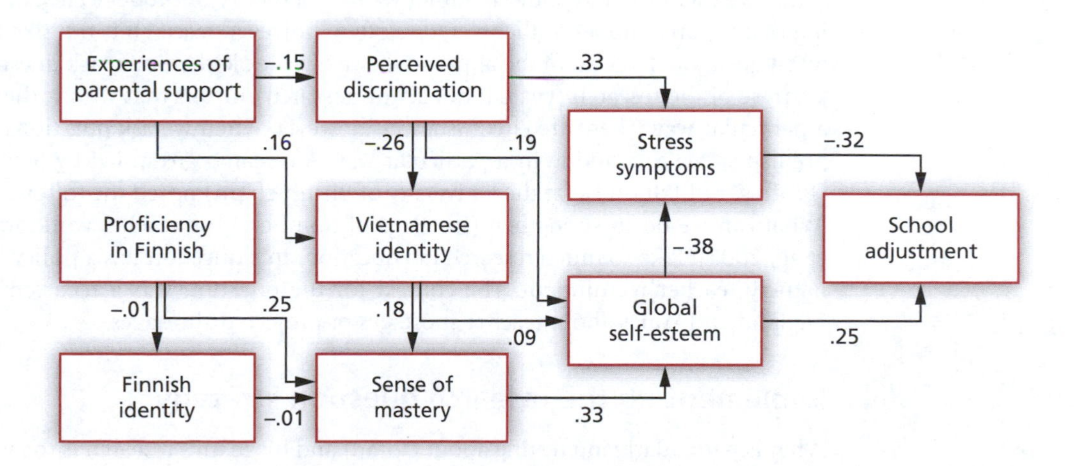

Figure 14.2 Inter-variable correlations for school adjustment

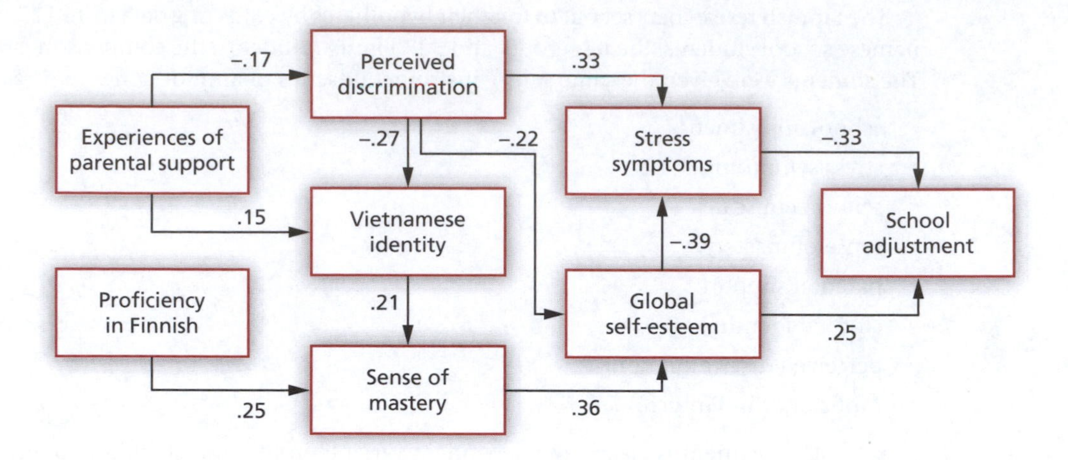

Figure 14.3 Revised model based on significant inter-variable correlations

Key features of hypothesis testing

- A hypothesis should test an existing theory or a model derived from a synthesis and assessment of research.
- A hypothesis should identify dependent and independent variables.
- All variables should be capable of being measured.
- Hypotheses are normally tested using quantitative methods of analysis.
- Statistical tests make assumptions about the data.
- Statistical tests assess the null hypothesis.
- Results of the tests should confirm, reject or reframe the theory or model.

14.8 Posing research questions

(i) Phrasing the research question

When we establish a hypothesis, either we have a theory or model to test or we are hoping to develop a model or theory. Quite often, however, research is not like this, there is just a question. Now all of the approaches we have looked at so far ask questions but the purpose of the research (evaluation, action research) means that we ask the question in a particular way. There are circumstances, however, when we ask questions that do not predispose us to working in a particular way. A research group led by Stephen Gorard (Professor of Education at the University of Birmingham) posed the following question: 'What can we do to strengthen (in terms of numbers) the teacher workforce?' (Gorard et al., 2007). Like so much research in education, this question has a policy implication, namely teacher recruitment. The context for the question was a recurrent concern in England and Wales about teacher shortages or projected shortages.

(ii) Implementing the research question strategy

What is particularly interesting about Gorard and his team's research is the way in which they looked at the broad question. The stimulus to this was their refusal to accept what was the popular view, that the 'teaching workforce appears to lurch from one crisis to another' (p. 420). In asking how far this assertion could be justified, they also explicitly questioned the extent to which it was not justified. This opened up the way into some interesting research and particularly interesting conclusions. But before we look at these, we should assess the options that were open to them in terms of data collection.

To do this we have to think about the circumstances that can give rise to a shortage of teachers. We can say that the problems are on the supply side, that is, not enough people are entering the teaching profession. Alternatively, the problem could be with the demand. Has this increased over time? A third model could see a combination of the two, a shortage of teacher supply in some subjects or areas in part due to an increased demand for teachers or an increase in the numbers leaving the profession. This analysis might direct us to identify the following data needs.

- We could conduct a survey of undergraduates (because these make up the majority of entrants into the profession) to understand their career intentions and the relative attractiveness of different areas of employment. This would give us a sense of the future supply of trainee teachers and whether there was anything that could be done to strengthen the supply.
- We could conduct a survey of teachers to understand what aspects of the work they disliked and what impact this might have on their career intentions. This would allow us to judge whether factors within the control of school management or government were contributing to people leaving the profession.
- We could survey those who have to recruit teachers (education authorities and schools) and ask what problems they are having with teacher recruitment and whether their need for teachers had changed in the recent past or was likely to change in the immediate future.

Gorard's team's solution was not to embrace the second and third of these approaches. Let us think why. The second accepts the assumption that there is a problem and does not question it. If there is not a problem, there is no need to survey. As well, they may have been suspicious of the quality of data they would get. If I wanted to improve my career lot, I might represent myself as more disenchanted than I really am. So the second solution would require an expensive survey for a problem that might not exist.

The third solution represents a difficult data collection problem. Where does responsibility for teacher employment lie? In some cases with the school and in some with a managing authority? Does this mean we survey authorities in respect of the schools they are responsible for and, separately, schools where responsibility for management lies with the school? This could be a sampling nightmare. It would almost certainly be a costly exercise identifying the two populations. Of course, we could always sample schools directly but against this we have to acknowledge that there will be an awful lot of them. In this situation time and cost are factors we must take account of.

The only survey the team did was of undergraduates and, even then, it was set in the context of a secondary data analysis. Obtaining primary research evidence ourselves (for a discussion of primary and secondary data see sections 4.6 and 4.7) is an expensive business, particularly so when the scale of our needs requires a national survey. In these circumstances we should always look to see what official data exist. Gorard and his team's focus was England and Wales. Because of devolved governance, this meant that data sources for England and Wales had to be used. Their secondary data sources for teacher recruitment, teacher vacancies, teachers in post, teachers in training, recruitment to training and outcomes were obtained from: the General Teaching Council for Wales, the Teacher Training Agency (now The Training and Development Agency for Schools), the Universities and Colleges Admission Service, the Universities Council for the Education of Teachers, the National Assembly for Wales, The Department for Education and Skills (now the Department for Children, School and Families and the Department for Innovation, Universities and Skills), National Statistics and the School Teachers' Review Body (responsible for advising the Government on teachers' salaries and conditions). The fragmentation of the data between these bodies was clearly an issue but it does put into perspective that the effort of bringing the data together and the loss of detail through having to use less than perfect data sets was still more cost effective than a mass primary data collection exercise. This data was supplemented with (a) a survey of students in higher education (to determine what proportion might consider teaching as a career and to profile their characteristics) and (b) focus groups with trainee teachers (to establish why they had taken the decision to train).

So what were the conclusions?

- 'There is no great crisis, either passing or looming and so no need for further major and headline-grabbing policy initiatives at a national level' (p. 434).
- 'Teacher training, in general, is an increasingly popular option for graduates' (p. 424).
- 'Most teacher trainees are . . . successful, in terms of qualifying and obtaining a post' (p. 424).
- 'Any problems tend to reflect the regional and subject dispersion of teaching staff rather than any national shortages' (p. 425).
- 'Almost none of the crisis account of teacher supply is well-founded' (p. 426).

And, in passing, Gorard et al. have some critical things to say about previous work in this area that has accepted, uncritically, the idea of a crisis.

What can we conclude from this in relation to how we plan and conduct our research? It is this. While some research questions will predispose us to adopt a particular strategy (such as action research or evaluation), there are many that just encapsulate an issue and set no conditions as to how we should approach the research. We are free agents. Of course, we have the possibility of rephrasing our research question (for example, into a null hypotheses) but this is just a consequence of our freedom to choose. It is how we choose to answer the question that is the key issue and while, from our perspective, this is a matter of obtaining data from here rather than there, using this method rather than that and analysing the data this way rather than that way, from the perspective of those who read our research, they will judge it in terms of 'Does it work?' and 'Is it convincing?' This is the test that all researchers have to pass.

Key features of a research question strategy

- The question determines the approach.
- The question usually arises from a prior awareness of an issue or field of knowledge. It comes about because of a researcher's critical assessment of a field of interest.
- Judge whether the research question could benefit from being addressed within another research strategy.
- The question determines data needs. Data does not necessarily have to be primary data.
- The methodology can be quantitative, qualitative or a mixture of the two.

14.9 Preparing a case for a research programme

As we have said many times, at the heart of good research is a well-planned programme. There are many occasions when this has to be done formally as part of the research procedure (for example, when submitting a proposal for an undergraduate or postgraduate project or a bid for externally funded research) but, even if the research is for our own personal satisfaction, planning is still an essential process. In this section we shall look at the process of preparing a research proposal. What will become apparent is that the process of preparing a proposal is a revision of the main themes in this text.

14.9.1 Getting an idea for research

In Chapter 2 we looked at how philosophy could affect our standpoint on research, considering specifically scientism, humanism, critical theory and postmodernism, and at sources of inspiration that could generate a research issue. Figure 14.4 shows the process at work. There are three sources of stimulus:

1. Literature – what others have researched or claimed (including theories and models to explain the educational process);
2. Policy about education goals and processes or influencing those goals and processes;
3. Our own experience of education, as a learner or as a teacher, and of the organisation of educational provision as well as of the classroom experience.

We engage with these stimuli. We think about them; we link up different strands and begin to question what we find. What should we be doing? What if we did things differently? The sorts of questions we ask and the type of engagement we have are influenced by our own values and perhaps even by a philosophical perspective.

This process should be going on in the background all the time. It should be embedded in the modules we take and in the courses we design. We should be constantly adding to our knowledge and then sorting it, sifting it and, finally, judging it. Without this background process, research ideas will not be generated. The process requires that we remain aware of trends in education and that our engagement with the material involves a debate with the author or producer. We should always understand where an author is coming from. The preface to a book will usually give us a clue (have you read the preface to this book?).

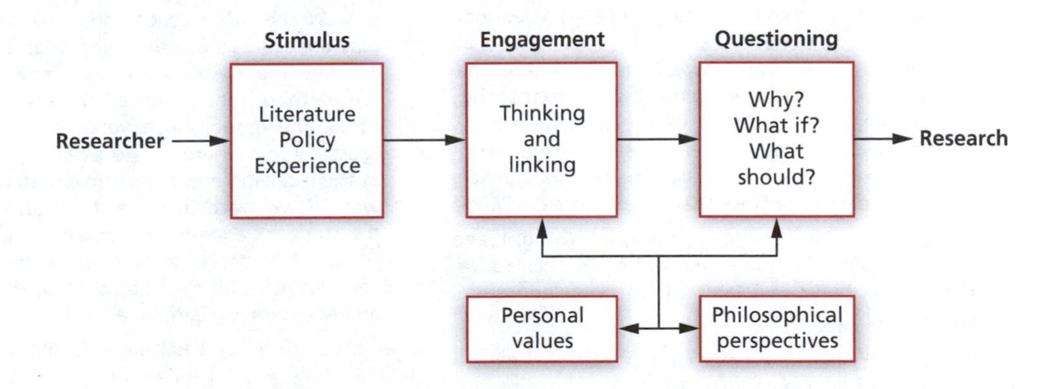

Figure 14.4 The background to research

Out of this process a research issue will emerge. Sometimes, however, we have to kick-start the process. Activity 14.1 is an attempt to do just this. Learning how this happened for others can also help us with the process. Geoffrey Walford, now Professor of Education at Oxford University, edited a book in which researchers reflected on the research process (Walford, 1991).

- Stephen Ball (Professor at the Institute of Education in London) explains that his research on the micropolitics of a school came out of a course on school organisation he taught. He found that there was little literature and that the literature that existed was poor quality.
- Barbara Tizard (Emeritus Professor at the Institute of Education in London) and Martin Hughes (Professor at Bristol University) describe a study they conducted with others into 4-year-old girls at home and later at school. They explain that their work had its origins in a debate about language and social class, its implications for language development and education and the wider issue of the benefit of pre-school education.
- Geoffrey Walford's stimulus to carrying out research on city technology colleges (state-funded schools in England and Wales that are independent of local political control) was their introduction as part of new Government policy.

Now look at Activity 14.2.

Activity 14.1 Identifying a research strategy

Below are contexts for a research question. Your tasks are:

- to identify which research strategies might be appropriate for the issue
- to select one which you would use and to explain why
- to set out the research question you would seek to answer.

At the end of each context statement is a reference to the paper from which it came and where you can see how the researcher(s) tackled the topic.

1. Training programmes for students wishing to become primary or secondary teachers are obviously quite different. This reflects the development differences in the children and a curriculum designed to meet the needs of each age group. There is always an issue over how effective a professional programme is in developing students so that they can meet the demands of the workplace. How would you assess whether courses for training primary teachers and those training secondary teachers developed professional competence?

Source: Wong, A., Chong, S., Choy, D., Wong, I. and Goh, K. (2008) *Australian Journal of Teacher Education*, 33(3), 77–93, available at http://ajte.education.edu.edu.au.

2. The story has had a place in the classroom experiences of young children for a great many years. The image of children sitting around the storyteller is one that many people will be able to conjure up. Listening, however, can cover a range of engagements from the quietly bored to a child actively experiencing the plot or place in their mind's eye. Do we know, though, how children engage with books? If there are differences are they due more to the type of book or to the child? What could you do to find out?

Source: Moschovahi, E. and Meadows, S. (2005) *Early Childhood Research and Practice*, 7(2), no page numbers, available at http://ecrp.uinc.edu/.

3. Individual performance is something that sports stars and musicians have in common, and the process of preparing for that outcome is long and arduous. Relationships are a crucial part of this process, the sports coach and music teacher both play the same role with their students. The learning and training process is also important; different methods may produce different results. Very often, the model we have of the development process is one where the student is a passive player at the receiving end of instruction and advice. But what if we were to understand and appreciate the student's experiences, emotions and feelings, could this improve development? Your task is to consider how this might be done with students at an early stage of learning a musical instrument.

Source: Creech, A. and Hallam, S. (2006) 'Every Picture Tells a Story: Pupil Representations of Learning the Violin', *Educate*, 6(1), 35–56, available at http://www.educatejournal.org.

Activity 14.2 Identifying research themes

Sometimes what a government thinks is important can help us focus on an area of interest and opportunity.

Go to the Scottish Government's website (www.scotland.gov.uk), follow the 'Topics' link and then the link to the research page. Choose either the 'Children and Young People' link or the 'Education and Lifelong Learning' link and then follow the link to 'publications'. Look through the publications for the last two years, categorise them and assess where the research priorities are.

Write a reflective review that brings out:

- the knowledge that you have gained;
- the areas/themes that you think are particularly important in educational terms;
- why you think they are important;
- which topic you might be interested in exploring.

14.9.2 Don't start if you cannot finish

With any research project we have to judge (a) whether the scale is sufficient for us to make the impact we need to make in order to be successful and (b) whether we have the wherewithal to deliver at this scale. Chapter 1 advised auditing the resources available and in section 2.4.4 we set out the types of resource that need to be considered. The question of impact depends in large part where we are in our research careers. For an undergraduate project, we have to convince our tutors that we have gone about our data collection and analysis in the right way. For a doctorate, it is our examiners that have to believe that not only is the way we have worked acceptable but also that our research results add something to the stock of knowledge. To achieve this impact, our project must have potential. But how do we assess potential and scale before we begin?

The key questions to ask ourselves are, 'Are the data available?' and 'Where are they?' To be able to answer these questions we should be aware of primary and secondary data sources (Chapter 4) and how we will identify primary sources (Chapter 6). If the answer to our question about data availability and location are, 'Yes, but they are hard to get at', we need to see if our resources are sufficient. If they are not and we cannot increase them, then the research is beyond us and we have to look for a new topic. Activity 14.3 will give you practice at preparing a case for a research project.

14.9.3 Arguing the case for the research

By this time we are beginning to get an idea of (a) whether the topic has the potential to convince our judges and (b) whether it is feasible for us to undertake it. Assuming that we have a green light on both counts, our next action is to produce a convincing argument that we should be permitted to do the research.

Activity 14.3 Arguing a case for research

Either for a theme you identified in Activity 14.2 or a topic that interests you, assess it against the following questions:

- What evidence can you produce that others will think that it is a significant issue?
- What data will you require in order to draw conclusions?
- Where are these data located? How will you assess them?
- How long will it take to collect the data?
- Are there any additional costs other than your time in collecting the data?
- What length of time is available for the project?

(i) The field of enquiry

There are two levels to the field of enquiry. First, we have to convince other educationalists of the importance in advancing the general field of enquiry. Second, we then have to persuade them that the question we want to answer is appropriate.

Let us now deal with the first of these two issues. On what basis can we justify research?

- *It has never been done before:* it is unlikely that this will be claimed by researchers undertaking their first project. If we are in this position and we do make this claim, then be sure, people will be looking for the mistakes in our thinking.
- *Testing out a general theory model or philosophical perspective in a specific context:* this is entirely feasible for new researchers and is what many actually do if they make a claim for originality.
- *Looking at the impact of policy in a local context:* again entirely appropriate because the context limits the scale of the investigation.
- *Seeking to replicate a finding found elsewhere:* a new piece of research should be validated with additional studies to assess whether it is generally applicable or a one-off instance or a mistake.
- *Picking up a theme in one area and applying it to another:* this could be finding a research theme in one country that has not been applied in one's own, or finding a theme in another subject or branch of education.
- *Extending existing research:* picking up where other researchers have finished by taking their assessment of what additional research needs to be done.

These are not the only justifications we can use but they are some of the most common. But justification for research has to have something going for it other than that it has never been done before. There has to be something in it that others will find valuable. For this we need to probe the justification. For example, if we wished to replicate a finding, the question to ask is, 'Why?' The most likely answer is that this would give us confidence in building some sort of theory and this certainly would be valuable. The reverse would be true if our goal were to test theory. A theory without explanatory or predictive power in the real world is of little value. And, if we were testing policy, we would want to know why it was or wasn't working. You may say that all of this is implicit in the original justification and while this may be true, our role as researchers is to make things *explicit* so that others can be convinced by *our reasoning* and not *their interpretation* of our argument. This is something that beginner researchers often fail to do well and while the importance of something can be clear in their minds, other people may be less insightful. If there is one piece of advice to offer it is 'spell it out!'

(ii) The research issue/question

Now let us turn to the second issue, convincing our audience that we have chosen the best question or issue to address. In essence what we have to do here is demonstrate that of all the aspects of our research issue that could be tackled, why the one we have chosen is the one to address first. What reasons can we put forward to support it?

- We are dealing with the most important element or factor first. 'Importance' can refer to explanatory power or to political significance or to something specific to the circumstances of the research.

- The nature of the environment in which we are carrying out the research could be an influence. It could be social concern about quality in a specific school or an educational concern, for instance differential rates of exclusion.
- We may focus on a specific aspect of an issue because that is manageable within the resource envelope available to us. This should not be the total argument for carrying out research but it is a reasonable supplementary argument for anyone with a restricted timescale for the work (such as an undergraduate student).

What else can we use in the argument to bolster our claim for the validity and value of our research theme? The answer to this is the claims made by other researchers. We use what they say about their research to support our claim for our own research. The danger of this is that the whole edifice of claims can become like a house of cards, liable to fall down when a foundation is undermined. What we have to do to prevent this is ensure that the claims are rooted in some incontrovertible evidence. Our literature search (see Chapter 5) should be used to provide support for our claim. As researchers we should enhance our skill in synthesising and shaping other people's work to help make our argument. Activity 14.4 provides an opportunity for this.

Activity 14.4 Using literature to present a case

There is, quite naturally, great interest in the trajectories people follow through their lives. If, in their background, people have a sound educational foundation, we often refer to their trajectories as 'career paths' or 'employment paths'. Because of the fast-moving nature of the twenty-first century economy, we know that we have to embrace new skills and ways of working and many employers as well as Government supports us with lifelong learning opportunities. But what if our original premise is not met, that there is no sound educational background, what then?

This is the question: 'Are there patterns in the lives of young people that will predispose them to a trajectory that leads to behavioural problems, antisocial behaviour and, ultimately, criminality?' Your task is to conduct a literature search to consider what evidence exists. You should assemble at least ten references, summarise their conclusions and write a report of 500–700 words.

After this, look at Sections 3 and 4 of the Research Report by Peter McCarthy's research team from the University of Newcastle upon Tyne, below.

Source: McCarthy, P., Laing, K. and Waller, J. (2004) 'Offenders of the Future? Assessing the Risk of Children and Young People Becoming Involved in Criminal or Antisocial Behaviour', *Research Report 545*, Department for Education and Skills, HMSO, available at http://www.dsf.gov.uk/research/data/uploadfiles/RR545.pdf (accessed January 2009).

14.9.4 Determining strategy and methods

Our selection of a strategy will be informed by:

- the phrasing of our research question (see section 2.1.5);
- the data that we need – and where those data are and how we are going to collect and process them;
- and, of course, the resources available to us.

We may have to go through several cycles of testing out options before we are able to select and plan a strategy. But once we have a strategy, that is not the end of the issue because it is not only ourselves who have to be convinced, it is the audience for our research output. In other words, as with the selection of the topic, we have to have an argument for what we have done that is as convincing for others as it is for ourselves.

To be successful at this stage we have to know about data sources, methods of collecting data and methods of describing and analysing what we have collected. This means that we have to be confident about everything from Chapters 6 through to 13! We have to be able to argue for this method in preference to that method. There are two things we can do to convince an audience:

- First, we can justify our selected methods (or non-use of methods) on the basis of their strengths, weaknesses and requirements – that is, on the basis of their suitability.
- Second, we can demonstrate that the methods we propose have been successfully used by others in similar circumstances. This is validatory evidence. And, once again, everything has to be explicit.

As part of this whole process it is good practice to prepare a plan that sets out a schedule of activities. If you are doing a project as part of a course, many institutions will require a plan as part of the project proposal. The reason for this is that they need to be sure that you understand what you are taking on. A plan is a clear demonstration that you understand what is required to make your strategy operational. If you do not appreciate what it takes to gather the data (and many people new to research underestimate the time required), this will be apparent in the plan. A plan, however, is more than an allocation of time for a process in the strategy because the process will inevitably have different elements to it. If data is going to be gathered through a questionnaire, the plan should show how much time is allocated to:

- developing the questionnaire;
- identifying the population;
- testing the questionnaire;
- revising the questionnaire;
- establishing the sample size required;
- determining the sampling method;
- drawing the sample;
- contacting the sample;
- administering the questionnaire.

And for each of these stages we would have to ask, 'What could go wrong?' and build in a contingency.

There should never be any time in a research programme when nothing is happening. Amongst activities that can always fill time are:

- ensuring that we have the skills to undertake an activity later in the schedule (for example, that we know how to input data into SPSS or any other program and that we are confident that we can interpret the results);
- continuing a literature search and review;
- drafting sections of the final report (for example, the argument for the research, how other people have approached the issue, the strategy and method adopted);
- reviewing the plan to see if our experience suggests we should make changes.

14.9.5 Making sense of what we have

Once we have our data, our task is then to extract meaning from it. How we do this depends on the data that we have. The broad goal, however, with all data is (a) to look for pattern and meaningful relationships and (b) to demonstrate the wider implications of what we have found. In most cases how we do this is fairly straightforward and will fit into one of the following categories:

- We can explain what we have found in theoretical or conceptual terms.
- We can judge whether an action or activity has met its objectives and how modifications to processes can improve outcomes.
- We can identify courses of action that should not be followed to avoid failure or that should be followed to ensure success.

With *statistical and numerical data* (both data that we have collected ourselves and data already published), we should begin by portraying it and describing it. Shape and pattern in our data are indicators of processes at work that we should seek to understand and explain. The methods we looked at in Chapter 10 allow us to do this and also to manipulate the data to explore relationships. While Chapter 10 introduced us to graphical methods, Chapter 12 introduced us to the idea of numerical descriptions of data (the ideas of central tendency, spread, peakedness and skew). Chapter 13 showed us how we could look for and assess association and relationships in our data.

With *non-numerical data* (observations, text, audio and visual recordings) we have to choose an approach that fits in with (a) our research position and (b) our research data. Are we neutral researchers seeking 'truth'? Do we believe that our task is to understand 'truth' as people themselves appreciate it? Do we think that how people respond to life opportunities is conditioned by where they sit in terms of social, political and economic relationships? And if we do, is our task as researchers to explain this to other researchers or to help people understand their situation and free them from their situation? All of these are positions that researchers can adopt and each pushes us towards a way of working and a way of interpreting what we find. Our data and our research question also influence our selection of a strategy. If our purpose is to see how people interact through talking, then conversation analysis may be the first approach we should look at. If our purpose is to see how organisations use words to present themselves, we may look at discourse analysis or semiotics as an approach in the first instance. If we want to build a model from our investigation, perhaps grounded theory should be what we consider first.

What we should take away from this is how similar qualitative and quantitative analysis of data actually are in their requirement that we understand the things that affect our choice of method before we start. With quantitative analysis, the research hypothesis and measurement scale are key influences. With qualitative analysis, we should understand the influence of our philosophical position and data. In both cases we are dealing with a research approach that is 'joined up', where what we do in one part of the investigation affects how we proceed in another. If we do not have this overview, we can find that we create problems for ourselves.

14.10 Benefiting from research

Undertaking a programme of research affects everyone who does it. There will be times when it is exciting and times when it is a burden. Sometimes this can affect our self-confidence. There will be people we can talk to if this happens, colleagues and tutors, but we should always remember that when we started out someone with experience thought that the research theme was a good idea.

There are, however, some things that we can do to sustain our commitment. We are driven forward by the goal of producing a report, dissertation or thesis. We recognise this as the output of all our work. It demonstrates how we have responded to an issue and embodies how we have intellectualised it. It is our product and its existence should be a matter of satisfaction and pride. If, however, we focus only on the end product of all our work, we will fail to appreciate the other benefits that doing research brings. Let's enumerate them.

- Research will inevitably take us into new areas. We will read new authors (and with the worldwide Web available to us these can be drawn from all parts of the globe). This process is stimulating. We begin to make connections, tie up things in different ways and find new patterns. The process advances our thinking and our understanding and, ultimately, puts us in a position to make real conceptual or practical advances that arise when our minds are stretched.
- Second, we become aware of new approaches (ways of collecting data, statistical tests) that we may substitute for others in our plan. Even if we do not do this, we have expanded our armoury of procedures.
- Third, we gain experience. We see what works and what does not. The changes we have to make to the way we conduct our research may be the result of a failure in planning or the result of something unforeseen. Either way, we have learnt something.

The great danger is that we will be so caught up with producing the end product that we will lose sight of how the research process is changing us. It is good practice to reflect on our work and to maintain an accurate analytical report or diary that identifies not only what we did but what we learnt from doing it.

14.11 The value of education research

Now that we are close to the end of our journey, it is worth reflecting on the value of research in and on education. The vast majority of education research has been done to make a difference. All research should enhance and increase our knowledge. Even if we show that a classroom teaching intervention has no effect or leads to poorer outcomes, the research has not been a wasted effort. We have increased our knowledge and, if the intention was to roll out a process to other teachers, we have at least saved resources and possibly saved the education world from a disaster. We should not, however, confuse the value of increasing our knowledge with the value that some people place upon that knowledge. Research that seems idiosyncratic or of no relevance to the lives we lead or research that develops theory for the sake of developing theory can be judged by people in one generation to be of no value, only for some of it to be found much later to be a springboard to innovations of a life-changing character.

But the vast bulk of research in education is not like this. Its value lies in its ability to have an effect, to change things or to confirm the value of changes that have been made. Research into classroom practice, into teaching methods, into behavioural management, into the organisation and leadership of educational institutions, into the life experiences of children and young people are all carried out with a purpose, and that is more than just 'to know'. Educational research is, at its core, practical and its broad purpose is to seek improvement. If we move our gaze from practice in the classroom to how education provision should be organised to achieve a specific purpose, that is, from practice to policy, we find that education research is still concerned with impact; why did or didn't this succeed? How can we deliver multi-agency working? Do schools with independent governance achieve more for their pupils? It would be hard to judge that this knowledge is not valuable.

But education research is valuable in another way too. Research is undertaken by students, by teachers, by lecturers and by research professionals. For each of these, every time they start a research project, they begin a journey of personal and professional learning and discovery. Research is an exercise in solving problems and this has an impact on the personal development of everyone who is or has been a researcher. As individuals create knowledge, they grow their understanding and their confidence to meet new challenges. This process has repercussions for the education sector. There is a willingness to accept and act on a weight of evidence. There is active debate on goals and methods, something that is absolutely necessary for the best ideas to emerge. All of this grows capacity and capability within education and means that education as a sector is more capable of meeting the challenge of change.

However, there are consequences in the way in which educational research happens that can make life difficult for the new researcher. The educational research production process is more like a cottage industry than anything else. This is not to say that the research output is not good but that there is a large quantity of it worldwide and, until recently, there was not a lot of joining up the massive research output taking place. For this reason, it is important that every researcher looks at books and journals whose goal is to synthesise research in particular fields, before starting any research enquiry. Because what we intend for our research may well have been done before.

Research is a messy business. It has to be because the issues we face and the questions we tackle are so varied and we have to address them in unique ways. As our knowledge and understanding of the research process grows, so will we gain in confidence to do it our way. The journey to become a good researcher is not short but it is satisfying. Research well done is exhilarating and always a satisfying element of any career.

Summary

In this chapter we have been concerned with the process of shaping a research approach. There are some key learning points to this.

- First, while we have terms like research strategy/approach, methodology and method, the way we use these terms to describe what we do is not necessarily stable. An evaluation, for example, can be of a case study, while a case study is an analytical description of a situation and an approach in its own right. We can set up an experiment without a hypothesis and we can establish a hypothesis and conclude that experimentation is the best way to collect the data. This is confusing at first but we have to realise that research is rarely about hard and fast rules and clear situations. Its principal concerns are, 'What is appropriate?' and 'What works?' This results in fuzzy situations and it is something we have to live with.
- This inevitably produces uncertainty amongst new researchers. The best way to combat this is to be confident in our knowledge of research procedure and research methods.

- Notwithstanding this, there are clearly ways of working within frameworks that others would recognise. If we work within these frameworks (case study, evaluation, ethnography, action research, experimentation and hypothesis testing), it is usually because we want to put a question in a particular way.
- The consequence of working within a framework is that it predisposes us to collect and/or analyse our data in a particular way. The implication of the way we ask our research question can, therefore, be far-reaching.
- Finally, the process of putting a research strategy together is conditioned by the issue, the way we would like to work, the resources available to us and the need to convince others with our results. There is no requirement that we should work within named strategies. These are merely islands of relative stability in a world where what works is the only real test of acceptability.

Further reading

Case study

Yin, R.K. (2003) *Case Study Research: Design and Methods,* Sage, London.

Case study research makes use of all of the data gathering and analysis techniques considered here. If we undertake a case study, we need to show (a) why it is appropriate and (b) how we would progress the study and assemble and process the data. The introduction to Robert Yin's book is convincing on both these counts.

Evaluation

Rossi, P., Lipsey, M.W. and Freeman, H.E. (2004) *Evaluation: A Systematic Approach,* Sage, London.

Many texts on evaluation spend much time on methods of data collection and analysis that are little different from what is found in this book. This text has some distinctive sections that give a real sense of why evaluation requires its own mindset. The authors identify different types of evaluation, the political dimensions to evaluation, the process of identifying evaluation questions (a skill in itself) and estimating programme effects (including cost-benefit analysis).

Research questions and proposals

Andrews, R. (2003) *Research Questions,* Continuum, London.

Punch, K. (2006) *Developing Effective Research Proposals,* Sage, London.

If you are struggling to develop a research question, Richard Andrews' book may well be what you are looking for. His approach is to see the main research question as being composed of a series of subsidiary questions. Chapter 2 (How Questions Emerge) will certainly be helpful to most new researchers.

There are many good books on preparing research proposals. I like this one by Keith Punch because it puts right in the foreground decisions that we have to make and gives examples.

Reflection

Shacklock, G. and Smyth, J. (eds) (1998) *Being Reflexive in Critical Educational and Social Research,* Falmer, London.

One of the themes of this chapter is that we should reflect upon our research activities in order to recognise and acknowledge our learning gains. Reflection is a difficult skill. Our experience becomes the object of our intellectualisation and while we can willingly acknowledge our successes, our failures can be more problematic. Actually doing it, however, can release us from our demons and enable us to attain an insight that yields greater inner strength. This book presents 11 studies within a broad paradigm of critical education and social research. I was particularly taken by Andrew Sparkes' chapter (5) in which he acknowledges the difficulty of a 'fair trade' between researcher and researched and struck by one sentence in Noreen Garman's chapter (8): 'I discovered that writing is a *method of enquiry,* a way of finding out about myself and my topic' (p. 130). On reflection, an appropriate sentiment on which to end!

References

Bates, M. (2008) 'Work-Integrated Curricula in University Programs', *Higher Education Research and Development*, 27(4), 305–317.

Bergendahl, C. (2003) 'Acton Research as a Means of Professional Development: Reflections on Research and Action in University Chemistry Education', *Journal of In-Service Education*, 29(3), 363–374.

Bowker, R. (2002) 'Evaluating Teaching and Learning Strategies at the Eden Project', *Evaluation and Research in Education*, 16(3), 123–135.

Creech, A. and Hallam, S. (2006) 'Every Picture Tells a Story: Pupil Representations of Learning the Violin', *Educate*, 6(1), 35–56.

Forsberg, L. (2007) 'Involving Parents Through School Letters: Mothers, Fathers and Teachers Negotiating Children's Education and Rearing', *Ethnography and Education*, 2(3), 273–288.

Gorard, S., See, B.H., Smith, E. and White, P. (2007) 'What Can We Do to Strengthen the Teacher Workforce?', *International Journal of Lifelong Education*, 26(4), 419–437.

Meeus, W., Van Petegem, P. and Meijer, J. (2008) 'Portfolio as a Means of Promoting Autonomous Learning in Teacher Education: A Quasi-experimental Study', *Educational Research*, 50(4), 361–386.

Moschovahi, E. and Meadows, S. (2005) 'Young Children's Cognitive Engagement during Classroom Book Reading: Differences According to Book, Text Genre, and Story Format', *Early Childhood Research and Practice*, 7(2), no page numbers (available at http://ecrp.uiuc.edu/v7n2/index.html).

Sandford, R., Duncombe, R. and Armour, K. (2008) 'The Role of Physical Activity/Sport in Tackling Youth Disaffection and Anti-Social Behaviour', *Educational Review*, 60(4), 419–435.

Tihanyi, K. and du Toit, S. (2005) 'Reconciliation Through Integration? An Examination of South Africa's Reconciliation Process in Racially Integrating High Schools', *Conflict Resolution Quarterly*, 23(1), 25–41.

Walford, G. (ed.) (1991 and 2003), *Doing Educational Research*, Routledge, London.

Westera, W., van den Henk, J. and van de Vrie, E. (2004) 'Strategic Alliances in Education; The Knowledge Engineering Web', *Innovations in Education & Teaching International*, 41(3), 317–328.

Wong, A., Chong, S., Choy, D., Wong, I. and Goh, K. (2008) 'A Comparison of Perceptions of Knowledge and Skills Held by Primary and Secondary Teachers: From the Entry to Exit of their Preservice Programme', *Australian Journal of Teacher Education*, 33(3), 77–93.

Appendix 1

Calculating sample size

In section 6.8 we saw how to calculate a sample size using on-line calculators. In this Appendix, we shall see how we can do this for ourselves. To understand, you should have read:

- Chapter 11 – calculation of the mean and standard deviation and standard error.
- Chapter 12 – derivation and use of z values.

How much error are we prepared to accept?

The first approach to determining the size of our sample is to ask, 'How accurate do we want our sample to be?' or, to put it another way, 'How much error are we prepared to accept?' To understand how we reach a decision, we have to return to something we first came across in Chapter 3. Here we looked at how many combinations of a given sample size there were in a population whose size was known. The answer, as the worked example in Case Study 3.3 showed, is an awful lot. Let us think about all of these possible samples for a moment and, to help understand the point, let us imagine that our research requires us to draw a sample of teachers from a single administrative area. The samples we can draw will have two extremes.

- On the one hand, we could draw samples that are composed of the *most typical teachers*. If we were to calculate the average age of the teachers in our samples, they would be very close to the average age of all teachers.
- On the other hand, we could draw samples of the *most atypical teachers*. At one extreme, there is a sample of the youngest teachers in the area and, at the other, an equally valid sample of the oldest teachers. Remember that we are talking about *all possible samples* that we might draw, so while the average age of all teachers might be 37 years and 8 months, there are *valid samples* that could represent the average age as 24 years and 2 months or 64 years and 9 months. While these are valid samples, they

are not particularly representative. There are, of course, many, many other samples lying between these two extremes and distributed around the population average. Fortunately for us, if we draw the sample randomly, then we are more likely to choose average teachers simply because there are more of them.

If we were to plot all of our possible samples on a graph, then we would finish up with a distribution like that in Figure A1. What this shows is that, on the extreme left and right of the curve is a single sample of all of the youngest (on the left) and all of the oldest (on the right) teachers in the area. In the centre of the distribution, around the average of the population, are many samples that generate an average teacher age close to the population average. This distribution is called the *sampling distribution*. It is a theoretical distribution that shows every possible sample of a given size.

One of the things we should note about this distribution is its shape. It is the same as the distribution we met in Chapter 12, the *normal distribution*. This sampling distribution is also a normal distribution. Whether we have a sample of 20 students, 50 students, 100 students or 1,000 students, the sampling distribution will *always* have this bell shape. The normal distribution has some important characteristics. First, it is symmetrical (around the population mean in our example). Second, we can define limits within which a given proportion of the distribution (in this case of all possible samples for a given size) will fall. These limits are called *standard deviations* (we met them in Chapter 12). In a normal distribution the following are constant:

- 68% of the values in the distribution fall within one standard deviation either side of the centre, 34% to the left and 34% to the right;
- 95% lie between two standard deviations of the central point, 47.5% to the left and 47.5% to the right;
- 99.7% lie between three standard deviations of the central point, 49.85% to the left and 49.85% to the right.

We can use this information about the characteristics of a normal distribution to calculate sample size. In essence, the question we shall be asking is, 'How accurately do we want to estimate the population average?'

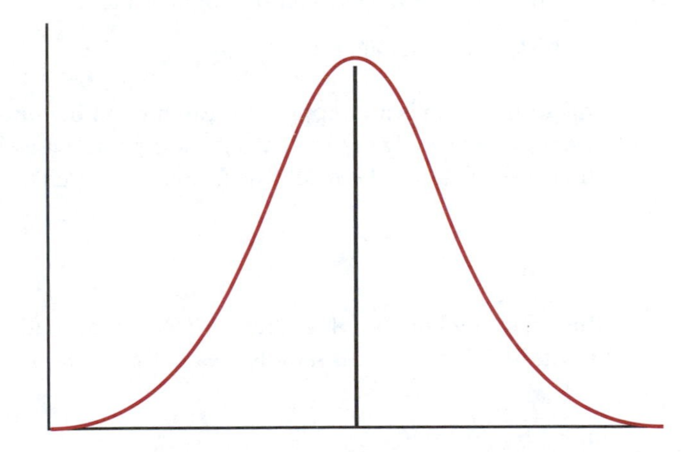

Figure A1 Sampling distribution: plot of mean values of all samples of a given size

Calculating sample size using standard error

Let us change our terminology a little and call the average the mean (see Chapter 12). It is a simple calculation that most of us are familiar with – add up all of the values and divide the total by the number of values. We can express it using a statistical equation:

$$\bar{x} = \sum_{1}^{n} \frac{x}{n}$$

where $\bar{x}$ is the mean of x

x is a single value

$\sum_{1}^{n}$ represents the process of summing all the values of x from the first (1) to the nth

— indicates the division process

n is the total number of x_s

If we turn back to our sampling distribution, it is clear that the accuracy with which the samples estimate the population mean decreases as the sample moves towards the extremes of the distribution. The implication of this is that when we calculate a sample mean, each and every one is likely to have an error in its estimate of the population mean. The scale of the possible error is derived from the sampling distribution. For example, there is a 68% chance that the sample is drawn from within one standard deviation of the population mean. Thus the standard deviation of the sampling distribution is the standard error of the mean. Again, we can express this as a simple statistical expression:

$$SE\,\bar{X} = \delta/\sqrt{n}$$

where $SE\,\bar{X}$ is the standard error of the sample mean

δ is the calculated standard deviation of the sample (that is, the value either side of the sample mean that defines the limits of 68% of the sample)

n is the total number of sample values

$\sqrt{\ }$ is the square root

This formulation is an important breakthrough because if we know δ from our sample, then we can specify the level of standard error that we are prepared to accept. Let us call this level of standard error *d*. The formula can then be rewritten:

$$n = \frac{\delta^2}{d}$$

Thus if, in our samples of teachers, δ is 22.4 years and we want the population mean to be within 5.0 years of our sample mean, the sample size n is given by:

$$n = \frac{(22.4)^2}{5} = 20.07$$

However, before we rush in and make contact with 20 teachers, we should think about the implications of this. How confident are we that we will get the results we want? The answer is that we can only be 68% confident because we only took one standard deviation. From a statistical point of view, this is a pretty risky situation. It would be better to be 95% confident, that is, two standard deviations. The formula then becomes:

$$n = \frac{(1.96 \times 22.4)^2}{5} = 77.1$$

The only value that we are not familiar with here is 1.96. This is called a *z score* and it is derived from the normal distribution (see Chapter 13). The z value identifies the proportion of the normal distribution that lies between the central point (0) and any z value. If we are concerned with both sides of the distribution, then the proportion is double. The z value for a 95% level of confidence is 1.96, that is, 95% of a normal distribution will fall ± 1.96.

Determining sample size using sequential estimation

An alternative approach to the determination of sample size is to use a method called *sequential estimation*. The origins of this approach are to be found in the work of an Austrian statistician, Abraham Wald, who fled his native country for the USA in 1938. Known for his work in economics, he moved into statistics while at the US Center for Naval Analyses at Columbia University. One of his achievements was to analyse patterns of bullet holes in aircraft in order to identify how best to reinforce them. This was an important issue because the extra weight of the reinforcement affected flight distance, so it was important not to over-armour a plane. Wald's work on quality control in factory production in the Second World War led to the development of a statistical test to evaluate interventions. But the principle on which Wald developed his test can also be applied to the problem of sampling.

Wald's approach was to monitor results and to use the test named after him to estimate whether an intervention was effective. The monitoring was continuous, so each analysis represented a new sub-sample added to the data. This can be applied directly to a sampling procedure. Imagine that we want to explore student performance on a final year assessment and the amount of tuition that they had received for each part of the course. We are fortunate enough to have access to all student records in a university. It would be easy enough for us to carry out a systematic sample but when should we stop? Sequential estimation would work in this way. We might decide to sample at the rate of 1 in 70. For the first sample, we would calculate the mean assessment score of all students. We would repeat this sample (that is, sample again at a rate of 1 in 70) and combine the results with the first sample and calculate the mean score. The process would continue and, after each sample and calculation, we would look to see how the new mean differed from the previous mean. We would expect initial variation to settle down and once this happened we could be reasonably sure that we had a sufficiently large sample of students based on their test scores. Wald's approach was considered so important that its circulation was restricted for fear that it would become known to enemy spies.

Appendix 2

Calculating critical values for the Kolmogorov-Smirnov test

These calculations are for a two-tailed test.

Test of goodness of fit (one sample test)

Critical value for D when sample is greater than 35:

90% (.10) $\frac{1.22}{\sqrt{n}}$ where n is sample size

95% (.05) $\frac{1.36}{\sqrt{n}}$

99% (.01) $\frac{1.63}{\sqrt{n}}$

For values below 35, refer to tables.

Test of difference (two sample test)

Critical value for D:

90% (.10) 1.22 $\frac{n_1 + n_2}{\sqrt{n_1 n_2}}$ where n_1 and n_2 are the two sample sizes

95% (.05) 1.36 $\frac{n_1 + n_2}{\sqrt{n_1 n_2}}$

99% (.01) 1.63 $\frac{n_1 + n_2}{\sqrt{n_1 n_2}}$

Glossary

Term	Definition	Section
Action research	A style of research in which an issue or problem is identified, a way forward is tried out and the outcome assessed in the context of the goal (the issue or problem resolution). This can give rise to another phase of action in resolving the issue or problem. The approach is used by professionals (including teachers) as a way of improving their own practice.	2.1.4 & 14.5
Analysis of variance (ANOVA)	A statistical test that seeks to establish whether two or more data sets are significantly different from each other. The test uses the variance in the data sets and apportions the variance to that within the individual sets of data, that within the combined sets of data and a residual (the difference between the sum of the individual sets and the combined set).	13.6.5
Asynchronous	A process or event that is not in time with another. For example, learning with tutor feedback subsequent to student activity is asynchronous as is an interview conducted by email.	
Attitude	A perspective held by a person in respect of an object, concept, idea, event or other person. The attitude is usually represented as being for or against.	
Attitude scale	A means of quantifying a person's attitude. The scale is usually a composite measure.	8.8 & 8.9
Bar Graph (chart)	A representation of the frequency of a categorical variable (such as ethnicity) in which the horizontal axis represents the variable and the vertical shows the frequency (see also histogram).	10.2.2
Benchmarking	This term is used in two ways. It refers to the comparison of, say a school or education authority, with another that has similar characteristics. It is also used in an evaluative study to assess the impact of an intervention. The benchmark is a description of the situation and outcomes before the intervention.	2.1.4
Bias	A process that generates data that are not representative of the parent population. Bias can occur through faults in sampling, poor practice in data collection and inappropriate (even deliberate) misinterpretation of evidence.	9.15

Term	Definition	Section
Bivariate	This means two variables. It is usually used where two variables (such as the number of children with free school meals and the index of deprivation for their community) are plotted against each other.	
Boolean	A form of algebra developed by George Boole and used in search engines. It allows us to include/or exclude items, to group terms and so on.	
Case Study	A study of an individual circumstance or situation (such as a failing school). The case can be selected because it is unusual or because it is typical.	2.1.4 & 6.6.5 & 14.2
Categorical data	Data that can be put into a group or category, such as independent and public schools and the grouping of people according to their lifestyles. The classification of data in this way enables some quantification (numbers of data units in the group) of data that is, inherently, not quantifiable. For this reason, categorical data is sometimes referred to as counted data.	
Cause	The idea that there are consequences when something occurs. The idea of a cause creating an effect is often central to social science research and certainly essential if we conduct experiments, construct hypotheses or develop theories or models.	
Cause and effect	A key approach in social science and educational research in which a researcher attempts to show that a variable (the cause) produces and impact (the effect) in a second variable or in a situation. The impact is usually measured as a quantity.	2.1.1
Census	A survey of a whole population. Most states conduct a population census, typically every ten years.	4.5.3
Central tendency	The idea that in any bundle of quantified data we can identify values or types of data that are most typical (see mean, median and mode).	12.3
Chernoff face	A visual depiction of many variables in the form of a face, with variables taking the form of the mouth, eyes, eyebrows, ears, nose and so on.	10.2.8
Chi-Square (χ^2)	A non-parametric statistical test that uses counted data to determine the significance of any difference between an observed distribution of data and a distribution that would be expected given specific assumptions.	13.6.2
Citation	The process of referencing academic and other work that has informed a researcher's own study.	5.3.5
Closed Question	A question that gives the respondent no freedom to respond other than with the categories pre-chosen by the researcher. Researchers can increase the flexibility of closed questions by adding a response category 'other' and asking respondents to give details.	8.1.1
Cluster sampling	A method of sampling that is useful for dealing with large data sets. The population is divided into groups (clusters), often on a geographical basis. The clusters are sampled as individual units and the members of the population within the selected cluster are the source of data.	6.5.4
Codes	The names given to themes selected for their significance to the research issue in qualitative research (see coding and tags).	11.3

Term	Definition	Section
Coding	The process of identifying concepts or themes from text, speech or behaviour. Codes are umbrella ideas that link together basic data units. The coding process links together similar words, ideas, actions or behaviour and progressively seeks to build them into an interpretative hierarchy.	11.3
Coding frame	This is the set of codes that have been devised to analyse data. The coding frame should be sufficiently well developed and clearly explained so that two different researchers will process the same data in the same way.	11.3
Coding Software	Software that can be used to handle qualitative data. It can be used to add codes, bring codes together, add comments about the coding process and, in modern versions, even predict the allocation of codes to data.	11.4
Coefficient of variation	A measure of the relationship between the mean and the standard deviation.	12.4.2
Cognitive Interview	An interview approach in which the interviewee is asked to place him or herself in situations or to remember situations about which the researcher wishes to collect data. The technique was developed for police witness interviewing.	9.5
Cohen's d	A statistic that measures effect size (see definition).	13.3.6
Cohort	A group in a sequence of groups. For instance, a cohort of students could be studied from the time they enter the educational system to the time they leave.	
Collective Interview	An interview with more than one person present and answering questions.	9.6
Compound Indicator	An indicator of a variable that consists of several parts brought together in a single measure.	7.4.2
Computer Assisted Telephone Interview	An interview conducted by phone in which the interviewer follows (often reading) a proforma. Data are often entered directly into a database.	9.2
Confidence interval	This is the range within which the true value of an estimate will lie. For example, if we sample voting intentions, we can say that 30% will vote for party A plus or minus 3%. The range 27% to 33% is the confidence interval. The level of accuracy we require (that is, a smaller rather than a larger interval) will increase sample size.	6.8
Confidence level	This is the proportion of times we would expect our sample to deliver an estimate with a specified confidence interval (see definition). Confidence levels are expressed in probabalistic terms. In social research 95% is commonly used, though 90% and 99% are also found. The higher the confidence level required, the larger will be the sample.	6.8
Connotation	Meanings that are attached to the literal meaning of a word by a group or individual. Connotative meaning can be the image we bring to mind or the meaning we ascribe to an image (see denotation).	11.10.4
Constructivism/ constructivist	A theoretical perspective that represents learning as process in which we build an understanding of the world (our reality) out of our experiences of functioning in that world. In terms of research it implies that we should adopt an interpretivist (see definition) approach to understand the world within which people operate.	

Term	Definition	Section
Content analysis	An approach to text analysis. It originated as a quantitative analysis of word or phrase counts but is becoming a more qualitative analysis in which the text is reduced to themes (much like coding) that are assessed in terms of their meaning and the way in which they associate with each other.	11.7
Continuous data	Data that can be measured either on a scale of infinite length or data that over a range can have an infinite number of measurement possibilities. For example, when measuring the height of adult males, there are an infinite number of measuring points.	3.2.3 (iii)c
Control group	In an experimental or quasi-experimental situation, the control group operates under non-experimental conditions. This means that the intervention (which is the subject of the experimental enquiry) is not applied to the control group.	3.2.4
Control variable	A lens through which we examine data to see if it produces any patterning in the character of the data. In survey research, for instance, we may use gender, age, ethnicity and social status as control variables to see whether they reveal differences in responses.	7.4.3
Convenience sampling	An approach to sampling in which data collection is based on ease of access to the data source.	6.6.4
Conversation analysis	A qualitative approach that explores the verbal interaction between two or more people. The emphasis is on the pace, lilt and tone as much as the meaning. Conversation analysis has a well developed framework for analysing verbal interaction.	11.10.2
Correlation	A means of measuring the degree of association between a pair of variables (see correlation coefficient).	13.7.1
Correlation coefficient	A calculated measure used to express the level of correlation between two variables. The association is measured on a scale ranging from −1 (a perfect negative correlation) through 0 (where there is no correlation) to +1 (a perfect positive correlation).	12.9
Critical theory	Within social science and in this book, critical theory is a philosophical perspective that informs the selection of a research issue and the analysis and interpretation of research data. In broad term its perspective is to remove or reduce inequalities in society.	2.1.1 & 1111.10.3
Cumulative frequency diagram	Also ogive	10.2.3
Data	Facts, numbers, opinions, attitudes, actions, appearances and so on that we use in any combination and from which we extract information that will help us answer a research question.	Chapter 4
Data Archive	A depository for primary research data. Data are usually stored in digital form.	4.5.3
Data visualisation	An approach to data analysis that portrays data so that shape, patterning and visual forms can be used to suggest processes at work.	Chapter 10

Term	Definition	Section
Deductive	A way of representing research in which the purpose of the activity is to test the appropriateness of a theory or model. With this approach, the researcher postulates what will or should happen and then collects data to test whether the world from which the data came fits the theory or model.	7.1
Degrees of freedom	A procedure used in statistical testing for taking account of sample size. Conceptually, degrees of freedom in statistical tests are the number of data values that can vary when we calculate the test statistic without changing that statistic. For the non-mathematician, this is confusing so it is easier to stick with the idea that they allow for the influence of sample size on the variability of our test statistic.	13.6.1(i)
Denotation	The literal meaning of a word (see connotation).	11.10.4
Dependent variable	In a process (cause/effect) relationship, the dependent variable is the one that changes as a result of a causative process (see independent variable).	7.4.1
Descriptive statistics	A range of statistical approaches that are used to describe the shape and characteristics of data. Conventionally the qualities that are described are averageness, spread, peakedness and skew. Form in data can, however, appear as sequences and patterns in time or space, so we should be aware of methods that describe data in these ways as well.	
Directional hypothesis	A positive hypothesis that specifies how variables differ, for instance that a is larger than b.	3.2.3(i)
Discourse analysis	A qualitative approach that explores how we use words to construct as well as convey meaning. The term has been used by several disciplines, which can create confusion because the approaches can be quite different.	11.9
Ecological fallacy	The assumption that a relationship that holds true for a group is equally applicable to a specific individual. This is a danger in correlational analyses.	3.2.3
Effect	An outcome of an event or action (see cause).	
Effect size	This is a quantification of the influence that one variable has on another. Particularly with small samples, it can be a better estimator of impact than a significance test.	13.3.6
Epistemology	The study of knowledge. In a research setting, an epistemological assessment would be concerned with how we could be concerned that the knowledge we acquire through our efforts is valid and true.	3.1
Ethics	A branch of philosophy that deals with what is right and wrong, good and bad. In a research context, ethics is concerned with the rights and protection of respondents and of researchers, the misuse of data and accuracy, honour and responsibility in reporting results.	9.8 & 9.15
Ethnography	An approach to data collection in which the researcher is immersed in the community from which the data is obtained.	2.1.4 & 14.4
Evaluation	An approach to research that seeks to identify whether goals, outputs and outcomes have been achieved, what processes lead to which outcomes and to assess the effectiveness of actions, programmes and interventions.	2.1.4 & 14.3

Term	Definition	Section
Existentialism	A flexible philosophical concept that can take on different nuances with different people. Central to most are the ideas that our experiences shape our lives and that our life choices are made on the basis of our freedom to choose. These ideas stand in contrast to those espoused by structuralists.	2.1.1
Experiential learning	A process of learning by doing (as opposed to rote learning or memorising). Experiential learning has become significant as societies have become more concerned with skills development and skill transfer from the learning environment to the work environment.	
Experiment	A research strategy that seeks to identify the effect of a single variable or a set of variables acting both individually and in combination upon a situation. The experimental condition seeks to ensure that the variables under test can vary but nothing else can.	3.2.4 & 14.6
Explanatory theory	Theory derived from observation in the real world which seeks to explain how that world operates.	2.2.1
Exploratory data analysis	An inductive approach to research in which data is analysed to assess whether there are patterns that require further investigation. Exploratory data analysis uses semi graphical approaches and often seeks to produce rapid conclusions as to the need for further investigation.	
Factor analysis	A quantitative approach for detecting order in associations between variables. The method seeks to identify which correlations between variables cluster together and calls these clusters 'factors'.	13.8
Factorial design	An experimental design used to test the effect of several variables at the same time or the same variable in different concentrations or, in the most complex situations, a combination of the two.	3.2.4
Fisher's Test	A statistical test for small samples cast as a contingency table.	13.6.4
Focus group	A means of collecting data from a group of people. Members are selected to represent a particular interest or set of interest that are significant to the research. The strength of the focus group approach is that discussion amongst members can reveal feelings and sensitivities that simply responding to a question will not.	9.6.2
Formative assessment	Used to describe a learning task whose purpose is to enhance understanding so that a student can progress to further learning challenges (see also summative assessment).	
Frequency distribution	A chart that shows the number of counts of a variable or a data range within a variable. We could construct, for instance, a frequency distribution of the ethnicity of children in a school and a frequency distribution of their ages. The former would show the number of children in each ethnic group and the latter the number of children in each age group.	12.4.2(ii)
Gantt Chart	A chart designed to show the sequencing and duration of activities in a process or programme (such as a research programme).	6.3
Glyph	A generic name for systems used to graphically portray data.	10.2.8

Term	Definition	Section
Grounded theory	The development of an explanation or theory that is grounded in the evidence. The data used as evidence is usually verbal and/or behavioural and is processed using a strict and rigorous procedure (see coding, tagging and theming).	11.8
Hawthorne effect	A specific intervention effect (see definition) in which subjects change their behaviour sometimes to confound the proposal being tested by the research. Named after a factory in the USA where the effect was first identified.	3.2.4
Hermeneutics	Hermeneutics is the discovery and study of meaning. To this extent it sits above ways of researching (such as positivism). It can be used as a method to develop other ways of discovering and studying meaning (for instance, the critique of positivism that has given rise to qualitative methodology in general and humanistic approaches in particular).	2.1.1
Histogram	A visual representation of continuous data grouped into categories (or classes). The horizontal axis of the histogram shows the class boundaries of the variable and the vertical axis the frequency of occurrence. Also called histograph. See bar chart.	10.2.2
Holistic	Referring to something that is looked at in its entirety. In a research context, it implies interdisciplinarity. Education as a research field is implicitly holistic because it will often look at the individual or organisation in a social, economic and political context.	3.3.3
Humanism	A broad class of philosophical standpoints that highlight the need to understand human experience. In terms of research practice, this becomes the focus of the research, and people are seen as individuals and not as contributors to a statistical description.	2.1.1
Hypothesis	A statement about the likely effect of a variable or variables on a situation. The hypothesis can be derived from a theory as to what an effect should be or from a situation observed elsewhere.	14.7
Independent variable	A variable that is the 'cause' in a cause/effect hypothesis or model.	7.4.1
In-depth interview	An interview format characterised by free-form questioning to probe a respondent's knowledge, understanding or viewpoint. The interviewer is able to use follow up questions to press the respondent on his or her answer.	9.4
Index number	A measure of an activity or quantity calculated in such a way that 100 is taken as the base. Index numbers are often calculated for time series.	10.1.6
Indicator	An indicator is a set of data that stand for a variable. For example, if our variable was 'boredom' (and our study was into factors that affected student attainment), we could use video evidence of student inattention or we could use self reports by students.	7.4.2
Inductive	A way of representing research in which the derivation of a theoretical statement or model arises out of the process of data analysis. Puzzled or intrigued by a situation or set of data, the approach of the researcher is to subject it to various analyses (the type of analysis depending on the nature of the data) in order to reveal order and pattern.	7.1

Term	Definition	Section
Inferential statistics	A set of statistical approaches through which we can identify statistically significant relationships between variables.	
Informed consent	The practice of ensuring that those who provide data are willing to do so under conditions that are acceptable to both the researcher and the researched. Informed consent is one of the mainstays of an ethical approach to research.	9.8.1
Intelligent design	An argument in relation to evolution, the creation of the world and of the universe that sees the order that exists as being the product of some supernatural process. Its significance educationally is the push to teach intelligent design as part of a scientific curriculum. Most scientists would argue that this is inappropriate as the underpinning theory is not testable but an expression of belief.	1.7.1
Interpetivism/ interpretivist	At one level all of what we know is the product of our interpreting the evidence. The concept, however, is used in a more specific way in social research to argue that only by examining the lives, actions and statements of people can we understand the world from their perspective. Interpretivism underpins the qualitative approach to research (see constructivism).	
Interquartile range	A quantitative measure of spread, being the range between the 25% of data values immediately above the median and the 25% immediately below the median when the whole data set is ranked from high to low or vice versa.	12.4.1
Interval scale	A measurement scale in which the difference between all scale points is the same. There is no zero which represents no quantity of the thing being measured.	4.4
Intervening variable	A variable which does not directly affect an independent variable but which impacts on the process by which the independent variable impacts on the dependent variable.	7.4.1
Intervention effect	The idea that the process of investigation can influence what is being investigated. This is of particular concern to researchers who believe that they should strive to be neutral and that their observations should be unsullied. There is, however, much evidence that this is not the case, from the well-known 'Hawthorn effect' (see reference) to the problem of preventing interviewees overidentifying with the interviewer and the objects of the investigation and shaping their responses to please the interviewer. At the other extreme there are researchers who believe that it is their task to create change, that is produce intervention effect in their subjects.	3.2.4
Kolmogorov-Smirnov test	A statistical test that compares the difference between two distributions (for instance, between the grades gained by boys and girls in a class test).	13.6.3
Kurtosis	An expression of the peakedness of a distribution (see platykurtic and leptokurtic).	12.6
Leptokurtic	A distribution that is more peaked than a normal distribution with the same mean.	12.6
Liberal	Both a political philosophy and an approach to education. At the heart of the concept is the idea of free choice tempered by social and economic responsibility. In educational terms, it implies a broad education as a means of producing a balanced individual capable of exercising a socially motivated (or constrained) choice.	

Term	Definition	Section
Lifeworld	This concept (linked with phenomenology) refers to the world as lived in and experienced by the people in our investigation. The lifeworld is therefore an individual and subjective idea (as compared with the idea that there is a 'real world' which most people experience in the same way) (see phenomenology).	2.1.1
Likert scale	A scale developed to represent the attitude or views of people. For example, if we wished to assess the attitude of teachers to teaching as a profession, we could construct a Likert scale. This would consist of a set of statements to which respondents would indicate their degree of agreement on a scale (of normally five scale positions from agree to disagree). The total of their scores for each statement would represent their overall attitude. There are procedures for ensuring that a statement is appropriate and that there is an appropriate balance of statements.	8.10.1
Line graph	A graph showing the relationship between two variables both measured on continuous scales. The points on the graph created by the two variables must fall on a continuous line. A time series is also a line graph.	10.2.5
Logarithm	A mathematical representation of number in which the value of a number is given by the power to which a base number is raised. A common number base is base 10. Every number can be expressed in base 10. So, for instance, the logarithm of 10 (in base 10) is 1 because 10 to the power 1 is 10, while the logarithm of 100 is 2 because 10 to the power 2 is 100.	3.2.3
Longitudinal study	A study in which changes over a long period of time (relative to the issue being researched) are one of the prime interests. Longitudinal studies are often concerned with the profiling of the characteristics of an age cohort over a period measured in decades.	
Matched group	An experimental design in which the test group and the control group are matched in terms of key characteristics. These might be having children of the same gender, age and social status or ensuring that the environment is the same for both test and control (e.g. by using the same space for both).	3.2.4
Matrix Chart	A way of portraying three or more variables on a grid. The computer programs that produce the visualisation are usually interactive and allow researchers to manipulate data.	10.2.8
Mean	A measure of the 'averageness' of a data set. The mean is usually calculated as the arithmetic mean (there are others) in which the total of all values in the data set is divided by the number of values in the data set.	12.3.1
Measurement scale	The basis against which things can be measured. In research we use the phrase in two ways, as a framework for describing types of measurement and as a term to describe a length of measurement. In the first case, the most used framework for representing measurement scales is nominal, ordinal, interval and ratio. In the second case we might ask someone how far they agree with a statement on a scale 1 to 5, where 1 is completely agree and 5 is completely disagree.	4.4
Median	A measure of the 'averageness' of a data set. The median is the middle item in a data set when the set has been ranked from high to low.	12.3.2

Term	Definition	Section
Metaphor map	A generic name for visual representations of data that take a recognisable form (see Chernoff face).	10.2.8
Methodology	The approaches we use or can use to collect and analyse data. A methodology can be just a collection of methods used in a specific instance though it is, more usually, an association of methods that are commonly used together.	2.1.4
Mixed method analysis	A combination of qualitative and quantitative methods of data collection and analysis in the same investigation. Mixed methods analysis stands apart because it is driven by the needs of the research and pragmatic in its orientation, whereas quantitative and qualitative approaches can be presented as being mutually exclusive.	2.1.2
Mixed method design	A research design that incorporates quantitative and qualitative approaches either in parallel or sequentially.	3.4.3
Mixed methodologies	The combination of research approaches (such as positivist and humanist) that purists in those areas argue should not be combined because it compromises underpinning principles.	3.4
Mixed model design	A research design in which quantitative and qualitative approaches are integrated throughout the enquiry.	3.4.3
Mode	A measure of the 'averageness' of a data set. The mode is the value that occurs most often. When applied to individual data values, it can produce a misleading estimate of 'averageness'. For this reason it is more often applied to grouped data, and the measure is referred to as 'modal class'.	12.3.3
Model	A representation of the key functional or process relationships in a situation (for example, bullying). A model can be constructed at the beginning or end of the research process (see also causal and soft system).	2.2.2
Modern (movement)	The period prior to the postmodern. Recognisable in art and design and in social studies. In the latter case it was typified by the identification of general processes and the search for theory that could describe the social world and which could be used to improve that world.	
Moving average	An approach for depicting the trend in a time series in which the value for any one time point is the average (arithmetic mean) of that point and points either side. For a three period calculation, we take the central value (time t) and add to that t−1 and t+1, divide by three and ascribe the value to time t. The method then moves forward a period and adds t, t+1 and t+2 and ascribes the value to t+1 – and so on.	12.8
Multilevel design	A research design in which one approach (quantitative or qualitative) dominates at a particular scale of analysis (for example, class group and pupil).	3.4.3
Multiple correlation	An approach to estimating the relationship between variables in which the influence of all variables is assessed. The correlation coefficient is interpreted as normal (see correlation coefficient).	13.7.2
Multi-Stage sampling	An approach which requires that the population is broken up into clusters whose individuals are then sampled. Those sampled are then assumed to be an adequate description of the cluster character.	6.5.5

Term	Definition	Section
Multivariate	This means many variables. It is used to describe a situation in which several variables (such as age, gender, socio-economic status and ethnicity) may be influencing a situation (such as the number of young people from an area entering higher education). A set of analytic procedures has been developed to allow us to assess the impact of such variables individually and in combination.	
Narrative analysis	An approach to analysing spoken or written data whose significance is that the data represent the authentic voice of the subject or of the subject as mediated by a third person (e.g. the transcript of a statement given to a policeman).	11.10.1
Neo-conservatism or neocon	A right wing political philosophy that believes in the primacy of the free market and the freedom of the individual to act in his or her own interest. The consequence of this is a belief in 'small government', that is minimum regulation.	2.1.1
Nominal data	Data that are measured on a nominal scale (see definition).	
Nominal scale	The simplest scale of measurement in which objects are placed in classes and their frequencies counted. Such data are also called 'counted data'.	4.4
Non-directional hypothesis	A positive hypothesis that specifies that two variables, a and b, are different and not how they are different.	3.2.3(i)
Non-parametric statistics	A family of statistical tests that makes no assumption about whether the data to be processed conform to a specific type of probability distribution. For this reason, these tests are referred to as distribution free. Because they make no assumption about the underlying nature of the research data, they are favoured by many social scientists.	13.4.1
Non-participant observation	A means of data collection in which the researcher observes the behaviour and lifestyle of the individual(s) or group(s) in which he or she is interested. Sometimes those being observed are aware of the observer's status (see visible researcher) and sometimes they are not (see invisible researcher). The observer does not participate in or influence the activities being observed.	9.13
Non-probability-based sampling	A family of methods of drawing samples for which the assumption that each unit of data has the same chance of being drawn as every other unit of data is relaxed or non-existent.	6.6
Non-response	The people who choose not to participate in the data collection process. As researchers we ought to assess whether the pattern of non-response introduces bias into the data we collect.	6.9.1
Normal distribution	A distribution established theoretically with specific characteristics that are (more or less) shared by many data sets studied by both natural and social scientists. The main characteristics are that the distribution is symmetrical about the mean and that known and immutable proportions of data are found at specific distances from the mean.	13.2.1
Normative theory	Theory derived from principles, which shows how the world would operate if it were ruled by those principles. In research terms, the world of normative theory is compared with the real world to assess how far the latter deviate from the former.	2.2.1

Term	Definition	Section
Null hypothesis	The hypothesis that is actually tested with a statistical test. The hypothesis is framed along the lines of 'there is no significant difference between a and b' for a two-tailed test or 'a is not larger than b' for a one-tailed test.	3.2.1 & 3.2.3
Observation	A unit of data or set of data observed at specific time or over a specific period (an observation). Also the process of collecting data by watching the source that generates the data.	
Observatory	Borrowed from the observation of stars and planets, it is now used to describe an organisation that collects information about an area or specific theme. Within the EU, observatories have been encouraged that will profile localities.	2.3.4
Ogive	See cumulative frequency diagram	
One-tailed test	The tail refers to a test distribution. In a one-tailed test, we examine the probabilities associated with test result in one tail of the distribution only. This requires us to have defined a directional positive or research hypotheses.	13.3.2 & 13.3.4
Open Question	A question that gives a respondent free reign in the formation of an answer.	8.1.2
Ordinal scale	A measurement scale in which data can be ranked according to some criteria. The rank value constitutes the measurement but the differences in rank may not be of equal size.	4.4
Outlier	In a set of data an individual unit or group of data that lies outside the broad pattern of data. Sometimes an outlier can be the result of a problem with sampling, other times it can be a valid but unusual outcome.	
P value	The p value is the probability of a specific test statistic under the null hypothesis. In the past social scientists used to compare their test statistic with the values of test statistics at critical values (such as 10%, 5%, 2.5%, 1%, .1%). With the advent of statistical packages, they calculate the actual probability of the test statistic under a null hypothesis, thus making it easier for the researcher to compare the test result with the critical value of acceptance/rejection of the null hypothesis selected at the outcome of the research.	
Paradigm	An idea that at any one point in time all those working in a particular area, field or subject adopt common ways of working and common ways of looking at issues.	2.1.2
Parametric statistics	A family of statistical tests that assumes the data conform to a normal distribution. While the assumption of normality can be challenging for educational researchers, there are ways of transforming data to bring them closer to a normal distribution.	13.4.1
Partial correlation	An approach to estimating the relationship between variables in which the influence of one variable is assessed while holding others constant. The correlation coefficient is interpreted as normal (see correlation coefficient).	13.7.2
Partial regression	A representation of the relationship between one variable and another while other variables are held constant.	13.8

Term	Definition	Section
Participant observation	A means of data collection in which the researcher observes the behaviour and lifestyle of the individual(s) or group(s) in which he or she is interested. Sometimes those being observed are aware of the observer's status (see visible researcher) and sometimes they are not (see invisible researcher). The observer participates in the activities being observed.	2.1.4 & 9.13
Percentile	A one percent division of a data set that has been ranked from high to low.	
Phenomenog-raphy	A research approach that seeks to provide a rich and detailed description of an individual's or individuals' experience. This description constitutes the data from which an understanding is constructed. Phenomenography is an interpretivist approach (see definition). Often confused with phenomenology, it differs in that it considers the specific experiences of research subjects, while phenomenology is more concerned with general experiences considered from the researcher's perspective.	11.10.5
Phenomenology	In social research phenomenology is an approach that seeks to understand how we understand the world. The focus is often the meanings we ascribe to our experiences (see lifeworld).	2.1.1
Pie Chart	A visual approach to the representation of data. Data are classified into mutually exclusive classes and the size of each class is expressed as a proportion of the whole data set. The proportions are used to construct segments of a circle (the 'pie').	10.2.4
Pilot (test/survey)	An investigation that takes place before the main investigation and which is designed to test and evaluate the effectiveness of the research procedures.	8.11
Platykurtic	A distribution that is more flat than a normal distribution with the same mean.	12.6
Point-biserial correlation	A correlation coefficient in which one of the data sets is continuous and the other is counted data, usually for two mutually exclusive categories.	13.7.3
Policy analysis	An approach to social research that either seeks to understand how policy was determined (research about policy) or to identify what policy is needed or why policy is failing or successful (research for policy). It makes use of a wide range of methodologies and methods.	1.4
Population	The totality of a group from which a sample is drawn. This totality can be people (the population of children in a schools), organisations (all schools in an administrative area) and objects (all of the computers in a school).	6.4.2
Positive hypothesis	See research hypothesis. The term positive hypothesis is used when we want to draw a contrast with the null hypothesis.	3.2.1 & 3.2.3
Positivism (positivist)	An approach to conducting social research that seeks to apply the principles developed by the natural sciences. The key principles are the neutrality of the researcher with respect to the problem and taking decisions about the results of the research out of the researcher's hands. Positivism seeks to emulate scientific research in seeking to develop theory. Its approach is to postulate hypotheses which, if proven, can constitute building blocks of a theory.	2.1.1 & 3.2.1

Term	Definition	Section
Postmodernism	The period after modernism. The transition can be seen in many fields including art and design and social studies. In the case of the latter, the broad indicator is the shift from the study of, search for and identification of the general to appreciating the significance of the individual, from the search for order to one of understanding why things are different, from implementing global solutions to problems to valuing local solutions.	2.1.1
Pragmatism/ pragmatics	A philosophical perspective that establishes the viability of a proposition (and thus establishes whether it is 'true') on the basis of what works. Pragmatism has been put forward as a philosophical underpinning for mixed methods research. It could equally apply to other research traditions.	2.1.2
Praxis	While the dictionary defines praxis as an habitual way of doing things, within the emerging field of work based learning and education more broadly, it is used to bring together the idea that work activity is a blending of theory with practice, that practice informs theory and theory then informs practice.	1.4
Primary data	Data that are collected first hand from original sources (such as people themselves) by the investigator and not statistics or data collected by others (see secondary data).	4.5.1
Probability based sampling	A method of drawing samples in which each unit of data has a specific chance (probability) of being selected. The usual selection process is equal probability, in which case the approach is also known as random sampling.	6.5
Probing	The process of pushing a source to clarify an answer or to reveal more in an answer to a question.	
Probing question	A question that is asked in order to clarify a previous response or whose purpose is to get the respondent to reveal more of an issue.	
Purposive sampling	Sampling which has a specific purpose aligned to the goals of the investigation. Purposive sampling is not probability based. Selection of a case study is purposive as is the identification of subjects with relevant characteristics or behaviours (such as gay teachers).	6.6
Qualitative Data	Often erroneously considered to be data that cannot be measured (see quantitative data), qualitative data are more properly data that reflect beliefs, attitudes, views. Such data can take the form of verbal statements, written accounts, behaviours, objects and relationships. The meaningfulness of qualitative data arises from an understanding of personal lives.	4.3
Qualitative research and analysis	A research approach whose principal concern is how an outcome comes about. It is more concerned with why 90% do this and 10% do that rather than the fact that they do.	2.1.2 & 3.3 & Chapter 10
Quantitative data	Data that are capable of being measured along one of several measurement scales. Such data are held to exist in the 'real' world.	4.3
Quantitative research and analysis	A research approach that seeks to identify pattern and association in numerical data. It is closely linked with positivism which makes assumptions about how research should be conducted.	2.1.2 & 3.2

Term	Definition	Section
Quartile	A quarter of a data set that has been ranked from high to low (or vice versa). These quarters are referred to as the upper quartile (the top 25%), the lower quartile (the bottom 25%), the upper middle quartile (26 to 50%) and the lower middle quartile (51 to 75%).	
Question bank	A repository of questions and questionnaires. Usually on-line.	8.4.1
Questionnaire administration	The process of presenting a questionnaire to a subject. There are various ways of administering a questionnaire, including face to face, self completion, drop and collect, telephone and computer assisted.	Chapter 8
Quota sampling	The specification of sample sizes (quotas) for specific groups. The sample sizes (quotas) are designed to meet specific research goals. In some cases the quotas can reflect relative proportions in a population (making them similar to stratified samples), in other cases the sizes may reflect the need to get a sample large enough to make meaningful quantitative statements. A distinguishing feature of many quota procedures is that respondents are approached and accepted only if they meet quota specifications.	6.6.1
Radical	Both a political philosophy and an approach to problem solving. In both cases it has connotations of thinking unconstrained by conventional solutions.	
Random	A process in which every event has the same probability as every other event. This situation is important in sampling if we wish to use statistical tests with our data. In this case, each unit in our population should have the same chance of being selected.	3.2.4
Random sampling	A way of drawing samples in each unit of data has the same chance of being drawn as every other unit of data. This approach is also referred to as probability based sampling.	6.5
Range	A quantitative measure of spread, being the difference between the greatest and the smallest in a data set.	12.4.1
Rating scale	A means of enabling subjects to express their level of agreement with a statement or indicate their position with respect to a linear scale defined by the researcher.	
Ratio scale	A measurement scale in which the difference between all scale points is the same. The scale has a zero which represents no quantity of the thing being measured.	4.4
Refereeing	The process or peer review of papers published by academic journals. Peer review of a paper by an independent and anonymous referee is a means of ensuring quality in academic publication.	1.7.3
Reflection	A high order analytic process through which to identify what has occurred and why. It is a core process in action research and in anchoring personal learning. In this regard experience and outcomes are assessed and reassessed in order to understand, learning processes, capture learning gains and establish ways of moving forward.	
Regression	A line used to represent the trend in a data plot (see scattergraph). The line can be inserted by eye but is more usually computed so that the total of the squares of the distance between any data point and the line is minimised.	12.9

Term	Definition	Section
Representative	In sampling, ensuring that the characteristics of the sample reflect those of the population from which it is drawn.	
Research agenda	This is the priority given to research problems and themes. A university department could have its research agenda but those with the power to influence what research is done are those of funding bodies such as research councils, national governments and the EU.	2.3
Research ethics	See ethics	2.1.3
Research hypothesis	The opposite of a null hypothesis and the issue that we are really investigating. The research hypothesis can be non-directional (there is a difference between a and b) or directional (a is larger than b).	3.2.1 & 3.2.3 & 13.3.2
Research issue	The area of interest to the researcher. The first task of a researcher is often to focus down the issue and isolate a research question or research questions.	2.3
Research methodology	See methodology	
Research philosophy	A term used to describe the principles governing research practice. What this description fails to convey, however, is that there is not just one research philosophy, so while we can use the term in a portfolio sense, we have to talk about the different principles that drive research practice. The study of these different sets of principles can also be referred to as research philosophy.	2.1.1
Research problem	More general than a research question, a research problem is an issue that requires further focus before it can be investigated.	2.3
Research question	A formulation of a research issue that isolates the specifics to be researched and to which an answer is required.	2.1.5 & 7.2 & Chapter 14
Research strategy	The overall approach to obtaining and processing data that will answer the research question. A research strategy is informed by whether a researcher chooses to work within a paradigm and the level of resources available. Essentially a research strategy is a combination of methodology and method designed to meet the needs of a particular research situation.	
Response rate	In survey research, the proportion of those contacted who take part. It is usually expressed as a percentage (of respondents) of the sample. The response rate is important in establishing the quality of the survey and in identifying the possibility of bias.	
Review Journal	A journal whose principal purpose is to summarise the latest developments in a field.	5.3.3
Running mean	See moving average	
Sample	A selection from a population (see probability and purposive sample).	6.4

Term	Definition	Section
Sample frame	The section or area of the population from which the sample will be drawn. In many cases the population will be the sample frame (for instance, if we want to interview a sample of a year group in a school, the year group would be both the population and sample frame). In other cases the sample frame will be a subset of the population. For example, if we were studying the problems faced by head teachers in schools that drew their pupils from socially deprived areas, it would be difficult to sample the whole population of head teachers in such schools in a country, so we could identify three areas with different levels of deprivation and sample the head teachers in these areas. In this case, the three deprived areas constitute the sample frame.	6.4.2
Sample size	The sample size is the number of people or bodies that participate in a survey. Sample size is expressed both as a number and a proportion of the population. The determination of sample size is important before a survey if data are to be processed to yield results that meet standards of statistical rigour.	6.8 & Appendix 1
Sampling fraction	The proportion of the population accounted for by the sample (that is the sample as a fraction or percentage of the population).	
Scale	Used in two ways in social research. (a) a framework for measurement (attitude scale) (b) a level at which data are presented and analysed. This level can be geographical (national, local) or hierarchical (expenditure on food, leisure or expenditure on pre-pepared food, on fruit and vegetable, on meat, on fish, on cereals etc.).	4.5.3
Scatter graph	A way of portraying the interaction of two variables on a graph. Each axis represents a variable. Data points are plotted against the two axes.	10.2.6
Scatterplot	See scatter graph	
Scientism	Both an approach to research and a belief about how research should be conducted. Scientism believes in the primacy of a scientific approach to research, with key principles being the neutrality of the researcher, the demonstration of the effect of an individual variable or set of variables upon a situation and the development of a model to reflect a particular circumstance or a theory to describe a general relationship.	2.1.1
Secondary data	Data used by the researcher or the research team but collected originally by another researcher.	4.5.2
Self-Selecting Sample	A sampling procedure in which a population identifies the survey opportunity and takes part.	6.6.6
Semantic differential	A rating scale based on adjectival opposites that can be used to profile respondent views about an issue.	
Semi Structured Interview	An interview in which themes are identified and lead questions specified but where the interviewer is given training to ask supplementary questions that will provide the data needed by the research programme.	9.3
Semiotics	An approach to qualitative research that seeks to identify the deeper meanings behind behaviour and the way text and objects are used.	11.10.4

Term	Definition	Section
Sign	The fundamental unit of semiotics. A sign stands for something. What it stands for is socially and/or culturally determined. What it stands for (its meaning) can be analysed (see connotation).	11.10.4
Significance level	This is the level of probability at which a researcher chooses to reject the null hypothesis. The most usual value selected is 5% but in some circumstances significance in social or educational research terms could be less than this (for instance 10 or 20%).	3.2.3
Skew	A pattern in data in which the data are not equally divided and balanced either side of a central value (usually the mean). When plotted as a frequency distribution, the appearance of the data set is that it leans to the left or to the right.	12.5
Smoothed mean	See moving average	
Snowball sampling	Developed as a purposive sampling approach and often sued for hard to reach populations. The researcher uses subjects already identified to identify new subjects, the assumption being that in hard to identify groups those already in the group are likely to know other group members.	6.6.2
Soft system	Whereas a system normally requires a quantitative relationship between inputs and outputs, a soft system is an expression of the relationship between broader variables for which there may not be a simple quantitative measure. For instance, if we were researching children's progress in pre-school, we might suggest that a contributory factor was the amount of time parents spent reading with them. Further investigation suggests that socio-economic status might be a factor that influences this. As well, we ought to consider whether one or both parents worked was something to take into consideration. We are exploring a process but, at this stage, in a non-quantitative way.	
Special educational needs	Conventionally this refers to the additional or special educational or care provision required by students with specific physical or learning disabilities. Theoretically it could also apply to those who are gifted in a general or specific context but it is now usual to describe these as 'gifted and talented'.	
Spectral analysis	A quantitative approach to the analysis of time series in which data plotted through time is decomposed into a series of sign waves of different amplitude and wavelength. When these curves are combined, they reproduce the original data set. The task of the researcher is to identify the significance of the individual curves in terms of processes at work.	12.8
Standard deviation	A measure of spread in a distribution based on the total of differences between every element in the distribution and the mean of the distribution.	12.4.2
Standard error	The idea that a characteristic of a sample reflects the characteristic of a population within known limits. The standard error is usually calculated for the mean of a sample. It is expressed as the sample mean plus or minus a value determined through calculation with a 68% (approximately) or 95% (approximately) likelihood.	12.4.2
Starplot	A way of portraying the sizes of a number of variables (usually more than 5). The variables are plotted in a circle on radii that are at equal angles from each other. The value of the variable is shown by the length of the radius.	10.2.8

Term	Definition	Section
Statistical significance	A way of assessing the likelihood that the difference between two distributions could be random in nature. The conventional critical level of significance adopted by statisticians is that an event occurring 1 time in 20 (5%) indicates that chance is unlikely to be a factor. However, for some investigations this level may be too strict and researchers should judge significance taking other factors into account.	13.3.1
Stem and leaf diagram	A means of visually representing the digits of a numeric data set. Numbers are broken down into component parts, such as tens and units. In this case the tens constitute the stem and are written as a column of figures from high to low or vice versa. The units constitute the leaf. These are written against the appropriate stem, thus the 2 of 52 is place against 50 and the 5 of 55 against 50.	10.2.1
Stepwise correlation	An approach to estimating the relationship between variables in which variables are introduced in turn into the correlation on the basis of their contribution to the value of the correlation coefficient. The correlation coefficient is interpreted as normal (see correlation coefficient).	13.7.2
Stratification	A procedure used in sampling that divides the population into groups (strata) and allocates the sample size according to the relative sizes of the strata. The effect of this is to reduce the sample size because we are sampling units of the population that are more homogeneous than the population overall.	6.5.3
Structuralism	A broad class of philosophical standpoints in social science that interprets situations in the context of power relationships, in particular the persistence of strong and weak, rich and poor.	2.1.1
Structured interview	An interview in which the themes to be covered are identified. A questionnaire interview is structured but there is no necessity to use a questionnaire approach. All that is required is that the themes are identified and covered in sequence (see unstructured interview).	9.2
Structured question	See closed question	
Student's t test	A statistical test for assessing whether two small samples are drawn from the same population.	13.6.1 & 13.7.1
Summative assessment	Used to describe the position a student has reached in terms of knowledge, understanding and learning at a point in time (see also formative assessment).	
Survey	A systematic collection of data through questionnaire, interview or observation. A systematic procedure is necessary in order to ensure that a representative set of data are collected.	
Synchronous	Something that happens at the same time as something else. Classroom teaching and learning, for instance, are synchronous activities.	
Synthetic phonics	A method of teaching reading in which the reader is taught the 'sounds' of letters and letter combinations then break-up the word into these sounds and assembles them to make the word. For example, SH – I – P to make ship.	1.3

Term	Definition	Section
System	A sequence of inputs and outputs that constitute a process. We can think of the number of undergraduates in a university academic year as a system in which the inputs were the number entering the year one plus any that were required to retake the year less those who failed the previous year and were required to leave.	7.3.1
Systematic sampling	A sampling approach in which a sample is drawn as a sequence according to a given sampling fraction. For example, if the sampling fraction is 1 in 50, one respondent is drawn out of every 50. If the first respondent is the third in sequence, the second is the fifty-third, the third is the one hundred and third and so on.	6.5.2
t test	See Student's t test	
Tagging	In grounded theory, the process of attaching a code to a piece of data (thereby effectively converting data to evidence).	11.3.5
Template analysis	Analysis of data according to a pre-existing framework. This framework can be a standard template, a template devised for another piece of research (which we might use to test previous results) or one devised to assess a theory or model.	11.6
Test statistic	All statistical tests compute a test statistic, which is assessed against its probability of occurrence under a null hypothesis. The test statistic is the outcome of the numerical processes required by the test itself.	
Theory	A statement about functional and process relationships that create cause and effect. Theories can be derived as a result of data analysis or prior to analysis and tested through data collection and analysis.	2.2.1 & 3.2.1 & 3.3.3
Think Aloud Interview	An interview approach in which a subject is asked to perform a task and, at the same time, describes the thinking process that underpins his or her actions.	9.5.2
Time series	A line graph that shows how a variable (such as birth rate or students in higher education) changes over time.	
Tree map	A tree map is a way of representing data with a hierarchical structure in two dimensions. The computer programs that produce the visualisation are usually interactive and allow researchers to manipulate data.	10.2.8
Triangulation	A process of verifying data. Data given by one source is confirmed by another and preferably a third. The sources can be people, documentation, statistics, reports and so on.	3.3.4 & 3.4.3
Two-tailed test	The tail refers to a test distribution. In a two-tailed test, we examine the probabilities associated with test result in both tails of the distribution. This requires us to have defined a non-directional positive or research hypotheses (that there is a difference).	13.3.2 & 13.3.3
Type 1 error	The incorrect rejection of a null hypothesis, that is when there is no difference between our samples, we conclude that there is.	13.3.4
Type 2 error	The failure to reject the null hypothesis when it should be rejected, that is when data sets are different, we conclude that they are not.	13.3.4

Term	Definition	Section
Univariate	This means one variable. It is usually used in the context of a distribution. A univariate distribution is one where one variable (such as age) is plotted in terms of frequency.	
Unstructured interview	A free form interview. Themes will have been identified by the researcher but there is freedom to follow up on new themes, to return to themes as new information is gathered and to probe for additional information. Unstructured interviews are particularly useful for scoping an issue before more detailed investigation is carried out. They are used extensively in policy analysis (see structured interview).	9.4
Unstructured question	See open question	
Variable	A factor that can influence an outcome or be influenced by an outcome. The concept of variable is important in modelling research situations.	7.4
Variance	The square of the standard deviation.	
Z score/value	Z scores are values for a unit of data standardised in relation to the data sets mean and standard deviation. Z scores associated with a research data set can be compared with scores for a normal distribution, where the proportions of a data set lying at specific distances from the mean are known. These known proportions are presented as a Z table and can also be computed. A Z table shows the proportion of a normal distribution that lies between the mean and a Z value, between Z values and below and above Z values.	13.2.1 & 13.2.2

Index